Human Sexuality Today

Human Sexuality Today **Fourth Edition**

Bruce M. King

University of New Orleans

Study Guide Included

Prentice
Hall

Upper Saddle River, New Jersey 07458

Library of Congress Cataloging-in-Publication Data

King, Bruce M.
    Human sexuality today / Bruce M. King. — 4th ed.
        p.   cm.
    Includes bibliographical references and index.
    ISBN   0-13-034072-3
        1. Sex instruction for youth—United States.   2. Sex.   3. Sex (Biology)   4. Sex
    (Philosophy)   5. Hygiene, Sexual—United States. I. Title.

HQ35.2 .K56 2001
306.7—dc21

2001021972

VP/Editorial Director: Laura Pearson
Acquisitions Editor: Jayme Heffler
Editorial Assistant: April Dawn Klemm
VP/Director of Production and Manufacturing: Barbara Kittle
Senior Managing Editor: Mary Rottino
Production Editor: Kathleen Sleys
Production Assistant: Elizabeth Best
Copyeditor: Mary Louise Byrd
Prepress and Manufacturing Manager: Nick Sklitsis
Prepress and Manufacturing Buyer: Tricia Kenny
Marketing Director: Beth Gillett Mejia
Senior Marketing Manager: Sharon Cosgrove
Image Permissions Coordinator: Michelina Viscusi
Creative Design Director: Leslie Osher
Interior and Cover Designer: Maria Lange/Kenny Beck
Cover Art: Tana Powell
Director, Image Resource Center: Melinda Reo
Photo Research Supervisor: Beth Boyd
Image Permissions Supervisor: Kay Dellosa
Photo Researcher: Abby Reip
Line Art Coordinator: Guy Ruggiero
Permissions Researcher: Marlene Gassler

This book was set in 11/11.75 Garamond by TSI Graphics
and was printed and bound by Von Hoffman.
Covers were printed by Phoenix Color Corp.

For permission to use copyrighted material, grateful acknowledgment
is made to the copyright holders listed on page 497, which is considered
an extension of this copyright page.

© 2002, 1999, 1996, 1991 by Pearson Education, Inc.
Upper Saddle River, New Jersey 07458

Printed in the United States of America
10   9   8   7   6   5   4   3   2   1

ISBN 0-13-034072-3

Pearson Education LTD.
Pearson Education Australia PTY, Limited
Pearson Education Singapore, Pte. Ltd
Pearson Education North Asia Ltd., Hong Kong
Pearson Education Canada, Ltd., Toronto
Pearson Educación de Mexico, S.A. de C.V.
Pearson Education—Japan, Tokyo
Pearson Education Malaysia, Pte. Ltd
Pearson Education, Upper Saddle River, New Jersey

TO GAIL

Without whom this book would never
have been possible

and

TO LESLIE, JOHN, KATIE,
AND COREY

May I always be a positive influence in
their lives.

Brief Contents

Contents

Preface

There has never been a greater need for human sexuality education than at the beginning of the 21st century. Unfortunately, with the AIDS crisis and high teenage pregnancy rate, a lot of important information has been presented in a negative way. Although one of my goals in writing this book is for students to understand the relevant facts in order to make responsible decisions in their daily lives, an equally important goal has been to present the information in a warm, nonthreatening way that leaves students with positive feelings about sex and their own sexuality.

When I began to write this text I recalled my students' complaints about the dryness, sterility, and length of books I had used previously. So with them in mind, I tried to create a book that was factual and thorough, yet readable and interesting. Thus I have included numerous case studies (most contributed by my own students!) to supplement and make more personal the substantial coverage of scientific studies. Although my writing style is purposely conversational, I have worked hard to maintain the scientific foundation of my presentation. This fourth edition has well over 2,000 references for students who wish to use the book as a resource. In addition, the section on HIV/AIDS is as thorough and up-to-date as can be found in any human sexuality textbook.

The final test for any textbook is whether or not students will read it, learn from it, and enjoy it. As a result of feedback from students and reviewers, the book has continually evolved in an attempt to create an ever-better product. The fourth edition includes a new chapter on sexuality as a social concept as well as new sections throughout the book on cross-cultural comparisons. The chapter on communication has been moved up so that students may benefit from it at an earlier part in the course.

The cost of textbooks to students has become an increasing concern to many. Besides the cost of the primary textbook, already prohibitive for some, there is the added cost of a student's study guide. However, because it has been the goal of Prentice Hall and myself to publish a high-quality textbook at the lowest possible expense to the students, the Student Study Guide is now included at the end of each chapter at no additional cost to the student.

ACKNOWLEDGMENTS

I offer my deepest gratitude to Dr. Cameron Camp, who helped write the classroom-testing versions and the first edition of the book. His friendship and support will always be appreciated. Thanks also to Anne Downey for her input on the first edition. Others who helped in the early development of the book include Vic Hughes, Cheryl Stout, Desiree Comeaux, Chantelle Boudreaux, Corbie Johnson, Teresa Weysham and Kathryn King. I thank Jim Pipitone, who typed the present edition.

Thanks to everyone at Prentice Hall who worked on this book. Special thanks to Bill Webber for having faith in me, Jayme Heffler for her guidance, Kathleen Sleys for her hard work in production, and Mary Louise Byrd for her excellent editing.

My sincere appreciation and thanks to the following colleagues for their valuable input and constructive feedback in reviewing this book: for the first edition, Susan Graham-Kresge, University of Southern Mississippi; Kendra Jeffcoat, Palomar College; Deborah R. McDonald, New Mexico State University; Ken Murdoff, Lane Community College; Janet A. Simons, University of Iowa; and Janice D. Yoder, University of Wisconsin-Milwaukee; for the second edition, Kendra Jeffcoat, Palomar College; Deborah R. McDonald, New Mexico State University; Ken Murdoff, Lane Community College; and Janet A. Simons, University of Iowa; for the third edition, Donna Ashcraft, Clarion University of Pennsylvania; Robert Clark/Labeff, Midwestern State University; Betty Dorr, Fort Lewis College; and Priscilla Hernandez, Washington State University; and for the fourth edition, Nanette Davis, Western Washington University; Xiaolin Xie, Cameron University; Betty Dorr, Fort Lewis College; Carrie Yang Costello, University of Wisconsin-Milwaukee; Lillian Rosado, New Jersey City University; and Judith A. Reitan, University of California—Davis.

Finally, I cannot thank enough the thousands of students who provided me with chapter reviews and/or case histories. This book was written with students in mind. I hope it helps them to lead healthier, happier, and more fulfilling lives.

Bruce M. King

ABOUT THE AUTHOR

Bruce King received his Ph.D. in biopsychology from the University of Chicago in 1978. He has taught human sexuality to over 34,000 students at the University of New Orleans since 1981. He has also conducted human sexuality workshops for physicians, public school teachers, staff members working with the mentally retarded, and parental groups. In addition to conducting research in the field of human sexuality, Dr. King has co-authored a textbook on statistics and has published over 60 papers on the biological basis of feeding behavior and obesity. He is a Fellow in the American Psychological Society and an honorary member of the Golden Key National Honor Society for excellence in teaching.

Human
Sexuality
Today

Chapter 1

Why a Course in Human Sexuality?

Amoebas at the start
Were not complex;
They tore themselves apart
And started sex.

(Arthur Guiterman)

Nearly all colleges and universities around the country now offer courses in human sexuality (Rodriguez et al., 1996). In many of them, the enrollment is over 400 students per semester. Why are so many students taking these courses? **Sexuality** is certainly an important part of our lives. We need only to look at the world population of over 6 billion people to see that sexual motivation is very strong. Although sex is necessary for procreation, it is doubtful that many people think of this on more than just an occasional basis when having sexual intercourse. Sex can be a source of great physical and emotional pleasure, enhancing our sense of health and well-being. It can relieve tensions and anxieties. It can boost self-esteem and make us feel more masculine or feminine. It is also the vehicle through which couples can express their affection for one another.

When you have finished studying this chapter, you should be able to:

1. Explain the need for, and benefit of, sexuality education;

2. Explain why, even though people may have extensive sexual experience, many know very little about human sexuality;

3. Describe cultural perspectives other than our own with regard to sexual behaviors and attitudes;

4. Describe what makes someone sexually attractive and how that can change over time or be different in other cultures;

5. Explain the historical influence of Judaism and Christianity on contemporary attitudes about sexuality;

6. Summarize the Victorian era's sexual views and its influence on our sexual values and behaviors today;

7. Explain the contributions of Sigmund Freud, Henry Havelock Ellis, Alfred Kinsey, and Masters and Johnson to the field of sexuality;

8. Understand the uses and limitations of surveys, correlational studies, direct observations, case studies, and experimental research;

9. Explain the problems that may occur in survey studies from the use of terms like "sex" and "had sex," and understand why researchers must be very specific in the questions they ask about people's behaviors; and

10. Understand the diversity of opinions regarding the content and nature of sexuality education programs in schools.

So why the need for a course in human sexuality? Surely someone in your life took the time and responsibility to educate you about this important topic. However, surveys in my course have consistently revealed that fewer than one-half (and often less than one-third) of the 1,000 students per semester have ever had a serious and meaningful discussion with their parents about sex (see King & LoRusso, 1997). Nationally, only 36 percent of teenagers say that they learned "a lot" from their parents about sex (Kaiser Family Foundation, 1996). For many teens whose parents did talk to them about sex, it was just a single discussion—one "birds and bees" talk that was supposed to prepare them for life. The students generally received little information from their parents apart from a description of intercourse and the fact that it can result in pregnancy. Here are a few comments that I have received from students regarding their prior sex education. These were selected, not because they are unusual, but because they are typical of the many comments I've gotten on end-of-semester course evaluations.

> "My father thinks this class is a waste because he feels people instinctively know how to deal with their sexuality. Maybe I'm just a freak of nature, but I've never had any instincts explaining any of this to me."
>
> "My boyfriend doesn't like me taking the course. He says, 'You don't need a classroom to teach you about sex. I'll teach you everything you need to know.'"
>
> "Until now my parents never spoke to me about sex. I'm from a very strict family. They made me feel as though it was a sinful subject to talk about."
>
> "I remember my mother finding a book my sister was reading and screaming at her, so everyone in the house could hear, about what an awful, dirty book it was. It wasn't pornography. It was a book on sex education. She just wanted to learn something correctly."
>
> "When I was young the word sex was never brought up. My mother had one short talk with me, and that was to explain what a period is."
> (All examples are from the author's files.)

Students also provided the following comments regarding the usefulness of a human sexuality course. Apparently, it's never too late to learn.

> "I'm glad I registered in the class. I sure thought I knew it all and found I knew very little. I've been married 6 years and knew little about my own body, much less about my husband's."
>
> "I am 32, divorced with an 8-year-old child. I was married 9 years. I am amazed at how much I did not know."

> "When selecting this course, the thought came to me that it would be a very easy class because I knew everything about sex because Mother told me. After all, there are 18 of us in the family. Boy, was I wrong. I've learned more in one semester than Mother could teach me in 20 years."
>
> "I was very surprised at the amount of material I learned. I thought it was going to be just about sex. There is a lot more to sex than just sex." (All examples are from the author's files.)

Where, then, did most of us learn about sex? According to a 1998 *Time* magazine/CNN survey, 74 percent of teenagers said that friends and television were their major sources of information, compared to only 10 percent who listed parents or sex education (Stodghill, 1998). During prime time on television, three-fourths of the shows contain talk about sex or show sexual behavior (Kaiser Family Foundation, 2001). Twelve percent contain scenes where sexual intercourse is depicted or implied. On soap operas, sexual references per hour have increased 35 percent since the mid-1980s (Greenberg & Woods, 1999). The typical viewer sees only one instance of preventive behavior for every 25 instances of sexual behavior. This, of course, would include pre-adult television viewers. Television has been called "the most powerful storyteller in American culture, one that continually repeats the myths and ideologies, the facts and patterns of relationships that define our world and legitimize the social order" (Brown & Steele, 1996, p. 6). In addition to television, many R-rated movies have sexually explicit scenes with full frontal nudity. Many stores have erotic magazines on open display. Television and magazine advertisements frequently use sex (e.g., seductively dressed models and/or physical contact) to sell products (Reichert et al., 1999). Sex is everywhere, and children are exposed to it all day long.

In the face of all this, many parents continue to be silent with their children on the subject of sex. However, this, too, is a source of sex education. Making something mysterious only makes adolescent children want to know more about it. With their parents remaining silent, who can teens turn to? Medical organizations recommend that physicians talk about sexual matters with their teenage patients, but most have not (Schuster et al., 1996). As a result, most young people turn to their friends and the media for their sexual information (Kaiser Family Foundation, 1996; *Time*/CNN poll, 1998). Much of this information is incorrect, and as a result a majority of Americans are amazingly ignorant about sexual behaviors and sexual health (Reinisch, 1990). Many believe, for example, that people over 60 do not have sex, that masturbation is physically harmful, or that you cannot get AIDS if you are heterosexual.

Sexuality All of the sexual attitudes, feelings, and behaviors associated with being human. The term does not refer specifically to a person's capacity for erotic response or to sexual acts, but rather to a dimension of one's personality.

From *The Times-Picayune* (New Orleans) January 31, 1996, page B-6. ©Tribune Media Services, Inc. All Rights Reserved. Reprinted with permission.

What all this adds up to is that many people do not fully understand or appreciate the consequences of engaging in sexual relations. Half of all high school students have had sexual intercourse, and over 8 percent started before the age of 13 (Centers for Disease Control and Prevention, 2000b). However only about one-third of sexually active teenagers use contraception on a regular basis (Piccinino & Mosher, 1998; Sonenstein et al., 1998). Each year, over 1 in 10 teenage girls aged 15 to 19 gets pregnant and over 1 in 4 sexually active teens contract a sexually transmitted disease (Centers for Disease Control and Prevention, 2000b; Ventura et al., 1999). Most young people do not know the symptoms of sexually transmitted diseases and do not know where to turn if they think they have one.

So, once again, why the need for a course in human sexuality? Probably because you desire to have factual information about a subject that plays, or will play, an important role in your life. Human sexuality courses are designed to do just that. If parents are not going to assume the responsibility, the next best alternative is the schools. Recent surveys consistently show that over 85 percent of Americans support the teaching of sexuality education in public high schools, and 75 to 85 percent support it in junior high schools (Kaiser Family Foundation, 2000; Phi Delta Kappa/ Gallup Poll, 1998; SIECUS/Advocates for Youth, 1999). These surveys also found that 80 percent of those questioned believed that sexuality education should not be limited to reproductive biology and venereal disease, but should include a discussion of birth control as well. Nearly 3 out of 5 teenagers say they have not been given enough information about birth control (Kaiser Family Foundation, 1996). Sexuality education curricula are available for elementary and secondary schools (SIECUS, 1996), yet far fewer than half the states require that public high schools offer any type of sexuality education (NARAL, 1995; see section on Sexuality Education Today).

Canada and most northern European countries have extensive sexuality education programs, and the teenage pregnancy rates are much lower in these countries than in the United States (Singh & Darroch, 2000). However, the purpose of taking human sexuality courses is much more than just learning about reproduction and sexually transmitted diseases. People want to feel comfortable with their own sexuality and to feel good about themselves. Knowing about their bodies and understanding their feelings and emotions can help people achieve this. No part of our bodies should be shrouded in mystery. Understanding our partners' bodies will help in verbal and nonverbal communication and prevent unnecessary problems. Appreciating that all people are sexual beings can give us a greater understanding of our children, parents, grandparents, and friends. Studies show that sexuality education courses in schools typically result in substantial gains in knowledge and a more tolerant attitude toward others (SIECUS, 1992). The tolerance that develops with sexuality education is particularly important. Understanding that people are different from ourselves without condemning them is an important part of getting along with others.

> *PERSONAL REFLECTIONS*
> *From whom (or from where) did you acquire most of your information about sex (e.g., parents, friends, the media, teachers, the Internet)? Did your parents discuss sexuality with you? If not, why do you suppose they did not? From whom do you hope your children will learn about sexuality?*

A SEXUAL KNOWLEDGE QUIZ

Many of you may already be sexually experienced, and as a result, you may think that you do not need a course in human sexuality. There is more to sexuality, however, than engaging in sexual intercourse. See how well you do on the following 50-question quiz. Do not be afraid to admit that you do not know the correct answer (don't guess)—no one except you is going to see the results. The answers are at the end of the quiz.

	True	False	Don't Know

1. Erections in men result, in part, from a bone that protrudes into the penis.

2. Sperm can be produced only in an environment several degrees lower than normal body temperature.

3. The hymen is a reliable indicator of whether or not a woman is a virgin.

4. The inner two-thirds of the vagina is highly sensitive to touch.

5. Many men experience nipple erection when they become sexually aroused.

6. Most men and women are capable of multiple orgasms.

7. Breast size in women is related to the number of mammary glands.

8. Before puberty, boys can reach orgasm, but they do not ejaculate.

9. During sexual intercourse, orgasm in women results from direct stimulation of the clitoris by the penis.

10. Menstrual discharge consists of sloughed off uterine tissue, blood, and cervical mucus.

11. For hygiene reasons, you should avoid sex during menstruation.

12. Ovulation generally occurs just before menstruation.

13. After a vasectomy, a man can reach orgasm but does not ejaculate.

14. AIDS is the diagnosis for people who have human immunodeficiency virus (HIV).

15. A girl can get pregnant as soon as she starts having menstrual periods.

16. The combination birth control pill works primarily by preventing implantation of a fertilized egg.

17. Taking the oral contraceptive pill results in fewer serious health problems than do pregnancy and childbirth.

18. Women show their highest levels of sexual desire at the time of ovulation.

19. There are about 12 million new cases of sexually transmitted diseases in the United States each year.

20. The major cause of AIDS is homosexuality.

21. If gonorrhea is not treated, it can sometimes turn into syphilis.

22. Most women do not show symptoms in the early stages of gonorrhea or chlamydia.

23. Gonorrhea, syphilis, and herpes can be successfully treated with antibiotics.

	True	False	Don't Know
24. In vitro fertilization involves a process where part of fetal development occurs in a test tube.	_____	_____	_____
25. It is usually safe to have sexual intercourse during the 7th and 8th months of pregnancy.	_____	_____	_____
26. "Prepared childbirth" (e.g., Lamaze) refers to delivering a baby without the use of drugs.	_____	_____	_____
27. Most healthy people in their 60s or older continue to engage in sexual behavior.	_____	_____	_____
28. Men's descriptions of orgasm are different from women's descriptions of orgasm.	_____	_____	_____
29. Excessive masturbation can cause serious medical problems.	_____	_____	_____
30. The birth control pill gives women some protection against sexually transmitted diseases.	_____	_____	_____
31. Women who masturbated to orgasm during adolescence generally have less difficulty reaching orgasm during intercourse than women who never masturbated.	_____	_____	_____
32. The frequency of sexual relations is highest for married couples aged 25 to 35.	_____	_____	_____
33. Adult male homosexuals have lower than normal levels of male hormones.	_____	_____	_____
34. Douching is an effective method of birth control.	_____	_____	_____
35. Recent evidence indicates that environmental factors are most important in determining one's sexual orientation.	_____	_____	_____
36. Prostitutes are generally hypersexual and have pathological sexual needs.	_____	_____	_____
37. Most convicted rapists committed their crimes because of an uncontrollable sex drive.	_____	_____	_____
38. There is a demonstrated link between the availability of pornography and sex crimes.	_____	_____	_____
39. It is against the law in many states for a married couple to engage in sexual behaviors other than penile-vaginal intercourse.	_____	_____	_____
40. Most cases of child molestation involve an acquaintance or relative of the child.	_____	_____	_____
41. A pregnant woman can transmit syphilis to the unborn baby.	_____	_____	_____
42. Exhibitionists and voyeurs often attempt to rape their victims.	_____	_____	_____
43. Nocturnal emissions ("wet dreams") are often an indication of a sexual problem.	_____	_____	_____
44. Alcohol is a central nervous system excitant that enhances sexual performance.	_____	_____	_____
45. Humans can crossbreed with animals with the use of artificial insemination techniques.	_____	_____	_____
46. Women's sexual desire decreases sharply after menopause.	_____	_____	_____

	True	False	Don't Know
47. Vaginal infections can be prevented by regular use of feminine hygiene products.	___	___	___
48. A woman's ability to have vaginal orgasms is related to penis size.	___	✔	___
49. Oral herpes can be transmitted to another person's genitals by oral-genital sexual relations.	✔	___	___
50. Unless testosterone is present during embryonic development, nature has programmed everyone to be born a girl.	✔	___	✗

ANSWERS—CHAPTER 1

1. false
2. true
3. false
4. false
5. true
6. false
7. false
8. true
9. false
10. true
11. false
12. false
13. false
14. false (only in the final stages)
15. true
16. false
17. true
18. false (no good evidence for this)
19. true
20. false (homosexuality does not cause AIDS)
21. false
22. true
23. false
24. false
25. true
26. false
27. true
28. false
29. false
30. false
31. true
32. true
33. false
34. false
35. false
36. false
37. false
38. false
39. true
40. true
41. true
42. false
43. false
44. false
45. false
46. false
47. false
48. false
49. true
50. true

These questions were not intended to be tricky or difficult. They are representative of the type of material that is covered in this book. How did you do? Fewer than one-fourth of the students in my classes are able to answer 40 or more questions correctly at the beginning of the semester. Fewer than half get 35 or more correct. Did you really know all the ones that you got right, or did you just make a good guess on some of them? If you were not certain of the answers to some of the questions, then that is sufficient reason to read this book.

CROSS-CULTURAL COMPARISONS

missionary position A face-to-face position of sexual intercourse in which the woman lies on her back and the man lies on top with his legs between hers. It was called this because Christian missionaries instructed people that other positions were unnatural.

ethnocentric The attitude that the behaviors and customs of one's own ethnic group or culture are superior to others.

It should come as no surprise that people are different. Some people like short hair, while others like it long. Some like blue eyes, while others prefer brown. Some people like to dress up; some like to dress down. People's sexual attitudes and behaviors differ as well. Some people, for example, have sexual intercourse only in the **missionary position** (i.e., the woman lying on her back with the man on top—so called because Christian missionaries instructed people that other positions were unnatural). Others prefer a variety of positions. Some people are most aroused by looking at breasts or a hairy chest. Other people become highly aroused by looking at legs or buttocks.

We learn to accept that other people in our own culture are different from ourselves, and we do not regard them as abnormal when their behavior falls within what we consider the "normal" range of responses. What is normal, however, is defined by the community in which we live. As different as we are, we share much in common. An outsider, such as a person from a different country, is often regarded as very strange by many people. Unfortunately, Americans have a reputation around the world of being **ethnocentric**—that is, viewing our own culture's behaviors and customs as correct or as the way things ought to be (a perception leading to the image of the "ugly American"). We must not lose sight of the fact that if we traveled to another country we would probably be regarded as strange. One country's customs and beliefs should not be regarded as correct or normal and another's as incorrect or abnormal. (In this book, I will make an exception in cases in which a culture sanctions sexual abuse.) Instead, the world can be viewed as one large community, with the behaviors and beliefs of all its peoples falling into the normal range of responses.

The topics covered in some chapters of this book are the same for all peoples of the world (e.g., anatomy, physiology, hormones). When the book discusses behaviors and attitudes, it will be primarily from the perspective of people in the United States. Behaviors of people in other cultures will be presented in special boxes, beginning with Box 1–A in this chapter. However, before going on, here is a brief introduction to sexual attitudes and behaviors in a few other cultures around the world. Some of them may seem funny, but remember, *we seem just as strange to them* as they seem strange to us.

SEXUAL ATTRACTIVENESS

Cultures differ with regard to which parts of the body they find to be erotic. In the United States, most people have negative thoughts about armpits, but Abkhazian men (Abkhaz was part of the former Soviet Union) are highly aroused at seeing women's armpits. The sight of a navel is considered highly arousing in Samoa. This generally is not true in the United States, but did you know that the TV censors would not allow actress Barbara Eden to have her navel exposed on the 1960s television show *I Dream of Jeannie?* A knee is considered to be erotic in New Guinea and the Celebes Islands. When anthropologist Martha Ward visited New Guinea in the early 1970s, she deboarded the plane wearing a miniskirt, blouse, and brassiere, customary clothing for American women at that time. She caused quite a ruckus. She wrote the following letter to one of her colleagues in the United States:

Dear Len,
I have had to change my manner of dressing. Thank goodness for the Sears Catalog. The minidresses and short skirts you all are wearing in the States cause quite a stir here. It seems that breasts are regarded as normal female equipment and useful only for feeding babies. Clothing for many women consists of a large towel or three yard length of brightly colored cloth. This is worn around the waist inside the house or in the yard. . . . [In public] if you have on a bra, you don't need a blouse. Bras are considered proper dress for women. Those black Maidenforms with the heavy stitched cups are particularly valued. When Americans are not around, it is sufficient to cover oneself only from the waist down. . . .

Breasts are not really erogenous, but legs are. Particularly that sexy area on the inside of the knee! No more miniskirts for me. Fitting in and observing local customs means that I have lengthened my skirts to below the knee. . . .

The American men watch women with nothing on above the waist. The Pohnpeian men comment on American women with short skirts. I am now dressed to please the standards of two cultures. . . . (From *Nest in the Wind: Adventures in Anthropology on a Tropical Island* by Martha C. Ward, © 1989 by Waveland Press, Inc. Reprinted with the permission of the publishers.)

Many groups of people find body weight to be an important determinant of sexual attractiveness. There is a great deal of pressure in our culture, for example, for men and women to remain thin. It is no coincidence that fashion models are very thin and that movie stars who are considered to be "sexy" have small waistlines. In many other countries, however, these people would not be considered attractive. For example, women who would be considered obese by most American men are found highly attractive in some other cultures. Adolescent girls are sometimes kept in huts and fed high-calorie diets in order to become more attractive (Gregersen, 1982).

What is considered to be sexually attractive can also change over time. Plump women, for example, were also considered to be very attractive in Western cultures a few centuries ago. If you don't believe this, just look at some famous paintings of nude women that were done 200 or 300 years ago (see Figure 1–1).

Figure 1–1 Rubens's *The Three Graces*, painted in 1630, is a good example of how cultural ideals change over time. Thinness is considered to be physically attractive today, but a thin woman in Rubens's time would have been considered unattractive.

American men find female breasts very sexually arousing. There are many areas of the world, however, where women's naked breasts have no erotic significance at all (see Figure 1–2). They are important only to hungry babies. On the other hand, Polynesian men are as fascinated with the size, shape, and consistency of women's genitals (particularly the mons veneris) as American men are with breasts (Marshall, 1971). In some African cultures, a woman's labia minora are considered to be the most erotic part of her body.

Although walking around naked in public would be considered highly deviant by most people in the United States, there are some cultures in New Guinea and Australia where people go about completely naked. They do, however, have firm rules about staring at other people's genitals. The Zulus of South Africa also have public rituals that call for people to be naked. They believe that a flabby body results from immoral behavior, and thus if someone refuses to undress for these rituals, it is taken as a sign that the person is trying to hide his or her immorality (Gregersen, 1982). These attitudes about the human body are in marked contrast to those that prevail in Islamic societies, where female sexuality is suppressed and women must cover their entire body and most of their face when they leave the privacy of their homes.

In some cultures people carve holes in their lips, while in others they stretch their lips or necks, or wear needles through their noses. In Borneo it is common for men to wear a rod through the end of their pierced penis. The rod, called a penis pin, has protuberances (e.g., gemstones, feathers, pig's bristles) at each end, which the men believe enhances women's pleasure during intercourse (Brown, 1990). Elaborate abdominal scars are considered to be very sexually attractive on women of the Kau culture in Sudan. It is obvious from the lack of universal standards that attitudes about the human body, and what is considered to be sexually attractive, are culturally learned responses.

SEXUAL BEHAVIORS AND ATTITUDES

Kissing is a highly erotic and romanticized part of sexual relations in Western cultures. You will probably be surprised to learn, therefore, that this practice is not shared by many cultures, including the Japanese, Hindus of India, and many groups in Africa and South America (Ford & Beach, 1951; Gregor, 1985). "When the Thonga first saw Europeans kissing they laughed, expressing this sentiment: 'Look at them—they eat each other's saliva and dirt'" (Ford & Beach, 1951). Foreplay before intercourse is entirely unheard of in some cultures.

Anthropologists believe that the most sexually permissive group of people in the world are the Mangaians, who live on the Cook Islands in the South Pacific (Marshall, 1971). Mangaian boys and girls play together until the age of 3 or 4, but after that they separate into age groups according to sex during the day. When the boys approach adolescence, the arrival of manhood is recognized by superincision of the penis (cutting the skin of the penis lengthwise on top). As the wound heals, the boy is instructed in all aspects of sex, including how to bring a girl to orgasm, which is considered important. Girls receive similar instructions from older women. The boy is then given to an experienced woman, who removes the superincision scab during intercourse and teaches the boy an array of sexual techniques. After that, the boy actively seeks out girls at night, having sex an average of 18 to 20 times a week. Mangaian adolescents are encouraged to have sex with many partners and engage in all types of sexual activities, including different positions of intercourse, oral-genital sex, anal sex, and axillary sex (i.e., placing the penis between the armpit or the breasts). Once they reach adulthood, Mangaian men and women become monogamous.

Many other societies in the South Pacific, including Samoa and Pohnpei, similarly encourage their teenage children to enjoy sexual relations (Ward, 1989). In some of these cultures, the boys go into the huts where teenage girls live and have sex with them while the girls' parents are present. The parents ignore them and act as if the children are invisible. In all of these societies, the physical pleasure of both sexes is emphasized (women have orgasm as often as men) and emotional attachments come later. They regard our custom of emphasizing love before sex as very strange.

The most sexually repressed society in the world is believed to be the Inis Baeg, a fictitious name (coined by anthropologists to preserve anonymity) for a group of people who live on an island off the coast of Ireland (Messenger, 1971). Any mention of sex is taboo, so that children are never told about things like menstruation and pregnancy, which are greatly feared. Nudity is strictly forbidden, to the extent that although they depend on fishing to survive, most of the Inis Baeg never learn how to swim (which requires taking off some clothing) and usually drown if they are in a boating accident. Children wear smocks, and their mothers do not entirely undress them during bathing, but instead wash one arm or leg at a time. Even married adults do not see each other completely naked—they do not bathe together and they wear smocks during sexual intercourse. Sexual relations are not regarded as something positive by either sex. Foreplay is unheard of, and intercourse, which is always done in the missionary position, is completed as quickly as possible because men consider it to be dangerous to their health (and, unlike Mangaian women, Inis Baeg women almost never have orgasm).

Between the two extremes of the Mangaians and the Inis Baeg is a large range of sexual attitudes and behaviors. You will find that many cultures are more

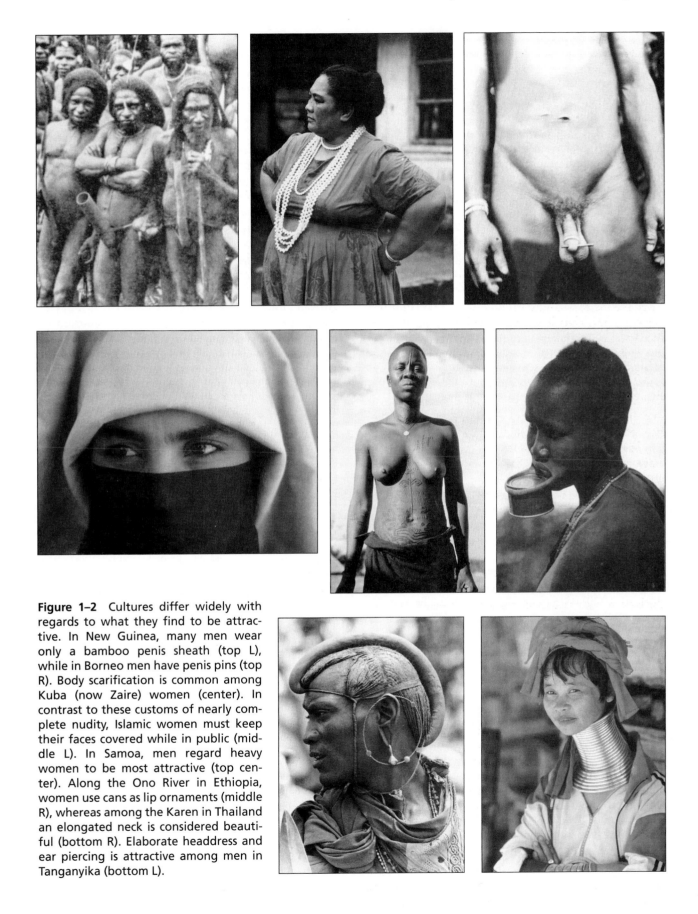

Figure 1–2 Cultures differ widely with regards to what they find to be attractive. In New Guinea, many men wear only a bamboo penis sheath (top L), while in Borneo men have penis pins (top R). Body scarification is common among Kuba (now Zaire) women (center). In contrast to these customs of nearly complete nudity, Islamic women must keep their faces covered while in public (middle L). In Samoa, men regard heavy women to be most attractive (top center). Along the Ono River in Ethiopia, women use cans as lip ornaments (middle R), whereas among the Karen in Thailand an elongated neck is considered beautiful (bottom R). Elaborate headdress and ear piercing is attractive among men in Tanganyika (bottom L).

restrictive (or repressed) than our own. For example, until very recently it was taboo to openly discuss sex in China, Japan, Russia, and many African cultures (Ecker, 1994; Kitazawa, 1994; Rivkin-Fish, 1999). Oral-genital sex is common in Western cultures, but most African cultures consider it to be disgusting (the same way they regard kissing, you recall). In many Islamic parts of the world, women's sexuality is suppressed by mutilation of the genitals during childhood (see Box 4–A).

On the other hand, many cultures are more permissive (or tolerant) than our own. In Chapter 11, for example, you will read about the Sambian culture where homosexual relations are expected among young boys and teenaged boys (Box 11–A). Sex with minors is a crime in Western culture, but in the Tiwi culture (Melville Island) girls are married to an adult man at age 7 and begin having sexual intercourse shortly afterwards. Incest is also a taboo in Western culture, but marriage between cousins or between uncles and nieces is often expected in other cultures (Box 17–C). Similarly, monogamy is the standard in Western cultures, while in many others polygamy is practiced (Box 14–A). Many of you have probably heard the story of the Hudson Bay Eskimos. It was once the custom for an Eskimo husband to share his wife with any traveler who stayed in the igloo overnight. Western men's eagerness to take advantage of this custom eventually brought it to an end.

Even the overall approach to sex can differ among cultures. For example, sex in Western cultures tends to focus on genital stimulation, orgasm, and physical gratification, whereas Eastern Tantric cultures emphasize spiritual union during sex (Box 15–A). On the other hand, in New Guinea there is a tribe called the Dugum Dani that expresses little interest in sex (Heider, 1979). Although they appear to be normal physically, husbands and wives sometimes go as long as 5 years without having sex. Unlike the Inis Baeg, they do not have a negative attitude about sex; they just do not regard sex as important.

CULTURAL DIVERSITY WITHIN THE UNITED STATES

To this point, I have referred to Western culture as if it were composed of a homogenous group of people. North America may originally have been settled primarily by Caucasian Christians of European descent, but the population today is much more diverse. In fact, it is predicted that during this century people whose ancestors came from Europe will become a minority in the United States. Today, a sizable proportion of the U.S. population is made up of African Americans, Latinos, and Asian Americans. However, even within these ethnic groups there are often distinct subgroups. Among Asian Americans, for ex-

ample, there are people whose ancestors came from Japan, China, Vietnam, Thailand, Korea, the Philippines, and South Pacific islands. Within each subculture there are several factors that can influence sexual attitudes and behaviors. These include religion, level of education, and socioeconomic status (see Hodes, 1999). In short, it is sometimes difficult to make generalizations even about cultural subgroups. With these cautions in mind, what generalizations can we make?

One example of cultural differences in sexual behavior in the United States is found when we examine oral-genital sexual relations. This has been a very common behavior among white middle-class (especially college-educated) Americans for at least 50 years (Kinsey et al., 1948, 1953). Today, it is also common among Latinos, but is practiced by only a minority of African Americans, with Asian Americans in between (Laumann et al., 1994). The small proportion of African Americans engaging in this behavior is explained in part by their African ancestry (remember, many African cultures have a very negative attitude about it) and also by the socioeconomic status of many black Americans. Oral-genital sex is less common among all low-educated, low-income groups, regardless of ethnic background. The sexual behavior of middle-class African Americans more closely resembles that of middle-class whites. As a whole, African Americans are also less likely than other cultural groups to masturbate, a behavior found more frequently in well-educated groups (Laumann et al., 1994).

In Mexico and other Latin-American countries, gender roles tend to be very stereotyped (Guerrero Pavich, 1986; Van Oss Marin & Gomez, 1994). As a general rule, men are allowed a great deal of liberty in their sexual behaviors. For women, on the other hand, there is considerable cultural pressure to remain a virgin before marriage. Thus, in Latin-American countries the percentage of women who have engaged in premarital sexual intercourse is much lower than for European-American and African-American women. This is partly the result of greater adherence to Roman Catholic values than is found in many other cultures. However, people of Latin-American heritage living in the United States tend to be less stereotyped in their relationships (Sanchez, 1997).

Among people living in the United States, Asian Americans are generally the least permissive in their sexual attitudes and behaviors. This is partly a reflection of restrictive attitudes about sex in Asian countries, but also results from the strong emphasis that people from many Asian countries place on family and social conformity. Asian Americans tend to have very low rates for both premarital intercourse and multiple sexual partners (Laumann et al., 1994). On the other hand, they have the highest rate (among the subcultures discussed) for abortions. This is a reflection not only of non-Western religious beliefs (that do not question the morality of abortion) but, often, also a result of having immigrated from overpopulated countries where the prevailing attitude is that it is best for the general good to limit the number of children one has.

Another factor that can influence sexual attitudes and behaviors is the number of generations that have passed since one's ancestors immigrated to the United States. The United States has been called the great melting pot. Throughout our history the descendants of numerous, different cultures have blended (melted) together to form a common culture. Our subcultures differ in some respects, but as a result of sharing similar experiences (e.g., schooling, exposure to TV and other media), we also have much in common. Today, interracial relationships, which were once taboo, help speed this process. Much of what you will read in the chapters ahead is true for nearly all subcultures in the United States. However, when there are major differences, you will read about them also.

> *PERSONAL REFLECTIONS*
> *Has your own cultural heritage affected your attitudes about sex? If so, how?*

HISTORICAL PERSPECTIVES

If the Mangaians and Inis Baeg represent the two extremes, where do we fall on this continuum? In many ways our behavior is permissive—we live during the so-called sexual revolution—but our attitudes about sex are often less than positive (evidenced, for example, by the fact that parents and children rarely talk about it together). The constant emphasis on sex on TV, in movies, in magazines, and on the radio gives children one type of message—sex is fun, sex is exciting, sex is great. At the same time, these same children get another type of message from their parents, school, and church—sex is not for you! Is it any wonder that many Americans have ambivalent attitudes about sex? Sex is something good on the one hand, yet bad on the other. We fall somewhere between the Mangaians and Inis Baeg. We are permissive, yet repressed. To see how we arrived at this point in the 2000s, we must examine the history of sexual attitudes in our own culture.

JUDAISM

Life for the biblical Jews was harsh. Living in nomadic tribes that roamed the desert areas of what is now referred to as the Middle East, they considered it a great advantage to have many children. The Jews were directed to do so in the first chapter of the first book of the Old Testament:

And God blessed them, and God said to them, "Be fruitful and multiply, and fill the earth and subdue it." (Genesis 1:28, Revised Standard Version)

Having many children assured the survival of the Jewish people. Thus, the Hebrews recognized that the primary purpose of sex was for *procreation* (to have children). Celibacy was looked upon as neglect of one's obligations and was regarded as sinful.

Sons were especially valued because of their dual roles as providers and defenders. In the strongly patriarchal Hebrew society, daughters and wives were regarded as property (of fathers or husbands), and there were many rules to guarantee that material property was passed on to legitimate offspring. Thus, the Hebrews were very concerned with the social consequences of sex. Sex outside of marriage, for example, was severely condemned and punished. A Jewish woman caught committing adultery was stoned to death, but a man who committed adultery was considered only to have violated another man's property rights. Rape, too, was considered to be a violation of property rights. The punishment for homosexuality and bestiality was death (Leviticus 18:22–29).

In contrast to those harsh views, the Old Testament presents a positive view of sex within a marriage. A good example of this can be found in the Song of Solomon (Song of Songs):

> *How graceful are your feet in sandals,*
> *O queenly maiden!*
> *Your rounded thighs are like jewels,*
> *the work of a master hand.*
> *Your navel is a rounded bowl*
> *that never lacks mixed wine.*
> *Your belly is a heap of wheat,*
> *encircled with lilies.*
> *Your two breasts are like two fawns,*
> *twins of a gazelle. . . .*
> *How fair and pleasant you are,*
> *O loved one, delectable maiden!*
> *You are stately as a palm tree,*
> *and your breasts are like its clusters.*
> *I say I will climb the palm tree*
> *and lay hold of its branches.* (Song of Solomon 7:1–8, Revised Standard Version)

The human body, including the genitals, was not considered to be obscene, for God had created Adam and Eve in his own image. Mutual sexual pleasure was very important to Hebrew couples. In fact, sex between husband and wife was cause for rejoicing, a gift from God. A married couple could engage in any sexual activity, with only one restriction—the husband had to ejaculate within his wife's vagina (not doing so was considered "spilling of seed" because it could not lead to having children). Although Jewish women had second-class status, a Jewish wife could take an active role in sexual relations. In fact, her sexual rights were guaranteed in the marriage contract. For example, husbands were not allowed to change jobs without the wife's consent if it meant a change in conjugal rights. The ancient Hebrews did not distinguish between physical and spiritual love.

> *PERSONAL REFLECTIONS*
> *The Hebrews of biblical times believed that humans were created in the image of God, and therefore they were not ashamed of any part of their bodies, including their genitals. What do you think about this? How do you feel about your own body? (Don't just respond "good" or "bad," but explain in some detail.)*

THE GREEKS AND ROMANS

The ancient Greeks and Romans, like the Jews, placed a strong emphasis on marriage and the family. Although procreation was viewed as the primary purpose of marital sex, a couple had children for the state, not God. Unlike the biblical Jews, Greek and Roman men were allowed considerable sexual freedom outside marriage. In Greece, sexual relations between men and adolescent boys in a teacher-student relationship were not only tolerated but were encouraged as part of the boy's intellectual, emotional, and moral development. Greek women were viewed as second-class citizens, bearers of children with little or no legal status. Roman women were considered to be the property of their husbands, but they enjoyed more social prominence than Greek women.

The Greeks idealized the human body and physical beauty (as is evident in their art), but in the latter part of the Greek era there was a strong emphasis on spiritual development and a denial of physical pleasures. The basis for this change was **dualism,** the belief that body and soul are separate (and antagonistic). Dualism gave rise to an *ascetic philosophy*, which taught that from wisdom came virtue, and that these could only be achieved by avoiding strong passions. Plato, for example, believed that a person could achieve immortality by avoiding sexual desire and striving for intellectual and spiritual love (thus the term *platonic* for sexless love). As you will see next, dualism was a major influence on early Christian leaders.

CHRISTIANITY

Like the theology of the latter-period Greeks, Christian theology separated physical love from spiritual love. The period of decline of the Roman empire, which coincided with the rise of Christianity, was marked by sexual excess and debauchery. The views of the early Chris-

dualism The belief that body and soul are separate and antagonistic.

tians regarding sex were partly the result of an attempt to keep order.

There is little written record about Jesus' views on sex. It is known that except for grounds of adultery, he forbade divorce. It is written in the Gospel of Matthew that Jesus said, "Everyone who looks at a woman lustfully has already committed adultery with her in his heart." (Matthew 5:27, Revised Standard Version). Thus, it was not enough for a Christian to conform behaviorally; there was to be purity of inner thoughts as well.

The teachings of the early Christian writers reflect their own personal struggles with sexual temptation. One of the most influential of the early writers was **St. Paul** (about A.D. 5–67), who was a fanatical persecutor of Christians until he had a vision and was converted to Christianity. St. Paul regarded the body as evil and struggled to control it:

> **For I know that nothing good dwells within me, that is, in my flesh. I can will what is right, but I cannot do it. For I do not do the good I want, but the evil I do not want is what I do. . . . For I delight in the law of God, in my inmost self, but I see in my members another law at war with the law of my mind and making me captive to the law of sin which dwells in my members.** (Romans 7:18, 7:22–23, Revised Standard Version)

St. Paul blamed Eve for the expulsion from the Garden of Eden and viewed women as temptresses. He strongly believed, as did many others, that the second coming of Christ (signifying the end of the world) would occur in his lifetime and preached that a celibate life-style was the way to heaven. Marriage was only for the weak-willed:

> **It is well for a man not to touch a woman. . . . To the unmarried and the widows I say that it is well for them to remain single as I do. But if they cannot exercise self-control, they should marry. For it is better to marry than to be aflame with passion . . . if you marry, you do not sin. . . . From now on, let those who have wives live as though they had none.** (Corinthians 7:1, 7:8–9, 7:28, 29, Revised Standard Version)

Some have interpreted these ambiguous passages to mean that Paul believed that sex within marriage was sinful. Scholars now say that Paul did not believe that marital sex was a sin, but that he was concerned that married couples who sexually desired one another would become too involved in worldly (physical) concerns (Deming, 1995; Poirier & Frankovic, 1996). Paul's argument was that celibacy was spiritually superior to marriage. Thus, Paul regarded marriage as a compromise (and a rather poor one at that) to deal with the problems of the flesh. His followers believed that women should be subordinate to men, and therefore should assume the bottom position during sexual intercourse.

St. Jerome (about A.D. 340–420), who spent years fasting in the desert trying to get rid of visions of dancing girls, said a man who loved his wife too passionately was guilty of adultery.

> **A wise man ought to love his wife with judgment not with passion. Let a man govern his voluptuous impulses, and not rush headlong into intercourse. . . . He who too ardently loves his own wife is an adulterer.** (Hunt, 1959, p. 115)

Pope John Paul II created some controversy within the Catholic Church when he appeared to echo the beliefs of St. Jerome:

> **Adultery in the heart is committed not only because a man looks in a certain way at a woman who is not his wife . . . but precisely because he is looking at a woman that way. Even if he were to look that way at his wife, he would be committing adultery.** (*New York Times*, October 10, 1980)

The major influence on Christian beliefs was **St. Augustine** (A.D. 354–430), whose life was full of conflict, beginning with his birth to a pagan father and a Christian mother (Figure 1–3). He had a mistress and a son at an early age and continued to have numerous sexual affairs into his early 30s, including some with male friends—"I muddied the stream of friendship with the filth of lewdness and clouded its clear waters with hell's black river of lust" (*The Confessions of St. Augustine*, Book III, chap. 1). He is reported to have prayed, "Give me chastity and continence, but do not give it yet" (*The Confessions*, Book VIII, chap. 7). After reading the works of St. Paul, he converted to Christianity and thereafter led an ascetic life.

It was Augustine, more than anyone else, who solidified the Church's antisexual attitude. Augustine believed that all sexual intercourse was sinful, and thus all children were born from the sin of their parents. As a result of the downfall of Adam and Eve, he argued, sex was shameful and equated with guilt. Augustine recognized that married couples had to engage in sexual intercourse for procreation, but denounced sex between a husband and wife for the purpose of pleasure. He even considered marital sex for the purpose of procreation to be an unpleasant necessity:

> **They who marry . . . if the means could be given them of having children without intercourse with their wives, would they not with joy unspeakable embrace so great a blessing? Would they not with great delight accept it?** (Cited in Goergen, 1975)

Augustine not only departed from the Hebrews in denying the pleasures of (marital) sex, but in the process also differed from them by showing complete disgust for the human body: "Between feces and urine we are born."

Figure 1–3 St. Augustine (A.D. 354–430). Augustine was the major influence on Christian attitudes about sex. He believed that all sexual acts were driven by lust and were therefore evil, including sex within marriage.

Although the New Testament allowed bishops and deacons to have wives (I Timothy 3:2, 3:12), celibacy became an official part of the Catholic Church with a decree by Gregory VII in 1074. Augustine's beliefs were systematized by St. Thomas Aquinas (1225–1274) and became doctrine in 1563. Any sexual behavior that was done for pleasure and excluded the possibility of procreation was considered lust and a sin against nature. In descending order of infamy, this included bestiality, homosexuality, intercourse in "unnatural" positions, and masturbation (Murray, 1998). The Catholic Church's view that the only reason married couples should engage in sex for procreation was confirmed by Pope John Paul II as recently as 1993 ("Veritatis Splendor") and 1995 ("Evangelium Vitae"). Although not all Christians today are of the same denomination, they all share the same early history, and thus they all have been influenced by the beliefs of St. Paul and St. Augustine.

> "I grew up being told my body was a filthy thing, sex was a sin, and I would burn in hell if I paid any attention to it. Everybody shoved the word 'sin' down my throat and showed disgust at the slightest infraction, real or imagined, of 'God's rules.' The result is that I had an extremely low

self-esteem during adolescence, as well as an inner struggle between mother nature and the expectations of 'God,' which about drove me nuts." (from the author's files)

In the 16th century, Martin Luther (1483–1546) and John Calvin (1509–1564) organized revolts against the Catholic Church. Some of their followers later came to be known as Puritans. The *Reformation* movement, as it was called, included opposition to celibacy. Luther believed, for example, that priests and nuns should be allowed to marry in order to solve the problem of lust. Adultery, homosexuality, and masturbation were still viewed as sinful and severely punished (because of the perceived threat to the family unit), but the linkage of sex with love in marital relationships was emphasized. Thus, the Puritans had a positive view of sex within marriage, and this attitude was brought to the New World with them. The Puritans proved their worthiness of going to heaven, not by denying the pleasurable aspects of marital sex but by living frugal and industrious lives.

> ### PERSONAL REFLECTIONS
> *Christian views about sex were strongly influenced by St. Augustine, who believed that the only legitimate reason to engage in sex was to have children. How do you feel about engaging in sex for pleasure? How do you feel about masturbation? With regard to sexual behavior, how has your religious upbringing affected your opinions about what is right or wrong?*

VICTORIANISM

The 19th century is often referred to as the **Victorian era,** after Queen Victoria (1819–1901), who reigned in England for most of the century. It was an era of public prudery and purity. All pleasurable aspects of sex were denied. Women, who just a few centuries before had been considered sexual temptresses, were now viewed as asexual (i.e., having no interest in sex) and as innocent as children. Men were the ones who were viewed as responsible for lust. According to Victorian moralists, a woman's place was in the home, and wives engaged in sex only to perform their "wifely duties." Women's dresses covered the neck, back, and ankles, and the prudery was carried to such an extreme that even piano legs were covered. At the dinner table, it was considered improper to ask for a "breast" of chicken.

The medical views of the 19th century generally supported the antisexuality of the era. A prominent Swiss physician named Tissot had published a book in 1741 in which he claimed that masturbation could lead to blindness, consumption, other physical disorders, and insanity. This view had numerous supporters in the medical community, includ-

Victorian era The period during the reign of Queen Victoria of England (1819–1901). With regard to sexuality, it was a time of great public prudery (the pleasurable aspects of sex were denied) and many incorrect medical beliefs.

"If sex is dirty and disgusting, why should I save it for someone I love?"

Reproduced by Special Permission of *Playboy* magazine: copyright © 1993 by Playboy.

ing Benjamin Rush (1745–1813), the father of American psychiatry. The eminent German neurologist Richard von Krafft-Ebing classified sexual disorders in his *Psychopathia Sexualis* (1886), in which the predominant theme was a link between sexuality and disease. To the Victorians, including the physicians of that era, loss of semen was thought to be as detrimental to a man's health as loss of blood, a belief that had originated with the Greek physician Hippocrates (Haller & Haller, 1977). As a result of these beliefs, parents often went to ridiculous lengths to prevent masturbation (Hall, 1992) and nocturnal emissions ("wet dreams," or spermatorrhea, as it was called then), including having their boys castrated or circumcised or making them wear antimasturbation devices to bed at night. Between 1856 and 1932, the U. S. government awarded at least 33 patents for sexual restraint devices (Schwartz, 1973); even more were awarded in England. Two such inventions are shown in Figure 1–4. The "spermatorrhea ring" was invented by a Dr. J. L. Milton in the 1800s, and the "surgical appliance" was patented by one J. E. Heyser in 1911. Patents were even issued for devices designed to prevent horses from masturbating.

The Victorians' concerns that "excess" sex was harmful to one's health were not limited to masturbation in children and adolescents. Adults were supposed to show restraint in their desires for sexual intercourse as well, even within marriage. Here's an example of the attitudes that prevailed during that time:

It is best to avoid marrying widows, who may have had one or more husbands, whose premature

Figure 1–4 Two antisex devices invented and patented during the Victorian era: (A) a spermatorrhea ring to prevent nocturnal emissions; (B) a "surgical appliance" made of leather straps and metal pockets to prevent masturbation.

deaths were caused by other than accident . . . for . . . they are likely to possess qualities in them, that in their exercise use up their husband's stock of vitality, rapidly weakening the system, and so causing premature death. (John Cowan, *The Science of a New Life*, 1869)

The amount of misinformation that was distributed by the medical community during the Victorian era is really quite appalling. For example, a group of British doctors claimed to have evidence that touching a menstruating woman could spoil hams (*British Medical Journal*, 1878). Consider also a book titled *Perfect Womanhood* by "Mary Melendy, M.D., Ph.D.," published in 1903. It was a book of advice for women, and in addition to the usual warnings about masturbation and excessive sex, it contained the following advice about when it was safest to have intercourse (to avoid pregnancy):

It is a law of nature—to which there may be some exceptions—that conception must take place at about the time of the menstrual flow. . . . It may be said with certainty, however, that from ten days after the cessation of the menstrual flow until three days preceding its return, there is little chance of conception, while the converse is equally true. . . . This law is to the effect that if the conception takes place in the early part of the menstrual period a female child will be the result; if in the latter part, a male child will be born.

These beliefs were based on the fact that most nonhuman mammalian females have a bloody discharge at the time of ovulation (the optimal time for conception to occur). As you will learn in Chapter 3, this is not true for women (ovulation occurs about two weeks before the menstrual discharge begins); yet some people still believe it.

The private lives of Victorians may not have been as repressed as the image of modesty and prudery they conveyed in public. A recently discovered questionnaire of 45 married women conducted by Dr. Clelia Mosher in 1892 reveals that most of the women desired and enjoyed sex (Jacob, 1981). There was also a great deal of hypocrisy during this era. Prostitution and pornography flourished, and extramarital affairs were common (Trudgill, 1976).

Although Queen Victoria died in 1901, the Victorian era of repressed sexuality continued well into the 20th century. For example, some television shows in the 1950s would show Elvis Presley only from the waist up. During this same time period, television hosts and actors were not even allowed to use the word "pregnant" ("with child" was considered to be the proper term). When Lucy of the *I Love Lucy* show first said "pregnant" on television, it caused a public outrage. With this degree of negativity and repressiveness regarding sex, how did Western culture enter into the sexual revolution?

THE SEXUAL REVOLUTION

It was not unusual for our great-great-grandfathers, whether they worked on the farm or in the city, to put in 12- to 16-hour days, often 6 days a week. Child labor was common, so that many children were also working these hours. In addition to puritanical Victorian ideals, the lack of leisure time limited opportunities for sexual relations.

The industrial revolution slowly changed all this. Mechanization and more efficient means of production eventually led to shorter workweeks, freeing people to engage in leisure activities. The invention of the automobile allowed young people to get away from the watchful eyes of their parents and neighbors. The Great Depression of the 1930s and then World War II in the 1940s again prevented most people from having much leisure time. The 1950s saw the first peacetime generation of American teens whose families were affluent enough to provide them with an automobile. For the first time, Americans had two things necessary to engage in leisure sex: time and mobility.

The growing women's rights movement eventually resulted in more equality for women, and they began to take an active role in sexual matters (they were not the passive, asexual creatures portrayed by Victorian moralists). With the introduction of penicillin in 1940, people worried less about sexually transmitted diseases such as syphilis and gonorrhea. If they got these diseases, they could now be cured.

In 1960, the birth control pill and the IUD became available, so that having sexual intercourse could be spontaneous and people did not have to worry about unwanted pregnancies. The major impact of this was that the pleasurable aspects of sex could be completely separated from the reproductive aspects. It did not take long before people began to think that one had nothing to do with the other.

As a result of these several factors, we entered the so-called **sexual revolution,** a time when more people than ever in the past were supposedly engaging in more sex, beginning at an earlier age, and with more partners. We have already discussed how movies, TV, and magazines portrayed sexual relations (including premarital and extramarital sex) as exciting and desirable. The newest generation of Americans to come of age was under pressure, not to abstain from premarital sex but to engage in it.

The sexual revolution continued unabated in the 1960s and 1970s, but the 1980s saw the emergence of HIV and AIDS as a worldwide life-threatening disease. However, when the large majority of new cases in the United States were diagnosed in gay men and intravenous drug users, Americans were slow to respond. The percentage of college students who had engaged in sexual intercourse did not decline during the 1980s, and may have even increased. By the mid-1990s more and more people were becoming aware that the virus leading to AIDS could be spread during heterosexual intercourse, and researchers began

---

sexual revolution A period in U.S. history, beginning about 1960, of increased sexual permissiveness.

---

to see evidence of what may be a more conservative attitude about sex. Not only were more sexually active young people using condoms than in the past (e.g., CDC, 2000b; Sonenstein et al., 1998), but there was also a decline in the number of teenagers who had had sexual intercourse (Centers for Disease Control and Prevention, 2000b; *Newsweek*, 2000b). As a result, there has also been a decline in teenage pregnancies, births and abortions.

We do not yet know whether these recent trends signal an end to, or a change in, the sexual revolution. Compared to past generations, behaviorally our society is still permissive, but many people still do not have a positive attitude about their own sexuality. Many of the negative attitudes of the early Christian church and the Victorian era are still with us. Even at the height of the sexual revolution, most parents could not bring themselves to have meaningful discussions with their children about sex. It is no wonder that so many people still have so many questions, doubts, and anxieties about sex.

SEX AS A SCIENCE

Until the last few centuries, religion was the primary influence in intellectual endeavors. The rise of science was slow and was met with much resistance. Galileo (1564–1642), for example, was forced to publicly recant his support for Copernicus's theory that the earth moved around the sun—and not vice versa, as stated in Church doctrine—or face excommunication. People's desire for facts and knowledge could not be stifled, however, and the following centuries saw great advances in the biological and physical sciences. Science slowly replaced religion as the authority on most subjects.

Unfortunately, sexual behavior as a subject for scientific investigation met with more resistance than most others. As we have already seen, even the medical professionals of the 19th and early 20th centuries were guilty of allowing their personal moral beliefs to interfere with their treatment of sexual subjects. Not until the last few decades have researchers interested in studying sexual behavior been able to apply the two tools necessary for scientific inquiry: observation and measurement. Let us take a brief look at a few individuals who were responsible for making sexual behavior a serious, objective field of study. Further details of their work will be discussed in later chapters.

SIGMUND FREUD (1856–1939)

Sigmund Freud, perhaps more than anyone else, is responsible for demonstrating the influence of sexuality in human life (Figure 1–5). It is all the more remarkable that he did so during the antisexual atmosphere of the Victorian era.

Figure 1–5 Sigmund Freud. Freud lived during the Victorian era, a period often described as being indiscriminately antisexual. He is given the major credit for showing the importance of sexuality in human behavior and motivations.

In actuality, Freud was not a sex researcher. Rather, he merely discussed sexuality as a primary motivation for behavior. Sexual energy—or *libido*, as Freud called it—was said to be channeled into particular areas of the body at different ages. First was the oral stage (in which the center of eroticism was the mouth), then the anal stage, followed by the phallic, latency, and genital stages. You will learn about these stages in greater detail in the chapter on development. Freud developed psychoanalysis as a means for evaluating and treating unconscious sexual motivations.

Although many people disagree with Freud's theory today (see, for example, Gray, 1993b), he remains important for his ideas on sexual motivation and sexuality in infants and children. However, like other Victorian doctors, Freud had many incorrect beliefs about sex, including the belief that loss of semen was as detrimental to a man's health as loss of blood.

HENRY HAVELOCK ELLIS (1859–1939)

When he was a young man in the 1800s, **Henry Havelock Ellis** (Figure 1–6) had frequent nocturnal emissions (wet dreams), which at the time was called spermatorrhea because Victorian physicians believed it was caused by the same thing that caused gonorrhea. The end result, Ellis was told, would be blindness, insanity, and eventual death. He wanted to commit suicide but was too fearful, so instead he kept a diary to document his death by

Figure 1–6 Henry Havelock Ellis. This English researcher published seven volumes about the psychology of sex between 1896 and 1928. His views were remarkably tolerant compared to those of most Victorian physicians and scientists.

this dreaded "disease." When his eyesight and reasoning did not deteriorate over the passing months, Ellis concluded that loss of semen did not really lead to death, and he became angry about the misconceptions held by the medical profession. In order to spare others the emotional trauma that he had suffered, Ellis devoted the remainder of his life to sexual research (although he reputedly remained a virgin himself).

As a physician practicing in Victorian England, Ellis collected a large amount of information about people's sexual behaviors from case histories and cross-cultural studies. He eventually published six volumes of a series titled *Studies in the Psychology of Sex* between 1896 and 1910, and a seventh in 1928. He argued that women were not asexual and that men's and women's orgasms were very similar. Ellis was particularly important for his emphasis on the wide range of human sexual behaviors and for his belief that behaviors such as masturbation and homosexuality should be considered normal. His tolerant view of sexuality was in marked contrast to that of the Victorian moralists and was a major influence on researchers for several generations.

ALFRED C. KINSEY (1894–1956)

The first formal exchange of information among sex researchers occurred in Berlin in 1926 at the First International Congress for Sex Research. However, the modern era of sex research did not begin until the publication of Alfred Kinsey's studies a quarter of a century later. Nearly everyone, of course, has heard of Kinsey's surveys on sexual behavior (1948, 1953). Similar to Ellis's boyhood fears of nocturnal emissions, as a boy Kinsey was greatly afraid he would go insane because he masturbated. Later in life he told a friend, "I decided I didn't want any young people going through the nonsense I went through" (Ericksen, 2000). When asked to teach a course on marriage at Indiana University in 1938, **Alfred C. Kinsey** was amazed to find how little objective data there were on sexual behavior. He started collecting his own data by giving questionnaires to his students, but he soon decided that personal interviews resulted in a greater amount of more detailed data. He was joined by Wardell Pomeroy, Clyde Martin, and Paul Gebhard (see Figure 1–7). Their final samples had a total of 5,300 men and 5,940 women.

Kinsey's work opened the door to a whole new field of research, but this did not come without a price. His findings that most people masturbated, that many people engaged in oral-genital sex, that

Figure 1–7   Alfred C. Kinsey and colleagues. This college professor's surveys of male sexual behaviors in 1948 and female sexual behaviors in 1953 marked the beginning of the modern era of sexuality research. From left to right: Clyde Martin, Paul Gebhard, Kinsey, Wardell Pomeroy.

women could have multiple orgasms, and that many men had had a homosexual experience shocked many people. He was accused of being antifamily and amoral. One Columbia University professor stated that "there should be a law against doing research dealing exclusively with sex" (*New York Times*, April 1, 1948). Some researchers believe that Kinsey was the major influence in changing 20th-century attitudes about sex (Bullough, 1998), and as a result his work is still the target of impassioned attacks today (e.g., Reisman & Eichel, 1990). Kinsey died an embittered man in 1956, but the Institute for Sex Research at Indiana University continues to be a major center for the study of human sexuality.

MASTERS AND JOHNSON

Kinsey paved the way for scientific behavioral studies of sexual behavior, but the study of functional anatomy and physiological studies of sex were still limited to experiments with laboratory animals. Dr. Denslow Lewis, a prominent Chicago gynecologist, presented the first frank discussion of the physiology of sex to the annual meeting of the American Medical Association in 1899. He graphically described erection and vaginal lubrication, and even noted that women could have multiple orgasms (and thus could enjoy sex). His paper was not well accepted. When Lewis had finished with his presentation, Dr. Howard Kelly, the leading gynecologist of the day, responded: "I do hope we shall not have to go into details in discussing this subject. Its discussion is attended with more or less filth and we besmirch ourselves by discussing it in public." Papers read at meetings of the American Medical

Association were routinely published in the *Journal of the American Medical Association*, but the journal refused to publish Lewis's.

More than half a century later, William Masters, a physician, and Virginia Johnson, a behavioral scientist (Figure 1–8), did not believe that experiments with rats could tell us a great deal about sexual behavior in people. Clellan Ford and Frank Beach (1951) had published a book a few years earlier in which they included observations of themselves having sexual intercourse with their wives, but it lacked objectivity. Therefore, in 1954, **Masters and Johnson** started to directly observe and record the physiological responses in humans engaged in sexual activity under laboratory conditions. Their results, which were based on over 10,000 episodes of sexual activity of 312 men and 382 women, were not published until 1966 *(Human Sexual Response)*. Although some people were shocked at Masters and Johnson's observational approach, calling them "scientific peeping Toms," most people in the medical community appreciated the importance of their findings.

As in all other areas of medical science, the understanding of anatomy and physiology led to methods for treating clinical problems and abnormalities. Masters and Johnson developed the first methods for treating sexual problems and opened a sexual therapy clinic in 1965. Their techniques were described in their 1970 book *Human Sexual Inadequacy*. The behavioral approach to treating sexual disorders, based on Masters and Johnson's work, has helped thousands of people to overcome sexual problems, thus improving their sexual relations and their overall satisfaction with life. William Masters died in 2001.

Figure 1–8   William Masters and Virginia Johnson. Their laboratory studies of the physiological responses that normally occur during sexual arousal led to the development of modern-day sexual therapy techniques.

Figure 1–9 Robert T. Michael, John H. Gagnon, Stuart Michaels, and Edward O. Laumann. They headed the most scientifically conducted sexual survey to date.

Social Life Survey was the most comprehensive nationally representative survey to date, as in-depth as the Kinsey surveys, but with scientifically sound sampling techniques. Since their initial work, Laumann's group has continued to publish results of their surveys (e.g., Laumann et al., 1997, 1999). However, the sample size was not large enough to allow the researchers to draw definite conclusions about small subgroups of the population. Similar national surveys were conducted in the early 1990s in England and France, thus allowing some accurate cross-cultural comparisons to be made.

THE NATIONAL HEALTH AND SOCIAL LIFE SURVEY

During the 1980s, there were calls from many sources to update what we know about sexual behavior of people in the United States. The Centers for Disease Control and Prevention argued the need for a new national survey (to combat AIDS) in the spring of 1988. In 1989, a panel of the National Academy of Science's National Research Council asked federal agencies to fund new surveys of sexual behavior in order to help with AIDS prevention. In the same year, the U.S. Department of Health and Human Services was getting ready to test a new survey designed to acquire information about the increase in teenage pregnancies, sexually transmitted diseases, and sexual abuse of children. The department initially approved $15 million for a large survey of 20,000 Americans that would be led by sociologist Edward Laumann. However, U.S. Senator Jesse Helms of North Carolina introduced an amendment in the Senate to eliminate funding for surveys of sexual behavior (saying that they were designed to "legitimize homosexual lifestyles"), and the White House Office of Management and Budget eventually blocked attempts to fund the survey.

Despite the new political obstacles, Laumann and his colleagues Robert Michael, John Gagnon, and Stuart Michaels (see Figure 1–9) eventually received $1.7 million from private foundations, and after scaling down their project, in 1992 they interviewed 3,432 adults (Laumann et al., 1994). Their random sample had a 79 percent participation rate (very high for this type of survey) and was a good representation of all English-speaking adults aged 18 to 59 living in the United States. Interviews were conducted face-to-face and lasted 90 minutes. In short, the National Health and

PERSONAL REFLECTIONS
How do you feel about sex as a subject for scientific study? Do you think researchers should ask people about their sexual behaviors? What about physiological studies in which researchers measure bodily responses while people actually engage in various sexual acts?

SCIENTIFIC METHODOLOGY

SURVEYS AND SAMPLES

Throughout this book you will see statistics about sexual behaviors (e.g., percentages of people, frequencies of behavior). In order to know such things, it was necessary for someone like Kinsey, for example, to ask people about their sexual attitudes and behaviors. This involves taking a survey. A **survey** is a study of people's attitudes, opinions, or behaviors. The researcher generally asks a standard set of questions, either in a face-to-face interview or on a paper-and-pencil questionnaire.

The researcher begins by specifying the **population**—the complete set of observations about which he or she wishes to draw conclusions. The population of interest may be quite large (e.g., all adults living in the United States), or it can be small (e.g., all adults living in a town). If the population of interest is large, it may not be possible to obtain responses from everyone. In this case, the researcher must take a **sample** (subset) from the population. There have been many such surveys, some of which you may have heard of: the Kinsey report, the Hunt report (done for *Playboy*), the Hite report, and surveys done by *Redbook*, *Cosmopolitan*, and

survey A study of people's attitudes, opinions, or behaviors. Responses are usually obtained either in a face-to-face interview or on a paper-and-pencil questionnaire.

population The complete set of observations about which a researcher wishes to draw conclusions.

sample A subset of a population of subjects.

other magazines. Sometimes the results of these surveys agree, but in other cases they disagree, sometimes considerably. Which ones should we trust to be true? Are any of them accurate?

It might seem to make sense to some of you that the accuracy of a survey would depend on the size of the sample (i.e., the number of people surveyed). Although sample size is important, there are other factors that, if not considered, can negate any advantage obtained by using a large sample. The classic example illustrating that bigger is not necessarily better is a survey conducted in 1936 by a magazine called *Literary Digest*. The magazine sent questionnaires to 10 million people whose names were gathered from lists of telephone and automobile owners. They asked these people whether they were going to vote for Franklin D. Roosevelt or Alfred M. Landon in the upcoming presidential election. Over 2 million people responded, and the results indicated that Landon, a Republican, would beat the Democratic incumbent Roosevelt by a landslide. In fact, Roosevelt beat Landon by a landslide. As a result, *Literary Digest* lost credibility and went out of business shortly thereafter.

How could a survey that included such a large number of people have been so wrong? The country was in the middle of the Great Depression, and most people were worrying about whether they could continue to buy food to feed their families. Only financially secure people could afford to own cars and have telephones, and they tended to vote Republican. However, most voters were registered Democrats. In other words, despite the large sample size, this survey was grossly inaccurate because of a built-in bias. It surveyed only a small subgroup of the population and was not representative of the entire country. For a sample to be accurate, it must be taken randomly.

What is random sampling? Does it mean blindly picking names from a phone book or stopping people on the street? No, because these types of samples might have the same built-in biases as the *Literary Digest* survey. A **random sample** is one in which observations are drawn so that all possible samples of the same size have an equal chance of being selected (see Minium et al., 1993). A special type of random sample is a **stratified random sample,** sometimes called a *representative sample* because it pretty accurately represents the target population. This is the type used by the Gallup and Harris polls to predict the outcome of presidential elections today. Before they take their surveys, these polls break the entire country down by sex, race, education, income, geographic location, and many other fac-

tors. They know, for example, exactly what percentage of the population is white, Protestant, college educated, and living in the Northeast. Their sample survey includes this percentage of people with these characteristics. As a result, the Gallup and Harris surveys are rarely off by more than a few percentage points (and because both are done scientifically, they generally agree with each other as well). Yet both polls survey only about 2,500 people out of an estimated 100 million voters.

Kinsey's two studies were quite large, but his samples were not randomly drawn from the U.S. population. They were what is known as *convenience samples*— samples made up of whatever group is available (such as students in a course). Kinsey's samples overrepresented midwestern, white, college-educated people, and also included a disproportionately large number of inmates from local prisons. Surveys conducted by magazines are also generally quite large, sometimes with over 100,000 respondents, but are they representative of the country as a whole? What kind of people read *Playboy* or *Hustler*? What kind of people read *Cosmopolitan* or *Ladies Home Journal*? One-third of the respondents to a 1982 *Playboy* magazine questionnaire said that they had engaged in group sex. Do you really believe this is true for the entire country?

There are more problems in taking a survey of people's sexual behavior than making sure it is representative of the population. Ask yourself the following questions:

1. How often do you masturbate?
2. How many sexual partners have you had in your lifetime?
3. Do you have sexual intercourse in different positions?
4. Do you engage in oral-genital sex?
5. Have you ever had a homosexual experience?
6. Have you ever had an extramarital affair?

Answering some of these questions may have made you feel uncomfortable, for these are very personal questions. How would we know that the people we are surveying are telling the truth? Some people might try to make themselves look good by lying when answering questions about their personal life, so some questionnaires contain "truth items," that is, questions such as "Have you ever told a lie?" It is assumed that everyone has told a lie in his or her life (maybe just a little one), so someone responding negatively to this item would be assumed to be not telling the truth.

Incorrect answers are not necessarily the result of intentional deceit, but can also be due to faulty recall. How well do you remember all the events of your childhood, for example? If couples are surveyed, what does the interviewer do if there are discrepancies in the

---

random sample A sample in which observations are drawn so that all other possible samples of the same size have an equal chance of being selected.

stratified random sample A sample in which subgroups are randomly selected in the same proportion as they exist in the population. Thus the sample is representative of the target population.

answers given by the two people? How can the interviewer decide who is telling the truth, or is it the case that they both recall events differently? For example, in one of my own surveys (King & LoRusso, 1997), we asked several hundred college students and their parents if they had ever had a meaningful discussion about sex while the students were growing up. Well over half of the students answered "no," but in 60 percent of these cases one or both of their parents said that there had been meaningful discussions.

With regard to sex surveys, two problems are particularly troublesome. Some people may exaggerate their sexual experiences, while others may try to hide certain aspects of their sexuality. Surveys often find, for example, that the number of female sexual partners reported by men is greater than the number of male partners reported by women (see Wiederman, 1997c). Problems like these can sometimes be minimized if the survey is done by questionnaire rather than by interview and the questions can be answered anonymously; that is, the respondent is assured that no one (including the person doing the survey) will ever know who he or she is (Durant & Carey, 2000). However, researchers have found that people sometimes give biased responses on sex surveys even when they are tested anonymously (Meston et al., 1998).

Okay, so now you know enough to design a good sex survey. First you stratify the population of people in which you are interested, and then you randomly sample a specified number of people from each of the subgroups. The questionnaires will be filled out anonymously and contain a few items to check for truthfulness. After all this, however, there is another major problem that plagues sex survey research. What do we do when people refuse to participate? In Morton Hunt's survey (1974), which was an attempt to update Kinsey's data (1948, 1953), only 20 percent of the people contacted agreed to participate. Shere Hite's often-cited surveys (1976, 1981, 1987) had only a 3–6 percent response rate. From a scientific point of view, it is necessary that everyone randomly selected to be in a survey participate in it, but it probably would not surprise you to learn that many people refuse to answer questions like those you just read. We cannot force people to do so. This is the problem of **volunteer bias.**

Are there differences between people who agree to participate in a sex survey and those who do not? Should we assume that people who refuse to answer are more conservative in their views and behavior than those who do answer? Or is it possible that the only difference in sexual behaviors between these two groups is that one regards sex as something very private and not to be shared with others? In fact, recent studies have found several differences between people who volunteer to participate in sexual studies and those who refuse. Volunteers had more sexual experi-

ences, were more interested in variety, had a more positive attitude about sex, and had less sexual guilt (Bogaert, 1996; Strassberg & Lowe, 1995). What this means is that the greater the number of people in a survey who refuse to participate, the more cautious we should be in making generalizations about the entire population.

AN EXAMPLE OF PROBLEMS IN SURVEY STUDIES: WHAT DOES "SEX," "HAD SEX," AND "SEXUAL RELATIONS" MEAN?

In 1998, when President Clinton appeared on national television to address accusations that he had had sexual relations with Monica Lewinsky, a White House intern, he claimed, "I did not have sexual relations with that woman." Many people assumed that he had lied when it was later discovered that the president and Ms. Lewinsky had engaged in oral-genital relations. But did he really lie?

In a study conducted by the Kinsey Institute, researchers asked students at a midwestern state university, "Would you say you 'had sex' with someone if the most intimate behavior you engaged in was . . . a person had oral (mouth) contact with your genitals?" or ". . . . you had oral (mouth) contact with a person's genitals?" (Sanders & Reinisch, 1999). Only 40 percent of the college students responded that they would say that they had "had sex." Students who had never engaged in penile-vaginal intercourse were the most likely not to regard oral-genital contact as having "had sex." Interestingly, 20 percent of the respondents did not regard penile-anal intercourse as having "had sex."

It should be noted that the Kinsey Institute's data were collected in 1991 (before the Clinton-Lewinsky episode), were limited to a single college campus, and the response rate was low. In 1998 (after the episode became public knowledge), five news organizations conducted telephone surveys (see Smith, 1999, for a review) in which they asked people if "sexual relations" included (a) more than sexual intercourse or (b) "oral sex." When phrased this way, 73 to 87 percent of respondents said yes, but this still means that 18 to 27 percent disagreed or were not sure. In a recent study, about half the students surveyed on a college campus did not regard oral sex as "sex" (Bogart et al., 2000).

> "... about a year into the relationship, after engaging in oral sex, we came very close to actually having sexual intercourse. I stopped because I didn't want to have sex until marriage ... " (from the author's files)

It is well established that on any survey of self-reported behavior, the wording of the questions can strongly influence results (Smith, 1999). The Kinsey Institute's study makes

volunteer bias A bias in research results that is caused by differences between people who agree to participate and others who refuse.

it very clear that sex researchers (and authors of sexuality textbooks) must be specific when they use terms such as "sex" or "had sex." Unless otherwise specified (e.g., vaginal intercourse, anal intercourse, oral-genital sex), in this book I will use the terms "sex" and "had sex" in the way as defined by the National Health and Social Life Survey (Laumann et al., 1994):

> . . . By "sex" or "sexual activity," we mean any mutually voluntary activity with another person that involves genital contact and sexual excitement or arousal, that is, feeling really turned on, even if intercourse or orgasm did not occur.

PERSONAL REFLECTIONS
Would you tell the truth on a survey about sexual behavior? What if you could answer anonymously? Why or why not?

CORRELATION

You are probably aware that there is a relationship between high school grade-point averages and grades earned during the first year of college. The same is true of performance on certain standardized tests (the SAT or ACT, for example) and freshman-year grades. **Correlation** is a mathematical measure of the degree of relationship between two variables. Correlations can be either *positive* (increases in one variable are associated with increases in the other) or *negative* (increases in one variable are associated with decreases in the other), or, for a case in which there is no relationship, zero.

The association between two variables is rarely perfect. We all know students who had mediocre scores on their SAT or ACT test but who did very well in college (perhaps because they are exceptionally motivated and worked hard). On the other hand, a few students who do very well on their entrance tests do rather poorly in college (perhaps because they are not motivated). Generally, however, the association is good enough so that colleges and universities can use the test scores to predict performance in school. The greater the correlation between two variables, the more accurately we can predict the standing in one from the standing in another.

Correlations are also found in studies of human sexuality. For example, in their nationally representative survey, Laumann and his colleagues (1994) found that the more sex a married person has, the more likely he or she is to masturbate (a positive correlation). This may be interesting, but there is a major limitation to the correlational method—correlation never proves causation. In the case of the relationship between sex and masturbation, we cannot tell whether frequent intercourse leads to (causes) frequent masturba-

correlation A mathematical measure of the degree of relationship between two variables.

direct observations Observing and recording the activity of subjects as they conduct their activities.

case studies An in-depth study of an individual.

tion or frequent masturbation leads to frequent intercourse. Or maybe there is a third variable that similarly affects both frequency of intercourse and frequency of masturbation. Laumann's group, for example, believed that frequency of intercourse and masturbation was a reflection of a person's overall sex drive. Although we must use caution in drawing conclusions from correlations, they are often very useful in pointing the way to more systematic research.

DIRECT OBSERVATIONS

You have just learned that one of the main problems with conducting a survey is ascertaining the truthfulness of responses. One way around this problem is to make **direct observations** of people's behavior. Anthropologists do this when they study the behavior of people of other cultures in their natural settings *(naturalistic observation* or *ethnographic research)*. This is the type of study that Marshall (1971) did of the Mangaians and Messenger (1971) did of the Inis Baeg. Of course, people may not behave normally if they know that they are being observed (the *observer effect)*, so it is necessary for the observer to take great care to interfere as little as possible.

For most people, sexual behavior is not done in the presence of others, so some researchers have used what is called the *participant-observer method,* in which the researcher observes while he or she participates. In an early study on "swinging," for example, anthropologist Gilbert Bartell (1970) and his wife attended swingers' parties and observed people engaging in group sex.

Direct observation studies can also be done in the lab. The classic example is the work of Masters and Johnson, who, you recall, observed over 10,000 episodes of sexual activity in their laboratory in St. Louis (Masters & Johnson, 1966). For Masters and Johnson, the advantage of observing behavior in the lab was that they could make close observations and also take measures with electrophysiological recording equipment. However, the same limitations apply here as with the previous methods. Were the people Masters and Johnson studied affected by the fact that they knew they were being observed (observer effect)? Are people who would volunteer to have sex under these conditions different from the general population (volunteer bias)? Masters and Johnson were interested in physiological responses, which are probably the same for most people, but we still must be cautious when making generalizations about the entire population.

CASE STUDIES

Clinical psychologists and psychiatrists commonly do in-depth studies of individuals, called **case studies.** They may gather information from questionnaires, interviews with other persons, and even public records, but most of what they learn usually comes from face-to-face interviews conducted over a long period of time. The goal of a case study is to understand a person's behavior and motivations as much as possible. Some of Freud's case studies—such as the case of Little Hans, a 5-year-old boy who had a great fear of horses—are still read today. Freud eventually concluded that Hans's fear of powerful animals grew out of his masturbatory behavior and was actually a disguise for his fear that his father might cut his penis off.

One potential problem with case studies is that the therapist's observations and conclusions might be biased by his or her own emotions and values (**observer bias**). During the Victorian era, for example, Freud and other physicians believed that masturbation was dangerous and would eventually lead to neurosis (Groenendijk, 1997). In today's world, self-exploration is regarded as normal for young children. Do you suppose that a therapist today would attach great importance to Hans's masturbation?

When working extensively with an individual, a therapist may try different and new techniques, and thus case studies are often the first published reports we have of potentially beneficial treatments. Again, however, great caution must be used in making generalizations about the effect of the treatment for others.

EXPERIMENTAL RESEARCH

The biggest limitation of the research methods you have just read about is that none of them can be used to demonstrate cause-and-effect relationships between two variables. To do so, we must use the **experimental method.** With this approach, the researcher systematically manipulates some variable, called an *independent variable*, while keeping all other variables the same. The variable that is measured is called the *dependent variable*. Typically, the researcher compares two groups (sometimes more). One group receives the experimental treatment and the other (called a control group) does not. If there is any difference between groups in the dependent variable, we can conclude that it was caused by manipulating the independent variable.

I will use one of my own studies as an example (King et al., 1993). As I mentioned earlier, few of my students say that they ever had a meaningful discussion about sex with their parents. The question of interest was whether completion of a college sexuality education course would increase the likelihood that students would talk to their own children about sex. Fifty-two former students with children who were at least 5 years old were surveyed 2½ to 3 years after they had taken the course. Their responses were compared to those given by a control group of 50 parents on the first day of the course. Here, the completion of a sexuality education course was the independent variable; the incidence of discussions with children about sex was the dependent variable. We found that while only 18 percent of the parents who had not yet begun the course had initiated discussions about sexuality with their children, 86.5 percent of the sexuality-educated parents said that they had done so. We therefore concluded that there was a cause-and-effect relationship: Comprehensive college sexuality education increases the likelihood that students will initiate discussions about sex with their children.

While experimental research has advantages over the other methods, it, too, often has limitations. This study, for example, still relied on self-reports. Although I was careful not to survey my former students myself, out of concern that some might give answers they thought would please me, we cannot be sure that everyone answered honestly. In addition, the two groups were convenience samples, so we must be cautious in making conclusions about the effects of college sexuality education courses nationwide. Moreover, researchers simply cannot use experimental designs to address some questions. We may believe, for example, that an infant's hormone levels shortly after birth strongly influence future sexual orientation, but we cannot purposely manipulate hormones in children in order to prove our hypothesis.

In the chapters ahead you will see references to hundreds of studies. Although each study has its limitations, it is often the case that a particular subject has been studied in numerous investigations using a variety of methods. The more agreement there is among the results of different studies, the safer we can feel about making general conclusions.

SEXUALITY EDUCATION TODAY

Kinsey's surveys (1948, 1953) were met with public outrage, but surveys of people's sexual behaviors and attitudes have since become commonplace, so that we now have a good idea of what can be considered normal sexual behaviors. Physiological studies with humans rather than animals have become accepted within the scientific community as well. As a result, we now have a large body of data on human sexual responses. The emerging field of sexual therapy has provided us with much information on sexual disorders.

For the first time in our history, we are in a position to give factual information about human sexuality to our children. However, more often than not, sexuality education has become a battleground among groups with different moral and political ideologies.

observer bias The prejudicing of observations and conclusions by the observer's own belief system.

experimental method A study in which an investigator attempts to establish a cause-and-effect relationship by manipulating a variable of interest (the independent variable) while keeping all other factors the same.

Even if sex educators do not openly talk about values, sex education cannot be value-free (Reiss, 1995), and conflict about values is probably inevitable in democratic societies in which there is a diversity of ethnic, religious, and sexual groups.

On one side of the debate are those who wish to guide their children toward their own view of the world and who regard sexuality education as the exclusive right of the family (thus protecting the children from other points of view). This group is guided by the belief that there has been a decline in morals within our society and that only a narrow set of sexual behaviors is normal and moral. They tend to view sexual diversity as part of the problem of moral decline, and their ideology with regard to sex education is to restrict the curriculum.

On the other side are those who favor what is called comprehensive sexuality education. They believe that children should be exposed to a wide variety of beliefs so that they can make their own choices as to what is best for them. Furthermore, they generally believe that it is the duty of the state to impose this education for the "public good."

Nowhere is the battle over curriculum more heated than with regard to the subject of how to prevent teenage pregnancy and sexually transmitted diseases. At the heart of this debate is the central issue of the purpose or goal of sexuality education. Those favoring comprehensive education argue (often passionately)

that students should be taught about birth control methods and the use of condoms (and often advocate making condoms available to teens) in the interest of public health. Most educators who favor a comprehensive curriculum believe that "sex education should reduce teenage pregnancy and help prevent transmission of HIV and other causes of sexually transmitted diseases" (Reiss, 1995). Those favoring a restrictive curriculum, on the other hand, see schools as agents of socialization that shape the moral and sexual norms of future generations, and they want sexuality education to promote family values and abstinence. They frequently cite an article that appeared in the *Atlantic Monthly*, titled "The Failure of Sex Education," which concluded that comprehensive sexuality programs have failed to reduce the number of teenage pregnancies and cases of sexually transmitted diseases (Whitehead, 1994). Advocates of comprehensive education point to other studies. For example, the National Institutes of Health's Consensus Panel on AIDS concluded that "abstinence-plus" programs (programs that teach abstinence, contraception, and the prevention of sexually transmitted diseases) are more effective than "abstinence-only" programs (NIH Consensus, 1997). A review of sexuality education programs done for the World Health Organization concluded that the programs did not increase sexual experimentation or activity, and that they often resulted in teens postponing sexual intercourse and/or initiating safer sex practices (Grunseit et al., 1997). Other studies have found that high school programs that make condoms available to students also do not lead to an increase in sexual activity (Kirby et al., 1999; Schuster et al., 1998).

The battle is now being fought in the political arena. In 1995, fewer than half the states required comprehensive sexuality education in schools, and 13 did not even require any education about sexually transmitted diseases (NARAL, 1995). During the 1997–1998 school year, opponents of comprehensive sexuality education introduced 135 measures in 33 states designed to further restrict the curriculum (Kempner, 1998). In 1996, Congress passed legislation, signed into law by President Clinton, that provided $250 million to fund abstinence-only programs from 1998 to 2002. Although this effectively ended teaching about other types of birth control, only California and New Hampshire refused to accept the federal funds.

The result of this battle for control of sexuality education is a great unevenness in programs. In some areas the curriculum reflects a single sexual philosophy, generally ignoring cultural and ideological diversity. Many, perhaps rightfully so, regard this as ideological indoctrination. Other programs, in an attempt to find common ground among differing ideologies, are stripped to the point of offering information only about reproductive biology and some basics of sexually

DUNAGIN'S PEOPLE

"DON'T WORRY. WHEN SEX EDUCATION IS PRESENTED IN A CLASSROOM SETTING, IT WILL BECOME AS FOREIGN TO THE STUDENTS AS MATH AND SCIENCE."

Box 1-A   CROSS-CULTURAL PERSPECTIVES

Sexuality Education

Children learn about sex from a variety of sources, including parents, brothers and sisters, friends, the media, and school. Parents' attitudes about the sexuality of their children vary considerably across cultures. In many cultures, parents are very permissive, either promoting sexual relations among adolescents and sometimes even among preadolescent children (as in the Mangaian culture or the Muria Gond of India) or at least tolerating it (as with the !Kung of Africa) (Elwin, 1968; Marshall, 1971; Shostak, 1981). In other cultures, parents are very restrictive, never mentioning sex or normal bodily functions such as menstruation to their children and severely restricting premarital sexual relations (as in the case of the Inis Baeg of Ireland and in most Islamic cultures) (Halstead, 1997; Messenger, 1971). In Russia, sex education has traditionally focused on morality and the control of sexual expression (Rivkin-Fish, 1999). Even among Western countries, attitudes about sex education differ substantially. In England (and to a large extent the United States) the prevailing attitude is that children must be protected from sexual knowledge, while countries such as Sweden and the Netherlands are much more accepting of young people's sexuality (West, 1999). In a survey of 141 societies, Broude and Greene (1976) found 25 percent to be highly permissive and another 25 percent highly restrictive.

In Europe and in the United States and other English-speaking countries, schools are increasingly becoming the primary source of information about sex. The country with probably the longest history of school sexuality education is Sweden, which made it compulsory for all children (starting at age 8) in 1956. Schools in Sweden, Denmark, France, Germany, and the Netherlands do not have special sexuality education classes, but instead integrate lessons about sexuality into the rest of the curriculum. In these countries teenage sexuality is not regarded as a political or religious issue, but instead as a health issue (Kelly & McGee, 1999). People in the United States generally believe that Sweden's sexually permissive culture is a result of Swedish openness, yet in fact, studies show that Swedish teens are not promiscuous and that the teenage pregnancy rate in Sweden is substantially lower than it is in the United States (Singh & Darroch, 2000).

In many parts of the world, government or international agencies are playing a role in sexuality education (Finger, 2000). In June 1988, then–U.S. Surgeon General Everett Koop's office mailed a brochure entitled "Understanding AIDS" to 107 million American households. In 1993, the World Health Organization called for more sex education in schools. As a result, government organizations have recently developed sexuality education programs in such countries as Colombia, Nigeria, and India (Mendez, 1996; Nayak & Bose, 1997; Shortridge, 1997).

The primary source of sexual information may vary from culture to culture, but there is a definite trend in the direction of enlightenment. Throughout the world, the sexual education of children has increasingly become an integrative responsibility shared by parents, schools, and the government.

transmitted diseases, and as a result omit important information about sexual health. Overall, in the U.S. there has been a marked decrease since the late 1980s in the amount of information about contraception given to teenagers in grades 7–12 (Darroch et al., 2000).

Almost always left out of the debate are the opinions of young people themselves, most of whom, according to a recent survey, say that they do not receive enough information about sex and birth control and that what they do get comes too late (Kaiser Family Foundation, 1996). Most teens want to receive sexual

health education in school. Here are some opinions of students in my own course:

"I believe human sexuality should be taught in public schools. The media exposes young people to every imaginable kinds of sexual topics already."

"I think that sex education should be included in public high schools.... I knew girls that actually thought urinating after sex or bathing after sex prevented pregnancy. I think it is vital that teens know the real truth about a very important issue."

"Yes, because it gives students, especially at that age, the ability to learn about sex without feeling stupid because their friends know more than they do."

"Ignoring the fact that teens have sex will never help them to be responsible. By giving them knowledge of the consequences and responsibilities that go along with having sex, they are more inclined to make a better decision."

Not everyone believed that all subjects should be taught in school:

"The one subject they should not discuss is positions."

"I think the issue of homosexuality should be left out."

"Oral sex shouldn't be taught, people should find out about that with experience."

How should we resolve these differences in ideology and construct a sexuality education curriculum? In a thoughtful essay, Alexander McKay (1997) argues for a democratic philosophy of sexuality education that is committed to freedom of belief:

In sum, a democratic sexuality education does not insist that students consider the moral dimensions of sexuality from the perspective of a particular sexual ideology. Rather, a democratic sexuality education encourages students to exercise their liberty of thought to deliberate critically between competing ideological perspectives in clarifying their own beliefs and at arriving at new ones. (p. 295)

As a student at a college or university, you were probably not required to take this course. When you enrolled, you exercised your freedom of choice. In this text, I will provide accurate information and attempt to make you aware of the diversity in sexual behavior and values. I do not advocate one life-style over another or one set of values over another. My goal for you is that, upon completion of this course, you feel more comfortable with your own sexuality, and at the same time find a tolerance and respect for the beliefs of others.

> *PERSONAL REFLECTIONS*
> *Do you believe that sexuality education should be taught in school? If not, why not? If so, beginning at what level? Why?*

Key Terms

ascetic philosophy 12	Alfred C. Kinsey 17	sex ("had sex") 21
case study 22	Masters and Johnson 18	sexuality 1
correlation 22	missionary position 6	sexual revolution 16
direct observation 22	observer bias 23	stratified random sample 20
dualism 12	population 19	St. Augustine 13
ethnocentric 6	procreation 11	St. Paul 12
Henry Havelock Ellis 17	random sampling 20	survey 19
experimental method 23	Reformation 14	Victorian era 14
Sigmund Freud 16	sample 19	volunteer bias 21

Suggested Readings

Bullough, V. L. (1998). Alfred Kinsey and the Kinsey report: Historical overview and lasting contributions. *Journal of Sex Research*, 35, 127–131. Puts Kinsey's contribution in proper perspective.

D'Emilio, J., & Freedman, E. (1988). *Intimate matters: A history of sexuality in America*. New York: Harper & Row. A very scholarly history.

Hodes, M. (Ed.) (1999). *Sex, love, race: Crossing boundaries in North American history*. New York: New York University Press. An excellent book that focuses on cultural differences within the United States.

Journal of Moral Education, 26(3), 1997. This issue is devoted exclusively to articles about the debate over sexuality education and how to arrive at a curriculum in a culture with a diversity of religious, ethnic, and sexual groups.

Laumann, E. O., & Michael, R. T. (2000). *Sex, love, and health in America*. Chicago: University of Chicago Press. Provides deeper research and analysis than the original 1994 report.

Marshall, D. S. (1971, February). Too much in Mangaia. *Psychology Today*.

Messenger, J. L. (1971, February). Sex and repression in an Irish folk community: The lack of the Irish. *Psychology Today*.

Michael, R. T., Gagnon, J. H., Laumann, E. O., & Kolata, G. (1994). *Sex in America: A definitive survey*. Boston: Little, Brown. The condensed, popularized version of the landmark survey conducted by the National Opinion Research Center.

Stodghill II, R. (1998). Where'd you learn that? *Time*, June 15, 52–59. An excellent article about where teenagers today are learning about sex.

Suggs, D. N., & Miracle, A. W. (1993). *Culture and human sexuality*. Pacific Grove, CA: Brooks/Cole. Cross-cultural essays about human sexuality.

Wiederman, M. W. (2001). *Understanding sexuality research*. Belmont, CA: Wadsworth Thomson Learning. A short, but excellent book on methodology problems in sex research with many real-world examples.

Study Guide

INTERACTIVE REVIEW

Some people feel that sexuality education should be the responsibility of parents, yet fewer than half of all college students report ever having a meaningful discussion about sex with their parents. Most young people turn to (1) _____ and (2) _____ for information about sex, but much of what they learn is incorrect. The best alternative would be for children to receive factual information in school. Surveys indicate that more than (3) _____ percent of Americans favor sexuality education in school, but fewer than half of all junior high schools and high schools in the United States presently offer such courses.

Sex is only a part of (4) _____, which encompasses all of the sexual attitudes, feelings, and behaviors associated with being human. Sexual behaviors and attitudes (such as what is considered to be sexually attractive) vary from culture to culture, and can even change within a culture over time. American sexual attitudes are both permissive and repressed, and as a result many people in the United States have ambivalent feelings about sex.

In order to understand how we arrived at our current values, we must examine the history of sexual attitudes in our culture. The idea that the primary purpose of sex is for procreation (to have children) originally came from (5) _____ , but they also had a very positive attitude about their bodies and sexual pleasure between husbands and wives. The early (6) _____ affirmed the procreational purpose of sex, but completely denied its pleasurable aspects. Sexual desire, even within marriage, was now associated with guilt. The biggest proponent of this view within Christianity was (7) _____ . In Western culture, negative attitudes about sex reached their zenith during the reign of (8) _____ of England. During this time, the medical profession contributed many incorrect negative beliefs about engaging in sex, including the belief that excess sex, particularly masturbation, could lead to serious medical problems and eventually insanity.

The industrial revolution slowly changed Americans' lives, including their sex lives. With shorter workdays and workweeks and greater mobility (e.g., automobiles) than in past generations, people now had more free time to spend together. With the availability of (9) _____ during World War II and the marketing of (10) _____ in 1960, the United States entered the sexual revolution.

Because of the antisexual attitudes of the Victorian era, scientific study of human sexuality was slow to develop. (11) _____, who emphasized the sexuality of all people, including children, and (12) _____, who published seven volumes about the psychology of sex, were two researchers of the Victorian era who attempted to counter antisexual attitudes. However, it has only been within the last 40 years that the scientific and medical communities have accepted sex as a subject for serious discussion and research. The first large-scale surveys were done by (13) _____ in the 1940s and early 1950s. (14) _____ published their physiological investigations of human sexual behavior in 1966. Even today, however, there is some resistance on the part of governmental agencies to fund research on human sexual behavior.

SELF-TEST

A. TRUE OR FALSE

T F 15. The Old Testament presents a positive view of sex within marriage.

T F 16. American sexual behaviors are considered to be the norm by the rest of the world.

T F 17. Because of AIDS, all states now require that public schools offer education about sexually transmitted diseases.

T F 18. The larger the number of people in a survey, the more accurate it always is.

|T|F| 19. All cultures consider women's breasts to be highly erotic.
|T|F| 20. The Puritans' sexual beliefs were a major influence on current American values.
|T|F| 21. Kissing is one sexual behavior that is done worldwide.
|T|F| 22. One good method of obtaining a random sample is to randomly pick names from a phone book.
|T|F| 23. Each year in the United States, 1 in 4 sexually active teens gets a sexually transmitted disease.
|T|F| 24. Among American subcultures, African Americans have the lowest rates for oral-genital sex and masturbation.
|T|F| 25. Over half of all American teenagers have had sexual intercourse before their 17th birthday.
|T|F| 26. The era of permissiveness known as the "sexual revolution" started during the Victorian era.
|T|F| 27. About one-fourth of all societies in the world encourage or openly tolerate children engaging in sex.
|T|F| 28. Kinsey's surveys are a good example of the use of random sampling techniques.
|T|F| 29. A strong positive correlation between two variables is evidence of a cause-and-effect relationship.
|T|F| 30. In the late 1990s, there was a decline in the percentage of teenagers engaging in sexual intercourse and in teenage pregnancies.
|T|F| 31. Americans' attitudes about sex tend to be ethnocentric.

B. MATCHING, PART 1

_____ 32. A Victorian-era physician who emphasized the sexuality of children and adults

_____ 33. He viewed sex for procreation as an unpleasant necessity and equated guilt with sexual desire

_____ 34. Conducted the first large-scale physiological study of human sexual behavior

_____ 35. He systematized Christian thought during the Middle Ages

_____ 36. They believed that the purpose of sex was for procreation, but had a very positive attitude about sexual relations between a husband and wife

_____ 37. Reformation leader who said that priests and nuns should be allowed to marry

_____ 38. They proved their worthiness, not by denying the pleasurable aspects of marital sex but by living frugal and industrious lives

_____ 39. They believed in an ascetic philosophy: wisdom and virtue come from denying physical pleasures

_____ 40. He conducted the first large-scale survey of American sexual attitudes and behaviors

_____ 41. The first major influence on Christian sexual values, he regarded bodily pleasures as evil and thought it "well for a man not to touch a woman"

_____ 42. A Victorian-era sex researcher with a tolerant attitude about sexuality

_____ 43. They held antisexual attitudes that were reinforced by the mistaken medical beliefs of that time

_____ 44. He headed a recent survey of a nationally representative sample of adults living in households

a. Henry Havelock Ellis
b. Edwardians
c. St. Paul
d. ancient Greeks
e. Jesus
f. Sigmund Freud
g. Masters and Johnson
h. biblical Hebrews
i. Puritans
j. Victorians
k. Morton Hunt
l. St. John
m. Martin Luther
n. St. Thomas Aquinas
o. Alfred Kinsey
p. St. Augustine
q. Edward Laumann

MATCHING, PART 2

_____ 45. The major method of investigation used by Masters and Johnson: _____.

_____ 46. In her laboratory, Professor Jones uses different groups of subjects to study the effects of different amounts of alcohol consumption on men's arousal from viewing sexually explicit films showing violence toward women. Her method of investigation is called _____.

a. population
b. sample
c. convenience sample
d. stratified random sample
e. survey

_____ 47. In question 46, the different amounts of alcohol consumption are the _____.

_____ 48. In question 46, the level of arousal is the _____.

_____ 49. Professor Jones's subjects are a _____.

_____ 50. If Professor Jones's subjects were volunteers from her class, they would be a _____.

_____ 51. Professor Jones finds that a group given alcohol shows more arousal than a control group that does not consume alcohol. If she kept all other factors the same, she can draw a conclusion based on _____.

_____ 52. Professor Jones finds a strong linear relationship between the amount of alcohol consumed and the degree of arousal. This is an example of the use of _____.

_____ 53 Professor Jones makes a conclusion about the effects of alcohol in all adult men. She has made a _____.

_____ 54. In Professor Jones's study, "all adult men" is the _____.

_____ 55. If the men who agreed to participate in Professor Jones's study did so because they enjoyed watching sexually violent movies more than other people do, this would be an example of _____.

_____ 56. The major method of investigation used by anthropologists: _____.

_____ 57. If an anthropologist's description of another culture's behaviors was influenced by his own (Western) values, this would be an example of _____.

_____ 58. Dr. Smith does an in-depth investigation and analysis of a serial rapist. His method of investigation is called a _____.

_____ 59. Professor Thomas gives a paper-and-pencil questionnaire to her class asking about their sexual attitudes. This is an example of a _____.

_____ 60. If a study samples randomly from targeted subgroups in the same proportion as they are found in the general population, the result is a _____.

f. correlation
g. direct observation
h. case study
i. experimental research
j. volunteer bias
k. observer bias
l. independent variable
m. dependent variable
n. generalization
o. cause and effect

C. FILL IN THE BLANKS

61. Anthropologists believe the most sexually repressed society in the world to be the _____.

62. Four important influences that led to the sexual revolution were (a) _____, (b) _____, (c) _____, and (d) _____.

63. A random sample is properly defined as a sample drawn from a population in a manner so that _____ has an equal chance of being selected.

64. _____ believed that intellectual love could lead to immortality.

65. The _____ had a positive view of sex within marriage and brought this view over to the colonies in the New World.

66. A democratic philosophy of sexuality education is committed to _____.

67. A major influence on early Christian thought was the Greek philosophy of dualism, which separated _____ and _____.

68. Victorian physicians called nocturnal emissions _____ because they believed they were caused by the same thing that causes gonorrhea.

69. The major influence on Christian attitudes about sex was _____.

70. In the National Health and Social Life Survey (Laumann et al., 1994), "sex" or "had sex" was defined as _____.

Chapter

Our Sexual and Reproductive Anatomy

So God created man in his own image, in the image of
God he created him; male and female he created them.

(Genesis 1:27, Revised Standard Version)

Many of the first words that we learn are anatomical terms. Parents often spend hours teaching their young children to point to and name different parts of the body, such as the mouth, eyes, ears, and nose. Unfortunately, when naming body parts, many parents simply skip from arms, chest, and "tummy" to legs, knees, and feet, completely omitting any mention of the genitals and anus. Other parents teach their children the correct anatomical words for all other parts of the body, but substitute such "cute" words as "weeney," "booty," "peanut," and "talleywacker" for the genitals. As for the functions of this mysterious body area, many of us are simply taught during toilet training to make "pee-pees" and "poo-poos." Although some adults became sexually experienced without ever knowing the correct anatomical terms, many others who know better nevertheless feel very uncomfortable about teaching their children to say the words "penis" and "vagina."

When you have finished studying this chapter, you should be able to:

1. Explain why learning correct anatomical terms is important;

2. Describe each part of the external female anatomy—mons veneris, labia majora, labia minora, clitoris, hymen, and vaginal and urethral openings—and explain its function(s);

3. Discuss attitudes about an intact hymen and their implications for women of different cultures;

4. Understand why early detection of breast cancer can save lives and explain how to perform a breast self-examination;

5. Explain the risks associated with breast augmentation operations;

6. Describe each of the female internal anatomical structures—vagina, uterus, Fallopian tubes, and ovaries—and explain its function(s);

7. Explain the importance of an annual pelvic examination and Pap smear for women's health;

8. Describe each of the structures of the external and internal male anatomy—penis, scrotum, testicles, epididymis, vas deferens, ejaculatory ducts, urethra, prostate gland, seminal vesicles, and Cowper's glands—and explain its function(s);

9. Discuss the advantages and disadvantages of circumcision of the penis;

10. Explain how to perform a testicular self-examination;

11. Identify the early signs of prostate problems and understand the importance of regular prostate examinations for men's health;

12. Explain what role the brain plays in sexual behavior; and

13. Describe how other parts of the body (lips, mouth, hair, buttocks, etc.) may also be considered part of our sexual anatomy.

As we grow older, we learn new words from our peers that describe our sexual anatomy and behavior, but quite often these are slang terms. Men are more likely than women to use slang terms when referring to their own **genitalia,** but many people use no words at all to refer to their partner's or their own genitals (Fischer, 1989). Very few people use the word *intercourse* when referring to the act of copulation. The use of slang terminology and the discomfort that many people feel about using the correct words reflect the ambivalent feelings they have about sex. There is perhaps no better example of the distorted negative attitudes that some people have toward sex than the common use of the word "fuck" instead of intercourse. It is frequently used to express displeasure ("What the fuck is going on here?"), trouble ("I got fucked over at work"), or aggression ("Fuck you!"). At many other times we think of sexual intercourse as a pleasurable experience. The word "fuck" probably originated from the Middle English word "fucken." At one time its use was not considered improper, but the word acquired negative connotations in the mid-1600s.

Many of the slang terms used to describe our sexual anatomy also have negative connotations. A commonly used term for women's genitalia, for example, is "pudendum," which is derived from a Latin word meaning "something to be ashamed of." Similarly, the slang term "prick" is often used in a derogatory manner.

Slang terms can result in misinformation about sexual anatomy and behavior. In response to an item on a questionnaire given on the first day of class in human sexuality, many students indicated that they believed that an erection in men occurs when a bone protrudes from the base of the penis. This belief should not be surprising, for after all, why else would an erection be called a "boner"? Slang terms such as "cherry," "nuts," and "pussy" can be misleading.

It is not my intent to teach "dirty" words or slang terminology. In fact, people who take courses in human sexuality often end up using the proper terms more frequently (Fischer, 1989). We must acknowledge the fact, however, that many of us come to class with a sexual vocabulary that consists almost entirely of slang words. The question that many students have, of course, is, "What good will it do to learn the correct anatomical terms, which are almost always Latin or Greek?" The lack of such knowledge obviously does not hinder most people from becoming sexually experienced. Knowledge of sexual anatomy may help dispel any misleading ideas acquired through use of slang terms, but will it help make us better sexual partners? Learning correct anatomical terms may be very helpful, particularly if it results in our becoming less inhibited about our own bodies and those of our partners. Many people have never even examined themselves (possibly because many parents discouraged or punished such behavior during childhood) and are ashamed of their genitals, rather than viewing them as a source of pleasure and a positive part of their anatomy. This is more often true of women than men (Reinholtz & Muehlenhard, 1995). Here are a few comments that I received from students when I was using a classroom-testing version of this book:

> "As for the illustrations in Chapter 2, I thought they were good and very well illustrated, but they were rather embarrassing to look at."

> "Figure 2–2 made me feel uncomfortable. I felt as if everyone could see me."

> "The pictures in this chapter were quite graphic. I wish they were on another separate page so that we wouldn't have to look at them the entire time we read a particular page. Even just reading this by myself was a little embarrassing."

> "I had difficulties looking at the pictures without embarrassment and shame. I should be able to look without any bad feelings."

No one should feel embarrassed or ashamed about any part of his or her own body, including the genitals. If you have never done so, I encourage you to examine yourself during this part of the course. By making us more aware of our own bodies and those of our partners (or future partners), a chapter on basic anatomy might result in our becoming more comfortable with exploring other aspects of our sexuality as well.

In the act of sexual intercourse, you share in mutual bodily stimulation with your partner. *Intercourse* means "communication" (*Webster's New World Dictionary*), but communication, whether verbal or tactile, is not possible without some basic knowledge. Should your sexual relations result in having children, it is hoped that someday you will teach them about their bodies without having to resort to slang or cute terminology that avoids the basic facts of life (see Chapter 8).

> *PERSONAL REFLECTIONS*
> *Do you use sexual slang terms (a) to refer to your genitalia, or (b) when you are upset? Why? If you do, list below the terms you use, then write down the correct word next to each. Say each correct term out loud a few times. Are you comfortable or uncomfortable doing this? Could you use these terms in normal conversation without being embarrassed or uncomfortable? (If you cannot, why not? After all, you probably use the slang terms.)*

EXTERNAL FEMALE ANATOMY

You can see the location of the female reproductive system in Figure 2–1. A picture of the external female genitalia, collectively known as the **vulva** (Latin for "covering"), is shown in Figure 2–2. The vulva consists of the mons veneris, the labia

genitalia The reproductive organs of the man or woman.

vulva The external female genitalia, including the mons veneris, labia majora, labia minora, clitoris, vaginal opening, and urethral opening.

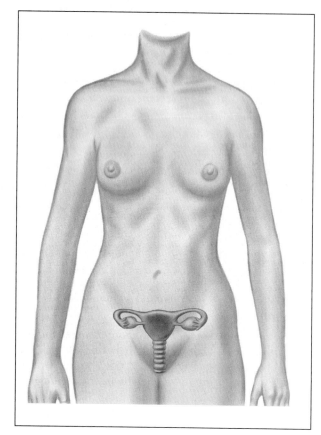

Figure 2–1 Anatomical location of the female repro-ductive system.

majora, the labia minora, the clitoris, and the vaginal and urethral openings. When examining herself (which re-quires use of a hand mirror), a woman should not con-sider herself to be abnormal if she does not look identical to the drawing in Figure 2–2. As with all other parts of the body, women's genitalia vary in appearance from per-son to person, differing in size, shape, and color (see Figure 2–3). Many women have nega-tive feelings about their geni-talia (remember the use of the term *pudendum*). The feelings that a woman has toward her genitalia are directly related to her participation in and en-joyment of sexual activity (Reinholtz & Muehlenhard, 1995).

THE MONS VENERIS

Translated from Latin, **mons veneris** means "mount of Venus." The term refers to the soft layer of fatty tissue over-

---

mons veneris The soft layer of fatty tissue that overlays the pubic bone in women. It becomes cov-ered with pubic hair during puberty.

labia majora Two elongated folds of skin extending from the mons to the perineum in women. Its outer surfaces become covered with pubic hair during puberty.

labia minora Two hairless elongated folds of skin located be-tween the labia majora in women. They meet above the clitoris to form the clitoral hood.

perineum Technically, the en-tire pelvic floor, but more com-monly used to refer to the hairless bit of skin between the anus and either the vaginal opening (in women) or the scrotum (in men).

---

laying the area where the pubic bones come together. Venus, of course, was the Roman goddess of love, and the mons area is considered to be very erotic after pu-berty, when it becomes covered with hair. Until the early 1970s, magazines such as *Playboy* and *Penthouse* considered *pubic hair* too explicitly erotic for publica-tion, and the hair was airbrushed out of photographs.

Our sensitivity to touch is dependent on the den-sity of nerve endings in a particular area of skin. Areas such as the lips and fingertips have a high density of nerve endings and thus are very sensitive to touch, while areas such as the back have a much lower den-sity of nerve endings and are much less sensitive to touch. Because of numerous nerve endings in the mons area, many women find gentle stimulation of the mons pleasurable.

Although the soft layer of fatty tissue cushions the pubic region during intercourse, one can only speculate as to what purpose nature intended pubic hair to serve. Some researchers believe that this pocket of hair on an otherwise mostly hairless body is meant to be sexually attractive. However, pubic hair also traps vaginal secre-tions. Males of most mammalian species find vaginal odors erotically stimulating, and similar results have been found for humans under laboratory conditions (Hassett, 1978). Many people in Western cultures, however, are conditioned to have negative feelings about such odors (see the section on the vagina).

THE LABIA

The labia consist of two outer (**labia majora,** or major lips) and two inner (**labia minora,** or minor lips) elon-gated folds of skin, which, in the sexually unstimulated state, cover (and thus protect) the vaginal and urethral openings. The outer surfaces of the labia majora be-come covered with hair at the time of puberty. The labia majora extend from the mons to the hairless bit of skin between the vaginal opening and the anus, called the **perineum.** Because the perineum often tears during childbirth, physicians commonly make an inci-sion in it (called an *episiotomy*) prior to delivery (see Chapter 7). When sewing up this area, some old-fashioned doctors add an extra stitch to tighten the vaginal opening (called a "husband's knot," as its only purpose is to increase the man's pleasure when sexual intercourse is resumed). After childbirth it is not un-common for the labia majora to remain separated to some extent in the unstimulated state.

The pinkish and hairless labia minora are lo-cated between, and sometimes protrude beyond, the labia majora. Among some African groups, particu-larly the Hottentots, elongation of the labia minora is considered to be highly erotic, and girls are taught to pull on them from early childhood. Some "Hottentot Aprons," as they are called, can protrude as much as 7 inches.

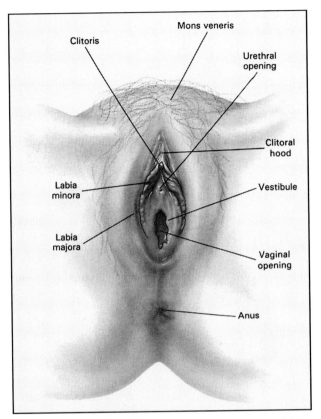

Figure 2–2 The female genitalia (vulva), with the labia parted to show the vaginal and urethral openings.

The labia minora, which meet at the top to form the **clitoral hood** (or *prepuce*), are very sensitive to touch. They have numerous blood vessels that become engorged with blood during sexual stimulation, causing them to swell and turn bright red or wine-colored.

Located at the base of the labia minora are the **Bartholin's glands,** which, during prolonged stimulation, contribute a few drops of an alkaline fluid to the inner surfaces via ducts. The small amount of fluid does not make a significant contribution to vaginal lubrication during sexual intercourse, but it does help to counteract the normal acidity of the outer vagina (sperm cannot live in an acidic environment). Infection or cysts of the Bartholin's glands sometimes occur, and a physician should be consulted if there is any local swelling or irritation.

THE CLITORIS

The **clitoris** (from a Greek word meaning "hill" or "slope") develops from the same embryonic tissue as the penis and has at least as many nerve endings as the much larger penis, making it extremely sensitive to touch. In fact, it is the only structure in either men or women with no known function other than to focus sexual sensations (Masters & Johnson, 1970). The only visible portion is the *glans*, which in a sexually

unaroused woman looks like a small, shiny button located just below the hood of skin formed where the two labia minora meet.

The body, or *shaft*, of the clitoris is located beneath the clitoral hood. It is about 1 inch long and one-quarter inch in diameter, but divides to form two much larger structures called *crura* (Latin for "legs"), which fan out and attach to the pubic bone. Like the penis, the clitoris contains two *corpora cavernosa*, made up of spongy tissue that becomes engorged with blood during sexual arousal. This causes the clitoris to increase in size; but because of the way it is attached to the pubic bone, the clitoris does not actually become erect like the penis. Any form of sexual arousal may result in engorgement and enlargement of the clitoris. If sexual stimulation continues, the previously visible clitoris pulls back against the pubic bone and the glans disappears from view beneath the clitoral hood.

Contrary to what some people may believe, the sexual pleasure of women is not related to the size of the clitoris (Money, 1970). Another popular myth is that women are more sexually responsive the shorter the distance between the vaginal opening and clitoral glans (so that the penis can more easily stimulate the clitoris); but this, too, is untrue. The penis, in fact, usually does not come into direct contact with the clitoris during sexual intercourse. The thrusting of the penis only indirectly stimulates the clitoris, by causing the clitoral hood to rub back and forth over the glans. Surgical removal of the clitoral hood (*clitoral circumcision*) in order to directly expose the clitoris was once a common practice, done in order to enhance responsivity in wives who were thought to be "frigid." However, problems with sexual desire and trouble attaining orgasm are only rarely the result of an anatomical problem.

Surgical removal of the clitoris was sometimes performed in the United States and Europe during Victorian times in order to prevent girls from masturbating and growing up "oversexed." *Clitoridectomy* is no longer legally performed in America, but it is very common in Northern African countries and parts of the Middle East, Malaysia, and Indonesia (see Box 4–A on page 88).

Thick secretions called *smegma* can accumulate beneath the clitoral hood and result in discomfort during sexual intercourse by causing the glans to stick to the clitoral hood. The secretions can generally be washed off, however, by bathing thoroughly.

THE VAGINAL OPENING

The vaginal and urethral openings are visible only if the labia minora are parted. The

clitoral hood The part of the labia minora that covers the clitoris in women.

Bartholin's glands Glands located at the base of the labia minora in women that contribute a small amount of an alkaline fluid to their inner surfaces during sexual arousal.

clitoris A small, elongated erectile structure in women that develops from the same embryonic tissue as the penis. It has no known reproductive function other than to focus sexual sensations.

Figure 2–3 Two variations in the appearance of female genitalia.

area between the two labia minora is sometimes referred to as the **vestibular area** (Latin for "entrance hall") and the vaginal opening as the *introitus* (Latin for "entrance"). The vaginal opening, which is very sensitive to stimulation, is not a permanently open orifice always ready for penetration by the penis. It is surrounded by the **bulbocavernosus muscle,** a ring of sphincter muscles similar to the sphincter muscles surrounding the anus. Sexually experienced women can learn to voluntarily contract or relax these muscles during intercourse, and during childbirth the vaginal opening expands enough to accommodate delivery of a baby. In sexually inexperienced women, on the other hand, these muscles may involuntarily contract as a result of extreme nervousness, making penetration very difficult. The **vestibular bulbs,** which are located underneath the sphincter muscles on both sides of the vaginal opening, also help the vagina grip the penis by swelling with blood during sexual arousal.

In sexually inexperienced women, a thin membrane called the **hymen** (named after the Greek god of marriage) may partially cover the opening to the vagina. This membrane is found only in human females. Until shortly before birth, the hymen separates the vagina from the urinary system. It ruptures after birth, but in humans remains as a fold of membrane around the vaginal opening. It is found in all normal newborn girls (Berenson, 1993). The hymen may have one opening (annular hymen), two openings (septate hymen), or several openings (cribriform hymen) that allow for passage of menstrual flow. In the rare instance that the hymen has no opening (imperforate hymen), a simple surgical incision can be made at the time of first menstruation. The vaginal opening of women who have given birth is sometimes referred to as the *parous introitus* ("passed through").

The hymen has no known physiological function, but the presence of the hymen has been used by men throughout history as proof of virginity. In the time of the biblical Hebrews, a newly wed woman who did not bleed during first intercourse was sometimes stoned to death.

> **But if the thing is true, that the tokens of virginity were not found in the young woman, then they shall bring out the young woman to the door of her father's house, and the men of her city shall stone her to death with stones, because she has wrought folly in Israel by playing the harlot in her father's house; so you shall purge the evil from the midst of you. (Deuteronomy 22:20–21, Revised Standard Version)**

Even today, in many parts of the world a newly wed wife can be divorced or exiled if her husband believes her to be unchaste. Many Muslims, Chinese, and Moroccans display a bloodstained sheet on the wedding night as proof of a new bride's chastity. It was

vestibular area A term used to refer to the area between the two labia minora.

bulbocavernosus muscle A ring of sphincter muscles that surrounds the vaginal opening in women or the root of the penis in men.

vestibular bulbs Structures surrounding the vaginal opening that fill with blood during sexual arousal, resulting in swelling of the tissues and a narrowing of the vaginal opening.

hymen The thin membrane that partially covers the vaginal opening in many sexually inexperienced women. Its presence or absence, however, is really a very poor indicator of prior sexual experience.

once the custom in some cultures for a priest to devirginate a woman. In other cultures, girls are ritually "deflowered" with stone phalluses or horns. Although these extreme customs are not found in Western culture, many American men nevertheless expect their female partners to bleed during first intercourse.

> "A girlfriend of mine, a few years ago, told me that she was a virgin, so naturally I figured that after we had sex she would bleed. Then, when she didn't I felt upset and betrayed."

> "When my girlfriend and I first had intercourse it was just understood by listening to my peers that she was supposed to bleed and I should see some kind of skin hanging (hymen). This didn't happen and for years it bothered me because I thought she lied to me when she told me that I was her first. It wasn't until after taking this course that I realized how ignorant my friends and I were."

> "Being very athletic came natural for me and by the time I was 12, I had won four athletic trophies and many certificates. My mother took me to a doctor right after I made 14 and he told her that I was not a virgin because my hymen was not in place. I cried for 2 weeks. It was not true. My life was very traumatic for the next 6 months. Now at 40 years old, I am still angry." (All examples are from the author's files.)

In actuality, the hymen is a very poor indicator of whether or not a women is sexually experienced, and there is often very little bleeding or discomfort during first sexual intercourse. In fact, pain during first intercourse often reflects a woman's attitudes about sex (Weis, 1985). The hymen sometimes ruptures during vigorous physical activity or insertion of a tampon, and in some women the opening in the hymen only stretches rather than tears during first intercourse (thus there would be no bleeding). It speaks poorly of our attitudes about sex that many newly wed women are expected to bleed and experience great discomfort and pain in order to please their husbands. Untold millions of women throughout history have probably suffered much grief (and even death) for failing to display what many men wrongly believe is the appropriate response to first intercourse.

THE URETHRAL OPENING

Urine passes from the bladder through a small tube called the **urethra** and out the urethral opening, which is located below the clitoris and above the vaginal opening. A man's urethra serves for the passage of sperm as well as urine, but a women's urinary system is not related to her reproductive system.

Cystitis is an inflammation of the bladder with symptoms of frequent and burning urination. Women are more susceptible to this than men. Many factors increase the risk, including recent sexual intercourse

and use of a diaphragm with spermicide (Hooton et al., 1996). Rectal bacteria can also cause cystitis. Thus, after a bowel movement, a woman should not wipe herself in the direction from the anus to the vulva (see Chapter 5). Some women suffer from chronic inflammation of the bladder, a condition called *interstitial cystitis*. Researchers are not sure what causes it (a protein is suspected), but there is a drug (Elmiron) that helps in some cases. If you suffer from this condition, you should avoid acidic foods, coffee and tea, and alcohol or carbonated drinks.

THE BREASTS

Although **breasts** are not part of a woman's reproductive system, they are considered to be highly erotic by most men in Western societies, and therefore we must consider them part of a woman's sexual anatomy. Recall from Chapter 1, however, that women's breasts have no erotic significance in many cultures around the world.

Breasts develop at puberty as a result of increasing levels of the hormone *estrogen*, which is produced by the ovaries. Thus, the breasts are really a secondary sex characteristic, just as pubic hair is. Interestingly, it is common for one breast (usually the left) to be slightly larger than the other. Boys also have a slight increase in estrogen levels after puberty, and many show a slight increase in breast size (called *gynecomastia*) as a result. This may cause embarrassment for some young teenage boys, but the condition usually disappears within a few years.

Each adult breast consists of 15 to 20 **mammary** (milk-producing) **glands** (see Figure 2–4). A separate duct connects each gland to the *nipple*, which is made up of smooth muscle fibers and also has lots of nerve fibers (making the nipples sensitive to touch). When a woman becomes sexually aroused, the smooth muscle fibers contract and the nipples become erect. The darkened area around the nipple, called the *areola*, becomes even darker during pregnancy. The small bumps on the areola are glands that secrete oil to keep the nipples lubricated during breast-feeding.

In the late stage of pregnancy, a hormone called *prolactin* from the pituitary gland (at the base of the brain) causes the mammary glands to start producing milk (called *lactation*). A baby's sucking on the nipple causes the pituitary to produce the hormone *oxytocin*, which results in the ejection of milk. There can also be secretions from the breasts at other times (a condition known as *galactorrhea*) as a result of certain drugs, birth control pills, stress, or rough fabrics rubbing against the breasts. Some

urethra The passageway from the bladder to the exterior of the body. In men, it also serves as a passageway for semen during ejaculation.

breasts In women, glands that provide milk for infants; located at the front of the chest.

mammary glands Milk-producing glands of the breast.

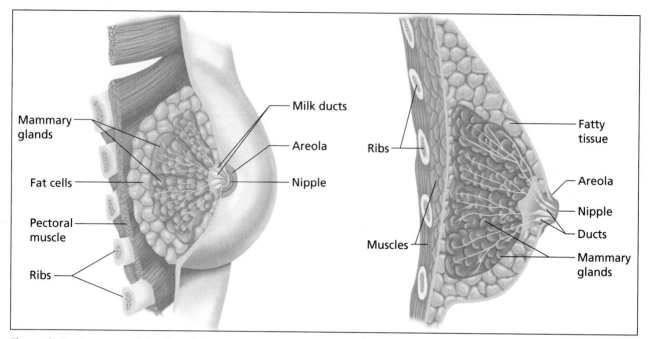

Figure 2–4 Anatomy of the female breast.

people, including men, have inverted nipples or an extra nipple, but this generally does not pose a health problem.

Breasts vary in size from woman to woman (see Figure 2–5). Breast size is not determined by the number of mammary glands, which is about the same for all women, but by the amount of fatty (adipose) tissue packed between the glands. This is determined primarily by heredity. Although some men believe that large-breasted women have a greater sexual capacity than small-breasted women, there is no relation between breast size and sensitivity to touch (Masters & Johnson, 1966). Large breasts do not have a greater number of nerve endings than small breasts. Nevertheless, because of the attention that many men give to breast size, some women attempt to enlarge their breasts.

Breast augmentation exercises and the lotions and mechanical devices advertised in women's magazines do not work (remember, breast size is determined by the amount of fatty tissue). In the 1960s, plastic surgeons began implanting soft pouches filled with silicone to increase the size of breasts. In 1999, the Institute of Medicine estimated that 1.5 million to 1.8 million American women had had their breasts enlarged in this manner, 70 percent of them for cosmetic purposes. However, complications are common. Sooner or later, nearly all implants rupture (Robinson et al., 1995). In about 17.5 percent of women who receive breast implants, a fibrous capsule forms around the implant, making the breast hard, tight, and unnatural in appearance (Gabriel et al., 1997).

Ruptured implants initially raised concerns about the possibility of implants causing cancer and autoimmune disease (antibodies attacking the body's own tissues, resulting in arthritis or lupus). However, numerous scientific studies have found no evidence that silicone implants cause cancer or connective tissue disease (see Brinton & Brown, 1997; Janowsky et al., 2000). Thousands of lawsuits have been filed by women against the manufacturers of implants, but in 1999 the Institute of Medicine also concluded that there is no evidence that implants cause these problems.

Although silicone implants apparently do not cause serious health problems, women who are considering implants should not forget about the many cases of painful hardening of the breasts. Talk-show host Jenny Jones has had six operations because of the damage her implants did to her breasts. She was quoted in *People* magazine as saying, "I hate my body a thousand times more now than I ever did before. . . . I would sell everything I own to be able to have the body back that I gave up." Students in my class have relayed similar experiences:

> "My mom had a breast augmentation job done about 2 years ago and has had nothing but problems. She started growing too much scar tissue and lumps in her breasts, and now, after all the pain and money and aggravation she went through, she's having them removed this summer. I know she did it for my dad, but she can never tell me enough times how sorry she is she ever did it."

In 1992, the Food and Drug Administration (FDA) severely restricted silicone implants for purely

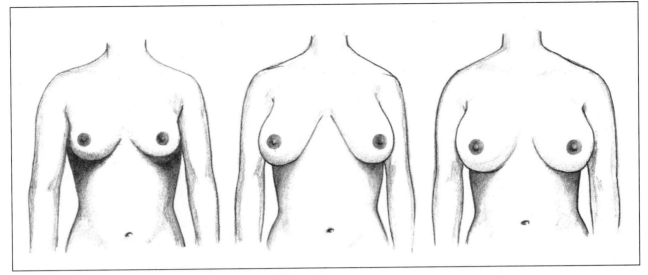

Figure 2–5 Some variations in the appearance of female breasts.

cosmetic purposes, but left them available for women with mastectomies (breast removal), for whom they felt the emotional benefits outweighed the other risks. Manufacturers are now making saline-filled implants (about 130,000 American women had them implanted in 1999). However, the FDA has warned that silicone-filled implants rupture at an "alarmingly high" rate, and these new implants do not eliminate the problem of fibrous capsules forming, causing hardening of the breasts.

Many naturally large-breasted women would like to be smaller. One major reason is that nearly all very large-breasted women suffer from bad back pain (Kerrigan, 1999):

> "I currently wear a DD cup. . . . My chest has become a large nuisance. It is hard for me to dance, jog, or do any kind of activity that involves moving around a lot. Finding clothes is very hard. . . . I just recently talked to a friend of mine who had a breast reduction. I really want to have this operation. It would make me feel better about myself."
> (from the author's files)

Breast reduction involves removing some of the fatty tissue; but, although it generally has fewer complications than breast augmentation, it can cause scars or leave numbness in parts of a breast.

Cancer of the breast is the second leading cause of death by cancer in women. Women are advised, therefore, to learn how to examine themselves in order to make an early, possibly life-saving, detection (see Box 2–A).

PERSONAL REFLECTIONS
Do you wish you had different-sized or different-shaped breasts? How would you like to be different? Why? Should a woman's breast size be an important factor in sexually pleasing a partner?

INTERNAL FEMALE ANATOMY

The vagina, uterus, Fallopian tubes, and ovaries are often referred to as a woman's reproductive system (see Figure 2–7). The vagina serves as a depository for the man's sperm. Eggs are produced by the ovaries. During a woman's reproductive years, one or more eggs will mature on a monthly basis and will be released from an ovary and picked up by one of the Fallopian tubes. It is in the Fallopian tube that an egg and a sperm unite to start a new living being. The fertilized egg then travels through the tube and implants itself within the uterus (see Chapter 7).

THE VAGINA

We have already discussed the vaginal opening as part of the genitalia or external anatomy, but the **vagina** (Latin for "sheath") is really an internal structure located behind the bladder and in front of the rectum. It serves not only as a depository for sperm during sexual intercourse but also as the birth canal, and thus is capable of expanding to about 4 inches in diameter. However, contrary to what some men may believe, the vagina is not an open orifice always ready to accommodate the insertion of a penis. In the unstimulated state, it is about 3 to 5 inches long and its walls are collapsed. It is not until a woman becomes sexually aroused that the walls of the inner two-thirds of the vagina begin to expand to accommodate a penis. The vaginal opening actually narrows during sexual arousal (see Chapter 4).

The vaginal walls have three layers. The inner layer has a soft mucosal surface similar to that of the inside of the mouth. Before puberty, the

vagina The sheathlike canal in a woman that extends from the vulva to the cervix and that receives the penis during intercourse.

Box 2-A **SEXUALITY AND HEALTH**

Breast Cancer and Examination

Apart from skin cancer, cancer of the breast is the most common type of cancer (and the second leading cause of cancer death) in women, with over 184,000 new cases and 41,000 deaths per year (American Cancer Society, 2000). The odds of getting breast cancer have increased over the last few decades, and the latest statistics show that 1 in 8 American women will develop breast cancer in her lifetime (Feuer et al., 1993). A fact that is less well known is that men can get breast cancer too (about 1,400 men will be diagnosed this year).

The cause or causes of most cases of breast cancer are unknown, but there are some factors that put a woman at high risk. These include a family history of breast cancer (as many as one-fourth of cases may be due to inherited factors), being older than 50 years, never giving birth or having the first child after age 30, starting menstruation before age 12, or undergoing menopause after age 55 (see Armstrong et al., 2000; Lichtenstein et al., 2000). About 5 to 10 percent of breast cancer cases are caused by an inherited gene mutation (Martin & Weber, 2000). Recently, researchers have discovered that Epstein-Barr virus is found in many breast tumors (Bonnet et al., 1999), but it is too early to understand what this means.

The rate of breast cancer in North America and northern Europe is much higher than in Asia or Africa, but children of immigrants from these low-incidence areas have rates of breast cancer similar to those of the high-incidence countries (Kliewer & Smith, 1995). This suggests that life-style and environment also play a role. Within the United States, breast cancer rates are highest for African-American women and lowest for Latino and Asian-American women. Some of the factors that have been implicated as risks are obesity and lack of exercise (Huang et al.,1997; Thune et al., 1997), alcohol consumption (Longnecker et al., 1992), and smoking (Calle et al., 1994). Breast-feeding offers very little protection against breast cancer (Lipworth et al., 2000). Estrogen (a hormone released by the ovaries) has long been thought to be a cause of breast cancer, but results of studies on the effects of birth control pills (which contain estrogen) or postmenopausal estrogen replacement therapy have been in-

consistent. Current consensus is that if the birth control pill or hormone replacement therapy does increase the risk, the increase is only very slight, and only with long-term use (Collaborative Group on Hormonal, 1996, 1997; Romieu et al., 1990; Stanford et al., 1995; Steinberg et al., 1991). How little is known about breast cancer is revealed by the fact that only about half of all cases are associated with any of the known risk factors.

Today, there is a preventive drug available for healthy women who have a high risk of eventually getting breast cancer. The drug, called tamoxifen, reduces the rate of breast cancer (by 45 percent) by preventing estrogen from getting into cells (Armstrong et al., 2000). Tamoxifen may increase the risk of endometrial cancer and cardiovascular problems, but another drug with fewer side effects (raloxifene) should be on the market soon.

About half of all cases of breast cancer have spread beyond the breast before they are discovered. However, with early detection, there is a 96 percent survival rate (American Cancer Society, 2000), and with a little instruction, the woman herself is the one most likely to make a life-saving early detection. Women should examine their breasts on a monthly basis. The best time is immediately after menstruation ends, when estrogen levels are low and the breasts are not tender or swollen. Women who are pregnant, postmenopausal, or do not menstruate regularly should examine themselves at a regular time each month. First look at yourself in front of a mirror. Do this with your hands at your sides, then with your hands on your hips, and finally with your hands raised above your head. Look for any bulging, flattening, dimpling, or redness. The symptoms are usually painless. In each position, examine one breast with the opposite hand. With fingers flat, press gently in small circular motions, starting at the top, and check the outermost part of the entire breast in clockwise fashion (see Figure 2–6). It is normal to have a ridge of firm tissue in the lower curve of each breast. After you have completed the circle, move your fingers an inch closer to the nipple and make another complete check around the breast. At least three to four complete circles around the breast will be required. Be sure to

Figure 2–6 Breast self-examination: The traditional method (top) and a new alternative method (bottom, right).

examine under your arms as well, because this is one of the most common areas for cancer to occur. In addition, examine the nipple by squeezing it and noting any discharge. Repeat the same procedure on the other breast. When you are done, examine yourself again during a bath or shower, as it is often easier to detect a lump, hard knot, or thickening when the skin is wet and slippery.

An alternative method of examining the breasts in which you examine yourself with vertical strips has been gaining in popularity (Barton et al., 1999). If you want to know more about this method, write to Mammacare Personal Learning System, P.O. Box 15748, Gainesville, FL 32604, or visit their Website at www.mammacare.com.

Whichever method you use, report any suspected abnormality to your doctor immediately.

"I am a 33-year-old nurse that has instructed many other women about self-examination, but unfortunately, did not practice what I preached. After one of your lectures I did examine my breasts and was horrified to find a small lump." (from the author's files)

Unfortunately, by the time many women discover a lump, the cancer has already spread to other parts of their bodies. As a result, the American Cancer Society strongly recommends that women have **mammograms** (breast X-ray) to find cancers that are too small to be felt by hand. They suggest a mammogram every 1 to 2 years between the ages of 40 to 49, and an annual breast X-ray after the age of 50. All leading medical organizations now endorse this schedule. The amount of radiation used in a mammogram is quite small, and the American Cancer Society believes that the long-term benefits far outweigh any potential risks (Mettler et al., 1996). The number of cancers detected by mammograms has doubled since the mid-1980s, and with the introduction of digital mammography in 2000, detection can be made even earlier.

mammogram Low-radiation X-rays used to detect breast tumors.

Eight out of 10 lumps that are discovered are benign (noncancerous) cysts (fluid-filled sacs) or fibroadenomas (solid tumors). They are known as *fibrocystic disease* and (because they are rare after menopause) are believed to be caused by hormones. Therefore, do not panic if you find a lump in your breast, as the chances are good that it is not malignant.

> "When I was 15 years old, I discovered a breast lump accidentally while bathing. That was one of the scariest days of my life. My doctors told me I had fibrocystic disease. The day before my 18th birthday, I had surgery to remove another lump."
> (from the author's files)

Biopsies are now being done by needle, which is faster, more exact, and less painful than the conventional surgical biopsy. Should you have a lump and it is diagnosed as cancerous, a number of surgical procedures might be performed: (1) radical *mastectomy*, in which the entire breast, underlying muscle, and lymph nodes are removed; (2) modified radical mastectomy, in which the breast and lymph nodes, but not the underlying muscles, are removed; (3) simple mastectomy, in which only the breast is removed; and (4) *lumpectomy*, in which only the lump and a small bit of surrounding tissue are removed, followed by radiation therapy. Studies show that with early detection, lumpectomy and radiation treatment are as effective as radical mastectomy (Fisher et al., 1995). In cases of cancer that have spread to the lymph nodes, the established procedure is mastectomy with chemotherapy. If one or both breasts have to be removed, breast reconstruction through plastic surgery is often possible (over 50,000 breast cancer patients choose to do this every year).

Whatever the therapy, it is not uncommon for women with breast cancer to experience sexual problems and the need to make adjustments (Meyerowitz et al., 1999; Moyer, 1997). The reaction of a woman's partner is important. For example, a woman who has had a breast removed needs to be reassured that she is not going to be desired or loved less than before. Would you expect your partner to love you less if you lost a toe, foot, leg, finger, hand, or arm? Of course not. So why should it be any different if she loses a breast? This may seem obvious to you, but your partner will probably want to hear you say it.

> "I came from a family consisting of five daughters and no one had ever been diagnosed with breast cancer. I had never given it a thought that I would be the one to have a lump in my breast. . . . I had a modified radical mastectomy of my left breast. . . . When my doctor told my husband and me my husband was wonderful about it. All you need to get over the shock is an understanding and supportive husband and family. Emotionally I was able to get over the surgery because he never made me feel like 'half' a woman." (from the author's files)

For more information and for help in finding the most appropriate tests and therapies, call the National Cancer Institute hotline: 1-800-4-CANCER.

PERSONAL REFLECTIONS
Do you regularly examine your breasts for abnormal lumps? If the answer is no, why not? The Centers for Disease Control and Prevention report that nearly 85 percent of women aged 40 or older have had a mammogram (Blackman et al., 1999). If you are in this age group and have not had one, why not?

---

walls of the vagina are thin and relatively inelastic. The rising levels of female hormones at puberty cause the vaginal walls to thicken and become more elastic and highly vascularized (i.e., having lots of blood vessels). Vaginal lubrication during sexual arousal results from the walls of the vagina becoming filled with blood, with the resulting pressure causing fluid (super-filtered blood plasma) to be secreted from the mucosal lining. At menopause (the time in life when a woman's reproductive capacity ends) the ovaries atrophy, and the consequent loss of hormones causes the walls of the vagina to again become thin and inelastic, similar to their condition before puberty. There is also a decrease in the blood supply to the vaginal walls after menopause, resulting in decreased vaginal lubrication, and

thus many older women may require a lubricant during sexual intercourse.

The vagina is a self-cleansing organ. Many potentially harmful bacteria from the outside environment are destroyed by other bacteria that are found naturally within the vagina. In addition, the walls of the vagina continually secrete fluids that help to maintain an acidic environment. A healthy vagina has a musky odor. Vaginal odors act as a sexual stimulant to the males in most mammalian species. Vaginal secretions from female rhesus monkeys, for example, contain fatty acids called copulins, which attract the male monkeys. A similar substance has been found in human vaginal secretions. In laboratory studies, most men do not find musky vaginal odors offensive (Hassett,

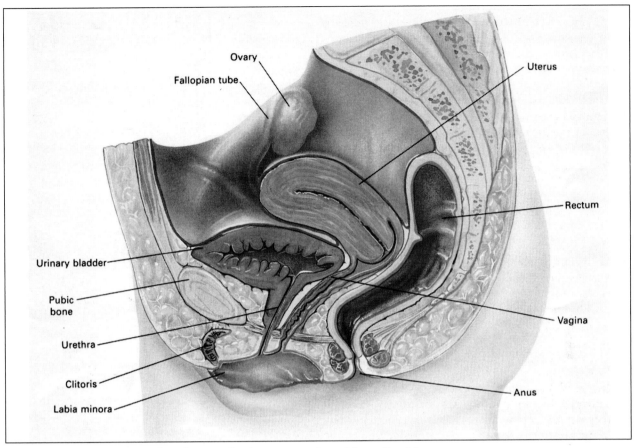

Figure 2–7(A)   The internal female reproductive system, viewed from the side.

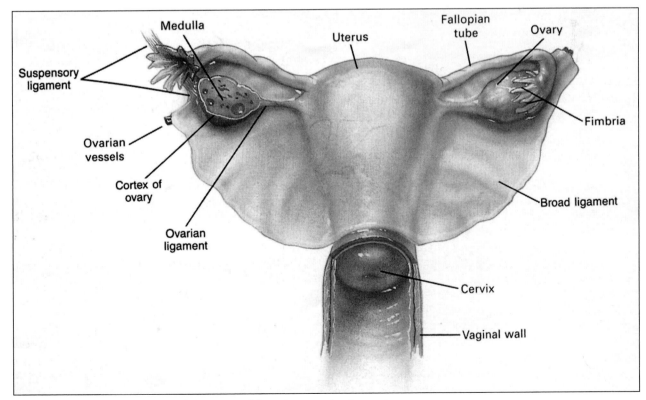

Figure 2–7(B)   A frontal view of the internal female reproductive system.

1978). However, often we are taught that vaginal odors are offensive. If a person hears enough dirty jokes and stories about vaginal odors before becoming sexually experienced, he or she will come to believe this, even though it is not true. How, then, did these stories get started? Probably because most women will occasionally get a vaginal infection that can be accompanied by a foul odor (see the discussion on vaginitis in Chapter 5). These infections can be easily and quickly cured. In order to sell their products, however, advertisers of feminine hygiene sprays and douches generally imply that vaginal odors are always offensive and must be masked with a perfumed substance. The fact is that these products do not cure vaginal infections; in fact, they generally make them worse by further changing the chemical environment of the vagina.

> "A year ago I started using a feminine hygiene deodorant spray. I had used this spray for an average of 5 months before I realized that my discharge was abnormal. After talking with my doctor I found that I had a yeast infection. All of this could have been avoided if I had only stayed away from feminine deodorant sprays." (from the author's files)

Recent studies have found that regular douching increases the risk of pelvic inflammatory disease (a serious infection of a woman's reproductive system; see Chapter 5), ectopic pregnancy, and perhaps even cervical cancer (Zhang et al., 1997). Women should avoid using douches unless told to do so by a physician.

PERSONAL REFLECTIONS
Women, do you have any anxieties or insecurities about whether your vaginal odors may be offensive? Do you use feminine hygiene products or douche regularly? If so, why? If you answered "yes," how did you acquire these negative feelings about the female body? Men, have you ever told a joke, or laughed at a joke, about offensive vaginal odors? If so, how would you feel (and how would it affect feelings about your own sexuality) if women commonly told jokes about offensive penis odors?

pubococcygeus (PC) muscle The major muscle in the pelvic region. In women, voluntary control over this muscle (to help prevent urinary incontinence or to enhance physical sensations during intercourse) is gained through Kegel exercises.

Kegel exercises Exercises that are designed to strengthen the pubococcygeus muscle that surrounds the bladder and vagina.

Grafenberg (G) spot A small, sensitive area on the front wall of the vagina found in about 10 percent of all women.

uterus The womb. The hollow, muscular organ in women where the fertilized egg normally implants.

Although the vaginal opening is very sensitive to touch, the walls of the inner two-thirds of the vagina are relatively insensitive to touch as a result of having few nerve endings. It has been demonstrated that some women cannot even tell when their inner vaginal walls are being touched by a probe (Kinsey et al., 1953). Does this mean that the presence of a penis in the vagina does not contribute to a woman's subjective feelings of pleasure during sexual in-

tercourse? Not necessarily. Although the vaginal walls are sparse in nerve endings, the vagina is surrounded by a large muscle, the **pubococcygeus (PC) muscle,** which is more richly innervated with nerves. It has been found that women who have little vaginal sensation during intercourse (some report that they cannot even feel the penis) have a weak pubococcygeus muscle (Kegel, 1952). As a result, some sex therapists have advocated daily exercises to strengthen this muscle in order to enhance pleasure during sexual intercourse (Barbach, 1976; Graber, 1982; Perry & Whipple, 1981). These exercises, called **Kegel exercises,** are the same ones that many physicians instruct women to do after having a baby, in order to regain urinary control. The pubococcygeus muscle controls urine flow, but it becomes stretched and weak during pregnancy, causing many women to suffer from urinary incontinence.

Here are the steps for doing Kegel exercises: (1) Learn what it feels like to contract the PC muscle by stopping yourself in the middle of urinating with your legs apart; (2) after you know what it feels like to contract the PC muscle, insert a finger into your vagina and bear down until you can feel the muscle squeeze your finger; and (3) once you can do this, start doing daily Kegels without a finger inserted. Physicians and therapists suggest practicing 10 contractions of 3 seconds each three times a day. The best thing about Kegel exercises is that they can be done anytime and anywhere, and no one else knows what you are doing.

There is an exception to the general statement that the vaginal walls are relatively insensitive to touch. Some women have a small sensitive spot on the front wall of the vagina at about the level of the top of the pubic bone (about a third or halfway in from the vaginal opening). This has been named the **Grafenberg (G) spot,** after the German doctor who first reported it in 1950 (Perry & Whipple, 1981). Stimulation of the G spot often leads to an orgasm that some women say feels different from an orgasm caused by clitoral stimulation (see Chapter 4). Originally it was claimed that all women had a G spot (Ladas et al., 1982), but later studies suggested that only 10 percent or fewer women have this area of heightened sensitivity (Alzate & Londono, 1984).

One in every 4,000 to 5,000 girls is born without a vagina (Harnish, 1988). When this occurs, physicians are usually able to surgically construct one.

THE UTERUS

It is within the **uterus,** or womb, that a fertilized egg will attach itself and become an embryo and then a fetus. Resembling a small, inverted pear, the uterus in women who have not had children measures only about 3 inches long and 3 inches across at its broadest portion, but it is capable of tremendous expansion.

The *cervix*, the narrow end of the uterus, projects into the back of the vagina and can be easily felt (as a slippery bump) by inserting a finger into the back of the vagina. The broad part of the uterus is called the *fundus*. Ligaments hold the uterus in the pelvic cavity at about a 90-degree angle to the vagina, although in some women it may tilt slightly forward or backward.

The uterus has three layers: the innermost **endometrium,** where the fertilized egg implants; a strong middle layer of muscles called the *myometrium*, which contracts during labor; and an external cover called the *perimetrium*. The endometrium thickens and becomes rich in blood vessels after ovulation, but it is sloughed off and discharged from the woman's body during menstruation if fertilization does not occur. Glands within the cervix secrete mucus throughout a woman's menstrual cycle, and a change in the consistency of this mucus is often used to tell when ovulation has occurred. The cervical opening, or *os* (Latin for "mouth"), is normally no wider than the diameter of a matchstick, but it dilates to 10 centimeters (about 4 inches) at childbirth to allow delivery of the baby.

Unfortunately, the cervix is the site of one of the most common types of cancer in women. It is extremely important, therefore, that all women, whether sexually inexperienced or sexually active, go to a physician for an annual examination and Pap smear (see Box 2–B).

THE FALLOPIAN TUBES

Extending 4 inches laterally from both sides of the uterus are the **Fallopian tubes,** or oviducts, as they are sometimes called. There is no direct physical connection between the Fallopian tubes and the ovaries, but the fingerlike projections at the end of the tubes (called *fimbria*) brush against the ovaries. After an egg is expelled from an ovary into the abdominal cavity at ovulation, it is picked up by one of the fimbria. If a sperm fertilizes the egg, it will usually do so within the tube. The fertilized egg then continues its 3- to 4-day trip through the tube and normally implants itself in the endometrium of the uterus. Anatomical abnormalities and infections can block the tube and cause sterility (sperm cannot meet egg) or a tubal pregnancy (a fertilized egg implants itself within the tube). The latter poses a serious health threat because the tubes are not capable of expanding like the uterus. Either tying off and cutting or cauterizing the tubes (*tubal ligation* or *laparoscopy*) is a popular means of birth control for couples who already have all the children they want (see Chapter 6).

THE OVARIES

The **ovaries** are the female gonads and develop from the same embryonic tissue as the male gonads, the testicles. They are suspended by ligaments on both sides of the uterus. The ovaries have two functions: to produce eggs, or *ova* (sing. *ovum*), and to produce female hormones (*estrogen* and *progesterone*). A girl has all the immature

eggs that she will ever have at birth, about 300,000 to 400,000 in each ovary. Each egg is surrounded by some other cells and contained within a thin capsule to form what is called a **primary follicle.** At puberty, one or more of the follicles is stimulated to mature on about a monthly basis (the menstrual cycle). When mature, the follicle is called a *Graafian follicle*. This process ends at menopause, and thus only about 400 of the several hundred thousand ova in a woman's ovaries will ever mature during her lifetime. In contrast, a man's testicles produce millions of new sperm every day.

EXTERNAL MALE ANATOMY

Generally speaking, men have a better idea than women of what their genitals look like. Not only is a man's genitalia more visible to him than a woman's genitalia is to her, but boys are taught at a very young age to hold the penis while urinating, and thus may be less inhibited than girls about touching and examining themselves. Although they differ in appearance, many of the male structures develop from the same embryonic tissue as female structures (the penis and clitoris, for example). The male reproductive system and genitalia are shown in Figures 2–9 and 2–10. Penises differ in appearance just like any other part of the body, and men should not consider themselves abnormal if they do not look identical to Figure 2–10.

> *PERSONAL REFLECTIONS*
> *What were your feelings when you first looked at Figures 2–2 and 2–10? If you experienced any discomfort or anxiety, why? As part of this chapter, I have suggested that you examine your own genitals. Were you able to do this without feelings of guilt or anxiety? If not, why do you think you have negative feelings about looking at this part of your body?*

THE PENIS: OUTER APPEARANCE

The **penis** (Latin for "tail") has both a reproductive and a urinary function. It serves to deposit sperm in a woman's vagina and also to eliminate urine from the bladder. When a man is unaroused, the penis is soft and hangs between the legs. It hardens and becomes erect during sexual stimulation, thus enabling penetration of the vagina. The average size of the penis in the unstimulated (flaccid) condition is 3.75 inches in length and 1.2 inches in diameter; it is about 6 inches in length and 1.5 inches in diameter when erect (Jamison & Gebhard,

endometrium The inner mucous membrane of the uterus where a fertilized egg implants. Its thickness varies with the phase of the menstrual cycle.

Fallopian tubes The passageways that eggs follow on their way to the uterus.

ovary The female gonad in which ova are produced.

primary follicle An immature ovum enclosed by a single layer of cells.

penis The male organ for sexual intercourse and the passageway for sperm and urine.

Box 2-B SEXUALITY AND HEALTH

Cancer of the Female Reproductive System

Cancer of the Cervix

The cervix is a common site for cancer in women. There are approximately 60,000 new cases of cervical cancer in the United States every year, of which 12,800 are invasive (have spread beyond the surface of the cervix) (American Cancer Society, 2000). It results in about 4,600 deaths a year. Women can have this cancer at almost any age. Women at high risk include those who began having sexual intercourse at an early age or who have had numerous sexual partners and those whose partners have had numerous sexual partners (Rosenberg & Gollub, 1992). Cancer of the cervix is rare among nuns and other celibate women. It is not sex itself that is the cause of cervical cancer but certain types of human papillomaviruses, a virus that is spread during sexual activity (see Chapter 5) (Walboomers et al., 1999). Regular use of barrier methods of contraception (such as condoms and diaphragms) reduces the risk of getting cervical cancer. Women who smoke also have a higher risk of cervical cancer (Gram et al., 1992), probably because smoking weakens the body's defenses, making it easier for the cancer-causing viruses to have their effect.

A pelvic exam and **Pap smear** test (named after Dr. George Papanicolaou, who developed the test) are a necessary part of female health care. The risk of developing cervical cancer is only about one-fourth as great for women who get Pap smears regularly as it is for women who do not (Shy et al., 1989). Most cervical cancer–related deaths occur in women who do not get regular Pap tests. Dr. Patricia Braley, who headed a National Institutes of Health panel on cervical cancer in 1996, said, "In theory, cervical cancer is a cancer we can completely prevent. If we could reach all the women in this country who are not getting regular Pap tests we could eradicate this type of cancer."

Many women are nevertheless reluctant to get a Pap smear because of embarrassment. The first step, therefore, is to find a doctor with whom you are comfortable and who shows concern for his or her patients (as by warming instruments to body temperature before using them). In the examination room, the woman lies flat on her back with her legs apart and her feet in footrests called stirrups. An instrument called a speculum, which is shaped like a duck's bill, is inserted into the vagina and gently opened so that the vaginal walls and cervix may be inspected. A cotton swab or thin wooden stick is used to gently skim the surface of the cervix in order to collect cells, which are then examined under a microscope for abnormalities. During the exam, the doctor will also check the vaginal walls and vulva for possible infections. Some doctors may include a rectal exam at this time. The entire process generally takes only a few minutes, and although some women may experience discomfort, it is generally not painful.

> "Human sexuality class has made me more educated about my body, and I became more aware. Before I entered this class I was very scared of going to the gynecologist for a visit (age 20). Recently I went for my first visit and found my fears were ridiculous. It was not bad at all and I even felt better to find out I was OK."

> "At the beginning of the semester you mentioned UNO's Health Services and I decided to check them out. When the results of my Pap smear came in, I had tested positive. I had stage II dysplasia. I had cryotherapy. . . . If it had not been for this class, I don't know how long I would have waited to get a Pap smear or what the results would have been." (All examples are from the author's files.)

Any detected abnormalities of cells are treated according to severity. An estimated 1 million women per year are found to have low-grade dysplasia (abnormal cellular changes). In the precancerous stage, the localized abnormal cells are often destroyed by extreme cold (cryotherapy) or intense heat (electrocoagulation). Because most precancerous abnormalities are slow to develop and have a low risk of becoming cancer, some physicians believe in a watch-and-wait strategy at this stage (Bergstrom et al., 1993). Precancerous abnormalities in cells often take as long as 8 years before they start to invade other tissues. If the cancer progresses, warning signs may include bleeding between menstrual periods, excessive bleeding during periods, and bleeding after menopause. However, sometimes there are no symptoms. If cancer of the cervix is found, a woman may have to have a *hysterectomy*

Pap smear A test for cancer of the cervix in women; named for Dr. Papanicolaou, who developed it.

(surgical removal of the uterus), which will end her reproductive capabilities. Some studies report that the surgery decreases vaginal lubrication and elasticity in about 25 percent of women (Bergmark et al., 1999), but the surgery does not interfere with sexual desire and may even improve some women's sex lives (Rhodes et al., 1999).

> "I thought after my hysterectomy my vagina would dry up and I would lose my sexual desire. It has been 5 years and I still take hormones but I haven't dried up and I have reached my sexual peak. Within these 5 years I have felt better about my self sexually."   (from the author's files)

The American Cancer Society advises women that regular checkups should begin when they start having sexual intercourse, or at age 18 even if they are sexually inexperienced. Annual checkups are required at first because the Pap smear test sometimes does not detect precancerous conditions. After three initial negative tests, your doctor may tell you to come back less often.

Pelvic exams are also done to fit a diaphragm or IUD, to check for vaginal infections, and to examine the uterus during pregnancy. Many women assume that their doctor routinely checks for sexually transmitted disease when taking a Pap smear, but most do not unless specifically asked to do so. If you have had multiple sexual partners (and are thus at high risk to get a sexually transmitted disease), you should consider these additional tests at this time.

PERSONAL REFLECTIONS
The Centers for Disease Control and Prevention report that 91–93 percent of women 18 years old or older have had a Pap smear test (Blackman et al., 1999). Have you? Have you had one within the last year? If not, why not?

Cancer of the Endometrium and Ovaries

Cancer of the endometrium is also very common, with an estimated 36,100 new cases and 6,500 deaths per year in the United States (American Cancer Society, 2000). Typically, the first symptom is abnormal vaginal bleeding, so if you should experience this, go to a physician immediately. He or she will make a diagnosis by dilation and curettage (D&C). Should cancer be found, your doctor will probably recommend a hysterectomy, but radiation, drug, or hormonal therapies are also used sometimes.

Ovarian cancer is a rare disease (lifetime risk of less than 1.5 percent), but a deadly one. It causes the death of more American women each year (approximately 14,000) than either cervical or endometrial cancer. Most cases are found in postmenopausal women or women approaching menopause (between 50 and 59 years old). It is more common in women who have never been pregnant, and less so in women who use oral contraceptives. The use of fertility drugs is also associated with an increased risk of ovarian cancer (Whittemore et al., 1992). However, the highest risk factor is a family history of ovarian cancer (Lynch & Lynch, 1992). Breast-feeding has been found to offer some protection against ovarian cancer (Siskind et al., 1997).

Cancer of the ovaries is usually painless in the early stages. Thus the tumors are often quite large by the time they are discovered, making effective treatment difficult. Today there is a blood test for women at high risk (it tests for CA-125, a protein produced by cancerous ovarian cells). Treatment usually involves removal of the ovaries and radiation.

Many ovarian cysts are benign (noncancerous), but these cysts can become quite large. Surgeons at Stanford University removed a cyst weighing 303 pounds (the woman herself weighed 210 pounds after the operation). Studies show that in the case of benign cysts, removal of the cyst alone results in fewer problems than does hysterectomy (surgical removal of the uterus).

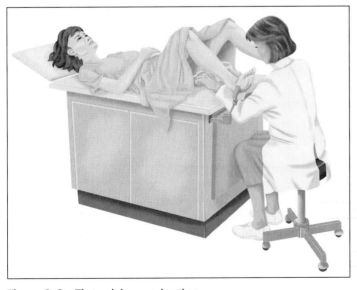

Figure 2–8   The pelvic examination.

Figure 2–9   Anatomical location of the male reproductive system.

1988; Sparling, 1997). Some penises are curved to the left or right, and others are curved up or down. In a rare condition called micropenis, the penis never develops to more than 1 inch in length (usually due to low levels of the male hormone testosterone; see Aaronson, 1994). In Chapter 4, we will consider whether penis size relates to sexual satisfaction in women.

The skin of the penis is very loose to allow for expansion during erection. At birth the *foreskin* folds over the glans, the smooth rounded end of the penis, but many men have had their foreskin cut off in a surgical procedure known as **circumcision** (see Figure 2–10). If you should have a son, be sure to teach him that good hygiene includes cleaning under the foreskin (see Box 2–C). However, when bathing a newborn, do not pull back forcibly on the foreskin for the first several months, because it is often partially adhered to the penis during this time. In some boys it is still adhered at 3 years of age (Williams et al., 1993).

THE PENIS: INTERNAL STRUCTURE

circumcision   In men, the removal of all or part of the foreskin of the penis. In women, the removal of the clitoral hood.

The penis has three parts: the body or shaft; the glans; and the root. Only the first two parts are visible (see Figure 2–11). In cross section, the

shaft of the penis can be seen to consist of three parallel cylinders of spongy tissue, two *corpora cavernosa* (or "cavernous bodies") on top and a *corpus spongiosum* (or "spongy body") on the bottom. Each is contained in its own fibrous sheath. The corpora cavernosa do not extend the full length of the penis. Instead, the spongy body expands greatly in front to form the round, smooth *glans*. The raised rim at the border of the shaft and glans is called the *corona* (and is the most sensitive to touch of any part of the penis). The *urethra*, which serves as the passageway for urine and sperm, runs through the corpus spongiosum, and thus the urethral opening (or meatus) is normally located at the tip of the glans. Occasionally it is located to one side of the glans, and although this usually poses no major problem, it can cause a man to have a negative perception of his own genitals. For reasons not yet determined, this condition (called *hypospadias*) has nearly doubled in frequency of occurrence since 1970, but it can be corrected by surgery (Paulozzi et al., 1997).

The *root* of the penis consists of the expanded ends of the cavernous bodies, which fan out to form *crura* and attach to the pubic bone (note the similarity in structure to the clitoris), and the expanded end of the spongy body (called the *bulb*). The root is surrounded by two muscles (the bulbocavernosus and the ischiocavernosus) that aid in urination and ejaculation.

In men, an erection does not result from a bone protruding into the penis, as in some mammalian species (e.g., dogs), nor does it result from voluntary contraction of a muscle. When a man becomes sexually aroused, the arteries going to the penis dilate and the many cavities of the cavernous and spongy bodies fill with blood. Valves in the veins that drain the penis simultaneously close. Expansion of the sinuses (cavities) and contraction of the muscles at the base of the penis may further aid this process by pressing against the veins and partially cutting off the drainage. In brief, an erection results from the

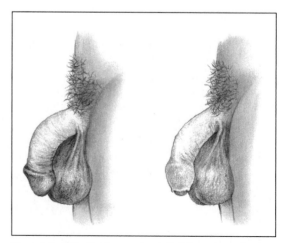

Figure 2–10   A circumcised (left) and uncircumcised (right) penis.

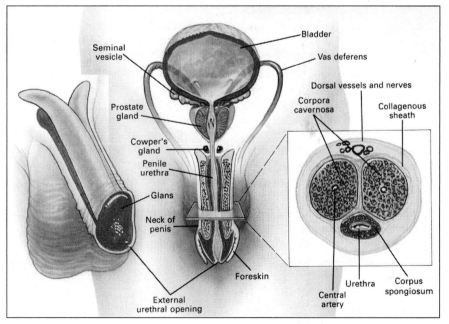

Figure 2–11 The internal male reproductive system: (top) from a side view and cross section of the penis; (bottom) from a frontal view.

Box 2-C CROSS-CULTURAL PERSPECTIVES/SEXUALITY AND HEALTH

Male Circumcision

Circumcision has been performed on boys since at least 4000 B.C. Egyptian mummies dating from this period give evidence of it, and the Greek historians and geographers Herodotus and Strabo later wrote about observing it in their travels (Manniche, 1987). The ancient Egyptians and Ethiopians performed circumcisions for cleanliness (Herodotus), and the practice was borrowed by the Hebrews at about the time of Abraham (the custom later fell into disuse but was revived by Moses). Today, Jewish boys are circumcised on the 8th day of life to symbolize the covenant with God made by Abraham (Genesis 17:9–27). Muslim boys are also circumcised as part of a religious ceremony, often at 13 years of age.

In many cultures today, the operation is performed as a puberty rite, and sometimes it involves more than the cutting away of the foreskin. It is often done with crude instruments and without anesthesia. The Mangaians and other South Pacific islanders cut lengthwise along the top of the penis (superincision) all the way to the stomach (Marshall, 1971). Primitive tribes in central Australia make a slit to the depth of the urethra along the entire length of the lower side of the penis (subincision) so that men urinate at the base of the penis, requiring that they sit like women (Gregersen, 1982). Still other cultures insert rods with gemstones, feathers, or bristles attached to the end (D. Brown, 1990: see Figure 1–2). Many anthropologists believe that these customs are performed as symbolic pledges of loyalty to the group.

In the United States and England, circumcision became popular during the 19th century because Victorian physicians believed that circumcised penises were less sensitive and that the operation would therefore prevent masturbation and hypersexuality. Circumcision reached its height in popularity between World Wars I and II, but then fell out of favor in most English-speaking countries. Nowadays only one-quarter or fewer of boys are routinely circumcised in countries such as England, Canada, New Zealand, and Australia, leaving the United States the only country in which circumcision is still performed for nonreligious reasons on a majority of boys. About 60 percent of all newborn boys are circumcised yearly in the United States (National Center for Health Statistics), but the practice is much more common among white men than other ethnic groups.

Circumcising boys' penises, of course, does not stop them from masturbating. In fact, a recent study found that circumcised men had greater sexual satisfaction and fewer sexual problems than uncircumcised men, and more of them masturbated (Laumann et al., 1997). Today, the reason for circumcision most commonly given by American physicians is to ensure proper hygiene, but there is considerable debate about this, even within the medical community. Glands located beneath the foreskin secrete an oily substance that gets mixed with dead cells to form a cheesy substance called **smegma,** which can cause the foreskin to adhere to the underlying glans of the penis. Without proper hygiene, the smegma serves as a possible breeding ground for bacteria. Several studies have found that many young boys have poor genital hygiene (Schoen, 1990). Cancer of the penis is more common in uncircumcised men, but it is very rare (found in only 9 out of 1 million American men). However, penile cancer is no more common among uncircumcised men who regularly clean under their foreskins than among circumcised men.

People who favor circumcision point out that the rate of urinary tract infections in uncircumcised infants is at least 4 times greater than in circumcised infants, but the overall rate of these infections is less than 1 percent in the United States and is usually easy to treat. Several studies have also found that uncircumcised men have about a 50 percent greater chance of getting HIV (the virus that causes AIDS) or other sexually transmitted diseases if they have unprotected intercourse with infected partners (see Weiss et al., 1999).

On the other side of the argument are the health risks associated with circumcision, including hemorrhage, infection, and (rarely) accidental amputation (Poland, 1990). In addition, circumcision is often done on infant boys without the use of anesthesia. Thus, for many infants circumcision is a painful operation that causes them to cry for hours (Howard et al., 1994).

smegma The cheesy secretion of sebaceous glands that can cause the clitoris to stick to the clitoral hood or the foreskin of the penis to stick to the glans.

"When I was 10 years old, I saw my baby brother get circumcised. I hated to see the pain that he was going through. I could not see why a baby should go through it at all. So I have decided to not let my baby boy go through that kind of pain. I just won't!" (from the author's files)

As a result of these concerns, in 1971 the American Academy of Pediatrics took a stand against the routine circumcision of newborns. Largely because of the urinary tract infection studies, in 1989 the academy decided to take a neutral stand on the matter, allowing parents and physicians to decide for themselves. After a review of 40 years of research about the benefits and risks, in 1999 the American Academy of Pediatrics again opposed the routine circumcision of newborns (American Academy of Pediatrics, 1999). The academy also came out in favor of doctors using a topical cream anesthetic when circumcision is performed. One consequence of the American Academy of Pediatrics' decision is that many in-surance companies now regard circumcision as an optional cosmetic procedure, and will no longer pay for the cost of the operation.

All of these medical arguments are no doubt very confusing to most parents. Many probably choose circumcision just so that their baby boys will look like Dad.

"I will have my son circumcised because I don't want him to feel different." (from the author's files)

My advice to parents is that you should educate yourself about both sides of the argument (I suggest consulting Poland, 1990, and the American Academy of Pediatrics Task Force Report, 1999, in addition to considering the information in this box) and then make a decision that feels right for you.

PERSONAL REFLECTIONS
If you should have a son, do you plan to have him circumcised? Why or why not?

---

spongy tissues of the penis becoming engorged (filled) with blood. *Detumescence*, or loss of erection, is not as well understood, but probably occurs as a result of the arteries beginning to constrict, thus removing pressure from the veins and allowing drainage.

Some men have a severe curvature of the penis. This is sometimes due to developmental abnormalities, but it is often due to injury to the fibrous sheath (elastic tissue) that holds the three parallel cylinders of spongy tissue—called *Peyronie's disease* (Gregory & Purcell, 1989). If the fibrous sheath is injured at any spot, the elastic tissue is replaced by hardened plaque which doesn't expand during erection, thus causing curvature of the penis. If the curvature is too extreme, it can cause pain during intercourse. In some positions of sexual intercourse, men can place too much pressure or weight on their penis, and this can result in a "fracture" (rupturing of the cavernous bodies), which may require surgery (Adducci & Ross, 1991).

THE SCROTUM

The sac located beneath the penis is called the **scrotum.** It holds the testicles outside of the body cavity. Sperm are produced in the testicles, but they can only be produced in an environment several degrees lower than the normal body temperature of 98.6 degrees Fahrenheit. Scrotal temperature is typically about 93 degrees Fahrenheit. The skin of the scrotum is sparsely covered with hair and has many sweat glands that aid in temperature regulation. The scrotum also has small muscle fibers that contract when it is cold to help draw the testicles closer to the body cavity for warmth. When it is hot, the muscle fibers relax and the testes are suspended farther away from the body cavity.

In tropical areas of the world, it is not uncommon for men to suffer from elephantiasis of the scrotum (caused by a parasite), a condition in which the scrotum can get as large as a basketball.

INTERNAL MALE ANATOMY

The male internal reproductive system consists of the testicles, a duct system to transport sperm out of the body, the prostate gland and seminal vesicles that produce the fluid in which the sperm are mixed, and the Cowper's gland (see Figure 2–11).

THE TESTICLES

The **testicles** (the male gonads, or *testes*) develop from the same embryonic tissue as the ovaries (the female gonads). Like the ovaries, the testicles have two functions: to produce *sperm* and to produce male hormones. Millions of new sperm start to be produced each day in several hundred *seminiferous tubules* (the entire process takes about 70 days). Each tubule is 1 to 3 feet in length, and if they were laid together end to end they would measure over one-quarter of a mile in length. In between the

scrotum The pouch beneath the penis that contains the testicles.

testicles The male gonads that produce sperm and male hormones.

seminiferous tubules are cells called *interstitial cells of Leydig,* which produce male hormones. Male (or masculinizing) hormones are called *androgens.* The most important is *testosterone* (you will find many references to this hormone in later chapters). Another hormone produced in the testicles (by Sertoli cells) is called *inhibin,* discussed in Chapter 3.

The testicles are in the abdominal cavity for most of fetal development, but about 2 months before birth they descend through the inguinal canal into the scrotum. They fail to descend in about 2 to 5 percent of male births, a condition known as *cryptorchidism* (Toppari & Kaleva, 1999). This usually corrects itself (only 1–2 percent have failed to descend by 3 months), but if it persists it can result in sterility and increased risk of hernia and cancer of the testicles.

Each testicle is suspended in the scrotum by the *spermatic cord,* a tubelike structure that contains blood vessels, nerves, the vas deferens, and a muscle that helps to raise and lower the testicles in response to changes in environmental temperature and level of sexual arousal (the testicles are drawn closer to the body during sexual arousal). Each testicle is enclosed in a tight fibrous sheath.

In right-handed men it is normal for the left testicle to hang lower than the right one, and vice versa in left-handed men (don't ask why). Both testicles, however, should be about the same size. The testicles are very sensitive to pressure, and men differ as to whether they like to have them touched during sexual relations.

Men and parents of boys should be aware of several health problems associated with the testicles. The virus that is responsible for mumps, for example, causes the testes to swell painfully, and the pressure against the fibrous sheath can crush the seminiferous tubules, resulting in sterility if mumps occurs after puberty. In an uncommon condition called *testicular torsion,* the spermatic cord twists and cuts off the blood supply to the testicles, necessitating their removal if the problem is not corrected in time. This condition is generally accompanied by severe pain, and men should go to a doctor immediately if such pain is experienced. The testes are also the site of a relatively rare form of cancer (see Box 2–D).

The word *testes,* by the way, is derived from a Latin word for *witness* ("to testify"). People shake hands when completing a deal or sealing a promise today, but in biblical times a man held the testicles of the man to whom he gave an oath. The idea was that if he broke his oath, the children of the other man had the right to take revenge.

THE DUCT SYSTEM

After sperm are produced in the seminiferous tubules, they pass through a four-part duct system (epididymis, vas deferens, ejaculatory duct, and urethra) before being expelled from the penis during an ejaculation. The seminiferous tubules converge to form the **epididymis,** coiled tubes (about 20 feet long if uncoiled) that can be felt on the top and back of each testicle. Sperm mature (become more fertile and achieve greater motility) as they travel through the epididymis, which takes up to 6 weeks (Orgebin-Crist, 1998). From here the sperm pass into the paired 14- to 16-inch **vas deferens.** The vas begin in the scrotum, then travel through the spermatic cord and enter the abdominal cavity through the inguinal canal. From there, they go up and over the bladder toward the prostate gland. Many sperm are stored in the expanded end of the vas, called the *ampulla,* prior to ejaculation. Tying off and cutting the vas (*vasectomy*), is a voluntary sterilization procedure performed in men.

During orgasm, rhythmic muscular contractions force the sperm into the **ejaculatory ducts,** short (about 1 inch long) paired tubes that run through the prostate gland, where they are mixed with fluids from the prostate and seminal vesicles to form *semen.* The two ejaculatory ducts open into the **urethra,** which passes through the spongy body of the penis. Sphincter muscles surround the part of the urethra coming from the bladder. These involuntarily contract during an erection so that urine does not get mixed with semen.

THE PROSTATE GLAND AND SEMINAL VESICLES

Although an average ejaculation contains about 200 million to 300 million sperm, they make up very little of the total volume. Most of the volume is seminal fluid from the **seminal vesicles** (accounting for about 70 percent of the fluid) and the prostate gland (about 30 percent). Among other substances, the seminal vesicles (misnamed because anatomists once thought that was where sperm were stored prior to ejaculation) secrete fructose, prostaglandins, and bases. Fructose (a sugar) activates the sperm and makes them mobile, while prostaglandins cause contractions of the uterus, aiding movement through that structure. Bases neutralize the normal acidity of the vagina so that sperm will not be destroyed on their way to the more favorable alkaline environment of the uterus. The **prostate gland** secretes all of these substances and another

---

epididymis   The elongated cordlike structure on the back of a testicle. It is the first part of the duct system tht transports sperm out of a man's body.

vas deferens   The second part of the duct system that transports sperm out of a man's body.

ejaculatory ducts   One-inch-long paired tubes that pass through the prostate gland. The third part of the duct system that transports sperm out of a man's body.

urethra   The passageway from the bladder to the exterior of the body. In men, it also serves as a passageway for semen during ejaculation.

seminal vesicles   Two structures in a man that contribute many substances to the seminal fluid.

prostate gland   A gland in men that surrounds the origins of the urethra and neck of the bladder and contributes many substances to the seminal fluid.

Box 2-D SEXUALITY AND HEALTH

Testicular Cancer and Self-Examination

Cancer of the testicles is not very common. About 6,900 new cases occur in the United States each year (American Cancer Society, 2000). However, it is the most common type of cancer in men aged 20 to 35 (Forman & Moller, 1994). This type of cancer recently received much attention when bicyclist Lance Armstrong (winner of the Tour de France in 1999 and 2000), comedian Tom Green, and Olympic Gold Medal–winning skater Scott Hamilton were diagnosed with it. Men at highest risk are those whose testicles did not descend into the scrotum before the age of 10, those who had an early puberty, and those with inguinal hernias (United Kingdom Testicular Cancer Study Group, 1994). White men have a higher incidence of this type of cancer than do African-American or Latino men. Cancer of the testicles is not related to masturbation, frequent sex, or sexually transmitted diseases.

The most common symptom of testicular cancer is a small lump or a testicle that is slightly enlarged. In the first stages of testicular cancer, the tumors are painless; thus it is important that all men (particularly those in a high-risk group) examine themselves regularly—once a month is advised.

Examine yourself after a warm bath or shower. This causes the testicles to descend and the skin of the scrotum to relax. Examine your testicles one at a time by placing both thumbs on top and the middle and index fingers on bottom (see Figure 2–12). Gently roll your testicle between the thumbs and fingers. When

Figure 2–12 Testicular self-examination.

doing so, you will also feel your epididymis, which feels like a spongy rope on the top and back of each testicle.

Not all abnormal lumps are cancerous, but if a lump should be, treatment usually involves surgical removal of the affected testicle and chemotherapy. The cancer rarely spreads to the other testicle, and the unaffected testicle can produce enough male hormones for normal sex drive and enough sperm to father a child. Synthetic implants can be inserted into the scrotum to give the man's genitals a normal appearance.

PERSONAL REFLECTIONS
Do you regularly examine your testicles for abnormal lumps? If not, why not? The self-exam takes only about 3 minutes.

---

substance (fibrinogenase) that causes semen to temporarily coagulate after ejaculation, thus helping to prevent spillage from the vagina. More recently, it has been found that the prostate also secretes a powerful antibiotic, possibly to protect the male and female reproductive systems from infection. The prostate is the site of the second most common type of cancer found in men and should be checked annually when they reach the age of 40 (see Box 2–E).

THE COWPER'S GLANDS

The **Cowper's**, or bulbourethral, **glands** are two pea-sized structures located beneath the prostate. They secrete a few drops of an alkaline fluid (a base) that may appear at the tip of the penis prior to orgasm. The fluid

neutralizes the normal acidity of the urethra, and thus sperm are not destroyed when passing through the penis during ejaculation. Many couples use withdrawal as a contraceptive technique (i.e., the man withdraws his penis from his partner's vagina just prior to orgasm), but the fluid from the Cowper's glands often contains sperm, making this an unreliable method of birth control (see Chapter 6).

THE BRAIN

The brain has been called the most sexual organ in the human body. This is probably

Cowper's glands Two pea-shaped structures located beneath the prostate gland in men that secrete a few drops of an alkaline fluid prior to orgasm.

true. It is the structure that translates nerve impulses from the skin into pleasurable sensations; controls the nerves and muscles used in sexual behavior; regulates the release of hormones necessary for reproduction; and last, but not least, is the origin of our sexual desires. You will read about the brain in many of the chapters to come. Here is a brief introduction to the parts of the brain most directly involved in sexual behavior and reproduction (see Figure 2–13).

The *cerebral cortex* is the outer layer of nerve cell bodies that covers most of the brain. In nonhuman mammals it is relatively smooth in appearance, but in humans it has numerous folds, or convolutions, that allow for more surface area (and therefore more cells). The cortex is the part of the brain that allows us to think and reason. It is also the anatomical origin of our sexual thoughts and fantasies.

Beneath the cortex are several groups of cell bodies and fiber systems that are known collectively as the *limbic system.* This includes structures with some rather peculiar names, such as the amygdala, hippocampus, cingulate gyrus, and septal area. The limbic system structures are where emotions and feelings originate. These structures apparently are also important for sexual behavior. For example, damage to the amygdala in monkeys, dogs, and cats causes hypersexuality. Male animals with this kind of brain damage will persistently mount not only females but also males and animals of other species. For obvious ethical reasons, researchers cannot destroy parts of the brain in humans, but in a few cases in which the amygdala has had to be removed for medical reasons, the patients afterwards engaged in persistent masturbation (Terzian & Ore, 1955).

Perhaps the most important part of the brain for sexual functioning is the **hypothalamus,** a small area at the base of the brain consisting of several groups of nerve cell bodies. The hypothalamus receives its major input from the limbic system structures. Destruction of certain areas of the hypothalamus completely eliminates sexual behavior in laboratory animals. On the other hand, if electrodes are placed in certain areas of the hypothalamus or limbic system of rats and the animals are allowed to press a lever to deliver electrical stimulation, they will press continuously for hours until they drop from exhaustion (Olds, 1958). Researchers have referred to these brain areas as "pleasure centers."

The hypothalamus is also important for sexual behavior and reproduction because of its relation with the **pituitary gland,** directly below it. The pituitary gland secretes chemical substances called hormones into the bloodstream. Some of these hormones are produced in the hypothalamus and others are produced in the pituitary gland, but release of

hypothalamus A part of the brain that regulates the release of hormones from the pituitary gland.

pituitary gland A gland located at the base of the brain that secretes eight hormones, including follicle-stimulating hormone and luteinizing hormone.

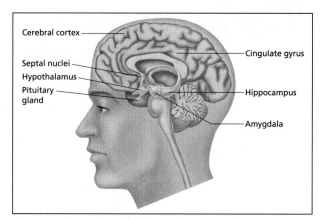

Figure 2–13   The human brain.

all of the pituitary hormones is controlled by the hypothalamus. You have already learned about two of the pituitary hormones: oxytocin and prolactin (see the section on the breasts). You will learn about two more pituitary hormones—follicle-stimulating hormone and luteinizing hormone—and their role in reproduction in Chapter 3.

OUR SEXUAL BODIES

Does our sexual anatomy include only the genitals and breasts? Of course not. Most of us are attracted to and aroused by many other parts of our partner's body. For example, the lips and mouth, which have numerous nerve endings, are very sensitive to touch and are certainly erogenous areas. Kissing is an important part of sexual relations for most people in Western culture, and it is no accident that women try to make themselves more attractive by wearing lipstick.

Although not sensitive to touch, hair is a very important part of our sexual anatomy, and people spend a great deal of money getting it groomed in the latest attractive styles. Many men love the touch and smell of women's soft and shiny hair. Many women find a man's hairy chest a sexual turn-on. Eyes, too, can be an erogenous part of the body. Do women spend a great deal of time putting on eye makeup because it will improve their eyesight? Eye contact between two people can be an initial and ongoing form of sexual communication (eyes have been called the "windows of our souls").

The buttocks are considered highly erotic by a lot of people. They are really just a large bunch of muscles covered by fat and skin with relatively few nerve endings, yet some people wear tight and skimpy bikini bottoms or swim trunks to the beach in order to look more attractive.

In addition to specific parts of the body, one's overall physical appearance is an important part of

Box 2-E SEXUALITY AND HEALTH

Prostate Problems and Examination

Cancer of the prostate is the most common nonskin cancer among men in the United States, with approximately 180,000 new cases and 32,000 deaths each year (American Cancer Society, 2000). An average of 1 in every 8 men will be diagnosed with prostate cancer by age 85. The rates are considerably higher among African-American men than among white men. Although the cause of prostate cancer is still unclear, two suspected risk factors are high testosterone levels and dietary fat. The good news is that cancer of the prostate is usually a very slow-growing type of cancer. If it is detected and treated early, before the tumor spreads outside the prostate, there is about a 90 percent chance that a man will live at least 15 years. However, many men show no symptoms in the early stages. As the cancer advances, symptoms may include difficulty in urination or a frequent need to urinate (especially at night), blood in the urine, and continuing pain in the lower back or pelvic region. By the time symptoms appear, there is only a 30 percent chance that the tumor is confined to the prostate and is curable.

Both the diagnosis and treatment of prostate cancer have undergone revolutionary changes. The traditional method to diagnose prostate cancer has been the rectal examination, in which a physician feels the prostate for any abnormalities. Although this method will continue to be widely used, nearly 70 percent of the cancers detected by it are already in an advanced stage. The good news is that there is now a blood test for detecting prostate cancer. The test measures levels of prostate-specific antigen (PSA), a substance produced by prostate cells. PSA levels are higher in men with prostate cancer. If a biopsy is necessary, it involves passing a fine needle from the rectum into the prostate. A recent review concluded that a combination of diagnostic techniques is better than any single technique (O'Dowd et al., 1997). The American Cancer Society recommends that all men have a yearly PSA test starting at age 50.

Prostate cancer traditionally has been treated by either radical prostatectomy (surgical removal of the prostate, seminal vesicles, and other tissues) and/or radiation (Shipley et al., 1999). However, side effects of these treatments often include impotence and urinary incontinence (inability to control the bladder), and many men feel that the cures are worse than the disease (Stanford et al., 2000). Because localized prostate cancer is slow to develop and surgery and radiation have limited benefits and unwanted side effects, many experts are now advising that the best treatment is "watchful waiting"—doing nothing except regular monitoring until there is a threat that the cancer will spread to surrounding tissue (Johansson et al.,1997).

Cancer is not the only problem a man can have with his prostate. Inflammatory infections (e.g., prostatitis), sometimes resulting from untreated sexually transmitted diseases, can occur. In addition, as men grow older it is common for the prostate to enlarge as a result of overgrowth of normal prostate tissue. This condition, called *benign prostatic hyperplasia* (often called BPH), affects up to 80 percent of men over the age of 60 (Roehrborn & McConnell, 1991). The overgrowth pinches off the urethra, causing increase in frequency of or difficulty in urination. The traditional treatment has been transurethral prostatectomy, in which the prostate tissue is removed by an instrument inserted through the urethra. However, about 10 to 15 percent of men who have had this operation suffer complications, including impotence (although some cases of impotence may be psychological in origin). Drugs are available to shrink the prostate, but the most promising new treatments are devices that use microwaves or radio waves to kill the excess tissue. Today an increasing number of physicians believe that unless the urethra is completely blocked or there are other bothersome symptoms (such as urinary difficulties), the best approach, again, is watchful waiting (Wasson et al., 1995).

If you are man, to be safe you should have a prostate exam at least once a year, starting at age 40.

PERSONAL REFLECTIONS
If you are over 40 years old, have you been to a doctor for a prostate examination? If not, why?

sexual attractiveness. How we feel about our bodies affects our self-esteem and behavior, and influences with whom and how we interact with others. Unfortunately, in today's society, magazines, television, and movies overemphasize a person's visual appearance to the point that people can't help but compare themselves to those who are considered physically beautiful. As a result, most Americans are unhappy with their bodies (Garner, 1997). Many Americans have become obsessed about their bodies and have become so image-conscious that they pay thousands of dollars for face-lifts, breast or penis enlargements, hair transplants, and even padding for their buttocks and legs. But is sex only for the very beautiful? Of course not. Physical appearance might make us sexually appealing to others at first, but a good healthy sexual life involves having *sensuality*, which encompasses all of our senses and who we are as a total person. A person's voice, feel, taste, smell, and personality can all be sensual and contribute to his or her sexuality. For example, an overweight person who appreciates the importance of touching and taking his or her time may be a much better sexual partner than one who physically may be a perfect "10."

Think how boring the world would be if we all looked the same, even if all our bodies were perfect. We each have different ideas and standards as to what we find sexually arousing. Some people are attracted to outdoorsy types, while others are more aroused by a person's intellect. Some men are preoccupied with becoming bald, but many women find

bald men sexy, so much that many young men shave their heads. We are all unique, and if we can appreciate that uniqueness and love ourselves, then we also have the capacity to truly care for others. Chances are that our partners have (or will have as they grow older) as many unique physical features as we do. By the way, the same survey that found that most Americans had a negative body image found that our partners' opinion about our appearance was a major factor in how we felt about ourselves (Garner, 1997). It also found that having good sexual experiences is a good way to start feeling good about your body. So, find a partner who appreciates you for who you are and how you look, and vice versa, and learn to feel good about yourself.

In the long run, human tenderness and caring, being interesting and interested, and loving and being loved are more important than physical appearance. In the excitement of sexual relations with someone we truly enjoy and care for, a paunchy midline, a bald spot, or a small penis or small breasts are not important. We all have the capacity to be sensual beings, and we all have bodies that are sexual.

PERSONAL REFLECTIONS
What body parts of others do you find to be most sexually arousing? Why? Do you think this is a learned response, or is it biologically determined? If the latter, how do you account for the fact that people in other cultures may not be aroused by parts of the body that you find to be arousing (see Chapter 1)?

Key Terms

Suggested Readings

Boston Women's Health Book Collective (1998). *Our bodies, ourselves for the new century* (4th ed.). New York: Simon & Schuster. For women, with an emphasis on health care.

Love, S. (1990). *Dr. Susan Love's breast book.* Reading, MA: Addison-Wesley. All about breast care, with many illustrations.

Morgentaler, A. (1993). *The male body: A physician's guide to what every man should know about his sexual health.* New York: Simon & Schuster. The title says it all.

Schover, L. R. (1997). *Sexuality and fertility after cancer.* New York: John Wiley & Sons. Many survivors of cancer suffer sexual problems. This book will help.

Zilbergeld, B. (1992). *The new male sexuality.* New York: Bantam Books. An excellent source of information about male sexuality and health, this book also provides information about female sexual anatomy.

Study Guide

INTERACTIVE REVIEW

When referring to their genitals or breasts, many people feel more comfortable using slang terms than the correct anatomical names. The use of sexual slang often reflects ambivalent feelings about sex and may lead to misinformation.

Women's external genitalia are collectively known as the (1) _____. This includes the (2) _____, (3) _____, (4) _____, (5) _____, (6) _____, and (7) _____. The (8) _____ and (9) _____ become covered with hair at puberty. The (10) _____ has no known function other than to focus pleasurable sensations. It is most similar in structure to a man's (11) _____. The (12) _____ meet at top to form the clitoral hood. The area between the labia minora is called the (13) _____. Many sexually inexperienced women have a thin membrane, called the (14) _____, that partially covers the vaginal opening. It has no known physiological function, but its presence or absence is used by men in many cultures to tell whether or not their partner is a virgin. In actuality, it is a poor indicator of prior sexual experience.

A woman's breasts are not part of her reproductive anatomy, but in cultures where men consider them to be erotic, they are part of her sexual anatomy. One in (15) _____ women will get breast cancer sometime in their lifetimes.

A woman's internal reproductive system includes the (16) _____, (17) _____, (18) _____, and (19) _____. The (20) _____ is the depository for sperm, the birth canal, and the exit route for menstrual fluids. It is a self-cleansing organ, and its odor is generally not offensive. The walls of the inner two-thirds of the (21) _____ are relatively insensitive to touch, but about 10 percent of all women have an area of heightened sensitivity on the front wall called the (22) _____. When a mature ovum (egg) is released from an (23) _____, it is picked up by a (24) _____, which then transports it to the (25) _____. If fertilized by a sperm, the egg usually implants in the (26) _____ of the uterus. Women should have an annual pelvic exam and Pap smear to test for (27) _____.

Men's external anatomy consists of the penis and the (28) _____, which contains the (29) _____. Erection of the penis occurs when the two (30) _____ and the (31) _____ become engorged with blood. The rounded end of the penis, called the (32) _____, is covered by the (33) _____ unless this excess skin has been surgically removed in an operation called (34) _____. The American Academy of Pediatrics opposes routine circumcision of newborns.

Men's internal reproductive system includes the (35) _____, which produce sperm and the male hormone (36) _____, and a four-part duct system (starting from the testicles) consisting of the (37) _____, (38) _____, (39) _____, and (40) _____, which transports sperm out of the body. During an ejaculation, sperm are mixed with fluids from the (41) _____ and (42) _____ to form (43) _____. A small amount of fluid is released by the (44) _____ before a man reaches orgasm. Cancer of the (45) _____ is the most common type of cancer in men aged 20 to 35. The most common cancer (other than skin cancer) among all men in the United States is cancer of the (46) _____.

SELF-TEST

A. TRUE OR FALSE

[T] [F]   47. The testicles in adult men normally produce millions of new sperm every day.

[T] [F]   48. It is normal for one testicle to hang lower in the scrotum than the other.

[T] [F]   49. Sperm can only be produced in an environment that is several degrees lower than normal body temperature.

[T] [F]   50. Most doctors routinely check for sexually transmitted diseases when they perform pelvic exams.

[T] [F]   51. Most women have a G spot.

[T] [F]   52. The American Cancer Society advises that women should have mammograms starting at age 40.

[T] [F]   53. The ovaries produce hundreds of new eggs every month during a woman's reproductive years.

[T] [F]   54. The American Academy of Pediatrics presently favors the routine circumcision of boys for health reasons.

[T] [F]   55. The use of feminine hygiene sprays and douches is a recommended part of normal feminine hygiene.

[T] [F]   56. Women can reduce their chances of getting a urinary tract infection (cystitis) by wiping themselves from front to back after a bowel movement.

[T] [F]   57. There is no direct physical pathway between the ovaries and the Fallopian tubes.

[T] [F]   58. The labia majora are hairless and meet at the top to form the clitoral hood.

[T] [F]   59. Deep, pleasurable vaginal sensations during intercourse are due to sensitive vaginal walls.

[T] [F]   60. Erections in men are due in part to a bone that protrudes into the penis.

[T] [F]   61. The hymen is a good indicator of whether or not a woman has had sexual intercourse.

[T] [F]   62. A woman's sexual responsiveness is related to breast size.

B. MATCHING

_____ 63. hypothalamus

_____ 64. areola

_____ 65. os

_____ 66. mammogram

_____ 67. mons veneris

_____ 68. cystitis

_____ 69. perineum

_____ 70. introitus

_____ 71. corpora cavernosa

_____ 72. bulbocavernosus muscle

_____ 73. corona

_____ 74. fimbria

a. inflammation of the bladder

b. term used to refer to the vaginal opening

c. darkened area around the nipple

d. opening to the cervix

e. X-ray procedure used for early detection of breast cancer

f. hairless area of skin between the vaginal opening and the anus

g. cheesy substance secreted by glands in the foreskin and clitoral hood

h. soft layer of fatty tissue overlaying the pubic bone

i. two spongy cylinders in the penis

j. large muscle that surrounds the vagina and the bladder

k. raised ridge where the glans and shaft of the penis meet

l. tiny fingerlike endings of the Fallopian tubes

m. smooth rounded end of the penis

n. two glands located at the base of the labia minora

o. surgical removal of the foreskin

_____ 75. glans

_____ 76. Bartholin's glands

_____ 77. smegma

_____ 78. pubococcygeus muscle

_____ 79. circumcision

_____ 80. vestibular bulbs

_____ 81. spermatic cord

_____ 82. pituitary

p. ring of sphincter muscles that surround the vaginal opening and root of the penis

q. structures located on both sides of the vaginal opening that become engorged with blood during sexual arousal

r. tubelike structure that suspends the testicles in the scrotum

s. area of the brain important for sexual functioning

t. gland located at the base of the brain

C. FILL IN THE BLANKS

83. The American Cancer Society advises all women aged 18 or over to have regular pelvic exams and _____ tests to check for _____ cancer.

84. All men over the age of 40 should have an annual examination to check for cancer of the _____.

85. In women, the two outer elongated folds of skin that extend from the mons to the perineum are called the _____.

86. The innermost layer of the uterus, which is sloughed off and discharged from the woman's body during menstruation, is called the _____.

87. In men, an erection results from the spongy tissues of the penis becoming engorged with _____.

88. When a man becomes sexually aroused, a few drops of a clear fluid produced by the _____ may appear at the tip of the penis.

89. Breast size in women is determined by the _____.

90. The best time for most women to examine their breasts for abnormal lumps is _____.

91. After sperm travel through the vas deferens, they enter the paired _____.

92. Most of the fluid in an ejaculation comes from the _____.

93. The best time for a man to examine his testicles for abnormal lumps is _____.

94. Two glands that secrete small amounts of alkaline fluid into ducts at the base of the labia minora are called _____.

95. Sperm are produced in the _____ of the testicles.

96. Both the penis and the _____ have corpora cavernosa.

97. The muscle surrounding the vagina and bladder is called the _____ muscle.

98. In women who have a G spot, it is located on the _____ wall of the vagina.

99. The pituitary hormone that causes production of milk is _____.

100. The gland at the base of the brain that releases hormones important for reproduction is the _____ gland.

Hormones and Sexuality

We live in a greeting card culture where, for [$2.50],
we purchase socially approved statements about childbirth, marriage, or death.
But Hallmark manufactures no cards that say,
"Best wishes on becoming a woman."
Rather than celebrate the coming-of-age in America,
we hide the fact of the menarche,
just as we are advised to deodorize, sanitize, and remove the evidence.

(Janice Delaney, Mary Jane Lupton, & Emily Toth, 1988)

What are hormones? Do you know what they do? Although most people have heard of hormones, very few are certain of their function. Here are some typical responses by students enrolled in my course. Many had no idea what hormones do:

"Before I was enrolled in this course I did not know what hormones were. All I knew was that they were part of our body and were there for some reason." (woman)

"I knew hormones made you grow and sweat. But I didn't know they had anything to do with menstruation. I didn't even know they had any purpose besides just being there." (woman)

"Because everyone talks about hormones 'kicking in' at puberty, I knew it had something to do with growing up, but not exactly the specific roles. I didn't even know that hormones were carried by the blood." (woman)

"I thought hormones were the building blocks of our body, like DNA, except hormones were related to attitudes of an individual." (man)

When you have finished studying this chapter, you should be able to:

1. Identify and describe the hormones of the endocrine system that are involved in reproduction;

2. Describe the four phases of the menstrual cycle;

3. Explain the difference between menstrual and estrous cycles;

4. Understand the reasoning behind negative attitudes about having sex during menstruation and realize their lack of factual basis;

5. Define and explain menstrual problems such as amenorrhea, premenstrual syndrome (PMS), dysmenorrhea, endometriosis, and toxic shock syndrome (TSS);

6. Explain the regulation of testosterone and sperm production in men;

7. Understand the dangerous effects of anabolic steroids; and

8. Understand the relationship between hormones and sexual desire.

Many thought that hormones controlled our moods:

> "I thought that hormones controlled my moods. Whenever I'm happy, sad, mad, angry, or even 'in the mood' it was all hormones. Any unusual behavior was because of hormones." (woman)

> "I believed that hormones were really only in women and they were only in use when a female was on her period. When women had cramps, I've always heard people say, 'She's on her period. Her hormones are acting up!'" (woman)

Others thought that hormones had only to do with sexual behavior:

> "I thought hormones made guys horny and go after girls. The girls would always tell us 'The hormones must be flowing' whenever we would do anything to try to impress them. So I figured only guys had them." (man)

> "I always thought hormones made a person horny. I always heard people say that when a person was interested in sex 'their hormones were going crazy.'" (woman)

> "I always thought that hormones determined how feminine or masculine someone can be. I thought it was what made people gay or straight or in-between." (man)

Let us now see what role hormones play in human sexuality.

THE ENDOCRINE SYSTEM

Hormones play a crucial role in both men and women. They are important for growth (growth hormone), metabolism (thyroid hormone), water retention (antidiuretic hormone), reaction to stress (cortisol), and many other functions. They are also important for the development and maintenance of our reproductive system, and they influence our sexual behavior.

Hormones are chemical substances that are released into our bloodstream by ductless glands found throughout the body. They are carried in the blood to other parts of the body, where they exert their effects. Hormones released by one gland often cause another gland to release its own hormones. This network of ductless glands is called the **endocrine system.**

Not all glands in the body are endocrine glands. Salivary glands and sweat glands, for example, are not endocrine glands. They secrete their products (saliva and sweat) through ducts to the surface. The testicles and ovaries, on the other hand, are part of the endocrine gland system. The testicles manufacture and release **testosterone,** which is often referred to as the "male hormone"; the ovaries produce the "female hormones" **estrogen** and **progesterone.** However, testosterone is also produced in small amounts by the ovaries, and estrogen in small amounts by the testicles. The *adrenal glands* (located near the kidneys) also produce small amounts of these hormones; thus, all three hormones are found in both men and women.

What causes the testicles and ovaries to secrete their hormones? The immediate answer is that it is the *pituitary gland,* which, you recall, is located at the base of the brain (see Figure 3–1). The pituitary gland releases eight different hormones into the bloodstream. Two of these have their effect on the ovaries and testicles, and are thus called *gonadotropins* ("gonad-seeking"). In women, **follicle-stimulating hormone (FSH)** stimulates the maturation of a *follicle* (an immature egg) in one of the ovaries. This was its first known function, and thus how it received its name. However, FSH is also released by a man's pituitary to stimulate the production of sperm in the testicles.

A second pituitary gonadotropin hormone is called **luteinizing hormone (LH).** In women, LH triggers *ovulation* (release of an egg). In men, it stimulates the testicles to produce male hormones.

The pituitary was once called the "master gland" of the body because many of its hormones (like FSH and LH) influence the activities of other glands (like the ovaries and testicles). We now know, however, that the brain controls the release of pituitary hormones, so maybe it is the brain that should be called the master gland. The release of gonadotropin hormones from the pituitary, for example, is under the control of another hormone, called **gonadotropin-releasing hormone (GnRH),** which is manufactured in the *hypothalamus* (see Figure 3–1).

---

hormones Chemical substances that are secreted by ductless glands into the bloodstream. They are carried in the blood to other parts of the body, where they exert their effects on other glands or target organs.

endocrine system A network of ductless glands that secrete their chemical substances, called hormones, directly into the bloodstream, where they are carried to other parts of the body to exert their effects.

testosterone A hormone that is produced by the testicles (and in very small amounts by the ovaries and adrenal glands).

estrogen A hormone that is produced by the ovaries (and in very small amounts by the testes and adrenal glands).

progesterone A hormone that is produced in large amounts by the ovaries after ovulation. It prepares the endometrium of the uterus to nourish a fertilized egg.

follicle-stimulating hormone (FSH) A gonadotropin hormone released by the pituitary gland that stimulates the development of a follicle in a woman's ovary and the production of sperm in a man's testicles.

luteinizing hormone (LH) A gonadotropin hormone released by the pituitary gland that triggers ovulation in women and stimulates the production of male hormones in men.

gonadotropin-releasing hormone (GnRH) A hormone released by the hypothalamus in the brain that causes the pituitary gland to release the hormones FSH and LH.

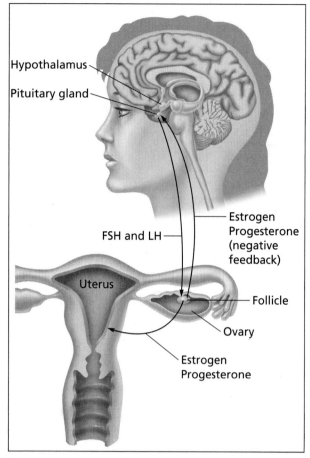

Hypothalamus

Pituitary gland

FSH and LH

Uterus

Estrogen
Progesterone
(negative
feedback)

Follicle

Ovary

Estrogen
Progesterone

Figure 3–1   The brain-pituitary-gonad feedback loop in women.

ample, another ovarian hormone, called **inhibin,** helps to regulate FSH production, and input from the brain affects release of GnRH. The feedback-loop model of hormonal regulation is made even more complicated by the fact a woman's pituitary and gonadal hormones vary cyclically on about a monthly basis. This is known as the **menstrual cycle,** which will now be described in more detail. We will consider the regulation of male hormones later in the chapter.

THE MENSTRUAL CYCLE

An ovum (egg), you recall, is surrounded by other cells within a thin capsule of tissue to form what is called a **follicle.** At birth, each ovary has about 300,000 to 400,000 immature (called primordial) follicles, and the ovaries do not produce any new follicles during a woman's lifetime. Instead, after birth about 1,000 follicles begin to mature every month. The entire growth phase of a follicle proceeds through several stages (primordial, primary, secondary, antral, and Graafian) and takes at least 220 days (McGee & Hsueh, 2000). However, during the first several years of life the follicles never complete their development beyond the antral stage and only about 200,000 primordial follicles remain in each ovary at the time of puberty. When a girl reaches puberty, follicle-stimulating hormone from her pituitary gland allows one or more antral follicles to enter the final stage of growth, which takes a little less than a month. During this phase of growth, called the menstrual cycle, the endometrium of the uterus thickens and becomes highly vascularized (supplied with lots of blood vessels) in preparation for implantation of a fertilized egg. If the egg is not fertilized by a sperm, uterine tissues are discharged from the body, accompanied by bleeding **(menstruation),** and a new follicle starts to mature. This process will end at *menopause,* when the ovaries shrivel up to the point that no follicles can mature (usually around the age of 50), and thus an average woman will have about 400 menstrual cycles in her lifetime.

The average length of an adult human menstrual cycle is about 28 days. I will describe the hormonal events that occur in a 28-day cycle as consisting of four phases. *In numbering the days, it is customary to refer to the start of menstruation as day 1.* This is because menstruation is the only event of the cycle that all women can recognize. In actuality, however, menstruation is really the last of the four phases of the cycle, so we will begin with the events that occur after menstruation, on about day 5 (see Figure 3–2). Try not to be confused by the system used for numbering days. As you will soon learn, consistent 28-day cycles are not very common, so the numbers of the days in parentheses will be different for shorter and longer cycles.

GnRH, the gonadotropins, and the gonadal hormones (testosterone, estrogen, and progesterone) are regulated by negative feedback loops. To better understand a negative feedback loop, think of how a thermostat works. When the room is cold, the thermostat triggers the furnace to go on. An increase in room temperature eventually causes the thermostat to turn the furnace off. Now look at Figure 3–1. In women, increases in blood levels of GnRH from the hypothalamus cause an increase in the release of FSH from the pituitary gland, which in turn results in increased blood levels of estrogen from the ovary. The increased estrogen levels then work to decrease the production of GnRH. There is a similar feedback loop among GnRH, LH, and progesterone.

These are just the basics. The complete story, of course, is more complicated. For ex-

inhibin A hormone produced by the testicles and ovaries that inhibits release of follicle-stimulating hormone from the pituitary gland.

menstrual cycle The monthly cycle of hormonal events in a woman that leads to ovulation and menstruation.

follicle A sac in the ovary containing an ovum and surrounding follicular cells.

menstruation The monthly discharge of endometrial tissue, blood, and other secretions from the uterus that occurs when an egg is not fertilized.

PREOVULATORY PHASE (DAYS 5 TO 13)

This phase is also referred to as the *follicular* or *proliferative phase*. The pituitary secretes relatively high levels of follicle-stimulating hormone (FSH), which, as the name indicates, stimulates the development of a follicle in the ovary. The growing follicle, in turn, becomes a temporary endocrine gland and secretes increasingly higher levels of estrogen. Estrogen is carried in the bloodstream back to the brain and pituitary, where it inhibits further release of FSH. Estrogen also stimulates release of luteinizing hormone (LH) from the pituitary and promotes proliferation (growth) of the endometrium of the uterus. Near the end of this phase, estrogen levels reach their peak, which triggers a release of LH from the pituitary (called the *LH surge*).

OVULATION (DAY 14)

The LH surge (along with a sharp increase in FSH) signals the onset of ovulation within 12 to 24 hours. By this time, the mature follicle (now called a *Graafian follicle*) has moved to the surface of the ovary (see Figure 3–3). At **ovulation,** the follicle ruptures and the ripe ovum is expelled into the abdominal cavity, where it will soon be picked up by a Fallopian tube. Only the ovum is expelled during ovulation. The cells that had surrounded it in the follicle remain in the ovary and now have a new name, the **corpus luteum.** In addition, the hormonal changes induce a change in the quantity and consistency of cervical mucus—from white and sticky to clear and slippery like an egg white—to provide a more hospitable environment for sperm.

Some women experience lower abdominal cramps for about a day during ovulation. This is sometimes referred to as *Mittelschmerz* (German for "middle pain"). It is more common among young women than older women.

POSTOVULATORY PHASE (DAYS 15 TO 28)

The postovulatory phase is also referred to as the *luteal* or *secretory phase*. The cells of the corpus luteum, which are already secreting estrogen, also begin to secrete large levels of progesterone after ovulation. Progesterone inhibits further release of LH from the pituitary and further prepares the thickened endometrium in case the egg is fertilized. The endometrium develops small blood vessels, and its glands secrete nourishing substances. If the egg is fertilized by a sperm, it continues its trip through the Fallopian tube and implants itself in the endometrium. The developing placenta produces the hormone *human chorionic gonadotropin (HCG),* which ensures that the corpus luteum will continue to secrete estrogen and progesterone to maintain the endometrium (thus, HCG serves the same role as the pituitary hormones).

But how often in a woman's reproductive lifetime will one of her eggs be fertilized and result in preg-

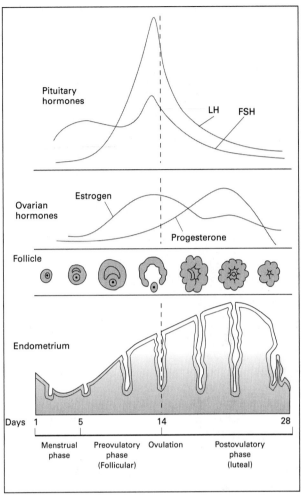

Figure 3–2 Hormonal, ovarian, and uterine changes during a 28-day menstrual cycle.

nancy? Not too often. Most of the time fertilization does not occur, and in the absence of implantation, the corpus luteum degenerates. There is a sharp decline in estrogen and progesterone near the end of this phase.

MENSTRUATION (DAYS 1 TO 4)

With the decline in levels of estrogen and progesterone, there is loss of the hormones that were responsible for the development and maintenance of the endometrium. The endometrium is sloughed off and shed over a 3- to 6-day period. Menstruation is the discharge of sloughed off endometrial tissue, cervical mucus, and blood (about 4–6 tablespoons over the entire menstrual period). The loss of estrogen (which was inhibiting the release of FSH, you recall) also results in the pituitary gland once again secreting FSH, and a new cycle begins.

ovulation The expulsion of an egg from one of the ovaries.

corpus luteum The follicular cells that remain in the ovary after the follicle expels the ovum during ovulation. They begin to secrete progesterone in large quantities in the postovulatory stage.

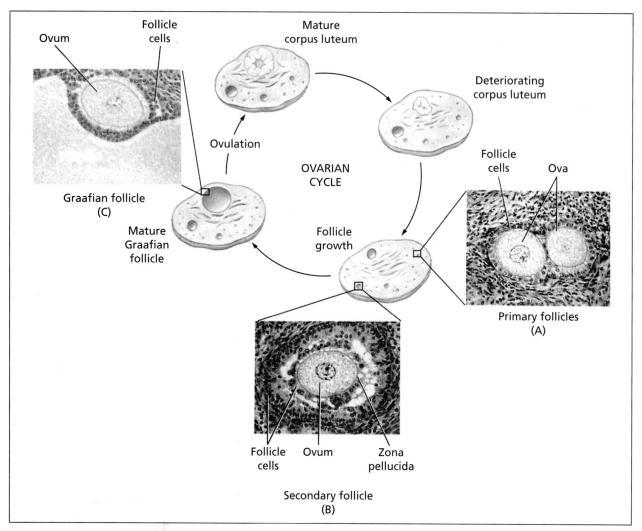

Figure 3–3 Changes that take place in the ovary during a menstrual cycle.

LENGTH OF THE MENSTRUAL CYCLE

In the previous section, you learned that the average length of a woman's menstrual cycle is 28 days. Actually, this is not true until women are full adults, often not until they are in their 30s (see Treloar et al., 1967). During adolescence, most girls' cycles average longer than 28 days. Even for adult women most cycles do not last exactly 28 days. There is considerable variability from woman to woman and from cycle to cycle in the same woman. Most women have cycles that vary in length by 8 days or more (Harlow & Ephross, 1995). The variability in cycle length is greatest during the 2 to 5 years after a girl's first menstruation and before a woman's menopause. There is more variability in the preovulatory (follicular) phase than in the postovulatory (luteal) phase. Many things can affect the length of the menstrual cycle, including stress, nutrition, illness, drugs, and—as you will see next—other women's cycles.

MENSTRUAL SYNCHRONY AND PHEROMONES

The sexual behavior of animals is greatly influenced by their sense of smell. If you have ever owned a female cat or dog, you know about this. When your pet was "in heat," male animals from all over the neighborhood started showing up in your yard. They were attracted by natural body scents called **pheromones.** In the scientific literature, pheromones are defined as "a substance secreted by an animal to the outside of that individual which is then received by another individual . . . of the same species, which then elicits some behavioral or developmental response in the latter" (Karlson & Luscher, 1959). The excretion of pheromones has been well established for many nonhuman species (Singer, 1991), and it has also been found that the receptor site is a structure called the vomeronasal organ, part of the olfactory (smell) system (see Cutler, 1999). Many people use perfumes and colognes to enhance their sexual attractiveness, but is there any evidence that human sexuality is influenced by natural body odors?

The answer might be yes. In a study of 135 college coeds, Martha McClintock (1971) found that roommates came to have similar menstrual cycles while living together over the course of a year. At the beginning of the year, their cycles were an average of 8.5 days apart, but by the end of the year their cycles were an average of only 4.9 days apart. Mothers and daughters who live together also display menstrual synchrony (Weller & Weller, 1993, 1997). McClintock suggested that some undetermined natural body odor synchronized women's cycles. Results of later studies support her hypothesis. Women who were regularly smeared under the nose with sweat collected from the underarms of other women began to have menstrual cycles that coincided with those of the sweat donors (Preti et al., 1986). More recently, it was found that women exposed to preovulatory underarm secretions of other women had shortened preovulatory phases, and women exposed to postovulatory secretions had longer preovulatory phases (Stern & McClintock, 1998). Studies also suggest that male pheromones may affect women's menstrual cycles. Several studies, for example, found that women who had regular sexual experiences with a man had more regular menstrual cycles (e.g., Cutler et al., 1985). Women with abnormal menstrual cycles who were regularly smeared under the nose with underarm secretions collected from men began to show more normal cycles (Cutler et al., 1986).

It should be noted that some studies have not found any evidence of menstrual synchrony among women (Wilson et al., 1991; Trevathan et al., 1993), but rather than disproving synchrony, these negative findings are actually an indication of the many complex factors that must come together for synchronization to occur (see McClintock, 1999, for a review).

MENSTRUAL VERSUS ESTROUS CYCLE

Does a woman's interest in sexual relations differ, depending on the phase of her menstrual cycle? Well, apparently some people think so:

Dear Abby:

You advised "Mismatched," the woman whose sexual appetite didn't match her husband's, to seek therapy. Bad advice, Abby. It's just another example of the guilt trip that has been laid on women ever since Freud and Kinsey came along with their crackpot theories about sex.

It is a biological truth that female mammals, which includes human beings, have a brief period of sexual desire when the ovum is ready for impregnation by the male.

This period is easily observed in wild mammals and is familiar to owners of female dogs and cats. We humans have chosen to ignore its existence, and try to make our females feel guilty because they desire sex far less frequently than males, whom nature created to be always ready for action.

Happily Married

Dear Married: The female of the human species need not be in her fertile phase to desire sex. The biological "truth" you cited is a misconception. (No pun intended.) (From the "Dear Abby" column by Abigail Van Buren. Copyright 1984, Universal Press Syndicate. Reprinted with permission. All rights reserved.)

That is correct, Abby! There are some obvious differences between women and cats and dogs. Women, for example, do not walk on all fours or bark or meow. So why is it so difficult for some people to believe that sexual desire in women may be determined differently than in nonhuman species? Only women and females of a few other primate species (mostly apes) have menstrual cycles. The females of other species, including cats and dogs, have **estrous cycles.** Although owners of female cats and dogs may have noticed some periodic estrous discharge, these animals do not have a menstrual period. The slight discharge (called spotting) occurs during ovulation, and it is only at this time that the female is sexually receptive ("in heat," or in estrus) to the male.

Numerous studies have investigated whether women's sexual interest changes with different stages of the menstrual cycle. Some found a slight peak at about the time of ovulation, but other studies reported peaks at other times of the cycle. Results are influenced by which aspect of sexual activity is measured (e.g., interest, fantasy, dreams, physiological arousal, masturbation, or intercourse). However, a comprehensive review of these studies concluded that the large majority found that peak sexual activity occurs somewhere between a few days after the end of menstruation and the ovulation phase of the cycle (Hedricks, 1995). In a recent study, researchers showed photos of men's faces to women during different times of their

pheromones Chemical substances secreted externally by animals that convey information to, and produce specific responses in, members of the same species.

estrous cycle The cycle of hormonal events that occurs in most nonhuman mammals. The females are sexually receptive ("in heat," or in estrus) to males only during ovulation.

cycles. They found that women preferred men with stereotypic rugged masculine features (hunks?) around the time of ovulation, and men with more "feminine" rounder faces (kindly providers?) during the other three weeks (Penton-Voak et al., 1999). Although there appears to be no consistent, distinct peak in sexual interest during any part of the menstrual cycle, the important point is that women, unlike the females of most other mammalian species, can become sexually aroused at any time of the cycle.

Why have a few species evolved so that the females of the species have menstrual rather than estrous cycles? What purpose does menstruation serve? It has been proposed that the adaptive significance of menstruation is to rid the body of bacteria carried into the uterus by sperm (Profet, 1993) or to eliminate abnormal embryos (Clarke, 1994), but there is little evidence yet to support either theory.

ATTITUDES ABOUT MENSTRUATION: HISTORICAL PERSPECTIVES

The biblical Hebrews regarded a menstruating woman (*Niddah* in Hebrew) as "unclean" or "impure," and believed that she could transfer her condition of uncleanliness to a man during sexual intercourse:

> When a woman has a discharge of blood which is her regular discharge from her body, she shall be in her impurity for seven days, and whoever touches her shall be unclean until the evening. And everything upon which she lies during her impurity shall be unclean; everything also upon which she sits shall be unclean. And whoever touches her bed shall wash his clothes, and bathe himself in water, and be unclean until the evening. . . . And if any man lies with her, and her impurity is on him, he shall be unclean seven days; and every bed on which he lies shall be unclean. (Leviticus 15:19–21, 24, Revised Standard Version)

Sexual intercourse was strictly forbidden for 7 days from the time a woman first noticed menstrual blood. If no blood was noticed on the 8th day, she immersed herself in a *mikvah* (ritual bath) and was again considered "pure." The menstrual taboo later was extended to all physical contact, and a *Niddah* was required to leave her home and stay in a special house called a house for uncleanliness. Orthodox Jews still adhere to a literal interpretation of the passages in Leviticus. (See also Box 3–A.)

Attitudes about menstruation were even more negative during the time of the Roman Empire. Consider, for example, this passage from the Roman historian Pliny (A.D. 77) describing the possible effects of menstrual blood (Delaney et al., 1988):

> Contact with it turns new wine sour, crops touched by it become barren, grafts die, seeds in gardens are dried up, the fruit of trees falls off. . . . the edge of steel and the gleam of ivory are dulled, hives of bees die, even bronze and iron are at once seized by rust, and a horrible smell fills the air, to taste it drives dogs mad and infects their bites with an incurable poison.

As you will see in the next section, many people in the United States still have very negative attitudes about menstruation today.

> *PERSONAL REFLECTIONS*
>
> *How was menstruation first described to you: as something positive (e.g., "becoming a woman"), as just a fact of life, or as something negative? What effect do you think these early experiences have had on your present attitudes about menstruation? Are you able to talk about menstruation in your family today? If not, why not?*

ATTITUDES ABOUT MENSTRUATION TODAY

Although our country no longer has formal menstrual taboos, there are still many people who have negative attitudes about menstruation. In its 1997 Body Image Survey, *Psychology Today* magazine found that three-fourths of women said that menstruation made them have negative feelings about themselves (Garner, 1997). Many people believe menstrual myths—that is, incorrect negative beliefs about menstruation. Here are a few of the many provided by students in my class:

> "When I was about 10, I was told that if a woman was on her menstrual cycle, she shouldn't visit friends who had infant boys because the baby would get a strain."

> "My mother told me to tie a piece of black thread around my baby's foot when I went out in public. She claimed that women menstruating would give the baby colic."

> "When you had your period not to cook or go around the stove while cooking red gravy because it would curdle."

> "All my mother said was, 'Never wash your hair when you are on your period. It will give you cramps.' Not being able to wash my hair for almost a week was pure torture."

Myths that women should avoid bathing, swimming, and exercise during menstruation are common (see Cumming et al., 1991). Bathing, washing their hair, and swimming are not the only things many women do without during menstruation. Results of a survey published in 1978 indicated that the vast majority of Americans aged 55 or older had never had sexual intercourse while the woman was menstruating

Box 3-A   CROSS-CULTURAL PERSPECTIVES

Attitudes about Menstruation: Menstrual Taboos vs. Menstrual Celebrations

A taboo is defined as "forbidden and excluded persons, acts, words, thoughts, and things that supposedly threaten a group's welfare and survival and are, therefore, used to that group's advantage" (Voight, 1984). In many cultures, menstruation is a taboo in that menstruating women are portrayed as sick, impure, or filthy.

In our own culture, we have a long history of negative attitudes about menstruation. The Bible instructed that no one touch a woman while she was in her "impurity," and as recently as the Victorian era physicians advised that menstruating women be kept away from the kitchen or pantry so that they would not spoil hams (*British Medical Journal*, 1878).

Today, **menstrual taboos** persist in many cultures around the world, including such geographically diverse places as central Africa, Alaska, and the South Pacific. For example, the Havik Brahmins of southern India believe that if a woman touches her husband while she is menstruating, it will shorten his life (Ullrich, 1992). This is similar to the belief held by Sambian (Melanesian) men that menstrual blood endangers their health (Herdt, 1993). The Lele of the Congo believe that if a menstruating woman enters the forest, it will ruin hunting for the men (Douglas, 1966), while the Thonga of South Africa believe that sex with a menstruating woman will cause the man to be weak in battle (Ford & Beach, 1951).

In order to ensure that a menstruating woman has no contact with men, many cultures require that she remain in a small menstrual hut, usually on the outskirts of the community, for an entire week. Figure 3–4 shows a group of such huts in New Guinea (Ward, 1989). This practice is carried to an extreme among the Kolish Indians of Alaska, who lock young girls in a small hut for as long as a year after their first menstruation (Delaney et al., 1988). Women of the Dyak tribe (Southeast Asia) must live for a year in a white cabin while wearing white clothes and eating nothing but white foods. Other cultures do not use special huts, but do require that a woman sleep outside of the house while she is menstruating (Ullrich, 1992).

Figure 3–4 Menstrual huts in New Guinea where menstruating women are isolated for 7 days.

It is a common practice in these cultures to introduce menstrual taboos to young girls during initiation ceremonies held about the time of their first menstruation (Schlegel & Barry, 1980). These ceremonies are rites of passage into adulthood, signifying that the girls are ready for sexual activity or marriage. Anthropologists believe that the taboos serve to emphasize the low status and inferiority of women in these cultures, where the social organization (including division of labor) is based on sex. Formal menstrual taboos are most frequently observed in small food-gathering or horticultural societies (Schlegel & Barry, 1980). The taboos decrease in importance with increased educational and professional opportunities for women. These changes can occur rather rapidly (over a period of only 20 years, for example, among the Havik Brahmin of India; Ullrich, 1992).

Larger societies generally do not have formal adolescent initiation ceremonies, and there are even some cultures in which people do not have negative attitudes about menstruation. In Japan, for example, parents celebrate a daughter's first menstruation in a positive manner (Delaney et al., 1988).

menstrual taboos Incorrect negative attitudes about menstruating women.

"Growing up, I was not told much about sex by my parents. As a result, I felt uncomfortable about beginning menstruation. My best friend's mom, on the other hand, who was from Japan, told her about menstruation early and openly. When she began menstruation, she felt comfortable telling her mom, and according to the custom of her native country, a celebration dinner was planned to celebrate her entrance into womanhood." (from the author's files)

Which girl do you suppose felt better about herself as a blossoming woman during adolescence?

Many Native American cultures also held celebrations at the time of a girl's first menstruation (Owen, 1993). Some tribes, such as the Mescalero Apaches, had annual celebrations for all the girls who had passed from childhood to womanhood. Others had newly menstruating girls go to a hut (called a "moonlodge"), but it was viewed as a positive experience, a time for spiritual reflection. However, cultures that view menstruation (or first menstruation) in positive terms are clearly in the minority. For most, it remains an event viewed with great negativity.

(Paige, 1978). More recent studies also find that American men and women seldom initiate sex during menstruation (Barnhart et al., 1995; see Hedricks, 1995, for a review), although initiating sex is more common among better-educated young white women than among others. This abstinence is a direct reflection of negative attitudes about menstruation. When people can be persuaded to try sexual intercourse during menstruation, they are often surprised by their reaction:

"My girlfriend sometimes wanted to have sex while she was menstruating. However, I was always reluctant. After taking this course I decided to give it a shot. Much to my surprise, I didn't mind it at all. In fact, she enjoys herself more than normal."

"The first time my girlfriend and I had sex during menstruation I told her that she was going to have to remove the condom afterwards without me looking. The thought of it disgusted me. But as we started, we found that we enjoyed it much more because we did not have to worry about getting her pregnant, it relaxed her afterwards, and because of the added fluids, she was much more lubricated. Now we look forward to sex during menstruation."

"I enjoy making love to my boyfriend while I'm having my periods. It might be messy, but it gives me pleasure, and most important it makes my period light the next day. Anyone who hasn't tried making love this way is crazy. If their only excuse is that it's messy, haven't they ever heard of a shower?" (All examples are from the author's files.)

A 1981 survey by the manufacturers of Tampax found that one-quarter of Americans believed that menstruation was not an acceptable topic of conversation in the home, and two-thirds believed it was not an acceptable topic in social situations (Delaney et al., 1988).

In her book *Outrageous Acts and Everyday Rebellions* (1983), feminist Gloria Steinem asked what our attitudes about this subject would be if men were the ones who menstruated:

Clearly, menstruation would become an enviable, boastworthy, masculine event: Men would brag about how long and how much.
Young boys would talk about it as the envied beginning of manhood. Gifts, religious ceremonies, family dinners, and stag parties would mark the day. . . .
Sanitary supplies would be federally funded and free. Of course, some men would still pay for the prestige of such commercial brands as Paul Newman Tampons, Muhammad Ali's Rope-a-Dope Pads, John Wayne Maxi-Pads, and Joe Namath Jock Shields— "For those Light Bachelor Days!" (Copyright © 1984 by East Toledo Productions, Inc. 1983, 1995 by Gloria Steinem. Reprinted with the permission of Henry Holt and Company, LLC.)

There is nothing dirty or nasty about menstruation, and with a little knowledge, it is not even mysterious, but rather a basic, important biological function.

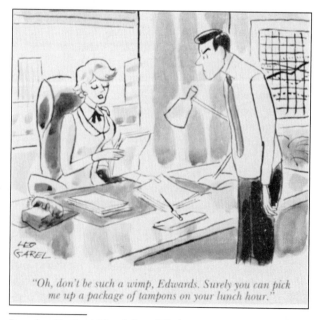

"Oh, don't be such a wimp, Edwards. Surely you can pick me up a package of tampons on your lunch hour."

Reproduced by Special Permission of *Playboy* magazine: copyright © 1985 by Playboy.

The discharge, you recall, consists of nothing more than some sloughed off endometrial tissue, mucus, and a small amount of blood. From a contraceptive perspective, menstruation is the safest phase of the cycle in which to have unprotected intercourse, although conception is still remotely possible.

If the messages in advertisements about menstrual products are any indication, attitudes about menstruation (and menstruating women) may slowly be changing (Merskin, 1999). From the 1930s through the 1980s the dominant message was fear, shame, guilt, and secrecy—menstruation was filthy and it would be humiliating if anyone knew you were menstruating. In the 1990s, ads still portrayed menstruation as messy, unpleasant, and embarrassing, but more and more they also tended to directly address young women's concerns and dispel menstrual myths.

> *PERSONAL REFLECTIONS*
> *What are your attitudes about menstruation? Do you regard it as a normal physiological event, or is it something about which you or your sexual partner feel ashamed or embarrassed? Test your attitude by answering one of the following two questions: (1) Women, would you feel comfortable asking your boyfriend or husband to buy you some tampons or sanitary napkins at the store? (2) Men, if your girlfriend or wife asked you to do so, would you feel comfortable buying her some tampons or sanitary napkins at the store? If not, why not?*

Some women not only would not ask a man to buy them tampons or sanitary napkins but are even embarrassed to buy them for themselves:

> "Before taking this class I didn't realize what effect attitudes in the U.S. had on me. When I went to the store to buy sanitary napkins I would try to hide them until I was getting ready to pay for them. I would not want a man to see me pay for them. I felt that they would think or say she's on her period." (from the author's files)

If you would be uncomfortable about buying tampons or sanitary napkins, ask yourself why. No one feels uncomfortable about buying toilet paper at the store. The reason for this, of course, is that we all know that everyone has bowel movements. It is a normal physiological event. Well, nearly all women will menstruate on a monthly basis for 30 to 40 years of their lives. Menstruation is also a normal physiological occurrence.

> "One class session you asked how many men would buy tampons for their girlfriend. I don't think that is a fair question, because I wouldn't ask my girlfriend to buy condoms for me." (from the author's files)

When a person buys condoms, it is with the intent of having sex. Tampons, sanitary napkins, and new products such as Instead are not used for sexual relations. In fact, menstruation has nothing to do with whether or not a women is sexually experienced. Sexually inexperienced women menstruate. No one should feel ashamed or embarrassed, or be made to feel so, about a normal bodily function.

MENSTRUAL PROBLEMS

Many women experience problems that are associated in some manner with the menstrual cycle.

AMENORRHEA

Amenorrhea refers to the *absence of menstruation* for 6 months or longer. Oligomenorrhea is the absence of menstruation for shorter intervals, or unevenly spaced menstrual periods. Amenorrhea is normal, of course, when a woman is pregnant, and it is not unusual during breast-feeding or in the first few months after a woman discontinues use of birth control pills. It is also common for menstrual cycles to be irregular during the first few years after **menarche** (a girl's first menstrual period). With the exception of these reasons, women should be having menstrual periods on about a monthly basis from their late teens until they approach menopause, at which time their cycles will again become irregular. However, about 3 percent of women in their reproductive years have amenorrhea, and oligomenorrhea is even more common (Harlow & Ephross, 1995; Schachter & Shoham, 1994).

As you will learn in Chapter 7, a failure to ovulate (and menstruate) may be due to pituitary or ovarian problems (Crosignani et al., 1999). However, a woman's health can also affect her hormone levels. There is a relationship between body fat levels and age of menarche. Girls with high body fat levels generally start menstruating at a younger age than girls with low levels of body fat. Amenorrhea is common among female athletes (Odden & Fick, 1998). Women with the eating disorder anorexia nervosa are often considerably underweight, and as a result rarely menstruate (Katz & Vollenhoven, 2000). On the other hand, extreme obesity can also result in amenorrhea (Friedman & Kim, 1985). Adult women who are not menstruating regularly should not assume, however, that this is due to diet or abnormal body fat levels.

While poor health can result in amenorrhea, amenorrhea can also affect a woman's health. For example, the low levels of estrogen usually associated with amenorrhea often result in long-term problems such as osteoporosis and cardiovascular disease (Schachter & Shoham, 1994). Thus, a premenopausal woman who is not menstruating regularly should consult a physician.

amenorrhea The absence of menstruation.

menarche The term for a girl's first menstrual period.

Figure 3–5 Menstrual products. Top: Examples of three types of tampons: with applicators (left) and without applicators (right). Bottom: Examples of two types of menstrual pads: underpant liner for light flow and larger one for heavier flow (left) and a newer product (Instead), a soft disposable cup that fits under the cervix, molds to a woman's body, and holds menstrual flow for up to 12 hours (right). Some companies now make reusable cotton menstrual pads (e.g., Glad Rags).

PREMENSTRUAL SYNDROME (PMS)

"I suffer from terrible PMS. . . . My boyfriend of 4 years broke up with me. I go from being angry, to upset, to having my feelings hurt by nothing, to crying. I have a terrible self-image during this time of the month, and I usually have a bubbly, vivacious personality." (from the author's files)

In recent years, **premenstrual syndrome (PMS)** has received more attention than any other menstrual problem. PMS refers to a group of physical and/or emotional changes that many women experience in the last 3 to 14 days *before the start of their menstrual period* (i.e., during the postovulatory, or luteal, phase of the cycle). Physical symptoms may include bloating, breast tenderness, abdominal swelling, swollen hands and feet, weight gain, constipation, and headaches. Emotional changes may include depression, anxiety, tension, irritability, and an inability to concentrate. Women with PMS usually do not have all of these symptoms. Some women are more bothered with the physical symptoms than the emotional changes, while for others it is just the reverse.

Katharina Dalton and others have published numerous articles claiming that marital conflicts, job absenteeism,

premenstrual syndrome (PMS) A group of physical and/or emotional changes that many women experience in the last 3 to 14 days before the start of a menstrual period.

premenstrual dysphoric disorder (PMDD) A severe form of PMS that markedly interferes with social relations, work, or education.

accidents, suicide attempts, and criminal acts are more common in the last several days before the start of menstruation than at other times of the menstrual cycle (e.g., Dalton, 1960, 1964, 1980; Hylan et al., 1999). However, research in this area is plagued with methodological flaws and inconsistencies, so some researchers believe that no conclusion can yet be reached (e.g., Bedeian & Phillips, 1998).

These inconsistencies have led some researchers to doubt whether or not there really is such a thing as PMS. In addition, some researchers say that the term PMS is widely overused—and misused (Hardie, 1997). They claim that most women who perceive themselves as having PMS do not really have a recurrent pattern of premenstrual mood changes and mistakenly attribute high stress, poor health, and work problems to PMS. When asked to complete surveys about these problems, men score just as high as most women who perceive themselves as having PMS (Hardie, 1997). So what distinguishes PMS from other conditions with similar symptoms? In order to be classified as true PMS, the symptoms must regularly occur in a cyclic fashion before menstruation and *must end within a few days after the start of menstruation*.

For some women, premenstrual mood changes are severe. In fact, the American Psychiatric Association recently decided to classify some of the more severe symptoms of PMS as **premenstrual dysphoric disorder,** or **PMDD** (1994 edition of the *Diagnostic and Statistical Manual of Mental Disorders*). To be diagnosed with PMDD, a woman's symptoms must "markedly interfere" with social relations, work, or education, and include at least one of the following symptoms: markedly depressed mood, marked anxiety or tension, persistent and marked irritability or anger, or "marked affective lability" (extreme changes in mood, such as sudden sadness) (see Endicott, 2000; Steiner, 2000). It is estimated that 3 to 8 percent of all women in their reproductive years have PMDD.

"I am a 29-year-old female who is suffering with PMS. It starts exactly 2 weeks before my menstrual period. I can tell when my PMS starts because I start to get very frustrated for no reason at all. Little things that I can normally handle seem impossible at this time. I start to regret that I have children and I desire a divorce from my husband. It seems like the walls are closing in on me and I suddenly get the urge to run away. I can't make any sense out of myself at this time and a lot of times I think of suicide. I know that I am going thru PMS but I have no control of my emotions and actions, and thinking. I hate myself at this time. As soon as a drop of blood is released from my body (menstruation) I feel like all my stress and anxieties are released with that blood. All of a sudden I feel like myself again." (from the author's files)

Women with PMS or PMDD generally have normal hormone levels and normal estrogen/progesterone ratios (Steiner, 2000). The current consensus of opinion is that the ovarian hormones act in combination with a brain chemical called serotonin to produce the symptoms. Several studies have found that the antidepressant drug Prozac (fluoxetine) substantially reduces the tension and irritability in many women with PMDD (e.g., Steiner, 2000). Prozac blocks the reuptake of serotonin into brain cells. Recently, selective serotonin reuptake–inhibiting drugs such as sertraline have proven to be very effective in reducing PMDD symptoms (Dimmock et al., 2000; Steiner, 2000).

Is there anything that women with milder symptoms of PMS can do? Some of the symptoms can often be relieved by medication and changes in diet. Diuretics ("water pills"), for example, can be prescribed to eliminate excess body fluid, which causes bloating and swelling; cutting down on salt intake can also achieve this. Caffeine (found in coffee, tea, many soft drinks, and chocolate) should be avoided because its stimulating effect will worsen problems like nervousness, irritability, and anxiety.

Although a hormonal basis for PMS is suspected, social and cultural factors can also play a role. Several researchers have noted that PMS is greatest in women who have a very negative attitude about menstruation. With so many people still treating menstruation as a taboo, is it any wonder that some women are depressed during the few days before it begins?

Feminists, who for years denied that menstruation makes any difference in behavior, worry that the new attention to PMS will revive allegations of biological inferiority and keep women out of positions of responsibility. Former vice president Hubert Humphrey's personal physician publicly stated that women were unfit to hold high public office because of their "raging hormonal influences," and during a United Nations debate a diplomat stated that the actions of Great Britain's (former) Prime Minister, Margaret Thatcher, could only be understood in the "context of the glandular system of women." At most, this would apply to only a small percentage of women (those with PMDD that cannot be helped with medication), and there are probably just as many men with severe emotional problems that would make them unfit for office. Generalizations about all women are certainly unfounded.

PERSONAL REFLECTIONS

Do you or your partner suffer from premenstrual syndrome? If the answer is "yes", is it possible that any negativity that you or your partner have about menstruation may contribute to it? What do you do about PMS?

DYSMENORRHEA

Many women experience *painful abdominal cramps during menstruation,* called **dysmenorrhea.** Symptoms can also include backaches, headaches, a feeling of being bloated, and nausea. Up to 60 percent of women of reproductive age have experienced menstrual pain, and in 7 to 15 percent it is severe. It is most common in young adult women 17 to 24 years old, and more common among women who smoke than those who do not (Harlow & Ephross, 1995).

There are two types of dysmenorrhea—primary and secondary. In *primary dysmenorrhea,* the symptoms are not associated with any pelvic abnormalities; whereas in *secondary dysmenorrhea* there are pelvic abnormalities. Secondary dysmenorrhea is often caused by endometriosis (see next section), pelvic inflammatory disease (see Chapter 5), or ovarian cysts.

Primary dysmenorrhea is not a psychological condition, as was once believed. It is the result of an overproduction of *prostaglandins,* substances that cause contractions of the uterus. The symptoms may be severe enough to cause many women to occasionally miss work or school.

"My periods used to ruin 5 days out of the month. I could barely get out of bed with extreme cramps to the point of nausea. Nothing helped, not even over-the-counter medicine. I have been on birth control pills for almost a year. It is the best thing that ever happened. I haven't experienced any pain."

"The cramps kept me doubled over for days at a time, feeling like I was going to die. Only recently did I find out about drugs like Advil."

"Sex actually seems to relieve the severity of the cramps for a while." (All examples are from the author's files.)

All three of these personal experiences reflect common (and usually successful) ways of alleviating primary dysmenorrhea. Drugs like ibuprofen (trade names Motrin, Advil, and others) inhibit the production of prostaglandins. Many physicians prescribe birth control pills for women who suffer from dysmenorrhea (Nabrink et al., 1990). Finally, Masters and Johnson (1966) reported that orgasms relieve the symptoms, at least temporarily.

ENDOMETRIOSIS

The endometrium of the uterus grows and thickens during each menstrual cycle and is then sloughed off and discharged during menstruation. **Endometriosis** refers to a condition in which the *endometrial tissue also grows outside the uterus.* It occurs in 2–20 percent of women with no symptoms, and in 40–60 percent of women with dysmenorrhea (Farquhar,

dysmenorrhea Painful menstruation.

endometriosis The growth of endometrial tissue outside of the uterus.

2000). Endometriosis may involve the Fallopian tubes, ovaries, external surface of the uterus, vagina, pelvic cavity, and other areas. Like endometrial tissue in the uterus, the out-of-place tissue grows and then breaks apart and bleeds during the menstrual cycle, but the blood cannot drain normally like the inner uterine lining. The abnormal bleeding becomes surrounded by inflammation, and scar tissue forms, in many cases causing adhesions (abnormal growth that binds organs together). Endometriosis is found in 25–40 percent of women who are examined for infertility (Lessey, 2000).

It is not fully understood how endometriosis develops, but those who have it suffer severe cramps and abdominal soreness, especially at menstruation, and often there is excessive menstrual bleeding. Some women experience deep pelvic pain during sexual intercourse as well:

"I have had problems with severe menstrual cramps since I was a junior in high school. The pain got worse and worse over the years. I would have to wear a tampon and two sanitary napkins just to catch the blood. It was awful. I remember missing many days of school because the pain was so severe I could not walk. Then it was discovered that I had endometriosis." (from the author's files)

For women who have painful symptoms, relief can often be achieved with hormone therapy that reduces estrogen levels (the birth control pill is often helpful) (Farquhar, 2000). In some cases, surgical removal of the abnormal abdominal tissue is required.

TOXIC SHOCK SYNDROME (TSS)

"I work at a local hospital. . . . One evening a patient came in with flu-like symptoms. The woman got progressively sicker as time went by and her color was actually turning purple in tint. The doctor looked her over from head to toe and then stated that he had found an old tampon in the back of her vagina. He diagnosed her with TSS. The patient's symptoms were getting worse so we went ahead with an emergency transfer by helicopter. After she left, the clerk answered the phone and told us it was the helicopter. Our patient had died." (from the author's files)

Toxic shock syndrome (TSS) is caused by toxins produced by a bacterium (*Staphylococcus aureus*). The symptoms, which are often mistaken for the flu, include a sudden high fever, vomiting, diarrhea, fainting or dizziness, low blood pressure, and a red rash that resembles a bad sunburn (Hanrahan, 1994). It sometimes results in death. Although children and men can get TSS, over 85 percent of all TSS cases are related to menstruation (Bryner, 1989).

toxic shock syndrome A syndrome with symptoms of high fever, vomiting, diarrhea, and dizziness; caused by toxins produced by the *Staphylococcus aureus* bacterium.

There were over 300 cases of TSS in 1980, when the Centers for Disease Control released the first published report of the disease. Most of the cases were in women who had used extra-absorbent tampons. The number of cases of TSS fell dramatically after highly absorbent tampons were removed from the market, but there are still close to 200 cases reported nationwide each year.

The acid level in the vagina drops during menstruation, and the air pockets in tampons contain oxygen. If the *Staphylococcus* bacteria are in the vagina and the person does not have antibodies to them (most people do by the time they are adults), the conditions are right for the development of toxic shock. Tampons do not cause toxic shock, but women who use tampons should change them three or four times a day and switch to sanitary napkins at night before going to bed. If any of the previously described symptoms should develop during menstruation, be sure to see a doctor immediately.

REGULATION OF MALE HORMONES

In men, the hypothalamus, pituitary gland, and testicles operate in a feedback loop (see Figure 3–6) much like the feedback loop in women. Let us first consider sperm production. Release of gonadotropin-releasing hormone (GnRH) from the hypothalamus causes release of follicle-stimulating hormone (FSH) from the pituitary. Increases in blood levels of FSH stimulate production of sperm in the seminiferous tubules of the testicles. FSH production is inhibited by increases in blood levels of inhibin, produced in men by Sertoli cells in the testicles (Plant et al., 1993).

Testosterone production increases when GnRH from the hypothalamus stimulates release of luteinizing hormone (LH) from the pituitary gland. Higher blood levels of testosterone (produced by the Leydig's cells in the testicles, you recall) then inhibit the production of GnRH.

Unlike what occurs in women during their reproductive years, the levels of FSH, LH, and testosterone in men are relatively stable. There is a diurnal rhythm of testosterone production (higher levels during the day than at night), but testosterone levels do not change dramatically in a monthly cycle.

What accounts for the fact that women of reproductive age have monthly cycles of fluctuating hormone levels while men do not? Are women's pituitary glands different from men's pituitary glands? Research with animals has shown that when male pituitary glands are transplanted into females, these glands also begin to secrete FSH and LH cyclically. Thus, the difference is in the hypothalamus of the brain, not in the pituitaries. A woman's hypothalamus is, in fact, different in both structure and connections from a man's

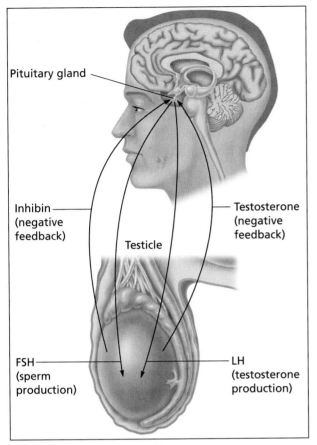

Pituitary gland

Inhibin
(negative
feedback)

Testicle

Testosterone
(negative
feedback)

FSH
(sperm
production)

LH
(testosterone
production)

Figure 3–6 The brain-pituitary-gonad feedback loop in men.

hypothalamus, and it is for this reason that women show cycles in FSH and LH (and consequently, the gonadal hormones) and men do not (Whalen 1977). I will have more to say about this later in the book.

HORMONES AND SEXUAL DESIRE

Is the degree of our sexual desire related to our hormone levels? Do people with high sex drives have high levels of hormones while people with low sex drives have low levels? Do some hormones influence sexual desire more than others?

Research on sex and hormones relies heavily on two types of studies: those investigating the effects of administering hormones and those investigating the effects of a loss of hormones (usually after surgical removal of the ovaries or testicles). We will restrict our discussion to human studies, because as you have already learned in reading about menstrual versus estrous cycles, the differences between human sexual behavior and the sexual behavior of most nonhuman mammalian species is so great as to make generalizations from studies with laboratory animals very questionable.

In humans, there is considerable evidence for testosterone playing a role in sexual desire. After puberty in boys, 6 to 8 milligrams of testosterone are produced every day (95 percent of it by the testicles and 5 percent by the adrenal glands), and among very young (12 to 14 years old) adolescent boys sexual activity increases as testosterone levels increase (Halpern et al., 1998). There is a gradual decline in testosterone production as a man grows older, but men who are sexually active often have high testosterone levels. However, we do not know which came first (the old chicken-and-egg question). Men exposed to sexually explicit pictures show a short-term increase in testosterone levels (Rowland et al., 1987).

Hypogonadal men (men who have abnormally low levels of testosterone) show very little interest in sex. Hormone replacement therapy generally restores sexual desire (Bancroft, 1984). It was once believed that elevating testosterone levels beyond a minimum threshold had no further effect on sexual desire, but more recent studies have found that administration of testosterone enhances sexual desire and activity, even in men with normal hormone levels (Anderson et al., 1997; Anderson et al., 1992; Bagatell et al., 1994).

In some parts of the world, men who were once used as harem attendants were forced to have their testicles removed (castration, or *orchiectomy*) so that they would not be interested in the women they were supposed to protect. In many cases this worked, especially if the men were not yet sexually experienced at the time of castration. However, there were also stories of some eunuchs (as they are called) having the time of their lives, like roosters guarding a henhouse. Modern studies of castrated men show, however, that sex drive and behavior are drastically or completely suppressed in a high percentage of cases. In most men, the decline is rapid, but castrated men may continue to show some interest in sex for years (Bancroft, 1984). One cannot rule out the possibility that a decrease in sexual interest after castration might be due in part to a negative psychological reaction to having mutilated genitals.

Castration has been performed on sex offenders in some European countries, and most of the subjects have shown a decrease in sexual desire and behavior. In Europe and in the United States, some judges now offer male sex offenders a choice between prison and chemical castration with an antiandrogen drug called Depo-Provera (medroxyprogesterone acetate). This drug and others like it severely reduce testosterone production, and often reduce interest in sex.

What about women? The loss of estrogen and progesterone at menopause (or after surgical removal of the ovaries) does not reduce sexual desire in most women. In those postmenopausal women who do show a decrease, estrogen replacement therapy alone generally has no effect (Myers et al., 1990). Administration

Box 3-B SEXUALITY AND HEALTH

Anabolic Steroids

In their pursuit to be the best, athletes are always looking for an edge over their competitors. Megavitamins, painkillers, stimulants—all have been used in the desire to win. Today there is another substance that is widely used for this purpose by athletes, from high school football players to world-class Olympians: synthetic **anabolic steroids** (the more correct name is *anabolic-androgenic steroids*). These steroid hormones are derivatives of testosterone. They have masculinizing (androgenic) effects and also promote growth by enhancing protein uptake by the muscle cell (the anabolic effect).

When administered in proper dosages by a physician, anabolic steroids often have therapeutic value for people recovering from illness or surgery. However, in an attempt to gain weight and build muscle mass and strength, many athletes started taking many times (often 100 times) the normal dose. In the United States, about 375,000 teenage boys have used steroids at least once, including many nonathletes who do it for cosmetic purposes (to look good) (Yesalis et al., 1997).

The misuse of anabolic steroids can have serious harmful effects. These include high blood pressure and other serious cardiovascular diseases; tumors of the liver and prostate gland; decrease in size of the testicles and impaired reproductive function in men; and lumps in the breast tissue. Steroids can also stunt growth in boys who have not yet reached their full height. Taking anabolic steroids will not make a man's penis bigger, and steroids are likely to cause acne.

Men are not the only ones that take anabolic steroids. Because of the increased emphasis on women's sports, use of anabolic steroids among women substantially increased during the 1990s (Yesalis et al., 1997). About 175,000 teenage girls have used them at least once. Women who take steroids risk sterilization, masculinization of the fetus should pregnancy occur, and a much greater than normal chance of breast cancer. Anabolic steroids also have a marked masculinizing effect in women (e.g., causing facial hair growth, male pattern baldness, and deepening of the voice), which is not reversed by discontinuing use of the drugs.

Although anabolic steroids often boost energy and self-esteem, at least temporarily, other behavior changes may include anxiety, irritability, depression, impaired judgment, and paranoid delusions. One study found that one-third of steroid abusers suffered mild to severe mental disorders as a result of using the synthetic hormones (Pope & Katz, 1988). Steroid use also increases aggressiveness and antisocial behavior (Yesalis et al., 1997).

Here are some personal experiences related by students taking my course:

"My friends and I worked out in high school. It was a goal of mine to be bigger and stronger than the others. I decided to take anabolic steroids. Not sure how to do it, I had another inexperienced friend help me inject it into my buttocks. About 2 weeks later I noticed my testicles were getting smaller. In another week I started to get severe abdominal pains."

"I am 19 years old and started using steroids last summer. I wanted to bench press 500 pounds. I gained about 40 pounds. These steroids tended to make me irritable and edgy. I occasionally got bad acne on my back and my testicles shrunk."

Many high school athletes and some college athletes probably take anabolic steroids without knowing much about their side effects, but many world-class athletes who know better continue to do so. In the most publicized case, Canadian sprinter Ben Johnson was stripped of his 1988 Olympic gold medal in the 100-meter dash for taking steroids. More recently, Randy Barnes, the 1996 Olympic gold-medal shot-put champion was banned for life, and Irish swimmer Michelle Smith, winner of three Olympic gold medals, was banned from competition for 4 years.

Many champions have earned their medals without ever taking steroids. Why, then, do some persist in light of the dangers? In addition to physical training, most athletes get themselves "psyched up" when competing. Some athletes are easily "psyched out," especially if they believe that the drugs their competitors are taking give them an edge. In two independent surveys, world-class athletes were asked if they would take a drug that would make them Olympic champions but kill them within 1 to 5 years. A majority responded that they would (Goldman et al., 1987; Mirkin & Hoffman, 1978). This may be a sad commentary on our attitude about winning. An anabolic steroid is not a miracle drug that will turn someone into a champion. It may, however, cause serious harm.

anabolic steriods Synthetic steroid hormones that combine the growth (anabolic) effects of adrenal steroids with the masculinizing effects of androgenic steroids.

of testosterone, on the other hand, enhances sexual desire (Bartlik et al., 1999). It appears, therefore, that testosterone is also the most important hormone for sexual desire in women. Small amounts of testosterone (0.5 milligram) are normally produced daily by a woman's ovaries and adrenal glands. Several studies have found that testosterone levels in women are directly related to measures of sexual behavior and desire (Alexander & Sherwin, 1993; Persky et al., 1982;

Sherwin, 1988). Administration of testosterone in sexually normal women produces an increase in genital arousal and sensations (Tuiten et al., 2000). A deficiency in testosterone produces a marked decrease in sexual desire and responsiveness in women (Kaplan & Owett, 1993). In conclusion, a stronger case can be made for the influence of testosterone on sexual desire in both sexes than for estrogen and progesterone.

Key Terms

adrenal glands   59
amenorrhea   67
anabolic steroids   72
corpus luteum   61
dysmenorrhea   69
endocrine system   59
endometriosis   69
estrogen   59
estrous cycle   63
follicle   42, 43, 60
follicle-stimulating hormone (FSH)   59
follicular (proliferative) phase   61

gonadotropin-releasing hormone (GnRH)   59
gonadotropins   59
hormones   59
human chorionic gonadotropin (HCG)   61
inhibin   60
luteal (secretory) phase   61
luteinizing hormone (LH)   59
menarche   67
menopause   60
menstrual cycle   60
menstrual taboo   65
menstruation   60, 61

Mittelschmerz   61
orchiectomy   71
ovaries   43, 59
ovulation   59, 61
pheromones   63
pituitary gland   52, 59
premenstrual dysphoric disorder (PMDD)   68
premenstrual syndrome (PMS)   68
progesterone   59
prostaglandins   69
testicles   49, 59
testosterone   59
toxic shock syndrome (TSS)   70

Suggested Readings

Anthony, J. (1996, May). Endometriosis: The hidden epidemic. *American Health*.

Boston Women's Health Book Collective. (1998). *Our bodies, ourselves for the new century* (4th ed.). New York: Simon & Schuster.

Delaney, J., Lupton, M. J., & Toth, E. (1988). *The curse: A cultural history of menstruation*. Urbana and Chicago: University of Illinois Press.

Golub, S. (1992). *Periods: From menarche to menopause*. Newbury Park, CA: Sage. Excellent and very thorough.

McClintock, M. K. (1999). Whither menstrual synchrony? In R. C. Rosen, C. M. Davis, and H. J. Ruppel Jr. (Eds.), *Annual Review of Sex Research* (vol. IX, 1998), pp. 77–95. By the person whose paper started it all in 1971. Examines all the complexities of menstrual synchronization.

Steinem, G. (1978, October). If men could menstruate. *Ms*. A humorous and political view of menstruation.

Study Guide

INTERACTIVE REVIEW

Hormones are chemical substances that are released into the bloodstream by ductless (1) _____ glands. The ovaries and testicles are part of this system. The testicles produce the "male hormone" (2) _____, and the ovaries produce the "female hormones" (3) _____ and (4) _____. Hormones from the (5) _____ cause the ovaries and testicles to produce their hormones.

In adult women, an egg matures on an average of every (6) _____ days. The pituitary hormone that starts the menstrual cycle is called (7) _____. This hormone stimulates the development of a (8) _____ in the ovary. During the preovulatory phase of the menstrual cycle (also called the (9) _____ phase), estrogen from the follicle promotes growth of the (10) _____, inhibits release of (11) _____, and stimulates release of (12) _____. The (13) _____ surge signals the onset of (14) _____, at which time the ovum is expelled into the (15) _____ and is picked up by a (16) _____. During the postovulatory phase of the cycle, also called the (17) _____ phase, the (18) _____ secretes progesterone in large amounts. If the egg is fertilized by a sperm, it normally implants in the (19) _____. If the egg is not fertilized, the corpus luteum degenerates and the (20) _____ is sloughed off and discharged in a normal physiological process called (21) _____. Although the average length of the menstrual cycle is 28 days, the large majority of women have cycles that vary in length by (22) _____. In most nonhuman mammalian species, this cycle of hormonal events is called the (23) _____ cycle. Unlike human women, females of species with this type of cycle are sexually receptive to males only during (24) _____. Some cultures have menstrual (25) _____ that prohibit contact with a menstruating woman. Even in our own culture many women and their partners avoid sexual intercourse during menstruation, but this generally reflects inaccurate information and/or negative culturally learned responses. Menstrual discharge consists simply of (26) _____, (27) _____, and (28) _____.

In men, FSH stimulates (29) _____, while (30) _____ stimulates the production of (31) _____ in the Leydig's cells of the testicles. Misuse of anabolic steroids, derivatives of testosterone, can cause serious harmful effects such as (32) _____ (name three effects).

Some women experience menstrual-related problems. The absence of menstruation is called (33) _____. Emotional and/or physical changes taking place (34) _____ days before the start of menstruation are referred to as (35) _____. What distinguishes this condition from other emotional states is that it ends (36) _____. The major cause of (37) _____, painful menstruation, is an overproduction of (38) _____. Endometriosis refers to a condition in which (39) _____. Women who use tampons but do not change them frequently risk getting a serious bacterial infection called (40) _____.

In men, sexual desire appears to be related to circulating levels of (41) _____. Studies of women after menopause, or after surgical removal of the ovaries, suggest that women's sexual desire is not strongly affected by the hormones (42) _____ or (43) _____. Other studies indicate that the hormone (44) _____ does influence sexual desire in women.

SELF-TEST

A. TRUE OR FALSE

[T] [F] 45. Hormones are important for women's sexual desire, but not for men's.

[T] [F] 46. Testosterone is found only in men, and estrogen is found only in women.

[T] [F] 47. All female mammals have menstrual cycles.

[T] [F] 48. Most women's menstrual cycles are 28 days in length.

[T] [F] 49. It is medically safe for a man to have sexual intercourse with a menstruating woman.

[T] [F] 50. Women who use tampons should change them three or four times a day, even if the tampons are advertised as long-lasting.

[T] [F] 51. Men can no longer have an interest in sex after castration.

[T] [F] 52. Women show a large increase in sexual desire around the time of ovulation.

[T] [F] 53. Women produce new eggs throughout their lifetimes.

[T] [F] 54. Near the end of the postovulatory phase of the menstrual cycle, there is an LH surge.

[T] [F] 55. Ovulation almost always occurs 14 days before the start of menstruation.

[T] [F] 56. There is some evidence suggesting that women's menstrual cycles can be altered by certain smells.

[T] [F] 57. Only women can get toxic shock syndrome.

[T] [F] 58. Estrogen, according to most research, is the primary hormone responsible for sexual desire in women.

B. MATCHING

_____ 59. endocrine system

_____ 60. testosterone

_____ 61. luteinizing hormone

_____ 62. estrogen

_____ 63. FSH

_____ 64. follicular phase

_____ 65. corpus luteum

_____ 66. amenorrhea

_____ 67. luteal phase

_____ 68. dysmenorrhea

_____ 69. *Mittelschmerz*

_____ 70. inhibin

_____ 71. ovulation

_____ 72. prostaglandins

_____ 73. premenstrual syndrome

_____ 74. endometriosis

a. substances that cause contractions of the uterus

b. cells surrounding the ovum that are left behind at ovulation

c. emotional and/or physical changes that precede menstruation

d. male hormone produced in testicles, ovaries, and adrenal glands

e. cramps experienced for about a day during ovulation

f. postovulatory phase when the corpus luteum begins to secrete large amounts of progesterone

g. endometrial tissue growing outside the uterus

h. network of ductless glands

i. rupture of the mature ovum into the abdominal cavity

j. female hormone produced in ovaries, testicles, and adrenal glands

k. preovulatory phase when the pituitary secretes FSH and the follicle secretes estrogen

l. pituitary hormone that stimulates production of sperm and maturation of ova

m. absence of menstruation

n. pituitary hormone that triggers ovulation in women and the production of testosterone in men

o. painful cramps during menstruation

p. substance produced in the ovaries and testicles that inhibits production of FSH

C. FILL IN THE BLANKS

75. The gland located at the base of the brain that secretes follicle-stimulating hormone and luteinizing hormone is the _____ gland.

76. Natural body scents that can affect the behavior of other members of the same species are called _____.

77. Each immature ovum is surrounded by other cells within a thin capsule of tissue to form what is called a _____.

78. During ovulation, the cells that surround the ovum in the follicle remain in the ovary, and are then referred to as the _____.

79. After ovulation, there is a large increase in circulating levels of the hormone _____.

80. _____ is the hormone most influential in influencing sexual desire in women.

81. If an egg is fertilized by a sperm and implantation occurs, the corpus luteum is maintained by a hormone from the developing placenta called _____.

82. The hypothalamic hormone that causes release of FSH and LH from the pituitary is called _____.

83. In the female hormone feedback loop, LH production is suppressed primarily by _____.

84. In the male hormone feedback loop, LH production is suppressed primarily by _____.

85. In the male hormone feedback loop, FSH production is suppressed by _____.

Chapter 4

Similarities and Differences in Our Sexual Responses

How can biologists, behaviorists, theologians, and educators insist in good conscience upon the continued existence of a massive state of ignorance of human sexual response, to the detriment of the well-being of millions of individuals? Why must the basics of human sexual physiology create such high levels of personal discomfort among the very men and women who are responsible for guiding our culture? There is no man or woman who does not face in his or her lifetime the concerns of sexual tensions. Can that one facet of our lives, affecting more people in more ways than any other physiologic response other than those necessary to our very existence, be allowed to continue without benefit of objective, scientific analysis?

(William Masters & Virginia Johnson, 1966)

The primary tools of behavioral scientists are observation and measurement. The mechanisms involved in most human behaviors have been under investigation since the 19th century, but because of the negative attitudes that have prevailed since the Victorian era, human sexual behavior was considered off limits as a subject for scientific inquiry. The first major surveys of human sexual behavior were not published until the mid-1900s (Kinsey et al., 1948, 1953). Then, in 1966, William Masters and Virginia Johnson published their book, *Human Sexual Response*, based on direct laboratory observation of hundreds of men and women engaged in sexual activity on thousands of occasions. Human sexuality as a topic for research was thereafter no longer taboo. In this chapter, you will learn about the physiological responses that occur during sexual arousal. The emotional and psychological aspects of sexuality will be discussed in later chapters.

When you have finished studying this chapter, you should be able to:

1. List and describe the four phases of Masters and Johnson's model of the sexual response cycle in order of their occurrence;

2. Explain why researchers after Masters and Johnson chose to add a desire phase;

3. Understand the process of vaginal lubrication and penile erection;

4. Describe the two stages of muscular contractions involved in men's orgasms and explain the male refractory period;

5. Differentiate among the various kinds of women's orgasms;

6. Explain and discuss several controversies about orgasm;

7. Understand the role of penis size in sexual pleasuring;

8. Discuss the validity of reputed aphrodisiacs;

9. Explain and discuss the practice of female genital mutilation in other cultures; and

10. Appreciate that people with disabilities, like everyone else, are sexual human beings.

Prior to Masters and Johnson, men and women were thought to be quite different in their sexual responses. Men, for example, were thought to heat up like light bulbs, whereas women, who many thought were incapable of orgasm, were believed to respond only after long periods of foreplay. Masters and Johnson focused on physiological responses during sexual activity and emphasized the similarities, rather than the differences, between the two sexes. Some researchers now believe, however, that Masters and Johnson were too intent on showing that men's and women's sexual responses were similar (Basson, 2000; Tiefer, 1991). Research conducted in the last 30 years has shown that although men's and women's sexual responses are a lot more similar than once believed, there are some important differences between the sexes, as well as some individual differences within each sex.

MEASUREMENT OF SEXUAL RESPONSES

You were introduced to the work of Masters and Johnson in Chapter 1, where you learned that they used the technique of direct observation to study sexual responses. But how did they actually make their observations and do their recording?

Masters and Johnson recruited their sample of 312 men and 382 women from the local community. The ages of their volunteers ranged from 18 to 89. The laboratory was a plain room that had a bed and recording equipment. The subjects were first allowed to have sex with no one else present so that they would feel comfortable, but after that there was always one or more investigators present. Masters and Johnson recorded over 10,000 sexual episodes leading to orgasm. This included people engaged in masturbation, intercourse, and oral-genital sex. Many subjects were observed dozens of times in order to determine the amount of variability in their responses.

The subjects were hooked up to equipment that measured physiological responses such as heart rate, blood pressure, muscle tension, respiration, and brain waves. Rather than rely on subjects' self-reports of degree of sexual arousal, Masters and Johnson had special equipment made to record the volume of blood in the genitals. Two of these devices are shown in Figure 4–1. The *penile strain gauge* is a thin rubber tube filled with mercury that fits over the base of the penis and transmits a small electric current that can record even a slight change in the circumference of the penis. The *vaginal photoplethysmograph* fits like a tampon into the vagina and has a light and photocell to record blood volume in the vaginal walls (by measuring changes in the reflection of light).

The main disadvantage of studies like those of Masters and Johnson is the unnatural setting of the laboratory. Were the subjects affected by the presence of observers or by the recording equipment? Furthermore, how normal were the subjects themselves? Would you volunteer to participate in a study like this? However, it is generally assumed in medical research that studies of normal physiological processes (digestion, for example) do not require a random sample of subjects because these processes will be more or less the same from person to person. Most importantly, Masters and Johnson's results have stood the test of time. Their findings have been applied with great success in sexual therapy, counseling, and other areas.

PERSONAL REFLECTIONS

Do you think it is important that we know the physiological responses that normally occur during sexual arousal? Is it important that physicians and therapists have this information? What do you think about studies, such as those by Masters and Johnson, that require observing and recording individuals engaged in sex? If your opinion is negative, how else could we learn about the normal physiological responses during sexual arousal?

Figure 4–1 A penile strain gauge (left, the Geer gauge) and a vaginal photoplethysmograph (right, the Barlow gauge) used to measure vasocongestion in the genitals.

MODELS OF SEXUAL RESPONSE

Masters and Johnson described the physiological responses that take place in men and women as occurring in four phases: (1) excitement, (2) plateau, (3) orgasm, and (4) resolution. They referred to this response pattern as the **sexual response cycle.** Although there is little argument concerning specific responses, it must be emphasized that the phases are only a convenient model. Even Masters and Johnson admitted that the phases are arbitrarily defined, and rather than indicating a noticeable shift, they often flow together. Hardly anyone, for example, would be aware of the precise moment of leaving the excitement phase and entering the plateau phase.

Other researchers and therapists have proposed models that divide the sexual responses into fewer or more phases than the model used by Masters and Johnson. Many sex therapists have found, for example, that some people never become sexually excited (the first phase in Masters and Johnson's model) because of a lack of sexual desire or an aversion to sex (see Chapter 15). As a result, some therapists have suggested that desire should be considered the first phase of the sexual response cycle. Helen Kaplan (1979), for example, proposed a model for sexual responses that has only three phases: desire, excitement, and orgasm. From a subjective point of view, her model is appealing because most people would be able to distinguish the change in these phases. However, because of the historical importance of Masters and Johnson's studies, this book will follow their four-phase model and simply add Kaplan's desire phase to the beginning. None of these models, however, should be viewed as being right or wrong. They are merely different ways of looking at the same experience.

The addition of a desire phase has been very popular with many sex therapists, particularly those who feel that the subjective aspects of sexual responsiveness (how one thinks and feels emotionally) are as important as the physiological responses. A person can have the physiological response (e.g., erection) without feeling aroused, or can feel highly aroused but fail to have the physiological responses. Recently, in an article about women's sexual responses, Rosemary Basson (2000) emphasized the mental and responsive aspects of desire. Clearly, emotional and cognitive factors play a strong role in sexual motivation. What about the need for intimacy and emotional connectedness as a driving force to have sexual relations?

Some researchers have distinguished between sexual desire (defined as a global, nonspecific sensation) and eight distinct sexual motivations that result in sexual expression (Hill, 1997; Hill & Preston, 1996). These are "desire for (a) feeling valued by one's partner, (b) showing value for one's partner, (c) obtaining relief from stress, (d) providing nurturance to one's partner, (e) enhancing feelings of personal power, (f) experiencing the power of one's partner, (g) experiencing pleasure, and (h) procreating." The investigators found that individuals differ in their level of interest in each motivation and that sexual arousal in response to different sexual scenarios was most strongly associated with an individual's specific sexual motivations rather than with global sexual desire.

Regardless of what specifically motivates an individual, once a person has sexual desire, the physiological responses that occur during excitement and the remaining phases do not differ with different stimuli. The responses are the same regardless of whether the source of arousal is another person, of the opposite sex or of the same sex, or oneself (fantasy and/or masturbation). We can describe most of the responses that occur in terms of two basic physiological processes: vasocongestion and myotonia. **Vasocongestion** refers to tissues becoming engorged (filled) with blood, and **myotonia** refers to a buildup of energy in nerves and muscles, resulting in involuntary contractions.

EXCITEMENT

MEN. The first physical sign of arousal in men, of course, is *erection of the penis* resulting from the spongy tissues of the corpora cavernosa and the corpus spongiosum becoming engorged with blood (see Figure 4–4). This vasocongestive response starts within 3 to 8 seconds after stimulation begins but usually does not result in a full erection right away. Many men, however, worry if they do not have a "steel-hard" erection immediately upon stimulation. Remember, the **excitement phase** is just the initial phase of the response cycle, and it is not unusual for men to be easily distracted at first by either mental or

---

sexual response cycle The physiological responses that occur during sexual arousal, which many therapists and researchers have arbitrarily divided into different phases.

desire A state that "is experienced as specific sensations which move the individual to seek out, or become receptive to, sexual experiences" (Kaplan, 1979).

vasocongestion The engorgement (filling) of tissues with blood.

myotonia A buildup of energy in nerves and muscles resulting in involuntary contractions.

excitement phase The first phase of the sexual response cycle as proposed by Masters and Johnson. The first signs are erection in men and vaginal lubrication in women.

THE SEXUAL RESPONSE CYCLE

DESIRE

Desire, according to Helen Kaplan (1979),

is experienced as specific sensations which move the individual to seek out, or become receptive to, sexual experiences. These sensations are produced by the physical activation of a specific neural system in the brain. When this system is active, a person is "horny"; he may feel genital sensations or he may feel vaguely sexy, interested in sex, open to sex, or even just restless.

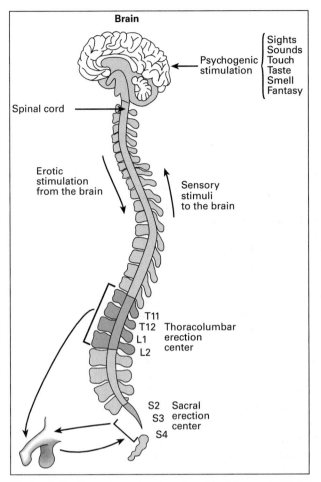

Figure 4–2 Neural mechanisms involved in an erection.

external stimuli, resulting in fluctuation in the firmness of the erection.

Vasocongestion of the penis results from nerve impulses causing dilation of the arteries that carry blood to the penis. To better understand this, look at Figure 4–2. There are two centers in the spinal cord responsible for erection. The more important of the two is located in the lowest (sacral) part of the spinal cord. Nerve impulses caused by stimulation of the penis travel to this center, which then sends nerve impulses back to the penis in a reflex action. The nerve impulses release a chemical in the penis (cyclic GMP) that causes the smooth muscles in the spongy tissue to relax, allowing dilation of the arteries (and vasocongestion). Many men with spinal cords cut above the sacral erection center can still get erections in this reflexive manner, although they cannot feel stimulation of the penis. This is true for quadriplegics as well as paraplegics (Alexander et al., 1993). In men with intact spinal cords, nerve impulses from the brain (generated by such things as sights, sounds, and fantasies) are carried to the erection center and result in vasocongestion. A second erection center, located higher in the spinal cord (thoracolumbar), also receives impulses originating in the brain, and thus it too contributes to psychologically caused erections. Although vasocongestion of the penis sounds like a mechanically easy process, a number of things can interfere with it, including physical or emotional stress and/or fatigue (see Chapter 15).

Vasocongestion of the penis is not the only response that happens in men during the excitement phase. Any time we become excited there is an increase in heart rate and blood pressure. During sexual excitement, the scrotum thickens (the muscle layer contracts) and the spermatic cord shortens, thus elevating the testicles toward the body. Late in the excitement phase, the testicles also start to become engorged with blood and slightly enlarge (see Figure 4–4). In addition, nipple erection occurs in some men, a reaction that is not related to a man's masculinity or femininity.

WOMEN. The first sign of sexual arousal in women is also a vasocongestive response, and just as in men, it begins within seconds after the start of stimulation. The vaginal walls become engorged with blood, and the pressure soon causes the walls to secrete drops of fluid (superfiltered blood plasma) on the inner surfaces. This is called *vaginal lubrication.* However, while it is difficult for a man not to notice that his penis is getting firm, many women may not be aware that their vagina is lubricating until several minutes have passed.

Many men mistake the presence of vaginal lubrication as a sign that their female partner is ready to begin intercourse. Although lubrication makes vaginal penetration easier and prevents irritation during thrusting, remember that this is just the first physiological response experienced by a woman and does not mean that she is emotionally, or even physically, ready to begin sexual intercourse. Recent studies have found that there is no relationship between vaginal vasocongestion (physiological arousal) and subjective sexual arousal. For example, nearly all women have genital arousal while watching erotic films, including those women who have a negative reaction or no feeling of being aroused (Laan & Everaerd, 1996).

In addition to vaginal lubrication, the labia majora, which normally cover and protect the vaginal opening, flatten and begin to move apart. The walls of the vagina, which are collapsed in the unstimulated state, begin to balloon out, and the cervix and uterus pull up, thus getting the vagina ready to accommodate a penis (see Figure 4–4). The clitoris, which is made up of two corpora cavernosa, becomes engorged with blood, resulting in an increase in diameter of the shaft (and length in 10 percent of women) and a slight increase in diameter of the glans. As a result, the clitoris is more prominent during the excitement phase than at any other time (see Figure 4–3).

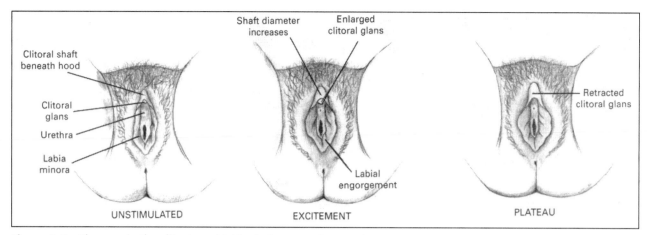

Figure 4–3 Changes in the clitoris and labia during sexual arousal.

The nipples also become erect during the excitement phase—a result of contraction of small muscle fibers, not vasocongestion. Vasocongestion of breast tissues is responsible, however, for a slight increase in breast size late in the excitement phase.

PLATEAU

The **plateau phase** is a period of high sexual arousal that potentially sets the stage for orgasm. In some people this phase may be quite short; in others it may last a long time and be as satisfying as orgasm.

MEN. In men, the diameter of the penis further increases during the plateau phase, especially near the corona. In addition, the testicles become fully engorged with blood (increasing in size by 50 to 100 percent) and continue to elevate and rotate until their back surfaces touch the perineum, an indication that orgasm is near (see Figure 4–4). The Cowper's glands secrete a few drops of clear fluid that may appear at the tip of the penis. About 25 percent of men experience a sex-tension flush on various areas of the skin (see next section).

WOMEN. In women, many events occur during this period that make the plateau phase distinct from the excitement phase (see Figure 4–4). While the inner two-thirds of the vagina continue to expand like an inflated balloon and the uterus continues to elevate (creating a "tenting effect" in the vaginal walls), something quite different happens in the tissues of the outer third of the vagina. These tissues become greatly engorged with blood and swell, a reaction that Masters and Johnson call the *orgasmic platform.* The swelling of tissues results in a narrowing of the vaginal opening by 30 to 50 percent. Thus, the tissues of the outer third of the vagina grip the penis during this stage

(negating the importance of penis size, according to Masters and Johnson).

Changes in blood flow cause a measleslike rash to appear on areas of the skin early in the plateau stage (or late in the excitement stage). This *sex-tension flush,* as it is called, occurs in 50 to 75 percent of all women and generally appears on the breasts, upper abdomen, and buttocks, although it can appear on any part of the body.

There are three additional responses occurring in women during the plateau phase that are sometimes misinterpreted by men to mean that the woman is no longer aroused, when in fact she is at a very heightened stage. First, the clitoris pulls back against the pubic bone and disappears beneath the clitoral hood (see Figure 4–3). Second, the breasts, and particularly the areola, become engorged with blood and swell, increasing in size by 20 to 25 percent in women who have not breast-fed a baby and to a lesser extent in those who have. This obscures the nipple erection that was so prominent in the excitement phase. Third, the secretion of fluids from the vaginal walls may slow down if the plateau phase is prolonged (the Bartholin's glands secrete a few drops of fluid during this stage, but not enough to contribute to lubrication). Some men may worry about the disappearance of some responses that were so prominent during the initial excitement phase, but once again, these are the normal physiological responses when women become highly aroused. The glans of the clitoris, for example, is extremely sensitive to touch at this stage, and indirect stimulation is generally sufficient to maintain arousal. In fact, some women find direct stimulation of the clitoris during this phase to be too intense and less pleasurable than indirect stimulation.

The labia minora also become greatly engorged with blood during the plateau phase, resulting in a doubling or tripling in thickness and a vivid color change (from pink to wine color). The thickening of

plateau phase The second phase of the sexual response cycle proposed by Masters and Johnson. Physiologically, it represents a high state of arousal.

the labia minora helps to further push the labia majora apart and expose the vaginal opening. Masters and Johnson claim that the color change in the labia minora means that a woman is very close to orgasm.

The changes that occur in the plateau phase in men obviously are not as distinct as the changes that occur in women. Although the responses that occur in women prior to orgasm can justifiably be divided into two phases, there are those who disagree with such a division for men. They claim that the plateau phase in men is really just an advanced stage of excitement, and that Masters and Johnson included a plateau phase for men only because they were determined to show the similarities between men and women.

> ### PERSONAL REFLECTIONS
> *List the physiological responses that you experience during sexual arousal (e.g., vaginal lubrication, nipple erection, secretion from Cowper's glands, sex-tension flush). How do you feel about your responses? Are you comfortable with them, or do some cause you anxiety? Why? What about your partner's responses?*

ORGASM

THE ESSENCE OF ORGASM. With continued and effective stimulation, many people experience intense physical sensations lasting a few seconds that are referred to collectively as **orgasm** (climax, or "coming"). Masters and Johnson define orgasm as a sudden discharge of the body's accumulated sexual tension, while *Webster's Dictionary* defines it as "the climax or culmination of a sexual act." But do either of these definitions describe the real essence of orgasm? If a Martian were to land on earth and ask you what an orgasm is, how would you describe it? Here are some responses students in my class gave me when I asked them to describe their orgasms for someone who had never had one:

> "It feels like all the tension that has been building and building is released with an explosion. It is the most pleasurable thing in the whole world. It makes my body tingle and I don't want to even move after; I just want to enjoy the rhythmic sensations." (woman)

> ". . . like a bomb but feels great. When you reach your max, you feel like you are going to burst open. Then you feel like you are floating in the sky." (man)

> ". . . like a roller coaster. At first you feel excited, your whole body feels tingly. My heart feels like it's falling in my chest. Then my stomach and leg muscles tighten up, and all tension is then released in a moment." (man)

> "It is at first a force that feels as if you're on a roller coaster ride and are about to be propelled off. Then come the contractions that feel as if the roller coaster ride is hitting every bump on the track." (woman)

> "A feeling that kind of feels like waves of electricity rushing through your whole entire body. It kind of ripples through and makes your toes and fingers curl." (woman)

> "Like a bolt of lightning strikes you in the back of your spine. You get stiff, curling your toes and making ludicrous faces." (man)

> ". . . like you have been drinking 10–15 beers on a road trip and the person driving won't pull over for you to relieve yourself. The feeling is like when they finally do pull over, and the first few seconds of relief." (man)

> ". . . like when you have to urinate extremely bad and when you finally relieve yourself, you sometimes shake. Compare this at 100 times greater and it feels like an orgasm." (woman)

Obviously, it is difficult to adequately describe orgasm in words. I guess that you have to have had one to really know what it is.

Interestingly, men and women describe orgasm similarly. When physicians and psychologists were presented with descriptions of orgasm such as those just cited, they were unable to distinguish those that had been written by men from those written by women (Vance & Wagner, 1976; Wiest, 1977).

Using electrophysiological recording equipment, Masters and Johnson (1966) found that orgasm consisted of rhythmic muscular contractions in specific parts of the body that initially occurred every 0.8 second, but then diminished in intensity and regularity. Others have reported that the first contractions are only 0.6 second apart (Bohlen et al., 1980), but the really important thing is that for the first time definite physiological responses could be identified in specific tissues.

Is an orgasm really nothing more than rhythmic muscular contractions in a few genital tissues? Did Masters and Johnson record what an orgasm actually is, or merely what it looks like? Later studies were unable to find a relationship between a person's perception of orgasm and the muscular contractions. Contractions often begin before a person's perception of orgasm begins and end before the person reports orgasm to be over. Moreover, strong contractions are sometimes seen with "mild" orgasms, whereas weak contractions are sometimes associated with orgasms that are perceived as intensely pleasurable (Bohlen et al., 1980, 1982; Levin & Wagner, 1985). In short, researchers can measure the contractions, but they can't measure the pleasure. The

orgasm The brief but intense sensation (focused largely in the genitals but really a whole body response) experienced during sexual arousal. During orgasm, rhythmic muscular contractions occur in certain tissues in both the man and woman. The third phase of the sexual response cycle proposed by Masters and Johnson.

perception of the orgasm can be measured only by the individual person. Subjectively, people report a feeling of pleasure focused initially in the genitals and then spreading throughout the entire body. This has led some experts to conclude that the essence of orgasm lies not in the genitals but in the brain (see Gallagher, 1986). Evidence for this is provided by the finding that some women can experience orgasm in response to imagery alone, in the absence of any physical stimulation (Whipple et al., 1992).

Additional proof lies in the fact that some paraplegics and quadriplegics, people whose spinal cord has been transected, report having orgasms (Alexander et al., 1993; Sipski et al., 1999; Whipple & Komisaruk, 1999). They display the typical heart rate changes, muscle tensions, and sex flushes that people with undamaged spines show. A male paraplegic might be capable of having erections during arousal but would not be able to feel them.

In summary, it appears that orgasm is a perceptual experience (generated in the brain, thus not always requiring genital stimulation) and that its occurrence is subjective.

MEN. In men, orgasm occurs in two stages. In the first stage, called *emission,* rhythmic muscular contractions in the vas deferens, prostate gland, and seminal vesicles force the sperm and the prostate and seminal fluids into the ejaculatory ducts, thus forming *semen.* Sphincter muscles (circular bands of muscle fibers) contract and close off the part of the urethra that goes through the prostate, and the semen causes it to swell to two to three times its normal size (called the urethral bulb). These initial contractions give men a feeling of ejaculatory inevitability (the famous "I'm coming")—the feeling that orgasm is about to happen and cannot be put off.

In the second stage, called *expulsion,* these contractions are joined by contractions in the urethra and muscles at the base of the penis to force the semen from the penis—**ejaculation.** During this stage, the sphincter muscles surrounding the part of the urethra coming from the bladder are tightly contracted so that urine is not mixed with semen. A few men have a medical problem known as *retrograde ejaculation* in which the sphincter muscle that allows passage of semen through the penile urethra closes (instead of opening) and the sphincter muscle surrounding the part of the urethra from the bladder opens (instead of closing), thus forcing semen into the bladder instead of out of the body.

Although ejaculation occurs at about the same time as orgasm in men, *they are really two different events.* Orgasm refers to the subjective pleasurable sensations, while ejaculation refers

ejaculation The expulsion of semen from the body.

to the release of semen from the body. The passage of semen through the penis has nothing to do with the sensation of orgasm or the intensity of orgasm. Think about it: If the passage of fluid through the uretha were the cause of the pleasurable sensations, at which other times during the day would men have a very intense orgasm (but do not)? Orgasm and ejaculation, in fact, do not always occur together. Before puberty, for example, boys can have orgasm, but do not ejaculate (the prostate and seminal vesicles do not enlarge until puberty). Ejaculation in the absence of orgasm has also been reported with some types of illness and medications.

WOMEN. Incredible as it may seem, until just a few decades ago many people (including many physicians and therapists) did not believe that women had orgasms. In fact, as late as 1976, a graduate school professor of mine was still telling students that women were not capable of orgasm. This mistaken belief was due in part to attitudes left over from the Victorian era. Women at that time were not supposed to enjoy sex and were thought to participate only to "do their wifely duties." Sex was something that men did to women when they could not control their own desires; thus, a woman's role was merely passive. This belief was also partly based on comparative studies. Symons (1979) found that nonhuman female primates living in the wild rarely, if ever, experience orgasm (even if they are physiologically capable of experiencing it, the males mate too quickly for it to occur). It was not until Masters and Johnson recorded electrophysiological responses from women that the debate was finally ended. Like men, women also had rhythmic muscular contractions in specific tissues that were initially 0.8 second apart. These tissues included the outer third of the vagina (the orgasmic platform), the uterus, and the anal sphincter muscles. Unlike men's orgasms, women's orgasms occur in a single stage, without the sense of inevitability (the sense of "coming") that men have.

Does orgasm in women serve any function other than pleasure? The answer may be "yes." Baker and Bellis (1995) found that if a woman has an orgasm after male ejaculation she retains more sperm than when her orgasm comes before her partner's ejaculation. The effect is observed up to 45 minutes after the man's ejaculation. Others have found that the more a woman desires to be pregnant, the more likely she is to have orgasm after her partner's orgasm (Singh et al., 1998). Baker and Ellis propose that this has value when a woman is having sexual intercourse with more than one man (as in ancestral environments). By (consciously or unconsciously) timing her orgasms, a woman can increase the chance of fertilization by a preferred man.

Figure 4–4 Comparison of men's and women's sexual responses.

Figure 4–5   Variations in the male and female sexual response cycle.

PERSONAL REFLECTIONS
Do you know what factors influence your continued arousal as you go through the excitement, plateau, and orgasm phases of the sexual response cycle? Do you know which kinds of stimulation will give you the most pleasure? Do you know what pleases your partner most? Is it assumption or fact? Have you talked with your partner about how best to please each other? If not, why not?

RESOLUTION

MEN. Resolution is defined as a return to the unaroused state. In men, this involves a loss of erection, a decrease in testicle size and movement of the testicles away from the body cavity, and disappearance of the sex flush in those who have it. Loss of erection (detumescence) is due to the return of normal blood flow to the penis. Some of the excess blood is pumped out by the orgasmic contractions, and normal blood flow then returns as the arteries begin to constrict and the veins open. The testicles had become swollen with blood during the plateau phase, and if orgasm is delayed or not achieved, men may now experience testicular aching (what is sometimes known as "blue balls").

The discomfort is only temporary and is not dangerous—and the testicles and scrotum do not turn blue.

Many men, of course, are capable of reaching orgasm two or more times while having sex. If emotional and/or physical stimulation continues after an orgasm, a man's physiological responses may not fall all the way to preexcitement-phase levels, but they will drop below plateau level for some period of time. Partial or full erection may be possible, but the man will be unable to have another orgasm until his responses build up to plateau level again. (Remember, it is not possible to have an orgasm until one's responses have built up to the high intensity level Masters and Johnson called plateau.) The period of time after an orgasm in which it is physiologically impossible for a man to achieve another orgasm is called the **refractory period** (see Figure 4–5). It is not a fixed amount of time; the refractory period differs from individual to individual. It tends to grow longer as men age, and also after each successive orgasm (should he have two or more orgasms). Of course, the most important factor is the amount of stimulation. For example, the refractory period may be very short if a man is having sex with a new partner. This is known as the "Coolidge effect," named after American President Calvin Coolidge. President and Mrs. Coolidge were being conducted on separate tours of a farm. When Mrs. Coolidge reached the henhouse, she asked the farmer whether the continuous and vigorous sexual activity of the hens was really the work of just one rooster. After the farmer acknowledged that it was, Mrs. Coolidge responded, "You might point that out to Mr. Coolidge." Her statement was relayed to the President, who then asked the farmer whether the rooster had sex with a new hen each time. When the farmer responded "Yes," Mr. Coolidge replied, "You might point that out to Mrs. Coolidge."

WOMEN. A woman's physiological responses, like those of men, generally drop below the plateau level after orgasm and return to the unaroused state (see the first solid line in Figure 4–5). Some women, however, are capable of having true **multiple orgasms**—two, three, four, or numerous (limited only by the point of physical exhaustion) full orgasms in quick succession without dropping below the plateau level (see the dotted line in Figure 4–5). They must be capable, of course, of having the first orgasm, and additional orgasms are possible only with continued sexual desire

resolution The fourth and final phase of the sexual response cycle proposed by Masters and Johnson. It refers to a return to the unaroused state.

refractory period In men, the period of time after an orgasm in which their physiological responses fall below the plateau level, thus making it impossible for them to have another orgasm (until the responses build back up to plateau).

multiple orgasms Having two or more successive orgasms without falling below the plateau level of physiological arousal.

and effective stimulation. As many as 10 percent of sexually experienced women have never had an orgasm (see the wavy line in Figure 4–5). Only about 14 to 16 percent of women regularly have multiple orgasms (Kinsey et al., 1953), but perhaps as many as 40 percent have experienced them occasionally (Darling et al., 1991). Thus, the female sexual response cycle is highly variable. In fact, it is best not to think of *the* human sexual response cycle (a universal model that applies to everybody on all occasions) but rather to *a* human sexual response cycle—one that differs from person to person and from occasion to occasion (Basson, 2000; Tiefer, 1991).

Among those women who have experienced multiple orgasms, only a few do so in all of their sexual encounters. Many women report that multiple orgasms are most easily experienced during masturbation, when they are not distracted by the partner and when sexual fantasy is maximal.

> "Sometimes [I get] two or three orgasms right after each other. I can have multiple orgasms as much as eight times in a row, but this is only during masturbation." (from the author's files)

Many physicians and psychoanalysts (mostly men) refused to believe Kinsey when he first reported multiple orgasms in women in 1953. In a book entitled *Kinsey's Myth of Female Sexuality,* for example, it was stated that "one of the most fantastic tales the female volunteers told Kinsey (who believed it) was that of multiple orgasm" (Bergler & Kroger, 1954). It was not until Masters and Johnson (1966) physiologically recorded multiple orgasms that many people accepted them as truth. Unfortunately, the pendulum may now have swung too far, with some people misinterpreting Masters and Johnson's findings to mean that all women who have learned to have single orgasms can (or should) have multiple orgasms.

Multiple orgasms, as well as simultaneous orgasms (orgasm at the same time as one's partner), have become the one and only goal in sex for some men and women. This can be self-defeating, as these people feel like failures when the goal is not achieved. Many individuals are completely satisfied by a single orgasm, and they should not put additional pressure on themselves by treating sex like an Olympic event. When people watch the Olympics, it never occurs to them that they should be able to run a 4-minute mile or perform incredible feats on the parallel bars. Many of the same people, however, feel that they have to go for a gold medal every time they have sex. This sexual Olympics mentality can only detract from having a good, healthy, and sexually satisfying experience and can lead to sexual problems as well (see Chapter 15).

At some point after a single orgasm or multiple orgasms, a woman's responses will start to fall below plateau level and return to normal. The blood drains from the breasts and the tissues of the outer third of the vagina, the sex flush disappears, the uterus comes down, and the vagina shortens in width and length. The clitoris returns to its normal position within seconds, but the glans may be extremely sensitive to touch for several minutes. Perspiration may appear on both the woman and man but is often unrelated to the degree of physical exertion.

> ### PERSONAL REFLECTIONS
> *Do you judge your sexual experiences by your ability to reach orgasms or your frequency of orgasm? Your partner's orgasm? Why? Many women do not experience orgasm during sexual intercourse. How do you think they feel about it? How would you feel if it were you? Is it necessary to have an orgasm to enjoy sex?*

CONTROVERSIES ABOUT ORGASMS

ARE ALL WOMEN CAPABLE OF ORGASM DURING SEXUAL INTERCOURSE?

> "I have had sex but never actually had an orgasm. If I have I did not know it. Sex feels good, but I think I never had one because of the way people say an orgasm feels."
>
> "Unfortunately, I have yet to learn how to have an orgasm with a partner during intercourse, but I have no problem reaching orgasm during oral sex." (All examples are from the author's files.)

About 5 to 10 percent of American women have never had an orgasm under any circumstances (Spector & Carey, 1990). Shere Hite (1976) reported that only 30 percent of adult women experienced orgasm regularly during intercourse without simultaneous stimulation of the clitoris. Kinsey's group put the figure at 40 to 50 percent. However, in their more recent, well-conducted study, Laumann and colleagues (1994) found that 75 percent of married women and 62 percent of single women usually or always had an orgasm during sexual intercourse. Even so, this still leaves a sizable minority of women who do not.

Both psychosocial and biological factors appear to play a role in women's ability to reach orgasm (Basson, 2000; Raboch & Raboch, 1992). From years of experience in her own clinical practice, sex therapist Helen Kaplan (1974) concluded; "There are millions of women who are sexually responsive, and often multiply orgasmic, but who cannot have an orgasm during [vaginal] intercourse unless they receive simultaneous clitoral stimulation." Kaplan and others reached this conclusion after interviewing many women who reported that they desired and enjoyed sex and became highly aroused, but had never had an orgasm with a male partner (and some reported having had many partners) without simultaneous clitoral stimulation. On the other hand, Masters and Johnson (1966) and others (e.g. Barbach, 1980) claimed to have successfully treated similar women and believe that all women in good health are capable of orgasm during intercourse without additional stimulation. We will return to this issue in Chapter 15.

HOW MANY TYPES OF FEMALE ORGASM ARE THERE?

Sigmund Freud, unlike many of his Victorian colleagues, not only believed that women had orgasms, but started another controversy when he said that there were two types of female orgasms, one due to clitoral stimulation and one resulting from vaginal sensations. Moreover, he claimed that clitoral orgasms were infantile and a sign of immaturity (because they were caused by noncoital acts), whereas vaginal orgasms were "authentic" and "mature" and a sign of normal psychosexual development (the result of stimulation by the penis). "The elimination of clitoral sexuality," he wrote, "is a necessary precondition for the development of femininity." Freud's views, which were made without any physiological data, have since been refuted by modern sex researchers.

Kinsey and colleagues (1953), who doubted the authenticity of vaginal orgasms, had five gynecologists touch the vaginal walls of 879 women with a probe. Most women could not tell when their vagina was being stimulated, but were very much aware when their clitoris was touched. Physiologically speaking, the inner two-thirds of the vagina has few nerve endings, but it is possible, of course, that the vagina is more sensitive to stimulation during sexual arousal, which Kinsey did not test.

Masters and Johnson (1966) later reported that all women's orgasms were physiologically the same. No matter whether the source of stimulation was clitoral or vaginal, identical rhythmic muscular contractions were recorded in the same structures, and the focus of subjective sensation was the clitoris. The clitoris is indirectly stimulated by the penis during vaginal penetration, you recall (by the clitoral hood), but the same contractions were recorded in women who had reached orgasm from breast stimulation alone. According to Masters and Johnson's early physiological research, an orgasm is an orgasm, regardless of the source of stimulation. In other words, Masters and Johnson initially denied the existence of vaginal orgasms.

As you learned earlier, while scientists can measure contractions, they can't measure pleasure. Several studies have found that women subjectively distinguish between orgasms caused by clitoral

Grafenberg (G) spot A small, sensitive area on the front wall of the vagina found in about 10 percent of all women.

stimulation during masturbation and orgasms during intercourse (which were described as "fuller, but not stronger," "more internal," and "deeper" [e.g., Bentler & Peeler, 1979; Butler, 1976]):

> "I believe I've had clitoral orgasms, vaginal orgasms, and the blended type. All of these feel different. . . . For me the best type of orgasm is the blended type because I feel it all over and when it is over my body trembles as if I had just stopped running." (from the author's files)

In fact, some women say that they have never had an orgasm from clitoral stimulation—that their orgasms always result from vaginal stimulation:

> "I am a 30 yr. old woman who has been sexually active since my late teens. I've always been very responsive sexually, resulting in multiple, intense orgasms during intercourse. The significant point is, I have orgasms during intercourse, but never during oral sex or direct clitoral stimulation. My orgasms are strictly vaginal, they are never clitoral. I'd always felt fine about this until I had a relationship with a man who said there was something wrong with me because I did not reach orgasm during oral sex. He made me feel so bad that I literally lost all of my self-esteem and self-confidence. I truly believed I was abnormal. It took me a long time to get over these feelings of inadequacy. I know now that I am okay. I may not be the same as most other women, but there is nothing 'wrong' with me. I consider myself lucky . . . not different." (from the author's files)

If the walls of the inner two-thirds of the vagina are so sparse in nerve endings, what could be the anatomical basis for vaginal orgasms? Recall from Chapter 2 that the muscle surrounding the vagina, the pubococcygeus (PC) muscle, is more richly innervated with nerve endings than the vaginal walls, and that women who report vaginal sensations during intercourse tend to have strong PC muscles (Kinsey et al., 1953). In 1982, Ladas, Whipple, and Perry suggested in their book, *The G Spot,* another possible basis for a vaginal orgasm. The **Grafenberg (G) spot** was first described by the German gynecologist Ernst Grafenberg (1950) in the 1940s. It was described as being a very sensitive area about the size of a dime located on the front wall of the vagina, about halfway between the back of the pubic bone and the front of the cervix (just under the bladder). It swells when stimulated, and a woman's first reaction (lasting a few seconds) may be an urge to urinate.

Ladas, Whipple, and Perry described three types of orgasm. In the *tenting type,* described by Masters and Johnson (1966) and Helen Kaplan (1974), orgasm results from clitoral stimulation (which travels via the pudendal nerve) and is characterized by the buildup and discharge of myotonia in the orgasmic platform (which closes) and the pubococcygeus muscle. In the *A-frame type,* orgasm results from stimulation of the Grafenberg spot (which travels via the pelvic nerve) and is characterized by the uterus pushing down instead of elevating, no orgasmic platform, and the buildup and discharge of myotonia in the deeper vaginal muscles. A third type was described as *blended.* Remember, though, that some studies suggest that only 10 percent or less of women even have a distinct G spot (Alzate & Londono, 1984). More recently, Whipple and Komisaruk (1999) found that stimulation of the cervix can result in orgasm, even in many women with spinal cord injury, and that sensations were carried by the vagus nerve.

Women's experiences of orgasm can also differ with regard to the duration of the orgasm. For example, Rosemary Basson (2000) found that for some women orgasm is not a short, intense release of sexual tension (as occurs in men, and as shown by a little blip on a curve like Figure 4–5), but can last for well over a minute.

Is all this just a question of semantics, that is, of people confusing the stimulus with the response? The most effective stimulus for erection in men is touching the glans of the penis (light pressure stimulates the pudendal nerve), but the orgasmic contractions come from the base of the penis and perineum (deep pressure stimulates the pelvic nerve). Yet no one argues whether there are glans or perineal orgasms in men. Instead, men are viewed as having a total-body orgasm, with different ranges of the same experience (some mild and others intense). Although most women do not have a distinct G spot, for many the front wall of the vagina is a more sensitive area than other parts of the vagina (Darling et al., 1990) and may be "part and parcel of the female's clitoral/vaginal sensory arm of the orgasmic reflex" (Schultz et al., 1989).

So do women have different types of orgasm, or do they experience different ranges of one orgasm that has both clitoral and vaginal components? Circumstances and emotional climate (e.g., masturbation versus having sex with a partner) can certainly affect the experience. As psychiatrist and sex therapist Helen Kaplan (who believed that there is just one type of orgasm) said: "You use the same muscles to eat a hamburger that you use to eat a dinner at Lutèce, but the experiences are very different" (Lutèce is a fancy, expensive New York restaurant); quoted by Gallagher, 1986). As for the opinion of the author of this text, a man, I prefer the view of William Masters, who said: "Physiologically, an orgasm is an orgasm, though there are degrees of intensity. But psychologically—don't ask me about women. I'm a man, and I know that I don't know" (Gallagher, 1986).

In conclusion, there appears to be a variety of orgasm responses by women that do not conform with the original Masters and Johnson model, which viewed

orgasm as a short, intense release of sexual tension (see Basson, 2000). There is one thing that all sex therapists agree on today—that one type should not be viewed as infantile, immature, or less important and another type as mature, authentic, or more important. In short, a woman should not worry about what kind of orgasm she has. As Barbara Seaman (1972) writes, "The liberated orgasm is any orgasm a woman likes."

DO WOMEN EJACULATE DURING ORGASM?

Adult men ejaculate during orgasm, but do women also ejaculate? Crude novelettes written for the purpose of arousing men often describe female orgasm as including "great gushes of fluid flowing down her thighs." References to female ejaculation have also appeared in some better-known fiction (e.g., D. H. Lawrence's *Lady Chatterley's Lover,* 1930) and in marriage manuals (Van de Velde, 1930). Actually, the emission of a fluid by some women during orgasm was noted as early as 300 years ago by the Dutch embryologist Regnier de Graff, who described the fluid as coming from the small glands surrounding the urethral opening. This was confirmed in the modern scientific literature by Ernst Grafenberg (after whom the G spot was named) in 1950. The emission of fluid in some women was described as a dribble and in others as a gushing stream.

> "I have always achieved vaginal orgasms with fluid. The fluid is clear and white. It has no odor and is not unpleasant. I thought all women have this type of orgasm."
>
> "The first time I emitted a fluid, I thought I had urinated on myself and my boyfriend. I mean it was all over. My boyfriend kept looking at me real strange and I couldn't explain it. After the first time I kept making sure that I went to the bathroom before we had intercourse. When it happened after I knew I couldn't have that much fluid in my bladder. I got a little worried, but my boyfriend enjoyed watching me 'let loose' and got very excited." (All examples are from the author's files.)

Prior to the 1980s, women who emitted a fluid during orgasm were almost always told by physicians that they suffered from urinary incontinence, which is the inability to control urination during stress. In 1981, however, three articles on female ejaculation appeared in *The Journal of Sex Research,* followed in 1982 by a book about the Grafenberg spot and ejaculation (Ladas, Whipple, & Perry, 1982). They confirmed that the fluid was emitted not from the vagina but from the **Skene's glands** located in the urethra (Belzer, 1981; Perry & Whipple, 1981). These glands were thought to develop from the same embryonic tissue as the men's prostate (Heath,

Skene's glands Glands located in the urethras of some women that are thought to develop from the same embryonic tissue as the man's prostate, and that may be the source of a fluid emitted by some women during orgasm.

Box 4-A **CROSS-CULTURAL PERSPECTIVES**

Female Genital Mutilation

Cutting of girls' genitals has been a common practice in many cultures since antiquity. The first record we have of it came from the Greek historian Herodotus in 450 B.C. (Joseph, 1996). In England and the United States, various forms of clitoral circumcision were used in the late 19th and early 20th centuries as a treatment for "nymphomania" and masturbation.

Today, cutting of girls' genitals is still performed in many parts of the world (see Figure 4–6). Some cultures practice *clitoridectomy* (removal of the clitoris), while many others subject girls to *excision* (removal of the clitoris, upper labia minora, and part of the labia majora) or *infibulation* (cutting away the entire clitoris, labia minora, and labia majora, and then sewing together, sometimes with thorns, the raw sides of the vulva except for a small opening for urine and menstrual flow) (Barstow, 1999). The procedures are often referred to as *female circumcision,* but this is not a very precise term and does not begin to describe the extensive mutilation that occurs with excision and infibulation.

Female genital cutting is usually performed by an older village woman ("midwife") with a knife or razor and without anesthesia, requiring that the girl be tied or held down. It is usually done during early childhood, but in some cases, as in Nigeria, it is carried out just prior to marriage (Messenger, 1971). Many of the girls suffer hemorrhage or shock, and some die. Long-term effects include chronic uterine, vaginal, and pelvic infections; cysts; abscesses; and difficult, painful, and sometimes fatal labor and childbirth (Barstow, 1999; Toubia, 1994).

> Once I was inside the hut, the women began to sing my praises, to which I turned a deaf ear, as I was overcome with terror. My throat was dry, and I was perspiring though it was early morning and not yet hot. "Lie down there," the excisor suddenly said to me, pointing to a mat stretched out on the ground. No sooner had I laid down than I felt my thin frail legs tightly grasped by heavy hands and pulled wide apart. I lifted my head. Two women on each side of me pinned me to the ground. My arms were also immobilized. Suddenly, I felt some strange substance being spread over my genital organs. My heart seemed

to miss a beat. I would have given anything at that moment to be a thousand miles away: then a shooting pain brought me back to reality from my thoughts of flight. I was already being excised: first of all I underwent the ablation [surgical removal] of the labia minor and then of the clitoris. The operation seemed to go on forever, as it had to be performed "to perfection." I was in the throes of endless agony, torn apart both physically and psychologically. It was the rule that girls of my age did not weep in this situation. I broke the rule. I reacted immediately with tears and screams of pain. I felt wet. I was bleeding. The blood flowed in torrents. Then they applied a mixture of butter and medicinal herbs which stopped the bleeding. Never had I felt such excruciating pain! (Joseph, 1996, pp. 3–4)

The World Health Organization estimates that 85 million to 114 million women have had their genitals cut away in this manner. This includes the large majority of women in Somalia, Ethiopia, Sudan, and Egypt and about half the women in Kenya, with smaller numbers in other African countries (El Hadi, 1997). The practice is also common in several Middle Eastern countries and in parts of Indonesia, Malaysia, and the India-Pakistan subcontinent. Most of the cultures in which genital cutting is performed are Muslim, but it is not an official Muslim practice (it is not mentioned in the Koran). Instead, it is a cultural custom that is also practiced by Christians and Jews that live in these areas.

Why are girls subjected to this mutilation? Many reasons have been given, including myths that the clitoris is dirty, or evil, or poisonous, or will grow like a penis (Barstow, 1999). However, these are not the major reasons. In the words of Raqiya Dualeh Abdalla, a Somali woman who denounced the practice in her 1982 book *Sisters in Affliction:*

> The various explanations and mystifications offered to justify the practice . . . all emanate from men's motive to control women economically and sexually and as personal objects.

Genital cutting substantially reduces sexual pleasure. Most genitally mutilated women do not enjoy sex, and for many sexual intercourse is painful (Barstow, 1999). The men in these cultures, for whom sexual pleasure is reserved

Figure 4–6 Seita Lengila, a 16-year-old Kenyan girl, is held down by village women as her clitoris is cut away with a razor. The wound was then cleaned with cow urine and smeared with goat fat to stop the bleeding.

exclusively, believe that the elimination of sexual desire in women "frees them to fulfill their real destiny as mothers." Proponents of genital mutilation often argue that the practice helps cultural cohesion and identity. Marriage and motherhood are generally the only roles allowed for women in cultures where genital cutting is performed, and for a girl to refuse to submit is to give up her place in society.

A second, but related, reason is economic. The countries where genital mutilation is practiced are strongly patriarchal, and thus there is great concern about guaranteeing the inheritance of property from fathers to legitimate sons. Women are regarded as property and are often sold in marriage. The sewing together of the vulva guarantees that a new wife is a virgin on the wedding night (the vulva is partially cut open by the man), and the elimination of sexual desire reduces infidelity, so that any offspring are almost assuredly the husband's. Infibulated women are fully cut open at childbirth and then partially restitched afterwards.

In 1992, the World Health Organization unanimously approved tougher action to end the practice of female genital cutting, as had the Organization of African Unity in 1990. The U.S. Centers for Disease Control and Prevention estimate that at least 168,000 girls of

African ancestry living in the United States have been cut or are at risk of being cut (Jones et al., 1997). In 1995, the American College of Obstetricians and Gynecologists officially opposed the performance of these procedures by physicians in the United States. A federal law went into effect in 1997 making it a crime (punishable by up to 5 years in prison) for parents to arrange to have this done to their children.

Attempts by outsiders to put an end to genital mutilations have resulted in a clash of cultural values. Westerners generally cite humanitarian and feminist values, but many in Western cultures ritually follow the practice of cutting away the foreskins of boys, usually without the use of anesthesia (see Box 2–C). There is legitimate concern that Western people's negative reaction to the practice will generalize to the cultures where it is practiced. In the words of Nahid Toubia, a Sudanese author:

Over the last decade the . . . West has acted as though they have suddenly discovered a dangerous epidemic which they then sensationalized in international women's forums creating a backlash of over-sensitivity in the concerned communities. They have portrayed it as irrefutable evidence of the barbarism and vulgarity of underdeveloped countries . . . [and the] primitiveness of Arabs, Muslims, and Africans all in one blow. (1988, p. 101)

Some African and Arabic groups have switched from extreme infibulations and clitoridectomies to more symbolic genital cuts (allowing group cohesiveness and identity without subjecting girls to the greater risks of the more severe procedures) (e.g., Gruenbaum, 1996). However, the practice will probably continue unabated in many areas. A survey conducted in the Sudan, for example, found that 90 percent of the women wanted their daughters' genitals cut, and half of them favored the extreme infibulation (Williams & Sobieszczyk, 1997).

PERSONAL REFLECTIONS
What was your reaction to reading about genital mutilation in African and Arab cultures? What is your view about male genital circumcision in the United States? We do not mutilate women's genitals in this country to deny them their sexuality. Do we deny women's sexuality in other ways? How?

1984), and the fluid, which was said to differ in color (clear to milky white) and odor from urine, was found to contain prostatic acid phosphatase, an enzyme found in prostate secretions (Addiego et al., 1981; Zaviacic et al., 1988). A few researchers have even begun to refer to the Skene's glands as the female prostate (Zaviacic & Whipple, 1993). Not all female ejaculators emit a fluid that is chemically different from urine (Whipple & Komisaruk, 1999). Female ejaculation, it is claimed, is seen most often with stimulation of the Grafenberg spot and in women who have a strong pubococcygeus muscle (Perry & Whipple, 1981; Zaviacic et al., 1988). However, as yet there is no evidence of an anatomical link between the front wall of the vagina and the Skene's glands, and ejaculation has also been seen with clitoral stimulation (Whipple & Komisaruk, 1999).

How many women emit a fluid (ejaculate) during orgasm? Perry and Whipple claimed in their initial article that "perhaps 10 percent of females" did so, but later claimed in their book that perhaps as many as 40 percent of women had experienced this on occasion. More recent studies agree with this (Darling et al., 1990; Zaviacic et al., 1988). It would appear, therefore, that while it can no longer be doubted that some women emit a fluid from the urethra during orgasm, there is some question as to the nature of the fluid. No doubt some women do suffer from stress-induced incontinence, but in others it may actually be a true ejaculation.

CAN MEN HAVE MULTIPLE ORGASMS?

Masters and Johnson originally took the position that only women could have true multiple orgasms—two or more orgasms within a short time without dropping below plateau. Whenever they recorded orgasm with ejaculation from men, it was always followed by a refractory period. Only when a man's level of arousal built back up to the plateau level could he have another orgasm. However, two survey studies question whether there is a true sex difference in the ability to have multiple orgasms. The first study reported 13 men who said that they had multiple dry "mini-orgasms" by withholding ejaculation before having a full wet orgasm (i.e., with ejaculation). The wet orgasm was always followed by a refractory period (Robbins & Jensen, 1978). In the second study, 21 men reported experiencing a variety of multiple orgasms (Dunn & Trost, 1989). Some had one or more dry orgasms before ejaculating, while others had an orgasm with ejaculation followed by one or more dry orgasms. As you have learned, scientists have always been the last ones to believe people's claims about experiencing different types of orgasm. Until someone records rhythmic muscular contractions during multiple dry orgasms, that will probably be the case here as well.

PENIS SIZE: DOES IT MATTER?

In an article written for *Cosmopolitan* (1984), Michael Barson stated that "for a man, the one emotion more disquieting than his own sense of not being big enough is the terror of finding himself in bed with a woman who shares his opinion." It should not be surprising that many men have anxieties about the size of their penis, for penis size has been a focus of attention throughout history. Priapus, the Greco-Roman god of procreation, was always displayed as having an enormous penis. Many writers have also described the penis in exaggerated terms. In the novel *Justine* by the Marquis de Sade, for example, the hero's penis was described as "of such length and exorbitant circumference that not only had I never clapped eyes upon anything comparable, but was absolutely convinced that nature had never fashioned another as prodigious; I could scarcely surround it with both hands, and its length matched that of my forearm." In D. H. Lawrence's *Lady Chatterley's Lover,* the gamekeeper's penis was even given its own name, "John Henry." More recently, penis size has been emphasized in magazine centerfolds and erotic X-rated movies. Bernie Zilbergeld (1978), a noted sex therapist, has said that "it is not much of an exaggeration to say that penises in fantasyland come in only three sizes—large, gigantic, and so big you can barely get through the front door." All of this tends to leave the impression that penis size is related to virility, that is, the ability of a man to sexually please a woman, so that even men with normal-sized penises may wish they were larger.

> Penises come in a variety of shapes and sizes . . . and about the only thing most penises have in common is that they are the wrong size or shape as far as their owners are concerned. In the many hours we have spent talking to men in and out of therapy, we have heard every conceivable complaint about penises. They are too small (the most common complaint), too large, too thin, too thick, stand up at too small (or great) an angle when erect, bend too much to the right, or left, or in the middle, or don't get hard enough when they are erect. (Zilbergeld, 1978)

> "I have an inferiority complex about my penis size. Even though my penis is larger than normal (about 7 inches) . . . no matter how many women tell me that my penis is large, I still have that complex." (from the author's files)

Breast size in women is relatively easy to assess, but for most heterosexual men the only opportunity to compare themselves to others is in the locker room, where they may get a false impression. The average size of a flaccid penis is about 3.5 to 3.75 inches in length and 1.0 to 1.2 inches in diameter. Researchers at the Kinsey Institute have found, however, that there is considerably more variation in penis size in the flaccid condition than in the erect state. Penises that appear small when flaccid display a proportionately greater increase in size upon erection than penises that appear large in the unaroused state (Jamison & Gebhard, 1988). Frequent intercourse does not cause a penis to get larger. Also, penis size is not related to height, weight, or build.

This is not to say that all penises are the same size when erect. Kinsey's group and others found that the average size of an erect penis (measured along the top) was 6.2 inches in length and 1.5 inches in diameter (Jamison & Gebhard, 1988; Richters et al., 1995). However, these studies relied on self-measurement, and some men probably exaggerated. Two, more recent studies that did not rely on self-reports found the average length of an erect penis to be smaller, with most men in the 4.5- to 5.75-inch range (Sparling, 1997; Wessells et al., 1996).

Are there ethnic differences? A recent paper concluded that Asian men may be smaller than Caucasian men (Han et al., 1999), but the averages recorded were no different than for the two studies I just cited. As for a comparison of white and black men, no study has found a substantial difference. See former Black Panther Eldridge Cleaver's book, *Soul on Ice*, for a discussion of how the story that black men have larger penises got started.

Today, some men are paying thousands of dollars to have their penises made larger by injecting fat from other parts of the body. However, the American Society for Aesthetic Plastic Surgery has issued a warning that the safety of this procedure has not yet been established. Before any man considers having this operation, let us examine whether the size of a man's penis really is important in pleasing a woman during sexual intercourse.

In order to answer this question, we must first reexamine some basic facts about female anatomy. A woman's vagina, you will recall, is neither a bottomless cavern nor an open hole always ready to accommodate a penis. In the unaroused state, the vagina measures 3 to 5 inches in length and its walls are collapsed. When a woman becomes sexually aroused, the walls of the inner two-thirds of the vagina expand and its depth averages 6 inches, which perhaps, not coincidentally, is about the same length as the average penis (isn't nature wonderful?). In its capacity to physically stimulate the vagina, therefore, there is no real advantage to having a penis any longer than about 6 inches, for there is no place for it to go. And don't forget that the walls of the inner two-thirds of the vagina are relatively sparse in nerve endings anyway. The tissues of the vaginal opening are highly sensitive to touch, but recall that the vaginal opening narrows when a woman is highly sexually aroused, minimizing the importance of penis size.

Figure 4–7 The fertility gods of the Greeks and Romans were always sculptured to have an enormous penis.

Most important, remember that the focus of physical sensations in most women is not the vagina, but the clitoris, which usually doesn't come into direct physical contact with the penis during intercourse. Thrusting of the penis stimulates the clitoris only indirectly by causing the clitoral hood to rub back and forth over the clitoral glans.

Do women consider the size of a penis important? In one study, it was found that depictions of large penises produced no more arousal in women than depictions of smaller ones (Fisher et al., 1983). In another study, several hundred women were asked what was most important to them during sexual intercourse. Not one mentioned penis size (Zilbergeld, 1978). In surveys conducted in my class, only once has a woman expressed a preference for large penises.

"I love men who have big dicks. They don't have to be huge or anything, but I much prefer the larger size."

For the large majority of women, penis size was not important. Here are some typical responses:

"Penis size—of course it doesn't matter!"

"And about penis size, we don't care!"

"Also, penis size doesn't mean anything, especially to women."

"It's not what you have that's so important, but how you use it."

"It is not the size of the ship that matters, but the motion of the ocean."

The women in these surveys were more concerned with their male partner taking his time and his total response to her during sexual intercourse. The quality of the entire sexual experience—not the length of the penis—was the important factor in sexual enjoyment and satisfaction.

> *PERSONAL REFLECTIONS*
> *Do you wish you had a different-sized or different-shaped penis? How would you like to be different? Why? Should the size of a man's penis be an important factor in sexually pleasing a partner?*

APHRODISIACS: DO THEY HELP?

"Many of my older friends believe that if you eat raw oysters before you have sex you can last for hours."

". . . As one of my friends ordered oysters, he commented on how it was such a good aphrodisiac. . . . He explained that every time he goes to a seafood restaurant and eats oysters he is ten times better in bed." (All examples are from the author's files.)

People have searched for **aphrodisiacs**—substances that enhance sexual desire or prolong sexual performance (named after the Greek goddess of love, Aphrodite)— for centuries. At one time or another, over 500 substances have been believed to be aphrodisiacs, including bull's testicles, powdered rhinoceros horn, elephant sperm, turtle eggs, ginseng roots, and vitamin E, as well as such common foods as bananas, potatoes, tomatoes, asparagus, garlic, and radishes (Castleman, 1997). Some people like to believe that oysters are an aphrodisiac. Many of these foods gained their reputation as aphrodisiacs during the Middle Ages when it was commonly thought that plants and foods announced their usefulness by the way they looked. Thus, phallic-looking things such as carrots, bananas, and the horns of animals, or soft moist foods that resembled women's genitals (such as oysters) became

aphrodisiacs Substances that enhance sexual desire or performance.

anaphrodisiacs Substances that suppress sexual functioning.

popular. However, the fact is that none of these substances has any physiological effect on sexual responsivity. Any temporary improvement in sexual functioning is purely a psychological effect (believing that something will work can be arousing), and the effect will wear off shortly.

Spanish fly *(cantharides)*, made from powdered beetles that are found in Spain, is perhaps the most famous reputed aphrodisiac. Taken orally, the active substance causes inflammation and irritation of the urinary and genital tracts, which some may interpret as lust. In men, Spanish fly can cause a painful, persistent erection (priapism), even when there is no desire for sex. This is a dangerous drug, a poison, that can result in ulcers of the digestive and urinary tracts, diarrhea, severe pain, and even death.

Alcohol is commonly believed to enhance sexual desire and responsivity. One of its initial effects is dilation of blood vessels in the skin, which gives a feeling of warmth and well-being. A drink or two depresses certain areas of your brain, making you less inhibited about engaging in sex or other behaviors that you might not ordinarily do (Crowe & George, 1989). In fact, many college students "let themselves drink more than normal in order to make it easier for them to have sex with someone" (Anderson & Mathieu, 1996). Although alcohol may make a person less inhibited about engaging in sex, anything more than a single drink can impair the nervous system responses needed for engaging in sex. As Shakespeare says of drink in *Macbeth*, "It provokes the desire, but it takes away from the performance." Alcohol, in fact, is an **anaphrodisiac,** a suppressant of sexual functioning. In even moderate amounts it can cause erectile problems in men (Rosen, 1991) and difficulty in reaching orgasm in both sexes (Malatesta, 1979, 1982).

Some illegal drugs also have reputations as sexual stimulants. Cocaine is a central nervous system stimulant, and thus may give the user a temporary burst of energy and a feeling of self-confidence, but the drug's effects are often equally due to heightened expectations and the social situation in which it is used (i.e., like alcohol, drugs give people an excuse that they can use afterwards for having had sex). The use of cocaine, however, can often result in erectile failures and difficulties reaching orgasm for both men and women (Cocores et al., 1986; Henderson et al., 1995). Heavy, chronic use of cocaine generally leads to nearly total sexual dysfunction (impotence and inability to reach orgasm), although abusers may still try to engage in sex compulsively (Washton, 1989).

Amphetamines ("speed" or "uppers") in low doses can also give the user a burst of energy (sometimes used for marathon sexual encounters), but will decrease sexual functioning in higher doses (Buffum et al., 1981) and can result in severe paranoia if used chronically. Amyl nitrate ("poppers" or "snappers"), which is used medically for treatment of coronary disease (it dilates blood vessels), is inhaled just prior to orgasm by some people in order to intensify the sensations (Cohen, 1979). This can be especially dangerous for people with heart or blood pressure problems.

Most marijuana users report that the drug improves sexual pleasure (Kolodny et al., 1979). It does not increase desire or arousal, nor does it intensify orgasm, but it enhances relaxation, thus allowing increased awareness of touch. Men who use marijuana chronically, however, may experience erectile problems, lowered testosterone levels, and decreased sperm production (Kolodny et al., 1974).

Among young people, a drug known as Ecstasy (3, 4-methylenedioxymethamphetamine, or MDMA) has become popular as an aphrodisiac. Proponents claim that it enhances a user's sensitivity, sense of well-being, and empathy without the visual distortions of other hallucinogens. MDMA was originally a "designer drug," created to be very similar to banned drugs but just different enough in structure to escape the law. However, it too is now outlawed. Research has shown that it causes permanent brain damage, and some users have experienced psychotic episodes (Leinwand & Fields, 2000).

Several studies have focused on pharmacological agents that affect central nervous system neurotransmitters—the chemical substances that allow brain cells to "talk" to one another. Of these, yohimbine hydrochloride, a substance derived from the sap of an African tree, has received the most attention because of a report that it caused intense sexual arousal in male rats (Clark et al., 1984). The results of several studies have shown that yohimbine has a positive effect on sexual desire and performance in men with psychologically caused impotence (Ernst & Pittler, 1998; Rowland et al., 1997). However, it appears to have little or no effect on men who do not have erectile problems.

Some of you may have heard of a commercially sold product called Libido (also sold as Ardorare, Erosom, Libid, and Libbido). It is a powder derived from fertilized eggs mixed with water or juice that, according to a preliminary report, increases sexual desire in men (Eskeland et al., 1997). You have also probably seen advertisements for pheromones or perfumes and colognes with pheromones added (e.g., Realm, Jovan) that promise increased sexual attention from others. (Remember pheromones? If not, look back at Chapter 3.) Researchers from one company that markets pheromones reported that men who added a synthesized non-odorous pheromone to their aftershave lotion showed increased levels of sexual intercourse and "sleeping" with a romantic partner compared to men in a control group with no pheromones (Cutler et al.,

1998; see also Berliner et al., 1996). These results are very interesting, but don't get too excited yet. Much more work needs to be done, including independent replication, before we can assume that all we need to do to attract others sexually is to slap on some pheromone-added perfume or cologne. The products are not magic elixirs that can guarantee you a sexual experience.

> "When I was 18 years old, I read about this pheromone spray which allegedly would attract women and make them desire sex with me. The pamphlet I got in the mail had several alleged true stories of the success of this stuff. I thought it was a fantastic breakthrough and immediately sent off my $65.00. In return I received a very small (2 fluid oz.) bottle of this spray which I excitedly sprayed on before I hit the town. Did I get laid? Hell no. I didn't even get a nice conversation." (from the author's files)

Despite the lack of scientific evidence that most of the chemicals tried as aphrodisiacs really work, some people will probably continue to search for a problem-free drug that enhances sexual performance. Their efforts would probably be better rewarded if they instead took the time to learn how to communicate and be intimate with their partners. We will discuss how to do this in later chapters.

AND AFTERWARDS?

You have just read Masters and Johnson's description of the sexual response cycle as ending with orgasm and the return of physiological responses to normal. However, an individual does not have to stop paying attention to his or her partner as soon as he or she reaches orgasm (e.g., by rolling over and going to sleep, or by lighting up a cigarette). This is one of the things that distinguishes human beings from other species. It is a rare couple who can experience simultaneous orgasms on any more than an occasional basis, which means that most of the time, someone will get there first. If it is the man, this will often mean loss of erection. Stimulation of one's partner, however, is not totally dependent on the functioning of the genitals. Sexual intimacy is a whole-body response, involving lips, tongue, hands, and emotional responsivity. Even if your partner has reached orgasm, the time afterwards can be a period of mutual touching, hugging, and emotional intimacy. When Ann Landers asked her female readers in 1985 if they would forgo "the act" if they could be held closely, 100,000 women responded, of whom 72,000 of them said "yes." Touching is necessary for a baby's emotional well-being, and we do not lose that need as we grow older. Sexual intimacy is more than genital thrusting and orgasm. It is having someone to touch and to touch you. It is a sense of closeness, a sense of partnership. This next section is a good example of that.

SEXUALITY AND PEOPLE WITH DISABILITIES

Is sexual pleasure reserved only for the young and beautiful? Judging by the number of jokes about the sexual behavior of the elderly and obese, and of other people whom our society often labels as "unattractive," many people apparently think so. These negative attitudes are often extreme in the case of people with disabilities. What about people who are blind, deaf, spinal cord–damaged, or suffer from other physical disabilities? What about the mentally retarded? Do these groups of people have sexual desires and feelings? If so, should they be allowed to express those desires?

In this chapter we focused on the physiological events that occur during sexual arousal. Masters and Johnson's model places emphasis on sex as a physical act. But is sexuality just physical? Look again at the definition of **sexuality** at the beginning of Chapter 1. Here is another definition, one that was given by a group of women with complete spinal cord injury:

> "It is a tremendous core of who I am. Everything else comes out of that. How I think and feel about my body, my physical body. How I would define myself as a woman. How I am in all my relationships, whether they are sexual or otherwise. How I decorate my house. It's everything that I am. I may not have another way . . . another component that is so strong that I could say sums up everything that I am. So it's the physical, it's spiritual, it's emotional, everything." (from Richards et al., 1997)

Earlier in the chapter you learned about the effects of one kind of physical disability on sexual functioning: the effects of spinal cord damage on the ability to achieve erection and/or orgasm (Alexander et al., 1993; Sipski et al., 1999; Whipple & Komisaruk, 1999). However, as difficult as a person's physical disabilities may make it to engage in sex, a greater barrier to most people with disabilities having a sexual relationship is society's attitude about them. For example, I recently received the following note from a spinal cord–damaged student:

> "Recently my boyfriend's mother wanted him to explain to me that she wants grandchildren. I guess she assumed that because I'm in a wheelchair that I'm incapable of having children. Her ignorance amazed me. People who are in wheelchairs, whether they be paraplegics or quadriplegics, are no less sexually able. Sexuality is basically psychologi-cal, in terms of its influence upon a person's overall behavior. Thus, the fact that one is paralyzed from the neck down or from the hips down doesn't discount from one's sexual drive or fertility."

sexuality All of the sexual attitudes, feelings, and behaviors associated with being human. The term does not refer specifically to a person's capacity for erotic response or to sexual acts, but rather to a dimension of one's personality.

Many people treat adults with physical or mental disabilities as if they were asexual or childlike and think it ridiculous that these groups should even have any interest in sex (Blackburn, 1995; Katz et al., 2000). Parents of children with disabilities sometimes try to "protect" them by withholding sexual information, and friends and acquaintances of handicapped adults often try to protect them by never discussing the subject in their presence. Even the medical profession, which has perfected many ways to ensure the reproductive capabilities of disabled persons, has only recently begun to realize the importance of a holistic approach in treating people with disabilities. People with recent disabilities want to learn (or relearn) more than just how to be capable. They also want to know how to love and be loved. Current rehabilitation approaches now include sexual counseling in helping patients and staff deal with the emotional, self-esteem, and social issues that may impair sexual functioning (Alexander et al., 1993; Burling et al., 1994).

The well-intended but incorrect assumption of those who would protect people with disabilities by denying their sexuality is that they have more important things to worry about. For example, in the case of spinal cord–damaged people, it is often assumed that they would (or should) not be interested in sex but instead be most concerned about physically rehabilitating the functional parts of their bodies.

Are sexual relations really so unimportant that they should be given such a low priority? To answer this question, we must first ask why it is that people engage in sex. Is it possible for a person to enjoy sexual relations even if he or she cannot have sexual intercourse? Is sexual pleasure restricted to genital sensations? (e.g., is a man's sexuality focused exclusively in his penis?) Recall that paralyzed individuals often become highly sensitive to touch in their functional body parts. There are many reasons that people engage in sexual relations besides the physical pleasure of genital sensations. Sexual relations are important to many people for the shared intimacy. Equally important to the physical intimacy is the opportunity for emotional intimacy provided by the closeness of sexual relations. Hugging, holding, kissing, and shared affection are as important in sexual relations as is intercourse for many people. Physical closeness can be very psychologically exciting (see Figure 4–8). Here is part of a letter from the husband of a woman who had undergone three years of surgeries and rehabilitation for severe spinal cord damage suffered in an automobile accident:

> "In July 'Susan' felt well enough to try once more. Sex was very good that day . . . we took it slow

Figure 4–8 We are all sexual beings.

and easy. . . . We compensated with lots of holding and touching, something that often had been lacking in our pre-accident relationship. Incredibly, just holding each other in bed became very satisfying, and it actually seemed to bring us closer together emotionally."

Approximately 200,000 people in the United States have severe spinal cord injuries, 20 percent of them women (National Spinal Cord Statistical Center, 1995). People with spinal cord damage usually show an initial "shutting down" and "shutting out" of sexuality after the injury, followed by relationship disconnection (avoidance of sex with a partner) (Richards et al., 1997). The sexual desire of the partner can help overcome this. With proper support, spinal cord–damaged people eventually go through a phase of sexual exploration (both giving and receiving sexual pleasure) and sexual reaffirmation (becoming comfortable with their own sexuality). Spinal cord–injured individuals may show a decrease in sexual intercourse, but often compensate for this with other sexual activities (Alexander et al., 1993). There are, in fact, many ways to enjoy sexual relations besides intercourse.

What about people with traumatic brain injury or severe mental retardation? They display sexual behavior, including touching, kissing, and masturbation, but are often unable to differentiate between appropriate times and places. This "inappropriate" (by normal standards) behavior results in many people, even special education teachers and administrators, having negative views of sexual behaviors in developmentally handicapped or brain-injured persons (e.g., Scotti et al., 1996; Wolfe, 1997). However, denial of sexuality

in (and for) the mentally impaired is not a realistic solution. "Regardless of their specific disabilities, persons with mental retardation are individuals with sexual feelings who develop physically at a rate comparable to that of normal young adults and respond to many of the same sexual stimuli and situations as do persons without mental retardation" (Scotti et al., 1996). A more realistic approach is to provide sexuality education to both persons with mental disabilities and to their service providers (Ames, 1991; Medlar, 1998).

People with hearing or vision impairments also have sexual desires and needs that should not be ignored by family, educators, and health-care providers (Gannon, 1998). Different handicaps present different problems in one's ability to have sexual relations, but none of the physical problems is as great an obstacle to healthy sexuality as society's attitude about handicapped people. Remember, regardless of what we look like or our physical or mental capabilities, we are all sexual beings.

Here are some helpful references regarding sexuality and the handicapped: See Chipouras et al. (1979) for a sexual bill of rights for disabled people. Two issues of *SIECUS Report* (March 1986 and April/May 1995) are devoted to meeting the needs of people with disabilities. For resources about sexuality and persons with spinal cord injuries, see Tepper and Lawless (1997).

PERSONAL REFLECTIONS

If you were to have an accident and become physically disabled, do you think you would still want to hug, hold, kiss, and share affection (and have sex, if possible) with your partner? How do you presently react when you see a person with disabilities engaging in these behaviors?

Key Terms

anaphrodisiac 92
aphrodisiac 92
clitoridectomy 88
desire 78
ejaculation 82
erection 78
excitement phase 78
Grafenberg (G) spot 42, 86

Helen Kaplan 78
Masters and Johnson 18, 76
multiple orgasms 84
myotonia 78
orgasm 81
orgasmic platform 80
plateau phase 80
refractory period 84

resolution 84
retrograde ejaculation 82
semen 50, 82
sex-tension flush 80
sexual response cycle 78
Skene's glands 87
vaginal lubrication 79
vasocongestion 78

Suggested Readings

Furlow, F. B., & Thornhill, R. (1996, January/February). The orgasm wars. *Psychology Today.* Considers the function of female orgasms from the view of evolutionary psychology.

Gallagher, W. (1986, February). The etiology of orgasm. *Discover.*

Kaufman, M. (1995). *Easy for you to say: Q & A's for teens living with chronic illness or disability.* Toronto: Key Porter Books. A lengthy, excellent chapter on sexuality.

Masters, W., & Johnson, V. (1966) *Human sexual response.* Boston: Little, Brown. The classic work.

Rowland, D. L. (1999). Issues in the laboratory study of human sexual response: A synthesis for the nontechnical sexologist.

Journal of Sex Research, 36, 3-15. An excellent review of the advantages and disadvantages of laboratory studies of human sexual responses.

Tiefer, L. (1995). *Sex is not a natural act and other essays.* Boulder, CO: Westview. Offers some criticisms of the Masters and Johnson model; well written.

Toubia, N. (1993). *Warrior marks: Female sexual mutilation and the sexual blinding of women.* New York: Harcourt Brace.

Study Guide

INTERACTIVE REVIEW

(1) _____ observed and recorded physiological responses from hundreds of people engaged in sexual activity. This work led them to conclude that men and women are (2) _____ in their responses than previously believed. They divided the physiological responses during sex into four phases: (3) _____, (4) _____, (5) _____, and (6) _____. This pattern of responses is often referred to as the (7) _____. Other researchers have organized the responses into fewer or more phases, and this chapter follows the model of sex therapist (8) _____ and includes (9) _____ as the first phase.

The first response in the excitement phase for both men and women is a (10) _____ response, which results in (11) _____ in men and (12) _____ in women. During the (13) _____ phase in women, the tissues of the outer third of the vagina become swollen with blood, causing the vaginal opening to narrow. This response is referred to as the (14) _____. Also during this phase, the clitoris (15) _____. Early in the plateau phase, (16) _____ percent of all women and about 25 percent of all men experience a rash on the skin called the (17) _____.

At the time of orgasm, both men and women have (18) _____ in specific tissues that initially occur every 0.8 second. However, recent studies indicate that the real essence of orgasm is not in the genitals, but in (19) _____. Men's and women's descriptions of orgasm are (20) _____. Men's orgasms occur in two stages, (21) _____ and (22) _____. The expulsion of semen from the penis is called (23) _____. After men have an orgasm, their physiological responses generally dip below plateau, during which time they cannot have another orgasm. This period of time is called the (24) _____. Unlike most men, some women can have (25) _____, defined as two or more orgasms in quick succession without dropping below the plateau level. The return to the unaroused state is called (26) _____.

By most estimates, only (27) _____ percent of adult women experience orgasm regularly during sexual intercourse. Masters and Johnson claimed that all women in good health are capable of reaching orgasm during intercourse, but Helen Kaplan and others believe that many women are incapable of reaching orgasm during intercourse without simultaneous (28) _____ stimulation.

Freud believed that there were two types of female orgasm, one caused by (29) _____ stimulation and another by (30) _____ sensations. Masters and Johnson originally claimed that all female orgasms were identical and were focused in the (31) _____. However, some women report having experienced different types of orgasms, and work conducted in the 1980s revealed that many of these women had a sensitive area on the (32) _____ wall of the vagina called the (33) _____. Stimulation of this area sometimes resulted in (34) _____ during orgasm. In some women the fluid was identified as urine, but in others it contained an enzyme found in secretions from men's (35) _____.

Most women say that the size of a partner's penis is (36) _____ for their pleasure during intercourse. Many people have tried to enhance their sexual desire or performance by taking substances called (37) _____, but there is little evidence that they have any real effect. In many places in the world, sexual pleasure is denied to women by mutilating their genitals in procedures called (38) _____ and (39) _____. The World Health Organization has had little luck in stopping these ancient cultural practices.

People with disabilities may have special problems communicating or engaging in the physical act of sex, but sexuality is more than just the physical responses described by Masters and Johnson. It includes emotional and spiritual feelings and how we relate to others. We are all sexual human beings.

SELF-TEST

A. TRUE OR FALSE

T F 40. The first physiological signs of arousal in men occur within seconds, but take several minutes to begin in women.

T F 41. Vaginal lubrication is actually superfiltered blood plasma.

T F 42. The presence of vaginal lubrication means that a woman is ready to begin sexual intercourse.

T F 43. Both men and women can experience nipple erection during the excitement phase.

T F 44. When the clitoris pulls back and disappears beneath the clitoral hood, it means that a woman is less sexually aroused than before.

T F 45. The secretion of fluids from the vaginal walls may slow down if the plateau phase is prolonged.

T F 46. Changes that occur during the plateau phase in men are not as distinct as the changes that occur in women.

T F 47. Generally speaking, descriptions of orgasm written by women can be easily distinguished from those written by men.

T F 48. Orgasm and ejaculation occur at the same time in men and are actually the same event.

T F 49. The rhythmic muscular contractions during orgasm recorded by Masters and Johnson are not strongly related to a person's subjective sensations of pleasure.

T F 50. A full orgasm for men, with ejaculation, is almost always followed by a refractory period.

T F 51. Some people who have suffered severe spinal cord injuries can experience orgasm.

T F 52. The walls of the inner two-thirds of the vagina are very sensitive to touch, thus making penis length an important factor during intercourse.

T F 53. There is more variation in penis length in the unaroused condition than in the erect state.

T F 54. Alcohol excites the central nervous system and enhances sexual performance.

T F 55. Regular long-term use of marijuana can lower testosterone levels and decrease sperm production.

T F 56. A man's penis size is related to his height, weight, and race.

T F 57. Regular use of cocaine often leads to erectile problems and difficulties reaching orgasm.

T F 58. There is a strong relationship between vaginal vasocongestion and a woman's subjective sense of sexual arousal.

B. MATCHING (SOME QUESTIONS HAVE MULTIPLE ANSWERS)

_____ 59. desire

_____ 60. excitement phase

_____ 61. plateau phase

_____ 62. orgasm phase

_____ 63. resolution phase

_____ 64. vasocongestive response

a. Cowper's glands secrete a few drops of clear fluid
b. penis starts to become erect
c. labia minora become engorged with blood
d. specific sensations cause the individual to seek out, or become receptive to, sexual experiences
e. rhythmic muscular contractions occur in outer vagina, uterus, and anal sphincter muscles
f. clitoris pulls back against the pubic bone
g. vaginal lubrication begins
h. blood drains from breasts, outer third of the vagina, labia minora, and clitoris
i. sex-tension flush appears
j. nipples become erect
k. clitoris is most prominent at this time
l. scrotum thickens and helps pull the testicles toward the body
m. blood drains from penis and testicles
n. walls of the inner two-thirds of the vagina begin to balloon out
o. return to the unaroused state
p. rhythmic muscular contractions in vas deferens, prostate gland, urethra, and anal sphincter muscles
q. outer third of the vagina becomes engorged with blood
r. nipples appear to be less erect
s. labia majora flatten and spread apart
t. testicles increase in size by 50–100 percent
u. in men, a fluid is emitted from the urethra

C. FILL IN THE BLANKS

65. The two basic physiological responses that occur during sexual arousal are called _____ and _____.

66. Some women emit a fluid during orgasm that comes from the _____.

67. Most women and many men get a skin rash called the _____ when they become highly sexually aroused.

68. _____ refers to the buildup of energy in nerves and muscles resulting in involuntary contractions.

69. The first stage of orgasm in men is called _____.

70. The engorgement and swelling of the outer third of the vagina was named the _____ by Masters and Johnson.

71. A sensitive area that is found on the front wall of the vagina in about 10 percent of all women is called the _____.

72. After ejaculating, most men have a period of time called the _____ during which it is impossible for them to have another orgasm.

73. In women, the _____ become greatly engorged with blood during the plateau phase, resulting in a doubling or tripling in their thickness and a vivid color change.

Sexually Transmitted and Sexually Related Diseases

When a person has sex, they're not having it just with that partner. They're having it with everybody that partner has had it with for the past ten years.

(Otis Bowen, former U.S. Secretary of Health and Human Services)

The National Institute of Medicine has declared that sexually transmitted diseases (STDs) are at epidemic proportions. Every year approximately 12 million Americans are diagnosed with an STD (see Table 5–1). In fact, 1 in 4 sexually active teenagers will contract at least one sexually transmitted disease (Alan Guttmacher Institute, 2001). Of the nation's 10 most frequently reported infections, 4 are STDs (chlamydia, gonorrhea, hepatitis B, and HIV). The total cost to the country is over $17 billion a year. It is to everyone's advantage, therefore, that we educate ourselves about the causes, symptoms, modes of transmission, and treatments for these diseases. If left untreated, some of these diseases can cause sterility, blindness, and even death, not to mention ruined relationships.

When you have finished studying this chapter, you should be able to:

1. Explain what causes sexually transmitted diseases, how they are spread, and who can get them;

2. Describe the symptoms of gonorrhea, chlamydia, syphilis, chancroid, herpes, hepatitis, venereal warts, HIV/AIDS, trichomoniasis, pubic lice, and scabies;

3. Understand that with many STDs it is possible to be infected and have no symptoms (for particular STDs, name whether men or women are more likely to be asymptomatic, and at what stage);

4. Describe the method of diagnosis and treatment for each STD;

5. Summarize the complications that can occur if STDs are not treated early;

6. Discuss the possible effects on the fetus and newborn if a pregnant woman has various STDs;

7. Describe the three types of vaginitis and discuss vaginal health care; and

8. Discuss safer sex practices.

Chapter 5

T ARE THEY, AND WHO GETS THEM?

Some people believe that sexually transmitted diseases are punishment for having sinful or immoral sex and that only promiscuous persons get STDs. They talk as if they believe that sexual behavior causes the diseases. These beliefs are not only incorrect, they are also cruel, for tens of thousands of loyal and faithful men and women have caught these diseases from unfaithful partners. A similar number of innocent newborns have contracted them from infected mothers.

TABLE 5–1	
STDS IN THE UNITED STATES	
Type of Sexually Transmitted Disease	Estimated New Cases per Year
Chlamydia	4,000,000+
Trichomoniasis	3,000,000+
Gonorrhea	800,000
Human papillomavirus infection	500,000–1,000,000
Genital herpes	1,000,000
Syphilis	<10,000
Hepatitis B (sexually transmitted)	50,000+
AIDS	50,000
HIV infection	?

Source: Centers for Disease Control and Prevention and studies cited in text

"I got gonorrhea from my boyfriend. I, myself, thought that I was engaged in a monogamous relationship. However, it was not monogamous for him."

"Over the past 2 years, I have had one steady boyfriend. I have never slept around and I thought he was faithful to me. I would have put my life on the line to prove this. During these 2 years I have contracted chlamydia three times, PID, and trichomoniasis."

"My first time having sex was at 16. My only fear was getting pregnant. My boyfriend said he was infertile so I couldn't get pregnant. We had sex. Approximately 1 month later I found out I had gonorrhea. I had no idea I could be a victim of an STD."

"I am a 48-year-old woman who contracted a sexually transmitted disease from my husband. As a result, I had to have a total hysterectomy." (All examples are from the author's files.)

bacteria Small, single-celled organisms that lack a nuclear membrane, but have all the genetic material (RNA and DNA) to reproduce themselves.

virus A protein shell around a nucleic acid core. Viruses have either RNA or DNA, but not both, and thus cannot reproduce themselves. They invade host cells that provide the material to manufacture new virus particles.

venereal diseases Term originally used to refer to gonorrhea, syphilis, and three other diseases that are spread almost exclusively by sexual contact.

sexually transmitted diseases (STDs) Diseases that can be, but are not necessarily always, transmitted by sexual contact. This term is generally preferred to the term *venereal diseases*.

These people were not promiscuous, yet they still became infected with sexually transmitted diseases. What causes STDs? It is not sexual behavior, per se; the behavior is merely the mode of transmission for bacteria, viruses, or parasites that must be present for the diseases to be transmitted. *Sexually transmitted diseases are spread, for the most part, by sexual contact* (including vaginal and anal intercourse and oral-genital contact) *with someone who has the bacteria, viruses, or parasites that cause the diseases.*

Bacteria are very small single-celled organisms. They lack a nuclear membrane but have all the genetic material (RNA and DNA) and metabolic machinery to reproduce themselves. **Viruses** are just a protein shell around a nucleic acid core. They have RNA or DNA, but not both, and thus cannot reproduce themselves. They invade host cells that provide the material to manufacture new virus particles. The bacteria and viruses responsible for STDs live outside the body for only a short period of time. The common belief that you can catch these diseases from a toilet seat is greatly exaggerated, although it might be possible to expose yourself to the bacteria or viruses by using a damp towel soon after someone with a disease uses it (and in this case, you are more likely to spread it to your eyes than to your genitals).

Some people believe (or at least would like to believe) that sexually transmitted diseases occur only in, or primarily in, the poor, the uneducated, and minority groups. Sexually transmitted diseases, however, are nondiscriminating. The bacteria or viruses that cause these diseases do not care whether you are white, black, yellow, or brown; whether you are on welfare or a millionaire; whether you bathe every day or only once a week; or whether you are a grade school dropout or college-educated. In fact, at least one of these diseases (chlamydia) is at epidemic proportions among college students today. The point, here and in the previous case histories, is that anyone having sex is at some risk for contracting a sexually transmitted disease.

Some of these diseases were once called **venereal diseases** (after the Roman goddess of love, Venus), but this term generally referred to diseases that are spread almost exclusively by sexual contact (gonorrhea, syphilis, and three other lesser known diseases). Today, the description **sexually transmitted diseases (STDs)** is generally preferred and refers to these diseases plus other infectious diseases that can be, but are not always, transmitted by sexual contact.

There are still other diseases of the sexual organs that are caused by overgrowths of yeast or fungal organisms found naturally in the body, and these too can sometimes be passed on during sex. I will refer to these as **sexually related diseases.** A few other sexually transmitted diseases are not really diseases at all, but rather infestations of parasites (pubic lice and scabies) that are transmitted from person to person during sexual contact.

PERSONAL REFLECTIONS

How would you feel if you found out you had a sexually transmitted disease (or, if you have been infected, how did you feel)? Would you feel differently than you would if you had contracted the flu? Why? How would you tell your partners of their possible infection?

WHERE DID THEY COME FROM?

Some people argue that humans first contracted sexually transmitted diseases by having sex with animals, but no animal species is known to have gonorrhea or syphilis. Later you will learn that the virus that causes AIDS originated in monkeys, but it was probably transmitted to humans by contact with blood, not by sex. It is more likely that previously harmless bacteria or viruses mutated (they are highly susceptible to change) into strains causing disease.

Although where and how STDs originated remain unknown, some of these sexually transmitted diseases have been around for at least a few thousand years, as many famous Greeks, Romans, and Egyptians (including Cleopatra) were described as having the symptoms. In fact, public kissing was banned for a period in Roman times because of an epidemic of a disease that was described as being identical to what we now know as herpes. An epidemic of syphilis also swept through Europe in the early 1500s, and it is still hotly debated whether Columbus and his sailors brought it back from the New World, or vice versa (e.g., Catterall, 1974; Luger, 1993). In fact, Columbus died of advanced syphilis.

The fact is that it does not really matter where or how STDs originated; they are here to stay and we must deal with them. In our own country, there have been major outbreaks of STDs from time to time, most recently after the start of the sexual revolution and the war in Vietnam. The present epidemic situation can probably be attributed to several factors:

1. The discovery of penicillin and other antibiotics (about the time of World War II), which made people less fearful about contracting an STD
2. A large drop between the end of World War II and 1955 in the amount of federal funds available for STD prevention (possibly due to overconfidence in antibiotics)
3. The new sexual freedom that many people believed possible as a result of the birth control pill and other reliable means of birth control
4. The shift from use of the condom to use of the birth control pill
5. A lack of education, or just plain ignorance

Surveys of teenagers indicate that many know very little about sexually transmitted diseases, although they believe themselves to be well informed. Many people are unaware, for example, that they can have an STD but show no symptoms and still be contagious. As a result, they do not seek treatment as early as they should. I will discuss some precautionary measures that can help you avoid contracting sexually transmitted diseases and will outline what to do in case you should get one. First, let us examine the symptoms and treatment for some of the most widely known diseases.

Note to students:

This chapter contains more information about STDs than is usually included in sexuality textbooks. I want the chapter to serve as an introduction to the subject of STDs, but I also want it to serve as a reference for those who want more than an introduction. If you ever contract an STD, you will want to know everything about it.

GONORRHEA

Gonorrhea (from the Greek *gonos*, "seed," and *rhoia*, "flow"; also known as "the clap" or "the drip") is probably the oldest of the STDs. Its symptoms are described in Leviticus in the Old Testament, which dates back to about 1500 B.C., and were also described in detail by Greek physicians. The number of reported cases of gonorrhea has declined to less than 400,000 a year, but many go unreported, and the Centers for Disease Control and Prevention estimates that there will be 800,000 new cases in the United States this year. The rate of infection is considerably higher among African Americans than it is among Latinos or whites (Stoner et al., 2000) and is 6 times more likely among teens aged 15 to 19 than among the general population. The rates for gonorrhea in the United States are dramatically higher (often 100 times higher) than in all other developed countries except Russia (Panchaud et al., 2000).

SYMPTOMS AND COMPLICATIONS

Gonorrhea is caused by a bacterium (*Neisseria gonorrhoeae*, often referred to as gonococcus)

---

sexually related diseases Diseases of the reproductive system or genitals that are not contracted through sexual activity. Often involve overgrowths of bacteria, yeasts, viruses, or fungal organisms that are found naturally in sexual and reproductive organs.

gonorrhea A sexually transmitted disease caused by the *Neisseria gonorrhoeae* bacterium (often referred to as "the gonococcus"), which lives on mucous membranes.

named after Albert Neisser, who discovered it in 1879. It lives on warm, moist mucous membranes in the urethra, vagina, rectum, mouth and throat, and eyes. A person gets gonorrhea by having his or her mucous membranes come into contact with another person's infected membranes. Because of the location of these membranes in the body, this normally occurs only during intimate contact. However, your chance of catching gonorrhea from having vaginal intercourse once with an infected person is not 100 percent. A man's risk of infection during intercourse with an infected woman is about 30 to 50 percent, whereas a woman has about a 50 to 60 percent chance of catching it the first time she has intercourse with an infected man (Platt et al., 1983). The gonococcus can also infect the anus and rectum (during anal intercourse) and the throat (during oral-genital sex, particularly fellatio), but less is known about the relative risk by these means of transmission. The bacteria have been found to survive for a short time outside the body, but your chances of picking them up from nonsexual contact, particularly a dry toilet seat, are extremely remote.

In men who become infected during sexual intercourse, the gonococcus bacteria invade and cause inflammation of the urethra *(gonococcal urethritis)*. This usually results in a thick, puslike white or yellowish discharge from the urethra ("the drip"), starting 2 to 10 days after infection (see Figure 5–1). There is generally an irritation or a burning sensation at the urethral opening, and urination is often frequent and painful. Because the symptoms are painful and obvious, most men seek treatment immediately. However, *about 5 to 20 percent of men show no symptoms (are asymptomatic)*, while in others the early symptoms disappear. These asymptomatic men are still infected and can pass the gonococcus to new partners. If left untreated, gonorrhea spreads up the man's reproductive system and causes inflammation of the prostate, seminal vesicles, bladder, and epididymis. By this time, he usually experiences severe pain and fever. In 1 to 2 percent of cases, the disease gets into the bloodstream and causes inflammation of the joints *(gonococcal arthritis)*, heart, or brain covering, as well as skin lesions (Brown et al., 1999). However, gonorrhea rarely results in death.

Figure 5–1   Urethral puslike discharge of gonorrhea.

In women, the gonococcus initially invades the cervix, but unlike men, *most women show no symptoms during the early stages.* They are often unaware of their infection unless told about it by an infected male partner, and thus can unknowingly pass gonorrhea on to new partners. In the 20 to 40 percent of women who show symptoms, there may be an abnormal vaginal discharge and irritation of the vulva and urethra, causing burning during urination. Because so many women are asymptomatic, they often go untreated, and the gonococcus spreads through the uterus into the Fallopian tubes. In up to 40 percent of untreated women, the tubes become swollen and inflamed, a condition known as **pelvic inflammatory disease (PID),** with symptoms of severe abdominal pain and fever (see page 104). Hospitalization may be necessary at this stage. PID can cause scarring of the Fallopian tubes, which blocks passage of the sperm and egg—a common cause of sterility and tubal pregnancies in women (see Chapter 7).

If a pregnant woman contracts gonorrhea, the fetus will not be infected because the gonococcus normally is not carried in the bloodstream. However, a baby's eyes can become infected at delivery as it passes through the infected cervix and vagina (a condition called *gonococcal opthalmia neonatorum;* see Figure 5–2). This can rapidly lead to blindness. In some developing countries, 3 to 15 percent of babies are at risk, but the rate for gonorrhea in pregnant women in the United States is less than 1 percent, and most states require that an antibiotic or silver nitrate drops be put into all babies' eyes at birth to prevent possible

pelvic inflammatory disease (PID) A bacterially caused inflammation of a woman's reproductive tract, particularly the Fallopian tubes, that can result in sterility. The most common (though not the only) cause is untreated gonorrhea and/or chlamydia.

Figure 5–2 Eye infections caused by gonorrhea (left) and herpes (right).

becoming resistant to it as well. To complicate matters, many people who are diagnosed with gonorrhea are also found to have another sexually transmitted disease called chlamydia, which is treated with tetracycline or an erythromycin. To combat these multiple problems, most physicians today treat gonorrhea with a drug called ceftriaxone (Brown et al., 1999). However, in 2000 the Centers for Disease Control and Prevention announced that gonorrhea is becoming resistant to many currently used drugs as well. This means that we are quickly running out of inexpensive antibiotics to treat gonorrhea, and that soon we may have to turn to expensive injectable antibiotics to fight the disease. In the future, it may be possible to combat the spread of gonorrhea by vaccinating people (Sparling et al., 1994).

Should you ever be diagnosed with gonorrhea, be sure to tell all your recent partners that they may have gonorrhea so that they, too, can be treated. Gonorrhea is not like chicken pox, where you become immune after having had the disease. You can catch gonorrhea again if you again have sex with someone infected with the gonococcus.

infections (Laga et al., 1989). Adults can also transmit the gonococcus to their eyes by a contaminated hand.

DIAGNOSIS AND TREATMENT

Most individuals with symptoms of gonorrhea will seek treatment immediately. Remember, however, that many people—particularly women—have no early symptoms. Therefore, if you suspect that you have had sex with someone who has gonorrhea, see a doctor as soon as possible. Until recently, a culture test was always used to test for gonorrhea. A cotton swab was inserted into the area of suspected infection, and the cells were grown in culture for a couple of days and then tested. However, this test is invasive, and a lot of people were reluctant to go to a doctor to be examined. Today, an accurate urine test is routinely used to test for gonorrhea (e.g., Jones et al., 2000).

Little could be done for people with gonorrhea prior to the discovery of antibiotics. The urethral inflammation caused by gonorrhea often caused blockage in men, and because a man's urethra also serves as the passageway for urine, it was often necessary to clean out an infected urethra with a pipe cleanerlike instrument. Fortunately, penicillin was discovered around the time of World War II and proved to be highly effective. Unfortunately, the bacterium developed resistance to penicillin over time. A dosage of 150,000 units was given to people for gonorrhea in the 1940s, but by the 1980s the standard dosage was nearly 5 million units, and there were some strains that could not be destroyed with any dose (*penicillinase Neisseria gonorrhoeae*). Many physicians had switched to tetracycline by the early 1980s, but by the end of the decade the bacterium was

CHLAMYDIA AND NONGONOCOCCAL URETHRITIS

Any inflammation of the urethra not caused by the gonococcus is called **nongonococcal** (or **nonspecific**) **urethritis (NGU)**. This term is often reserved for men with an inflamed urethra, but the organisms that cause it cause infection in women (*cervicitis*) as well. Several organisms can cause infection (including *Ureaplasma urealyticum* and *Trichomonas vaginalis*), but the one that is most frequently responsible today is *Chlamydia trachomatis*. The infection caused by this sexually transmitted bacterium is called **chlamydia.**

Chlamydia is much more common than gonorrhea, with an estimated 4 million new cases in the United States this year (Centers for Disease Control and Prevention). It is especially prevalent in teenagers and young adults and is more common among whites than

nongonococcal (nonspecific) urethritis (NGU) Any inflammation of the urethra that is not caused by the *Neisseria gonorrhoeae* (gonococcus) bacterium.

chlamydia A sexually transmitted disease caused by the *Chlamydia trachomatis* bacterium, which lives on mucous membranes.

African Americans (Stoner et al., 2000). Similar to gonorrhea, the rates for chlamydia are much higher in the United States than in all other developed countries except Russia (Panchaud et al., 2000). A study of nearly 150,000 sexually active American girls aged 15–19 years found that 10 percent of them had chlamydia (Mosure et al., 1997).

Because many students have never heard of chlamydia, they think that it cannot be all that bad. In fact, although its initial symptoms are usually milder than those of gonorrhea, if left untreated it is more likely than gonorrhea to cause damage to the reproductive organs.

SYMPTOMS AND COMPLICATIONS

Like the gonococcus, *Chlamydia trachomatis* lives only on mucous membranes. Chlamydia is spread when the infected membranes of one person come into contact with the membranes of another person.

If a person with chlamydia shows early symptoms, he or she will start doing so within 1 to 3 weeks after infection. The early symptoms are milder than, but similar to and sometimes mistaken for, those of gonorrhea: irritation and burning of the urethra (although usually not painful) and a discharge (usually thin and clear rather than puslike). However, most women and a large proportion of men have no symptoms at all in the initial stage.

> "I found out that I had chlamydia when my girlfriend handed me a bottle of pills and told me to follow the instructions. I didn't even know what chlamydia was. . . . I had no idea I had an STD."

> "When I was attending LSU, I went to see the doctor for a regular gynecological exam. The nurse suggested that I consider some other tests for STDs because some of them had few or no symptoms. At first I declined, thinking that I had not slept with many people and, also, that if I had anything I would surely know from symptoms. But I changed my mind and was tested. When I called for results, I was shocked to find out that I was positive for chlamydia." (All examples are from the author's files.)

If left untreated, chlamydia spreads through the reproductive system, which in men can cause infection of the prostate and epididymis and possibly sterility (Greendale et al., 1993). In women the spread of chlamydia can cause pelvic inflammatory disease, which can leave the Fallopian tubes scarred and result in sterility or increased risk of tubal pregnancy (see next section). At this stage the infection can be quite painful and may require hospitalization. Research has shown that *a single attack of chlamydia is about 3 times more likely than gonorrhea to cause sterility in women.* Babies born to women who have chlamydia at the

time of delivery can get eye infections *(chlamydia conjunctivitis)* and/or nose-throat infections, or even pneumonia (an estimated 182,000 cases per year) (Schachter et al., 1986). There is an increased risk of stillbirths, premature deliveries, and death as well. In underdeveloped countries, the chlamydia bacterium often causes an eye infection called *trachoma,* which is spread to other people's eyes by flies. It is the leading cause of blindness in those areas. In tropical countries, certain subtypes of chlamydia are also responsible for a serious sexually transmitted disease called **lymphogranuloma venereum (LGV)** (there are fewer than 150 cases annually in the United States). If left untreated, LGV causes the inguinal lymph nodes to swell, followed by swelling of the penis, labia, or clitoris (sometimes enormously so, resulting in elephantiasis of the external genitalia) (Brown et al., 1999).

DIAGNOSIS AND TREATMENT

As with gonorrhea, the culture test for chlamydia has been replaced with a noninvasive urine test (Jones et al., 2000). If chlamydia is confirmed, it is usually treated with tetracycline, doxycycline, or erythromycin. Remember, many people have no symptoms in the early stages, so if you think someone you have had sex with has chlamydia, seek treatment immediately.

PELVIC INFLAMMATORY DISEASE (PID) IN WOMEN: A LIKELY CONSEQUENCE OF UNTREATED CHLAMYDIA OR GONORRHEA

In the discussion of gonorrhea and chlamydia, I referred to pelvic inflammatory disease in women as a possible consequence if the diseases went untreated. PID is a general term for an infection that travels from the lower genital tract (vagina and cervix) to the Fallopian tubes and sometimes to surrounding structures such as the ovaries and pelvic cavity (Berger, et al., 1992). It results from infection with a variety of organisms, but 50 to 75 percent of cases are caused by *Chlamydia trachomatis* or *Neisseria gonorrhoeae* (Brunham et al., 1988; Rice & Schachter, 1991).

Over 1 million cases of PID occur each year in the United States (Donovan, 1997), requiring about 182,000 hospitalizations. One in 7 women of reproductive age has had PID (Aral et al., 1991).

Symptoms may include tenderness or pain in the lower abdomen (sometimes to the extent that standing up straight is impossible), high fever, and chills. However, 3 times as many women experience a persistent low-grade infection, either with no symptoms or with intermittent abdominal cramps (Wolner-Hanssen et al., 1990). In these "silent" infections (i.e., the women do not go to a physician for diagnosis), the long-term inflammation can result in pelvic adhesions and abscesses.

The inside diameter of a Fallopian tube is only about that of a human hair; thus, even a small amount

---

lymphogranuloma venereum (LGV) A sexually transmitted disease common in tropical countries that is caused by chlamydia. If left untreated, it causes swelling of the inguinal lymph nodes, penis, labia, or clitoris.

of scar tissue can result in a life-threatening ectopic (tubal) pregnancy or in permanent sterility (Weinstock et al., 1994). The chances of sterility increase from 11 percent of women after one case of PID to 54 percent of women with three episodes (Weström, 1980). Largely because of the increase in sexually transmitted diseases, the rates for ectopic pregnancies and infertility have increased dramatically in young women during the last 2 decades. Over 40 percent of ectopic pregnancies are directly related to STDs and pelvic inflammatory disease (Coste et al., 1994).

Because PID is so closely associated with the acquisition of chlamydia and gonorrhea, it should not be surprising that the major risk factors for PID are related to sexual behavior: early age for first experience of intercourse and history of multiple partners (Aral et al., 1991). Interestingly, there is also an increased risk from douching (probably by forcing the bacteria into the uterus) and smoking (by impaired tubal ciliary function or impaired immune response) (Wolner-Hanssen et al., 1990; Scholes et al., 1992).

Is there anything that women can do to minimize the chances of getting PID? One option, of course, is to reduce the number of one's sexual partners. But many of us may be sexually monogamous and still have several (monogamous) partners over time. Spermicides and barrier methods of contraception, such as male or female condoms and the diaphragm, reduce the risk of PID by reducing the risk of sexually transmitted diseases (Washington et al., 1991; see Box 6–A). The birth control pill increases the risk of chlamydial infections of the lower genital tract, but decreases the risk of PID, while IUDs increase the risk of PID (see Chapter 6). It is very important that women having sexual relations have regular pelvic examinations (and perhaps ask their doctor to test for gonorrhea and chlamydia if they have had new partners since their last exam).

SYPHILIS

The consequences of untreated gonorrhea or chlamydia can be serious, but untreated **syphilis** is far worse, being responsible for the deaths of over 100 million people worldwide in the 20th century (Chiappa & Forish, 1976). As stated earlier, some people have speculated that Columbus brought the disease back from the New World (Catterall, 1974; but see Luger, 1993, for another explanation), while others have thought that the disease evolved from the treponema organism, which causes the skin disease yaws in tropical areas. They believe that when humans migrated to cooler climates, the skin provided a less desirable environment and the organism retreated to the genitals and anus, becoming a sexually transmitted disease. Whatever the

origin, there is no written description of the disease's symptoms prior to the time of Columbus.

It was once thought that gonorrhea and syphilis were the same disease. In the 1700s, an English doctor named John Hunter tried to prove this by inoculating his own penis with the pus from a patient with gonorrhea. He thought he had proven his hypothesis when he developed the symptoms of both diseases, but in fact the patient simply had had both diseases. *Treponema pallidum,* the spiral-shaped bacterium (spirochete) that causes syphilis, was finally identified in 1905.

In the United States, outbreaks of syphilis have tended to occur in 10-year cycles. The disease last peaked in 1990, when 50,578 cases were reported. Only 6,993 cases were reported in 1998 (CDC, 1999c). Similar declines have been observed in all other developed countries except for Russia, where it is in epidemic proportions (Panchaud et al., 2000). Here, the disease is found mainly in southern states and large urban areas and is 30 to 40 times more common among African Americans than whites (Kilmarx et al., 1997). These ethnic differences are not direct risk factors for syphilis, but are instead related to more specific risks. Syphilis is particularly bad in the inner cities because of widespread unemployment, poor education and health care, prostitution, and in particular, the use of crack cocaine and the practice of exchanging sex for drugs.

SYMPTOMS AND COMPLICATIONS

Almost all cases of syphilis are transmitted by sexual contact. However, unlike the bacteria that cause gonorrhea and chlamydia, which require contact of mucous membranes for transmission, the spirochete that causes syphilis can also pass directly through any little cut or scrape of the skin into the bloodstream. This means that one could potentially get syphilis by merely touching the sores of another person, as has happened to some dentists and physicians. If a person has been infected by the spirochete, the first symptoms generally appear 2 to 4 weeks later. If many bacteria are transmitted, the incubation period can be as short as 10 days; but if only a few are transmitted, the sores can take as long as 90 days to appear.

The symptoms of syphilis generally occur in four stages (Brown et al., 1999). The **primary stage** begins with the appearance of a very ugly ulcerlike (raised edges with a crater) sore called a *chancre* (see Figure 5–3) at the site where the spirochete entered the body (usually the penis, cervix, lips, tongue, or anus). The chancre is full of bacteria and highly infectious, but even though the chancre looks awful, it is usually painless, and thus some

syphilis A sexually transmitted disease caused by the *Treponema pallidum* bacterium (spirochete), which can also pass directly through any cut or scrape into the bloodstream.

Figure 5–3 A primary-stage syphilis chancre on the penis (top) and labia (bottom).

als remain infected *and* infectious even after the chancre disappears.

Symptoms of the **secondary stage** of syphilis usually appear within 4 to 6 weeks after the chancre heals. The main symptom is an *itchless, painless rash* that appears all over the body, including the palms of the hands and the soles of the feet (see Figure 5–4). In the moist areas around the genitals, the rash appears as large sores called *condylomata lata,* which break and ooze a highly infectious fluid full of bacteria. Other symptoms can include a sore throat, a persistent low-grade fever, nausea, loss of appetite, aches and pains, and sometimes even hair loss. These symptoms are bothersome enough that many infected people will seek treatment, but many people mistake the symptoms for the measles, an allergic reaction, or some other disease (syphilis is sometimes called "the great imitator"). If treatment is not obtained, these symptoms, like the chancre of the primary stage, will also disappear (within several weeks to 1 year) and not return.

An infected person now enters the symptomless **latent stage,** and after about a year is generally no longer contagious because the spirochete is no longer found on the mucous membrane surfaces. This stage may last for years with no noticeable signs, but all the while the bacteria are attacking the internal organs of the body, particularly the heart and blood vessels and the brain and spinal cord.

About two-thirds of the people with untreated syphilis will not experience any more problems with the disease, but one-third will develop serious complications as a result of the accumulated organ damage. They are now in the **late (or tertiary) stage.** Large ulcers called *gummas* often appear on the skin and bones. Damage to the heart and blood vessels frequently results in death, while damage to the central nervous system can lead to paralysis, insanity, and/or deafness.

Particularly heartbreaking is the fact that an *unborn baby can catch syphilis from an infected mothe*r. This happens because the spirochete travels from the pregnant woman's blood into the placental blood system. If it is not diagnosed and treated, the fetus will be aborted, stillborn, or born with a rather advanced stage of the disease called **congenital**

people do not seek treatment. Because the painless chancre generally appears on the cervix in women, they usually are unaware that they are infected during the initial stage unless they get a pelvic exam. Even if a person is not treated, the sore will usually disappear in 10 to 14 days. However, the spirochete continues to be carried in the person's bloodstream, and thus individu-

Figure 5–4 Secondary-stage syphilis rash on the palms and abdomen.

syphilis. There were 801 reported cases in the United States in 1998 (CDC, 1999b). Complications of congenital syphilis can include deformation of the bones and teeth, blindness, deafness, and other abnormalities that can result in an early death (see Figure 5–5). Blood tests for syphilis are done routinely during pregnancy tests, and if detected the disease can be treated.

DIAGNOSIS AND TREATMENT

The spirochete taken from a chancre or sore can be identified under a microscope, but blood tests are almost always done as well (some conditions, such as lupus and some types of arthritis, and some flu vaccines can cause a false positive test result). The saddest thing about any suffering or death that occur from syphilis is that the spirochetes are so easily eradicated with antibiotics. Penicillin G is very effective, with the amount and duration of treatment depending on the stage of infection (Augenbraun & Rolfs, 1999). Although antibiotics can eradi-

cate the bacteria at any stage, they cannot reverse any organ damage that may have already occurred if the disease was left untreated until the late stage. It is important, therefore, that people seek treatment as early as possible.

The director of the Centers for Disease Control and Prevention has created the National Plan to Eliminate Syphilis from the United States (Koplan, 2000). The goal is to reduce the number of cases to less than 1,000 by 2005. Scientists have mapped the entire genetic pattern of the bacterium that causes syphilis, and this may eventually lead to a vaccine that could help to eliminate the disease (Fraser et al., 1998).

LESS COMMON BACTERIAL STDS

There are other types of bacterially caused STDs that are common in tropical climates but rare in the United States. I have already mentioned lymphogranuloma venereum (see the section on chlamydia); two additional examples are chancroid and granuloma inguinale. **Chancroid** is caused by *Haemophilus ducreyi* and is characterized by small bumps on the genitals or other sites that rupture into soft, craterlike sores (see Figure 5–6). The incubation period from the time of infection to the appearance of the first sores is only 3 to 14 days. Unlike the syphilis chancre, chancroid is painful. The lymph nodes in the groin area often become inflamed and swollen. Only about 250 new cases of chancroid are reported each year in the United States, but in many parts of the world it is more common than syphilis. Chancroid can be treated with several different antibiotics (Brown et al., 1999).

Granuloma inguinale is rare in the United States, with fewer than 50 cases per year, but is much more common in tropical areas of the world. The main symptom is a painless pimple that ulcerates and spreads to surrounding areas, permanently destroying the tissue and causing death if not treated. It is treated with doxycycline and trimethroprim-sulfamethoxazole (Brown et al., 1999).

Shigellosis is another uncommon sexually transmitted disease. It is contracted from exposure to feces infected with the *Shigella* bacteria (a result of behavior such as oral stimulation of the anus). Symptoms include acute diarrhea, fever, and

Figure 5–5 A baby born with congenital syphilis.

chancroid A sexually transmitted disease, caused by the *Haemophilus ducreyi* bacterium, which is characterized by small, painful bumps.

granuloma inguinale A rare (in the United States) sexually transmitted disease that is characterized by ulceration of tissue.

shigellosis A disease that can be contracted during sexual activity by exposure to feces containing the *Shigella* bacterium.

Figure 5–6 Two adjacent chancroid lesions on the penis.

pain. Thirty percent of the cases in the United States occur in male homosexuals. Shigellosis is treated with tetracycline or ampicillin.

> ### PERSONAL REFLECTIONS
> *How would you feel if your best friend told you that he or she had an STD? Your teenage son told you that he had an STD? Your teenage daughter told you that she had an STD? Your partner told you that he or she had an STD acquired from a previous relationship?*

HERPES

Before all the attention given to AIDS, herpes was the media's favorite STD, appearing on the covers of *Time* and *Newsweek* and even the subject of a feature article in *Rolling Stone* magazine. Although it does not receive the attention it used to, genital herpes is still with us, infecting as many as 1 million Americans every year. Unlike gonorrhea, chlamydia, and syphilis, there is no cure for herpes. The men and women infected this year will be added to those who already have it, making the total number of genital herpes sufferers at least 45 million—1 in 5 Americans age 12 or older (Fleming et al., 1997). This is a 30 percent increase since the late 1970s. While genital herpes is much more common among blacks than whites or Latinos, the incidence rate has quintupled among white teens since the late 1970s.

Herpes (from a Greek word meaning "to creep") has been around for a long time. It is *spread by direct skin-to-skin contact* (from the infected site on one person to the site of contact on another person). A terrible epidemic in Roman times led the emperor Tiberius to ban public

kissing. Herpes was finally identified as a virus in the 1940s, with two different types (1 and 2) of the virus identified in the mid-1960s. The type 1 virus is much more common than type 2, with two-thirds of Americans older than 12 infected (Centers for Disease Control and Prevention). Both types cause painful blisters, but in the mid-1960s there was a 95 percent site specificity: 95 percent of people with fever blisters or a cold sore around the mouth had *herpes simplex virus type 1* (and thus this type was called "oral herpes"), and 95 percent of people with blisters around the genitals had *herpes simplex virus type 2* (which thus came to be called "genital herpes"). Only 5 percent of individuals with blisters on the mouth had type 2, and vice versa. Thus, it was commonly believed that HSV type 1 was acquired by kissing and HSV type 2 only by sexual intercourse.

Today, there is no longer a strong site specificity, particularly in young people. Among sexually active adults, the type 1 herpes virus causes just as many genital infections as it does infections of the mouth (Langenberg et al., 1999). Some believe that this is due to the increased popularity of oral-genital sexual behavior in recent decades. Whether or not this is true, it is certain that both *the type 1 and type 2 viruses can be transferred from mouth to genitals, and vice versa*. The two viruses are not different clinically, as both cause the same painful symptoms. Nevertheless, many people persist in their mistaken belief that oral herpes can only be caught by kissing and genital herpes only through intercourse. Perhaps this letter to Ann Landers will be more persuasive:

> Dear Ann Landers:
>   I got genital herpes from my boyfriend of two years from an innocent fever blister on his lip. I could not believe a woman could get a venereal disease from indulging in oral sex with someone who had a simple cold sore. My doctor cultured it and sure enough it came back Herpes Simplex Type I (the oral kind). But now I have genital herpes.
>   I developed a high fever after being exposed to the virus on his lip. That virus caused two fever blisters on my genitals. They reappear every two months and are quite painful.
>   My boyfriend dumped me when he learned I was infected. He remains "pure" and does not come down with a sexually transmitted disease, while I am alone and scared. There is no justice! Please, Ann Landers, inform the public at once. Tell them what can happen if a person has contact with those innocent-looking sores near the mouth.
>   Sign Me Dumb and Angry
>
>   Dear Angry: I have printed this information in my column more than once. Several readers wrote to say I was ill-informed, stupid, and just plain nuts. Thanks for your testimony. (Reprinted with permission of Ann Landers and Creators Syndicate.)

A person with blisters on the mouth not only can transfer the virus to another person's genitals, and vice

Figure 5–7 Herpes blisters on the mouth (left) and penis (center). Photo (right) shows ulcerated herpes lesions on the penis.

versa, but a person with herpes can transfer it by touch to other parts of his or her own body—including the eyes—as well. This is referred to as *autoinoculation*. I will refer to herpes blisters or ulcerations on the mouth as **oral herpes** and blisters or ulcerations on the genitals as **genital herpes,** without worrying whether the blisters were caused by the type 1 or type 2 virus (see Figure 5–7). Although oral herpes can be contracted through oral-genital sex, experts believe most cases of oral herpes in adults to be reactivations of latent infections acquired during childhood (see Fleming et al., 1997). The virus can be easily spread by even a quick, casual kiss, and thus *it should not be assumed that a person suffering an attack of oral herpes was recently involved in sexual activity.* By the way, not all mouth ulcers are caused by the herpes virus; they can also be caused by bacteria, allergic reactions, or autoimmune responses. Canker sores, for example, are not caused by herpes virus. However, "fever blisters" and most cold sores are herpes.

There are actually eight human herpes viruses, but only types 1, 2, and 8 are sexually spread. The herpes simplex virus types 1 and 2 are very closely related to the viruses that cause chicken pox in children and shingles in adults (varicella zoster virus), infectious mononucleosis (Epstein-Barr virus), cytomegalic ("large-cell") inclusion disease in infants (cytomegalovirus), and Kaposi's sarcoma. Kaposi's sarcoma is a cancer of the capillary system that is common in AIDS patients. It is caused by herpesvirus 8, which is sexually transmitted (Martin et al., 1998).

SYMPTOMS—PRIMARY ATTACK

Symptoms of the initial herpes attack normally appear about 2 to 20 days after contact with an infected person, with an average of 6 days. The symptoms occur in three stages. In stage one, the **prodromal stage,** the person feels a tingling, burning, itching, or anestheticlike sensation on the skin surface where he or she came into contact with the virus. Sometimes the symptoms are more diffuse; in the case of genital herpes, for example, the in-

fected person may feel pain running down the buttocks and thighs. These initial signs indicate the beginning of viral *replication and shedding* (i.e., viruses traveling from the source, free to incorporate themselves into other cells). Therefore, the individual should immediately cease all intimate contact involving the infected area.

Within a few hours the skin surface will break into a rash, which is followed a short time later by the appearance of fluid-filled *blisters* called *vesicles* (see Figure 5–7). These can be excruciatingly painful. After a while, the vesicles break open, resembling pustules and then ulcerated running sores. Although herpes lesions generally resemble blisters, many people have sores that are more ulcerative in appearance. These symptoms mark the second, or **vesicle stage,** which can last from 2 to 3 weeks. The first, or primary, herpes attack includes more than just painful blisters, however. The person often has flulike symptoms, suffering muscle aches and pains, headache, fever, and swollen lymph glands. Urination can be quite painful for those with genital herpes (catheterization is sometimes required), and even walking or sitting can be extremely painful sometimes.

The sores eventually begin to develop scales and form scabs. This is the third, or **crusting-over stage.** Concomitant bacterial infection of the sores sometimes occurs during this stage, but the lesions eventually heal without leaving scars. Viruses are still being shed during the crusting-over stage; thus, intimate contact with the infected area should be avoided until all the sores are fully healed. The average duration of a primary attack is about 16 days (Beutner, 1996).

The primary attack is severe because the person has not yet built up antibodies to the virus. A person can have more than one primary attack of herpes, however. An individual could have a primary attack after exposure to the type 1 virus, for example, and later be exposed to the type 2

oral herpes A herpes infection in or around the mouth. It can be caused by herpes simplex virus types 1 or 2.

genital herpes Herpes infection in the genital region. It can be caused by herpes simplex virus types 1 or 2.

virus and have another primary attack. Primary attacks to different strains of the same virus are also possible. A person with genital herpes, therefore, should not assume that it is safe to have intercourse with someone who also has herpes.

RECURRENT ATTACKS

During the primary herpes attack, some viruses migrate up sensory nerves from the infected site to the nerve's ganglion (the nerve cell center): the sacral nerve ganglion in the case of genital herpes and the trigeminal nerve ganglion in the case of oral herpes. The viruses become dormant (inactive) when they reach the ganglion. About one-third of those who have suffered primary herpes symptoms never again have another attack, but the remaining cases are evenly divided between those who suffer occasional attacks and those who suffer regular recurrent attacks. A recurrent attack occurs as a result of the virus reactivating and traveling down the sensory nerve to or near the same area as the initial sores, where it again starts multiplying. Genital herpes infections are twice as likely as oral herpes to recur again within 1 year of the primary attack, and people with type 2 herpes suffer an average of four recurrent attacks a year, compared with one a year for those with type 1 herpes (Brown et al., 1999). Recurrent attacks are usually less severe than the primary attack (because the individual now produces antibodies) and generally last only from 5 to 10 days.

What causes recurrent attacks? *Stress* to the immune system, either of a physical or emotional nature, seems to be the major cause. A recurrent attack can be brought on by illness, fatigue, menstruation, too much sunlight, and/or anxiety.

ASYMPTOMATIC AND UNRECOGNIZED INFECTIONS

The herpes viruses are easily spread when sores (blisters or ulcerations) are present. The sores are an obvious sign of viral shedding, and infected persons should take measures to prevent the spread of the virus to other persons at this time. However, in many people the symptoms are mild, while still other individuals are asymptomatic shedders of the virus. In fact, as many as 75 to 90 percent of people infected with herpes simplex type 2 in the genital region are unaware that they are infected (Fleming et al., 1997; Wald et al., 2000). Half or more of these individuals have clinically recognizable symptoms, but the symptoms are so mild that the individuals do not recognize them as herpes. Experts now believe that most transmission of genital herpes occurs during periods when there are no recognizable symptoms (Brown et al., 1999).

"The guy I had been dating for two years told me that he had 'jock itch' and showed me a sore at the base of his penis. I didn't know what jock itch even looked like, much less herpes, so I believed him. His sore went away. About a month later another sore came up, so he went to the doctor . . . [who] told him he had herpes. Two days later I had a sore on my labia. . . . The doctor diagnosed the sore as herpes." (from the author's files)

SERIOUS COMPLICATIONS

We generally think of herpes blisters as occurring only on the mouth and the genitals or anal area, but *the blisters may appear on any part of the body.* The virus can be spread to the eyes (by touching blisters that appear elsewhere on the body and then rubbing the eyes, or by using saliva to insert contact lenses), resulting in *herpes keratitis,* or ocular herpes. This is the *leading cause of blindness resulting from infection* in the United States today (see Figure 5–2). Symptoms escalate from feeling as if you have something in your eye to marked irritation and pain, often accompanied by conjunctivitis (inflammation of the mucous membrane). Small lesions are often visible on the eyeball and will always result in scarring as they heal (it is the scars that eventually cause blindness). So if you have herpes, be sure to wash your hands if you touch the sores.

Occasionally, dormant oral or facial herpes migrates to the brain rather than to the face, resulting in *herpes encephalitis,* a rare but often fatal condition. Primary attacks of herpes sometimes include inflammation of the membranes covering the brain and spinal cord *(herpes meningitis),* but full recovery usually follows.

Herpes can result in serious complications during pregnancy. A primary attack during pregnancy is generally more severe than usual, and recurrent attacks tend to occur more frequently. The stress of delivery may also bring on a recurrent attack. The greatest risk is to the unborn or newborn baby, particularly for women who have a primary attack near the time of labor (Brown et al., 1997). The virus ordinarily does not get into the bloodstream, but there is a higher than normal rate of premature births, spontaneous abortions, and congenital malformations (e.g., brain damage or mental retardation), suggesting the possibility that the virus can cross the placenta (Stone et al., 1989).

Neonatal herpes is devastating. If a woman has an active case of genital herpes during delivery, there is at least a 50 percent chance that the baby will catch it. The first signs appear 4 to 21 days after birth. Many babies who get herpes at birth die or suffer permanent and severe neurological problems (see Brown et al., 1997). Eye infections, widespread skin eruptions, and damage to internal organs can occur as well. The disease is so virulent in newborns because they have no defenses to fight off the infection. Unfortunately, it is not possible to assess the risk of spreading infection to the baby by looking for symptoms in the mother prior to birth. Most babies who become infected are born to mothers who do not display genital blisters at the time of delivery (Stone et al., 1989). It is for these reasons that most doctors prefer to deliver babies by cesarean section to women with genital herpes. Because many people with the herpes virus have no symptoms, or have symptoms they do not recognize to be herpes (see previous section), pregnant women are advised to get a blood test (Kulhanjian et al., 1992). An active case of oral herpes is not a risk factor at the time of delivery, but parents (or anyone else) with an active case of oral herpes should avoid kissing or fondling a baby.

DIAGNOSIS AND TREATMENT

First, the bad news: As yet, there is no cure for herpes. Nothing you can do or take will rid your body of the herpes virus. The virus lies dormant in the ganglion cells between active outbreaks, and the potential for another attack is always there. Herpes sufferers nevertheless remain persistent in their attempts to find a home cure. Treatments such as applying baking soda, bleach, ether, yogurt compresses, seaweed, and even peanut butter or snake venom to the blisters have been tried. None of these has proven effective in scientific tests, but just attempting to do something probably makes people feel better. However, some of these home remedies (e.g., ether) have proven to make matters even worse in some cases. Creams and ointments should also be avoided because they help to spread the virus to adjacent areas and prevent the skin from drying. Many people attempt to control herpes through diet, such as eating foods high in L-lysine (e.g., fish, meat, milk, beans, cheese, eggs) and avoiding foods high in arginine (e.g., nuts, chocolate, whole wheat bread, raisins, oatmeal, brown rice). The Centers for Disease Control and Prevention indicates that there is no merit to these specific diet claims.

Now the good news. Although there is no known cure for herpes, antiviral drugs are available that relieve symptoms and speed up the healing process during the primary attack (see Brown et al., 1999; Wald, 1999). One drug is called *acyclovir* (marketed under the name Zovirax) and is available both as an ointment and as a tablet. People who have frequent recurrent attacks can take tablets 5 times daily. Two newer, equally effective, antiviral drugs, valacyclovir and famciclovir, require that you take only two pills a day. Another antiviral cream, penciclovir, helps heal cold sores (oral herpes) (Spruance et al., 1997). Still another antiviral drug is available to help treat ocular herpes. These drugs are not a cure, however, and recurrent attacks will return once they are discontinued.

There is real hope for a herpes vaccine in the near future (Stanberry, 1998). Several vaccines are in various stages of testing. The one that has proceeded the furthest works only in women and is not 100 percent effective, so we still have a long way to go. In the meantime, it is rec-ommended that sufferers avoid stress, wash their hands regularly to prevent autoinoculation, and avoid wearing nylon or tight-fitting underwear. Furthermore, because the herpes virus can live outside the body for a while, such items as towels and toothbrushes should not be shared. Intimate contact with the infected area should certainly be avoided during an active attack; and because some people shed the virus when they have no symptoms, the use of condoms for those with genital herpes (or for individuals whose partner has herpes) is recommended between active attacks. A blood test (for herpes antibodies) is available, and can help identify individuals who are at risk for transmitting herpes (Wald, 1999).

THE PERSONAL SIDE OF HERPES

Most people with oral herpes continue to lead normal lives. A person with oral herpes can engage in sexual intercourse without worrying about infecting his or her partner, but kissing and oral-genital relations during an active attack should be avoided, of course.

Genital herpes is almost always contracted by intimate sexual contact. Recall, too, that people with genital herpes usually have frequent recurrent attacks. Besides the physical symptoms, individuals suffering with genital herpes almost always have some psychological difficulties adjusting to their infection. They often pass through several stages: shock, emotional numbing, isolation and loneliness, and sometimes severe depression and impotence. After the initial shock, many genital herpes sufferers have feelings of ugliness, self-loathing, and guilt. The reactions of others may make them feel like "social lepers." As a result, some may have sexual problems, and others may just swear off sex. A 1993 survey of readers of *the helper* (a magazine for people with herpes) found that in the previous 12 months, 52 percent had suffered depression and fear of rejection, 36 percent had feelings of isolation, and 10 percent had self-destructive feelings (Catotti et al., 1993).

> "In my early 20's I felt a painful sore on my vagina. I had no idea what it was. At the time I hadn't had many partners. Later I had another eruption. My doctor told me I had herpes. Needless to say, I was shocked. I went through a denial phase that followed many nights of wet pillows. It took me years to accept it." (from the author's files)

So how should you deal with personal relationships if you have herpes? Accept the fact that although there is no cure, you do not have the plague. *The use of condoms will reduce the chances of infecting a partner* (in case there is viral shedding without symptoms). You should try to minimize the stress in your life, and if you have frequent or long-lasting attacks, talk to your doctor about taking acyclovir. Contact the American Social Health Association. They will provide you with current up-to-date information on herpes research, therapy, and care.

HEPATITIS

Hepatitis is an inflammation of the liver that can have many causes. We will address three types caused by viruses. The incubation period (time period before symptoms appear) is 2 to 6 weeks for hepatitis A and 6 weeks to 6 months for hepatitis B. The symptoms can range from mild (poor appetite, diarrhea) to severe (fever; vomiting; pain; fatigue; jaundiced, or yellow-tinged, skin and eyes; dark urine).

Hepatitis A (infectious hepatitis) is caused by a small virus (HAV) that is spread by direct or indirect oral contact with contaminated feces. There are about 180,000 new cases each year in the United States (Bell et al., 1999). The disease can be spread sexually (by contact with the anus of an infected person during sex) and has a higher incidence in male homosexuals than in other groups. However, it is most often contracted through nonsexual means, such as eating food handled by infected individuals, or shellfish taken from contaminated waters. The Centers for Disease Control and Prevention recommends routine vaccination of children to reduce the prevalence of this disease.

Hepatitis B (serum hepatitis) is caused by a different, larger virus (HBV) and is transmitted by infected blood or body fluids such as saliva, semen, and vaginal secretions. It can cause a number of liver diseases, including cancer and cirrhosis. More than 350 million people worldwide are infected with this virus, which causes 1 million deaths a year (Kane, 1995). At least 25 percent, and perhaps as many as 50 percent, of the 200,000 to 300,000 new cases each year in the United States are spread during sex (Centers for Disease Control and Prevention, 1996). The disease is most common in African Americans, male homosexuals (particularly those who engage in anal sex), and drug users who share needles (McQuillan et al., 1999). One can also get the virus during a blood transfusion, and over two-thirds of all pregnant women infected with hepatitis B pass the infection to their babies. In fact, each year at least 20,000 babies exposed to hepatitis B at birth will be at risk for chronic infection (CDC, 1996). The antiviral drug interferon is effective in many cases (Brown et al., 1999). About 90 percent of those with hepatitis recover, but up to 10 percent remain chronically infected and thus become carriers of the disease. The Centers for Disease Control and Prevention (1999a) has recommended that *all* children (babies as well as adolescents) be vaccinated against the hepatitis B virus.

Hepatitis C, which is caused by still another virus (HCV), was not identified as a specific virus until 1988. At least 300 million people are infected worldwide, including 4 million (1.8 percent) Americans (Alter et al., 1999). About 75 percent of them remain chronically infected, although many go 10 to 20 years or longer before they show any symptoms. About one-fifth will develop cirrhosis of the liver and/or liver cancer, resulting in 8,000 to 10,000 deaths a year (National Institute on Drug Abuse, 2000). The number of deaths are expected to double or triple over the next 10 to 20 years. The hepatitis C virus is most commonly spread through contact with contaminated blood (blood-to-blood contact), and thus it is frequently found in people who inject illicit drugs and share needles. The virus can be spread during sex, but not near as easily as hepatitis B. Sexual transmission accounts for less than 20 percent of cases. The highest risk is for individuals with multiple partners and who engage in behaviors resulting in blood exposure (Brown et al., 1999; National Institute on Drug Abuse, 2000). There is no vaccine available for protection against hepatitis C. The disease is treated with interferon in combination with ribavirin, but this is effective in only 30 to 40 percent of cases (NIDA, 2000).

GENITAL HUMAN PAPILLOMAVIRUS INFECTION

Have you ever heard of genital human papillomavirus (HPV) infection? Most college students haven't, yet this is a very common and often life-threatening sexually transmitted disease. It is estimated that 24 million Americans are already infected with HPV and that there are 500,000 to 1 million new cases every year (Institute of Medicine, 1997). Perhaps as many as 1 in 3 sexually active adults have HPV (Brown et al., 1999).

Human papillomaviruses infect epithelial cells (the covering of internal and external surfaces of the body). Over 70 different types have been identified (de Villiers, 1989). HPV infections are called *clinical infections* if there are symptoms visible to the naked eye, and *subclinical infections* if there are no visible symptoms. Subclinical HPV infections are at least 10 times more common than clinical infections (Rudlinger & Norval, 1996).

hepatitis A, B, and C Liver infections caused by viruses. Type A is spread by direct or indirect contact with contaminated feces. Type B is transmitted by infected blood or body fluids, with 25 to 50 percent of the cases contracted during sex. Type C is spread mainly by contaminated blood, but may possibly be spread during sexual intercourse in some cases.

human papillomaviruses Viruses that cause abnormal growths in epithelial cells. There are over 70 types. A few (types 6 and 11) cause genital warts, while others (types 16, 18, 31, 33, and 45) can lead to cancer of the cervix.

Figure 5–8 Venereal warts on the penis caused by human papillomavirus.

We can separate clinical HPV cases into three broad categories: (1) those that cause a rare skin condition (epidermodysplasia verruciformis) that appears as reddish plaques, (2) those that cause nongenital warts (including common, plantar, and flat warts), and (3) those that cause warts in the genital and anal area (although these can also cause problems in the mouth, pharynx, and larynx). There are about 25 different human papillomaviruses that can cause anogenital warts, but the large majority of genital warts are caused by HPV types 6 and 11. It was once thought that the only type of genital wart was *condyloma acuminata,* the type shown in Figure 5–8, but recent studies have shown that HPV can result in a wide variety of anogenital lesions and that a single individual can have many different-appearing warts (e.g., papular, macular) (Brown et al., 1999).

For those people who develop **genital (venereal) warts,** the first symptoms generally appear anywhere from 3 weeks to 8 months after contact with an infected person. The warts can cause itching, irritation, or bleeding. In men, the warts generally appear on the penis, scrotum, and/or anus, but they can also grow within the urethra. In women, the warts can appear on the cervix and walls of the vagina as well as the vulva and anus, and thus the virus can be transmitted to a baby during vaginal delivery. Women are much more likely than men to develop visible warts (and serious complications—see below) because the cervix has a zone of cells that are continually undergoing cell division (which makes it easier for the viruses to exploit them). The skin of the penis, on the other hand, resists transformation by the virus.

"I contracted venereal warts from a married woman I frequently slept with. I then gave them to my girlfriend. I did not know I had the affliction until she was diagnosed during a semi-annual exam with her gynecologist. The removal procedure for me as a man was rather simple as opposed to her treatment. Her first treatment involved cryogenically freezing her cervix. After that unsuccessful attempt they resorted to laser surgery. She is still not cured. If I could change things I would. We're not together anymore, but I still pray for her. I surely will never forget and I practice safe sex with my new girlfriend."

"When I was 17 years old I went to the doctor for a Pap smear. He found pre-malignant warts on my cervix. When he informed me that they were sexually transmitted, I didn't want to believe him. I went to an all-girls Catholic high school and the guys I slept with were usually from a boy's Catholic high school. I would never think that I would get a STD. I always thought STDs happened to lower class people.

"My doctor performed laser surgery to get rid of the warts. A year and a half later I had another outbreak, had surgery, and within seven weeks after the surgery they came back. These last two times they weren't just on the cervix, they spread all the way to the vulva. . . . I have abstained from sex since the beginning of the second outbreak." (All examples are from the author's files.)

Women with HPV infections have a greatly increased risk of developing cervical and/or vulvar cancer. In fact, nearly all women with cervical cancer are found to have HPV infections (Schiffman et al., 2000; Walboomers et al., 1999). The latency period between infection with HPV and detection of cancer is 5 to 25 years (Schiffman & Brinton, 1995). However, only a few kinds of human papillomaviruses are found in cervical cancers: HPV 31, HPV 33, HPV 45, HPV 18 (in 10 to 20 percent of cases), and, in particular, HPV 16 (in at least 40 to 60 percent of cases). Note that these types of HPV are different from the two types that cause most genital warts (types 6 and 11). What this means, of course, is that *most women with HPV infections who are at risk of developing cervical cancer will have no visible symptoms.* Because of this, a regular pelvic exam and Pap smear are an essential part of female health care. Women who test positive for HPV should have Pap smears at least every 6 months. Although HPV has been associated with cancer of the penis, it is much less likely that the viruses will lead to cancer in men (as is the case for visible warts, you recall).

Two of the major risk factors for HPV infection in young women are the number of lifetime male sexual partners and the male partner's number of lifetime sexual partners (Burk et al., 1996). Eighty percent of the male partners of infected women have no visible symptoms (Rudlinger & Norval, 1996).

genital warts Warts in the genital and anal regions caused by human papillomaviruses (mainly types 6 and 11). The warts are cauliflowerlike growths.

Recall that most HPV infections are subclinical (no visible symptoms) and that most disappear on their own—i.e., the individuals eventually test HPV negative (e.g., Carter et al., 1996). For individuals who have anogenital warts, various treatments are available, but none is ideal for all patients (Brown et al., 1999). Small external warts can be treated by applying a solution of podophyllin (sold in stores as Condylox), which causes them to dry up. Larger warts can be removed by cauterization or minor surgery. Internal warts are often removed by laser surgery. For HPV infections of the cervix, cryotherapy (freezing) is the preferred therapy. However, none of these methods attacks the virus directly, so recurrences of the warts are common (see previous case histories). Injection with antiviral or immunomodulatory drugs has shown some promise.

Because millions of Americans infected with HPV have no symptoms, they are unaware that they can infect others. The best way to eliminate the disease would be to vaccinate people before they are exposed to the virus (see Frazer, 1996). The first tests of a vaccine in humans began in 1997, but it will probably take at least 6 years before a vaccine is ready for large-scale use.

> ### PERSONAL REFLECTIONS
> *Have you ever engaged in sex with a new partner while under the influence of alcohol? If your answer is "yes," did your use of alcohol result in your engaging in unprotected sex? If it did, what will you do in the future to prevent this?*

MOLLUSCUM CONTAGIOSUM

Molluscum contagiosum is a painless growth that is caused by a pox virus. The virus is spread by direct skin-to-skin contact, and thus among adults it is often transmitted during sex. The number of cases in sexually active adults has increased dramatically during the sexual revolution, from only about 10,000 cases a year in the mid-1960s to well over 100,000 cases a year today. Infected individuals can easily spread it to other parts of their bodies. The virus incubates for 2 weeks to 6 months and then erupts into dome-shaped growths that are usually 1 to 5 mm in diameter and look like small pimples filled with kernels of corn. Molluscum contagiosum is easily diagnosed by the appearance of the growths, and is usually treated by removing

molluscum contagiosum A sexually transmitted virus whose symptoms look like small pimples filled with kernels of corn.

(acquired immunodeficiency syndrome) AIDS An often fatal disease caused by a virus (HIV) that destroys the immune system. It is spread by intimate sexual activity (the exchange of bodily fluids) or contaminated blood.

human immunodeficiency virus (HIV) A virus that kills CD4+ cells, eventually resulting in AIDS.

immune system The bodily mechanisms involved in the production of antibodies in response to bacteria, viruses, and cancerous cells.

the growths (Brown et al., 1999). However, they usually disappear on their own within 6 to 9 months.

HIV INFECTION AND AIDS

In the early 1980s, doctors in California were puzzled when five men were diagnosed with *Pneumocystis carinii pneumonia,* a rare respiratory infection usually seen only in people with depressed immune systems. Several young men in Miami were simultaneously diagnosed as having *Kaposi's sarcoma,* a rare cancer of the capillary system that appears as purple blotches on the skin (see Figure 5–9). It, too, is a sign of a depressed immune system. More and more cases of depressed immune systems began to appear, but it was not until 1982 that the new disease was given a name: **acquired immunodeficiency syndrome (AIDS).** It was not until 1984 that the cause of AIDS was identified as a virus, named **human immunodeficiency virus,** or **HIV.** There is controversy about which group discovered the virus first, but after 2 decades in which several million people have died of AIDS, that hardly seems important anymore.

In technical terms, HIV is a Lentivirus, a subfamily of retroviruses. Retroviruses reverse the normal pattern of reproduction in cells. There are two major types of HIV: HIV-1, which is the most common type worldwide, and HIV-2, found mainly in West Africa. HIV-2 wasn't observed in the United States until 1987. HIV displays considerable genetic variability (Peeters & Sharp, 2000). To date, researchers have identified 13 major HIV-1 subtypes (classified as group M subtypes A, B, C, D, F, G, H, J, K and four recombinant forms) and two very aberrant subtypes (groups N and O). The most common subtypes found in Africa are A, C, and D; the most common subtype found in the United States is B. However, different subtypes can be found in different people living in the same area, and even within one infected individual. HIV has obviously undergone extensive mutation, but examination of the genetic makeup of various subtypes suggests that all the subtypes evolved from a single virus.

HIV AND THE BODY'S IMMUNE SYSTEM

The **immune system** is that part of your body that defends against bacteria, viruses, fungi, and cancerous cells. White blood cells, or *lymphocytes,* are the main line of defense in this system. There are several types. One type, called *CD4+ lymphocytes* (also called *helper T cells* and *T4 lymphocytes*), has the job of recognizing the disease-causing agents and then signaling another type of white blood cell (*B cells*) to produce antibodies. The antibodies bind to the recognized agents so that they can be identified by yet another type of white blood cell, the *killer T cells* (T is for the thymus gland, where the cells develop). The CD4+ cells then signal the killer T cells to destroy the identified disease-causing agents. In addition to CD4+ cells, there are also *suppressor T cells* that suppress the activity of the B cells and killer T cells. A person normally has twice as many CD4+ (helper) cells as suppressor T cells.

Recall now that viruses must invade and live in normal body cells (called host cells) in order to replicate themselves. The human immunodeficiency virus infects CD4+ cells and reproduces itself, causing death of the cell in about 1½ days and the release of more of the virus. The replicated virus then invades other CD4+ cells. As many as 2 billion CD4+ cells are killed each day (Perelson et al., 1996). Thus, HIV destroys the cells that ordinarily would work to fight it off. The body tries to replace the dead cells, but the number of CD4+ cells begins to decline early in the course of HIV infection. The victim eventually has fewer helper (CD4+) T cells than suppressor T cells, leaving the body defenseless against viruses, bacteria, and other infection-causing agents.

CD4+ white blood cells are not the only body cells invaded by HIV. The virus has also been found in cells of the brain, gastrointestinal tract, kidney, lungs, cerebrospinal fluid, and other blood and plasma cells. However, it is the destruction of CD4+ cells that leads to the disease we call AIDS.

PROGRESSION OF HIV INFECTION

After invading the body, HIV reproduces unchecked at first, reaching enormous levels in the bloodstream. Between 50 and 75 percent of newly infected persons experience flulike symptoms (e.g., fever, headache, diarrhea, tiredness, skin rash) during this time. This is called **primary HIV infection** and can last for several weeks to a few months (Cates et al., 1997). The body's immune system then launches a huge counterattack that kills the virus by the billions, reducing it to very low levels. In time, however, the virus regains the upper hand by slowly killing off the CD4+ cells.

A normal, healthy person has between 1,000 and 1,200 CD4+ cells per cubic millimeter of blood. Although CD4+ cell counts decline with time, people with HIV show no visible symptoms in the first stage of the chronic infection, called **asymptomatic HIV infection.** This stage often lasts for years.

Infected persons generally start to show symptoms of a weakened immune system when their CD4+ cell count falls below 500 per cubic millimeter of blood. Symptoms may include fatigue, persistent headaches, loss of appetite, recurrent diarrhea, loss of body weight, low-grade fever (often accompanied by "night sweats"), swollen lymph nodes, and "colds," "flus," and yeast infections that linger on and on. At this point, the infection is called **symptomatic HIV infection** (formerly called *AIDS related complex*, or *ARC*).

Figure 5–9 Kaposi's sarcoma lesions on a patient with AIDS.

HIV infection is not called **AIDS** until it has become life-threatening. As the CD4+ cell count approaches 200 per cubic millimeter of blood, infected persons' immune systems have become so weakened that they fall prey to what are referred to as *opportunistic infections*—diseases such as lymphomas, Kaposi's sarcoma (see Figure 5–9), *Pneumocystis carinii* pneumonia, recurrent bacterial pneumonia, pulmonary tuberculosis, cryptococcal meningitis, wasting syndrome, and invasive cervical cancer (Katlama & Dickinson, 1993). These are often accompanied by a severe decline in mental ability, referred to as HIV-associated dementia (Clifford, 2000). In 1993, the Centers for Disease Control and Prevention expanded the definition of AIDS to include a *CD4+ cell count below 200*, whether or not the person had yet fallen victim to an opportunistic disease. Some people whose CD4+ cell counts have dropped below 200 have gone 3 years or longer without developing AIDS-related illnesses (Hoover et al., 1995). In the end, however, AIDS patients die as a result of the opportunistic infections (not as a direct result of HIV).

Once an individual is infected with HIV, how long does it take to develop a full-blown case of AIDS? About 5 percent will develop AIDS within the first 3 years after infection with HIV-1; about 20 percent within 5 years; and 50 percent in 10 years. Only 12 percent of infected persons will not yet have been diagnosed with AIDS after 20 years (Buchbinder et al., 1994; Munoz & Xu, 1996; Rutherford et al., 1990). About 2 to 4 percent of HIV-infected individuals are called *long-term nonprogressors*. Despite their infection, they maintain high

primary HIV infection The first few weeks of HIV infection, during which HIV reaches enormous levels in the blood and 50 to 75 percent of infected individuals experience flulike symptoms.

asymptomatic Showing no symptoms.

symptomatic HIV infection Formerly called AIDS-related complex (ARC); the early symptoms of HIV infections, which eventually lead to AIDS.

AIDS (acquired immunodeficiency syndrome) An often fatal disease caused by a virus (HIV) that destroys the immune system. It is spread by intimate sexual activity (the exchange of bodily fluids) or contaminated blood.

CD4+ levels and do not develop symptoms (e.g., Petrucci et al., 1997). It is believed that they have a slower progression rather than no progression.

What accounts for the fact that some HIV-infected people progress to AIDS in just a few years while others take many years? The type of HIV may be one factor. For example, persons infected with HIV-2 take much longer to develop AIDS than those infected with HIV-1 (and many are long-term nonprogressors) (van der Loeff & Aaby, 1999). People who already have a weakened immune system (as a result of age or illness, for example) have a more rapid progression to AIDS. Individuals who experience acute primary HIV infection (flulike symptoms or worse upon initial exposure) are more likely to develop AIDS earlier than people who are asymptomatic upon initial infection (Sinicco et al., 1993). A review of several studies found no difference between men and women in the progression of infection (Suligoi, 1997).

Several recent studies have shown that the best single predictor for progression to AIDS is not an individual's CD4+ cell count but his or her plasma HIV RNA levels, which show the amount of virus in the blood (Mellors et al., 1996; O'Brien et al., 1996). This is called the *viral load*. The higher the viral load, the sooner the person will develop AIDS. HIV-infected persons can have the same CD4+ cell count but very different levels of the virus; and if the viral load is high, infected persons can have AIDS symptoms even if their CD4 + count is well above 200 (Hennessey et al., 2000). The combination of HIV RNA levels and CD4+ cell count is an even better predictor of the progression to AIDS (Mellors et al., 1997). Today, drug therapies have been designed to lower the viral load, and thus in the future it should take longer for an HIV-infected person to develop AIDS.

How long can an HIV-infected person expect to live after being diagnosed with AIDS? Without medication, the survival time is only about 1 year. In one of the last studies of long-term survival after HIV infection (the study was conducted before the introduction of the new highly effective drug therapy), the median survival time was 12.1 years (Koblin et al., 1999). However, new drug therapies have allowed many HIV and AIDS patients to live longer, productive lives (see section on treatment).

WHERE AND WHEN DID HUMAN IMMUNO-DEFICIENCY VIRUS ORIGINATE?

There is no question that HIV-1 and HIV-2 are new to the human species, but where did they come from? "Conspiracy" theories are popular. At one time, the Soviets blamed it on U.S. biological experiments gone awry. Filmmaker Spike Lee publicly said that AIDS was "a government-engineered disease targeted at gays, African Americans, and Hispanics" (November 1992). Another person circulated a booklet claiming that WHO, the World Health Organization, "murdered Africa with the AIDS virus" (Douglass, 1988). He, as well as others, said that the virus was injected into people with various vaccines. The most common claim is that HIV was introduced to humans during testing of a polio vaccine in Africa in the late 1950s (the polio virus was grown in monkey kidney cells, and the article suggested that the cells were contaminated with a monkey virus).

Scientific studies of the origins of HIV have indeed implicated nonhuman primates but do not support conspiracy theories (see Gao et al., 1992). There is a diverse genetic pool of nonhuman *simian* (primate) *immunodeficiency viruses (SIV)*. The viruses are found in rhesus monkeys, sooty mangabeys, African green monkeys, and chimpanzees. The SIV in sooty mangabeys has been clearly identified as the origin of HIV-2 (Chen et al., 1997; Gao et al., 1992). In other words, humans acquired HIV-2 through cross-species transmission, i.e., the virus is a "simian immunodeficiency virus residing in and adapting to a human host" (Myers et al., 1992).

HIV-2 is responsible for only 1 percent of the world's AIDS cases. What about HIV-1, which is responsible for the other 99 percent? Recent studies have now definitely established that this virus was transmitted to humans from chimpanzees (Gao et al., 1999; Hahn et al., 2000). Considerable evidence indicates that this first occurred in colonial French Equatorial Africa around 1930, long before there were polio vaccinations (Chitnis et al., 2000; Hahn et al., 2000; Korber et al., 2000).

The chimp-to-human transmission probably occurred by exposure of humans to primate blood during food preparation (Hahn et al., 2000). The virus was probably isolated for sometime, but with big increases in the population more and more people came to rely on bushmeat (including chimpanzee meat). After World War II, there were rapid changes in the social structure in Africa, including mass movement to large cities and forced labor camps. This resulted in a breakdown of families and an increase in prostitution. Though not the cause of HIV, the use of nonsterilized needles for injections and vaccinations may have helped to spread the disease (see Hahn et al., 2000, for a full history). Tests of stored blood samples show that HIV-1 was definitely starting to spread by 1959 (Zhu et al., 1998), and by the 1970s high rates of Kaposi's sarcoma were being reported in central Africa. The rest is history. Features of modern society such as worldwide travel, promiscuous sexual activities, and sharing of syringes and hypodermic needles probably greatly helped the spread of the virus.

HOW IS HIV SPREAD?

What is the evidence concerning the transmission of HIV? Some people worry about catching it from just breathing the same air as, or touching objects previously held by, AIDS victims. Some neighbors of AIDS victims worry about mosquitoes. Some people have even quit donating blood. Can you get AIDS by casual contact with an HIV-infected person?

If HIV could be contracted from casual contact, you would expect that family members living with AIDS patients would be at great risk. However, no family member of an AIDS patient has ever become infected by sharing household facilities and items, and no child has ever become infected by just playing with or living with an AIDS-infected brother or sister. HIV has sometimes been found in body fluids such as tears and saliva, but not in high enough concentrations to pose a threat. A protein found in saliva helps block HIV from infecting human cells (Shugars et al., 1999). In fact, the concentrations in saliva are so low that your chance of acquiring the virus by being bitten by an HIV-infected individual is extremely slim (Richman & Rickman, 1993).

In the final stages of AIDS, patients cannot hold food down, often have uncontrollable diarrhea, and generally sweat profusely. Yet except for a few people who accidentally stuck themselves with a contaminated needle and a few others whose skin was exposed to a large amount of contaminated blood (which may have entered the body through a small cut), none of the doctors, nurses, or other medical personnel who have cared for the most seriously ill AIDS patients on a daily basis have ever developed an HIV infection (Ippolito et al., 1999).

Malaria and some other diseases are spread by mosquitoes, but it is certain that HIV is not spread in this manner (Castro et al., 1988). If it were, we would be seeing a much larger number of children and elderly people with AIDS.

There is no need for panic—*HIV is not spread by casual contact.* There are three main ways in which HIV is transmitted: (1) sexual contact with an infected person; (2) exposure to infected blood (mainly needle sharing among intravenous drug users); and (3) mother-to-infant transmission. Thus, HIV is transmitted almost exclusively by intimate sexual contact and contaminated blood. Let us examine each of these means of transmission.

There are still some researchers and other individuals who claim that it is a myth that HIV causes AIDS, or that HIV can be spread by sex between heterosexuals (Brody, 1995; Duesberg & Ellison, 1996; France, 2000). Recently, South Africa's President Thabo Mbeki caused great controversy when he supported this theory (Masland & King, 2000). Believe me, it is no myth. HIV is found in the semen and vaginal fluids of HIV-infected individuals (see Mostad & Kreiss, 1996). The risk of transmission of HIV during sex is directly related to the infected person's viral load (Quinn et al., 2000). Remember, the concentrations of HIV are

greatest at the very beginning of the infection, then decrease dramatically, and then increase again as the disease progresses toward the AIDS stage. This means that the risk of transmission of HIV is greatest in the first 60 days and then later in the symptomatic HIV and AIDS stages.

A major factor is whether HIV is transmitted onto an uninfected person's mucous membranes or directly into his or her blood. Any sexual activity in which bleeding occurs would greatly increase the risk. Because of this, anal intercourse is one of the easiest ways to spread HIV from an infected person to another. Many male homosexuals engage in anal intercourse, but it is also common among heterosexual couples (Halperin, 1999). Sores on the genitals caused by other sexually transmitted diseases such as syphilis, chancroid, or herpes also greatly increase the risk of HIV transmission (see Vernazza et al., 1999). Studies show that during vaginal intercourse HIV is at least twice as easy to transmit from an infected man to a female partner than vice versa (see Vernazza et al., 1999). However, when there are sores on the genitals, transmission is easier from woman to man.

Although there have been a few isolated reports of heterosexual or male homosexual partners becoming infected during oral sex, most experts believe that the risk of HIV transmission through oral-genital sex is very small (see Vernazza et al., 1999). Again, this is because of inhibiting substances found in saliva. There has been only one case of transmission by kissing, and this was through the man's blood, not saliva (both partners had gum disease) (CDC press release, 1997).

Let me summarize what we know about HIV transmission during sex (see Vernazza et al., 1999): Stage of infection and bleeding are factors that increase the risk. In terms of behavior, HIV is spread most easily during anal intercourse (because of bleeding), followed by vaginal intercourse (especially when there are open sores), and occasionally during oral sex.

As previously mentioned, a second major way in which HIV is transmitted is by exposure to contaminated blood. Needle-sharing drug users are at especially high risk (Des Jarlais et al., 1996). But what about our chances of getting HIV from a blood transfusion? At one time this was a major concern. Several thousand people contracted HIV from blood transfusions before screening tests were begun in 1985. Today, because all blood is tested, only 1 of every 677,000 units is likely to be infected with HIV (Glynn et al., 2000). A few units of infected blood still get through because the test cannot detect HIV if the blood donor has just been infected (see page 120). Unfortunately, many people in the United States have stopped donating blood out of fear of getting AIDS, and as a result, there is a severe shortage of blood in many parts of the country. At blood donation centers in the United

States, needles are sterilized and used only once. You will not get AIDS from donating blood!

The third major way that HIV is transmitted is from an infected mother to her infant (see John & Kreiss, 1996). Worldwide, more than 1,000 children are born with HIV every day (Sharland et al., 1997). The Centers for Disease Control and Prevention estimates that, in the United States 8,000 women a year who become pregnant are infected with HIV. Without antiviral drug therapy, the transmission rate is about 20 to 25 percent (Lindegren et al., 1999). The infections can occur either very late in pregnancy, during delivery, or by breast-feeding (European Collaborative Study, 1992, 1994). The risk is greatest in women who have high levels of the virus in their blood and when fetal membranes rupture several hours before delivery (Landesman et al., 1996; Mofenson et al., 1999). The frequency of transmission of HIV-1 by breast-feeding is about 16 percent (Nduati et al., 2000). This is so high that in 1998 the United Nations recommended that women with HIV not breast-feed their babies.

The rapidity with which children infected with HIV progress to AIDS is directly related to their viral load (Shearer et al., 1997). Most infected children show symptoms of HIV infection by 6 months of age (European Collaborative Study, 1991). By 1 year of age, about a fourth have AIDS and many have died. With immature and weakened immune systems, nearly all eventually fall prey to various opportunistic diseases.

What about your risk of contracting HIV from a health care professional (e.g., a physician or dentist)? Studies of thousands of patients of HIV-infected surgeons and dentists reveal that the risk is practically nonexistent (Dickinson et al., 1993; Mishu et al., 1990; Rogers et al., 1993). Nevertheless, because chemical disinfectants do not always kill the virus, surgeons and dentists are now required to steam-clean their instruments and wear protective gloves. Expert review panels will decide on a case-by-case basis whether HIV-infected health professionals may continue performing surgical procedures (American College of Physicians, 1994). Conclusion: There is no good reason to avoid getting regular health and dental checkups.

WHO HAS HIV/AIDS?

HIV infection is a true pandemic disease. Currently, worldwide there are about 16,000 new infections a day (5.3 million a year) and about 36.1 million people currently living with HIV. This includes 600,000 children under the age of 15. About 3 million people die of AIDS every year (United Nations Programme, 2000).

The U.S. Census Bureau's World Population Profile estimated that 121 million people could be infected by the year 2020. The really bad news is that the experts continue to underestimate how rapidly the disease is spreading. For example, the number of people presently infected with AIDS in Africa is 3 times greater than experts predicted just 10 years ago.

At present, 90 percent of persons infected with HIV live in developing countries (Bartholet et al., 2000). More than two-thirds of the world's cases are in sub-Saharan Africa, where HIV originated; countries such as Uganda, Zambia, and Rwanda have been devastated (see Figure 5–10). In some places, as many as 1 out of every 4 people are infected with HIV, resulting in an average reduction in life expectancy of over 20 years (see Box 5–A).

HIV may have originated in Africa, but the World Health Organization says that "the most alarming trends of HIV infection are in Southeast Asia where the disease is spreading in some areas as fast as it was a decade ago in sub-Saharan Africa." India is another country where HIV has reached epidemic proportions (at least 4 million people infected with HIV). In fact, while Africa is bearing the burden of the epidemic now, experts believe that because of the dense populations and sexual practices, Southeast Asia and the Indian subcontinent will be hit the hardest during this century (e.g., Fauci, 1999).

What about the United States? The Centers for Disease Control and Prevention reported that there were 46,400 new cases of AIDS in 1999 (HIV/AIDS Surveillance Report). This is an underestimate, due to delays in reporting and unreported cases. Nevertheless, the number of new AIDS cases for 1999 represents a

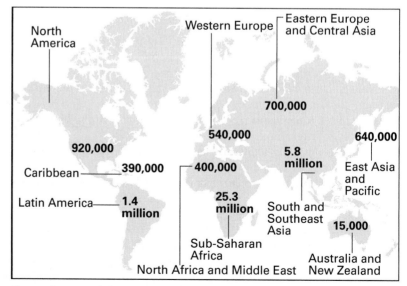

Figure 5–10 Adults and children living with HIV/AIDS at the start of 2001. *Source:* UNAIDS Programme.

decrease of about one-third from the number of reported cases in 1993. This may mean that the number of new cases is leveling off, but part of the decrease is certainly due to new drug therapies that have slowed the progression of the disease before it becomes AIDS.

At the start of June 2000, there had been a cumulative total of 753,907 reported cases of AIDS in the United States. Nearly 60 percent of these had already died. The Centers for Disease Control and Prevention estimates that 650,000 to 900,000 more Americans are presently infected with the human immunodeficiency virus. By the mid-1990s, AIDS had become the *leading cause of death among Americans aged 25 to 44*, ahead of accidents, cancer, and heart disease (Centers for Disease Control and Prevention).

Of the cases reported to the CDC in 1999, 33.5 percent of the new cases of AIDS in adolescents and adults occurred among homosexual or bisexual men, 21.9 percent occurred among intravenous (injecting) drug users, and 3.9 percent occurred among homosexual or bisexual men who also injected drugs.

Why have so many cases in the United States shown up in the male homosexual community? Political commentator Patrick Buchanan was quoted as saying: "The poor homosexuals. They have declared war on nature, and now nature is exacting an awful retribution." However, you have already learned that a person's sexual behavior or sexual orientation does not cause HIV infection. To become infected, you must come into contact with the human immunodeficiency virus. The virus cannot tell whether you are homosexual or heterosexual. The reason it first spread so rapidly among the male homosexual community here is three-fold: Many gay men had numerous, often hundreds, of sexual partners; the practice of unprotected anal intercourse was common; and AIDS was a new disease with a long incubation period. Before anyone even knew that HIV or AIDS existed, the virus had already been spread to tens of thousands of male homosexuals.

A disproportionate number of the new AIDS cases in 1999 occurred among African-Americans (47.1 percent) and Latinos (about 19.4 percent), particularly those in low-income groups. Among women diagnosed with AIDS, 81 percent were African American or Latina. Of the newly reported HIV cases in 1999, 77 percent of the women and 59 percent of the men were African American or Latino. U.S. Surgeon General David Satcher said in 1998, "I don't think there is any question that the epidemic in this country is becoming increasingly an epidemic of color."

Worldwide, the largest proportion of new HIV infections is acquired by heterosexual transmission (see Figure 5–11). In Africa, for example, nearly half of the millions of people infected with HIV are women (Fauci, 1999; United Nations Programme, 2000), but many heterosexuals in the United States still do not be-

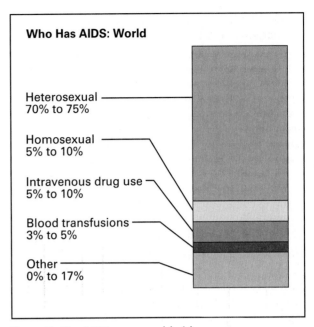

Figure 5–11 AIDS cases worldwide.

lieve that they can get HIV. However, the most dramatic change in new HIV and AIDS cases has been among heterosexuals. Only 7 percent of new AIDS cases in 1985 were women, but in 1999, 23.4 percent of newly diagnosed AIDS patients were women, probably half of whom acquired HIV during heterosexual intercourse. The CDC reports that among new HIV cases in 1999, 32 percent of them were women (49 percent in the 13- to 24-year-old group). More than 50,000 U.S. children have been left motherless because of AIDS.

If you still are not convinced, there is no better evidence than what happened in Haiti, where, as one researcher stated, you can see "how rapidly and dramatically the AIDS virus can spread in a promiscuous heterosexual population." In 1983, 71 percent of the cases of AIDS in Haiti occurred among male homosexuals and intravenous drug users. By the late 1980s, the large majority of new AIDS patients were heterosexuals (Pape & Warren, 1993). One of the reasons HIV spread so rapidly in Haiti is the common acceptance of multiple sexual partners, along with the common practice of prostitution (Pape et al., 1990).

In the United States, the most likely pathways by which HIV first spread into the heterosexual community were through bisexual men and intravenous drug users infecting their heterosexual partners (Chu et al., 1992; Lewis et al., 1990). Another likely route of infection was through prostitutes, many of whom are intravenous drug users. By the mid-1990s, in some cities the infection rate was already as high as 25 percent for female prostitutes and 50 percent or higher for male homosexual prostitutes (Boles & Elifson, 1994; McKeganey, 1994).

In 2000, the Centers for Disease Control and Prevention warned that 5 million Americans were at high risk for catching HIV (Gayle, 2000). This number includes individuals who have six or more sexual partners a year, men who engage in unprotected sex with men, prostitutes and individuals who engage in sex with prostitutes, users of intravenous drugs or crack cocaine, and those who have sex with a person known to have HIV. In July 2000, the San Francisco Department of Public Health reported that there had been a dramatic increase in new HIV infections in that city. After a period of stabilization, are new HIV infections about to increase again?

THE HUMAN SIDE OF AIDS

With each passing year, more and more of us do not have to read a newspaper to get a firsthand experience with AIDS. AIDS is more than a disease; it is a personal tragedy, not only for the patient but for the patient's family and loved ones as well. Some students in my course have asked me to share their experiences. Here are a few:

> "My reaction to a low T-cell test was devastating. It was like a bomb exploding inside or a knife through the heart. My time is near and each day is a gift to cherish. . . . Finding out I was HIV positive was not as shocking as finding out that what I have changed to improve the quality of my life makes little difference in my life expectancy."

> "My father has AIDS. You really don't know the severity of a problem until you're faced with it. Watching my father die has been extremely painful and stressful."

> "I still believe that most students don't think that AIDS can happen to them. I have seen AIDS happen firsthand. I learned in one of the most painful ways I can imagine. Two years ago my older brother died of AIDS. I was only 19, he was 24. It had been said that everyone's lives would be touched by AIDS, and when I was younger I didn't believe it. Now I do."

The emotional impact of finding out that you have AIDS or are infected with HIV can be devastating (Derlega & Barbee, 1998). Severe depression is common in the early phases of HIV infection and again at the symptomatic stage, and the suicide rate is 17 to 66 times greater in individuals diagnosed with AIDS than in the general population (see Kalichman & Sikkema, 1994). On the other hand, many people have led productive lives for years after being diagnosed with AIDS. There is increasing evidence that stressful life events can speed up the progression of HIV infection (Leserman et al., 2000). It is important, therefore, that HIV-infected individuals not give up hope and that they receive as much positive support as possible.

TESTING FOR HIV

The standard tests for HIV do not test for the virus directly, but instead detect antibodies to the virus that are produced by an infected person's immune system. Blood is first checked with the ELISA (enzyme-linked immunosorbent assay) test. However, the test can result in "false positives" (i.e., uninfected blood testing positive). A recent flu vaccination can sometimes produce a false positive, for example (Mac Kenzie et al., 1992). To ensure against false positives, the ELISA test is repeated if the results are positive. If there is a second positive indication, the blood is tested again with either the Western Blot or IFA (immunofluorescent assay) tests. These are more expensive and demanding tests that give information about particular antibodies. A negative test result means only that a person *probably* has not been infected with HIV. Remember, it often takes several months for an infected person's body to start producing antibodies to the virus; a person who has just recently been infected will not test positive.

New tests are now available that measure the presence of antibodies to HIV in saliva or urine. The sample is checked with the ELISA test and positive results are then confirmed with the Western Blot blood test. These tests are less accurate than the blood test, but may be more appealing to some people than blood tests.

The HIV-antibody tests are very effective in detecting HIV infection in individuals who are already showing symptoms (and thus have high levels of HIV and antibodies to HIV). They are not as reliable in screening HIV-infected persons who are still healthy. Today, there is a technique that directly tests for HIV RNA. Called the polymerase chain reaction (PCR), it can detect a single HIV-infected white blood cell among 100,000 healthy ones (Piatuk et al., 1993). However, this technique is expensive. In mid-2000, the Food and Drug Administration was considering approval of several rapid HIV tests that are inexpensive and provide results within minutes.

TREATMENT FOR HIV/ AIDS: HOPE AND LIMITATIONS

Many drugs have been approved for treating patients with HIV (see Cohn, 1997). One group of antiretroviral drugs is technically called *nucleoside reverse transcriptase inhibitors* (e.g., zidovudine). They slow the progression of HIV infection by blocking an essential enzyme (called reverse transcriptase) needed for the virus to replicate itself (this occurs at step 2 in Figure 5–12). A second group is called *non-nucleoside reverse transcriptase inhibitors* (e.g., nevirapine). These drugs block the same enzymes as the nucleoside drugs, but in a different manner. The newest drugs available to fight HIV are called *protease inhibitors*. The drugs block an enzyme called

Box 5-A CROSS-CULTURAL PERSPECTIVES/SEXUALITY AND HEALTH

AIDS in Africa: A Look into the Future?

Newsweek magazine says that to take a trip to sub-Saharan Africa is to "peer through the portals of hell and glimpse the holocaust to come" (Bartholet et al., 2000). In the United States, about 650,000 to 900,000 people have HIV, about 0.18 percent of the population. In many parts of sub-Saharan Africa, more than 25 percent of adults are infected with HIV (see Bartholet et al., 2000; United Nations Programme, 2000). In Botswana, more than a third of all adults are infected. The result is devastating: 2.3 million deaths and over 5.3 million new cases of HIV each year, and the numbers keep increasing yearly. In the United States, life expectancy increased by 30 years during the 1900s. In Africa, it dropped from 59 in 1990 to 37–41 in many areas in just 10 years (United Nations, 1999). The devastation caused by HIV in Africa rivals that caused by the Black Death in Europe during the Middle Ages, when one-fourth of the population was lost.

In actuality, the situation is even worse because the previous statistics are for all adults. The percentage of infected persons is even higher for adults in the 15- to 40-year-old age group. Two-thirds of Botswanans aged 15 today are expected to die of AIDS before they are 50. In most of sub-Saharan Africa, there are more elderly people than young adults.

What about the children? Have you ever read *Lord of the Flies*? At the end of 2000, there were 13 million AIDS orphans in sub-Saharan Africa. Over half of the children in Zambia have lost one or both parents. With income normally very low even before AIDS, the elderly are unable to care for the orphaned children, and there is not enough funds to support all the orphanages. As a result, an undeterminable number roam the streets, malnourished and often infected themselves. To make matters worse, there is a commonly held myth among African men that you can be cured of AIDS by having sex with a virgin, so many young girls are preyed upon. Within 10 years, the number of African AIDS orphans is likely to double, or even triple (Masland & Nordland, 2000).

It takes more than introduction of a new virus to result in an epidemic of this magnitude. Certain demographic and social conditions also have to be present (Fauci, 1999). Massive migration from rural areas to large cities, the resulting breakups of traditional family units, sexual promiscuity (including frequent use of prostitutes)—all have contributed to the epidemic. A potent strain of HIV (type C) is common in Africa, and transmission of the virus is helped by high numbers of cases of other sexually transmitted diseases that cause genital ulcerations (Vernazza et al., 1999). Ignorance has also contributed. Most African leaders refuse to talk about the problem. None showed up for the 11th International Conference on AIDS in Zambia in 1998, and at the 13th International Conference in South Africa in 2000, South African President Thabo Mbeki denied that HIV causes AIDS (Masland & King, 2000). Among the African people, AIDS victims are stigmatized.

Economies are collapsing under the weight of the epidemic. Low-level use of antiretroviral drugs might slow the disease (Wood et al., 2000), but African nations have little money to pay for health services. Each year, a greater proportion of children go uneducated (and uncared for), giving little hope for the future.

Most African men still refuse to use condoms (Cowley, 2000a; United Nations Programme, 2000). The best hope is for an effective vaccine, but there has been controversy about using African people in clinical trials of drugs and vaccines (e.g., Annas & Grodin, 1998). Even without opposition, an effective vaccine may be many years away.

In the 2 minutes it took you to read this box, 20 more people in Africa became infected with HIV. Since the time you woke up yesterday morning, more than 6,000 African men and women have died of AIDS. HIV spread through Africa many years before it appeared in the United States. If we do not take the necessary precautions, could the same fate that has befallen Africa happen here? Perhaps Dr. Ward Cates of the Centers for Disease Control and Prevention put it best: "Anyone who has the least ability to look into the future can already see the potential for this disease being much worse than anything mankind has seen before."

HIV survives by invading white blood cells and turning them into virus factories. The process involves several steps, and each offers a potential target for therapy. This shows how HIV does its work, and how antiviral drugs do theirs.

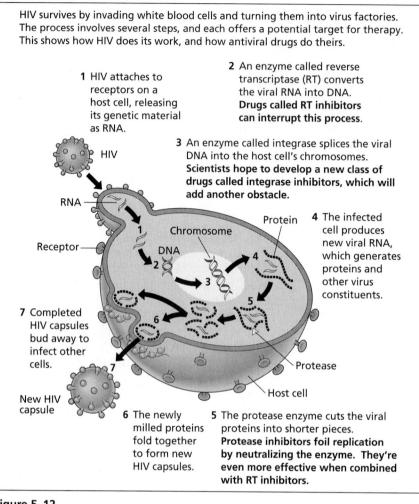

1 HIV attaches to receptors on a host cell, releasing its genetic material as RNA.

2 An enzyme called reverse transcriptase (RT) converts the viral RNA into DNA. **Drugs called RT inhibitors can interrupt this process.**

3 An enzyme called integrase splices the viral DNA into the host cell's chromosomes. **Scientists hope to develop a new class of drugs called integrase inhibitors, which will add another obstacle.**

4 The infected cell produces new viral RNA, which generates proteins and other virus constituents.

7 Completed HIV capsules bud away to infect other cells.

6 The newly milled proteins fold together to form new HIV capsules.

5 The protease enzyme cuts the viral proteins into shorter pieces. **Protease inhibitors foil replication by neutralizing the enzyme. They're even more effective when combined with RT inhibitors.**

HIV · RNA · Receptor · Chromosome · DNA · Protein · Protease · Host cell · New HIV capsule

Figure 5–12

protease that is critical to the last stages of HIV replication (step 5 in Figure 5–12) (see Cohn, 1997). Recall that a variety of opportunistic diseases develop as HIV destroys the body's immune system. Over 40 drugs have been approved to treat these AIDS-related infections.

The first antiviral drug used was zidovudine (AZT). The initial studies were very promising, indicating that the drug delayed the onset of AIDS (e.g., Fischl et al., 1989), but subsequent studies delivered more sobering news. For many HIV-infected patients, AZT's side effects (e.g., anemia) made them so ill that it offset any advantage to postponing the onset of AIDS. Several large-scale studies found that while AZT delayed the onset of AIDS when given early, it did not prolong life (Hamilton et al., 1992). It is now the general consensus that the benefits of AZT, when used alone, fade very rapidly. In fact, the virus quickly becomes resistant to any of the drugs used alone (Cohn, 1997).

Zidovudine has proven to be much more successful in treating HIV-infected pregnant women. You learned earlier that worldwide over 1,000 babies a day catch HIV from their mothers. However, in the United States, treatment of HIV-infected pregnant women with zidovudine reduced the transmission of the virus to babies from 1,650 cases in 1991 (about 24 percent) to about 400 cases (about 6–7 percent) in 1997 (Lindegren et al., 1999). A newer drug, nevirapine, reduces the transmission rate even further (Guay et al., 1999), and a transmission rate of less than 2 percent can be achieved if the mother uses the HIV drugs and has a cesarean delivery (International Perinatal HIV Group, 1999). Nevirapine is so cheap compared to AZT and other drugs that it is hoped it can be used effectively in Africa. Because of these successes, the Centers for Disease Control and Prevention has recommended that all pregnant women be tested for HIV. Zidovudine, didanosine, or both are also used to slow the progression of HIV infection in children (Englund et al., 1997).

The most exciting advance in the treatment of HIV has been use of a drug "cocktail"— the use of several drugs in combination (see Carpenter et al., 1997; Deeks et al., 1997). Administration of nucleoside inhibitors and/or non-nucleoside inhibitors, in combination with protease inhibitors, simultaneously attacks the replication of HIV at two different places (early in the process at step 2 and late in the process at step 5; see Figure 5–12). In many patients, this approach initially knocks blood HIV levels down to undetectable levels, raises CD4+ cell counts, and partially restores immune responses. Restored immune response is important for protecting against opportunistic diseases (Lederman & Valdez, 2000). As a result of this new combination drug therapy, deaths from AIDS in the United States have dropped dramatically since 1996 (by over 60 percent).

The initial optimism that the combination drug approach might be a cure for HIV infection has been followed quickly by some sobering reality (see Fauci, 1999; Hirschel & Opravil, 1999, for reviews). Many patients cannot tolerate the side effects, and many others cannot afford the treatment. Long-term use results in increased body fat and insulin resistance (Eron, 2000). The real Achilles heel of the new "cocktail approach" antiretroviral therapy is adherence to the medication schedule (Rabkin & Chesney, 1999). To be effective, dozens of pills must be taken every day at precise times. Most studies have found that fewer than 50 percent adhere to this schedule in the long run. When the schedule is not followed, the result is multidrug resistance. With so many people failing to stick to their drug schedule, the number of drug-resistant cases is increasing.

Now the worst news. For most HIV/AIDS patients, *the new antiretroviral drug therapy is not a cure!* Numerous studies have shown that although the therapy lowers HIV levels to extremely low levels, HIV can still exist in places where the drugs do not affect it (e.g., Dornadula et al., 1999; Furtado et al., 1999). If patients decide to stop the drug therapy, HIV levels increase dramatically within days (e.g., Chun et al, 1999; Davey et al., 1999). Even when drug therapy is not stopped, some patients who initially had a dramatic decrease in their viral loads start to show increases after several months (Deeks et al., 1997; Finzi et al., 1997; Wong et al., 1997). There is some hope. A recent small study with eight patients found that if the antiretroviral drug cocktail is started *shortly after people become infected*, the virus may be completely eliminated (Walker & Goulder, 2000). Even if combination therapy should not prove to be a cure, it will certainly allow HIV-infected individuals to lead much longer and more productive lives.

People with HIV, and particularly those with AIDS, require a lot of medical care. Unfortunately, not everyone in the United States is provided good medical care. Members of ethnic minorities and individuals who are uninsured or who have only Medicaid are the most likely to receive inferior care (Shapiro et al., 1999). The average direct cost for the care of an HIV-infected adult in the United States is about $20,000 per year (Bozzette et al., 1998), but it is certainly higher for those who have AIDS and require more care. Indirect costs, such as lost productivity, are estimated to be at least 10 times higher. In addition, AIDS affects everyone in the household, not just the patient. Many middle-class households will be pushed into poverty, while households already in poverty will be pushed to the edge of survival.

Health experts agree that the use of antiretroviral drugs will not bring an end to the HIV pandemic. Even if the problems could be overcome, people in developing countries simply cannot afford the drugs (Cochrane, 2000). An ideal way to combat HIV would be to develop a vaccine (see Esparza & Bhamarapravati, 2000; Klein, 1999). About 30 vaccines are presently being tested with humans, but as of mid-2000 only two have advanced to the large-scale phase III trials necessary for approval.

Unfortunately, there are some major problems with developing an HIV vaccine. First, it will be difficult to develop a vaccine that is effective against all the different genetic subtypes of HIV. Second, because the virus continues to mutate, a vaccine developed today may become ineffective over time. Dr. Anthony Fauci (1999) of the National Institutes of Health said, however, that the threat of AIDS is so great that a less than perfect vaccine would be acceptable. The best hope presently is that one of the vaccines undergoing testing might prove to be 85 percent effective.

PUBLIC REACTIONS TO AIDS

Despite the laws of the land, discrimination continues to play a brutal and important role in the lives of those infected with HIV. The extent and the cruelty of such discrimination have been brought forth in heartrending testimony to the National Commission at each of its many hearings. As a colleague and I wrote recently, "The pain, suffering and despair of the disease alone are dreadful enough. The added stigma makes it virtually unbearable. You lose not only your life, but also your pride, your job, your insurance, your friends and your family. Posterity remembers you for dying of AIDS, not for having lived." (Dr. David Rogers [1992], vice chair of the National Commission on AIDS)

HIV-positive individuals have to deal with more than the fact that they have a deadly disease. They must also deal with the stigma of having HIV/AIDS. A majority of the public have feelings of anger, disgust, or fear toward persons with AIDS, and over a third of Americans feel that people with AIDS should be separated from the rest of society (Kalichman, 1995). The public's fear of AIDS has been fueled by well-publicized cases of individuals who knowingly put others at risk. In 1992, health officials in Michigan confined a woman after she was accused of having sex with six men without telling them she was infected with HIV. In 1997, police in New York arrested a 21-year-old HIV-positive man who may have infected over 100 female sexual partners (Gegax, 1997).

But the negativity directed at people with AIDS is not limited to the few who would knowingly spread the disease. Some young children who contracted AIDS have been temporarily barred from attending school. In Florida, the home of three hemophiliac children with AIDS was burned to the ground when they attempted to go to public school.

How should we as a society deal with the HIV epidemic? First of all, it is important to educate the public that the virus is not spread by any type of casual contact, and thus there is no medical basis for avoiding nonsexual interactions with infected individuals. Most states now have laws that protect HIV-infected persons against discrimination in the workplace and in housing.

Box 5-B   SEXUALITY AND HEALTH

Assessing Your Risk for Getting HIV/AIDS and Other Sexually Transmitted Diseases

This year there will be close to 12 million newly diagnosed cases of sexually transmitted diseases in the United States. One in four American teenagers will contract at least one STD (Alan Guttmacher Institue, 2001). Ask yourself, "Am I at risk of getting a sexually transmitted disease?" What precautions do you take to prevent it from ever happening? Surveys conducted on college campuses indicate that most students do nothing more than look for symptoms in potential new partners. However, many infected individuals, including those with the virus that causes AIDS, do not show any symptoms. We must, therefore, do more than just look for symptoms. As a first step, you should have some idea of your level of risk. Everyone who has sexual relations is at some risk, some more than others. The following questions are designed to help you assess your own level of risk. Be honest when you answer the questions; the questionnaire cannot be of any use to you if you have not answered each item truthfully.

1. How many sexual partners (intercourse or oral-genital sex) have you had (a) in the last 7 years, if you have not had an HIV antibody test; or (b) since your last HIV antibody test that proved negative?

   4 points _____ 42 or more (an average of 6 or more per year)
   3 points _____ 8–41
   2 points _____ 2–7
   1 point _____ 1
   0 points _____ none

2. Do you use drugs intravenously?

   4 points _____ yes
   0 points _____ no

Note: If you scored zero on the first two questions, you are at extremely low risk of being infected with the human immunodeficiency virus or any other virus, bacterium, or parasite discussed in this chapter. You may stop here. If you scored greater than zero, complete the questionnaire.

3. How many sexual partners have you had in the last year?

   4 points _____ 6 or more
   3 points _____ 3–5
   2 points _____ 2
   1 point _____ 1
   0 points _____ none

4. What kinds of sexual contacts have you had? (*Note:* Working from top to bottom, give yourself the points *only* for the *first* category you check.)

   4 points _____ "one-night stands" with relative strangers, sex with a prostitute, or group sex
   3 points _____ (a) "casual sex" (i.e., sex with acquaintances or friends with whom you do not have a "steady" relationship) or (b) steady relationship(s), but you have "cheated" on at least one occasion
   1 point _____ steady relationship(s) without cheating during relationship
   0 points _____ you have not yet had sexual intercourse or oral-genital sex

5. What is your sexual orientation?

   4 points _____ male homosexual, male bisexual, or male heterosexual with occasional male homosexual experiences (*Note:* Homosexuality does not cause STDs, but STDs are very prevalent in these groups.)
   1 point _____ (a) exclusively male or female heterosexual, or (b) female homosexual
   0 points _____ you have not yet had sexual intercourse or oral-genital sex

6. Have you been a victim of forced sexual activity in the last 7 years?

   4 points _____ yes, and you have not been tested for STDs (including an HIV antibody test)
   1 point _____ yes, but subsequent STD tests, including an HIV antibody test, were negative
   0 points _____ no

7. What kinds of sexual activities do you usually engage in? (*Note:* Working from top to bottom, give yourself the points *only* for the *first* category you check.)

   4 points _____ anal intercourse, fisting, oral-anal, or any other activities involving contact with feces or urine
   3 points _____ unprotected (no condom) vaginal intercourse
   2 points _____ unprotected oral-genital sex
   1 point _____ protected (condom) vaginal and/or oral-genital sex
   0 points _____ kissing, caressing, massage, masturbation

8. How often have you had sex after using alcohol or drugs?
   - 4 points ____ very often
   - 3 points ____ usually at parties only
   - 2 points ____ sometimes
   - 1 point ____ hardly ever
   - 0 points ____ never

9. Where do most of your sexual partners live?
   - 1 point ____ in a large city or immediate suburb
   - 0 points ____ in a small city or town
   - 0 points ____ you have not yet had sexual intercourse or oral-genital sex

10. In the last year, how often have you or your sexual partners used condoms?
    - 4 points ____ never or rarely, and you have had more than one partner
    - 3 points ____ usually, but sometimes you have taken chances
    - 2 points ____ never or rarely, but you have had only one steady partner
    - 1 point ____ every time (for each act of penetration), including the first time with a new partner
    - 0 points ____ (a) you have not yet had sexual intercourse or oral-genital sex, or (b) you are an exclusively homosexual female

11. How many sexual partners has your current (or last) partner had prior to you?
    - 4 points ____ many
    - 3 points ____ several
    - 2 points ____ one or a few
    - 1 point ____ none (you think)
    - 0 points ____ you have not yet had sexual intercourse or oral-genital sex

12. How certain are you that your current (or last) sexual partner has not had sex with anyone else since you and he or she started having sex?
    - 4 points ____ you are certain your partner has had sex with others during your relationship
    - 3 points ____ you suspect your partner of having sex with others during your relationship
    - 2 points ____ you are uncertain
    - 1 point ____ you are relatively certain that he or she has not (*Note:* No one can be 100 percent certain.)
    - 0 points ____ you have not yet had sexual intercourse or oral-genital sex

(*Note:* Answer question 13 only if you are not a homosexual or bisexual male.)

13. Have any of your sexual partners had male homosexual experiences or had sex with someone who has? (*Note:* Homosexuality, per se, does not cause STDs.)

- 4 points ____ definitely yes
- 3 points ____ possibly
- 1 point ____ do not know
- 0 points ____ you are relatively certain that he or she has not

14. Have any of your sexual partners used drugs intravenously?
    - 4 points ____ yes
    - 2 points ____ you do not know
    - 0 points ____ no

15. Do you and your sexual partner(s) discuss sexually transmitted diseases and "safer sex"?
    - 2 points ____ rarely
    - 1 point ____ yes, but you have not been tested
    - 0 points ____ (a) yes, and you have both been tested, or (b) you have not yet had sexual intercourse or oral-genital sex

How to Score

If you use condoms every time during vaginal or anal intercourse (be honest—it must be *every time*) for questions 3, 4, 5, 8, 11, 12, and 13, subtract 1 point for each question for which you scored a "2," and subtract 2 points for each question for which you scored a "3" or a "4." If you and your partner are in a monogamous relationship lasting several years and neither of you has ever cheated, you may subtract 2 points if you scored "2" or more for question 7.

Add up your adjusted total points for the 15 questions (a maximum of 4 points on questions 1–8 and 10–14; 2 points on question 15; and 1 point on question 9).

15 points or less	Unless you take drugs intravenously (an automatic high risk), you are at low risk of contracting a sexually transmitted disease.
16–29 points	You are at moderate risk and should adjust your life-style.
30 points or more	You are at high risk. You are strongly advised to change your life-style. If you take drugs intravenously, you are at high risk regardless of your point total.

If you are at moderate or high risk, how can you adjust your life-style? Look back at the questions and see where simple changes would result in subtracting points. The easiest way is by limiting the number of sexual partners you have and/or by always using condoms. Think about it—it could save your life.

Ensuring the privacy and equal treatment of persons with HIV infection is essential to the success of testing, treatment, and outreach programs. Public health officials will not gain the confidence and cooperation of infected individuals if these persons are not legally protected from stigma and irrational prejudice. As former President Ronald Reagan said, "It is the disease that is frightening, not the people who have it."

Some medical journals have argued that there should be more routine testing of people's blood for HIV (e.g., testing of all hospital patients, health care workers, pregnant women, and newborns; Angell, 1991). Others have called for more widespread testing (Kutchinsky, 1996). National surveys have found that 40 percent of adult Americans have been tested for HIV, up from only 16 percent in 1987 (Anderson et al., 2000). Routine testing is already done for syphilis (e.g., when people apply for a marriage license and during prenatal exams). However, some people oppose mandatory testing because of possible civil rights violations (positive test results might be passed on to employers and insurance companies).

Some communities have initiated needle exchange programs in order to eliminate HIV among injecting drug users. Although well-intentioned, these programs have had only limited success (Strathdee et al., 1997).

One likely way to reduce the spread of HIV is education, but there is even controversy about that. Former U.S. Surgeon General C. Everett Koop, a noted conservative, startled many people when he advocated the teaching of sex education, including facts about AIDS and condoms, in all public schools. Former U.S. Secretary of Education William Bennett, on the other hand, opposed Koop and wanted to stress moral values and abstinence from sex until marriage.

A big question, of course, is whether or not education about AIDS will convince people to change their life-styles. The surgeon general's office has been educating and warning people about the long-term dangers of smoking since 1964 (is there really anyone who hasn't heard that smoking can cause lung cancer?), yet many people continue to smoke.

THE EFFECT OF AIDS ON SEXUAL BEHAVIOR

Have AIDS and AIDS prevention programs resulted in long-term changes in sexual behavior in the general population? Some reviews have concluded that the answer is yes (e.g., Carey, 1999; Kalichman et al., 1996). But how widespread have the changes been? Use of condoms increased dramatically from the mid-1980s to the mid-1990s (e.g., Bankole et al., 1999; Sonenstein et al., 1998). The greatest increases in use were observed among African-American and Latino men and women (Catania et al., 1993; Piccinino &

pubic lice An infestation of the parasite *Phthirus pubis*, which attach themselves to pubic hair and feed on blood. Also known as "crabs."

Mosher, 1998; Soler et al., 2000). Still, only about one-third of sexually active teens use condoms consistently (Piccinino & Mosher, 1998). Another review of 27 studies concluded that HIV counseling has had little effect in getting HIV-negative individuals to adopt safer sex behaviors (Weinhardt et al., 1999).

Several studies have reported some very disturbing trends. For example, in the male homosexual community there has been a considerable relapse from safer sex practices, particularly among young gay men (Stall et al., 2000; Valleroy et al., 2000). The real concern is that some infected individuals on the new cocktail antiretroviral therapy have become complacent and returned to high-risk sexual behaviors (Miller et al., 2000). Homosexuals are not the only ones engaging in risky sex. As many as 30 to 40 percent of 21-year-old heterosexuals have had six or more sexual partners (Santelli et al., 1998).

Most disturbing are findings that some people apparently have no regard for their own health or for the health of others. For example, many people who have had a sexually transmitted disease in the past still do not take precautions to prevent another infection (O'Campo et al., 1992). In fact, a sizable minority of people who discover that they are infected with HIV continue to engage in unsafe sexual activity (Diamond & Buskin, 1999). Many people keep their infections secret from their partners (Marks et al., 1991). King and Anderson (1994) reported that some people might be willing to accept death by AIDS for an opportunity to engage in a few years of having unlimited sexual partners. Results like these indicate strongly that HIV will continue to spread for some time to come.

PERSONAL REFLECTIONS
What do you do to protect yourself from sexually transmitted diseases? Now that you have learned more about STDs, what changes in your sexual life-style do you plan to make to better protect yourself?

PARASITIC INFESTATIONS

Viral and bacterial diseases are not the only things that can be transmitted from one person to another during sex. It is also possible to pick up parasites from an infested person. Condoms will do little good in preventing these types of infestations.

Pubic lice (*Phthirus pubis*, the crab louse, or "crabs") are 1 to 2 mm long, grayish (or dusky red after a meal of blood), six-legged parasites that attach themselves to pubic hair and feed on human blood (see Figure 5–13). Infestation with the lice is technically

Figure 5–13 Top: *Phthirus pubis* (crab lice). Bottom: Gravid female *Sarcoptes scabiei mite*. (David Toplin & Terry Meinking: Scabies, lice, and fungal infections. *Primary Care*, 16(3), 551–568. Dept. of Dermatology and Cutaneous Surgery, and Epidemiology and Public Health, University of Miami School of Medicine, Miami, Florida.)

called *pediculosis pubis*. The lice travel very slowly, so it is almost always transmitted by skin-to-skin contact. Your chance of getting them during sex with an infected partner is about 95 percent (Brown et al., 1999). The lice cause intense itching.

> "I was a senior in high school and I was sleeping with a guy who I had been involved with for a year. For about 2 weeks I had been itching in the pubic area. The longer it went on, the more irritating it got. Finally, I examined my pubic hair and found little crab-looking things. I was shocked and disgusted."

> "I noticed an itching down in my pubic area. It got extensively annoying so I took a look to see what was happening down there. I almost started to scream when I noticed little flat insects crawling around that area." (All examples are from the author's files.)

The lice typically do not live for more than 24 hours away from the human body, but any eggs that fall off can survive and hatch up to 10 days later (Meinking & Taplin, 1996). You could, therefore, pick them up from the sheets, towels, or clothing of an infested person. Normal bathing will not wash the lice off, but you can eliminate them by applying pyrethrin products (e.g., 1 percent permethrin cream rinse) or 1 percent lindane (Kwell) lotion, cream, or shampoo to the infested area *and all other hairy body areas*. Repeat the treatment in 7 to 10 days. Be sure also to clean all clothing, sheets, and towels that might be infested in very hot water to avoid reinfestation.

Scabies is a contagious infestation of 0.3 to 0.4 mm long, pearly white, parasitic itch mites (*Sarcoptes scabiei*; see Figure 5–13). The eight-legged mites burrow under the skin to lay their eggs, resulting at first in extremely itchy, red, pimple-like bumps when the eggs hatch. Large patches of scaling skin result if the mites are not immediately destroyed. Secondary bacterial infection is common. The itch mite is acquired by close contact with infested persons (the mites survive 24 to 36 hours off the body), and thus is most common in people living and sleeping in crowded conditions. Sexual contact is not necessary, but sexual transmission is common among adults (Brown et al., 1999). The mite "is notorious for its lack of respect for person, age, sex or race, whether it be in the epidermis of an emperor or a slave, a centurion or a nursling, it makes itself perfectly at home with undiscriminating impudence and equal obnoxiousness" (Friedman, 1947). Scabies has traditionally been treated with 1 percent lindane lotion or permethrin 5 percent cream, but recent studies have found that a single oral dose of ivermectin is also highly effective (Meinking et al., 1995). Should you ever get scabies, be sure that you also wash all your sheets, towels, and clothing to avoid reinfestation.

Pinworms (*Enterobius vermicularis*) live in the large intestine and are generally gotten through nonsexual contact with the eggs. The female pinworms leave the rectum at night and lay their eggs around the anus, which causes intense itching (see Weber, 1993). Pinworms are common in children, who pass them from one to another by hand-to-mouth contact while playing. Pinworms can also be transmitted sexually in adults by manual or oral contact with the anus of an infected person. This mode of transmission occurs most commonly

scabies A contagious infestation of parasitic mites (*Sarcoptes scabiei*) that burrow under the skin to lay their eggs.

pinworms Small worms (*Enterobius vermicularis*) that live in the large intestine and are generally transmitted through nonsexual contact with the worms' eggs, but which can be transmitted sexually by manual or oral contact with the anus of an infected person.

among homosexual men. Such sexual practices can also result in the transmission of a one-celled animal (*Entamoeba histolytica*) that causes intestinal **amebiasis**, or amebic dysentery (Petri & Singh, 1999).

VAGINITIS

Vaginitis is a general term that refers to any inflammation of the vagina. There are basically three types, and it is rare that a woman does not experience at least one of them in her lifetime. Vaginitis has many causes, including hormone imbalances, allergic reactions, chemical irritation, and infection. Symptoms generally include discomfort or pain during urination, along with a vaginal discharge that often has a disagreeable odor.

TRICHOMONIASIS (TRICHOMONAL VAGINITIS)

Only one type of vaginitis, trichomoniasis, is usually contracted by sexual contact. Worldwide, there are about 170 million new cases every year, but it is most common in undeveloped areas (Bowden & Garnett, 2000). In the U.S., there will be at least 3 million new cases of "trich" this year, which is more than gonorrhea, syphilis, and genital herpes combined.

Trichomoniasis is caused by a one-cell protozoan named *Trichomonas vaginalis* that lives in the vagina and urethra. Symptoms in women generally appear from 4 days to 1 month after exposure and include a copious, foamy, yellowish-green discharge with a foul odor accompanied by severe vaginal itching. However, about half of infected women show no symptoms (Bowden & Garnett, 2000).

> "About 2 weeks after becoming sexually involved with my boyfriend, I began to have severe pain during intercourse. Soon I noticed a discharge, itching, and an extremely foul odor. After many weeks of shame I finally went to the infirmary with my roommate, who was having urinary problems. Imagine how surprised we were to find out that we both had trichomoniasis. How could we catch such a thing? The only person she had sex with was her boyfriend and the only person I had sex with was my boyfriend! In the end we found out that our boyfriends went out together one night and had unprotected sex with a girl that they had known less than 6 hours!" (from the author's files)

T. vaginalis can survive in urine or tap water for hours or sometimes days, so it is possible to pick it up by using a wet toilet seat or by sharing towels. Nonetheless, the vast majority of cases are transmitted by sexual intercourse. Until recently, it was believed that infected men show little or no symptoms. However, it is now known that at least half infected with trich show mild to moderately severe urethral irritation and discharge (thus making it a type of nongonococcal urethritis) (Bowden & Garnett, 2000; Krieger, 2000). Still, *many men act as asymptomatic carriers,* spreading it to new female partners—just the opposite of what we often see in the early stages of gonorrhea, chlamydia, and syphilis.

Trichomoniasis can be very irritating (due to itching and burning), but until recently most authorities did not believe that there were any serious long-term consequences if it was left untreated, and thus regarded trich as a "minor" STD. However, studies have found that trichomoniasis can lead to infertility, premature labor in pregnant woman, and facilitates transmission of HIV from an infected partner (Bowden & Garnett, 2000).

The diagnosis of trich is made by examining any discharge and growing the parasite in culture. However, the tests have not been totally reliable. If trichomoniasis is suspected, both the infected woman and her partner should be treated. Otherwise, he will just reinfect her when intercourse resumes. Trich is easily eradicated by a drug called metronidazole (its trade name is Flagyl), but it should not be taken during pregnancy.

MONILIASIS (OR CANDIDIASIS)

Moniliasis is caused by an overgrowth of a microorganism that is normally found in the vagina (*Candida albicans* in 80 percent of cases and other *Candida* species in 20 percent). It is a fungus or yeast infection that is very common in women. Three-fourths of women will experience it at least once in their lifetimes, and 40 to 45 percent will experience it at least twice. About 10 to 20 percent of women have what is called *recurrent candidiasis*—four or more episodes a year (see Lauper, 1996).

Symptoms include a thick, white, cheesy discharge accompanied by intense itching. Unfortunately, many women do not realize how common normal yeast infections are, and feel alone or dirty when it happens to them.

> "The first time I got a yeast infection I was terrified. I didn't know what it was. All I knew was that the itching was intolerable and I had this discharge that wasn't normal."

> "The first time I had it was when I was 16. I started to have an uneasy itchy feeling. I took a shower and thought it would go away. It not only continued, but it became worse. The itchiness was now accompanied by a foul smelling discharge. . . . I felt very dirty." (All examples are from the author's files.)

amebiasis Dysentery caused by infestation of amoebae, one-celled organisms.

vaginitis A general term that refers to any inflammation of the vagina. There are three general types: trichomoniasis, moniliasis, and bacterial vaginosis.

trichomoniasis A type of vaginitis caused by a one-cell protozoan that is usually transmitted during sexual intercourse.

moniliasis Sometimes called candidiasis. A type of vaginitis caused by the overgrowth of a microorganism (*Candida albicans*) that is normally found in the vagina. Moniliasis is a fungus or yeast infection and usually is a sexually related, rather than a sexually transmitted, disease.

Box 5-C SEXUALITY AND HEALTH

Vaginal Health Care

For women, vaginal infections are probably second in frequency only to the common cold. Here are some hygiene tips to help minimize your chances of getting vaginitis:

- Bathe regularly, avoiding deodorant soaps and bubble baths, and do not share washcloths and towels.
- Dry the vulva thoroughly and wear cotton panties (synthetic fabrics retain heat and moisture, conditions in which bacteria thrive).

"I used to get yeast infections several times a year. Every time I would visit or call my doctor. . . . I finally figured it out on my own with a little help from one of the hottest days in June. I would always wear silk or polyester blend underpants and nylon hosiery. Do any of these materials allow absorption? Of course not. I ran out and bought cotton underpants and hosiery with garter belts. Five years have passed and not one yeast infection yet."
(from the author's files)

Certainly never wear synthetic underpants to bed. Also, the yeast that results in monilial infections can survive normal laundering in hot water. As a result, a recent study suggested that women put their laundered but damp cotton underwear in a microwave for 5 minutes (do not try this with dry or synthetic fabrics).

- Avoid feminine hygiene products.
- After a bowel movement, wipe the anus from front to back, not back to front, as this can spread rectal bacteria to the vagina.
- Allow time for adequate vaginal lubrication during intercourse, and if you use a lubricant, use a water-soluble one such as K-Y jelly (petroleum-based lubricants not only harbor bacteria but disintegrate condoms as well).
- If you and your partner engage in any type of anal stimulation during sex, be sure to wash the hands or penis before touching the vaginal area again.
- If your partner has sexual relationships with people other than yourself, make sure he uses a condom during intercourse.
- If you have frequent yeast infections, ask your doctor about douching with a mild acidic solution.
- Keep stress to a minimum, eat well, and get adequate sleep.
- See a doctor as soon as you notice any of the previously mentioned symptoms. Remember, vaginal infections are very common and nothing to be ashamed of. They can be treated very easily.

Yeast infections are sometimes transmitted sexually, but the vast majority of cases are not contracted in this manner. *Children, even babies, can get this, too* (Robinson & Ridgway, 1994). Thus, monilial infections are not really considered a sexually transmitted disease, such as trichomoniasis, but are a sexually related disease. The microbe can also invade the mouth (where it is called thrush), anus, and skin, as well as internal organs. Thrush is often caused by high blood sugar, a weakened immune system, or use of steroids.

Anything that changes the normal chemical environment of the vagina can result in an overgrowth. This includes hormone changes, diabetes, heavy use of antibiotics (which kill off the "friendly" bacteria in the vagina that keep the yeast in check), and even overly zealous hygiene (e.g., the use of perfumed feminine hygiene products). Many women first experience a monilial infection during pregnancy, for example, or when they first start taking oral contraceptives.

"Once when I had an infected tooth, my dentist prescribed an antibiotic. About the third day I developed a yeast infection. No one had ever told me I could get a yeast infection from an antibiotic. When I told some of my friends, they told me this had happened to at least two of them before."

"I had my first yeast infection when I was pregnant with my first child. I was so embarrassed about having this terrible itch in the genital area that I couldn't tell anyone. Finally it was time for my regular prenatal checkup, and when the doctor examined me and saw that I had scratched myself raw he wanted to know why I had not called him. I was just too embarrassed to say I had an itch in the genital area." (All examples are from the author's files.)

Women with immune deficiencies (e.g., HIV infection and AIDS) are particularly susceptible to yeast infections. The question of what causes recurrent infections is still controversial (see Lauper, 1996). Reduction of intestinal sources of *Candida albicans* and treatment of partners do not prevent recurrences. Some people believe that women can suffer from a chronic candidiasis syndrome (also called candidiasis hypersensitivity syndrome or the "yeast connection"), characterized by severe PMS, gastrointestinal problems, depression and anxiety, and fatigue (Crook, 1983). However, this has been challenged by the American Academy of Allergy and Immunology (1986).

Yeast infections are often treated with antifungal creams or suppositories. There are over-the-counter drugs that you can purchase in the drugstore (e.g., Monistat and Gyne-Lotrimin). Drugs that you can take by mouth (Fluconazole, Itraconazole) are also available (Lauper, 1996). However, if the symptoms do not go away within a few days, see your doctor immediately, for you might have one of the other types of vaginitis.

BACTERIAL VAGINOSIS

Bacterial vaginosis is the most common of the three types of vaginitis. It is caused by the interaction of several vaginal bacteria (particularly *Gardnerella vaginalis*) that can also live in the man's urethra. Bacterial vaginosis used to be called by a variety of names (haemophilus, Gardnerella, or nonspecific vaginitis), but the current name more correctly reflects what we now know about the microbiology of the disease (Eschenbach, 1993). Whether or not bacterial vaginosis can be transmitted sexually is still controversial. It is more common in women with many sexual partners, but treating partners does not prevent recurrences of the disease (see Joesoef et al., 1999).

The main complaint of patients is a vaginal odor (sometimes described as fishy), but there is also an abnormal discharge (grayish and nonclumpy). We now know that this type of infection can lead to serious upper reproductive tract infection (Eschenbach, 1993). The antibiotics of choice are metronidazole or clindamycin, but the recurrence rate is very high (Joesoef et al., 1999).

CYSTITIS AND PROSTATITIS

Cystitis refers to a bacterial infection of the bladder. Because a woman's urethra is considerably shorter than a man's, and thus bacteria have a shorter distance to travel, cystitis is much more common in women than men. It is especially common in sexually active young women and is strongly associated with recent intercourse, especially after using a diaphragm with spermicide (Hooton et al., 1996). However, many cases are unrelated to sexual activity. The bacterium *Escherichia coli*, for example, is often transmitted from the rectum to the urethral opening by wiping forward from the anus after a bowel movement. Women should always wipe themselves from front to back. Cystitis can also be caused by the *N. gonorrhoeae* and *Chlamydia trachomatis* bacteria, but it is generally not considered a sexually transmitted disease.

Symptoms may include a frequent urge to urinate, painful urination, and lower abdominal pains. Cystitis is treated with either sulfa drugs or antibiotics. Vigorous intercourse, especially in women first becoming sexually active, can also result in urinary tract infection (hence the term *honeymoon cystitis*) by causing inward friction on the urethra, allowing nonsexually transmitted bacteria to ascend. For those women who experience postcoital urinary tract infection, trimethoprim and sulfamethoxazole taken together within 2 hours of intercourse prevents infections (Stapleton et al., 1990).

The *E. coli* bacteria can also be transmitted to a man's prostate during sexual activity, resulting in **prostatitis.** Symptoms may include lower back and/or groin pain, fever, and burning during ejaculation. This, too, is treated with antibiotics.

PRACTICING SAFER SEX

Add them up: at least 4 million new cases of chlamydia per year, at least 3 million new cases of trichomoniasis, nearly 1 million new cases of gonorrhea, one-half million to 1 million new cases of human papillomavirus infection, 1 million new cases of herpes, an unknown number of new HIV infections—plus syphilis, sexually transmitted cases of hepatitis, chancroid, and others. There will be about 12 million new cases of sexually transmitted diseases this year—about 33,000 new cases every day—with most cases occurring within your age group (late teens through 40). Of course, some people who are sexually active will be infected with the same STD two or more times in a single year, or even get two or more different STDs at once. Yes, having one does not prevent you from getting others, so it is possible to hit the jackpot and have more than one at once.

What are you doing to avoid sexually transmitted diseases? It appears that many college students are doing little or nothing. In fact, many continue to engage in high-risk behaviors. There is a strong association between number of sexual partners and having, or having already had, a sexually transmitted disease (e.g., a woman with five or more lifetime partners is eight times more likely to have had an STD than a woman with only one partner; Joffe et al., 1992); yet, according to surveys, many young people have had multiple lifetime sexual partners. A national survey of heterosexuals living in large cities found

---

bacterial vaginosis A type of vaginitis caused by the interaction of several bacteria (particularly *Gardnerella vaginalis*).

cystitis A bacterial infection of the bladder (often caused by the bacterium *Escherichia coli*).

prostatitis Inflammation of the prostate gland.

that 39 percent reported having multiple sexual partners (Catania et al., 1995). Another national survey found that among 21-year-olds, 31 percent of women and 45 percent of men had had six or more lifetime partners (Santelli et al., 1998). Thirty-eight percent of young homosexual men have engaged in unprotected anal intercourse (CDC press release, 1996).

Why do so many people continue to engage in high-risk sexual behaviors (see Box 5–D)? Many young men and women who have had multiple sexual partners believe "it won't happen to me" (Kusseling et al., 1996). Recall, however, that it *will* happen to 1 in 4 American teens (Alan Guttmacher Institute, 2001). So let's get serious and consider how you can minimize the chances of it ever happening to you.

The only way to completely avoid any chance of ever getting an STD is never to have sex, but few of us wish to live the life of a Tibetan monk. There is no such thing as safe sex with another person; anyone having sex is at some risk. We can, however, practice **"safer sex"**—behaviors that minimize the chances of contracting an STD.

One safer sex solution is to *restrict your sexual activity to a mutually faithful, long-term monogamous relationship*. If neither you nor your partner has an STD at the start of the relationship and neither of you has other partners, you do not have to worry about STDs. However, there are problems with this approach. First, while many of us limit our sexual behavior to monogamous relationships, most monogamous relationships do not last forever. Many of us have life-styles of what is commonly called *serial monogamy*. We break up and eventually enter into another monogamous relationship. You may have been having sex with only one person for a certain period of your life, but how many monogamous relationships have you had in your lifetime? If just one of those partners had an STD, he or she could have transmitted it to you. When we have new sexual partners, we can rarely be sure of their sexual history. One study, for example, found that many people have lied to new partners about their past sexual experiences (Cochran & Mays, 1990).

> "A friend of mine was going out with a guy from _____. They had a sexual relationship and used condoms most of the time. He only recently mentioned that he had tested positive for the AIDS virus in the past. My friend is under tremendous psychological distress." (from the author's files)

A second problem is that few of us can be 100 percent certain that our partner will remain monogamous. Read again the personal case histories at the beginning of the chapter.

A second solution is to *always use condoms*. A study of 256 heterosexual couples in which one partner was infected with HIV found that for those couples who used condoms consistently, none of the noninfected

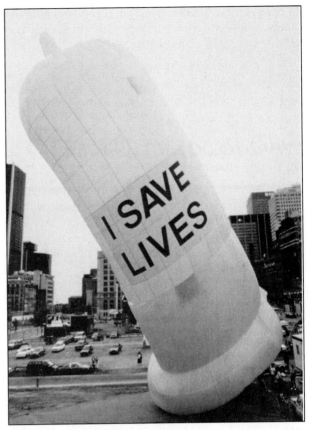

Figure 5–14 A giant condom displayed at the Fifth International AIDS Conference in Montreal.

partners became infected during a total of 15,000 episodes of intercourse (De Vincenzi et al., 1994). It is certainly best to use condoms if you are going to engage in "casual" sex. For women whose partners refuse to wear condoms, there are some birth control techniques that reduce the risk of HIV (or other STD) infection (see Box 6–A in Chapter 6).

There are problems with condoms (as STD prevention) as well. Even if you and your partner or partners use them consistently and properly, they sometimes tear (see Chapter 6). Even microscopic tears are large enough to allow the passage of viruses. In other words, as is the case with practicing monogamy, condoms cannot guarantee that you will never get a sexually transmitted disease.

Which method is better? In a study that used probability modeling to test the amount of risk reduction, the authors concluded that "consistent and careful condom use is a far more effective method of reducing HIV infection than is reducing the number of sexual partners" (Reiss & Leik, 1989). Whichever behavioral strategy you use—condoms

safer sex Sexual behaviors involving a low risk of contracting a sexually transmitted disease. These include consistent use of condoms and/or abstaining from sex until one enters a long-term monogamous relationship.

or the practice of monogamy (in a *long-term* relationship)— you will greatly reduce your chances of ever getting a sexually transmitted disease.

WHAT TO DO AND WHERE TO GO IF YOU HAVE AN STD

You would think it would be obvious to people what to do if they thought they might have, or thought they were at risk for, a sexually transmitted disease—go to a doctor! However, many people hesitate to do this out of fear, shame, guilt, or just plain denial. Now that you know the consequences of untreated STDs, I hope that this will not include you. So, if you think you have an STD (or if you have put yourself at high risk of getting one):

1. See a physician immediately.
2. If he or she diagnoses you as having an STD, abstain from having sex until you are cured (or use condoms if there is no cure).
3. If you have an STD, tell your partner or partners so that they, too, can be treated and not infect others or yourself again. You do not want to play STD Ping-Pong with your partner!

"It's not that I don't trust you, Kevin, I just don't trust the women who've been with the men who've been with the women who've been with the men who've been with the women you've been with."

Reproduced by Special Permission of *Playboy* magazine: copyright © 1990 by Playboy.

There are two other reasons that someone might not go to a doctor immediately. Some (e.g., poor college students) may not be able to afford the doctor's charges and lab test costs, and others might not know where to go even if they had the money (they might not have a doctor, or they may wish to avoid the family doctor). Fortunately, the U.S. Public Health Service provides clinics for the diagnosis and treatment of sexually transmitted diseases—often free of charge! The government is committed to eradicating STDs. So there is no excuse not to be treated. Contact the Public Health Service clinic in your area.

The Centers for Disease Control and Prevention also has an STD informational National Hotline toll-free number: 1-800-227-8922.

POSITIVE SEXUALITY IN THE ERA OF AIDS

AIDS, human papillomavirus infections, herpes—the attention being given to these and other sexually transmitted diseases is making many people afraid of sex. My intent in this chapter has been to educate you about some of the *possible* consequences of sexual behavior, not to scare you so badly that you will want to avoid ever having sexual relations.

There are many activities human beings engage in that involve risk. Take skiing, for example. No one has to tell us that going down a snow-and-ice-covered mountain on a pair of skis is a dangerous activity. If trees, boulders, and other skiers are not avoided, the result can be terrible injury, yet this doesn't detract from the tremendous enjoyment many people derive from this winter sport. Those who ski learn that there are limitations to how they seek that pleasure. Skiing out of control has its consequences.

The same is true of driving an automobile. Many people own sports cars, and many others would like to. They get a certain thrill by accelerating quickly and driving fast. But, again, there are limitations. Taking a corner at too high a speed can be fatal. At high speeds, we must be able to react to unanticipated events (e.g., another car cutting in front of us) in a fraction of a second. Driving while having impaired judgment

Box 5-D   SEXUALITY AND HEALTH

Impediments to Practicing Safer Sex

Until an effective vaccine is developed, health officials must rely on convincing people to change their behavior in order to prevent the spread of HIV. For most of the population, this means convincing them to practice safer sex behaviors. During the 1980s, it was hoped that educating people about AIDS and the transmission of HIV would lead them to practice safer sex. Schools began teaching about HIV; the surgeon general mailed an informational brochure to all U.S. households; and hardly a day went by that newspapers did not include an article about HIV or AIDS.

Studies in the 1990s found that most young people today are, in fact, knowledgeable about HIV and AIDS. However, AIDS and sex education programs have had, at best, only a modest success in convincing people to reduce their number of sexual partners and/or to use condoms regularly (e.g., Weinhardt et al., 1999). Even scare tactics have not produced behavior change (Sherr, 1990). In fact, researchers find that there is no relationship at all between people's knowledge of AIDS and their sexual behavior (DiClemente et al., 1990; Klepinger et al., 1993). This has led many researchers to conclude that, by itself, knowledge is "not sufficient for compliance to safer-sex guidelines" (Ahia, 1991; Helwig-Larsen & Collins, 1997; Sheeran et al., 1999).

If it is not lack of knowledge that prevents many people from practicing safer sex, what is it? Actually, there are many reasons. We will consider a few of the most important.

One of the most common reasons that men give for not using condoms is that one was not available when they were in the mood to have sex (Carter et al., 1999). Many men are embarrassed about buying condoms (Murphy & Boggess, 1998). Young people are also less likely to use condoms, and more likely to have had multiple partners, if they frequently used alcohol or drugs prior to sex (Ku et al., 1993; Santelli et al., 1998). People are more likely to have a condom available if they have used them in the past, especially if they are with a partner with whom they have agreed to use condoms.

The major problem here is that to have come to an agreement, a couple has to have talked about using condoms, and most people, including those who are college educated, do not know how to initiate and engage in conversation about condoms (Sheeran et al., 1999). Practicing safer sex means that you must be able to talk with partners about using condoms, as well as about their sexual history, and that you must be able to put a stop to sexual activity if your partner will not use one. This requires some degree of assertiveness. Young people who have these behavioral skills are much more likely to practice safer sex (Fisher & Fisher, 1992; Wingood & DiClemente, 1998).

One factor that prevents some women from acting in their own best interest is the perceived power difference between men and women. If a woman's predominant experience of relations between men and women is of men exerting power over women and always getting their way, they are not likely to insist that a man use a condom if he doesn't want to (Browne & Minichiello, 1996; Seal, 1996). This may be common in cultures that emphasize the ideal that men are virile and macho.

Even when there is little or no power difference, communication between a man and a woman about safer sex is often hindered by cultural double standards and sexual "scripts" (Ehrhardt, 1992; Metts & Fitzpatrick, 1992). In American culture, men are given more sexual freedom than are women. Thus, a woman may be viewed negatively by a partner and by others if she openly expresses a desire for sex or if she carries condoms (Hillier et al., 1998), and she may be considered respectable only if she refuses a partner's sexual advances. Women who believe that their partners endorse this standard are not likely to provide a condom or suggest that their partner use one. As you will learn in Chapter 17, many women engage in "scripted refusal" with new partners—first telling them no (in order to appear respectable) and then consenting (Muehlenhard & McCoy, 1991). Women who engage in this behavior are very unlikely to look after themselves by carrying and providing their partners with condoms.

One of the most common HIV-prevention behaviors used by college students, especially coeds, is to have sex only with individuals they believe to be "safe" (Carter et al., 1999). They look for partners who appear to have no symptoms (Baldwin & Baldwin, 1988) and then restrict their sexual relations to a monogamous relationship. Many have life-styles of what I have previously referred to as serial monogamy. However, many women are unaware of their partner's past (or current) risky sexual behavior, including sex with other men (Ellen et al., 1998).

Another problem is that sexual scripts often work against the use of condoms when one starts dating a "respectable" and "safe" partner where the goal is the formation of a relationship (Afifi, 1999; Browne & Minichiello, 1996; Hynie et al., 1998). There is a negative relational significance associated with condoms: if they are not being used for birth control, their only other use is for the prevention of STDs with an "unsafe" partner. When the focus of "getting to know you" is on the other person's suitability as a relational partner, the subject of condoms may be viewed negatively, suggesting promiscuity and possible infection (by oneself or the other) and increasing the likelihood of rejection (see Choi et al., 1994). In such situations, a couple are likely to avoid directly asking each other about past sexual behavior or the use of condoms and just talk about AIDS and safer sex in general rather than in terms of the relationship. People (incorrectly) take a partner's willingness to talk about AIDS as a sign that he or she is safe. Even when condoms are used during early sexual episodes, they are likely to be abandoned once the two individuals perceive themselves as starting a relationship (Crosby et al., 2000). But

without previous explicit, honest discussion about prior sexual experiences, you cannot be certain. Or, put another way, "You know if you're using a condom or you're not. You don't know if you're picking the right partner" (Heterosexual AIDS, 1988).

Our culture also has a taboo against seriously discussing any sexual topic (Wight, 1992). For example, dating partners generally do not ask each other directly if the other wishes to have sex, but instead communicate their intentions to one another indirectly via ambiguous body language and other behaviors (Hickman & Muehlenhard, 1999). The use of alcohol further lowers communication skills (Gordon et al., 1997). Indirect communication also serves as a way of avoiding rejection—cues and signals that go unacknowledged are generally considered to be less rejecting than a direct refusal to verbal requests (O'Sullivan & Byers, 1992). But you can't communicate about the use of condoms with indirect gestures.

In conclusion, the number of individuals practicing safer sex will probably not increase substantially beyond the present levels until health educators begin to teach behavioral skills and address gender issues. If you ever wanted to talk about condoms with a potential new sex partner but could not bring yourself to do so, it might help you to know that a recent study found that sexual partners feel more positively about partners who insist on using condoms (Hocking et al., 1999).

---

and motor coordination due to alcohol consumption is certainly an often fatal high-risk behavior. The fact that each year thousands of people are injured or killed because they foolishly took that risk does not detract from the pleasure that the rest of us often get from driving our cars.

AIDS is not the first sexually transmitted disease, only the most recent. Syphilis and gonorrhea were greatly feared before the discovery of antibiotics. Many millions more have died of syphilis than of AIDS, yet this hasn't stopped people from enjoying sex. Why? *Because sex, by itself, does not cause any of these diseases.* Like driving an automobile, if we avoid foolish, high-

risk behaviors, we can still enjoy the pleasures of sexual relations. The few seconds it takes to put on a seat belt does not detract from your enjoying your automobile. Similarly, the few seconds it would take you or your partner to put on a condom will not detract from the enjoyment of sex. Like drinking and driving, making sexual decisions while under the influence of alcohol is also foolish.

AIDS does not strike randomly—it only affects those who are exposed to the virus. If you make just a few adjustments to reduce the risk of exposure, sex can be as pleasurable and exciting as always.

Key Terms

acquired immunodeficiency
   syndrome (AIDS) 114
amebiasis 128
asymptomatic 102
autoinoculation 109
bacteria 100
bacterial vaginosis 130
cervicitis 103
chancre 105
chancroid 107
chlamydia 103
cystitis 130
genital herpes 109
genital (venereal) warts 113
gonorrhea 101
granuloma inguinale 107
gummas 106

hepatitis A 112
hepatitis B 112
hepatitis C 112
human immunodeficiency virus
   (HIV) 114
human papillomavirus (HPV) infection 112
immune system 114
lymphogranuloma venereum (LGV)
   104
molluscum contagiosum 114
moniliasis 128
nongonococcal (nonspecific) urethritis (NGU) 103
opportunistic infections 115
oral herpes 109

pelvic inflammatory disease (PID)
   102, 104
pinworms 127
prostatitis 130
pubic lice 126
safer sex 131
scabies 127
sexually related disease 101
sexually transmitted disease (STD)
   100
shigellosis 107
syphilis 105
trichomoniasis 128
vaginitis 128
venereal disease 100
virus 100

Suggested Readings

Anderson, P. B., de Mauro, D., and Noonan, R. J. (Eds.) (1996). *Does anyone remember when sex was fun? Positive sexuality in the age of AIDS.* Dubuque, IA. Essays on positive sexuality from many different perspectives.

Boston Women's Health Book Collective. (1998). *Our bodies, ourselves for the new century* (4th ed.) New York: Simon & Schuster. The landmark book on women's sexuality and health.

Brandt, A. M. (1987). *No magic bullet: A social history of venereal disease in the United States since 1880.* New York: Oxford University Press.

Ebel, C. (1996). *Managing herpes: How to live and love with a chronic STD.* Research Triangle Park, NC. The best book ever written about herpes.

Fauci, A.S. (1999). The AIDS epidemic: Considerations for the 21st century. *New England Journal of Medicine,* 341, 1046–1050.

Masland, T., and Norland, R. (2000). 10 million orphans. *Newsweek,* January 17, 42–45.

Planned Parenthood. *Vaginitis: Questions and answers.* 16 pages.

Shute, N. (1998). Hepatitis C: A silent killer. *U.S. News & World Report,* June 22. Five times as many Americans have hepatitis C than HIV, and it can be deadly.

Time. (1997, January 7). Several articles devoted to the AIDS pandemic and new treatments.

United Nations Programme on HIV/AIDS (December, 2000). Report on the global HIV/AIDS epidemic. Geneva, Switzerland: United Nations.

Study Guide

INTERACTIVE REVIEW

There are about 12 million new cases of sexually transmitted diseases in the United States every year. For sexually active American teens, about 1 in (1) _____ will have at least one STD sometime in their life.

Sexual behavior does not cause STDs. The behavior is merely the mode of transmission for (2) _____, (3) _____, and/or (4) _____ that must be present for the diseases to be transmitted. These causative agents are nondiscriminating—anyone having sex with an infected partner can get a sexually transmitted disease.

The three most common STDs (in the United States) caused by bacteria are (5) _____, (6) _____, and (7) _____. In the early stages of (8) _____ and (9) _____, most women and many men show no symptoms. If they are not treated, the bacteria that cause these two STDs can invade the upper reproductive tract and cause prostatitis and epididymitis in men and (10) _____ in women.

(11) _____ passes through several stages, and if left untreated can cause organ damage and death. These types of STDs can be cured with (12) _____.

Sexually transmitted diseases caused by viruses are generally incurable because the viruses live inside normal body cells. Herpes has been around since biblical times and is spread by direct (13) _____-to- _____ contact. Genital herpes is almost always transmitted by genital-to-genital or mouth-to-genital contact; oral herpes is often spread by more casual contact. After the primary attack, many herpes sufferers experience (14) _____ attacks when the virus replicates and sheds. The virus is most easily transmitted during active attacks, but can be transmitted at other times.

Hepatitis is an inflammation of the (15) _____ that can be caused by contact with contaminated (16) _____ (hepatitis A) or infected (17) _____ (hepatitis B). One-fourth to one-half of all cases of hepatitis B are sexually transmitted. Four million Americans are infected with hepatitis C.

Warts in the genital and anal areas are caused by a few types of the (18) _____ virus. Other types of the virus are associated with cancer of the cervix and penis. Physicians can attempt to remove the warts or abnormal cervical cells, but they cannot attack the viruses directly; thus, in many cases, the condition reappears.

AIDS is caused by the (19) _____. HIV invades and destroys (20) _____ (also called helper T) cells, white blood cells that are a critical part of the body's (21) _____ system. Most people infected with HIV remain asymptomatic for several years. HIV infection is not called AIDS until the immune system is so weakened that the individual's life is threatened. People with AIDS eventually die from a variety of (22) _____ infections. Without medication, about half of all individuals who become infected with HIV will develop AIDS within (23) _____ years. HIV originated in Africa from simian (nonhuman primate) immunodeficiency viruses. It is transmitted by (24) _____ and exposure to infected (25) _____. It is not spread by (26) _____. HIV infection is a true pandemic, with at least 120 million cases expected worldwide by the year 2020. Worldwide, most cases are spread by sexual activity between (27) _____. Presently, there is no cure, but there are several antiretroviral drugs that slow the progression of the infection.

Pubic lice and scabies are not really diseases, but (28) _____. Pubic lice attach themselves to pubic hair and feed on blood. Scabies is caused by a mite that burrows under the skin to lay its eggs.

Vaginitis is a general term that refers to any inflammation of the vagina. There are three types. (29) _____ is caused by a one-celled protozoan that is transmitted during sexual intercourse. The other two types of vaginitis are not considered STDs because most cases are not acquired during sexual relations. (30) _____ vaginitis is a fungus or yeast infection that is very common in women. Anything that changes the chemical environment of the vagina can cause a yeast infection. Probably the most common type of vaginitis is (31) _____, caused by the interaction of several vaginal bacteria. Vaginal infections are very common and nothing to be ashamed of.

STDs do not strike randomly—they only affect those who are exposed to the bacteria or viruses. You can greatly reduce your chances of ever contracting a sexually transmitted disease by practicing safer sex. This means making one of two choices: (1) using condoms (preferably with spermicide) properly and consistently, or (2) abstaining from sexual relations until you are reasonably confident that you are in a long-term monogamous relationship. See the self-assessment questionnaire (Box 5–B).

SELF-TEST

A. TRUE OR FALSE

| T | F | 32. People who have had a sexually transmitted disease in the past are immune to getting that type of STD again.

| T | F | 33. Cold sores and fever blisters are symptoms of herpes.

| T | F | 34. Homosexuality is one of the causes of AIDS.

| T | F | 35. If left untreated, gonorrhea can turn into syphilis.

| T | F | 36. Yeast infections (monilial vaginitis) can usually be prevented by using feminine hygiene products.

| T | F | 37. A person with a cold sore on the mouth can give his or her partner genital herpes during oral-genital sex.

| T | F | 38. Gonorrhea, chlamydia, and syphilis are often contracted by people who use toilet seats previously used by infected individuals.

[T] [F]   39. Chlamydia is more common than gonorrhea.

[T] [F]   40. It is possible to contract HIV by hugging, touching, or being close to an infected person.

[T] [F]   41. The large majority of women do not show any symptoms in the early stages of gonorrhea or chlamydia.

[T] [F]   42. Herpes can sometimes be cured with antibiotics.

[T] [F]   43. A person can have only one type of sexually transmitted disease at a time.

[T] [F]   44. HIV, the virus that causes AIDS, is sometimes spread by mosquitoes.

[T] [F]   45. Pelvic inflammatory disease can be caused by infections that were not contracted during sex.

[T] [F]   46. Condoms are generally ineffective against the human immunodeficiency virus.

[T] [F]   47. The eggs of pubic lice can survive for days on towels or sheets.

[T] [F]   48. A person who has no symptoms does not have to worry about having gonorrhea, chlamydia, or syphilis.

[T] [F]   49. Only women can contract trichomoniasis and monilial infections.

[T] [F]   50. Herpes can be cured with a drug called acyclovir.

[T] [F]   51. The human papillomaviruses that cause cervical cancer are the same as those that cause genital warts.

[T] [F]   52. Regular douching decreases the risk of pelvic inflammatory disease.

[T] [F]   53. Recurrent herpes attacks are generally more painful, and last longer, than the first (primary) attack.

[T] [F]   54. Herpes is the leading infectious cause of blindness in the United States.

[T] [F]   55. Hepatitis A is most often spread by nonsexual means.

[T] [F]   56. Worldwide, most cases of HIV infection (infection with the virus that causes AIDS) are contracted by sex between heterosexuals.

[T] [F]   57. Generally speaking, people who get AIDS this year are those who became infected with HIV 5 to 15 years ago.

[T] [F]   58. To minimize their chance of a vaginal infection, women should wear panties made of synthetic fabrics.

[T] [F]   59. People who get HIV are extremely contagious in the first 60 days after exposure.

[T] [F]   60. Hepatitis C is 5 times more common than HIV in the United States.

[T] [F]   61. HIV/AIDS can be considered cured when drug therapy reduces HIV to nondetectable levels.

B. MATCHING

Symptoms

_____ 62. painful, craterlike sores

_____ 63. itchless, painless rash all over the body

_____ 64. puslike discharge and/or burning during urination

_____ 65. intense itching caused by grayish, six-legged parasites

_____ 66. thick, white, cheesy vaginal discharge and intense itching

_____ 67. loss of appetite, fatigue, slow recovery from colds and flus, continual yeast infections, purple blotches on skin, pneumonia

_____ 68. cauliflowerlike growths

_____ 69. severe abdominal pain and fever

_____ 70. scaling skin caused by pearly mites

_____ 71. large, ulcerlike, painless sore

_____ 72. fluid-filled blisters

_____ 73. copious, foamy, yellowish-green vaginal discharge and odor

Infection (or Infestation)

a. chancroid
b. chlamydia
c. gonorrhea
d. hepatitis
e. herpes
f. HIV infection (AIDS)
g. molluscum contagiosum
h. moniliasis (yeast infection)
i. PID
j. primary stage syphilis
k. cystitis
l. secondary stage syphilis
m. scabies
n. trichomoniasis
o. venereal warts (human papillomavirus infection)

_____ 74. wartlike growths that look like small pimples filled with a kernel of corn

p. late-stage syphilis
q. pubic lice

_____ 75. thin, clear discharge and irritation of the urethra

_____ 76. jaundiced or yellow tinge of skin and eyes

_____ 77. large ulcers (gummas) on the skin and bones; damage to the heart and nervous system

_____ 78. inflammation of the bladder

C. FILL IN THE BLANKS

79. Trichomoniasis, pubic lice, and scabies are all caused by _____.

80. Inflammation of the vagina is referred to as _____.

81. In women, untreated gonorrhea or chlamydia can lead to _____.

82. A woman who has had _____ is at high risk of getting cancer of the cervix.

83. The sexually transmitted disease that impairs the immune system is called _____.

84. Trichomoniasis, moniliasis, and bacterial vaginosis are all _____.

85. A viral liver infection that can be sexually transmitted is _____.

86. A drug that is prescribed to relieve the symptoms of herpes is _____.

87. Two serious possible consequences of PID are _____ and _____.

88. Three sexually transmitted diseases that can be passed from an infected pregnant female to the fetus are _____, _____, and _____.

89. _____ is the most common thing that brings on recurrent herpes attacks.

90. The bacteria that cause gonorrhea and chlamydia live on _____.

91. Any inflammation of the urethra not caused by the gonococcus is called _____.

92. Antibiotics commonly lead to _____ infections.

93. _____ live in the large intestine and can be transmitted during sex, but are generally acquired by children through nonsexual means.

94. Many people diagnosed with gonorrhea are also found to have _____.

95. HIV attacks immune system cells called _____.

96. People with HIV are most contagious (when) _____.

97. The most common AIDS test tests for _____.

98. Gonorrhea, chlamydia, syphilis, herpes, HPV infection, HIV infection, trichomoniasis—for which of these diseases do women usually not have visible symptoms in the initial stage? _____

99. For which of the diseases listed in the previous question do men usually not show symptoms in the initial stage? _____

100. The best ways to avoid sexually transmitted diseases are _____ and _____.

Chapter 6

Birth Control

We should not delude ourselves: the population explosion will come to an end before very long. The only remaining question is whether it will be halted through the humane method of birth control, or by nature wiping out the surplus.

(Paul and Anne Ehrlich, 1990)

The teenage pregnancy rate in the United States is the second highest of any developed country in the world (see Table 6–1). This is not a recent phenomenon. Births to teenagers in the United States reached a peak in 1957 and have declined a bit since then. What is new is the proportion of births to unwed teens. Only 15 percent of teenage births were out of wedlock in 1960, but this figure rose to 49 percent by 1980, and reached a peak of 76 percent in 1991. The greatest increase in pregnancy rates has been among young teens aged 14 to 17 without a high school education. About 80 percent of pregnancies to teens are unintended, and nearly half of these are terminated by abortion (Henshaw, 1998a).

Recently there has been some improvement. The teenage pregnancy and birth rates declined after 1991, and by the late 1990s had reached their lowest levels since 1976 (Ventura et al., 1999, 2000). Nevertheless, the teenage pregnancy rate in the United States is still nearly twice as high as in England and Canada, and 8 times as high as in Japan (Singh & Darroch, 2000; see Table 6–1).

When you have finished studying this chapter, you should be able to:

1. Discuss the teenage pregnancy problem in the United States;

2. Understand the worldwide need for effective contraceptive techniques;

3. List some contraceptive myths and relatively ineffective methods of birth control and discuss why they are not effective;

4. Explain how the various fertility awareness methods of contraception are supposed to work;

5. Compare and contrast the various barrier methods of birth control and their effectiveness;

6. Discuss the latest developments in intrauterine devices;

7. Describe the various hormonal methods of contraception, how they work, and their potential side effects;

8. Describe the various sterilization procedures and explain their advantages and disadvantages;

9. Discuss the various methods of abortion;

10. Discuss the contraceptive methods that also help to prevent sexually transmitted diseases; and

11. Determine which contraceptive technique is right for you.

The birth rate is much higher for African-American and Latino teenagers than it is for white or Asian-American teens (Ventura et al., 2000). However, the birth rate for African-American teens has decreased substantially since 1991, and the rate for unmarried black teens is the lowest it has been in 40 years. On the other hand, the rate for Latino teens is increasing. White teens are much more likely than black or Latino teens to "hide" an unintended pregnancy by getting married. Because the divorce rate for couples married as teenagers is much higher than average, many of these prematurely married white teens end up as young single parents anyway (see Coley & Chase-Lansdale, 1998).

The high pregnancy rate among U.S. teens reflects widespread nonuse of **contraception.** One-third of American teenagers use no contraceptive method at first intercourse, and the rate is even higher for young teens (Abma et al., 1997). Only one-third of sexually active teens aged 15 to 19 years old use contraception on a consistent basis (Piccinino & Mosher, 1998; Sonenstein et al., 1998). Teens' self-esteem, ego development, and educational aspirations often predict whether or not they use contraception (Goodson et al., 1997). Teens with repeat pregnancies generally have a history of behavior problems (school problems, drug and alcohol use, etc.) (Gillmore et al., 1997).

Among young teens, ignorance about reproduction and contraception is common.

> "As a Paramedic I've delivered more babies than I can count. Once I responded to a person with 'rectal bleeding.' To my surprise, a young girl greeted me saying that 'she has something coming out her rectum and she is bleeding all over.' The 15-year-old was scared to death, still clothed in underwear, bleeding, with a large mass between her legs, inside the underwear. I gained information from the family that no one had any inclination that this 15-year-old was even pregnant. What an education for a 15-year-old. Is this really what we want for our children, or do we want to provide the availability of more classes such as Human Sexuality. I vote for the latter." (from the author's files)

However, most teens know about contraception, and also know that if they have sex without contraception they are taking a chance. But if they have already taken that chance without having it result in pregnancy, they are likely to take the chance again. Eventually, they begin to feel that they can't get pregnant—that it won't happen to them.

> "I have been having sex since I was 16. I have had different partners and unprotected sex with all of them. I always believed that I couldn't get pregnant. It only happens to bad girls and people who wanted it to happen. There were a couple of late periods and worrying, but it never made me want to try birth control. . . . I found out I was 2 months pregnant. I was completely shocked." (from the author's files)

contraception The prevention of conception.

TABLE 6–1	
YEARLY TEENAGE PREGNANCY RATE (PER 1,000 WOMEN) IN DEVELOPED NATIONS	
Russian Federation	101.7
United States	83.6
England and Wales	46.9
Canada	45.4
Australia	43.7
Norway	32.3
Sweden	24.9
Denmark	22.7
Finland	20.5
France	20.2
Germany	16.1
Spain	12.3
Netherlands	12.0
Italy	12.0
Japan	10.1

Source: Singh & Darroch (2000). Reprinted with permission of the publishers.

Who are the male partners responsible for these teenage pregnancies? Half of the fathers of babies born to girls aged 14 to 17 are at least 20 years old, and 27 percent are at least 5 years older (Lindberg et al., 1997; Taylor et al., 1997). Nevertheless, many male teenagers also become fathers. Only about half of these fathers spend any time with their children and only one-fifth contribute money (Rangarajan & Gleason, 1998). Men who do poorly in school, lack long-term goals, come from impoverished backgrounds, and engage in other socially deviant behaviors (e.g., drugs) have the most irresponsible attitudes about reproduction. In fact, many of these men consider getting a woman pregnant a sign of masculinity. This attitude is more common among African-American men than among whites (Marsiglio, 1993a). Another problem is that many men take no responsibility if they consider their partner an acquaintance (as opposed to a girlfriend): Oftentimes, "girls think they have boyfriends. Boys think they have acquaintances" (L. Smith, 1993).

> "I am an admitted 'serial monogomist.' One of these types of relationships led to pregnancy right after high school. . . . My ex and I no longer speak to each other and he has never been a part of his own child's life (by choice)." (from the author's files)

Margulies/*The Journal*, VA/Rothco.

The teens most likely to have babies are generally the ones least prepared to take care of them—teens who are already living in poverty and with low educational aspirations (Coley & Chase-Lansdale, 1998). The cost to the nation is staggering. The U.S. government spends over $30 billion a year on welfare support for families started by teenagers (Center for Population Options, 1992). The cost would be even higher if it were not for publicly funded expenditures for contraceptive services. But the cost to the individual can be even more tragic. Teenage mothers are much more likely to have high-risk babies with health problems, problems often made worse because many pregnant teens never seek prenatal care (Hein et al., 1990). As a result, the United States has one of the highest infant mortality rates among developed countries (Singh & Yu,1995). Some of these problems can be attributed to the socioeconomic status of teen mothers. In addition to not being economically or physically ready to have children, teenagers are generally not emotionally ready to have children either. Children of teenage parents are much more likely than other children to be victims of child abuse and neglect (Goerge & Lee, 1997).

Being an unwed teenage mother does not guarantee that she will be locked into poverty with no job skills and little education, but most will experience long periods of hardship because of early childbearing (see F. Coley & Chase-Lansdale, 1998, for a review). Girls born to teenage mothers are even more likely to experience economic dependence and inability to escape poverty (Horwitz et al., 1991). The children of teen parents who later become young teen parents themselves often report that they experienced emotional deprivation at an early age, have had significant depressive symptoms, and "seek emotional closeness through sexual activity and early parenthood" (Horwitz et al., 1991).

Perhaps the most unfortunate part of all this is that the high rate of births to teens continues to occur in a day and age when highly effective means of birth control are available. This was not always the case. The prevailing attitude toward sex during Victorian times and throughout the history of the Christian church, as you recall, was that it was for procreation only, and thus birth control was opposed. In many states it was against the law to sell or distribute contraceptive devices. As a result, women generally had several or even many children, and many poor women who worried that they could not feed another child died during crude and often self-attempted abortions. It was as a result of watching one of these poor tenement women die from a self-induced abortion attempt in 1912 that Margaret Sanger gave up a nursing career and founded Planned Parenthood. The work of the reformers and the changing attitude about the role of women in general gradually had their effect.

Two-thirds of Americans surveyed in a 1936 Gallup poll said that information about birth control should be available to those who wanted it. The last of the state laws prohibiting the sale of contraceptive devices to married couples was finally repealed in 1965 (by a U.S. Supreme Court decision in the case of *Griswold v. Connecticut*), and laws preventing the sale to unmarried persons were struck down in 1972 (*Eisenstadt V. Baird*). By then, 81 percent of the public approved of the availability of birth control information. The birth control pill was introduced in 1960, but until recently condoms and other birth control devices that did not require a visit to the doctor were kept behind the counter in

Figure 6–1 Margaret Sanger, a founder of the birth control movement, was forbidden to talk about birth control, so in 1929 she voluntarily had her mouth taped and wrote about the subject on a blackboard.

drugstores, which inhibited many people from purchasing them. Today, male and female condoms, contraceptive sponges, and spermicides are sold openly, yet the number of teenage pregnancies continues to be high.

PERSONAL REFLECTIONS
Are you prepared at the present time to assume the responsibilities of being a parent? Why or why not? How would your life change if you or your partner were pregnant (consider your relationship, finances, career goals, etc.)?

WORLD POPULATION

In addition to personal reasons, there are other reasons why a society as a whole should practice birth control. Imagine two shipwrecked couples on a small South Pacific island in the year 1700. The island has a small supply of fresh water, some animal life but no predators, edible vegetation, and a small amount of land suitable for farming. For these four people, the island is Utopia—it has more than they will ever need. Each couple is fertile and has four children (probably an underestimate without birth control), and the children in turn pair off in their late teens to form four couples, each of which has four more children. Thus, in each generation there would be twice as many people as in the previous generation. If there were no accidental deaths and the people lived until age 65, there would be at least 224 people living on the island by the year 1800. For those people, the island is no longer Utopia. The animals have all been killed, the edible plant life is consumed within days of becoming ripe, and there is not nearly enough farmland to support a population of this size. What's worse, even the water supply must be rationed, and the population continues to increase. Soon there will be large-scale death from starvation and dehydration.

Wildlife experts are used to seeing this happen to populations of deer in areas where there are no predators, but is this scenario too far-fetched for humans? Consider that the world is really just an island. We have a limited amount of natural resources, including water. Should they become exhausted, we would find ourselves in the same situation as the inhabitants of our hypothetical island. The world population has been increasing at an alarming rate (see Figure 6–2), and it is now more than 25 times greater than in the year A.D. 1. It was about 800 million in 1760, reached 5 billion in 1987, and reached 6 billion at the end of 1999. Each year, 78 million people are born. The United Nations (Population Division) es-

timates that the total world population could rise to 9 billion to 10 billion people by 2050.

Many experts predict that unless this world population explosion is substantially slowed, the end result will be widespread starvation. Already, half the children born today are at poverty levels. Robert Repetto of the World Resources Institute estimates that if the present population doubles, all of the current cropland in the world would have to produce 2.8 tons of grain per acre per year, equivalent to the most productive American farms. Read again the warning by Paul and Anne Ehrlich, authors of *The Population Explosion* (1990), at the beginning of the chapter. They add:

We realize that religious and cultural opposition to birth control exists throughout the world; but we believe that people simply do not understand the choice that such opposition implies. Today, anyone opposing birth control is unknowingly voting to have the human population size controlled by a massive increase in early deaths.

David Pimentel (1998) of Cornell University adds that unless something is done soon, by 2100 "12 billion miserable humans will suffer a difficult life on Earth."

In some parts of the world, mass starvation is no longer hypothetical, but already a reality. Most recently, attention has been focused on Ethiopia and Somalia,

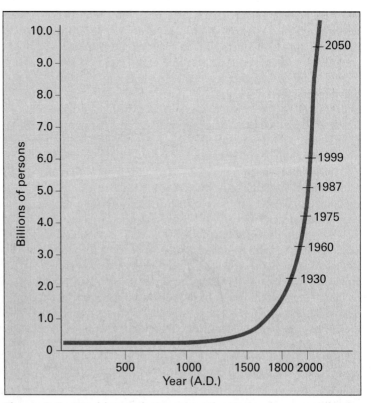

Figure 6–2 World population growth. Notice how rapidly the world population has increased since the beginning of the 20th century.

where thousands of people have died of starvation because the land can no longer support the population. The sight on TV of little children dying a slow, horrible death is not pretty, but it is not just happening in Somalia and Ethiopia. It is happening in many other parts of Africa and in Asia; and in Brazil alone an estimated 2 million children have been abandoned by their parents. In India, infanticide (the killing of children, especially newborn girls) is not uncommon (Cohen, 2000).

China, the world's most populated country with about 1 billion people, has much less farmland than the United States. There is only one-fifth of an acre of land per person, which is just enough to provide food for one person. Any additional increase in the population will mean starvation for millions. As a result, the Chinese government was forced in 1982 to order mandatory birth control. For the next 100 years, couples will be told not to have more than one child. To oversee this policy, each district and town has a family planning council. Birth control courses are given before marriage. Newlywed couples then sign a contract limiting themselves to one child, and those who adhere to the policy earn "model worker" status in their factory, which entitles them to many benefits, including bonus income and free education for their children. Factories with 100 percent participation become "model factories." Older women are assigned to "look after" small groups of women in each neighborhood. If a second pregnancy is detected, tremendous pressure from community leaders is put on the couple to have an abortion and sterilization. As a result of this policy, China's fertility rate has fallen dramatically from about 6 children per woman in 1970 to about 1.8–2.1 children in 1997 (Attané, 2000).

These measures seem very harsh in terms of our own standards of freedom, and with an abundance of farmland in America it is hard for us to imagine such a thing ever happening here. During the "baby boom" years (following the end of World War II through the mid-1950s), there was an average of 3.5 babies born to each American couple. If that rate had continued, the population of the United States today would have been around 500 million, nearly twice what it actually is. Just imagine what the congestion and pollution would have been like. Would our natural resources have been strained? I do not know, but our life-style could not possibly have been as good as it is today.

What prevented the United States from having this population explosion? Quite simply, it was the use of birth control, which has made it possible for people to limit the number of children they have. The birth rate started to fall in the early 1960s, and by 1970 the average American woman had 2.0 births in her lifetime, the same as it is today (Ventura et al., 1999). As a

result, the population of the United States has stabilized, with only a small increase due to immigration. The fertility rate is now below the replacement level in 20 developed countries, and as low as 1.3 in southern and central Europe (Foster, 2000). In eastern and western Africa, on the other hand, the fertility rate is 6.2, and 3.8 to 4.2 in western and south-central Asia (Potts, 2000).

Stop and think about it for a minute: Would you really like to see us in a situation where our population doubles every generation? We might be able to continue to live comfortably during our lifetime, but what would life be like for our grandchildren?

EVALUATING DIFFERENT BIRTH CONTROL METHODS

If all fertile couples practiced unprotected sexual intercourse (no pills, condoms, diaphragms, etc.) and did not abstain from having sex at any time of the month (no fertility awareness methods), 85 to 90 percent of them would conceive within a year. In judging the effectiveness of the various birth control techniques, we need to know how many couples using a particular contraceptive method would conceive in a year's time. There are actually two figures here that are important: the perfect-use pregnancy rate and the typical-use pregnancy rate. Older studies use the term "failure rates." A failure rate is not the same as pregnancy rate, and it has been recommended that the term not be used (Steiner et al., 1996), but I occasionally will have to use it when referring to results of older studies.

For a particular contraceptive technique, the **perfect-use pregnancy rate** is the percentage of couples who would conceive if all couples who were using the technique used it consistently and properly. The **typical-use pregnancy rate** is usually higher than the perfect-use rate because not all people use a method consistently or properly. The birth control pill, for example, was designed to be taken every day, but not all women remember to do so, and this results in some pregnancies. Although all the birth control techniques that you will learn about are better than using nothing at all, some are more effective than others. Ideally, a couple wishing to postpone or prevent pregnancy would like their birth control technique to be 100 percent effective (zero pregnancies in a year's time). Some contraceptive methods approach this, but others do not.

perfect-use pregnancy rate For a particular birth control technique, the percentage of pregnancies during the first year of use by couples who use the technique properly and consistently.

typical-use pregnancy rate For a particular birth control technique, the percentage of pregnancies during the first year of use by all couples who use the technique, regardless of whether or not they use it properly or consistently.

Pregnancy rates are almost always stated in terms of the number of pregnancies that occur *in the first year of use* for every 100 couples using the technique (see Table 6–2). Although I will follow that tradition, most young people want to have several years of sexual relations before their first planned birth. If their chosen contraceptive technique has a pregnancy rate of 5 percent in the first year of use, what are the chances of an unplanned pregnancy if they continue to use the technique over a much longer time period?

Estimates differ, depending on whether one assumes that the pregnancy rate remains constant or declines over time, but even the most conservative estimates show that over a long period of time the risk of pregnancy is high for most contraceptive techniques (Ross, 1989). For a technique with a first-year pregnancy rate of only 5 percent, for example, the 10-year pregnancy rate is between 23 percent (this assumes that the risk will have declined to zero by the end of that time span) and 40 percent (this assumes that the risk remains constant). For a contraceptive technique with a first-year pregnancy rate of 10 percent, the

TABLE 6–2

NUMBER OF PREGNANCIES PER 100 WOMEN DURING THE FIRST YEAR OF CONTINUOUS USE

Method	Perfect Use	Typical Use
Male sterilization	0.1	0.15
Female sterilization	0.2	0.4
Norplant (5-year implant)	0.2	0.2
Implanon (3-year implant)	0.1	0.1
Depo-Provera (3-month shot)	0.3	0.3
Lunelle (1-month shot)	0.1	0.1
Combination birth control pill	0.1	3.0
Progestin only (mini) pill	0.5	4.0
IUD (copper)	0.8	1.0
IUD (Progestasert)	1.5	2.0
Male condom (with spermicide)	<1.0	12.0
Male condom (without spermicide)	3.0	12.0
Female condom	5.0	21.0
Diaphragm (with spermicide)	6.0	15.0+
Cervical cap (for women who have not given birth)	8.0–10.0	18.0
Contraceptive sponge (for women who have not given birth)	9.0–10.0	17.0–20.00
Spermicides alone	6.0	26.0
Withdrawal	4.0	18.0
Fertility awareness:		
Calendar	9.0	25.0
BBT	3.2	25.0
Billings	3.2	20.0
Emergency contraception (Yuzpe)		25.0
Emergency contraception (levonorgestrel)		<10.0
No method	85.0	85.0

Source: Various sources cited in text.

10-year pregnancy rate is between 40 and 66 percent. Some of the contraceptive techniques that we will consider have a first-year pregnancy rate of 20 percent. Over a 10-year time period, the chance of having an unplanned pregnancy while using these techniques is between 67 and 90 percent. Thus, while contraceptive methods reduce the number of unplanned pregnancies, most are far from being 100 percent effective over a long period of time.

In evaluating birth control techniques, we must look at more than just their effectiveness. Some techniques are more suitable for certain subgroups of the population than others. The birth control pill is highly effective, but it is not recommended for women with diabetes or cardiovascular problems, for example. Some people only wish to postpone pregnancy and therefore require a reversible technique (i.e., one that can be discontinued at any time), while others wish to totally prevent any more pregnancies and require a permanent technique. Factors such as

spontaneity and aesthetics sometimes play a role, and some people may be looking for simultaneous protection against sexually transmitted diseases. In many cases, religious beliefs must be considered. I will provide as much information about each of the techniques as possible, pro and con, so that whenever you decide to use birth control, you will be able to decide which method is best for you.

PERSONAL REFLECTIONS
If you are having sexual relations, what do you do about contraception?

CONTRACEPTIVE MYTHS

"In high school I heard that if a male drinks Mountain Dew or Surge cold drinks they would have a low sperm count and could have sex and not get the girl pregnant."

There is a lot of peer pressure to engage in sex during the adolescent years. In addition to the pressure to conform, teens are often given a great deal of misinformation about contraception by friends and potential partners. Some of the information is so incorrect that it can be considered myth. For example, some of you may have heard that if a man drinks Mountain Dew before sex it reduces his sperm count, or that if a woman douches with Coca-Cola or ice water afterwards she cannot get pregnant. How many of you were told, "You can't get pregnant the first time you have sex" or "You can't get pregnant if you don't kiss"? Well, these stories are just not true. A girl is capable of reproduction as soon as she starts having menstrual cycles (recall that in the United States, the first menstrual period occurs at an average age of 12½). This is evidence that she is ovulating, i.e., producing eggs. Some of you may have been told that a woman cannot get pregnant if she is on top or if she has sex while standing up (because of gravity), but these statements are also untrue. It is also not true that a woman must have an orgasm during sex in order to get pregnant. No doubt there are other stories that you have heard, but unless they are included in the remainder of the chapter (i.e., they have a basis in fact), chances are they just are not true.

RELATIVELY INEFFECTIVE METHODS

One of the most popular ways in which young people try to prevent pregnancy is **withdrawal (coitus interruptus),** where the man withdraws his penis just before reaching orgasm and ejaculates outside his partner's vagina. In recent years the use of withdrawal has decreased as use of condoms has increased, but 13 percent of high school students still rely on it (Everett et al., 2000). It sounds logical, for if the man does not ejaculate in the woman's vagina, there will be no sperm there—right? Wrong! The Cowper's glands, you recall, secrete a few drops of fluid before a man reaches orgasm, and this fluid can contain stray sperm. Most studies find that nearly 20 out of every 100 couples using the withdrawal method conceive within the first year of use (see Hatcher et al., 1998).

"An ex-boyfriend of mine thought if he pulled out before 'he came,' then a girl wouldn't get pregnant. He was shocked when he found out his current girlfriend was pregnant. He claimed he couldn't be the father because he didn't 'come'." (from the author's files)

Withdrawal is better than nothing, but it is ineffective compared to some other types of contraception. What's more, withdrawal may not be very physically or emotionally satisfying to the man or his partner. Even in cases where a couple does not actually begin intercourse, if the man ejaculates on or near his partner's vaginal opening (during heavy petting, for example), it is possible that some sperm could get into the vaginal secretions and make their way into the vagina.

Some women believe that **douching** is an effective method of birth control.

"I was told that douching and/or using the bathroom right after sex would get rid of the sperm and you would not get pregnant." (from the author's files)

Again, it sounds logical. If you wash out the contents of the vagina, there should be no sperm. The problem is that no matter how quickly a woman douches after intercourse, some sperm will have already made it into the cervix. In fact, the pressure caused by douching can actually force sperm into the cervical opening. Over 40 out of every 100 couples who use douching as their only means of birth control will conceive in a year's time. In addition, recall from Chapter 2 that frequent douching can increase the likelihood of pelvic inflammatory disease and also ectopic pregnancy (Zhang et al., 1997).

It is commonly believed that **breast-feeding** a newborn baby protects a woman from getting pregnant. Breast-feeding has been called "nature's contraceptive." There is some truth to this. The sucking response of the baby on the mother's nipple inhibits the release of gonadotropin hormones (FSH and LH) from the pituitary, thus preventing normal menstrual cycles and ovulation. Before modern contraceptive techniques were introduced, breast-feeding was the major factor that determined the length of the interval between pregnancies. Studies in rural areas of China and India have found that when breast-feeding is frequent and prolonged, the birth interval is 5 to 10 months longer than for women who do not breast-feed (Jain, 1969). Two recent large-scale studies found that if a mother is fully breast-feeding *and is not menstruating*, the chance of pregnancy during the first 6 months is less than 2 percent (Labbok et al., 1997; World Health Organization, 1999). *The risk of ovulation rises if a woman continues breast-feeding beyond 6 months.*

The problem is that for this method to work, the baby must be fed "on demand," that is, whenever it wants to feed, at any hour of the day or

withdrawal (coitus interruptus) Withdrawal of the man's penis from his partner's vagina before ejaculation in order to avoid conception. It is sometimes ineffective because fluids from the Cowper's glands may contain sperm.

douching A feminine hygiene practice of rinsing out the vagina, usually with specifically prepared solutions.

breast-feeding In reference to contraception, the sucking response by a baby on the mother's nipple that inhibits release of follicle-stimulating hormone, thus preventing ovulation.

night. There can be no substituting a bottle (not even with water), and even a pacifier must be avoided as it might satisfy the baby's need to suck. Breast-feeding has been shown to work in less developed countries, where women remain at home all the time or can breast-feed in public (Jain, 1969), but the typical-use pregnancy rate in the United States (where most women cannot feed on demand) is very high (Hatcher et al., 1998). In other words, American couples who rely on this method quite often have babies 10 to 12 months apart.

ABSTAINING FROM SEX

The most effective way to avoid an unwanted pregnancy is to abstain from sex. Individuals who make this decision can be 100 percent worry free about getting pregnant or getting someone pregnant.

What about sex education programs that teach abstinence-only as birth control? In 1996 the U.S. government provided $250 million to the states to start abstinence-only programs. This approach is popular with many Americans, most of whom believe that unplanned pregnancies are a big problem and that a decline in moral standards has contributed to the problem (Mauldon & Delbanco, 1997). But how effective are these programs? California has led the way in implementing abstinence-only programs. The largest statewide program, called Education Now and Babies Later, encouraged preteens to abstain from sex until they were older. Despite the good intentions of its founders and teachers, evaluation of the program has found it to have no influence on teens' sexual decisions (Kirby et al., 1997; see Roan, 1995). "Abstinence-plus" programs that teach abstinence *and* contraception, on the other hand, have often proved to be very effective in reducing teenage pregnancy rates (e.g., NIH Consensus, 1997; Tiezzi et al., 1997). Recall from Chapter 1 that most teens say they do not have enough information about birth control and that what information they do receive comes too late (Kaiser Family Foundation, 1996).

Some comparisons with other countries might be helpful here. Denmark, for example, has comprehensive sexuality education in its schools. Danish teenagers become sexually active at as young an age as American teens (half by age 17), but the vast majority use contraception, and the teenage birth rate in Denmark is among the lowest in the world (Singh & Darroch, 2000; Wielandt & Knudsen, 1997). Switzerland recently promoted condoms for teens to combat AIDS. Condom use increased dramatically and did not lead to any major changes in number of sexual partners or frequency of sex (Dubois-Arber et al., 1997).

fertility awareness methods Methods of birth control that attempt to prevent conception by having a couple abstain from sexual intercourse during the woman's ovulation.

Although abstinence-only programs have not proven to be very successful, it remains true that individuals who choose to abstain will avoid unwanted pregnancies. Apparently, more teens are, in fact, making that choice. Results of recent national surveys show that there has been a decline in the number of teenagers engaging in sexual intercourse (Centers for Disease Control and Prevention, 2000b; *Newsweek*, 2000).

FERTILITY AWARENESS: ABSTAINING FROM SEX DURING OVULATION

The **fertility awareness method** (also called the *rhythm method* or *natural family planning*) may be the only method acceptable to many of you because of your religious beliefs. These are the only birth control methods that are not opposed by the Catholic Church and evangelical Protestant denominations. There are three variations to this method, but all are based on predicting when ovulation occurs. *A woman can only get pregnant when an egg is present during the first 24 hours or so after ovulation.* After that, the egg is overly ripe and a sperm cannot fertilize it. Rhythm methods involve the identification of "safe days" in a woman's menstrual cycle and the abstinence of sex during the "unsafe period." It would be almost impossible for a woman who is not having regular menstrual cycles to use these techniques. For those who do cycle regularly, they require a great deal of training and motivation.

CALENDAR METHOD

Sperm can live in a Fallopian tube for several days. Although most do not live for more than 3 days, some can live for as long as 5 days. Wilcox, Weinberg, and Baird (1995) calculated the following probabilities of conception (in relation to the day of ovulation):

Day	Probability
−5	0.10
−4	0.16
−3	0.14
−2	0.27
−1	0.31
0	0.33

Even if you do have intercourse on the day of ovulation, it results in pregnancy only 12 percent of the time (Steiner et al., 1998).

In a woman with perfect 28-day cycles, ovulation would be at midcycle, and the safest time to have sex to avoid pregnancy would be during menstruation (yet 20 percent of college women in a recent Gallup poll believed it was dangerous to have sex during menstruation). The problem is that few women have cycles of the same length month after month. It is normal for a woman's cycle to differ in length over time by several days (see Chapter 3). Most of the differences are due to fluctuations in the preovulatory phase of the cycle. Ovulation generally occurs about 14 days before the start of menstruation, but it doesn't do any good to count back 14 days from the start of menstruation (it is too late by then, anyway). We need to know when ovulation is going to occur.

So the first thing a woman must do to use this method is to keep track of the length of her menstrual cycles for a minimum of eight cycles (more would be better). Let us take a hypothetical example of a woman who has kept track of 10 cycles and found that although her average cycle length was 28 days, she had one that was only 24 days and another that lasted 32 days. The **calendar method** uses a formula to calculate the unsafe period. Subtract 18 from the length of the shortest cycle (24 − 18 = 6) and 11 from the length of the longest cycle (32 − 11 = 21). The unsafe period would thus be from days 6 through 21 (by the numbering system explained in Chapter 3; day 1 is the start of menstruation). This is a period of over 2 weeks that the woman and her partner must abstain from having sexual intercourse. If the woman had had a cycle shorter than 24 days or longer than 32 days (which is not unusual), the period of abstinence would have been even longer.

The calendar method has proved to be very unreliable, with some studies reporting a typical-use failure rate as high as 40 to 45 percent in one year. Most studies report that the typical-use failure rate is about 25 percent per year (Hatcher et al., 1998; Trussell et al., 1990). The calendar method has been called the Russian roulette of birth control: The losers get pregnant right away, and the winners get pregnant later and worry in the meantime. In addition to severely testing human motivation, all it takes for the method to fail is just one cycle that is shorter or longer than previously observed.

There are two variations of the rhythm method that use biological markers to better identify the time of ovulation.

BASAL BODY TEMPERATURE METHOD

A woman's basal (resting) body temperature rises by a few tenths of one degree Fahrenheit 24 to 72 hours after ovulation. In the **basal body temperature method,** couples abstain from having sexual intercourse from the end of menstruation until about 4 days after a temperature rise is noted. The basal body temperature should be taken at the same time every day, preferably first thing in the morning (before going to the bathroom, eating, drinking, or smoking). Note that this method still involves a long

period of abstinence, so it again severely tests human willpower. Even those women who attempt to use it properly often get pregnant, for its success depends on being able to detect a very small temperature increase (and, more importantly, is based on the assumption that the increase in body temperature is due to ovulation). If no increase is noted, a couple must go an entire cycle without sexual relations. What's more, small temperature increases of a few tenths of a degree are often caused by low-grade infections that we are not even aware of, by stress, or by other factors. Some women have a history of irregular basal body temperature. The typical-use failure rate is about 25 pregnancies per every 100 couples per year (Hatcher et al., 1998; Trussell et al., 1990).

BILLINGS METHOD (CERVICAL MUCUS OR OVULATION METHOD)

The fertility awareness method that is most widely used today is the **Billings method,** which attempts to pinpoint the time of ovulation by noting changes in the consistency of a woman's **cervical mucus.** It is named after two Australian doctors who developed it (Billings et al., 1974). Mucus is discharged from the cervix throughout a woman's menstrual cycle, and its appearance changes from white (or cloudy) and sticky to clear and slippery (like that of an egg white) a day or two before ovulation. Until recently, the only way to note this change was a finger test, that is, placing a finger in the vagina and then examining the mucus. Women who use this method should not douche, for that makes it more difficult to notice the changes in consistency of the mucus. A couple is instructed to abstain from sexual intercourse from the end of menstruation until 4 days after the mucus has changed consistency.

If you wish to use this method, do not rely on the preceding simple instructions. There are organizations that will give you more detailed instructions. Be warned, however, that some of these are advocate organizations (i.e., they strongly favor this form of birth control over others) that may exaggerate the effectiveness of the Billings method. Theoretically, it has only a 3 percent pregnancy rate (Dominik et al., 2000), but the typical-use failure rate is much higher. The Alan Guttmacher Institute reported that the accidental failure rate for married women is 16 percent, but most studies have found about 20 pregnancies per year for every 100 couples using this method (Hatcher et al., 1998; Trussell et al., 1990). Similar high failure rates obtained in carefully designed studies done in five

calendar method A fertility awareness method of birth control that attempts to determine a woman's fertile period by use of a mathematical formula.

basal body temperature The temperature of the body while resting. It rises slightly after ovulation.

Billings method A fertility awareness method of birth control in which changes in the consistency and quantity of cervical mucus are used to tell when ovulation has occurred.

cervical mucus The slimy secretion of mucous membranes located inside the cervix.

different countries led the World Health Organization to conclude that the Billings method was "relatively ineffective in general use for preventing pregnancy" (Seventh Annual Report, 1978; see also World Health Organization, 1981).

Advocate groups generally dismiss these high failure rates as due to improper instructions and unmotivated participants (i.e., user failures due to people having sex during unsafe periods). Most of the pregnancies do, in fact, result from conscious deviations from the rules (World Health Organization, 1981), no doubt because the average period of abstinence is 17 days per cycle. A later study from a World Health Organization clinical trial indicated that the first-year failure rate is, in fact, only 3.1 percent during *perfect use if women also abstain from sex during stress*, but 86.4 percent during imperfect use (Trussell & Grummer-Strawn, 1990). Thus, the Billings method can be very effective if used perfectly, but perfect compliance is difficult for many couples who desire sexual intercourse.

Some couples combine the basal body temperature and Billings methods (along with other signs of ovulation, such as ovulatory pain) to enhance the effectiveness of these fertility awareness methods. This is often referred to as the *sympto-thermal method* and has a lower pregnancy rate than any of the other methods used alone. However, one of the problems with any method based on changes in cervical mucus is that perhaps as many as one-third of all women do not have the typical mucus pattern. Even for those who do, the finger test is obviously not very scientific. Not surprisingly, only about 2 percent of all American women use fertility awareness for birth control (Hatcher et al., 1998).

There is real hope for those who want to use the fertility awareness method. Chemical testing kits that will more accurately pinpoint the time of ovulation may soon be available in stores for home use. Because sperm can live in the Fallopian tubes for 2 to 5 days, the chemical tests would have to predict ovulation at least 5 days in advance to be useful as a contraceptive technique (there are already some products available that predict ovulation 12 to 36 hours in advance, but these are useful only for couples who want to conceive). A method that measures hormones called PERSONA is presently being tested by an English Company (Severy & Spieler, 2000).

SPERMICIDES: SUBSTANCES THAT KILL SPERM

spermicides Chemicals that kill sperm. In most products, the chemical is nonoxynol-9.

Spermicides are chemicals that kill sperm (nonoxynol-9 or octoxinol-9). They are sold in a variety of forms. Spermicidal foams, jellies, creams, and film (VCF, or *vaginal contraceptive film,* is a square of film that is placed over the cervix) help hold sperm-killing chemicals in the vagina against the cervix and simultaneously act as a barrier to sperm. Suppositories and tablets are also available. Specific instructions differ for each type of spermicide, but all of them must be placed in the back of the vagina shortly before sexual intercourse begins. They lose their effectiveness over time, so new spermicide must be inserted shortly before each time a woman has intercourse. Be very careful not to confuse spermicidal products with feminine hygiene products. They are often displayed together in drugstores, so if you want the contraceptive material, be sure that the package says "spermicide" or specifies that the product "kills sperm."

Spermicides came on the market before companies were required to prove the effectiveness of new drugs. In 1996 the Food and Drug Administration threatened to make manufacturers prove the effectiveness of spermicides. To date, surveys have found the typical-use rate to be about 26 pregnancies per 100 couples per year (Hatcher et al., 1998), but many of these pregnancies are due to improper or inconsistent use (user rather than method failures). One survey found that when spermicides are used consistently and properly, the failure rate can be as low as 6 percent (Harrison & Rosenfield, 1996). However, it is believed (but not proven) that foams and suppositories are more effective than jellies and creams. Women should consider using spermicides in combination with a blockade or barrier method (diaphragm or condom). Some brands of condoms already contain a spermicide.

In addition to their contraceptive benefit, spermicides containing *nonoxynol-9* reduce the risk of contracting gonorrhea and chlamydia by killing the bacteria that cause them. The use of spermicides may also reduce the risk of cervical cancer, probably by helping to kill human papillomavirus (see Chapter 5). However, there are concerns that spermicides may increase the risk of catching HIV from an infected partner (see Box 6–A).

On the negative side, several studies have found that spermicides containing nonoxynol-9 (including condoms with spermicide) increase the risk of urinary tract infection (e.g. Hooton et al., 1996). However, another study found that condoms with spermicide reduced the risk compared to unlubricated condoms (Foxman et al., 1997). Even if it should turn out to be true that spermicides increase the risk of urinary tract infections in women, avoiding spermicides for this reason must be weighed against the risk of unwanted pregnancy and exposure to sexually transmitted diseases. Although there were some early concerns, studies have shown that spermicides do not cause birth defects (Einarson et al., 1990).

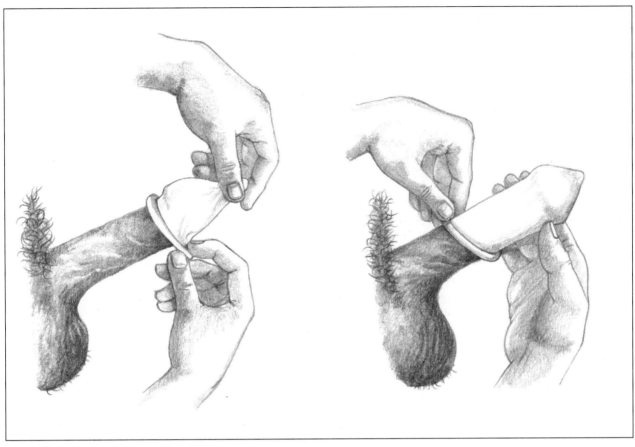

Figure 6–3   Use of the condom.

Most college women rate spermicides as one of their least preferred types of contraception (Sarvela et al., 1992). The most common complaint is that, like the condom and the diaphragm, inserting the spermicidal material just before intercourse interferes with the spontaneity of sexual relations and detracts from the mood. Others complain that spermicides are messy or detract from oral-genital sex. A few people (1 in 20) find that spermicides burn or irritate the vagina or penis. However, as a backup to barrier techniques, and because of their antiviral and antibacterial activity, spermicides have advantages that for many women may outweigh the disadvantages.

BARRIER METHODS: PREVENTING SPERM FROM MEETING EGG

Barrier methods of birth control are designed to prevent pregnancy by placing a blockade between the penis and cervix so that sperm cannot reach the egg if ovulation has occurred. Thus, these methods do not require you to abstain from sexual intercourse, but they may interfere with the spontaneity of sexual relations by requiring you to stop and put something on or put something in.

MALE CONDOMS

Condoms ("rubbers," "safes," or prophylactics) are thin sheaths made of latex rubber, lamb intestine, polyurethane, or synthetic elastomers that fit over the penis and thus trap the sperm (see Figure 6–3). They also serve as a barrier between the man's membranes and woman's membranes, and therefore *are also highly effective in preventing the spread of sexually transmitted diseases* (SIECUS, 1998). In fact, condoms were originally invented for this purpose in the 1500s. A French writer in 1761 described condoms as "armor against love, gossamer against infection." Mass production of condoms became possible in the mid-1800s with the discovery of how to make rubber more flexible and durable. Today, condoms are the most frequently used method of birth control in Japan, England, and some northern European countries, but for a variety of reasons (to be discussed later), American men have been reluctant to use them.

Condoms come rolled up, dry or lubricated, and until

barrier (blockade) method General term for contraceptive methods that block the passage of sperm.

condom For men, a thin sheath made of latex rubber, lamb intestine, or polyurethane that fits over the penis. For women, a polyurethane intravaginal pouch held in place by two flexible rings. Condoms are effective as contraception and for prevention of sexually transmitted diseases.

recently they came in only one size. However, there is now a large size for men who find the usual type too tight. (American manufacturers had been reluctant to make different-sized condoms for fear of insulting a man's ego—can you imagine a man asking for a small condom?)

As a birth control technique, condoms are highly effective. They present no major health hazards and are available without a prescription. What's more, their use requires no mathematical calculations and no subjective evaluation of biological processes. There are only a few simple rules to remember:

1. Put the condom on before you start having intercourse. Otherwise, it is no more effective than withdrawal. *Unroll it on the penis; do not try to yank it on like a sock.* If the condom does not have a nipple tip, leave a little extra space at the tip of the penis to catch the ejaculate. If you are uncircumcised, pull back the foreskin while putting on the condom.
2. Hold on to the base of the condom when you are finished and withdraw. Otherwise, you might leave it and its contents in the woman's vagina.
3. Use a condom only once. If you have intercourse more than one time while having sex, use a new condom each time. Some people say that you can wash and dry them, powder them with cornstarch, and then roll them up for reuse, but they will eventually tear, so for maximal effectiveness use them only once. After all, even condoms made from animal membranes are not terribly expensive.
4. Check the expiration date. Do not store rubber condoms for long periods of time in a warm place (such as your wallet) or where they are exposed to light. This will eventually deteriorate them. Store them someplace cool, dark, and dry. Also, *do not use rubber condoms in combination with mineral oil, baby oil, vegetable oil, hand lotions, Vaseline, or other petroleum jellies,* for these, too, can damage them.

"During a recent sexual experience, my partner and I used oil from one of those fancy 'bath and body stores' for lubrication in conjunction with a condom. During intercourse, the condom disintegrated." (from the author's files)

A man should never begin intercourse until his partner is lubricating, but if additional lubricant is needed, use a water-based one (do not confuse "water-based" with "water-soluble") like K-Y Jelly or Today Personal Lubricant. Better yet, use a spermicide. (The new polyurethane condoms can be used with oil-based lubricants.)

If these very simple instructions are followed, the theoretical failure rate is only about 2 to 3 percent (SIECUS, 1998; Trussell et al., 1990). If always used with a spermicide, the theoretical failure rate is less than 1 percent (Kestelman & Trussell, 1991). When used with a spermicide, condoms are the most effective of the nonprescription birth control techniques. However, the typical-use rate is about 12 pregnancies per 100 couples per year. Most of these pregnancies are due to inconsistent use, and teens are more likely than older persons to use condoms inconsistently.

Not all pregnancies are due to user failures. *Consumer Reports* found that several brands of condoms failed its laboratory strength tests. Many brands, however, were sufficiently strong (May, 1995). Several studies have found that during human use, the breakage rate is about 1–3 percent during vaginal intercourse (e.g., Macaluso et al., 1999; Messiah et al., 1997), but others have reported breakage rates of over 5 percent (Trussell et al., 1992). The breakage rate may be considerably higher during anal intercourse (Silverman & Gross, 1997). It must be noted that condom failure due to breakage is most common among men who do not use condoms regularly (Messiah et al., 1997), or who have experienced condom breakage before (Spruyt et al., 1998). Both of these facts are indicators that some men are not putting them on properly. The use of two condoms during sex reduces the breakage rate to near zero (Rugpao et al., 1997). Slippage of condoms occurs in about 1 percent of cases (Macaluso et al., 1999; Messiah et al., 1997), often due to penetration beyond the end ring or improper withdrawal (see rule 2). The breakage and slippage rates for the new polyurethane condoms are about the same as for rubber condoms (Rosenberg et al., 1996).

Condom use by teenagers increased dramatically during the early and mid-1990s, but still only a minority use them consistently during intercourse (Piccinino & Mosher, 1998; Sonenstein et al., 1998).

If condoms are so effective, why aren't all sexually active men using them? Here are some lines that women in my class have told me that men commonly use to keep from using a condom (Oncale & King, 2001):

"I promise I will not come in you."

"I will pull out before I nut."

"It doesn't feel the same."

"I can't feel anything with it on."

"I don't have a disease."

"If you're not having sex with anybody else, why should I use it? If you trust me, you wouldn't make me use it."

Before they have ever tried one, most men have heard many times that condoms will reduce sensitivity. Their preconceived notions probably exaggerate the problem. Condoms will reduce a man's sensitivity—slightly—but *Consumer Reports* (1989) found that many men eventually find this to be something positive because it makes sex last longer. The new polyurethane condoms are only half as thick as rubber condoms and transmit heat better than rubber. Men generally prefer these to rubber condoms in regard to comfort, sensitivity, lack of smell, and natural feel (Rosenberg et al., 1996).

Others complain that they are allergic to rubber. About 1 to 3 percent of men and women are allergic (Hatcher et al., 1998), but again, some condoms are made of natural animal membranes or polyurethane. Still others complain about the loss of spontaneity, that it is a nuisance to stop and put a condom on in the middle of having sex. How long does it take to put on a condom? The answer is, only a few seconds. These reasons for not wearing condoms are in many cases just excuses. The real reason many men won't use condoms is that they are too embarrassed to go into a store and purchase them.

> "During high school, I was actually embarrassed to buy condoms. I only would get them in those bathroom machines. Perhaps if they were discretely available, then more teens would buy them." (from the author's files)

A few women in my classes have said that they have talked a partner out of using a condom, but the large majority have to talk partners into using them. By the way, here are some lines that women say they have used successfully to get a male partner to use a condom (Oncale & King, 2001):

> "No condom, no sex."
>
> "If you choose not to use a condom, you're choosing not to have sex with me."
>
> "If you don't use one, you won't get none."
>
> "Boy, I'm not having your baby."
>
> "It's not that I don't trust you; I don't trust who you've been with."
>
> "There will be no action in the ballpark until the player with the bat puts his glove on."

However, if a man refuses to use condoms or get a vasectomy (usually done only on older men who want no more children), this generally means that his female partner must assume the responsibility for birth control. In fact, 40 to 50 percent of condoms are purchased by women today. Putting on a condom takes less time than putting in a diaphragm or cervical cap, and it isn't as messy as most vaginally used spermicides. The latter three must be purchased at a store just like condoms, and use of a diaphragm requires that a woman have a pelvic exam. Although many men may complain about loss of spontaneity and reduced sensi-

tivity, these are just minor annoyances compared to the side effects often associated with use of the pill or an IUD. Whatever excuses may be used, there is no excuse for not using a condom if the only alternative is unprotected intercourse that may result in unwanted pregnancy or sexually transmitted diseases.

There are certain subgroups of the population for which I highly recommend use of the condom. If you are sexually active and have multiple partners over time, or if your partner has had multiple partners or is an intravenous drug user, you are in a high-risk category for contracting a sexually transmitted disease. STDs are in epidemic proportions today. The walls of latex condoms prevent the bacteria and viruses that cause sexually transmitted diseases from passing through them. Although skin condoms are stronger (and thus are very effective for contraception), they have small pores that may allow passage of the hepatitis B virus and the virus that causes AIDS. Thus, the latex condom is highly effective for both birth control and STD prevention (see Chapter 5 and Box 6–A for additional information).

> *PERSONAL REFLECTIONS*
> *Whose responsibility is it for birth control—your responsibility or your partner's? Why? If you answered that it is your partner's responsibility, do you think that you share any of the responsibility for the consequences of engaging in sexual intercourse?*

THE FEMALE CONDOM

It was not until 1993 that we saw the introduction of the first woman-controlled barrier method of contraception designed to give simultaneous protection against sexually transmitted diseases. The **female condom** (trade name: Reality), as it is called, is actually an intravaginal pouch—a 7-inch-long polyurethane bag that is held in place in the vagina by two flexible rings (see Figure 6–4). A woman inserts it with her fingers by pushing the closed-ended ring against the cervix, as she would a diaphragm. It is held in place by the outer ring, which fits on the outside of the vagina, partially covering the labia (see Figure 6–5). It can be inserted up to 8 hours before having sexual intercourse.

Many people are put off by the appearance of the female condom, but it is thinner than male condoms, feels softer than rubber, and transfers heat. Thus many of those who try it say that it feels more like unprotected intercourse than sex with male condoms.

> "It looked so unromantic I was sure I wasn't going to like it. Were we surprised! My boyfriend quit using male condoms now. There's a lot more friction and it feels more natural." (from the author's files)

As with the diaphragm, the female condom raises no major health concerns and does not have adverse

Figure 6–4 Male condoms (left and middle) are sold rolled and in two sizes. Female condoms (right) are intravaginal pouches that are held in place by two flexible rings.

effects on the vaginal wall. However, female condoms are considerably more expensive than male condoms and, like male condoms, are used for only one act of intercourse.

Many women know about HIV and other sexually transmitted diseases, but are nevertheless reluctant to talk about safer sex (e.g., using condoms) on dates. For those women, and for those whose partners refuse to wear a male condom, the female condom provides them with the opportunity to protect their own health (see Gollub, 2000). Studies have found that the pregnancy rate during typical use is the same as for the diaphragm, sponge, or cervical cap (Farr et al., 1994; Trussell et al., 1994). For those who use the female condom correctly, the current first-year pregnancy rate is about 5 percent or less (see Gollub, 2000).

The Reality female condom is just the first of several new female barrier techniques to reach the market. Many

diaphragm A dome-shaped rubber cup with a flexible rim that fits over the cervix and thus acts as a contraceptive device by serving as a barrier to the passage of sperm into the uterus.

others are in various stages of development (see section on future technology).

THE DIAPHRAGM

A **diaphragm** is a large, dome-shaped rubber cup with a flexible rim that fits over the cervix. It works by preventing the passage of sperm into the uterus. In biblical times, women sometimes inserted camel or crocodile dung into the back of the vagina to prevent the sperm's passage. Fortunately for today's women, the rubber cup was invented in 1882 in Germany. However, because of laws that prohibited the mailing or transportation of "obscene" materials (this included birth control devices), the diaphragm was not used in the United States until the 1920s. By the 1930s, the diaphragm was being used by one-third of all couples who practiced birth control. With the introduction of the birth control pill in 1960, the use of the diaphragm became almost nonexistent. There was a small resurgence in its popularity in the 1970s, but its use among single women declined sharply again in the 1980s. Presently, only about 1.7 percent of American women rely on it (Hatcher et al., 1998).

A woman has to be fitted for a diaphragm by a physician or health care worker (the distance between the cervix and pubic bone is measured). She will then be given a prescription for a diaphragm that fits her. It is not something you borrow from a girlfriend for a date. You may have to be refitted if your body undergoes any major changes (e.g., pregnancy or weight changes of 10 pounds or more). A woman getting her first diaphragm is also going to need instructions and coaching on how to insert it properly and quickly (see Figure 6–5). This may be one reason why there was a decrease in the use of the diaphragm, for it was easier for doctors to prescribe pills than to take time to teach a patient how to use a diaphragm.

After you have learned to insert your diaphragm properly, there are only a few simple rules to remember:

1. As with condoms, diaphragms should be used with a spermicidal jelly. This recommendation is almost universal (Hatcher et al., 1998). Spermicides are also beneficial in helping to kill bacteria and viruses that cause sexually transmitted diseases (see Box 6–A). Spread spermicidal jelly on the inside part of the diaphragm (the part in contact with the cervix) and rim before insertion.

2. Insert the diaphragm no more than 2 hours in advance of starting intercourse. Otherwise, the spermicide dissipates and adds little additional protection. For maximal effectiveness, the diaphragm should be put in immediately prior to intercourse, although this may interfere with spontaneity.

3. Leave the diaphragm in for 6 to 8 hours after intercourse to make sure that there are no more live sperm. If you have intercourse more than once

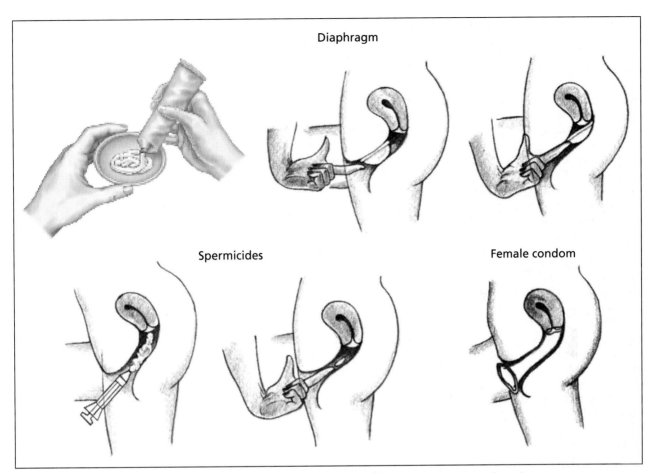

Figure 6–5 Use of the diaphragm (with spermicide), spermicides (foam and suppository), and female condom.

while having sex, place more spermicide in the vagina before each time. Do not remove the diaphragm to do this (sperm may get into the cervix while the diaphragm is removed), but instead use a plunger or some other means of application. Do not leave a diaphragm in for more than 12 hours.

When used in combination with a spermicide, the perfect-use pregnancy rate for the diaphragm is usually stated as about 6 percent per year (Harrison & Rosenfield, 1996). The typical-use pregnancy rate is about 15 percent per year (Trussell et al., 1993). Most of these pregnancies, particularly among young women, are due to inconsistent use. Some of the failures are also due to improper insertion or to the diaphragm's becoming dislodged during vigorous intercourse (this happens most often when the woman is on top).

Women with a history of urinary tract infections should not use a diaphragm, especially with a spermicide (Hooton et al., 1996). The diaphragm also should not be used during menstruation or periods of abnormal vaginal discharge. A few women may have allergies to rubber or spermicide. The most common complaint about the

diaphragm is aesthetics. Some complain that insertion is a nuisance, interfering with spontaneity, and that spermicides can be messy and detract from such sexual behaviors as oral-genital sexual relations. These complaints are not heard as often, however, in women who are sexually experienced and in a monogamous relationship.

"For years I used a diaphragm. My partners always said that they could not feel it in me and that it did not take away from their pleasure." (from the author's files)

The most important thing to consider is that the diaphragm offers an inexpensive, safe, and relatively effective means of birth control when used consistently and properly.

THE CERVICAL CAP

The **cervical cap** is another barrier device that is designed to prevent passage of sperm from the vagina into the uterus. Made of latex rubber or plastic, it is smaller and more compact than a diaphragm and

cervical cap A contraceptive device that fits over the cervix by suction, thus blocking the passage of sperm into the uterus.

Figure 6–6 The diaphragm.   The cervical cap.   The contraceptive sponge.

resembles a large rubber thimble (see Figure 6–6). *It is used with a small amount of spermicide* (for added effectiveness) and fits over the cervix by suction. Insertion and removal of the cap are more difficult than for the diaphragm, but once in place it is more comfortable than the diaphragm and can be left in for 24 hours. Women should check each time after having sexual intercourse to make sure that the cap has not been dislodged.

Although the cervical cap has been popular in England for years, it has not been used very much in this country. In fact, it did not receive approval for marketing in the United States until 1988 because of concerns about prolonged exposure to secretions trapped by the cap (including cervical mucus and menstrual flow). It has been recommended that the cap be used only by women who have normal Pap smears, because of possible adverse effects on cervical tissue (Mishell, 1989).

The first-year typical-use failure rate for the cervical cap is listed as 18 pregnancies per 100 women, but the cap offers substantially better protection to women who have not yet given birth (Trussell et al., 1993). For these women, the pregnancy rate is only 8 to 10 percent when the cervical cap is used correctly.

THE CONTRACEPTIVE SPONGE

In 1995, the manufacturer of the Today contraceptive sponge stopped producing the product because of problems in its manufacturing plant (the sponge itself was not an issue). At the time, it was the most popular over-the-counter female contraceptive technique. You may recall that the character Elaine on TV's *Seinfeld* bought all the remaining sponges in New York and then judged prospective lovers as to whether or not they were "sponge-worthy." Well, it's back! A new company is now marketing an identical sponge. The polyurethane **contraceptive sponge** is 2 inches in diameter and 1 inch thick, and

contraceptive sponge A contraceptive device made of polyurethane sponge that contains enough spermicide to be effective for 24 hours after being inserted into the vagina.

contains spermicide (nonoxynol-9). It works by blocking the cervical opening and killing sperm (see Figure 6–6).

The sponge has several advantages over the diaphragm. First, it does not require a pelvic exam. It is sold in one size without a prescription. Second, users report that it is very easy to insert. A woman simply moistens it with tap water and inserts it deep in the vagina. One side has a concave dimple that fits over the cervix to decrease the chance of it being dislodged. Last, but not least, it can be left in for 24 hours, during which period the woman may have intercourse as many times as she wishes without having to add more spermicide. The sponge has a small loop on one side for removal, and is thrown away when the woman is done. Its easy availability and ease of use are what attracted women to the sponge (Beckman et al., 1992). It must be noted, however, that a few users (about 6 percent) sometimes have difficulty removing the sponge. A few women report some mild irritation during intercourse as a result of excessive absorption of vaginal secretions.

Studies of the effectiveness of the sponge show an actual-use pregnancy rate of about 17 to 20 percent (Hatcher et al., 1998; Trussell et al., 1993), higher than for the diaphragm. The sponge is most effective in preventing pregnancy among women who have not given birth, for whom the pregnancy rate is about 9–10 percent.

BARRIER METHODS AND SPONTANEITY

All of us, I suppose, would like our sexual relations to be passionate and spontaneous, with no interruptions. Putting on a condom or inserting a diaphragm, contraceptive sponge, or spermicide does not take very long for many sexually experienced people. Some individuals even integrate the use of barrier methods (e.g., putting on a condom) as part of foreplay. But some couples occasionally take chances and have unprotected intercourse because they do not want to stop and possibly ruin the mood. This is probably the most common cause of failure for barrier methods. The contraceptive techniques that we will cover next get around this problem by not requiring anything be done at the time when you want to have sex (except getting your partner in the mood, of course).

THE IUD

The **IUD (intrauterine device)**, like the birth control pill, came on the market in the 1960s and helped to open a new era of what people thought was going to be spontaneous and worry-free sex. However, there were numerous health problems caused by a few of the early IUDs, and as a result of the subsequent lawsuits, most were taken off the market. Before we continue with this part of the story, let us examine how the IUD works.

The IUD is a small plastic and/or metal device (of various shapes) that is placed into the uterus by a physician (see Figure 6–7). This is actually a very old idea—camel drivers used to insert a stone into a female camel's uterus to prevent pregnancy (don't ask me how they came up with this idea). It has long been believed that IUDs work as birth control by preventing implantation of a fertilized egg, and thus this method was not acceptable to Roman Catholics and others for moral reasons. However, several studies have found that IUDs work primarily by preventing fertilization,

Figure 6–7 An IUD (intrauterine device), inserted.

mostly by their effect on sperm transit through the uterus (Bromham, 1993; Senanayake, 1990; Sivin, 1989). It is very possible that IUDs work for both of these reasons (Spinnato, 1997). The IUDs sold in the United States today have either a copper or progesterone coating, both of which further impair the passage of sperm. These IUDs are highly effective, with typical-use pregnancy rates of less than 2 percent per year (Hatcher et al., 1998). The copper T 380 A IUD can be used effectively for 10 years (Population Council, 1994).

Now back to the story of the early IUDs. Once inserted, the woman's uterus often attempted to expel the foreign object. Because some women did not notice that their IUD had been expelled, manufacturers added a thread to the IUD that protruded from the cervix into the vagina so that women could check to see if their IUD was still in place. However, the thread served as an easy path for bacteria and viruses to follow. The spread of gonorrhea and chlamydia into the upper reproductive tract, causing pelvic inflammatory disease (PID), was especially rapid in women with IUDs. Pelvic inflammatory disease left many women sterile or with an increased chance of a tubal pregnancy. The most common complaint of users of some older types of IUDs was heavier and longer menstrual flow, with more cramps and spotting.

Most of these health risks were limited to one type of IUD, the Dalkon Shield (see Sivin, 1993). The company that manufactured it had no previous experience in contraceptive technology, and despite early warnings from physicians that it was difficult to insert and complaints from users, the company marketed it anyway. Many pregnancies and infections, and even some fatalities, followed. The company filed for bankruptcy after hundreds of millions of dollars in lawsuits were filed. Most of the other IUDs available then were not associated with major health problems, but their manufacturers nevertheless removed them from the market.

The two types of IUDs on the market today are regarded by physicians and researchers to be safe products (e.g., Grimes, 1992; Petitti, 1992). The progesterone (Progestasert T) and copper-coated (Copper T) IUDs used today have a single-filament polyethylene string and are not associated with an increased risk of pelvic inflammatory disease, ectopic pregnancy, endometrial cancer, infertility, or increased bleeding or pain, and there have been no fatalities (Chi, 1993b; Ebi et al., 1996; Rosenblatt et al., 1996). They also have a lower expulsion rate.

Despite these advances, many women still have concerns about the IUD. Its popularity has dropped from 7.1 percent of contraceptive users in 1982 to only 0.8 percent in

intrauterine device (IUD) A birth control device, usually made of plastic with either a copper or progesterone coating, that is placed in the uterus to prevent conception and implantation.

1995 (Piccinino & Mosher, 1998). Of those women who use an IUD, most have a favorable opinion about it (Rosenfield et al., 1993).

> "After the birth of my second child, my doctor strongly advised no more children for a while. I was only 24 years old, so my doctor suggested a three-year IUD. It was very easily done in the doctor's office and my doctor advised me it was safe to have sex right away. It was a wonderful method of birth control." (from the author's files)

To be absolutely safe, many physicians advise women who have multiple sexual partners over time to use a contraceptive technique other than the IUD (Mishell, 1989). The IUD cannot protect a woman from her own, or her partner's, sexual behavior. But for women in a stable, monogamous relationship who have completed their families, the IUD is a safe, highly effective method of contraception that also permits spontaneity in sexual relations.

HORMONAL METHODS OF CONTRACEPTION

THE BIRTH CONTROL PILL (ORAL CONTRACEPTION)

The birth control pill is the most popular of the reversible methods of contraception. The pill is most popular among women in their 20s (well over one-third of sexually active women rely on it). It is still the most popular method among teenage girls as well, but in recent years it has decreased in popularity as more girls rely on use of the male condom (which, unlike the pill, offers protection against sexually transmitted diseases) (Everett et al., 2000; Piccinino & Mosher, 1998).

The pill is the most effective of reversible nonsurgical techniques, with a perfect-use pregnancy rate of close to zero. The typical-use pregnancy rate is three pregnancies per year for every 100 couples using the pill (Hatcher et al., 1998; Trussell et al., 1990). Most of the pregnancies that do occur are due to user, not method, failures. If a woman consistently follows just one simple rule, she really does not need to worry about getting pregnant. What is that? Take the pill every day. However, one study found that 16 percent of women who use the pill do not take it consistently (Peterson et al., 1998).

The birth control pill is not effective immediately, and a backup method of birth control should be used during the first month of use. After that, even if a woman forgets occasionally, taking two pills the next day will probably compensate for the missed pill, but any further forgetfulness will certainly result in unpro-

---

combination pill An oral contraceptive that contains both synthetic estrogen and synthetic progesterone.

minipill An oral contraceptive that contains only progestins.

---

tected intercourse. If you forget to take the pill for a few days, you again must use a backup method of birth control until you have taken daily an entire package of pills. Women, as well as their doctors, should also be aware that *the pill is rendered less effective by simultaneous use of many types of antibiotics, barbiturates, analgesics, and tranquilizers.*

> "During our senior year in high school, my cousin came to me because she was afraid that she was pregnant. She was on the pill, and she was taking them correctly. We could not figure out what went wrong. . . . About a month before she became pregnant, she went to the doctor for a bad cold. It turned out that the medicine which was prescribed for the cold made the birth control less effective." (from the author's files)

There is really not just one pill, but several different types. In fact, there are over 30 types marketed in the United States. The most widely used and most effective are the **combination pills,** which contain synthetic estrogen and synthetic progesterone *(progestins).* Most contain a fixed amount of the two hormones in each capsule, but there are also combination pills that adjust the levels of progestins in an attempt to mimic the natural hormonal phases of the menstrual cycle (although different manufacturers of this type of pill cannot agree on what is "natural"). Regardless of the type, the pill is taken for 21 days and then discontinued for 7 days to permit menstrual bleeding. Most companies package the 21 pills containing hormones with 7 additional pills that contain no hormones (placebos), so that women will not get out of the habit of taking a pill every day.

The combination pill works primarily by preventing ovulation. The hormones in the pill prevent the pituitary from releasing FSH and LH (see Figure 6–8). Without an egg present, it is impossible to get pregnant. Even if ovulation should somehow occur, the progestin inhibits the development of the uterine lining (making implantation difficult) and keeps the cervical mucus thick (making passage of the sperm difficult). When a woman decides to stop using the pill, her menstrual cycles may not become regular immediately, but there is no long-term effect on fertility (Chasen-Taber et al., 1997).

There is also a **minipill** that contains only progestins. It works primarily by inhibiting development of the endometrium and by keeping cervical mucus thick. This pill is for women who are breast-feeding (estrogen inhibits milk production), or who cannot tolerate the side effects of the estrogen-containing pill. It is less effective than the combination pill (1.4–4.3 pregnancies per 100 women in a year) but just as safe, if not safer (Chi, 1993a). However, in some women these pills may cause menstrual problems.

There was a decline in the use of the combination pill during the 1970s and early 1980s when discoveries of serious health risks were reported. However, many of

Inhibition of
pituitary hormones

Stimulation of uterus

Figure 6–8 How oral contraceptives work.

these studies were conducted with the first-generation, high-dosage pill containing more than 150 micrograms of estrogen. Manufacturers of oral contraceptives stopped marketing high-dosage pills in 1988. Today's third-generation pills have less than 50 micrograms of estrogen, and therefore have less risk associated with them.

The combination pill also has some significant health benefits. Nevertheless, there are specific subgroups of women who should not use the combination pill. Let us examine the risks and benefits in detail.

NEGATIVE SIDE EFFECTS AND HEALTH RISKS.

There were some early reports of a few women showing decreased sex drive as a result of taking the combi-

nation pill (Masters & Johnson, 1970). These reports have been questioned, and more recent studies have found that pill users engage in sex more frequently, have greater sexual interest, and report more sexual satisfaction than do nonusers (Alexander et al., 1990; McCoy & Matyas, 1996). Some women do not use the birth control pill because they have heard that they might gain weight, but in a recent study none of the 128 women who began taking the pill gained weight (Rosenberg, 1998).

It is not uncommon for women who are first starting to take the pill to experience some symptoms that mimic those of early pregnancy. These may include nausea, constipation, breast tenderness, a bloated feeling, and emotional depression. These responses usually occur only during the first few days of each cycle and usually diminish within a few months. If they continue or are bothersome, the woman's doctor may be able to adjust the dosage of the hormones. Because the hormones in the pill alter the chemical environment of the vagina, there is also an increased susceptibility to yeast infection. As a result of the lowered dose of hormones in today's pill, breakthrough bleeding (i.e., bleeding during the 21 days of hormone use) sometimes occurs, but it usually disappears during the first 4 months of use. Despite these problems, the large majority of women who use the pill have a very favorable opinion of it as a contraceptive technique (Rosenfield et al., 1993).

The previously mentioned problems may be bothersome, but they are not considered serious health risks. However, there are other, more serious problems that have been associated with use of the pill. Studies conducted in the 1970s, when the dosage of estrogen in the birth control pill was much higher than it is today, showed use of the pill to be associated with (though not necessarily the cause of) high blood pressure (4 percent of users), diabetes (1 percent), migraine headaches (0.5 percent), and liver cancer (rare) (Rinehart & Piotrow, 1979). The pill was once thought to be the cause of gallbladder disease, but recent studies do not support this belief (Vessey & Painter, 1994).

Older studies with pills that contained high dosages of estrogen suggested that their use could cause serious cardiovascular problems such as blood clots, heart attacks, and strokes (see Mishell, 1999). Users of the pill who were in their 30s and smoked, for example, were 7 times more likely to have a heart attack than users who did not smoke. Later studies showed that other risk factors, primarily smoking, accounted for most of the cardiovascular problems (Mishell, 1999). In fact, the Food and Drug Administration voted in late 1989 to allow women over the age of 40 who do not smoke to continue taking the pill (Kaeser, 1989).

What about today's third-generation low-dose pills? Pill users who are younger than 35, do not smoke, and do not have high blood pressure have very little or no risk of stroke or heart attack (Mishell, 1999; WHO Collaborative Study, 1996). The newest pills slightly increase the risk of a nonfatal blood clot, but reduce the risk of heart attacks as compared to the risk for users of the second-generation pill. The authors of the blood clot studies said that their findings were "no cause for alarm," and the risk is only half of that caused by pregnancy (Mishell, 1999). Oral contraceptive users over the age of 35 who smoke still have an unacceptably high risk of heart attack and stroke and should not use the combination pill.

Users of the birth control pill may have an increased risk of cervical cancer (Ursin et al., 1994), but there is a great deal of uncertainty as to whether this is due to the pill or to other risk factors (see Mishell, 1989). There were also concerns for many years that use of birth control pills containing estrogen would increase the risk of breast cancer. Breast cancer is the second most common type of cancer in women, affecting 1 in 8 women at some point in their life (see Box 2–A). Although some studies claimed to have found a link between the pill and breast cancer, some 20 other studies, including one by the Centers for Disease Control and Prevention, have found that pill users are at little or no greater risk than nonusers (e.g., Romieu et al., 1990; Sattin et al., 1986; Stanford et al., 1995; Steinberg et al., 1991). A review of 54 studies found that women currently taking the combination pill have only a slightly increased risk of breast cancer and that there was no increase in risk 10 years after stopping the pill (Collaborative Group on Hormonal Factors, 1996, 1997).

When discussing the health risks associated with use of the pill, you should put things into proper perspective and compare the risks to what would happen if nobody used the pill. For women who do not smoke, the health risks (including deaths) *are significantly less than those caused by pregnancy and childbirth* (Hatcher et al., 1998; see Table 6–3).

HEALTH BENEFITS.   After 40 years of use, it is now known that women who take the birth control pill are at less risk for some health problems than nonusers. Some of these findings were unexpected and could properly be called fringe benefits. The

TABLE 6–3

RISK OF DEATH IN A YEAR'S TIME RESULTING FROM SELECTED ACTIVITIES

Activity	Chance of Dying
Motorcycling	1 in 1000
Automobile driving	1 in 5,900
Power boating	1 in 5,900
Playing football	1 in 25,000
Using tampons (toxic shock), age 15–44	1 in 350,000
Having sexual intercourse (pelvic infection), age 15–44	1 in 50,000
Using contraception	
Oral contraception—nonsmoker	1 in 66,700
Oral contraception—heavy smoker	1 in 1,700
Using IUDs	1 in 10,000,000
Using diaphragm, condom, or spermicides	none
Laparoscopic tubal ligation	1 in 38,500
Vasectomy	1 in 1,000,000
Deciding about pregnancy	
Continuing pregnancy	1 in 11,000
Legal abortion	
Before 9 weeks	1 in 262,800
9–12 weeks	1 in 100,100
13–15 weeks	1 in 34,400
After 15 weeks	1 in 10,200

Source: Hatcher et al. (1998). Reprinted with permission of the publishers.

major benefits include a decreased risk of cancer of the endometrium and cancer of the ovaries (Hulka et al., 1982; Ness et al., 2000). Not only is there no reliable evidence that use of the birth control pill is linked to breast cancer, but in fact there is a substantial decrease in the number of benign breast tumors (one-fourth as likely). Use of the pill also results in reduced rates of ovarian cysts (one-fourth as likely), rheum-atoid arthritis (one-half as likely; Ory et al., 1980), and pelvic inflammatory disease (one-half as likely; Panser & Phipps, 1991). The birth control pill is also known to reduce premenstrual syndrome, reduce menstrual pain and bleeding (anemia is only two-thirds as likely; Milsom et al., 1990), and improve acne. In fact, some doctors prescribe the pill to women primarily to reduce menstrual problems, and only secondarily as a contraceptive technique.

"I am now on the birth control pill. . . . My cramps were minimized a great deal and so was the length and heaviness of my period."   (from the author's files)

For older women who do not smoke, are not obese, and do not have hypertension or cardiovascular problems, today's low-dosage pills are also being prescribed to regulate menstrual cycle disturbances that are common before menopause (Volpe et al., 1993).

"THE SHOT"

In early 1993, a new type of contraception became available to women in the United States: **Depo-Provera,** an injectable drug containing a progestin (medroxyprogesterone acetate, or DMPA, a synthetic form of progesterone). The injectable contraceptive has been used by more than 30 million women in 90 different countries. The injection is good for 3 months and prevents the problem of pregnancies resulting from missing a daily dose, as with the pill. It works by preventing ovulation (by blocking the pituitary hormones FSH and LH) and has a yearly pregnancy rate of less than 1 percent (Bigrigg et al., 1999). After a woman stops injections, it takes from several months to a year for fertility to return.

There are some possible side effects that might cause some women to discontinue this method. These include menstrual irregularities (including an increase or decrease in menstrual bleeding), weight gain (an average of 15 pounds), tiredness, weakness, nervousness, dizziness, and/or headaches. In fact, these problems are so bothersome that only about one-third of women who try "the shot" are still using it after a year (Sangi-Haghpeykar et al., 1996; Westfall et al., 1996).

In 1993, the World Health Organization also approved injectable contraceptives that contain both estrogen and progestin. They are injected once a month and are nearly 100 percent effective. One of these, called **Lunelle,** was approved for use in the United States in 2000. Because it contains estrogen, there are fewer problems with irregular vaginal bleeding than with Depo-Provera and Norplant (see below). If you are interested, ask your doctor.

NORPLANT: THE 5-YEAR HORMONE IMPLANT

Norplant, the hormonal implant, offers contraceptive protection for up to 5 years. In fact, recent studies demonstrate that it is highly effective for 7 years (Sivin et al., 2000). Approved for use in the United States in 1990, it consists of six flexible silicone tubes, each about the size of a match, that are inserted under the skin in a fanlike pattern on the inside of a woman's upper arm (see Figure 6–9). The tubes are non-biodegradable and can be removed at any time. The procedure takes only 15 to 30 minutes and costs about the same as a 5-year supply of birth control pills. The tubes contain a progestin (levonorgestrel), a synthetic form of progesterone that is slowly released over time and prevents pregnancy by inhibiting the LH surge and thus ovulation (see Chapter 3). The implant only partially inhibits FSH activity, so that there is some follicular development and estrogen secretion. The advantage of this is that Norplant does not require estrogen (as in the birth control pill), but the disadvantage is that there is irregular, unpredictable vaginal bleeding.

Figure 6–9 Norplant.

Norplant's pregnancy rate is said to be about 2 in 1,000 (Trussell et al., 1990), as compared to 30 in 1,000 for the pill (most of which are user failures). This makes it nearly as reliable as sterilization. Only about 15 percent of women who choose Norplant decide to have it removed by the end of 1 year, some because they plan to have another child, but many because of unhappiness with the side effects (Clarke et al., 1998; Kirkman et al., 1999). About three-fourths of women with Norplant implants experience side effects in the first year. The most common side effects (as with all progestin forms of contraception) are spotting or irregular bleeding (this can include prolonged menstrual bleeding or no bleeding at all), weight gain, and headaches. Some other side effects include nervousness, dizziness, nausea, breast tenderness, and acne (Clarke et al., 1998). However, only one-third of the women who experience side effects are bothered by them. Over three-fourths of Norplant users are very satisfied (Clarke et al., 1998).

"I chose the Norplant birth control method after I had my first child at age 20. My life, of course, changed 100 percent, something I was not ready for, mentally or financially. I am now back in school as a single mother. I decided to try Norplant when I was still married and didn't want any more 'accidents.' . . . The in-office procedure lasted only thirty minutes. . . . I felt no pain. . . . I started to gain a little weight and had some slight dizziness. Then my menstrual periods stopped. Now 10 months later they are normal again and I have no other symptoms. My Norplant will last for 5 years. This is just enough time for me to finish school. I would recommend this method of birth control to anyone." (from the author's files)

Depo-Provera Market name for medroxyprogesterone acetate, a chemical that when injected suppresses ovulation for 3 months.

Norplant Six flexible silicone tubes containing a progestin that are implanted under the skin to prevent conception; they remain effective for 5 years.

Box 6-A ▸ SEXUALITY AND HEALTH

Contraceptive Methods That Help Prevent Sexually Transmitted Diseases

*S*exually active individuals who are not in monogamous relationships must (and should) worry about sexually transmitted diseases in addition to pregnancy. Unfortunately, contraceptive development has concentrated almost entirely on preventing pregnancy and has ignored STDs. What do we know about the effectiveness of currently available contraceptive devices in preventing STDs?

Fertility awareness methods, sterilization, Norplant, Depo-Provera, the IUD, and the birth control pill offer no protection against STDs (Cates & Stone, 1992b). The IUD, you recall, increases a woman's chances of getting pelvic inflammatory disease should she get a bacterial infection of the lower genital tract (e.g., gonorrhea or chlamydia). The birth control pill offers some protection against pelvic inflammatory disease (e.g., Panser & Phipps, 1991) but increases replication of HIV in the vagina (Mostad et al., 1997).

That leaves barrier methods and spermicides. Let us consider spermicides first. The active ingredient in most spermicides, nonoxynol-9, not only kills sperm but also is effective against most of the bacteria and viruses that cause STDs, including gonorrhea, chlamydia, trichomonas, and hepatitis. There are not enough data to make conclusions about whether spermicides protect against herpes, syphilis, or chancroid. While spermicides reduce the risk, *they do not reduce the risk to zero*, and may actually increase women's risk of catching HIV (see below). At best, there is a reduction in risk of about 50 percent. (There are far too many studies to cite here; for an excellent review, see Rosenberg & Gollub, 1992; or see Howe et al., 1994, for a review specific to HIV.)

For men, of course, use of rubber condoms will reduce their risk of getting an STD; "skins" (condoms made of sheep intestine) have pores that are large enough for the passage of HIV and other viruses. However, not all the news is reassuring. Rubber condoms may not have any holes before use, but under conditions that resemble intercourse, about a third of these condoms develop very small holes that might be large enough to allow passage of HIV (Carey et al., 1992). What's more, condoms break about 1 to 3 percent of the time during vaginal intercourse, and more often during anal intercourse (Messiah et al., 1997; Silverman & Gross, 1997; see Cates & Stone, 1992a, for a review of numerous studies). Of course, we would expect that if condoms were always used correctly and consistently, and always in combination with a spermicide, their effectiveness at STD prevention would be much greater. In one study of 124 serodiscordant couples (only one member was HIV positive) who used condoms consistently, none of the HIV-negative partners became infected during a total of 15,000 acts of intercourse (De Vincenzi et al., 1994).

What about women? Women are at a higher risk of contracting HIV and other STDs because of the greater mucosal surface in the vagina and the secret high-risk behavior of many of their partners. What contraceptive methods can women use that will simultaneously reduce the risk of contracting STDs? At first glance, an obvious choice might be to have their partners always wear condoms, but this "may be unrealistic because traditional sex roles in most cultures do not encourage a woman to talk about sex or to initiate sexual practices or otherwise control an intimate heterosexual encounter" (Rosenberg & Gollub, 1992). Among women at high risk for getting an STD, the female condom would appear to be a good alternative (Gollub, 2000). However, while most women at high risk are willing to try it, only a minority like it well enough to use it consistently. (Haignere et al., 2000; Macaluso et al., 2000).

Michael Rosenberg and his colleagues (1992) reported that under actual use, women using the diaphragm had lower rates of infection for gonorrhea and trichomonas than women whose partners used condoms. The diaphragm was also more effective than condoms against chlamydia. Other researchers believe that the authors "overstated the scientific case for these methods, especially in comparison with the condom" (Cates et al., 1992). However, there is no question that the barrier contraceptives (diaphragm and the new female condom), if used consistently, properly, and with spermicide, offer women some protection against many STDs (Cates & Stone, 1992a; Rosenberg & Gollub, 1992).

You have already learned that spermicides help kill many of the bacteria and viruses that cause STDs. What about HIV? Spermicides kill HIV in a test tube, but studies suggest that they may actually increase women's chances of catching HIV from an infected partner by irritating the vaginal walls and making transmission of HIV easier (Bird, 1991; Cates et al., 1992; Van Damme et al., 2000). The real hope for the future may lay in development of a *vaginal microbicide*, a bacteria-and-virus-killing cream or gel that women can apply vaginally before intercourse (Harrison, 2000; Van Damme & Rosenberg, 1999). Over 60 types are now undergoing testing. When these become available, women will indeed be able to take measures to protect themselves.

The Food and Drug Administration and the World Health Organization believe Norplant is a safe form of contraception because it contains no estrogen. Norplant had already been used by 500,000 women worldwide before it was approved for use in the United States. Nevertheless, Norplant should not be used by women with liver disease or tumors, breast cancer, or a history of blood clots.

A new implant, called Implanon, is currently undergoing the final stages of testing (Bennink, 1998; Croxatto & Makarainen, 1998). It is a single rod that contains progestin and completely inhibits ovulation for 3 years. During testing, no pregnancies were reported, which would make it the best contraceptive device ever developed. As with all progestin-only techniques, the major side effect is irregular vaginal bleeding.

EMERGENCY CONTRACEPTION

There are three methods of **emergency contraception** that can be used to prevent pregnancy when no other type of contraception was used at the time of intercourse (Glasier, 1997; Trussell et al., 1997). One is called the Yuzpe method. A woman first takes a pill containing 100 μg of ethinyl estradiol (synthetic estrogen) and 0.5 mg levonorgestrel *within 72 hours of intercourse*, and then takes a second dosage of the same pill 12 hours later. This procedure is about 75 percent effective in preventing pregnancy (Trussell et al., 1999). It does not cause an abortion! You may be interested in knowing that many birth control pills contain the same hormones, and if taken in the proper dosage could be safely used for this short period (see Trussell et al., 1997).

Some pharmaceutical companies now offer a progestin-only (.75 mg levonorgestrel) emergency contraception product. A recent study indicates that it is at least 90 percent effective (United Nations Development Programme, 2000).

Probably the most effective method of emergency contraception is implantation of a copper IUD (within 7 days after intercourse). However, it may be very difficult to find a doctor willing to do this because of the time it takes to implant an IUD (Reuter, 1999).

Many women have difficulties finding a doctor who will prescribe emergency contraception pills (Trussel et al., 2000). It is believed that if emergency contraception were readily available, it could prevent as many as 1 million to 2 million unintended pregnancies each year (Trussell & Stewart, 1992). As a result, in 2000 the American Medical Association recommended that the Food and Drug Administration make emergency contraception pills available over the counter.

VOLUNTARY STERILIZATION

Over 1 million **sterilization** procedures are performed in the United States every year. In fact, more Americans rely on sterilization for birth control than on any other birth control technique (Piccinino & Mosher, 1998). For a couple to rely on this method, it is not necessary that they both be sterilized, so this figure is derived by adding male and female sterilizations (28 percent of contraceptive users rely on female sterilization and 11 percent on male sterilization). In fact, more than half of all married couples eventually use sterilization after the birth of their last planned child. Sterilization has recently become very popular among unmarried (especially African-American) women as well (Bumpass et al., 2000).

In men, the sterilization procedure is called **vasectomy.** In Western cultures, it has traditionally been done by making a small incision or two in the scrotum (under local anesthesia), then tying off and cutting the vas deferens (see Figure 6–10). The entire procedure takes only about 20 minutes. As an alternative, a "no-scalpel" vasectomy has been introduced from China, where it has been performed safely on millions of men. With this technique, the skin of the scrotum is

emergency contraception Methods that prevent contraception when used in the first few days *after* sexual intercourse.

sterilization A general term for surgical techniques that render an individual infertile.

vasectomy The male sterilization technique in which the vas deferens is tied off and cut, thus preventing passage of sperm through the reproductive tract.

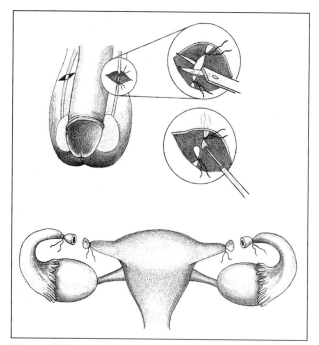

Figure 6–10 A vasectomy and a tubal ligation.

simply pierced with a sharp instrument. It takes less than 10 minutes, produces less bleeding, and results in fewer infections (Jow & Goldstein, 1994).

A vasectomy does not interfere with the production of hormones or sperm in the testicles. New sperm simply cannot get past the point where the vas have been tied and cut, and eventually they are destroyed by other cells called phagocytes. Sperm that are already past this point at the time of operation, however, must be eliminated before a man is "safe." Other means of contraception should be used until the man has had 12 to 16 ejaculations. Some men are reluctant to get a vasectomy because they think that they will no longer be able to ejaculate (obviously confusing ejaculation with orgasm), but recall from Chapter 2 that nearly all of the fluid in a man's ejaculation comes from the prostate gland and seminal vesicles, which are unaffected by the procedure. A man with a vasectomy will still ejaculate during orgasm, but his ejaculation will contain no sperm.

In women, the term **tubal ligation** is often used for a variety of techniques, but it really refers just to the tying of the Fallopian tubes. More commonly, the procedure involves cutting as well as tying the tubes (see Figure 6–10). Both methods, of course, prevent passage of the egg and

tubal ligation A female sterilization technique that originally referred only to the tying of Fallopian tubes, but which is now often used as a general term for a variety of female sterilization techniques.

laparoscopy A technique that involves inserting a slender, tubelike instrument (laparoscope) into a woman's abdomen to examine (via fiberoptics) her reproductive organs or a fetus. The procedure is often used to perform female sterilizations.

sperm. The egg is absorbed by the woman's body. In the past, these procedures required hospitalization, general anesthesia, and large abdominal incisions.

Today, most tubal ligations involve small incisions. In a *minilaparotomy*, 1-inch incisions are made in the abdomen and the Fallopian tubes are pulled to the opening and cut, tied, or blocked with clips. A **laparoscopy** is a procedure in which a laparoscope, a long, tubelike instrument that transmits TV pictures, is inserted through a small incision in the navel. Once the tubes are located, surgical instruments are inserted through the laparoscope (or other tiny incisions) and the tubes are cut or cauterized. Both procedures are usually done with general anesthesia, but do not require lengthy hospitalization. Most women go home the same day. Unlike the male technique, a woman may safely engage in sexual intercourse as soon as she feels the desire to do so. Instead of using abdominal incisions, some physicians approach the Fallopian tubes through small incisions in the vagina (a procedure called *culpotomy*). However, minor complications (infection or hemorrhage) are twice as high as with the other procedures.

COMPLICATIONS. Surgical complications resulting from vasectomy are uncommon (less than 5 percent) and generally minor. Early, postsurgical complications depend, in large part, on the experience of the surgeon (Schwingl & Guess, 2000). However, there have been some concerns about the long-term effects. Rather than being destroyed, some sperm leak into the bloodstream, and as a result, at least half of the men who have had a vasectomy produce antibodies to their own sperm. Some initial research with monkeys suggested that this could lead to accelerated arteriosclerosis (hardening of the arteries), and a small study with humans suggested a link between vasectomy and testicular cancer. However, several large studies conducted with thousands of humans have found no link between the surgery and later development of arteriosclerosis, immune problems, or testicular cancer (see Schwingl & Guess, 2000).

More recently, some studies have raised concerns that vasectomy may increase men's risk of prostate cancer (Giovannucci et al., 1993; see Klitsch, 1993). However, after a scientific panel at the National Institutes of Health met to discuss these findings, they concluded that the evidence was not strong. Subsequent studies supported this conclusion (see Schwingl & Guess, 2000). An accompanying editorial stated: "There is no known biologic mechanism to explain a causal relationship." In spite of these (unfounded) concerns, the prevalence of vasectomy remained unchanged during the 1990s, with about 500,000 performed each year in the United States (Magnani et al., 1999).

Some physicians have suggested that there is a "post–tubal ligation syndrome" characterized by heavier-than -normal menstrual bleeding and more severe menstrual cramps. This has sometimes been used as a justification for performing hysterectomies (Goldhaber et al., 1993); and in fact, women who have had a tubal sterilization are more likely than nonsterilized women to eventually have a hysterectomy (Hillis et al., 1998). However, studies conducted by the World Health Organization found no increase in menstrual bleeding associated with sterilization (World Health Organization, 1984, 1985), and a recent large-scale study found that most women experienced no change or a decrease in menstrual and inter menstrual bleeding (Peterson et al., 2000). Most studies find that the large majority of women are satisfied with their choice of surgical contraception. In fact, a recent study found that women's satisfaction with sterilization was greater than for any other type of birth control (Oddens, 1999). What's more, sterilization in women has some definite health benefits: It substantially decreases their risk of getting cancer of the ovaries (Miracle-McMahill et al., 1997). Overall, the long-term benefits outweigh the risks (Kawachi et al., 1994).

CAN STERILIZATIONS BE REVERSED? Sterilization procedures are highly effective, with failure rates of less than 1 percent (Schwingl & Guess, 2000). Today, they should also be considered permanent. Few people who decide to be sterilized ever wish to have the procedure reversed (about 4 percent change their mind), but for those who do there is no guarantee of success. The problem is that the sewing together of the vas deferens or Fallopian tubes requires very skilled microsurgery techniques (the inside diameter of a Fallopian tube, for example, is no greater than a human hair). The success rate for vasectomy reversal has been steadily improving (a new technique using laser surgery appears to be very promising), with some doctors now reporting restored sperm flow in over 50 percent of their patients. However, even with restored sperm flow, the chance of a man impregnating a woman decreases markedly if the reversal is not performed within a year or two. This is probably due to the increased levels of the man's antibodies to his own sperm. The pregnancy rate after a reversal is about 50 percent (Hatcher et al., 1998). Successful reconstruction of the Fallopian tubes is very difficult because the slightest scarring can impair passage of the egg (and result in tubal pregnancy even if fertilization occurs). Success rates range from 43 to 88 percent (Hatcher et al., 1998; Kim et al., 1997). So, while there have been successful reversals in both men and women, the success rates are still far less than 100 percent. Therefore, only people who are quite sure that they do not want any more children should opt for these procedures.

WHICH PARTNER SHOULD BE STERILIZED? Remember, if a couple agrees that they do not wish to have any more children and choose sterilization as their contraceptive technique, only one of them need have surgery. Which one should it be—the man or the woman? One study that compared expenses, complication rates, and the number of people who regretted their operations concluded that the male sterilization technique was preferable in every way (Kjersgaard et al., 1989). Vasectomy is considered less popular among African Americans and Latinos than among white Americans, but even among white couples more choose tubal sterilization than vasectomy (Bumpass et al., 2000). Whatever the choice may be, it is important that the couple make an educated decision so that both persons will be happy with the decision.

PERSONAL REFLECTIONS
Considering all factors (including your sexual life-style), which birth control technique is best for you? If you are not presently using it, how can you obtain it?

UNWANTED PREGNANCIES: THE FINAL OPTIONS

There is no reversible method of contraception that is 100 percent effective (although Norplant, Depo-Provera, and the pill come close); thus, unwanted pregnancies sometime occur even for couples who are using the most reliable forms of contraception. If an unwanted pregnancy should occur, a woman (or a couple) really has only three options: to continue with the pregnancy and keep the baby; to continue with the pregnancy and put the baby up for adoption; or to terminate the pregnancy (abortion). In many cases, none of these is an easy choice.

The responsibilities involved with **keeping and raising a baby** force many women to drop out of school and remain uneducated and unskilled, locking them into a lifetime of poverty and reliance on state funds and services to raise the child. The rate of child abuse resulting from the emotional frustration in these situations is much higher than normal (Goerge & Lee, 1997).

Some women or couples choose to put an unplanned baby up for **adoption** by others who are better able to care for it. In many cases, this may be best for the child, but nevertheless, it often results in long-lasting adjustment problems for those who have surrendered their child. The following is a typical case:

"I was one of the teenage pregnancies. I was 14 years old and was pregnant. My boyfriend, now my husband, was also 14 years old and thought

adoption Taking a child into one's family by legal process and raising the child as one's own.

that he could not produce sperm yet, and I believed him. It has caused me a very hard life because of the guilt I feel for having to give up my child. We now have two more children, but it still doesn't fill the void. I only wish we both could have been aware of this then. All of the agony could have been spared." (from the author's files)

For many women or couples, **abortion** is no less difficult a choice.

"At the age of 18 I became pregnant. My boyfriend of 4 years and I had recently broken up, so I was alone. I suppose I could have told my parents, but I was too scared of their reactions. At three months I terminated my pregnancy. It hurt very badly emotionally. Occasionally I think of how old my baby, boy or girl, would be today." (from the author's files)

However, the large majority of women who have first-trimester abortions do not experience emotional or psychological problems afterwards (Adler et al., 1990; Major et al., 2000). Many feel a sense of relief because of compelling health or economic considerations (see Lewis, 1997). The few women who do suffer emotionally after an abortion generally had emotional problems before (Russo & Dabul, 1997).

Of these three options, only abortion can be considered a method of birth control. However, many people have strong negative views of the use of abortion as a method of birth control. Let us discuss this topic in more detail.

ABORTION

The World Health Organization estimates that there are about 50 million abortions performed annually throughout the world, of which only about 30 million are performed under safe conditions by trained providers (Berer, 2000). Worldwide, at least 13 percent of deaths during pregnancy are the result of unsafe abortions. Abortion is the main form of birth control in Russia, with the average Russian woman having about three abortions in her lifetime (Goldberg et al., 1998). Although the U.S. abortion rate is well below the worldwide rate (20 versus 37 to 55 per 1,000 women aged 15 to 44), over one-fourth of all pregnancies end in abortion (Henshaw, 1998b). Most abortions performed in this country are for middle-class white women (Henshaw & Kost, 1996). Fewer than 1.2 million legal abortions were performed in the United States in 1997, which is not only down from the high of 1.43 million in 1990 but the lowest since 1978 (Centers for Disease Control and Prevention, 2000).

Nearly 90 percent of all women who obtain abortions

abortion Termination of pregnancy. Depending on how far the pregnancy has advanced, this can be done by taking a pill (RU 486); scraping the uterine lining (dilation and curettage); removing the uterine lining by suction (dilation and evacuation); or inducing labor (by injecting hypertonic saline or prostaglandins).

do so within 12 weeks of conception (CDC, 2000). Death resulting from a legal abortion is very uncommon—less than 1 per 100,000 abortions—and, in fact, is much less common than deaths resulting from childbirth. Modern legal abortions do not increase a woman's subsequent risk of infertility, miscarriage, ectopic pregnancy, or having a low-birthweight baby (Frank et al., 1993; Holt et al., 1989; Melbye et al., 1997).

What are some of the possible consequences of legalizing abortion? Of abolishing abortion? If abortion were made illegal in the United States, it would result in an increase of 440,000 births per year (Levine et al., 1999). In Romania, the abolishment of legalized abortion led to the highest maternal mortality rate in Europe and the abandonment of tens of thousands of children in institutions (Stephenson et al., 1992).

There are several methods used to terminate a pregnancy:

1. *Medical (nonsurgical) abortion:* In 1988, the French government approved a pill (*RU 486*, or *mifepristone*, made by the French company Roussel-Uclaf) that can be used to chemically induce an abortion up to 8 weeks after a woman's last menstrual period. It is presently being used in France, England, Sweden, China, Israel, and several developing countries. One-third of all abortions performed in France are presently done by this method. It is about 95 to 97 percent effective when taken in combination with oral prostaglandins (misoprostol, which causes contractions of the uterus that expel the embryo) within the first 7 weeks after implantation (Kahn et al., 2000; Schaff et al., 2000). RU 486 works by blocking the body's use of progesterone, the hormone necessary for maintaining the endometrium of the uterus, thus causing shedding of the uterine lining (France & Rosenberg, 2000). Another drug combination (methotrexate and misoprostol) has proven to be equally effective in terminating early pregnancies (Kahn et al., 2000). In both cases, a woman takes the first drug at a doctor's office and the second drug at home 2 days later. The main side effects are nausea, cramping, and prolonged uterine bleeding (see Grimes, 1997). For these reasons, many women may prefer the surgical abortion (D & E), which is completed in 1 day. Of course, the advantage of chemical abortion is greater privacy; a woman does not have to go to an abortion clinic.

    The Food and Drug Administration approved use of mifepristone in the United States in late 2000. It is distributed under the name Mifeprex by Danco Laboratories in New York. However, in 2001 newly elected President George Bush said that he would review the FDA's decision to approve RU 486.

2. *Dilation and curettage (D & C):* Once the standard procedure for unwanted pregnancies of 15 weeks

or less, D & C procedures are now used less and less for purposes of abortion. Under general anesthesia, a woman's cervix is dilated, and the lining of the uterus is then scraped with a metal instrument called a curette. In addition to the risks associated with general anesthesia, this procedure results in more bleeding and discomfort than D&E (see below) procedures.

3. *Dilation and evacuation (D & E):* In this procedure, which does not require general anesthesia, a tube is inserted through the cervix and the fetal material is removed by suction. About 98 percent of all legal abortions in the United States are now performed by this method (CDC, 2000). Today, with use of a hand-held vacuum syringe, the procedure can be done 8 days after conception, and it takes only 5 minutes (Painter, 1999). For early abortions, most women prefer D&E over medical abortions because of the ease, quickness, and less bleeding and discomfort (Jensen et al., 1999; Painter, 1999). D&E can be done without anesthesia in the first 4 to 6 weeks of pregnancy, but requires local anesthesia and dilation of the cervix for pregnancies terminated during weeks 7 through 12. Later-stage abortions may require gentle scraping of the uterine walls in addition to suction. The older D&C procedure was associated with a risk of subsequent sterility, but early first-trimester abortions performed by the vacuum technique do not appear to have this risk (Frank et al., 1993).

4. *Induced labor:* This method is used exclusively for termination of pregnancies that have proceeded beyond 16 weeks (which accounts for only 5 percent of all abortions). A solution of hypertonic saline or prostaglandins (hormones which cause smooth muscle contractions) is injected into the amniotic sac and induces labor within 12 to 36 hours. The fetus is born dead.

5. *Intact dilation and evacuation (intact D&E):* This procedure, also known as *dilation and extraction (D&X)*, is performed in very-late-term pregnancies and supposedly only when the mother's health is in danger. The fetus's head is partially delivered and its brain is then removed by suction (thus the frequently used description "partial-birth abortion"). The Centers for Disease Control and Prevention estimate that about 1.3 percent of abortions are by intact D&E (see *AMA Bulletin*, March 3, 1997).

THE PRESENT STATUS AND FUTURE OF ABORTION IN THE UNITED STATES.

Abortion is a subject that has polarized people throughout the nation. Those opposed to abortion ("right-to-lifers") express concerns about protecting human life. "Pro-choicers," on the other hand, wish to retain the right of individuals to make decisions about something that will have a major impact on their own lives. In a national survey conducted in 2001 by ABC News and the Washington Post, 57 percent of the respondents said abortion should be legal in most or all cases, and 90 percent supported a woman's right to abortion in at least some circumstances. A 1998 *New York Times*/CBS News Poll found that while a majority of the American public still supports legalized abortion, they also feel that it should be harder to get and less readily chosen (Goldberg & Elder, 1998).

The laws regarding abortion have been in a state of transition for over two decades. Prior to 1973, each state could allow or prohibit abortion as it wished, but in that year a 7–2 Supreme Court decision (*Roe v. Wade*) prohibited the states from interfering with decisions made between a woman and her doctor during the first 3 months of pregnancy. The ruling also prevented states from prohibiting abortion in the second trimester of pregnancy, but did allow for more regulations designed to protect a woman's health (hospitalization, e.g.). Antiabortion forces won a victory in 1977 when the Supreme Court upheld the Hyde Amendment, which disallowed the use of federal Medicaid money to pay for abortions. Without public funding, obtaining a legal abortion became difficult for women with limited incomes. The number of abortion providers also decreased substantially during the 1990s, and about 86 percent of counties in the United States have no provider (Henshaw, 1998b).

Although the decision in *Roe v. Wade* giving a woman the right to choose is still the law, subsequent court decisions have given states greater leeway in regulating abortion. In 1989, a sharply divided Supreme Court upheld by a 5–4 vote (*Webster v. Reproductive Health Services*) a Missouri law that further restricted public funds and facilities for abortions and that also required physicians to test for fetal viability (the potential for the fetus to survive) at 20 weeks. The earliest point of fetal viability is 24 weeks (the law allowed for a 4-week margin of error in determining the time of conception), and the vast majority of abortions have already been performed before the 20th week. In 1990, the Court voted 6–3 to uphold state laws that ban abortions for girls under the age of 18 unless a parent is notified. In a 1992 case (*Planned Parenthood v. Casey*), the Court, in another 5–4 vote, upheld a Pennsylvania law that imposed a 24-hour waiting period, required doctors to tell women about other options, and also required parental notification in the case of minors. In 2000 the Supreme Court (in another 5-4 vote) overturned state laws that attempted to ban intact D&E. Legal decisions regarding abortion are likely to continue to change as the members of the Supreme Court are replaced, either by more conservative or more liberal justices.

Religious beliefs regarding abortion have often changed as well. Within the Catholic Church, for example, the first pope to declare that abortion was murder was Sixtus V in 1588, but that was reversed just 3 years later by Pope Gregory XIV. For the next 300 years, abortion was allowed up to the time of what was termed "animation by a rational soul" (up to 40 days after conception in the case of a male embryo and for the first 80 days in the case of a female fetus; Connery, 1977; Grisez, 1970). In 1869, however, Pope Pius IX again declared that abortion was murder, and this has remained the belief of every pope since.

With the diversity of opinion regarding this subject, religious and legal beliefs about abortion will probably continue to change for many decades to come.

FUTURE TECHNOLOGY

In more and more societies, rich with technological diversity and replete with seemingly endless permutations of consumer goods, it is odd indeed that [the present array of contraceptive technologies], central to the lives of so many individuals, families and societies, is so limited. (Harrison and Rosenfield, 1996. Reprinted with permission of the publisher.)

The female condom became available to women in the United States in 1993. This probably was the first of what will be a whole new generation of female barrier contraceptives. In addition to the condom, two other vaginal pouches are under development. The *Woman's Choice Female Condomme* is inserted into the vagina with an applicator and has a latex rubber umbrellalike cap that is about a third thicker than the male condom. The *unisex condom garment* is a polyurethane item resembling a bikini bottom with an attached sheath that can be worn by either men or women (as a vaginal liner or a penis covering) for contraception and protection against sexually transmitted diseases.

Researchers are also testing variations of the cervical cap. The *Lea's Shield* is made of silicone rubber and has a loop that makes it easy to insert and remove. It is a one-size-fits-all barrier contraceptive that allows passage of cervical secretions and is intended to be sold over the counter (Mauck et al., 1996). The *Fem Cap* is also made of silicone rubber. It conforms to the vaginal walls by means of a surrounding "brim." The *Oves Cervical Cap*, unlike the others, is disposable, and will probably be available across the counter.

Research into a *male pill* continues, but do not expect it on the market any time soon (see Comhaire, 1994). The problem is trying to find a pill that inhibits sperm production without simultaneously lowering sexual desire or a man's ability to get and maintain an erection. There was some success with gossypol, a Chinese derivative of cottonseed oil that disables sperm-producing testicular cells, but acceptance is unlikely because as many as 20 percent of men who take it remain permanently sterile (Coutinho et al., 2000). Present research is focusing on the administration of hormones to block the pituitary hormones responsible for sperm production (see Chapter 3), while simultaneously delivering other hormones to assure that there will be no loss of sex drive (Meriggiola et al., 1997; Harrison & Rosenfield, 1996).

Perhaps the most promising future means of birth control is *vaccination* (Alexander, 1994; Naz, 1999). It might be possible to prevent pregnancy the same way you can the flu. Researchers are trying to develop vaccines that will cause the body to produce antibodies to proteins in either sperm or eggs. Scientists in India are already clinically testing a vaccine that stimulates the production of antibodies to HCG (human chorionic gonadotropin), a hormone necessary to maintain pregnancy. With this vaccine, a fertilized egg cannot implant and is discharged during menstruation. U.S. scientists are also working on a contraceptive vaccine. For example, if women could be inoculated with a vaccine that triggered production of antibodies to a protein found only in sperm, this would prevent fertilization. A booster shot would be needed every couple of years to continue the effectiveness of such vaccines.

A report issued in 1990 by the National Research Council's Institute of Medicine warned that the United States is far behind other countries in offering choices of birth control. The biggest deterrent to new contraceptive methods is not technology or lack of research, but an insurance–product liability problem. American consumers are accepting of the fact that contraceptive methods sometimes fail to prevent pregnancy, but they are less forgiving about side effects. However, as Dr. Carl Djerassi (one of the developers of the birth control pill) stated to a congressional committee in 1978, "there is no such thing as a wholly safe contraceptive." Some methods, such as Depo-Provera, went through more than 20 years of FDA hearings before they won final approval, yet were available to people around the world all during that time. Women in Europe are presently using two new types of IUDs (including one that releases hormones) and a hand-held computer that tells when it is safe to have intercourse, but they still are not approved for use in the United States.

When a legal case involves an individual versus a large corporation, juries often award large settlements to the individual in the belief that the corporation can afford it. A jury awarded $5 million, for example, to a couple who claimed that their child's birth defects were caused by spermicides, even though the authors of the study that claimed to link spermicides with birth defects had repudiated their own results. Lawsuits have been filed by 50,000 users of Norplant, but thousands have been dismissed and the only one to go to court was decided in favor of the manufacturer. However, a few more cases like this and we may see the end of spermicides, the diaphragm and contraceptive sponge, and all hormonal methods of contraception. There has never been a contraceptive device that was not associated with some risk, but unless consumers change their attitudes and stop unrealistically expecting perfection, we may retreat to the days when there was nothing available except the condom.

CHOOSING A CONTRACEPTIVE METHOD

It is important that men and women choose a method of birth control with which they and their partner are comfortable. A woman may like the diaphragm, but it will not be good if her partner resents her stopping in the middle of having sex to put it in. A man may prefer that his female partner take the pill, but it will not be

good for the couple's relationship if she resents having to suffer possible side effects. A couple can work these kinds of problems out only by talking about the matter and communicating with each other on a regular basis.

Choosing a particular birth control method does not mean that you have to stick with it if you are unhappy about it for any reason. As you know by now, there are many alternatives. For example, about 1 out of 7 married women attempting to avoid pregnancy decide to abandon their chosen method within the first year of use. Unfortunately, half of these women use no type of contraception at all for at least a month afterwards (Grady et al., 1988). If you do not presently wish to have children and are unhappy with the birth control method you use, decide on an alternative method *before* you stop using your present one.

When deciding which type of birth control to use, ask yourself the following questions; they were developed to help you decide whether the method you are considering is a good choice or a poor choice *for you* (adapted from Robert Hatcher et al. (1998). Reprinted with permission of the publishers.)

Method of birth control you are considering using: _____

Length of time you used this method in the past: _____

Answer "yes" or "no" to the following questions:	**Yes**	**No**
1. Have I had problems using this method before?	____	____
2. Have I ever become pregnant while using this method?	____	____
3. Am I afraid of using this method?	____	____
4. Would I really rather not use this method?	____	____
5. Will I have trouble remembering to use this method?	____	____
6. Will I have trouble using this method correctly?	____	____
7. Do I still have unanswered questions about this method?	____	____
8. Does this method make menstrual periods longer or more painful?	____	____
9. Does this method cost more than I can afford?	____	____
10. Could this method cause me to have serious complications?	____	____
11. Am I opposed to this method because of any religious or moral beliefs?	____	____
12. Is my partner opposed to this method?	____	____
13. Am I using this method without my partner's knowledge?	____	____
14. Will using this method embarrass my partner?	____	____
15. Will using this method embarrass me?	____	____
16. Will I enjoy intercourse less because of this method?	____	____
17. If this method interrupts lovemaking, will I avoid using it?	____	____
18. Has a nurse or doctor ever told me *not* to use this method?	____	____
19. Is there anything about my personality that could lead me to use this method incorrectly?	____	____
20. Am I at any risk of being exposed to HIV (the AIDS virus) or other sexually transmitted infections if I use this method.	____	____
Total Number of "Yes" Answers:	____	____

Most individuals will have a few "yes" answers. "Yes" answers mean that potential problems may lie in store. If you have more than a few "yes" responses, you may want to talk to your physician, counselor, partner, or friend. Talking it over can help you to decide whether to use this method, or how to use it so it will really be effective for you. In general, the more "yes" answers you have, the less likely you are to use this method consistently and correctly.

This chapter has only introduced the various contraceptive methods. If additional information is desired, you are urged to contact your local Planned Parenthood organization or your state family planning clinic. The people who work there will be glad to help you.

Sex is for people who are ready and willing to take a lifetime responsibility for the outcome of sex. (Sue Finn, as quoted by L. Smith, 1993)

Many parents are opposed to the teaching of contraception in school because they worry that it will lead to sexual activity. Research has shown, however, that young people who have had sex education are no more likely to engage in sexual intercourse than those who have not had it—and, more importantly, that they are less likely to get pregnant. Look again at Table 6–1. Danish, Dutch, and Swedish children have sex just as much as American teens, but far fewer get pregnant or get someone pregnant (e.g., Singh & Darroch, 2000; Wielandt & Knudsen, 1997). In those countries, children are taught about contraception at an early age, in an open and frank manner. Teenage pregnancies are treated not as a moral issue, but as a public health issue (see Box 1–A).

Key Terms

abortion   164
adoption   163
barrier method   149
basal body temperature method   147
Billings method   147
breast-feeding   145
calendar method   146
cervical cap   153
cervical mucus   147
combination pill   156
condom   149
contraception   140
contraceptive sponge   154

Depo-Provera   159
diaphragm   152
dilation and curettage (D&C)   164
dilation and evacuation (D&E)   165
douching   145
emergency contraception   161
female condom   151
fertility awareness method   146
IUD (intrauterine device)   155
laparoscopy   162
Lunelle   159
minilaparotomy   162

minipill   156
nonoxynol-9   148
Norplant   159
perfect-use pregnancy rate   143
progestins   156
RU 486   164
spermicides   148
sterilization   161
sympto-thermal method   148
tubal ligation   43, 162
typical-use pregnancy rate   143
vasectomy   50, 161
withdrawal (coitus interruptus)   145

Suggested Readings

Consumer Reports. (1995, May). How reliable are condoms? Tests the strength of over 40 types of condoms, along with giving consumer ratings.

Gordon, L. (1990). *Woman's body, woman's right: A social history of birth control.* New York: Penguin. An excellent history of birth control.

Hatcher, R., et al. (1998). *Contraceptive technology.* New York: Irvington. This is the most comprehensive and technical review of contraceptive methods. It is revised every 2 to 3 years.

Nordenberg, T. (1997, April). Protecting against unintended pregnancy: A guide to contraceptive choice. *FDA Consumer.* A short article, but hits the major points.

Potts, M. (2000). The unmet need for family planning. *Scientific American,* January, 88–93. Looks at the high fertility rate in many parts of the world.

Tribe, L. (1992). *Abortion: The clash of absolutes.* New York: W. W. Norton. An even-handed treatment of the controversy over abortion.

Winikoff, B., & Wymelenberg, S. (1997). *The whole truth about contraception.* Washington, DC: National Academy of Sciences. It is easy to read, and accurate (after all, it's from the National Academy of Sciences).

Study Guide

INTERACTIVE REVIEW

The teen pregnancy rate in the United States is (1) _____ as high as in most other developed countries. About 80 percent of pregnancies to teenagers in the United States are unintended, and (2) _____ are terminated by abortion. Unfortunately, the teens most likely to have babies are those least prepared to take care of them.

Worldwide, there is need for effective contraceptive technology. World population is expected to nearly double by the middle of this century, yet already there are many parts of the world experiencing food shortages and mass starvation.

While all the methods of birth control discussed in this chapter are better than using nothing, some are more effective than others. Relatively ineffective methods include withdrawal, douching, and breast-feeding. Fertility awareness methods—the (3) _____, (4) _____, and (5) _____ methods—rely on calculating when (6) _____ will occur and abstaining from intercourse during that period. The pregnancy rates for these methods are higher than for most others. (7) _____ work by killing sperm and are generally used in combination with a barrier method of contraception—(8) _____, (9) _____, (10) _____, or (11) _____. Barrier methods block sperm from getting into the (12) _____. Spermicides and barrier methods often interfere with spontaneity, but for people who are not in a monogamous relationship, a major advantage of these methods (not offered by other methods) is that they (13) _____.

Intrauterine devices (IUDs) have had a reputation for causing serious problems, but today's IUDs are safe as well as highly effective. However, they are recommended only for women in long-term monogamous relationships who have completed their families. The combination birth control pill contains synthetic (14) _____ and (15) _____ and works by preventing ovulation. The pills used today contain low dosages of estrogen and are safer than the high-dosage pills used in the past. Nevertheless, there are certain groups of women who, for medical reasons, should not take the pill. (16) _____ (the shot good for 3 months) and (17) _____ (the implant good for 5 years) contain only progestin and are believed to be safer than the pill. All three hormonal methods of contraception have theoretical failure rates of less than 1 percent. For women who have had unprotected intercourse, emergency contraception pills are effective when taken within (18) _____ hours of intercourse, or an IUD may be implanted within 7 days.

If you consider male and female sterilization techniques together, more Americans rely on sterilization for birth control than any other method. In a vasectomy, the (19) _____ is tied off and cut. Afterwards, the man still ejaculates during orgasm, but his ejaculation contains no sperm. For a (20) _____ or (21) _____, a woman's Fallopian tubes are cut, cauterized, or blocked by clips. The failure rate is close to zero.

For women who have an unplanned or unwanted pregnancy, one option is abortion. Various techniques can be used to terminate pregnancy, including chemicals, scraping or suctioning away of the endometrium, and induced labor. The Supreme Court has recently made several decisions affecting the availability of abortion in the United States.

It is important for you to choose an effective contraceptive technique *before* you have sexual intercourse. A questionnaire is provided at the end of the chapter that is designed to help you decide which method is best for you.

SELF-TEST

A. TRUE OR FALSE

- [T] [F] 22. The contraceptive sponge is effective for 24 hours.
- [T] [F] 23. The rates for births to teenage girls have decreased since 1970 because of increased use of contraceptives.
- [T] [F] 24. The world population is expected to stabilize by the year 2010 because of increased use of birth control.
- [T] [F] 25. The U.S. fertility rate is presently about 2.0 births per woman.
- [T] [F] 26. If the perfect-use pregnancy rate for a contraceptive method is 20 percent, then for 100 couples who start using the method, about 20 of them will have conceived after 3 years.

T F	27.	In order for a woman to get pregnant, she must have an orgasm.
T F	28.	More couples rely on sterilization than on the birth control pill.
T F	29.	It is possible for a girl to get pregnant as soon as she starts having menstrual periods.
T F	30.	A relatively effective method of birth control for women is to wash out the contents of the vagina immediately after sexual intercourse.
T F	31.	The birth control pill reduces the risk of getting a sexually transmitted disease.
T F	32.	A vasectomy works as birth control by preventing ejaculation.
T F	33.	If carefully washed and dried, condoms can be used safely on more than one occasion.
T F	34.	Most women gain weight when they start taking the birth control pill.
T F	35.	The contraceptive sponge is more effective than the diaphragm.
T F	36.	Taking antibiotics makes the birth control pill less effective.
T F	37.	Legal abortions do not increase a woman's later risk of infertility, miscarriage, or a low-birth-weight baby.
T F	38.	Because IUDs are so effective, they are highly recommended for young, sexually active women.
T F	39.	The major difference between the cervical cap and the diaphragm is that the cervical cap does not need to be used with spermicide.
T F	40.	Emergency contraceptive techniques work by causing abortion.
T F	41.	Breast-feeding a baby inhibits the release of follicle-stimulating hormone from a woman's pituitary gland.
T F	42.	With perfect use, fertility awareness methods are as effective as the birth control pill.
T F	43.	Spermicides help to kill HIV, the virus that causes AIDS.
T F	44.	Pregnancy and childbirth result in more maternal deaths than the birth control pill.
T F	45.	In the future, it will probably be possible to be vaccinated to prevent pregnancy (as is done for the flu).
T F	46.	Rubber condoms are more effective than "skin" condoms for prevention of STDs.
T F	47.	The female condom is actually an intravaginal pouch.
T F	48.	In high dosages, combination birth control pills can be used as emergency birth control.
T F	49.	Most women over the age of 40 can continue to take the combination birth control pill.
T F	50.	Once inserted under the skin, Norplant must remain in place for 5 years.
T F	51.	The diaphragm offers women some protection against gonorrhea and chlamydia.

B. MATCHING (SOME ANSWERS CAN BE USED MORE THAN ONCE)

Contraceptive Method

_____ 52. breast-feeding
_____ 53. calendar method
_____ 54. basal body temperature method
_____ 55. Billings method
_____ 56. spermicides
_____ 57. male condom
_____ 58. female condom
_____ 59. diaphragm
_____ 60. cervical cap
_____ 61. contraceptive sponge
_____ 62. emergency contraception

a. once believed to work by preventing implantation, but now known also to work by preventing fertilization
b. active ingredient kills sperm
c. prevents release of FSH
d. involves noting changes in cervical mucus in order to determine when to abstain from intercourse
e. prevents sperm deposited in the vagina from getting into the uterus
f. involves tying, cutting, or cauterizing Fallopian tubes, or blocking them by clips
g. contains enough spermicide to be effective for 24 hours
h. blocks sperm from getting into the vagina
i. uses simple mathematical formula to determine when to abstain from intercourse

_____ 63. IUD
_____ 64. combination pill
_____ 65. Depo-Provera
_____ 66. Norplant
_____ 67. vasectomy
_____ 68. tubal ligation
_____ 69. laparoscopy

j. progestins prevent ovulation
k. uses changes in resting temperature to determine when to abstain from intercourse
l. involves tying or cutting off vas deferens
m. synthetic estrogen helps to prevent ovulation
n. prevents implantation

C. FILL IN THE BLANKS

70. Withdrawal is not a highly effective method of birth control because of secretions from _____.

71. After a vasectomy, a man is not sterile until _____.

72. If a woman's shortest recorded menstrual cycle is 25 days and her longest is 31 days, by the calendar method she should abstain from intercourse from day _____ to day _____.

73. Women's basal body temperature _____ 24 to 72 hours after ovulation.

74. Women's cervical mucus becomes _____ at the time of ovulation.

75. Rubber condoms should not be used in combination with _____ lubricants.

76. The IUD is regarded as a safe contraceptive method for women _____.

77. Three nonprescription barrier types of contraception are the _____, _____, and the _____.

78. The most common side effect of Depo-Provera and Norplant is _____.

79. Four birth control techniques that offer women some protection against STDs are _____, _____, _____ and _____.

80. In cases of rape, emergency contraception can be provided within the first few days by _____.

81. If used properly and consistently, the most effective nonprescription nonsurgical method of birth control is _____.

82. Sperm can live in a Fallopian tube for as long as _____.

83. The best way to avoid an unwanted pregnancy is _____.

Pregnancy and Childbirth

Sex is separateness: a division of reproductive labor into specialized cells, organs, and organisms. The sexes of a species are the classes of reproductively incomplete individuals. In order for a sex member to contribute to the physical foundations of its species, to reproduce part of itself into the next generation, it must remedy its incompleteness. The remedy is found in the union of incomplete parts from complementary complete organisms: eggs and sperm cells unite.

(Gordon Bermant and Julian Davidson, 1974)

Pregnancy and childbirth are intense experiences, remembered for a lifetime. The most potent human emotions—hope, fear, love, loneliness, depression, and joy—are often felt at their maximum levels. The first time that a woman feels a baby move inside her, her first labor contractions, the first time that a child is viewed by its parents after birth—these are often the things that make life worth experiencing. Giving birth means assuming a great responsibility, for the newborn is totally dependent upon his or her parents. Relationships change with the addition of a new life and new responsibilities within a family. This requires that many adjustments in living be made. As you will see, it is important to begin making these adjustments before the baby is born—sometimes even before the baby is conceived.

When you have finished studying this chapter, you should be able to:

1. Explain the process of conception, including the terms primary follicle, Graafian follicle, capacitation, and zygote;

2. Trace the process of development from the zygote through implantation, and discuss some problems that sometimes occur with implantation;

3. Describe what occurs in each trimester of pregnancy for both mother and embryo/fetus;

4. Summarize the possible effects of smoking, alcohol, drug use, environmental hazards, and diseases in the embryo and fetus;

5. Compare and contrast several methods for detecting fetal abnormalities;

6. Discuss traditional and alternative birthing practices, including Lamaze, Bradley, home births, and the use of midwives;

7. Explain the three stages of labor and the events that occur in each;

8. Identify and explain the problems that can occur during breech deliveries, cesareans, and preterm deliveries;

9. Describe the hormones necessary to produce milk for breast-feeding and discuss the benefits of breast-feeding;

10. Discuss recommendations concerning sexual intercourse during and following pregnancy; and

11. Compare and contrast the various methods for dealing with infertility.

CONCEPTION AND IMPLANTATION

As you learned in Chapters 2 and 3, the ovaries store eggs (**ova**). Each egg is surrounded by a small sac, forming what is called a **primary follicle.** As a result of the release of follicle-stimulating hormone (FSH) from the pituitary gland, one (or more) of these primary follicles matures to become a **Graafian follicle.** About midway through a 28-day menstrual cycle, the Graafian follicle breaks open and the ovum is released into the abdominal cavity, where it is picked up by one of the Fallopian tubes. The **ovum** moves through the Fallopian tube to the uterus. It will take 3 to 7 days to reach the uterus, but *the ovum can only be fertilized during the first 24 hours after it leaves an ovary* (Moore, 1993). If a sperm does not penetrate the ovum during this time, the ovum becomes overly "ripe" and eventually disintegrates in the uterus, leaving the woman's body during her menstrual flow.

At orgasm during sexual intercourse, a man will ejaculate 200–300 million **sperm** into the vagina. The sperm then attempt to pass through the cervix and uterus to the Fallopian tubes. This is not an easy journey. Some sperm are stopped by the force of gravity, some by the acidity of the woman's reproductive tract, some by clumping, and some simply by taking wrong turns (because usually only one egg is released, only one Fallopian tube will be the right path for the sperm to follow). Only a few thousand will live long enough to reach the Fallopian tubes, and fewer than 50 will reach the egg within the Fallopian tube (Moore, 1993). Most sperm live for only 3 days inside a woman's reproductive tract, but a few may live for as long as 5 days (Wilcox et al., 1995). Thus, intercourse can result in conception only 6 days out of every 28-day menstrual cycle (5 days before ovulation and the day of ovulation). If you want to know the probability of conception on any one of these 6 days, go back to the section on fertility awareness methods in Chapter 6.

While the sperm are in the female's reproductive tract, they undergo a process called **capacitation** in which their membranes become thin enough so that an enzyme (called hyaluronidase) can be released to soften the egg's outer layers. Only sperm that undergo capacitation are able to unite with an egg. For capacitation to finish, sperm need to spend several hours in the reproductive tract. The egg sends out tiny projections

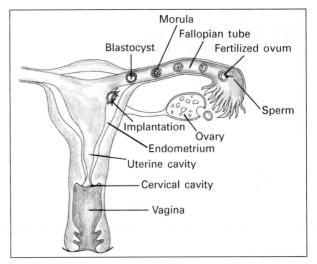

Figure 7–1 Ovulation, fertilization, and implantation.

and pulls one sperm to its surface, the *zona pellucida.* That sperm secretes the enzyme and penetrates the egg's surface, and **conception** takes place. An instantaneous chemical reaction within the ovum then prevents other sperm from penetrating the ovum. Within 24–30 hours, the nuclei of the sperm and the ovum fuse to form a one-celled organism called a **zygote.** This single cell contains the complete genetic code, or blueprint, for a new human being.

Shortly afterward, the zygote splits into two separate cells, then four, then eight, and so on. As cell division occurs, each individual cell gets smaller. This collection of cells is called a **morula.** While cell division is rapidly taking place, the morula is slowly continuing its trip toward the uterus. When the conceptus has about 100 cells, it has developed a fluid-filled center and is then called a **blastocyst.** After the blastocyst reaches the uterus, it may float there for several days. At this point it is still smaller than the head of a pin.

The endometrium is receptive to **implantation** for a 4- or 5-day period. At about 8 to 11 days after ovulation, the blastocyst attaches itself to the endometrium via hairlike roots called *villi* (Wilcox et al., 1999) (see Figure 7-1). By this time the endometrium has a large supply of blood that can serve as a source of nutrients and oxygen. The blastocyst is now called an embryo; it is called a fetus at about 8 weeks (see section below on pregnancy).

---

ovum (ova, pl.) An egg; the female reproductive cell.

primary follicle An immature ovum enclosed by a single layer of cells.

Graafian follicle A mature follicle.

sperm The germ cell of a man.

capacitation A process that sperm undergo while traveling through the woman's reproductive tract in which their membranes become thin enough so that an enzyme necessary for softening the ovum's membrane can be released.

conception The union of an egg and a sperm.

zygote The one-celled organism created from the fusion of a sperm and egg.

morula The collection of cells formed when the zygote begins rapid cell division.

blastocyst The fluid-filled sphere that reaches the uterus after fertilization and which was created by the transformation of the morula through continued, rapid cell division.

implantation The process by which the blastocyst attaches itself to the wall of the uterus.

The outer cell layers of the embryo are called the **trophoblast** (from the Greek *trophe,* meaning "to nourish"). The trophoblast begins to grow rapidly and forms four protective layers or membranes, each with a special function. One produces blood cells for the embryo until it can produce its own. Another cell layer forms the **umbilical cord**—the major link between the developing embryo and its mother. The third membrane is called the **amnion.** It is a thick-skinned sac filled with water that surrounds the embryo. By surrounding the developing embryo with liquid, protection is provided against bumps, sudden movements by the mother, and changes in temperature. The fourth membrane, called the **chorion,** will develop into the lining of the placenta. The **placenta** is an organ that serves as a connection or interface between the embryo's systems and those of the mother. The embryo is connected to the placenta by the umbilical cord. Through it, the embryo receives nourishment from its mother. It also receives antibodies for protection against infection. Wastes from the embryo's system travel from the umbilical cord to the placenta, and from there are taken up by the mother's excretory system.

Over 98 percent of term pregnancies result in the birth of a single baby. What causes twins (or other multiple births)? If two different ova are fertilized by two different sperm, the result is *dizygotic* (fraternal or nonidentical) twins. *Monozygotic* (identical) twins result when a fertilized ovum subdivides before it implants in the uterus. Interestingly, the chance of having multiple births increases with the age of the mother (Lazar, 1996).

PERSONAL REFLECTIONS
What qualities do you possess that will make you a good parent? Do you have any qualities that might not make you a good parent? What things can you do to prepare yourself to be a good parent? How well suited is your partner to be the mother or father of your child?

---

trophoblast The outer four cell layers of the embryo.

umbilical cord The cord that connects an embryo or fetus to the mother's placenta.

amnion A thick-skinned sac filled with water that surrounds the fetus.

chorion The fourth membrane of the trophoblast; it develops into the lining of the placenta.

placenta An organ that serves as a connection or interface between the fetus's systems and those of the mother.

ectopic pregnancy The implantation of a fertilized egg outside of the endometrium of the uterus.

PROBLEMS WITH IMPLANTATION

It has been estimated that about three-fourths of conceptions either fail to implant or are spontaneously aborted within the first 6 weeks (Wilcox et al., 1999). Over 20 percent fail before pregnancy can be detected by chemical tests (Wilcox et al., 1988). Failure to implant may be a means of "weeding out" or preventing the further development of blastocysts that are not completely healthy or normal.

One type of problem with implantation is called **ectopic pregnancy** (from the Greek *ektopos,* meaning "out of place"). In this case, conception is successful, but implantation takes place outside the uterus. In about 96 percent of these cases, implantation occurs in a Fallopian tube. In rarer cases, implantation can occur on an ovary, on the cervix, or in the abdomen. When implantation occurs in a Fallopian tube (often called a *tubal pregnancy*), there is simply not enough room for the embryo to grow. Unlike the uterus, the Fallopian tubes are not capable of much expansion. The embryo may be dissolved by the body's immunological system, but if it continues to grow after the 8th week, it may break the tube. This is a serious complication of pregnancy, and it can be fatal. Although the mortality rate has been dropping due to earlier detection, ectopic pregnancies still account for up to 10 percent of all pregnancy-related deaths (Kamwendo et al., 2000).

The rate of ectopic pregnancies increased fourfold from 1970 to the mid-1980s, and they now account for about 1.5 percent of all pregnancies (Kamwendo et al., 2000). Ectopic pregnancies are caused by conditions that block or slow passage of the conceptus to the uterus. The most common cause is scarring of the Fallopian tubes due to pelvic inflammatory disease resulting from untreated chlamydia or gonorrhea (Kamwendo et al, 2000; Tay et al., 2000). Because they reduce the risk of sexually transmitted diseases, use of condoms also reduces the risk of tubal pregnancies in sexually active women. Other factors include previous ectopic pregnancy, anatomical malformations of the tubes, use of (older types of) intrauterine devices, increasing age at time of conception, smoking, and douching. If a woman has an ectopic pregnancy, she has an increased risk of having more ectopic pregnancies in the future, because many of the causes of the original problem, such as scarring, will still be present in later pregnancies (Tay et al., 2000).

"I got pregnant only to learn it was tubular. . . . One year later I got pregnant again and again it was tubular. The specialist told me I needed surgery to remove scar tissue that was choking my Fallopian tube." (from the author's files)

Today, the vast majority of ectopic pregnancies can be diagnosed by transvaginal sonography (which uses sound waves to create a picture of the inside of a woman's reproductive tract) in combination with blood HCG levels (Tay et al., 2000). In the past, women diagnosed with tubal pregnancy always had part of the affected tube surgically removed, which greatly reduced the chances of pregnancy in the future. Now, if an ectopic pregnancy is confirmed, it can be treated by laparoscopic surgery rather than tubal sectioning. The probability of subsequent successful pregnancies is just as high with the conservative therapy as

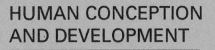

A close-up photo of sperm on the surface of an ovum

Many sperm attempting to penetrate the membrane of an ovum. Only one will be successful.

A FIBEROPTIC VIEW OF EMBRYONIC AND FETAL DEVELOPMENT

(a) One day (two cells)

(b) 3 1/2 days

(c) 21 days (note the primitive spinal cord)

(d) Four weeks

(e) Eight weeks

(f) Twelve weeks

(g) Sixteen weeks

Stages of prenatal development. The heart and nervous system begin to function by the end of four weeks. The fetus is recognizably human by 16 weeks, but will stand very little chance of survival if born before 24 weeks. Note the umbilical cord connection with the placenta in the photo taken at eight weeks.

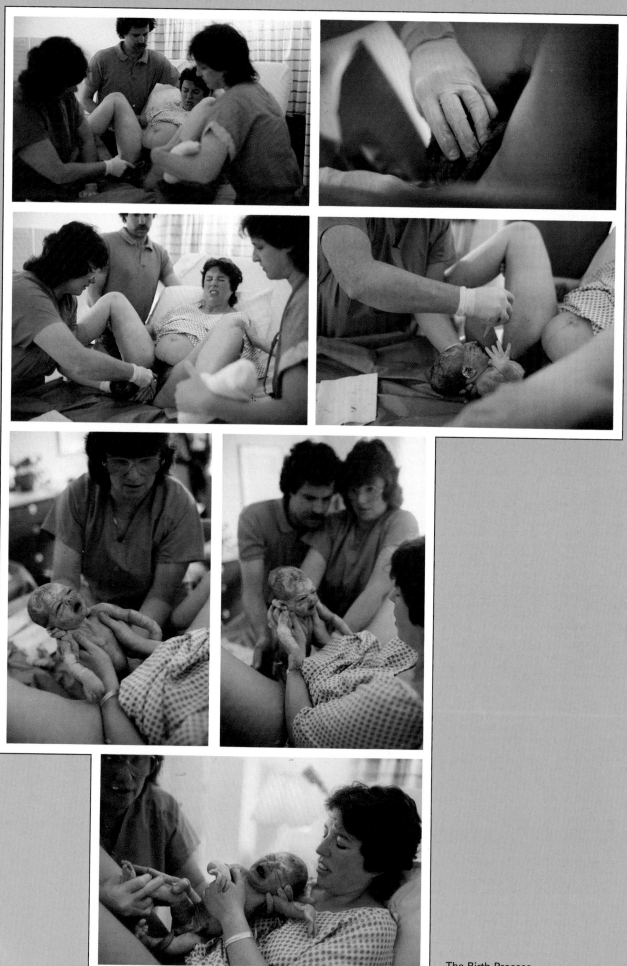

The Birth Process

with the radical therapy. Alternatively, some physicians are treating ectopic pregnancies by administering a drug called methotrexate (see Tay et al., 2000). This field is undergoing rapid change, and there is increasing optimism that more and more women will be treated with these conservative procedures.

PREGNANCY

Pregnancy lasts an average of 260 to 270 days. "Due dates," the dates that physicians set as the "expected time of arrival" for babies, are rarely the dates of actual birth. This is because the exact date of conception is hard to measure with complete accuracy and because there is great variability among births, even with the same parents. Because pregnancy lasts about 9 months, this time is divided into 3-month periods, called **trimesters,** for descriptive purposes.

THE FIRST TRIMESTER—THE MOTHER

Recall from Chapter 3 that a missed menstrual period is not a sure sign of the start of pregnancy. Many things can cause a missed period, including stress and illness. In fact, a woman can miss a period without knowing it, because implantation of the blastocyst into the uterine wall can cause bleeding that may be mistaken for menstruation.

When a period is missed, women often want quick and accurate information about whether or not they are actually pregnant. To get this information, they take a "pregnancy test." These tests are conducted by physicians and medical technicians; some are even sold in drugstores for use at home. They work by determining if a hormone secreted by the placenta (**human chorionic gonadotropin,** or **HCG**) is present in a woman's urine. This test is most accurate (95–98 percent) 2 weeks or more after a missed period. Tests that measure HCG in blood can detect if a woman is pregnant even sooner than this.

The most common symptom of early pregnancy is nausea. It is called **"morning sickness"** (medically referred to as *nausea and vomiting of pregnancy*), though it can occur at any time of the day. Seventy to 90 percent of pregnant women experience mild or moderate morning sickness. It generally begins 4 to 6 weeks after conception, reaches its peak by 8 to 12 weeks, and then usually (although not always) spontaneously disappears by the 20th week (Zhou et al., 1999). Although there are a number of speculations as to its cause (particularly rising estrogen levels), nothing has been proven conclusively (Deuchar, 1995). Some women eat crackers, drink soda water, and try a variety of other home remedies to cope with morning sickness, but there is no known safe yet effective way of treating it. Many men experience some of the same

symptoms of pregnancy as their partners. In the United States this is sometimes called "sympathy pains," but the medical term for it is **couvade syndrome** (from a French term for the birthing process).

Other symptoms that women may exhibit during the first trimester include enlarged and tender breasts, prominent veins on the breasts, darkened areolas, enlarged nipples, increased frequency of urination, and irregular bowel movements. In addition, many women feel tired and run-down.

THE FIRST TRIMESTER—THE EMBRYO/FETUS

In the first trimester of pregnancy, a substantial amount of development takes place (see Figure 7–2). When the blastocyst implants, it is less than one-third of an inch in diameter. After implantation, it is known as an **embryo.** Cell differentiation begins to take place now, and development occurs in orderly ways. Growth in the embryo occurs from the head downward and from the center (spine) outward. As mentioned earlier, the outer layers of the blastocyst form structures designed to nourish and protect it. In the embryo, three inner cell layers will form specific parts of the body: The *ectoderm* forms the nervous system, skin, and teeth. The *mesoderm* forms the muscles, skeleton, and blood vessels. The *endoderm* forms the internal organs (lungs, liver, digestive system, etc).

In the 3rd week of pregnancy, a central structure called a neural tube becomes a dominant feature. The neural tube will become the central nervous system. By the end of the 4th week, the umbilical cord, heart, and digestive system begin to form. At 6 weeks, the embryo has a "tail," which will become the tip of the spine. It also has structures that look like gills but are actually parts of the neck and face that have not yet fully developed. At 8 weeks, the embryo is about 1⅛ inches long. All organs have begun to develop. The heart is pumping, and the stomach has begun to produce some digestive juices. The embryo, although small, is well on its way toward developing into a unique human being. After 8 weeks and until birth, the developing organism is called a **fetus.**

THE SECOND TRIMESTER— THE MOTHER

In the 4h or 5th month of pregnancy, the movements of the fetus can be felt by its mother. This first experience of movement is called **quickening.**

trimesters Three-month periods of pregnancy (months 1–3, 4–6, and 7–9), so labeled for descriptive purposes.

human chorionic gonadotropin (HCG) A hormone secreted by the chorion that stimulates the ovaries during pregnancy.

morning sickness A symptom of early pregnancy involving nausea.

couvade syndrome The experiencing of pregnancy symptoms by male partners; sometimes called "sympathy pains."

embryo The term given to the blastocyst after it has implanted.

fetus The term given to the embryo after the 8th week of pregnancy.

quickening The first time a pregnant woman experiences movement of the fetus, usually in the 5th month.

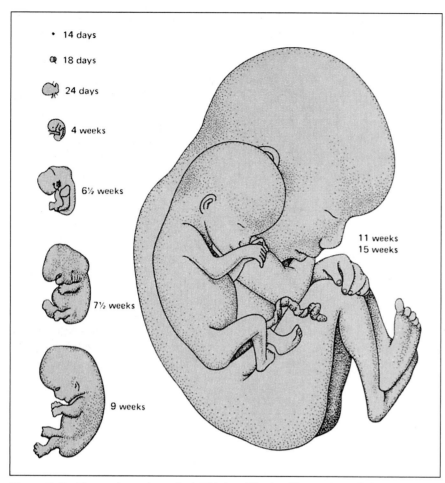

- 14 days
- 18 days
- 24 days
- 4 weeks
- 6½ weeks
- 7½ weeks
- 9 weeks

11 weeks
15 weeks

Figure 7–2 The embryonic period. This is a life-size illustration of the growth of the human embryo and fetus from 14 days to 15 weeks.

that is produced before milk starts to flow. Water retention may cause edema (swelling) in the ankles, feet, and hands. Women may begin to develop varicose veins and/or hemorrhoids. The cessation of morning sickness often brings an increase in appetite.

THE SECOND TRIMESTER—THE FETUS

At this time, the fetus begins to make sucking motions with its mouth. In the 5th month, the fetus has a detectable heartbeat (see Figure 7–4). It will respond to sound, and it begins to show definite periods of sleep and wakefulness. If born at this time, the fetus has only a 1-in-10,000 chance of survival. In the 6th month, the fetus can open its eyes. It will suck its thumb and respond to light. At the end of the second trimester, the fetus is about 1 foot long and weighs about 1 pound.

THE THIRD TRIMESTER— THE MOTHER

For the expectant mother, walking, sitting, and rising become more difficult. Pregnant women often have to learn new ways to sit down and to get up out of a chair. Expectant mothers often experience back pain from carrying a new weight load in front of them, which shifts their center of gravity. The uterus, enlarging with the rapidly growing fetus, puts pressure on the bladder and stomach. As a result, urination becomes more frequent—a woman may have to urinate four or five times a night. Indigestion, heartburn, gas, and constipation are also common complaints. Finding a comfortable sleeping position is not easy, and a woman may have to change positions several times each night. Leg cramps may occur, a condition sometimes treated by taking extra calcium. The woman's navel may push out. Often she experiences a low energy level.

Although a woman generally knows by this time that she is pregnant, this knowledge is usually an abstract or "intellectual" thing. Once a woman begins to feel a new life moving inside her, the fetus begins to be viewed as a person, and an emotional attachment to her unborn baby generally begins to form.

> "During my 5th month of pregnancy, I felt the baby move for the first time. It almost felt like the rumbling a stomach makes when you're hungry. It could be described as a 'fluttering,' and it is very exciting. Unfortunately, it doesn't happen that often at first, so you have to 'catch it' if you want your partner to share in the experience." (from the author's files)

Women generally begin to get over their morning sickness in the second trimester. They also notice that their figures are changing, and they may worry about no longer being attractive to their partners. As her abdomen expands, red lines, or "stretch marks," may develop on a mother-to-be. The breasts begin to swell and may start to leak *colostrum*, a thick, sticky liquid

In 1990, the Institute of Medicine made the following recommendations for weight gain during pregnancy based on initial weight and height: 28–40 pounds for underweight women, 25–35 pounds for normal-weight women, 15–25 pounds for overweight women, and at least 15 pounds for obese women. If weight gain is too low, there is concern about the fetus having proper levels of nourishment. If weight gain is too high, blood pressure may rise and there is an increased risk of a difficult labor and the need for emergency cesarean delivery (Johnson et al., 1992). Also, excess weight may be hard to lose after the baby is born. It is advisable to have weekly checkups by a physician when the due date gets close.

THE THIRD TRIMESTER—THE FETUS

By the end of the 7th month of pregnancy, the fetus is about 15 inches long and weighs about 1½ pounds (see Figure 7–5). Fatty tissues begin to develop under the skin. A lack of these tissues is what causes premature infants to look so skinny. In the 8th month, the fetus's weight begins to increase dramatically. At the end of the 8th month, it will weigh about 4 pounds and will be 16 to 17 inches long. From this point on, the fetus will gain about ½ pound per week. In the 9th month, the fetus will grow to about 20 inches in length and weigh an average of 7 to 7½ pounds (see Figure 7–6). There is considerable variation in these measurements, however.

The fetus is covered with light hair **(lanugo)** and a waxy bluish substance **(vernix caseosa).** These will make the newborn look very interesting, but they serve as protective devices. Today, the vernix is often allowed to be absorbed into the skin after birth rather than being immediately washed off.

SEXUAL INTERCOURSE DURING PREGNANCY

Feelings about sexual behavior during pregnancy vary from culture to culture. In North America, two patterns of sexual activity have been observed during pregnancy. One is a steady decline in sexual activity throughout pregnancy (Call et al., 1995). However, a large-scale study found that 90 percent of couples were still having intercourse in the 5th month of pregnancy (Hyde et al., 1996).

> "The fact that it's impossible to get any more pregnant, it makes sex during pregnancy very exciting. My senses seemed much more heightened and both my husband and I found it to be extremely pleasurable." (from the author's files)

The second pattern, discussed by Masters and Johnson (1966), is an increase in sexual activity from the first to the second trimester. Freed of the worry about getting pregnant, some women begin to express their sexuality fully for the first time. This is followed by a decreased interest in sex during the third trimester (von Sydow, 1999). As you might expect, attitudes about sex during pregnancy are related to attitudes about sex before pregnancy (Fisher & Gray, 1988).

Women (and men) list three general reasons for a declining interest in sexual intercourse during pregnancy. One reason is physical discomfort. The tradi- tional man-on-top position can be increasingly uncomfortable for the woman as pregnancy progresses. This discomfort can be alleviated through the use of alternate positions that lessen pressure on the woman's abdomen during intercourse. The woman-on-top position is probably most comfortable. After the fetus drops, the penis can make contact with an unyielding cervix during sexual intercourse, so shallow penetration is recommended for intercourse late in pregnancy.

A second reason for decreased interest in sex is that women may feel that they no longer appear attractive. They fear that their partners will see them as "ugly," lose interest, and begin to look for new sex partners. Interestingly, men generally do not list this as a cause of decreased sexual activity.

> "We never had sexual intercourse after the first 5 months. I felt disgusted, embarrassed and upset with the way my body had changed." (from the author's files)

The third reason is fear about the pregnancy or about the possibility of harming the fetus (Bogren, 1991).

> "At about the middle of my pregnancy, my husband had a decrease of interest in sex while my interest had increased. I was already feeling fat and ugly, and this just made things worse. Many nights I stayed up crying because not only did I think I was fat and ugly, but I thought my husband did too. Then I realized his problem was that he was scared he was going to hurt me or the baby. I tried to convince him that he wouldn't, but I guess he just couldn't stop thinking about it while we were having sex." (from the author's files)

This leads to an important question: How far into pregnancy is it safe to engage in sexual intercourse? A recent review of 59 studies found that if there are no other risk factors, sexual intercourse during pregnancy does not harm the fetus (von Sydow, 1999). The consensus of opinion is summed up in the highly regarded *Williams Obstetrics*: "It has been generally accepted that in healthy pregnant women, sexual intercourse usually does no harm before the last four weeks or so of pregnancy" (Cunningham et al., 1997). What about the last 4 weeks? Here, there is some debate and you should consult with your doctor.

In any case, sexual behavior is not limited to intercourse, and in the latter stages of pregnancy alternative forms of sexual stimulation may be preferred. Hugging, touching, and other displays of affection are important ways of communi- cating attraction. It is impor- tant to speak to a pregnant woman about love and devo- tion and to express pride in her and hope for the future.

lanugo Light hair that covers a newborn baby.

vernix caseosa A waxy bluish substance that covers a newborn baby.

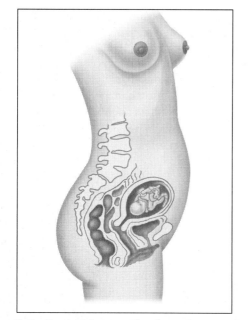

Figure 7–3 THIRD MONTH. The fetus is now about 3 inches long and weighs about 1 ounce. It may continue to develop in the position shown or may turn or rotate frequently. The uterus begins to enlarge with the growing fetus and can now be felt extending about halfway up to the umbilicus.

Figure 7–4 FIFTH MONTH. The fetus measures about 10–12 inches long and weighs from ½ to 1 pound. It is still bright red. Its increased size now brings the dome of the uterus to the level of the umbilicus. The internal organs are maturing at astonishing speed, but the lungs are insufficiently developed to cope with conditions outside of the uterus.

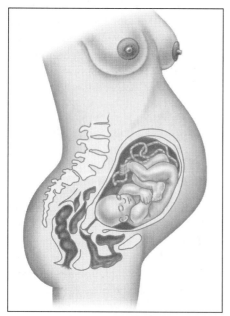

Figure 7–5 SEVENTH MONTH. The fetus's weight has about doubled since last month, and it is about 3 inches longer. However, it still looks quite red and is covered with wrinkles that will eventually be erased by fat. At 7 months the premature baby has a fair chance for survival in nurseries cared for by skilled physicians and nurses.

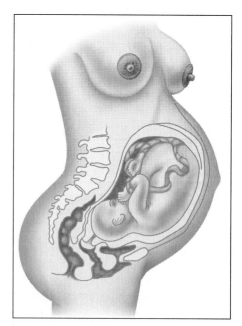

Figure 7–6 NINTH MONTH. At birth or full term the baby weighs on average about 7¼ pounds if a girl and 7½ if a boy. Its length is about 20 inches. Its skin is coated with a creamy coating. The fine downy hair has largely disappeared. Fingernails may protrude beyond the ends of the fingers.

Telling her that she is beautiful may be a far more effective way for her partner to show that he cares than having sexual intercourse (see Figure 7–7).

COMPLICATIONS OF PREGNANCY

Although pregnancy is a complex process, about 97 percent of all births result in a healthy, normal infant. However, complications of pregnancy can occur. Many of these can be prevented if parents-to-be are aware of them.

Substances that can harm an embryo or fetus are called **teratogens** (from the Greek word *tera*, meaning "monster"). Until recently, the placenta was thought to be a perfect filter that kept out all harmful substances. Now we know of hundreds of teratogens that can cross the placental barrier. Three things determine the harm caused by teratogens—the amount of the teratogen, the duration (amount of time) of exposure to the teratogen, and the age of the embryo or fetus. Each part of the developing body has a time, called a **critical period,** when it is most susceptible to damage. These are the times when it is undergoing most of its formation. During critical periods, body parts are sensitive to "signals" or "messages" about how to develop. Usually, these signals come from the genetic code that guides normal development. However, this sensitivity means that the developing embryo or fetus can be easily influenced by teratogens. Although teratogens should be avoided at all times, most body parts are maximally susceptible to damage during the first 8 weeks of development (see Figure 7–8).

Remember that in the first 8 weeks of pregnancy, many women won't be sure if they are pregnant. There is an important lesson to be learned from this. If a woman wants to change her behavior to improve the chances of having a healthy baby (e.g, to stop drinking alcoholic beverages), it's better for her to do this when she is trying to become pregnant rather than after she finds out that she is pregnant. Still, if a woman wants to change, it is better to do so late rather than never. The woman's partner can encourage healthier habits by also changing his habits at the same time.

DISEASES

Some strains of the flu, mumps, chicken pox, and other common diseases can cause harm to the embryo or fetus. One of the first teratogens to be discovered was the **rubella** virus, or "German measles." A baby exposed prenatally to rubella may be born blind, deaf, and/or intellectually impaired. This is especially true if the mother contracts this virus in the first 3 months of pregnancy. (Michaels and Mellin, 1960). During an outbreak in 1964–1965, 20,000 women gave birth

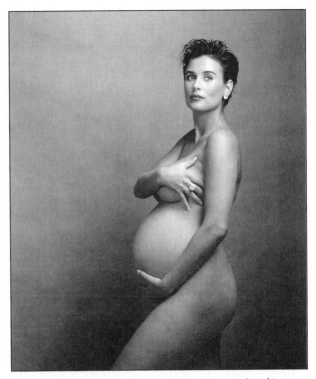

Figure 7–7 In a pose for *Vanity Fair* magazine (August 1991), actress Demi Moore shows that pregnancy is a time when a woman can still be proud of her body.

to abnormal infants, and another 11,000 had abortions after contracting the illness (Franklin, 1984). Administering a rubella vaccine to schoolchildren has greatly decreased the prevalence of the disease, and the number of cases has been reduced by about 99 percent since 1969 (CDC, 1997b).

> "Unbeknown to the doctor or myself, I had chlamydia. Since the baby was in the birth canal he contracted it in the eyes. It was bad! He almost went blind." (from the author's files)

As you learned in Chapter 5, most types of *sexually transmitted diseases* can affect a fetus or newborn baby. There is a 1-in-5 chance that a pregnant woman with an HIV infection (the virus that causes AIDS) will pass the virus to the fetus. If a woman has an active case of genital herpes at delivery, it can result in the death of or neurological damage in the newborn. Blindness in newborns can result if the mother has either gonorrhea or chlamydia at the time of childbirth. Untreated syphilis is particularly bad, because it can be passed to the fetus, resulting in considerable damage by the time the baby is born.

teratogens Substances that can harm an embryo or fetus.

critical period In relation to teratogens, the time during embryonic or fetal development during which a particular part of the body is most susceptible to damage.

rubella A disease, also known as German measles, caused by a virus. If contracted during pregnancy, it can cause fetal abnormalities.

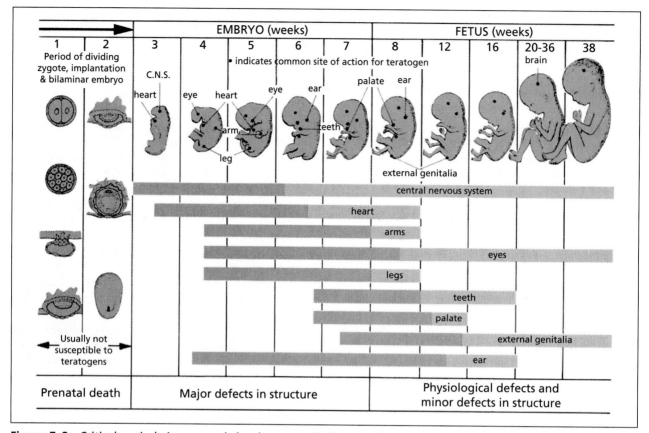

Figure 7–8   Critical periods in prenatal development. Darker shading represents highly sensitive periods; lighter shading represents less-sensitive periods.

TOXEMIA OF PREGNANCY

A pregnant woman can also have a disease called **toxemia of pregnancy.** In its early stages, this disease is called *preeclampsia,* and up to 10 percent of pregnant women will experience it. Its symptoms include protein in the urine (which allows it to be detected by physicians), high blood pressure, weight gain, and swollen joints due to excessive water retention. The high blood pressure results from overactivity of what is known as the sympathetic nervous system (Schobel et al., 1996). In about 3 percent of cases, the disease advances to *eclampsia,* characterized by convulsions and coma. In the Western world, eclampsia is a major cause of maternal death.

"During my first pregnancy, they discovered that I had toxemia. I was immediately put on a low-sodium diet and had to stay in bed for the rest of my pregnancy. When she was born, my baby weighed only 4 lbs. 10 oz. and her weight then fell to 4 lbs. 1 oz. She had respiratory problems and severe jaundice. They kept her in an incubator for about 4 weeks. She was a very pretty baby, but took a long time to start crawling, walking, and talking. I didn't get toxemia in my second or third pregnancies."   (from the author's files)

Toxemia generally occurs in the last trimester of pregnancy. It is most likely to occur in younger women, especially if it is the first birth. Women who develop toxemia in their first pregnancy often do not have it in later pregnancies. Also, women who used barrier contraceptives (e.g., condoms, diaphragms) prior to pregnancy have a much higher risk of preeclampsia (Klonoff-Cohen et al., 1989). In other words, these findings indicate that the greater the exposure to semen, the less likelihood a woman will develop preeclampsia. These results suggest that the disease is due to altered immune responses (see Li & Wi, 2000). Calcium supplementation and bed rest are the usual treatments for preeclampsia (Witlin & Sibai, 1997). However, if eclampsia still develops, labor will be induced prematurely in order to keep the disease from being life-threatening.

SMOKING

About 12 percent of all pregnant women smoke (Ebrahim et al., 2000). Cigarette smoking during pregnancy is a concern because it is associated with a

toxemia of pregnancy   A disease of pregnancy characterized in its early stage (preeclampsia) by high blood pressure, weight gain, swollen joints, and protein in the urine. Unless it is corrected, it can lead to convulsions and coma.

substantial increase in the risk of having a low-birth-weight baby (Nordentoft et al., 1996) and increases the risk of miscarriages, ectopic pregnancies, preterm births, and infant mortality (see DiFranza & Lew, 1995, for a review). Babies born to women who smoked while pregnant have decreased respiratory function (Stick et al., 1996). Mothers who smoke during pregnancy double (9 cigarettes or less a day) or triple (10 cigarettes or more a day) the risk that their baby will die of sudden infant death syndrome ("crib death") (Haglund et al., 1990). You should know that even if you do not smoke during pregnancy, passively inhaling cigarette smoke from others can have bad effects on the baby (Dejin-Karlsson et al., 1998).

ALCOHOL

A survey from the Centers for Disease Control and Prevention found that in recent years there has been a big increase in drinking by pregnant women (CDC, 1997a). About 16 percent of pregnant women report having had a drink in the previous month. Drinking during pregnancy can have dire consequences, and binge drinking (five or more drinks) is especially bad for the fetus (Nanson, 1997). Approximately 2 out of every 1,000 children born in the United States have physical deformities and/or mental retardation because of damage caused by the mother's use of alcohol during pregnancy (*Newsweek*, 1989). The condition is known as **fetal alcohol syndrome (FAS)** and is 6 times more common now than it was in 1979 (CDC, 1997a). Children born with FAS are underdeveloped and have facial deformities, abnormally spaced eyes, and small heads. They also have damage to the central nervous system, and occasionally they have damage to other organs. FAS is the leading cause of mental retardation in the United States (Abel & Sokol, 1987).

Research with animals indicates that alcohol probably has its maximum effect on the developing fetus in the 3rd week of pregnancy (Sulik et al., 1981), but it can have negative effects throughout pregnancy. Animal research also shows that alcohol can cause the umbilical cord to collapse temporarily, cutting off oxygen to the fetus and causing a condition known as *minimal brain damage* (Mukherjee & Hodgen, 1982), which has been associated with hyperactivity and learning disabilities in humans. Even moderate alcohol consumption can result in children with emotional problems and inability to cope in school (known as *fetal alcohol effect*). These data indicate that *it is probably best to avoid alcohol entirely during pregnancy*. If you wouldn't give your newborn baby an alcoholic drink, why would you give it one before it is even born? In fact, because maximal damage might occur before a woman knows that she is pregnant (the 3rd week), it might be best for a woman to stop drinking if she is trying to become pregnant. Even after the baby is born, a mother should not drink if she is

breast-feeding, because this can result in the baby having a low rate of motor development and coordination (Little et al., 1989).

COCAINE

The use of cocaine, especially crack cocaine, increased dramatically during the 1980s. Sadly, many of the casualties of this epidemic are children born to women who used cocaine during pregnancy. Ten to 15 percent of babies born in large urban areas are affected by their mothers' use of cocaine—over 100,000 babies a year (U.S. General Accounting Office, 1990). The immediate hospital costs alone (at time of delivery) are $5,000 to $12,000 more per child than for unexposed babies (Behnke et al., 1997).

The most widely reported effects of cocaine exposure during pregnancy are diminished growth and preterm birth (both resulting in low birth weight) and decreased head circumference (Eyler et al., 1998; Sprauve et al., 1997). "Crack babies" have a variety of sensory-motor and behavioral deficits, including irritability and disorientation. There is also a real potential of later learning problems and behavioral disorders (see Singer et al., 1992, for a review).

OTHER DRUGS

Many drugs can cross the placental barrier. These include illegal drugs, prescription drugs, and over-the-counter drugs. Women who are addicted to heroin (or methadone) while pregnant will give birth to infants who are addicted as well. These infants must go through withdrawal after being born, showing symptoms such as fever, tremors, convulsions, and difficulty in breathing. Withdrawal is extremely painful and can be life-threatening (Brazelton, 1970). Also, heavy use of marijuana during pregnancy can result in problems that resemble fetal alcohol syndrome (Hingson et al.,1982).

Numerous prescription drugs, such as antibiotics and tranquilizers, are clearly harmful to the fetus. In addition, commonly used drugs such as antihistamines (in allergy medication and cough medicine) and megadoses of certain vitamins have proven to have harmful effects. Even aspirin can be harmful. The Food and Drug Administration has issued a warning against taking over-the-counter aspirin products during the last 3 months of pregnancy because they can affect fetal circulation and cause complications during delivery. Caffeine (found in coffee, tea, many soft drinks, and chocolate) has been found to result in reduced birth weights (Vlajinac et al., 1997). Even too much vitamin A during pregnancy can cause birth defects (Rothman et al., 1995). The best advice, which is being given by increasingly large numbers of physicians, is not to take any drugs during pregnancy if at all possible.

fetal alcohol syndrome (FAS) A condition common to infants born to alcoholic mothers, involving physical and nervous system abnormalities.

RH INCOMPATIBILITY

There is a protein in the blood of a majority of people called the **Rh factor.** It got its name from the rhesus monkey, the species in which this blood protein was first discovered. If a person has the protein, he or she is "Rh positive." If not, the person is "Rh negative." A blood type of "O positive" means that the person is blood type O and has the Rh factor. Each person has two genes—one gene is received from each parent—that determine whether or not he or she has the protein. The Rh positive gene is dominant, which means that if a person has one Rh positive and one Rh negative gene, the blood will have this protein. A person can have Rh negative blood only when both genes are Rh negative.

In about 8 percent of all pregnancies in the United States, the mother will be Rh negative and the fetus will be Rh positive. When this occurs, there is an Rh compatibility problem. For the first birth, this situation usually isn't dangerous. But during labor and delivery, blood of the fetus and the mother, kept separate in the placenta during pregnancy, may mix together. If this happens, the mother's blood treats the Rh factor in the baby's blood as if it were a dangerous foreign substance, forming antibodies that will attack and destroy the "invader" in the future. If the mother then has another Rh positive fetus, these antibodies can cross the placental barrier and attack the fetus's blood supply, causing a miscarriage, possible brain defects in the fetus, or even death.

Fortunately, there is an injection that can be given to the mother to prevent these antibodies from forming. The drug used for this is called *Rhogam*. It consists of Rh negative blood that already has these antibodies in it. Because Rhogam already has antibodies, the mother's system doesn't produce very many of its own. The antibodies in Rhogam eventually die off, leaving the mother capable of carrying another Rh positive fetus. It is important that this drug be given immediately after the birth of the first child or after a first mis-carriage of a fetus with Rh positive blood. If there is a delay, the mother's body will build up too many antibodies of its own, making the drug ineffective.

DETECTION OF PROBLEMS IN PREGNANCY

In addition to X-rays, which are generally used only late in pregnancy, if at all, there are several other techniques for detecting problems in the fetus while it is inside the uterus. One is called **chorionic sampling** or *chorionic villus biopsy.* As you learned earlier, the chorion surrounds the embryo and develops early in pregnancy. In chorionic sampling, a small tube is inserted through the vagina and cervix. Guided by ultrasound, the tube will remove some hairlike cells (villi) from the chorion by gentle vacuum suction. These cells can be examined to detect chromosomal problems (such as Down syndrome), abnormalities in the fetus, or to look for evidence of certain diseases. One of the major advantages of chorionic sampling is that it can be used to detect problems early in pregnancy (from the 8th to 10th week of pregnancy), but after 12 weeks of pregnancy all of the villi of the chorion are gone. Although the safety of chorionic sampling compares favorably with that of other methods of detecting fetal abnormalities, serious complications, including fetal or neonatal death, can occasionally result. Doctors are currently using a newer, "safer" prenatal technique called **celocentesis** in which a needle is inserted between the placenta and amniotic sac to retrieve cells (Jurkovic et al., 1993).

Another technique that provides similar information is **amniocentesis** (Wilson, 1998). This technique has been in use longer than chorionic sampling. In amniocentesis, a hollow needle is inserted through the abdomen and uterus of the mother, through the membrane of the amniotic sac, and into the amniotic fluid surrounding the fetus. Ultrasound is often used to guide the needle. Some of the amniotic fluid is then extracted, and fetal cells that have dropped off and have been floating in the fluid are examined for evidence of abnormalities. This procedure can only be used after the 14th week of pregnancy, because before that time there may not be enough fetal cells in the amniotic fluid to make it useful and the fetus may take up too much room in the amniotic sac for the procedure to be used safely. Even so, there is a 1 percent chance that the procedure will cause a spontaneous abortion.

A relatively new technique is called **fetoscopy.** A tube that contains fiber optic strands—wires that can

---

Rh factor A protein in the blood of most individuals. If a mother does not have it and the fetus she carries does, she can develop antibodies against the Rh factor. This is called an *Rh incompatibility problem.*

chorionic sampling A technique used for detecting problems in a fetus during the 8th to 10th weeks of pregnancy. Hairlike projections (villi) of the chorion are collected and examined.

celocentesis A technique used for detecting fetal abnormalities in which a needle is inserted between the placenta and the amniotic sac to retrieve cells.

amniocentesis A technique for detecting fetal problems, involving collection of amniotic fluid after the 14th week of pregnancy.

fetoscopy A procedure in which a tube containing fiberoptic strands is inserted into the amniotic sac to allow inspection of the fetus.

send back "pictures"—is inserted into the amniotic sac. The "fetus-scope" can inspect the skin of the fetus and can be used to get a blood sample from the fetus. This technique also carries a risk of damaging the fetus, however.

X-rays, chorionic sampling, amniocentesis, and fetoscopy are called "invasive" techniques, meaning that they invade, or get inside of, the uterus and/or the fetus. **Ultrasound** is considered a "noninvasive" technique because it only bounces sound waves off the uterus and fetus. Ultrasound can be used to diagnose problems such as a malformation of the skeletal system of the mother or fetus. It cannot detect genetic defects as amniocentesis can. An ultrasound is recommended *only if the expectant mother has an increased risk factor for a problem* with a pregnancy or delivery. Use of ultrasound as a routine screening procedure has no clinical benefits (Ewigman et al., 1993). A balance must be found between detecting potential problems and creating new problems when these procedures are used.

FETAL SURGERY

One of the newest methods in treating a problem pregnancy is **fetal surgery**—performing an operation on the fetus while it is still in the uterus of the mother. The first fetal surgeries were performed for urinary tract obstruction and diaphragmatic hernia. With urinary tract obstruction, urine backs up into the kidneys and damages them. When this problem is detected through ultrasound, the surgeon can insert a needle through the mother's abdomen to help place a little tube (catheter) into the fetus's bladder. Urine then drains through the catheter and bypasses the urinary tract. A newer technique involves making a surgical incision through the fetus's abdomen directly to the bladder. The use of surgical incisions rather than catheters is called *open fetal surgery*. The technological advances in this field have been rapid. In 1989, physicians performed the first successful major surgery on a fetus, repairing a hernia of the diaphragm that if left untreated probably would have resulted in death shortly after birth (Harrison et al., 1990). In 1996, a 4-month-old fetus was given a bone marrow transplant while still in the uterus (Flake et al., 1996). More recently, doctors have corrected spina bifida on 23-week-old fetuses (Adzick et al., 1998). As the technology of fetal surgery evolves, it is expected that risks associated with the procedures will decline and that a greater variety of problems will be remedied in this way.

In the near future, doctors will be able to use *in utero gene therapy* (Zanjani & Anderson, 1999). Here, doctors inject healthy genes into the cells of an organ of a patient with a genetic disease (e.g., neurologic or immunologic genetic diseases). The injected genes kill off the bad cells. This is already done in children and adults, but the advantage of doing it to the fetus while still in the uterus is that a disease can be eliminated before the appearance of any clinical symptoms. Scientists say that by injecting the genes into a fertilized egg, genetic diseases could also be avoided in later generations (see Designer Babies, 1998).

MISCARRIAGES (SPONTANEOUS ABORTIONS)

Earlier in this chapter you learned that about three-fourths of all conceptions fail to survive beyond 6 weeks. Of the remaining quarter, about 10 percent fail to survive to term (Wilcox et al., 1999). There are many possible causes for **miscarriage,** including genetic, anatomic, and hormonal causes; infections; maternal autoimmune responses; and smoking cigarettes or use of cocaine (e.g., Ness et al., 1999). Usually, physicians will not attempt to diagnose causes of miscarriage until the woman has had three of them. *Recurrent miscarriages*, as these are called, occur in 0.5–1.0 percent of women (Alberman, 1988). There are two major reasons for this. The first is that most women who have a miscarriage will carry the next fetus to full term. (Some insurance companies don't want to pay for tests after only one or two miscarriages.) The second is that even after three miscarriages have occurred, 60 percent of these women will later have healthy babies, even without treatment.

For many couples, a miscarriage can be a heavy emotional disappointment:

> "I have been married for 14 years. I conceived 7 times, and every time I had a miscarriage at about 4½ months. My doctor diagnosed that my uterus is too weak to carry the baby after 4 months and no matter what and how I try I cannot have a baby of my own. I get very depressed sometimes and cry. Lately I feel very uncomfortable around other people's babies."

> "Some people may think only women are upset because of losing a baby due to miscarriage . . . but this hurt me in ways unimaginable. . . . First of all, I felt as if it was my fault for not being there. It hurt the most because a part of us had not yet had a chance to grow and mature into our baby. Our relationship is just now returning to normal." (All examples are from the author's files.)

It is important to allow adults who experience miscarriage to express their emotions and grieve (Cole, 1987). It often takes several months to recover.

At this point I would like to emphasize that hundreds of millions of babies are born without serious problems. A fetus is incredibly resistant to harm. It is important that you eat well, avoid toxic substances, get early and regular care from a physician, and prepare for the birth of your child through

ultrasound A noninvasive technique for examining the internal organs of a fetus; it uses sound waves like a radar or sonar scan to create a picture.

fetal surgery A surgical operation on the fetus while it is still in the uterus.

miscarriage A spontaneous abortion.

study and training (which I will describe shortly). These all go a long way toward making pregnancy, labor, and birth an enriching, happy experience.

NUTRITION AND EXERCISE DURING PREGNANCY

One of the best ways to increase the chances of having a healthy baby is to eat well during pregnancy. A poor diet can increase the risk of complications such as toxemia, anemia, and low birth weight.

Remember, if you are pregnant, you are now eating for two. You will need to eat more *good-quality* foods than you usually do. This especially applies if you are a teenager because of the high incidence of low-birth-weight babies in this age group. Anyone expecting twins must also eat plenty of healthy foods. Here are some suggestions for foods you should eat every day to assure a healthy diet (Brewer & Brewer, 1985):

- Four glasses of any kind of milk (e.g., whole, low fat, skim). If you do not like milk, substitute yogurt
- Two eggs
- Two servings of meat, including chicken or fish. If you are a vegetarian, substitute beans and rice
- One serving of leafy green vegetables
- One yellow vegetable (five times a week)
- Five servings of whole breads or cereals (part of your milk intake can be with cereal)
- One potato
- Two pieces of fresh fruit

Although this diet will provide you with most of the necessary nutrients, the U.S. Public Health Service recommends that pregnant women *supplement their intake of folic acid* by taking a multivitamin. Your physician may make additional recommendations if you have certain conditions (such as adjusting salt intake to ease toxemia). Some women have negative feelings about gaining weight during pregnancy, but remember, this is not only normal but necessary. Never put yourself on a low-calorie diet during pregnancy.

There has been some concern that vigorous exercise during pregnancy might cause premature labor and delivery. A recent large-scale study not only found no evidence to support this but also, that regular exercisers who were in good condition had timely deliveries (reduced the chance of a preterm birth) (Hatch et al., 1998).

PREPARING FOR CHILDBIRTH

prenatal examination A health checkup by a physician during pregnancy.

In the United States, nearly 20 percent of pregnant women never bother to have a prenatal examination (Rosenberg et al., 1996). Prenatal exams are an essential part of health care during pregnancy. However, there is more to giving birth than assuring the safety of the mother and baby. What about a woman's psychological well-being and emotional adjustment? Modern maternity care in developed countries is aided by many technological advances, but, as Ulla Waldenström (1996) asks, "Does safety have to take the meaning out of birth?" In this section you will learn about several alternatives to the traditional medical model of birthing—methods that are concerned with safety but also try to make childbirth a meaningful experience.

The use of general anesthesia, labor rooms where women waited for hours (usually separated from their male partners) before giving birth, delivery rooms, waiting rooms for men, and other aspects of "modern" birth techniques were all instituted to make it easier for health professionals to deliver their services (Mead, 1975). Women and their male partners were usually given very little education about what was to come, with only the expectation that it would be painful. For many women, labor and delivery were not positive experiences.

"At age 20 I prepared to give birth to my first child. 'Induced labor' was a convenient form of delivery for the physician, and widely practiced in the 70s. At my last visit to his office, he 'broke the water bag,' handed me five Kotex pads, and told me to walk across the street to _____ hospital and admit myself. He said he would check on me later that evening. After having called my husband for me at the hospital, the delivery room nurse started a 'drip' to begin contractions. I now know why the old _____ hospital had bars on the labor room windows. I cannot describe that intense pain, especially not having been prepared for natural childbirth. To jump would have been a blessing."

"My experience with childbirth was very traumatic. The pain I had to endure. . . . I remember reaching out to punch the nurse because the prepping solution she used on me was so cold. The next thing I knew, the gas mask covered my face and I was out cold."

"It is good the way births are being handled now. When I had babies the hospital treated you like the baby belonged to them. My second child wasn't even in the same building with me and I wasn't allowed to see her until the next day. It was torment wondering how she looked." (All examples are from the author's files.)

Fathers were generally the forgotten person when a baby was born. They seldom were allowed to be with their wives during any part of labor or delivery.

"I went out of the room to get a candy bar while the nurse gave my wife an exam (neither I nor my wife had ever heard of Lamaze then). When I re-turned to her room, I saw my wife being taken away. The nurse explained that my wife was giving birth. I'd been awake for several nights with my wife, so I laid down on her bed to rest and fell asleep. Shortly after 6 P.M., the phone next to the bed rang and the nurse told me I was the father of a baby girl." (from the author's files)

In 1932, a British physician named Grantly Dick-Read wrote a book in which he advocated the practice of *natural childbirth* (Dick-Read, 1972). He became the founder of a movement away from "modern" tech-niques, a movement that has become increasingly popular in America. Dick-Read came to the conclu-sion that modern birthing techniques, in which preg-nant women were regarded as "patients" (implying that pregnancy is an illness to be treated), led to a **fear-tension-pain cycle.** He reasoned that women were being put into strange environments, not know-ing what was going to happen next and surrounded by strangers, and that this created fear. He believed that fear could cause physiological changes associated with tension, such as tightened muscles. These things were believed to increase substantially the sensation of pain felt by mothers during labor and delivery. Instead, he advocated educating mothers-to-be about pregnancy, labor, birth, and birth procedures to relieve fear of the unknown (see Larimore, 1995, for a history). He also advocated training in relaxation techniques to relieve the physiological effects of tension. Drugs were per-missible if thought necessary, but were to be avoided if possible. Today, people more properly refer to these techniques as **prepared childbirth** rather than natural childbirth (Bing, 1990).

THE LAMAZE METHOD

A French physician, Fernand Lamaze, traveled to the Soviet Union in 1951 to study birthing techniques in that country. The Soviets had extended the condition-ing techniques of Ivan Pavlov into the area of labor and delivery. They had reasoned that if conditioning could create new associations between food and bells, associ-ations between labor and pain could be replaced with new associations. Women were conditioned to learn pleasant new associations for the sensations of labor and birth. They were also taught relaxation and breathing techniques to aid in making labor easier. Throughout the Soviet Union, Lamaze saw that women were giving birth without using anesthetics or experiencing great pain. This was stunning to Lamaze. He returned to France, modified the Soviet techniques slightly, and began using this new approach to child-birth in his practice (Lamaze, 1970). An American woman, Marjorie Karmel, used this approach under Lamaze's guidance and wrote about her experience in a best-selling 1959 book titled *Thank You, Dr. Lamaze.*

Since then, the *Lamaze method* has become the most popular form of childbirth in the United States. Compare the following childbirth experiences from two individuals who went through Lamaze training with the three case histories that were presented at the beginning of this section. Which persons do you think remember giving birth as a positive experience?

"I have gone through three different ways of giv-ing birth—the first being totally drugged out. I didn't get to see my baby until the next morning. The next two deliveries were natural childbirth using a birthing room and I didn't have any re-straints on me. You are given the freedom and dig-nity of childbirth. I used a birthing chair with my last baby. It was a more natural way of delivery and I found pushing to be less of an effort. The re-laxation and breathing techniques taught with Lamaze training really kept me focused and pre-pared. You know what you want—this is the way you have chosen to give birth. . . . My husband was there the whole time encouraging me. It was such a joy to see what love had produced. The smile on my husband's face. We could hold the baby after its birth—there bonding begins."

"We had our children using Lamaze. The thing I remember most is how in control my wife was, even at the very end. She had drawn her own focal point a few weeks before and concentrated on it every contraction while doing her breathing and effleurage. The absolutely best thing about the births was both of us being there to see our chil-dren the moment they were born. Each of them were so wide-awake and looking all around. My wife was yelling, 'It's a girl! It's a girl!' To be able to hold them right away was great. When the last child was born, her big brother and big sister were able to put on gowns and hold her after she was born. It was important to be there when my wife was giving birth, to be part of the experience. I cannot remember any other moment when I felt so connected to her and so alive." (All examples are from the author's files.)

The Lamaze approach resembles that of Dick-Read and other forms of prepared childbirth in that it tries to determine the specific causes of pain and provides meth-ods for dealing with each cause. What are the causes of perceived pain in childbirth? Basically, these break down into (1) anxiety and fear; (2) muscle tension; (3) stretch-ing of muscles; (4) too little oxygen getting to muscles; and (5) pressure on nerves. Here are some ways that Lamaze train-ing deals with each of these.

1. **Anxiety and fear.** There are a variety of factors that increase the sensation of pain. It is important to

fear-tension-pain cycle
According to prepared childbirth advocates, the cycle of events that women experience during labor when they are not properly edu-cated about labor and childbirth.

prepared childbirth
Courses or techniques that pre-pare women for labor and child-birth, with the goal of making it a positive experience.

remember that pain is a subjective experience. A football player may break an arm or leg and yet be unaware of it and continue to play until after the game is over (when the pain may suddenly become unbearable). Some people, on the other hand, wince and scream when they get a blood test before the needle even touches them. These examples illustrate two things that influence the experience of pain. The first is the anxiety and fear associated with the experience, and the second is the attention paid to the source of pain.

In Lamaze training, fear and anxiety are first dealt with through education. The unknown is always frightening, and if a woman in labor does not know what to expect, her anxiety will increase her experience of pain. This is counteracted by teaching expectant mothers about pregnancy and childbirth. They learn about the different stages of labor and medical procedures associated with childbirth. They also are encouraged to preregister at the hospital (so that this doesn't have to be done later when the mother-to-be has more important things on her mind) and to take a tour of the maternity ward and birthing facilities. In this way, the expectant mother knows what to expect and is more familiar with the environment where labor and birth will take place.

Expectant mothers also are not left alone during labor and birth. Throughout their training, labor, and delivery they are accompanied by a "coach." The coach is often the father of the baby but can also be a friend. The coach helps the mother utilize her training, providing support, encouragement, and instruction. It is the coach's responsibility to keep the mother-to-be as comfortable as possible, while at the same time keeping her concentration focused and her spirits up. The coach learns all of the exercises that the expectant mother does, practices with her, and "paces" her during labor.

Another way that the subjective experience of pain is reduced is through learning to focus attention or concentration. The mother-to-be picks out something outside her body, such as a favorite doll or a piece of furniture, and learns to focus all her attention on that thing, or "focal point." By concentrating on the focal point, she is not concentrating on her pain, and so the perception or subjective experience of pain is reduced.

2. **Muscle tension.** When people are anxious or fearful, muscles tighten up. This is a natural reaction and can be adaptive, because it allows quick movement in a "fight or flight" situation. However, keeping muscles tense over long time periods can cause them to ache and be used inefficiently. Labor is just such a situation, lasting several hours, with long periods of inactivity between contractions when tense muscles serve no useful purpose. One of the first exercises in Lamaze training involves learning to know when muscles are tense and how to relax them. Expectant mothers will be told to tighten the muscles in one arm, keeping the muscles in the other arm and the legs relaxed. They are told to notice the difference between the tensed arm and the other limbs. Then the coach lightly strokes the tensed arm saying "relax, relax" while the mother-to-be slowly relaxes the arm. The coach also learns to distinguish between the relaxed and tensed muscles of the mother. This does two things. First, expectant mothers and coaches learn to control the tension of the woman's muscles to prevent her from tensing up, especially between contractions. Second, through lots of practice and repetition, the woman is conditioned to immediately relax her muscles when the coach says the word "relax."

3. **Stretching of muscles.** The muscles used in labor have to go through many hours of exertion. Like any set of muscles, they will get tired and begin to ache if they are overworked, especially if they are out of condition. In Lamaze training, women are taught a number of exercises so that muscles to be used in labor and delivery can be toned up and strong when the baby decides to arrive.

4. **Too little oxygen getting to muscles.** Muscles use so much energy during vigorous exercise that they often cannot get enough oxygen, and so they begin to ache. The same is true in labor. In order to help deal with this, expectant mothers and coaches learn a variety of breathing techniques. These different types of breathing are generally used during contractions, while the woman's attention is fixed on her focal point, as previously described. During the first part of labor, when contractions are mild and far apart, the expectant mother breathes deeply and slowly (called "low-slow" breathing). During transition, she uses a type of breathing called "shallow-chest" or "pant-blow," which keeps the diaphragm (the muscle under the lungs) from pressing down on the top of the uterus during contractions, thus reducing pain. There is even a type of breathing that keeps her from being able to push if the urge to push comes too early or if the physician needs more time. In addition to helping keep oxygen supplied to muscles, these breathing exercises also force the expectant mother to think about something other than the source of pain. This, like using a focal point, reduces the subjective experience of pain.

5. **Pressure on nerves.** Pressure on nerves caused by the fetus moving through the birth canal is dealt

with through the use of *effleurage,* or massage. One type of effleurage involves having the expectant mother lightly touch her abdomen with her fingertips, tracing large ovals on her skin during contractions. This light massage generally is a pleasant sensation, and by continually pairing the discomforts of contractions with a pleasant sensation, the subjective experience of pain is reduced. More recently, light massage is being replaced by deep muscle massage. The back, especially the small of the back, is also massaged. If the baby is coming through the birth canal face first rather than crown (back of the head) first, pressure is put on nerves in the lower back (back labor). By applying counterpressure to the lower back, a coach can reduce some of this discomfort.

These techniques are a sample of some of the components of Lamaze training. The shared training and birth experience can help bring a couple closer together. However, while Lamaze's techniques were a major advance—especially in allowing women and their partners more control over an important event in their lives—he is not without his critics. Some, for example, feel that even his methods are too controlling and that the end result is that women give birth "by direction, as if it were a flight plan" (Armstrong & Feldman, 1990). Today, there are several other birthing techniques that couples can use in place of the traditional hospital–general anesthesia approach. Here are a few of them.

THE BRADLEY METHOD

The second most popular type of prepared childbirth in the United States is based on the work of Robert Bradley in the 1940s. He, too, was inspired by Dick-Read and believed that pain during childbirth resulted from culturally learned fear. He argued against the "meddlesome interference with nature's instinctual conduct and plans" and felt that women could learn to deal with labor pain in the same manner as animals do (Bradley, 1981). He emphasized childbirth without medication and had husbands play an even greater role than in Lamaze. Compared to women who have received Lamaze training, women trained in the *Bradley method* are more likely to be critical of the conventional medical model of hospital birth, more likely to question the judgment of their doctors, and more likely to experience less medical intervention during childbirth (Monto, 1996).

THE LEBOYER METHOD

Another French physician, Frederick Leboyer, wrote an influential book in 1975 called *Birth without Violence.* He felt that traditional techniques of delivery were traumatic for babies, and instead advocated "gentle birth." In the *Leboyer method*, the baby is delivered and immediately placed on the mother's abdomen. The room is dimly lit to simulate the lighting inside the mother's body. The umbilical cord is not cut for several minutes, until it stops pulsating. The baby is then put in a warm bath (to simulate the amniotic fluid). The idea behind these procedures is to allow the transition of the baby from life inside the mother's body to life in the outside world to be as smooth as possible. Leboyer claims that babies born in this manner immediately smile, are calm, and even develop more rapidly. Critics claim that babies at this age are incapable of experiencing trauma, that dim lighting can interfere with the ability of hospital staff to detect problems in the baby or mother, and that there are no data to confirm Leboyer's claims. At present, it is much more difficult to find a physician willing to use this method as opposed to the Lamaze approach.

HOME BIRTH, BIRTHING ROOMS AND CENTERS, AND MODERN MIDWIFERY

In 1870, fewer than 1 percent of women gave birth in hospitals (Tew, 1990). In the late 1990s, only about 1 percent of women gave birth outside of a hospital (Curtin, 1999). Today, in Europe and the United States, there is a growing movement back to having births in the home. This movement has been driven, in part, by economic considerations. Because of the cost of malpractice insurance, 1 in 8 obstetricians has stopped delivering babies, and one-fourth of the counties in the United States do not have a clinic to provide prenatal care (Nazario, 1990). Of course, home births are also much less expensive. There are also personal considerations. Many couples feel that having a baby in familiar surroundings is more natural than a hospital birth. It also provides an opportunity for the entire family to be present and participate. For pregnant women who are at low risk for complications, home birth is a safe alternative to hospital delivery (Olsen, 1997).

To compete with this movement, many hospitals have "birthing rooms," which are designed to look like bedrooms rather than hospital rooms. Labor and delivery take place in the same bed, and often a crib is present so that the baby can sleep in the room with the mother after birth. In some areas, a closely related option is *birthing centers*, institutions that offer delivery in a homelike atmosphere with the assistance of skilled individuals such as midwives or physicians. They have proved to be just as safe for women as traditional hospital care (Waldenström & Nilsson, 1997), but this may be partly because birthing centers are really an option only to women with no foreseeable complications. Although popular in Europe, birthing centers are still a novelty in the United States.

Whether the choice is to deliver at home, in a birthing center, or in a hospital, there is also a growing trend to use **nurse-midwives** rather than physicians. In many European countries, over two-thirds of all babies are delivered by midwives (Nazario, 1990), but only about 7 percent of births in the United States are attended by nurse-midwives (and most of these are in hospitals) (Curtin, 1999). Midwives are generally registered nurses trained in obstetrical techniques who are well qualified for normal deliveries (and minor emergencies). They are less expensive than physicians, and they provide personal care during the latter parts of pregnancy, labor, and delivery. Studies indicate that the outcome for babies (and mothers) is just as good when they are attended by nurse-midwives as when they are attended by physicians (Saunders, 1997). Nurse-midwives are certified by the American College of Nurse-Midwives, and from state to state there is a fairly uniform set of regulations. The use of lay midwives (persons who are not nurses and are generally trained by nurse-midwives) is also increasing in popularity, but the regulations are not as uniform and some states outlaw the practice. So it is important to learn about the midwife's background, years of experience, and references.

ANESTHETICS OR "NATURAL" CHILDBIRTH?

In the Book of Genesis, God punishes women for Eve's transgression (eating the forbidden fruit) by making childbirth painful:

> **I will greatly multiply your pain in childbearing; In pain you shall bring forth children. (Genesis 3:16, Revised Standard Version)**

When painkillers were first used for childbirth in the 1800s, the British clergy opposed it, arguing that it was against God's will. It was Queen Victoria who decisively argued in favor of painkillers.

Many people reading this book came into the world in a drugged state. This is because anesthetics were used during their mother's labor to relieve pain. Under general anesthesia, a woman is unable to push during contractions. As a result, the infant has to be pulled into the world with forceps, which resemble tongs. Anesthetics cross the placental barrier and enter the fetus. Because the fetus's organs are not all fully developed at birth, it cannot get rid of drugs from its system as quickly as its mother. This is one reason why some infants have to be slapped in order to get them to cry and begin breathing. Babies born without the use of anesthetics generally come into the world with eyes open and ready to breathe without having to be slapped into consciousness.

Today, most births in which anesthetics are used do not involve general anesthetics. The mother-to-be can be given an *epidural*, a spinal anesthetic that deadens all sensations from the waist down. Thus, it is possible to be anesthetized and still be conscious. However, epidurals are associated with some complications. Labor tends to last longer, the chance of fever is 5 times as great, and there is a much greater risk of hypotension (Halpern et al., 1998). Some people argue that epidurals increase the chance of a cesarean section, but studies do not support this. Babies born to mothers who used epidurals are generally healthier afterward than babies born to mothers who used narcotic injections.

About 40 percent of American women who gave birth in 1992 received an epidural (Hawkins et al., 1997), but another survey indicates that the number of women choosing an epidural may have increased dramatically in recent years (see Pan, 1999). In fact, some women who do not have to are choosing to have a cesarean section (see later section).

These trends greatly concern proponents of "natural" (prepared) childbirth. As one midwife put it, "We have a culture that pops a pill whenever we feel pain" (Pan, 1999). Women who have some form of prepared childbirth and/or who are assisted during labor and delivery by a midwife generally require less medication for pain, need fewer cesarean sections, and have more positive feelings about the experience (Butler et al., 1993; Turnbull et al., 1996). However, a word of caution: Do not start thinking of childbirth as a contest to see if you can get through with the least amount of medical help. This attitude can make the use of anesthetics or a C-section seem like a "failure." That should not be the case. Any birth that results in a healthy mother and baby is a good one, regardless of the technique used. That is always the goal of childbirth, and should not be forgotten.

> *PERSONAL REFLECTIONS*
> *Make a list of all the words that come to your mind when you think of childbirth, labor, and delivery. Examine your list for negative stereotypical concepts. Are there alternatives?*

CHILDBIRTH

Before birth, the fetus will generally rotate its position so that its head is downward. This can happen weeks or hours before birth and is what is meant when people say "the baby dropped." It is also called **"lightening"** because once the fetus's head (its largest part) has lowered in the uterus, pressure on the mother's

nurse-midwife A registered nurse, trained in obstetrical techniques, who delivers babies, often at the expectant mother's home.

lightening Rotation of the fetus prior to childbirth so that its head is downward, resulting in decreased pressure on the mother's abdomen.

abdomen and diaphragm is greatly reduced. Being able to breathe more easily makes a mother feel like the load that she has been carrying (the fetus) weighs less (is "lighter").

Shortly before a woman begins to give birth ("goes into labor"), she may experience a burst of energy. A woman may feel better than she has in months, and may start to clean house or do some other type of work as a means of "burning off" this energy. It is probably a good idea to save some of this energy for later, when it certainly will be needed.

TRUE VERSUS FALSE LABOR

Throughout the latter stages of pregnancy, the uterus will undergo contractions—tightenings and relaxations of the muscles. These are involuntary, and for most of the pregnancy will go unnoticed. These contractions, called **Braxton-Hicks contractions,** are a type of natural "exercise program" for the uterus. Sometimes these contractions become so strong that they are noticed and mistaken for true labor. Parents-to-be sometimes worry and go to a hospital, only to be told that they have had a **false labor** and should return when the woman is in "real" labor. Here are some rules of thumb that help distinguish false labor from true labor.

One important sign of labor is the time between contractions. The uterus is basically a muscle in the shape of a bag. Its job is to push the fetus into the world. Like most muscles engaged in prolonged, heavy labor, it must repeatedly contract, or tighten. If contractions are coming 10 minutes apart on a regular basis, this is a good sign that labor has begun. False labor contractions are usually less regular and will eventually cease. The duration of each contraction also should be measured. If contractions are 30 seconds long on a regular basis, this is a good sign that labor has begun. False labor contractions are usually shorter than contractions marking true labor. With true labor, discomfort caused by contractions is usually felt in the back and abdomen. With false labor, discomfort is more likely to be felt in the groin and lower abdomen.

Two important signs of the beginning of labor involve the cervix. The first sign is **dilation.** In the last month of pregnancy, the cervix will dilate to about 1 centimeter in diameter. When a woman goes into labor, the uterine contractions help cause the cervix to dilate more. It must eventually dilate to 10 centimeters (about 4 inches) in diameter before the baby can be born. In the first stage of labor, the cervix will dilate to about 2 or 3 centimeters. The second sign is **effacement.** The cervix must stretch until it is "thinned out," or "effaced," so that it won't block the baby's passage into the birth canal (vagina). A good sign of true labor is that the cervix is 70 percent or more effaced. At birth, it will be 100 percent effaced. Although both of these cervical changes are good signs that labor has begun, they are only general rules of thumb.

Labor for the first child is usually longer than labor for subsequent children. A mother who has had many children may be asked to go to the hospital when contractions are still 20 minutes apart, because she could go directly from 20 minutes apart to a much shorter interval. It is not uncommon for women to wait too long before going to a hospital and to give birth in taxis, hospital parking lots, or hospital elevators.

STAGES OF LABOR

There is an abundance of evidence suggesting that it is the fetus that determines when labor begins, although the exact mechanism is still unknown (Norwitz et al., 1999). Once it begins, labor is divided into three stages. The initial stage of labor is a **start-up stage** and involves the woman's body making preparations to expel the fetus from the uterus into the outside world. This stage usually lasts from 6 to 13 hours. At this time, uterine contractions begin to push the fetus downward toward the cervix. The cervix begins to dilate and efface, as described earlier. At first, contractions are far apart (one every 10 to 20 minutes) and don't last long (15 to 20 seconds), but eventually they begin to come closer together (1 to 2 minutes) and last longer (45 to 60 seconds or longer).

During pregnancy, the cervix becomes plugged up with a thick layer of mucus. This prevents the amniotic sac (bag of water) and the fetus from having direct contact with the outside environment (through the vagina). During labor, this mucous plug will come out. A discharge of mucus and blood (known as a "bloody show") is a sign of labor. However, for some women the mucus comes out a little at a time, so that this sign is not clearly seen. In other women, the plug literally pops out like the cork in a bottle of champagne. As usual, every variation in between is also seen.

For about 10 percent of pregnancies, the amniotic sac will break before labor begins. In some women, the break is a small tear and the fluid seeps out. In other women, the water gushes out. This is what happens when a woman's *"water breaks."* Labor usually begins within a day after the amniotic sac breaks. If not, most physicians will induce labor through use of drugs in order to prevent contact with the outside world from causing infection in the fetus. A woman can also go into labor without having the water break. Physicians sometimes

Braxton-Hicks contractions Uterine contractions experienced during the last trimester of pregnancy that are often incorrectly interpreted as the beginning of labor; also called *false labor.*

false labor A set of temporary contractions of the uterus that resemble the start of labor.

dilation Becoming wider or larger.

effacement The thinning of the cervix during labor.

start-up stage The stage of labor that begins with uterine contractions pushing the fetus downward toward the cervix and ends when the cervix is fully dilated.

break the amniotic sac on purpose in order to speed up labor. It is even possible to give birth with the fetus enclosed in an unbroken amniotic sac. Physicians in this country don't allow this to happen and will break the sac first. However, in the Far East, children born in this manner are believed to be blessed with good fortune.

The last part of the first stage of labor is called the **transition phase,** so called because it marks the end of the initial stage of labor and the beginning of the next (birth) stage. This phase takes place when the cervix is almost fully dilated (8–10 cm). Contractions are severe, and the woman may feel nauseated, chilled, and very uncomfortable. She will often start to think that there is no end to this process, and many women at this point

Figure 7–9   The stages of childbirth.

will announce that they quit and are going home. Fortunately, transition usually lasts 40 minutes or less (compared to the often hours-long duration of the earlier part of the first stage).

During labor, it is important to monitor the fetus's vital signs. A sudden drop in heart rate may indicate a life-threatening situation. Nurses or physicians can monitor heart rate with a stethoscope or by a device called a fetal monitor. With a monitor, a recording device is placed on the expectant mother's abdomen (or, in the second stage of labor, directly on the fetus's scalp) and the fetus's heart rate is shown on a machine. However, fetal monitors are no better than stethoscopes in detecting fetal distress and reducing the incidence of perinatal deaths. In addition, they sometimes give false indications of abnormal heartbeats that can lead doctors to perform cesarean sections unnecessarily (Parer & King, 2000).

The **second stage** of labor begins when the cervix is fully dilated and the fetus begins moving through the birth canal (Figure 7–9). It ends with birth. Contractions during this stage of labor are accompanied by an intense desire to push or "bear down." The contractions cause the opening of the vagina to expand, and expectant mothers often get a "second wind" because they now can see an end to their work. Expectant mothers (and fathers) begin to

get excited about the fact that they will soon be able to see their baby, and this makes the contractions a little easier to bear. This stage lasts from 30 to 80 minutes on the average, depending on whether it is the first child or a later child. Just before the actual birth, physicians often use a surgical procedure called an episiotomy (see next section).

The first sign of the fetus is usually the sight of its head at the opening of the vagina. This is called **crowning,** because ideally the crown of the head is leading the way. If the head is turned around so that its nose and forehead are leading, it is called a "back labor" because this will cause the crown of the fetus's head to put pressure on nerves in the lower back, making the labor more painful than normal. The person (usually a physician) delivering the baby will tell the expectant mother when and how hard to push during contractions in order to get the baby into the world. The head is delivered first, with the physician reaching beneath the infant's chin to be sure that the umbilical cord is not wrapped around the baby's neck before the head is brought out. Once the head is delivered, suction is applied to the mouth and nose with a small rubber bulb so that the baby can breathe more easily. The head then turns, and the shoulders and rest of the body come out rather quickly. The mouth and nose are suctioned again.

A newborn will usually cry at birth. If not, the baby's back will be rubbed to start the baby breathing. The umbilical cord will be clamped and cut about 1½ inches from the baby's body. This stub will fall off in a few days, leaving the navel. (The navel is either an "inny" or an

transition phase The last part of the start-up stage of labor, during which the cervix dilates to 10 cm in order for baby to be able to enter the birth canal.

second stage of labor The stage of labor that begins when the cervix is fully dilated and the fetus begins moving through the birth canal. It ends with birth.

crowning The appearance of the fetus's head at the vaginal opening during childbirth.

"outty," but the type of navel you have seems to depend on heredity, not on how the umbilical cord was cut.)

In the **third stage** of labor, the placenta detaches from the uterus and leaves the mother's body (along with the other materials). This is what is called the **afterbirth.** This stage usually lasts only from 10 to 12 minutes. The physician examines the afterbirth to make sure that it is in one piece; then it is discarded. If even small pieces of the placenta stay in the uterus, infection and bleeding can occur. When this takes place, physicians use a procedure called *D&C* (dilation and curettage), in which the cervix is dilated to allow access to the uterus, which is then scraped clean. If any tears in the vagina have occurred, they are repaired at this time.

After the third stage of labor, the uterus should contract and remain constricted. To help this happen, the abdomen is sometimes massaged, and/or drugs may be given. This helps prevent excess bleeding (hemorrhaging) in the uterus.

EPISIOTOMY AND PREPPING

In the United States, about 43 percent of women who deliver vaginally in hospitals are given an **episiotomy** just before they give birth (Curtin, 1999). An episiotomy is an incision made from the bottom of the vagina (through the perineum) toward the anus, thus enlarging the vaginal opening. An episiotomy is a useful procedure if the baby is in distress. Although the number of episiotomies has dropped substantially since the end of the 1980s (57 percent then), many authorities still believe that most episiotomies are unnecessary and are done routinely only for the benefit of the physician (Lede et al., 1996). Episiotomies are uncommon in midwife-assisted deliveries (see Henriksen et al., 1994). In fact, several studies have found that women having vaginal deliveries who did not have episiotomies had fewer problems, including less damage to the perineum and less likelihood of urinary incontinence, than women who did have them (Foldspang et al., 1999; Low et al., 2000). When sewing up the incision, a few physicians add a "honeymoon stitch" (or "husband's stitch") in the lower part of the vaginal opening in order to make it tighter during intercourse. Both of these procedures should be abandoned as routine birthing practices.

Another procedure that is done less frequently than in the past is **prepping,** that is, shaving the pubic hair prior to delivery. Many physicians now think that this is unnecessary and can even be a source of infection.

PROBLEMS WITH CHILDBIRTH

Pregnancy and childbirth do not always go as planned. The World Health Organization estimates that worldwide nearly 600,000 women a year die as a result of childbirth (WHO, 1996). Although the maternal mortality rate in the United States is only 8.4 per 100,000 live births, it is still higher than in Canada (5.2 per 100,000) and many other Western countries (Hoyert et al., 2000). The major causes of death are blood clots, hypertension, and hemorrhage.

Deaths may be uncommon, but there are other complications that occur much more frequently. Let us examine a few of the most common ones.

BREECH BIRTHS

Babies, you recall, are generally born head first. This occurs in about 96 percent of all births, and ideally the back of the head, or crown, leads the way. Sometimes, a fetus will try to come through the birth canal feet or buttocks first. This is called a **breech birth** and occurs in 2 to 4 percent of all births. A fetus can even try to come out back first, shoulder first, or in any other conceivable position, but these cases are rare. Sometimes a fetus will spontaneously shift from feet to head first just before delivery. Sometimes during labor a woman will be asked to try lying in different positions, such as on her side, in the hope that this will cause the fetus to change to a head-first position. A physician can sometimes turn the fetus by grasping the mother's abdomen and manually change the fetus's position.

Today, some physicians may try to perform a vaginal ("normal") delivery even if a breech birth is unpreventable. This will depend on the circumstances and the physician. If the physician feels that the risks of a vaginal delivery are too great, he or she may perform a cesarean section.

PLACENTA PREVIA

The blastocyst normally implants in the upper part of the uterus. However, for about 1 out of every 200 pregnant women, implantation occurs in the lower uterus (Iyasu et al., 1993). As the placenta grows, it often blocks the cervical opening, a condition called **placenta previa.** This does not affect the fetus, but it may prevent a vaginal delivery.

CESAREAN SECTIONS

A **cesarean section** (also spelled *caesarean*), or *C-section*, is an incision through the abdominal and uterine walls to deliver a baby. Although the name is often attributed to the way in which Julius Caesar was born, in actuality it is derived from

third stage of labor Detachment and expulsion of the placenta from the uterus after childbirth.

afterbirth The expulsion of the placenta from the uterus after a baby is born.

episiotomy A surgical procedure performed on women just before giving birth to reduce the risk of tearing the perineum.

prepping The shaving of a woman's pubic hair prior to delivery of a baby.

breech birth A birth in which the baby is born feet or buttocks first.

placenta previa A condition in which the placenta blocks the cervical opening.

cesarean section (C-section) The surgical removal of a fetus through the mother's abdomen.

lex cesarea, a Roman law (715 B.C.) that allowed a fetus to be saved in the case of its mother's death.

There are many legitimate reasons for performing a cesarean section. These include *some* cases of breech birth or placenta previa; the baby's head being too big for the mother's pelvis; maternal illness or stress; and fetal stress. However, the World Health Organization has suggested that the upper limit for cesarean section deliveries be no greater than 15 percent (see Flamm, 2000). Cesarean sections accounted for 5 percent of live births in the United States in 1970, 14 percent in 1979, and reached a peak of 24.7 percent in 1988. The rate has since declined a bit, to 21 percent in 1997 (Curtin, 1999). Many individuals, including many health professionals, have begun to call for changes in the way physicians decide when to use this procedure (Flamm et al., 1998). Although cesareans are supposedly done to reduce the risk to the mother or baby, most are done on middle- and upper-income women. Thus, there has been a suspicion that many C-sections have been performed for the economic benefit of the physician or the hospital, or to avoid the risk of malpractice lawsuits in case of complications during vaginal deliveries.

It used to be that once a woman had a C-section, all later pregnancies would have to end with C-section deliveries (because the cuts were made vertically through the horizontal abdominal muscles and through the contracting part of the uterus). These repeat cesarean sections accounted for about a third of the C-sections performed each year (Curtin, 1999). Today, however, incisions are made horizontally through the abdomen and then through the noncontracting part of the uterus. In most cases, it is considered safe for a woman who has had a cesarean section to deliver vaginally (Rosen et al., 1991), with only a small (but higher than usual) risk of major complications (McMahon et al., 1996). Obstetricians have been slow to respond, but the number of vaginal births after a C-section has substantially increased since the mid-1980s (Curtin, 1999). However, C-sections are still the most frequently performed major operation in the United States. Interestingly, if given a choice, many women today say they would prefer a C-section over a vaginal delivery (31 percent in one survey). The new president of the American College of Obstetricians and Gynecologists was quoted as saying, "The time is coming, if not already here, for the maternal choice cesarean" (Torassa, 2000).

Because C-sections are so common, it is advisable for a pregnant woman to talk with her physician about his or her attitudes regarding their use before she goes into labor. She should also talk with the physi-

preterm infant An infant born weighing less than 5½ pounds and before week 37 of pregnancy.

respiratory distress syndrome An illness common in premature infants; caused by insufficient levels of surfactin.

cian about episiotomies, anesthetics, attitudes about prepared or "natural" childbirth, and all other details of the birth process at this time. This talk should take place when the expectant woman first begins to see the physician. If she doesn't like what she hears, she should find a new doctor.

PRETERM INFANTS

Nine out of every 1,000 births in the United States result in the death of the baby after it is delivered. The leading cause of infant mortality is from preterm birth. An infant is considered preterm if it weighs less than 5½ pounds and the mother was pregnant for less than 37 weeks. Sometimes people use the term "premature infants" to describe such children, but others prefer an alternative term, such as "low-birth-weight infants." I will compromise and use the phrase **preterm infants.** Preterm births account for about 7 to 10 percent of all U.S. births (Norwitz et al., 1999). Conditions such as malnutrition and toxemia increase the risk of having a preterm birth; other risk factors include a previous preterm birth, a short cervix, and bacterial vaginosis (Goldenberg et al., 1998). If a woman goes into labor prematurely, drugs can be given to relax the uterus and postpone labor. This must be done early in labor to be effective, however.

Advances in neonatology (the care of newborn babies) have reduced the limit of viability to about 23 to 24 weeks after conception (Allen et al., 1993). One of the biggest problems facing a fetus born at this time is that it has great trouble breathing. Before the age of 23 weeks (around 5 1/2 months), the fetus cannot produce a liquid called *surfactin*. Surfactin lets the lungs transmit oxygen from the atmosphere to the blood. After 4 months of age, the fetus can produce some surfactin, but it cannot maintain the liquid at the necessary levels until about 8 or 9 months of age. Newborns who cannot maintain proper levels of surfactin develop **respiratory distress syndrome** and die.

"When I was exactly 8 months pregnant my amniotic sac broke and labor was induced. When I saw my baby in the nursery, she was under oxygen, had all kinds of wires connected to her, an IV in her foot, and she had a lot of trouble breathing. I wasn't ready for this. However, I feel that if I was more informed about premature births I would have understood better." (from the author's files)

Before 1980, there was little hope of survival for babies born weighing less than 2 pounds. Today, about 17,000 infants per year born weighing less than 2 pounds are placed in *intensive care nurseries* (ICNs), where new techniques and equipment allow these infants a good chance of survival. Infants weighing just over 1 pound have about a 20 to 30 percent chance of survival, while those weighing about 2½ pounds have about an 80 percent chance of survival (Draper et al., 1999; Phelps et al., 1991). The cost of such technology is very high. For example, the cost of caring for a 4-month premature baby can be over $300,000. In addition, premature infants run a high risk of having disabilities that can require treatment for many years. Babies born weighing less than 750 grams (a little over 1½ pounds) are much more likely than others to have poor psychomotor skills, very low IQ scores, and poor performance in school (Hack et al., 1994). Early childhood intervention improves the IQ and verbal performance of preterm infants born weighing 4½ pounds or more, but is of little or no help to very-low-birth-weight babies. Most of them remain cognitively and behaviorally impaired (McCarton et al., 1997), and are much less likely to graduate from high school by age 19 than their normal-birth-weight brothers and sisters (Dalton & Bennett, 2000).

AFTERWARDS

In 1980, the average stay in a hospital room was 3.2 days for a vaginal delivery. This dropped to 1.7 days in the early 1990s, when most insurance companies refused to pay for more than one day. In a revolt against these "drive-by deliveries," many states passed laws in 1995–1996 requiring insurance companies to pay for at least 2 days. As a result, the average woman giving birth vaginally now stays 2.1 days (Raube & Merrell, 1999).

BREAST-FEEDING THE BABY

Milk production (lactation) begins about 3 days after a woman gives birth (Figure 7–10). Recall from Chapter 2 that two hormones produced by the pituitary gland are responsible for milk production. **Prolactin** stimulates the breasts to produce milk, while **oxytocin** causes the breasts to eject milk. When the baby sucks on the breasts, a milk-flow reflex is created. In fact, over time merely hearing the baby cry can cause the breasts to begin ejecting milk. At first, the breasts give out **colostrum,** mentioned earlier, which is high in protein and also helps immunize the infant against diseases. After about 3 days, milk begins to flow. The average amount of milk produced is 2½–3 cups per day, but there is a lot of variation among individuals. Some women do not produce enough milk, and some produce too much.

Mother's milk contains many infection-fighting proteins that protect the infant from gastrointestinal illnesses (e.g., diarrhea), respiratory infections, meningitis, skin diseases, and other problems (e.g., Raisler et al., 1999). Breast-feeding has benefits to mothers as well. When a mother begins nursing, a hormone is released that helps the uterus to contract and helps stop internal bleeding. You should know that both the American Academy of Pediatrics and the Institute of

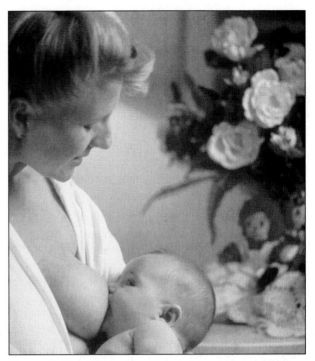

Figure 7–10 Mother's milk contains many infection-fighting proteins and is easier for a baby to digest than cow's milk.

Medicine (1991) endorse breast-feeding. The World Health Organization recommends that children should be breast-fed until they are at least 2 years old (along with the introduction of nutritionally safe foods at about 6 months) (World Health Organization, 1995). A nursing mother may not begin her menstrual cycle for several months after birth, which gives her some protection against pregnancy (see Chapter 6). Information about the benefits of breast-feeding must be spreading because the rates of breast-feeding in the United States have increased substantially since 1990 (Ryan, 1997). Keep in mind, however, that drugs and pollutants can be transmitted to the infant through mother's milk. Before taking any medication (including birth control pills), therefore, it is important for nursing mothers to consult their physicians or pharmacists.

Despite the benefits, many women choose not to breast-feed their babies, often because of a career outside the home. If a woman stops breast-feeding (or never begins), milk production will stop within days. This can be speeded up by an injection of estrogen. Be aware, however, that human milk is much easier to digest than cow's milk, and if bottle-fed, a baby should be given formula.

prolactin A hormone released from the pituitary gland that stimulates milk production in the breasts.

oxytocin A hormone released from the pituitary gland that causes the breasts to eject milk.

colostrum A thick, sticky liquid produced by a mother's breasts before milk starts to flow.

Whether a baby is breast-fed or bottle-fed, fathers should not ignore this new responsibility. A father can sit with his partner while she breast-feeds in the middle of the night, or a mother can use a breast pump to extract her milk for a later feeding (allowing her to sleep while the father feeds the baby).

POSTPARTUM DEPRESSION

The first 3 months after childbirth are called the *postpartum period*. Although most women look forward to having a baby, many experience a period of negative emotions during this time. In some cases their distress can be extreme:

> "After I had my son I spent weeks upon weeks of sitting alone on the kitchen floor with him on my lap and crying and crying uncontrollably."

> "I was so depressed after giving birth to a little girl. If somebody touched her, I screamed. When my baby was 3 days old I had a fight with my mother-in-law and husband. Actually, they tried to help me out, but I was so depressed that I always fought with them. Things got worse and I thought I was going to get divorced. . . . My doctor explained to me it is because of hormone changes. . . . I am thankful to my husband, who always tried to understand me at that time."

> "I can remember being depressed for a couple of months. . . . I felt so helpless. . . . Sometimes I resented my baby because I felt so bad and was so exhausted. I hated myself for having these feelings." (All examples are from the author's files.)

There is a range of negative emotions that women can experience after childbirth, and it is customary to distinguish three types of depression on the basis of severity (O'Hara, 1997). Many women experience a letdown in the first week or two after delivery, called **postpartum blues.** Symptoms may include a depressed mood, confusion, anxiety, and crying, but the condition is mild and does not last long. However, about 10 percent of women experience **postpartum depression,** characterized by a deeper depression and anxiety, guilt, fatigue, and often obsessive-compulsiveness. The stricken mother may feel that she cannot face daily events, is overwhelmed by child care, and feels ashamed and guilty about her inadequacy as a mother. About 1 in 1,000 women experience **postpartum psychosis,** characterized by affective (mood) symptoms and hallucinations in what often resembles a manic depressive state. I will focus here on postpartum depression.

Biological factors, particularly hormone changes, may contribute to postpartum depression (O'Hara, 1997). The placenta secretes high levels of estrogen and progesterone during pregnancy, and there is a sudden drop in the levels of these hormones after birth. But social and psychological factors certainly play a major role.

Marital unhappiness and lack of support by the spouse and family, for example, can contribute to the depression (Hagan, 1999). Newborn infants need frequent feeding, which can cause mothers to lose lots of sleep. A woman can feel abandoned if she feels she is not receiving support from her partner. High levels of stress during pregnancy and afterwards also contribute. Stress factors include low socioeconomic status, unemployment and financial problems, and multiple children (Righetti-Veltema et al., 1998).

Many studies indicate that if postpartum depression lasts several weeks, it can affect the infant's emotional, behavioral, and cognitive development (e.g., Murray, 1992). It is probably a mother's style of interacting with her child (brought on by the depression) that results in these negative consequences (Murray & Cooper, 1997). A simple screening questionnaire has been developed to identify mothers with postpartum depression and is a useful tool to suggest who might need support during this difficult time (Cox et al., 1987). Women with postpartum depression generally are treated in the same manner as other depressed patients (O'Hara, 1997).

SEXUAL INTERCOURSE AFTER BIRTH

> "We tried to make love again when our first baby was about 3 1/2 weeks old. The pain from the episiotomy made this impossible and we both wound up very frustrated and wondering if our sex life would ever be back to normal. We finally did succeed at about 6 weeks but still it wasn't very comfortable. After a while we got used to the new normal. . . . After my second and third babies were born everything was very different. I didn't have an episiotomy, or tear at all, even though they were both very large. We made love just a few weeks later without any discomfort whatsoever." (from the author's files)

Labor often leaves a woman tired and sore for some time, and stitches from an episiotomy may leave her uncomfortable. Vaginal bleeding continues for 2 to 6 weeks in most women (Marchant et al., 1999). The loss of estrogen results in vaginal dryness and irritation during intercourse for some time. Most physicians advise that sexual intercourse not be resumed until 4 to 6 weeks after the birth.

Women also may worry about their sexuality because of stretch marks, extra weight left over from pregnancy, and "flabby" stomach muscles. The stretch marks soon become paler, and problems with weight and stomach muscles can be helped through exercise.

postpartum blues A mild, transient emotional letdown experienced by a majority of women after giving birth.

postpartum depression A deep depression experienced by about 10 percent of women in the first few months after giving birth.

postpartum psychosis A psychotic state experienced by about 1 in 1,000 women after giving birth.

"Pretend you're carrying your golf clubs, and you won't mind it."

Reprinted courtesy of Bunny Hoest and Parade Magazine © 1987.

Some women also worry that their vagina has become too large after birth, but the vaginal muscles generally become firm and tight again, especially if the woman continues to practice Kegel exercises (see Chapter 2).

The best time to resume sexual relations depends on many factors. In all cases, however, a man and a woman must learn to relate to each other as both sexual partners *and* as parents. Making this adjustment to new roles and feelings requires time and patience. Differences in sleep patterns with an infant that must be fed at night, demands on time and energy made on parents by children, and difficulty finding periods of privacy all force couples to make adjustments in their sexual behaviors.

Despite these concerns, couples do resume sexual intercourse an average of 7 weeks after childbirth (Hyde et al., 1996). However, sexual activity tends to be lower than before pregnancy for several months, and sexual problems (e.g., painful intercourse, decreased desire, vaginal dryness) during this time are common (von Sydow, 1999). Women who are breast-feeding show less sexual activity than others (Visness & Kennedy, 1997), and women who had a cesarean delivery tend to start earlier than those who delivered vaginally. As you might expect, sexual attitudes in general play a role. Couples who had a positive attitude about sex before pregnancy tend to resume sexual relations earlier than couples with a less than totally positive attitude (Fisher & Gray, 1988).

NEW RESPONSIBILITIES

Becoming a parent is like being asked to start a new job with little or no training. Just because someone has given birth or fathered a child does not mean that she or he has natural parenting ability. Learning how to deal with children effectively and to provide the right balance of discipline and love is not easy. Although 80 percent of women say they would choose to be a parent again if they had it to do all over again (Genevie & Margolies, 1987), most find the demands of new (and multiple) roles in their lives to be stressful (Ventura, 1987). Studies find that after the transition to parenthood, happiness within the marriage is directly related to the sharing of child care and housekeeping responsibilities (Hackel & Ruble, 1992). Many new fathers, for example, complain about a diminished sex life and their wives' mood swings, yet do little to relieve their partners in their new responsibilities. Men, do you value your relationship enough to share these responsibilities?

It is useful to acquire some training and knowledge about parenting, just as it is useful to acquire training and knowledge about giving birth. Some excellent references are listed at the end of the chapter. In addition, the Family Resource Coalition has published a listing of programs to improve parenting skills and strengthen families. To learn about such programs in your area, contact the Family Resource Coalition at 200 South Michigan Avenue, 16th floor, Chicago, IL 60604.

> *PERSONAL REFLECTIONS*
> *Will pregnancy affect your sexual relationship with your partner? How? Why? Will being parents affect your sexual relationship? How? Why? What steps can you and your partner take to ensure that as parents your sexual relationship will continue to be fulfilling?*

SPACING PREGNANCIES

How much time in between pregnancies is best for producing a healthy, full-term baby? In a large-scale study by the Centers for Disease Control and Prevention (Zhu et al., 1999), it was found that a woman should wait 18 to 23 months after giving birth before getting pregnant again. Getting pregnant sooner than this, or waiting a long time, greatly increases the chance of a premature (and undersized) baby. Waiting 18 to 23 months apart has an added advantage for mom and dad as well—you won't have two babies in diapers at the same time.

INFERTILITY AND IMPAIRED FECUNDITY

Infertility is defined as the inability of a couple to conceive. The ability of a couple to conceive within a certain period of time is called **fecundity.** For

infertility The inability of a couple to conceive.

fecundity The ability of a couple to conceive within a certain period of time.

most studies, fecundity is measured over a year's time. Notice that these two terms have different meanings. A person can be fertile, but not very fecund. For example, as people age from their early 20s to their late 30s, most are still fertile, but they become less fecund.

Most people think of an infertile couple as a couple who have never been able to conceive, called *primary infertility*. However, the inability to conceive after having had one child, called *secondary infertility*, is even more common (Mosher & Pratt, 1991). Many people believe that infertility is increasing, and popular magazines make reference to an infertility "epidemic." There has, in fact, been an increase in problems with couples conceiving. Infertility increased from about 8 percent of couples in the 1980s to 10 percent in the mid-1900s, but much of the increase is due to many people delaying childbearing (problems with fecundity due to an increase in age) (Chandra & Stephen, 1998). What there has also been a big increase in is the number of couples seeking help for infertility, which has led to the perception of an epidemic (Stephen & Chandra, 2000).

The causes of infertility are many and varied because so many organs of both sexes must function properly for conception to take place. About 40 percent of the problems involved with infertility are due to the man, with another 40 percent due to the woman. About 20 percent of the cases result from problems in both partners (Hudson et al., 1987; Moore, 1993).

Before we proceed, you should be aware that there is a national organization that offers updated information and support to infertile couples. If interested, contact RESOLVE, 1310 Broadway, Somerville, MA 02144–1731, or call 617–623–0744.

INFERTILITY IN MEN

It has been known for a long time that fecundity in women decreases with age (van Noord-Zaadstra et al., 1991). Recently, it has been found that this is true for men as well (Ford et al., 2000). The probability that it would take longer than a year to conceive is only 8 percent for men under 25 years of age, but nearly doubles to 15 percent for men over 35. This is due to declining numbers and quality of sperm.

As you may remember, only a very few of the millions of sperm cells released during ejaculation survive the trip to the egg. If a man's reproductive system cannot produce enough sperm, and/or if the sperm he produces are too slow or too weak, the probability that fertilization can occur is substantially reduced. Low numbers of sperm are caused by a variety of factors, including endocrine problems (low levels of pituitary or gonadal hormones), drugs (including alcohol and many antibiotics), marijuana, radiation, and infections. If a man gets mumps after puberty, for example, it often spreads to the testicles and causes severe swelling that destroys the seminiferous tubules where

sperm are produced. Other infections, including some sexually transmitted diseases, can result in blockage of a man's duct system (just as some STDs can lead to blockage of the Fallopian tubes in women). Varicosity of the veins in the spermatic cord (*varicocele*) can also lead to a low sperm count (Howards, 1995; see Kamischke & Nieschlag, 1999, for a review of the many possible causes).

Because sperm can only be produced at a temperature several degrees lower than normal body temperature, sperm count is sensitive to temperature variations. For example, athletes who regularly wear athletic supporters or metal cup protectors for long periods of time (resulting in increased testicular temperatures) risk having a temporarily low sperm count. Frequent use of saunas or hot tubs can also cause a temporarily low sperm count. If a couple is trying to conceive, the man may be told to switch to loose-fitting underwear so that his testicles will hang farther from his body and thus have less exposure to body heat.

A review of 61 studies conducted worldwide concluded that the average sperm count per ejaculation had dropped by more than half in the last 50 years (Carlsen et al., 1992). What could cause such a dramatic change? Neils Skakkeback, one of the authors of the paper, said, "It would have to be something in the environment or life style. Changes that occur within a generation could hardly be due to a change in genetic background" (quoted by Epstein in AP release, September 1992). Further evidence is found in the fact that the rates for testicular cancer tripled during the same time period. Could industrial chemical pollutants have such effects? Boys born to (and breast-fed by) mothers exposed to high levels of pollutants can have testicular malformations and dramatically undersized penises, and the same is true for many species in the wild (see Begley & Glick, 1994). Many of the suspected pollutants resemble the female sex hormone estrogen in structure. Since the initial report, some scientists have found no evidence that sperm counts are lower than in the past (Bromwich et al., 1994; Farrow, 1994; Fisch et al., 1995; Paulsen et al., 1996), while others confirm that there has been a substantial decline (Auger et al., 1995; Irvine et al., 1996). There will certainly be much research in this area in the future.

Infertility is not just a physical problem; it also affects men emotionally:

"Several months ago we began trying to have kids unsuccessfully. When I was younger I had an . . . operation and my doctor said that because of this I would not be able to have children. My wife and I wanted children, and this situation has really put a strain on our marriage."

"Being sterile is not an easy thing to discuss. On top of diminishing dreams and goals, it has made finding the right girl to begin a lifelong relationship with very difficult. . . . My future wife and I will never be able to have children of our own. . . . I've always wanted to teach my son to play sports or take my daughter to dancing lessons. . . . Hopefully someday I will find the right woman and we can adopt." (All examples are from the author's files.)

What are the medical treatments for male infertility? Infertility due to varicose veins in the spermatic cord (8–23 percent of cases) can often be corrected with surgery (Howards, 1995; Kamischke & Nieschlag, 1999). If the cause is hormonal, treatment with pituitary hormones (or brain hormones that cause release of pituitary hormones) or gonadal hormones (androgens) is often successful. A blocked duct system in men is much easier to correct through surgery than are blocked tubes in women.

When a man is found to have a low sperm count, a procedure called **artificial insemination** is often used. In this procedure, sperm are collected via masturbation and inserted into the female partner's uterus immediately after ovulation. Several ejaculations are usually collected and stored by freezing (frozen semen is just as effective as fresh). For example, if a man's average ejaculation were found to contain 50 million sperm, six to eight ejaculations (totaling 300 million to 400 million sperm) might be collected and frozen. When enough sperm have been collected, they are gathered together for a single insertion. The success rate is close to 20 percent, but this can be improved to about 33 percent if fertility drugs are also given to the women to induce "superovulation" (Guzick et al., 1999). Sperm can be safely preserved for more than 10 years, and some men make deposits in sperm banks before having a vasectomy, undergoing chemotherapy, working a hazardous job, or going off to war.

If a man's sperm count is so low that combining several ejaculations will not help, a couple can choose to use sperm from another, usually anonymous, man. In these cases, artificial insemination is often called *donor insemination*. Donors are usually matched with the physical characteristics of the man. At one time, over 30,000 babies a year were conceived by this method in the United States (see Barratt et al., 1990).

The newest and most successful technique involves injecting a single sperm directly into an egg (called **intracytoplasmic sperm injection**). The first U.S. baby conceived by this technique was born in 1993. This procedure is now being used more and more frequently and with good results, and has resulted in decreased demand for donor insemination (Dozortsev et al., 1995).

Sperm with X or Y chromosomes can be partially separated by filtering them through liquid albumin, a protein. Thus, artificial insemination also allows couples who wish to do so to attempt to select the sex of their child (Beernink et al., 1993). Sex selection can also be done by genetic diagnosis during in vitro fertilization (see next section, but this is generally regarded as unethical (Ethics Committee, 1999).

INFERTILITY IN WOMEN

The discovery that she is infertile can be emotionally devastating to a woman and her partner:

"My husband and I have been unsuccessful in our attempts to have children. We started trying to have a family 7 years ago. We waited a year and a half before even seeing a doctor. My doctor did the preliminary infertility workup and gave me some low doses of Clomid. After 6 months of no success I went to a specialist. He gave me some industrial strength fertility drugs and after about 4 months I got pregnant and miscarried. We tried the same drugs again with no success and finally threw in the towel. All of this took about 5 years.

"The experience is terribly isolating. People don't understand what you're upset about—after all, you didn't lose anything that they can see. All of our friends have had their kids. That's a lot of baby showers and first birthday parties that we didn't show up for. The funny thing about new parents is that it is perfectly normal for them to shamelessly go on and on about their new kids and problems—so even when we got together with our friends for other reasons the main topics were breast-feeding and details about their pregnancy and delivery. It was heartbreaking not to be able to be happy for them because at the time we just happened to be in a lot of pain. You can also add to the list the ignorant people who think you are selfish and self-centered for not having any kids. You don't tell them you are having problems because it's none of their business and they get to assume the worst. Dr. King—I just think most people don't realize that when you come to realize that you can't have your own kids . . . the couple really does grieve about an imaginary child that everyone has dreamed about. . . . We plan on adopting this summer." (from the author's files)

For women of reproductive age, problems with fertilization generally come from two sources—structural problems in the Fallopian tubes or uterus and failure to release eggs (ova). Blockage of the Fallopian tubes accounts for about 25 to 35 percent of all cases (Honoré et al., 1999). Blockage can be due to anatomical malformations, growths (e.g., polyps), endometriosis (see below), infections, and scar tissue. Cigarette smoking and douching also increase the risk of infertility by increasing the risk of pelvic inflammatory disease and blocked tubes (Baird et al., 1996; Buck et al., 1997). Scar

artificial insemination A method of treating infertility caused by a low sperm count in men. Sperm are collected during several ejaculations and then inserted into the partner's vagina at the time of ovulation.

intracytoplasmic sperm injection A procedure used to treat men who have a low sperm count; injection of a single sperm directly into an egg.

tissue from sexually transmitted diseases, especially chlamydia and gonorrhea (resulting in pelvic inflammatory disease), accounts for at least half the cases of infertility from blocked tubes. Given the epidemic levels of these diseases, this will continue to be a primary cause for both ectopic pregnancies and infertility in the near future (see Chapter 5).

The diameter of the passageway that an egg takes through the Fallopian tube is only about half that of a human hair. Sometimes surgeons are able to reopen these tiny structures, but the success rate for microsurgery is only about 50 percent, (Honoré et al., 1999). In recent years, laser beams have been used successfully to unblock tubes. An even newer surgical technique to reopen blocked Fallopian tubes involves inserting a small balloon into the tubes and then inflating it (balloon tuboplasty). A similar technique has previously been used to unclog arteries leading to the heart.

About 25 to 40 percent of infertile women have endometriosis to some degree (see Lessey, 2000, for a review). Endometriosis can cause infertility by the growth of endometrial tissue in the Fallopian tubes and/or around the ovaries. Many women today are postponing pregnancy, and endometriosis is known as the "career women's disease" because it is most common in women in their mid-20s and over, especially if they have postponed childbirth. Hormone treatment to control the growth of endometrial tissue or surgery to remove it has commonly been used. Today, laparoscopic surgery (with cauterization) is being used with greater frequency for endometriosis-related infertility.

The major cause of infertility in women is a failure to ovulate, which can be due to several hormone irregularities (Crosignani et al., 1999). Some infertile women have too much of a hormone called prolactin, while others have too little or too much of what are called gonadotrophic hormones (hormones that stimulate the ovaries). Low levels of gonadotrophic hormones are commonly due to extreme emotional stress or being very underweight. Perhaps the most common cause of failure to ovulate is polycystic ovarian syndrome, in which eggs only partially develop within the ovary and there is an excess of male hormones.

Women who are infertile because of a failure to ovulate are treated with drugs (see Crosignani et al., 1999). In the case of too much prolactin, prolactin-lowering drugs are used. More commonly, if a woman is having problems becoming pregnant because she is not having regular menstrual cycles, and thus eggs are not being released, her physician will try **fertility drugs.** There are two major types. One type stimulates the pituitary gland to secrete FSH and LH, the hormones necessary to start the cycle (see Chapter 3). Clomiphene is an example of this type of drug. A second type stimulates the ovaries directly (HMG, or human menopausal gonadotropin, is an example). The success rate for fertility drugs is about 50 to 70 percent in cases where the problem is entirely hormonal.

Although they are often successful, there have been two major concerns with the use of fertility drugs. First, they increase the chance of multiple births from 1 or 2 percent to 10–20 percent. From the early 1970s to the mid-1990s, twin births rose 65 percent and multiple births of three or more increased by nearly 400 percent, largely because of fertility drugs (Luke et al., 1994; Ventura et al., 1997). In 1999, a woman gave birth to eight babies after being treated with fertility drugs. Multiple births pose medical risks both to the babies (being born prematurely and of having low birth weight) and to the pregnant woman (Elster et al., 2000). If very underweight, they may end up with major health problems as well as learning disabilities. Second, there has been some concern that fertility drugs may increase the risk of ovarian cancer (Whittemore et al., 1992). However, rates for ovarian cancer are already much higher in women who have never given birth, and when this is taken into account there is little evidence that fertility drugs increase the risk (Bristow & Karlan, 1996; Mosgaard et al., 1997).

ASSISTED REPRODUCTIVE TECHNOLOGY

The techniques for overcoming infertility entered a new era with the development of **in vitro** ("in glass") **fertilization (IVF)** in England in the 1970s. Here eggs and sperm are combined in a Petri dish, and after fertilization takes place, several fertilized eggs (usually at about the four-cell stage) are placed into the woman's uterus with the hope that at least one will then attach itself to the uterine wall. Fertility drugs are often used to stimulate egg production; the eggs are then surgically removed from the ovaries when mature and sperm is collected via masturbation. The first baby born through use of this technique was Louise Brown of England in 1978 (Steptoe & Edwards, 1978). Children conceived with in vitro fertilization are often called "test-tube babies" by the press and others, but as you can see, the procedure does not even use test tubes.

The overall success rate for in vitro fertilization in 1994 was only 20.7 percent (Society for Assisted Reproductive Technology et al., 1997). Since then, the success rate has improved to 36–43 percent for women under 35 years of age by transferring two fertilized eggs (rather than one) to a woman's uterus. However, this

fertility drugs Drugs that improve the chance of conception in women who are infertile owing to hormone deficiencies. The drugs either stimulate the pituitary gland to secrete FSH and LH or stimulate the ovaries directly.

in vitro fertilization (IVF) A process in which a mature ovum is surgically removed from a woman's ovary, placed in a medium with sperm until fertilization occurs, and then placed in the woman's uterus. This is usually done in women who cannot conceive because of blocked Fallopian tubes.

also has increased the chances of a multiple birth to 20–23 percent for women under 35 (Schieve et al., 1999). By waiting 4 to 5 days before placing the conceptus into a woman's uterus (by this time it is a blastocyst) instead of the usual 2 to 3 days, pregnancy rates have improved even further to about 50 percent. The average cost of a successful procedure is $68,000 to $85,000 (Mol et al., 2000). Many institutes were freezing fertilized eggs in case the first attempt failed, but research has shown that the success rate is higher with fresh fertilized eggs (Levran et al., 1990). The major problem, however, was that eggs fertilized outside a woman's Fallopian tubes simply did not attach to the uterine walls as often as eggs fertilized in a normal manner (i.e., within a Fallopian tube).

In the mid-1980s Ricardo Asch and his colleagues modified the IVF procedure (Asch et al., 1984). They bypassed the Petri dish by putting eggs and sperm into a pipette and inserting them directly into a Fallopian tube. They called the technique **gamete intrafallopian transfer (GIFT).** The fertilized eggs implant in the uterus at a higher rate than with IVF, and the overall success rate is about 27 percent—40–50 percent in the best clinics (Society for Assisted Reproductive Technology, 1993). But that is not the end of the story. In order to assure fertilization, Asch's group had fertilization take place in a Petri dish (as with IVF) and then placed the fertilized eggs directly into a Fallopian tube, a procedure called **zygote intrafallopian transfer (ZIFT).** The success rate is presently slightly lower than for GIFT. However, after several years, the pregnancy rates for GIFT and ZIFT have not proved to be much better than for in vitro fertilization. Because GIFT and ZIFT require major surgery, most physicians have returned to the simpler, less invasive IVF procedure (Menezo & Janny, 1996).

These techniques can also be used to screen potential embryos (preembryos) for genetic defects. In 1993, for example, eight-cell preembryos were tested for the deadly Tay-Sachs disease by removing one cell, and three "clean" fertilized eggs were then placed back in the mother. The couple's first child had died of the disease, but they now know that their new baby, born in 1994, is free of the disease.

These techniques are used for a variety of infertility problems, male or female. If it is necessary, donated eggs or sperm can be used for any of the procedures. However, there are some problems. As with fertility drugs, IVF, GIFT, and ZIFT all involve an increased chance of multiple births (Elster et al., 2000). And in the end, at least half of all couples who undergo assisted reproductive techniques still will not conceive.

More than 60,000 couples a year undergo some form of assisted reproductive technology in the United States (Schieve et al., 1999). However, the biggest obstacle to advancement in this field is social, political, and legal. Many people oppose these procedures to treat infertility. The Roman Catholic Church, for example, rejects both artificial insemination and in vitro fertilization, proclaiming that procreation must be "a physically embodied love act." Many physicians believe that GIFT will be ethically acceptable to most religious groups (see Mastroyannis, 1993), but that remains to be seen. The U.S. government has refused to fund research on IVF. Joseph Schulman, a former section director at the National Institutes of Health, said, "I can think of no other examples where for a decade and a half a whole area of investigation that has in fact proven itself to be of massive value to thousands and thousands of couples has been pigeonholed" (quoted in Baker, 1990). Studies indicate that most people have favorable opinions of infertility treatments that produce a child that is biologically related to both members of the couple (they have less favorable opinions of interventions that use donor eggs, donor sperm, or surrogacy; Halman et al., 1992). How do you feel about this?

> *PERSONAL REFLECTIONS*
> *Imagine that you and your partner have tried to conceive for 5 years. You both have gone through innumerable tests, but nothing seems to work. How do you feel? What would you do next? What options would you consider? What options would you never consider? Why or why not?*

SURROGATE MOTHERS

One of the most controversial fertility solutions is **surrogate motherhood,** sometimes resorted to when a woman cannot conceive or carry a fetus during pregnancy. In such a case, a couple may create a zygote through in vitro fertilization and then have the fertilized egg implanted in the uterus of another woman. In a second method, the surrogate mother is impregnated with the male partner's sperm, usually through artificial insemination. The surrogate mother gives birth, and the infant is raised by the infertile couple. The couple will generally pay for the surrogate mother's medical expenses, along with necessary legal fees. They also will pay the surrogate mother a fee for providing this "service." However, some surrogate mothers have changed their minds after delivery, and a 1987 case involved the rights of surrogate mothers to "back

gamete intrafallopian transfer (GIFT) A procedure for treating female infertility in which sperm and eggs are gathered and placed directly into a Fallopian tube.

zygote intrafallopian transfer (ZIFT) A method of treating infertility caused by blocked Fallopian tubes. An ovum taken from the infertile woman is fertilized by sperm from her partner and then transferred to the unblocked portion of a Fallopian tube.

surrogate mother A woman who carries a fetus to full term for another couple, agreeing to give the infant to the other couple after it is born. The infant generally represents a union of the sperm from the man and either his partner's ovum or the ovum of the surrogate mother.

out of" such contracts (the judge awarded custody to the infertile couple). Some states have passed laws that allow surrogacy, while others have attempted to outlaw it. Court tests of these laws continue to-day. This is certainly one area where laws have not kept pace with the new technology (Foote, 1998).

DELAYED CHILDBEARING AND ASSISTED REPRODUCTIVE TECHNOLOGY

As women grow older, their fecundity declines. For most women, this starts happening when they are as young as 31 years of age (van Noord-Zaadstra et al., 1991). After age 30, the chances of having a healthy baby decrease by more than 3 percent each year. The problem is not with the uterus but with the decreased number and quality of eggs as women age. Recall from Chapter 3 that about 1,000 follicles mature (and are then lost for good) every month (McGee & Hsueh, 2000). At menopause, you recall, the ovaries stop working entirely and women are no longer capable of reproduction—or at least that was what was thought until recently.

As more and more women have entered careers and chosen to delay pregnancy, they have often been faced with fertility problems when they do decide they are ready for motherhood. Today, however, in vitro fertilization and the related procedures have allowed even some postmenopausal women to become pregnant and have children. Eggs are donated by a young woman (and thus are usually of high quality), and then in vitro fertilization is attempted to achieve fertilization and implantation. The uterus is kept functional with injections of estrogen and progesterone. One of the first women to become pregnant with this technology was a 42-year-old former cancer patient who had lost her ovaries because of chemotherapy (see Sauer et al., 1992).

More recently, postmenopausal women over the age of 50 have elected to have children by egg donation and in vitro fertilization (see Sauer et al., 1993). In 1994, a 62-year-old Italian woman gave birth after receiving donated eggs, followed in 1997 by a 63-year-old California woman (Kalb, 1997). In the words of Marcia Angell, executive editor of the *New England Journal of Medicine*, "The limits on the childbearing years are now anyone's guess."

Many people, including many physicians, are debating the ethics and health-related issues of assisted delayed childbearing. The older a woman is during pregnancy, the greater the risk of a low-birth-weight baby. There are also risks to the woman herself—diabetes, high blood pressure, and increased likelihood of having to have a cesarean section (Gilbert et al., 1999). These problems might be minimized by careful screening, but what about the ethical considerations? For those who oppose assisted reproductive technology, proponents offer two arguments. First, there is often a double standard, with many people admiring older men who father children. Why shouldn't women have the same opportunity? Second, qualities like love, experience, and responsibility are more important than age in determining who will be a good mother. As the chairperson of the Council of the British Medical Association said, it is better to have "a fit, healthy 59-year-old than an unfit, unhealthy 19-year-old" mother. What qualities do you think make a good mother?

ADOPTION

When a couple cannot conceive and medical technology cannot correct the problem, there are still some options available. Many couples become parents by adopting a child. One difficulty with the option of **adoption** is that the demand for children to be adopted is very high. Long waits—sometimes months or even years—may be required before a couple is able to find and adopt a healthy child. Some couples choose not to wait and adopt children of other nationalities or disabled children. For caring people, adoption benefits everyone—the couple who so badly want a child and a child who needs a home, love, and affection.

For information about adoption (including a bimonthly magazine called *Ours*) and support, you can contact the National Council for Adoption (see Resources at the end of the book).

SUPERFERTILITY

For some women, having children is, apparently, very easy. According to the *Guinness Book of World Records*, the most prolific mother alive is Leontina Albina of Chile, who gave birth to 59 children—always triplets or twins. She was one of three triplets sent to an orphanage, but while her two brothers were adopted, she was not. She promised herself that if she ever had children, she would never give them away. Leontina married at age 12 and continued to have children into her 50s.

A word of caution: Studies show that women who have had six or more pregnancies are at higher risk for coronary heart disease and cardiovascular disease (Ness et al., 1993). Please take this into consideration if you are planning a large family.

adoption Taking a child into one's family by legal process and raising the child as one's own.

Key Terms

Suggested Readings

Bing, E. (1988). Yes, you can. *Childbirth '88*, vol. 5. Discusses sexual intercourse during pregnancy, assuring women that it is okay. If you want more information, see Bing, E., & Coleman, L. (1983). *Making love during pregnancy*. New York: Bantam.

Cowan, C. , & Cowan, P. (1992). *When partners become parents*. New York: Basic Books. Addresses the many challenges that couples will face when they become parents. An excellent book that is based on 10 years of research.

Kime, R. (1992). *Wellness: Pregnancy, childbirth and parenting*. Guilford, CT: Dushkin. Aimed at teaching parents-to-be to think about health.

Kitzinger, S. (1997). *The complete book of pregnancy and childbirth*. New York: Knopf. From one of the leaders in midwifery.

Marrs, R., Bloch, L. F., & Silverman, K. K. (1998). *Dr. Richard Marrs' fertility book*. New York: Knopf. For infertile couples.

Pryor, K., & Pryor, G. (1999). *Nursing your baby*. New York: Pocket Books. For those considering breast-feeding.

Study Guide

INTERACTIVE REVIEW

Sexual intercourse can result in conception on only about 6 days of the menstrual cycle (from about (1) _____ days before (2) _____ to about (3) _____ days afterwards). Fertilization usually occurs within a (4) _____, and implantation normally occurs in the (5) _____ of the uterus. Implantation of a fertilized egg at any other location is called an (6) _____ pregnancy, and the most common cause is scarring of the Fallopian tubes due to (7) _____. Pregnancy tests are positive if a woman's urine or blood contains a hormone secreted by the developing placenta called (8) _____.

Pregnancy is divided into three 3-month intervals called (9) _____. After implantation, the conceptus is called an (10) _____ for the first (11) _____ months and then a (12) _____ for the last (13) _____ months of pregnancy. An expectant mother can first feel her unborn baby moving, an experience called (14) _____, during the (15) _____ month of pregnancy. Sexual intercourse during pregnancy is generally thought not to be harmful to the fetus, although some health professionals recommend that a pregnant woman not engage in intercourse during the 9th month of pregnancy.

There are many possible causes of complications of pregnancy. Substances that can cross the placental barrier and harm the unborn baby are called (16) _____. Examples include viruses, smoking, alcohol, cocaine and other drugs. Fetal abnormalities can often be detected by ultrasound or by a variety of invasive techniques such as chorionic sampling, (17) _____, celocentesis, and fetoscopy. Today, it is sometimes possible to perform surgery on a fetus while it is still in the uterus.

Prepared childbirth courses attempt to break the (18) _____ cycle through education and preparation. Lamaze and other techniques generally include a "coach" (usually the woman's partner) to help the expectant mother through labor and delivery. These methods hold to a philosophy that the mother-to-be and the coach should be in control of the birthing process and that anesthetics should not be used unless absolutely necessary. Today, there is a growing movement advocating going back to giving birth in the home (or in a homelike environment), usually with the aid of a nurse- (19) _____ rather than a physician.

The actual birthing experience is known as labor. Before giving birth, many women experience false labor. True labor is distinguished from false labor by the timing and length of (20) _____ and by the (21) _____ of the cervix. Labor proceeds in three stages. The initial or (22) _____ stage usually lasts from 6 to 13 hours, although each stage of labor varies a great deal from woman to woman and even from birth to birth in the same woman. The (23) _____ breaks (or is broken by the physician) just prior to or during this stage. The last part of the first stage of labor is called the (24) _____. It marks the beginning of the birth process. In the second stage of labor, the cervix is (25) _____ and the fetus begins moving through the birth canal. The baby usually enters the world (26) _____ first, and after delivery the (27) _____ is cut. In the third stage of labor the (28) _____ detaches from the uterus and leaves the mother's body. If complications develop during childbirth, the baby can be delivered surgically through the mother's abdomen by a (29) _____. Today, in most cases, it is considered safe for women who have previously had a C-section to deliver vaginally during subsequent deliveries.

An increasing number of U.S. women are breast-feeding their babies. Mother's milk contains many infection-fighting (30) _____ and is easier to digest than cow's milk. After giving birth, many women experience negative emotions, called (31) _____. Hormone changes, lack of sleep, and new demands can all contribute to this. Most physicians advise that women not resume sexual intercourse for (32) _____ weeks after delivery. Studies find that after the transition to parenthood, happiness within a relationship is related to (33) _____.

Infertility or impaired fecundity affects about one in (34) _____ couples in the United States. About (35) _____ percent of these cases are due to problems with the man, (36) _____ percent to problems with the woman, and about (37) _____ percent to problems with both partners. In men, infertility is usually caused either by blockage of the duct system or (38) _____. For the latter, a procedure called (39) _____ is often used. In women, infertility is usually the result of blocked (40) _____ or a failure to (41) _____.

Today, infertile couples can be helped by a variety of assisted reproductive procedures in which an egg is fertilized outside of a woman's body and then placed into her uterus (called (42) _____) or Fallopian tube (called (43) _____), or in which both eggs and sperm are placed into a Fallopian tube (called (44) _____). These techniques have allowed some postmenopausal women to have children as well. For many infertile couples, adoption has proved to be a rewarding alternative.

SELF-TEST

A. TRUE OR FALSE

- T F 45. At conception, the one-celled organism is called an embryo.
- T F 46. A primary follicle first begins to mature under stimulation of luteinizing hormone.
- T F 47. About 75 percent of all conceptions either fail to implant or are spontaneously aborted within the first 6 weeks.
- T F 48. "Morning sickness" is most common during the last trimester of pregnancy.
- T F 49. An expectant mother cannot feel her unborn baby moving inside her ("quickening") until the second trimester.
- T F 50. Sexual intercourse during the 7th and 8th months of pregnancy is often harmful to the mother and/or fetus.
- T F 51. Drugs can adversely affect the fetus, but smoking, while hazardous to the mother, has little effect.
- T F 52. If a woman is Rh positive and her fetus is Rh negative, the condition is called Rh incompatibility.
- T F 53. One beer or one glass of wine a day is thought to be acceptable when a woman is pregnant.
- T F 54. One of the most common causes of scarring of the Fallopian tubes is untreated gonorrhea and chlamydia.
- T F 55. "Prepared childbirth" means having a baby without the use of anesthetics.
- T F 56. A baby is born during the third stage of labor.
- T F 57. If a woman has an ectopic pregnancy, there is an increased risk that her future pregnancies will also be ectopic.
- T F 58. Women who have delivered babies by cesarean section usually can deliver vaginally in subsequent pregnancies.
- T F 59. Natural filters protect the baby from alcohol, drugs, and pollutants during breast-feeding.
- T F 60. The expression "test-tube babies" refers to the process whereby conception and embryonic development (i.e., the first 2 months) occur outside the mother's body.
- T F 61. Artificial insemination refers to the fertilization of an egg by synthetically manufactured sperm.
- T F 62. With assisted reproductive techniques, women over the age of 60 can have babies if they wish to.
- T F 63. "Morning sickness" can be effectively treated with hormones.
- T F 64. True labor is marked by the onset of Braxton-Hicks contractions.

B. MATCHING (MATCH THE PROBLEM WITH THE TREATMENT OR SOLUTION)

Treatment or solution
- _____ 65. artificial insemination
- _____ 66. balloon tuboplasty
- _____ 67. cesarean section
- _____ 68. chorionic sampling (or amniocentesis, or fetoscopy)
- _____ 69. episiotomy
- _____ 70. fertility drugs
- _____ 71. fetal monitor

Problem
a. Susan has a tubal (ectopic) pregnancy.
b. Sherry and John cannot conceive because she is not having regular menstrual cycles.
c. Harriet's physician is worried that her perineum might tear during delivery.
d. Carol and David cannot conceive because he has a low sperm count.
e. Maria and John cannot conceive. Eggs taken from Maria are fertilized by sperm from John and the fertilized eggs are placed into one of Maria's Fallopian tubes.

_____ 72. fetal surgery

_____ 73. gamete intrafallopian transfer

_____ 74. in vitro fertilization

_____ 75. laparoscopic surgery

_____ 76. surrogate mother

_____ 77. zygote intrafallopian transfer

_____ 78. intracytoplasmic sperm injection

f. Phyllis is not yet fully dilated and her baby is in distress.

g. Diane cannot carry a fetus during pregnancy, but she and Frank want to have a baby that is biologically theirs.

h. Mary is in labor and her physician wishes to keep track of the unborn baby's vital signs.

i. Shelly and Mark cannot conceive. Eggs taken from Shelly are fertilized by sperm from Mark and then placed into Shelly's uterus.

j. Cindy and Bert cannot conceive because she has blocked Fallopian tubes, but they have ruled out assisted reproductive techniques.

k. Linda and Walter's unborn baby has a life-threatening urinary tract infection.

l. Joan and Tom are worried that their unborn baby may have an abnormality.

m. Betty and Sam cannot conceive. Eggs taken from Betty and sperm taken from Sam are placed directly into one of her Fallopian tubes.

C. FILL IN THE BLANKS

79. Zygote, _____, _____, embryo, fetus.

80. The major link between the developing baby and the mother is the _____.

81. A pregnant woman who has gained excessive weight and has high blood pressure and swollen joints may have _____.

82. Before birth, the fetus's head drops lower in the uterus. This is called _____.

83. Three rules of thumb to determine if labor has begun are _____, _____, and _____.

84. The _____ trimester is when a developing fetus is generally most susceptible to harmful substances.

85. The vast majority of ectopic pregnancies are _____ pregnancies.

86. In 1990, the Institute of Medicine recommended that normal-weight women gain _____ pounds during pregnancy.

87. By the time a fertilized egg has reached the uterus, it is a fluid-filled sphere called a _____.

88. The part of a baby that normally comes into the birth canal first is _____.

89. The cervix becomes fully dilated during the _____ stage of labor.

90. An egg remains ripe only for about _____ after ovulation.

91. The fetus is protected in a thick-skinned sac called the _____.

92. _____, _____, and _____ are three procedures used by physicians during labor and childbirth that many experts feel are done far too routinely (and unnecessarily).

93. For a baby to have any chance of surviving, it must develop in the uterus for at least _____ weeks.

94. The World Health Organization recommends that babies breast-feed until they are at least _____ years old.

95. To best assure the chances of a healthy baby, a woman should wait _____ months after giving birth before getting pregnant again.

96. The major cause of infertility in women is _____.

Chapter 8

Communicating about Sex

Why do Americans find it easier to have sex than to talk about it?

(Peggy Clarke, 1996/1997)

Communication is the act of making information known, the exchange of thoughts or ideas (to paraphrase the *American Heritage Dictionary*). Until now, you may have lacked factual information about a wide variety of topics in human sexuality. However, when it comes to talking about the topic of sex, it is not enough to have factual information. Many people have trouble talking about sex, even with their partner.

In this chapter I will present some guidelines to help you communicate better about sexual matters. There are a variety of situations in which people might communicate about sexually related matters, including interactions with a new or short-term partner (dating, initiating sexual activities, contraception, and safer sex); making one's needs and desires known to a long-term partner; and conveying information and values to children. Because I cannot possibly cover them all, I have chosen to limit this chapter to sexual communication between long-term partners and communication between parents and their children about sexuality. *In Chapter 5 you can find some advice on initiating discussions about safer sex with a dating partner.*

When you have finished studying this chapter, you should be able to:

1. Take steps that enable you and your partner to become more comfortable talking about your sexual relationship (including agreement on a sexual vocabulary);

2. Take responsibility for your own sexual pleasure;

3. Understand the importance of positive reinforcement and "I" language;

4. Become a better listener;

5. Understand the importance of nonverbal communication;

6. Know how to properly convey your emotions to your partner when you are angry so that he or she clearly understands why you feel the way you do;

7. Understand why the sex education of children should be an ongoing process rather than a single "birds and bees" talk;

8. Know at what age children should be told about certain sexuality-related topics by their parents; and

9. Know how to speak to your children in a manner so that they are likely to value your opinion.

The first half of this chapter deals with communication between two people who have made a commitment to a long-term relationship. It assumes that each person genuinely cares for the other, that there is trust and intimacy. As you will learn in Chapter 15, most couples experience sexual differences or problems in their relationship (Frank et al., 1978; Laumann et al., 1999). How they work those problems out—how they communicate with one another about their differences and problems—will affect their sexual adjustment. In cohabiting couples, sexual satisfaction is associated with understanding (particularly by men) their partner's sexual preferences (Purnine & Carey, 1997). "In many cases, sexual dysfunction problems cannot be addressed until communication improves" (Wincze & Carey, 1991, p. 110). Good communication also leads to a better relationship, and a better relationship generally leads to better sex (Cupach & Metts, 1991). The second half of the chapter is designed to help parents (and future parents) take what they learn in this course and teach it to their children.

In order to better communicate with you about communication, I have elected to abandon the usual academic style of textbook writing. I present to you a few guidelines about improving your communication skills in a question-and-answer format.

TALKING WITH YOUR PARTNER ABOUT SEXUAL DIFFERENCES AND PROBLEMS

WHY IS IT DIFFICULT TO TALK ABOUT SEX?

"I have a tendency to be the only person in a relationship that realizes that the other person is not psychic. I tell the other person what I want but usually I can never get accurate feedback." (from the author's files)

Intercourse means "communication," but there are few topics that people have more difficulty talking about than sex. One of the major reasons for this is that most people have little experience talking about sex in an intelligent and mature manner. Surveys in my own course consistently indicate that fewer than half of the 1,000 students I teach every semester have ever had a serious discussion with their parents about sex (King & LoRusso, 1997). Very few ever had a course in sex education during junior high or high school. This means, of course, that most people's only experience with discussing sex is locker room conversation and jokes, usually with individuals of the same sex. Much of this is crude and vulgar and contains misinformation. Adolescents often

communication The exchange of information, thoughts, ideas, or feelings.

Figure 8–1 Most couples are going to experience sexual problems or differences in their relationship. If they do not communicate well, the problems as well as their relationship will only grow worse.

avoid talking to members of the opposite sex about sex because they fear that this will be interpreted as an invitation or come-on. Thus, men generally have some experience talking about sex with other men, and women with other women, but many people reach adulthood with little or no experience in talking to the opposite sex. Even conversations with people of the same sex may be limited to nonthreatening sexual topics, for to talk about a sexual problem is to admit that you have one. Many people, particularly adolescents, are unwilling to do this because of worries that their friends might think less of them and tell others what they have said. As adults, some people are afraid to talk with their partners about a sexual problem because they are afraid it will threaten the relationship.

Are there any gender differences that may contribute to communication difficulties in heterosexual relationships? In the popular book *Men Are from Mars, Women Are from Venus* (Gray, 1992), it is claimed that "not only do men and women communicate differently but they think, feel, perceive, react, respond, love, need, and appreciate differently. They almost seem to be from different planets, speaking different languages" (p. 5). Deborah Tannen's best-seller *You Just Don't Understand: Women and Men in Conversation* (1990) also portrays men and women as polarized in their conversation styles.

Research has shown that although there are gender differences in communication, the differences are not as large as popular books would have us believe (see Aries, 1998, for a review). For example, a review of 256 studies found that women self-disclose more than men, but that the difference is not that great. The authors concluded: "It's time to stop perpetuating the myth that there are large differences in men's and women's self-disclosure" (Dindia & Allen, 1992).

Nevertheless, there are some gender differences in communication styles. Men may be less likely to maintain eye contact during conversation, be less clear or neutral in their responses, and be more likely to withdraw (Klinetrob & Smith, 1996). During arguments, women are more likely to set the emotional tone (we will return to communication during arguments later). Many people believe that it is not masculine for a man to express his feelings and emotions (including during sex). All people of both sexes need to express their feelings and emotions and be able to communicate them. The image of a man as "strong and silent" robs him of a fundamental part of his humanity and robs his partner of a true companion.

Communication about sex can also be hampered when a couple is locked into stereotypic behavioral gender roles. For example, one harmful stereotype is that men are experts at sex. This is simply not true. Women and men both *learn* about sex. Individuals differ greatly in the types of sexual experiences that they enjoy. Each person must explore and learn what brings the greatest pleasure to his or her sexual partner. Because sexual behaviors are learned, anyone can become an "expert" if that person is willing to read, to try new behaviors, to listen to feedback and direction from a partner, and to learn as well as to teach.

Finally, power differences in a relationship can affect communication (Quadagno et al., 1998). We are

---

Box 8–A CROSS-CULTURAL PERSPECTIVES

Ethnic Differences in Communication Patterns

Are there differences among ethnic groups in the way people communicate? The answer is yes. For example, compared to most white Americans, African Americans are more expressive and emotional in their interactions (Parham et al., 1999). Their verbal communications may be very animated in style. Asian Americans and Latinos, on the other hand, are less inclined than white Americans to engage in direct verbal communication, especially confrontation (Chang & Holt, 1991; Hecht et al., 1990). In white American culture great emphasis is placed on the individual (and individualism), whereas Asian Americans and traditional Latinos tend to place greater emphasis on the group (Gudykunst et al., 1996).

Differences in power between men and women also affect communication patterns. As a general rule, the greater the economic equality between partners, and when traditional gender roles do not dictate that women are subordinate to men, communication about sex is more open and direct (Weinberg & Williams, 1988). Among white couples, women are often financially dependent on men, whereas in African-American relationships frequently there is greater economic equality. As a result, African-American women are more comfortable in their discussions with men about sex, and are much more likely than women in other ethnic groups to make the decisions about when and what type of sex will occur (Quadagno et al., 1998).

In traditional Latino and Asian cultures, men are much more dominant in relationships, even in marriage (e.g., Queen et al., 1985), and this is true of less acculterated groups in the United States as well (Marin & Van Oss Marin, 1991). In Latino culture, for example, great value is attached to male *machismo*, and women are not supposed to bring up the subject of sex (Van Oss Marin & Gomez, 1994). Latino men feel that wives are supposed to learn about sex from their husbands.

As a result of the difference in gender roles, Latino and Asian-American couples are less likely than African-American or white couples to discuss sex openly and may avoid the subject altogether (Bradshaw, 1994; Guerrero Pavich, 1986; Van Oss Marin & Gomez, 1994). Confrontation and any negativity about sexual relations are avoided if at all possible. Instead, Latinos and Asian Americans rely heavily on nonverbal communication (e.g., body language, avoidance of eye contact, silence). They may not only be less likely to admit and discuss a sexual problem within a relationship but are also much less likely to seek help from a counselor or therapist (see Box 15–A).

The guidelines offered in this chapter about communication are intended to help everyone. However, I recognize that depending on your ethnic background, you may have more difficulties than some others incorporating them into your relationships.

most likely to express an opinion, particularly a difference of opinion, to those persons we perceive as having equal status. In some relationships, there is a power imbalance; in heterosexual relationships, it is usually in favor of the man. Although the following suggestions for improving communication should be helpful to everyone, they will be most useful to individuals in an egalitarian relationship. (To resolve a major power imbalance in a relationship may require professional counseling.)

HOW CAN MY PARTNER AND I GET USED TO TALKING ABOUT SEX?

One of the best ways to get used to talking with your partner about sex is to discuss together any sexuality-related topics in your daily newspaper. Hardly a day goes by when there isn't at least one article (and there are often many) in the paper about sexuality—AIDS, birth control, fertility research, and, best of all, results of sex surveys. The "Dear Abby" and "Ann Landers" columns often are about sexually related matters. Show your partner some selected topic in this book and start off with a statement like "I didn't know this" or "This is really interesting."

When you both become more comfortable talking about sex together, then you can more safely talk about your own sexual relationship. Often a good place to start is to talk about why it is difficult for you both to talk about sex. If, for example, your parents had a negative attitude about talking about sex, talk about that and how you would like to be different. Next you might talk about normal bodily functions related to sexuality and how they affect your sexual relationship. Try talking about menstruation, for example. Many people have *learned* (and thus can unlearn) negative attitudes about that (see Chapter 3 for an extensive discussion of learned negative attitudes about menstruation and how they affect sexual relations).

When you and your partner are comfortable enough to talk about sexual differences (in attitudes, preferred behaviors, etc.), you might want to discuss when and how to talk about such matters. For couples interested in exploring their attitudes about different sexual behaviors, looking at a sex manual together might be helpful (e.g., Alex Comfort's *The New Joy of Sex*).

WHAT IF I AM UNCOMFORTABLE WITH THE LANGUAGE OF SEX— WHAT WORDS SHOULD I USE?

Many of the commonly used words for our sexual anatomy and functions reflect the negativity that has prevailed in Western culture since early Christianity. Words like *prick, cock, cunt, pussy, screw,* and *fuck* may be common in conversations among men (Fischer,

1989), but many women (and men) might feel uncomfortable using such words with their partners, particularly if they wish to express positive emotions (Geer & Bellard, 1996). Medically correct terms such as *penis, vagina,* and *sexual intercourse* may not have any negative connotations but are so unerotic that they, too, may seem inappropriate in conversations between two people in a deeply emotional relationship. Euphemisms such as "go to bed with," "sleeping with," and "making love" may seem more erotic to some and convey that there is a relationship, but they are often inappropriate as well. Do we always "make love" when we have sex? Some couples develop a private vocabulary for body parts that is used only in conversations between themselves.

It is not for me to tell you what words to use with your partner when talking about sex. However, it is important that you both be comfortable with a sexual vocabulary. Therefore, as part of the process of getting used to talking about sex, be sure to discuss this with your partner until you both agree on a vocabulary that is explicit and specific enough to convey your feelings and desires and that you also find nonoffensive (yet still erotic).

WHEN (AND WHERE) SHOULD I TRY TO TALK TO MY PARTNER?

When is a good time to tell your partner that you prefer different behaviors, or wish to be touched or made love to in a different manner (or any other preference)? If you do it right after sex, you run the risk of making your comments sound like a report card or performance rating, and perhaps not a very good one at that. If you do it during sex, you might distract or frustrate your partner, and if you express your dissatisfaction before you start, that might cause performance anxiety.

Perhaps a neutral time would be best. Recall from the previous section that one of the general topics you and your partner might first discuss is when to talk about sexual differences. Whenever you do it, make sure you are not frustrated, angry, or highly emotional at the time. It is not so much *when* you discuss your differences but *how* you go about it, and your concerns may not be well received if you begin in a negative emotional state. Try to judge when your partner would be most receptive to talking about your concerns.

Finally, if you have most of your sexual relations in the bedroom, never worry about or discuss your sexual problems while in bed. If you do this too often, the bed can become a stimulus for sexual tension and anxiety; that is, just being in bed can cause you to start worrying. Save the bed for pleasant experiences and pick a neutral site like the living room for worrying about problems.

HOW SHOULD I APPROACH MY PARTNER WITH CONCERNS ABOUT OUR SEXUAL RELATIONSHIP?

Because of their inexperience in talking about sex—particularly sexual problems—many people say nothing and allow a problem to continue, with the end result often being increasingly greater frustration and/or anger. When they finally do get around to saying something, many people begin with statements like "I don't like it when you . . ." or "You don't. . . ." These types of statements accentuate the negative and are often met with defensive reactions and counteraccusations. This can quickly escalate into a full-scale argument.

There are few things that easily insult a person's ego as criticizing his or her sexual expression or interaction. Nearly everyone would like to believe that he or she is a good sexual partner. To try to solve your own frustrations by criticizing your partner, therefore, is asking for trouble. Sometimes people ask for feedback about sex and then get upset with the response. Some people, for example, ask questions like "How was it?" "Did you like it?" or "Wasn't that great?" after having sex. Sometimes they are really looking for a pat on the back or ego reinforcement rather than an honest answer, so this is really not a good time to express any negative reactions. Whenever possible, *accentuate the positive rather than the negative*. This is the most important advice that I can give you. Rather than beginning the conversation with "I don't like it when you . . . ," try "I like it when you. . . ." Your partner must do something that you like while having sex, so give him or her some positive reinforcement. Thousands of studies have shown that behaviors increase when they are reinforced, and praise is generally a powerful reinforcer for human beings.

> *PERSONAL REFLECTIONS*
>
> *Suppose that you are unsure of your partner's sexual desires and preferences, and you are unsure whether he or she is totally aware of yours. How might you communicate with one another? Suppose your desires and preferences are not exactly the same?*

WHAT IF I THINK THAT MY PARTNER IS TO BLAME—CAN I EVER COMPLAIN?

If you haven't expressed your concerns to your partner in a clear, specific manner (because you are uncomfortable talking about sex or for any other reason), do not lay the blame entirely on your partner. The problem has continued because you have allowed it to. Your partner cannot know what you want unless you tell him or her. It is wrong for you to think, or expect, that your partner should know what you want or how to please you. *You must take the responsibility for your own pleasure,* and you can do this only if you tell your partner of your needs and desires.

> "My husband and I are very open about our sexual ideas and feelings. When I don't like something he's doing I tell him and he does the same. We are at our sexual peak and communicating openly is very important." (from the author's files)

Although I emphasized the use of positive reinforcement in the previous section, that does not mean that you can never complain or express anger. However, when you are angry, learn to control your anger. Express it only after you have calmed down. (Remember, highly emotional negative accusations will probably be met with similar responses on the part of your partner.) Ask yourself what your motivation is for expressing complaints. Is it to hurt your partner, or is it for constructive change? Couples with good relationships accept that there will be differences, and sometimes even conflict, but they resolve those differences and conflicts in constructive, not destructive, ways. If you criticize your partner, make sure you criticize his or her behavior, not his or her character. There is a big difference between saying "You don't show me often enough how much you care" and saying "You are an uncaring person." If you must criticize your partner's behavior, be sure to praise other aspects of his or her behavior as well.

HOW SHOULD I EXPRESS MY NEEDS AND DESIRES?

Most communications experts suggest that individuals use *"I" language* when expressing desires to their partners. That means beginning sentences with "I," followed by an expression of *your* feelings, desires, or thoughts. There are some important advantages to this. By directly stating your feelings, you are taking the responsibility for your own well-being. In addition, "I" sentences avoid the blaming or accusatory tone common in statements that begin with "You." Statements such as "You don't like to hug me anymore" or "You don't love me" attack the other person's character and may well be met with a defensive response. The statement "I would like you to hug me more often" more directly expresses your feelings and desires and is less likely to elicit a defensive negative response.

Questions that begin with "Why" ("Why don't you . . . ?") are also often used to criticize a partner. Avoid those as well. Even sentences that begin with "We" can cause problems because they make assumptions about your partner's desires, moods, thoughts, or feelings. Don't talk for your partner.

Harold Bloomfield and Sirah Vettese, marriage partners and co-authors of *Lifemates: The Love Fitness Program for a Lasting Relationship* (1989; reprinted with permission), suggest "sexual heart talks" to enhance sexual intimacy. They ask couples to take turns completing the following statements with their spouse:

"The best thing about our sex life is . . ."

"What I find sexually attractive about you is . . ."

"A sexual delight I would like to indulge with you is . . ."

"A sexual fantasy I would like to act out with you is . . ."

"The way I would like to be touched is . . ."

"When I would like to be sexually romantic and you don't respond I . . ."

"I feel like withdrawing from sex when . . ."

"Three sexual fears I have are . . ."

"I feel sexually frustrated when . . ."

HOW CAN I FIND OUT ABOUT MY PARTNER'S DESIRES AND NEEDS?

Yes, it's important that you know and understand your partner's sexual desires and needs, but as a preliminary step, be sure that you are aware of your own. Once you are certain, a good place to start is with self-disclosure. Studies show that the more sexual self-disclosure there is in a relationship, there is usually greater sexual and relationship satisfaction (Byers & Demmons, 1999; Derlega et al., 1993).

> "Two years into the marriage our relationship took a downward spiral. Sex began to get boring and felt like just another chore. We finally began to talk openly about what we wanted from one another sexually. After much discussion, we are more attentive to each other's sexual needs. When I think back to our 'down' times I am sorry we didn't talk openly earlier. Sex is once again pleasurable."
>
> "My boyfriend and I of 2 years had never really talked about sex in a serious manner . . . we both felt really open that night so we played a game of 20 questions. The questions all had to deal with sexuality. For example, what we enjoyed, what he liked done to him, what I liked done to me, fantasies, etc. That one night opened the door for us to be able to talk about our sexual relationship in a serious manner. I felt more comfortable about what we were doing and why. It also brought us closer together as a couple. He told me after the conversation that night that he felt much closer to me than ever before." (All examples are from the author's files.)

Reveal to your partner (using "I" language) your thoughts, feelings, desires, and needs. This creates an environment of trust and understanding, and most people will self-disclose in return. Compare and discuss how each of you feels about different behaviors. Learn each other's preferences. Here again, a sex manual might be helpful.

Of course, you can also ask your partner about his or her preferences, but make sure that you *ask questions*

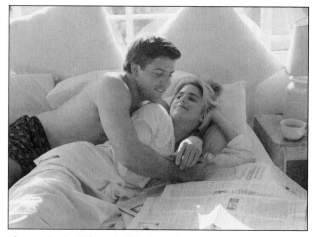

Figure 8–2 When talking with your partner, disclose your own feelings and desires by using "I" language, accentuate the positive, and (like this couple) make eye contact.

that are open-ended (e.g., "How do you like me to touch you when . . ."). Avoid questions that can be answered with one word (yes-or-no questions such as "Did you like it?" or "Do you like me to kiss your neck?").

IS LISTENING IMPORTANT? IF SO, HOW CAN I BECOME A BETTER LISTENER?

Effective communication is what holds close relationships together and enables them to grow. However, many people forget that communication requires not just talking, but listening as well. This is as true for sexual relations as it is for any other behavior. How well do you listen?

We may hear with our ears, but *we show how attentive we are with body language*—body position (Do you face your partner while he or she talks to you?), eye contact, facial expressions. Be supportive of your partner's attempts to communicate with you. In addition to positive body language, interact with him or her in a constructive manner. Make comments or paraphrase what your partner is saying so that you both are sure what the other is trying to say—not everyone conveys messages clearly.

To improve your listening skills, try giving your partner a massage. Giving one another a massage strengthens relationships by promoting better communication (Comiskey, 1989). Use some oil and make it a good massage. When starting the massage, it is normal to assume that what feels best to you will feel best to others as well. If you like your shoulders and neck massaged with a lot of pressure, for example, it is only natural that you will start off by attempting to please your partner in this manner. However, not everyone likes the same things you do. Your partner may prefer gentle massaging of the lower back. How will he or she communicate this to you? He or she may tell you, but it is important to realize that a person does not have to use words to communicate. When a massage really feels good, most people emit little noises like "ooh" and "aah." These responses should be just as effective as words in letting you know that what you are doing feels good.

When giving your partner a massage, vary the pressure and explore different areas of your partner's body. Avoid touching genitals and breasts, for the purpose of the massage is not your own sexual pleasure but to learn how to listen (you may discover, however, that massage is a great form of foreplay and you may want to use it for that purpose in the future). Listen to your partner's responses while you are massaging. If you listen well and care about your partner, you can modify your behavior and give a massage that pleases him or her instead of giving one that might please only you.

If you are a good enough listener to adjust a massage to please your partner, you can easily do the same while having sex. All of us want to believe we are (or will be) a good sexual partner, but to be one we must first be a good listener.

PERSONAL REFLECTIONS
Suppose that you are in a long-term monogamous relationship that includes sexual relations. Suppose also that your partner often does not take as much time during foreplay as you would like and does not spend much time holding and touching you afterwards. This often leaves you sexually unfulfilled and frustrated. How would you go about correcting this situation? Be as specific as possible.

IS IT POSSIBLE TO COMMUNICATE NONVERBALLY?

The answer, of course, is yes. Actually, I have already partially answered this question in my answer to the last question. Things like eye contact, facial expressions, and interpersonal distance (how close you stand or sit next to someone) all express messages. Single persons commonly use these types of messages to convey interest, or lack of interest, in another person. Silence can convey a message (e.g., anger, anxiety). Touch, in particular, is a very powerful means of *nonverbal communication*. As one person who studies communication and intimacy puts it, "If intimacy is proximity, then nothing comes closer than touch, the most intimate knowledge of another" (Thayer, 1986). For example, the manner in which you and your partner go about giving each other a massage may well reflect how much you care about the other.

Perhaps the biggest problem with nonverbal signals is that, because they are not as precise as verbal messages, they can be misinterpreted. This frequently happens in the singles' world.

When two people are communicating verbally, it is important for there to be agreement between the verbal and nonverbal aspects of the communication. How do you suppose your partner would feel if, while telling him or her how much you care, you were inattentive, with little or no eye contact?

DEALING WITH ANGER AND CONFLICT: AN EXAMPLE

Admittedly, the preceding guidelines about communication are somewhat fairy taleish. In the real world, couples are going to have moments of anger and conflict. No section on communication would be complete without some advice about how to deal with our own anger and that of our partner. The guidelines also focused on features of individual communication, independent of the partner. But communication is interactive, so we must also examine communication patterns between partners.

One of the best predictors of long-term success in a relationship is the manner in which couples handle their disagreements (Notarius & Markman, 1993). During a disagreement, couples can display three different patterns of communication: mutual constructive communication, avoidance of communication, or demand/withdraw (Christensen, 1988). The *demand/withdraw pattern* can be particularly damaging, and is frequently observed in distressed (e.g., divorcing) couples (Gottman & Krokoff, 1989; Heavey et al., 1995). Studies have found that men are more likely to practice withdrawal, especially if their partners are expressing negative emotions and complaints (demand), but it can work the other way as well (Vogel et al., 1999).

> "My ex-girlfriend would get upset and demand to be left alone and would block me out if I tried to ask and understand what was bothering her. She pulled back into her shell for days and this behavior caused me stress because I did not know what was wrong, or if I could help. After several days she would open up but not discuss what it was that she had been upset about. She would just try and pick up where we left off like nothing happened. This occurred several times throughout our relationship. Notice I refer to her as my ex-girlfriend." (from the author's files)

In place of withdraw, or demand/withdraw, what can we do? The following metaphor is provided by Notarius, Lashley, and Sullivan (1997) to help couples deal better with their anger:

We ask partners to imagine a scenario in which one person is in the kitchen cutting up some vegetables for dinner right after the partners have had a huge fight and are not talking to each other. The anger in the relationship is palpable. Just as one partner happens into the kitchen, the person cutting the vegetables slips and badly cuts

a finger. There is blood spurting everywhere. At this point we ask both partners to state what would happen. With no exception to date, all couples report that there would be caretaking—every effort would be made to do whatever was necessary to take care of the wounded partner. In this scenario, there is a physical wound, and the wounded partner's body is taking care of alerting the other that attention is required. When one partner bleeds, the other takes care of him or her. If the other stood by and watched him or her bleed without providing care, this would be a powerful message indeed.

Now we ask couples to consider a similar scenario in which a partner suffers a psychological wound that causes "internal bleeding." The hurt is not visible to the world, and therefore support will not be immediately forthcoming. Instead, the injured party must "emotionally bleed" in order to get support. The likelihood of getting support in this scenario will be directly related to the clarity of the "emotional bleeding." If the wounded person decides to bare his or her teeth as some wounded animals do, then this is likely to keep away a potential caretaker. If, on the other hand, the wounded person decides to show the wound plainly to another, to "bleed," then caretaking will most likely follow. Thus, the advice we offer to couples is for partners to "bleed" when they are psychologically hurt. We say, "Show your wounds to your partner, and just as if you were physically bleeding, more often than not you will receive the caretaking you desire."

There are two other aspects of this metaphor to consider. The primary difference between cutting oneself while slicing vegetables and suffering an emotional wound is that in the latter case, the other partner is usually held responsible for the injury. And in this case, the "emotional bleeding" that we encourage will be directed at the person blamed for the injury, who is *also* the potential caregiver. We find it useful to have the "bleeding" partner focus primarily on his or her own wound rather than on blaming the other for the injury. We remind couples that the goal is caretaking, and that at the moment anything that interferes with it will be self-destructive.

Second, we encourage couples to think through the scenario in which the injured partner plays the role of a hurt animal and snarls at anyone who attempts to provide care. Such behavior certainly minimizes the opportunity for another to provide care, but it need not preclude caregiving. Accordingly, if a partner finds that his or her wounded mate is pushing others away, successful approach and caregiving under these adverse circumstances can be an opportunity to show an extra amount of caring. In essence, it conveys this message: "I love you in spite of all your efforts to suffer alone and to push me away. I will not be pushed away." Of course, if this becomes a predictable pattern in the relationship rather than an infrequent opportunity for showing extra caring, it may be difficult for the caregiver to keep overcoming the initial barriers to providing care. It is hard enough to be a caregiver without having to overcome the obstacles of a partner in need who rejects succor. (from *Satisfaction in Close Relationships,* pp. 236–237. Guilford Press. Reprinted with permission.)

Notice that in resolving their conflict and anger, the couple would employ several of the good communication tools that you have learned. These include "I" language, self disclosure, listening, and attentiveness.

> *PERSONAL REFLECTIONS*
> *What communication style do you use when you are angry with your partner? Is it the best style for clearly conveying your emotions to your partner?*

IF I WANT MY PARTNER TO CHANGE AND I FOLLOW THESE GUIDELINES, HOW SOON CAN I EXPECT TO SEE A CHANGE?

Even when there is good communication, neither you nor your partner can be expected to change overnight. If there are several things about your partner's attitude or behavior that bother you, do not address them all at once. Attempt to change only one thing at a time. If you present your partner with a long list of criticisms, it will probably be met with defensiveness and retaliatory criticism.

WHAT IF WE CANNOT AGREE?

No one person will always be able to satisfy all the needs and desires of another. That is true even in the best of relationships. People simply have differences of opinion and different preferences. When this happens, good communication can only lead to an understanding of those things that the two of you disagree about. It is often helpful to agree that you disagree. However, if either you or your partner is greatly bothered because your needs and desires are going unfulfilled, then it would be wise to seek professional counseling. Chapter 15 provides the names and addresses of two organizations that will help you locate qualified professionals in your area.

IN THE FUTURE: TALKING WITH YOUR CHILDREN ABOUT SEX

When asked where he received his education, Mark Twain answered, "Throughout my life, except for the years I attended school." This is generally true for most people when it comes to learning about sexually related matters. Sex education courses are really just an intervention—a *formal* attempt to provide knowledge. The few people who take comprehensive sex education courses generally do not take them until they are in high school or college. However,

Courtesy of Family Planning Centers of Hawaii.

sexual learning begins in infancy and continues throughout childhood and adolescence. It is informal and is received from family, friends, the media, and the rest of the general environment.

During the preadolescent years, a child's parents are the most powerful influence on his or her beliefs and behavior. Even if parents never discuss sex with their children—and most do not—by their behavior and their attitudes, they still serve as role models from which their children learn.

As children approach their teenage years, the media (primarily television) and their peer groups come to have a greater influence on their behaviors and attitudes than their parents (Kaiser Family Foundation, 1996; Stodghill, 1998). The average child watches several hours of TV every day and is exposed to hundreds of references to sex in a year (Kunkel et al., 1999). Between the amount of time that their children spend with peers and watching TV, it is obvious that parents have a difficult time competing as a source of sexual knowledge and values. Unfortunately, the peer group is often misinformed, and TV and movies often display irresponsible sex (e.g., couples having sex without any mention of birth control).

Today, with the threat of AIDS, there has never been a better reason to teach our children responsibility about their health and their bodies. Yet, despite all the public debate about AIDS and other sexually related matters, most parents continue to remain silent (Stodghill, 1998).

> "Sex was never a topic in my home when I was growing up. It led to embarrassment when I finally had to ask questions, but I could only ask my friends, never my parents. It shouldn't be like that, it shouldn't be embarrassing and I should have been able to talk to my parents." (from the author's files)

Surveys show that the vast majority of Americans favor sex education in schools (Kaiser Family Foundation, 2000; Phi Delta Kappa/Gallup Poll, 1998; SIECUS/Advocates for Youth, 1999). So why is there reluctance to teach it at home? Probably because most parents never received sex education themselves and thus are uncomfortable with their own sexual knowledge and feelings.

> "Due to lack of knowledge, I could not elaborate enough."

> "I always hoped I would be able to handle such topics with my children, but I guess I was unable because it was never really discussed with me."

> "If I had been educated earlier, beginning at age 9 or 10, I would have been able to help myself and my children with facts of life much better and much earlier." (All examples are from King & LoRusso, 1997.)

Some parents will not discuss sex because they do not want to think about the possibility of their children being sexually active. I even know of some parents who have never talked to their children about sex because of fear that the children would then suspect that they have sexual relations, as if that were wrong.

When you complete this book, you should be ready to put an end to the cycle of noncommunication that has existed between parents and each new generation of children. I realize, however, that although you may have learned the necessary information, you may still feel uncomfortable about discussing sex with someone else. This part of the chapter is intended to help you initiate discussions of sexuality with your children so that they too may acquire factual information. I will try to answer some of the questions that often concern parents.

WHICH PARENT SHOULD TALK WITH THE CHILDREN?

Most children would like to turn to their parents for information about sex. Unfortunately, only about a third learn "a lot" about sex from their parents (Kaiser Family Foundation, 1996), and once they become teenagers, fewer than 10 percent list their parents as their major source of information (Stodghill, 1998). When a parent does make the attempt to open communications about sexuality, it is almost always

sexual learning Knowledge about sex that is received (usually informally) from family, friends, the media, and society in general.

the mother (e.g., K. Miller et al., 1998a; Rosenthal & Feldman, 1999). This is true for sons as well as daughters. Fathers are notoriously silent!

One thing that prevents discussions between parents and children about sexuality is a defensive climate in the household (Rozema, 1986). When one or both parents have reacted negatively to the subject of sex in the past, children are less likely to open up or approach them with questions. Family communication about sexuality is most likely to occur in households that have an openness in the communication process and when parents have talked to their children about other personal topics as well (K. Miller et al., 1998a; Raffaelli et al., 1998). Children may be more likely to discuss sex with their mothers than their fathers because mothers are often viewed as more emotionally expressive, more likely to answer questions about intimacy, and, as a result, more approachable.

Fathers are doing a disservice to their children by remaining emotionally distant and appearing (to their children) to be unapproachable on the subject. Both parents should make the attempt to open lines of communication, and as you will soon learn, the earlier the better.

DOES TELLING CHILDREN ABOUT SEX LEAD THEM TO DO IT?

Some of you may worry that if you educate your children about sex, they will try it and get pregnant or get someone else pregnant. Does driver's education cause automobile accidents? Surveys show that most people engage in premarital sex. The average age of first intercourse today is 16, and in some large metropolitan areas it is much younger (Centers for Disease Control and Prevention, 2000; Laumann et al., 1994). Most of these teens have never had formal sexuality education, at school or at home, so sexuality education can hardly be blamed. Studies have shown, you may recall, that children who have had sexuality education are no more likely (and perhaps are less likely) to have sexual relations, to get pregnant, or to contract a sexually transmitted disease than those who have not had sexuality education (Grunseit et al., 1997).

As for discussions at home, when parents talk openly and *comfortably* with their teens about sex and sexual risks (including use of condoms), teens are more likely to discuss these matters with their own partners and are also much more likely to use condoms. This is especially true when parents have these talks *before* their teens begin having sexual intercourse (K. Miller et al., 1998b; Whitaker et al., 1999). Furthermore, in families that have developed strong loving relationships in which parents give their children much positive attention (including the quality of communication), children are less likely to begin sexual intercourse at a young age (B. Miller et al., 1998; Resnick et al, 1997). Do you need better reasons to talk to your children about sex?

WHY SHOULD I TALK TO MY CHILD ABOUT SEX?

Unless you are willing to keep your children locked up in a closet until they reach adulthood, *there is no avoiding their learning about sex.* As I have already said, even if they stay home all the time and do nothing but watch TV and listen to the radio, your children will still see and hear thousands of references to sex every year. Do you really want to leave it to the soap operas and "shock jocks" to educate your children about this important subject? What kind of values do you suppose they will learn? Also, don't fool yourself. Children (in all likelihood your own as well) do talk about sex with their friends. Not only may your child's friends be misinformed, but do you want to leave it to your child's peer group to teach sexual values? Even formal sex education courses are generally value-free. By assuming the primary responsibility for your children's sex education, you not only can make certain that they are getting factual information, but at the same time you can stress the social and emotional aspects of sex and teach them values that you consider important. June Reinisch, former director of the Kinsey Institute, said, "If parents are comfortable and have good information, they can be wonderful sex educators. They can contextualize the sexual information into the fabric of family values, ethics, morals and religious beliefs. Sex is embedded in all of these" (quoted by Henderson, 1990).

> *PERSONAL REFLECTIONS*
> *Some day you will probably be a parent (if you aren't one already). Do you plan to educate your children about sexuality? If so, how? When will you begin?*

WILL A SINGLE "BIRDS AND BEES" TALK SUFFICE?

Do you really believe that one talk will prepare your child for a lifetime of sexual relations and problems? The answer is no! Experts say that it is a mistake to think that talking about sex means sitting down for one long, serious conversation (see Roan, 1993). Even if you could fit all the necessary information and values into one talk, that one talk can hardly compete with the hundreds of hours of exposure to sexually related matters your child will receive while growing up. As Mark Twain said, education is a lifelong thing. Communication between parents and children about sex and anything else should also be lifelong.

WHEN SHOULD I START TALKING WITH MY CHILD ABOUT SEXUALITY?

When asked why she had not yet begun talking to her 13-year-old daughter about sex, a mother said, "I kept waiting for the right time. But I'm just too afraid to bring it up. I'm not sure what to say" (Roan, 1993).

As I hope you have learned by now, sex education is more than just explaining sexual intercourse. Children should be properly educated about their bodies. For example, you should teach them the correct anatomical terms for their genitals at the same time you teach them the names of the other parts of their bodies. "Penis" and "vagina" are not too difficult for young children to pronounce. American parents are notoriously silent about this. The following comments were written by a student in my course:

> "I disagree strongly with teaching children about sexuality starting from preschool to third grade. Kids at this age don't even know the ABC's. . . . I just don't believe that kids under grade 4 should be told the terms 'penis' and 'vagina.' I do feel that kids under the age of 10 should be taught to know when a stranger is touching them wrong." (from the author's files)

Think about this for a moment. How will this woman tell her children about inappropriate touching without using the proper words? Will she use cutesy words (e.g., "pee-wee" or "weeney") or make vague references (e.g., "Don't let anyone touch your bottom")? Either of these approaches may convey an attitude to the child that these parts of his or her body are naughty or dirty, and may eventually cause the child to think that the functions of these body parts are also dirty. Teaching boys that they have a penis and girls that they have a vagina is honest and helps them attain a healthy attitude about sexuality.

> "My mom never spoke with me about sex. This ignorance caused many misconceptions in my teenage years. When I was 10 I began menstruating. I told my mom and she laughed and gave me a box of maxipads. No explanation, no lessons, nothing. . . . So as a young, married adult I changed my attitude. No longer would I follow in the steps of my mother. I have 4- and 5-year-old boys now. They know the proper names for every part of their bodies. They know about exploring their bodies and when it is not appropriate for anyone to touch them. My mom says those words like 'wee wee' and 'petie.' That to me is just as disgusting as saying 'dick.' She becomes angry when I correct her, but she understands." (from the author's files)

It is also very important to discuss with your children the physiological changes that start at puberty before they actually begin puberty. Some parents don't talk to their daughters about the menstrual cycle or to their sons about "wet dreams" until after they occur (see Chapter 12). This is very wrong. These changes can be frightening to children, who may think that they are sick or dying.

> "There is one thing I would personally put more emphasis on [in the book]. That is the importance of explaining menstruation in advance. From personal experience, I feel this is critical. I had no idea what was happening to me when I started menstruating for the first time. I can remember that I couldn't stop the bleeding and was scared to death and was afraid and embarrassed to tell anyone. I finally told a friend who was in the dark just as I was. She then told her mother. Her mother gave me a pad and said this would happen every month. That was the extent of communication on the subject." (from the author's files)

It is also important to explain the changes associated with puberty in girls to boys and the changes in boys to girls. Men should be able to relate to women with empathy and understanding, and vice versa. Ignorance about the physiological and emotional changes being experienced by the opposite sex is not a good basis on which to build relationships.

Children themselves are often the best guides as to when to initiate talks about a particular topic. It is common, for example, for young children to ask where babies come from. If they are curious enough to ask questions about some sexually related matter, don't avoid discussing it. Never brush them off. If you do, they may avoid coming to you in the future and may rely instead on getting their information from somewhere else.

Some guidelines for when to start talking about specific topics within human sexuality and family living are presented in Table 8-1. The guidelines are a condensed composite of those suggested by the Sex Information and Education Council of the U.S. (SIECUS National Guidelines Task Force, 1996) and Planned Parenthood (1991). These are only general guidelines for just a few of the many things your child may want to know about. Remember, if your child asks questions before the age level indicated here, don't wait to respond.

WHAT SHOULD I TELL MY CHILDREN ABOUT AIDS AND OTHER STDS?

With all the attention devoted to AIDS by the media today, children are naturally going to be curious about it. The first question about sexuality that my son asked me was about AIDS. If you hear your child mention AIDS, be sure to take the opportunity to ask what he or she knows about it. Clear up any myths or misunderstandings. If your child never mentions AIDS, do not ignore the subject, for this is a very serious disease that everyone needs to be educated about. Initiate the discussion yourself. Remember, however, that you must teach your child about sexuality on a level that he or she can understand. Whatever their age, teach your children respect for individual differences and acceptance of others.

Most parents fear that in order to explain about AIDS, they must explain behaviors like anal and oral sex. This is really not necessary for preschool and elementary school children. Most preadolescent children

TABLE 8–1

GUIDELINES FOR TEACHING CHILDREN ABOUT SEX

Age (School) Level	Concepts to Be Learned
3–5 (preschool)	Correct names for body parts (e.g., penis, vagina); differences between boys and girls; both boys' and girls' bodies are special and each of us can be proud of our special body; adults kiss and hug each other to show how much they care; respect for the privacy of others; their bodies belong to themselves and they have a right to say "no" if they don't want to be touched; how to respond if a stranger offers candy or a ride.
6–9 (early elementary school)	Continue to use a proper vocabulary when talking about body parts; continue to promote self-esteem (their bodies are special); people have body parts that feel good when touched; touching those body parts should be done in private; "sex talk" is done at home; the basics of reproduction and that our genitals and reproductive organs enable this; a fetus is inside the uterus and a baby usually comes out of the vagina; milk comes from breasts; people can have babies only after puberty; meaning of heterosexual and homosexual; awareness of sexuality of people of all ages (parents and grandparents); understanding that there are different types of caring homes and families (e.g., single-parent families); promote nonstereotyped gender roles both inside and outside the home (both mothers and fathers have important jobs and there are no jobs just for boys or just for girls); good hygiene.
9–13 (upper elementary school)	Changes in *both* boys and girls during puberty (e.g., girls menstruate; boys ejaculate and have wet dreams) and that the changes occur at different ages in different people; the idea that human sexuality is natural and that sexual feelings are normal; sex is not just for reproduction, but is also pleasurable; masturbation (many people do it, it's not harmful, often a child's first experience with sexual pleasure); intercourse can cause pregnancy and having children is a long-term responsibility that should be planned (include basics on contraception); children are not ready for sexual intercourse; physical appearance does not determine a person's value—liking yourself; communication and assertiveness skills; people can disagree and have different values but still be friends; men and women have equal talents and strengths; recognition of the potential of sexual abuse (including that it is most often committed by someone the child knows) and how to react to it; continued encouragement of good hygiene; encouragement that it is okay to talk to parents about sexuality (*even if our opinions differ*).
13–15 (junior high school)	It is normal to have sexual feelings, desires, and fantasies; sex is pleasurable; the size of one's penis or breasts does not determine whether one will be a good sexual partner; people of all body shapes (including the disabled) have sexual feelings and desire; understanding the differences in sexual behavior (sexual orientation, abstinence, marriage); love is not the same as sexual attraction or desire; understanding the possible consequences of unprotected sexual intercourse (pregnancy); contraception; young teens are not yet ready for sexual intercourse; dating (why, when, how) and relationships (e.g., going steady); peer pressure and your right to say "no" and to disagree with your friends; respecting the limits that are set by your partners; awareness of exploitive relationships (psychological coercion, alcohol, physical force, date rape); physical health (e.g., breast and testicular self-exams); establishing a value system (and consideration of the above topics within that system).
15–18 (high school)	People of all ages are sexual beings; sexuality is only one part of your total personality; integration of sexuality into your value system; feeling good about your body, sexuality, and sexual orientation; how to express your sexual feelings in appropriate ways; communicating your sexual feelings, desires, and limits to partners in an open and honest manner; expressing your sexual feelings without intercourse; further understanding of sexual exploitation among adolescents; for those who engage in sexual intercourse, choosing a method of contraception that will be used consistently; knowledge of the responsibilities of parenthood and child care; understanding that long-term commitments (including marriage and parenthood) require work and that people's sexual and emotional needs change over time.

are not going to understand anal or oral sex. Young children can be taught to be in charge of their own bodies—sexual responsibility—without being told what anal sex is.

What kind of questions is your child likely to ask? Valentich and Gripton (1989) have listed many questions about AIDS that are frequently asked by children. Early elementary school–age children may want to know answers to questions like: What is AIDS? Can I get AIDS? Can I get it by playing with friends or by touching someone at school? Will it make me sick? Is there medicine I can take to make it go away?

Children aged 9–12 will want to know more about how AIDS is transmitted (e.g., whether they can get AIDS by holding hands, hugging, kissing, having sexual intercourse, or being in the same classroom with someone who has AIDS) and how they can tell if someone has it. Children at this age can also be taught about STDs such as gonorrhea, chlamydia, syphilis, and herpes (and told that they are caused by bacteria and viruses) (SIECUS, 1996). Teenagers will probably want answers to more explicit questions about transmission (e.g., whether they can get AIDS by French kissing, masturbation, genital touching, or sexual intercourse) and prevention (including the use and reliability of condoms). Be sure to include further discussion of other sexually transmitted diseases at this time as well.

You should prepare yourself for questions like these so that you can give your child factual information about means of transmission, prevention, and treatment appropriate for his or her age. When answering questions, you can also discuss values with your child. No matter what your child's age, *you should not deny the pleasures of sex or resort to scare tactics.* Teaching children that sex is something good and pleasurable is as important as teaching that it must be handled responsibly.

Figure 8–3 When a pet gives birth, parents have a great opportunity to teach their children about sexuality.

HOW DETAILED SHOULD SEX DISCUSSIONS BE?

Your discussions should be frank and explicit. Children do not want "birds and bees" analogies; they want factual information using real terms. In fact, euphemisms and analogies will only confuse them. At the same time, do not make things too detailed for your child's age level. *Make your answer age-appropriate.* Always check to see if your child understands what you have said. You may have to rephrase your answer to make it clear. Sometimes we give great answers, but not to the question the child asked. Remember, a child may not know what to ask or how to ask it correctly. When a 6-year-old asks where babies come from, for example, many parents worry that they must explain sexual intercourse in detail. Your 6-year-old is not really asking about that. Keep your answer uncomplicated and tell the child only what he or she wants to know. In this case, you could explain that the baby is in a special part of the mother called a uterus (do not avoid explicitness by saying "tummy"—this is incorrect anyway) and that when it is ready to be born it comes out through an opening called the vagina.

Remember that young children are curious about *everything* and that sex is only one part of their world. Also, children don't think about sex the way adults do. Children have not had sexual intercourse (unless they were molested), have not had babies, and may not look at sex as a special topic of conversation. (In fact, chances are you are making a bigger deal about it than your child.)

Discussions with your teenage children should definitely be frank and explicit. In a recent study, I asked students and their parents if they had ever had a "meaningful" discussion about sex with one another (King & LoRusso, 1997). Over half of the students responded "no," yet for 60 percent of them one or both parents said that there had been meaningful discussions. Here are some responses by parents who believed that they had had meaningful discussions (but whose children disagreed):

> "I believe children should be taught that total abstinence is the best way. . . . This is so because of God's law and the design for total inner peace and joy."

> "My discussion with _____ dealt with one's soul. A soul is not to be fragmented—not to be given away in bits and pieces. A soul is sacred—sex is sacred."

> "They [the children] knew what was expected, and they behaved accordingly. . . . If you asked about teaching morality to my children, the answer is yes, and if you teach and live a good, healthy, moral life, it usually works."

There is nothing wrong with teaching your children values. However, do not substitute morality for factual information.

WHAT IF I FEEL EMBARRASSED?

Parents' talks with their children about sexuality are most effective when the parents are open, skilled, and comfortable (Whitaker et al., 1999). Many of you will not be able to avoid embarrassment at times, but the result—your child's education—is worth the initial discomfort of using real terms and direct language. Be honest. Let your children know that you are a bit embarrassed, but that you are glad they asked to talk with you, that you'll be happy to answer all of their questions, and that it's okay to talk to you about the subject. What you say to your children is important, *but how you say it is just as important.* Let them know that you are willing to (and want to) listen to their questions.

HOW SHOULD I TALK WITH MY CHILD?

Most important, *discuss—never lecture.* Also, be sure not to grill your child about his or her behavior or attitudes. Parents who try to dominate and assert themselves will probably be met with passivity (e.g., Lefkowitz et al., 2000), while those who take an open, collaborative approach will probably find that their children actively engage in discussions (K. Miller et al., 1998a; Whitaker et al., 1999). In other words, allow your child to have his or her input. Your tone of voice is particularly important, for your child learns attitudes from your tone. Try to sound calm and relaxed at all times. Sol Gordon, author of *Raising Your Child Conservatively in a Sexually Permissive World* (1989), says, "The most important message is that nothing a child does will be made worse by talking to the parent about it. There is no way of dealing with sexuality unless the parent has created the atmosphere of love and caring. Unless that atmosphere is there, nothing works. The child will lie" (quoted by Roan, 1993).

Also, it is not necessary always to have formal talks; this may create tension. You can break the ice by briefly explaining and discussing sexually related matters that your child sees on TV (try watching *Friends* with your teenage child), hears on the radio, or reads in "Dear Abby." Recall, too, that parent-child talks about sexuality are easier when the parents have a history of talking with their children about other personal topics (Raffaelli et al., 1998).

Remember, *avoid scare tactics.* You must teach sexual responsibility without making your child afraid of sex—children should learn that sex is something good and positive, and not something to feel ashamed or guilty about. Scare tactics probably will not work anyway, and they may cause emotional and psychological problems.

PERSONAL REFLECTIONS
How do you suppose you would react if . . . ?

1. *Your 5-year-old child asked you where babies come from*
2. *Your 9-year-old child asked you what sex is*
3. *Your 10-year-old child asked you what "French kissing" is*
4. *Your 12-year-old son came home from school saying that he had to watch a "gross" movie about girls having their period*
5. *Your 15-year-old son asked you about birth control*
6. *Your 15-year-old daughter asked you about birth control*

Would your reactions to any of these situations discourage your child from coming to you in the future and talking to you about sex?

WHAT ABOUT MORALS? AREN'T THEY IMPORTANT TOO?

Most formal sex education is value-free, and that is why it is so important for parents to assume some responsibility for their children's education, even if their children are receiving sex education at school. Sex is more than a biological function. If you want your children to share your beliefs and values about sex, you must talk about them. However, your success in imposing your values upon your children will depend, in large part, on your overall relationship with them. Parents who generally have good loving interactions with their children are more successful in transmitting values than are parents who generally have poor interactions with their children (Resnick et al., 1997; Taris & Semin, 1997b).

When you discuss moral values with your child, there are some important guidelines you should follow. Most important, *you can emphasize your values, but don't preach or try to dominate.* It is not wrong for you to say how you feel, but if your child has developed some values that are different from yours, you must learn to discuss your differences rather than dictate. Remember, you want to create an atmosphere that allows your child to be comfortable so that he or she will come to you when they have questions. If you always preach and pass judgment, your child may be reluctant to discuss sexuality with you at all, and then you will have no input.

One of the biggest dilemmas facing parents when discussing sexuality with their children is whether to emphasize global moralities or situational ethics. *Global moralities* are values that are supposed to apply to all people under all circumstances. An example is when parents tell their children that sexual relations should be reserved for marriage. As you recall, however, surveys show that well over half of all adolescents engage in premarital intercourse. Can you safely assume that your children will never have premarital sexual relations and that you can thus avoid the topic of birth control? Many parents are reluctant to talk about birth control with their children because they think that it promotes promiscuity. The consequences of not talking about it, however, can be devastating (e.g., unwanted pregnancies and/or sexually transmitted diseases).

Situational ethics emphasize the proper thing to do in particular situations (i.e., "We prefer that you not do it, but if you're going to do it anyway, then . . ."). In this case, for example, it could be explained to an adolescent child that condoms substantially reduce the risk of both unwanted pregnancy and sexually transmitted diseases. I cannot tell you which of these two approaches to use. Only you can make that choice.

CAN MY BEHAVIOR AFFECT MY CHILD'S ATTITUDES AND BEHAVIOR?

You should also be aware that *your own behavior can play a role* in your child's sexuality and moral values. It is important for children to learn that their parents share affection for each other. Hugging between parents and between parents and children teaches youngsters that the open display of affection is appropriate and appreciated.

> "My husband and I have always tended to be very private about showing affection. I guess that's because our parents were that way. However, as a result of what I've learned in this class we've been hugging and kissing in front of our kids—who are both teenagers. They've noticed the changes and have even asked us about it, which has given us wonderful opportunities for open and frank discussions with them. Hopefully, it's not too late." (from the author's files)

Parents who wait until they are alone to kiss or hug are teaching their children that there is something wrong about physical contact between the sexes. *Don't confuse affection with sex.*

At the same time, we live in a day when many parents are divorced and have boyfriends and girlfriends of their own. You must avoid appearing to be hypocritical. If you want your child to abstain from premarital sexual relations, for example, you must avoid premarital sexual relations or be very discreet yourself. What message do you suppose you are sending your children if you tell them it is wrong to engage in sex and they know that you are having premarital sexual relations?

Even if you never discuss sexuality with your children, your behavior will still serve as a role model. Unfortunately, many children acquire negative attitudes about sexuality by watching and listening to their parents. Many adults, for example, enjoy "dirty" jokes. What attitude do you suppose is conveyed when children overhear their parents laughing and snickering at jokes involving sex or body parts? Learning that there are "clean" and "dirty" jokes can lead to beliefs that sex is dirty, especially if other sources of information about

Figure 8–4 When talking to your children about sex, discuss—never lecture. Let them have their input.

sex are unavailable. Also, laughing at a child's use of obscenity or joking about it will only reinforce the behavior, making it increase in frequency (remember, you are a role model). If your child uses an obscenity, don't go overboard. Calmly explain what the word means. Often the child will not know. Reacting calmly tells children that they can discuss anything with you.

HOW DO I KNOW IF I HAVE SUCCEEDED?

You can judge the success of your attempts to educate your children about sexuality only by their willingness to come to you when they have questions and problems.

> "I am a non-traditional student with three kids. I didn't know that I should start talking with them about sex at such a young age. My boys are 7 and 9 and my daughter is 5 years old. They are very receptive to our talks. And now they always want to talk to me about anything. 'Open lines of communications.' Thanks." (from the author's files)

All normal adolescents will have an interest in sex and will continue to need information about their sexuality as long as they live. They will want to know about dating, courtship, marriage, living together, starting a family, and many different things at different times in their lives. They will seek information about these and other matters from a variety of sources, and you will want to be one of them. This will only happen, however, if communication between children and parents is open and continuous.

HOPE FOR THE FUTURE

At the beginning of this chapter, I said that fewer than half of the more than 1,000 students who have taken my course each semester had ever had a serious

Box 8-B   CROSS-CULTURAL PERSPECTIVES

Ethnic Differences within the United States in Parent-Child Communication

Recall from the text that in most families the mother assumes the primary responsibility of communicating with young children and teenagers about sex (K. Miller et al., 1998a; Rosenthal & Feldman, 1999). Recall also that regardless of which parent attempts to communicate, their influence with teenage children depends not only on what they say but how they say it (K. Miller et al., 1998a; Whitaker et al., 1999). Parents who are open and comfortable in their discussions are generally more successful. What about cultural differences? Do parents of different ethnic groups have different styles of communicating with their children? Keep in mind that what you are about to read are just generalities. Within any group, there is a whole range of behaviors.

Research has shown that parents of different ethnic groups tend to be different in their general parenting styles (Forehand & Kotchick, 1996). Regardless of their general style differences, mothers are still the primary communicators about sex in white, African-American, and Latino families (K. Miller et al., 1998a). Studies have been inconsistent in their findings of how often parents of different ethnic groups talk with their children. African-American parents have been reported to discuss sex with their teens both more often and less often than white parents (Furstenberg et al., 1984; Inazu & Fox, 1980), while Latino parents have been reported to discuss sex both less than and as much as white parents (Leland

& Barth, 1993; Sigelman et al., 1995). A recent study found that discussions about sex were equally likely in African-American and Latino families (K. Miller et al., 1998a).

Nevertheless, some major differences in the style, or structure, of the conversations have been found. Compared to white or African-American mothers, Latina mothers tend to dominate the conversations about sex with their children (Lefkowitz et al., 2000). This was independent of both socioeconomic status and cultural background (e.g., Mexican, Cuban, South American). As a result of this dominating style (e.g., allowing fewer comments or questions from children), adolescent children of Latina mothers are less open and less satisfied about their parent-child discussions, and tend to seek discussions with others more often. Latina mothers are not more negative than mothers of other groups. Instead, the dominating style has been attributed to a culture that emphasizes close family ties, in which children are expected to be respectful and obedient (Lefkowitz et al., 2000). When parents of other ethnic groups are dominant and demanding in their conversations, the outcomes of the talks are also less successful (Whitaker et al., 1999). Regardless of their ethnicity, if parents want their children to open up to them, the parents must not only talk openly but also be willing to listen and try to understand the feelings that are behind their children's questions (K. Miller et al., 1998a).

---

discussion with their parents about sex. For those who have had one, in many cases it was just a single "birds and bees" talk explaining sexual intercourse. You have learned how this lack of knowledge has been costly to both individuals and society in terms of births to young teens and sexually transmitted diseases. Misinformation about sexual matters is often a contributing factor in sexual disorders, relationship problems, and sexual abuse as well.

I hope that by expanding people's knowledge, courses like this will result in greater sexual responsibility and fewer problems. I hope, too, that this book will help you feel more comfortable with your sexuality so

that you are not ashamed of your body or embarrassed by its functions. Most of all, I hope that when you have children you will be able to discuss sexual matters with them. I've found that students who have completed my course are much more likely to discuss sexuality with their children than are former college students who had not taken a comprehensive human sexuality course (see King et al., 1993).

Let us hope that in the years to come, when I ask my students on the first day of class if they have had discussions with their parents about sex, most of them will say "yes."

Key Terms

Suggested Readings for Couples

A Couple's Guide to Communication by John Gottman. Champaign, IL: Research Press, 1976. The book most recommended by members of the Society for the Scientific Study of Sex (Althrop & Kingsberg, 1992).

For Each Other: Sharing Sexual Intimacy by Lonnie Barbach. Garden City, New York: Anchor, 1982.

He Says, She Says by Lillian Glass. New York: G. P. Putnam's Sons, 1992. Designed to break the communications barrier between men and women.

The Love Fitness Program for a Lasting Relationship by Harold Bloomfield and Sirah Vettese. New York: New American Library, 1989. This married couple suggests "sexual heart talks" to enhance sexual intimacy.

Why Marriages Succeed or Fail by John Gottman. New York: Simon & Schuster, 1994. Designed to help couples with communication.

You Just Don't Understand: Women and Men in Conversation by Deborah Tannen. New York: William Morrow, 1990 (paperback: Ballantine, 1991). Explains the different styles of conversation used by men and women and gives advice on how to talk to the other sex.

Suggested Sex Education References to Help Parents

All about Sex: A Family Resource on Sex and Sexuality by Planned Parenthood Federation of America. New York: Three Rivers Press, 1997. Written at an intermediate level and intended for the whole family.

Ask Me Anything by Marty Klein. New York: Simon & Schuster, 1992. Prepares parents to give straightforward answers to anything their children might ask.

Before She Gets Her Period: Talking with Your Daughter about Menstruation by Jessica Gillouly. Los Angeles: Perspective Pub., 1998.

The Family Book about Sexuality by Mary Calderone and Eric Johnson. New York, Harper & Row, 1990. Very humanistic approach.

How to Talk to Your Children about AIDS by the Sexuality Information and Education Council of the United States (SIECUS), 1994.

How to Talk with Your Child about Sexuality: A Parent's Guide by Planned Parenthood: Faye Wattleton with Elizabeth Keiffer. New York: Doubleday, 1986.

Now What Do I Do? by the Sexuality Information and Education Council of the United States (SIECUS), 1996. Designed to help parents of preteens.

Talking with Your Child about Sex: Questions and Answers for Children from Birth to Puberty by Mary Calderone and James Ramey. New York: Ballantine Books, 1984.

"What Kids Need to Know," article by Sol Gordon in *Psychology Today*, October 1986.

What We Told Our Kids about Sex by Betsy and Michael Weisman. San Diego: Harcourt Brace Jovanovich, 1987. Gives answers to 102 questions typically asked by preadolescent children.

Suggested Sex Education References for Children

For Young Children

Where Did I Come From? by P. Mayle and A. Robins. Secaucus, NJ: Carol Publishing, 1999. For young children.

Where Did I Come From? by Peter Mayle. New World. A 27-minute animated videocassette version of the book. Many video rental stores carry it.

Babies Come from People by George and Ann Carpenter. Salt Lake City, UT: Goldstream, 1975. For preschoolers.

Puberty

What's Happening to Me? by Peter Mayle and Arthur Robins. New York: Carol Publishing, 1992. For children approaching puberty.

Are You There, God? It's Me, Margaret by Judy Blume. New York: Dell, 1970, 1999. An educational story about a girl going through puberty.

It's Perfectly Normal: Changing Bodies, Growing Up, Sex and Sexual Health by Robbie Harris. Cambridge, MA: Candlewick Press, 1996.

Dr. Ruth Talks to Kids by Dr. Ruth Westheimer. New York: Aladdin Paperbacks, 1998. Aimed at children aged 8 through 14. *Time* magazine (May 24, 1993) says that Dr. Ruth's book provides an excellent middle ground between books that teach abstinence only and those that favor a more comprehensive approach.

The What's Happening to My Body? Book For Girls: The New Growing-Up Guide For Parents and Daughters by Lynda and Area Madaras. New York: Newmarket Press, 2000.

The What's Happening to My Body? Book For Boys: The New Growing-Up Guide For Parents and Sons by Lynda and Area Madaras. New York: Newmarket Press, 2000.

Teenagers

All about Sex: A Family Resource on Sex and Sexuality by Planned Parenthood Federation of America. New York: Three Rivers Press, 1997. Written at an intermediate level and intended for the whole family.

Caution: Do Not Open until Puberty: An Introduction to Sexuality for Young Adults with Disabilities by Rick Enright. London,

Ont.: Thames Valley Children's Centre, 1996. Presented in a funny, yet straightforward manner for teens with disabilities.

Deal with It! A Whole New Approach to Your Body, Brain, and Life as a Gurl by Esther Drill, Heather McDonald, and Rebecca Odes. New York: Pocket Books, 1999. The "Our bodies, Ourselves" for teenagers.

Girltalk: All the Stuff Your Sister Never Told You by Carol Westin. New York: Harper Perennial, 1997. Straightforward, doesn't avoid any topic.

Teensex? It's OK to Say: No Way! by Planned Parenthood (16 pages, also available on VHS videocassette).

Talk about Sex by SIECUS. For teens, this 46-page booklet "offers clear, honest, straightforward information and instruction about relationships, communication skills, and safer sex behaviors in a very engaging, youth-friendly" manner. 1–4 copies, $2 each. SIECUS, 130 West 42 Street, Suite 2500, New York, NY 10036.

Out with It: Gay and Straight Teens Write about Homosexuality, edited by Philip Kay, Andrea Estepa, and Al Desetta. New York: Youth Communication, 1996. Articles (e.g., "Coming out to mom") by teens.

Study Guide

INTERACTIVE REVIEW

Communication is the exchange of information. Because of our culture's negative attitudes about sex and the negativity communicated by most parents, many people feel uncomfortable talking about sex, even with their sexual partners. Cultural differences affect communication about sex. White-American and African-American couples are more open to talking about sexual relations, while traditional Latino and Asian-American couples generally avoid the subject altogether. (1) _____ and power differences in a relationship also contribute to this difficulty.

You and your partner can get used to talking about sex together by discussing sexuality-related articles in newspapers, books, and magazines. One of the first things you must do is agree on a comfortable (2) _____ to use when talking about sex. When talking about sexual differences or problems, be sure to emphasize the (3) _____ rather than the (4) _____ things that your partner does. That doesn't mean that you can never complain, but when you do, focus on your partner's behavior rather than on his or her character.

Take responsibility for your own pleasure by expressing your feelings and desires to your partner in a clear, specific manner. Whenever possible, begin sentences with "I" rather than (5) _____, (6) _____, or (7) _____. It is often easier to find out about your partner's sexual desires and needs if you first (8) _____. However, good communication is a two-way street; it requires that you also become a good (9) _____. In addition to communicating verbally, we also communicate nonverbally with (give four examples) (10) _____, (11) _____, (12) _____, and (13) _____. Even with good communication skills, people will not always agree, but it is possible to agree that you disagree.

It is equally important for parents to learn to communicate with their children about sexuality in a positive manner. Your children will learn about sex whether or not you ever talk to them about it. (14) _____ begins in infancy, and children receive it from their peers, the media, and your own behaviors. Children who have had sex education are (15) _____ likely to have sexual relations than those who have not. Avoid that one long "birds and bees talk" approach; communication between parents and their children about sexuality should begin (16) _____ and be ongoing. This chapter presents guidelines for age-appropriate discussions about sexuality-related topics.

Discussions with your children about sexuality should be frank and explicit. When talking to your children about sex, (17) _____ is just as important as what you say. You should strive to create an atmosphere of love and caring, so avoid (18) _____ and do not lecture to them. You can emphasize your own sexual values, but do not preach. Your own behavior will affect your child's attitudes and moral values, so don't let them overhear you use "dirty" language or tell "dirty" jokes—and teach them, by example, that affection is something positive. The only way you will be able to know whether or not your attempts to educate your children about sexuality have been successful is by their (19)_____ .

SELF-TEST

A. TRUE OR FALSE

- [T] [F] 20. Parents should teach the words *penis* and *vagina* to their children at the same time they teach them the names for other body parts.
- [T] [F] 21. When discussing sex with their children, parents should insist that the children reveal their sexual attitudes and behavior.
- [T] [F] 22. In most families, mothers are the primary communicators about sexuality (with both sons and daughters).
- [T] [F] 23. Research has shown that gender differences in communication exist, but are not as great as some popular books would have us believe.
- [T] [F] 24. White mothers tend to be more dominating in their communication styles with children than mothers of other ethnic groups.
- [T] [F] 25. Demand/withdraw is the best way to deal with anger or conflict with a partner.
- [T] [F] 26. In order to dissuade your child from engaging in sex, you should emphasize the possible negative consequences (e.g., AIDS).
- [T] [F] 27. It is okay to teach your children about values while giving them factual information.
- [T] [F] 28. You should avoid open displays of affection with your partner (e.g., hugging or kissing) when your children are present.
- [T] [F] 29. Your own sexual behavior and attitudes will likely serve as a role model for your children, whether or not you discuss sexuality with them.
- [T] [F] 30. When talking to your partner about sex, use of the term "making love" is always better than saying "having sex" or "sexual intercourse."
- [T] [F] 31. The best time to talk about a sexual problem or difference with your partner is immediately after sex.
- [T] [F] 32. The best place to discuss a sexual problem or difference with your partner is in bed.
- [T] [F] 33. When you have a sexual difference or problem with your partner, you should never complain or express your anger.
- [T] [F] 34. When talking to your partner about your sexual attitudes and preferences, it is good to begin sentences with "we" because it emphasizes the relationship.
- [T] [F] 35. Giving your partner a massage can strengthen communication by making you a better listener.
- [T] [F] 36. When approaching your partner about differences in sexual attitudes or preferences, it is best to present all your criticisms at once.

B. MATCHING: AT WHAT AGE (GRADE LEVEL) SHOULD YOU BEGIN TO TALK TO YOUR CHILD ABOUT THE FOLLOWING TOPICS?

- _____ 37. the changes that occur in boys and girls at puberty
- _____ 38. correct names for genitals
- _____ 39. the idea that human sexuality is natural and that sexual feelings are normal
- _____ 40. peer pressure and the right to say "no"
- _____ 41. an explanation of AIDS and how it is transmitted
- _____ 42. promotion of nonstereotyped gender roles

a. preschool
b. early elementary
c. upper elementary
d. junior high
e. high school

_____ 43. basics of reproduction and the role of our genitals and reproductive organs in enabling it

_____ 44. integration of sexuality into an individual's value system

_____ 45. awareness of exploitive relations

_____ 46. how to express sexual feelings in appropriate ways

_____ 47. the fact that certain body parts feel good when touched

C. FILL IN THE BLANKS

48. When expressing your desires to your partner, you should try to begin sentences with _____.

49. The word *intercourse* means _____.

50. When communicating with another, it is important that there be agreement between the _____ and _____ aspects of communication.

51. When answering your child's questions about sex, be sure to make your answers _____ appropriate.

52. If you must criticize your partner, make sure you criticize his or her _____, not his or her _____.

53. With regards to sexual relations, you must take responsibility for _____.

54. If you want your child to actively engage in your attempts to discuss sex, you should take a _____ approach.

55. During a disagreement, couples generally display one of three patterns of communication: _____, _____, or _____.

56. One of the best predictors of long-term success in a relationship is the manner in which couples handle _____.

57. Teenagers are most likely to practice safer sex if their parents' talks with them have been _____.

58. During arguments, women are more likely to _____ while men are more likely to _____.

Chapter 9

SEXUALITY AS A SOCIAL CONCEPT

The nature of sexuality depends on how its irreducible biological basis is interpreted by a particular society at a particular time.

(Michael Parsons, 2000)

The emphasis in Chapters 2 through 7 was on biology and physiology. The information was presented as facts. But what is a fact? Can something deemed factual change over time, or be viewed differently in different cultures? The information you read about in those chapters was presented in the context of present-day Western ideology. **Ideology** has been defined as "the mental frameworks—the languages, concepts, categories, imagery of thought, and the systems of representation—which different classes and social groups deploy in order to make sense of, define, figure out, and render intelligible the way society works" (Hall, 1986). It determines the manner in which we see ourselves and our world, and also what we call "normal" or "natural."

You have already read some examples of how biological "facts" are interpreted differently, depending on the ideology of a culture. For example, menstruation is a biological fact. All women in good health between the ages of puberty and menopause menstruate. However, as you have learned (Chapter 3), in some cultures menstruation is a greatly feared event, while in others a girl's first menstruation is cause for celebration.

When you have finished studying this chapter, you should be able to:

1. Understand that the meaning of sexuality is shaped by society;

2. Explain how Western culture's concept of the sexuality of women has changed over time;

3. Grasp how "childhood" and childhood sexuality are concepts;

4. Describe how sex education has changed over the decades to reflect our society's concept of sexuality;

5. Explain the process of socialization and define a socializing agent;

6. Explain the role of sex education and religion as socializing agents; and

7. Understand how the media have become omnipresent agents for sexual socialization in today's world.

In Victorian times, it was an accepted "fact" that masturbation was harmful and would lead to insanity. Thus, it became the standard practice to circumcise boys' penises so that they would be less likely to masturbate (Box 2–C). Today, masturbation is considered by many people to be "normal" and a form of safer sex.

These examples show that "events and objects in life do not, inherently, have meaning. Rather, through social agreement, meaning is created" (Merskin, 1999). This is certainly true of sexuality. **Sexuality** is not a fact. It is a concept whose meaning is shaped by society and which will continue to change and evolve as the society that has defined it changes and evolves.

I will begin this chapter with three examples of how the concept of sexuality has changed and evolved in our culture. We will then focus on the major factors influencing sexual socialization of young people today.

SEXUALITY AS AN EVOLVING CONCEPT

SEXUALITY OF WOMEN

The biblical Hebrews, you recall from Chapter 1, had no shame about the human body or sexual relations *within* marriage. Hebrew wives rejoiced in their sexuality. However, in Hebrew folklore, God also created Lilith at the same time Adam was created. Lilith refused to obey Adam and ran off, and became an evil spirit that seduced married men (Reineke, 1995). (More recently, Lilith has become viewed as a spirit of independence.)

In Western culture, it was the early Christians that came to view sex as sinful. Alarmed by the sexual excesses of Romans, and influenced by the Greek concept of dualism (separation of body and soul), early Church leaders such as St. Paul argued that celibacy was necessary for spiritual development (see Chapter 1). St. Augustine, the major influence on early Christian beliefs about sex, believed that lust was the original sin of Adam and Eve and, consequently, that sex was sinful (St. Augustine, *City of God,* 4). He blamed Eve for the fall from grace, and in the 2 centuries that followed it was women who came to be viewed as temptresses.

> **. . . . she took of its fruit and ate; and she also gave some to her husband, and he ate. Then the eyes of both were opened, and they knew that they were naked;** (Genesis 3:6–7, Revised Standard Version)

ideology The mental frameworks that different classes and social groups use to make sense of the way society works.

sexuality All of the sexual attitudes, feelings, and behaviors associated with being human. The term does not refer specifically to a person's capacity for erotic response or to sexual acts, but rather to a dimension of one's personality.

Thus, in both Hebrew culture (Lilith) and Christianity (Eve), women were viewed as seducing men. Augustine believed that if Eve had not tempted Adam, there would have been no lust.

> **The husband, exempt from all seductive goading of passion, could have come to rest on his wife's bosom with peace of mind undisturbed and pristine state of body intact.** (St. Augustine, *City of God*)

The prevailing view of women's sexuality began to change at the time of the Crusades and the elevation of Mary in the Roman Catholic Church. The Virgin Mary was perceived as compassionate and pure, and thus a dichotomous view of women evolved: virgins as asexual and pure, and sexually experienced women who expressed sexual desire as evil temptresses. This virgin/whore dichotomy is still very prevalent in traditional Latino cultures (Espín, 1984).

The general view during the Middle Ages was still that men were ruled by reason and had more control of their sexual impulses, while women were ruled by animal appetites (Murray, 1995, 1998). When men had anxieties about their bodies and sexual impulses, women were blamed for causing (often passively) their lust. Negative attitudes about women reached a fever pitch in the 1500s and 1600s, when tens of thousands of women were executed (generally burned at the stake to "purify" them) as witches.

With the rise of courtly love, which reached its peak in the 1600s, women (at least upper-class women) came to be admired and romanticized, but in a nonsexual way (Tannahill, 1980). During the Victorian era, we saw a complete turnabout in the way women were viewed (see Chapter 1). Rather than temptresses, the majority of Victorian moralists considered women to be asexual, and it was men who were now viewed as sexual aggressors who could not control their desires.

> **Ordinarily the normal young girl has no undue sexual propensities, amorous thoughts or feelings. . . . Girls . . . should be aware of giving way to advances on the part of young men which have only one object in view: the gratification of their animal passion.** (Henry Stanton, 1922)

Women's gender roles were very stereotyped at this time, and they were expected to be subservient to men and fulfill their roles as wives and mothers. The noted psychologist G. Stanley Hall was of this opinion (Hall, 1904).

The sexual dichotomy of women was not completely abandoned in the Victorian era. With the rise of modern medicine, psychiatrists simply replaced the concept of whore with nymphomania. Women who did not restrict their sexual behavior to marriage could now be labeled with a medical diagnosis.

Nymphomania may be defined as excessive vene-real impulse in the female. . . . It is found in the most cultured, in the most modest, and in the most religious, almost to the same degree as in those less carefully educated . . . many of the nymphomaniacs are given to masturbation and . . . many of these cases end up as prostitutes (Max Huhner, M.D., 1916)

The 1900s witnessed the advancement of the feminist movement, greater autonomy for women, and finally, with the start of the sexual revolution (about 1960, see Chapter 1), sexual freedom and equality. In the time span from St. Augustine to the present, the prevailing view of woman had gone from temptresses, to asexual, to sexual equals.

The sexuality of women as a social concept can be easily seen if we compare modern Western attitudes with those of other cultures. For example, perhaps the most negative view of women and female sexuality today is found in Islamic culture (see Unger & Crawford, 1992). A woman's place is in the home, and if she must go out in public her entire body must be veiled from head to toe (see Figure 1–2). You have already read that in wide parts of the Islamic world, women's genitals are mutilated to deprive them of their sexuality (Box 4–A). Islamic men's fear of female sexuality is also emphasized in their image of Paradise—a cool garden with fountains, fruit, and 70 *hur* (virgins). The hur are always good-tempered, never menstruate, and are always virgins—even after a man has already had intercourse with them (Smith, 1987; Smith & Haddad, 1975).

PERSONAL REFLECTIONS

How has society (e.g., parents, school, religion, the media) shaped your attitudes about women, femininity, and female sexuality? Do you suppose your attitudes would be different if you had been raised in another culture?

SEXUALITY OF CHILDREN

According to historian Phillippe Ariès (1962), "in medieval society the idea of childhood did not exist." Young children were treated as miniature adults and expected to start working in the fields shortly after they learned to walk. The idea of a separate category called childhood, different from adults, did not arise until the mid-1700s. Although other scholars disagree with Ariès, they agree that the concept of childhood was different than the way we view it in Western culture today. In England during the 1600s, for example, children were believed to be carriers of original sin, prone to evil impulses, and thus childhood was the time of life in which parents and society had to instill control. During the 1700s, this view gave way to the modern view of children as vulnerable and needing protection (Hockey & James, 1993). However, at that time children were considered asexual. Just a century later Freud argued that even young children between the ages of 3 and 5 were sexual:

In boys, as we know, this phase is marked by the fact that they have learnt how to derive pleasurable sensations from their small penis and connect its excited state with their ideas of sexual intercourse. Little girls do the same thing with their still smaller clitoris. (Freud, 1933/1965)

Children now had to be protected from their own sexuality, and as a result of urging from the medical community, Victorian era parents resorted to circumcision and protective belts and gadgets in an attempt to prevent their children from masturbating (see Figure 1–4).

The biological immaturity of children is an irrefutable fact, but "childhood is a concept,

Figure 9–1 In Western culture, women's sexuality has been viewed differently at different times. Women were viewed as temptresses in early Christianity, but during the Victorian era marriageable women were regarded as asexual.

and it is determined by how a society interprets that biological fact, and by the meanings it attaches to it" (Parsons, 2000). Children of the 1600s, 1700s, and 1800s were understood differently because the concept of childhood was different for each of those time periods.

Again, we can see verification of this by examining how other cultures interpret childhood. In Chapter 11 you will read about the Sambian culture in the South Pacific where young boys (starting at age 7) are expected to perform oral-genital sex on adolescent boys (Herdt, 1993). Among the Azande of Sudan, boys perform the role of wives to adult warriors (Ford & Beach, 1951). In the Hausa culture of Nigeria, childhood for girls ends abruptly at age 10 when they are married (James et al., 1998). In Chapter 1 you learned about the Tiwi culture, where girls are married and begin having intercourse at age 7. In other cultures (e.g., Chewoy in Malaysia) girls are not regarded as women until they give birth. In our own culture, a person is generally not recognized as an adult until he or she turns 18. Different cultures attach different meanings to childhood and being a child.

> *PERSONAL REFLECTIONS*
> *What is your concept of childhood? Adulthood? At what point (e.g., age, event) is it okay for young people to engage in "adult" sexual behaviors? Is your opinion influenced by biological maturation or social concepts? How do you reconcile your opinion with what is expected of young people in the Hausa, Tiwi, or Sambian culture?*

SEX EDUCATION

Most of us assume that sex educators teach factual information. But as you have just learned, what is believed to be factual about male and female sexuality, and children's sexuality, depends on the culture and the era. What do you suppose sex educators (parents, others) in Mangaia, the most sexually permissive culture in the world, teach children about sexuality? How do you suppose this would differ from what the sex educators among the Inis Baeg, the most sexually repressed culture in the world, teach children? (See Chapter 1 for a review of the Mangaians and Inis Baeg.)

In the United States, sex education in schools originated as part of a social hygiene movement to prevent rising levels of sexually transmitted diseases (Imber, 1994). The first printed matter for sex education appeared in the early 1900s (see Fitz-Gerald & Fitz-Gerald, 1998). The "education" (lectures and printed matter) was in actuality moralistic and anti-sex, designed to repress sexual behavior (Kyman, 1998). Why? In addition to STDs, recall that the medical profession of that era also believed that loss of semen was

harmful to men's health (Hall, 1992). Masturbation, for example, was called "self abuse," and physicians believed it to be the cause of insanity. Thus, for sex educators the prevailing philosophy of the day was prophylactics—protection from "distorted knowledge" by teaching restraint (Penland, 1981). Girls, in particular, were to be protected because of their delicate and asexual (pure) nature.

The following guidelines for sex education were presented in 1905 at the meeting of the American Society of Sanitary & Moral Prophylactics (Penland, 1981):

1. Sexual physiology and hygiene need not be formally taught to girls.
2. Sexual physiology and hygiene should be taught to every boy, when mental and sexual puberty make him capable of beneficially utilizing the knowledge.
3. The nature and scope of instruction on sexual subjects should be regulated according to each pupil's ability properly to appreciate the warnings inseparable therefrom.
4. The age at which a person may safely be instructed in sexual subjects is the age at which, in each individual case, such instruction becomes necessary for the purposes of moral and physical prophylactics.
5. Textbooks on elementary hygiene should not contain chapters on sexual physiology. Those charged with imparting instruction on sexual subjects should be provided with separately printed chapters on the physiology and hygiene of these matters. These separately printed chapters could then be given with the greatest discretion to such pupils only whose mental development would preclude their misusing the information derived therefrom.

By 1940, the focus of sex education in the United States was changing from prophylactics to personal relationships and long-term adjustment. The curriculum now included a biological component, but the basic approach was still moralistic, focusing on sex within marriage and family life (Penland, 1981). The U.S. Public Health Service published the following recommendation in that year:

"Educators must . . . ask themselves whether they are not neglecting their duty in disregarding for those reasons young people's problems of adjustment to sex and family life. As teachers they may be puzzled, but silence only complicates the adjustment problems for students.

The change in philosophy over a two-generation period has been attributed to a longer life expectancy, a change from a rural agricultural society to an industrial society, and a need for managing larger numbers of people in cities by compulsory schooling and health laws (Fitz-Gerald & Fitz-Gerald, 1998). Normal, healthy sexuality was supposed to be expressed only in marriage. The American Psychiatric Association considered homosexuality to be a mental illness, and masturbation and premarital sex were still not considered to be normal and were discouraged. Girls were now allowed to take sex education, but classes were almost always segregated by sex (Fine, 1988).

Another generation later the sexual revolution was in full swing. By the mid-1960s, numerous scientific surveys and studies had been conducted (e.g., Kinsey and colleagues and Masters and Johnson). The philosophy that emerged among sex educators was a comprehensive sex education presented in a nonjudgmental, impartial manner with open discussion (Kyman, 1998). Girls were now included in the same classes as boys. In addition to sexual anatomy and sexual health, a variety of behaviors were presented as normal, so that people could now engage in masturbation, oral-genital sex, and homosexual relations (to name a few examples) without guilt or shame.

It should be obvious from this brief history that what is taught in sex education reflects the prevailing concepts of male, female, and child sexuality of the time. However, sex education is also a powerful socializing agent for children and adolescents (and as such is the subject of much debate among different political and religious groups; see end of Chapter 1). It is not the only socializing agent, and we will now turn our attention to other major agents that help shape our culture's attitudes and beliefs about sex and our own sexuality.

SEXUAL SOCIALIZATION: AGENTS

Socialization refers to the manner in which a society shapes individual behaviors and expectations of behaviors (norms). The social influences that shape behaviors are often referred to as **socializing agents.** These include parents, peers, school, religion, and the media. The extent of influence of parents and peers is limited to a few individuals, and you will learn about their roles in the socialization process in Chapters 10 (gender identity and gender roles) and 12 (development). In this chapter we focus on socializing agents that have the capability to influence large numbers of people about sexual behaviors and attitudes. You have already read about school-based sexuality education programs in Chapter 1 and the preceding section.

RELIGION

"The media has always shown that everyone is having sex, no matter what type or what age. I have never followed the example of the media and that is mainly because of my religious beliefs. I don't believe that sex is wrong. I have just been taught that you wait until marriage."

"The media makes sex look so wonderful and perfect and I became curious. But I had the thought that I had to wait to fall in love before I could have sex because my religion and church believes that sex is only for marriage."

"I was raised in a Catholic home and I have been taught to wait until marriage, etc. Just because I see something on TV or in a magazine does not want to make me go out and try something." (All examples are from the author's files.)

Just two or three generations ago a large majority of Americans believed that premarital sex was wrong and immoral (Reiss, 1980). Today, the majority of teens have engaged in sexual intercourse (Centers for Disease Control and Prevention, 2000b). However, a person's religion and the strength of his or her religious belief still influence decisions about sexual behavior (Laumann et al., 1994). Look, for example, at Table 9–1 (Janus & Janus, 1993). It shows that for people who consider themselves to be very religious it is "very important" or "important" that their sexual behavior be in harmony with their religious beliefs.

In a recent study of teenage girls between 15 and 19, it was found that (after controlling for demographic and socioeconomic differences) fundamentalist Protestants and Catholics who went to church frequently were less likely than others to have had premarital sexual intercourse (Brewster et al., 1998). Similar results have been found for teenage boys (Halpern et al., 1994). Nevertheless, the same study also revealed that 40 percent of fundamentalist teenage girls and over half of Catholic teen girls were sexually active. This is apparently true even of many very religiously conservative individuals. For example, a survey found that 40 percent of people who regularly read the very conservative magazine *Christianity Today* admitted to having had premarital intercourse (Robinson, 1992). In addition, religious affiliation and beliefs have very little effect on whether or not people use birth control. The Catholic Church opposes contraception, but practicing Catholics are only slightly less likely than others to actually use contraception (Brewster et al., 1998). What these results mean is that while many people consider religion to be an important

socialization The process of internalizing society's beliefs; the manner in which a society shapes individual behaviors and expectations of behaviors.

socializing agent The social influences (e.g., parents, peers, the media) that shape behaviors.

TABLE 9–1

RELATION BETWEEN DEGREE OF RELIGIOUS BELIEFS AND ATTITUDES ABOUT OWN SEXUAL BEHAVIOR

	Very Religious	Religious	Slightly Religious	Not Religious
That My Sex Practices Are in Harmony with My Religion is:				
Very important	45%	18%	2%	3%
Important	36	38	24	8
Not sure	7	24	26	15
Unimportant	5	17	37	37
Very unimportant	7	3	11	37

Source: From S. S. Janus and C. L. Janus, *The Janus Report on Sexual Behavior.* Copyright © 1993 John Wiley & Sons, Inc. Reprinted by permission of John Wiley & Sons, Inc.

part of their lives, other socializing agents must play a major role in shaping their sexual attitudes and behaviors. Let us examine some of them.

PERSONAL REFLECTIONS
What role has your religion and church played in the development of your sexual attitudes and behaviors?

Figure 9–2 Publishers of popular magazines frequently use sex appeal on the covers in order to sell their products.

THE MEDIA

Probably no other socializing agent has as much of an impact on young children's and teenagers' sexual attitudes and behaviors as the media. When considered together, the sexually related messages received by young people from different branches of the media—television, movies, radio, music, magazines, and tabloids—are omnipresent and pervasive, and generally overwhelm the input received from parents, peers, and school-based sex education (Huston et al., 1998).

> "I would see on television and movies that everyone had sex. That's when I would say I used television to overcome my fear of sleeping with other people."
>
> "To me it's never a question of when to become sexually active. It's always how to become sexually active. What I really mean is that when you are watching television you see some love scenes and they make you want to try the same thing."
>
> "I was raised in a very religious household, which made me kind of sexually repressed. My parents and my church made me think my innermost thoughts were dirty. However, when I got about 16 and saw the same things I discussed with my parents were on television, I realized I wasn't strange. It was normal to have fantasies and occasional dirty thoughts. The songs on the radio echoed my feelings."
>
> "From a young age seeing sexual references and acts on TV clued me in on sex being a lot of fun and highly enjoyable. So sex was something I greatly anticipated. I watched women on shows or movies who were considered sexy and I wanted to be like them."
>
> "I had a very negative attitude towards sex and my body. I was raised with *everything* being a taboo. Now since I am so into television and movies and magazines, my whole sexual attitude has changed. I have dropped all of the negative attitudes that I was taught and I try a lot of the things that I see in the media." (All examples are from the author's files.)

MAGAZINES AND TABLOIDS. You do not have to go to XXX bookstores to find magazines that use sex to make sales. *Playboy, Penthouse, Hustler,* and other magazines for men are openly sold in drugstores and newsstands. And sell they do, with (in double-digit) millions sold every month. In addition to the Playmates or Pets-of-the-Month foldouts and other nude pictorials, most of the articles and cartoons are about sex. Even if you do not read (look at?) these magazines yourself, you are very aware of them simply because they are sold openly everywhere and you cannot avoid seeing the covers. Although not as explicit, magazines such as *Maxim,* which emphasizes cleavage and large breasts, are becoming increasingly popular with young men. Recent issues included articles with titles such as "The sex olympics (. . . a list of sex acts in public places that'll score you and your girl points)" and "Cook her pants off (do it right and you'll be dessert)."

Even more mainstream magazines sometimes increase their sexual content to boost sales. *Sports Illustrated* normally sells over 2 million copies a week, but its annual swimsuit issue sells over 5 million. Newsmagazines such as *Newsweek* and *Time* have more than tripled their references to sex since the start of the sexual revolution.

Many magazines for women also emphasize sex. Nearly all the articles in *Cosmopolitan* are about sex. As an example, the cover of a recent issue emphasized articles on multiple orgasms ("Yes! Yes! Yes! Cosmo's come-again guide to help you climax over and over. Read this, grab him, and head to bed"), men's attitudes on swimsuits ("Is your thong wrong? Is your itsy too bitsy? Does your tank turn him on?"), and sex skin secrets ("Fake perfect post—'O' glow"). *Redbook* and *Mademoiselle* also have a heavy dose of articles related to sex (e.g., "35 sexy new ways to touch your man"). Photographs in these magazines are frequently of partially (or totally) undressed couples in "romantic" poses. Even magazines that target young teen and preteen girls, such as *YM,* often have sexually related articles ("Look summer sexy").

Tabloids, of course, are full of sexually related and sexually stimulating material. This includes scantily clothed people (usually women), as well as stories with sexual content (e.g., "Big girls make better lovers," "Hollywood's craze with lesbian lovers"). Romance novels, sexual advice books, and novels with sexual plots occupy much of the space on store bookshelves.

PERSONAL REFLECTIONS
What effect has the sexual content in magazines and magazine advertisements had on your attitudes about physical attractiveness? Masculinity? Femininity? Sex, and what is sexually normal?

MUSIC. In today's music world, it is common for groups and performers to release CDs with sexually explicit lyrics. Just 10 years ago the lyrics to some of Madonna's songs were considered scandalous, but now they pale in comparison to songs by Hot Boyz, Trina, Sisqo, Eminem, Kid Rock, Blink 182, Link, Bloodhound, and Nine Inch Heels, to name just a

Figure 9–3 Rock and pop stars such as Jennifer Lopez (left), Ricky Martin (middle), and Britney Spears (right) commonly use sex in music videos and on stage to promote themselves.

few. Much of this isn't even played on the radio because it is so explicit, but it is readily available to teens at stores. The videos that accompany release of singles are also often provocative. Two-thirds of music videos contain sexual imagery (Pardun & McKee, 1995). Britney Spears proclaims her virginity, but what message does she send teens when she is nearly lap-dancing half-naked in videos and on stage? Vivid sexual imagery is sometimes true even of the conservative country music field. For example, the video for Faith Hill's "Breathe" had her singing in bed while partially wrapped in a sheet. One study found that teens who watched

Figure 9–4   Many radio and TV personalities appeal to young people's interest in sex. Howard Stern (left) emphasizes the crude and vulgar aspects of sex, whereas Dr. Drew Pinsky (right) of MTV's *Loveline* teaches sexual responsibility.

music videos a lot were generally more sexually permissive than teens who did not (Strouse et al., 1995).

RADIO. As a means of mass communication, radio serves more than just music. Howard Stern became a national celebrity as a radio talk-show "shock jock." We don't hear that term much anymore because almost every large urban area has a local disc jockey who focuses on sexual jokes, stories, and innuendoes. It is no longer shocking. Nor is it regulated; children of any age can turn on the radio in the morning and listen to adults make constant references about sex.

PERSONAL REFLECTIONS
What effect have references to sex in music, and disc jockey talk about sex, had on your attitudes about sex? Have you ever wanted to be a rock star? Are rock stars sexier than other people? Why?

MOVIES. The movie industry continues to push the limits of what is considered acceptable. Hollywood did not show women's breasts until the mid-1960s, but by the 1990s films showing women in full frontal nudity were commonplace. Sharon Stone's leg-crossing scene in 1992's *Basic Instinct* caused quite a stir, but since then films with male genitals (e.g., *Boogie Nights,* 1997; *The Full Monty,* 1997) have become common as well. *Eyes Wide Shut* (1999), starring Nicole Kidman and Tom Cruise, was full of steamy sex scenes, including

group sex. In 2000, Hilary Swank won an academy award for her performance in *Boys Don't Cry,* which featured several explicit lesbian scenes. Hollywood has also recently released movies that focused on autoeroticism (*American Pie,* 1999), mother-son incest (*Spanking the Monkey,* 1994) and necrophilia (*Kissed,* 1997). Summer movies that target teens often show sex used in an exploitative manner (e.g., *Wild Things,* 1998; *Cruel Intentions,* 1999). Are the sex scenes always an integral part of the story, or are they included for gratuitous reasons, to arouse and titillate? Well, according to people who were present when *Basic Instinct* was being filmed, director Paul Verhoeven arrived on the set one day and loudly asked, "How can we put more tits and p— into this movie?" (Zevin, 1992).

TELEVISION.

> Life does not imitate art; it only imitates bad television.   (from Woody Allen's *Husbands and Wives*)

Three-fourths of teenagers today list television and friends as their major sources of information about sex (Stodghill, 1998). The average American child watches television for several hours a day, and nearly two-thirds have their own television in the bedroom (M. Edwards, 1996). Recall from Chapter 1 that two experts on communication have described television as "the most powerful storyteller in American culture, one that continually repeats the myths and ideologies, the facts and patterns of relationships that define our world and legitimize the social order" (Brown & Steele, 1996, p. 6). And what is the primary message that television presents about sex? Two other prominent researchers have stated: "TV presents sex as a distorted, realistic oriented, exploitive, casual activity without dealing with the consequences" (Strouse & Fabes, 1985, p. 255).

Are these researchers exaggerating? Three-fourths of the programs shown at evening prime time have sexual content, with an average of 5.3 scenes per hour (Kunkel et al., 1999; Kaiser Family Foundation 2001). Mostly it is talk about sex, but about 10 percent of prime-time shows have scenes in which sexual intercourse is depicted or strongly implied. Scenes about unmarried intercourse outnumber those about married intercourse by a 5 to 1 ratio (see Greenberg & Hofschire, 2000). Less than 10 percent of scenes with sexually related behavior on prime time make any reference to sexual responsibility (e.g., birth control) or risks. Situational comedies have the greatest amount of sexual content. For example, *Friends, Sex and the City, Undressed, Seinfeld* and many other shows frequently focus on sexual topics. Even once what was called the "family hour" isn't exempt, with sexually suggestive sitcoms like *Just Shoot Me, Spin City,* and *Norm.* Here is a scene from the very popular *Seinfeld* show:

> Jerry, George, and Elaine are among a crowd in a church, awaiting the start of a friend's wedding ceremony. Earlier in the day, George learned that Jerry had previously slept with George's date for the wedding, a woman named Nina. As they all sit and wait for the ceremony to begin, George grows angry thinking about the situation, and says quietly to Jerry that he demands "reparations" to even the score. Since Jerry has slept with Nina, and Nina is George's date, George insists that he should be allowed to sleep with Jerry's date, Elaine. Elaine then joins the conversation and says she absolutely will not sleep with George, and what is the difference who slept with who? Elaine whispers to George, "Nina slept with him, he slept with me, and I slept with Pinter," referring to the man getting married. "Nobody cares," adds Elaine. George responds at the top of his voice, "You slept with the groom?" The crowd gasps in shock and the wedding is disrupted. (*Seinfeld,* NBC, November 20, 1997, from Kunkel et al., 1999)

Prime-time dramas such as *NYPD Blue* typically use slang terminology and have also included scenes with nudity and sexual intercourse. Late-night television includes many shows such as *Howard Stern, The Man Show, Strip Poker,* and *The X Show,* which focus on sex. Even morning news-talk shows get in the act. In 1998 viewers of the *Today* show were treated to several days of discussion and comments about President Clinton, Monica Lewinsky, and a sexual act involving a cigar. The History Channel's *History of Sex* was its highest-ever watched program.

Daytime television is awash in programs with heavy sexual content. Of all the topics discussed on talk shows, sexual themes are the second most common (Greenberg & Hofschire, 2000). *Jerry Springer, Ricki Lake,* and *Jenny Jones* rarely talk about anything except sexually related topics. Forty million people watch soap operas on any given day (Greenberg & Woods, 1999). This includes at least 3 million to 5 million adolescent viewers. In order to attract younger audiences, soaps are including younger and younger characters in these sexual activities There are about 6.6 sexual acts either shown or referred to every hour on the soap operas (Greenberg & Buselle, 1996; Greenberg & Woods, 1999). Intercourse between two unmarried persons is the most commonly shown (or referred to) activity (2.4 times per hour), followed by rape (1.4 times per hour). Safe sex (e.g., contraception) is almost never mentioned. Sexual intercourse may not be explicitly shown, but it is often strongly implied:

> Michael and Kimberly, two young lovers, are in bed together, apparently naked but with their bodies discreetly covered by disheveled sheets. He sighs and says, "What a great way to spend an afternoon." She replies, "Do you realize that's all we've been doing lately?" Kimberly tells Michael she is concerned that he might find sex with her boring because he has had so many previous lovers. She asks how they could spice things up. Michael explains a fantasy he would like to act out with him as a plumber and Kimberly as a "hot-to-trot" housewife. They agree to act out the fantasy tomorrow. (*Melrose Place,* Fox, March 4, 1996, from Kunkel et al., 1999)

Parents may attempt to regulate which programs their children watch, but parents are not always home. Many teens and preadolescents do not watch the same programs when they are alone that they do when their parents are around (Edwards, 1996).

PERSONAL REFLECTIONS
How many of the movies and TV shows that you see contain sexual content (behaviors and talk about sex)? How many references a year do you think you see? What effect do you think this has had on your own sexual attitudes and behaviors?

ADVERTISEMENTS. Sex sells, or at least manufacturers of perfumes and colognes, liquor and beer, cigarettes, and clothing think so (Reichert et al., 1999). In my own metropolitan area there is a weekly magazine with hundreds of photographs of used cars for sale that always has a cover photo of a young woman in a bikini

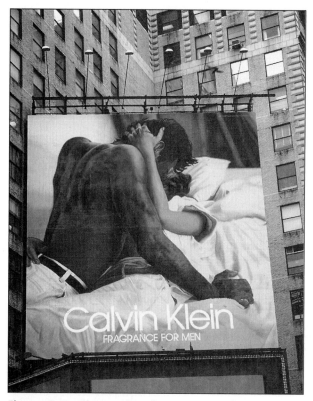

Figure 9–5 Many advertisers use sex (in a process called identification) rather than product information to sell their product.

sitting on or standing next to a car. The advertisements by Calvin Klein, particularly for underwear, have frequently come under attack, for both the poses and the young age of the models. Parents, churches, and others attempt to tell young adolescents that they are not ready for sex, but advertisements direct the attitudes and beliefs of young people in a different direction. As one researcher put it, coming of age has become a "process to be worked out in the market place rather than at home" (Brumberg, 1997, p. 41).

The aim of sexy or romantic themes in advertisements is **identification,** not product information. The message of using young attractive models in sexy or romantic poses is that if you use this product, you too can be sexy and have exciting and romantic interactions. Advertisers argue that the use of models in ads merely reflects the present cultural attitudes. However, recall from Chapter 3 how the messages in advertisements for feminine hygiene products have helped shape people's attitudes about menstruation (Merskin, 1999).

SEXUALLY EXPLICIT MATERIAL. I have made little mention of very sexually explicit material, (i.e., the type of magazines, videos, and so on that many people consider to be pornographic). This material is readily available, and try as they might, many parents have diffi-

culties preventing their children from obtaining it. This material, too, serves as a socializing agent. However, in this chapter we focus on mainstream magazines, movies, and television programs. You will learn about the effects of pornographic material in Chapter 18.

SEXUAL SOCIALIZATION: CAUSE AND EFFECT?

It is not uncommon for a publisher of a magazine, or a producer of a particular television show, to deny that his or her product could possibly, by itself, influence the attitudes and behaviors of large numbers of people. They are probably correct, yet at the same time they are missing the point. Kunkel et al. (1999) have summed up the process of socialization very nicely:

> As with most aspects of media influence, the effect of viewing sexual content . . . . is not thought to be direct and powerful, with a single exposure to a particular program [movie, or magazine] leading a viewer to think or act in any given way. Rather, the effects of messages about sex are conceptualized more as the product of a slow and cumulative process. Because such influence tends to be gradual in nature, it is the overall pattern of messages across the [media] landscape that is of primary interest for explaining the effects of long-term exposure." (p. 235)

Sexual content is prevalent in all branches of the media (Huston et al., 1998). What is the long-term cumulative message? By watching television and movies, looking at magazines, and listening to the radio, children eventually develop attitudes and answers to questions such as "When is it okay for me to start having sex?" ; "With whom is it okay for me to have sex?" ; "What sexual behaviors are okay to engage in?" ; and "Why is it okay?" In other words, the cumulative effect is that children take what they see and hear in the media to learn social norms (Brown et al., 1990). The visual messages do not have to be explicit. Just listening to talk about sex helps teenagers form their opinions about sex, love, and relationships (Ward & Rivadeneyra, 1999). Teens are most influenced by media contact when they see or hear people they relate to— "people like them" (Steele, 1999).

What specific evidence is there to support the idea that the media play a major role in sexual socialization? For one, many teens say that they have used what they see or hear in the media to get ideas about how to talk to boyfriends or girlfriends (Kaiser Family Foundation, 1998). Children who watch television shows with a lot of sexual content are more likely to begin having sexual intercourse earlier than other children (Brown & Newcomer, 1991; Peterson et al., 1991). In a controlled experiment, teenagers who had just watched television shows with a lot of sexual content gave more positive ratings to casual sex than teenagers who had not been shown the programs (Bryant & Rockwell, 1994). In a review of many studies, Greenberg and Hofschire (2000) concluded that frequent sexual content on television has four major effects on viewers: (1) overestimation of the prevalence of certain sexual activities in the general public; (2) disinhibition—a more liberal attitude about sex; (3) increased interest in sexual issues; and (4) learning about sexual topics.

One of the biggest problems is that the input to children from the media begins much earlier than input from schools and churches, and often years before parents start to talk to their children about sex. The early exposure to media, and the huge quantity of information that children receive from the media, simply overwhelm the input from other socializing agents. In order to have any chance of balancing the media's sexual messages, parents and school-based sex education programs need to find ways to incorporate what is shown on television and in movies and heard on the radio and CDs into their discussions (Kyman, 1998).

There can be little doubt that the avalanche of sexual content in the media contributes to the sexual socialization of children and adolescents. But can heavy sexual content in the media explain all the sexual attitudes and behaviors of American teenagers? The answer may not be that simple. European television, magazines, and advertisements contain a great deal more nudity than their American counterparts, yet European teens do not begin sex at a younger age than American teens, and the teenage pregnancy rate in most European countries is much lower than it is in the United States (Singh & Darroch, 2000). Obviously, it is not just the amount of sexual content that is important. Perhaps the nature of the sexual content (e.g., types of behaviors shown) in the media is equally important. European media may show more nudity, but the sexual behaviors portrayed tend to be less exploitative and birth control techniques are advertised openly. Recall, for example, that the second most common theme on American soaps is rape. Keep in mind, too, that the media do not work in splendid iso-

lation. Recent studies have found that the messages and practices shown or talked about in the media intersect with the influences of school, family, and friends (Steele, 1999). Europeans generally receive a more balanced approach from all the various agents of sexual socialization. Parents are more open about sex, and school-based sex education begins early in life for most European children. What do you suppose accounts for the difference?

The heavy sexual content in the media today cannot entirely account for teenagers interest in sex. For example, guess the year for which the teenage pregnancy rate was the highest ever for the United States? Sometime in the 1990s? 1980s? 1970s? Would you believe 1957? The sexual content on television at that time was practically zero. Top-rated programs included *Ozzie and Harriet, Leave It to Beaver,* and *Father Knows Best.* The point is that young people are going to have an interest in sex regardless of the media content. However, the quantity and nature of the sexual content make the media major socializing agents in shaping attitudes about love, relationships, and sexual behaviors (e.g., premarital sex). Compared to 1957, the unwed teenage pregnancy rate is much higher today. Do you suppose that the media's heavy portrayal of nonmarital sex has contributed to this?

In this chapter we have focused on the effects of the media and religion on sexual behavior. However, religion, magazines, music, movies, television, and advertisements also are major socializing agents in establishing and reinforcing gender roles. You will read about this in the next chapter.

PERSONAL REFLECTIONS

In the three previous Personal Reflections, you were asked about the effects of specific branches of the media on your sexual attitudes and behaviors. You may have denied or minimized the effect of any one branch. Now consider them all together, and the fact that you have been bombarded with messages about sex since early childhood. Do you suppose your attitudes about sex would be any different if you had been raised in a culture with no radio, movies, or television, or if the media presented a negative portrayal of sex?

Key Terms

Suggested Readings

D'Emilio, J. & Freedman, E. B. (1998). *Intimate matters: A history of sexuality in America.* New York: Harper & Row. The title explains it well.

Douglas, S. J. (1994). *Where the girls are: Growing up female with the mass media.* New York: Random House. Looks at how television, advertising, and music shape our attitudes about girls and women.

Greenberg, B. S., & Hofschire, L. (2000). Sex on entertainment television. In D. Zillman & P. Vorderer (Eds.), *Media entertain-ment: The psychology of its appeal* (pp. 93–111). Mahwah, NJ: Lawrence Erlbaum.

Stodghill II, R. (1998). Where'd you learn that? *Time,* June 15,

Strasburger, V. (1995). *Adolescents and the media.* Thousand Oaks, CA: Sage. A review of the research on the media's effect on teenage sexuality.

Study Guide

INTERACTIVE REVIEW

Sex is based in biology, but it does not have inherent meaning. (1) _____ is a concept whose meaning is shaped by (2) _____. Its meaning will continue to evolve as the society that had defined it changes and evolves. The sexuality of women is an example. St. Augustine believed that the original sin of Adam and Eve was lust, and early Christians viewed women as (3) _____. During the Crusades a dichotomous view of women evolved: (4) _____ / _____. At the height of the Victorian era women were thought to be (5) _____. The sexuality of children offers another example. In the 1600s, children were thought of as carriers of original sin, but in the 1700s children came to be viewed as vulnerable, needing protection, and asexual. During the Victorian era, it was (6) _____ who argued that young children are sexual beings. (7) _____ generally reflect society's concepts of adult and child sexuality.

The manner in which society shapes behaviors and attitudes is called (8) _____. In our own culture, the major (9) _____ for sexual behaviors and attitudes include parents, (10) _____, (11) _____, (12) _____, and the media. For many people it is very important that their sexual behavior be in harmony with their (13) _____. Nevertheless, there is probably no other socializing agent with as much of an impact on young people's sexual attitudes and behaviors as (14) _____. This includes (15) _____, (16) _____, (17) _____, (18) _____, and especially television. (19) _____ of teenagers list television and friends as their major sources of information about sex. Many advertisements, whether on television or in magazines, provide little product information, but instead use sex to sell their products in a process called (20) _____.

Sexual socialization does not occur as a result of a single exposure, but instead is a slow and cumulative process. The sexual content in the media is omnipresent, but the manner in which sex is portrayed may be just as important as the quantity. The media in (21) _____ show more nudity than in the United States, but the teenage pregnancy rate is much lower.

SELF-TEST

A. TRUE OR FALSE

- [T] [F] 22. Sex is a biological fact, and thus must be viewed the same in all societies.
- [T] [F] 23. Sexuality is not a fact, but rather a concept whose meaning is shaped by society.
- [T] [F] 24. According to historian Phillippe Ariès, the idea of childhood did not exist in medieval society.
- [T] [F] 25. In Western culture, women have always been viewed as less sexual than men.
- [T] [F] 26. The biological immaturity of children is an irrefutable fact, but childhood is a social concept.
- [T] [F] 27. Freud believed that children as young as 3 to 5 years were sexual.
- [T] [F] 28. In some cultures girls are expected to marry and begin having intercourse before puberty.

☐ T ☐ F   29. The first school-based sex education in the United States was moralistic and anti-sex.

☐ T ☐ F   30. School-based sex education is a socializing agent.

☐ T ☐ F   31. Among girls aged 15 to 19, those who are very religious are just as likely to have begun sexual intercourse as others.

☐ T ☐ F   32. Teens who watch a lot of music videos are generally more sexually permissive than teens who do not.

☐ T ☐ F   33. Three-fourths of the programs shown during evening prime time have sexual contact.

☐ T ☐ F   34. Children who watch a lot of television shows with sexual content are no more likely than others to have begun sexual intercourse.

☐ T ☐ F   35. In a controlled experiment, teenagers who had just watched television shows with a lot of sexual content gave more negative ratings to casual sex than teens who had not watched the programs.

☐ T ☐ F   36. Just listening to talk about sex on the television or radio helps teenagers form their opinions.

☐ T ☐ F   37. The amount of sexual content in the media is directly rated to the teenage pregnancy rate.

B. FILL IN THE BLANKS

38. _____ is "the mental frameworks . . . which different classes and social groups deploy in order to make sense of, define, figure out, and render intelligible the way society works" (Hall, 1986).

39. _____ is all of the sexual attitudes, feelings, and behaviors associated with being human; a dimension of one's personality.

40. During the Victorian era, the sexual dichotomy of women as virgin/whore was replaced by _____.

41. Today, the culture with the most negative view of female sexuality is _____.

42. _____ has been called "the most powerful storyteller in American culture, one that continually repeats the myths and ideologies, the facts and patterns of relationships that define our world and legitimize the social order" (Brown & Steele, 1996).

43. On the afternoon soap operas, there are about _____ sexual acts either shown or referred to every hour.

Chapter 10

Becoming a Woman/Becoming a Man: Gender Identity and Gender Roles

Our theoretical position is that gender is a social construction, that a world of "two sexes" is a result of the socially shared, taken-for-granted methods which members use to construct reality.

(Suzanne Kessler and Wendy McKenna, 1978)

What determines whether we are born with male or female anatomy? How do we learn that we are a boy or a girl? What does it mean to be "masculine" or "feminine"? Is it appropriate for a woman to ask a man for a date? If a father sees his son playing with a doll, what should the father do? Where do our ideas about "acting like a woman" or "acting like a man" come from? Before these questions can be answered, you must learn the distinction between two terms—*gender identity* and *gender role*.

Gender identity is your sense of self as a man (or boy) or a woman (or girl), while **gender role** includes everything you feel, think, say, and do that shows to yourself and others that you are, in fact, a man or a woman. In other words, gender role is the way you express your gender identity. Gender identity and gender role are not two different things, but rather two different aspects of the same thing. Gender identity is the inward experience of your gender role, and gender role is the outward expression of your gender identity.

When you have finished studying this chapter, you should be able to:

1. Define gender identity and gender role;

2. Explain various biological influences on sexual anatomy and gender identity;

3. Describe the various types of intersexed individuals;

4. Define and differentiate the concepts of gender identity disorder, transsexuality, homosexuality, transvestism, and gender dysphoria;

5. Explain how gender is a social concept;

6. Explain the Freudian, social learning, and cognitive-developmental theories of gender identity development;

7. Discuss the dualistic and unidimensional models of masculinity and femininity and the concept of androgyny;

8. Summarize the development of gender roles in childhood and adulthood; and

9. Describe, from a microstructural viewpoint, how gender roles have evolved in the United States.

Kelly and Worell (1977) view gender roles as involving two different traits or sets of characteristics—"masculinity" and "femininity." These two characteristics were once viewed as bipolar (opposite ends on a scale), and psychological tests for masculinity and femininity measured people along this one scale. It was believed that if an individual scored high on masculine traits, he or she would not show any feminine traits (see Spence & Helmreich, 1978).

Today, researchers believe that the characteristics of masculinity and femininity are present in both men and women, but to different degrees (Spence et. al., 1974). Sandra Bem (1974) developed the Bem Sex-Role Inventory to measure the amount of masculinity and femininity within an individual's gender role. She noted that individuals could be characterized as masculine or feminine if they scored high on one dimension and low on the other. For example, a high score on the femininity dimension and a low score on masculinity would classify a person as "feminine." A person having high scores on both dimensions would be classified as *androgynous.* The term **androgyny** comes from the Greek words *andro,* for "male," and *gyn,* for "female." Many see this combination as socially desirable (Spence et al., 1975). The concept of androgyny implies that it is possible for a person to be both assertive and compassionate, logical and emotional, depending on what is most appropriate for a particular situation. In addition, Bem claimed that some people scored low on both dimensions. Such individuals would be labeled *undifferentiated.* These combinations of femininity and masculinity are summarized in Table 10–1.

Gender-role stereotypes are oversimplified, rigid beliefs that all members of a particular sex have distinct behavioral, psychological, and emotional characteristics. A person is considered stereotyped if he or she exhibits a relatively high number of characteristics associated with one gender and claims not to have or not to value the other type of characteristics. For example, a man would be stereotyped if he chose only to display masculinity in himself and preferred not to show signs of femininity. In contrast to the gender-role stereotyped individual is the androgynous person. An androgynous person is capable of integrating both traditionally masculine characteristics and traditionally feminine characteristics into his or her gender role.

In this chapter, you will learn about the forces that shape both gender identity and gender roles.

TABLE 10–1
BEM'S SEX-ROLE CLASSIFICATIONS

	High Femininity	Low Femininity
High Masculinity	Androgynous	Masculine
Low Masculinity	Feminine	Undifferentiated

These forces are biological and social, internal and external, involving both genetics and learning. Theorists differ in the importance they give to the influence of these different forces. As always, it seems that most theorists agree that it is the interaction of such forces that ultimately determines gender identity and gender role. I will begin the chapter with a discussion of how gender identity is formed, focusing first on biological aspects of this process. The issue of "nature versus nurture" in the formation of gender identity will be explored. You will learn of instances where an individual's gender identity conflicts with his or her biological sex. Psychological theories of gender identity formation are elaborated upon, including Freudian theory, learning theory, and cognitive-developmental theory. Finally, we will discuss the development of gender roles, and the forces shaping our concepts of masculinity and femininity.

> *PERSONAL REFLECTIONS*
> *In your opinion, what traits (other than physical characteristics) make a man masculine? What traits make a woman feminine? Why? Were there any traits shared by both men and women? Why or why not? Can a man be gentle, caring, affectionate, emotional, and nurturing to his children, and still be masculine? Why or why not? Can a woman be assertive, independent, ambitious in a career, and still be feminine? Why or why not?*

BIOLOGICAL INFLUENCES ON GENDER IDENTITY

How do we end up as a boy or girl at birth? Genetics certainly plays an important role, but hormones are equally important.

---

gender identity One's subjective sense of being a man (or boy) or a woman (or girl). This sense is usually acquired by the age of 3.

gender role A set of culturally specific norms concerning the expected behaviors and attitudes of men and women.

androgyny The ability of an individual to display a variety of personality characteristics, both masculine and feminine, depending on whether a trait or behavior is appropriate in a given situation. It is often viewed as a positive characteristic that gives an individual greater adaptability.

gender-role stereotypes Oversimplified, preconceived beliefs about the gender roles of men and women.

THE ROLE OF CHROMOSOMES

A human cell normally has 23 pairs of **chromosomes,** rod-shaped structures that determine a person's inherited characteristics. Eggs and sperm have only half the normal genetic material (one chromosome from each of the 23 pairs). Thus, when an egg and sperm unite (called *conception*), the resultant single cell will again have the normal 23 pairs. One of these pairs determines whether at birth the baby will be genetically a boy or a girl. *Girls usually have two X chromosomes (XX), while boys usually have one X and one Y chromosome (XY).* Thus, it is the sperm from the father that determines the genetic sex of the child, and this is determined at the moment of conception. However, sometimes individuals with an XX combination have male anatomy and other individuals with an XY combination have female anatomy. How is this possible? Researchers have determined that a smidgen of the Y chromosome—a gene called SRY (sex-determining region of the Y chromosome)—determines maleness (Sinclair et al., 1990). This piece is missing from XY girls' Y, and it is present on XX boys' X. In addition, it has been found that a gene on the X chromosome—a gene called DSS (dosage-sensitive sex reversal)—may help determine femaleness (Bardoni et al., 1994).

THE ROLE OF HORMONES

As two researchers put it, "Nature's rule is, it would appear, that to masculinize, something must be added" (Money & Ehrhardt, 1972). This something is *testosterone*, which must be produced at a critical stage of embryonic development (i.e., during the first 2 months after conception) in order for an XY combination to result in a baby with male anatomy.

Embryos cannot be distinguished anatomically as either male or female for the first few weeks of development. A pair of primitive gonads develops during the 5th and 6th weeks that have the potential for developing into either ovaries or testes. At this stage, the embryo also has two duct systems: (1) the **Wolffian duct system,** which if allowed to develop will become male structures; and (2) the **Mullerian duct system,** which if allowed to develop will become female structures (see Figure 10–1). If the primitive gonads were removed at this stage of development, the baby would always be born anatomically a girl, even if it were genetically XY. Why?

chromosomes Rod-shaped structures containing the genetic material that determines a person's inherited characteristics.

Wolffian duct system A primitive duct system found in embryos that, if allowed to develop, becomes the male reproductive system.

Mullerian duct system A primitive duct system formed in embryos, which, if allowed to develop, becomes the female reproductive system.

Mullerian-duct-inhibiting substance A chemical secreted by the testes during embryonic development that causes the Mullerian ducts to shrink and disappear.

Normally, the SRY gene on the Y chromosome triggers the transformation of the primitive gonads into testicles during the 7th week of gestation (Hiort & Holterhus, 2000). The newly developed testicles begin to secrete testosterone, which promotes the development of the Wolffian duct system into the male internal reproductive system. The masculinizing hormone is also responsible for the development of the external genitalia a few weeks later. What happens to the Mullerian duct system in these male embryos? The SRY gene activates the testicles to secrete an additional substance called **Mullerian duct–inhibiting substance,** which causes these ducts to shrink.

What happens to embryos with an XX combination (genetically female)? If there is no Y chromosome (and thus no chemical substance to convert the primitive gonads into testicles), the primitive gonads will eventually develop into ovaries. The absence of large levels of testosterone results in the shrinkage of the Wolffian duct system and the development of the Mullerian duct system into the female reproductive system.

In summary, it would appear that *unless there are high levels of male hormones at a critical stage of prenatal development, nature has programmed everyone for female development.* In the vast majority of births, the baby's genetic and anatomical sex are matched. Occasionally, however, a different pattern of development may be seen.

SEXUAL DIFFERENTIATION IN THE BRAIN

Are men's brains different from women's brains, and if so, could this account for differences in behavior? In the 1970s, it was discovered that parts of an area of the brain called the hypothalamus (see Chapter 2) were different in male and female rats (see Kelly et al., 1999, for a review). The difference wasn't noticeable at birth but became apparent shortly thereafter as a result of differences in testosterone levels. Studies of humans show that men's and women's hypothalamuses also differ (e.g., Swaab et al., 1992). Experiments with rats demonstrated that administration of testosterone to females shortly after birth masculinized the brain. Obviously, sex hormones very early in life affect not only the anatomy of the genitals but the anatomy of the brain as well.

Now for an important question. Is the purpose of chromosomes and embryonic and fetal hormones limited to determining the anatomical characteristics of men and women, or do they also contribute to an individual's gender identity and gender role? One way of examining this question is by looking at individuals whose chromosomes or embryonic/fetal hormone levels differed from the usual pattern.

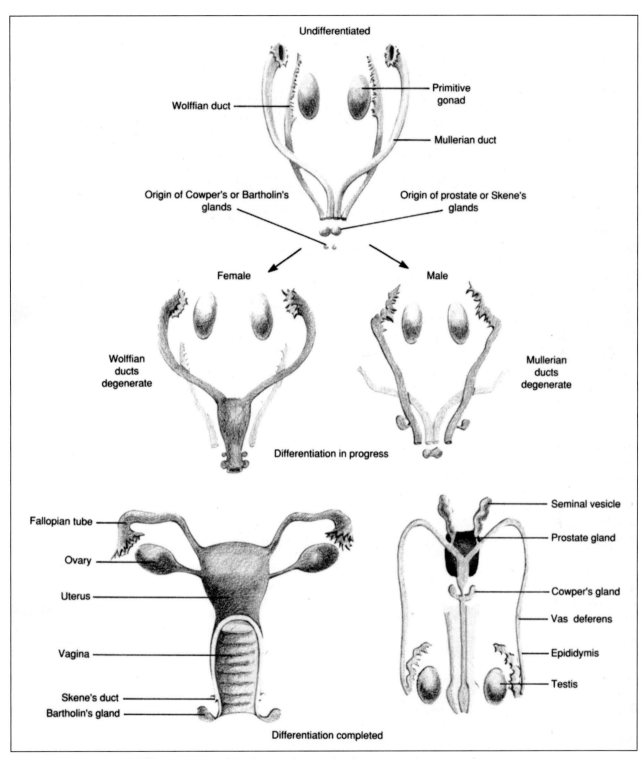

Figure 10–1 Prenatal differentiation of the internal reproductive systems in men and women.

VARIATIONS IN DEVELOPMENT: INTERSEXED INDIVIDUALS

Due to some irregularities in prenatal development, some individuals are born with anatomical features not usually associated with being a boy or a girl. Often, but not always, this includes ambiguous genitals. These individuals are called **intersexuals.** Let us look at some of the causes.

CHROMOSOME VARIATIONS

There are over 70 known irregularities involving the sex chromosomes, and approximately 1 in every 426 people is born with unusual sex chromosome combinations (Nielson & Wohlert, 1991). For example, in 1 out of every 500 live male births, there is one or more extra X chromosomes (XXY or XXXY), a condition known as *Klinefelter's syndrome.* These biological men have both masculine characteristics, because of the Y chromosome, and feminine characteristics, because of the XX chromosome combination. They tend to be tall with long arms and have poor muscular development, enlarged breasts and hips, a small penis with shrunken testes, and low sexual desire (Mandoki et al., 1991). Klinefelter men are generally given testosterone so that they can have secondary male characteristics (e.g., body hair), but they are often confused about their gender identity.

Turner's syndrome is a condition in which there is only one X chromosome (XO). It occurs in about 1 in every 2,000 to 3,000 live births (Gravholt et al., 1996). Because women with Turner's syndrome are missing a chromosome, the ovaries never develop properly; and in the absence of ovarian hormones, they also do not menstruate or develop breasts at puberty. These women are generally short, infertile, and often have skeletal abnormalities, but they have normal intelligence. Because the ovaries are nonfunctional, women with Turner's syndrome are generally given estrogen to produce female secondary sex characteristics. However, because there is no Y chromosome, there are no masculine characteristics. Thus, although these women often have problems with self-concept (frequently associated with being infertile), they generally do not have problems with gender identity (Kagan-Krieger, 1998).

One of the most interesting sex chromosome patterns involved Stella Walsh, an internationally renowned athlete who won an Olympic gold medal in the women's 100-meter dash in 1932 and a national pentathlon in 1954 (see Figure 10–2). After her death

intersexual Individuals with a combination of male and female anatomical features.

hermaphrodite A person with both male and female reproductive systems as a result of failure of the primitive gonads to differentiate properly during embryonic development.

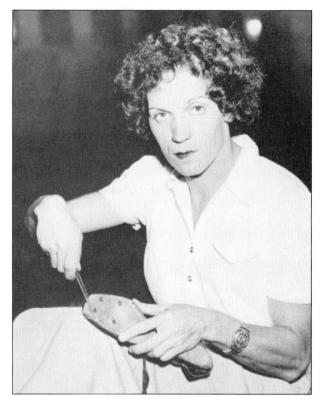

Figure 10–2 Stella Walsh won an Olympic gold medal in the women's 100-meter dash in 1932. After her death, it was discovered that she had both XX and XY cells.

in 1980, it was found that some of the cells in her body were XX and others were XY. She had been raised and lived as a woman, but had nonfunctional male sex organs.

The vast majority of us are born with the correct number and combination of sex chromosomes. However, as you have learned, having an XY chromosome combination does not guarantee that a baby will be anatomically a boy at birth. Hormones are also critically important in the determination of one's sex.

HORMONAL VARIATIONS

Hermaphroditism is a condition in which a person is born with both male and female reproductive systems as a result of the primitive gonads failing to differentiate properly during the embryonic stage (see Blyth & Duckett, 1991). The term *hermaphrodite* is derived from the Greek mythological figure Hermaphroditus, who merged with the nymph Salmacis to form a single body with male and female genitals. Hermaphrodites are usually genetic females, and even though a uterus is almost always present, they often have an ovary and Fallopian tube on one side and a testicle and a vas deferens and/or epididymis on the other (see Figure 10–3). The external genitalia are usually ambiguous in appearance, but because the phallus is often enlarged, nearly two-thirds of these individuals are raised as boys, with complications arising at puberty when they begin to develop breasts and to menstruate. This is a rare condition, occurring in about only 1 in every 65,000 births (Intersexual Society of North America).

More common is a condition known as **pseudohermaphroditism,** in which a person with an XX or XY chromosome pattern is born with the proper set of gonads (ovaries or testicles, respectively), but whose external genitalia are either ambiguous or that of the other sex. In women, the most common cause is known as **adrenogenital syndrome (AGS),** also known as *congenital adrenal hyperplasia,* in which the adrenal glands secrete too much masculinizing hormone during fetal development (Clarnette et al., 1997). The internal organs are normal, but the genitals are masculinized (i.e., the clitoris and labia are enlarged), so that even physicians sometimes mistake these individuals for boys at birth (see Figure 10–4) This condition occurs in about 1 in 20,000 births. If the problem is not recognized and corrected early, the excess adrenal hormones will continue to masculinize the individual during subsequent development.

The first treatment for this condition, developed in the 1950s, included administration of the adrenal hormone cortisone and surgery to correct the appearance of the genitals. Initial studies concluded that early treatment, combined with being raised as a girl, generally leads masculinized girls to develop female gender identity. Later work has shown that many have problems with gender identity and gender roles (Slijper et al., 1998). For example, many of them are reported to show tomboyish behavior as children and to have fewer fantasies about motherhood during adolescence. As adults, they often score like men on personality tests (see Collaer & Hines, 1995, for a review). Nevertheless, most have a heterosexual orientation as adults, and some who receive treatment later marry and have children.

The most common cause of pseudohermaphroditism in men is known as **androgen insensitivity syndrome** (some-times called *testicular feminization syndrome*), in which the testicles secrete normal amounts of testosterone but the body tissues do not respond to it (Kaplan & Owett, 1993). As a result, a clitoris, a short vagina, and labia develop, but the internal female structures fail to develop because the testicles still secrete Mullerian duct–inhibiting substance (see Figure 10–5). This happens in about 1 in 20,000 births. These individuals are generally raised as girls, and because of their insensitivity to testosterone, their estrogen causes them to develop breasts and hips at puberty. In fact, unless the undescended testicles are felt in the groin during infancy, the condition is often not discovered until the individual fails to start menstruat-

Figure 10–3 Hermaphroditism. This individual is genetically a woman (XX chromosomes), has one ovary and one testicle, and has always lived as a man.

Figure 10–4 Adrenogenital syndrome in an infant girl.

Figure 10–5 Androgen insensitivity syndrome in an individual who is genetically a man (XY chromosomes)

ing as a teenager. These individuals can be very feminine in appearance and behavior, and despite the fact that they cannot conceive, they have made excellent adoptive mothers. They are attracted to male sexual partners and clearly have a female gender identity (Hines & Collaer, 1993; Money, 1994).

In 1974, 38 boys in the Dominican Republic were discovered who suffered from a type of androgen insensitivity syndrome. They had an XY chromosome combination and prenatally their testicles had produced testosterone and Mullerian duct–inhibiting substance, so that their internal structures were male. However, because of an inherited enzyme deficiency, the testosterone was not converted into dihydrotestosterone, which is necessary for proper

pseudohermaphroditism A condition in which a person is born with ambiguous genitalia as a result of a hormonal abnormality.

adrenogenital syndrome A condition in girls in which the adrenal glands excrete too much testosterone during fetal development, causing masculinization. This includes enlargement of the clitoris and labia, so that at birth the genitals are sometimes mistaken for those of a boy. Also called *congenital adrenal hyperplasia.*

androgen insensitivity syndrome A condition in which the testicles secrete normal amounts of testosterone during male embryonic development, but the tissues do not respond to it. As a result, a clitoris, labia, and a short vagina develop, but the internal female structures do not develop because the testicles still secrete Mullerian duct-inhibitory substances.

formation of the external genitals (the condition is therefore called **DHT deficiency syndrome**). As a result, they had a very small penis that looked like a clitoris, an incomplete scrotum that looked like labia, undescended testicles, and a short, closed vaginal cavity.

Eighteen of these children were reared as girls, but at puberty, when their testicles started secreting large amounts of testosterone, their voices deepened, muscles developed, the testicles descended, and their "clitoris" grew to become a penis. Although the urethral opening was located on the perineum and not the tip of the penis, they were capable of ejaculating sperm.

How do you think you would feel if you were being raised as a girl, but suddenly started growing a penis at puberty? The culture in these remote villages has a strong patriarchal "macho" bias. Girls are forced to stay home and do chores, while boys are given considerable freedom, including sexual freedom as adults. Parents of these children generally rejoiced when they discovered that they had an unexpected son. The villagers called them *quevote* ("penis at twelve"). Under these circumstances, it is probably not surprising that 16 of these 18 children decided to become boys and subsequently developed a strong sexual interest in girls (Imperato-McGinley et al., 1979).

It should be noted that anthropologist Gilbert Herdt (1990) believes that this interpretation of the adjustment by the DHT-deficient children is an example of observer bias (see Chapter 1). Western culture categorizes people by two sexes, but the culture in which the children were raised believes in three sexes. In this case, adjustment is easier.

Do you suppose that the transition would have been as easy in a country like the United States? In fact, most American children with this disorder choose to remain girls when their bodies become masculinized (Rubin et al., 1981).

ATTEMPTS TO REASSIGN SEX AT BIRTH

Is gender identity determined mostly by biology or mostly by teaching the values of society (socialization) through child-rearing practices? Much debate has taken place over this question, but recent studies suggest that biology plays a much stronger role than previously believed. Consider, for example, the following case history.

Identical twin brothers were circumcised at 8 months of age, but due to a surgical mistake, one of the twins lost his penis. After considerable deliberation, and upon the recommendation of doctors, the boy's parents decided to raise the child as a girl. They were encouraged to

DHT deficiency syndrome
A type of androgen insensitivity syndrome in which, because testosterone is not converted into dihydrotestosterone, boys' external genitals do not develop properly. Development occurs at puberty with the rise in testosterone.

do so because at that time it was believed that at birth people are psychosexually neutral and that normal psychosexual development depends on the appearance of one's genitals.

When the child was 1 year old, his name was changed and surgical procedures were done to reconstruct the genitals in order to make them female. The child was dressed in girls' clothing and was encouraged to play with girls' toys and engage in girls' activities.

The published reports during this person's childhood concluded that the sex reassignment had been a success. According to Money (1975), the child readily achieved a female gender identity and gender role. The twin brother developed traditional masculine traits. Largely as a result of the "success" of this often cited case, thousands of children born with ambiguous genitals were given sex reassignment surgery (see Colapinto, 1997).

Notice that up to this point the underlying assumption in the medical treatment for children with ambiguous genitals (whatever the cause) was that sex was dichotomous—an individual was either a boy or a girl. Furthermore, the standard practice was to define a person's sex on the appearance of his or her genitals. It was believed that in the case of babies with ambiguous genitals, all doctors had to do was surgically change them to be more male or female in appearance. The child could then be raised successfully as a boy or girl, and would have a gender identity that corresponded to the surgically altered anatomy.

In the case of the twin who had been sexually reassigned at birth to be a girl, later interviews revealed many problems. The psychiatrist following "her" development found that "she" had great difficulty in her attempt to become a woman. She rejected girls' clothes and toys, preferring boys' clothes and toys. She imitated her father and was regarded as a tomboy. She frequently urinated (or tried to) while standing up. As she entered adolescence, she became depressed and suicidal, which finally resulted in her parents' telling her the truth—"she" was a boy. He chose to have a mastectomy, receive male hormone shots, and undergo surgery to partially restore his penis. Afterwards, he adjusted well, married, and adopted his wife's children. When asked why he had rejected all the attempts to raise him as a girl, he said that being a girl "did not feel right" (Diamond, 1997).

Here is another example (Dittman, 1998). A baby boy (XY chromosomes) was born with an extremely rare condition called *penile agenesis,* in which the testicles develop but the penis does not. He was castrated at age 3 and thereafter was raised as a girl, and began hormone treatment to develop breasts at age 14. In his late teens, he rejected these attempts at sex reassignment and had surgery to reconstruct a penis. He fully regarded himself as a man and later married.

These are not isolated cases. Many individuals who underwent sex reassignment as infants because of ambiguous or injured genitals have rejected the socialization process (Diamond, 1997; Cowley et al., 1997). Pediatric endocrinologist Bruce Wilson expressed what is becoming the prevailing view in medicine: "We have had to listen to what our former patients are saying. For a lot of us, it has become clear that current practices were causing problems, that we were doing more harm than good, and that we couldn't predict the outcome with any sort of accuracy" (cited in Palmer, 1999).

What can be concluded from these cases? According to Diamond (1997), they show that nature sets a predisposition for gender identity and that "one's sexual identity is not fixed by the gender of rearing." In other words, we cannot always define a person's sex (or make assumptions about his or her gender identity) simply on the basis of the appearance of the genitals. Obviously, biology (genetics and hormones) plays a major role. For example, in the cases of children with surgically altered genitals or children with DHT-deficiency syndrome, it may very well be that although their genitals did not develop properly, fetal hormones altered the brain in the manner appropriate for their chromosomal pattern.

We must be cautious before we accept this idea without hesitation. In both of these case histories, the children were not operated on at birth, so some socialization occurred. Also, because the differences in brain anatomy are not noticeable in newborns, some interesting questions are raised. Do biological (brain) influences determine behavior, or do social stimuli (i.e., the different manner in which people interact with boys and girls) alter both psychology and biology (see Breedlove, 1994, for a review)? This is a fascinating new area of research, and we will return to it in Chapter 11, but it is too early to come to definite conclusions.

GENDER IDENTITY "DISORDER"

You have just read about a few individuals who had sex reassignment surgery in infancy because of ambiguous-looking or injured genitals. Attempts to raise them as persons of the opposite sex were not successful. Are there ever cases in which individuals with normal genitals are not happy with their sex? The answer is yes.

Some people's gender identity does not match their biological sex. These individuals have normal anatomy, both internally and externally, and yet feel that they are actually a member of the opposite sex. They feel intense distress with their anatomy, a condition known as **gender dysphoria** (American Psychiatric Association, DSM-IV, 1994). People with gender dysphoria feel that they are "trapped in the wrong anatomic body" (Pauly, 1985). This feeling of a mis-

match between gender identity and anatomy often begins at a very early age, although in some cases it does not arise until adulthood.

> "Ever since I can remember anything at all I could never think of myself as a girl and I was in perpetual trouble, with this as the real reason. When I was 5 or 6 years old I began to say to myself that, whatever, anyone said, if I was not a boy at any rate I was not a girl. This has been my unchanged conviction all through my life." ("Miss D," from Henry Havelock Ellis, 1918)

> "My friend Kelly believes himself to be a male, when in fact he is really a female. Kelly has everyone call him a he. He's a girl, I know, but I call him a he and always have. He gets a lot of torment, so we try not to tell anyone the truth. He wants a sex change, but he doesn't have the money. He lives life as a guy. He has an auto mechanic job and a girlfriend, but I don't think he's gay. It was really weird at first, but I don't even notice it any more." (from the author's files)

Adults with this condition are generally referred to as **transsexuals**, and children with the condition are diagnosed as having gender identity disorder of childhood. However, in the American Psychiatric Association's latest diagnostic manual, DSM-IV, all conditions have been collapsed into a single diagnosis—**gender identity disorder (GID)** (Bradley & Zucker, 1997). The criteria for gender identity disorder are (a) behaviors that indicate identification with the opposite gender and (b) behaviors that indicate discomfort with one's own anatomy and gender roles. Thus, people with gender identity disorder have an intense desire to belong to the opposite sex, prefer to cross-dress, and want to participate in the games and pastimes of the opposite sex. Persistent discomfort with their bodies and bodily functions is almost always the case (e.g., boys are disgusted with their penises and testicles and distressed about facial and body hair; girls do not want to grow breasts, menstruate, or urinate in a sitting position).

Among children, boys in therapy for GID outnumber girls 7 to 1, but this may be because our culture has a higher tolerance for girls who display cross-gender behavior (Bradley & Zucker, 1997). The ratio becomes less one-sided in adolescence. Nevertheless, researchers often report that even among adults, male-to-female transsexuals are 3 to 6 times more common than female-to-male transsexuals (Stockard & Johnson, 1980). Among genetic males, transsexualism is found in both heterosexual individuals

gender dysphoria The feelings of being trapped in a body of the opposite sex.

transsexual An adult whose gender identity does not match his or her biological sex.

gender identity disorder A disorder whose criteria are (a) behaviors that indicate identification with the opposite gender, and (b) behaviors that indicate discomfort with one's own anatomy and gender roles.

(most commonly) and homosexual individuals. Among women, it is rare for a heterosexual individual (someone attracted to men) to be transsexual (Dickey & Stephens, 1995). Most female transsexuals attracted to men have a fantasy of being gay.

In the late 19th and early 20th centuries, sexologists like Richard von Krafft–Ebing (1927) explained transsexualism as "sexual inversion" and related it to homosexuality (which then was considered a perversion). According to this explanation, sexual attraction was "natural" only if it was directed toward members of the opposite sex. It is important to understand that transsexualism has to do with gender identity, not sexual orientation—it is not the same as homosexuality. Homosexuals have gender identities that agree with their anatomical sex just as often as heterosexuals. Most male-to-female transsexuals, for example, are attracted to men because they wish to be desired and loved as a woman by a heterosexual man.

Transsexuality is also not the same as transvestism. A transvestite, as you will learn in Chapter 16, dresses in the clothing of the opposite sex in order to achieve sexual arousal. However, a transvestite does not want to change his or her biological sex and does not experience gender dysphoria. In contrast, transsexuals cross-dress as a means of attempting to be more comfortable psychologically with their appearance, not for sexual arousal. Some men are sexually aroused by the thought of themselves with female attributes and may even undergo breast augmentation (Blanchard, 1993), but this is not the same as gender dysphoria either.

The cause(s) of gender identity disorder has not been determined. Children with GID tend to have internalizing psychopathology (e.g., depression, low self-esteem) (Bradley & Zucker, 1997). Recent studies have found that while adult transsexuals were dysphoric, they do not show signs of other psychopathology and are "normal" in the desired gender (Cohen-Kettenis & Gooren, 1999). With regard to biological factors, autopsy studies have revealed that the brains (more specifically, the hypothalamus) of male-to-female transsexuals are similar to brains of women (Zhou et al., 1995). Thus, it is likely (though unproven) that hormones before birth or shortly afterwards may have had effects on later behavior and gender identity (see previous sections; see also Collaer & Hines, 1995). Psychosexual factors, particularly the parents' preference for a boy or a girl and parent-child interactions (e.g., whether or not parents discourage cross-sex behavior), may also play a role (Bradley & Zucker, 1997; Cohen-Kettenis & Gooren, 1999).

Until very recently, the medical profession viewed transsexualism as a problem that needed to be corrected. The medical model, you recall, assumed that there were only two sexes and that sex was defined by the anatomy of the genitals. We will question this in the next section, but for the moment let us examine the medical model. What treatment is available? For children with GID, approaches that discourage cross-gender behavior, promote same-sex identification, and encourage parental involvement have had some success (Zucker & Bradley, 1995). In any case, many children with GID do not become transsexuals as adults (Green, 1987; Meyenburg, 1999). As for adult transsexuals, many have turned to surgery to deal with the problem (Cohen-Kettenis & Gooren, 1999).

Prior to undergoing sex reassignment surgery (a "sex-change operation"), individuals are carefully screened by psychological testing. In addition, they are usually required to live for 1 or 2 years as a member of the "opposite" (anatomical) sex before undergoing surgery. For example, a female-to-male transsexual would take on a male identity and wear men's clothing. Sex hormones are also administered to stimulate the growth of secondary sex characteristics of the opposite sex. The male-to-female transsexual is given estrogen, which will result in the development of breasts, the formation of fatty deposits in the hips, and a change in skin tone. The female-to-male transsexual is given testosterone, which will cause a deeper voice, increase facial and body hair, and inhibit menstruation.

During this period, the transsexual can prepare family, friends, and acquaintances for the planned sex change. It is common for there to be a great deal of anxiety, apprehension, and discomfort in the way that family members and friends react to the idea of transsexual surgery. It is best for these feelings to be confronted and dealt with before the surgery. Likewise, obtaining legal recognition of a sex change can be attempted during this try-out period. Many courts in the United States have refused to recognize individuals as really being of the other sex (different from their chromosomal or anatomical sex) after a sex reassignment operation. Marriages following the operation may also not be legally recognized if the marriage partner is of the same sex as the transsexual was before the surgery.

The male-to-female transformation can be done in one surgery (Bouman, 1988). The penis and testicles are removed first. Next, a vagina is created using pelvic tissue. Sensory nerves in the skin of the penis are relocated to the inside of the new vagina. Sexual intercourse is possible after the operation, though lubricants may have to be used. Male-to-female surgery is a much simpler procedure than female-to-male surgery.

In female-to-male surgery, the uterus, ovaries, and breasts are removed. Some individuals have no further changes made, while others decide to have an artificial penis created. The new penis is made using flaps of skin and muscle (from the groin, forearm, or other places) or by clitoral enlargement (Hage et al., 1993).

Figure 10–6 Tennis player Renee Richards as she appeared after a sex reassignment operation (right) and before as Dr. Richard Raskind (left).

It is incapable of normal erection, although artificial means of creating erections are possible, such as those used in treating erectile disorders.

One of the most famous cases of sexual reassignment was that of an ophthalmologist named Richard Raskind (Richards & Ames, 1983). Raskind had attended college and medical school, become a highly ranked tennis player, and married. He hated his maleness and genitalia and reported the agony that he felt in his presurgery dilemma. "As a child . . . I would pray every night that I could be a girl. I knew then that I wanted Renee as my name. It means reborn" (*People* magazine, 1976). He eventually decided to have sex reassignment surgery and become Renee Richards (Figure 10–6).

After the operation, Renee felt more comfortable with her gender identity, but found that female tennis players did not want to let her compete in the top professional tournaments. They claimed that Renee's physical abilities gave her an unfair advantage. However, a judge ruled that Renee could compete on the professional women's circuit. She did so for several years and later became a tennis coach, most notably for Wimbledon tennis champion Martina Navratilova. In another case (Docter, 1985), a man decided to undergo transsexual surgery at the age of 74. He had been happily married for 37 years, but had had lifelong fantasies of becoming a woman. He finally decided to become a woman after his wife had been dead for several years.

The purpose of sex reassignment surgery is to lessen the feeling of gender dysphoria in the transsexual and to contribute to his or her emotional health and well-being. Most studies have found that the vast majority of transsexuals achieve satisfactory results with the procedure, with only a few expressing feelings of regret (see Cohen-Kettenis & Gooren, 1999; Green & Fleming, 1990, for reviews). It is important to remember that the *surgery is used to help confirm an individual's previously established gender identity.* Such gender confirmation can be heavily influenced by the society within which the transsexual lives. The need for external validation of a person's sense of self varies from individual to individual, with the social acceptance of transsexuality varying across settings and times. It seems reasonable to state that surgery will most help those who can find both internal and external confirmation of their gender identities after the operation.

GENDER AND SEX AS SOCIAL CONSTRUCTS

Consider the following scenario and question:

> **A person who does not start menstruating as expected during adolescence goes to a physician to find out why. The physician discovers that this person—whose outward appearance [including no penis] and sense of self are both female—has no uterus or ovaries, but instead has male (XY) chromosomes. Is this person female or male?** (McKain, 1996. Reprinted with permission of the publisher.)

Did you hesitate to answer? Most people do. Why? Probably because being a boy or a girl is more complicated than having a single characteristic. More importantly, "Hesitation in answering the above question suggests how committed people are to the notion that everyone is *either* female *or* male, period. If people were not so wedded to this notion, they would simply respond that the person described above is female in some ways and male in others" (McKain, 1996).

Before we pursue this further, let us first reconsider what we mean by the terms *sex* and *gender* (see Laner, 2000). When people hear the word *sex,* most think of biological features (genitalia, reproductive organs, chromosomes, etc.) or an act (lovemaking, having sex). But what is *gender*? **Gender** (from the Latin *genus* and the Old French *gendre,* meaning "kind" or "sort"), according to Joan Scott (1986),

> **is a constitutive element of social relationships based on perceived differences between the sexes. (p. 1067)**

One text (Doyle, 1985) states that we may use the term gender

> *only* **when discussing social, cultural, and psychological aspects that pertain to the traits, norms, stereotypes and roles considered typical and desirable for those whom society has designated as male or female. (p. 9)**

Sandra Harding (1986) adds:

In virtually every culture, gender difference is a pivotal way in which humans identify themselves as persons, organize social relations, and symbolize meaningful natural and social events and processes. (p. 18)

In a point of view called *biological determinism,* biological influences are believed to set predetermined limits to the effects of cultural influences. The theory holds that there are two sexes, men and women, and thus two possible gender identities.

The concept of gender was adopted "to distinguish culturally specific characteristics associated with masculinity and femininity from biological features," and thus was used to repudiate biological determinism (Hawkesworth, 1997). In short, gender is not a natural category, but instead is the social construction of femininity and masculinity (Kessler & McKenna, 1978).

The important lesson from the first part of this chapter is that there is no direct relationship between sex and gender. You have been introduced to individuals with ambiguous genitalia and to others with unambiguous genitalia but whose gender identity did not correspond with their anatomical sex. Some other cultures recognize three sexes (Herdt, 1990), and at least one scholar has argued that we should recognize five different sexes (Fausto-Sterling, 1993). Today, use of the term *intersexed individuals* recognizes that sex is not dichotomous. In fact, Judith Butler (1990) has convinced many that sex, like gender, is also a social construct. She argues that both concepts can be challenged and changed in any manner.

The dualistic categories in biological determinism define individuals by their genitals. Quite simply, men have penises and women do not. All other sex/gender characteristics (e.g., lesbian, gay, masculine, feminine, transsexual) derive from this dichotomy. Today, the foremost proponent of this viewpoint is the medical profession. If you are not unambiguously a man or a woman in anatomy and have what society considers to be an appropriate gender identity, you are "abnormal." Consider again individuals born with ambiguous genitals. Well-intentioned physicians believed it was necessary to "assign" these individuals to one sex or the other and then perform "corrective" surgery.

Transsexualism offers another example. Even the official medical term, gender identity "disorder," implies a mistake that must be corrected to conform with the dichotomous model and the expectations of society (including doctors)—the expectation of sexual stereotypes (see Denny, 1998). To correct this, medicine offers sex "reassignment" surgery, so that an individual's anatomy and gender identity are in accord with society's expectations. Kessler and McKenna (1978)

transgender An individual whose gender roles are opposite of those that society expects based on his or her anatomy.

raise an interesting question: Is one's sex primary and gender secondary, or is it the other way around? Most people would probably agree with the former, but Kessler and McKenna point out that when transsexuals choose to "correct" their condition they change their body (their sex), not their gender (also see Diamond, 1998).

The medical field would counter that they are only trying to make transsexuals more comfortable, i.e., they surgically reassign only those individuals who ask to have it done. Many feminists and others counter that it is society and doctors that make transsexuals uncomfortable in the first place. Today, there are some organizations that actively work on helping intersexed and transsexual individuals accept themselves (e.g., Harry Benjamin International Gender Dysphoria Association; Intersexual Society of North America). In fact, more and more intersexed and transsexual individuals are choosing not to have genital-altering surgery (Palmer, 1999). Many of these individuals prefer to be described as **transgendered** because they believe it better describes themselves (i.e., someone having a gender role in a body opposite to society's expectations) (Denny, 1997). Most now agree that children born with ambiguous genitals should also be allowed to grow to an age when they can choose for themselves rather than have doctors assign them at birth. Why? Because, as Diamond (1998) puts it, "One's sexual identity is prenatally organized as a function of the genetic-endocrine forces," regardless of the appearance of the genitals. Perhaps Carla Golden (2000) sums it up best: "The natural attitude would certainly be . . . knowing that there are women with penises, and men with vulvas (p. 33)."

PSYCHOLOGICAL THEORIES OF GENDER IDENTITY DEVELOPMENT

In the previous sections, you learned that biology plays a major role in establishing one's gender identity. This is not to say that the environment has no effect. The two interact. It is likely that "nature sets a predisposition for these sexual developments and within such limits the environment works" (Diamond, 1997). Parents are obviously an important part of a child's environment. Three major psychological theories of development claim that the parent is an important role model who influences the development of gender identity.

FREUDIAN THEORY

Sigmund Freud believed that psychological development was influenced primarily by sexual development. He called sexual energy *libido* and thought that the location of the libido (the area of the body responsible for sexual pleasure) changed over time. The part of the body where the libido is focused is called an "erogenous zone." The primary erogenous zone, according to Freud, depends on which *stage of psychosexual development* the individual has reached. In the 1st year of life, the mouth is the primary erogenous zone, so Freud called this the *oral stage*. Pleasure is derived from sucking and from exploring things with the mouth.

The second stage is called the *anal stage,* which lasts from age 1½ to about age 3. According to Freud, the primary source of pleasure in this stage comes from holding in and expelling feces. Conflicts arise when parents attempt to teach their children to control their bowel movements in ways that are socially acceptable. Children at this time may fight parental control and toilet training.

The third stage, called the *phallic stage,* lasts from about age 3 to 5. Freud believed that gender identity is learned at this time. It is during this stage, according to Freud, that boys begin to derive pleasure through masturbation, and as they do so, they begin to sexually desire their mothers and come to view their fathers as powerful rivals who might punish them for these desires by taking away their penises. This fear is called "castration anxiety" and is based on the fact that previous sources of pleasure have already been taken away through weaning and toilet training. In addition, because girls and women do not have a penis, this further suggests to children that the penis may be taken away. Gender identity formation for boys takes place by resolving these conflicts, known as the *male Oedipus complex* (named after the principal character in the Greek play *Oedipus Rex,* in which a man kills the king of Thebes and then marries his queen, who turns out to be his own mother). Following the rule "If you can't beat them, join them," boys try to become like their fathers and adopt their fathers' gender identity. This process occurs unconsciously and is called **identification.** In this way, boys try to ensure that for the future, they, too, will be able to fulfill their sexual desires, just like their fathers.

Freud has a more complicated explanation for how gender identity is learned in girls. In the *female Oedipus complex,* according to Freud, when a girl realizes that she has no penis, she feels envious and angry, a state that he referred to as "penis envy." The girl blames her mother for this and wants to possess her father in order to replace the mother. Once she realizes that this cannot happen, she unconsciously identifies with her mother as a means of ensuring that she, too, will be able to fulfill her sexual desires in the future.

Most psychologists do not believe that Freud's theories are accurate descriptions of development. Many feel that his ideas are blatantly sexist and were the result of thinking founded on Victorian ideas of morality and sex roles (e.g., Lerman, 1986). Nevertheless, Freud was one of the first modern thinkers to discuss the possibility that children were sexual and to relate this to gender identity development.

SOCIAL LEARNING THEORY

Social learning theory emphasizes the acquisition of new associations. An important type of learning that may be involved in acquiring gender roles is that of **operant conditioning,** which is based on the principle that an individual's behavior is modified by the consequences of the behavior. For example, a boy may be praised by a parent for "acting like a man" and not crying after he falls down; he may be yelled at or punished for putting on his mother's lipstick; or he may be allowed to stop doing his homework in order to help his father fix the car. In each of these three examples, the boy is being reinforced to behave in a "masculine manner." He is learning a gender identity and a gender role, and he will associate good things with "masculine behavior" and negative things (even punishment) with "feminine behavior." For a girl, encouragement and praise may follow the display of "feminine behavior," while "boyish behavior" may result in being ignored or being shown disapproval by parents. Thus, behaviors that are reinforced will continue, and behaviors that are not reinforced will eventually stop.

Research with children shows that they do not alway have to perform a behavior to learn it (Bandura & Walters, 1963). Most young boys observe their mothers putting on lipstick, but may never do it themselves because they learn from observing others that such behavior in boys is met with ridicule or other punishment.

According to social learning theorists, another way children learn gender stereotyped behavior is by **imitating models** of people of their own sex. For example, children love to imitate their parents and learn what "daddy" and "mommy" do simply by watching their parents. It is always interesting to ask children, "What kinds of things are daddies supposed to do?" and "What kinds of things do mommies do?" "Do daddies wash dishes?" "Do mommies use a saw and hammer nails?" Answers to these questions will tell a lot about the gender roles that children learn from their parents. (How did you answer these questions?) Children also will try to do the things that their parents and other role models do (i.e., imitate them), although the amount of time between when the behavior is observed and when they eventually imitate it can be long (Figure 10–7).

Operant conditioning and social learning theory do not have to be competing theories. Imitation may cause a child to

identification The adoption of the sex roles of the same-sex parent by a child. In Freudian theory, identification resolves the Oedipus complex.

operant conditioning A type of learning in which an individual's behavior is modified by the consequences of the behavior.

imitation Following the behaviors of someone taken as one's model.

Figure 10–7 Children often learn gender roles and a gender identity by observing and imitating their same-sex parents.

try a specific behavior for the first time, but the rewards or punishments that follow that behavior will determine whether the child attempts the behavior again (B. F. Skinner, personal communication).

COGNITIVE-DEVELOPMENTAL THEORY

Cognitive theory views infants as "information seekers." Rather than talking about an "oral stage of psychosexual development" to explain why crawling infants put things into their mouths, cognitive theory claims that this is done because infants can "know" things and acquire information about the world this way. To a crawling infant without language, the world can be divided into things that can and cannot be put in the mouth. It can also be known in terms of things that taste good, bad, or have no taste. Sex is another category into which children can sort themselves.

This theory (Kohlberg, 1966) states that the concept of "male" is first learned by observing others. For example, a boy's father is a man, and because a boy is more like his father than his mother, he begins to think of himself and his father as males. Boys become motivated to seek out information about what boys and men should do and how he should behave, imitating a ready source of information about male conduct from their fathers. The mother becomes the prime source of information about what is appropriate "female behavior" for girls.

At this early age, children's idea of gender is "concrete," based on physical cues like hair-style and dress. Cognitive theorists say that while most children have learned that they are a "boy" or a "girl" by the age of 3, they do not yet have an understanding of gender constancy. **Gender constancy** is the knowledge that one's sex is constant and will not change. For example, a 4-year-old boy may think that since girls have long hair, if he lets his hair grow long he will change into a girl. A 4-year-old girl may believe that when she wears jeans and a football helmet, she is a boy, but when she takes them off, she changes back into a girl again. Because they do not yet have an understanding of gender constancy, young boys may say that they will become mommies when they grow up and girls may say they'll be daddies. This is a natural thing to believe until gender constancy has been acquired, which *usually happens by age 6 or 7*. According to cognitive developmentalists, once a child has acquired the concept of gender constancy, he or she actively seeks information about his or her own gender.

Stagnor and Ruble (1987) point out that cognitive theory is similar to psychoanalytic theory in that both describe development as occurring in stages. Both describe a "motivation" to complete development. In psychoanalytic theory, identification is driven by the need to reduce anxiety and maintain a good self-image. In cognitive theory, the motivation is a need to attain mastery over the behaviors typical of one's gender.

Both cognitive theory and social learning theory claim that imitation is extremely important in development. But social learning theory states that behavior is based on the rewards that will follow. Cognitive theory

gender constancy The knowledge that one's sex is constant and will not change. This knowledge is usually acquired by age 6 or 7.

claims that people behave in certain ways because the behavior is rewarding in itself. In other words, social learning theory states that gender understanding occurs because of the learning process. Cognitive theory states that a need to understand one's gender causes a child to want to learn (Stagnor & Ruble, 1987).

GENDER ROLES

THEORIES OF GENDER ROLE

Recall that **gender role** is a set of *culturally specific* norms about the expected behaviors and attitudes of men and women. Gender roles vary from culture to culture (see Box 10–A). Another term you will see in this section is **gender-role identity**—"a concept devised to capture the extent to which a person approves of and participates in feelings and behaviors deemed to be appropriate to his or her culturally constituted gender" (Hawkesworth, 1997). For example, girls with adrenogenital syndrome might have a clear sense of themselves as girls (gender identity), but be unhappy with and refuse to behave in accord with our culture's norms of femininity.

Risman and Schwartz (1989) describe two major perspectives on gender-role development: individualist theory and microstructural theory. **Individualist theory** is based on the idea that an individual's personality is created relatively early in life. There is a set of personality traits developed early on that do not change much over the life cycle; these traits then determine an individual's expression of masculine or feminine behavior. Thus, a woman may choose not to enter a "masculine" career, such as welding, because she cannot be motivated to start such a career. Her personality structure and self-concept prevent her from making such a choice.

Microstructural theory, on the other hand, is based on the notion that it is society's expectations of male and female behavior that predict how people will behave. Thus, rather than believing that masculinity or femininity is expressed because of internal forces such as rigid personality traits, microstructural theory assumes that men and women would behave identically if society had identical expectations of them. Gender-role differences are therefore constructed by the way men and women interact within their environment and with each other. Furthermore, the nature of these interactions can change over time and in different settings.

In the introduction to this chapter, you learned that prior to the 1970s, masculinity and femininity were viewed as opposite ends of a unidimensional continuum (Hathaway & McKinley, 1943; Strong, 1936; Terman & Miles, 1936). In this bipolar model, a person who was high in masculinity would have to be low in femininity, and vice versa.

This conceptualization of masculinity and femininity was revolutionized in 1973 by Anne Constantinople, who proposed that masculinity and femininity were independent constructs. This led to the theory of androgyny, which said that a person could be both masculine and feminine, and that this was the healthiest of all gender roles (Bem, 1974; Spence et al., 1975). As Bohan (1993) put it, "Thus, none of us is feminine or masculine or fails to be either of those. In particular contexts, people do feminine; in others, they do masculine." According to Sandra Bem (1974), "Both historically and cross-culturally, masculinity and femininity seem to have represented two complementary domains of positive traits and behaviors, a cognitive focus on 'getting the job done' (a masculine or *instrumental* orientation) and 'an affective concern for the welfare of others' (a feminine or *expressive* orientation)."

Androgynous individuals are viewed by these researchers as being healthy because of their flexibility, demonstrating instrumental or expressive orientations as the situation demands. They are described as being

> **behaviorally flexible with respect to all manner of gender related phenomena. As such, they are willing and able to exhibit masculine behaviors, feminine behaviors, or both as situationally appropriate. Individuals with sex-typed personalities, on the other hand, will tend to avoid or exhibit lower levels of cross-sex-typed behaviors.** (Helmreich et al., 1979)

More recently there have been some challenges to the dualistic theory of gender and some questions about androgyny. One study, for example, found support for both the dualistic and unidimensional models. Biernat (1991) studied the development of gender stereotypes in social judgments about others and concluded that young children view gender in dualistic terms, but that as they grow older they come to view gender as a unidimensional construct. Others have even questioned the Bem Sex-Role Inventory, the most popular measure of androgyny. One study found that while the items on the inventory did, in fact, measure two different personality characteristics, the two characteristics no longer had anything to do with masculinity and femininity—the authors of the study suggested the terms **instrumental** and **expressive** (Ballard-Reisch & Elton, 1992). One possibility is that people's perceptions of gender roles have changed over the last 20 years. Recent studies have, in fact, found that while the Bem Sex-Role Inventory is still valid, perceptions of traditional gender

gender The social construction of femininity and masculinity.

gender-role identity The extent to which a person approves of and participates in feelings and behaviors deemed to be appropriate to his or her culturally constituted gender.

individualist theory The theory that personality traits develop early in life and do not change much over the life cycle; these traits then determine an individual's expression of masculine or feminine behavior.

microstructural theory A theory that stresses the role of the external environment in shaping gender roles.

instrumental A personality characteristic; a cognitive focus on "getting the job done."

expressive A personality characteristic; a cognitive focus on "an affective concern for the welfare of others."

roles have weakened a bit (Holt & Ellis, 1998). Interestingly, Bem (1979) predicted the destruction of the concept of androgyny:

> If there is a moral to the concept of psychological androgyny, it is that behavior should have no gender. But there is an irony here, for the concept of androgyny contains an inner contradiction and hence the seeds of its own destruction. Thus, as the etymology of the word implies, the concept of androgyny necessarily presupposes that the concepts

of femininity and masculinity themselves have distinct and substantive content. But to the extent that the androgynous message is absorbed by the culture, the concepts of femininity and masculinity will cease to have such content and the distinctions to which they refer will blur into invisibility. Thus, when androgyny becomes a reality, the concept of androgyny will have been transcended.

A quick reading of Box 10–A makes it obvious that when it comes to "acting like a man" or "acting

Box 10–A CROSS-CULTURAL PERSPECTIVES

Gender Roles

Today in the United States, boys and girls are often treated differently beginning at birth. Consider, for example, the blue or pink name tags that many hospitals use to designate a baby boy or girl. However, this was not always the case. Until the early part of the 20th century, infant boys and girls were treated very much alike in things like dress (both wore gowns) and hairstyle (long curls). The socialization process of emphasizing masculine or feminine qualities did not begin until the age of 2 or 3 (Garber, 1991).

Some other cultures do not emphasize differences between boys and girls for several years after birth. Some African cultures even have nonmasculine titles (e.g., "woman-child") for boys (Whiting, 1979). In these cultures there is usually a ritualized initiation ceremony for boys (generally between the ages of 7 and 12) to eliminate any identification with female gender roles and to emphasize male alliance and gender roles (Munroe, 1980). These rituals often include painful practices such as circumcision of the penis (see Box 2–C). Some of these cultures have rituals for girls as well, and usually focus on their role in fertility (Schlegel & Barry, 1980). However, there are other cultures that allow even grown men to express their "feminine" side, often in a practice called *couvade* in which men are secluded (like women) and act out giving birth (Paige & Paige, 1981; Whiting, 1979).

Completely opposite gender roles can sometimes be found in cultures living in close proximity to one another. Margaret Mead (1935, 1975), for example, described a tribe in New Guinea, the Tchambuli, in which men were considered too weak to do hard physical labor; were emotional, gossipy, and easily embarrassed; and

were primarily artistic in their activities. In that culture, women were independent, aggressive, and made all the important tribal decisions. In another New Guinea culture, the Arapesh, qualities that many Americans would consider "feminine" are reinforced in both men and women. As a result, Arapesh men and women are peaceful, cooperative, and nurturing. Just 80 miles away, in the Mundugumor society, "both men and women are expected to be violent, competitive, aggressively sexed, jealous, and ready to see and avenge insult, delighting in display, in action, in fighting" (Mead, 1935). What did Mead conclude?

> Many, if not all, of the personality traits which we have called masculine or feminine are as lightly linked to sex as are the clothing, the manners, and the form of head-dress that a society at a given period assigned to either sex. . . . The evidence is overwhelmingly in favor of social conditioning.

Admittedly, to this point I have selected a few extreme examples. In nearly all cultures, whether emphasis of differences begins in infancy or later in childhood, the large majority emphasize nurturant behavior in women and achievement and self-reliance in men. In a study of 24 culturally diverse countries, Williams and Best (1990) found that 5-year-old children from all countries believed that men were strong and aggressive and women were weak and softhearted. By the time they were 8, their beliefs were even more stereotyped. The conclusion: belief in gender stereotypes not only increases with age in all countries, but the same stereotypes can be found in nearly all countries (though to different degrees) (see Gibbons, 2000, for a review).

like a woman," there is a wide range of behaviors that can be affected by culture. In this section you will learn how one's culture works to shape gender.

GENDER-ROLE DEVELOPMENT DURING CHILDHOOD

Regardless of the particular theory that researchers support on how gender identity and gender roles are acquired, they do agree that this process occurs and that society's expectations become a part of the individual's own set of attitudes and behaviors. The process of internalizing society's beliefs is called **socialization,** which begins at birth (e.g., different colors are used to represent a baby boy and a baby girl).

What kinds of attitudes do children learn from our society about gender roles? Cognitive theory, described earlier, shows that young children have difficulty understanding complex concepts. Their early learning often consists of dual categories, such as "good and bad" or "big and small." It is not surprising, then, that young children's ideas about gender roles reflect concrete, simple ideas, dividing behaviors or traits into either "masculine" or "feminine." In our society, there are *gender-role stereotypes.* **Stereotypes,** you recall, are oversimplified, preconceived beliefs that supposedly apply to anyone in a given group.

The stereotype for the female gender role is that of a person who nurtures and cares for others; is passive, dependent, and cooperative; seeks social approval; and is expressive in showing her emotions. The male gender-role stereotype emphasizes independence, dominance, competition, aggression, success, achievement, and emotional repression (recall the belief that "big boys don't cry" and the expression "the strong, silent type") (Murray, 1999). Most people believe that men and women differ in these ways (Doyle & Paludi, 1991).

Harvard psychologist Jerome Kagan has said, "If I showed you a hundred kids aged 2, and you couldn't tell the sex by the haircuts, you couldn't tell if they were boys or girls" (quoted in Shapiro, 1990). If this is true, when do gender roles start developing, and what (or who) is responsible?

Parents who assume "traditional" (stereotypic) gender roles behave differently toward their children (Ex & Janssens, 1998). In these families, mothers act as the caregivers, while the fathers act as playmates to their infants. Fathers, however, may be more likely to treat their children in gender-stereotyped ways (Leve & Fagot, 1997). Fathers emphasize the strength and coordination of their newborn sons and the beauty and softness of their newborn daughters (Krieger, 1976). This is

done in spite of there being little difference between the behavior of newborn boys and girls. Fathers are also more likely to offer toys that are stereotypically male to their newborn sons (Jacklin & Maccoby, 1983).

In one study, preschoolers were presented with stereotypic gender-role toys. In one condition, children were given toys that matched stereotypic toys for their own gender. However, in another condition boys were asked to play with dolls or kitchen sets the way girls would, while girls were asked to play with army war toys or cowboy outfits the way boys would. This was done while parents were out of the room. The experimenters were interested in studying how the parents would react when they entered the room and saw the types of toys the children were playing with. Mothers reacted similarly, regardless of whether the toys fit gender-role stereotypes or not, but fathers showed markedly more negative reactions when they found their children playing with toys that did not fit gender roles. This was especially true when boys were playing with "girls'" toys: the fathers often interfered with their sons' play and showed other signs of negative emotions in those situations (Langlois & Downs, 1980) (see Figure 10–8).

"My godson, Mikey, will definitely grow up with the idea that men are the head of the households and that women are 'under' them. My uncle encourages Mikey to play football and run around in the house, yet when he and his sister dance around it is not acceptable. Mikey is only allowed to play 'boy' games. He is not allowed to cook, because that is what a girl does."

"For as far back as I can remember my father only allowed us to do 'masculine' type things. Sports, cars, outdoor activities, etc. He never allowed us to play with girls. On one occasion I distinctly remember playing with two girl neighbors. My father came looking for me and found his son playing with dolls. For quite a while after that I was known as his 'faggot son.' I couldn't have been more than 10. I never became the 'faggot' son, but I did leave that day with a low self-esteem that I carried with me for quite some time."   (All examples are from the author's files.)

Other adults treat boys and girls in different ways as well. In another study, individuals were shown an infant and asked to make observations about its appearance and behavior. The types of comments

socialization The process of internalizing society's beliefs; the manner in which a society shapes individual behaviors and expectations of behaviors.

stereotypes Oversimplified, preconceived beliefs that supposedly apply to anyone in a given group.

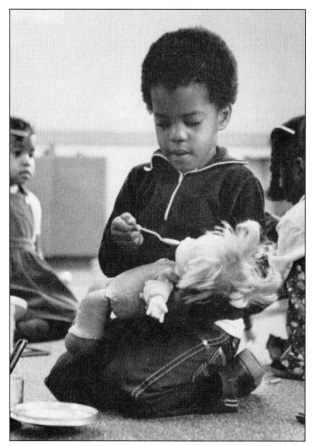

Figure 10–8 How would you react if you found your young son playing with a doll? Do you think that playing with dolls can teach boys behaviors that will be useful when they become adults?

made were very different, depending on whether they were told the infant was a boy or a girl (Condry & Condry, 1977). The socialization process in gender-role development is seen everywhere in the child's environment. Children's toy catalogs often use pink pages to show toys for girls' and blue pages for boys' toys (Haffner & Casselman, 1996). The toys available for boys are often action-oriented, while girls are given more passive playthings. Take a walk through a toy store and look at the toys being offered. It is interesting to see how toys are packaged. Many have pictures of children playing with the product on the front of the box. How many toys have pictures of both boys and girls playing with the same toy? (Very few.) Have you ever wondered why boys' bicycles have to be different from girls' bicycles? (They don't.)

Here is a little experiment that you can try on your own. Ask a boy playing with a toy soldier or a plastic model of a superhero if he is playing with dolls. He probably will say "no." (Boys in our culture

gender schemas Ideas about gender roles that children create from their interactions with their environment.

don't often play with dolls, but they do play with "action figures.") Give the boy a toy soldier and a male "fashion figure," such as the one who usually serves as a "boyfriend" to a famous female doll, and then ask the boy to point to the toys that are dolls. He will probably point to the "fashion figure." Now give the soldier's clothes (and weapons) to the "fashion figure" and have the soldier wear the other toy's clothes (and accessories). Then ask the question again. Which one will the boy now think is the doll? What do you think? Why?

Some psychologists think that boys should learn at an early age how to care for infants by playing with baby dolls. Learning at an early age how to put on diapers and the like can help make a man respond in a more useful way after a real baby is born. Some fathers refuse to change diapers because (1) it is disgusting work, and (2) it is "women's work." It is true that changing diapers can sometimes be disgusting, but it is also necessary. It is not true that this is "women's work." If a man can change the dirty oil in his car, he should be able to manage changing a dirty diaper. Women should also remember that the same holds true for them. Girls can learn to use tools and change the car oil just as easily as they can learn to change diapers. Dirty oil and dirty diapers are neither masculine nor feminine. They just need to be changed.

The socialization process begins at an early age. As early as 14 months of age, infants play with toys that are gender stereotyped more often than with other toys (O'Brien & Huston, 1985). In one study, it was found that boys aged 2½ believed that girls don't fight and that they like to clean house. Girls of the same age believed that boys don't cry and that they like to fight. Boys and girls aged 2 and 3 believed that boys like to help their dads, like to hit, and like to break the rules. They thought that girls liked to help their moms and didn't hit (Kuhn et al., 1978). Thus, children show gender-stereotyped behavior even before they have a firm grasp of gender identity or gender constancy.

Sandra Bem (1981, 1983) has proposed that children cognitively organize the world according to gender. She calls this a **gender schema**—a set of ideas about gender roles that children create from their interactions with their environment. Objects in the environment are often treated as masculine or feminine. Why, for example, do we often regard dogs as masculine and cats as feminine? Languages such as French or Spanish classify all nouns as either masculine or feminine. Gender schemas can influence decisions about what activities to take part in or learn about, including things like affection, which really has nothing to do with one's sexual anatomy. Unfortunately, many American men regard displays of affection as effeminate, even toward their own children (see Salt, 1991):

"I know my father cares about his children, but he never displays any kind of affection toward me (male) or my brother, only to my sisters. I think that is one big experience that I missed during my childhood." (from the author's files)

Children organize their world according to gender starting at age 2 or 3 (Hort et al., 1991). In fact, it may be the first social category used by children (Kohlberg & Ullian, 1974). Bem (1983) concludes that "gender has come to have cognitive primacy over many other social categories because the culture has made it so."

Gender roles are usually learned first in the home, but when children reach school age peers and teachers

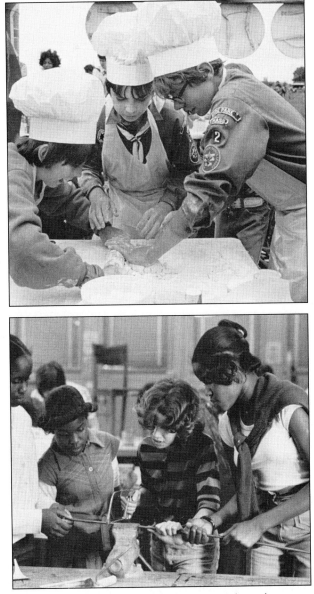

Figure 10–9 In the past, traditional gender-role expectations would never have allowed these boys and girls to enjoy these experiences.

become powerful reinforcers of the process of socialization and gender-role development (Fagot, 1995; Moller et al., 1992). The activities and chores that teachers assign to children in the classroom are often determined by stereotypic gender roles (Sadker & Sadker, 1994). Children quickly identify individuals who act "different." Boys or girls who do not display behaviors similar to the gender roles adopted by most of their peers may be singled out for teasing or ridicule. Interestingly, "tomboy" behavior in girls is usually far more tolerated by peers, teachers, and parents than "effeminate" behavior in boys. It is much easier to carry the label of a "tomboy" than that of a "sissy." Peers will apply great social pressure against boys who show "girlish" behavior (Birns & Sternglanz, 1983). Children generally prefer playmates of the same sex (Powlishta et al., 1993), but if they have to choose, boys prefer girls with masculine play styles to boys with feminine play styles (Alexander & Hines, 1994). As boys and girls approach junior high school age, they tend to participate less in girl-dominated activities and more in male-dominated activities (Sandberg & Meyer-Bahlburg, 1994).

Textbooks and history books in particular have emphasized the central, dominant role of men and the supporting role of women, but there has been some change in recent years. A recent analysis of third-grade basal readers found that male characters are still portrayed as having mostly masculine traits, but that female characters have evolved from having mostly feminine traits to having a balance of masculine and feminine traits (Witt, 1996). Organized religion also acts as a socializing agent about gender roles (Eitzen & Zinn, 2000). In almost all religions there is an underlying philosophy of male superiority, and church leadership is almost always dominated by men.

Gender roles in adolescents have begun to change in recent years. For example, it is now more common for girls to ask boys out. One study found that while it was once rare (and considered improper) for girls to call boys on the telephone, it is now very common (Anderson et al., 1995). The authors were able to identify 1965–1980 as the period in which this gender role changed.

In spite of some changes away from the traditional gender-role expectations, stereotypic gender roles are often still in force during puberty and are reinforced by peer pressure (Doyle, 1985). For example, many teenage girls still view being popular and attractive to boys as the primary way to enhance their self-worth. For many teenage boys, achievement in athletics and/or in career-related activities is the primary means of gaining self-esteem .

Recently it was proposed that many of the gender differences in social behavior are due to a difference in *self-construals* (the manner in which men and women view themselves) (Cross & Madson, 1997). Men, the authors claimed, view themselves as independent, while women define themselves in terms of their relationships with others (interdependency). Others, however, have pointed out that children begin displaying gender-related behaviors before they develop a sense of self (Martin & Ruble, 1997).

PERSONAL REFLECTIONS
How would you react if your teenage son wanted to take home economics instead of machine shop or auto mechanics? Why? How would you react if your teenage daughter wanted to take machine shop or auto mechanics instead of home economics? Why?

I will refer to two recent studies to help summarize what we know about the development of gender roles in childhood and adolescence. There may be little noticeable difference between boys and girls before the age of 2, but there is no question that most children have embraced gender stereotypes by the age of 4. By the age of 3 or 4, children know sex stereotypes about clothing, toys, games, and work, and by the age of 4 or 5 most have stereotyped occupational goals (Huston, 1983). According to Yale psychiatrist Kyle Pruett, "There are rules about being feminine and there are rules about being masculine. You can argue until the cows come home about whether those are good or bad societal influences, but when you look at the children, they love to know the differences. It solidifies who they are" (quoted in Shapiro, 1990).

However, Pruett's own work shows that children don't necessarily have to develop strongly stereotyped views (see Shapiro, 1990, for a review). He followed the development of children in 16 families where the mothers worked full-time and the fathers were mostly responsible for caring for the children. The children had strong gender identities of being a boy or a girl, but more relaxed views of gender roles than their friends. Pruett commented, "I saw the boys really enjoy their nurturing skills. They knew what to do with a baby, they didn't see that as a girl's job, they saw it as a human job. I saw the girls have very active images of the outside world and what their mothers were doing in the workplace." (quoted in Shapiro, 1990).

Pruett also feels that fathers benefit by assuming more responsibility in raising their children. He says, "The more involved father tends to feel differently about his own life. A lot of men, if they're on the fast track, know a lot about competitive relationships, but they don't know much about intimate relationships. Children are experts at intimacy. After a while the wives in my study would say, 'He's just a nicer guy'" (Shapiro, 1990).

The second study investigated how, and to what extent, young children and adolescents use gender stereotypes to make judgments about the characteristics of male and female individuals (Biernat, 1991). It was found that young people rely on gender labels as judgment cues to the same degree from kindergarten to the college years, but that as they grow older, they increasingly rely on more individuating information as well. In other words, as people grow older, they are more able to rely on information about an individual to make judgments, even when the information is not consistent with stereotyped gender roles.

GENDER-ROLE DEVELOPMENT IN CHILDREN RAISED IN SINGLE-PARENT HOUSEHOLDS

The traditional American family has been declining in number since the 1960s. In 1970, 87 percent of children lived with two parents, but in 1996 less than 70 percent did so. This was especially true among African Americans. One-third of all black children lived with one parent in 1970, but by 1996 nearly two-thirds lived with one parent—their mother in all but a few cases (Bianchi & Spain, 1996).

What happens to the development of gender roles in children raised by a single parent? Several early studies concluded that a critical factor in gender-role development was the identification of children with their fathers, by either interacting with their fathers or by watching their parents interact (Biller & Bahm, 1971; Roberts et al., 1987). Recall, too, that fathers are more concerned than mothers that their children act in gender-stereotyped ways. Adults in single-parent families have less traditional (less stereotyped) attitudes than adults in two-parent families (Leve & Fagot, 1997). So what happens to children raised in a household in which the father is absent? In brief, children who are raised in single-parent households are more likely than those raised in "intact" households to become androgynous (Russell & Ellis, 1991). This is true not only for boys but for girls as well.

Androgyny is generally considered to be a positive characteristic (see next section). If so, one study concluded that "parents who model adaptive yet nontraditional roles may play an important role in the healthy development of their children" (Russell & Ellis, 1991).

ROLE OF THE MEDIA

All television is educational; the only question is : what is it teaching? (Federal Communications Commissioner Nicholas Johnson)

In Chapter 9 you learned that the media, particularly television, are powerful socializing agents in shaping our culture's attitudes about sex. What about gender roles? Do the media contribute to gender-role stereotypes? The answer is definitely yes.

Exposure to stereotypes on television begins in early childhood. For several decades television cartoons have portrayed boy characters as active, noisy, and aggressive, and girl characters as concerned about their appearance, domestic, attracted to boys, and often in need of rescue (Streicher, 1974; Barcus, 1983). What's more, young children are aware of these differences and perceive the characters in stereotypical ways (Thompson & Zerbinos, 1997).

Sex-role stereotyping is common even in FCC-mandated children's educational television (Barner, 1999). This includes *Sesame Street* (Media Report to Women, 1993). Most of the central characters are active, dominant boys or men who carry out plans and who receive consequences for their behavior. Women and girls, on the other hand, are commonly portrayed as dependent and nurturing and receive no consequences for their behavior (i.e., they are ignored).

These same stereotypes are common in prime-time television shows targeted for teenagers and adult audiences. A 1997 survey by the Kaiser Family Foundation and Children Now found that female roles on television typically emphasize romance more than work, and beauty more than intelligence, as the main thing by which women are valued. TV shows such as *ER, Law and Order,* and *The X-Files* have women in lead roles that are strong and dominant, but these tend to be the exception rather than the rule.

Television advertisements frequently use stereotyped characters (Furnham & Mak, 1999). Men are much more likely to be shown as the authoritative central figure (and white men more so than black men), while women generally assume dependent rules. Even the settings are stereotypical. Men are often shown in outdoor leisure activities, while women are most likely to be shown at home.

Does television's portrayal of characters in stereotyped roles affect viewers? You might not be surprised to learn that people who watch a lot of TV generally believe in more stereotyped gender roles (Lips, 1992).

> *PERSONAL REFLECTIONS*
> *Watch several television shows. Notice the gender roles that are presented for men and for women. What do you feel should be changed, if anything?*

WHAT CAUSES DEVELOPMENTAL GENDER DIFFERENCES?

There is little question that boys and girls differ and that these developmental gender differences appear early in childhood. What causes these differences? For this question, there is considerable debate. On one side are the "social structuralists" (there is no agreed-upon name for this group), who claim that the social structure leads to psychological sex differences (Eagly & Wood, 1999). The basis of this theory was stated as early as 1903 by psychologist Helen Bradford Thompson:

> The psychological differences of sex seem to be largely due, not to difference of average capacity, nor to difference in type of mental activity, but to differences in the social influences brought to bear on the developing individual from early infancy to adult years. (p. 102)

Eagly and Wood (1999) conclude that behavioral differences between boys and girls result from physical differences, which are then influenced by social factors (social structure, cultural beliefs, etc.).

There can be no denying that there are basic physical differences between men and women. This includes not only bone structure and muscle mass but hormonal differences as well. For example, men have much higher levels of testosterone than women, which is related to aggression and dominance (Mazur & Booth, 1998).

Sociobiologists and evolutionary psychologists believe that behavioral differences have evolutionary value. In Chapter 12, for example, you will learn that, regardless of culture, men and women prefer different qualities in a long-term mate (Buss, 1989). Men prefer physical attractiveness, whereas women prefer good providers (see Box 12–A). According to sociobiologists, this has adaptive value in evolution. Geary (1999) has proposed that gender differences in childhood also have adaptive value from an evolutionary perspective. He says, for example, that rough and tumble (and competitive) play among boys prepares them for male-male competition for women as adults. Girls, on the other hand, engage in play parenting and developing social skills, attributes that will aid them as adults. In other words, according to Geary the function of childhood is to develop competencies that will aid them in reproduction and survival as adults.

Far more research has been conducted by the social structuralists, and this chapter focuses on that approach. However, before we leave this subject of gender differences, perhaps a third voice should be heard:

> As long as the categories 'female' and 'male' present themselves to people in everyday life as external, objective, dichotomous, physical facts, there will be scientific and naive searches for differences, and differences will be found. Where there are dichotomies it is difficult to avoid evaluating one in relation to the other, a firm foundation for discrimination and oppression. (Kessler & McKenna, 1978)

GENDER-ROLE DEVELOPMENT IN ADULTHOOD

Among adults today, gender roles are in transition. Women have not only entered the work force in larger numbers but have gained entry into careers and attained access to higher-level positions previously dominated by men. In 1960, fewer than 20 percent of all women with children under the age of 6 were employed outside the home, but in 1996, two-thirds of women with young children were in the labor force and 80 percent of all

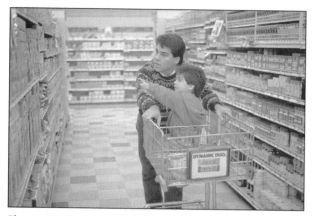

Figure 10–10 Husbands devote more time to domestic duties today than in the past, but they still do less than their wives (even when the wives are employed outside the home).

mothers with school-age children had jobs outside the home (Bianchi & Spain, 1996). In addition, over half of the bachelor's and master's degrees awarded today are to women; 38 percent of all Ph.D.'s are awarded to women, up from only 11 percent in 1960 (Bianchi & Spain, 1996). As a result of this movement by large numbers of women into the work force, attitudes about men and women and jobs/careers have become much more egalitarian, especially among younger generations (Brewster & Padavic, 2000; Spence & Hahn, 1997). Thus, the idea that being a mother means not having a career is no longer true and is not influencing women to the extent it did in the past.

Nonetheless, gender stereotypes may not have changed much since the 1960s, and double standards often still exist, even in two-career families. For example, even if a woman works outside the home, she generally assumes much more responsibility for housecleaning, meals, and child care than does her male partner (Baxter & Western, 1998; Bianchi & Spain, 1996). While some men, especially African-American men, are spending more time doing housework than in the past (John & Shelton, 1997), overall the contribution made by men has not changed in 20 years (Bird, 1999). When husbands do participate in domestic chores, women are happier with them (Baxter & Western, 1998), but men with traditional stereotyped attitudes are likely to evaluate their marriages negatively if "forced" into egalitarian roles (McHale & Crouter, 1992).

PERSONAL REFLECTIONS
Men: Your wife has decided to resume postgraduate studies leading to a career. This will require that she be away from home more than before and that you assume more responsibilities for care of the house and children. Your reaction?

Women: Your husband has decided to pass up a career opportunity (leading to higher rank and salary) to spend more time at home with the children. Your reaction?

Women who work in the home may not have the same chance for self-gratification or self-fulfillment as men, who often serve as both breadwinners and heads of households. Many people still consider work in the home to be "not as important" as work outside the home. Younger and more educated women are especially likely to find little satisfaction in housework (Baxter & Western, 1998). In 1990, for example, students at Wellesley College objected to then–First Lady Barbara Bush giving the commencement address because she had been a stay-at-home wife and mother. According to a 1990 survey conducted for *Time* magazine, 86 percent of the young men surveyed wanted a mate who was hardworking and ambitious (Gibbs et al., 1990). While the same survey found that nearly half of the young men wanted to spend more time at home to raise their children, the number of "house-husbands," whose primary responsibility is work in the home, remains small. Career achievement is still used to determine the worth of individuals, rather than the ability to maintain a home and care for others.

What is considered to be masculine and feminine in adult gender roles is becoming far less rigid and distinct than was true for past generations. Some researchers see these trends as a movement toward androgyny. As you recall, androgyny is the ability of individuals, regardless of gender, to display a variety of personality characteristics, so that the same person can be both assertive and compassionate, both instrumental and expressive, and both masculine and feminine, depending on whether a trait or behavior is appropriate for a given situation. Thus, androgyny is often viewed as a positive characteristic that gives an individual greater adaptability (Spence et al., 1975).

Taylor and Hall (1982) concluded that in American society, androgynous or masculine individuals show greater social adaptation and adjustment, regardless of their gender. They believe, for example, that women who show masculine characteristics may initially not be rewarded for acting that way, but those who continue to do so are eventually given greater rewards and prestige than women with mostly feminine characteristics. In a now classic study, Spence and Helmreich (1972) found that people liked women best who were competent and doing "masculine" things. In a recent review of numerous studies, it was found that the difference between men and women on measurements of masculinity and femininity had, in fact, decreased since the early 1970s (Twenge, 1997). However, the change was not due to men becoming more androgynous (having more feminine traits), but had resulted from women displaying more masculine-stereotyped traits than in the past.

Nevertheless, the push for gender equality has taken its toll on some individuals. Rotheram and Weiner (1983) found that among dual-career couples, dual-career status increased satisfaction with the relationship, but also increased personal stress. By 1990, 80 percent of those in a *Time* magazine survey believed that it was "difficult" or "very difficult" to balance marriage, children, and a career (the 1980s "superwoman" ideal), and, in a shift from previous surveys, many women rated a happy marriage as more important to them than a successful career (see Gibbs et al., 1990). It is obvious that different women can have the same roles (mother, wife, worker), yet have different experiences of the quality of each (Baruch & Barnett, 1986).

Some researchers have noted that as individuals develop as adults, they acquire more complex sets of gender roles. For example, the fact of fatherhood may force men to acquire more experience in being nurturing, while working outside the home may force women to become more assertive and independent. The more complexity there is in gender-role patterns of behavior, the greater the chance for integration of gender roles (Labouvie-Vief, 1990). Although men and women arrive at developmental complexity by different routes, the adaptive end point for both genders is an integration of gender roles; that is, gender roles tend to converge in adulthood (see Blanchard-Fields & Suhrer-Roussel, 1992). Thus, gender-role development extends well into adulthood with cross-gender-role characteristics (i.e., behavior of the opposite sex) often emerging among both older men and women. Individuals with a large number of both masculine and feminine characteristics will then be better able to cope with a wide range of life challenges and social situations than will those individuals with a more rigid or narrow range of gender-role patterns of behavior.

> *PERSONAL REFLECTIONS*
> *Have you ever considered marriage? If so, what traits do you want in a husband or wife? Are these the same traits you will want in your partner after you become parents? Is your answer consistent with your answers to the previous questions?*

GENDER ROLES AND SEXUAL RELATIONS

Victorian-era physicians and sexologists such as Sigmund Freud and Henry Havelock Ellis believed that male and female sexuality were very different. Female sexuality was viewed as more passive, weaker, and less fulfilling than male sexuality. Many Victorian physicians did not even believe that women had orgasms, as you may recall (see Chapter 4). More recently, Kinsey's surveys (1948, 1953) and the physiological studies by Masters and Johnson (1966) have emphasized that male and female sexuality are very similar. However, there is still some debate. A recent review concluded that women have a milder sex drive than men (Baumeister, 2000). As evidence, the

author provided studies showing that, compared to men, women thought of sex less often, had fewer sexual fantasies, and masturbated less frequently. However, this could be due to being raised in a repressive culture. In another review of numerous mammalian species, it was found that the females are highly sexual, and promiscuous (Birkhead, 2000). Female chimpanzees, for example, have sex up to 1,000 times for each pregnancy, with multiple partners. Among humans, another study found that there were, in fact, no gender differences in sexual satisfaction (Oliver & Hyde, 1993).

Everyone agrees that there are still some gender differences. As a general rule, men have considerably more permissive attitudes about casual sex than do most women (Oliver & Hyde, 1993). As might be expected, women with egalitarian gender-role attributes (i.e., those who would show some "masculine" personality traits on the Bem Sex-Role Inventory) tend to have more sexual partners than women with stereotyped attitudes (Lucke, 1998; Mikach & Bailey, 1999). When people have stereotypic views that men ought to be more sexual than women, it can result in negative labeling of those who don't conform. If a man does not appear to engage in sex as often as others, he may be viewed as inadequate and "unmanly." Conversely, if a woman demonstrates that she really enjoys sex and likes having sex frequently, she may be considered by some to be "easy" or a "slut." Clearly, there is a wide range of individual differences in the way both men and women feel and act with regard to sex. There is no "right" amount of sex drive and/or sexual activity for either men or women.

Many studies have found that men are more interested in the purely physical aspects of sex than are women (Baldwin & Baldwin, 1997; Laumann et al., 1994). Women, on the other hand, are more likely than men to value love and a nurturing relationship. Not surprisingly, then, is the finding that men desire a physically attractive marriage partner more than women do (Regan & Berscheid, 1997), or that women are more likely than men to have sex for emotional intimacy and men are more likely to do so to relieve sexual tensions (Brigman & Knox, 1992). Can we make any general conclusions about men's and women's sexual behavior? A recent review concluded that in general, men's sexual desires were unaffected by the social context, whereas women's sexual desires were greatly affected by sociocultural factors. In other words, women's sexual desires are more flexible and adaptive than men's (Baumeister, 2000).

One commonly held stereotype is that women are more emotional, loving, and accepting, while men should not express deep feelings and emotions (Plant et al., 2000):

Box 10–B CROSS-CULTURAL PERSPECTIVES

The Native American Two-Spirit

Before the influence of Western culture led to their disappearance, there existed among many North American Indian tribes individuals, known until recently as berdaches, who had special gender status. According to Callender and Kochems (1987), a *berdache* was "a person, usually male, who was anatomically normal but assumed the dress, occupations, and behavior of the other sex to effect a change in gender status." Accounts of berdaches date back to the 1500s (Katz, 1976,) and they existed in at least 113 groups that extended from California to the Mississippi Valley and upper Great Lakes (list compiled by Callender and Kochems, 1987).

Early observations were heavily influenced by Western values and perceptions and focused primarily on the homosexuality or bisexuality of many of the berdaches. In fact, the word *berdache* is not an Indian term but rather a medieval French term meaning "male homosexual." According to Callender and Kochems, homosexuality didn't bestow the status of berdache on an individual, but many berdaches became homosexual. Translations of the Indian terms give "halfman-halfwoman" or "man-woman," with no insinuation about sexuality. Native Americans, as well as anthropologists, are presently urging that scholars use the term **two-spirit** or terms within native languages when referring to these individuals (see Jacobs & Thomas, 1994).

The two-spirits were held in awe and highly revered, but were not chiefs or religious leaders (they were not shamans). Individuals became two-spirits by showing a strong interest in the work of the opposite sex during childhood and/or (and more commonly) by having a supernatural vision during adolescence that confirmed the change in gender status. In almost all groups, a male two-spirit dressed and fixed his hair like a woman and assumed a woman's occupations, at which he excelled—part of the reason he was admired. On certain occasions, he dressed like and assumed the role of a man. He was generally responsible for burial rituals, but because he could cross back and forth between genders, he was especially valued as a go-between for men and women. It was these exceptional gender-mixing abilities that led to his being greatly admired. But, as noted, Western values intervened. Lurie (1953), who studied the Winnebago Indians, reported, for example, that "most informants felt that the two-spirit was at one time a highly honored and respected person, but that the Winnebago had become ashamed of the custom because the white people thought it was amusing or evil."

Figure 10–11 We'wha, a 19th-century two-spirit from the Zuni tribe.

two-spirit In North American Indian tribes of past centuries, a person, usually a man, who assumed the dress, occupations, and behavior of the other sex in order to effect a change in gender status. The term now preferred by Native Americans and anthropologists over *berdache*.

"Recently I was involved in a relationship with a very 'sex-typed' guy. . . . Every time I would try to talk to him about how I felt about things or let him know how my emotional needs were going unfulfilled, he would change the subject or dismiss the whole discussion as being 'sissified.'" (from the author's files)

All people, men and women, need to express their feelings and emotions and be able to communicate them. The image of a man as "strong and silent" robs him of a fundamental part of his humanity and robs his partner of a true companion. Herb Goldberg (1979), author of the book *The New Male,* has written extensively about the harmful effects of men trying to live up to the so-called male role. He states that the entire male socialization process is contrary to the human needs of men and is hazardous to their health and well-being. Good communication leads to happier, healthier, and often more satisfying sexual relations and to greater intimacy (Rubin et al., 1980). Furthermore, people's beliefs about the likelihood of a person becoming angry or sad during a personal challenge could lead to inferences about their leadership skills, which could ultimately channel people into different career paths and social roles (Plant et al., 2000).

In Chapter 12 you will learn that many parents deny their sexuality by hiding it from their children. As a result, some people view parents, and parenthood, as less sexual than others. For people with extremely stereotyped views of gender roles, this can create a conflict when their own partner becomes a parent:

"My husband and I were in what seemed an ideal marriage. Not only was our coupling wonderful, but we also shared an extremely intense sexual relationship as well. Two years into our marriage we were informed that we were going to be parents. My husband was great; he was so attentive and supportive during the time I carried our child. . . .

"He was a proud father. However, things were never the same between us after the birth of our daughter. My husband insisted I stay home and raise her as he did not want her brought up in nurseries or with babysitters. Soon, he was obsessed with work. . . . He was working 18–20 hrs. a day, 6 days a week. . . . There had been little sex between us since the baby, but I attributed it to his long hours. . . .

"I started sensing that my husband was distant. I told him he was growing away from us instead of with us. I asked him what was wrong. . . . He said that ever since I became a mother that he no longer could see me as a sexual partner. I was a mom and that was something sacred that should be put on a pedestal. He said it was impossible to think of me in a sexual way anymore." (from the author's files)

Recall from Chapter 4 that in some cultures, women's genitals are mutilated, in part because men view women's sexual desire as being inconsistent with their roles as wives and mothers. In our own culture, childbearing often symbolizes the acceptance of traditional gender roles (Nock, 1987). An androgynous person is less likely to have conflicting views about sexuality and parenthood, and more likely to view his or her partner as both nurturant (whether a man or a woman) and sexual.

MICROSTRUCTURAL THEORIES OF GENDER-ROLE DEVELOPMENT

Many adults today were raised with traditional role expectations through socialization in their childhood and adolescence, but are currently being influenced by recent trends in society toward more androgynous gender roles. Such mixed signals can result in confusion about what is truly masculine or feminine, with some people claiming that even making such a distinction is unnecessary. In order to better understand how individuals react in times of transition to major social changes that influence traditional gender roles, we shall examine the research based on microstructural theory within the sociological literature.

Sociologists are interested in the processes of group dynamics and change. Microstructural theory, like learning theory in psychology, stresses the role of the external environment in shaping attitudes and behavior. The focus of this type of research is less on the individual and more on large-scale social institutions. In looking at how gender roles have evolved in our country's past, we may better understand what is happening today.

Cancian (1989) and Kimmel (1989) have examined the way in which gender roles have evolved in America. Cancian (1989) argues that love became feminized during the 1800s, when the United States was becoming industrialized. Early American society did not have different gender roles for the expression of love, nurturance, or dependency. According to Cancian (1989), this was because the home was the center of the educational, economic, and social activities of the family, where both men and women shared in all aspects of family life. The church admonished men and women to be nurturant and loving to each other, as this ensured a stable home environment.

With increased industrialization, men began to earn their livings away from home, and the economic activities of men and women began to split. Men were viewed as breadwinners who left the home to compete in a harsh outside world filled with competition and danger. Women continued to stay at home, and the home began to be viewed as a retreat for the husband after finishing his day's labors. The home became an idealized place of peace and affection, in contrast to the business world. Because the woman maintained the home, the qualities of nurturance, love, and devotion became associated with being feminine. The work that a wife did at home was either ignored or not considered to be as important or meaningful as work done outside the home. Perhaps this was due to the fact that women failed to receive monetary compensation for their labors within the household. Independence, success, achievement, competition, and self-control came to be valued as masculine characteristics as the man pursued work outside the home.

Cancian (1989) believes that our present gender roles evolved as a means of achieving control. Workers in industrial settings were dependent upon companies for their wages, while the individual man was viewed as being independent, tough-minded, and thriving in an impersonal, affection-free business world. This fostered the illusion that the individual man still had control over his life through the display of masculine characteristics, especially in the home. Women were dependent upon wage-earning husbands, but this dependency was hidden by the feminine gender role of women in the form of being nurturant, emotional, passive, and physically weak, though morally pure. Women who worked outside of the home were almost always single, and once married would retire to do the housework of the feminine wife and/or mother. It should be noted that the 1800s saw the opening of the American frontier, and this was seen as a man's job, calling for independence, self-reliance, and the ability to do without female influence.

Kimmel (1989) points out that the end of the 1800s saw a great deal of challenge to traditional masculine and feminine gender roles. Kimmel argues that social changes in the late 1800s gave rise to the "New Woman," who was single, economically independent, and highly educated, and who did not believe that a woman should have to become dependent on a man in order to be feminine. The New Woman was part of a growing women's movement that attempted to challenge traditional gender roles and create a more equal distribution of power within American society. In an attempt to combat traditional gender roles, some women tried to act and dress in a less restrictive manner.

According to Kimmel (1989), men reacted to the rise of the women's movement in one of three ways. The first way was an antifeminist response, with an emphasis on the need to return the woman to the home. A second reaction was a pro-man reaction, which involved segregating boys and girls in separate schools and other social institutions in order to "preserve" boys' masculinity from the corrupting influence of feminism. The third reaction was pro-feminist. Some men joined with feminists to promote equality among the sexes. Kimmel notes that past definitions of masculinity and femininity help reproduce power relationships between the sexes, and when those power relationships are challenged, gender roles are questioned as well and may begin to change.

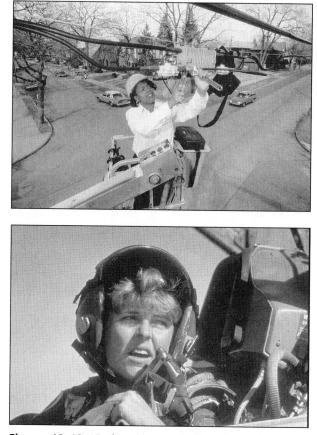

Figure 10–12 Today, the majority of women contribute to their family's income, often in nontraditional roles such as electrical repair and fighter pilot.

We have similar forces at work in our society today. Women are seeking more control over job opportunities, the same amount of pay as men receive for comparable work, more freedom in the conduct of their personal affairs, and, in general, more equality between the sexes. Reactions to today's feminist movement are similar to the ones described at the turn of the 20th century, for gender roles are still being seriously questioned and redefined within our society. Qualities that are believed to characterize men and women appear to be undergoing a dramatic change. The initial force behind the changes has come from the women's movement, which asserts that the traditional system of sex-role differentiation is outmoded and destructive. Pleck (1976), a leading authority on the male gender role, notes that women are challenging their traditional gender-role patterns and redefining their roles and their place in society. In turn, men in our society have begun to reexamine their own gender roles. This can cause a conflict within a man between what he was taught was appropriate for his gender role when he was a boy and society's current expectations for the "New Man."

Box 10-C   OPPOSING POINTS OF VIEW

Author's note: The following two essays are included to stimulate thought. When reading them, ask yourself if you are guilty of having any of these sex-stereotyped attitudes.

Why I Want a Wife

I belong to that classification of people known as wives. I am a wife. And, not altogether incidentally, I am a mother.

Not too long ago a male friend of mine appeared on the scene fresh from a recent divorce. He had one child, who is, of course, with his ex-wife. He is obviously looking for another wife. As I thought about him while I was ironing one evening, it suddenly occurred to me that I, too, would like to have a wife. Why do I want a wife?

I would like to go back to school so that I can become economically independent, support myself, and, if need be, support those dependent on me. I want a wife who will work and send me to school. And while I am going to school, I want a wife to take care of my children. I want a wife to keep track of the children's doctor and dentist appointments. And to keep track of mine, too. I want a wife to make sure that my children eat properly and are kept clean. I want a wife who will wash the children's clothes and keep them mended. I want a wife who is a good nurturant attendant to my children, who arranges for their schooling, makes sure that they have an adequate social life with their peers, takes them to the park, the zoo, etc. I want a wife who takes care of the children when they are sick, a wife who arranges to be around when the children need special care, because, of course, I cannot miss classes at school. My wife must arrange to lose time at work and not lose the job. It may mean a small cut in my wife's income from time to time, but I guess I can tolerate that. Needless to say, my wife will arrange and pay for the care of the children while my wife is working.

I want a wife who will take care of *my* physical needs. I want a wife who will keep my house clean. A wife who will pick up after me. I want a wife who will keep my clothes clean, ironed, mended, replaced when need be, and who will see to it that my personal things are kept in their proper place so that I can find what I need the minute I need it. I want a wife who cooks the meals, a wife who is a *good* cook. I want a wife who will plan the menus, do the necessary grocery shopping, prepare the meals, serve them pleasantly, and then do the cleaning up while I do my studying. I want a wife who will care for me when I am sick and sympathize with my pain and loss of time from school. I want a wife to go along when our family takes a vacation so that someone can continue to care for me and my children when I need a rest and change of scene.

I want a wife who will not bother me with rambling complaints about a wife's duties. But I want a wife who will listen to me when I feel the need to explain a rather difficult point I have come across in my course of studies. And I want a wife who will type my papers for me when I have written them.

I want a wife who will take care of the details of my social life. When my wife and I are invited out by my friends, I want a wife who will take care of the babysitting arrangements. When I meet people at school that I like and want to entertain, I want a wife who will have the house clean, will prepare a special meal, serve it to me and my friends, and not interrupt when I talk about the things that interest me and my friends. I want a wife who will have arranged that the children are fed and ready for bed before my guests arrive so that the children do not bother us.

And I want a wife who knows that sometimes I need a night out by myself.

I want a wife who is sensitive to my sexual needs, a wife who makes love passionately and eagerly when I feel like it, a wife who makes sure that I am satisfied. And, of course, I want a wife who will not demand sexual attention when I am not in the mood for it. I want a wife who assumes the complete responsibility for birth control, because I do not want more children. I want a wife who will remain sexually faithful to me so that I do not have to clutter up my intellectual life with jealousies. And I want a wife who understands that *my* sexual needs may entail more than strict adherence to monogamy. I must, after all, be able to relate to people as fully as possible.

If, by chance, I find another person more suitable as a wife than the wife I already have, I want the liberty to replace my present wife with another one. Naturally, I will expect a fresh, new life; my wife will take the children and be solely responsible for them so that I am left free.

When I am through with school and have a job, I want my wife to quit working and remain at home so that my wife can more fully and completely take care of a wife's duties.

My God, who *wouldn't* want a wife?

Judy Syfers

Why I Want a Husband

I am not a husband. I am, however, a male, and have a father who is a husband. I am also fortunate enough to know a great many men who are husbands and will probably become a husband myself someday.

I recently read Judy Syfers' essay "Why I Want a Wife" and decided a reply was in order. Though not the most qualified author for such an undertaking, I felt it my duty to make an effort. For I now realize that just as Judy Syfers wants a wife, I want a husband.

I want a husband who brings home the bacon. I mean really rakes in the bucks. After all, I certainly can't have anything less than the best. My husband must be driven to succeed; he must climb the corporate ladder quickly and efficiently. He must make every payroll and meet every deadline. Anything less would be completely unacceptable.

And I want a husband who bears the burden of being the wage earner without complaint. He must deal with the stresses of his job without bringing his problems home from the office so as not to upset me. I want a husband who deals patiently and lovingly with screaming, fighting kids even after a tough day. I want a husband who, for fairness sake, does the dishes (even sometimes the wash) for me so that I can put my feet up after dinner. And, I want a husband who will leave the office during a busy day of work to check on a sick child while I'm out on the town shopping.

I want a husband who will gladly eat cold leftovers for a week while I am relaxing with a friend in sunny California. My husband will have to sit through boring PTA meetings and ice-cream socials after a rough day at work. My husband must, of course, be courteous and kind to meddling, gossiping friends. (After all, I am entitled to my friends, too.) I want a husband who listens patiently to my panic about the oversudsing washing machine while he silently sweats about the thousands of dollars he just borrowed from the bank.

I want a husband who keeps the house and lawn looking beautiful in his spare time. He must be willing to spend his Saturday afternoons weeding my garden, and he must give up that tee time with the guys when I decide the grass is a little too long. I want one who makes sure the car is fixed (engines are so complicated and dirty!), and takes care of all the "little" chores around the house—raking leaves in the fall, shoveling snow in the winter, painting the house in the spring. And I want one who will take out the garbage. When he's done with these chores, he can take the kids to the zoo or the park or the ballgame because these are things a father should share with his children.

I want a husband who gladly pays for his wife's shopping sprees without ever asking her where all the money goes. He will understand that women need to spend time with their friends. I want a husband who will watch the kids on vacation so my wife can shop and work on her tan. (He must accept the fact that after traveling so many miles, a shopping trip is the only way to wind down.)

And I want my husband to be completely receptive to my sexual needs. He must completely understand when I have a "headache." He will be sensitive to my problems and respect my private life. I want a husband who understands that I must have my freedom. He will be ready to accept the possibility that I may need to "find myself" and may walk out at any time. He will understand, of course, that I will take half of everything we own. He would keep the kids, however, because I would need to start a brand new life for myself.

I want a husband who will do all these things for me forever or until I decide we have enough money to retire, or until he has a heart attack and collapses in a heap. Yes, I want a husband.

How could anyone live without one?

Kurt Fernsler

Pleck (1976) refers to this as the *gender* or *sex-role strain perspective*. This perspective contends that the problem with the male gender role is that men in our society are confronted by contradictory demands and expectations from their early socialization process and their adult life experience. For example, men were conditioned to control their emotions and be unexpressive in order to be strong and to be so-called real men, whereas the adult male role (i.e., marital role, parental role) calls for the ability to express feelings and to share affection with their spouses and children.

Perhaps it is more difficult for men to adopt non-traditional role behaviors, as it is harder for men who wish to act in ways that may be labeled feminine. In order for men to move away from traditional gender-role behavior, it has been noted that men not only need to feel such change is desirable and beneficial as far as improving the quality of their lives, but they also need to receive support from their spouses, from other men, and in the workplace (Canavan & Haskell, 1977). Pleck (1976) believes that in redefining their gender roles, men need to make changes in their relationships to women, other men, and their children and to their work environment.

Many forces have contributed to challenging such traditional attitudes as "a woman's place is in the home" and "a man's home is his castle." These include the rise in the divorce rate, the availability of contraceptives, the large number of women in the work force (especially working mothers), and increased sensitivity to civil rights and personal freedoms. Despite the many gains women have made personally and professionally, feminists are sometimes still considered radical by individuals who are satisfied with the gender roles received from previous generations. Additionally, women often still get paid less to do the same work as men, have fewer opportunities for higher-level leadership roles in corporate or government settings, and must contend many times with conflicting sets of expectations from parents, friends, bosses, and other people about what is appropriate feminine behavior.

Microstructural theories see gender roles as based on gender relationships and power. Reactions to attempts to redistribute power are similar, whether from the turn of the 20th century or today. Risman and Schwartz (1989) argue that the way to change gender roles is not to retrain individuals, but to restructure the social environment. Women will become assertive if their jobs demand it and when they are rewarded for acting assertively. Men will become nurturant when they are held responsible for taking care of others.

Key Terms

adrenogenital syndrome (AGS)   243

androgen insensitivity syndrome   243

androgyny   239

biological determinism   248

chromosomes   240

DHT deficiency syndrome   244

expressive   251

gender   247

gender constancy   250

gender dysphoria   245

gender identity   238

gender identity disorder (GID)   245

gender role   238, 251

gender-role identity   251

gender-role stereotype   239

gender schema   254

hermaphroditism   242

identification   249

imitation   249

individualist theory   251

instrumental   251

intersexual   242

Klinefelter's syndrome   242

microstructural theory   251

Mullerian duct system   240

Mullerian duct–inhibiting substance   240

Oedipus complex   249

operant conditioning   249

phallic stage   249

pseudohermaphroditism   243

socialization   253

stereotype   239, 253

testosterone   59, 240

transgender   245

transsexual   245

Turner's syndrome   242

two-spirit   260

undifferentiated   239

Wolffian duct system   240

Suggested Readings

Cowley, G., Gideonse, T., & Underwood, A. (1997, May 19). Gender limbo. *Newsweek.* Good article on the lack of success of sex reassignment surgery at birth.

Fagot, B. I. (1995). Psychosocial and cognitive determinants of early gender-role development. *Annual review of sex research,* vol. VI. Mount Vernon, IA: Society for the Scientific Study of Sexuality. The title says it all; a very thorough review.

Hyde, J. S. (1996). *Half the human experience: The psychology of women* (5th ed.). Boston: Houghton Mifflin. Comprehensive and well-written review of women and gender roles.

Kessler, S. J. (1998). *Lessons from the intersexed.* New Brunswick, NJ: Rutgers University Press.

Laqueur, T. (1992). *Making sex: Body and gender from the Greeks to Freud.* Cambridge, MA: Harvard University Press (paperback).

Lips, H. (1992). *Sex and gender.* Mountain View, CA: Mayfield. This is a good, easy-to-read introduction to gender roles.

Morris, J. *Conundrum* (1974). New York: Harcourt Brace Jovanovich. The story of a transsexual's experiences.

Schwartz, P,. & Rutter, V. (1998). *The gender of sexuality.* Thousand Oaks, CA: Pine Forge Press.

Shapiro, L. (1990, May 28). Guns and dolls. *Newsweek.* An excellent article on the development of gender roles during childhood.

Swann Jr., W. B., Langlois, J. H., & Gilbert, L. A. (Eds.). (1998). *Sexism and stereotypes in modern society: The gender science of Janet Taylor Spence.* Washington, DC: American Psychological Association.

Study Guide

INTERACTIVE REVIEW

(1) _____ is your subjective sense of being a man or a woman. It is influenced by both biological and social factors. A person's genetic sex is determined at conception by the combination of an egg, which has an X chromosome for sex, and a sperm, which can have either an X or a Y chromosome. (2) _____ combinations usually result in girls, while (3) _____ combinations usually produce boys. There are over 70 known irregularities in chromosome combinations. These include men with one or more extra X chromosomes, (4) _____ syndrome, and women with only one X chromosome, (5) _____ syndrome.

Hormones determine whether an embryo will develop anatomically to be a boy or girl. Unless there are high levels of (6) _____ at this critical stage of prenatal development, nature has programmed the body to develop into a (7) _____. Hormone abnormalities before birth can result in a mismatch between genetic and anatomical sex, or a baby whose external genitalia are ambiguous in appearance. These individuals are called (8) _____. Some individuals feel that they are trapped inside a body of the wrong sex, a feeling called (9) _____. Persons whose gender identity does not match their biological sex are said to have (10) _____. They often elect to undergo sex reassignment surgery.

Three psychological theories, though very different in their explanations, suggest that gender identity is learned. (11) _____ theory emphasizes unconscious identification with the parent of the same sex, while (12) _____ theory emphasizes the role of reinforcement and imitation. Cognitive-developmental theory states that children do not acquire the concept of (13) _____ until the age of (14) _____.

(15) _____ are norms (what is considered appropriate) about the behaviors and attitudes of men and women. They vary from culture to culture and can change over time within the same culture. (16) _____ theory emphasizes how gender roles are integrated within the individual early in life as part of the individual's personality. The development of gender roles begins before a child develops gender identity or gender constancy. (17) _____ theory emphasizes the role of the environment or social context in influencing the way gender roles develop over the life span.

Masculinity and femininity were once viewed as opposite ends of a unidimensional continuum, but today they are generally viewed as (18) _____ constructs. This has led to the theory of (19) _____, which says that a person can be both masculine and feminine and that this is the healthiest of all gender roles because of the flexibility it gives individuals in different situations.

Parents, teachers, the media, and peers are all powerful influences on the process of socialization and gender-role development. Gender is possibly the first social category learned by children. When children cognitively organize the world according to gender, they create gender (20) _____. Children raised in single-parent households tend to be more (21) _____ than children raised in two-parent households. As individuals become adults, they generally acquire more complex sets of gender roles, and for both sexes there is an integration of gender roles. Continued belief in stereotypic gender roles can adversely affect one's personal and sexual relations with a partner.

Traditional gender roles in our culture evolved over time in response to social forces. Those forces have been changing (an example has been the increased presence of women in the work force), and as a result, gender roles are in a state of transition. This may encourage individuals to base their behaviors, beliefs, and attitudes on human roles rather than being limited by rigid gender-role expectations.

SELF-TEST

A. TRUE OR FALSE

[T] [F] 22. Transgendered and transsexual mean the same thing.

[T] [F] 23. Hormone levels around the time of birth alter brain anatomy to be either "male" or "female."

[T] [F] 24. By the age of 3, children know whether they are a boy or a girl, but do not understand that this cannot change.

[T] [F] 25. In the absence of testosterone during embryonic development, we would all be born anatomically a girl.

[T] [F] 26. Fathers tend to treat their children in more gender-stereotypic ways than do mothers.

[T] [F] 27. According to microstructural theory, the way to change gender roles is not to retrain individuals but to restructure the social environment.

[T] [F] 28. Transsexual is a term for a type of homosexual.

[T] [F] 29. "Tomboy" behavior in girls is usually better tolerated by peers, parents, and teachers than is "effeminate" behavior in boys.

[T] [F] 30. According to social learning theory, imitation is a process by which children may learn gender identity and gender roles.

[T] [F] 31. Parents who assume "traditional" gender roles behave differently toward their male and female children.

[T] [F] 32. The rise of industrialization helped create the male gender role of being independent and unemotional.

[T] [F] 33. Gender role is the way you express your gender identity.

[T] [F] 34. The most common cause of pseudohermaphroditism in men is androgen insensitivity syndrome.

[T] [F] 35. Men's and women's hypothalamuses are different.

[T] [F] 36. A transsexual is someone who cross-dresses for sexual arousal.

[T] [F] 37. Children do not show gender-stereotyped behavior until they have developed gender constancy.

[T] [F] 38. A recent study found that young children view gender in dualistic terms, but as they grow older they come to view gender as a unidimensional construct.

[T] [F] 39. There is little noticeable difference between the behavior of boys and the behavior of girls before the age of 2.

[T] [F] 40. As people grow older, they are more able to rely on information about an individual to make judgments, even when the information is not consistent with stereotyped gender roles.

[T] [F] 41. As a result of converging gender roles, men and women no longer differ with regard to permissive attitudes about casual sex.

B. MATCHING (SOME QUESTIONS HAVE MORE THAN ONE ANSWER)

_____ 42. Tom believes he is a woman but is anatomically a man, and does not want sex reassignment surgery.

_____ 43. Bob is low in instrumental orientation ("getting the job done") and has great affective concern for the welfare of others.

_____ 44. Frank prefers men as sexual partners.

_____ 45. Susan cannot reproduce; she is short, infertile; and has one X chromosome.

_____ 46. Joe is neither instrumental nor expressive, neither assertive nor emotional.

a. adrenogenital syndrome
b. androgen insensitivity syndrome
c. androgynous individual
d. DHT-deficient individual
e. "feminine" on Bem Sex-Role Inventory
f. gender dysphoric
g. gender identity disorder
h. hermaphrodite
i. homosexual
j. intersexual
k. Klinefelter's syndrome

_____ 47. David's body did not respond to testosterone during prenatal development; he has female genitalia and undescended testes.

_____ 48. Sam was born with a very small penis that looked like a clitoris, an incomplete scrotum, and a short, closed vaginal cavity. At puberty his voice deepened, his testes descended, and his "clitoris" grew to become a penis.

_____ 49. Wayne is both instrumental and expressive, assertive and emotional.

_____ 50. Phillip believes he is a woman trapped in a male body and wishes to have sex reassignment surgery.

_____ 51. Carol has an enlarged clitoris and labia because of too much masculinizing hormone during her fetal development.

_____ 52. Mike believes that men should be assertive, aggressive, success-oriented, unemotional, and play little role in housekeeping and child-care responsibilities.

_____ 53. Harold is tall, with long arms; he has a small penis, shrunken testes, low sexual desire, and an extra X chromosome.

_____ 54. Barbara is genetically a woman, but has both male and female reproductive systems as a result of the failure of her primitive gonads to differentiate during the embryonic stage.

l. pseudohermaphrodite
m. stereotyped individual
n. transgendered person
o. transsexual
p. Turner's syndrome
q. undifferentiated individual

C. FILL IN THE BLANKS

55. A child's knowledge that his or her sex does not change is called _____ in cognitive-developmental theory.

56. According to Cancian, gender roles for men and women did not start to differ until the _____.

57. According to _____ theory, an individual's gender role results from society's expectations of male and female behavior.

58. According to Freud, children acquire the gender identity of the same-sex parent through the process of _____.

59. The process of internalizing society's beliefs is called _____.

60. Oversimplified, rigid beliefs that all members of a particular gender have distinct behavioral and emotional characteristics are called _____.

61. On Bem's Sex-Role Inventory, a person who scores low on both dimensions is called _____.

62. According to Freud, children acquire their gender identity in the _____ stage of psychosexual development.

63. If an individual scores high on both the femininity dimension and the masculine dimension of the Bem Sex-Role Inventory, he or she would be called _____.

64. Money and Ehrhardt (1972) stated, "Nature's rule is, it would appear, that to masculinize, something must be added." That something is _____.

65. According to Freud, gender identity is acquired when children resolve the _____ complex.

66. _____ cross-dress for sexual arousal and gratification, whereas _____ cross-dress because they truly believe they are members of the opposite sex.

67. In social learning explanations of gender identity development, when children watch their mothers and fathers and copy them, it is called _____.

68. The _____ view of gender-role development holds that biological influences establish predetermined limits to the effects of cultural influences.

69. According to Bem, masculine is to instrumental as feminine is to _____.

70. According to Kagan, boys' and girls' behaviors do not differ at the age of _____.

71. Some languages classify all nouns as either masculine or feminine. This is an example of _____.

72. The presence of _____ shortly before and after birth changes the brain to male anatomy.

73. As a general rule, men have considerably more permissive attitudes about _____ than women do.

74. Among early North American Indian tribes, a _____ was a highly respected man who cross-dressed and assumed the behaviors of a woman.

Sexual Orientation

It doesn't really matter why people are gay or not gay. That's not the important question. What's really important is how they're treated. I haven't spent that much time thinking about where my sexuality comes from. I've spent a lot more time thinking about how I fit into this world I have to live in.

(David Barr, quoted by Angier, 1991)

Are you sexually attracted to men? To women? To both men and women? These are questions about **sexual orientation**—one's sexual attraction to members of the opposite sex, the same sex, or both sexes. Attraction to members of the opposite sex is called **heterosexuality,** while attraction to same-sex individuals is called **homosexuality. Bisexuality** refers to sexual attraction to people of either sex.

At one time it was believed that people were either one or the other: heterosexual or homosexual (Gordon & Snyder, 1989). However, dichotomous scales are not accurate. As Kinsey et al. (1948) stated, "Not all things are black nor all things white." Today, sexual orientation is viewed as a continuum, with people who are exclusively heterosexual at one end and those who are exclusively homosexual at the other end. Kinsey and his colleagues (1948) devised a 7-point rating scale to measure sexual orientation, with 0 representing people who are exclusively heterosexual and 6 representing people who are exclusively homosexual (see Table 11–1). Kinsey's group regarded anyone as bisexual who had a rating of 2, 3, or 4. Kinsey's scale relied heavily on overt behavior, but there are problems with defining

When you have finished studying this chapter, you should be able to:

1. Define the terms *sexual orientation, heterosexual, homosexual, and bisexual;*

2. Summarize what we know about the prevalence of homosexuality and bisexuality in the United States;

3. Understand the difference between sexual orientation, gender identity, and gender roles;

4. Discuss the origins of sexual orientation, including psychoanalytic, social learning, and biological explanations;

5. Trace the history of attitudes about homosexuality in Western culture as well as the prevalence of sexual prejudice today;

6. Compare our attitudes about homosexuality with those in other cultures;

7. Understand what it involves for an individual to "come out"; and

8. Understand homosexual life-styles and the ability of homosexuals to parent.

TABLE 11–1

KINSEY AND COLLEAGUES' (1948) RATING SCALE FOR SEXUAL ORIENTATION

0	1	2	3	4	5	6
Exclusively heterosexual	Predominantly heterosexual; only incidentally homosexual	Predominantly heterosexual; more than incidentally homosexual	Equally heterosexual and homosexual	Predominantly homosexual; more than incidentally heterosexual	Predominantly homosexual; only incidentally heterosexual	Exclusively homosexual

Reprinted with permission of The Kinsey Institute for Research in Sex, Gender, and Reproduction, Inc.

a heterosexuality–homosexuality continuum only in terms of behavior. However, before we address these problems, let us examine the results of surveys by Kinsey and others regarding behavior.

PREVALENCE OF HOMOSEXUALITY AND BISEXUALITY

The large-scale surveys by Kinsey and his associates discussed in Chapter 1 (Kinsey et al., 1948, 1953) were the first source of information about the prevalence of homosexuality in the United States. They found that 4 percent of their sample of white men had been exclusively homosexual for life, 10 percent had been exclusively homosexual for at least a 3-year period in their lives, and 37 percent had had at least one same-sex sexual experience to orgasm. This last figure shocked America, and Kinsey's survey was attacked as either biased or totally false (e.g., see Reisman & Eichel, 1990). An associate of Kinsey later claimed that the 37 percent figure was, in fact, too high, but lowered the estimate only to 25–33 percent (Pomeroy, 1972). For women, Kinsey's group found that 13–19 percent had had at least one same-sex sexual experience and that 1–3 percent were predominantly or exclusively homosexual after age 15.

A survey taken over 20 years later by Morton Hunt (1974) for *Playboy* magazine found that 20–25 percent of the men surveyed had had at least one same-sex sexual experience in their lifetimes. However, only 12–13 percent had had a same-sex sexual experience after age 15, and only 2–3 percent were found to be predominantly or exclusively homosexual after that age. A survey taken by the Kinsey Institute at about the same time (1970) found that 3.3 percent of adult men had same-sex sexual experiences "occasionally" or "fairly often" (Fay et al., 1989). Hunt found that 20 percent of single women reported having had at least one same-sex sexual experience in their lifetimes, but only 10–12 percent had done so after age 15. About 2 percent of single women were predominantly homosexual. For married women, 10–11 percent of Hunt's

sample said that they had had at least one same-sex sexual experience, but only 3 percent of them said they had had a same-sex sexual experience after age 15, and fewer than 1 percent were predominantly homosexual. Thus, in the case of both men and women, most people who said that they had had a same-sex sexual experience or experiences had done so as adolescents and were exclusively heterosexual as adults.

> "At the age of about 12, I experienced an act of homosexuality. My cousins and I performed anal intercourse with each other. It never occurred to me that I might be gay when I got older. I am now grown up and am not a homosexual. Maybe because it was just a game to me or exploring different functions." (from the author's files)

Hunt, like many others, felt that Kinsey overestimated the prevalence of homosexuality in the United States, but at the same time he felt that his own survey may have underestimated the number of homosexual people. What do more recent surveys indicate? In a national cross-sectional survey, Janus and Janus (1993) found that 22 percent of the men and 17 percent of the women surveyed said that they had had same-sex sexual experiences, and that for 9 percent of the men and 5 percent of the women, the experiences were either "frequent" or "ongoing." However, a survey done for *Parade* magazine found that only 3 percent of the men and 1 percent of the women identified themselves as homosexual, and another 3 percent of the men and 0.4 percent of the women said they were bisexual (Clements, 1994). In another national survey, 1.6 percent of sexually active individuals reported that they had had a same-sex sexual partner in the previous year (Cochran & Mays, 2000).

In the most scientifically conducted sexual survey to date (see Chapter 1), Laumann and colleagues (1994) found that 2.8 percent of the men and 1.4 percent of the women surveyed identified themselves

sexual orientation A distinct preference for sexual partners of a particular sex in the presence of clear alternatives.

heterosexual An individual with a sexual orientation primarily to members of the opposite sex.

homosexual An individual with a sexual orientation primarily to members of the same sex.

bisexual An individual with a sexual orientation toward both men and women as homosexual or bisexual. This was consistent with behavior: 2.7 percent of the men and 1.3 percent of the women in the survey said that they had had sex with someone of their own sex in the past year. In a large national survey done in France at about the same time, the numbers were even smaller (Messiah et al., 1995). However, Laumann's study found that in large urban areas, more than 9 percent of men identified themselves as homosexual.

Two other reviews are especially relevant here. One reviewed three surveys conducted by the National Opinion Research Center in 1988, 1989, and 1990 (Rogers & Turner, 1991). The other relied on seven surveys, including five conducted after 1987 (Seidman & Rieder, 1994). What did they conclude? As many as 20 percent of men have had a same-sex sexual experience, but only about 5 percent since the age of 18, and only 1–6 percent have done so in the last 12 months (most of the surveys put this last figure at around 2 percent).

After all this research, what is the overall conclusion? *About 3–5 percent of adult American men and about 1 percent of adult American women are homosexual.* Many more people, however, have had sexual experiences with individuals of the same sex at one time in their lives.

DEFINING SEXUAL ORIENTATION: ANOTHER LOOK

In studies of sexual orientation, many do not distinguish between behavior and the "psychological" component (see Sell, 1997). Many individuals who have had same-sex sexual experiences do not classify themselves as homosexual. Obviously, we must look at more than behavior when characterizing people as heterosexual, homosexual, or bisexual. For example, what about sexual fantasies? Most heterosexuals have had fantasies of homosexual experiences (and vice versa; Bell & Weinberg, 1978). What sexual orientation is a person who has been exclusively heterosexual in behavior, but whose sexual fantasies are *predominantly* homosexual in content?

What about a person's sexual self-identity—how someone *feels* about himself or herself? In fact, you do not have to have ever had sex to consider yourself heterosexual or homosexual. Also, some people who are predominantly heterosexual in behavior may feel that they are homosexual or bisexual, but limit themselves because of perceived social constraints and engage in same-sex sexual experiences only on an occasional basis. For example, in Laumann et al.'s (1994) survey, 5.5 percent of women and 6 percent of men found the idea of having sex with someone of their own sex appealing. This was twice as many as had actually engaged in same-sex sexual behavior in the past year or who identified themselves as homosexual or bisexual.

Figure 11–1 Millions of American men and women are either predominantly or exclusively homosexual.

Other studies have found that 8–12 percent of heterosexuals report awareness of some attraction to the same sex (McConaghy et al., 1994; Sell et al., 1995).

How, then, shall we define **sexual orientation?** I will use a modification of the definition by Ellis and Ames (1987): *distinct preferences consistently made after adolescence in the presence of clear alternatives.* Preferences can be reflected in desire and/or behavior, and, as noted by Ellis and Ames, "isolated instances of sexual behavior may or may not reflect one's sexual orientation."

Kinsey et al.'s 7-point measurement scale was an improvement over a dichotomous scale. Others have tried to improve on their scale (the Klein Scale, the Shively and DeCecco scale). All are unsatisfactory to some degree because of the inability to distinguish completely between behavioral and psychological components (see Sell, 1997). In this chapter, I shall attempt to distinguish between *same-sex sexual behavior* and *same-sex sexual orientation.* Only the latter will be referred to as homosexuality.

Perhaps the biggest confusion, and controversy, is with the term *bisexual.* Many people still insist on viewing sexual orientation as a dichotomous choice (either/or) and have difficulty accepting a third orientation. Many homosexuals (as well as heterosexuals) view people who have engaged in bisexual behavior as really homosexuals who have not yet "come out of the closet" (Gordon & Snyder, 1989; Lever, 1994). One study found that people's bisexual activity remained relatively stable over time (McKirnan et al., 1995). However, several other studies have found that among young people, sexual self-identification as gay, lesbian, or bisexual can change over time. One study found that about one-third of male bisexuals moved toward homosexuality over time (Stokes et al., 1997). Another study found that it was also not uncommon for lesbian and bisexual women to change their self-identity (Diamond, 2000). A third study reported that more than half of young people who identified themselves as lesbian or gay in the past now regarded themselves to be bisexual, or vice versa (Rosario et al., 1996).

Is bisexuality a behavior, a feeling, or an identity? In a study of nearly 7,000 men who acknowledged sexual experiences with both men and women, it was found that 2 percent described themselves as homosexual, 69 percent as heterosexual, and only 29 percent as bisexual (Lever et al., 1992). In the survey by Janus and Janus (1993), 22 percent of the men surveyed said that they had had a same-sex sexual experience, but only 4 percent regarded themselves as homosexual and another 5 percent as bisexual. Thus, most people who have had sexual experiences with both opposite- and same-sex individuals do not regard themselves as bisexual. For example, in an interesting study, Humphreys (1970) examined a behavior called "tearoom trade." This involves men giving oral sex to other men in public restrooms, often without exchanging names. He found that a majority of those who allowed oral sex to be performed on them viewed themselves as heterosex-

ual (54 percent were married and had children), and many did not believe that they had engaged in a homosexual act because they had only been the passive partner. In the study by Lever et al. (1992), those men who identified themselves as bisexual said that they were predominantly or sometimes homosexual, whereas those who identified themselves as heterosexual were predominantly heterosexual in behavior. Yet another example is teenage male prostitutes ("hustlers") who solicit male customers. Most are runaway or throwaway children who do this only part time for the money, and do not regard themselves as homosexual (see Chapter 18). These studies point out the shortcomings of relying exclusively on either behavior or self-identity as a definition.

A commonly used definition of **bisexuality** was suggested by MacDonald (1981, 1982):

> **To be bisexual means that a person can enjoy and engage in sexual activity with members of both sexes, or recognizes a desire to do so. Also, although the strength and direction of preference may be constant for some bisexuals, it may vary considerably for others with respect to time of life and specific partners.**

Recall that by Kinsey's definition (1948), the sexual behavior (or desire to behave) must be more than incidental. However, Kinsey's scale implies that the farther away an individual gets from one of the extremes (exclusively heterosexual or exclusively homosexual), the weaker that orientation becomes. A bisexual person, therefore, would have only moderate degrees of both orientations. This may not be true. One study found that bisexuals had the same amount of opposite-sex fantasies as heterosexuals and the same amount of same-sex fantasies as homosexuals (Storms, 1980). In conclusion, most researchers today agree that bisexuality is a legitimate classification of sexual orientation, distinct from both heterosexuality and homosexuality.

PERSONAL REFLECTIONS
How would you react if someone at work told you that he or she was homosexual? What if your best friend told you that he or she was homosexual? Your brother or sister? Your teenage son or daughter? Why?

SEXUAL ORIENTATION, GENDER IDENTITY, AND GENDER ROLES

It has been my experience that many students are uncertain (or mistaken) about the relationship between a person's sexual orientation and his or her gender identity and gender roles. The latter two are independent of sexual orientation (Lips, 1992). The *gender identity* of the vast majority of homosexuals and

sexual orientation A distinct preference for sexual partners of a particular sex in the presence of clear alternatives.

bisexuals is just as strong and consistent with their anatomical sex as is found among heterosexuals. Homosexuality and bisexuality are not the result of gender dysphoria, and being homosexual is not the same as being transsexual (see Chapter 10). Also, do not confuse homosexuality or bisexuality with transvestism; as you will learn in Chapter 16, most transvestites are heterosexual men.

The real misunderstanding concerns *sexual orientation* and *gender roles.* Early sexologists like Freud and Henry Havelock Ellis thought that homosexuality resulted from reversed gender roles. Many people today still hold to this belief, which is reinforced often by the media's portraying male homosexuals as effeminate and female homosexuals as masculine. While many homosexuals do not conform to gender roles that society considers "normal" for their sex, that is also true for many heterosexuals (Bell et al., 1981). Whether a person conforms or does not conform to gender stereotypes does not always predict sexual orientation.

However, because of these beliefs, many people are quick to label others who do not appear to be "typical." Many people assume that if a man is masculine he must be heterosexual, and that if a man is feminine he must be homosexual (Smith et al., 1998). For example, people are much more likely to assume that a man is homosexual if he works as a nurse or secretary, or if his face has some "feminine" features (Deaux & Lewis, 1983; Dunkle & Francis, 1990). Conversely, many people are quick to attribute feminine characteristics to a man they are told is homosexual (Madon, 1997).

Probably the major reason for beliefs like these is that for many people, masculinity and femininity are basic assumptions of heterosexuality: Men are masculine and attracted to women, women are feminine and attracted to men. If you believe this, then it follows that the less "masculine" a man is, the more likely that he will be perceived as homosexual; and if a man is homosexual, it is more likely that he will be perceived as "feminine." However, as you learned in the previous chapter, gender roles change over time, and this is true within the homosexual community as well as the heterosexual community. Before the 1970s, for example, effeminate qualities were emphasized in the male homosexual community, but in the 1980s masculinity was emphasized (Garber, 1991). Consider, too, the butch and femme roles assumed by many female homosexuals (behavior most prevalent prior to 1960)—their behaviors were quite different, but their sexual orientation was the same. Again, there is no strong evidence that a homosexual or bisexual orientation must be associated with atypical gender roles. A great many homosexuals and bisexuals do not walk, talk, dress, or act any differently than anyone else (Kirk & Madsen, 1989). Consider the following:

He had attended a Catholic high school, was a star athlete on school teams, and was engaged to be married to his high school sweetheart. They had been going steady for several years. He was handsome, masculine looking, well-liked—an "All American" type of young man. Raised in a supportive family environment along with a younger brother and sister, he had come from as normal a background as could be imagined. He, too, had always thought of himself as normal.

His first awareness of his attraction to men came in adolescence. . . . He felt as if he was the only person in the world with this "problem." He loved his girlfriend, but he knew that something wasn't right and after high school he broke off the engagement. . . . He does not apologize for his homosexuality, for he feels that there is absolutely nothing to apologize for (it would be like apologizing for breathing or the color of his eyes).

He does not explain his homosexuality as the result of following role models, for he had none. He felt that he alone had these feelings during his adolescence. He does not think that he acted out of rebellion against his parents. They were a close, warm family and his parents treated his brother and sister in a similar manner. Neither of them are homosexual. He knows of no close relative who is homosexual. He was just like everyone else in high school and today is indistinguishable from any of the other male students in college. (from the author's files)

THE ORIGINS OF SEXUAL ORIENTATION

Why are some people heterosexual, others homosexual, and still others bisexual? Researchers and clinicians used to direct their efforts to the question "What causes homosexuality?" However, any study of the causes of homosexuality is inevitably about the causes of heterosexuality, and vice versa—you can't consider one without considering the other.

Is sexual orientation biologically determined? Is it the result of the environment (family background, peers, etc.) shaping individuals? There are probably few topics in the study of human characteristics in which the nature-versus-nurture question has been so strongly debated. I will review this work and then come to two conclusions, which I give in advance: (1) Neither heterosexuality nor homosexuality nor bisexuality has a single cause; and (2) biological, psychological, and social/cultural influences interact to produce sexual orientation (see Byne & Parsons, 1993).

PSYCHOANALYTIC EXPLANATIONS

Sigmund Freud (1905) viewed all people as capable of becoming either heterosexual or homosexual—neither orientation was assumed to be innate. He believed that a person's sexual orientation depended on how the *Oedipus complex* was resolved (see Chapter 10) and that heterosexuality was the "normal" outcome (see Friedman & Downey, 1995). Homosexuality was the result of fixation at (or regression to) this stage of development, when a particular set of circumstances occurred.

More specifically, Freud believed that male homosexuality resulted when a boy had a domineering, rejecting mother and turned to his father for love, and later to men in general. According to Freud, female homosexuality develops when a girl loves her mother and identifies with her father and becomes fixated at this stage. Classical psychoanalytic theory attributes homosexual desires in women to masculine identification and penis envy, and assumes that it is almost always associated with global character pathology (Downey & Friedman, 1998). Freud also felt that some individuals managed to keep their homosexual tendencies hidden from their conscious mind, or "repressed," until these tendencies emerged sometime later. He called these persons latent homosexuals.

In support of Freud, Bieber and colleagues (1962) studied male homosexuals and claimed that they typically had domineering, overly protective mothers and weak, detached fathers who did not provide masculine models. The mothers were seductive (in that they were jealous of, and discouraged, any interest their boys had in girls) and destroyed their boys' masculine behavior. Bieber claimed that the boys became fearful of heterosexual relations and turned to men for the love that they never received from their fathers. In a related study in support of Freud, Wolff (1971) claimed that female homosexuals came from homes with absent fathers and cold and rejecting mothers. The girls then spent the remainder of their lives searching for the love that their mothers never gave them by having other women as sexual partners.

These studies were done with a small number of people who were in therapy. While some other studies have found similar results (Evans, 1969; Whitam et al., 1995), a much larger study of better-adjusted persons failed to support their findings. Bell, Weinberg, and Hammersmith (1981) could find little evidence that male homosexuals had dominant mothers and weak fathers, or that female homosexuals had chosen their fathers as role models.

What can we conclude? Although there is some evidence that persons with a family background like those described by Bieber or Wolff "have a greater than average likelihood of becoming homosexual" (Marmor, 1980), it is important to keep in mind that homosexuals have all kinds of parents, both good and bad, caring and cold (Masters & Johnson, 1979). The same is true of heterosexuals. The psychoanalytic theories cannot possibly begin to explain the sexual orientation of all individuals (Downey & Friedman, 1998).

Interestingly, although Freud's followers viewed homosexuality as a mental illness (see section on homosexuality), Freud himself apparently had a less harsh attitude, as evidenced by this letter to the mother of a homosexual son:

> **Dear Mrs. _____,**
> **I gather from your letter that your son is a homosexual. . . . Homosexuality is assuredly no advantage, but it is nothing to be ashamed of, no vice, no degradation, it cannot be classified as an illness; we consider it to be a variation of the sexual function produced by a certain arrest of sexual development.**
> **Many highly respectable individuals of ancient and modern times have been homosexuals, several of the greatest men among them (Plato, Michelangelo, Leonardo da Vinci, etc.).**
> **It is a great injustice to persecute homosexuality as a crime, and cruelty, too.**

OTHER PSYCHOSOCIAL EXPLANATIONS

Social learning theory explains homosexuality and heterosexuality as learned behaviors (Gagnon & Simon, 1973; Masters & Johnson, 1979). This theory would therefore treat homosexuality and heterosexuality similarly, with each type of sexual orientation being dependent on the learning history of an individual. Homosexuals would be expected to have had good or rewarding experiences with same-sex individuals and bad experiences with members of the opposite sex in their early social experiences. Once initiated, the sexual act itself, being pleasurable, becomes rewarding. Over time, they would therefore learn to associate homosexuality with more pleasure than heterosexuality. Also, they may have had role models to pattern themselves after in their youth.

What is the evidence in support of this explanation? Many people assume that homosexuals are people who are not attractive (or masculine or feminine) enough to "make it" with the opposite sex. However, the data do not support this. Most lesbians, for example, have had pleasurable sexual relations with men (Diamant et al., 1999). They simply prefer sexual relations with women. In their study, Bell, Weinberg, and Hammersmith (1981) found that "homosexual orientation among females reflects neither a lack of heterosexual experience nor a history of particularly unpleasant heterosexual experiences." However, there is some evidence that an extremely bad negative experience, such as being the victim of rape, can result in an individual's avoiding heterosexual relations (Grundlach, 1977).

There is also some evidence that if a person's first adolescent (or preadolescent) sexual experiences, such as mutual masturbation, are with an individual of the same sex, then there is a greater than usual chance that the person's sexual orientation will be homosexual (Van Wyk, 1984; but see Box 11–A). Storms (1980) has suggested that children who begin puberty early are particularly more likely than others to experiment with adolescent same-sex sexual experiences (for which there are more opportunities than opposite-sex sexual experiences), and these early pleasurable experiences make it more than likely that a homosexual orientation will develop. As a general rule, male homosexuals do begin puberty at an earlier age than heterosexual men (Blanchard & Bogaert, 1996a). There is no evidence to support the myth that adolescents became homosexual because they were seduced by an older homosexual (Bell et al., 1981).

Even if the studies about adolescent same-sex sexual experimentation are true, that still leaves the question of which came first: Did same-sex sexual experimentation lead to a homosexual orientation, or did homosexual tendencies lead to same-sex sexual experimentation? Bell et al. (1981) found that a person's sexual orientation was usually well established by adolescence and that gender (role) nonconformity during childhood was often, but not always, associated later with a homosexual orientation. Similar results have been reported by others (Phillips & Over, 1995).

The relation between childhood gender nonconformity and later homosexuality is greater for boys than it is for girls ("tomboyish" behavior by girls is accepted more than "sissy" behavior by boys). One study found that for boys, the absence of masculine traits was a better predictor of later homosexuality than the presence of feminine traits (Hockenberry & Billingham, 1987). Another study found that for boys who persistently play with girls' dolls and display other stereotypically feminine traits, there is about a 75 percent chance of their being homosexual as adults (Bailey & Zucker, 1995).

Richard Green (1987) studied a small sample of extremely effeminate boys (who he called "sissy boys") over a 15-year period. A few families reinforced the behavior, but most of the families simply tolerated (rather than initiated) it. The boys had poor relations with their fathers, but this could be the result of the boys' "unmasculine" behavior rather than a cause. Most of the boys engaged in homosexual fantasizing and behavior as adolescents, but some developed a clear heterosexual orientation. Thus, even in cases of extreme childhood gender-role nonconformity, one cannot absolutely predict future sexual orientation. Also, keep in mind that homosexual men who were "sissies" as boys are only a portion of homosexuals; many showed typical gender-role behavior as children (Bell et al., 1981; see section on gender roles).

Green's subjects had been different since early childhood. Bell et al. (1981) suggested that their results, along with those of Green (1987) and others, indicated a possible biological basis for sexual orientation. Let's now consider the evidence for that.

DEMOGRAPHICS

Several studies have found that, on average, homosexual men had a later birth order than heterosexual men (Blanchard & Bogaert, 1996a, 1996b; Purcell et al., 2000). Moreover, effeminate homosexuality was also associated with a greater number of older brothers, but not older sisters (see Blanchard & Bogaert, 1996b). No birth order effect was observed in homosexual women (Bogaert, 1997). Birth order effects are observed for many personality characteristics, but not in families where children are adopted (Beer & Horn, 1999). This suggests that birth order effects are the result of biological influences. Blanchard and Bogaert (1996b) have suggested that the birth order effect for sexual orientation in men may be due to a reaction of the mother's immune system (to the X chromosome chemicals) triggered by the previous male fetuses. This, they say, might affect differentiation of the brain.

BIOLOGICAL EXPLANATIONS

There is no question that men and women are structurally different. In Chapter 10, you learned that there are also some differences in male and female brains. Is it possible that brain difference could account for differences in sexual orientation?

GENETIC FACTORS. In 1952, Kallman found nearly 100 percent concordance for homosexual orientation in identical twins (i.e., if one twin was homosexual, the other almost always was too). The concordance for fraternal (nonidentical) twins was only about 10 percent. Similar results were found by a German researcher (Schlegel, 1962), and together these findings challenged the prevailing view that homosexuality was determined by social influences.

The results of these first studies with twins were questioned when several reports appeared in the 1960s and 1970s of single cases or small numbers of identical twins who were discordant for homosexual orientation (see Whitam et al., 1993, for a review). However, several recent larger-scale studies have reestablished a possible genetic basis for sexual orientation. Bailey and Pillard (1991) studied 167 pairs of brothers and found that 52 percent of the identical twin brothers of homosexual men in the study were also homosexual, compared with 22 percent of nonidentical twins and 11 percent of adoptive brothers. In another study of 143 pairs of sisters, they found that 48 percent of identical twins of homosexual women were also homosexual, compared to 16 percent of nonidentical twins and 6 percent of adoptive sisters (Bailey et al., 1993). Two more recent studies found a slightly lower concordance rate (Bailey et al., 2000; Kendler et al., 2000), but another study found a higher concordance rate (65.8 percent) for homosexual orientation in identical twin brothers (Whitam et al., 1993). However, not everyone obtains similar results. A recent study found a high concordance rate in female identical twins (60 percent) but not in male twins (Hershberger, 1997). A small study has suggested that in cases where male homosexuality is inherited, it is associated with childhood gender nonconformity (Dawood et al., 2000).

Still another group of researchers found that 33 of 40 pairs of homosexual brothers shared the identical DNA pattern on the tip of one arm of their X chromosomes (inherited from the mother; Hamer et al., 1993), but another group of scientists could not duplicate Hamer's findings (Rice et al., 1999). More recently, researchers have presented evidence that male (but not female) homosexuality is determined by a gene in a specific region of the X chromosome (Hu et al., 1995; Turner, 1995).

What does all this mean? Although the studies suffered from several methodological flaws, they leave little doubt of a biological contribution to sexual orientation. But how much? Remember, not all of the identical twins were homosexual, and in the study by Hamer et al. (1993), seven pairs of homosexual brothers did not share the same gene pattern. Michael Bailey, author of several twin studies, concluded that "the degree of the genetic contribution (to homosexuality) could range from 30 percent to 70 percent depending on the assumptions used." Even if his upper estimate is correct, that still leaves a lot of room for the influence of social and environmental factors. Social interactions might well mediate aspects of any genetic role in sexual orientation (Byne & Parsons, 1993). Recall, for example, the extreme gender nonconformity displayed by children in the "sissy boy" syndrome (see previous section). Even if this is due to genetics, treating the children differently from other children could reinforce later nonconformity in gender roles (Hines & Green, 1991).

ANATOMICAL FACTORS. At about the same time that researchers were finding a genetic component to sexual orientation, others were reporting differences between the brains of heterosexuals and homosexuals. Simon LeVay, a neuroscientist, performed autopsies on the brains of 19 homosexual men and 16 heterosexual men. He found that a part of the hypothalamus (at the base of the brain) known to influence sexual behavior was more than twice as large in heterosexuals (LeVay, 1991). This area of the hypothalamus is affected by sex hormones (see next section).

LeVay's study followed a report that another part of the hypothalamus, the suprachiasmatic nucleus, had twice as many cells in homosexual men as in heterosexual men (Swaab & Hofman, 1990). A subsequent study found that a major fiber bundle that connects the two halves of the brain (the anterior commissure)

was 34 percent larger in homosexual men than in heterosexual men and no different from the relative size of the same structure in the brains of heterosexual women (when brain weight differences between men and women were adjusted; Allen & Gorski, 1992). The anatomy of the inner ear in lesbians has been found to be nearly identical to those of men, suggesting that their anatomy has been masculinized in some way (McFadden & Pasanen, 1998).

Men and women differ in performance on several neurological tests of verbal, spatial, and mechanical skills. This is usually interpreted as being due to differences in cerebral asymmetry. If heterosexuals' and homosexuals' brain anatomy differs, you might expect that they would also differ in these tests. Do they? Initial results indicate that homosexual men perform very similar to heterosexual women, but no differences in cognitive performances have been found between heterosexual and homosexual women (Sanders & Wright, 1997; Wegesin, 1998; see Lalumiere et al., 2000).

What do the anatomical findings mean, and how are they related to the genetic research? Dean Heimer of the National Institutes of Health concluded, "The simplest interpretation would be that there is a gene, or genes, that control the growth of [the INAH-3 and other brain structures]. Both point to the same idea, that there is a biological component of sexual orientation" (cited by Maugh in the *Los Angeles Times,* 1991). However, these results do not prove causation; a recent study found that adult sexual behavior in rats can change the anatomy of the brain (Breedlove, 1997).

HORMONAL FACTORS. How might genes affect brain anatomy; and if that can be determined, when? Before birth? Shortly after birth? During childhood? At puberty?

It is likely that the critical link is hormones. Gorski and colleagues (1978) were the first to show differences in brain (hypothalamus) structure between male and female rats. Gorski's group later manipulated the levels of sex hormones in newborn rats and, as a result, were able to get male rats that exhibited the sexual behavior of female rats. Several studies with nonhuman species have shown that treatment with hormones prenatally (before birth) can result in homosexual behavior (see Kelly et al., 1999, for a review).

In humans, one thing we do know is that the level of circulating male sex hormones (testosterone) in adult heterosexual and homosexual men does not differ (see Gladue, 1988). Furthermore, giving sex hormones to adult homosexuals (e.g., testosterone to homosexual men, for example) does not change their sexual orientation. However, there is evidence for differences in hormonal responses. When injected with the female hormone estrogen, women show an elevation of the pituitary hormone LH (luteinizing hormone; see Chapter 3), while men normally show no elevation. Studies have found that male homosexuals show an intermediate elevation in LH after an injection of estrogen (Dorner et al., 1975; Gladue et al., 1984). Does this mean that homosexual men have a "female" hypothalamus? These and other studies suggest that if hormones do cause a difference in brain structure, it would have to be caused early in life.

Ethical considerations do not allow manipulation of hormones in human fetuses or infants, but there is some evidence that what has been found in nonhuman species is also true in humans. For example, studies have found that women who were exposed to high levels of masculinizing hormones before birth (see the discussion of congenital adrenal hyperplasia in Chapter 10) are much more likely than others to prefer boys' toys and activities as children (Berenbaum & Snyder, 1995) and develop a homosexual or bisexual orientation as adults (Meyer-Bahlburg et al., 1995; Money & Schwartz, 1977).

We also know that certain anatomical features occur early in embryonic/fetal development, and if the same hormones affected sexual orientation, we might expect to see a relationship. Recent studies have, in fact, found a relationship in men between sexual orientation and handedness (Lalumiere et al., 2000), finger length (Breedlove, 2000), and penis size (Bogaert & Hershberger, 1999). The associations were generally small but suggest (contrary to most expectations) that the men were exposed to high levels of adrogens at some point during pregnancy.

Ellis and Ames (1987), in an extensive review of both human and animal research, concluded that sexual orientation is primarily determined before birth. According to their theory, all mammals begin life with a single sexual orientation. It is the presence of certain (though yet undetermined) amounts of hormonal factors that directs sexual development and creates a variety of sexual orientations, heterosexuality being the most frequent orientation. The presence of testosterone during the 2nd month of embryonic development, you recall, is critical for determining one's sexual anatomy (see Chapter 10). Ellis and Ames claim that the critical period for the development of sexual orientation comes between the middle of the 2nd month and the middle of the 5th month of pregnancy; others claim that hormones have their effect in the first year or two after birth (recall the work by Gorski). But notice that all agree that the effect of hormones on sexual orientation occurs very early. Ellis and Ames list several potential factors that could influence an unborn child's development of sexual orientation, including genetic-hormonal factors, drugs, stress in the mother, and immune system dysfunctions.

CONCLUSIONS

Although there is a growing body of evidence for a biological contribution to sexual orientation, this does not mean that one's sexual orientation is destined by biology (Byne & Parsons, 1993; Gladue, 1994). The studies with identical twins point strongly to a biological factor, but the fact that about half the twins were discordant (in spite of the fact that they had identical genes) shows that environment also plays a role.

Most researchers today agree that biological and social influences *both* contribute to the development of sexual orientation. The question is no longer nature versus nurture, but to what extent each influences orientation. They certainly interact in some complex yet undetermined manner. At the moment, the most we can say for biological factors is that they probably *predispose* (this is not the same as cause) an individual to a particular sexual orientation. What this means is that given a certain genetic background and a particular set of social and environmental influences, it is more likely than not that a person will assume a heterosexual or homosexual orientation.

Psychologist Daryl Bem (1996) presented an intriguing hypothesis. He proposed that biology (genes, anatomy, hormones) "[does] not code for sexual orientation per se but for childhood temperaments that influence a child's preferences for sex-typical or sex-atypical activities and peers." For example, boys typically prefer rough-and-tumble play, but a boy who is temperamentally not aggressive may shy away from these activities and prefer girl-typical activities. In other words, biology does not code for sexual orientation directly but for temperaments which the environment then steers in the direction of a particular orientation.

Miller (2000) has offered a sociobiological explanation that is somewhat similar. He proposes that male sexual orientation is a trait influenced by several genes that have effects during development (e.g., on the brain). Inheritance of some of these genes allows heterosexual men to be sensitive, understanding, and kind, and as men inherit more of these genes there is a greater shift in the feminine direction.

The recent genetic and anatomical findings have created debate in the homosexual community. On the one hand, there are those who feel that proof of a biological determinant of sexual orientation will lead to greater tolerance. As stated by Richard Pillard, coauthor of the twin studies, "A genetic component in sexual orientation says, 'This is not a fault, and it's not your fault'" (quoted in Gelman et al., 1992). Or, as stated by George Neighbors, Jr., of the Federation of Parents and Friends of Lesbians and Gays, "It may help people look at this as a genetic issue. . . . If you believe in God or nature, that's what homosexuality develops from" (quoted by Recur, 1993). On the other hand, Neighbors and others worry that if a biological basis can be found, some people with an anti-homosexual bias will press for medical changes in sexual orientation, as was tried in the recent past (Byne & Stein, 1997).

It is certainly the case that gays and lesbians are often treated negatively by others. Let us examine what it means to be homosexual in our culture.

HOMOSEXUALITY

Homosexuality is a word derived from the Greek *homo,* meaning "same" (do not confuse this with the Latin *homo,* meaning "man"). The term was first used by a Hungarian physician in a pamphlet published in Germany in 1869 (Gregersen, 1982) and was popularized in the English language two decades later by Henry Havelock Ellis. The prefix *hetero-,* by the way, is also derived from a Greek word and means "different."

Homosexual behavior has been reported in nearly all cultures throughout the world (see Box 11–A). Same-sex sexual behavior (male-male or female-female mounting) has also been observed and studied in a variety of nonhuman species, including many primates and dolphins. Among male animals, it is often done as a display of dominance, and otherwise generally serves as a social function (reinforcing relations) rather than a sexual one (see Denniston, 1980; Ford & Beach, 1951).

Over the years there have been many derogatory terms used to describe homosexuals (e.g., "faggot," "queer," "fairy," "dyke"). Most homosexuals prefer the term **gay** for a male homosexual (although in some places the term is used for homosexuals of either sex) and **lesbian** for a female homosexual (derived from the name of the Greek island Lesbos, where, in about 600 B.C., the poet Sappho led a circle of young female disciples). Heterosexuals are often referred to as **"straights."** Among some gay and lesbian organizations, the term *homophile* is preferred when referring to a homosexual person.

HISTORY OF ATTITUDES ABOUT HOMOSEXUALITY

Western attitudes about homosexuality have varied considerably throughout history. In ancient Greece, same-sex sexual behavior between adult men and boys (called **pederasty**) was widely accepted as an alternative to heterosexuality (Boswell, 1980). Cantarella (1992) wrote that in ancient Greece pederasty had "become in practice an absolutely normal relationship, socially accepted, engaged in with total freedom, and celebrated by the poets." Plato praised homosexual relations in his

Figure 11–2 Socrates. This Greek philosopher and teacher believed that any evil committed by human beings is done out of ignorance. He devoted his life completely to seeking truth and goodness.

Symposium. Homosexual relations between Greek scholars (e.g., Socrates, Plato) and their students were considered to be a natural part of the young boys' education. Marriage between individuals of the same sex was legal among the upper class during the time of the Roman Empire, but the most common type of same-sex behavior engaged in was also pederasty (see Rind, 1998).

Same-sex sexual activities were practiced—often as part of religious rituals—by many groups of Hebrews prior to the 7th century B.C. As part of a reformation movement designed to unify the many Hebrew groups, homosexuality was thereafter condemned (along with other acts that had been part of older rituals) and was made punishable by death:

If a man lies with a male as with a woman, both of them have committed an abomination; they shall be put to death, their blood is upon them. (Leviticus 20:13, Revised Standard Version)

Female homosexuality was dealt with less harshly by the Jews because it didn't involve "spillage of seed" or violation of male property rights.

European Christians, following the Roman tradition, initially were tolerant of same-sex sexual behaviors, especially pederasty (Boswell, 1980; Rind, 1998). It wasn't until the time of St. Thomas Aquinas (A.D. 1225–1274), who emphasized the view of St. Augustine that the only purpose of sex was procreation, that homosexuality came to be viewed as unnatural or "against the laws of nature." However, Boswell (1980) notes that while same-sex sexual behavior was considered a sin in the Middle Ages, people who committed the sin were not then viewed as a type of person who was different from others. This remained true during the 1600s and 1700s, when homosexual acts became a crime as well as a sin.

It wasn't until the late 1800s and the rise of modern medicine (particularly psychiatry) that people who engaged in homosexual acts came to be viewed as a particular class of people—people with a mental illness. Freud (1924) referred to homosexuals as "perverts" in his academic teaching. As a result, there has never been a period in

gay A term generally used to refer to male homosexuals, although in some places it is used to refer to homosexuals of either sex.

lesbian A female homosexual.

straight A term used by homosexuals for a heterosexual.

pederasty A same-sex sexual behavior between adult men and boys.

Western culture with as much intolerance of homosexuality as there was in the 20th century. Because they were viewed as mentally ill, the medical profession subjected homosexuals to frontal lobotomies, forced castrations or hysterectomies, electric shock treatments, hormone injections, and endless hours of psychotherapy (Katz, 1976).

Until the 1960s, homosexuals had never been studied outside of a medical or prison setting. Then, in 1957, Evelyn Hooker published a paper showing that nonclinical heterosexual and homosexual men could not be distinguished by the best psychological tests (i.e., the homosexual men were as well adjusted as the heterosexual men). Even Freud had recognized this to be true:

> **Often, though not always, they are men and women who otherwise have reached an irreproachably high standard of mental growth and development, intellectually and ethnically, and are only afflicted with this one fateful peculiarity.** (Freud, 1924, p. 313)

Finally, in 1973, the American Psychiatric Association decided to discontinue classifying homosexuality as a mental illness (see Hooker, 1993, for a review of some of the events leading to this decision). The decision was not unanimously applauded; 37 percent of APA members were opposed to change, and some are still opposed (e.g., Socarides, 1996).

The APA decision has had far-reaching implications. If homosexuality is no longer considered an illness, there is no need to cure it. As you can see, the way individuals deal with homosexuality is based on what they believe. However, attitudes often change very slowly. Simply being homosexual is no longer a criminal offense, but many states still have old laws on the books that prohibit the sexual expression of homosexuality. For example, in 18 states there are laws against anal or oral sex that are used usually only to prosecute homosexuals (see Chapter 18). A police raid on the Stonewall Inn in Greenwich Village, New York City, in 1969 led to 3 days of public demonstrations, an event that many say was the beginning of the gay rights movement.

Similarly, the Catholic Church no longer considers homosexuality, per se, a sin, but it continues to condemn homosexual behavior. A letter to bishops worldwide written by Cardinal Joseph Ratzinger and approved by Pope John Paul II stressed that homosexual acts are sins. Homosexuals instead were urged to lead "a chaste life." In another letter to U.S. Catholic bishops in 1992, the Vatican called homosexuality "an objective disorder" and encouraged discrimination against homosexuals in public housing, family health benefits, and the hiring of teachers. The June 1988 convention of the Southern Baptists adopted a resolution that said that homosexuals,

"like all sinners, can receive forgiveness through personal faith in Jesus Christ," but added that homosexuality "is not a normal lifestyle and is an abomination in the eyes of God." Similarly, at their once-a-decade meeting in 1998, Anglican Church leaders said that gays and lesbians are "loved by God," but that homosexuality is "incompatible with scripture." While there are some exceptions, most Christian churches continue to have a rejecting or punitive attitude toward homosexuality.

During World War II and the Korean War, gays were as likely to have served in the military as heterosexual men (Black et al., 2000). However, the U.S. military has always banned and discharged homosexuals. In 1992, for example, Colonel Margarethe Cammermeyer, a 26-year career officer and Vietnam veteran, was discharged for admitting that she was a lesbian. At the urging of President Clinton, a "compromise" was enacted in 1993. Under the "don't ask, don't tell" policy, new recruits could no longer be asked if they were homosexual, but they could still be discharged for disclosing their orientation or for engaging in homosexual acts. The military opposed the policy, and by 1999, antigay behavior by military personnel had doubled and discharges of homosexuals from the military had increased by 73 percent (Vistica, 2000). In 1999, President Clinton called the "don't ask, don't tell" policy a failure.

SEXUAL PREJUDICE TODAY

Views by students in my class about homosexuality and homosexuals are greatly mixed:

> "During my junior year in high school I made a new male friend. The more I got to know him, the more I began to suspect that he was gay. This scared me. As a result of my growing fears I discontinued our friendship."

> "My feeling is that homosexuality is disgusting. . . . Just thinking about it gives me the creeps."

> "A few of my closest friends are homosexuals. At first, I admit, it was a shock when they told me, but that never stopped me from being their friend. My boyfriend is definitely homophobic and it aggravates me every time he says something negative."

> "To be really honest, if anyone is a homosexual, I don't care, as long as they are good people. . . . I believe that homosexuals should be legally accepted."

> "I believe that homosexuality is morally wrong. While I try hard not to judge the feelings of others, I do not agree with acting out these feelings."

> "When I was in high school I worked at a flower shop. I didn't realize the owner's son was gay until my junior year. He acted totally normal. . . . One

afternoon I saw him driving somewhere with his boyfriend. Ever since that day I am kind of afraid and don't like to even have conversation with him. I don't know why I fear him so much because he has never done any harm to me."

Many people are prejudiced against others whom they perceive to be different. People discriminate on the basis of skin color, gender, and religion, but hostility toward homosexuals is probably far more accepted among Americans than any other type of bias (Goleman, 1990). For example, in 1966 the editors of the highly respected *Time* magazine wrote a two-page editorial on homosexuals, which concluded with the following statement:

> [Homosexuality is] "a pathetic little second-rate substitute for reality, a pitiable flight from life. As such it deserves fairness, compassion, understanding and, when possible, treatment. But it deserves no encouragement, no glamorization, no rationalization, no fake status as minority martyrdom, no sophistry about simple differences in taste—and, above all, no pretense that it is anything but a pernicious sickness." (*Time*, 1966, p. 41)

Negative attitudes about homosexuals reached a peak among the American public in the 1980s. In a survey conducted in the early 1990s, 89 percent of 15- to 19-year-old teenaged boys believed that sex between two men was "disgusting" (Marsiglio, 1993b). Only 12 percent said they could be friends with a gay person. Surveys conducted in the mid-1990s, on the other hand, found that about 60 percent of all Americans felt that sex between two adults of the same sex is always wrong (Yang, 1997).

More recent surveys indicate that the American public continues to become more tolerant. *Newsweek* found that 46 percent of Americans regard homosexuality to be a sin, down from 54 percent in 1998 (Leland, 2000a). Over 80 percent said that gays and lesbians deserve job protection and 78 percent were for equal rights in housing. And for the first time, a majority were in favor of gay and lesbian spouses receiving health insurance benefits and social security. In 2000, the major automakers did, in fact, offer medical and dental benefits to the same-sex partners of their employees. (Attitudes about marriage and parenting were more harsh; see later section.) Interestingly, knowledge that homosexuality has, in part, a biological basis has made some people more tolerant and others more negative (Oldham & Kasser, 1999).

Despite some advances, there is still a sizable proportion of Americans with strongly negative attitudes about homosexuality. In 1998, Senate Majority Leader Trent Lott called homosexuality a sickness and a sin and compared it to alcoholism and kleptomania. One of the leaders in the antigay movement is radio and TV talk-show host Dr. Laura Schlessinger, who calls homosexuality a "biological error" and homosexuals "de-

viants" (Gates & Miller, 2000). Her broadcasts reach 20 million listeners. These widespread negative attitudes are sometimes displayed in the voting booth. By 1993, more than 130 states, counties, and cities had passed laws to protect gays and lesbians against discrimination, but there has been a backlash. Oregon voters narrowly rejected an anti-homosexual measure in 1992, but a similar ballot measure in Colorado passed in the same year (the Colorado Supreme Court subsequently overturned it). In 1998, voters in Maine became the first to repeal a homosexual rights law.

There is also considerable controversy regarding even teaching about homosexuality in schools. When the New York City school board proposed a "Children of the Rainbow" curriculum in 1992 that included the young children's books *Daddy's Roommate* (about a boy who spends weekends with his father and his father's male lover) and *Heather Has Two Mommies*, it ignited a public outcry. In a debate in the U.S. Senate about whether or not to withhold funds from school districts that "promote" homosexuality, Senator Robert Smith asked, "Do we really want our youngsters subjected to [homosexuality].... Do we want to educate them to it just to make sure that they have a good shot at becoming lesbian or homosexual?" (Petrovic, 1999). Nearly half of Americans are opposed to homosexuals even teaching in elementary schools (Yang, 1997), and scholars in the field argue about whether or not teachers should be allowed to express any negative views of homosexuality (Petrovic, 1999; Reiss, 1999).

Homosexuals are also often victims of hate crimes. Hate crimes are defined by the FBI as "crime motivated by preformed, negative bias against persons, property, or organizations based solely on race, religion, ethnicity/national origin, sexual orientation, or disability" (U.S. Department of Justice, 1996). Every year in the United States there are well over 1,000 reported hate crimes directed at individuals because of their sexual orientation (Herek, 2000). In many cases, the antigay violence is quite extreme. In October 1998, Matthew Shepard, a gay college student in Wyoming, was beaten into a coma by two men, who then tied him crucifixion-style to a fence. Matthew died 5 days later from a smashed skull. Six months later, Billy Jack Gaither, a factory worker, was beaten to death in Alabama because he made a sexual overture to one of his two assailants.

Hate crimes are just an extreme of the negative behavior that is often directly targeted toward homosexuals. Over 90 percent of gay men have been verbally abused or threatened (Herek, 1989). In a recent study, one-third of a sample of men at a reputedly liberal and tolerant college admitted to having used physical violence or name-calling directed at homosexuals (Franklin, 2000). In such a harsh world, is it any wonder that many homosexuals suffer from major depression and alcohol or substance abuse, and that 18 to 28 percent of young gays and lesbians have attempted suicide (Bradford et al., 1994; Cochran & Mays, 2000).

The most widely used term to describe negative attitudes toward homosexuals is **homophobia,** a term first used in the 1960s. However, homophobia generally implies that negative attitudes are the result of irrational fears that reflect individual psychopathology. Psychologist Gregory Herek (2000a) has proposed that a better term is sexual prejudice. **Sexual prejudice** is socially reinforced and includes negative attitudes toward individuals, communities, and homosexual behaviors. Sexual prejudice is greater among men than it is among women, and prejudiced men generally have a more negative attitude about gay men than they do lesbians (Herek, 2000b; Kite & Whitley, 1996).

Why do some people have such fear of and hostility toward homosexuals? Studies find that among men, homophobic views are greatest in those with stereotypic male gender-role attitudes (i.e., men who strongly believe in a masculinist ideology), a religious fundamentalist attitude, little education, and who score high on measures of authoritarianism (Herek, 2000; Marsiglio, 1993b). Among women, authoritarian attitudes are strongly associated with sexual prejudice (Basow & Johnson, 2000). However, this tells us nothing of the psychological basis of sexual prejudice.

Some psychologists believe that antigay behavior and attitudes stem from "self-righteousness in which homosexuals are perceived as contemptible threats to the moral universe" (Goleman, 1990). Some antigay heterosexuals do, in fact, view themselves as enforcers of social and moral norms (Franklin, 2000). However, there is a major problem with this as an explanation for all sexual prejudice by men. Recall that heterosexual men generally have much more negative attitudes toward male homosexuals than they do toward female homosexuals (Herek, 2000b; Kite & Whitley, 1996). In fact, many sexually explicit male-oriented magazines regularly devote several pages to women-on-women sexual activity, and female homosexual sex scenes are often shown in hard-core porno films made for male heterosexual audiences. Why? Publishers and producers of this material would not include it if they weren't certain that a great many heterosexual men are aroused by it. In fact, research has shown that many heterosexual men find lesbianism highly erotic and that this improves their attitudes toward lesbians (Louderback & Whitley, 1997). If the basics of sexual prejudice by men was morality only, there should be no difference in heterosexual attitudes toward gays and lesbians.

Obviously, male homosexuality must be more threatening to many men than female homosexuality. Some of Freud's

© 1977 Dayton Daily News and Tribune Media Services, Inc. Courtesy of Grimmy, Inc.

homophobia An irrational fear of homosexual individuals and homosexuality.

sexual prejudice Socially reinforced negative attitudes toward homosexuals, homosexual communities, and homosexual behaviors.

followers believe that it is the result of remnants of homosexuality in the "normal" (i.e., heterosexual) resolution of the Oedipus complex—identification with one's father involves love for one's father (de Kuyper, 1993). Some homophobic men, in fact, are physically aroused (show penile enlargement) when shown male homosexual videos (Adams et al., 1996).

Most researchers have a different explanation. For most people, adolescence is a confusing time as they try to establish their own identity and sexual orientation. Gregory Herek, the leading authority on homophobia, believes that antigay prejudice is an attempt to suppress any attraction to the same sex (see Herek, 1988). Herek says, "The teens and early 20's [are] a time of identity consolidation, struggling with issues of manhood and masculinity, how one becomes a man. By attacking a gay man or a lesbian, these guys are trying symbolically to affirm their manhood" (Associated Press, July 1993). Acts of sexual prejudice are most common among men whose peer group has very negative attitudes about homosexuality (Franklin, 2000; Herek, 2000). In other words, overt acts of sexual prejudice are often committed as a way of proving one's masculinity to one's peers. Heterosexuals tend to be much less prejudiced when they know gay and lesbian individuals personally (Herek, 2000).

Sexual prejudice affects relations among heterosexuals as well. Many Americans were probably shocked at seeing Eastern European and Asian male athletes hug and kiss each other in international competitions such as the Olympics. Such behavior is normal in their countries, where they have learned to differentiate affection from sex. Here, sexual prejudice is so widespread that it prevents many same-sex family members (most commonly, fathers and sons) and friends from being affectionate with one another. It prevents many people, especially men, from enjoying intimate relations with others. Are you able to hug your same-sex parent? Good friends of the same sex? If not, examine which fears prevent you from doing so. Sexual prejudice hurts everyone, including those who display it.

> *PERSONAL REFLECTIONS*
> *Do you ever judge others exclusively, or almost exclusively, by their sexual orientation? How do you suppose you would feel if others ignored your accomplishments in school, in your career, in your sports and hobbies, and in your community, and judged you on just your sex life?*

COMING OUT

With so many people in our society having negative attitudes about homosexuality, it should come as no surprise that acknowledging to oneself that one is homosexual, and then publicly declaring it, is often very difficult. The process of disclosing one's homosexuality is called **coming out.** There are several stages to this process. I will follow the stages outlined by the Boston Women's Health Book Collective (1984).

The first stage is *admitting to oneself that one has a homosexual orientation.* Some researchers believe that sexual orientation is established by the age of 4 (Gordon & Snyder, 1989), and many gays and lesbians knew that they were "different" at a very young age. Attraction to individuals of the same sex generally occurs well before sexual activity begins (Bell et al., 1981).

> "I discovered my sexuality at a surprising 6 years old. Naturally I didn't know at that young age that I was a lesbian, but I can remember having 'crushes' on my teachers and female upperclassmen."

> "I think that the most important thing you lectured on was the predisposition of sexual orientation before birth. I, too, felt different as a child as early as by 10." (All examples are from the author's files.)

For others, self-recognition is often a confusing and anxiety-producing discovery. Some do not recognize their sexual orientation until well into adolescence, or even later (recall the case history in the section on gender roles). Because so many people have a negative opinion of it, recognizing that one is gay or lesbian is often a lonely and painful experience.

> "As a young gay person, you feel all of the things every other young person feels. You feel all of the normal doubts, uncertainties, questions and frustrations common to that time of life. And you also begin to have feelings and thoughts as precious and deep as any can be: of self, and worth, and love, and life, and purpose. But when you are young and gay, you also face a world of pain and isolation few people have to face.

> "We all know how vulnerable and fragile a life can be in those early years. And yet few people seem ready or willing to consider how it must feel to be young and gay. In a time when nurturing and affirmation are so important, the young gay person is told by his church that he is evil. The law says that she is a criminal. Society says that they are misfits. The media displays freaks. And the world seems to say they are less than a whole person. And so, when you are young and gay, you can feel so much hatred, so much rejection, so unwanted, so unwelcome, so worthless, so unaccepted and so misunderstood.

> "Other people throughout time have known the kind of pain and persecution which reaches deep into a person's heart. There have always been people who were made to feel hated and demeaned because of their color, their religion, their heritage, or their gender. But as much pain and suffering as these people have known, they also knew they were not alone. They always had someone else they could see who was just like them; someone to identify with. And most important of all, they had someone to talk to; someone to share the pain with.

> "When you are young and gay, you feel the same terrible depth of pain. But you look around and there is no one to talk to; no one to share the pain with. There is no one who has feelings like yours or who understands how deeply you hurt. You feel so isolated and so alone. And at times, that vulnerability and pain and isolation can be so terribly overwhelming." (Steve L., personal communication, New Orleans)

In the next stage, the individual *gets to know other homosexuals,* thus ending the sense of isolation. It is easier to come out if the individual finds acceptance in others, and those most likely to be accepting are other homosexuals. Most gays and lesbians were raised in the same anti-homosexual environment as others, and by coming into contact with other homosexuals, they can replace these negative stereotypes with a more positive attitude about homosexuality—and about themselves.

> "As I was growing up, I heard all of the jokes and stories about the lives gays lived. I saw all of the negative images that the media could dish up for public consumption. . . . I wanted to find someone I could share the rest of my life with.

> "And then I looked for that life and tried to find it. . . . The only place society had allowed gays to meet was in one small bar-filled pocket of the city. And so I turned to where I was accepted and where I could breathe. But then I heard society condemn me because of the life-style I 'chose' to lead.

> "In time, I grew to learn that there was more of a life to be had than just the narrow world which society tries to impose upon gays. I met many happy and healthy

coming out Disclosing to others one's homosexual orientation, from the expression "coming out of the closet."

gay people who helped me to understand and learn and grow." (Steve L., personal communication, New Orleans)

Once contact is made with other gays and lesbians, a new way of expressing sexuality has to be developed. In many ways, what happens next is quite similar to what happens when heterosexuals begin to date. There are initial relationships and breakups, and often lasting relationships are eventually formed. Contact with other homosexuals may also lead to an increased interest in gay rights and other political activities to support the rights of homosexuals.

In the third, very difficult, stage, the individual *tells family and friends of his or her sexual orientation.* Many hide their sexual orientation from others for long periods.

"But as bad as you hurt, you keep the pain to yourself. You fear being discovered by the people you love and need the most; for everything your world has taught you makes you afraid you will lose their love and friendship if they find out you are gay. The world gives you the pain, and then makes it impossible for you to talk about it because of fear.

"So not only does the world isolate you from learning about your feelings and others who are like you, but you begin to isolate a part of yourself from family and friends. You begin to develop techniques of telling half-truths and skirting around questions. You learn how to hide inside of yourself and smother feelings. You learn how to be around other people without letting them get too close. You learn how to survive.

"And then, you grow tired of hiding. You grow tired of not being able to share the beauty as

well as the pain that fills your life. You grow tired of not being as close as you want to be to the people you care most about.

"But the fear is still very strong. You find it is easier to avoid the questions by just staying away more often. And you don't have to find as much strength to hide and be silent. So you drift further and further from the people you love the most and you feel the pain and isolation building up inside." (Steve L., personal communication, New Orleans)

Some, because of social constraints and possible punitive actions, feel that they must keep their orientation a secret.

"I've come to terms with my sexuality and live with it. However, I don't choose to show that side of me. I am in the military and must remain discreet. As a matter of fact, I'm in charge of a number of troops. Some members of my unit are in this class, which keeps me from relaxing. Although the new policy in the military is 'Don't ask,' 'Don't tell,' 'Don't pursue,' if found to be gay I would be discharged." (from the author's files)

When an individual does finally disclose his or her homosexuality to the family, it often creates a crisis. Parents have raised their children with the expectations that they will be heterosexual. Thus, verbal and physical abuse by parents (especially by fathers) and other family members is common (D'Augelli et al., 1998).

"My parents became aware of my sexual preference when I was 18. Since that time, I have endured numerous nasty conflicts with them. My mother told me that she would rather me be a prostitute, and my father told me I would never be anyone as long I was a 'faggot.' They threw me out immediately after graduation from high school and forbade me to enter their house. They took me back on their terms—that I would go straight and live what is in their opinion a good, decent, moral life-style. I agreed and abided for a few months, but found myself extremely unhappy. I ended up moving out after a fight with my father.

"The continual attempts to persuade me to change drove me to a feeling of no self-worth. My parents do not understand that my life-style is not something I can just change—turn on and off like a light switch. They think that if they make me miserable enough, that I'll want to change." (from the author's files)

Family counseling can be very helpful here (Coenen, 1998). According to PFLAG, in most cases the family eventually adjusts and accepts their family member's homosexuality (Henderson, 1998). Usually, after the family has been told, the next step is to tell friends, but this too is often met with different reactions.

"I am a 25-year-old female. I've been close friends with 'Darla' since 7th grade. 'Darla' and I used to

Figure 11–3 Leonardo da Vinci. This Italian Renaissance painter *(Mona Lisa, The Last Supper),* anatomist, astronomer, and engineer was one of the most versatile geniuses in history.

talk about girl things all the time (boys, dating, sex). I felt there was nothing we couldn't discuss.

"Two years after high school graduation, 'Darla' and I along with another mutual friend got together for pizza and to catch up on old times. 'Darla' then said she had something very important to tell us. She told us she was gay. She said she had those feelings since she was a child and only recently acted on them. I handled her news supportively, but our other friend told 'Darla' that she was 'disgusting' and 'gross.' I'm sure without a doubt that was the hardest day in 'Darla's' life." (from the author's files)

For those of you who are homosexual and have not yet revealed your orientation to your family, contact PFLAG for help as to how best to go about it (Henderson, 1998).

The final stage is *complete openness about one's homosexuality.* This includes telling people at work; it completes the process, making one's homosexuality a total life-style. The important task for all adults, regardless of their sexual orientation, is to develop an acceptance of their sexuality (i.e., of themselves), to find acceptable ways to express it, and to learn to incorporate their sexuality into their total life-style and personality.

> *PERSONAL REFLECTIONS*
> *Gays, lesbians, and bisexuals: Have you told your family and friends of your sexual orientation? Why or why not?*

HOMOSEXUAL LIFE-STYLES AND RELATIONS

Finding companions and sexual partners can be difficult for many gays and lesbians, especially in rural areas and small towns where there may be little tolerance of homosexuals meeting together in public. In large urban areas there is usually a much larger number of people who are homosexual, as well as a much greater acceptance of their life-style. In fact, 60 percent of gay men with partners live in one of 20 cities (San Francisco, Washington, D.C., Los Angeles, Atlanta, and New York are the most popular) (Black et al., 2000). Lesbian couples are less likely to be concentrated in large cities. Prior to the 1970s, gays and lesbians met in "secret" bars, bathhouses, or public restrooms. Over time, gay bars became more than places in which to have sex. Because homosexuality was not openly tolerated, the bars provided an atmosphere where one's sexual orientation was accepted without criticism.

Over the last three decades, the gay and lesbian urban community has grown from a small collection of bars and bathhouses to entire neighborhoods of gay and lesbian stores, restaurants and coffeehouses, churches, and counseling and activity centers. The typical member of the gay community today is well educated, in a professional career position, and openly

homosexual (Black et al., 2000). In San Francisco, gays and lesbians have achieved positions of political leadership as well. This description, however, fits only those who are openly homosexual. For gay and lesbian individuals who have not yet come out, homosexual relations are still dominated by secret meetings in bars and bathrooms, often with strangers (see Humphreys, 1970, for a description of this "tearoom trade" lifestyle). Bisexuals, in particular, are unlikely to participate openly in the homosexual community (McKirnan et al., 1995).

In a 1978 study of gays and lesbians in the San Francisco Bay Area, Bell and Weinberg found that 71 percent of gay and lesbian life-styles fell into one of the following five categories:

1. **Close-coupled** (men—10 percent, women—28 percent): In this relationship, individuals have only one partner and generally report that they are happy with their sexual orientation.
2. **Open-coupled** (men—18 percent, women—17 percent): In this relationship there is a primary partner but additional sexual partners are sought outside the relationship. These people are generally happy with their sexual orientation.
3. **Functional** (men—15 percent, women—10 percent): This relationship resembles the "swinging single." Individuals are comfortable with their homosexuality, enjoy their independence, and have multiple partners.
4. **Dysfunctional** (men—12 percent, women—5 percent): These people are sexually active, but are not happy with their homosexuality and often have sexual problems.
5. **Asexual** (men—16 percent, women—11 percent): These people are single, have few partners, and are not interested in seeking partners.

The types of relationships found by Bell and Weinberg for gays and lesbians are similar to the types of relationships found among heterosexuals. Many heterosexuals believe that homosexual couples are less committed than heterosexual couples, but studies have found no differences in the amount of satisfaction and personal commitment between cohabiting heterosexuals and cohabiting homosexuals (Kurdek, 1995). In fact, gay and lesbian couples may be better at being "best friends" than heterosexual couples (Peplau, 1988). The smaller number of close-coupled pairs (in the Bell and Weinberg study) as compared to married heterosexuals may be a function of the negative attitudes that our society often has regarding homosexual couples. How would you feel if a gay or lesbian couple who were openly affectionate with each other moved next door to you? Many people would have negative or even hostile reactions. Also, young gays are not likely to see role models of monogamous, close-coupled relationships in gay bars (just as married heterosexual couples are rarely seen in "swinging singles" bars together). Furthermore, TV and the other media of our society do not give monogamous homosexual relationships much coverage or encouragement.

We will now focus specifically on the sexual relations of gays and lesbians. Before we begin, let me put things in proper perspective. The term *homosexual* tends to focus attention only on a person's sex life. However, gays and lesbians spend only a very small part of their lives engaged in sexual activities. The same is true of heterosexuals. Homosexuals and heterosexuals alike spend the large majority of their lives pursuing careers, enjoying recreational activities with family and friends, and exploring social, cultural, and political interests. Most heterosexuals would not want to be judged solely on their sexual behavior! The same is true for homosexuals.

Let us consider men first. Bell and Weinberg (1978) found that over 50 percent of their sample of openly gay men living in San Francisco had had at least 500 sexual partners in their lifetimes and 28 percent said that they'd had over 1,000 partners. Their data have been criticized for not being representative of all homosexuals, and, in fact, two earlier studies found that only 22 percent (Kinsey et al., 1948) or 8 percent (Hunt, 1974) of gays had had more than 11 sexual partners in their lifetimes. Still, the sexual life-style reported by Bell and Weinberg may not have been atypical for openly gay men living in a large urban homosexual community in 1978 (before we knew about AIDS). Many researchers have found that men, as a general rule, seek physical gratification and do not place as high a value on monogamy as do women. When large numbers of male homosexuals share this set of beliefs and have easy opportunities to meet, the large numbers of partners reported by Bell and Weinberg may not seem surprising. However, again, Bell and Weinberg's study (1978) was before anyone knew about AIDS. Unfortunately, recent surveys have found that many young gay men have abandoned safer sex practices (Stall et al., 2000; Valleroy et al., 2000).

The Kinsey (1953) survey found that only 4 percent of the lesbians sampled had had more than 11 partners, and the Hunt survey found only 1 percent. Even in the Bell and Weinberg survey (1978), a majority (70 percent) of lesbians reported having had fewer than 10 partners, while 50 percent said that they did not like to have one-night stands. Women, whether straight or lesbian, seem to value commitment and romantic love. This is reflected in the longer-lasting relationships they have compared to men (Leigh, 1989). As

Figure 11–4 Walt Whitman. Many scholars consider his *Leaves of Grass* to be the greatest collection of poems ever written by an American.

usual, men and women are very different in their sexual behaviors and attitudes, regardless of their sexual orientations.

In their sexual relations, gay and lesbian couples do everything that heterosexual couples do (Blumstein & Schwartz 1983; Masters & Johnson, 1979). They kiss, caress, engage in oral-genital sex, and, in the case of men, engage in anal intercourse (very few lesbians practice this). Lesbian couples generally take a great deal more time touching and caressing one another than heterosexual couples, for whom sexual relations are often dominated by the goal-oriented man (Hite, 1976; Masters & Johnson, 1979). Manual stimulation of the genitals and oral-genital sex are the preferred ways of reaching orgasm for lesbians (Bell & Weinberg, 1978; Masters & Johnson, 1979). Many lesbians engage in tribadism, the rubbing of genitals against another's genitals or other body parts, but very few use dildos (objects shaped like a penis). Perhaps because they take more time and understand each other's bodies better, lesbians have orgasms far more regularly during sex than do married heterosexual women (Kinsey et al., 1953). Among gays, oral-genital sex was once the most common sexual practice, followed by manual stimulation; anal intercourse was least common (Bell & Weinberg, 1978). Most men who engage in anal intercourse do so only once or twice a month, but there are a few who do it much more often (Coxon & McManus, 2000).

A common stereotype that many heterosexuals have of gays and lesbians is that they adopt a single role in a sexual relationship, with one being the "masculine" partner and the other being the "feminine" partner. This, of course, is based on their own heterosexual relations, but in fact it is not true. Most homosexuals change positions and roles or use simultaneous stimulation during sex. Hooker (1965) found, for example, that only 20 percent of male homosexuals preferred only one sexual role.

HOMOSEXUALS AND MARRIAGE

Studies estimate that at least one-fourth of all gay men and 40 percent of all lesbians are married or have been married (Black et al., 2000; Hewitt, 2000). Millions of homosexual or bisexual men and women are partners in heterosexual marriages (Binder, 1998). While some of these men and women were not aware of their sexual orientations when they married, many others were aware. Why would someone who knows he or she is homosexual or bisexual choose to marry a heterosexual? There are many possible reasons, including societal or family pressures, affection for the partner, desire to have children, or even negative feelings about leading a homosexual life-style (Bozett, 1987; Isay, 1998).

Of those married people who are consciously aware of their homosexuality or bisexuality, very few admit it to their partners (Stokes et al., 1996). Many experts find that there is little chance of a married homosexual or bisexual person being monogamous with a heterosexual partner (Clark, 1987). The secret life led by the homosexual or bisexual partner can cause him or her considerable anxiety and stress. When the heterosexual partner does discover the truth, he or she often experiences considerable pain and anger, which is heightened by feeling stupid and deceived. Most say they would have never married had they known the truth (Hays & Samuels, 1989).

What about openly gay or lesbian couples? Many gays and lesbians establish long-lasting relationships. Should they be allowed to legally marry? In two separate polls conducted by *Newsweek* and the *Los Angeles Times,* it was found that as many as two-thirds of Americans oppose the idea of legal homosexual marriage (Leland, 1998, 2000a). Why? Most heterosexuals believe that sexual relations between two people of the same sex is morally wrong. Most also believe that there is no point to it because homosexual couples can't have children (but see next section). Is the only purpose of marriage to have children?

The U.S. Constitution requires that states honor each other's laws, but in 1996 President Clinton signed the Defense of Marriage Act that defines marriage (in federal law) as the union of a man and a woman and allows states to refuse to honor same-sex marriages performed elsewhere. At the start of 2001, 32 states had banned same-sex marriages. In 2000, Vermont recognized marriage-like "civil unions," but not legally sanctioned marriages. The next few years will probably see many legal challenges, both pro and con, related to this issue.

HOMOSEXUALS AS PARENTS

There are, of course, several million married or formerly married gay or lesbian (or bisexual) people who also are parents. In fact, over 5 percent of partnered gays and nearly 22 percent of partnered lesbians have children currently living in the home (Black et al., 2000). Once the "secret" is unveiled, should an openly gay or lesbian person and his or her partner be allowed to raise a child? Should an openly gay or lesbian couple be allowed to adopt a child? Before we continue, read the following real-life story of Kerry and Val, a lesbian couple. It is told in Kerry's own words.

"Val and I have been together for 6 years. We have two children, a daughter, 5, Nicole, and a son, 2, Nicholas. We both wanted a family but were a little afraid of the effects that our life-style would have on the children. We finally decided that in spite of our sexual orientation, we would still be loving, caring parents with much to offer our children.

"Next arose the problem of how to go about it. (We could not very well do it on our own.) We ended up choosing a mutual friend of ours to father the children. Val took care of me while I was pregnant. We experienced all of the changes together: hearing the unborn baby's heartbeat, feeling it move, staying up with me when it was too uncomfortable to sleep. Val was with me all through labor and delivery. She got to see the babies being born and was the first to hold them. She was there from beginning to end. It was a wonderful experience for us to share and it brought us much closer.

"We both believe that a lot of love and a lot of time spent with our children is the key. We try to never be too busy to listen to them. We both are involved with Nicole's school (Val especially, she is a room parent for Nicole's class), friends, and activities. This is very difficult because we both work. I am self-employed and attend school full-time, and Val is planning to return to school next semester. We also spend a lot of time involved in family activities such as going to the park or zoo, bike riding, camping, etc. We almost always include the kids in everything we do.

"We are very happy together and can't imagine life without one another. We both wish that legally we could be recognized as a couple. It would be nice to be able to get insurance as a family, file taxes together, etc., but most importantly are the kids. If anything ever happens to me, what will happen to them? Val loves them as if they were her own and they love her and are very attached to her. I would want them to stay with her, but there is nothing I can do legally.

"My parents both know my wishes (they are divorced and both remarried). My dad adores Val and is very proud of the life we have made together and the stable home we have provided for our children. He would do his best to assure that the children remain with Val. On the other hand, my mom hates my life-style. She refuses to have anything to do with Val and because of this we rarely speak. If anything ever happened to me, she would try her best to take the children from Val and would raise the children to hate me (she has told me this).

"Val and I believe that as far as the children are concerned, we will never lie or hide any information about our life-style or their pasts. Along with their everyday education, we will also include the information about our life-style as they are able to understand it. We do not sexually do anything in front of the children—no parents should. We do hug, hold hands and kiss goodbye. It is healthy for the children to see people displaying affection for each other.

"We are honest with everyone about our life-style. Our friends, families, and employers and co-workers all know we are gay. To us, honesty is the best policy. We do not flaunt anything in front of them or do anything to embarrass anyone, nor would we, but we don't lie about it either. For the most part we have gotten nothing but respect from our straight friends. Sometimes they are curious, but that is natural. Mostly they respect our privacy and admire our honesty. Once people really get to know us they realize that we are no different from anyone else." (from the author's files)

The topic of gays and lesbians as parents is viewed very negatively by many heterosexuals. In a 2000 poll conducted for *Newsweek,* only 39 percent of the Americans surveyed said they were in favor of adoption rights for gay or lesbian partners (Leland et al., 2000a). Even many people who profess to be understanding and tolerant of homosexuality are opposed to gay and lesbian couples raising children:

> "My feelings on homosexuals are the same as my feelings on heterosexuals. I have no problems with it. . . . I do have doubts about them having children"

> "I think that homosexuality is the business of that person. Society should let them do their own thing. . . . I don't know if they should have children." (All examples are from the author's files.)

This negativity has been reflected in court custody cases as well. In a highly publicized case *(Bottoms v. Bottoms),* a Virginia judge denied a woman custody of her 2-year-old son because her lesbian relationship was "immoral" and illegal. The Virginia Supreme Court upheld the decision in 1995, saying that the mother was an unfit parent (see Swisher & Cook, 1996). Many other gays and lesbians have had similar experiences in court. Why the negativity? According to child psychiatrist Betty Ann June Muller, who debated on the subject at the 1994 annual meeting of the American Bar Association, "Judges often have cited long-held stereotypes in justifying awarding custody to the heterosexual parent. Those myths include the view that gays and lesbians are mentally ill, have weak parental instincts or are more likely to raise children who will be homosexual or be sexually abused" (Theim, 1994).

What does the scientific literature show? Of all the topics regarding homosexuality, this is probably the most controversial (see Clarke, 2000). On the antigay side are individuals such as psychologist Paul Cameron (1999) and law professor Lynn Wardle (1997), who argue that studies and court cases show that homosexual parenting has bad effects on children. On the pro-gay side are individuals such as psychologist Gregory Herek (1998) and Charlotte Patterson (1997), who argue that children of homosexual couples suffer no bad effects. Both sides attack each other for "bad research," bias and political motivations (Clarke, 2000). I will attempt to be objective in my review of the numerous studies.

I have already reviewed the literature on mental illness; most homosexuals are as well adjusted as heterosexuals. As for sexual abuse, several studies have found that very few cases of parental sexual abuse are committed by homosexuals; most are committed by heterosexuals. What about openly homosexual parents serving as role models for their children's gender identity and gender-role development? Children raised in a household where the parent is openly homosexual do not show gender identity conflicts, do not have problems with emotional or social adjustment, and have a heterosexual orientation as often as children raised by heterosexual parents (see Brewaeys & van Hall, 1997; Fitzgerald, 1999; and Patterson, 1992, for reviews of many studies). (This last finding is perhaps further evidence for the importance of biology in determining sexual orientation.) Some studies have found that some children of openly gay and lesbian couples are subject to harassment by peers, but overall their social adjustment is normal. Even the subcommittee on child custody issues of the once antigay American Psychiatric Association has recommended that "sexual orientation should not be used as the sole or primary factor in child custody cases" (Binder, 1998).

If one wanted to, one could find cases where gay or lesbian couples were bad parents and their children suffered serious problems. The same is true of heterosexual couples. Here is the important question: Should good parenting be based on sexual orientation, or are there other qualities that make a person a good or bad parent?

MEDIA PORTRAYAL OF HOMOSEXUALS

The top male box office star in Hollywood in the late 1950s was Rock Hudson, who was generally cast in leading romantic roles but who in his personal life was exclusively homosexual. But to admit that one was homosexual in those days was the kiss of death for one's career, so Hudson's studio arranged a marriage (on paper only) so he could keep his orientation secret. Montgomery Clift, another 1950s' actor in many romantic roles, was also homosexual. Other leading actors of that day, including Cary Grant and James Dean, were also known to have had sex with men, but they were always portrayed (on screen and off screen) as straight (Leland, 1995).

When Hollywood did star a person as being homosexual, he or she was almost always portrayed as a stereotype, still sometimes seen today in movies such as 1996's *Birdcage.* However, the media and arts have slowly begun to deal with the subject more honestly. In the 1980s, two Broadway plays, *Torch Song Trilogy* and *La Cage Aux Folles,* and movies such as *Kiss of the Spider Woman* and *Welcome Home, Bobby* dealt openly and sympathetically with the lives of male homosexuals. This was followed in 1993 by *Philadelphia,* starring

Box 11–A CROSS-CULTURAL PERSPECTIVES

Homosexuality in Other Cultures

Homosexuality is viewed very differently in different cultures. In Western culture, sexuality is an essential part of one's identity, and sexual orientation is generally considered to be fixed. In many other cultures we find a range of sexualities that cannot easily be classified by Western standards.

In a review of anthropological studies of 294 societies, Gregersen (1982) found that of 59 societies that had a clear opinion of homosexuality, 69 percent approved of it and only 31 percent condemned it. In an earlier study that included 76 societies in which homosexuality was noted, Ford and Beach (1951) found that 64 percent approved and 36 percent did not. In a more recent survey of 24 developed countries, in 18 more than 50 percent of people regarded adult homosexual relations to be "always wrong." However, on average, the attitudes were less disapproving than for extramarital sex or teen sex (Widmer et al., 1998). Among major Western industrialized countries, only the United States and Britain bar known homosexuals from the military. Canada, Australia, Germany, France, and the Netherlands are all more tolerant. On the other hand, the psychiatric organizations in China, India, Brazil, Poland, and Belarus still consider homosexuality to be a mental illness (Sleek, 1998b).

Recall that in ancient Greece sexual relations between men and adolescent boys was highly idealized (Plato's *Symposium*). It was believed that a boy could acquire knowledge by swallowing semen from an intellectual tutor. Pederasty, same-sex sexual activity with an older man during childhood and adolescence, is common in many cultures throughout the world. This includes at least 50 Melanesian (part of the South Pacific islands) societies and societies around the Mediterranean, the Middle East, Africa, Asia, and South America (Dykes, 2000; Gebhard, 1985; Herdt, 1991; Rind, 1998). In perhaps the most studied group, the Sambians (Herdt, 1993), boys are separated from their mothers about the age of 7 and live only with other boys and men. They regularly perform oral sex on older (but not yet adult) boys; swallowing semen is a practice that the Sambians believe assures maleness (makes them strong, virile, and good warriors and hunters). The boys continue this for 6 to 8 years and then reverse roles, becoming semen donors to younger boys. At 16 years of age, a Sambian boy marries, and for the next year or two is given oral sex by his new bride as well as by younger boys. Once his wife gives birth, however, the same-sex behavior stops, and the new Sambian adult is exclusively heterosexual (in desire as well as behavior) thereafter.

In another example of pederasty, male warriors of the Azande in Sudan take boys as "wives" (Murray, 1992). The boys perform all the usual tasks of women and are passive partners in anal intercourse. When they grow older, the boys then take on the role of "husbands." Many of them later marry women. In the Siwan culture in Africa, all boys are expected to be passive partners in anal intercourse with adult men. Married men loan their sons to one another and openly talk of their same-sex sexual relations with boys (Ford & Beach, 1951).

What about women? Female same-sex practices have not been studied as extensively as men's, but one study found examples of such behaviors in 95 native cultures (Blackwood, 2000). The types of behavior ranged from adolescent sex play to intimate friendships to erotic ritual practices.

Several important points can be learned from these cross-cultural studies. First, we must distinguish between same-sex sexual behaviors and a homosexual orientation. For example, although all Sambian men engage in same-sex practices during a specified time of their lives, Herdt (1987) estimates that fewer than 5 percent have a homosexual orientation as adults. In Mexico, Brazil, Turkey, Greece, and Morocco and other northern African countries, it is not uncommon for men to engage in oral-genital sex or anal intercourse, but only the passive partner is regarded as homosexual (Carrier, 1980). Thus, what is considered homosexuality is, in part, culturally defined. The fact that fewer than 5 percent of Sambian men develop a homosexual orientation as adults also says much about the role of the environment and biology. If environment were more important than biological factors, you would certainly expect to see a larger proportion of homosexual adults. On the other hand, the fact that same-sex sexual behavior is very age-structured demonstrates the role of the culture and the social surroundings in sexual orientation.

Some evidence has been found to support a role for the environment as a cause of homosexuality. One study found that homosexuality is uncommon in small societies that rely on gathering of food to survive, and becomes more common in larger, more complex societies that rely on agriculture, and particularly where there is much psychological stress in the lives of women (Barber, 1998). Nevertheless,

the percentage of homosexuals across cultures that have been extensively studied is about the same: from 1 to 7 percent (Diamond, 1993; Whitam, 1983). Homosexuals in different cultures greatly resemble one another in life-style as well, further evidence for a biological basis (Whitam & Mathy, 1986). What does vary from culture to culture are attitudes about homosexuality. That is a learned response, and what is learned depends on the time and the place in which a person is raised.

Tom Hanks. In the 1997 hit movie *In & Out,* actors Tom Selleck and Kevin Kline were shown engaging in a passionate kiss. Lesbianism as a subject for movies or television has met greater resistance, but when actress Ellen DeGeneres's character declared her homosexuality on the April 30, 1997, episode of *Ellen,* the TV show became the first to be built around (and star) a lesbian. In 2000, Hillary Swank won an Academy Award for her role in *Boys Don't Cry.*

Television has been slower to actually show romantic or sexual behavior between homosexuals, but even that is changing. Two actresses playing the role of attorneys kissed on NBC's *LA Law* in 1991, followed by Roseanne kissing another woman on her show in 1994. Gay and lesbian couples were portrayed on episodes of *Roseanne* and *Friends* in 1996, and by 2000 there were 13 openly homosexual characters appearing in original roles on network television shows (e.g., NBC's *Will & Grace,* Showtime's *Queer as Folk*). Things may have been slow to change but today, "The mass media that tell most of the stories to most of the people most of the time are slowly becoming more inclusive and accepting of diversity" (Gross, 1996).

CAN (SHOULD) SEXUAL ORIENTATION BE CHANGED?

Recall that in the not-too-distant past, homosexuality was viewed by the psychiatric profession as a form of psychopathology that required medical treatment. Many homosexuals were involuntarily subjected to "treatments" such as lobotomies, castration, and electroconvulsive shock therapy. Rejection of the psychopathology model of homosexuality led to the abandonment of the idea that all homosexuals should be "cured," whether voluntarily or involuntarily.

Over half of all Americans believe that homosexuals can change their sexual orientation by willpower, therapy, or religion (Leland & Miller, 1998). However, only 11 percent of gays and lesbians believe that sexual

orientation can be changed. When homosexuals were asked if they would choose to take a "magic heterosexual pill" to change their sexual orientation, only 14 percent of gays and 5 percent of lesbians said that they would do so (Bell & Weinberg, 1978). Note that these results indicate that the large majority of homosexuals feel comfortable with their sexual orientation and do not wish to change. It is a myth held by heterosexuals that most homosexuals want to change.

For those homosexual individuals who choose to change their orientation, there are therapists who practice a variety of techniques (see Murphy, 1992, for a review). Today, most attempts to "cure" homosexuals are conducted by religious fundamentalist groups (Leland & Miller, 1998). For example, Exodus International, a nondenominational Christian group with at least 83 chapters in 35 states, takes out full-page ads in newspapers promising gays that they can change by following strict biblical readings. The groups claim success rates

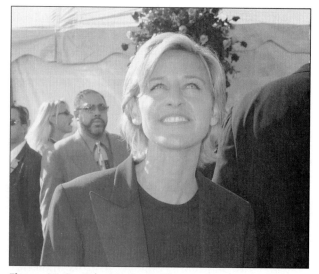

Figure 11–5 Television star Ellen DeGeneres in the television show *Ellen* was the first to portray a homosexual in a leading role.

of between 30 and 70 percent (Leland & Miller, 1998; Schaeffer et al., 1999), but "success" is generally defined as behavioral abstinence, and there have been no really long-term studies. The facts that two of Exodus International's ("cured") founders left the group because they fell in love, and over a dozen ministries have closed because the directors resumed their homosexuality, suggest that the long-term "success" rate is not high.

Almost all experts agree that changing an individual's sexual orientation is not possible (Edwards, 1996; Haldeman, 1994). This conclusion has gained strength with the recent findings of a possible biological role in sexual orientation.

Although homosexuals no longer have to fear unwanted medical treatment, it is still questionable whether those gays and lesbians who seek reorientation truly do so "voluntarily" (Murphy, 1992). Most probably do so because of years of dealing with family pressure, job discrimination, legal hassles, and other experiences resulting in shame and self-loathing (Allen & Oleson, 1999). According to Murphy (1992), "If this is true, it would appear that 'treating' the 'homosexual' would still be a form of blaming the victim, i.e., treating the person who suffers rather than ameliorating those social forces which devalue homoeroticism."

In 1994, the American Medical Association finally reversed a long-standing policy of recommending that physicians make efforts to turn unhappy homosexuals into heterosexuals. The American Psychological Association followed in 1997, calling "reparative therapy" harmful. The new policy states that most of the emotional problems of homosexuals are "due more to a sense of alienation in an unaccepting environment" and that "through psychotherapy, gay men and lesbians can become comfortable with their sexual orientation and understand the social responses to it" (AMA, 1994).

NATIONAL SUPPORT GROUPS

You will find the addresses and phone numbers of several organizations in the "Resources" section following the text. Also, be sure to contact local support groups and organizations. Most college campuses, for example, have gay and lesbian alliances.

PERSONAL REFLECTIONS
Are you comfortable with your sexual orientation? If not, why not? What steps can you take to become more comfortable?

Key Terms

bisexual   270, 273
coming out   283
gay   279
gender identity   238, 273
gender roles   251, 274

heterosexual   270, 273
homophobia   282
homosexual   270, 273
lesbian   279
Oedipus complex   249, 275

pederasty   279
sexual orientation   270, 273
sexual prejudice   282
straight   279

Suggested Readings

Bailey, J. M., & Pillard, R. C. (1995). Genetics of human sexual orientation. In R. C. Rosen, C. M. Davis, & H. J. Ruppel, Jr. (Eds.), *Annual Review of Sex Research*, vol. VI. Mount Vernon, IA: Society for the Scientific Study of Sexuality.

Clark, D. H. (1987). *The new loving someone gay.* Berkeley, CA: Celestial Arts. Written for parents of gays.

De Cecco, J. (Ed.). (1990). *Gay relationships.* New York: Haworth Press. Essays on many aspects of gay relations.

Gladue, B. A. (1994, October). The biopsychology of sexual orientation. *Current Directions in Psychological Science*, 3. An excellent review of the biology of sexual orientation.

Helminiak, D. A. (1994). *What the Bible really says about homosexuality.* San Francisco: Alamo Square Press. Many people are convinced that God condemned homosexuality, but this scholarly work shows that He really did not.

Herek, G. M. (Ed.) (1998). *Stigma and sexual orientation: Understanding prejudice against lesbians, gay men, and bisexuals.* Newsbury Park, CA: Sage.

Kantrowitz, B. (1996, November 4). Gay families come out. *Newsweek.* Discusses the controversy about homosexuals as parents.

Leland, J. (1995, July 17). Bisexuality. *Newsweek.* Many personal experiences.

Leland, J., & Miller, M. (1998, August 17). Can gays "convert"? *Newsweek*, pp. 45-52. Cover story about the controversy in attempts to convert homosexuals.

Newsweek, (2000, March 20) Special report, "Gay Today," includes several articles on homosexuals and American attitudes.

Study Guide

INTERACTIVE REVIEW

In this chapter, sexual orientation is defined as (1) _____ consistently made after adolescence in the presence of clear alternatives. Isolated instances of sexual behavior may or may not reflect one's sexual orientation. Recent surveys indicate that (2) _____ percent of the adult male population and about (3) _____ percent of the adult female population have a homosexual orientation. About 20 percent of all men (and a lower percentage of women) have had sex with a same-sex individual on at least one occasion, but fewer than 5 percent regard themselves as bisexual. A true bisexual would have a rating of (4) _____ on Kinsey's 7-point rating scale.

The (5) _____ of the vast majority of homosexuals and bisexuals are just as strong and consistent with their anatomical sex as among heterosexuals. Conformity or nonconformity with gender (6) _____ does not predict one's sexual orientation. A great many homosexuals and bisexuals do not walk, talk, dress, or act any differently than anyone else.

There are three major explanations for the origins of sexual orientation. Psychoanalytic explanations state that heterosexuality is the "normal" outcome and that homosexuality results from problems in resolving the (7) _____ complex. Some of Freud's followers believed that homosexual men had (8) _____ mothers and (9) _____ fathers, while homosexual women had (10) _____ fathers and (11) _____ mothers. However, later research does not generally support these claims. Homosexuals, as well as heterosexuals, have all kinds of parents, both good and bad, caring and cold. (12) _____ regards homosexuality and heterosexuality as learned behaviors; good or rewarding experiences with individuals of one sex and/or bad experiences with individuals of the other sex (particularly during adolescence) would lead to a particular orientation. However, social and cultural studies show that environment alone cannot explain sexual orientation. In the (13) _____ society in Melanesia, all boys engage in same-sex sexual behaviors for many years, yet the large majority grow up to have a heterosexual orientation.

Recent studies suggest that biology plays a major role in the origin of sexual orientation. Studies with twins indicate a (14) _____ factor, while anatomical studies have found differences in the (15) _____ of heterosexuals and homosexuals. Many researchers believe that differences in (16) _____ before or shortly after we are born predispose us to a particular sexual orientation. Nearly all agree that biological and social/cultural influences (17) _____ to produce sexual orientation.

Anthropologists find that most societies are (18) _____ tolerant of homosexuality than prevailing attitudes in the United States. Attitudes about homosexuality have varied considerably in Western culture. The (19) _____ and (20) _____ accepted homosexuality, as did the early Christians. It was not until St. (21) _____ that homosexuality came to be viewed as unnatural or "against the laws of nature," and not until the 1600s and 1700s that it was regarded as criminal. In the 1800s, the medical (psychiatric) model regarded homosexuality as an illness, and homosexual individuals were regarded as having pathological conditions in need of being "cured." It was not until 1973 that the American Psychiatric Association removed homosexuality as an official mental illness. Nevertheless, most people in the United States continue to have a harsh and negative attitude.

The process of (22) _____, or identifying oneself as homosexual, involves several often painful stages. The first stage is (23) _____. In the final stages, the individual attempts to gain the acceptance and understanding of friends, family, and co-workers. This is difficult in a society filled with (24) _____, socially reinforced negative attitudes toward individuals, communities, and homosexual behaviors.

Prior to the 1970s, opportunities for homosexuals to meet were limited to a few bars, bathhouses, and public restrooms. Today, most metropolitan areas have well-established homosexual communities where individuals can openly associate. Women, whether straight or lesbian, tend to value (25) _____ in their relations. Prior to the 1980s, many gays engaged in impersonal sex with numerous partners, but today there is a greater emphasis in the gay community on establishing relationships.

At the time this book was written, homosexual marriages were illegal in all 50 states. Most Americans oppose the idea of openly homosexual individuals raising children (even their own), yet research shows that most parental sexual abuse is committed by heterosexuals and that children raised by homosexual parents grow up to have normal gender identities and gender roles, and almost always have a heterosexual orientation. This last finding again suggests a greater role for biology than environment in the origin of sexual orientation, and it is the hope of the researchers conducting biological studies that their findings will promote greater understanding and tolerance.

SELF-TEST

A. TRUE OR FALSE

T	F	
☐	☐	26. In some cultures, same-sex sexual behavior is considered normal for boys during adolescence.
☐	☐	27. Homosexuals usually act and/or dress differently from heterosexuals.
☐	☐	28. Bisexuals are people who are afraid to admit to themselves their real homosexuality.
☐	☐	29. Most homosexuals are unhappy with their sexual orientation and would like to become heterosexual.
☐	☐	30. A homosexual orientation indicates a gender identity problem.
☐	☐	31. A male homosexual can be made heterosexual by administering large doses of testosterone.
☐	☐	32. People who have had same-sex sexual experiences are by definition homosexual in orientation.
☐	☐	33. Although being homosexual is no longer criminal, in many states it is against the law to engage in homosexual behaviors.
☐	☐	34. Freud believed that all people were capable of becoming either heterosexual or homosexual, depending on their early childhood experiences.
☐	☐	35. Researchers have found a higher rate of concordance for homosexuality between identical twins than between nonidentical twins.
☐	☐	36. A bisexual is anyone who has had sex with both men and women.
☐	☐	37. More recent studies support Kinsey's findings that 10 percent of all American men are predominantly homosexual.
☐	☐	38. Same-sex sexual experiences before age 15 are a good predictor of adult sexual orientation.
☐	☐	39. Bisexuals have fewer opposite-sex fantasies than heterosexuals and fewer same-sex fantasies than homosexuals.
☐	☐	40. Many homosexuals and bisexuals have gender dysphoria.
☐	☐	41. Most lesbians have not had pleasurable sexual relations with men.
☐	☐	42. Sexual orientation is usually well established by adolescence.
☐	☐	43. Extremely effeminate ("sissy") boys always develop a homosexual orientation.
☐	☐	44. If one identical twin is homosexual, the other twin always is too.
☐	☐	45. Studies have found that areas of the hypothalamus (in the brain) are different in heterosexuals and homosexuals.
☐	☐	46. Most homosexuals adopt a single role ("masculine" or "feminine") in sexual relationships.
☐	☐	47. Children raised by openly homosexual parents are more likely to develop a homosexual orientation than children raised by heterosexual parents.
☐	☐	48. On average, homosexual men had a later birth order than heterosexual men.
☐	☐	49. Homophobic men generally have equally negative attitudes about male and female homosexuals.

B. MATCHING

_____ 50. George is a zero on Kinsey's rating scale.

_____ 51. Henry has had a few same-sex sexual experiences, but has had sex only with women since he turned 15 ten years ago.

_____ 52. Joyce has been married and enjoyed sexual relations with her husband, but now prefers sexual relations with women.

_____ 53. Frank has had sex with both men and women.

_____ 54. Michael believes he is a woman and has sex only with men.

_____ 55. Carl sometimes enjoys sex with women, but prefers sexual relations with men.

_____ 56. Tom is 12 years old and his few sexual experiences have been exclusively with boys his age.

a. probably heterosexual
b. probably homosexual
c. probably bisexual
d. probably transsexual
e. not enough information to make a guess

_____ 57. Alice enjoys sex with men most of the time, but she often enjoys sex with women as well.

_____ 58. Diane has had sex only with men, but occasionally has homosexual fantasies.

_____ 59. Matthew occasionally goes to bathhouses and lets other men give him oral-genital sex.

_____ 60. Mary's gender identity is not consistent with her anatomical sex.

_____ 61. Steve is 19 years old and his only sexual experiences have been with women, but all his sexual fantasies are about men.

C. FILL IN THE BLANKS

62. In this book, sexual orientation is defined as distinct preferences consistently made after _____ in the presence of clear alternatives.

63. _____ and _____ believed (incorrectly) that homosexuality resulted from reversed gender roles.

64. Freud called individuals who kept their homosexual tendencies hidden from their conscious mind _____.

65. Simon LeVay found that a part of the brain called the _____ was different in heterosexual and homosexual men.

66. Researchers believe that hormones may affect sexual orientation during which time of life? _____

67. According to this chapter, biological factors probably _____ individuals to a particular sexual orientation.

68. The four stages of the coming-out process are (a) _____, (b) _____ (c) _____, and (d) _____.

69. Bell and Weinberg (1978) described homosexuals who were happy in their sexual orientation and in a monogamous relationship as _____.

70. Name four nonliving homosexuals who made significant contributions to humankind: (a) _____, (b) _____, (c) _____, and (d) _____.

Chapter 12

Life-Span Sexual Development

*The first debate I won was when, at 11, I persuaded a group of school friends
that there was no truth in the exciting idea that penises could be put into girls to
create babies. Their use as water pistols was accepted, but this new use had a
strange attraction. The argument was decided when we realized that if it were
true, our parents must have done this—which we all realized was inconceivable.
After all, our parents were "old people."*

(John Kellett, 2000)

People are sexual beings. To deny our sexuality is to deny our humanity. It should
come as no surprise, therefore, that our sexuality begins from the moment of birth
(and perhaps before) and lasts until our death, even if we live a very long life.

EARLY INFANCY (AGES 0–1)

Sexuality starts in the womb. Ultrasound recordings have discovered that male fetuses
have erections months before they are born (Calderone, 1983b). After birth, baby boys
often have erections before the umbilical cord is cut. Similarly, baby girls can have vaginal
lubrication in the first 24 hours after birth (Langfeldt, 1981).

When you have finished studying this chapter, you should be able to:

1. Explain infants' exploration of their bodies and their need for close physical comfort;

2. Discuss genital exploration and sex play in young children;

3. Summarize the changes that occur in boys' and girls' bodies at puberty and identify the hormones that are responsible;

4. Discuss sexual behavior among adolescents and the effects of peer pressure;

5. Explain how the sexual behavior of emerging adults often differs from that of younger and older age groups;

6. Discuss the sexual life-styles of adults, including marriage, cohabitation, and extramarital sex;

7. Describe the characteristics that men and women look for when choosing a short-term or long-term mate;

8. Describe the sexual behavior of middle-aged individuals and the physical changes that come with aging; and

9. Explain the realities of aging that can directly affect sexuality in the elderly, and discuss the prevalence of sexual relations among healthy elderly couples.

An important part of sexual development involves the amount of hugging and cuddling that an infant has with its caregivers. Many physicians and psychologists strongly encourage parents to hold their babies immediately after birth and to continue to give large amounts of hugging and cuddling throughout childhood. Lots of hugging and cuddling between parent and infant allows a strong attachment to be formed between them. This process is called *bonding*.

Monkeys raised in isolation and deprived of the opportunity of close physical comfort have difficulty forming relationships later (Harlow, 1959). The same seems to be true for children. Fifty years ago, a physician reported that 1 in 3 human infants in foundling homes died during the first year of life, even though they were well fed and provided with adequate medical care. What these babies were not receiving was cuddling, hugging, fondling, and kissing—they apparently died from emotional neglect (Spitz, 1945, 1946). Today, some hospitals are recruiting volunteers to hold and talk to babies (especially premature ones) so that they will not be deprived of early physical contact if their parents cannot provide it. When nursing, infant boys may get an erection and infant girls may display vaginal lubrication. These are normal reflexive reactions, and parents should not be alarmed when they happen.

As soon as infants gain sufficient control over their movements, they begin to touch all parts of their bodies. As part of this exploration, infants also touch their genitals. Infant boys and girls can feel pleasure from this and may continue to stimulate themselves. This happens because the nerve endings in the genitals are already developed at birth and transmit sensations of pleasure when stimulated. However, it is important to remember that infants do not comprehend adult sexual behavior. Their behavior is aimed at finding pleasurable physical sensations, not expressing sexual desire.

Although the initial sexual self-stimulation of children may be random, once they discover its pleasurable component, such stimulation quickly becomes purposeful (Lidster & Horsburgh, 1994). Taking a child's hand away from his or her genitals may cause the child to make a face or noises (indicating irritation), and the child may quickly try to resume self-stimulation. Kinsey and his colleagues reported that 32 percent of boys less than 1 year of age were able to have orgasms (though ejaculation during orgasm is not possible until puberty is reached). He also reported a number of cases of girls 3 years old or younger masturbating to orgasm (Kinsey et al., 1948, 1953).

EARLY CHILDHOOD (AGES 2–6)

Before age 2, children are highly *egocentric*, a term coined by psychologist Jean Piaget in his theory of cognitive development (the growth of knowledge in

human beings). This means that they cannot consider other people's points of view. Egocentric children do not play games together, because most play requires cooperation, and cooperation in turn requires respecting or anticipating someone else's point of view. Bodily exploration during this time is confined mainly to self-exploration (Figure 12–1). After the age of 2, however, children increasingly play together, and their natural curiosity now extends not only to their own bodies but to those of others.

Studies have shown that sexualized behaviors increase dramatically in children after age 2 and reach a peak period from 3 to 5, and then decrease until puberty (Friedrich et al., 1991). Interest in the genitals is very common for boys and girls in this age group, as are undressing and sexual exploration games that involve showing one's body and genitals to others, or vice versa (see Heiman et al., 1998; Ryan, 2000). Let us examine some of the common, normal behaviors frequently observed in young children.

As just mentioned, by the age of 2, children are very interested in their bodies. Because of this, they will try to watch their siblings and parents bathing and urinating.

> "When I was a very young girl, my parents brought me with them to visit some friends of theirs who had two young boys. One boy was my age and one was a couple of years older. I went to the bathroom with them and watched them urinate. My mother got very, very angry. This totally surprised, shocked, and confused me. Maybe if she had had a course like this one, she could have handled the situation a little better." (from the author's files)

The fact that boys stand and girls sit while urinating is fascinating to children. They will also take their clothes off together and will play games that allow for sexual exploration, such as "playing doctor" and "playing house." Most of the time, these games are limited to viewing and touching genitals. More aggressive sexual behaviors like oral-genital contact and inserting objects into the vagina or anus are uncommon and may be an indication of abuse (Friedrich et al., 1991; Heiman et al., 1998; Ryan, 2000). Sexual exploration games will not harm a child's development. What may be harmful is parents reacting too strongly when they "catch" their children engaging in sex play.

> "I can still remember the day my mother caught me playing 'doctor' with my neighbor. I was 5 years old. She got so mad at me that she locked me up in the bathroom. I don't remember how long I was in there. I didn't understand what I had done wrong. I ended up crying myself to sleep on the bathroom floor."

> "When I was 4, my cousin (age 5) and sister (age 3) had a slumber party. When we were all laying down we started asking questions and being curious. We then started 'playing doctor.' Well, my

parents caught us and I was spanked and punished for a long time. I have very vivid memories of this event and now I do not have very positive feelings about sex or my sexuality." (All examples are from the author's files.)

Sexual exploration games are often played with playmates of the same sex (Heiman et al., 1998). This is probably more common than sexual contact between sexes, because even at this age children usually play more with playmates of the same sex. Engaging in same-sex contact at this age does not mean that a child will become homosexual as an adult. Adult homosexuals may or may not have been involved in same-sex play in early childhood. The same is true of heterosexual adults.

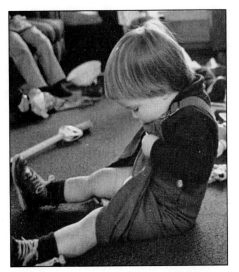

Figure 12–1 It is normal for children to explore their own bodies.

Recall that Freud said the genitals were the focus of children's pleasure during the *phallic stage* (approximately ages 3–7) of psychosexual development (see Chapter 10). It is true that nearly all young children touch and explore their genitals, although young boys engage in genital touching more often than young girls (probably because the male genitals are more visible; Friedrich et al., 1991). Here, too, the way parents respond is very important.

"My sister has a 5-year-old little boy. . . . She was all worried that something was wrong with him. He would constantly play with his penis. She scolded him one day and told him that if little boys play with themselves like that it would fall off. . . . I am afraid that this could scar him for life."

"I was raised in a strict Catholic family. I remember distinctly how my initially unhealthy attitude towards my sexuality and that of others began. As a small child, I used to masturbate. My mother would hit the ceiling when she would catch me because my favorite time to do this was at nap time. She would yell and scream and slap my hands and tell me that it was nasty. Her contempt for my actions was so obvious that I could not help but develop a negative attitude towards my sexuality. I worried for a long time that I was the only person who did this and felt very guilty about it." (All examples are from the author's files.)

Most parents respond negatively to finding their young child exploring and touching his or her genitals (Gagnon, 1985). However, when you become a parent, try not to overreact. Allowing children to explore and satisfy their curiosity enables them to become comfortable with their bodies, both as a child and as

an adult. Punishment or negative messages may lead to a poor body image and later sexual problems (Masters & Johnson, 1970). It is okay to teach your children that it is not appropriate (as opposed to "bad") to touch their genitals in certain situations; in public, for example. According to one child expert, "The attitude of the parent should be to socialize for privacy rather than to punish or forbid" (Calderone, 1983a). If your child touches herself or himself at home, the best thing to do is ignore it. If you feel that you have to stop the behavior because it bothers you, do not scold; simply distract your child by getting her (or him) involved in another activity.

By now, you should understand that parents' responses to normal behaviors have very important consequences for children's later sexual development and their attitudes about their bodies. According to one group of researchers, "From the earliest period in life, the child's family will reciprocally influence the sexual characteristics of the child. The family establishes a 'psychosexual equilibrium' that is a function of the parents' sexual adjustment, the child's developing sexuality, and the impact of the child's sexual development on parental sexual development" (Friedrich et al., 1991). The way parents react to the sexuality of their children is often an indication of the way they feel about their own sexuality.

PERSONAL REFLECTIONS
Does the thought of young children examining and touching their own genitals make you uncomfortable? If so, why? How would you feel if you found your 5-year-old boy with his pants down playing "doctor"? Why? Would your reaction be any different if you found your 5-year-old girl with her pants down playing "doctor"? Why?

THE INITIAL SCHOOL-AGE YEARS (AGES 7–11)

Freud believed that this time of life was a period of "latency," when children were not concerned with sexuality. Studies have found that American children in fact do engage in less overt sexual behavior at this time (Friedrich et al., 1991). This is probably due to their learning negative cultural standards. Studies in more primitive cultures reveal lots more sexual activity and interest by children prior to puberty. However, our culture has a long history of denying childhood

Figure 12–2 Children will attempt to satisfy their natural curiosity about the human body whenever they get a chance. If this were your child, would you pull her away, or would you let her explore and try to answer any questions she might have about the difference between boys and girls?

sexuality, so that most parents and teachers believe that sexual interest at this age is unusual or a problem (Ryan, 2000). By the time they begin kindergarten or first grade, children generally have developed a sense of modesty and inhibition about exposing their bodies in public. They may be very shy about undressing in front of their parents, and for the first time may start demanding privacy in the bathroom.

Some researchers believe that the amount of sex play by American children does not slow down at this stage but is simply hidden more from parents (Kinsey et al., 1948, 1953). Several recent studies of recollections by adults found that the large majority of adults recalled sexual interactions with other children prior to puberty (see Heiman et al., 1998; Ryan, 2000). This included exposing oneself for others, looking at others, touching, fondling, and various sexual games. A majority could even recall being aroused or sexually excited. Activities involving any kind of penetration are still uncommon at this age.

Children tend to segregate by sex by age 9. Thus, again,

puberty The time in life when an individual first shows sexual attraction and becomes capable of reproduction.

much of their sexual play is with same-sex children (Heiman et al., 1998). This is a normal part of growing up, and parents should not interpret it as homosexual activity as they would activity between two adults.

Almost all parents react negatively when they catch their children engaging in sexual exploration games. Thus, it is not surprising that sexual activity becomes less overt and that most adults remember feeling "guilty," "curious," or "confused" during their childhood experiences (Ryan, 2000). Girls are often treated more harshly than boys. This establishes a double standard—as a general rule, boys are allowed more freedom to explore their sexuality than girls.

Although the amount of overtly sexual play may decrease during the initial school-age years, curiosity about sex does not, and children will ask their parents questions such as "Where do babies come from?" However, American children still receive very little information from their parents (Ryan, 2000). Again, how parents respond will affect their children's responses (and willingness to ask questions of their parents about sex) in the future. Unfortunately, many parents are evasive or even negative.

> "My mother damaged my attitude about sexuality by responding to my question about the origins of babies by telling me that when a man and a woman kiss, it's called making love and this is where babies come from. Even today, she still refuses to discuss sex or sexuality." (from the author's files)

Chapter 8 described how to talk to children of different ages about sexuality. The ability to communicate with your children about sex and other topics is a critical part of good parenting.

In summary, contrary to our culture's expectations, there is an abundance of evidence that sexuality develops steadily throughout childhood. One researcher concluded that we live in "a culture at odds with the bulk of evolutionary, developmental, and cross-cultural evidence demonstrating that children are sexual beings, whose exploration of sexual knowledge and play, is an integral part of their development as fully functioning human beings" (Frayser, 1994, p. 210).

PUBERTY (AGES 7–15)

Puberty (from the Latin *puber,* meaning "of ripe age, adult") is the time of life when we first show sexual attraction and become capable of reproduction. It does not happen overnight, but instead is a *process lasting several years.* In fact, recent studies have found that puberty begins earlier and lasts longer than previously believed.

Traditionally, the physical and sexual changes that occur during puberty have been attributed to the maturation of the testicles or ovaries. However, puberty is at creased levels of hormones lead to a variety of physiological changes in girls and boys (e.g., breast development, facial hair).

These are often referred to as **secondary sex characteristics.** The changes in physical appearance create psychological changes in the way children think about themselves and others. Let us examine these changes in more detail and discuss how they affect adolescents' behavior.

CHANGES IN GIRLS

One of the first noticeable changes in girls is a growth spurt starting at about the age of 12. Many sixth- and seventh-grade boys suddenly realize one day that a lot of the girls in their classroom are taller than they are (a fact they may not discover until those first school dances). The reason for this is that the growth spurt in boys does not start, on average, until about age 14. Most of the boys eventually catch up with and pass the girls, because girls generally stop growing by age 16 and boys keep growing until about 18, but those first couple of years can be awkward.

The development of breasts in girls during puberty (a result of increased levels of estrogen) is viewed with great attention by both girls and boys. Many girls rush out to purchase training bras, which probably do nothing except make them feel mature. Girls worry that if they are not as "stacked" as their friends, they will be left behind in the rush to be popular with boys. Not all girls develop at the same rate, so insecurities may develop early. Some decide to speed things up on their own, as 11-year-old Margaret did in Judy Blume's novel *Are You There God? It's Me, Margaret*:

> I tiptoed back to my room and closed the door. I stepped into my closet and stood in one corner. I shoved three cotton balls into each side of my bra. Well, so what if it was cheating! Probably other girls did it too. I'd look a lot better, wouldn't I? So why not!
>
> I came out of the closet and got back up on my chair. This time when I turned sideways I looked like I'd grown. I liked it!

The increase in estrogen levels also causes an increase in fatty deposits in the hips and buttocks.

Pubic hair generally starts to appear shortly after breast development begins, followed in a couple of years by the appearance of axillary (underarm) hair. The growth of hair on new parts of the body results from increased levels of male hormones (mainly from the adrenal gland). These hormones also cause the sweat glands and sebaceous glands to develop, so that body odor and acne often become new sources of concern.

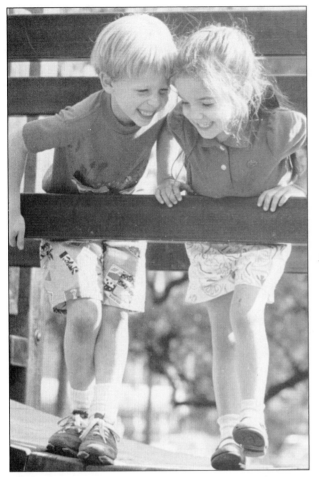

Figure 12–3 Boys and girls often play together during early childhood, but tend to segregate by sex by age 9.

least a two-part maturational process (see McClintock & Herdt, 1996). In the first part, the adrenal glands start to mature (called *adrenarche*) when children are between the ages of 6 and 8. The adrenal glands secrete the androgen hormone DHEA (dehydroepiandrosterone), which is then converted to testosterone and estrogen. Thus, the first increase in sex hormones is not due to the maturing gonads but to the maturing adrenals. Notice that at this stage girls as well as boys experience an increase in androgens ("male" hormones).

In the second stage, the testicles and ovaries mature (called *gonadarche*), usually several years after adrenarche. In this stage, the pituitary gland begins to secrete FSH in high doses, stimulating the production of sperm in seminiferous tubules in boys and the maturation of ova in girls (see Chapter 3). Prior to this time, boys do not ejaculate (though they can have orgasms) and girls do not have menstrual cycles. In girls, the maturing ovary produces estrogen and progesterone, while increased levels of luteinizing hormone from a boy's pituitary stimulates production of testosterone in the testes. The in-

secondary sex characteristics Bodily changes that occur during puberty and differentiate men and women.

Puberty may be a process that takes several years, but in many people's minds, a girl's first menstruation marks a turning point in her maturity. The vagina and uterus begin to enlarge about the time that pubic hair appears. The first menstrual period (called **menarche**) occurs at an average age of between 12 and 13 (Brooks-Gunn & Paikoff, 1997; Herman-Giddens et al., 1997). There is considerable variability, however, and it is normal for the cycles to be very irregular during the first couple of years after menarche. The rise in estrogen levels causes the vaginal walls to become thicker and more elastic and also results in lubrication during sexual arousal.

The average age for menarche has been dropping over the last few centuries. A study of New York City girls in 1934 found that the average age was 13.5 years, while the average age in Western Europe in the early 1800s was at least 14.5 years (Bullough, 1981). Many researchers believe that the reason for this decline is better nutrition resulting in an earlier acquisition of some minimally required amount of body fat (the putative signal that tells the brain to start releasing FSH).

The reaction of a young woman to her first menstrual cycle will be influenced primarily by what she has been told. Menarche can be viewed as something very positive (a sign of "becoming a woman"), "a simple fact of nature," or "a curse" and something disgusting. Mothers generally discuss menstruation with their daughters and pass on their own attitudes and beliefs about it.

"My mother told me that menstruation was a 'nasty' experience. As a result, I always did my utmost to totally hide the fact that I was menstruating. I didn't even want other women to know that I was having my period. I would refuse to purchase sanitary products out of the machines in restrooms if anyone else was in the restroom."

"Then, when my big moment came, instead of treating me as though something natural and exciting were happening, my mother reacted with embarrassment. I was very hurt when she told me to get my sister to show me how to wear a sanitary napkin. We never talked about any of these things. The sanitary napkins were even kept locked . . . and whenever any of us needed one we would slip it under our shirt and scurry into the bathroom."

"My mother told me when I was very young that I would have a period around age 13 or so. . . . Finally, one month before my 15th birthday, I started my period. I remember being so excited 'it' finally came. I called my mom in the bathroom and told her. Well, she was so excited she started calling my grandmothers and her friends. When my dad came home he got all excited too. They were so proud I'd finally 'become a woman.'" (All examples are from the author's files.)

menarche The term for a girl's first menstrual period.

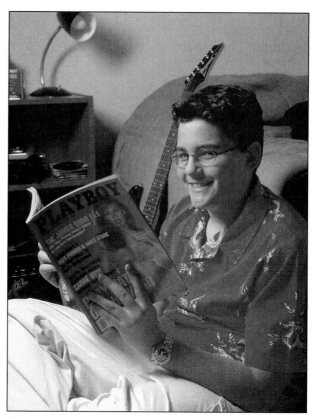

Figure 12–4 Early adolescence is a time of great curiosity about sex. Most boys, and many girls, have begun masturbating by age 15.

Which of these girls do you suppose began adolescence with good self-esteem about her body?

Older sisters, friends, sex education courses in schools, and fathers may also give information about menstruation. As you can see from the previous case histories, for some parents the subject is still a taboo, and some girls are never told anything about menstruation until it happens. In a study done by the Tampax Corporation in 1981, it was found that one-fourth of all people surveyed felt that menstruation was an unacceptable topic for discussion, even in the home (Delaney et al., 1988). Thus, some girls experience menarche with no prior knowledge, which makes it a frightening experience.

For boys, menarche is rarely a topic of discussion with their parents. Most learn about it "on the street," and it seems to be another mysterious difference between men and women. Menarche often is viewed as the topic of crude jokes, though most boys remain ignorant about the basic facts regarding menstruation until they reach adulthood (if then).

CHANGES IN BOYS

As mentioned earlier, pubertal development in boys lags about 2 years behind development in girls. The first noticeable change in boys is usually growth of the testes and scrotum, the result of increased levels of testosterone. Testosterone then stimulates growth of the penis, prostate gland, and seminal vesicles. The growth of the genitals begins, on average, about the age of 11½ and is completed, on average, by about the age of 15. Boys generally become capable of ejaculation about a year after the penis begins to grow.

© Lynn Johnston Productions Inc. Reproduced with permission. Distributed by United Feature Syndicate, Inc.

The first experience many boys have with ejaculation is a **nocturnal emission,** or "wet dream." Some boys have nocturnal emissions frequently, while others have only a few experiences. Fewer fathers prepare their sons for nocturnal emissions than mothers prepare girls for menstruation, and as a result many boys are ashamed, or even frightened, by these experiences.

> "When I was 13 years old, I had a 'wet dream' for the first time. I was shocked to later find out that I did not have a disease. I honestly thought I had one." (from the author's files)

Because they are ashamed, some boys may hide their underwear and sheets or try other ways to "hide the evidence." Because nocturnal emissions are not under voluntary control, there is no reason for shame. It is therefore important to educate children about nocturnal emissions (and for other aspects of puberty) *before* they begin to occur.

Many boys may also be initially frightened by the emission of a strange fluid from the penis that now occurs during masturbation. A case cited by sex therapist Bernie Zilbergeld (1978) is probably not unusual:

> "I kept stroking, my penis got hard, and the sensations felt better and better. Then I was overcome with feelings I had never before felt and, God help me, white stuff came spurting out the end of my cock. I wasn't sure if I had sprung a leak or what. I was afraid but calmed down when I thought that since it wasn't red it couldn't be blood. I kept on stroking and it hurt. I didn't know if the hurt was connected with the white stuff (had I really injured myself?) or if the event was over and my penis needed a rest. But I decided to stop for the moment. Of course, I returned the next day and did it again."

Many boys also develop temporarily enlarged breasts during puberty, called **gynecomastia.** This results from increased levels of estrogen (Mathur & Braunstein, 1997).

> "When I was about 13-years-old something started to happen to my chest. It seemed as though I was beginning to grow breasts. I went to my mother and showed her so she brought me to the doctor. I was a wrestler in middle school and all I could think about was how could I avoid taking off my shirt in public for one to two years." (from the author's files)

Gynecomastia usually disappears by the mid-teens, but unless boys are told why this is happening and that it is a normal, temporary condition, they may feel confused, embarrassed, or ashamed. Some fear that they are turning into girls and may stop swimming in public because they are embarrassed to display their male "breasts."

Pubic hair starts to grow about the same time as the genitals start to develop, the result of increasing testosterone levels, but underarm and facial hair generally do not appear for another 2 years. The amount of body hair, however, is also determined by heredity. As in girls, testosterone also causes development of the sebaceous and sweat glands with their accompanying problems (acne, body odor).

The appearance of facial hair is often as important to boys as the development of breasts is to young girls, for it is one of the few outward signs that they are becoming men. They often start shaving long before it is necessary, only to wish a few years later that they could avoid it altogether. Another change that is obvious to others is a deepening of the voice, a result of testosterone stimulating the growth of the larynx (voice box). This occurs today at an average age of about 13½, but it may have occurred at a later age in past centuries. It was not uncommon in Europe at one time for boys who sang in the great church choirs to be castrated before puberty (with parental approval) in order to preserve their soprano voices. (If castration is done after puberty, by the way, it does not substantially raise a male's voice because the larynx has already undergone its change.)

PRECOCIOUS AND DELAYED PUBERTY

Although the changes that occur during puberty generally begin about the age of 11

nocturnal emission An ejaculation that occurs during sleep in teenaged boys and men; a "wet dream."

gynecomastia Excessive development of the male breasts.

or 12, they have been known to occur much earlier. When sexual development begins before the age of 9, it is called **precocious puberty.** The youngest girl known to have given birth was only 5 years old: a Peruvian Indian girl who delivered a baby by cesarean section in 1939. This means, of course, that she was ovulating and having menstrual periods by the age of 4 or 5. The youngest couple on record who became parents were a Chinese boy and girl, aged 9 and 8, respectively.

There have been isolated outbreaks around the world of very young children developing breasts. This has happened to boys and girls as young as 6 months old. A recent study of thousands of American children found that nearly half of the black girls and 15 percent of the white girls studied had begun to develop breasts, pubic hair, or both by age 8 (Herman-Giddens et al., 1997). First menstruation still occurred after they had turned 12. It is speculated that the early development of secondary sex characteristics is due to early weight gain, hormones in meat and milk, or to what are called environmental estrogens, chemical pollutants that resemble the female hormone estrogen (Lemonick, 2000).

In some children, the appearance of secondary sex characteristics and physical growth do not begin at the same age as in most children. This is called **delayed puberty.** Most clinical referrals are boys who have failed to grow (Kulin, 1996). The usual treatment is to administer gonadotropin-releasing hormone or androgens (male hormones).

> *PERSONAL REFLECTIONS*
> *Try to recall the feelings you experienced during puberty as your body changed. Would better understanding of these events (via parents or sex education classes) have made it a more positive experience?*

SEXUAL BEHAVIOR

Along with an increase in hormones during puberty, major changes are also occurring in the brain. These changes occur in many mammalian species and happen in areas of the brain that make it more likely that adolescents will engage in risk-taking behaviors (Spear, 2000). This could have evolutionary value by resulting in adolescents exploring new territories and moving toward independence. Sexual behavior is certainly a part of this.

Several studies have found that children's first sexual attraction occurs at age 10, about the fourth or fifth grade (Herdt & McClintock, 2000; Pattatucci & Hamer, 1995). This is well before gonadarche and is true for both heterosex-

precocious puberty A condition in which puberty begins before the age of 9.

delayed puberty A condition in which the appearance of secondary sex characteristics and physical growth do not begin until well after they have begun in most children.

adolescence The time of life between puberty and adulthood.

ual and homosexual attraction. It coincides with rising androgen levels due to the maturation of the adrenal glands (Herdt & McClintock, 2000; McClintock & Herdt, 1996). This is further evidence that Freud's conception of a latency period between the ages of 6 and 11 is incorrect. A recent study of adult professionals' childhood recollections found that over half of both men and women had masturbated to orgasm by age 12 (Ryan, 2000).

In the developmental process, sexual attraction is followed in order by sexual fantasy and sexual behavior. By age 13, the sexual exploration games commonly played by young teens (such as "spin the bottle" and "post office") have a greater erotic content than the games of early childhood.

ADOLESCENCE (AGES 13–17)

Adolescence (from the Latin *adolescens*) refers to the time of life between puberty and adulthood. The term was first used in the English academic literature in 1904 by psychologist G. Stanley Hall. In many nonindustrial cultures individuals are considered to be adults when they reach puberty. In our culture, adolescence is a transition period before adulthood, and a rather extended one at that.

For most adolescent boys and girls, the most important issue in their lives is self-identity (Erikson, 1968). Because of their rapidly changing bodies, the search for self-identity first focuses on body image and physical characteristics. According to Maddock et al. (1983), "There is an intensification of body awareness . . . based upon the fact that the body is a primary 'symbol of self' in which feelings of personal worth, security, and competence are rooted." An adolescent's self-esteem is generally based on his or her subjective views of physical attractiveness. This is also true of teens' sexual esteem (Wiederman & Hurst, 1998). Broad-based self-esteem derived from one's accomplishments develops later. Thus, in the adolescent world there is usually a strong relationship between one's body image and one's overall quality of life (McCabe & Cummins, 1998). This may be especially true of girls, as men greatly prefer partners who are physically attractive (Regan & Berscheid, 1997; see Box 12–A). For those adolescents who fit the football star or prom queen image, adolescence is often a positive experience. For the rest of us, it is a difficult time, and more and more so if you fall farther and farther away from what is considered attractive. We will return to this issue shortly.

MASTURBATION

For most (but certainly not all) people, the first experience with orgasm occurs during masturbation (for others it occurs during mutual touching, petting, sexual intercourse, or dreams). The first data on masturbation during adolescence came from Kinsey's group (1948, 1953). He found that by age 15, 82 percent of boys and 20 percent of girls had masturbated to orgasm. By the age 20, these figures had risen to 92 percent for men and 33 percent for women. The frequency of masturbation by age 15 was 1.8 times per week on the average for boys and 0.5 times per week on the average for girls. A recent study found that three-fourths of adult men and women recollected having masturbated by age 18, and for most of them it was sporadic or continuous throughout adolescence (Ryan, 2000).

What do these numbers tell us? For one thing, most adults have masturbated and started doing so during adolescence. This is more true for men than women, but there seems to be a trend indicating that more women also are masturbating to orgasm during adolescence. Nevertheless, men still have more experience with orgasm by the time they become adults, as a result of their higher frequency of masturbation. There may be cultural differences as well. Studies indicate, for example, that masturbation is more common among white adolescents than among African-American teens (Belcastro, 1985; Laumann et al., 1994).

Although most teens masturbate, nearly half feel that it is "harmful," "sinful," or "wrong," and feel guilty about it (Laumann et al., 1994; Ryan, 2000). Nevertheless, many sex therapists believe that masturbation serves important functions in adolescence. Because sexual activity among adolescents is not condoned in our society, masturbation can serve as an outlet for sexual tensions. Masturbation also can serve as a way to sexually experiment, gain sexual self-confidence, and control sexual impulses (Barbach, 1980). Kinsey thought that masturbation to orgasm was especially important for girls. He felt that familiarity with orgasm during masturbation made it easier for them to experience orgasm during sexual intercourse as adults.

John Gagnon (1977), a sociologist and psychologist who studies communication between generations, notes that masturbation is the single most powerful predictor of adult sexuality. People who masturbated during adolescence generally engage in sexual activity more frequently and have more positive attitudes about sex (and better sexual self-esteem) than people who did not (see Smith et al., 1996). However, there are few programs, or parents, attempting to communicate anything positive about masturbation or other forms of sexual expression. Most communication about sex is negative ("Don't do this"; "Don't let this happen to you"). Gagnon's point is that parents should at least stop attaching guilt to the practice of masturbation in their children. If nothing else, it is surely the "safest" sexual outlet available. However, attitudes are hard to change; former U.S. Surgeon General Joycelyn Elders was fired for expressing similar views about masturbation.

PETTING

Kinsey's team of researchers defined *petting* as physical contact between men and women attempting to produce erotic stimulation without sexual intercourse. Such a definition would include a variety of behaviors, such as kissing, deep (French) kissing, stimulation of the woman's breasts, touching of the genitals, and oral-genital sex. Many sex researchers today define *petting* as noncoital sexual contact below the waist. Any other physical contact is called *necking*. Kinsey et al. (1953) found that by age 18, over 80 percent of the boys and girls in their sample had engaged in petting. Twenty-one percent of the boys and 15 percent of the girls had petted to orgasm by this age. A more recent study found that about half of high school students were virgins, but of these, nearly a third had engaged in genital stimulation with a partner in the past year and about 10 percent had engaged in oral-genital sex (Schuster et al., 1996).

SEXUAL INTERCOURSE

During the last two generations, the number of adolescents engaging in sexual intercourse has increased, and the average age at first intercourse has decreased. Kinsey's group, in 1953, found that only 3 percent of 15-year-old girls had engaged in sexual intercourse. In 1999, half of American high school students had engaged in sexual intercourse, 8.3 percent before the age of 13 (Centers for Disease Control and Prevention, 2000b). Nearly one-third of adolescent girls have had voluntary intercourse by age 15 (Leitenberg & Saltzman, 2000), and 40 percent of girls aged 15–19 have had sexual intercourse in the last three months (Singh & Darroch, 1999). About 16 percent of teens have had four or more sexual partners (CDC, 2000). However, there are major gender and ethnic differences (Upchurch et al., 1998). Among boys, the average age of first intercourse is much younger for African Americans and much older for Asian Americans. Among girls, Hispanic and Asian-American teens are less likely to have had intercourse than white or African-American teens. About 7 to 10 percent of teenage girls have their first voluntary intercourse with male partners who are at least 5 years older (Leitenberg & Saltzman, 2000). About the same percentage have a current partner who is at least 5 years older (Darroch et al., 1999). Overall, the percentage of American teens having intercourse is smaller than for teenagers in some countries, but greater than for most (Singh et al., 2000).

Attitudes about premarital sex are mixed. Interestingly, in their nationally representative survey Laumann et al., (1994) found that 58 percent of the people who believed that premarital sex was "always wrong" had engaged in premarital sex themselves.

Surveys show that the number of sexually active teens decreased during the 1990s (CDC, 2000; Ku et al., 1998). In addition, fewer young people now believe that it is okay to have premarital intercourse than was true in the 1980s (Ku et al., 1998). As a result of this change in attitudes, and an increased use of condoms by those teens who are having intercourse, the teenage pregnancy and birth rates also declined during the 1990s (Ventura et al., 1999, 2000). We do not yet know whether this change is just a momentary dip or the start of a long-term trend. Keep in mind also that of the teens not engaging in sexual intercourse, many are having oral-genital sex and/or anal sex, activities that many teens do not regard as sex (Gates & Somenstein, 2000; see Chapter 1).

Teenage boys and girls generally have different reasons for engaging in sex. For teenage girls, love and a committed relationship that is supposed to last are important before engaging in sex, but these things are not important for most teenage boys, for whom it is more important that they "never miss an opportunity" (Taris & Semin, 1997a).

How do teenagers feel about their first experiences of sexual intercourse? About one-fourth of teenage girls who engage in their first experience of sexual intercourse say that they did not really want to engage in it (Abma, Driscoll, & Moore, 1998). This was particularly true when first intercourse was with a much older partner. Not surprisingly, therefore, Weis (1983) found that women experience a range of emotions during their first sexual intercourse. About one-third have strongly negative emotional reactions (e.g., guilt, anxiety, shame, fear, regret), while another third have highly positive emotional experiences. For the final third, their experience is

neither positive nor negative, but a "Is that all there is?" response (e.g., disappointment, boredom). Men generally have more pleasure and less guilt than women during first intercourse, perhaps because they are more likely to have an orgasm (Sprecher et al., 1995).

Another study found that about one-third of the women surveyed suffered severe physical pain at first intercourse, while 28 percent said they had experienced no pain (Weis, 1985). Women with positive experiences and minimal pain generally had an extensive childhood and adolescent history of sex play (kissing, petting, masturbation, and often oral sex), had positive attitudes about their sex play, and had their first intercourse in a safe environment (no fear of discovery) with a caring partner. Those who had negative reactions and pain had little previous experience with sex play, had not planned it, and "gave in" to the man's pressure (see also Thompson, 1990).

Women who have feelings of guilt after first intercourse are more likely than others to be sexually dissatisfied (e.g., have less enjoyment) as adults (Moore & Davidson, 1997). In contrast, individuals who had positive feelings about their early sexual experiences have greater enjoyment of sex as adults (Bauserman & Davis, 1996).

What about those teens who choose not to engage in premarital intercourse (who now may account for more than 50 percent of teens aged 15–19)? What differentiates them from teens who do engage in sexual intercourse? Many abstain because of fears about pregnancy and sexually transmitted diseases. Teens who abstain are less likely to engage in other risky behaviors as well (e.g., drinking, drugs, etc.) (Kandel, 1990; Whitbeck, Conger, & Simons, 1993). However, parental involvement also plays a role. The *quality* of the communication between parents and teenage children (not just lectures; see Chapter 8) is positively related to the teenagers' values about sexual abstinence (K. Miller et al., 1998a).

PERSONAL REFLECTIONS
What would you tell a young teenager about sex? Why? Pretend you have an adolescent child who has just told you he or she is considering having sexual intercourse. What is your reaction? Does your answer change depending on the sex of the child? Why?

Figure 12–5 The biological changes that occur in adolescence lead to an interest in, and the development of, sexual behavior and sexual identity.

PEER PRESSURE

Studies have shown that about half of all boys are motivated by curiosity the first time they have sex, while nearly one-fourth to one-third of girls say they "went along" with it or that it was "voluntary but not wanted" (Abma et al., 1998; Laumann et al., 1994). Although many teens engage in sex because they have positive feelings about it, many others who are sexually active are motivated by a desire to boost self-esteem and a desire for acceptance (Hajcak & Garwood, 1988). For most teens there is enormous peer pressure to engage in sex. What is **peer pressure?** It is your peer group's expectations of how you are supposed to behave.

If a teenager believes that most of his or her friends are having sex, there can be intense pressure—internally as well as externally—to conform. Gender roles tend to be very rigid in adolescence, and peer pressure makes failure to conform even more difficult. Most young people believe that the average person engages in sexual intercourse after several dates (Cohen & Shotland, 1996), and many overestimate how many of their peers are actually having sex (Whitley, 1998). According to sociologist Donna Elder, "There's quite a bit of research that adolescent males use sex as another arena to achieve and score. They take the competitive sense and move it into the realm of sexuality" (quoted in Gelman & Rogers, 1993). What about those young men who don't wish to become sexually active yet?

> "You were right about the fact that there is great pressure to engage in sex. I didn't have sex until I got married at the age of 22. My friends thought it was dumb for me to want to wait so I lied to them and told them that I had sex and made up a bunch of lies about it. I realize now it was dumb of me. If they were really my friends they would have understood my decision to wait."

> "I am a 19-year-old sophomore and I have not yet had sexual relations. I made a promise to myself long ago that I would not have sex until I am married. I made this promise because of my own moral convictions and I am content with it. I have been the target of a great deal of laughter and ridicule because of this decision. . . . I have been accused of being gay by some and of being sexually repressed by others. I don't see what the fuss is all about. If I am content with my sexuality and I decide to wait until I'm married to have sex, why should I be considered abnormal?" (All examples are from the author's files.)

Many teenage girls also feel pressured to engage in sex:

> "I had sex at 17 in my senior year. . . . So many of my girlfriends would talk about doing it with and for their boyfriends, and would ask me about my experience. I was so ashamed for never having done anything throughout my entire life. . . ."

> "My first sexual experience was when I was 15. Everyone else was 'doing it' so I figured I should too. When it was over I cried. I wish I would have waited. Maybe not till I was married, but until I was more mature."

> "I had my first sexual relationships at 14. . . . I realize now that my reason for these relationships was to be accepted, wanted, have a boyfriend and pleasing him to keep him." (All examples are from the author's files.)

For many girls, the need for emotional intimacy is an important part of finding their self-identity (see Shaughnessy & Shakesby, 1992). Unfortunately, many mistake sexual intimacy for emotional intimacy. In many peer groups there is a double standard that also results in a negative sexual experience for many girls. While men the world over enjoy female promiscuity, in most cultures men prefer women (as mates) who are virgins (Buss & Schmitt, 1993, see Box 12–A).

> "I would let some of the guys from school touch my breasts because of the attention I got from them. I only got a bad reputation instead."

> "Please talk about labelling women. When I was 15, I had some experiences with some older guys around 17. Well, I did some things that I regret. Word got around at my all-girl Catholic high school that I was a slut. You don't know what it is like to walk down a hall and have girls call you a slut. Guys wanted to go out with me for just one thing. I am 21 and have a 'steady' boyfriend who does not know what I did six years ago. I still feel guilty. When I see girls from my high school, some of them still call me a slut." (All examples are from the author's files.)

Just as is the case with some teenage boys, many teenage girls decide not to have sexual relations until they are older and are content with their decision:

> "I am writing this letter to let others like myself know that it is okay to be a virgin. I am a 19-year-old college student and a virgin. There is nothing wrong or strange about it. . . . You do not have to give in to sex just to please others or to simply fit in. . . . You should feel good about yourself, whatever and whenever you decide. When the moment is right, so will you be ready." (from the author's files)

To this point, you may have concluded that the only peer pressure among teens is to engage in sex. However, you have also just learned that the number of teens engaging in sexual intercourse declined during the 1990s (CDC, 2000; Ku et al., 1998). Some experts are giving the credit to positive peer pressure (Alan Guttmacher Institute, 1999). "Many groups want to take credit for the drop in teenage pregnancy, but the credit truly goes to teen-agers," said Jacqueline Darroch of the Guttmacher Institute. The reasoning is that when fewer teens engage in sexual intercourse, they set examples for close friends.

If you engage in sex it should be for the right reasons, and you should feel good about yourself afterwards. Elizabeth Allgeier (1985) designed a questionnaire to get teens to think about whether they are engaging (or about to engage) in sex for the right reasons. You are ready for sex if . . .

1. **You feel guiltless and comfortable about your present level of involvement.**

peer pressure Expectations by one's peer group about how one is supposed to behave.

2. **You are confident that you will not be humiliated and that your reputation will not be hurt.**
3. **Neither partner is pressuring the other for sex.**
4. **You are not trying to:**
   a. **prove your love for the other person;**
   b. **increase your self-worth;**
   c. **prove that you are mature;**
   d. **show that you can attract a sexual partner;**
   e. **get attention, affection, or love;**
   f. **rebel against parents, society, etc.**
5. **It will be an expression of your current feelings rather than an attempt to improve a poor relationship or one that is growing cold.**
6. **You can discuss and agree on an effective method of contraception and share the details, responsibilities, and costs of the use of the method.**
7. **You can discuss the potential of contracting or transmitting sexually transmitted diseases.**
8. **You have discussed and agreed on what both of you will do if conception occurs, because no contraception method is 100 percent effective.**

(Reprinted with permission of SIECUS.)

PERSONAL REFLECTIONS
What kinds of pressure to engage in sex have you experienced (from dates, friends, the media, etc.)? Have you ever engaged in sex because of pressure (to please a boyfriend or girlfriend, to feel older, to be "like everyone else," etc.)? How have you dealt with the pressure? How could you deal better with the pressure?

EMERGING ADULTHOOD (AGES 18–25)

"When our mothers were our age, they were engaged. . . . They at least had some idea what they were going to do with their lives. . . . I, on the other hand, will have a dual degree in majors that are ambiguous at best and impractical at worst (English and political science), no ring on my finger and no idea who I am, much less what I want to do. . . . Under duress, I will admit that this is a pretty exciting time. Sometimes, when I look out across the wide expanse that is my future, I can see beyond the void. I realize that having nothing ahead to count on means I now have to count on myself; that having no direction means forging one of my own." (Kristen, age 22, in Page, 1999, pp. 18, 20)

The average age at marriage has increased dramatically in recent decades. The U.S. Census Bureau reported that the median age at which people first got married in 1996 was 25 for women and 27 for men, the highest levels in the 20th century. This is an increase of more than 2 years of age since 1980 and more than 4 years since 1960. The percentage of young Americans going on to higher education has also in-

emerging adulthood A developmental stage of life; an extended period of being a single adult that occurs between adolescence and young adulthood.

creased substantially, from 14 percent in 1940 to over 60 percent now (Bianchi & Spain, 1996). As a result, psychologist Jeffrey Arnett (2000) has proposed that a new developmental stage of life has emerged in today's society—**emerging adulthood.** This is an extended period of being a single adult that occurs between adolescence and young adulthood. Emerging adults have more freedom from parental restraints and more opportunity for privacy than in the past.

Arnett (2000) argues that this developmental stage is distinct from both adolescence and young adulthood, and not just in terms of demographics. Most individuals in this age group are ambiguous about whether or not they are adults; they say yes in some respects and no in other respects. This age period generally includes frequent change as individuals explore for their own identities in love, work, and worldviews. Dating, relationships, and love generally become more serious than during adolescence. There is often an increase in risk behavior as well as individuals search for their own identity. This developmental stage is not found in all cultures, but is common in advanced cultures where young people are allowed an extended period of independence and role exploration.

According to Seidman and Rieder (1994), who reviewed the results of numerous recent sexual surveys, the sexual activity of emerging adults is generally different from that of younger and older age groups. By the age of 20, approximately 90 percent of emerging adults are sexually experienced and having sex regularly, and most emerging adults have had multiple serial sexual partners during their short lifetimes. Let us review some of these studies.

Kinsey and his colleagues (1948) found that 68 percent of men surveyed with a college education, 85 percent of men with a high school education, and 98 percent of men with only an elementary school education had had premarital sex. The numbers for women were much lower, but more recent data indicate a striking increase in the number of women who have had premarital sex. Surveys have found that among unmarried persons aged 18–24, over 80 percent of the men and women had engaged in premarital sex with a heterosexual partner (Anderson & Dahlberg, 1992). Janus and Janus (1993) found that 91 percent of the men and 83 percent of the women they studied had had premarital sex. Nationally, nearly 20 percent of unmarried women have had four or more partners in the past 4 years (U.S. Department of Health and Human Services, 1997). Men are much more likely than women to have permissive attitudes about premarital sex, especially casual sex (Oliver & Hyde, 1993).

Many of these surveys focused on women in particular. These studies found that the earlier a woman becomes sexually experienced, the more likely it is that she will have had multiple sexual partners. Also, the more experienced she becomes, the less time she

Figure 12–6 Emerging adulthood is an extended period of being a single adult. The large majority of emerging adults are sexually experienced and have sex regularly.

Thus, for many emerging adults, their sexual life-style can be called **serial monogamy**—a series of relationships in which sex is reserved for just one other person.

The period of emerging adulthood is also a time in which most people gradually become less influenced by peer pressure and gain a better understanding of their own sexual motivations.

> "I now make my own choices and give my opinions without being intimidated about what someone else might think. But most of all I have stopped confusing sex for the attention I was striving for. For example, I used to think that if I give him sex then that means he must like me or is my friend." (from the author's files)

By the end of this stage, individuals have generally established *cognitive* views about sexual aspects of themselves (Andersen et al., 1999; Cyranowski & Andersen, 1998). Researchers call these views **sexual self-schemas.** Individuals with positive self-schemas look at sex more positively than those with negative schemas, and tend to engage in sex more often and have a wider range of experiences. Again, sexual self-schemas are cognitive views. What about emotions? Researchers refer to positive emotions about one's sexuality as **erotophilia,** and negative emotions as **erotophobia** (Fisher, 1986). One might expect that a person's sexual self-schemas and emotional responses to sex are closely related, and in fact erotophiliacs do seek out and enjoy sex more than do erotophobic persons. Of course, a person's cognitive views and emotions developed from past experiences and can change with future experiences.

YOUNG ADULTHOOD (ADULTS AGED 26–39)

spends between sexual relationships (Seidman et al., 1992; Tanfer & Schoorl, 1992). Less religious women are more likely to have had multiple partners than religious women, especially Catholic women, and less educated women were found to have had more lifetime partners than college-educated women (except for divorced or separated white women, for whom the reverse was true).

In summary, for adolescents and young adults, the number of sexual partners steadily increases the longer the individual has been sexually experienced (see Tanfer & Schoorl, 1992). For some young adults, this is a period of sexual experimentation in which they engage in "one-night stands" or even group sex:

> "This past year I have become very sexually active. I have a steady boyfriend. We love one another to death, but are involved in threesomes and sometimes foursomes. We enjoy sex and have tried everything imaginable. The persons involved in our 'parties' are his roommates. We consider ourselves 'one big happy family'." (from the author's files)

However, many adolescents and young adults probably begin a sexual relationship with the hope and expectation that it will last. Clements (1994) reported that 86 percent of the women and 71 percent of the men he surveyed said that it was difficult for them to have sex without emotional involvement.

> "Dates often leave me feeling bad that I don't engage in the one night stand scenes. . . . I prefer to make love. Sex is not a sport to me. Personally, it's too emotional to take it that lightly." (from the author's files)

In their review of sexual surveys, Seidman and Rieder (1994) concluded that relatively long-lasting monogamy was the norm for most adults aged 25 and older. For people in this age group, about 80 percent of sexually active heterosexual men and 90 percent of sexually active heterosexual women report having had only one sex partner within

serial monogamy The practice of having a series of monogamous sexual relationships.

sexual self-schemas Cognitive views by individuals about sexual aspects of themselves.

erotophilia Having positive emotions about one's own sexuality.

erotophobia Having negative emotions about one's own sexuality.

the last year. Nearly identical findings were reported by Laumann's group (1994).

For this age group, the best predictors of having more than one partner are marital status, sex, age, and race. Not only are men, particularly younger unmarried men, more likely than women to have had multiple partners in the preceding year, but for unmarried women abstinence becomes more common with increasing age (see Seidman & Rieder, 1994).

MARRIAGE

As mentioned in the introduction to this section, many people today are postponing marriage. Still others never marry. This is much truer for African Americans than it is for Americans in general (Laumann et al., 1994; Tucker et al., 1993). However, because of the history of negative attitudes about sexuality in Western culture (see Chapter 1), for many people sexual relations are legitimized only within marriage. Moreover, numerous studies have found that adults who get and stay married have higher levels of psychological well-being (and, in the case of men, less depression) than individuals who stay single (e.g., Horwitz et al., 1996).

The frequency of sexual intercourse in the first year of marriage is usually high, an average of about 15 times a month in the first year (Greenblatt, 1983). The frequency of sexual relations generally declines thereafter. However, for the entire population, the frequency of sexual relations is highest for married couples in their mid-20s to mid-30s (Clements, 1994; Janus & Janus, 1993; Laumann et al., 1994). Married women are also more likely than single women to have orgasms during sexual intercourse (Laumann et al., 1994).

The decrease in sexual relations after the first year or two of marriage occurs for a variety of reasons. Sex has to compete with other time demands, such as career advancement. Parenthood means less privacy and more demands, and often results in exhaustion at the end of the day. It is also normal for sexual relations to decrease somewhat as the novelty wears off and individuals within a relationship become accustomed to one another (Blumstein & Schwartz, 1983).

Studies find that married couples today are more likely to use a variety of sexual techniques than in the past. This is true for positions of sexual intercourse and for oral-genital sex (Hunt, 1974). Hunt found that a majority of young people also continue to masturbate after getting married. In fact, people with sexual partners are much more likely to masturbate than people who do not have a partner (Laumann et al., 1994; see

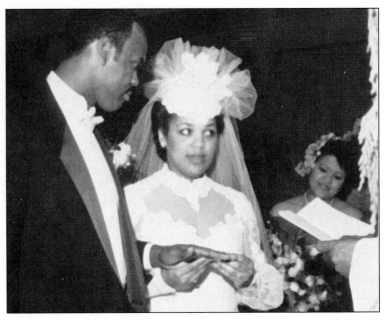

Figure 12–7 Relatively long-lasting monogamy is the norm for most adults aged 25 and older.

Chapter 13). However, a majority of both men and women report marital sex to be very satisfying, more so than do singles (Clements, 1994; Laumann et al., 1994). I will have more to say about marriage and sex in a later section of the chapter.

LIVING TOGETHER (COHABITATION)

Nearly half of all American women aged 25 to 39 years old have cohabited with a man outside of marriage at some time in their lives (Bumpass & Lu, 2000). About one-fourth of unmarried women aged 25 to 39 are currently cohabitating. The percentages are the same for whites and African Americans, and slightly lower for Latinos. This represents an increase in *cohabitation* of over 700 percent since the 1970 census. Forty percent of children live for some period of time in a cohabitating family. The increase in the number of couples living together may be one reason for the older age of couples today who marry for the first time.

> "I totally believe that it is a good idea to live with someone first if you plan to marry them. . . . I was very uncertain on where our relationship was and where it was headed. I know now after living with someone, just for three months, that he and I had totally different needs in our lives." (from the author's files)

Living together can be a test or trial period before marriage (there is much more to living together happily and successfully than simply enjoying sex). Fifty-four percent of all first marriages begin as cohabitation (Bumpass & Lu, 2000). Living together can also be an alternative to marriage. The amount of commitment that couples make to each other while living together can vary a great deal (Bumpass et al., 1991). As cohabitation has become more acceptable, a greater number of couples who cohabitate are doing so for temporary convenience (Bumpass & Lu, 2000). Studies show that in cohabitation there is generally less certainty about the relationship than in marriage (Bumpass et al., 1991). One advantage people claim for living together instead of marrying is that since there has been no formal contract, such as a marriage license, it is easy to simply walk away from a relationship that does not seem to be working. One disadvantage in living together is that it is easy to walk out on a relationship that does not seem to be working. (Think about it.) In actuality, cohabitation unions are very unstable; over half end within 5 years (Bumpass & Lu, 2000).

Although most people think that cohabitation is something done mostly by college students, cohabitation is most common among the least educated people in the population, particularly those from less religious families (Bumpass & Lu, 2000).

Interestingly, studies find that couples who live together before getting married are more likely than others to get divorced (Axinn & Thornton, 1992; Bumpass & Lu, 2000; Bumpass & Sweet, 1989). The higher divorce rate is not due to the greater time that cohabitors have spent together (DeMaris & Rao, 1992), but instead is the result of a lowered enthusiasm about marriage and a greater tolerance of divorce (Axinn & Barber, 1997). Axinn and Thornton (1992) believe that cohabitation "may reinforce the idea that intimate relationships are fragile and temporary" and this might "reduce the expectation that marriage is a lifetime relationship." Living together, they said, "probably attracts people who are, on average, more accepting of the termination of intimate relationships." Although more research is needed to determine why people who live together premaritally are more likely than others to divorce when married, we are able to conclude that cohabitation is not the answer to a stable relationship that many have hoped it would be.

SINGLE PARENTHOOD

In 1994, there were 11.4 million single parents raising children (9.9 million women and 1.5 million men), nearly triple the number in 1970 (U.S. Census Bureau).

About 25 percent of white children and 65 percent of black children lived with a single parent. Some adults become single parents through divorce or separation, but nearly 25 percent of never-married women are also mothers. This trend cuts across all socioeconomic groups. For example, among never-married managerial or professional women, the proportion who were mothers increased from 3.1 percent in 1981 to 8.2 percent in 1992.

I discussed the effects of single parenthood on children's gender identities and gender roles in Chapter 10. There has been very little research on the sexual behavior of single parents as a group.

EXTRAMARITAL SEX—IN SUPPOSEDLY MONOGAMOUS MARRIAGES

In their original surveys (1948, 1953), Kinsey and his colleagues found that about 50 percent of married men and 24 percent of married women had engaged in extramarital sex on at least one occasion. Surveys by magazines such as *Cosmopolitan, Playboy, Woman's Day,* and *Redbook* have found equally high, and often higher (especially for women), percentages. However, the Kinsey surveys have been criticized for being nonrepresentative, and magazine surveys are almost always nonrepresentative (see Chapter 1).

What do more scientifically conducted current surveys indicate? In its 1990 "New Report on Sex," the Kinsey Institute found that 37 percent of the husbands and 29 percent of the wives surveyed had had at least one extramarital affair (Reinisch, 1990). Janus and Janus (1993) found that 35 percent of married men (and 56 percent of divorced men) and 26 percent of married women (and 59 percent of divorced women) in their survey admitted to extramarital affairs. Other surveys find a lower percentage of people who admit to having been unfaithful to their spouses (Choi, Catania, & Dolcini, 1994; Clements, 1994; Laumann et al., 1994). In their nationally representative sample, Laumann's group found that 25 percent of men and 15 percent of women admitted to having had an affair. This agrees with another recent nationally representative sample (Wiederman, 1997b). Keep in mind, however, that if we look only at middle-aged persons (who have had more opportunity), the percentages increase to about 35 percent of married men and 20 percent of married women. By the way, the rate of extrarelational affairs is just as high for cohabitating couples as it is for married couples (Blumstein & Schwartz, 1983).

These statistics on adultery refer to extramarital *sexual* relations. But, according to psychologist Shirley Glass, "That's a male definition [of adultery]. If you look at emotional involvement and sexual involvement short of intercourse, you add another 20 percent" (quoted in Mehren, 1991). For

Reprinted with special permission of King Features Syndicate.

Box 12–A CROSS-CULTURAL PERSPECTIVES

How Do People Select a Mate?

The boxes on cross-cultural perspectives presented throughout this book generally show that cultures differ widely in their attitudes and behaviors regarding sexuality. Recently, however, David Buss and David Schmitt (1993) surveyed people throughout the world, from Zambia to China, and found that people's mating preferences and attitudes were very much alike. The only major differences were between men's and women's desires and whether or not people were interested in a short-term relationship (casual sex) or a long-term mate.

Short-term relationships dominate human mating patterns, but men and women engage in short-term liaisons for different reasons, according to the authors of the study. Men tend to engage in casual sex to test their virility, whereas a woman's short-term relationships are largely experimental in nature, either to test her market value (to see how desirable she is) or to determine what her desires are. On average, men wanted about 18 women as sexual partners in their lifetime, while the average woman wanted 4 men.

Other studies confirm that, as a general rule, men are much more likely than women to engage in casual sex with someone they hardly know, or don't know at all (see Oliver & Hyde, 1993). In one study, for example, researchers had an attractive man or an attractive woman approach college students and ask them if they would have sex with him or her (Clark & Hatfield, 1989). Three-fourths of the men said yes, but none of the women agreed to have sex with an attractive stranger. Buss and Schmitt found that most men were willing to have sex with a woman after knowing her for only a week, whereas the typical woman preferred to wait 6 months.

Buss and Schmitt found that in all cultures the idealistic goal was a lasting relationship. Across all cultures, over 90 percent of people eventually marry (Buss, 1985; Epstein & Guttman, 1984). However, this does not mean that people spend their lives with one partner. Many cultures allow people to have more than one mate, a practice called **polygamy.** In fact, about 80 percent of all societies allow **polygyny**—men to have multiple wives or mistresses (although only about 10 to 20 percent of men actually do so at any one time) (Buss, 1999; Fisher, 1989). About 2 percent allow **polyandry**—women to have more than one mate (Frayser, 1985). According to Buss and Schmitt, Western cultures may have outlawed polygamy, but people get around this by having serial marriages (divorce and remarriage) and by having extramarital affairs. In the United States, the divorce rate is around 50 percent (H. Fisher, 1987), and from 25 to 50 percent of people are estimated to have engaged in adultery (H. E. Fisher, 1987; Hite, 1987; Kinsey et al., 1948, 1953).

Buss and Schmitt believe that, for men, promiscuity is a primal instinct that maximizes reproduction potential. How do men balance their short- and long-term desires? Buss says, "If a man could have his fantasy, he would sequester and monopolize all the attractive women in the country. Indeed, men who are in a position to get what they want—kings, tycoons, celebrities—often do things like that" (quoted by Gura, 1994). Men may enjoy female promiscuity in a short-term relationship, but when looking for a long-term mate they seek a chaste woman, someone who has not yet had sex. Of 37 countries studied by Buss and Schmitt, in more than two-thirds of them the men valued chastity in choosing a mate more than the women did. This was especially true among Palestinian Arabs, Iranians, and Indonesians.

"I am of Mexican descent. In our culture, it is 'okay' for boys to engage in sex before marriage. In fact, it is encouraged. Girls, however, are not to have sex until after marriage. We are made to believe that a man will not want to marry a girl who is not a virgin. In most cases, it turns out to be true." (from the author's files)

Remember from Box 4–A that in many parts of northern Africa and the Middle East, girls' genitals are sewn together to assure chastity at the time of marriage. According to the study, chastity at marriage was not important to most men in Scandinavia and the Netherlands. However, regardless of culture, men placed a high value on physical attractiveness in choosing a long-term mate (Buss, 1989; Buss & Barnes, 1987; Regan & Berscheid, 1997) and preferred mates who were younger than they were (Buss, 1989; Kendrick & Keefe, 1992). Zambian men

polygamy The practice of allowing men or women to have more than one mate at the same time.

polygyny The practice of allowing men to have two or more wives at the same time.

polyandry The practice of allowing women to have more than one husband at the same time.

preferred wives who were at least 7 years younger, while Italian men preferred an age difference of 3 years and U.S. men a difference of about 2 years. Why this strong preference for physical attractiveness? Evolutionary scientists have found evidence that women's facial and bodily attractiveness signals hormonal and developmental (i.e., reproductive) health (Thornhill & Grammer, 1999).

Women's mating strategies are different from men's, according to Buss and Schmitt. Because a woman has a limited number of reproductive years and must invest time and energy in childbearing, women prefer mates who can offer them economic and physical protection. Women, more so than men, prefer men who are good financial prospects (Buss, 1989). Some researchers believe that dating and marriage frequently involve an exchange of sex for financial support (e.g., Muehlenhard & Schrag, 1990). Factors like a promising career, ambition, and education are important in women's decisions across all cultures. Women prefer older mates, and are not as concerned about physical attractiveness as are men. Chastity of a potential mate is important to women only in some Oriental cultures.

In line with their mating strategies, men and women use different strategies to keep a mate interested (Buss & Shackelford, 1997). Women are more likely to make themselves more attractive, while men are more likely to spend money on a mate and give gifts.

Buss and Schmitt believe that there is evolutionary value for what men and women seek in a relationship. Whether or not you agree with this, one thing is clear from this large cross-cultural study—love is not really blind.

---

example, it is not uncommon for married persons to have emotional affairs over the telephone or the Internet (see Shaw, 1997). Indeed, Thompson (1984) found that extramarital affairs that involved a deep emotional involvement, but were nonsexual, were about half as common as sexual affairs.

Throughout the world, nearly 90 percent of people believe that extramarital sex is "always" or "almost always" wrong (Widmer et al., 1998). In a 1996 survey done for *Newsweek,* only 22 percent believed that affairs can sometimes be good (Adler et al., 1996). There is also a sex difference. In a recent survey for *Modern Maturity,* a majority of American men aged 45 and older said that they did not believe it was wrong to have sex outside of marriage (Jacoby, 1999). Interestingly, Kinsey and his colleagues found that men were more likely to rate affairs as harmful to a relationship—if their wives were unfaithful to them. Men are more upset at the idea of their partner's getting physical with someone else than they are about an emotional attachment. Women, on the other hand, are more concerned about emotional infidelity on the part of their mates and are much more likely than men to forgive a partner for sexual infidelity (Buss et al., 1992; Wiederman & Kendall, 1999).

Why do so many people engage in extramarital sex (or sex outside of any supposedly monogamous relationship)? Some are simply curious to see what sex with another person would be like, while some want more variety in their lives. Some may seek out other partners in order to prove that they are still desirable or young (the famous "midlife crisis" or "middle-aged crazy" cause of extramarital sex), while others may be looking for the companionship no longer found in their marriages. Evolutionary psychologists believe that the primary drives for women are acquisition of a better mate and accumulation of resources (Greiling & Buss, 2000). Of course, there is also the excitement factor. As John Gagnon (1977) points out,

> **Most people find their extramarital relationships highly exciting, especially in the early stages. This is a result of psychological compression: the couple gets together; they are both very aroused (desire, guilt, expectation); they have only three hours to be together. . . . Another source of attraction is that the other person is always seen when he or she looks good and is on best behavior, never when feeling tired or grubby, or when taking care of children, or when cooking dinner. . . . Each time, all the minutes that the couple has together are special because they have been stolen from all these other relationships. The resulting combination of guilt and excitement has a heightening effect.**

Blumstein and Schwartz (1983) found that men generally look for casual sex and have more extramarital partners than women. Women are perceived as being more likely to seek an emotional attachment with their new partner (Sprecher et al., 1998). Still, in most cases affairs are primarily short term, or "one-night stands" (Gagnon, 1977).

There is very little relationship between social background—including political leaning (ultraconservative vs. ultraliberal) and religion or lack of it—and whether or not one engages in extramarital affairs (Janus & Janus, 1993). Whitehurst (1972) indicates that two things contribute to having "outside sex." One is simply opportunity. For example, Levin and

Figure 12–8 The addition of children may change the pattern of sexual relations, but not necessarily the frequency. Married couples in their mid-20s to mid-30s have sex more often than any other group.

Levin (1975) found that while 27 percent of all housewives surveyed reported having had an extramarital affair, 47 percent of married women who worked at least part time away from home had had sex outside of marriage. Women who work have more opportunity to meet other men and to have affairs than women who stay at home all day (Adler et al., 1996). As psychotherapist Marcella Weiner puts it, "Women are in the work force to stay now, and they have many more opportunities [to meet men]. It has always been okay with men, but it is becoming more and more a phenomenon with women" (quoted in Mehren, 1991). With the rising number of wives entering the work force outside of the home, the number of women having extramarital sex may continue to increase. The second contributor mentioned by Whitehurst is alienation. People can grow apart and develop different interests over time. Thus, if you meet someone else who shares your interests, seems attractive, and seems attracted to you, this can lead to sharing other parts of your life as well (see Chapter 14). An interesting

open marriage A marital relationship in which the couple agrees that it is permissible to have sexual relations outside the marriage.

swinging A type of open marriage relationship in which a couple has extramarital relations together with other couples.

thing about Whitehurst's argument is that situational factors are seen as responsible for the likelihood of extramarital sex, rather than some personality flaw. This would also explain why married individuals generally have affairs in the daytime—it is simply easier to get away and cover one's tracks during the day than at night.

EXTRAMARITAL SEX—CONSENSUAL ARRANGEMENTS

Some couples agree to have sex outside of the marital relationship. One such arrangement is **open marriage,** where both partners agree that it is okay to have sex with others. Even here, however, there are usually some agreed-upon restrictions, such as not having sex with a mutual friend or not having sex with the same person twice (Blumstein & Schwartz, 1983). Couples make these restrictions so that their primary commitment is to the marriage and thus the nonmarital partner will not be viewed as competition. According to Nena and George O'Neill, authors of the 1972 best-seller *Open Marriage,* this type of marriage challenges the idea that a single partner can meet all of a person's needs and allows personal growth for both individuals. Blumstein & Schwartz (1983) found that perhaps as many as 15 percent of married couples had some sort of "understanding" that allowed for extramarital sexual relations under some conditions. Although this type of extramarital arrangement is supposed to add role equality and flexibility to a marriage (O'Neill & O'Neill, 1972), the divorce rate among open-marriage couples is just as high as for sexually monogamous couples (Rubin & Adams, 1986). However, for those open-marriage couples that did break up, sexual jealousy was rarely the reason.

Another arrangement that allows consensual extramarital sex is **swinging** (often called "wife swapping" or the "lifestyle"), where a married couple has extramarital relations together. Couples get together by answering ads in newspapers or swingers' magazines, or by going to commercial clubs that encourage recreational sex. In some cases, several couples get together for swinging parties. The sexual activity often includes sex between the women while the husbands watch, but male homosexual activity is much less common, and in many cases forbidden. Swinging reached its peak in popularity in the 1970s, declined during the 1980s, but has since rebounded. Although there has been an increase in the number of swing clubs nationally, no recent research has been done to establish the overall prevalence (Jenks, 1998). Some couples abandon swinging after giving it a short try, usually because they find that it creates feelings of jealousy, sexual inadequacy, or rejection for them (Murstein, 1978). Except for the fact that they tend to be white, less religious than others, and to have had more premarital sexual experience, swingers are no different from other couples, and many are middle class and conservative (Jenks, 1998). There is no evidence to support the belief that they are unhappier (with themselves or their marriages) than others.

PERSONAL REFLECTIONS
Does the thought of your parents enjoying sexual relations make you comfortable or uncomfortable? Why? If you have difficulty viewing your parents as sexual human beings, what effect do you think that will have on your own sexual relationship when you and your partner become parents (and view one another as parents)? When you become a parent, will you be embarrassed if your children know that you and your partner enjoy sexual relations? Why?

MIDDLE AGE (AGES 40–59)

Christian and Victorian views of sex emphasized that sex within a marriage was for procreation only, and excluded sexual activities for pleasure. Thus Western culture came to view older individuals who were through conceiving children as asexual. For example, many students believe that their own parents and grandparents love each other, but how many students think of their parents and grandparents as being sexually active? Studies have found that many college students have difficulty accepting their parents' sexuality and underestimate how often their parents have sex by about half (Allgeier & Murnen, 1985; Pocs & Godow, 1977). Here are a variety of responses from students in my course:

"I was about 14 when my mom told me she and my dad have sex. I was shocked and thought it was disgusting. I didn't want to hear it any more."

"My parents don't have sex. They have other things to do."

"The thought of my parents actually possessing sexuality or having sex mortified me."

"And plus they are in their late 40's and early 50's—I just can't imagine them having sex."

"When I was a teenager, it would make me uncomfortable when they would go in their room and shut and lock the door because I knew what they were going to be doing and I just felt it was weird because to me, they were 'old.' Now that I'm in my 20s, it makes me feel good to know that my parents still love and care about each other, and it helps me to believe that I will have a positive sexual attitude well into my 40's and 50's."

"Sometimes I tease them a little when I catch my dad home late in the morning because I know he stayed home so they could have sex. I think it's great that they still love each other and express themselves sexually after being married for 25 years."

Pocs and Godow (1977) concluded that "many parents may appear to be nonsexual because they hesitate to discuss the topic of sexuality in any way with their children or because they are not inclined to exhibit loving, affectionate responses, let alone sexual behavior, in the presence of their children." Allgeier and Murnen (1985) later found that students whose parents had discussed sex with them gave more accurate estimates of their parents' sexual frequency.

Ask yourself these questions: "Do my parents enjoy sexual intercourse? How often? Do they enjoy using different positions? Do they enjoy oral-genital sex? Do my grandparents enjoy sex? How often? Do they enjoy using different positions? Do they enjoy oral-genital sex?"

Think about how you answered these questions, and then ask yourself: "What are my attitudes about sex? Is it something good that two people share?" For those of you who are sexually experienced, also ask yourself, "Do I like sex? How often do I enjoy it?" If you enjoy sex, why wouldn't your parents or grandparents? Sex therapists have found that the way that you feel about sex now is the best estimate of how you will feel about it in the future (Bretschneider & McCoy, 1988; Masters & Johnson, 1966). If you enjoy sex now, why should you stop enjoying sex later in life? *Adults of all ages are sexual beings.* Sex can be healthy and enjoyable throughout life. Problems with fully enjoying sex are more often due to one's beliefs and attitudes than to physiological changes (Kellett, 1991). If you want to have a good, healthy sex life in the future, you need to be aware now that older adults are still enjoying the pleasurable aspects of sex. From the previous case histories, which students do you think will enter parenthood with more positive attitudes about sexuality?

Older people are aware that young people have unfavorable attitudes about them having sexual relations. These negative attitudes can create many unnecessary barriers for people. Today, for example, people are not surprised when two young people decide to live together without getting married. However, the same

"Actually, Dad knows quite a bit about sex for a man his age."

Reprinted from *Good Housekeeping* by permission of Rex May.

young people might be shocked if a widowed parent or grandparent decided to date, or to move in with an older adult. Barring a tragedy, we will all grow old someday. These negative attitudes must change if today's young people want to be treated decently when they are older.

FREQUENCY OF SEXUAL INTERCOURSE

It is a common belief that sexual activity is highest for young people and that by middle age sexual relations have become stale as people cease to be sexy. However, the baby-boomer generation is now hitting their 50s and, having been raised during the sexual revolution, they do not accept the old stereotypes of aging and sexuality. There is a genuine *generation gap* between the attitudes of the previous generation and the baby boomers (Jacoby, 1999). Many people in their 50s and older are now regarded as sexy: Sean Connery, Susan Sarandon, Richard Gere, Tina Turner, Tom Selleck, Sophia Loren, Harrison Ford, Pam Grier, and the list goes on and on. How sexually active are the baby boomers?

As mentioned earlier, two national cross-sectional surveys found that sexual activity was highest for people in their mid-20s to mid-30s (Clements, 1994; Janus & Janus, 1993). Is there a sharp drop-off after that? Not really, at least not until the 60s. Although most surveys do show a decline in sexual activity for people in their 40s and a further decline in the 50s, the drop-off is very gradual (Clements, 1994; Segraves & Segraves, 1995; Seidman & Rieder, 1994). At most, the frequency of sexual intercourse for married couples decreases by only a couple of times a month from the 30s through the 50s (from 7–8 times a month to 5–6 times a month). A recent survey by *Modern Maturity* found that over half of 45- to 54-year-old people with partners were having sexual intercourse at least once a week (Jacoby, 1999). In fact, Janus and Janus (1993) found very little evidence of any decline in sexual activity through the early 60s.

A lot of people also believe that the sex lives of older married people are dull compared to those of singles. Actually, the surveys indicate that married people have sex more often than singles (never married or divorced) and are happier with their sex lives than are singles (Clements, 1994; Laumann et al., 1994). When asked if sex is important to them, more people in their 30s, 40s, and early 50s say yes than do people in their late teens or early 20s (Clements, 1994).

Not everyone in their 50s is having sex regularly. Some are not because of ill health, sexual disorders, or simply because they do not have a partner (see following sections). However, the major factors that affect sexual desire in middle age are an individual's cognitions about sex (beliefs/values about the sexuality of people in one's group) and his or her motivation. Within a relationship, sexual motivation and the quality of sex are highly associated with the overall quality of the relationship (Jacoby, 1999; Kingsberg, 2000). Relationship quality is

Figure 12–9 Over half of 45 to 54-year-old people with partners have sexual intercourse at least once a week. Do you believe that your parents still enjoy sex? When you become a parent, will you be embarrassed if your children know that you and your partner enjoy sexual relations?

high when there is *emotional* intimacy, some independence without too much distance, and stress is under control. There must also be a sexual equilibrium, i.e., "a balance of sexual capacities between two people and their perceptions of those capacities" (Kingsberg, 2000).

In the *Modern Maturity* survey (Jacoby, 1999), the percentage of people who said that their sex lives were "extremely" or "very" satisfying was almost identical to the percentage who said that their emotional relationship was highly satisfying. As for sexual equilibrium, women say that as their male partners grow older they tend to become more romantic (Jacoby, 1999). Thus, couples tend to regard such behaviors as hugging and kissing as much more important and pleasurable than they did when they were younger (Clements, 1994).

LOSS OF A MATE BY DIVORCE OR DEATH

Over half of all marriages in the United States now end in divorce (Saluter, 1996). Other people become single again as a result of their partner's death. When this happens, reentry into the singles world and dating are often difficult, particularly if the relationship had been a long-lasting one. Many divorced and widowed persons have no idea of what the current expectations are in dating, and thus, learning how to interact with potential partners may take some time and at first may be very awkward. New rules have to be created or discovered. For example, should a 45-year-old divorced woman have sex with her date on the first date, after they've gone out a few times, only after she thinks they love each other, or not at all?

The early sex surveys by Kinsey and colleagues (1953) and Hunt (1974) reported that divorced individuals were very sexually active. Resuming sexual activity is often an important part of letting go of the former bonds. However, more recent studies have found that three-fourths of divorced persons have either a single sexual partner or no partner in the first year (Stack & Gundlach, 1992).

Among divorced or widowed men and women, there are more opportunities for men. By the time people reach their early 40s, there are over 200 single women for every 100 single men (Blumstein & Schwartz, 1983). The survey by *Modern Maturity* found that among people aged 55 to 59, about 90 percent of men have sexual partners, but only about 70 percent of women do (Jacoby, 1999). It used to be the case that for middle-aged women, divorce or widowhood was the end of their sex lives because societal norms did not allow for nonmarital sex. As part of the new generation gap in sexual attitudes, baby-boomer women are much less likely to accept celibacy (Jacoby, 1999).

There is also a double standard in our society. While many people frown upon women having sexual relationships with men much younger than themselves, most feel that it is okay for men to have relationships with younger women. Have you noticed that whenever Hollywood puts a middle-aged leading man in a romantic role it is almost always with a woman 10 to 20 years younger (or even more) than he is? Because of the man-woman ratio and the double standard, women over age 40 generally have a more difficult time finding new partners than older men.

About three-fourths of divorced people remarry, usually within 3 to 4 years (Coleman & Ganong, 1991; Lown & Dolan, 1988), but do they do a better job of choosing a partner? Apparently not, for half or more of second marriages also end in divorce (Blumstein & Schwartz, 1983; Ganong & Coleman, 1989). Since the early 1970s, the percentage of people who have married three or more times has doubled, from 4 percent to 8 percent (National Center for Health Statistics). For some, marriage is just another form of serial monogamy.

FEMALE SEXUALITY: PHYSICAL CHANGES WITH AGE

Recall from Chapter 3 that girls are born with a few hundred thousand ova (follicles) at birth, and that several hundred begin to mature every month (McGee & Hsueh, 2000). As a woman ages into her 40s, her supply of ova is nearing exhaustion. Her ovaries do not respond as well to the pituitary hormones FSH and LH (see Fig. 12–10), so that menstrual cycle irregularities are common after the age of 35 (cycles become more frequent or less frequent than before). Eventually her ovaries atrophy (wither) and she quits having menstrual cycles entirely, thus ending her ability to have

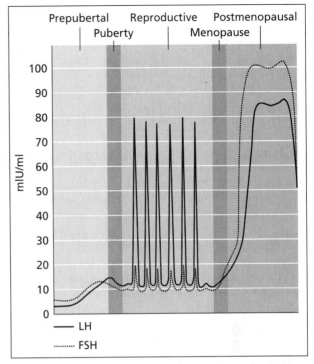

Figure 12–10 The pattern of secretion of pituitary hormones during a woman's lifetime. The large increases in FSH and LH after menopause are due to the loss of estrogen and progesterone from the ovaries.

children. The cessation of menstruation is referred to as **menopause.** The changes that occur in the few years that precede and the first year that follows menopause are called the **climacteric** (also called the *perimenopause*) (see Sowers, 2000).

Menopause usually occurs in a woman's late 40s or early 50s with the average age being 51.5 (Bromberger et al., 1997). This is a delay of about 4 years over the past century, probably due to improvements in health and socioeconomic status (Flint, 1997). Researchers have concluded that menopause is just a natural result of aging, and that the older a woman is when she experiences menopause the more likely it is that she will live a long life (Sowers, 2000). Some of the factors that can cause early menopause include cigarette smoking, a history of short menstrual cycles, and perhaps depressive disorders (Harlow & Signorello, 2000).

As the ovaries atrophy, they produce less and less gonadal hormones, and eventually produce no progesterone and only minute amounts of estrogen. Testosterone levels often decrease as well. Most women will experience some symptoms as a result of these hormonal changes. How a woman and her partner react to these changes can affect other aspects of a relationship,

menopause The term for a woman's last menstrual period.
climacteric The changes that occur in women in the few years that precede and the first year that follows menopause.

so it is important for everyone to understand their physical basis (see Nachtigall, 1994, for a review).

Estrogen and progesterone, you recall, inhibit release of FSH and LH from the pituitary. At menopause, the pituitary hormones are no longer inhibited and are released in large amounts. In addition to their reproductive role, these hormones affect the diameter of blood vessels, causing them to dilate. Subjectively, this physiological change is perceived as a *hot flash,* a sudden sensation of warmth or intense heat that spreads over the upper body, face, and head (see Kronenberg, 1994). The hot flash is usually accompanied by flushing and sweating and is often followed by a feeling of being chilled. Pressure in the head or chest, nausea, or feelings of suffocation can also be experienced during a hot flash. The sensations last from a few seconds to 15 minutes or more and are very common at night, thus interfering with sleep. This can lead to fatigue, irritability, and depression. Hot flashes generally disappear within a few years, but 20 percent of affected women may experience hot flashes for 5 years or longer.

The loss of estrogen also causes the vagina to become thinner and less elastic, with a marked *decrease in the amount of vaginal lubrication* during sexual arousal. If the vagina is not properly lubricated, sexual intercourse will be painful, so that some postmenopausal women may start avoiding sexual relations. This is unnecessary, however, if a woman and her partner accept vaginal dryness after menopause as a normal physiological response and not as an indication of lack of desire. The dryness can be countered with estrogen-based cream (Fonda, 1994) or a lubricant, such as K-Y jelly.

A lot of attention has recently been given to the role of decreased estrogen levels in *osteoporosis,* a condition in which the bones become more brittle with age (see Rozenberg et al., 1994). There are over 250,000 hip fractures a year due to osteoporosis, resulting in up to 50,000 premature deaths in women.

As women grow older, a few will experience severe weakening of the ligaments that hold the vagina and uterus in place, a condition called *prolapse.* Prolapse can usually be corrected, most commonly by reconstructive surgery.

THE MEDICALIZATION OF MENOPAUSE. In 2000, there were approximately 19 million American women in their menopause years, with another 30 million in their postmenopausal years. Thus, postmenopausal women have become a large segment of society that seeks health care, or, depending on your perspective, that is targeted by health care professionals.

Today, the medical profession treats osteoporosis, hot flashes, vaginal dryness, and other less common problems associated with menopause (e.g., decreased clitoral sensitivity, recurrent urinary tract infections), with *hormone (estrogen) replacement therapy* (in pill,

cream, or skin-patch form). Numerous studies have shown that estrogen is beneficial for preventing osteoporosis (e.g., Schneider et al., 1997; Writing Group, 1997). It may also offer protection against colon cancer (Crandall, 1999) and aging of the skin (Brincat, 2000). Initial studies indicated that estrogen replacement therapy also offers protection against heart disease (e.g., Stampfer et al., 1991; Grodstein et al., 1996) and Alzheimer's disease (e.g., Kawas et al., 1997; Tang et al., 1996). However, more recent large-scale studies have found no benefit for these aging problems (Herrington et al., 2000; Mulnard et al., 2000; Women's Health Initiative, see Begley, 2000). On the down side, there is concern that estrogen replacement therapy might increase the risks of breast and endometrial cancer. Progestins are given with estrogen to protect against endometrial cancer, but several studies have reported an increased risk for breast cancer with long-term use, and the addition of progestin may further increase the risk (e.g., Colditz et al., 1995; Collaborative Group, 1997; Schairer et al., 2000; Steinberg et al., 1991).

What about the increase in sexual problems that is seen in postmenopausal women? The painful intercourse due to vaginal dryness can be corrected with estrogen pills or vaginal estrogen cream. For those women who show a drop in sexual desire, estrogen pills help some and testosterone replacement therapy helps many others (see Gelfand 2000; Sarrel, 2000).

When considering estrogen therapy, a woman must weigh the risks against the benefits. The overall death rate for elderly women taking estrogen is lower than for elderly women not taking estrogen (Grodstein et al., 1997). More women die each year from broken hips, for example, than from cancer of the endometrium. Women on hormone replacement therapy also rate their health-related quality of life higher than women who are not on therapy (Tosteson et al., 2000). Estrogen should not be given indiscriminately, but many medical experts believe that the benefits outweigh the risks when it is prescribed in small doses for a short period of time (Armstrong et al., 2000). (Note: These conclusions were made before the latest heart study results were released.)

Medical intervention in treating menopause has not been universally applauded. Rather than medicinal hormone replacement therapy, some women are turning to "natural" alternatives, i.e., herbal supplements that contain plant estrogens (phytoestrogens) (see Waldman, 1998). Many other physicians and feminists argue that menopause is a natural part of being a woman that should be allowed to run its course (see van Hall, 1997).

The "mysteries" of a woman's body—puberty, menstruation, pregnancy, lactation, and menopause—are seen as times of power and growth. Menopause is an opportunity for conscious change, not a disease to be treated. (Weed, 1999).

Box 12–B CROSS-CULTURAL PERSPECTIVES

Menopause in Different Cultures

Menopause as a biological event is universal—all women worldwide will eventually stop having menstrual cycles and experience a decrease in estrogen levels. But what about the experience of menopause? Western health practitioners have medicalized menopause and portray the postmenopausal years negatively, as a time in which the body breaks down (but can be repaired by hormone replacement therapy). Western feminists, on the other hand, portray menopause not as a disease but as a normal part of aging that can bring liberation and joy. Which of these views is more realistic?

Richters (1997) reviewed cross-cultural studies of menopause and found many differences. For example, while a majority of American and European women experience hot flashes after menopause, hot flashes are uncommon among postmenopausal women in Japan or the Mayans of Mexico (Beyne, 1989; Lock, 1994). The Mayans do not even have a word for it. In some areas of Greece, women experience hot flashes, but do not think of them as medical symptoms that require going to a physician (Beyne, 1989). Like the Mayans, traditional Navajo women apparently do not experience the same symptoms as Western women and view menopause as a positive change of life status (e.g., being free of menstrual taboos) (Wright, 1983). Women in northeastern Thailand also view menopause positively as a natural event (Chirawatkul & Manderson, 1994).

Some, but not all, of these differences can be explained by the social position of women in different cultures (Richters, 1997). In cultures where women gain prestige and power in middle age, menopause may likely be viewed positively, in contrast to the United States, where older persons are often viewed as a burden. Migration from one country to another can rapidly change the perception of menopause. Older women in Italy generally have positive roles, but Italian women who migrated to Australia came to view menopause negatively when those roles were no longer valid (Gifford, 1994).

There are ethnic variations in the experience of menopause within our own country. The average age at menopause among African-American women is 2 years younger than for white women, with psychosocial stress being the main predictor (Bromberger et al., 1997). African-American women are also more likely to have hot flashes, while Hispanic women are more likely to experience a racing heart. Asian-American women, on the other hand, experience few symptoms (see De Angelis, 1997). This may reflect ethnic differences in the social status of aging women, but may also be due to diet (Adlercreutz et al., 1992). Smokers in all ethnic groups experienced greater symptoms.

Richters (1997) concluded that many factors might result in the differences in menopausal symptoms. However, one thing can be concluded—the experience of menopause is not the same for all women, either across or within cultures.

They point out that the large majority of women go through menopause without hormone replacement therapy and with few or no complaints. In fact, a 1997 Gallup poll found that a majority of women aged 45 to 60 regarded menopause as the start of a new and fulfilling stage of life (Utian, 1997). While most women experience a decline in well-being in the first 2 years after menopause, feelings improve spontaneously after that (Dennerstein et al., 1997). Women in some other cultures or ethnic groups report few problems during menopause (see Box 12–B).

So why the big push in our culture to "treat" women during and after menopause? Some claim that postmenopausal women have become a targeted consumer group aimed at making profits for pharmaceutical companies. *Medicalization* refers to "the process whereby the normal processes of pregnancy, childbirth, menstruation and menopause have been claimed and redefined by medicine" (Kaufert & Lock, 1997). Opponents of the medicalization of menopause claim that the negative expectations of deteriorating health are the result of culturally determined attitudes, promotions by drug companies, and media pressure, and point out (correctly) that older women in our country are already healthier than older men and outlive men by many years (van Hall, 1997).

Figure 12–11 For middle-aged couples, sexual motivation is highly associated with the quality of the relationship.

These many conflicting results and opinions have left many women confused about what to do. In the midst of all this, I will dare to offer an opinion. Hormone replacement therapy should not be mass-marketed as beneficial to all, but instead, the decision about its use should be individualized based on a woman's own family history and personal risk factors.

FEMALE SEXUALITY: BEHAVIOR

Does a woman's sexual desire end with menopause? I have found that many students believe that women no longer have any interest in sex after menopause. This is generally untrue.

> "I was surprised to find out that a woman still had a sexual desire after menopause. I always believed it to be a time of depression and no sex. Well, you learn something new every day."

> "I was totally surprised by the fact that older people still have sex. I often wondered what I was going to do at that age because I enjoy sex tremendously." (All examples are from the author's files.)

For most women, menopause causes no change in interest in sex (Hallstrom & Samuelsson, 1990; Segraves & Segraves, 1995). Some women actually show an increased interest in sex after menopause, possibly because they no longer have to worry about getting pregnant. Others show no change, but some do show a decline in both interest and orgasmic capacity, often due to changes like vaginal dryness, as previously noted.

The best predictor of sexual activity for middle-aged women is their sexual activity when younger. Positive personal attitudes about sexuality and past positive experiences regarding the importance of sex are important determinants of sexual functioning in aging women (Haavio-Mannila & Kontula, 1997). Some studies have found that women who have regular sexual activity throughout life experience less vaginal atrophy, and thus less of a decline in vaginal lubrication during sexual arousal after menopause (Bachman, 1989; Leiblum et al., 1983). However, data on sexual activity in middle-aged and older women are limited. Many middle-aged women do not have a sexual partner. Thus, many researchers feel that frequency of masturbation is the best index to use in measuring female sexuality in the middle-aged and elderly years. Janus and Janus (1993) obtained the following results for the relation between female masturbation and age:

	Age			
Frequency	**18–26**	**27–38**	**39–50**	**51–64**
Daily	2%	3%	2%	1%
Several times weekly	6	11	12	7
Weekly	10	16	16	12
Monthly	9	17	17	16
Rarely	29	33	37	34
Never	44	20	16	30

Reprinted with permission of John Wiley & Sons, Inc.

As you can see, there is very little change through the mid-60s.

Estimates of the percentage of older women (and men) who masturbate are probably much lower than the true numbers because many older adults do not want to give this information, even if they are willing to divulge the frequency with which they have sexual intercourse. (How would *you* answer a survey question such as "How often do you masturbate in a week?")

For those few middle-aged women who do show a loss of interest in sex, it may not be due to lack of opportunity or any physiological change. Some women suffer from nonsexually related anxiety and depression at about the time of menopause and this, of course, can affect a person's interest in sex. Sociologist Pauline Bart (1971) has pointed out, for example, that this is about the age that most women have to adjust to their children growing up and leaving home. Bart found that it is the traditional "supermother" type who is most affected by this problem of the "empty nest." It is also a time when a previously family-oriented woman may find that a lack of skills prohibits her from finding meaningful employment. An individual's occupation or avocation greatly affects his or her feeling of self-esteem and self-worth (Kingsberg, 2000). Moreover, some women may feel that they have grown apart from their husbands over the years and may not be interested in having sex with their husbands (remember, the overall quality of a relationship affects the quality of sex). In short, it is difficult to determine whether a decline of interest in sex is due to a hormonal change or to other changes in a woman's life.

MALE SEXUALITY: PHYSICAL CHANGES WITH AGE

Men normally do not experience menopause. Except in cases where men lose their testicles from surgery (in which case they do show symptoms, including fatigue and hot flashes), there is no *sudden* loss of hormones as experienced by women. Although the term *male menopause* is commonly used, this generally refers to the midlife psychological and emotional reactions that some men have as a response to changing family relationships (e.g., children growing up) and/or an inability to achieve earlier career goals. Society's attitudes may contribute to this, for many people in our culture treat elderly people like little kids or as nuisances. In cultures where elderly people are highly respected and revered (e.g., Oriental cultures), there is no term that is equivalent to male menopause.

Men do show a gradual decline in testosterone levels that begins in their late teens (Sternbach, 1998). By age 55, 20 to 50 percent of men have testosterone levels that are below the normal range for young adult men. This decrease in testosterone will result in some physiological changes as men age. The changes include decreased sensitivity of the penis, a longer time to become erect and a less firm erection, shrinkage of the testicles, less forceful ejaculation (often resembling a dribble), and a longer refractory period after orgasm (the length of time before a man is able to have another orgasm), a decline in muscle mass and strength, a reduction in bone calcium, sparse beards, and slightly higher voices (Rowland, 1998; Sternbach, 1998). If the drop in testosterone is large enough, it will also affect a man's interest in sex.

The production of sperm continues into old age, but it, too, declines after age 40. Nevertheless, many men in their 70s and 80s have fathered children.

Many men show a decline in erectile capacity as they reach late middle and old age (Kennedy et al., 1997). This is often true even when there is no decrease in health or other impairment. Although this, too, can be related to decreasing testosterone levels, some studies have found no relation between testosterone levels and sexual function and behavior (Schiavi, 1990). One study suggested that a decline in erectile capacity may also be related to decreased sensory/neural and autonomic functioning (Rowland, 1998).

In the mid-1990s there was new interest in the age-related changes in men and calls for medical treatment of the previously described "male climacterium problems." Testosterone replacement therapy can restore sexual desire, but because of the many side effects should be reserved only for men with a definite deficiency in testosterone (Sternbach, 1998). However, it is probably the case that other men will begin asking for it as well. A 1996 cover article in *Newsweek*, for example, was about whether testosterone replacement therapy can keep men young and virile (Cowley et al., 1996). Health food stores began pushing DHEA (dehydroepiandrosterone, a hormone that declines with age) to build muscle mass and increase energy and libido. We may be on the verge of a medicalization of the male "climacterium" similar to what has happened with women (see Oudshoorn, 1997).

If a man is not aware that the previously mentioned changes are normal, he may overreact to them and start to doubt his sexuality, and this performance anxiety can lead to serious problems. Paul Costa, Jr., of the National Institute on Aging, said, "Some older men may say their erections aren't as big as they recall them once being. But then their partners say, 'Well, dear, you overestimated them back then, too'" (quoted in Angier, 1992).

MALE SEXUALITY: BEHAVIOR

For most men, there is a gradual decline in sexual activity and interest after age 50 (see Segraves & Segraves, 1995). A man's sexual performance can be affected by many things, including declining health, anxiety over performance, and various medications. However, as with women, *the best predictor of a middle-aged man's level of sexual activity is his level of activity when younger* (e.g., Haavio-Mannila & Kontula, 1997).

As was the case with women, frequency of masturbation can be used as one indicator of sexual activity. Janus and Janus (1993) found very little change in the masturbatory behavior of men up through their mid-60s:

Frequency	Age			
	18–26	27–38	39–50	51–64
Daily	6%	9%	7%	9%
Several times weekly	18	19	16	23
Weekly	19	25	19	22
Monthly	8	9	12	4
Rarely	23	26	30	18
Never	26	12	16	24

Reprinted with permission of John Wiley & Sons, Inc.

Remember, for many men orgasms experienced during masturbation are in addition to orgasms experienced during sex with a partner (see previous section). Still, some researchers have found that the frequency of orgasm does drop off for some men in their 50s and 60s. However, this could be due to being accustomed to one's long-term partner (Blumstein & Schwartz, 1983). There is no decline with age in the number of erections men experience at night.

For those middle-aged and elderly men who are showing physiological changes, such as a longer time to become fully erect, there is a positive side—more time spent in foreplay, which generally translates into greater sexual happiness for the partner. Even if age interferes with quantity, there is no reason it has to interfere with quality. Sexual relations involve more than just using the penis; they include using the lips, tongue, hands, and other body parts, as well as one's emotional responsivity. Many men who experience declining erectile capacity with age report that their overall sex life is still just as good. Good sexual communication is a total human sexual response.

PERSONAL REFLECTIONS

Does the thought of elderly people enjoying sexual relations make you comfortable or uncomfortable? Why? Do you hope to still enjoy sexual relations when you are in your 50s and older? If not, at what age do you think that you will stop enjoying sex? Why?

THE ELDERLY YEARS (AGE 60+)

"I didn't think that elderly people thought about sex. I thought when you got older you just lost all interest." (from the author's files)

In our culture elderly people are regarded as asexual human beings—neuters. Sex is something enjoyed only by the young and healthy (Gochros et al., 1986). According to Rose and Soares (1993), "Evidence of sexuality among the aged is often joked about, dismissed, or defined as troublesome behavior. A sexually active older man is seen as a 'dirty old man' and a sexually active older woman is considered preposterous or embarrassing. This culturally embedded denial may be rooted in people's difficulty accepting the sexuality of their own parents."

What is the truth? Is it really unusual for elderly people to have an interest in sex? Recently, there have been two national surveys, one for *Modern Maturity* magazine (Jacoby, 1999) and the other by the National Council on the Aging (see Dunn & Cutler, 2000). Let's see what they found.

Among people in their 60s *who have partners,* over 70 percent are having sex regularly. Over 50 percent of them have sexual intercourse at least once a week. In their 70s, about one-third of men and women with partners are having sexual intercourse at least once a week. In their 80s, only about one-fourth of men and women are having sex at least once a month.

Other large-scale studies have also found a steady decline in sexual activity with age (see Segraves & Segraves, 1995, for a review). Marsiglio and Donnelly (1991) found that two-thirds of the people they studied aged 60–65 had had sex during the previous month, as compared to 45 percent of people aged 71–75 and 24 percent of people aged 76 and older. Clements (1996) reported that 55 percent of people aged 65–69 were sexually active, compared to 28 percent of people aged 75–79 and 13 percent of people over 85. Another study of people over 70 found that 30 percent had had sex in the last month (Matthias et al., 1997). Similar results were reported for elderly homosexual individuals (e.g., Berger, 1982; Raphael & Robinson, 1980).

Notice that even in the most elderly group there was still a sizable minority who were having sexual relations regularly. Is there any age at which sexual activity stops? Although it was not a representative sample, a study of 202 *healthy* men and women aged 80–102 found that three-fourths of them still fantasized about sexual relations and enjoyed touching and caressing their partners. Nearly half were having sexual intercourse and a third were engaging in oral-genital sex (Bretschneider & McCoy, 1988). Sexual activity was limited by living arrangements and the availability of partners, not by a lack of interest. Here is something to think about: Studies with animals have found that sexually active rats live a great deal longer than sexually inactive rats (Knoll, 1997), and a recent study reported the same for men (Smith et al., 1997). Could it be that these very elderly people lived as long as they did partly because they enjoyed sex regularly?

Now you know about frequency of sexual relations among the elderly, but what about quality? In the *Modern Maturity* and NCOA surveys (Jacoby 1999; Dunn & Culter, 2000), about two-thirds said their sexual relations were extremely or very satisfactory, as good or better than when they were younger. Women described their male partners as more "romantic" than when they were younger, and perhaps as a result a greater percentage of women were reaching orgasm regularly. Very few elderly people said they wanted less frequent sex.

Most other cultures have a much more positive attitude about the elderly as sexual human beings. In a study of attitudes in 106 different societies, Winn and Newton (1982) found: "Although some decline in the sexual activity of aged males is recorded in a significant proportion of the societies studies, many cultural groups have expectations for continued sexual activity for older men that imply little, if any, loss of their sexual powers until very late in life." What about elderly women? The researchers concluded: "Older women frequently express

Box 12-C SEXUALITY AND HEALTH

Sex and Heart Attacks

Victorian-era physicians, you recall, believed that sex was harmful to one's health (see Chapter 1). Even Freud believed that loss of semen was as detrimental to a man's health as loss of blood (Haller & Haller, 1977). We now know, of course, that this is not true, but are there other sex-related health problems? An article in a 1986 issue of *National Safety and Health News* startled many people, particularly older ones. The article reported the results of a Japanese study in which investigators looked at the autopsies of 5,000 people who had died suddenly. Thirty-four had died during intercourse. Are people with heart disease, especially former heart attack victims, putting themselves at risk by having sex?

Many people apparently think so. About one-quarter of all men who have had heart attacks never resume sexual activity, and half do so only occasionally (Kolodny et al., 1979). However, physicians and sex therapists say the greatest barrier is not the physical condition of the heart patient, but anxiety and fear. Wives of former heart attack victims also worry that sex might cause another attack (Gould, 1989). This kind of anxiety and stress can cause sexual problems. Female heart patients are less likely than men to cease sexual activity or develop sexual problems (Kolodny et al., 1979; Schover & Jensen, 1988).

A study from Harvard Medical School of nearly 2,000 patients who had suffered heart attacks found that the chance of having another heart attack resulting from sex was extremely small, only 20 in 1 million (Muller et al., 1996). During sex with one's usual partner, the maximum heart rate increases to about 120

beats per minute. This is no greater, and perhaps less, of an increase than one would experience during a brisk walk or some other form of moderate exercise (Masur, 1979). Extreme physical or emotional stress and things like alcohol or drugs might be risks, and so might sex involving emotional tension or extreme physical exertion. It must be noted, therefore, that of the 34 people that the Japanese study found to have died during sexual intercourse, all were intoxicated or near intoxication and 30 were having extramarital relations with a partner who, on average, was 18 years younger.

Most physicians believe that sexual activities can be resumed within a few weeks after a heart attack (see Tardif, 1989). Generally, masturbation can be resumed first. A general rule of thumb used by some physicians is that sexual activity should not be resumed until the patient can engage in moderate physical exercise (such as climbing two flights of stairs) without exhaustion.

For most people, daily exercise in moderate amounts is recommended for strengthening cardiovascular endurance. A daily brisk walk of at least 20 minutes is highly recommended for older people (Kligman & Pepin, 1992). Regular exercise also improves mental health. The American College of Sports Medicine recommends any physical activity that raises heart rate at least to 60 to 80 percent of your range. Sexual activity with one's usual partner produces heart rate changes like this. It is very possible, therefore, that regular sexual activity is beneficial in maintaining cardiovascular endurance. Sounds like a lot more fun to me than a stationary bike.

---

strong sexual desires and interests, . . . engage in sexual activity in many instances until extreme old age, . . . and may form liaisons with much younger men."

The conclusion reached by the behavioral scientists who conducted these studies was a very positive one—sexuality does not have to end at any given age. In the words of Myrna Lewis and Robert Butler (1994), authors of *Love and Sex after 60,* "Relatively healthy older people who enjoy sex are capable of experiencing it often until very late in life." Therapist David Schnarch adds, "The older population really has

the better deal. This is a time when people have the best sex in their lives, and it all has to do with maturity" (quoted in Mathias-Riegel, 1999).

So which is correct—the American cultural stereotype of the aged as sexless, or the optimistic picture painted by the recent surveys of the elderly as a still sexually active group? The truth may be somewhere in between. One recent report, for example, accused the earlier reports and their conclusions of sounding like "pep talks," trying to convince everyone that there would be no loss of sexual pleasure with aging (Rose &

Soares, 1993). The authors said the earlier reports "glossed over certain realities of aging which directly affect sexuality": the much greater ratio of women to men, the greater number of people suffering from chronic illness and disability, and the greater number of people dependent on others for daily personal care. Let us consider these problems.

The ratio of single women to single men that we discussed in the section on middle age becomes even more unfavorable to women over the age of 60. In the United States, women outlive men by an average of 7 years (78.9 years vs. 72 years) (Gelfand, 2000). For people aged 65 to 74, there are 123 women for every 100 men, and 100 single women for every 27 single men. At ages 75–84, there are 151 women for every man, and at ages 85 and older there are 241 women per 100 men (Guralnik et al., 2000; Weg, 1996). The *Modern Maturity* survey found that half of women aged 60–74 and 80 percent of women aged 75 and older have no partner (Jacoby, 1999). Thus, for women, there is a real "partner gap." Many women may be interested in sex, but there is no opportunity. Widows are often forced into involuntary retirement. Clements (1996) found that of those elderly persons not having sex, two-thirds of the men and nearly a third of the women say they would like to have sex. The *Modern Maturity* survey found that only 35 percent of women aged 75 and older said they would be happy if they never again had sex.

In the survey of people aged 80 to 102, the people were in good health (Bretschneider & McCoy, 1988). However, many people experience serious medical problems and disabilities as they grow older. Heart disease, stroke, arthritis, diabetes, prostate problems, and problems due to alcohol, smoking, and overeating are common (Giampaoli, 2000; Segraves & Segraves, 1995; Weg, 1996). In the *Modern Maturity* survey, women listed "better health for their partner" as the number one item that would most improve their sex lives (Jacoby,

1999). In the NCOA survey (Dunn & Cutler, 2000), 47 percent of elderly men said, "I have a medical condition that prevents us from having sex," and 43 percent of the women said, "My partner has a medical condition that prevents us from having sex." A sizable proportion of the medical conditions is associated with erection problems (impotence). Laumann et al.'s (1999) nationally representative survey found that 11 percent of men aged 40–49 and 18 percent aged 50–59 have erectile disorders. The *Modern Maturity* survey found that 16 percent of men aged 60–74 were completely impotent (and another 23 percent moderately so), and the number rose to 37 percent for men aged 75 and older (Jacoby, 1999).

One in 10 elderly men have tried Viagra, or testosterone patches, or other sex-enhancement medications (Jacoby, 1999). You may have seen the Viagra advertisements featuring former presidential candidate Robert Dole. But what about these men's partners? Over half of them say that their partner's treatment has resulted in increased pleasure for them as well. However, medical treatment for impotency can also suddenly change the sexual equilibrium in a relationship (Kingsberg, 2000). A few women report that their male partners' treatment had decreased their pleasure. Remember, female sexual pleasure is more complex than mens' erection and release pattern (see Leland, 2000a). For most women, their sexual pleasure is directly related to the quality of the overall relationship (Jacoby, 1999; Kingsberg, 2000: Leland, 2000).

The third major factor preventing some elderly people from enjoying sexual relations is opportunities for privacy when one is dependent on others for care. This particularly affects the very elderly. Nowhere is our culture's negative attitude about sexuality and the elderly more apparent than in nursing homes (Nay & Gorman, 1999). In the early 1990s, about 13 percent of all persons living in nursing homes and over the age of 65 were married (Kaplan, 1996). However, opportunities for sexual relations are very limited for elderly people with disabilities who are dependent on others for their care. Administrators and staff in most nursing homes are interested in institutional efficiency and tend to view the elderly as sexless (Kaplan, 1996; Weg, 1996). Some nursing homes require married couples to live in separate rooms (when both are institutionalized), and most deny them privacy when the healthy partner of an institutionalized spouse comes to visit (Kaplan, 1996; Wasow & Loeb, 1979). Nursing home residents often say that a lack of privacy prevents them from sexual relations, or even opportunities for masturbation (Spector & Fremeth, 1996). In short, elderly people with sexual needs who live in nursing homes are "truly members of a forgotten, neglected population" (Wasow & Loeb, 1979). Nay and Gorman (1999) have recommended several changes by nursing home staffs, including respect for clients' orientation, and opportunities for privacy and sexual expression.

Figure 12–12 From the moment of birth to the day we die, we are all sexual beings.

tinue throughout life if they had a positive attitude about sex when they were younger. Sexual interests may continue even for those with serious medical problems and disabilities. Sex surveys tend to measure sexual behavior in terms of physical acts such as sexual intercourse and masturbation, but there is more to sexuality than this. Elderly people often report great sexual satisfaction with emotionally erotic experiences (Shaw, 1994). Sexual pleasure, for example, includes touching, caressing, physical closeness, and intimacy. These can often be achieved even in the most extreme cases:

> Mr. N was deaf, blind, and unable to talk due to a recent laryngotomy. He was quite dependent on Mrs. N who had severe arthritis and had a mastectomy years ago. They typically sat close together, in part to aid communication due to Mr. N's impairments. But the way they held hands revealed great tenderness and affection. They slept in twin beds and indicated they no longer engaged in intercourse. Yet, they had a nightly ritual in which Mr. N helped his wife bathe and then gave her a massage in bed, which they described with some embarrassment and blushing. Interestingly, through this sensual routine, Mr. N, usually the more dependent of the two, was able to offer something of value to his wife. (From Rose and Soares, 1993. Reprinted with permission of Madeline Rose and the publisher.)

Other factors can also affect sexual desire in the elderly. These include education (more educated people tend to remain more active), religion (more religious people tend to be less sexually active), societal pressures to conform to (asexual) stereotypes, and, of course, one's attitude about sex when younger. This last point is very important. Remember the generation gap? Today's middle-aged population, all of whom grew up in the sexual revolution, are much less likely than today's elderly population to allow illness, disabilities, menopause, or erectile disorders to end their own sexual pleasure in the future (Jacoby, 1999).

So what can we conclude about sexuality in the elderly years? Sexual opportunities are limited for single women, but for healthy men and women with healthy partners, sexual activity will probably con-

Perhaps the biggest problem for elderly people interested in physical relations is our culture's negative stereotypes of the aged as sexless (Barrow & Smith, 1992). Many people poke fun at, or discriminate against, other people who are different from themselves, and this often includes the elderly. But unless there is a tragedy, all of us will be elderly some day. Do you enjoy sexual relations now? Do you ever want to give it up? If not, how do you think you will feel if one day younger people think you are silly, preposterous, or even lecherous or perverted for wanting the pleasure of someone else's touch? The time to address these attitudes is now, not later. We are all sexual human beings, from birth to death.

Key Terms

Suggested Readings

Alan Guttmacher Institute (1994). *Sex and American teenagers.* New York: Author. A comprehensive survey of the sexual behavior of teens.

Barbach, L. (1994). *The pause.* New York: Signet Books. All about menopause.

Beck, M., et al. (1992, May 25). Menopause: The search for straight talk and safe treatment. *Newsweek. Newsweek's* cover story covers both the medical and feminist perspectives on menopause.

Clements, M. (1996, March 17). Sex after 65. *Parade Magazine.* Discusses sexual activity and satisfaction in the elderly.

Gordon, S. (1986, October). What kids need to know. *Psychology Today.* Discusses some topics about sexuality that children need to know and gives advice to parents and schools about how to teach these subjects.

Jacoby, S. (1999). Great sex: What's age got to do with it? *Modern Maturity,* September–October, 41–45, 91.

Janus, S., & Janus, C. (1993). *The Janus report.* New York: John Wiley. Results of a nationwide survey of sexual behavior.

Michael, R., et al. (1994). *Sex in America.* Boston: Little, Brown. Results of the Laumann et al. survey, the most scientifically conducted survey ever done. Written for the general public.

Segraves, R. T., & Segraves, K. B. (1995). Human sexuality and aging. *Journal of Sex Education and Therapy,* 21. A very thorough review of sexuality and health in aging persons.

Smith, A. M. A., Rosenthal, D. A., & Reichler, H. (1996). High schoolers' masturbatory practices: Their relationship to sexual intercourse and personal characteristics. *Psychological Reports,* 76, 499–509. The title explains it all.

Study Guide

INTERACTIVE REVIEW

People are sexual beings from the moment of birth. In infancy, self-stimulation of the genitals is motivated by a general attempt to explore the body and seek pleasure. As children grow, their curiosity about their bodies continues and, during early childhood, reaches a peak in the age period from (1) _____ years old. Early childhood games such as "house" or "doctor" allow exploration of same-sex and opposite-sex individuals. In the initial school-age years, children develop a sense of (2) _____. Although overt sexual play may decrease, curiosity about the human body and sexuality does not.

(3) _____ is the time in life in which an individual first shows sexual attraction and becomes capable of (4) _____. Many bodily changes occur, the result of changing (5) _____ levels, and these physical changes require many adjustments for young adolescents. Unfortunately, many young teens acquire a negative attitude about their bodies as a result of their parents' reactions to normal events such as menstruation and nocturnal emissions.

Interest in sex increases dramatically at puberty, and earlier childhood games evolve into more erotic and consciously sexual games such as "spin the bottle." The most important issue in the lives of most adolescents is (6) _____, and during these years there is a focus on body image and physical characteristics. Almost all teenage boys and a majority of girls masturbate, which is usually accompanied by sexual fantasies. Sex therapists feel that masturbation is a safe and healthy sexual outlet for teenagers. Surveys find that (7) _____ of American high school students have engaged in sexual intercourse. For some teens, however, having sexual relations is not a positive experience, yet many engage in it because of (8) _____. The teenage pregnancy rate in the United States has decreased in recent years, but still is one of the highest among industrialized countries.

The average age at marriage has steadily increased and is now in the mid-20s. Most young adults believe that premarital sex, especially in a "serious" relationship, is acceptable. Most have also had two or more sexual partners, often in a life-style pattern called (9) _____.

By the time people are in their mid-20s, most people's sexual life-style is characterized by (10) _____, either in marriage or by cohabitation. In all cultures, the idealistic goal is a (11) _____. Throughout the world, men value female promiscuity when pursuing short-term relationships, but when choosing a long-term mate, men in most cultures value (12) _____. When choosing a long-term mate, women generally prefer men who can offer them (13) _____. Despite the ideal, about a third of all married men and about a fifth of all married women eventually engage in extramarital relations. Some do so with the consent of their mate.

Most young adults underestimate the frequency of sex practiced by older adults. Sexual activity is highest for people in their (14) _____, and only gradually declines up through the late 50s. Surveys indicate that married people have sex more often than singles and are happier with their sex lives than are singles. Still, over half of all marriages in the United States end in divorce. About three-fourths of all divorced people remarry, and for some marriage is just another form of serial monogamy.

As women grow older, their menstrual cycles become irregular and eventually stop entirely, which is called (15) _____. This usually occurs in a woman's late 40s or early 50s, and the change in hormones can result in hot flashes, a decrease in (16) _____, and osteoporosis. These conditions can be reversed with (17) _____ replacement therapy. Experts feel that men normally do not experience menopause, but they do show a gradual decline in (18) _____ beginning in their late teens. This also results in some physical changes, such as a decline in muscle mass and strength, less firm erections, less forceful ejaculations, and longer (19) _____ periods. However, most elderly people continue to enjoy sexual relations as long as they remain otherwise healthy and have a partner. For healthy couples, the best predictor of whether or not they will enjoy sex in old age is (20) _____.

SELF-TEST

A. TRUE OR FALSE

- T ⬜ F ⬜ 21. Ultrasound recordings have found that male fetuses have erections while still inside the uterus.
- T ⬜ F ⬜ 22. Children cannot masturbate to orgasm until they reach puberty.
- T ⬜ F ⬜ 23. The growth of pubic hair on girls is the result of increased levels of testosterone.
- T ⬜ F ⬜ 24. If a child is found engaging in sexual exploration games with another child of the same sex before age 7, it means the child is probably gay.
- T ⬜ F ⬜ 25. Gagnon believes that teenage masturbation is the single most powerful predictor of adult sexuality.
- T ⬜ F ⬜ 26. Couples who lived together before marriage are less likely than other couples to get divorced.
- T ⬜ F ⬜ 27. In a study of 202 men and women aged 80 to 102, it was found that nearly half still engaged in sexual intercourse.
- T ⬜ F ⬜ 28. The lack of vaginal lubrication in women who have undergone menopause is an indicator that their sex life is coming to an end.
- T ⬜ F ⬜ 29. The average married couple in their 20s or 30s have sex more often than young singles.
- T ⬜ F ⬜ 30. Adults almost always quit masturbating after they are married.
- T ⬜ F ⬜ 31. The average age at which girls have their first menstrual cycle has been decreasing over the last two centuries.
- T ⬜ F ⬜ 32. "Hot flashes" are due, in part, to increasing levels of pituitary hormones.
- T ⬜ F ⬜ 33. The best predictor of sexual activity for older women is the amount of vaginal lubrication they had when they were younger.
- T ⬜ F ⬜ 34. A heart attack almost always causes older men to become impotent.
- T ⬜ F ⬜ 35. Boys often develop enlarged breasts during puberty.
- T ⬜ F ⬜ 36. In early childhood it is normal for children to engage in sexual behaviors that imitate adults.
- T ⬜ F ⬜ 37. The way parents react to the sexuality of their children is generally an indication of the way they feel about their own sexuality.
- T ⬜ F ⬜ 38. There is no physical reason why elderly couples cannot continue to have sexual intercourse.
- T ⬜ F ⬜ 39. In terms of hormone changes with aging, men and women are very much alike.
- T ⬜ F ⬜ 40. In men, the production of sperm generally stops by the early 50s.
- T ⬜ F ⬜ 41. Most women show a decreased interest in sex after menopause.
- T ⬜ F ⬜ 42. In some cultures, hot flashes are uncommon among postmenopausal women.
- T ⬜ F ⬜ 43. Pubertal development in boys lags about 2 years behind development in girls.
- T ⬜ F ⬜ 44. If an adult man is castrated, it substantially raises his voice.
- T ⬜ F ⬜ 45. Girls as young as 6 or 7 have given birth.
- T ⬜ F ⬜ 46. Most teenage girls experience severe pain during their first sexual intercourse.

T   F   47. The sexual activity of emerging adults is generally different from the activity of younger and older age groups.

T   F   48. Men and women are more likely to be upset by their partner's having a sexual relationship with someone else than they are about their having an emotional attachment.

T   F   49. There is a strong relationship between social background (religious and political views) and whether or not one engages in extramarital affairs.

T   F   50. The divorce rate for open-marriage couples is lower than that for sexually monogamous couples.

T   F   51. Children's first sexual attractions occur around age 10.

B. MATCHING: WHICH HORMONE CHANGES ARE MOST LIKELY TO BE ASSOCIATED WITH THE FOLLOWING PHYSICAL OR BEHAVIORAL CHANGES?

_____ 52. breast development in girls

_____ 53. vaginal dryness at menopause

_____ 54. hot flashes in women

_____ 55. development of sweat glands (body odor, acne)

_____ 56. gynecomastia

_____ 57. pubic hair and body hair

_____ 58. menarche

_____ 59. less firm erection and longer refractory period

_____ 60. reversal of effects of menopause

_____ 61. decreased sexual desire in women (review from Chapter 3)

_____ 62. decreased sexual desire in men (review from Chapter 3)

_____ 63. children's first sexual attractions

a. increase in estrogen
b. decrease in estrogen
c. increase in testosterone
d. decrease in testosterone
e. increase in FSH and LH
f. increase in DHEA from adrenal glands

C. FILL IN THE BLANKS

64. The decline in sexual activity among older single women is most often due to _____.

65. The changes that occur in women in the few years that precede and follow menopause are called _____.

66. Before age 2, bodily exploration is usually confined to _____.

67. Freud referred to what this chapter calls the initial school-age years as the _____ stage of psycho-sexual development.

68. Development of breasts and growth of facial hair are examples of _____.

69. For many teenage girls, the need for _____ is an important part of finding their self-identity.

70. Throughout the world, men tend to engage in casual sex to _____.

71. About 80 percent of all societies allow men to _____.

72. Women are most concerned about _____ infidelity by their mates.

73. Whitehurst believes that the two things most likely to lead to extramarital sex are _____ and _____.

74. From a person's late 30s to the early 60s, the frequency of sexual intercourse _____.

75. Puberty is at least a two-part maturational process. The two parts are called _____ and _____.

Adult Sexual Behaviors and Attitudes

*. . . never before in history
has there been such a huge disparity
between the open display of eroticism
in a society and that society's
great reluctance to speak
about private sexual practices.*

(Robert Michael, John Gagnon, Edward Laumann, & Gina Kolata, 1994)

For the human species to survive, men and women must have sexual intercourse. We need only look at the large number of people in the world to know that this is not an uncommon sexual practice. But what about other sexual behaviors—that is, behaviors that are not necessary for procreation? How many people engage in oral-genital sex? Is your partner unusual for wanting to try different positions? Is it normal to have sexual fantasies? Is masturbation unnatural and bad for your health? Many people are unsure about the answers to these questions, and thus may have anxieties about whether the sexual behaviors they or their partners wish to engage in are "normal."

When you have finished studying this chapter, you should be able to:

1. Explain what is meant by "normal" sexual behaviors;

2. Identify the major historical, as well as current, sources of negative attitudes toward masturbation, and discuss recent findings about this sexual activity;

3. Describe what occurs during the normal sleep cycle that can result in nocturnal orgasms;

4. Summarize the research findings about the frequency, quality, and role of sexual fantasies in enhancing sexual expression;

5. Explain why different cultures, as well as individuals within a culture, use different positions of sexual intercourse;

6. Discuss ways to keep the sexual aspects of a relationship from becoming ritualized;

7. Define fellatio and cunnilingus and describe the current research findings on these activities;

8. Appreciate that the incidence of some of the sexual behaviors covered in this chapter often differs among whites, African Americans, Latinos, and Asian Americans; and

9. Define a sexually healthy person.

WHAT IS NORMAL?

Just what is "normal" sexual behavior? The answer is, it depends. Many factors are involved, including the age of the individual and the society and period in history in which the person lives. As you will soon learn, until recently most people in Western culture considered all the behaviors covered in this chapter to be unnatural and sinful. What is considered normal changes over the life span of an individual and from generation to generation.

In this chapter you will read about several sexual behaviors that can be considered normal from a statistical point of view. If a behavior is *statistically normal*, it means that a large number of people engage in it. Notice that for a behavior to be called "normal" it does not require that everybody engage in (or even approve of) it. Therefore, you should not consider yourself to be "abnormal" if you have not engaged in all of the behaviors discussed here. It is best to think of normal behavior as a *range of behaviors*. Today, sexual intercourse, masturbation, and oral-genital sex (to name a few examples) are considered to be within the range of behaviors labeled normal for adults by mental health professionals.

For any particular behavior, there is also the question of how frequently people engage in it. How often is normal? Averages can be (and are) computed, but you should not interpret "normal" as meaning only the average value. Again, normal involves a *range of values*. For example, what is the normal number of times per month that married women masturbate? The answer is a range (from zero to some higher number). Most behaviors are considered normal as long as the individual does not suffer physical and/or psychological damage, does not inflict physical and/or psychological damage on others, and the behavior does not interfere with being able to deal with the activities of daily life.

The incidence and frequency of the various sexual behaviors you will read about in this chapter were obtained by taking sex surveys. Be sure to review the section on surveys and sampling procedures in Chapter 1.

> *PERSONAL REFLECTIONS*
> *What was your emotional reaction, if any, when you first saw the drawings for this chapter? If your reaction was anxiety or disgust, why? Do you regard the behaviors shown as normal?*

MASTURBATION

"Until I became sexually active with a partner, I masturbated every day. Even after marriage, I continue to masturbate." (man)

"The guilt I feel right after masturbating is so painful that I cry at times." (man)

masturbation Self-stimulation of one's genitals.

"I have a steady girlfriend who satisfies my sexual needs. But sometimes I am not able to satisfy hers. This is the primary reason why I enjoy masturbating—because I don't have to worry about trying to satisfy anyone but me." (man)

"I didn't masturbate until after I was sexually active, which was in college. In between sex with my boyfriends, I didn't know there were ways I could 'pleasure' myself with sex—and without a partner. Now, after finding it, I truly enjoy it." (woman)

"I had masturbated long before I became sexually active and, as long as I kept it to myself, I never seemed to have a problem with it. Now, when my boyfriend asks me if I ever masturbated, I can't help but feel guilty." (woman)

"I've masturbated since about the age of 14. I still do, with and without my husband present. I have no guilty feelings about it, not even when I was younger. There are times when I would rather masturbate than make love. Not that I would give up intercourse. It's just nicer sometimes." (woman)

"All through my childhood I thought that masturbation was something only guys could do. But Cosmo started printing all kinds of articles telling women to masturbate so they can show their partner what to do, and I got confused. I know I shouldn't be ashamed of my body, but I still can't bring myself to do it." (woman)

"I am 36 years old and never in my wildest dreams would I have thought I would be masturbating, but I did and I think it's great because I can stimulate parts that a male partner would not have the slightest idea about." (woman) (All examples are from the author's files.)

ATTITUDES ABOUT MASTURBATION

When you were growing up, what kinds of things did you hear might happen to you if you masturbated? Many of us were told (by friends, acquaintances, and sometimes parents) that **masturbation** could cause us to go blind or deaf; have nosebleeds, heart murmurs, acne, or painful menstruation; cause hair to grow on the palms of our hands; and finally, if we didn't stop, result in insanity. Others of us were simply told that we had better not do it to excess. The consequences of doing it to excess were never quite spelled out, but the possibilities that it was bad for our health or could lead to insanity were always implied. And scarier yet, what was considered excessive? Whatever it was, most of us convinced ourselves that it was more than we did it.

It is obvious that masturbation is considered bad by some people, but where did these stories come from? Negative attitudes about masturbation have, in fact, been handed down from generation to generation for centuries. The Greek physician Hippocrates believed that overindulging in sex was harmful to one's health. Ancient Chinese cultures condemned male masturbation as a waste of *yang* (male essence), while the biblical Hebrews considered it "spillage of seed," punishable by death (recall, from the Bible, the divine slaying of Onan for spilling his seed). The early Roman Catholic Church considered the only legitimate purpose of sex to be for procreation (St. Augustine called intercourse an unpleasant necessity), and sexual behaviors that did not have this as a goal (i.e., sex performed for pleasure) were considered immoral. The Church's negative view of masturbation was formalized in the 1200s by Thomas Aquinas, who included it as one of the four categories of unnatural acts (Aquinas, 1968). Many scholars believe that the word *masturbation* is derived from the Latin words *manus* ("hand") and *sturpore* ("to defile") or *tubare* ("to disturb").

In 1741, a Swiss physician named S. Tissot published a book entitled *Onania, or a Treatise upon the Disorders Produced by Masturbation,* in which he expanded upon the negative medical views of Hippocrates. In his book, Tissot claimed that excessive sex (especially masturbation) was dangerous because it deprived vital tissues of blood and led to insanity. As proof of this, he said, one only had to look at the many men in insane asylums who sat around openly masturbating. Tissot's views were accepted by many physicians. In Victorian times (the 1800s and early 1900s), many physicians also believed that loss of semen was as detrimental to a man's health as loss of blood. In the "seminal theory," as it came to be called, semen was believed to contain the essence of life, and that during ejaculation these "seeds" were absorbed through the bloodstream and lost (Fitz-Gerald & Fitz-Gerald, 1998). Freud, for example, believed that the loss of 1 ounce of semen produced the same degree of fatigue as the loss of 40 ounces of blood. He also believed that people who masturbated had "poisoned" themselves and that masturbation caused nervous disorders or neurosis ("neurasthenia") (Groenendijk, 1997).

The Victorians, you recall, vehemently denied any pleasurable component of sex and were particularly concerned about masturbation (see Hall, 1992). Not only were many Victorian-era children forced to wear chastity belts and metal gloves to bed (see Figure 1–4), but castration, circumcision, and clitoridectomy became popular during this time as means by which parents tried to prevent their children from masturbating. For an example of extreme Victorian beliefs, read the following passages from a book titled *Perfect Womanhood* written in 1903 by "Mary Melendy, M.D., Ph.D.," which contains the following advice to women about what to tell their male children about masturbation:

> Impress upon him that if these organs are abused, or if they are put to any use besides that for which God made them . . . they will bring disease and ruin upon those who abuse [them]. . . . He will not grow up happy, healthy and strong.

> Teach him that when he handles or excites the sexual organs, all parts of the body suffer, because they are connected by nerves that run throughout the system, this is why it is called "self-abuse.". . .
> . . . The sin is terrible, and is, in fact, worse than lying or stealing!
> If the sexual organs are handled it brings too much blood to these parts, and this produces a diseased condition, it also causes disease in other organs of the body, because they are left with a less amount of blood than they ought to have. . . .
> It lays the foundation for consumption, paralysis and heart disease. It weakens the memory, makes a boy careless, negligent and listless.
> It even makes many lose their minds; others when grown, commit suicide.

Similarly, Dr. J. H. Kellogg (1887) wrote the following about the effects of masturbation in girls:

> Wide observations have convinced us that a great many of the backaches, sideaches, and other aches and pains of which girls complain, are attributable to this injurious habit. Much of the nervousness, hysteria, neuralgia, and general worthlessness of girls originates in this cause alone.
> The period of puberty is one at which thousands of girls break down in health. The constitution, already weakened by a debilitating, debasing vice, is not prepared for the strain, and the poor victim drops into a premature grave.

He wrote the following about masturbation in boys:

> In solitude he pollutes himself, and with his own hand blights all his prospects for both this world and the next. Even after being solemnly warned, he will often continue this worse than beastly practice, deliberately forfeiting his right to health and happiness for a moment's mad sensuality.
> (J. H. Kellogg, *Plain Facts for Old and Young*)

This is the same J. H. Kellogg associated with the breakfast cereals. He invented cornflakes to be used as a breakfast food that would curb youthful lust. Graham crackers were invented by Dr. Sylvester Graham for much the same purpose. In his 1834 book, Graham wrote that if a boy masturbated, he would turn into "a confirmed and degraded idiot."

Although not all cultures have had negative attitudes about masturbation (e.g., the ancient Egyptians believed that the world was created when the God Atum ejaculated), negative attitudes are still widely found in Western societies. For example, the Catholic Church called it an "intrinsically and seriously disturbed act" in 1975 (Patton, 1986), and this view was repeated by Pope John Paul II in 1993. Orthodox Jews still regard it as one of the worst sins mentioned in the Torah.

When former Surgeon General Joycelyn Elders was fired in 1994 for talking about masturbation at a

"Now they tell us masturbation is harmless!"

Reproduced by special permission of *Playboy* magazine: copyright © 1971 by Playboy.

conference on AIDS, sociologist John Gagnon was quoted as saying, "It remains a puzzle for me why a relatively innocuous behavior evokes tides of anxiety and fear in otherwise well adjusted people."

INCIDENCE OF MASTURBATION

With this long history of scare tactics, you would expect, then, that very few people masturbate. In fact, the large majority of human beings masturbate. Kinsey and colleagues (1948, 1953) found that 92 percent of the men he surveyed had masturbated by age 20. It was generally the first sexual experience to orgasm for adolescent boys. Only a third of the women in Kinsey's study reported that they had masturbated by age 20, but another third had done so by age 40 (a total of 62 percent). Nearly identical results were found 20 years later by Hunt (1974). In other words, men are more likely to start masturbating before they experience sexual intercourse, whereas many women do not start masturbating until after they start engaging in sexual intercourse.

Not all people who have masturbated continue to do so regularly. Laumann and colleagues (1994) found that for Americans under the age of 60, only 63 percent of men and 42 percent of women had masturbated in the past year (the percentages were higher in the 25- to 39-year-old group). Both Kinsey's and Laumann's groups found that the better educated a person was, the more likely it was that he or she masturbated (see Box 13–A). Among today's college students, about twice as many men as women masturbate (Leitenberg et al., 1993), again reflecting the gender and age differences found by Kinsey (1948, 1953). On the average, men who masturbate do so two or three times more frequently than women who masturbate

(Kinsey et al., 1953; Hunt, 1974; Leitenberg et al., 1993). Interestingly, in a review of many studies, it was found that although women report a much lower incidence of masturbation than do men, their attitudes toward masturbation do not differ from those of men (Oliver & Hyde, 1993).

Are all of these people risking their health or sanity? No. Masturbation, whether done once a month or three times a day, does not cause any of the problems mentioned previously, and few doctors today, if any, would make such claims. *It is a perfectly normal human behavior.* How can I be so confident as to call it normal when historically it has been so condemned? Just look at the statistics—when the vast majority of people engage in a particular behavior, it has to be considered normal. Still, there are some who continue to feel guilty or wrong about it—nearly half of all people who masturbate, according to Laumann et al. (1994).

METHODS OF MASTURBATION

People differ in the way they masturbate, but men display less variation than do women. Almost all men masturbate by rhythmically stroking up and down the body and glans of the penis with one hand (Hite, 1981). They may differ in how much of the penis they stimulate, and in the rhythm and pressure applied, but it is generally still a stroking motion. Very few thrust. Many men simultaneously stimulate their testicles and other parts of their bodies as well. In order to enhance arousal, many men fantasize and/or look at sexually explicit pictures while masturbating. Hunt (1974) found, for example, that 75 percent of the men he surveyed had fantasies of sexual intercourse with a loved person during masturbation.

Some individuals (mostly adolescent boys) try to make their orgasms more intense by performing activities that deprive them of oxygen, such as placing plastic bags over the head or hanging by the neck (Saunders, 1989). This is called *autoerotic asphyxiation.* Although masturbation, per se, does not cause health problems, these behaviors are dangerous, and 500 to 1,000 people die each year while engaging in them. Aside from simply holding your breath, you should not engage in any behavior that deprives you of oxygen—during sex or at any other time.

Most women who masturbate do so by stimulating the clitoris, labia minora, and/or the entire vulva. Only 20 percent or fewer insert a finger or anything else into their vaginas while masturbating (Hite, 1976; Kinsey et al., 1953). Those who do should not consider themselves abnormal, for remember, "normal" encompasses a wide range of behaviors, not just a single behavior. The manner in which women stimulate themselves is diverse. Many prefer to lie on their backs while masturbating, while some prefer a face-down position, with considerable individual preferences in the position of the legs. Some use a single finger, while others use their entire hand to apply pressure to a wider area. Kinsey's group (1953) found that about 11 percent of women stimulate their breasts during masturbation. Although only a few women in his sample reported using a vibrator, the number who do so today no doubt has increased because of the easy availability of these products now. Two percent of the women surveyed in Laumann et al.'s study (1994) said that they had purchased a vibrator or dildo in the past year.

> "In the masturbation section I believe you should emphasize the importance of a vibrator for women. Methods of masturbation seem apparent to males, but I think women need more guidance in this area. In my experience a vibrator is the most intensely pleasurable way to masturbate." (from the author's files)

Like men, most women enhance their arousal by fantasizing during masturbation (Hunt, 1974).

FUNCTIONS OF MASTURBATION

Why do people masturbate? Quite simply, because it feels good. The genitals have lots of nerve endings and thus are very sensitive to touch. As you learned in the chapter on development, almost all young children touch their genitals when they have the opportunity (e.g., in the bathtub) because it gives them physical pleasure (Lidster & Horsburgh, 1994). By the early teens, however, genital touching is not just physical. It is often accompanied by erotic thoughts. Although masturbation allows for sexual release when a partner is not available, it does not necessarily cease when one forms a sexual relationship with someone. Hunt (1974) found that 72 percent of the men and 68 percent of the women he studied continued to masturbate after marriage. More recently, Janus and Janus (1993) reported that 66 percent of the men and 67 percent of the women they surveyed agreed or strongly agreed that "masturbation is a natural part of life and continues on in marriage." In fact, Laumann et al. (1994) found high rates of masturbation among young people with sexual partners, and that the more sex a person has, the more likely he or she is to masturbate. In other words, masturbation is not so much an outlet for lack of sex as it is a reflection of a sexually active life-style.

Why do people with sexual partners masturbate? *Variety*—it is a sexual experience that is different (not necessarily better) than sex with their partner.

> "I masturbated a lot when I was without a partner, and now I still do. The orgasm is so different than those I get during intercourse. . . . My boyfriend doesn't understand . . . but I love making love with him." (from the author's files)

Freud thought that adult masturbation was immature. Even today, some people argue that it may be habit-forming and prevent development of "normal" adult sexual relations. However, Kinsey's group (1953) found that women who were able to masturbate to orgasm without guilt or shame during adolescence generally had the least difficulty in making the transition to enjoying sex with a partner. More recent studies report that not only is masturbation during adolescence not harmful to sexual adjustment in young adulthood, but that masturbation during marriage is often associated with a greater degree of marital and sexual satisfaction (Hurlbert & Whittaker, 1991; Leitenberg et al., 1993). So if you suspect your partner of masturbating occasionally, do not assume that he or she is unhappy with your sex life. There would only be a problem if your partner was masturbating (indicating a need for a sexual outlet) but showing little or no interest or sexual desire for you.

Today, some therapists prescribe masturbation as part of their treatment for orgasm problems in women and for greater ejaculatory control in men (Barbach, 1980; Kaplan, 1974; LoPiccolo & Stock, 1986). Thus, what was once a taboo is now often used as part of sexual therapy. This is not to imply, however, that everyone should masturbate, particularly if they are comfortable with their sexuality. Just as it was once wrong to make people feel bad because they masturbated, it would be equally wrong to make people feel abnormal if they did not. The important point is that those who have a desire to masturbate should be able to do so without feelings of guilt or worries about their health.

> *PERSONAL REFLECTIONS*
>
> *What are your feelings about masturbation? If they are negative, why? Do you have negative feelings when you pleasure yourself by touching (e.g., rubbing, massaging, scratching) other parts of your body? Consider masturbation in context of a larger question: Are genitals reserved only for procreation (to have children), or are they also a source of pleasure?*

NOCTURNAL ORGASMS

> "During wet dreams I always seem to wake up when I reach climax and am greeted with a puddle of sperm. I am not embarrassed by such occurrences—it just forces me to wash my sheets." (man)

> "I was 17 years old, and one morning I woke up finding my sheets wet. I thought I urinated in bed at first until I realized it wasn't urine. I was ashamed and didn't want anyone to know what happened. I quickly changed my sheets and took a bath." (man)

> "I experience nocturnal orgasms 5–6 times a month on the average. They are always corresponding to a sexual dream I am having. The orgasm wakes me up. I consider it a blessing." (woman)

Box 13–A CROSS-CULTURAL PERSPECTIVES

Ethnic Differences in Sexual Behavior

In this chapter you will read about several behaviors that are considered normal in American culture today. However, the statistics given for each behavior generally do not take ethnicity into account. Are the behaviors discussed normal for all ethnic groups?

As an example, let us consider masturbation. In their nationally representative sample, Laumann and colleagues (1994) found that two-thirds of white and Latino men and a slightly smaller proportion of Asian-American men had masturbated within the past year. Only 40 percent of African-American men had masturbated in the last year. As for women, whites were more likely to have masturbated than African Americans or Latinas (see Table 13–1).

Ethnic differences have frequently been found for oral-genital sex as well. African Americans, especially women, are much less likely than others to have engaged in this type of sexual behavior (Belcastro, 1985; Laumann et al., 1994; Quadagno et al., 1998; Weinberg & Williams, 1988). White men and women show the highest percentage of people engaging in this behavior, while Latinos and Asian Americans are intermediate between these two groups.

On the other hand, Latino men and women are more likely than people of other ethnic groups to have engaged in anal intercourse (Laumann et al., 1994; Van Oss Marin & Gomez, 1994). This behavior is highly prevalent among heterosexuals in Latin America, where the percentage may be as high as 50 to 60 percent in some countries (Halperin, 1998).

These ethnic differences in sexual behaviors can be partly attributed to differences in power between men and women in relationships and the resulting differences in communication patterns (see Quadagno et al., 1998; see also Box 8–A). The gender dichotomy in power is most notable for traditional Latinos. In some studies of anal intercourse, for example, only 16 percent of experienced Latina women found it pleasurable, but 80 percent said that the decision to engage in anal intercourse was always or almost always made by the man (Halperin, 1999).

TABLE 13–1

INCIDENCE IN SEXUAL BEHAVIORS AMONG ETHNIC GROUPS IN THE UNITED STATES

	Whites	African Americans	Latinos	Asian Americans
Masturbation (in past year)				
Men	67%	40%	67%	61
Women	44	32	35	no data
Oral-genital sex				
Men	81	50	71	64
Women	75	34	60	no data
Anal intercourse				
Men	26	23	34	15
Women	23	10	17	no data

	Less Than High School	High School Graduates	Some College	College Graduates	Graduate Degree
Masturbation (in past year)					
Men	45%	55%	67%	76%	81%
Women	25	32	49	52	59
Oral-genital sex					
Men	59	75	80	84	80
Women	41	60	78	79	79
Anal intercourse					
Men	21	23	26	30	29
Women	13	17	25	22	29

Source: Adapted from *The Social Organization of Sexuality* by Edward O. Laumann et al. (1994). Reprinted with the permission of the University of Chicago Press.

I introduced some of these ethnic differences in sexual behavior in Chapter 1. Recall that there are factors other than ethnicity that may account for differences in sexual behavior. In addition to communication patterns, these include age, education, marital status, economic status, and degree of acculteration. For example, while the lowest rates for oral-genital sex are found among African-American women, it is especially low for older African-American women (Quadagno et al., 1998). Ethnic differences become less apparent as people become more acculterated (Marin & Van Oss Marin, 1991). Look at the bottom half of Table 13–1. As you can see, mas-

turbation and oral-genital sex are more common among higher-educated groups. Do ethnic differences still appear when researchers control for these other factors (i.e., looking at white, African-American, Latino, and Asian-American people of the same age, marital status, education, income levels, etc.)? Here, there is some difference of opinion. Some studies find ethnic differences regardless of other factors (Laumann et al., 1994), but others do not (Quadagno et al., 1998). While more research is needed, it is probably safe to conclude that ethnic differences are not as great when we compare people of the same socioeconomic status.

"I heard, when I was growing up, about 'wet dreams' but thought that only applied to males. It wasn't until recently I awoke from a deep sleep, very sexually aroused, my heart beating rapidly, my body sweating, and vaginal lubrication had already begun. I don't remember the dream I was having." (woman) (All examples are from the author's files.)

Many people have **nocturnal orgasms** in their sleep. There are five stages of sleep. Stages I and II are light sleep, and stages III and IV are deep sleep. Adults enter a fifth stage about every 90 minutes. This is called REM. REM stands for "rapid eye movement" (our eyes move around under the eyelids during this stage). Many physiological events normally occur during this stage of sleep, including penile erection in men and vaginal lubrication in women. It is normal! In fact, when people do not show these responses, it is an indication that something physiologically is wrong. This is also the stage of sleep in which we have our most vivid dreams; but do not assume that the dreams have a sexual theme just because people are experiencing erection or lubrication. Most nocturnal orgasms are not associated with sexual dreams (Wells, 1986).

As with attitudes about masturbation, there is a long history of negative opinions about nocturnal orgasms. The biblical Hebrews believed that a man who had nocturnal emissions was unclean and had to undergo ritual washing before being allowed back into his community.

And if a man has an emission of semen, he shall bathe his whole body in water, and be unclean until the evening. And every garment and every skin on which the semen comes shall be washed with water, and be unclean until the evening. (Leviticus 15:16–17, Revised Standard Version)

If there is among you any man who is not clean by reason of what chances to him by night, then he shall go outside the camp, he shall not come within the camp, but when evening comes on, he shall bathe himself in water, and when the sun is down, he may come within the camp. (Deuteronomy 23: 10–11; Revised Standard Version)

St. Augustine did not regard nocturnal emissions as a sin (*The City of God*, 20.23), and this view was upheld in the 1200s by Thomas Aquinas (*Summa theologiae*). However, after this time medieval canonists and moralists unanimously came to view nocturnal emissions as sinful and requiring penance (Murray, 1998). In medieval times, it was also believed that male demons (incubi) had sex with women at night, while female demons (succubi) had sex with men while they slept. In the early 1800s, a French physician named Claude François l'Allernand believed that male nocturnal emissions ("wet dreams") were caused by the same thing that caused gonorrhea. Thus, in the Victorian era, nocturnal emissions were called *spermatorrhea*. Recall from Chapter 1 that as a young man, pioneering sexologist Henry Havelock Ellis thought he was going to die from spermatorrhea. Some Victorian parents made their male children wear spiked "spermatorrhea rings" to bed at night to prevent emissions (see Figure 1–4).

A lot of unfortunate Victorian boys must have experienced punctures. Kinsey et al. (1948) found that 83 percent of the men they surveyed reported having had nocturnal emissions. This occurs most frequently during the teen years and declines substantially after that, but these emissions can occur at any age. Many teenage boys are embarrassed by the wet spot on the sheets, especially if they have not been told in advance by their parents that this may (and is likely to) occur (see Chapter 12 for a more detailed discussion). Parents should not embarrass or ridicule their teenage boys for having wet dreams, particularly since it is a behavior over which they have no control

nocturnal orgasm An orgasm that occurs during sleep (sometimes called "wet dreams" in men).

(wet dreams occur during sleep). In fact, many men do not remember having had an orgasm in their sleep and are only aware that they did because of the wet spot.

Forty percent of the women in Kinsey's sample (1953) and 37 percent in a later study (Wells, 1986) also reported having nocturnal orgasms. However, the disparity between the responses of the two sexes may not really be this great. Women do not have a wet spot on the sheets in the morning as proof of a nocturnal orgasm, so only those women who are awakened by the orgasmic contractions can report them.

It is also normal for people to have sexually explicit dreams. Nearly 100 percent of the men and 70 percent of the women in Kinsey's studies reported having such dreams, although in some cases they caused distress. Keep in mind, however, that dreaming about something is not the same as doing it.

SEXUAL FANTASIES

"My sister, who was much older than I, would always have friends over and I would fantasize about making love to them while masturbating." (man)

"They [fantasies] almost always include my wife. It may also include another female." (man)

"I enjoy being male, but have occasionally fantasized about what it is like to be female during lovemaking." (man)

"During sex I have sexual fantasies about making love to a woman. . . . I would view my husband as a woman." (woman)

"My sexual fantasy has been the same since age 16. The man uses me, sometimes beats me, and bring his other female partners around me. This fantasy bothers me." (woman)

"I have sexual fantasies while making love to my husband, usually about men I'm attracted to from work. I think about how it would be and when I come, it's stronger and harder than it usually is." (woman)   (All examples are from the author's files.)

Recall from Chapter 1 that within Christianity there is a long history of condemnation of sexual thoughts, even if the thoughts are not accompanied by sexual behaviors (and even if the thoughts are of one's husband or wife). In the Victorian era it was thought that only men had sexual fantasies (because women were believed to be less interested in sex), but this is not true. Nearly everyone has sexual fantasies from time to time. Sometimes the fantasy may be a warm thought of a romantic interaction with a special person, but often the fantasies are very sexually explicit. Although most men think about sex more often than women—54 percent of men say they do so every day, as compared with

19 percent of women (Laumann et al., 1994)—the large majority of women do have sexual fantasies. In fact, more than 90 percent of women have had sexual fantasies (Leitenberg & Henning, 1995; Pelletier & Harold, 1988). Women's sexual fantasies tend to be more romantic and emotional, while men's fantasies tend to have more explicit and visual imagery. The frequency, length, and explicitness of an individual's sexual fantasies are related to the person's level of sexual experience (Leitenberg & Henning, 1995).

Sexual fantasies can occur at any time. Men have more sexual fantasies than women during nonsexual activity and masturbation, but there are no differences between the sexes during intercourse (Leitenberg & Henning, 1995). One of the most common fantasies during intercourse is the replacement fantasy, where one imagines oneself having sex with someone other than one's sexual partner (Cado & Leitenberg, 1990). If you have ever felt guilty about having these fantasies, as some people do (believing them to be immoral or socially unacceptable), you should be aware that they are so common that chances are that your partner has had them too. The fantasized partner can be a friend, a neighbor, a former partner, a celebrity (e.g., a movie star or a musician), or anyone else. Sharing fantasies with one's partner may enhance intimacy and sexual interest in some cases, but could also lead to jealousy and self-doubt. Most people prefer to keep their fantasies private.

The specific content of sexual fantasies is almost limitless, but we can group fantasies into four general categories: (1) exploratory (experimentation with never-before-tried behaviors such as group sex or same-sex activities), (2) intimacy (sexual activities with a known partner), (3) impersonal sex (sex with strangers or watching others have sex; fetishes), and (4) dominance-submission themes (Leitenberg & Henning, 1995; Meuwissen & Over, 1991). For both men and women, fantasies of intimacy with a present, former, or imaginary partner are most common. Dominance fantasies are more common for men, but submission fantasies of being overpowered or forced into having sex are not at all uncommon for women as well, especially among more experienced women who have little or no guilty feelings about sex (Strassberg & Lockerd, 1998).

The content of sexual fantasies does not indicate sexual unhappiness, nor does it signify personality or psychological problems. In fact, sexual fantasies are most common in those individuals who have the fewest number of sexual problems (Leitenberg & Henning, 1995). Most sex therapists view sexual fantasies as something positive to be enjoyed rather than as something bad for one's sexual health. Having a sexual fantasy does not mean that a person actually wants to experience it in real life. Fantasies also provide a safe and private outlet for thoughts that, if actually engaged in, might be considered improper and/or illegal. In fact, in most cases where people have acted out their fantasies, the result has been disappointment. One reason for this is that we are totally in control of the sequence of events in our fantasies, so that they proceed just to our liking; but this is seldom true in real life, where partners can cause distractions and have desires and demands of their own.

Although fantasies are generally viewed as positive, about one-fourth of all people who fantasize feel guilty about it (Leitenberg & Henning, 1995). For the most part, however, fantasies are harmless. Because the vast majority of people have them, they are also in the range of normal behavior.

PERSONAL REFLECTIONS

Do you have sexual fantasies? (Most people do.) Are you comfortable or uncomfortable with your fantasies—that is, do they cause anxiety or guilt? If your partner told you that he or she had sexual fantasies, what would your feelings be? Analyze the nature of your fantasies (e.g., their content, when they occur). What purpose do you think your fantasies serve?

COITAL POSITIONS AND LOCATIONS

"Before I became sexually active, I believed that everyone who engaged in sexual intercourse did so in the missionary position in the privacy of their own bedroom. Now I look forward to new positions." (woman)

"[Our sex] was boring me. We always used the same position—his favorite one." (woman)

"My boyfriend has the concept that men should be in control of sex. Well, I say 'What about my pleasure?' My favorite position is 'me on top' because I'm guaranteed to receive an orgasm." (woman)

". . . And also I like having sex standing up with my legs wrapped around the male's waist and walking around at the same time." (woman)

"I am a mature, responsible, middle-aged female. I am also an experienced diver with a mate who is equally comfortable under water. In my opinion, the most stimulating, exciting, and extraordinary sex on earth happens beneath the surface of the water. Complete sex beyond the grasp of gravity in a quiet, sensuous, foreign world is beyond our limited language to describe." (woman) (All examples are from the author's files.)

Of those Americans who are having sex, about 95 percent say that the sexual activity always or usually includes vaginal intercourse (Laumann et al., 1994). For most Americans, the first experience with sexual intercourse is in the **missionary position,** that is, a face-to-face position in which the woman lies on her back and the man lies on top with his legs between hers. It is called the missionary position because Christian missionaries in foreign countries used to instruct natives that this was the only "proper" way to have sexual intercourse. St. Paul believed that women should be subordinate to men during intercourse (i.e., on the bottom), and St. Augustine said that any other position was unnatural and a sin against nature (see Chapter 1). In the 1200s, the attitude of the Christian Church, that any other position of sexual intercourse was unnatural, was formalized by Thomas Aquinas in his *Summa theologiae* (1968), and this view then became the standard within Christianity (Brundage, 1984).

For many couples, man-on-top may be the only position in which they ever have sexual intercourse (**coitus**). Kinsey et al. (1948) found, for example, that over two-thirds of the population had never attempted any other position. The preference for this position by many American couples, however, appears to be culturally rather than biologically determined. The woman-on-top position is most popular in some other cultures, especially those in which women enjoy high status (see Box 13–B). In most nonhuman primate species, the male inserts his penis into the female's vagina from the rear.

Later surveys suggest that American couples are practicing a greater variety of sexual positions during intercourse

missionary position A face-to-face position of sexual intercourse in which the woman lies on her back and the man lies on top with his legs between hers. It was called this because Christian missionaries instructed people that other positions were unnatural.

coitus Sexual intercourse.

than in Kinsey's time. Hunt (1974), for example, found that of the married people he surveyed, 75 percent had tried woman-on-top, 50 percent had tried side-by-side, 40 percent had tried rear vaginal entry, and 25 percent had had intercourse while sitting. In fact, in a recent survey of college students it was found that 45 percent of men preferred the woman-on-top position (25 percent preferred man on top and 25 percent preferred man from behind), while a third of women preferred woman on top (48 percent said man on top and 15 percent preferred man from behind) (Elliott & Brantley, 1997).

Why do couples experiment with different positions? After all, the missionary position is perfectly adequate for procreational purposes. Well, to answer this, let's first examine the advantages and disadvantages of the missionary position. Perhaps the nicest thing about this position is that it allows for intimacy while having sex. A couple is face-to-face. But for most women, the benefits stop right there. In most couples, the man is considerably heavier than the woman, which means that she has to support a great deal of weight in the man-on-top position (and more and more so as the man gets tired). Some women may even have trouble breathing in this position. Women in my class have additionally pointed out that they receive very little touching or fondling in this position because their male partners are too busy supporting themselves. With a woman's hips "pinned to the mat," the man is in total control (probably the major reason that American men like this position), and it is often difficult to fully enjoy sex when you have little or no control over the movement or tempo.

There are other positions that still involve eye-to-eye contact but allow greater freedom and involvement for the woman. As you will see in a later chapter, woman-on-top is a position that is recommended by many therapists for optimal sexual arousal in both people. It is generally a lot easier for the man to support the woman, and it is also a position in which it is easy for the man or the woman herself to manually stimulate the clitoris (and most other parts of a partner's body) during intercourse..

Although these considerations are important, probably the main reason that most couples have sexual intercourse in different positions is to bring variety to their sex lives. Many a sexual relationship has become stale and boring by allowing it to become *ritualized*, that is, by only having sex at the same time of day, in the same place, in the same position. Even the manner in which many couples have sex is highly ritualized. Therapists report that it often proceeds in the following predictable manner: a few fleeting moments of kissing followed very quickly by the man touching and/or kissing the woman's breasts, followed directly by genital touching, followed by intercourse as soon as vaginal lubrication is detected.

Couples try different positions to keep their sex lives exciting, fresh, and fun—the way it was at the beginning of the relationship. Sex manuals show drawings of couples in what appears to be hundreds of different positions, but there are really just a few major variations that a couple can try: They can face each other or the woman can turn her back, and they can lie down, sit, or stand up. However, couples should try different positions only because they want to, and not because they feel pressured to do so.

Whether or not a couple ever try different sexual positions while having intercourse, it is important that they not allow their sex life to become a standardized ritual. The secret to that is to allow your sexual relations to be spontaneous, creative, and fun whenever possible. Some people get locked into a habit of never having sex until right before they go to sleep at night. If you and your partner are in the mood in the morning or afternoon, have sex then. Don't postpone it until later, when you might be tired. It is also normal for couples to have sex in a variety of places, for example, on the couch, on the rug, in different rooms, or in any other place. There is no rule that states you can have sex only in bed.

> Dear Ann Landers:
> My wife and I have been married 20 years. We have two sweet children and consider ourselves very fortunate. The problem is one we cannot discuss with our minister.
> My wife believes that sex anywhere but in the bedroom is sinful according to the Bible. I say a change of setting can add extra pleasure, and so long as there is complete privacy, it is perfectly moral.
> The place I have in mind is the car. We have a garage with a sturdy lock on the door. No one could possibly get in.
> We are good Christians and want to know what the Bible says about this. Can you contact a religious scholar? Strictly Confidential in Kentucky
>
> Dear Strictly: Since the Bible predates the automobile by a couple of thousand years, there is no point in bothering a Christian scholar.
> If you will settle for my opinion, here it is: It is perfectly all right for a married couple to make love anywhere they choose, providing it is private, safe, and reasonably comfortable. (Reprinted with permission of Ann Landers and Creators Syndicate.)

If you and your partner are on the couch and get in the mood to have sex, there is nothing immoral, sinful, or indecent in spontaneously doing so right there (assuming, of course, that the shades are pulled, there are no children around, and you are using contraception if pregnancy is unwanted). One of Ann Landers's readers felt compelled to respond to the letter by "Strictly Confidential":

Figure 13–1

Figure 13–2

Figure 13–3

Figure 13–4

Dear Ann Landers:

I was interested in the letter from the man who enjoyed making love in the car. His wife felt guilty and wanted to know if it was the "Christian" thing to do. You said so long as it was private, not dangerous, and reasonably comfortable, it was nobody's business.

I married one in a million. She was totally uninhibited, willing, and eager to make love any place at any time. I must say, we dreamed up some mighty unusual situations. We traveled quite a bit, and it was not unusual for us to pull off the road in the middle of the day if we ran into a wooded area, a vacant house, a sandy beach, a calm lake, or an inviting motel. On occasion, when the mood came upon us and none of the above was available, we just used the car.

This kept up until we were in our 60s, when my beloved wife passed away. I always felt as if we had the healthiest sex life of anyone I knew because we never stopped turning each other on. Sex was always unpredictable, imaginative, and fun.

Our sexual compatibility spilled over into all areas of our life and we were divinely happy.

You can print this letter if you want to but no name or city, please. Just call me . . . Beautiful Memories

Dear Beautiful: How lucky you were to find each other. It was a perfect match. Lots of readers will be envious. (Reprinted with permission of Ann Landers and Creators Syndicate.)

However, whenever, and wherever you decide to do it, try to make your sexual relations spontaneous, exciting, enjoyable, and fulfilling. A healthy and satisfying sex life can contribute to our overall physical and emotional well-being.

PERSONAL REFLECTIONS
How do you expect to keep your sexual relationship from becoming ritualized after 6 months, 6 years, 20 years, 60 years? The brain is your largest sex organ. Make sure you continue to use it to your advantage.

Box 13–B CROSS-CULTURAL PERSPECTIVES

Positions of Sexual Intercourse

The males of other primate species always mount the female from behind during sexual intercourse. The buttocks of the females become swollen and red when she is sexually receptive, which acts as a sexual stimulant to the males. With evolution of the two-legged stance in humans, mating occurred primarily face-to-face, with greater opportunity for emotional interaction and communication via facial gestures and vocalization (Lambert, 1995). Some researchers believe that one of the reasons many men find women's breasts sexually arousing is that breasts mimic the round contour of the buttocks (Diamond & Karlen, 1980).

Face-to-face is the preferred manner of sexual intercourse in all known cultures, but not necessarily man-on-top. In many African cultures, the most common position is with the partners lying side by side, while in Polynesian and many Asian cultures the most common position is with the woman lying on her back and the man squatting or kneeling between her legs (Gregersen, 1982). (By the way, it was the Polynesians who originally called the man-on-top position taught to them by European missionaries the "missionary position.") Actually, in most cultures there is more than one preferred

position. Mangaians, for example, practice a variety of positions while preferring some variety of man-on-top, but use the man-from-behind position more often when their partner is pregnant (Marshall, 1971).

Some researchers believe that a culture's preferred position of intercourse is a reflection of women's social status (Goldstein, 1976). In cultures where a woman's sexual satisfaction is considered to be as important as the man's, woman-on-top is usually preferred. The ancient Romans preferred this position. In male-dominated cultures, however, the reverse is true (Langmyhr, 1976). There may be no better reflection of the relation between women's social status and coital position than in our own culture. Here, women's gender roles have changed dramatically since World War II. In the 1940s, Kinsey et al. (1948) found that over two-thirds of the couples studied had never attempted any position other than man-on-top. More and more women began to enter the work force after that, and women's rights evolved rapidly in all areas. Twenty-five years later, Hunt (1974) found that the large majority of couples in the United States had tried the woman-on-top position.

Figure 13–5

ORAL-GENITAL SEX

"I was highly against oral sex because I thought it was so nasty and demeaning. But when I experienced it, my attitude changed. I didn't realize what I was against could feel so damn good." (woman)

". . . What did surprise me was the fact that I enjoyed giving more than receiving. I think it is a great way for two people to share very intimate moments." (man)

"It is a great way to relax, feel unpressured and not worry about pregnancy or how good you perform." (man)

"I do engage in oral-genital sex, but really prefer it as foreplay. I don't like the idea of a guy coming in my mouth—it gags me!" (woman)

"Oral sex is by far the most pleasurable sexual experience I have ever engaged in. It has produced some of the most intense orgasms that I have ever experienced, especially in the 69 position. I also very much enjoy orally stimulating my partner individually as much as being stimulated myself." (woman)   (All examples are from the author's files.)

fellatio Oral stimulation of a man's genitals.
cunnilingus Oral stimulation of a woman's genitals.

Sexual relations generally include a great deal of oral stimulation. One of the first sexual behaviors that most people engage in is kissing, which, of course, involves mouth-to-mouth stimulation. This usually progresses from "dry" kissing (lip to lip) to "wet" kissing (also known as "French" or "soul" kissing, involving the tongue) within a short time. It is also normal while having sex for people to kiss and lick other parts of their partner's body (the neck, for example). For many people, this includes their partner's genitals.

Oral stimulation of the penis is called **fellatio** (from the Latin *fellare*, meaning "to suck"), and oral stimulation of the vulva (clitoris, labia, vaginal opening) is called **cunnilingus** (from the Latin words for "vulva" and "licking"). These can be done either as part of foreplay or as the preferred sexual behavior, either by one partner at a time or by both at the same time (the latter is sometimes referred to as "69"). Although the slang term for fellatio is "blow job," the large majority of men prefer a sucking action to blowing. Many women report oral stimulation of the area around the clitoris to be more pleasurable than intercourse (the vaginal walls, you recall, have few nerve endings), and many men find fellatio (particularly orgasm during fellatio) to be more intense than intercourse (Janus & Janus, 1993). The pleasure, however, is not always reserved entirely for the recipient. While it is true that many people prefer receiving oral sex to giving it (Laumann et al., 1994), many others enjoy

Figure 13–6

orally stimulating their partner (and observing their partner's reaction) nearly or equally as much as being stimulated themselves. For many people, giving oral sex represents a moment of extreme intimacy.

How common are these behaviors? Kinsey's group (1948, 1953) found that about 50 to 60 percent of the married people they studied had engaged in oral-genital sex. However, only 15 percent of singles and only 10 percent of adolescents reported having engaged in it. More recent surveys indicate that about 70 to 90 percent of sexually active teens and young adults engage in oral-genital relations (e.g., Gates & Sonenstein, 2000; Janus & Janus, 1993; Laumann et al., 1994). Although no other behavior has increased as much in popularity since Kinsey's time as oral-genital stimulation, there are some notable differences among ethnic groups (see Box 13–A). The appeal of this behavior is positively associated with level of education and negatively associated with how religious one is.

Some individuals consider oral-genital sex disgusting, and no one should feel pressured to engage in a behavior just because a lot of other people do it. On the other hand, if you expect your partner to do it for you, then you should not have a double standard about doing it for him or her. Double standards in sexual relations can lead to serious problems in other aspects of the relationship.

"My girlfriend refuses to have oral sex with me, but thinks that it is just fine for me to do it to her! Even though I enjoy doing this to her, I don't think it is fair that she would not even try it." (man)

"My boyfriend and I are compatible emotionally, physically, and intellectually. But there is one flaw that tortures me daily: our oral-genital sex relations to this point have been very one-sided, and I am bewildered. My personal hygiene is wonderful but when I finally got the courage to ask him to give me cunnilingus he was mortified. Yet from the beginning I have not hesitated to give him fellatio when he requests. I felt like his pleasure was my reward. When he refused me I felt insulted and I cried for an hour. I just can't lose the feeling of very deep, very personal humiliation." (woman) (All examples are from the author's files.)

People often become more accepting of a sexual behavior when they learn that it is not abnormal (or that their partner is not abnormal or kinky for wanting to try it). As an example, try to remember your reaction when you first heard about French kissing. For many of us it seemed disgusting, but we later learned to enjoy it. Nevertheless, some people may have reservations about engaging in oral-genital sex because of cleanliness. Certainly, people ought to bathe regularly if they expect their partners to give them oral-genital stimulation (or engage in sexual relations of any kind, for that matter).

Even if a couple has good hygiene habits, however, there may be reservations about the cleanliness and odors of genital secretions. As I mentioned in the chapter on anatomy, the odor of a healthy vagina is not offensive. Some women do not like the taste of semen, but it, too, is relatively clean. In fact, mouth-genital contact is no less hygienic than mouth-to-mouth contact—the mouth harbors as many germs as the genital orifices. This assumes, of course, that neither person has a sexually transmitted disease, for these can be transmitted during oral-genital stimulation as well as during intercourse. On the other hand, there are no health benefits to swallowing genital secretions (such as curing acne or prolonging youthfulness), as some individuals mistakenly believe.

Try to recall your reactions when someone first told you about French kissing (also called "wet kissing" and "soul kissing"). Was your reaction somewhat negative? Could you really imagine allowing someone else to put his or her tongue in your mouth? How did your attitude change as you began to realize that most people engage in this behavior? Might this same process eventually change your attitude about any of the behaviors discussed in this chapter to which you presently have negative reactions?

ANAL STIMULATION

"The first time I had ever heard of anal sex was in 1987. A girl I worked with told me that she and her boyfriend had used this. I knew that male homosexuals had intercourse in that manner, but it never once occurred to me that heterosexuals did also!" (woman)

"Last summer my boyfriend decided he wanted to try some of the different types of things. . . . I will never try sex again in the anus because it was so painful." (woman)

"I do very much enjoy anal stimulation, if done properly. For me, anal stimulation during oral sex has produced the 'ultimate' orgasm . . . if it is done gently and not forcefully." (woman)

"I like anal sex, probably a lot more than most females. When I first had anal sex, I didn't like it. . . . The difference is in how fast or slow the guy is in penetrating and also how turned on I am before he goes in." (woman)

"My boyfriend and I sometimes use a mini-vibrator while making love. While we're in the missionary position, I insert the vibrator through the anus. At the same time, he continues to penetrate. I receive the ultimate feeling in sexual pleasure." (woman)
(All examples are from the author's files.)

The anus has numerous nerve endings and is very sensitive to touch. Many people enjoy having their anus manually stimulated by their partner's fingers during sexual intercourse. The anal sphincter muscle undergoes rhythmic muscular contractions during orgasm in both men and women, and thus anal stimulation can further enhance the pleasure. Although there is a physical basis for this pleasure, many people feel very negatively about anal sex and consider it abnormal, perverted, or kinky (Janus & Janus, 1993).

Anal intercourse is common among male homosexuals, but how common is it among heterosexual couples? Kinsey et al. (1948) found that 11 percent of the people he surveyed had attempted this behavior (only 8 percent successfully), but results of two more recent nationally representative surveys indicate that about 20 to 26 percent of young adults have tried anal intercourse (Catania et al., 1995; see Halperin, 1999; Laumann et al., 1994). Other recent surveys have found similar results (Baldwin & Baldwin, 2000). One in 10 American women engage in anal intercourse somewhat regularly (Voeller, 1991; Halperin, 1999). Among many heterosexuals, anal intercourse is a highly stigmatized behavior, and some people may deny having engaged in it. So how common is anal intercourse? In one study, many women denied having engaged in anal intercourse at first, but by the third interview 72 percent said they had tried it at least once (Bolling, 1988, see Voeller, 1991). This was not a nationally representative survey, but the point is that among heterosexuals, anal intercourse may be more common than reported in many surveys.

Interestingly, Laumann's group reported that only 5 percent of women found anal intercourse "very" or "somewhat" appealing. When asked why they participate, many women say that it is their least favorite sexual behavior, although they occasionally engage in it for variety or to please their partners. But as you can see from the personal testimonials at the beginning of this section, others enjoy it.

Why do heterosexual men engage in anal intercourse? Fourteen percent of American men say that anal intercourse is "very" or "somewhat" appealing (Laumann et al., 1994). Some prefer it because it gives them a "tighter" sensation (Halperin, 1998). However, for others it is an opportunity to display dominance or power:

"It (anal sex) is a conquest because women never want to give there. . . . When you do it there [people say], 'he did her over again,' like a virgin again. I got something that is difficult to get. When friends talk and say, 'I got to do EVERYTHING with that woman,' EVERYTHING doesn't mean normal sex because normal sex isn't everything. . . . Anal sex is the ultimate, the final barrier." (Goldstein, 1994)

How do people who have engaged in anal intercourse differ from others? A recent survey of college students found that those who had engaged in anal intercourse were generally younger (compared to those who had not) when they had their first experience of vaginal intercourse, were more erotophilic, and were less likely to use condoms in their present sexual relationships. Thus, as a group they appear to take more sexual risks than others (Baldwin & Baldwin, 2000).

For those who engage in this behavior, some words of caution are necessary. First, the anal sphincter muscle contracts in response to attempted penetration, and attempts to force the penis into the anus can result in injury. A water-soluble lubricant (like K-Y Jelly) should be used if you engage in this behavior. The muscle spasms do not relax until 30 to 60 seconds after penetration, so the woman often experiences some initial discomfort, even if her male partner proceeds slowly and gently. Even so, this behavior will almost certainly result in rupturing of small capillaries (unlike the vagina, the rectum does not readily accommodate this kind of stimulation; Agnew, 1986). Anal intercourse itself does not cause AIDS, but the ruptured capillaries maximize the chances of contracting HIV (the virus that causes AIDS) from an *infected* partner. If you are not in a monogamous relationship, use condoms. It is probably the case, however, that condoms tear more often during anal intercourse than during vaginal intercourse (Silverman & Gross, 1997). In addition, bacteria that are normally found in the anus can easily cause infection if introduced into the vagina. Couples who engage in anal stimulation, therefore, should never put anything (finger, penis, objects) into the vagina that has been in contact with the anus unless it has been washed first.

PREFERRED SEXUAL BEHAVIORS

What are the preferred behaviors for most Americans? In their well-conducted nationally representative study, Laumann and colleagues (1994) found that most Americans aged 18 to 44 were rather traditional. All but 5 percent of the people in their survey had engaged in vaginal intercourse the last time they had sex. It was by far the most preferred behavior. Among white men and women, receiving oral sex was the second most preferred behavior, followed very closely by watching their partner undress; and giving oral sex was fourth (though twice as many men as women found it "very appealing"). Among African Americans, watching their partner undress was the second most appealing behavior, and receiving oral sex was a distant third. Giving oral sex was a very distant fourth (see Box 13–A). Latino men ranked watching their partner undress as their second most preferred behavior, followed by receiving and giving oral sex. Latina women much

preferred receiving oral sex to watching a partner undress. Asian Americans also ranked receiving oral sex higher than watching a partner undress. In terms of it being "very appealing," anal sex was ranked very low by all groups.

Did you notice that watching a partner undress was a "very appealing" behavior among all groups? In fact, overall it ranked second. So, the next time you want to get your partner highly aroused, try undressing a little more slowly and seductively.

> *PERSONAL REFLECTIONS*
> *What sexual behaviors do you enjoy the most? The least? Why?*

THE SEXUALLY HEALTHY PERSON

You have now read about several sexual behaviors that a large number of people engage in. They are normal from a statistical perspective. Does this mean that you should try all these behaviors just because a large number of other people practice them? Do we judge sexual normality by the variety of sexual experiences or number of partners a person has had? No, not at all. Sexual health should not be judged like a decathlon event in the Olympics. A **sexually healthy person** is someone who (a) feels comfortable with his or her sexuality (i.e., does not view sex as something naughty, bad, improper, or sinful, and can engage in it without feeling guilty or anxious), and (b) feels free to choose whether or not he or she wishes to try a variety of sexual behaviors. "Feels free" means free of peer pressure, partner pressure, and social pressure. In today's world of epidemic sexually transmitted diseases, sexual health also means freedom from life-threatening diseases. Individuals should not engage in sex simply because they are being pressured by peers or a potential partner. A person can be sexually healthy and still say "no." Always saying "yes" does not prove that one is sexually healthy, any more than it proves that one is a "real man" or a "real woman."

By this definition, someone who has engaged in a wide variety of behaviors with numerous partners, but who gets little fulfillment from his or her sexual relations or who regards sex as dirty, would not be considered sexually healthy. Sometimes we can tell someone's real attitude about sex by how that person regards his or her partner or partners. For example, some people claim to have a positive attitude about sex, but they view their partners as dirty or bad for engaging in sex with them. On the other hand, a person could be sexually inexperienced and still be considered sexually healthy if he or she regarded sex as something good and positive

sexually healthy person Someone who feels comfortable with is or her sexuality and who feels free to choose whether or not to try a variety of sexual behaviors.

and was choosing not to engage in it for other reasons (e.g., saving sexual relations for someone he or she loved or cared for).

There are many behaviors that a couple can engage in that have not been mentioned. This chapter has discussed only the most common ones. (I am reminded of the couple who told Dr. Ruth Westheimer [*Playboy,* 1986] that among their favorite practices was having the woman toss onion rings over her partner's erect penis from various distances.) If a couple view their sexual relationship as something good and satisfying and want to experiment with different techniques, should they or anyone else have any concerns? Remember, most therapists take the view that any behavior between consenting adults done in private that does not cause physical, emotional, or psychological harm to anyone involved is okay.

Key Terms

anal intercourse   342
autoerotic asphyxiation   330
coitus   335
cunnilingus   340

fellatio   340
masturbation   302, 329
missionary position   6, 335
nocturnal orgasms   301, 333

range of behaviors or values   328
sexually healthy person   343
spermatorrhea   14, 333
statistically normal   328

Suggested Readings

Atwood, J. D., & Gagnon, J. (1987, Fall/Winter). Masturbatory behavior in college youth. *Journal of Sex Education and Therapy.*

Comfort, A. (1991). *The new joy of sex.* New York: Crown. A revised edition of a nicely illustrated, well-written sex manual. A best-seller since it was first published in 1972.

Friday, N. (1980). *Men in love.* New York: Delacorte Press. All about male sexual fantasies.

Halperin, D. T. (1999). Heterosexual anal intercourse: Prevalence, cultural factors, and HIV infection and other health risks, Part I. *AIDS Patient Care and STDs,* 13, 717–730. A thorough review of results of survey studies about anal intercourse.

Janus, S., & Janus, C. (1993). *The Janus report.* New York: John Wiley. Results of a nationwide survey of sexual behavior.

Maltz, W., & Boss, S. (1997). *In the garden of desire: The intimate world of women's sexual fantasies.* New York: Broadway Books. All about female sexual fantasies.

Michael, R., et al. (1994). *Sex in America: A definitive survey.* Boston: Little, Brown. A thinner version of the Laumann et al., (1994) study, adapted for the general public. Probably the most scientifically conducted sex survey ever.

Study Guide

INTERACTIVE REVIEW

This chapter presents several normal adult sexual behaviors. "Normal" is defined from a statistical point of view, and is best thought of as a (1) _____ of behaviors or values. Thus, you should not regard yourself as abnormal if you have not engaged in all the behaviors discussed here.

Historically, masturbation has been presented as unnatural, immoral, and bad for one's physical and mental health. In his landmark surveys of 1948 and 1953, (2) _____ found that (3) _____ percent of the men and (4) _____ percent of the women surveyed had masturbated, thus demonstrating that masturbation is, in fact, a very normal human sexual behavior. Modern medicine has also shown that masturbation has no negative medical consequences. Most men and women masturbate even when they are in sexual relationships. Most men, and probably most women, have also experienced orgasms during sleep, called (5) _____. They occur during a stage of sleep called (6) _____, during which all men in good health (7) _____ and women experience (8) _____.

Compared to those of men, sexual fantasies of women tend to be more (9) _____. Although at times a fantasy can be very sexually explicit, that does not mean that a person would actually want to do what he or she has fantasized. Fantasies are usually not an indication of sexual unhappiness or personality or psychological disorders.

The most common position for sexual intercourse in the United States is (10) _____-on-top, also called the (11) _____ position. However, there is no "correct" way of having sexual intercourse except what is right for you and your partner. Making your sexual encounters spontaneous, exciting, fulfilling, and not ritualized may mean exploring a variety of times, places, and positions.

Oral-genital sexual relations, properly referred to as (12) _____ and (13) _____, as a form of sexual expression have increased tremendously in popularity since Kinsey's time. In addition, a considerable number of heterosexual couples have tried anal intercourse on at least one occasion. However, the popularity of these behaviors differs among ethnic groups in the United States. (14) _____ Americans are more likely than other groups to engage in masturbation and oral-genital sex, while (15) _____ are most likely to engage in anal intercourse. Masturbation and oral-genital sex are the least popular among (16) _____.

A healthy and satisfying sexual relationship can contribute to one's overall physical and emotional well-being. (17) _____ individuals consider sex to be a positive and good thing, and feel free to choose when, where, and with whom to engage in a particular sexual activity. Just because many people may be exploring a particular form of expression does not mean it fits into everyone's value system.

SELF-TEST

A. TRUE OR FALSE

- [T] [F] 18. Women do not have nocturnal orgasms.
- [T] [F] 19. Substantially more men have sexual fantasies than women.
- [T] [F] 20. A person can be sexually healthy and choose not to have oral-genital sex, or even sexual intercourse.
- [T] [F] 21. Man-on-top is the preferred position of intercourse in all cultures.
- [T] [F] 22. Masturbation is normal for men, but not for women.
- [T] [F] 23. Studies have found that men masturbate in more varieties of ways than do women.
- [T] [F] 24. Assuming that neither person has a sexually transmitted disease, oral-genital sex is no less hygienic than kissing.
- [T] [F] 25. Most married people who masturbate do so because they are unhappy in their sexual relationships.
- [T] [F] 26. The content of sexual fantasies usually does not indicate sexual unhappiness or personality or psychological problems.
- [T] [F] 27. "Wet dreams" are dreams with a sexual theme.
- [T] [F] 28. Fantasizing about another person while having sex with your partner is usually an indication of a serious relationship problem.
- [T] [F] 29. Hunt's survey found that most couples have had sexual intercourse in more than one position.
- [T] [F] 30. No other behavior has increased as much in popularity since Kinsey's time as oral-genital sex.
- [T] [F] 31. Women's sexual fantasies are just as explicit as men's.
- [T] [F] 32. Generally speaking, men have sexual fantasies more often than women.
- [T] [F] 33. More people with sexual partners masturbate than people who do not have a sexual partner.
- [T] [F] 34. At least 20–26 percent of young adults have attempted anal intercourse.

B. MATCHING (ALL QUESTIONS HAVE MULTIPLE ANSWERS)

_____ 35. probably a sexually healthy person

_____ 36. probably a sexually unhealthy person

_____ 37. not enough information to tell

a. a 24-year-old man who has never had sexual relations
b. a 20-year-old woman who has had 15 sexual partners
c. a 20-year-old woman who is abstaining from sex, but is looking forward to sexual relations in a long-term relationship
d. a 20-year-old man who has had 15 sexual partners
e. someone who has had oral-genital sex and sexual intercourse in many positions
f. a man who engages in sex with many partners to prove his sexuality to his peers
g. someone who refuses to try oral-genital sex
h. a man who has had many sexual partners and regards them as sluts
i. someone who doesn't like oral-genital sex but always agrees to it
j. someone who engages in sex because of low self-esteem
k. someone who has had many partners and regards his or her experiences positively
l. someone who masturbates every day
m. someone who has always been faithful to his or her partner but feels guilty about desiring to have sex with him or her
n. someone who enjoys trying new sexual experiences with his or her partner, but chooses not to engage in anal sex

C. FILL IN THE BLANKS

38. Approximately every 90 minutes during sleep, women experience _____ and men experience _____.

39. Couples should not engage in anal and vaginal intercourse without washing in between because of _____.

40. Perhaps the most common type of fantasy during sexual intercourse is _____.

41. The main reason that many people continue to masturbate after forming a sexual relationship is _____.

42. Couples who always have sex in the same place and in the same manner risk letting their sex lives become _____.

43. Laumann and his colleagues (1994) found that the two sexual behaviors most preferred by Americans are _____ and _____.

44. Laumann and his colleagues also found that masturbation is mostly a reflection of _____.

45. The preferred manner of sexual intercourse in all known cultures is _____.

46. _____ is the position of intercourse usually preferred in cultures where a woman's sexual satisfaction is considered to be as important as the man's.

47. A sexually healthy person is someone who (a) _____ and (b) _____.

48. Oral-genital sex is most common among _____ Americans (ethnic group) and _____ -educated people.

Chapter 14

Love and Relationships

My bounty is as boundless as the sea,
My love as deep; the more I give to thee,
The more I have, for both are infinite

(Shakespeare, *Romeo and Juliet*, II, ii)

Poets write words to rhyme with it. Novelists glorify it in prose. Lyricists praise it in song. Philosophers wonder about its meaning, and politicians all support it.

What is this ubiquitous subject? Why, it's love, of course. Have I exaggerated? Think about it for a moment. How many popular songs that you hear are about love (first love, new love, broken hearts)? In fact, you may have to listen for quite a while before you find one that is not about love. When was the last time that you read a novel that didn't include at least one romantic subplot?

Love is obviously an emotion that most humans consider to be extremely important to their lives. But what is love? There have probably been as many definitions and thoughts about love as there have been philosophers, behavioral scientists, theologians, and biologists. Freud (1933/1953) believed that love was an emotional feeling that resulted from "aim-inhibited sexual desire." It originates with sexual desire, and when that desire cannot be expressed, the person idealizes the desired one and falls in love (notice the Victorian-era view of the role of sex in relationships). Others have viewed love as a social

When you have finished studying this chapter, you should be able to:

1. Discuss the history of romantic love and the role of sexual desire in romantic love;

2. Describe the characteristics that romantic love and friendship have in common, and the characteristics that distinguish romantic love from friendship;

3. Describe companionate love and its relation to romantic (and passionate) love;

4. Discuss the prerequisites for love;

5. Explain how attachment styles might affect romantic relationships;

6. Discuss Sternberg's triangular theory of love and how different combinations of three components lead to different kinds of liking and loving;

7. Describe Lee's different styles of love and his advice on how to find a compatible love relationship;

8. Explain what causes jealousy and how best to deal with it;

9. Discuss love in other cultures;

10. Explain how a couple can maintain a loving relationship; and

11. Discuss how couples can achieve greater intimacy.

instinct that satisfies a need for companionship with others. In *The Origins of Love and Hate* (1952), Ian Suttie expressed the belief that "the specific origin of love, in time, was at the moment the infant recognizes the existence of others." In contrast, others have expressed the belief that love results from conditioning (i.e., that it is a learned response). By this account, people come to be desired or loved when others have positive experiences in their presence. Love has also been viewed as a mania (Plato, in *Phaedrus*), a neurosis (Askew, 1965), an addiction (Peele, 1988), a disease (Burton, 1651/1963), and the enshrinement of suffering and death (de Rougement, 1969).

Christian ideals of love are found in St. Augustine's definition: "Love means: I want you to be." Viewing love simply as a desire for another person "to be" honors his or her existence. It transcends sexual desire and acknowledges that this emotion can be felt for a lover, a parent, a child, or a friend of the opposite or the same sex. Noted psychoanalyst Erich Fromm has echoed similar beliefs about love:

> **I want the loved person to grow and unfold for his own sake, and in his own ways, and not for the purpose of serving me. (Erich Fromm, 1956, pp. 23–24)**

HISTORY OF ROMANTIC LOVE

A history of love? You probably believe that love has always been a part of the human experience, so why do you need to read about its history? You may be surprised, then, to learn that many scholars believe that romantic love is a relatively recent phenomenon, or that it exists only in Western culture. You will also learn that love is, in part, a social concept (see Chapter 9) whose meaning has changed over time. Let us take a look.

The first thing we must do is identify the nature of romantic love. We do not experience romantic love for a calculated reason (e.g., because the other is a good provider or mate). From culture to culture, and in different time periods, the concept of **romantic love** has one thing in common—*idealization of another*. In the words of anthropologist Charles Lindholm (1998), romantic love is "experienced as spontaneous, total and boundless in its actual devotion to . . . the other—to love 'for a reason' is not to love at all. We love because we love, and not because of anything that the beloved other has to offer us beyond themselves" (p. 248). Lindholm adds, ". . . falling in love is an act of imagination in which the other is invested with absolute value; the beloved can even be loved for their very faults. . . . As such, it is . . . akin to the experience of religious ecstasy" (p. 258).

romantic love The idealization of another; the combination of passion and liking (intimacy).

Early, very influential anthropologists not only dismissed love as a subject for study but even doubted its very existence. Ralph Linton (1936) wrote:

> **The hero of the modern American movie is always a romantic lover, just as the hero of an old Arab epic is always an epileptic. A cynic may suspect that in any ordinary population the percentage of individuals with capacity for romantic love of the Hollywood type was about as large as that of persons able to throw genuine epileptic fits. However, given a little social encouragement, either one can be adequately imitated without the performer admitting even to himself that the performance is not genuine. (p. 175)**

Similarly, anthropologist Robert Lowie (1931) wrote:

> **Love exists for the savage as it does for ourselves—in adolescence, in fiction, among the poetically minded. (p. 146)**

When anthropologists finally acknowledged the existence of romantic love among ordinary people, many believed that it existed solely in Western culture (e.g., Hsu, 1983; Endelman, 1989). Their argument was that romantic love is unnecessary, and not valued, in primitive clans where there is shared intimacy. As Hunt (1959, p. 10) put it, ". . . by and large the clanship structure and social life of most primitive societies provide a wholesale intimacy and broad distribution of affection; Western love . . . is neither possible nor needed." Individuals achieve their identity through the group and close family and religious ties. The same has been said of modern societies that emphasize collectivism over individualism. An example would be China:

> **To an American in love, his/her emotions tend to overshadow everything else. . . . To a Chinese in love, his/her love occupies a place among other considerations. (Hsu, 1983, p. 50)**

According to these scholars, romantic love, with its idealization of another, was possible only in a fluid society that emphasized individualism (e.g., in modern Western culture). Romantic love was considered to be a way for isolated individuals to achieve identity and meaning in a society that no longer provided meaning through a fixed social structure, religion, or family relations (Beck, 1995).

Several scholars have successfully challenged the belief that romantic love is limited to modern Western culture. There are many accounts of homoerotic romantic love in classical Greece (Evans, 1998). Lindholm (1998) has pointed out that idealization of another occurred among the literate elite in Japan's Tokugawa period (as evidenced in love-suicide plays) and also in the myths and legends of ancient India. In clanships and modern collective societies, marriages are arranged and romantic love is generally prohibited (see Box 13–A). However, even in these societies romantic love is found (see Lindholm,

Figure 14–1 *Cupid and Psyche* by François Gérard conveys many people's idealistic view of romantic love.

Sexuality was deemphasized, and thus Christians came to believe "not only that God is love but also that love is God" (Singer, 1984, p. 340).

Romantic love as idealization of another really emerged in medieval times (beginning in the 12th century) when men returning from the Crusades transformed the cult of the Virgin Mary into *courtly love.* Here, courtiers expressed their undying love for a beloved (always a married woman), who they worshiped from afar as the epidemy of virtue (Lindholm, 1998). Sexual relations were never even considered, and this romantic love was not expressed within marriage. It was not until the 16th or 17th century that romantic love began to be linked with marriage (Evans, 1998). Eventually, in Western culture, the erotic aspects have come to be regarded as equally, if not more, important than the idealization of another (see next section).

There is a relatively new field of science called *sociobiology* that not only claims that romantic love is universal but also says that sexual desire and romance have always been linked together (see Fisher, 1992; Schopenhaver, 1966). To them, romantic love is an evolutionary mechanism that keeps men with their mates so that they can offer the protection and provisions necessary to raise children. However, this theory ignores the fact that in most cultures the beloved is not one's mate in marriage, nor the mother of the lover's children (see Lindholm, 1998).

We will study love in the remainder of this chapter from a Western perspective. However, keep in mind that in most cultures romantic love does not have the erotic aspects that it now has here, but that the aspect which is common in all cultures (yesterday and today) is idealization of another.

1998). It is never with one's spouse, it is secret and conducted at great risk, and it is generally not sexual in nature but always involves idealization of another. Lindholm adds that in these cultures "romantic love may offer a way of imagining a different and more fulfilling life" (p. 254). In the most comprehensive cross-cultural study to date, Jankowiak and Fischer (1992) studied 166 cultures and found evidence of romantic love in 147 of them, including many that had strong rules against it (pp. 153–54). Romantic marriages may not be universal, but love is apparently "a very primitive, basic human emotion, as basic as fear, anger, or joy" (anthropologist Helen Fisher, quoted by Gray, 1993a)—one that escapes all the restrictions and barriers imposed by numerous cultures.

Let us now focus on Western culture. Romantic love may not be a modern phenomenon, but what has changed in modern times is the way people in Western culture view the nature of romantic love. There are instances in antiquity in which romantic love and sexual desire were linked, such as the homoerotic love in classical Greece (Evans, 1998) or between patrician men and slaves in imperial Rome (Grimal, 1986). However, love as spiritual and intellectual idealization of another has its beginnings in Christianity and God's love for humans.

FRIENDSHIP VERSUS ROMANTIC LOVE

Studies conducted nearly 1,600 years after St. Augustine ("love means: I want you to be") confirm his belief that the structure of love is very similar for various types of close relationships (Sternberg & Grajek, 1984). Let us first ask what distinguishes love from friendship. Nearly 2,000 years ago, the Roman statesman and philosopher Seneca wrote, "Friendship always benefits; love sometimes injures." Is this true? Are love and friendship qualitatively different feelings, or is love just a more intense form of the emotion felt in friendship?

Studies by Keith Davis (1985) of the University of South Carolina have revealed several characteristics that are essential for **friendship:** (1) *enjoyment* of each other's

> **friendship** A relationship that includes (a) enjoyment of each other's company, (b) acceptance of one another, (c) mutual trust, (d) respect for one another, (e) mutual assistance when needed, (f) confiding in one another, (g) understanding, and (h) spontaneity.

Figure 14–2 Compared to friendship, romantic love rates high in fascination (a preoccupation with the other person), exclusiveness, sexual desire, and giving the utmost when the other is in need.

company most of the time (although periods of temporary annoyance or anger may occur); (2) *acceptance of one another* as is; (3) a *mutual trust* that each will act in his or her friend's best interest; (4) a *respect for each other* (an assumption that each will use good judgment in making life choices); (5) *mutual assistance* of one another during times of need; (6) *confiding* in one another; (7) an understanding of each other's behavior; and (8) *spontaneity* (the freedom to be oneself rather than playing a role). Generally speaking, men and women experience friendship in the same way (Bleske & Buss, 2000).

Davis found that people rated their "spouse/lover" and best friend nearly the same for all of these characteristics except for enjoyment, which more people attributed to their relationship with a lover than to the company of their best friend. What about close friends (rather than best friends)? People tended to rate spouses and lovers higher for enjoyment, respect, mutual assistance, and understanding. Still, close friends also generally fared well on these characteristics. Other researchers have also found considerable overlap in the characteristics that people desire for spouses/lovers and friends (Hendrick & Hendrick, 1993; Laner & Russell, 1998).

Are there some characteristics unique to spouses and lovers? Davis found that people generally rated romantic love relationships much higher (compared to friends) in *fascination* (a preoccupation with the other person, even when one should be doing other things), *exclusiveness* (not having the same relationship with another person), *sexual desire* (a desire for physical intimacy), and *giving the utmost* when the other is in need.

These feelings can be extremely intense. The loved one is perceived as able (and often solely able) to satisfy needs, fulfill expectations, and provide rewards and pleasure.

Notice again that romantic love includes a high degree of sexual desire (see Regan, 1998). (However, recall from the section on history that sexual desire as a major component of romantic love is relatively new in Western culture.) That brings us to an interesting question: "What is the difference between the word *love* and the expression *'in love'?*" "The word love is bandied about more promiscuously than almost any other word in the English language," according to Murstein (1988, p. 13). Nevertheless, Meyers and Berscheid (1997) found that a large majority perceives a difference between love and "being in love." When they had people place their social relationships into categories, they found that people put far many more people in the "love" category than in the "in love" category, and that people placed in the "in love" category (but not the "love" category) were also included within a "sexual attraction/desire" category. Meyers and Berscheid found that almost all of their subjects knew what it meant if someone told them "I love you, but I'm not in love with you." To them, it meant "I like you, I care about you, I think you're a marvelous person with wonderful qualities and so forth, but I don't find you sexually desirable." Their findings agree with Davis's that the major differences between friendship (love) and romantic love (being "in love") are fascination, exclusiveness, and sexual desire.

Davis and others report that most lovers find that their mood depends more on reciprocation of their feelings in romantic relationships than it does in friendships. Lovers tend to view their relationships as more under the control of social rules and expectations. Romantic relationships also rate much higher in ambivalence (mutually existing but conflicting feelings) than friendships. Thus, while romantic relationships are generally more rewarding than friendships, they are also more volatile and frustrating than friendships.

Most people have had at least one experience of *unreciprocated love* (loving another person who is not in love with you) (Aron et al., 1998). Many people remain in unreciprocated relationships even though it causes high levels of distress. Why? These individuals are driven by their perceived benefits of having a relationship with the beloved as well as the desirability of the relationship (Aron et al., 1998). In extreme cases it is called *obsessive relational intrusion,* defined as "repeated and unwanted pursuit and invasion of one's sense of physical or symbolic privacy by another person . . . who desires or presumes an intimate relationship," and may include stalking behavior (Cupach & Spitzberg, 1998). For most people, however, their pursuit of the beloved (as well as their feelings) eventually stops when love is not reciprocated.

HOW DO I KNOW IF THIS IS REALLY LOVE?

In addition to a preoccupation with the loved person, it has been argued that romantic love involves physiological arousal and the cognitive interpretation of that as being caused by the other person (Berscheid & Walster, 1974). Consider, for example, the following hypothetical scenario:

> **Susan was in her first year of college. She had gone out a few times, but too many weekend nights had been spent with girlfriends, and she generally felt lonely and bored. She was surprised when David, a handsome junior who had sat next to her in sociology class, called and asked her to go to a movie Friday night. They had a good time and studied together on Sunday. However, David didn't sit next to her in class on Tuesday, and Susan worried all that day and the next if he would call again. She could hardly contain herself when he called Wednesday evening and asked her to a big party at his fraternity.**
>
> **Susan and David spent a lot of time together during the next two weeks. She was no longer lonely or bored, and, in fact, her girlfriends let her know that they envied her. On the other hand, when she and David were apart, she worried if and when he would call, and her growing sexual attraction to David was keeping her aroused and agitated.**

Is Susan in love? She has feelings of extreme happiness (sometimes elation), periods of anxiety and frustration, and sexual desire, and she finds herself thinking about David when she should be concentrating on other things. David fulfills needs and satisfies desires (sexual, physical, and ego). There is no question that she is better off than before. But is this really love, or just infatuation?

Romantic love almost always includes certain *physiological responses,* such as heavy breathing, a pounding heart and increased blood pressure, sweaty palms, and a dry mouth when we are close to or thinking about the loved one. Michael Liebowitz (1983) has found that feelings of romantic love are associated with an increase in three brain chemicals called dopamine, norepinephrine, and phenylethylamine, the last of which is chemically similar to amphetamines. Falling in love, with the release of these chemicals, literally gives the person a natural high. (Some people are known to eat large amounts of chocolate, which is high in phenylethylamine, when suffering the heartache of a broken romance.)

The problem is, of course, that almost any kind of excitement or stress will cause a pounding heart and other physiological responses. A *cognitive component* is necessary before one can interpret these responses as a particular type of emotion (Hatfield & Rapson, 1993). To prove this, psychologists Stanley Schacter and Jerome Singer (1962) administered adrenalin, which causes increased heart rate and other signs of physiological arousal, to volunteer subjects who were told it was a vitamin shot. The subjects were then instructed to wait in another room with a fellow subject. This other subject, however, was really working for the researchers, and in half the cases acted very happy and in the other half very angry. The real subjects were experiencing strange physiological responses of arousal due to the adrenalin, but it was the environmental cues that determined how they interpreted them. The subjects with the happy person acted happy, while those with the angry person acted angry. When subjects were warned in advance of the physiological changes they would experience, they were not affected by the phony subject's behavior.

If Susan's friends are having similar experiences and say they are "in love," the chances are good that Susan, too, will interpret her newly aroused state as love. Under other circumstances, she might not.

Will Susan's feelings of love for David last? Initially, Susan certainly loves the way David makes her feel. But as many of you have discovered, that initial high usually doesn't last, at least not at the peak it first was at. Just as with amphetamines, the body builds up resistance to phenylethylamine, so that it takes larger amounts to experience the same high. Some people—call them "love junkies" if you like—go from relationship to relationship, ending each one as the initial high (passion) begins to subside. If love is to last for Susan, she must come to love David for who he is, and not just for what he causes her to experience.

COMPANIONATE LOVE

Companionate love has been defined as "the affection we feel for those with whom our lives are deeply entwined" (Walster & Walster, 1978). It is based on togetherness, trust, sharing, affection, and a concern for the welfare of the other (more so than passion). For example, the love between a parent and a child is usually the type we refer to as companionate love. It is also a stable kind of love that is characteristic of lasting adult relationships, for few relationships can sustain the initial level of excitement and sexual passion.

> **Young love is a flame; very pretty, often very hot and fierce but still only light and flickering. The love of the older and disciplined heart is as coals, deep burning, unquenchable.**   (Henry Ward Beecher)

Scientists have discovered that the continued presence of a partner increases the production of endorphins, natural opiate-like chemicals found in the brain (Fisher, 1992; see Toufexis, 1993). More recent research has found that oxytocin—the hormone released during breast-feeding, labor, and orgasm—might be important for mediating the stage in which couples settle down in a long-term relationship (Fisher, 1997). Perhaps it is these substances that give long-term lovers a sense of calm, peace, and security (in contrast to the high produced by the initial surge of amphetamine-like chemicals).

We have already seen that most people attach different meanings to the terms *love* and *in love* (Meyers & Berscheid, 1997). Researchers equate the word *love* with companionate love, and the expression *in love* with passionate love (Berscheid & Walster, 1978; Hendrick & Hendrick, 1989). **Passionate love** is defined as "a state of intense longing for union with another. . . . A state of profound physiological arousal" (Hatfield, 1988, p. 193). In this sense, it is similar to what we have called romantic love. The two kinds of love are usually described as a dichotomy. However, Meyers and Berscheid (1997) found that people can experience both simultaneously, and propose instead that the more accurate distinction is passionate/companionate love versus companionate love.

companionate love Love based on togetherness, trust, sharing, and affection rather than passion.

passionate love "A state of intense longing for union with another . . . A state of profound physiological arousal" (Hatfield, 1988).

attachment Two meanings: (a) A drab, mundane form of companionship where one's partner gives few positive rewards, other than predictability, for remaining in the relationship; (b) the emotional tie between a parent and child, or between two adults.

Passionate love is more sexualized than companionate love and tends to decline with time (Sprecher & Regan, 1998). Companionate love, however, does not always come later in a relationship, for some people do not consider romance to be their most important goal when establishing a relationship. Some people desire companionship more than anything else. Companionate love very often includes a good, satisfying sexual relationship as well. This is understandable in that a good overall relationship often leads to a healthy and good sexual relationship. Many people refer to this type of relationship as *realistic love* because it is not based on the fantasies and ideals of romantic love. The predictability (and avoidance of extreme highs and lows) of companionate love offers security, so that people may enjoy their lives outside of the relationship as well as in.

A drab, mundane form of companionship might be called **attachment** (Berscheid, 1982), where one's partner gives few positive rewards for remaining in the relationship aside from predictability (a different use of the term *attachment* is given in a later section). For most people, familiarity is comforting, and this can also be true even when all other aspects of a relationship are poor.

> "I confronted my boyfriend about growing up before we were supposed to get married. I said to him what he had ignored for 29 years of his life—he needs to leave mom and move out on his own. He acted as though I had spoiled all of his high hopes when I told him this. I, like five women before me, chose to confront the issue, yet he is totally bewildered about why his longest relationship with a woman has been merely 3 months long. No matter what confidences I shared with him, he would always have to spill the beans to mom. Any time there was a problem he would slip back into his comfort zone with mom there to cuddle him."
> (from the author's files)

Knowing what to expect may cause less anxiety for some than the thought of leaving and venturing into an unknown future. An extreme example of this is the devotion displayed by some battered wives toward abusive husbands on whom they are economically dependent. The fear of having to support themselves on their own may seem worse than the abuse. I will return to the subject of companionate love in the section on maintaining a relationship.

SEX WITHOUT LOVE

Is it possible to have a life-style of sex without love and still be happy? In the movie *Annie Hall*, Diane Keaton says to Woody Allen, "Sex without love is an empty experience." Woody responds, "Yes, but as empty experiences go, it's one of the best." In his book *Sex without*

Love (1980), Russell Vannoy argues that love is unnecessary and that sex should be enjoyed for its own sake. Masters and Johnson reported that they worked with hundreds of people who weren't in love but who deeply enjoyed sex. In fact, throughout history there have been many famous people who were noted for their sexual relations with hundreds, often thousands, of partners (e.g., Cleopatra, Empress Theodora, Catherine the Great, Sarah Bernhardt, King Solomon, King Ibn-Saud).

Love and sex share many things in common, including the fact that both may be intensely exciting experiences involving physiological changes that may be expressed in many ways. Feelings of love, however, tend to be more selective than sexual desires, and while the experience of being in love is generally felt all over, sexual sensations are generally confined to a few body parts.

In the United States, most people feel that sexual relations should be reserved for strongly affectionate relationships (Laumann et al., 1994; McCabe, 1987). Women in particular are apt to find sex unenjoyable unless it is within a loving relationship (McCabe, 1987):

> "I find it much more pleasurable and rewarding to make love with my partner. We have times when we have sex but I enjoy making love much more. My partner caresses me and makes me feel more special and loved."   (from the author's files)

Men, on the other hand, are much more likely than women to enjoy sex without emotional involvement (Leigh, 1989). In a study of people's private wishes (Ehrlichman & Eichenstein, 1992), many more men than women wished "to have sex with anyone I choose." Evolutionary theorists say that because women are the ones who bear children, they have an innate need for (and seek) male partners who will invest in their offspring. Anthropologist John Townsend (1995) found that even highly sexually active women who engage in nonemotionally involved sex are more likely than men to feel emotionally vulnerable and to have anxieties about their partners' willingness to invest.

For most people in our culture, sex without love is a passing stage in relationships. Eventually a large majority of women, and a small majority of men, wish "to deeply love a person who deeply loves me" (Ehrlichman & Eichenstein, 1992). However, this doesn't mean that a person cannot enjoy a life-style of sex without love. Some people may simply prefer their independence to emotional involvement. And remember, the emphasis in the United States of sex within a loving relationship is a culturally learned value. In some other cultures, people put considerable more emphasis on sexual pleasure (and think that Americans' attitude of "love first" is peculiar) and encourage sexual relations with many partners (see Chapter 1).

LOVE WITHOUT SEX

Keith Davis (1985), you recall, included sexual desire as one of the characteristics that distinguished romantic love from friendship. Other researchers agree. However, you have already learned that in other cultures romantic love may not include sexual desire, and that sexual desire may be a relatively new component of romantic love, even in Western culture. Is it possible for people living in Western culture today to experience romantic love without engaging in sexual relations?

Love is a feeling, not an act. Therefore, people who have a loving relationship may or may not choose to express their closeness with sex, even when there is sexual desire. Although attitudes toward premarital or nonmarital sexual relations are not as stringent as in previous generations, many couples still prefer to reserve their sexuality for marriage (Laumann et al., 1994). This period of voluntary celibacy allows them to devote time and energy to other aspects of their relationship (and allows the intimacy component to grow), perhaps resulting in their finding many nonsexual ways to express their love for one another. Even in sexually consummated relationships, sexual relations may have to be interrupted for long periods of time because of illness or physical separation (e.g. due to military duty), but this doesn't mean that feelings of romantic love are also interrupted.

> *PERSONAL REFLECTIONS*
> *How important to you is loving and being loved? Do you believe that you could enjoy sex without love? Why or why not? Could you enjoy being in a romantic love relationship for an extended period of time if the relationship did not include sex? Why or why not?*

UNCONDITIONAL LOVE

So far, most of our discussion about love has centered on romantic love, which tends to be **conditional love,** or what Maslow (1968) called *deficiency love* (or D-love). We fall in love with someone and remain in love because he or she satisfies certain needs and fulfills desires, and because it is positively reinforcing to be with him or her. We tend to fall out of love when our expectations and needs are no longer met. Our feelings for the other person depend to some extent, perhaps to a large extent, on how he or she makes us feel and contributes to our happiness.

Distinguished from conditional love is **unconditional love** (what Maslow called *being love* or B-love), in which one's

conditional love Feelings of love that depend on the loved one satisfying needs and fulfilling desires.

unconditional love Feelings of love that do not depend on the loved one meeting certain expectations or desires.

Box 14—A CROSS-CULTURAL PERSPECTIVES

Love and Marriage

Romantic love, the idealization of another, is not something new; there are references to it throughout history. Recall from the section on the history of love that in Western culture love became idealized during the Middle Ages with the rise of courtly love (a young man devoting himself to a married noblewoman). However, romantic love had never been viewed as a basis for marriage. For example, the Roman Seneca wrote, "To love one's wife with an ardent passion is to commit adultery" (Grimal, 1986, p. 252). Romantic love did not begin to be linked with marriage until the 16th or 17th century (Evans, 1998), and even then it was uncommon. In colonial times, Americans agreed to marry more or less by arrangement, the main purpose of marriage being to have children (Rothman, 1984). Romantic love was not considered a good reason to enter into marriage until the 1800s.

In fact, in a study conducted in the early to mid-1960s, about one-third of the U.S. men and three-fourths of the women surveyed indicated that being "in love" was not a necessity for marriage (Kephart, 1967). By 1976, this had changed; all but about 15 percent of the men and women in one study said that romantic love was a necessary prerequisite for marriage, and the same results were found in 1984 (Simpson et al., 1986) and again in 1995 (Levine et al., 1995). The change in attitude, mostly by women, was attributed to better economic status—financial independence allowed people to make relationship decisions based on romance.

Anthropologists initially believed that the linkage of romantic love and marriage was a peculiar American phenomenon. As Linton (1936) put it, "Our present American culture is practically the only one which has attempted to . . . make . . . [emotional attachments] . . . the basis for marriage" (p. 175).

Anthropologists have found that rules about marriage are, in fact, influenced by economics and politics (Barry & Schlegel, 1984; Hsu, 1981). In industrialized countries, where importance is attached to individuals, monogamy is the standard. In simpler societies, where less importance is given to individuals and more to situations, *polygyny* (allowing a man to have more than one wife) is often the rule. A few societies even allow *polyandry* (woman with more than one husband) (Frayser, 1985). In a study of 862 cultures, 83 percent permitted polygyny and only 16 percent were monogamous (Murdock, 1967). In some countries, over 40 percent of women are in polygynous marriages (Effah, 1999). Polygyny is very common in societies with strong fraternal interests (with dowries given at marriage), or where there is warfare for the capture of women, or where there are no constraints on expansion into new lands (White & Burton, 1988).

There are many differences among cultures in the relationship between a husband and a wife. In a great many cultures, marriages are arranged by parents, sometimes at birth. In contrast to the highly romantic beginnings of marriages in the United States, Japanese arranged marriages start off with very little love, but there is no difference in the amount of love within the two types of marriages after 10 years (due largely to the decrease in romantic love over time in American marriages; Blood, 1967). Marriages in India are arranged according to caste, age, and other factors. Many Islamic societies require that a young man marry his father's brother's daughter (first cousin), and husband-wife relations are generally without affection, and are often very hostile (Lindholm & Lindholm, 1980). Pacific Islanders and people in Southeast Asia are often required to marry their mother's brother's daughter. Some cultures require the man to capture a wife from an enemy village (Barnes, 1999), as in the case of the Gusii of Kenya, who rape their wives whenever they wish to have sex (Levine, 1974). Marriage by capture was common in the early Indo-European world (Dumézil, 1979). A man of the Marind Anim of New Guinea must first share his newlywed wife with all the other men of his clan before he is allowed to consummate the marriage (Money & Ehrhardt, 1972).

So, is romantic love as the basis for marriage restricted to Western culture? The answer is no. Lindholm (1998) cites several simple hunting and gathering societies (including the western Apache, !Kung, and the Hottentot) that link marriage with romance. Recently, two other studies have similarly identified many non-Western cultures that rate romantic love highly when choosing a mate (de Munck & Korotayev, 1999; Levine et al., 1995). Do they have anything in common? Romantic love as a basis for marriage is generally found in cultures that do not have strong sanctions against female sexuality, and that have a permissive attitude about premarital sex (de Munck & Korotayev, 1999). Love may be found in collective cultures, but as a basis for marriage it is still found predominantly in individualistic cultures (cultures that place emphasis on individuals rather than the group) (Levine et al., 1995). As the influence of Western culture spreads, this will include more and more cultures in which love as the basis for marriage was once prohibited.

---

feelings do not depend on the loved one meeting certain expectations and desires (Fromm, 1956). Unconditional love is the type of love that many mothers feel for their children (Fromm believed that love is conditional for most fathers), that many grown-up children continue to feel for their parents, and that many people feel for other individuals of the same or opposite sex. How one feels about his or her romantic partner can also eventually transcend the ability of the partner to satisfy needs and fulfill expectations. This is perhaps most closely approximated by what is called companionate love and which is expressed so well in St. Augustine's definition of love, "I want you to be."

PREREQUISITES FOR LOVE

SELF-ACCEPTANCE

In order to love another, it is first necessary that one be able to love oneself. As Erich Fromm once stated, "If an individual is able to love productively, he loves himself, too; if he can love only others, he cannot love at all" (1956, p. 60). The first prerequisite for a loving relationship, therefore, is a *positive self-concept* (good **self-esteem**).

Why is a positive self-concept so important? A comedian once said, "I wouldn't want to be a member of any organization that would let me be a member." If you cannot accept and love yourself, it will be impossible for you to accept that someone else might love you. And, like the comedian, people who cannot accept themselves generally reject other people.

People who feel positive about themselves are confident and self-sufficient—they do not require continual external validation. A positive self-concept does not mean that someone is self-centered or believes that he or she is always correct, good, and moral and can do no wrong. To accept oneself is to accept one's shortcomings as well as one's strengths—that is, "to accept myself for what I am" (Coutts, 1973). *The manner in which one is raised is important for acquiring a positive self-concept.*

"I think the reason I don't like myself is because of all the problems I had in the past . . . the absence of Mom and Dad, and when they were around so was abuse. I feel that since my parents couldn't accept me, why should I? I felt like a failure, the ugliest person alive, and basically trash. I had tried to kill myself." (from the author's files)

It is not unusual for children who have been neglected or abused to have negative self-concepts as adults and sometimes to be unable to be loving to others (in fact, abused children often become abusive parents). Having loving, caring parents during infancy and childhood teaches us not only that other people do nice things that make us feel good (and thus, that they are good), but that we are worthy of having someone else care about us. The trust that is gained by this experience generalizes to other people as we grow older.

PERSONAL REFLECTIONS
Do you have positive self-esteem? Why or why not? If your self-esteem is less than totally positive, what effects do you think this has on your ability to participate in a loving relationship?

SELF-DISCLOSURE

Self-acceptance and trust in ourselves give us the potential to trust and love others, but for love to really develop, there must be **self-disclosure** by both parties, resulting in an exchange of vulnerabilities (Derlega et al., 1993; Rubin et al., 1980). You cannot really love a person whom you do not really know, and, of course, the same is true for other people. They cannot really love you until they get to know the real you. This is what distinguishes love from infatuation.

Letting others get to know the real you is not always easy. In fact, for some people, emotional intimacy may be more difficult than sexual intimacy. We initially try to look and act our best, but for another person to really get to know you requires that you reveal your needs, feelings, emotions, and values. Unfortunately, some people

self-esteem The feeling one has about oneself.

self-disclosure Revealing one's thoughts, feelings, and emotions to another.

Figure 14–3 For a loving relationship to develop, each person must have good self-esteem and there must be an exchange of vulnerabilities.

go through life wearing a mask, never allowing themselves to be known by others. A study conducted in the 1950s found that women were much more willing than men to disclose personal information to friends or strangers under laboratory conditions (Jourard & Lasakow, 1958). This is what might be expected in a society where gender roles have traditionally favored emotional repressiveness for men and emotional expressiveness for women, but, as you learned in Chapter 10, gender roles have been changing. Nevertheless, a review of 205 studies of self-disclosure found that there was still a gender difference in disclosure—women disclose slightly more than men in relationships (Dindia & Allen, 1992).

People may be reluctant to reveal what they really think or feel out of fear that other people might judge them or might have less respect for them, or even worse, no longer want them as a lover or a friend. This requires trust, and sometimes that trust is misplaced. Some people may even use another person's trust to fulfill their own selfish desires. If John, for example, feels lust for Joanne, he may show her a lot of attention with the goal of having sex with her. Joanne, on the other hand, may actually be fond of John, interpret his attention to her as love, and subsequently reveal her feelings. John may then say "I love you" to Joanne just to fulfill his own selfish sexual goal. After satisfying his sexual curiosity, John may dump Joanne to pursue other sexual con-

quests, leaving Joanne emotionally devastated. She may also be more reluctant to trust again.

All of us need the perceptive ability to avoid placing our trust in those who would abuse it, but for love to develop, we must occasionally take that chance or risk. Relationships develop best when two people self-disclose to one another at about the same time. If Joe reveals some of his true thoughts and feelings to Mary, for example, it is expected that she will reciprocate. Well-timed self-disclosure makes a person more likable in beginning and maintaining social relationships (Collins & Miller, 1994; Vittengl & Holt, 2000). Emotional intimacy is achieved only after a couple has shared a reasonable level of self-disclosure (an exchange of vulnerabilities) and each has accepted his or her partner's state of awareness. At this point, they can be said to be interdependent.

THEORIES OF LOVE

Any textbook that includes the topic of love must—as an obligation, I suppose—present some coverage of the theories of love. But which ones? There are as many theories of love as there are definitions, maybe more. Moreover, the theorists cannot even agree on how to organize love. In his preface to a book containing articles by many theorists, Rubin (1988) states:

> **Many of the contributors to this volume have developed their own taxonomies of love. Each categorizing scheme differs from the next, and there are no ready translation rules from one chapter's formulation to another's. Just as partners with different views of love may find themselves talking past each other . . . I suspect that some of the contributors to this volume may find it difficult to relate to others' perspectives. (p. ix)**

Most theorists touch on only certain aspects of love, and few take the time to support their ideas and conclusions with empirical data. Popular books on love such as Leo Buscaglia's (1972) *Love* or M. Scott Peck's (1978) *The Road Less Traveled* rarely support their claims with any evidence at all. The works of some of the great thinkers (Plato, Aristotle, Kant), on the other hand, treat love as an academic subject and are often lacking in sensitivity.

Experimental social psychologists are the newest group to offer theories of love. As examples of this approach to love, I have selected the works of three pioneers in the field: Cindy Hazen and Phillip Shaver, Robert Sternberg, and John Lee. Other texts may have chosen different theories, but these will give you a good idea of how social psychologists perceive this complex topic we call love.

ATTACHMENT THEORY OF LOVE

How secure and protected did you feel as a child? How do you think your feelings of security (or insecurity) have affected your adult relationships? Questions like these are at the basis of what is called the *attachment theory of love*. Let us examine it in more detail.

The theory developed from early studies which showed that the strength of the infant-caregiver (parent) attachment bond depends on the amount of security offered to the child (i.e., how accessible and responsive the parents are to the child's needs) (Ainsworth et al., 1978; Bowlby, 1969). In young children, separation from the caregiver often causes anxiety and fear, and the researchers looked at how children reacted to this experience. From these studies, Ainsworth et al. (1978) identified three styles of **attachment:** (1) *secure* (children who learn that parents are a source of security and trust); (2) *anxious-ambivalent* (children whose parents are inconsistent, which eventually leads to uncertainty and a variety of emotional reactions that may include actively seeking to be near the parent, ambivalence, and angry outbursts); and (3) *avoidant* (children develop negative attitudes of others because their parents neglect them or either understimulate them or overstimulate them).

Hazen and Shaver (1987) proposed that these attachment styles could be extended to adult romantic relationships. Not only were the frequencies of the different attachment styles in infancy similar to those found in adults, but adults' experiences in romantic relationships were related to their attachment style. Adults with a *secure* attachment style do not fear abandonment and find it easy to get close to others. They have positive views of themselves and others, are well liked by others, and strive for a balance of closeness and independence. Adults with an *anxious-ambivalent* attachment style generally have negative attitudes about themselves and are insecure in their relationships. They fear rejection and try desperately to get close to their partners, in the process giving up much of their independence. Anxious-ambivalent lovers tend to fall easily in love and are very intense in their emotions, but their efforts often scare their partners away.

Avoidants have negative views of others and therefore have difficulties with feelings of intimacy and letting someone get close to them. They desire independence. Individuals with a positive view of others regard relationships to be rewarding, whereas individuals with a negative view of others regard relationships as unrewarding or unnecessary. Studies have shown that slightly more than half of all adults can be called secure, while about one-fourth are avoidant and one-fifth are anxious-ambivalent (Shaver et al., 1998).

More recently, some researchers have expanded the model to four attachment styles (Bartholomew & Horowitz, 1991): *secure, preoccupied* (similar to anxious-ambivalent), and two variations of the avoidant style. *Dismissives* have negative attitudes about others, but positive attitudes about themselves, whereas *fearful avoidants* have negative attitudes about both themselves and others.

What is the evidence to support attachment styles as a legitimate model for love? Among seriously committed couples, there is a high proportion of secure individuals, while among uncommitted individuals there is a much higher proportion of people with other attachment styles (e.g., Kirkpatrick & Davis, 1994). The most common pairing is a secure-secure matching. This is not surprising, as people have more positive responses to secure people, and prefer them as romantic partners, compared to any other style (Chappell & Davis, 1998). When they were not paired with a secure partner, persons with an anxious-avoidant attachment style are most likely to be paired with an avoidant partner. They are also more likely than others to experience unreciprocated love (Aron et al., 1998).

These pairings are consistent with the finding that people with different attachment styles differ in their communication styles. People who are secure or preoccupied give more hugs and other physical comfort to their partners, and also show more involvement and positive responses during conversations (Guerrero, 1996; Kunce & Shaver, 1994). Dismissives and fearful avoidants are less fluent and tend to sit farther away from their partners. They are also much less likely to self-disclose to partners during conversation (Mikulincer & Nachshon, 1991).

Much more work needs to be done with this new theory of love. But with what we have already learned, there appears to be a most interesting relation between adult attachment style and the nature and quality of romantic relationships.

PERSONAL REFLECTIONS
What type of attachment style do you display in your romantic relations? Do you have negative or positive views of yourself? Of others? How has this affected the nature and quality of your romantic relations?

ROBERT STERNBERG'S TRIANGULAR THEORY OF LOVE

Although most people rate their spouse or lover higher for some characteristics than they do their friends (Davis, 1985), this still does not tell us whether liking and loving are qualitatively different emotions or different regions along a single continuum of emotions. Robert Sternberg (1986, 1987) has proposed a *triangular theory of love* in which he takes a broader view of liking and loving. He suggests that all the different positive emotions that people can have for other individuals can be understood by the combination of three components. In his model, each component is viewed as the vertex of a triangle, as shown in Figure 14–4. The triangle should not be viewed as a geometric model, but rather as a useful metaphor for visualizing the way in which the three components are related.

The top vertex of the triangle is **intimacy.** Intimacy refers to those feelings in a relationship that promote closeness or bondedness and the experience of warmth. There are many signs of intimacy, including a desire to promote the welfare of the other, experiencing happiness with and having a high regard for the other, receiving and giving emotional support, having mutual understanding, and valuing the other person in your life (Sternberg & Grajek, 1984). The left-hand vertex represents the experience of **passion,** or those drives leading to physical attraction, sexual relations, and romance. The right-hand vertex is **decision/commitment,** which includes the decision to love another person and the commitment to maintain the relationship over time. More recent studies have verified that people's concepts of love are made up of these three components (Aron & Westbay, 1996).

Sternberg says that the different combinations of these three components result in different kinds of emotions. When all three components are absent, the result is *nonlove.* This characterizes most of our casual relationships, where there is no love or friendship in any meaningful way. If the intimacy component is expressed alone without passion or decision/commitment, it results in *liking.* The word *liking* is not used in a trivial manner to refer to casual acquaintances, but instead refers to the feelings of closeness, bondedness, and warmth in true friendships. When passion is felt in the absence of the other two components, the result is *infatuated love,* or what we call "love at first sight." A person feeling

intimacy Those feelings in a relationship that promote closeness or bondedness and the experience of warmth.

passion The drive leading to physical attraction, sexual relations, and romance.

decision/commitment One of the three basic components in Sternberg's theory of love; the decision that one loves another person and the commitment to maintain the relationship.

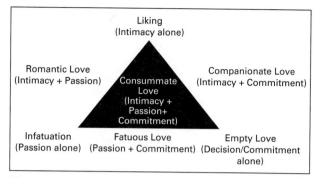

Figure 14–4 Sternberg's triangular model of love. All the different positive emotions that people can have for others are understood by the combinations of intimacy, passion, and decision/commitment.

passion alone is obsessed with the other person as an ideal, rather than as the individual he or she is in reality. The decision and commitment to love another person without intimacy or passion is experienced as *empty love.* In our society, empty love often occurs at the end of stagnant long-term relationships, but in other cultures where marriages are arranged, it may be the first stage in a long-term relationship.

If you look at the triangle, you can see that there are four possible combinations of the components. If you add passionate arousal to liking (the intimacy component alone), the result is *romantic love.* It results from two people being drawn together both physically and emotionally. There is no commitment, and the lovers may even know that a permanent relationship is not possible, as in "summer love." This is the Romeo-and-Juliet type of love that poets, playwrights, and novelists are so fond of writing about.

The combination of intimacy and decision/commitment without passion leads to *companionate love,* a long-term committed friendship. Sternberg (1988) believes that most romantic love relationships that survive do so by eventually turning into companionate love relationships.

When a commitment is made on the basis of passion without the experience of intimacy, the result is *fatuous love.* This leads to whirlwind romances, the type we often read about involving Hollywood stars. Without intimacy, there is a high risk that the relationship will end once the passion starts to fade (these romances are often over so quickly that there has been no chance for the intimacy component to develop).

Sternberg believes that complete love, what he calls *consummate love,* is found only in relationships that include all three components—passion, intimacy, and commitment. It is his belief that this is the type of love that most of us strive for in our romantic relationships. Thus, other types of relationships are viewed as lacking something (i.e., one or more of the three components).

JOHN LEE'S "MANY COLORS OF LOVE"

The English language gives us only one word—love—to describe a number of interpersonal relationships. Words such as liking, affection, and infatuation are not considered to be synonymous with love. As a result, our different experiences of love tend to be measured as differences in quantity: "Tell me *how much* you love me" or "I love you *more* than I've ever loved anybody." In our search for a partner, we hope to find someone who loves us *as much as* we love them. When relationships do not work out, we often deny any experience of love (e.g., "After a while, I realized I really didn't love Suzy," or "Suzy really didn't love me"). It's as if our experiences of love are measured in black and white and shades of gray.

Sociologist John Lee (1974, 1976, 1988) believes that there is more than one type of partnering love, with no one of them being singled out as "true love." Rather than black and white, Lee uses the analogy of colors to explain love. Different styles of love are portrayed by different colors. According to Lee, mutual love results from two styles or colors (not intensities) that make a good match.

Just as different colors result from blending red, yellow, and blue, the three primary pigment colors, Lee proposes that different styles of loving arise from blending three primary love-styles—eros, storge, and ludus. Let us look at each of these and their various combinations and then see what makes a good match.

THE PRIMARY COLORS

Eros (named after the Greek mythological figure) is a highly idealized love based on physical beauty. According to Lee, every erotic lover has a specific ideal physical type that turns him or her on. Erotic lovers look for physical perfection, knowing it is rare, and when they find someone who embodies their ideal, they quickly feel a strong physical attraction and emotions they perceive as love. It is as if they have always known this person that they have just met—their romantic ideal. Thus, the erotic lover is inclined to feel "love at first sight" and wants to have an intimate relationship immediately. Erotic lovers are very affectionate and openly communicate with their idealized partners. However, they are usually quick to find flaws and shortcomings in their new partners, so that many of their relationships are quick to fizzle out because the partner cannot live up to their unrealistic ideal. Therefore, erotic love is generally very transient, and erotic lovers tend to fall in love very often. Erotic lovers desire to have an exclusive relationship with their partners, but they are not jealous and do not try to possess them.

Lee's eros is very similar to the "passionate love" described by Berscheid and Walster (1978). It is quite different from the eros of Plato's *Symposium,* which was totally good and wholesome. Lee's choice of terms here is perhaps unfortunate.

Ludus (from the Latin word for "play" and pronounced "loo'-dus") is a self-centered type of love. The ludic lover avoids commitment and treats love like a game, often viewing the chase as more pleasurable than the prize.

> "I'm a 23 year old male in your MWF Sex Class. . . . I first had intercourse at age 13. . . . As of this writing, I have had intercourse with 508 women. I have done it 1,823 times in the last 9 1/2 years. My goal is 2,000 times by 1989. I've devoted a notebook strictly for recording names, dates, and places of sexual encounters. . . . I can say that I honestly love all women." (from the author's files)

Ludus is similar to Sternberg's fatuous love. Ludic lovers have no romantic ideal and never see any one person often enough to become dependent on them, or vice versa. Sex is had for fun, not for expressing commitment, for ludic lovers are not very emotional and do not have feelings of falling in love. They avoid jealous partners who might spoil the fun and see nothing wrong with having more than one partner at the same time. They are also more likely than people with other love-styles to use verbal coercion to obtain sex (Sarwer et al., 1993). Ludic lovers can be deceptive with their partners, like Don Juan, but many play the game honestly in order to avoid having feelings of guilt (and thus their partners know exactly what they are getting). This promiscuous type of love-style may seem empty to people with other love-styles, but most ludic lovers look back on their relationships with pleasure.

Storge (from the Greek, and pronounced stor'-gay) is an affectionate type of love that develops from friendship slowly over time. It is essentially the same as Sternberg's companionate love. The storgic lover does not have a physical ideal and does not go looking for love, but instead develops feelings of affection and commitment with a partner through experiencing activities that they both enjoy. Storgic lovers generally cannot recall a specific point in time when they fell in love. They are more practical than emotional, and their relationships lack the passionate emotional highs (but also avoid the dramatic downturns). In fact, storgic lovers would be embarrassed by having to say "I love you," or by excessive shows of emotion from their partners. They are more interested in talking about their shared interests

eros A highly idealized type of romantic love that is based mainly on physical beauty. Erotic lovers look for physical perfection.

ludus A self-centered type of love. Ludic lovers avoid commitment and treat love as a game, often viewing the chase as more pleasurable than the prize.

storge An affectionate type of love that grows from friendship.

than their mutual love. A true storgic lover would probably find this whole chapter very silly.

THE SECONDARY COLORS

How many different love-styles are there? You can get numerous colors by blending red, yellow, and blue, and the same is true for mixing the primary love-styles. Look at the color wheel in Figure 14–5. The apexes of the large triangle within the circle represent the three primary colors. Each pair can be combined by either going around the circle or along the edge of the triangle. When you combine two things, new properties may emerge and others may be lost. No one, for example, could have predicted the properties of water by looking at the properties of hydrogen and oxygen. Let us now look at a few of the numerous combinations that can result from mixing the primary love-styles.

Pragma (from the Greek, for "pragmatic") is a rational or practical style of loving resulting from combining ludus and storge. Pragmatic lovers have the manipulative confidence of ludic lovers and consciously look for a compatible mate. They are not looking for an exciting romance or affair, but instead (like the storgic lover) wants love to grow out of friendship. However, unlike the storgic lover, the person with a pragmatic love-style has a shopping list of qualities he or she is looking for in a mate and consciously and carefully sorts candidates to see if they have all the desired qualities. Women, for example, give more weight than men to socioeconomic status, ambitiousness, and intelligence in choosing a mate (Feingold, 1992). If a suitable mate cannot be found at work or in the community, the pragmatic lover may join organizations (e.g., church, club) or even try computer dating services to find a compatible partner. Pragmatic lovers want their partners to reciprocate signs of thoughtfulness and commitment, but do not like excessive displays of emotion or jealousy. Sexual compatibility is not unimportant, but it is treated more as a technical skill that can be improved upon if need be rather than as the result of chemistry. A person with this love-style views herself or himself as "in love" and tends to remain loyal and faithful as long as the partner continues to be a good match.

Mania (from the Greek, meaning love that hits like a lightning bolt) is a love-style characterized by an intense, obsessive emotional dependency on the attention and affection of one's partner. People with manic love-styles are "in love with love" (the excitement of falling in love). Dorothy Tennov (1979) coined the term *limerence* to describe extreme "head over heels" love in which one is obsessed with the loved one (i.e., extreme pre-

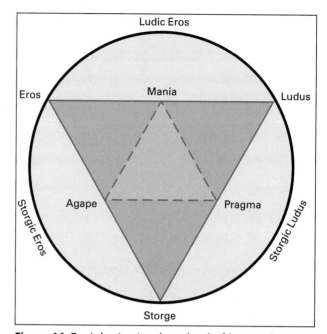

Figure 14–5 John Lee's color wheel of love-styles.

occupation and acute longing for exclusivity). Mania is also similar to Sternberg's (1987) infatuated love. The manic lover is intensely jealous and repeatedly needs to be assured of being loved. The feelings of mania are so intense that this kind of love can be like an addiction, with the manic lover often not even liking the partner, but at the same time unable to break off the relationship. As a result, manic lovers ride an emotional roller coaster: extreme highs when the partner is showing them attention, and extreme lows when he or she is not.

This love-style results from mixing eros and ludus. The manic lover wants an intense, physically stimulating relationship, but usually chooses inappropriate partners and madly projects desired qualities onto them. Everyone but the manic lover can see that the partner does not really have those qualities. The manic lover attempts to manipulate the relationship (e.g., by pulling back and not calling the partner), but is too dependent on the partner's love to remain confidently detached like the ludic lover (guess who ends up breaking down and calling first?). Because the manic lover is unable to break off the relationship, it is usually the partner who does so, leaving the manic lover devastated. Although many people have had an experience of manic love, the true manic lover is apt to repeat the same type of relationship again and again.

Agape (from the Greek, and pronounced ah-gah′-pay) is a selfless, altruistic love-style that puts the interest of the loved person ahead of the lover's own interest, even if it means great sacrifice. It is similar to Maslow's

pragma A rational or practical type of love. Pragmatic lovers actively look for a "good match."

mania A type of love characterized by an intense emotional dependency on the attention and affection of one's lover.

agape A type of romantic love that puts the interest of the loved person ahead of one's own, even if it means great sacrifice.

(1968) "being love" and Sternberg's empty love. This is the style of loving proposed by St. Augustine ("Love means: I want you to be") as a goal for all Christians, and the kind of love to aspire to, according to Fromm (1956). It is the result of combining eros and storge. Rather than yearning to find the perfect partner, the agapic lover submits to the perfect will of God and becomes the devoted friend of those who need his or her love. Agapic lovers believe it is their duty to love, but the feelings are often not directed toward a specific person, but instead to all who need their love.

Lee believes that agape is the least common love-style, and he is probably correct. In fact, some have questioned whether humans even have the capacity to feel true agape, which is selfless (see Nygren's *Agape and Eros,* 1982, and Singer's trilogy *The Nature of Love,* 1984–1987). An example that is often given is found in Charles Dickens's novel *A Tale of Two Cities,* a love story that takes place during the French Revolution. The hero, Sidney Carton, is in love with Lucie Manette, who is in love with Charles Darnay. At the end of the story, Charles Darnay is sentenced to die by guillotine. Sidney's love for Lucie is so strong that he takes Darnay's place and is guillotined so that Lucie can be with the man she loves. But Sidney probably would not have done this if he hadn't felt passionately about her. He certainly would not have done it for anyone else. However, there is no passion or any other type of self-interest in agape. Humans may not be able to achieve agape, but they can strive to achieve a love-style that approaches it.

OTHER COMBINATIONS. Pragma, mania, and agape are not the only possible outcomes of mixing the primary colors. Lee's analogy is mixing flour and water. Try mixing them when the water is hot, and then try it again when the water is cold. You are mixing the same ingredients, but the results are different. Other combinations are possible (e.g., storgic eros, storgic ludus, ludic eros). For a full description of these, see Lee (1988).

FINDING A GOOD MATCH

Lee's theory has received support from the results of a large-scale study (Hendrick & Hendrick, 1986). Over 1,300 students were asked to agree or disagree with various statements about love. Their responses clustered into six different groups that closely fit the six categories just reviewed. There were some interesting gender and ethnic differences as well. Men tended to be more ludic than women, who tended to be more pragmatic, storgic, and manic. Asian Americans tended to be more pragmatic and storgic than other ethnic groups.

Did you recognize your love-style from the preceding list? There are tests you can take to determine your love-style preference (Hendrick & Hendrick, 1986) but Lee (1988) suggests that you just review your own experiences. When doing this, keep in mind that love-styles are not necessarily fixed. We are not born with a particular love-style that we are stuck with for life, but instead we can learn from our experiences and change our preferences (we cannot learn from our experiences if we look at love as black and white and dismiss failed love as due simply to differences in intensity of feelings). Thus, you may have experienced more than one of the preceding styles. It is not unusual, for example, for a person's first love-style to be mania, or for a person to experience mania for the first time in midlife after a storgic marriage has become dull and uninteresting (conversely, one may prefer a comfortable storgic relationship after experiencing mania).

Lee believes that the secret to finding mutual love is to find a good match, not in the amount of love each person gives, but in the style of loving. There are some obvious bad matches—a manic lover with a ludic lover, for example. The ludic lover's vanity will enjoy all the attention given by the manic lover, but the possessiveness and jealousy of the manic lover are not desired. Manic lovers thrive on problems, and the ludic lover is guaranteed to provide them. It is not uncommon, however, to find this pairing, and while not very happy and ultimately doomed, a manic-ludic relationship is always interesting.

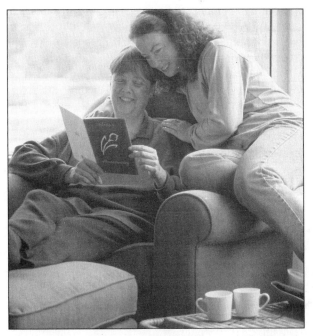

Figure 14–6 Christian ideals of love as a desire for another person "to be" acknowledge that love can be felt for a lover, a parent, a child, or a friend of the opposite or the same sex.

With the exception of mania and ludus, *a good match generally results from two styles that are close on the chart* (see Figure 14–5). A pragmatic love-style and storgic love-style make a good match, for example. The farther apart two love-styles are, the less likely it is that they would make a good match. The erotic or manic lover, for example, is likely to find the storgic love-style dull and regard it as friendship without passion and not love at all. The storgic lover will similarly accuse the behavior of the erotic or manic lover as not being love. A relationship between two people with these two different styles is probably doomed within a short time. In the end, each may accuse the other of not having really loved, but in reality both will have loved in his or her own way. It simply was not a good match in love-styles.

Studies have shown that whether or not a relationship is successful can, in fact, be partially predicted by the compatibility of Lee's love-styles (Davis & Latty-Mann, 1987; Hendrick et al., 1988). For example, it has been found that college students prefer dating partners who have love-styles similar to their own (Hahn & Blass, 1997). One exception noted by this and other studies is the attraction between people with mania and agape love-styles, suggesting that these two types may not be as different as Lee originally believed. As a general rule, individuals who score high in the positive love-styles (eros, agape, storge) show greater relationship satisfaction than others (Meeks et al., 1998). The ludus love-style is a strong negative predictor of satisfaction.

So the next time you find yourself attracted to someone, do not ask yourself how much this person loves you, but instead ask yourself how (in what style of love) he or she loves you and whether or not your colors make a good match. Lee (1988) warns us, however, not to define mutual love in terms of longevity. Two people may have a mutually satisfying relationship, but just because it ends because one of them has a change in love-style does not mean it wasn't wonderful while it lasted.

> *PERSONAL REFLECTIONS*
> *How do you define love? Which of Lee's love-styles best describes you in your present or last relationship? Do you think that you are locked into this love-style for future relationships? Why or why not?*

WHICH THEORY IS CORRECT?

jealousy An emotional state that is aroused by a perceived threat to a valued relationship or position.

At this point you may be very confused. Of the theories of love you have read about in this chapter, some have characterized love as a single dimension (Freud, 1933/1953; Tennov, 1979). Others have viewed love as resulting from two or more factors—Maslow's (1968) D-love and B-love; Hatfield's (1988) and Walster and Walster's (1978) passionate and companionate love; Sternberg's (1987) triangular theory. All of these focus on the structure of love. Still others focus on the processes of love—Lee's (1974, 1976, 1988) colors of love; Hazen and Shaver's (1987) attachment styles. Is any one of them correct? If so, does that mean the others are wrong?

Barnes and Sternberg (1997) have proposed a *hierarchical model* to explain the structure of love, and say that the other theories appear to differ because they are looking at different levels of the hierarchy. At the top of the hierarchy is a single entity we call love. Underlying this are several related entities (the second level), which in turn are made up of even smaller entities (the third level). These entities can be broken down into even smaller features.

In a series of studies, Barnes and Sternberg identified eight clusters of features (the third level) that contribute to our feeling of love. The individual clusters were different, depending on how they collected the data, but included things such as sexuality, trust, sincerity, compatibility, fulfillment, mutual need, and intimacy. When they looked at how these clusters were related, two main clusters (the second level) emerged—a "hot" cluster, which some have called passionate love, and a "warm" cluster, which has been called companionate love. Eros and agape would also be a good comparison, as would Sternberg's passion and intimacy components in his triangular theory. Together, these two main clusters, in turn, form what we call love.

In summary, Barnes and Sternberg find evidence that the many structural theories only appear to be different because they are looking at different levels of the features that make up what we call love.

JEALOUSY

Shakespeare, in *Othello*, described it as "the green-eyed monster which doth mock the meat it feeds on." He was referring, of course, to the emotion we call jealousy. How would you feel if your partner appeared to be forming an emotional attachment to a co-worker and has been spending a great deal of time with him or her? How would you feel if your partner and another person appeared to be sexually interested in one another? These are situations that typically cause many people to feel jealous. **Jealousy** is an emotional state "that is aroused by a perceived threat to a valued relationship or position and motivates behavior aimed at countering the threat" (Daly et al., 1982). The perceived threat can involve more than the actual loss of a partner; it can also include loss of face, loss of self-esteem, and loss of feeling special (Cano & O'Leary, 1997). Jealousy is a negative emotion that is hard to describe, but it usually involves anger, humiliation, fear, depression, and a sense of helplessness (Guerrero & Anderson, 1998).

At least 50 percent of people tend to be jealous (Pines & Aronson, 1983), but in only about 1 percent is it delusional or pathological (see Cano & O'Leary, 1997). Thus some researchers look at jealousy as a dispositional (personality) variable. Some people become jealous if their partner has even casual interactions with other persons. What type of person is most likely to become jealous? Research has shown that people with low self-esteem who are personally unhappy with their lives (Pines & Aronson, 1983) and those who place great value on things like popularity, wealth, fame, and physical attractiveness are more likely than others to be jealous individuals (Salovey & Rodin, 1985). Not surprisingly, attachment style is related to feelings of jealousy (Guerrero, 1998). People with preoccupied attachment styles are the most likely to have negative emotions and engage in watching and checking on their partners.

However, cultural and situational factors also play a major role (Cano & O'Leary, 1997). Jealousy is most likely to occur in cultures that consider marriage as a means for guilt-free sex, security, and social recognition (Hupka, 1981). This is true of American culture (as well as many others), and in the United States sexual jealousy by men is one of the leading causes of beating and murder of wives (Guerrero & Anderson, 1998).

Research shows that just as many women as men have feelings of jealousy (Bringle & Buunk, 1985). However, there are important gender differences in jealousy as well. Men are much more likely to become jealous to the perception of a partner's *sexual* infidelity, whereas women are much more likely to experience jealousy as a result of a partner's *emotional* infidelity (Buss et al., 1992; Wiederman & Kendall, 1999). Evolutionary psychologists argue that this difference between men and women is innate, resulting from men's need for certainty about paternity (after the energy spent in courting and mating, he wants to know that he is the father) and women's need for male investment in the children (Buss et al., 1992). Others question the evolutionary explanation and point out that the two types of infidelity, sexual and emotional, are not independent (DeSteno & Salovey, 1996; Harris & Christenfeld, 1996). Men, for example, may be likely to think that if a partner is emotionally involved, she is also having sex. In fact, in a recent study with college undergraduates, both men and women were more upset at the idea of sexual infidelity than they were about emotional infidelity (Nannini & Meyers, 2000).

Men's and women's reactions to jealousy also tend to differ (Sharpsteen, 1991; White, 1981). Women tend to experience jealousy when feeling inadequate, and they tend to respond by making themselves more attractive to their partner. Men, on the other hand, tend to initially experience jealous feelings and then have feelings of inadequacy, and they tend to seek solace in outside relationships.

Paradoxically, while jealousy is an emotional reaction to a perceived threat to a relationship and self-esteem, the expression of jealousy is likely to further damage both (Cano & O'Leary, 1997). Withdrawing from or attacking one's partner, for example, may cause him or her to withdraw or attack, thus increasing the fear of loss, which, in turn, may increase or prolong the feeling of jealousy.

How, then, should you deal with occasional bouts of jealousy? Acknowledge your feelings to your partner and describe what caused them (Anderson et al., 1995). If you choose to go to counseling (probably a good idea), go together—seek therapy as a couple (Cano & O'Leary, 1997). Conversely, never purposely try to make your partner jealous, as a few people do in order to get attention (White, 1980). Establish mutual trust, while at the same time respecting your partner's need for some personal freedom. If you can do this, your chances are good of keeping that green-eyed monster at bay.

> *PERSONAL REFLECTIONS*
>
> *Do you ever have feelings of jealousy? Are they so strong that they interfere with your relationship(s)? What are the conditions that usually cause you to become jealous? Does your partner ever try to make you jealous? What things might you do to control these feelings?*

MAINTAINING A RELATIONSHIP

There is hardly any activity, any enterprise, which is started with such tremendous hopes and expectations and yet which fails so regularly as love.
(Erich Fromm, 1956)

Many factors play a role in the initiation of a relationship. These include (a) physical attractiveness—men generally attach more importance to this than women (Buss, 1989; Sangrador & Yela, 2000; Walster et al., 1966); (b) proximity—people are most likely to fall in love with someone they interact with often (at work, school, etc.) (Berscheid & Walster, 1978); (c) similarity—people tend to be attracted to others who have similar love-styles (Lee, 1988), interests, values, intellectual abilities, personality traits, and degrees of attractiveness (there is no evidence to support the old saying that "opposites attract") (Arrindell & Luteijn, 2000; Byrne et al., 1986; Wetzel & Insko, 1982); and (d) reciprocity—we tend to like people who show that they like us (no one likes rejection) (Berscheid & Walster, 1978; Curtis & Miller, 1988).

Let us return for a moment to our hypothetical example of Susan and David (see "How Do I Know if This Is Really Love?"). All four factors have played a role in encouraging these two people to begin a relationship. Susan—and David, let's suppose—have experienced physiological arousal in each other's presence and have interpreted their responses as "being in love." The relationship continues to develop if there is mutual self-disclosure, equity in what each wishes to gain from (and give to) the relationship, and finally, commitment. But will it last?

Couples who experience a great level of love at the beginning of a relationship are more likely to stay together than couples who were not as much in love (Hill & Peplau, 1998). Relationships tend to last when partners idealize one another (Murray et al., 1996). Other studies show that personality characteristics are also important in determining whether or not a relationship lasts. People who are similar are not only attracted to one another, they are also more likely to stay together (Weber, 1998). However, even when a couple is well matched, they are going to have to learn to deal with change.

> The divorce rate is so high not because people make foolish choices, but because they are drawn together for reasons that matter less as time goes on. (Robert Sternberg, 1985)

If there is anything that is unavoidable in life, it is change. Couples will be faced with a variety of new challenges in life, including parenthood, financial crises, career-related stress, and, inevitably, aging. Two people who believe themselves to be in complete harmony during the dating, passion, and romantic loving periods are often surprised to find themselves in disagreement on how to handle these matters. Many couples, for example, report the child-rearing years to be the most stressful and least satisfying in their marriages (Hendrick & Hendrick, 1983; Morgan et al., 1988). Fixed gender roles—or, conversely, changing gender roles—may contribute to this (see Chapter 10). Today, there are the added challenges of two-job families and job-related moves far away from family and friends.

THE DECLINE OF PASSION

The challenges in life are not the only things that change. People also change over time. One of the things that normally occur in a relationship, leading to changes in how we interact with our partners, is **habituation.** Think of your favorite food. What makes it your favorite food? The taste and smell are no doubt important, but I am willing to bet that another factor is that you

habituation Responding less positively to a stimulus with repeated exposure to it.

do not have it very often. If you were served your favorite food every day for a month, do you think it would remain your favorite? Would we look forward to Thanksgiving turkey if we ate turkey every week? It's doubtful. When organisms, including humans, are repeatedly exposed to a stimulus that is initially very positive, it becomes less positive over time. This is why popular weekly TV shows eventually go off the air and why hit songs eventually drop off the Billboard "Top 10" list. We grow tired of seeing and hearing them. The same is true of the ability of other people to stimulate us—socially, emotionally, intellectually, and alas, sexually. Of all the challenges that a couple face in a relationship, habituation is certainly one of the greatest ones (Byrne & Murnen, 1988).

The decline of passion is almost inevitable, for a large component of passion is novelty and fantasy. A new partner cannot continue to arouse strong emotions, and with the passage of time it takes greater and greater stimulation to cause the same response that once was brought about by a mere glance or touch. As the passion subsides and fantasy is replaced with reality, the result is often disappointment. In a study of 62 cultures, Fisher (1992) found that the divorce rate peaked around the fourth year of marriage (7 years if a couple has another child 2 or 3 years after the first). The reason most frequently given by couples in the process of divorce is that they had "fallen out of (romantic) love" and were bored (see Roberts, 1992). (Abuse by men and emotional instability by women are additional frequently given reasons; see Shackelford & Buss, 1997.) Marital therapy has traditionally focused on improving communication and helping the development of rational skills, and only recently have therapists realized the importance of addressing emotional problems—the loss of sexual attraction and the ebbing of romantic love (Roberts, 1992). Many couples make the mistake of allowing their sex lives to become ritualized, but even when the passion has subsided, a sexual relationship can remain exciting, fun, and fulfilling if the couple work for variety and spontaneity (see Chapter 13).

Although passion will decline with time due to familiarity and habituation, there is no need for *intimacy* (those feelings and experiences that promote closeness and bondedness) to decline. The key to maintaining a relationship is replacing passion with those things that lead to companionate love.

GROWING TOGETHER/GROWING APART: WILL COMPANIONATE LOVE DEVELOP?

To maintain their relationship, Susan and David must simultaneously deal with the need for similarity in the relationship, the inevitable changes that occur (e.g., they will not always be in school together), and the natural process of habituation. Similarity, so important in establishing their relationship, can be maintained and habituation can be kept to a minimum by embarking on new activities together (Byrne & Murnen, 1988). For example, they may find it stimulating to engage in new sports and games together, share new hobbies, *try new sexual experiences together* (see Chapter 13), join dinner groups, plan vacations together, and/or seek new educational opportunities together. One of the major predictors of marital success is the number of shared pleasurable activities (Ogden & Bradburn, 1968).

Couples in happy, long-lasting relationships frequently say that they regard their partner as their best friend. As stated by Schwartz (1994, p. 28), "The possibility of achieving a deep friendship with a spouse represents the most exciting goal of marriage." Couples who are unhappy in their relationships often report that their children are their only or their greatest source of satisfaction together (Luckey & Bain, 1970). Whether or not Susan and David develop intimacy and companionate love will depend, of course, on their commitment (the third component necessary in Sternberg's model for consummate love). Couples who successfully accomplish this grow together; those who do not grow apart.

Married lovers grow within love; they develop into better human beings. (Erich Fromm, 1965)

What is meant by growing together or growing apart? I will try to demonstrate this with the use of intersecting circles (Levinger, 1988). Each person in the relationship is represented by a circle; the degree of intimacy shared is shown by the amount of overlap. The amount of passion felt by one person for the other is represented by plus (+) signs within the circle at the periphery of the intersection.

Look now at Figure 14–7. At the beginning of Susan and David's relationship (two circles at top), both are going to college. Their interests are shown within the circles, and each has a different set of friends: C, D, E, F, and G for Susan, and H, I, J, K, L, and M for David. Susan and David met and began to date, you recall, while taking the same course. Because they have a great deal in common, they have a lot to talk about when they are together: their college courses; their good, bad, and peculiar professors; their campus activities and sporting events; and, of course, their career goals. Let us suppose that they both play tennis and that dancing is their favorite activity on dates. David even goes bowling with Susan, although he doesn't like it much. Over time they establish a mutual set of friends, including other couples (C-D and K-L) and singles (N). They each still have their own sets of friends as

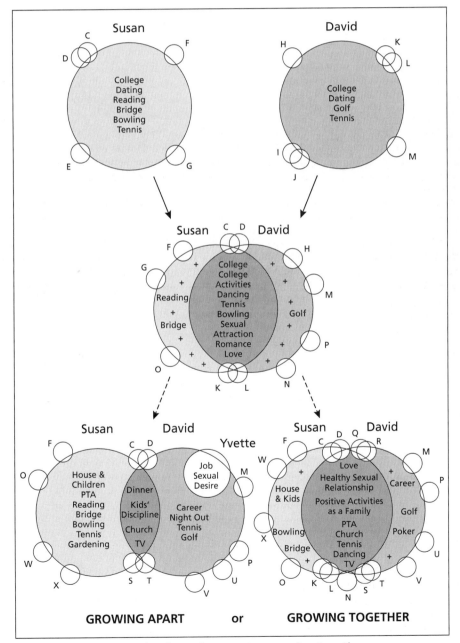

Figure 14–7 An example of growing apart or growing together.

well (each has lost contact with some, retained some, and gained some new ones, and each enjoys some activities not shared by the other—bridge and reading for Susan and golf for David). There is a great deal of passion felt by both Susan and David, and before long they tell one another that they are in love (decision). Dating is now more than just a good time, for there is a romantic component to being together. They realize that they share a great deal of each other's lives (i.e., there is a strong intimacy component, as shown by the amount of overlap in the circles in the middle), and neither can imagine life without the other. They make the commitment to have a lifelong relationship.

Let us now jump several years ahead and see what has happened to our imaginary couple. They no longer have the opportunity to spend most of the day together, for college is now just a distant memory. Instead, one of them is pursuing a career and spends 8 to 10 hours a day in an office (in today's world, it could be either Susan or David, but let us assume here that it is David), while the other is a full-time house-and-child caretaker. Yes, our imaginary couple now have children, and they only see each other briefly in the morning, in the evening before they go to sleep, and on the weekends (assuming that our career person does not work weekends as well). How they adjust to this big change will determine whether the relationship remains positive or turns negative.

Unfortunately, many couples **grow apart** over time. Let's assume, for example, that Susan now goes to bowling league, plays bridge and tennis with friends, and enjoys reading and gardening, all without David. David, on the other hand, plays golf and tennis with friends and enjoys an occasional night out with friends, all without Susan. They rarely go dancing anymore, and most of their time together is spent watching TV (with a minimal amount of conversation). Susan and David have children, but they do very little together as a family. David considers it Susan's duty to go to the PTA and drive the children to and from all their activities, even when he is home. Susan and David and their children eat dinner together (quickly) and go to church together, but most of Susan and David's conversations about their children involve school and discipline problems. Raising their children is treated more as a responsibility than as a blessing. Although Susan and David live together and have children, they actually share less now than when they were dating (there is less intimacy, indicated by less overlap in the circles at the lower left in Figure 14–7). There is no passion left, and very little affection (e.g., hugging, kissing, holding hands) is ever displayed between them. They have grown apart. This is not uncommon.

> "I am married, yet feel as if I do not have a husband. He goes hunting every weekend during hunting season, and goes fishing a lot too. Between his softball league and poker games at the club, most weeknights are taken as well. Most of my time is taken up by the kids' activities and what social life I have is spent with other wives. Most of the time I am too tired to make love when my husband is in the mood, which is not very often. A friend recently described our marriage as 'married singles.'" (from the author's files)

People generally grow apart very slowly, and by the time they realize it, they may have little left in common. At this point, some people may think that it is easier to form a new relationship than to work at their present one. For example, let us suppose that David spends a great deal of time with Yvette while at work (see Figure 14–7). They are together all day at least 5 days a week. They talk about the boss, fellow workers, job-related problems, and career goals. They even start telling each other about their personal problems at home. Add sexual attraction and feelings of passion, and David may conclude that he has as much in common with Yvette as he once had with Susan when they were in college together. David may decide to have an affair with Yvette, or leave Susan for Yvette. Unless David learns to work at keeping a relationship strong, however, this will just be a short-term solution, for over time David's passionate feelings for Yvette will subside as well and they, too, will grow apart.

Let us now look at another possible outcome for David and Susan. People change over time, but a couple who **grow together** substitute new common interests as old ones drop out (see Figure 14–7). In place of college, which once gave them both a great deal to talk about together, our couple view their children and family activities as something very positive. They go to movies as a family, have picnics together, go to the zoo together, and both are involved in Little League, the swimming team, the Boy Scouts and Girl Scouts, the PTA, and church and church social activities. Because they view their children's activities as positive experiences, our two adults have a great deal to talk about. They have substituted new shared activities for some of the ones they used to do together. They still find time (or *make time*) to play tennis on the weekends and go to movies, and they still enjoy dancing together as they did when they were dating. They also have a large number of mutual friends. It is not necessary for Susan and David to do everything together in order to be happy. In addition to being apart during weekdays, David still plays golf regularly and enjoys an occasional evening of poker with friends, while Susan has joined a bowling league (David refuses to bowl anymore) and

growing apart Having fewer common interests over time.

growing together Maintaining common interests over time.

"*When I fell in love with you, suddenly your eyes didn't seem close together. Now they seem close together again.*"

plays bridge with friends. They are different from the way they were when they were dating, but the amount of shared interests is just as great as then. Their feelings of passion for one another have declined, of course (hearts don't beat faster, breathing doesn't get heavier, and palms don't sweat when they see each other), but their sexual interest in one another remains strong. They enjoy each other's bodies and seek variety in the way they stimulate one another. There has been no decline in intimacy. They have grown together.

PERSONAL REFLECTIONS

For those presently in a long-lasting relationship: Have the activities you share with your partner changed since you first began dating? Have new shared activities replaced old ones? Are you growing together or growing apart? If you feel that you are growing apart, what can you do to change this?

COPING WITH BREAKUPS

Undo it, take it back, make every day the previous one until I am returned to the day before the one that made you gone. (Rapoport, 1994, p. 24)

We do not enter into a romantic relationship with expectations that it will end. Thus, breaking up is one of life's most painful experiences, but something that most of us have experienced. Many things commonly occur during the breakup process. Let us examine three of them (Weber, 1998; Weiss, 1975).

One thing that almost everyone engages in during a breakup is *obsessive review*, a "constant, absorbing,

sometimes maddening preoccupation [of the other and the situation] that refuses to accept any conclusion" (Weiss, 1975, p. 79). We review, again and again, the relationship and the breakup, searching for reasons. "Why?" "What did I do that caused this?" This process can detract from all other endeavors, but can be useful if it helps prevent breakups in future relationships.

Breaking up almost always includes *emotional and social loneliness* as well. Emotionally, you feel isolated, missing your ex-partner and everything that he or she brought to your life. But you can also end up socially isolated as well. Friends you had in common with your ex-partner may have to pick sides, or, because they feel awkward, may avoid both of you. You may be left wondering who your friends are and where you fit in.

The third, common experience that people often have to deal with is that their *ex-partner is still around*. If you are the one who was left, he or she is a constant reminder of the rejection (and possibly a reminder to others that you are rejectable). On the other hand, if you are the one who broke off the relationship, your ex may be telling everyone of how much you are to blame. Part of the process, then, is trying to "save face" (Weber, 1998).

To make matters worse, breaking up is usually a process, not limited to a clean break at a single point in time. When it is finally over, we want to believe that our ex-partner once felt as we did (do), that we will be remembered.

Psychologist Ann Weber (1998) has offered several suggestions to help the brokenhearted deal with their loss: (1) express your emotions (sorrow, anger) to someone who is a sympathetic listener, or write down your thoughts; (2) try to figure out what happened, and again, it may help to write it down; (3) do not idealize your ex, but instead focus on the real person, including his or her faults and shortcomings; (4) prepare to feel better (e.g., find what is funny or ironic in your experience) and expect to heal (think back on other physical or emotional injuries in your life and realize that you have always healed); (5) do not shut yourself off from others and let them know what you need from them at this time; and (6) take the perspective that your life is about to change and look at it as a new start. Do something new that you have always wanted to try—traveling, writing, entertainment, anything!

And so, we take our lessons to heart. We take this heart, this new heart and self, full of hope, humor, and irony, and we face the world—a new world with uncharted possibilities and dangers. Perhaps we try once again, explore a new love, although it will not be the same. Then again, the pain reminds us we do not want it to be exactly the same. We have some memories and fantasies to cherish, some sense of hard-won meaning, the moral of the story. Together these help to forge a sense of promise. Thus, silly to risk it, but crazy not to, we try again, and we take heart. (Weber, 1998, p. 304)

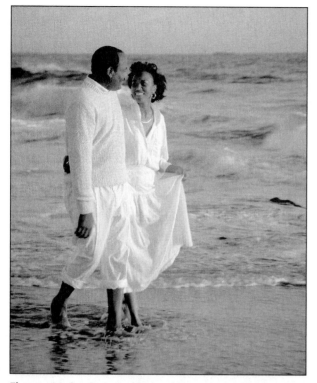

Figure 14–8 Companionate love is a stable kind of love based on togetherness, trust, sharing, affection, and a concern for the welfare of the other.

BECOMING MORE INTIMATE

For most couples, the passion component is generally greatest early in a relationship and then declines over time. Therefore, one of the most important things in maintaining a relationship is developing and maintaining intimacy. Sternberg (1986, 1988) defined intimacy as those feelings in a relationship that promote closeness or bondedness and the experience of warmth. Similarly, Elaine Hatfield (1984) defines it as "a process in which people attempt to get close to another; to explore similarities (and differences) in the way they think, feel, and behave."

True intimacy requires mutual understanding. It is easy to share our similarities and positive feelings, but what about our differences and negative feelings? In order to become really intimate with someone, you must share your differences as well. Hatfield (1988) has made several suggestions designed to teach couples to become more intimate. Let us briefly examine these.

1. Both individuals in a relationship need to *accept themselves as they are*. I have discussed this earlier in the chapter, but the need for self-acceptance bears repeating. *Your* best may not be *the* best, but it is all that anyone, including yourself, can ask of you. Learn to accept your ideas and feelings as legitimate.

2. Each individual in a relationship needs to *recognize his or her partner for what that person is*. As hard as we may be on ourselves, we are often harder on our partners because they are not everything we would want them to be, and we cannot understand why they will not change. Intimacy is not possible with an imaginary "perfect" partner. It can only occur when one recognizes one's mate for what he or she really is— weaknesses as well as strengths.

3. Each individual must *feel comfortable to express himself or herself*. People are often hesitant to express any doubts, irritation, or anger to their partners in a loving relationship. To do so requires that an individual be capable of independence, for independence and intimacy go hand in hand (Hatfield, 1988). An individual who is totally dependent on his or her mate is unlikely to express any anxieties or fears. It is important that we express positive feelings for our partners, for the ratio of positive to negative interactions is a key factor in maintaining a happy relationship (Byrne & Murnen, 1988). Positive feelings for one's partner can and should be communicated in many ways (e.g., by eye contact, holding hands and other physical closeness, thoughtful phone calls, and cards or gifts, as well as sexual interest and verbal responses). However, we must also be able to express our anxieties, fears, and anger to our partners (see Chapter 8). If we cannot, then we are not really intimate.

PERSONAL REFLECTIONS
Do you reveal your true needs, feelings, emotions, and values to your partner? Why or why not? Do you think that your partner reveals his or her true needs, feelings, emotions, and values to you? Why or why not? Do you deal with your partner's reactions when he or she does not like you to express your true feelings, or do you back up and/or apologize? Why or why not?

4. Learn to *deal with your partner's reactions*. If you express your feelings to your partner, he or she may not like what you say. Your partner may become angry or feel very hurt, but you must learn not to automatically back up or apologize for expressing feelings. Instead, keep calm and keep reminding yourself that your feelings are legitimate and that you are entitled to express them. In other words, keep trying. Only when both of you can express your own feelings and allow the other to do the same is there a chance for real intimacy.

The more intimate two people become, the greater the chance that the relationship will be maintained.

> **Love is an active power in man; a power which breaks through the walls which separate man from his fellow men. . . . In love the paradox occurs that two beings become one yet remain two. (Erich Fromm, 1956)**

Key Terms

agape   360
anxious-ambivalent   357
attachment   352, 357
attachment theory of love   357
avoidant   357
companionate love   352, 358
conditional love   353
consummate love   358
courtly love   349
decision/commitment   358
empty love   358
eros   359
fatuous love   358

friendship   349
growing apart   366
growing together   366
habituation   364
hierarchical model of love   362
infatuated love   358
"in love"   350
intimacy   358, 368
jealousy   362
liking   358
limerence   360
love   348, 350
ludus   359

mania   360
nonlove   358
passion   358
passionate love   352
polygyny   310, 354
pragma   360
romantic love   348, 350, 358
secure   357
self-disclosure   355
self-esteem (self-acceptance)   355
storge   359
triangular theory of love   358
unconditional love   353

Suggested Readings

Avery, C. S. (1989, May). How do you build intimacy in an age of divorce? *Psychology Today*.

Davis, K. E. (1985, February). Near and dear: Friendship and love compared. *Psychology Today*.

Fromm, E. (1956). *The art of loving*. New York: Harper & Row. An oldie, but a classic.

Gray, P. (1993, February 15). What is love? *Time* magazine.

Hatfield, E., & Rapson, R. L. (1996). *Love & sex: Cross-cultural perspectives*. Needham Heights, MA: Allyn & Bacon.

Kayser, K. (1993). *When love dies: The process of marital disaffection*. New York: Guilford Press. Explains marital disaffection as going through five phases: disillusionment, hurt, anger, ambivalence, and disaffection.

Lindholm, C. (1998). Love and structure. *Theory, Culture & Society*, 15, 243–263. The best short article on the history of love that I have seen.

Regan, P. C. (2000). Love relationships. In L. T. Szuchman and F. Muscarella (Eds.), *Psychological perspectives on human sexuality* (pp. 232–282). New York: John Wiley. Good discussion of the various theories of love.

Thayer, S. (1988, March). Close encounters. *Psychology Today*. Discusses the importance of touch in establishing intimacy and examines some gender and cultural differences.

Trotter, R. J. (1986, September). The three faces of love. *Psychology Today*. An easy-to read review of Sternberg's triangular theory of love.

Study Guide

INTERACTIVE REVIEW

There have probably been as many definitions and descriptions of love as there have been poets, philosophers, and scientists who study love. For many years, anthropologists believed that romantic love, the (1) _____ of another, was a recent phenomenon and existed only in Western culture. However, evidence of romantic love has been found in nearly all cultures, although it is rarely accepted as a good reason for (2) _____. What is relatively new in Western culture is that our concept of romantic love includes the element of (3) _____.

Recent work has shown that although friendship and romantic love share many characteristics, romantic lovers differ from friends in terms of their (4) _____, (5) _____, (6) _____, and willingness to give the utmost when the other is in need. The feeling of romantic love initially includes physiological arousal, but a (7) _____ is required to interpret the responses as love. Feelings of passion almost always decrease with time, and long-term happy relationships are based more on togetherness, trust, sharing, and affection, or what is called (8) _____ love.

The ability to love another person requires (9) _____ and (10) _____. Love and sex share many things in common, but it is possible to enjoy sex without emotional involvement, and it is also possible to love without having sexual relations. Love can be (11) _____ and depend on another person's ability to satisfy our needs and desires, or it can be (12) _____ and not dependent on the loved one meeting certain expectations and desires. (13) _____ is an emotional state that is aroused by a perceived threat to a valued relationship. It is more common in people who have low (14) _____ and/or who are personally unhappy in their lives, or who put great value on things like (15) _____.

Hazen and Shaver have proposed that one's experiences in romantic relationships are related to his or her (16) _____ style. People with a (17) _____ style have positive views of themselves and others and find it easy to form relationships, whereas individuals with anxious-ambivalent or (18) _____ styles find it more difficult to form relations.

Robert Sternberg has suggested that liking, loving, and all the other positive emotions we feel for other individuals can be understood by the combination of three components: intimacy, passion, and decision/commitment. According to this triangular theory, (19) _____ is intimacy alone, without passion or commitment. (20) _____ is liking plus feelings of passion without commitment, while (21) _____ is intimacy and commitment without passion. (22) _____, which Sternberg believes to be true love, requires the presence of all three components together.

In contrast to Sternberg, John Lee does not believe that there is only one type of love that should be viewed as true love. He proposes that there are many styles of loving. (23) _____ is based on an ideal of physical perfection; (24) _____ grows from friendship; (25) _____ is rational and practical; (26) _____ involves intense emotional dependency; (27) _____ is self-centered; and (28) _____ puts the interest of the loved person first. According to Lee, the degree of happiness an individual feels in a loving relationship depends greatly on how well his or her love-style (29) _____ that of the loved one.

Relationships that last are generally more realistic than idealistic and based more on companionship and affection than on passion. In order to maintain a relationship, a couple must substitute new shared activities for old ones as their lives change, and they also must develop skills to achieve greater (30) _____, those feelings and experiences that promote closeness and bondedness.

SELF-TEST

A. TRUE OR FALSE

T	F	
☐	☐	31. Romantic love is the basis for marriage in most cultures.
☐	☐	32. In Western culture, romantic love is separate from sexual desire.
☐	☐	33. In terms of attachment styles, the most common romantic pairing is a secure-secure matching.
☐	☐	34. The least common attachment style is the avoidant style.
☐	☐	35. People rate best friends and lovers similarly on characteristics such as acceptance, trust, respect, mutual assistance, and understanding.
☐	☐	36. According to Lee, love-styles are fixed and repetitive.
☐	☐	37. As a general rule, people are most attracted to opposites.
☐	☐	38. The decision and commitment to love another person without intimacy or passion is experienced as empty love, according to Sternberg.
☐	☐	39. In the initiation of a relationship, men attach greater importance to physical attractiveness than do women.
☐	☐	40. One of the major predictors of marital success is the number of pleasurable activities the couple shares.
☐	☐	41. Within a monogamous relationship, sexual intercourse and affection are synonymous.
☐	☐	42. The ludus love-style is a strong negative predictor of relationship satisfaction.
☐	☐	43. Feelings of romantic love are associated with the release of amphetaminelike chemicals in the brain.
☐	☐	44. The manner in which one is raised is important for acquiring a positive self-concept.
☐	☐	45. Self-disclosure is always important in a relationship, but it is not necessary that both individuals self-disclose.

T F   46. Men and women are most likely to become jealous if they perceive a partner to be sexually unfaithful.

T F   47. Romantic love tends to be unconditional.

T F   48. Anthropologists have found that romantic love is an idealized notion that is found almost exclusively in industrialized cultures where emphasis is on the individual.

T F   49. In order for a couple to become more intimate, it is important for them to withhold their negative feelings about each other.

T F   50. Theoretically, humans are probably not capable of true agape.

B. MATCHING

_____ 51. agapic love

_____ 52. anxious-ambivalent attachment style

_____ 53. attachment

_____ 54. avoidant attachment style

_____ 55. companionate love

_____ 56. conditional love

_____ 57. consummate love

_____ 58. empty love

_____ 59. erotic love

_____ 60. fatuous love

_____ 61. infatuated love

_____ 62. ludic love

_____ 63. manic love

_____ 64. pragmatic love

_____ 65. romantic love

_____ 66. secure attachment style

_____ 67. storgic love

_____ 68. unconditional love

a. highly idealized love based on physical beauty; these type of lovers are inclined to feel "love at first sight," but it usually doesn't last long

b. a love based on the partner satisfying certain needs and desires; Maslow called it "deficiency love"

c. an affectionate type of love that develops from friendship slowly over time

d. the love that results when commitment is made on the basis of passion without the experience of intimacy; leads to whirlwind romances that usually end when the passion starts to fade

e. do not fear abandonment and find it easy to get close to others

f. a selfless love-style that puts the interest of the loved person ahead of the lover's own, even if it means great sacrifice

g. a love that does not depend on the loved one meeting certain expectations and desires; Maslow called it "being love"

h. commitment without intimacy or passion; often the first stage in arranged marriages

i. a love in which one's partner gives few positive rewards, other than predictability, for remaining in the relationship

j. a self-centered love in which the lover avoids commitment and treats love like a game

k. have negative views of others and have difficulties with feelings of intimacy

l. a love characterized by passionate arousal and liking without commitment; the idealization of another

m. a love that results when passion is felt in the absence of intimacy and commitment, where the lover is obsessed with the other person as an ideal; similar to what Lee calls erotic love

n. love characterized by an intense emotional dependency on the attention and affection of the partner; "head over heels" love in which one is obsessed with the loved one

o. have negative attitudes about themselves, fear rejection, and desperately try to get close to their partners

p. a love found only in relationships that include intimacy, passion, and commitment

q. the combination of intimacy and commitment without passion; based on togetherness, trust, sharing, and affection

r. a rational or practical style of love; this type of lover consciously looks for a compatible mate (a "good match")

C. FILL IN THE BLANKS

69. Fatuous love in Sternberg's model most closely resembles _____ in Lee's theoretical model.

70. Companionate love in Sternberg's model most closely resembles _____ in Lee's theoretical model.

71. Infatuated love in Sternberg's model most closely resembles _____ in Lee's theoretical model.

72. St. Augustine's idea of love ("I want you to be") is probably closest to _____ in Lee's theoretical model.

73. Companionate love is often referred to as _____ love because it is not based on the fantasies and ideals of romantic love.

74. As a general rule, women are much more likely than men to experience jealousy in response to a partner's _____ infidelity.

75. Elaine Hatfield has suggested that couples can achieve greater intimacy by (a) _____, (b) _____, (c) _____, and (d) _____.

76. A large component of passion is novelty and fantasy. The decline of passion in a relationship is almost inevitable because of _____.

77. Meyers and Berscheid found that when people placed their social relationships into categories, people placed in the "in love" category were also included within the _____ category.

78. From culture to culture, and in different time periods, the concept of romantic love has one thing in common: the _____ of another.

79. _____ is defined as "a state of intense longing for union with another . . . a state of profound physiological arousal."

80. Barnes and Sternberg's hierarchical model says that love is composed of two main clusters of features, which they identify as _____ and _____.

81. Schwartz says that "the possibility of achieving _____ with a spouse represents the most exciting goal of marriage."

82. Three things that commonly occur during breakups are _____, _____, and having to deal with the fact that your ex-partner is still around.

Chapter 15

Sexual Problems and Therapy

In the fantasy world of sex, nothing ever hurts, nothing rubs or chafes, nobody is anxious, no one is tired, there are no menstrual cramps, strange viruses, or pregnancy fears, nothing bad ever happens and everything fits perfectly; in the fantasy world of sex, erections function, orgasms are easy, desire surges, birth-control methods don't interfere with spontaneity, and bodies melt. In the real world, it doesn't always happen this way.

(From *What Really Happens in Bed* by Steven Carter and Julia Sokol. Copyright © 1989 by Steven Carter and Julia Sokol. Reprinted with permission of the publisher, M. Evans and Company, Inc., New York.)

Several studies have found that half or more of all couples have had, or will eventually have, sexual problems at some time in their relationship. In their nationally representative survey, Laumann, Paik, and Rosen (1999) found that many Americans had experienced sexual problems lasting several months in just the previous year (see also Frank et al., 1978). Nearly one-third of the women reported a lack of interest in sex, nearly one-fifth of men aged 50 to 59 said they were impotent, and nearly 30 percent of men reported continual problems with premature ejaculation, to name just three examples. What does this mean? Laumann concluded that "everyone is at risk of sexual dysfunction, sooner or later. It's a myth that young, healthy people aren't going to have sexual problems" (quoted in Leland, 1999, p. 47).

In this chapter you will learn about the types of sexual problems that men and women may experience. In some cases, individuals have sexual problems regardless of who their partner is. Within a relationship, however, sexual problems frequently arise

When you have finished studying this chapter, you should be able to:

1. Discuss the common sexual differences couples may encounter in their relationship;

2. Describe some commonly used sexual therapy techniques (the medical history, the sexual history, systematic desensitization, sensate focus, self-awareness, psychosexual therapy, and the PLISSIT model of therapy);

3. Describe sexual problems that can affect both men and women (hypoactive sexual desire, hypersexuality, and dyspareunia);

4. Describe the sexual problems that occur in men (erectile disorder, premature ejaculation, orgasmic disorder, benign coital cephalalgia, and priapism);

5. Explain the sexual problems that occur in women (orgasmic disorder and vaginismus); and

6. Discuss what is meant by the "medicalization" of sexual disorders.

simply because of individual differences—people are different in what they want and how often they want it. I will begin with a discussion of the types of differences that can lead to sexual problems within a relationship.

INDIVIDUAL DIFFERENCES

DIFFERENT EXPECTATIONS

Men and women often have different ideas about sex and love, and therefore often differ on why they have sex. Many women are looking for affection and are interested in what their partner thinks, while most men engage in sex because of their partner's looks, body, and sexual attractiveness (Baldwin & Baldwin, 1997). As a result, many men are goal- (orgasm) directed during sex, whereas many women are pleasure-directed (Whipple & Komisaruk, 1999). Many men equate intimacy with sex. When asked to give six responses to the question "What things do you personally like best in a sexual partner?" for a survey in my course, most of the men listed specific anatomical characteristics (e.g., "nice ass," "big breasts," "sexy legs") or behaviors (e.g., positions, oral sex, no inhibitions). Women, on the other hand, were less concerned about anatomy ("attractive" and "good build" were the only two responses) and specific behaviors and much more concerned about being in a relationship in which they felt cared for, loved, and/or respected. Nearly every woman expressed the desire for her male partner to take his time. In fact, this was often expressed as a complaint —the male partners (who are goal-directed) were not taking their time. These different expectations about a sexual relationship can lead to problems.

> "I got married at a very early age. Sex to me was usually just wifely duties because it was demanded. I used to make up excuses just so I didn't have to do it. Our marriage finally broke up."
> (from the author's files)

> Dear Ann Landers:
> Two years ago I found out that my wife of 27 years was having an affair with another man. She was driving 40 miles to a motel twice a week to meet him for "lunch."
> When I learned what was going on, I asked her, "Why? It seemed to me you were getting more than enough sex at home."
> Her reply was, "What I am getting at home is just that. SEX. And sex is no substitute for love."
> Her answer made me stop and think. I had to admit she was right.
> I am writing this letter to all you husbands out there who are making the same mistake. Ask yourselves this question, "Am I making love to my wife, or am I just having sex with her?"
> Glad I Got Smart
> (Reprinted with permission of Ann Landers and Creators Syndicate.)

DIFFERENT ASSUMPTIONS

Men and women often have different initial sexual experiences, which can lead to incorrect assumptions about the opposite sex. The first sexual experience to orgasm for most men is masturbation. Most men masturbate by moving a hand up and down the penis at a continually accelerating rate as they approach orgasm. Kinsey et al. (1948) found that, on average, men took only 2 to 3 minutes to reach orgasm during masturbation (extremely orgasm-oriented). Women are more variable in their masturbation techniques, but most prefer indirect stimulation of the clitoris. Only 20 percent or less of women masturbate by inserting a finger in the vagina (Hite 1976; Kinsey et al., 1953). It takes women longer to masturbate to orgasm on the average than it does for men (Kinsey et al., 1953).

Without any evidence to the contrary, it is logical for people to assume that what feels best for them must feel best for others as well. Men often assume that women greatly enjoy having their genitals vigorously stimulated (as by rapid thrusting of a finger in and out of the vagina) during foreplay, when in fact this may not be the case. Similarly, on the basis of her own masturbatory experiences, a woman might assume that her male partner prefers gentle indirect stimulation, when in fact this may not be the case.

DIFFERENCES IN DESIRE

One of the most common types of problems that a couple might encounter is a difference in the frequency with which sex is desired (Zilbergeld & Kilmann, 1984). It is also a problem that can have a very negative effect on relationship satisfaction (Davies et al., 1999). To illustrate what is meant by differences in desire, I will begin with an example.

In the 1970s movie *Annie Hall* there is a scene where a man, played by Woody Allen, and a woman, played by Diane Keaton, are shown talking to their respective therapists. Woody says that he and his girlfriend (Diane Keaton) hardly ever have sex, perhaps three times a week. Diane Keaton tells her therapist that they have sex all the time, maybe three times a week. Who has the problem? Is the woman played by Diane Keaton undersexed and to blame, or is the problem that Woody is oversexed?

In many relationships, it does no good to point the finger and put the blame on one person or the other. People are generally only oversexed or undersexed relative to their partners' desires. *It is the couple that has the problem.* If the woman played by Diane Keaton instead had had a relationship with someone who also wanted sex once or twice a week, there would be no problem; and the same would be true if Woody had had a relationship with someone who also wanted sex every day.

Figure 15–1 Studies have shown that one-half or more of all couples have had, or eventually will have, sexual problems at some time in their relationship.

Sexual desire is not necessarily set at a fixed level. An individual's desire for sex often varies, depending on the circumstances. For example, stress and fatigue can greatly affect interest in sex. If your partner is showing less interest in sex than he or she once did, this may be due to other things that are happening in your partner's life. Our understanding of the other person's feelings would be greatly enhanced, of course, if we could only switch places for a little while.

"When I stayed home and my husband worked, I did not understand his seeming lack of desire. Not that he didn't enjoy it, but it could be placed low on a list of priorities. "He would say things like, 'Wait, let me finish watching the ball game,' or 'I don't feel well,' or, 'I'm tired.' He would tell me about his problems at work, and I was really interested in making love then. I didn't want to hear how obnoxious, rude, or unintelligent his boss could be.

"I took all of these 'excuses' as a personal put-down. I would say, 'You're home now, forget what happened in the day.' Little did I realize then, he could not separate them. A bad day could not be erased by a few hugs and kisses. "After a while, he started telling me that maybe he would be more interested if I didn't push him. After that, I began to let up and things went along fair. I still felt as though I wanted more than he was willing to give. Whenever I would tell him so, he would answer with, 'Quality, not quantity.' Then I would get mad and say, 'You don't understand me and what I need.'

"This period was heightened by his decision to quit his job of 25 years. When he finally decided to do this, I said I would go out to work and became a Kelly Girl. I really only wanted temporary work, but I'd go on short assignments of 2 or 3 weeks and stay 3 or 4 months. I never turned down an assignment and gave it my all. Now I am receiving tension, problems with bosses, and plain being physically and mentally tired.

"When I came home from work, I'd look for dinner, make remarks about the house, or want to know if he checked on the children's homework. He would be ready to be cuddly and kiss and I had a barrage of questions. I'd also start telling him about problems I had during the day. At first, I realized these were things he said to me, and I didn't say any more. Finally, I told him, 'I can't believe I'm doing and saying the same things you did to me.'

"After a while it became a joke, and I'd say these things and we'd laugh about it. He then knew how it felt and so did I. Well, this same attitude spilled over to the bedroom. I realized I was now telling him, 'I'm tired,' 'I have to get up early,' 'Why didn't you start this earlier?'—all things he had said to me. I knew how he was feeling and he knew how I was feeling. It was not that we didn't want to make love, but we used other issues to cloud our minds. We now are more understanding of each other's feelings, because we know where they are coming from. Even though I'm in school now, my time is even more used up, because of studying, but we are conscious of each other's needs.

"Every so often my mother takes care of the two younger ones and we get away for a few days without any responsibilities or pressures. Just like two lovers on a lost weekend." (from the author's files)

PERSONAL REFLECTIONS
What do you do when your partner desires sex and you are not in the mood? What would you expect your partner to do if you desired sex and he or she wasn't in the mood? Why? Have you ever pretended to be tired or feeling poorly in order to avoid sex with your partner? Have you ever faked an orgasm? If so, why? Do you think that responses like these are the best way to communicate with your partner about sexual needs?

DIFFERENCES IN PREFERRED BEHAVIORS

Differences in the type of sexual activities each person wants to engage in can also lead to problems. Suppose, for example, that person A (who can be either a man or a woman) wants to have sex only in the missionary position and is in a relationship with person B, who wants to have sexual intercourse in a variety of positions and locations.

> "My girlfriend and I are sexually active. I am tired of doing the same old missionary position. Whenever I mention a new position, she doesn't want to do it. I am so tired of the same old position I lose interest in sex. I don't want to even have sex sometimes." (from the author's files)

Who is to blame for the problem here? Is A inhibited or repressed, or is B perverted? Once again, it is all relative. It does no good to point a finger. Suppose that instead of having a relationship with A, person B was in a relationship with person C, who wanted to try bondage and anal intercourse (which B does not want to try). Should person B now be viewed as inhibited? Again, *it is the couple that has the problem,* not any one individual.

WHO NEEDS THERAPY?

In summary, there are many differences two people can have that can cause sexual problems. When this happens, it is far too common for one person to get upset and blame the other. It is generally best, however, that a couple view these types of problems as *their* problem, rather than as a particular individual's problem. This means working together to resolve it.

Sexual relations, of course, are only part of a couple's overall relationship. As you learned in the previous chapter, if a couple's overall relationship is good and positive, this generally carries over to sexual relations. Conversely, if a couple is experiencing relationship problems, this generally will affect sexual relations as well.

To work out sexual differences or relationship problems requires that a couple be able to talk about their differences. Most people do not know how to talk about sex comfortably, and Chapter 8 provided you with some guidelines. When couples cannot work out individual differences or relationship problems by themselves, they may need the aid of a counselor. When choosing a counselor, it is important to check his or her credentials. Be sure that you pick one who is properly trained and certified. In addition, just as you should do when choosing a doctor, shop around until you find one that you like. Some couples may prefer male and female co-therapists. The names and addresses of certified marriage and family therapists in your area can be obtained by writing to the American Association for Marriage and Family Therapy (AAMFT), 1133 15th Street, NW, Suite 300, Washington, DC 20005.

Not all sexual problems are the result of individual differences within a relationship. Rather than focusing exclusively on behavioral criteria (e.g., frequency of intercourse), we must also look at a person's basic beliefs, self-concept, and inner feelings and emotions. If a particular sexual behavior is causing an individual a great deal of stress and anxiety and possibly interfering with his or her ability to function in a relationship, then that person may be regarded (and probably regards himself or herself) as having a problem. In this case, the individual would probably benefit by seeing a sex therapist.

SEXUAL THERAPY

What is a sex therapist? What do they do? Some of my students believe that sex therapists have sex with their clients. When you have a toothache you go to a dentist, but does the dentist drill his or her own teeth while you're there? When you have an eye infection you go to an ophthalmologist, and when you have a chest pain you go to a cardiologist. Just as physicians specialize in different kinds of medical problems, therapists often specialize as well. A sex therapist is someone who specializes in helping people with sexual problems. Like any other specialist, a sex therapist has had several years of training before beginning practice.

Sex therapists consider it highly unethical for a therapist to have sex with a client (Lazarus, 1992). The following is an example of an unethical therapist. If anything like this ever happens to you, leave immediately and report the therapist.

> "Six years ago I willingly went to a psychiatrist feeling that I needed someone to talk to that could maybe relinquish some of the thoughts I had about sex that were very disturbing. After two visits the doctor proceeded to show me different sexual positions in his books. The next visit he showed me the positions using me as his partner. I never went back." (from the author's files)

Sex therapy is a relatively new field. In fact, the American Psychiatric Association's *Diagnostic and Statistical Manual* (DSM-IV, 1994) did not even list psychosexual disorders until 1980. Until the pioneering work by Masters and Johnson, which was published in 1970, most people with sexual problems went to their family doctor, to a urologist, or, if they could afford one, to a psychoanalyst. Most physicians were not prepared to deal with such problems. In fact, sex education was not even offered in most medical schools at that time. **Psychoanalysis** generally involved long-term treatment (sometimes years) and attempted to "cure" the problem by resolving childhood conflicts (believed to be unconscious), viewing the behavioral problem as merely a symptom of some other deeper conflict.

Masters and Johnson (1970) originally believed that most sexual problems were the result of faulty learning and could be undone in a relatively short period of time (often 2 weeks) by using **cognitive-behavioral therapy.** This kind of therapy focuses on specific behavioral problems, and most therapists work with couples rather than individuals. Psychoanalysts often charge that behavioral therapies only treat the symptoms. They claim that if the underlying cause of the problem is not determined, the problem will eventually manifest itself in another manner. No one can deny, however, that behavioral approaches have been enormously successful in treating sexual problems, such as erectile problems in men and orgasmic problems, in women.

Sex therapy is still refining its techniques, and in the years since Masters and Johnson began their clinical practice it has become clear that **psychosexual therapy,** designed to give insight into the historical cause of clients' problems, is often more successful for some types of problems (e.g., low sexual desire or sexual aversion; Kaplan, 1974, 1983). Perhaps the most controversial change in the treatment of sexual problems today has to do with the role of the medical field (see Tiefer, 2000). In the **medical model,** physicians have increasingly attributed sexual problems to organic causes and are treating them with medical techniques (medications, surgery). I will describe and critique medical approaches in the sections on specific sexual problems later in this chapter.

Sexual therapy programs generally have many things in common. Most follow what is called the **PLISSIT model** (Annon, 1974). PLISSIT is an acronym for *permission, limited information, specific suggestions, and intensive therapy*—the four levels of therapy. Each represents a successively deeper level of therapy. In the first level, the therapist "gives permission" for the client to feel and behave sexually. This is important, because many people and institutions (e.g., parents, some religions) cause people to suppress or repress their sexuality while growing up. In the second level, the therapist gives information to the client (educates him or her about the sexual problem by providing information that relates to the problem, such as teaching the client about clitoral stimulation or discussing the effects of alcohol). This is done in such a manner that the client continues to acquire a positive attitude about sexuality. At the specific suggestion (third) stage, the therapist gives the client exercises to do at home that will help with the specific problem. If the client is still experiencing problems after completing the specific suggestions, then intensive psychosexual therapy will be employed. Only about 10 percent of people who go to sex therapy require this last step.

If you ever think that you may need the help of a sex therapist, be sure to check the credentials of therapists first. In some places, almost anyone can advertise as a "counselor." The names and addresses of certified sex counselors and therapists in your area can be ob-

tained by writing to the American Association of Sex Educators, Counselors and Therapists (AASECT), 106 East Cary Street, Richmond, VA 23219.

SEXUAL THERAPY TECHNIQUES

MEDICAL HISTORY

Sexual problems are sometimes caused by physical or medical problems. Circulatory problems (e.g., arteriosclerosis), hormone abnormalities (e.g., low testosterone levels), or anything that causes damage to the central nervous system (e.g., diabetes, spinal cord injury) can cause a sexual problem. Alcohol and drugs often cause sexual impairment as well. One common cause of impotence in men, for example, is some prescription medications used to treat hypertension and heart disease. It is important, therefore, that a therapist take a complete *medical history* of the patient (and possibly refer the patient to a physician for a medical exam) before beginning therapy in order to rule out any physiologic basis for the presenting problem. Behavioral therapy will do little good if the problem has an organic cause.

SEXUAL HISTORY

Nearly all sex therapists will take a complete *sexual history* of the client before treatment begins. These histories are very thorough, and the length of time devoted to a history will depend on how candid the client is about his or her past experiences. Some therapists, like Masters and Johnson, prefer to work with couples, because, as they say, "There is no such thing as an uninvolved partner." A person's partner (or partners) is involved in the problem in some manner, and even when he or she is not the initial cause (e.g., in those cases where the problem existed before the relationship started), when one partner has a sexual problem, it is common for the other partner to develop one as well.

SYSTEMATIC DESENSITIZATION

Many patients have severe anxieties about sex in certain situations. Therapists often attempt to reduce this anxiety through **systematic desensitization,** involving muscle relaxation exercises or stress reduction techniques. A series of anxiety-producing scenes is presented to the patient, and he or she is told to try to imagine the scene. If this causes anxiety, the relaxation exercises

cognitive-behavioral therapy Therapy that views problems as resulting from faulty learning and that focuses on specific behavioral problems.

psychosexual therapy Therapy that attempts to provide insight into the historical cause of a client's problem.

medical model Attributing sexual problems to organic causes and treating them with medical techniques.

PLISSIT model An acronym for the four levels of treatment in sexual therapy: permission, limited information, specific suggestions, and intensive therapy.

systematic desensitization A therapy technique used to reduce anxiety by slowly introducing elements of the anxiety-producing theme.

are used until the scene can be imagined without anxiety. The therapist then proceeds to the next scene and repeats the procedure until the patient can complete the entire series without anxiety.

SELF-AWARENESS AND MASTURBATION

As you learned in Chapter 2, some people have never explored their own bodies. As a result, they lack **self-awareness** and are totally out of touch with their own physical responses. If you don't know what your body looks like and how it responds, it will be difficult to communicate your needs and feelings to a partner. Therapists are likely to tell those who are not in touch with their bodies to spend time examining themselves. Some therapists give their clients instructions on how to masturbate (LoPiccolo & Stock, 1986). Some therapists find that the use of erotica is helpful. Helen Kaplan called erotic videos "non-chemical aphrodisiacs" (Striar & Bartlik, 1999). Isn't it interesting that what once was taboo is now sometimes used as a therapeutic technique?

SENSATE FOCUS

Many people are goal- or performance-oriented during sexual relations (e.g., they focus on orgasm). Others have guilt or anxieties about enjoying sex. As a result, many people never really learn how to give or receive physical pleasure. Most therapists, therefore, instruct couples to use *nondemand mutual pleasuring techniques* when touching each other. They are instructed to go home, get undressed, and take turns touching each other without thinking about the goal of having intercourse or having an orgasm. Touching the breasts and genitals is forbidden at first, but all other areas of the body are to be explored (see Figure 15–2). The receiver is instructed to focus on the sensations produced by the giver and to provide feedback as to what feels good and what does not. The giver learns what makes his or her partner feel good while simultaneously learning the pleasure of touching. The couple learns to be sensual in a nondemanding situation.

Masters and Johnson, who created these **sensate focus exercises,** often have patients spend several days doing this non-genital-oriented touching. The purpose is to reduce anxiety and teach nonverbal communication skills. Eventually, the couple is instructed to include breast and genital stimulation in their touching but to avoid orgasm-oriented touching. More and more is slowly added, including mutual touching and *hand-riding techniques* in which the receiver places his or her hand over the giver's hand and guides it over his or her own body (touching the hand lightly at body spots where gentle stimulation is wanted and pressing harder at spots

where firm pressure is preferred). A successful outcome for the treatment of sexual problems is often directly related to the amount of sensate focus that is completed during therapy (Sarwer & Durlak, 1996).

> *PERSONAL REFLECTIONS*
> *Stop and reflect on the physical interactions you have with your partner(s). In most of your interactions, are you able to engage in extended nongenital touching and caressing of your partner, or are you usually in a hurry to achieve some immediate genital or breast touching? Is your partner able to caress your arms, legs, neck, and so on, without you quickly attempting to steer the behavior toward sexual play? Why or why not?*

SEXUAL SURROGATES

Sensate focus exercises require a cooperative partner who is willing to devote a great deal of time to them (and also be willing to postpone intercourse and orgasm). What about the client who has no steady partner? What does he or she do? Remember, sexual contact between therapist and client is considered unethical by professional standards, and most prostitutes are not likely to show much sympathetic interest. Some sex therapists, therefore, employ surrogate partners who are trained and skilled in sensate focus techniques (as well as being cooperative and sympathetic). *Sexual surrogates* do not advertise their services and do not solicit clients (clients are referred by therapists), and thus their work is not illegal (Nhu, 1997).

SPECIFIC EXERCISES

After the sensate focus exercises are successfully completed, therapists generally assign specific exercises to help with the problem for which the person came for treatment. These will be described as we discuss some of the most common types of problems. These exercises usually precede sexual intercourse. When the therapist does allow sexual intercourse, it is almost always in a woman-on-top or side-by-side position, where neither partner is in total control. Therapists believe that these positions have much more erotic potential than the missionary position frequently used by many couples.

SEXUAL PROBLEMS AFFECTING BOTH MEN AND WOMEN

HYPOACTIVE SEXUAL DESIRE AND SEXUAL AVERSION

> "I am 35 years old, my wife is 25, and we have been married for 6 years. From the outside we look like the perfect couple—clean-cut, church-going, the works. The problem is my wife. She devotes all her time to cleaning, cooking, and doing volunteer work for the church. However, we have had sex

self-awareness In sexual therapy, getting in touch with one's own physical responses.

sensate focus exercises Exercises designed to reduce anxiety and teach mutual pleasuring through nongenital touching in nondemanding situations.

Figure 15–2 Sensate focus is a nondemand mutual pleasuring technique in which a couple learns how to touch and be touched without worrying about performing or reaching a goal.

three times in the last 12 months. She says that I should be happy with everything else she does for me. It has even gotten to the point where she wants separate vacations because a hotel room with me is too much pressure for her to stand. I love my wife but can't continue to live this way." (from the author's files)

Hypoactive sexual desire was first reported in the 1970s (Kaplan, 1977; Lief, 1977), and today many therapists believe that it is the most common problem of couples going into sex therapy. In fact, Laumann et al.'s (1999) national survey found that nearly a third of the women studied reported a lack of interest in sex in the previous year. About 15 percent of the men reported the same. As a result, 20 percent of couples have a nonsexual marriage (defined as having sex less than 10 times a year).

Before we proceed with hypoactive sexual desire, let us first review what is meant by the term *sexual desire*. You were introduced to this term in Chapter 4. Recall that Helen Kaplan (1979) included it as the first phase of the sexual response cycle. Since then, researchers have attempted to show that desire is composed of three components (e.g., Levine, 1995): (1) sexual drive—the biological component; (2) sexual "wish"—the subjective, psychological component; and (3) sexual motivation—an individual's willingness to engage in sexual *behavior* with a person. A person may willingly engage in sex with a partner (e.g., because he or she wishes to please the partner), but have little subjective desire. Because of this, we will focus on the subjective aspect of desire.

So, how do we define **hypoactive sexual desire?** The DSM-IV (American Psychiatric Association, 1994) defines a lack of interest in sex as a problem when there is persistent or recurrent absence of sexual fantasies and

hypoactive sexual desire
A sexual problem characterized by a persisting and pervasive inhibition of sexual desire.

sexual desire. People with hypoactive (or inhibited) sexual desire show decreased frequencies of sexual arousal, self-initiated sexual activity, and sexual fantasy.

The problem in diagnosing hypoactive sexual desire, of course, is defining what is meant by "persistent." What is the normal frequency of sexual desire? Note also that *inhibited* is a relative term that must take into account the partner's frequency of desire (see the section on individual differences) and the level of desire of other people in the community. Some therapists classify a person as having hypoactive desire if he or she initiates an average of two or fewer sexual experiences a month (Schover et al., 1982). This does not have to mean intercourse; it can include masturbation and sex play.

Hypoactive sexual desire is more than just a lack of sexual activity, however. These individuals do not desire sex and avoid it even when there is an opportunity to engage in it. Sexually hypoactive persons display less physiological and subjective sexual arousal in response to erotic stimuli than do normal people (Palace & Gorzalka, 1992). Therapist Helen Kaplan's studies (1979) suggest that on some level, inhibited persons suppress their desire because they do not want to feel sexual. Another therapist has called it "sexual anorexia nervosa." In its most extreme form, the avoidance of sex becomes phobic in nature and is called **sexual aversion** (Kaplan, 1987). The anticipation of any kind of sexual interaction (even conversation about sex) causes great anxiety, so persons with sexual aversion simply "turn it off" at a very early stage.

It is difficult for people who enjoy sex to imagine that others find it unpleasant. What could cause such a lack of interest in sex? *Primary hypoactive sexual desire* (the case with people who have never had sexual feelings) is much more common in women than men (Wincze & Carey, 1991). *Secondary* or *acquired hypoactive sexual desire* can be attributed to organic factors, such as hormone deficiencies or tumors, in some cases, but the vast majority of cases are believed to be due to psychological factors (Leiblum & Rosen, 1988). Some cases may be due to a past trauma, such as rape or sexual molestation during childhood. Laumann et al. (1999) found that women who have ever been "sexually forced" by a man were twice as likely as others to have a lack of interest in sex. A person doesn't have to have been a victim of sexual abuse, however, to acquire a negative attitude about sex. Some people simply may never have learned to associate sex with pleasure because of a selfish partner or partners.

"My husband was drunk on our wedding night. He could hardly walk and practically tore my clothes off. I wanted to kiss and hug and feel like I was loved, but all he wanted was to screw. I wasn't ready and it hurt real bad. He made me do things I didn't want to do. Afterwards he threw up in the bathroom and passed out. I cried all night. Now I still don't want him to touch me." (from the author's files)

Sometimes, an unwanted pregnancy or contracting (or fear of contracting) a sexually transmitted disease can cause a person to have a negative attitude about sex.

"When I was 15 I had sex with a prostitute. My friends encouraged me to do so. One week later I noticed two sores on my penis. I couldn't tell my parents, they would kill me. I couldn't sleep. I asked a friend for help. I remember how he looked at me. I felt rejected. . . . I was horrified. . . . His father was a doctor and he treated me. I remember the anxiety when he told me I had chancroid. I didn't know if it was curable. . . . Today, I'm afraid of having sex with anyone. I have not had relations with a woman in nearly 5 years." (from the author's files)

As might be expected, sexual disorders are more common among individuals whose life histories have resulted in them having negative sexual self-schemas (a negative cognitive view of sex) (Cyranowski et al., 1999). Hypoactive sexual desire is often associated with a sexually repressive upbringing, or an aversion to female genitals or common sexual behaviors (Donahey & Carroll, 1993; LoPiccolo, 1980). Interestingly, many women with anorexia or other eating disorders have very low sexual functioning and satisfaction (Rothschild et al., 1991).

We must not ignore the biological component. For example, many antidepressant drugs (e.g., Prozac, Paxil, Zoloft, Luvox) cause many patients to lose their sexual desire (Rosen et al., 1999). Recall from Chapter 12 that some postmenopausal women show a loss of desire. The same is true of women who are testosterone deficient due to other reasons. In these cases, hormone replacement therapy that includes testosterone is often successful in restoring desire (Rako, 1996).

Today, many therapists believe that problems in a relationship are one of the most important factors contributing to hypoactive sexual desire (McCarthy, 1997, 1999). Hypoactive women are generally very unhappy with the quality of their relationship with their partner, particularly concerning the expression of affection, while hypoactive men tend to be overly reliant emotionally on their partner and to have anxieties about finding the right combination of sexual passion and emotional intimacy (Apt et al., 1993; Donahey & Carroll, 1993). For probably half or more of the couples who go into therapy for sexual desire problems, one partner or the other has a coexisting sexual problem (see Leiblum & Rosen, 1988). In some cases, hypoactive sexual desire may be a way of avoiding the sexual failure due to the other problem.

sexual aversion An extreme form of hypoactive sexual desire in which an individual's avoidance of sex becomes phobic.

Hypoactive sexual desire is probably the most difficult sexual problem to treat (Hawton et al., 1991; Kaplan, 1987). Many therapists report only a 10 to 20 percent success rate with conventional sex therapy techniques. Today, most therapists begin with behavioral and cognitive techniques that are designed to increase pleasure and communication and decrease anxiety, but add couples therapy (to resolve relationship problems and rebuild intimacy) and individual psychosexual therapy (to help the person understand what it is that is causing anxieties about sex) (e.g., LoPiccolo & Friedman, 1988; McCarthy, 1997).

HYPERSEXUALITY: COMPULSION, ADDICTION, OR MYTH?

At the beginning of this chapter, you learned that two people in a relationship often differ in the frequency with which they desire sex, but that ordinarily neither one should be considered hyposexual or hypersexual. By how much would one's sexual desire have to differ from that of most other people before he or she would be considered extraordinary? This is a matter of subjective judgment, which (as usual) varies across different cultures and times. As you have just read, some people can be classified as having hypoactive (inhibited) sexual desire. Can we make the same distinction at the other extreme? Can people be classified as "hypersexual"? Because diminished sexual desire is classified as a disorder, it seems logical that individuals at the other extreme could be considered as having a disorder (Vroege et al., 1998). However, many therapists say no, and in fact, the American Psychiatric Association's diagnostic manual DSM-IV (1994) has no such category. On the other hand, the World Health Organization's *International Classification of Diseases* (1992) does recognize excessive sexual drive. Let us explore this controversial issue further.

History is full of stories of famous people who reportedly had hundreds of sexual partners and often had sex many times a day: Cleopatra, Empress Theodora, Casanova, Catherine the Great, Rasputin, and King Solomon, to name a few. Terms like *nymphomania* and *satyriasis* have long been used to describe people with seemingly insatiable sexual appetites. However, therapists who favor a new classification for hypersexuality say that hypersexuality is more than just numbers. Patrick Carnes (1983, 1991) was the first to use the designation sexual addiction. Many therapists objected to this term, saying that there was no evidence of physical addiction as in the case of alcohol or drugs. Goodman (1992) redefined *sexual addiction* as follows:

A disorder in which a behavior that can function both to produce pleasure and to provide escape from internal discomfort is employed in a pattern characterized by (1) recurrent failure to control the behavior, and (2) continuation of the behavior despite significant harmful consequences.

This definition includes aspects of both dependency ("behavior motivated by an attempt to achieve a pleasurable internal state") and compulsivity ("behavior motivated by an attempt to evade or avoid an unpleasurable/aversive internal state") and is similar to the definition in DSM-IV for psychoactive substance addiction. The difference is that " 'addictiveness' is more a property of individual persons than a property of behaviors or substances" (Goodman, 1998).

Opponents of the designation "sexual addiction" argue that it is based on a repressive morality that can be used against anyone engaged in nonmonogamous sex (e.g., Coleman & Edwards, 1986; Levine & Troiden, 1988). As Coleman and Edwards (1986) note, "This concept can potentially be used to oppress sexual minorities . . . because they do not conform to the moral values of the prevailing culture (or therapist). Mental health professionals using such conceptualizations have become simply instruments of such conservative political views and have made people who do not fit into a narrow, traditional sexual life-style feel bad, immoral, and, now mentally ill." These therapists prefer to regard people who show a lack of sexual control as having a *sexual compulsion*.

Note that there is some common ground: Both sides admit that it is possible to engage in sex compulsively. I will use the purely descriptive term *hypersexual* to describe such individuals.

A **hypersexual individual** is distinguished from other people by the compulsiveness with which he or she engages in sex. Hypersexuals engage in sex repeatedly and compulsively to reduce anxiety and distress, usually finding little or no emotional satisfaction. Coleman (1991) and others choose to divide hypersexual (compulsive sexual) behavior into two types: paraphilic and nonparaphilic. I will discuss paraphilic behaviors in the next chapter; this section is devoted to nonparaphilic hypersexuality.

Hypersexual individuals feel driven to have sex, looking for something in sex that they can never find. They have excessive numbers of sexual partners and/or engage in excessive masturbation (Goodman, 1998). If they fall in love and establish a relationship, they often cannot stop their promiscuous behavior. Hypersexuality interferes with the ability to carry out normal daily living and results in unhappiness, lack of fulfillment, and the inability to break a pattern of compulsive behavior.

Here are two examples. Let's examine them from both sides of the controversy.

hypersexuality A term reserved for people who engage in sex compulsively, with little or no emotional satisfaction. Sometimes called *sexual addiction*.

"A few years ago, I dated a girl who I believe had hypersexual sexual desire. She wanted sex all the time no matter where we were. At first I enjoyed her 'disorder' but soon it got very out of hand. She would want sex while we were in public, while I was driving, in my mother's house. . . . When I began to refuse sex in these places we broke up and I haven't seen her since." (from the author's files)

Can we conclude from this case history that this woman is hypersexual? The answer is "no." All we can determine from this is that she wanted sex more often than he did, and that she was also less inhibited about where she had sex. This is the problem with labeling people by someone else's standards. The *couple* obviously had a problem, but it is the type called "differences in desire" discussed at the beginning of the chapter.

Dear Ann Landers:

I am a 20-year-old woman with a problem that could destroy my life. I've been living with a 23-year-old man for two years and I love him very much, but I have an obsession to go to bed with other men. It seems that I just can't be satisfied with one.

My guy and I have a great relationship. He's a terrific lover but I am always looking for others. Some of my lovers are married men, others I've been involved with have been close friends of mine. I've slept with men I barely knew. This problem has been with me since I was 16.

I once had an affair with a married high school teacher. It became public and caused him to lose his job. I felt awful about it but it didn't stop me from going to bed with another teacher the following year.

I think my guy knows I am sleeping around, but he says nothing because he doesn't want to lose me. Please tell me what to do. I don't want to behave like a tramp for the rest of my life.

Never Satisfied
(Reprinted with permission of Ann Landers and Creator's Syndicate.)

For this case history, we can make a better case that the individual might be hypersexual. Her sexual behavior has caused great harm to herself and others and causes her great distress, yet she is unable to change.

The threat of possibly contracting a sexually transmitted disease, including HIV infection and AIDS, does not stop hypersexual people. Although the term *sexual addiction* may be controversial, it has been found that some hypersexual individuals also display excessive dependence on alcohol or drugs to satisfy emotional needs. It is not uncommon, for example, for people who use cocaine to engage in high-risk sexual behaviors (e.g., new partners) when taking the drug (Washton,

dyspareunia Painful intercourse, usually resulting from organic factors (e.g., vaginal, prostate, or bladder infections).

phimosis A condition in uncircumcised men in which the foreskin of the penis is too tight, causing pain during erection.

1989). The dual addiction becomes a vicious cycle, with one addiction leading to the other.

Coleman believes that hypersexuality ("sexual compulsivity") results from "intimacy dysfunction" during childhood (Coleman & Edwards, 1986). This can occur, for example, if a child is neglected or abused. Such children often have low self-esteem and feelings of inadequacy and unworthiness as adults. They are often very lonely, and their emotional pain causes them to engage in behaviors (e.g., alcohol, drugs, food, sex) that give them pleasure and help them evade their internal discomfort. The relief is only momentary and is followed by a need to engage in the behavior again. However, engaging in the behavior results in greater feelings of unworthiness and shame, which makes it more likely that the person will engage in the behaviors in order to avoid the negative feelings felt at present. Coleman (1991) describes one form of hypersexuality common in women as "compulsive love affairs." These women compulsively lure potential partners to fall in love, but once the partner is "caught" there is no more appeal, and she breaks it off and relentlessly goes looking for the "right" partner.

How would one distinguish hypersexuality from a healthy interest in sex? Remember, it is not so much the frequency of sex as it is one's life-style. Ask yourself some questions as guidelines. Do you *frequently* use sex to alleviate depression or anxiety? Could your sexual behavior abuse or cause injury (physically or emotionally) to yourself or to someone else? Could it possibly damage your relationship, your career, your health, or your self-respect? Have you ever wanted to stop but not been able to do so? A positive response to these questions may make you a candidate for therapy.

Therapy is often twofold: (1) treating the internal discomfort (perhaps initially with antidepressants or stabilizing drugs), and (2) helping the individual find healthy, adaptive ways of dealing with his or her emotions and needs (psychotherapy will probably be used here) (Coleman, 1991). Those therapists favoring the addictive viewpoint probably will also teach cognitive-behavioral strategies to help the individual abstain from the addictive behavior (Goodman, 1992). While therapists continue to argue the validity of the concept of sexual addiction, a number of self-help organizations similar to Alcoholics Anonymous (e.g., Sexaholics Anonymous, Sex Addicts Anonymous) have been created for people who think they need help.

PAINFUL INTERCOURSE

Painful intercourse is called **dyspareunia.** It usually, but not always, is caused by a physical problem. In men, the most common causes are a prostate, bladder, or urethral infection, or the foreskin of the penis being too tight (a condition called **phimosis**). In rare cases, fibrous tissue deposits around the corpora cavernosa of the penis cause curvature of the penis (known as

Peyronie's disease) and pain during erection (Gregory & Purcell, 1989). In a very rare condition, some men experience persistent and recurring pain in the genitals during or immediately after ejaculation. This is called *postejaculatory pain syndrome,* and is caused by involuntary spasms of the genitals that are triggered by psychological conflicts (Kaplan, 1993).

Painful intercourse is much more common in women than men. It has been estimated that 1 to 2 percent of women suffer from chronic dyspareunia, with as many as 21 percent of young women (aged 18–29) and 15 percent of women aged 30–49 experiencing problems lasting several months or longer (Laumann et al., 1999). What this means is that nearly 1 in 5 women under the age of 50 do not find sex to be pleasurable. One of the most common causes is vaginal dryness. If a woman is not fully lubricated when intercourse begins, the thrusting of the penis will severely irritate the dry vaginal walls. Lack of sufficient lubrication can be due to a partner who doesn't take his time, but it can also be the result of fear or anxiety, which interferes with the vasocongestive process (vaginal lubrication, you recall, is the result of the walls of the vagina becoming engorged with blood). Vaginal dryness can also result from hormonal changes (which occur at menopause), the use of antihistamines and other medications, or even tampons. Use of a lubricant can often substantially alleviate this problem.

Another common cause in women is inflammation of the vestibular bulbs. This can often be alleviated with surgery (Bergeron et al., 1997). Dyspareunia in women can also be caused by endometriosis (growth of the endometrium outside the uterus), pelvic inflammatory disease, yeast and other vaginal infections, Bartholin's gland infections, and urinary tract infections. Allergies to semen, feminine hygiene products (deodorants and scented douches), powders, and spermicides can also make sexual intercourse painful (Erard, 1988).

If the physical factors responsible for dyspareunia are not quickly taken care of, dyspareunia can lead to other sexual problems. The anticipation of pain, for example, can become so great that it can lead to erectile problems in men, vaginismus in women, or loss of sexual desire in either sex. The resultant psychological stress can also damage relationships. Remember, pain during intercourse is generally an indication that there is something physically wrong, so see a physician immediately before there are greater problems.

MALE SEXUAL PROBLEMS

ERECTILE DISORDER

The term **erectile disorder** refers to a man's inability to get or maintain an erection. This condition is sometimes called impotence, but this is an unfortunate term

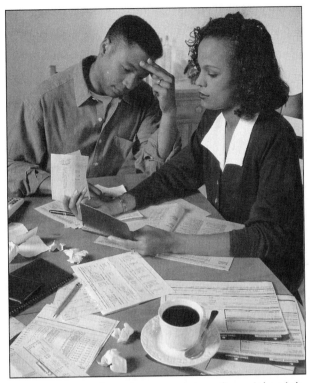

Figure 15–3 Serious stressors, such as financial or job-related problems, can lead to erectile problems or a loss of interest in sex.

because it has negative connotations about a man's masculinity. Most therapists prefer the purely descriptive term (National Institutes of Health Consensus Statement, 1992). Erectile disorders can be *primary* (i.e., the man has always had problems) or *secondary* (i.e., the individual has not had erectile problems in the past); and *global* (i.e., the problem occurs in all situations) or *situational* (e.g., a man cannot get an erection with his usual partner, but can with other women or during masturbation).

Historically, and in many cultures, an erect phallis has been a symbol of male power and virility. Having an erectile problem, therefore, can be psychologically devastating. But the disorder can affect more than the man. It often destroys the self-esteem of the female partner as well, because she often feels as if she is doing something wrong.

Billy and Karen were in their mid-30s and had been married for 3 years. They had no children and both worked full-time; he as the manager of a small insurance office and she as a lab technician in a hospital. Their sexual relationship, which began while they were dating, had always been "wonderful."

In their 3rd year of marriage, Karen was promoted to a job selling hospital equipment. About 6 months later, Billy began

erectile disorder A sexual problem in which a man has difficulty getting and maintaining an erection.

to have erectile difficulties. At first, Billy would lose his erection after intercourse had begun, but after about 2 months he began to have difficulty during foreplay as well. Sometimes he couldn't get an erection at all. He was embarrassed by this (calling himself a "failure") and began reacting by rolling over and going to sleep.

When the problem started, Karen tried to be supportive and didn't say anything, but as Billy's problem worsened she became angered at his silent withdrawal and lack of attempts to satisfy her through other means. As things progressed, Karen, who had been regularly orgasmic in the past, found that she could no longer reach orgasm. Now when they had sex Karen worried so much that Billy would get upset that she, too, lost all focus on sexual pleasure. Billy also began to rush her through foreplay to try and see if he would be able to perform in the "main event." Karen not only missed the intercourse and her own orgasms, but also the tenderness and closeness. Both felt inadequate because they both had sexual difficulty and could not figure out what was causing it. (Case history courtesy of Dr. David M. Schnarch.)

How common are erectile problems? It is a rare man who will not experience an erectile problem at least once in his life. An erection results from the spongy tissues of the penis becoming engorged with blood (the penile arteries dilate and valves in the veins close). Any number of things can impair functioning, including fatigue, stress, alcohol, and drugs. A drink or two loosens our inhibitions, but most men are unaware that alcohol is also a central nervous system depressant, and it is quite common to experience erectile problems after drinking too much (which sometimes may be only a couple of drinks; Rosen 1991).

So should we say that all men have erectile problems? No, but it is somewhat arbitrary as to where we draw the line. Masters and Johnson (1970) classified a man as having an erectile disorder if he was having problems in at least 25 percent of his sexual encounters. The American Psychiatric Associations DSM-IV's diagnostic criteria is that the problem must be *persistent or recurrent and causes distress or interpersonal difficulty.* Erectile disorder refers to more than a total inability to get an erection; it includes any inability to get or maintain an erection adequate for "satisfactory sexual performance." By this definition, Laumann et al. (1999) in their national survey found that about 10 percent of men aged 30–49 and 18 percent of men aged 50–59 had erectile problems lasting at least a few months during the previous year. The figures are much higher for older men (Jacoby, 1999). Thus, the National Institutes of Health estimate that 30 million American men have erectile problems. However, erectile problems are *not* inevitable with advancing age (i.e., age alone is not the cause), and the problem can be treated with a variety of therapies (NIH Consensus Statement, 1992).

What is responsible for the fact that so many men have an erectile disorder? Masters and Johnson once argued that as many as 80 percent of all cases are due to psychological factors, but physicians now estimate that the large majority of cases have a physical basis (NIH Consensus Statement, 1992). In fact, the biggest change in the treatment of erectile disorders in the past 10 years has been its *medicalization*—whereby erectile disorders are viewed as a medical problem resulting from organic causes that should be treated with medical solutions (drugs, devices, or surgery). We will focus on the medical approach first, then return to treatment for psychogenic disorders.

Circulatory problems (e.g., arteriosclerosis or sickle cell anemia), neurological disorders (e.g., resulting from accidents or pelvic surgery), prostate surgery, hormone imbalances (primary abnormalities or secondary complications due to diabetes), and groin injuries often result in erectile disorders. Men with erectile disorders often have decreased penile sensitivity (Rowland, 1998). One-fourth of all erectile problems are due to medications prescribed for other conditions, particularly antidepressants and the beta-blocking medications used to treat blood pressure and heart disease (NIH Consensus Statement, 1992). Men who drink alcohol every day have nearly twice as high rates of erectile disorders as other men (Laumann et al., 1999). Eighty percent of alcoholics are impaired. Smokers are 50 percent more likely than nonsmokers to suffer from erectile problems (Mannino et al., 1994). It is important, therefore, that a client with an erectile problem have a complete medical exam before treatment begins.

Actually, there is an easy test that can often (but not always) determine whether the cause of an erectile disorder is physical or psychological. Men, you remember, get erections at night during REM sleep. If a man gets normal erections during REM sleep, then the problem is most likely psychological. If not, then it is physical (see Ackerman & Carey, 1995).

One solution to erectile disorder is the use of a vacuum device that forces blood into the penis, thus causing it to become erect (Witherington, 1990). An elastic ring at the base of the penis keeps it erect. There are few side effects, but this device is clumsy and not very romantic.

Another medical solution is injection of drugs directly into the penis. Self-injections of phentolamine, alprostadil, or papaverine hydrochloride, drugs that cause expansion of vessels that supply blood to the penis and constriction in vessels that carry blood away from the penis, have proven to be successful for many men in reversing erectile problems due to circulatory problems (Rowland & Burnett, 2000). On the down side, injections can sometimes be painful, cause long-lasting erections, or cause fibrosis (scarring of the soft tissue).

Oral medications (pills) are the biggest break-through (see Leland et al., 1997 and Rowland & Burnett, 2000). The first such medication, Viagra (sildenafil), became available in 1998 and is about 70 percent effective (Goldstein et al., 1998). It works by relaxing smooth muscles in the penis, thus allowing arteries to expand and blood to rush into the penis. The pills work directly on the penis (not the brain) and work only when a man is sexually stimulated. However, Viagra can cause headaches and blurred vision. A survey for *Modern Maturity* magazine of men aged 45 and older found that 10 percent of men had tried Viagra (Jacoby, 1999). Now there is a new pill for erectile problems. Called Uprima, it works on the brain and takes effect faster than Viagra (see Cowley, 2000b). It is effective for about 56 percent of men. In some men with erectile disorders, testosterone is effective (Rakic et al., 1997).

For those men for whom medications and therapy do not work, such as those who have suffered permanent nerve or vascular damage, *penile implants* can be used. There are three types. One is made of semirigid plastic rods and is inserted into the erectile chambers of the penis. It is stiff enough to permit intercourse, but flexible enough to be bent downward during daily activity. A second, more sophisticated type of implant is made of two soft tubes that are implanted in the erectile chambers. They are connected by other tubes to a small pouch containing a saline solution that is implanted under the muscles in the pubic region. The pouch, in turn, is connected to a tiny pump located inside the scrotum. When a man wants to have sex, he gently presses the pump, which forces the saline solution into the tubes in the penis and causes an erection. When he wants to, he can squeeze another valve to reverse the process. A third type of implant is a silicone sack that is also inflated by a pump. Tens of thousands of American men are presently using these implants, and although postsurgical levels of sexual satisfaction do not always match presurgical expectations, a large majority of the patients and their partners are satisfied with the results (Chiang et al., 2000).

The medical model for the treatment of erectile disorders has failed to address some important issues. For example, quite often it is not easy to attribute an erectile problem solely to organic or psychological factors (Ackerman & Carey, 1995; NIH Consensus Statement, 1992). If a man has a problem due to a physical cause (or a temporary problem due to medication), he can become so apprehensive that he becomes completely impaired. Many physicians maintain that the use of injections or pills will reduce psychologically caused problems, but the evidence shows that few men using medical solutions are "cured" (see Schover & Leiblum, 1994). Lastly, it is easier for many men to view themselves as having a disease that can be cured

"Do those pills seem to be working, sweetie?"

with a magic pill or injection than it is to accept that they have psychological or sexual problems that may require seeing a sex therapist—even though short-term therapy may result in better long-term adjustment. There are probably psychological and/or relationship problems associated with all erectile problems, even those that are clearly caused by physical problems, and most patients would probably benefit from a combination of medication and therapy (see Ackerman & Carey, 1995; Rowland & Burnett, 2000). Let us now focus on traditional sexual therapy techniques.

If the cause of an erectile problem is determined to be psychological, the success rate during therapy depends largely on whether it is primary or secondary. Men with primary (psychological) erectile disorders are often found to have had a strict religious upbringing in which sex was equated with sin and guilt (Masters & Johnson, 1970).

"I was raised a _____ throughout my life. . . . I do remember in the seventh or ninth grade my father and I were talking about sex and he told me not to have sex until I was married or I would go to hell—I thought that for the longest time. Then when I discovered masturbation I felt terribly guilty, so I went to talk to a priest. He told me how wrong it was and gave me some prayers to say. From that time on I felt very guilty every time I did it. . . . I haven't had a full erection in 10 years (I'm 26)." (from the author's files)

An early traumatic experience might also result in long-term erectile problems:

> "At 16 years old . . . my best friend thought it was a shame I was still a virgin. . . . In a drunken stupor I was goaded into going downtown to pick up a hooker with my friend. The next day I walked tall and proud (although I felt no different), that is until I noticed a week later a greenish-yellow discharge on my underwear. A doctor diagnosed gonorrhea. I brought it up with my father, who became enraged, and to this day he still teases me about it. My brother laughed at me. . . . I did not date anyone for 3 years. Once I began, it took me 3 or 4 years to have sex. . . . I would get to the point of intercourse, then I would lose my erection." (from the author's files)

Men who were victims of adult-child sexual contact experience erectile problems three times more often than other men (Laumann et al., 1999). Therapists find that these primary disorders are much more difficult to treat than secondary disorders. Masters and Johnson report a 60 percent success rate, but many other therapists believe that only about 20 percent can be successfully treated (Kaplan, 1979). Men with a primary psychological disorder may be treated by having penile implants.

Situational erectile disorders are quite clearly psychological in origin:

> "My husband doesn't stay hard when we make love. Everything is OK at the start, but then he gets soft in a minute or two. He stays hard when I give him oral sex or masturbate him." (from the author's files)

If this man's erectile problem were caused by something physically wrong with him, he would be unable to maintain an erection with any type of sexual activity.

For men with a secondary erectile disorder due to psychological factors, the most common cause is **performance anxiety.** Performance anxiety is a fear of failure.

> "My girlfriend and I are sexually active. Since we first started having sex, I would have an orgasm but she wouldn't. She still hasn't had one, and we have had sex plenty of times. I feel that I am not doing my job as a man. I also feel embarrassed. It makes me feel I do not know much about sex. Lately . . . I have trouble getting an erection." (from the author's files)

performance anxiety A fear of failure during sexual relations that can lead to erectile disorder in men and inhibited orgasm in women.

spectatoring Observing and evaluating one's own sexual responses. This generally causes distraction, with subsequent erectile and/or orgasm problems.

Men who judge their sexual experiences like Olympic events (e.g., they are unhappy unless their partner has multiple orgasms) put enormous pressure on themselves. The same is true of men who feel they are competing with a real or imagined suitor.

Another common cause is a life change. For example, the stress caused by unemployment frequently leads to erectile problems (Morokoff & Gilliland, 1993). According to Levine and Althof (1991), "Typically, the man does not fully appreciate his response to these life changes, for example, his affects, defenses, coping devices, and adaptational shifts. Neither does he fully realize that the trigger mechanism for his arousal problem is contained in these responses. He avoids recognizing what these affect-laden events mean to him and only focuses on his loss of sexual confidence—that is, performance anxiety. He remains baffled by how he became dysfunctional."

Recall, for example, the case history of Billy and Karen. Let us continue with their story:

> When Billy and Karen started therapy, they still had no idea what was causing the problem. They felt they were doing everything the same as before. In actuality, Billy was threatened by Karen's impressive career advancement. Although he tried hard to be a liberated male, he was threatened by her increased income and status and the time she spent entertaining the various physicians and hospital administrators in her territory.
>
> During sexual relations, Billy had begun to worry if Karen found him as appealing as she had when she was more "naive and unworldly." He also had the secret fear that Karen was having an affair, and although she wasn't, he had begun to compete with his own fantasy of Karen's other partner. As with many men, this was sufficient to produce Billy's initial difficulty in maintaining an erection. Once the difficulty began, Billy's anticipation of it happening made it begin to occur earlier in each subsequent sexual encounter. (Case history courtesy of Dr. David Schnarch.)

Although an erectile problem in any of the previously mentioned situations is normal, many men are not aware of that and begin to worry about being "impotent." The next time they have sex, the anxiety caused by fear of failure can result in what is called **spectatoring**—observing and evaluating their own responses rather than experiencing sexual pleasures. Spectatoring is distracting, resulting in a loss of intimacy, and it can lead to loss of an erection, which results in even greater anxiety the next time. The behavior becomes a vicious cycle, and what started as a normal response to fatigue, alcohol, drugs, or other factors can become a chronic psychological disorder.

What is the best therapy for a man with a psychologically caused erectile problem (performance anxiety)? Today, many therapists are emphasizing the importance of the couple's dynamics and interpersonal issues in the cause and treatment of erectile problems. Many therapists worry that the medical solution of popping pills (e.g., Viagra) focuses on fixing the

Figure 15–4 A commonly used training technique for men.

mechanics of erectile disorder, while ignoring the personal and relationship problems that may have caused it. Other therapists add, "Clinical experience suggests that couples with strong, committed and supportive relationships generally develop effective coping strategies in the face of even the most severe sexual problems. In contrast, uncommitted couples with unresolved marital conflicts appear to derive little or no benefit from even the most advanced medical, surgical or psychological interventions" (Leiblum & Rosen, 1991). Initial assessment of a couple's motivation and interactions is important in choosing a therapy approach.

After their medical and sexual histories are taken, men with an erectile disorder are usually assigned sensate focus exercises. Many men are amazed to find that they are able to get a full erection during these initial sessions. The reason, of course, is that the touching in sensate focus exercises involves nondemand pleasuring—the man does not have to perform, but instead learns (or relearns) how to experience pleasure. When genital touching is allowed, the female partner is instructed to stop fondling the penis after the man gets an erection (see Figure 15–4). This is intended to teach the man that he does not have to use his erection immediately (many men with erection problems rush their performance for fear that they will lose their erection). With this *"teasing" procedure,* the man's erection comes and goes, and thus he also learns that loss of erection does not mean that he has failed, for it will come back again. When intercourse is finally allowed,

it is always in a woman-on-top or side-by-side position, and the woman is the one who inserts the penis into her vagina. Thus, the man is not put in a position of feeling that he has to perform.

Erectile problems can be so psychologically devastating that many men try to deal with their problem alone. However, there is now an organization called Impotents Anonymous, with 35 chapters nationwide that offer information and support (call 800-669-1603). Wives of men with erectile problems are also welcome to attend meetings.

> *PERSONAL REFLECTIONS*
> *Have you ever experienced performance anxiety during sexual relations (e.g., anxiety about pleasing your partner, maintaining an erection, reaching orgasm)? If so, what do you think is the cause of the anxiety?*

PREMATURE EJACULATION

> "I have a problem with premature ejaculation. As soon as I start to have sex I ejaculate. I feel like the whole world is laughing at me. . . . All my other friends are having sex and doing it right." (from the author's files)

When many people think of someone who prematurely ejaculates, they think of a man who reaches orgasm before intercourse even begins. Although this does sometimes happen, it is more often the case that a man ejaculates shortly after the couple begins intercourse. Laumann et al. (1999) reported that 30 percent of the men in their national survey said that they had had problems with premature ejaculation in the previous year. This was across all age groups and makes it the most common male sexual problem. Men who are concerned only with their own orgasms, of course, may not regard this as a problem. In fact, in some cultures where men are very dominant and the sexual pleasure of women is denied, the ability to ejaculate quickly is considered very masculine. It is estimated that only 20 percent of all premature ejaculators in the United States ever seek therapy.

How, then, do we define **premature ejaculation?** The American Psychiatric Association (DSM-IV, 1994) says that its essential feature is "the *persistent or recurrent* onset of orgasm and ejaculation with minimal sexual stimulation before, on, or shortly after penetration and before the person wishes it," accompanied by *"marked distress or interpersonal difficulty."* The DSM-IV cautions that one must also consider factors such as age and the novelty of the sexual situation or partner.

How long does a man have to continue in intercourse without being classified as a premature ejaculator? At various times in the past, premature ejaculation has been defined by a specified minimal number of thrusts, a minimal amount of time engaged in intercourse, or in terms of whether or not the female partner reaches orgasm at least 50 percent of the time (see Rowland et al., 2000). The problem with the first two types of definition is that they do not consider the partner. Suppose a man always reaches orgasm in only 1½ minutes after beginning intercourse, but that his female partner always reaches orgasm within that time period as well. Should he be considered as having a problem? The trouble with the last definition is that it depends exclusively on the partner's responses. What if the partner has difficulties reaching orgasm regardless of who her partner is? A man could continue intercourse until he's blue in the face and still be classified as a premature ejaculator. Most therapists choose to view premature ejaculation in terms of *absence of reasonable voluntary control* of ejaculation (Kaplan, 1974). By this definition, orgasm should not be a totally involuntary event, and a man should be able to have some control over when it occurs. A man who regularly reaches orgasm before he wants to, therefore, would be a candidate for sexual therapy.

A man who is disturbed by his own inability to exert any control over when he ejaculates may develop low self-esteem and performance anxiety (Kaplan, 1989). This, in turn, can lead to an erectile problem (and commonly does). Others may avoid dating new partners because of fear of embarrassment.

What causes some men to ejaculate too quickly? Tradi-tionally, it has been believed that in most cases premature ejaculation is due to psychological factors or interpersonal problems (e.g., anger at one's partner). In addition, many therapists believe that the early sexual experiences of many men actually teach them to rush during sex. Male masturbatory behavior is generally orgasm-oriented anyway, but a man may hurry it even more in situations where he fears being caught. Early heterosexual experiences often occur in places like a car, a parent's or friend's house, or some other place where there is a possibility of discovery, and thus sexual intercourse is hurried.

Recent studies indicate that there may be two different types of premature ejaculation: one caused by psychological factors and another caused by organic factors (Metz et al., 1997; Tiefer, 1994). Some types of injuries have been known to cause premature ejaculation, as do some medications and withdrawal from some narcotics (see Metz et al., 1997). Moreover, there are several pharmacological agents that delay ejaculation (antidepressants, benzodiazepine anxiolytics, dopamine antagonists). In fact, several studies have found that clomipramine (a tricyclic antidepressant) and various serotonin reuptake inhibitors can be used to increase ejaculatory latency in men with premature ejaculation (Rowland & Burnett, 2000).

The following therapeutic exercises are designed to teach a man not to hurry during sexual relations. After a couple has completed the sensate focus exercises described earlier, the woman is instructed to manually stimulate the man's penis until he gets close to orgasm. She then squeezes his penis firmly between her thumb and first and second fingers for 3 to 5 seconds and discontinues stimulation until he calms down. She repeats this three to four times before finally bringing him to orgasm. This *squeeze technique* was developed by Masters and Johnson (1970) and is still regarded as the most effective treatment. In a variation of this, called *stop-start,* the female partner simply stops manual stimulation and then starts again after the man's feeling of impending ejaculation has diminished (Semans, 1956). Both of these techniques teach the man that he can delay ejaculation, and he can also practice them during masturbation. When intercourse resumes, it is in a side-by-side or woman-on-top position (it generally takes longer to reach orgasm if you are not in total control).

Masters and Johnson (1970) have reported success rates of 95 percent. However, long-term follow-up studies show disappointing results. Most men who complete therapy successfully later regress to pretreatment levels (Metz et al., 1997; Schover & Leiblum, 1994). At this point, we do not know whether this means that traditional therapies should be changed (e.g., that follow-up therapy should be instituted) or whether greater effort should be made to identify and treat organic factors.

---

premature ejaculation A recurrent and persistent absence of reasonable voluntary control of ejaculation.

MALE ORGASMIC DISORDER

This problem can be thought of as just the opposite of premature ejaculation. **Male orgasmic disorder** (formerly called inhibited male orgasm or inhibited ejaculation) refers to a difficulty reaching orgasm and ejaculating in a woman's vagina, and it can be either *primary* or *secondary*. It used to be thought that only 1 or 2 percent of all men suffered from this problem (Masters & Johnson, 1970), but more recent studies indicate that perhaps as many as 7 to 9 percent of all men have this disorder on more than just an occasional basis (Laumann et al., 1999; Spector & Carey, 1990). It is often referred to as **ejaculatory incompetence** if the man is totally unable to ejaculate in a woman's vagina. Although a few cases can be traced to organic causes (e.g., drugs, alcohol, or neurological disorders; see Munjack & Kanno, 1979), most of these men are able to reach orgasm either during masturbation or during manual or oral stimulation by the partner (Kaplan, 1979), indicating that the usual cause is psychological and not physical.

Masters and Johnson (1970) reported that primary orgasmic disorder was often associated with a strict religious upbringing, a fear of getting a woman pregnant, negativity and hostility toward the partner, and/or maternal dominance. Secondary problems are less common and are often associated with some kind of previous trauma. Apfelbaum (1989) found that men with orgasmic disorder focus too much on performance and pleasing their partners, and as a result are subjectively not as aroused (as they are during masturbation, for example).

Inhibited ejaculation is often treated by what's called a *bridge maneuver*. The man is first taught to masturbate to orgasm while alone, and then in the presence of the partner. Once this is successfully completed, the partner manually stimulates the man to orgasm. When this is consistently successful, the female partner stimulates the man until he is very close to orgasm and then quickly inserts his penis into her vagina. The idea is that if this can be done several times, the man will overcome his fears of ejaculating inside her vagina. Apfelbaum additionally encourages men to be more assertive with partners in letting them know what they find to be arousing.

HEADACHES AFTER ORGASM

Several studies have brought attention to a problem suffered by some men (and a few women) during sex: severe headaches that start during or slightly after orgasm (see Diamond & Maliszewski, 1992, for several articles). This condition is called **benign coital cephalalgia** ("be-

nign orgasmic/sex headache"; alternative spelling: *cephalgia*). This is not a new problem, and in fact was first reported by Hippocrates, the father of modern medicine, in the fifth century B.C. It has been estimated that as many as 250,000 Americans may presently suffer from this problem. Most are men who are middle-aged, mildly obese, and somewhat hypertensive. The severe headaches resemble a migraine and may last for minutes or hours. They are not related to type of sexual activity, and although physicians sometimes mistake the pains as the sign of an imminent stroke, they are usually not associated with any other serious disorder. The headaches are in the general category of "exertional headaches" and are generally caused by contraction of scalp muscles and increased blood flow to the head, neck, or upper body during intercourse. For reasons that are not understood, the headaches often disappear for weeks or months at a time and then suddenly reappear. Another study found that the headaches eventually stop recurring in men who do not also suffer tension headaches or migraines (Ostergaard & Kraft, 1992). Treatment may include the teaching of relaxation techniques or medication for high blood pressure.

PRIAPISM

> "Sometimes my erection will stay for hours, which is kind of uncomfortable." (from the author's files)

To many men, the idea of having a *long-lasting erection* might seem appealing. **Priapism** is a rare condition in which the penis remains erect for prolonged periods of time, sometimes days. It results from damage to the valves regulating penile blood flow and can be caused by tumors, infection, or chemical irritants (such as Spanish fly; see Chapter 4). It is not usually accompanied by a desire for sex. Priapism is often painful, not to mention inconvenient, and men with this condition would gladly trade it for a normal erection. Many different treatments have been tried, ranging from ice packs to general anesthesia, but results from one study suggest that administration of the beta-agonist drug terbutaline is most effective (Shantha et al., 1990).

> *PERSONAL REFLECTIONS*
> *Are you able to comfortably communicate your sexual values and needs to your sexual partner or your potential partner? If not, what barriers are preventing you from doing so? Do you create any barriers that may prevent your partner from comfortably communicating his or her sexual values and needs to you?*

male orgasmic disorder A condition in which a man has difficulty reaching orgasm and ejaculating in a woman's vagina.

ejaculatory incompetence A condition in which a man is totally unable to ejaculate in a woman's vagina during sexual intercourse.

benign coital cephalalgia Severe headaches that start during or slightly after orgasm, usually in men.

priapism A condition in which the penis remains erect for a prolonged period of time, sometimes days.

FEMALE SEXUAL PROBLEMS

VAGINISMUS

Vaginismus refers to pain experienced during attempted sexual intercourse (intromission). It is caused by *involuntary contractions* of the muscles that surround the outer third of the vagina. Sometimes it is situational and occurs only during attempted intercourse, but in many cases vaginismus occurs at attempts to insert anything into the vagina (e.g., a finger or tampon). A pelvic examination may be impossible for women with this condition. To a man attempting intercourse, it feels like his penis is hitting a wall, and forceful attempts at penetration can be quite painful for the woman.

> "I was glad to see this topic addressed in your textbook and to know that it actually had a name. I was a virgin until I was 20 and when I did attempt intercourse, I encountered severe pain. My boyfriend at the time tried to be understanding, but it ended up tearing us apart. No matter how often we tried, we could not get it right. . . . I saw my OB/GYN and she gave me three different-sized vaginal dilators. I used these with KY Jelly but this was extremely humiliating. . . . I was helped over my fear by a much older man who took his time and made me feel extremely relaxed." (from the author's files)

About 2 percent of all women have vaginismus (Renshaw, 1990). Some therapists believe that vaginismus is a form of dyspareunia (de Kruiff et al., 2000). What often distinguishes the two is that the cause of vaginismus is usually *psychological* (Kaplan, 1974; Kleinplatz, 1998). It is normal for inexperienced women to have anxieties before intercourse that may result in some degree of involuntary muscle contraction, but the vast majority of women soon learn to relax (and even gain voluntary control over these muscles). Persistent and recurrent involuntary muscle spasms are often associated with past trauma (e.g., rape, abortion) or negative first sexual experiences, a religious upbringing (where sex is equated with sin), or hostility toward or fear of men (Masters & Johnson, 1970; Kleinplatz, 1998). Treatment usually consists of sensate focus relaxation exercises followed by systematic desensitization by *gradual dilation of the vagina* (with a set of dilators). The use of dilators in an atmosphere that is free of sexual demand, so that there is no performance anxiety, allows the woman to slowly overcome her anxieties about having an object in her vagina. The success rate approaches 100 percent (Masters & Johnson, 1970; Schnyder et al., 1998). Psychotherapy may have to be used as well in order to deal with past sexual trauma, guilt about sex, or relationship problems (Leiblum et al., 1989). Recently, an alternate humanistic approach has been suggested that emphasizes an integration of mind and body (Kleinplatz, 1998).

vaginismus A sexual problem in women in which pain is experienced during attempted intercourse because of involuntary spasms in the muscles surrounding the outer third of the vagina.

female orgasmic disorder A persistent or recurrent delay in, or absence of, orgasm following a normal sexual excitement phase.

FEMALE ORGASMIC DISORDER

The vast majority of women who seek sexual therapy do so because of problems in reaching orgasm. In their national survey, Laumann et al. (1999) found that about 27 percent of women aged 18–39 and over 22 percent of women aged 40–59 said that they had been unable to achieve orgasm for at least several months of the previous year. Many women have pretended to have an orgasm during sexual intercourse (Wiederman, 1997a). As with erectile problems, **female orgasmic disorder** can be *primary* or *absolute* (never having had an orgasm under any circumstances), *secondary* (having once been regularly orgasmic), or *situational* (e.g., able to reach orgasm during masturbation, but not during intercourse). Some men use the term *frigid* to describe such women, but this is an unfortunate term because it has negative connotations about a woman's emotional responsivity. Most women who have orgasm problems are emotionally responsive to sexual stimulation and otherwise enjoy sex.

One of the first questions to ask, of course, is whether a woman with problems reaching orgasm during sexual intercourse is receiving sufficient stimulation from her partner. Has there been enough time and foreplay?

> "My problem seems like one that some of my friends have—short foreplay. It takes me a long time to reach orgasm. When we take a long time and work up slowly to lovemaking, I have intense orgasms. It is wonderful for both of us. But this happens very rarely. Because 'John' works a 9-hour work day and usually comes home exhausted, our lovemaking is short and to the point. He's satisfied and I lay there feeling nothing because I faked an orgasm for him. Then, when I insist on continuing, I start to feel guilty for wasting his time." (from the author's files)

Remember that in response to a survey question asked in my course ("What things do you personally like best in a sexual partner?"), well over half of the women who indicated that they were sexually experienced answered that they wanted their partner (or partners) to take his time. Here are some examples:

> "Doesn't rush, and takes his time."

> "Lover takes his time and is as concerned with fondling and foreplay as he is intercourse."

> "Unhurried attitude toward sex and lovemaking in general."

> "Partner who likes to take time with foreplay and not rush into intercourse. A caring and sensitive person who is not out just to get a 'piece of ass.'"

A man's first physiological sexual response, you recall, is erection of the penis, which allows him to perform sexually almost immediately, even if he is experiencing very little emotionally. It generally takes women longer to reach orgasm than men (Kinsey et al., 1953), and many need additional emotional involvement as well, so that lengthy foreplay is very important for most women.

Even if her partner takes his time, many women may still have difficulties reaching orgasm during intercourse. The key for many women is the degree of stimulation to the clitoris. Most women prefer clitoral stimulation to reach orgasm, with or without vaginal stimulation (Darling et al., 1991). During sexual intercourse, the penis only indirectly stimulates the clitoris by causing the clitoral hood to rub back and forth over the clitoral glans. Helen Kaplan (1974) and Shere Hite (1976) have estimated, however, that fewer than half of all women are capable of reaching orgasm regularly during intercourse without more direct stimulation of the clitoris. I have seen numerous letters to magazine advice columns written by women who were concerned about their lack of physical sensations during intercourse, particularly in the missionary position. None could reach orgasm during intercourse, but they had no trouble during masturbation (with more clitoral stimulation), which indicates that there was nothing physically wrong. A letter to the *Playboy* "Advisor" was written by a woman whose partner refused to give her any type of clitoral stimulation so that she could "learn" how to have a vaginal orgasm.

Unfortunately, many men take the attitude that what feels good to the gander must also feel good to the goose—if it feels good to the man to have his penis in his partner's vagina, then it must also feel equally good to the woman. The stimulation provided by the vaginal walls to the penis during intercourse is similar to that experienced by men during masturbation, but the reverse is not true for women. The inner two-thirds of the vagina have relatively few nerve endings. Most women who masturbate do so by stimulating their clitoris. Men should not feel inadequate if their female partners require manual stimulation of the clitoris during intercourse to reach orgasm.

"Your class has also taught me how to talk to my boyfriend about sex. By stimulation of the clitoris manually it has brought great joy to my sex life. I now even reach orgasm from it during sex." (from the author's files)

Figure 15–5 A commonly used training technique for women.

If a man cares for his partner, he will do (or let her do) whatever she says feels best, not what he believes ought to feel best. *Therapists agree that clitoral stimulation during intercourse is not cheating.*

Not all cases of female orgasm problems can be blamed on insufficient stimulation. Sex is more than just the physical rubbing together of tissues. A healthy, positive attitude about sex and pleasure is also very important. Interestingly, Laumann et al. (1999) found that the prevalence of orgasm problems among women decreased as their education level increased, and education is associated with more positive attitudes about sex. Many cases of primary orgasmic disorder are associated with negative attitudes about sex or feelings of guilt about sex (often due to a very strict religious upbringing, where sexual feelings are associated with sin rather than something positive) (Kelly et al., 1990; Masters & Johnson, 1970).

> "I grew up sexually in marriage. In those days no one discussed sex, and my husband and I both only knew bits and pieces. I understood it to be very natural for women not to have orgasms, therefore, if I did, my private Catholic girl school upbringing made me feel ashamed of my own natural desires and pleasures."

> "I was a Catholic girl all my life. Throughout school there was always a hidden notion that sex was bad and dirty. Those views and ideas were always instilled in me. It made me feel as if I would die if I engaged in any sexual behavior." (All examples are from the author's files.)

Even if sex is not associated with sin, it is a fact that most parents allow their daughters less sexual freedom during adolescence than they allow their sons. Female sexuality is more likely to be suppressed during this period than is male sexuality.

> "I was told my whole life as a child and as an adolescent that because I was a woman, I was not supposed to feel sexual, or be sexual. My daddy told me that good women who wanted to be loved by a man did not feel sexual. A good man did not look for a woman who was sexual." (from the author's files)

Sexual suppression generally leads to passivity in sexual relations with a partner. But studies have found that sexually assertive women (those who are active in initiating sex and who communicate with their partners about their likes and dislikes) have higher frequencies of orgasms than less assertive women (Hurlbert, 1991). They also generally report greater satisfaction in their relationships. Women often get more assertive in their sexual relations as they grow older (Jacoby, 1999) and perhaps this is why more older women have orgasms than younger women (Laumann et al., 1999). Multiorgasmic women are generally more explorative in their sexual activities and more aware of pleasurable

sensations of the clitoris via masturbation than are other women (Darling et al., 1991).

In addition, sex involves sweating, underarm and vaginal odors (and often vaginal noises), and facial grimaces that many women were taught are unfeminine. To fully enjoy sex and experience the pleasures of orgasm, one must "let go." Simply telling a young woman that sex is now okay is not going to change these attitudes overnight. It may take years to overcome inhibitions about sex.

> "I was raised as good girls don't, and if you do you are used property. After getting married, the morals were supposed to change. I had great difficulty in the transition of why it is OK now, after marriage. I am now divorced. I wish I would have had your class prior to marriage. It would have made the transition a lot easier." (from the author's files)

Kinsey's group (1953) found that half of all women who masturbated did not start doing so until after the age of 20 (and thus probably after they were already sexually experienced). More recent studies have found that married women who have masturbated to orgasm have more orgasms and greater marital and sexual satisfaction than married women who have not masturbated to orgasm (Hurlbert & Whittaker, 1991). In fact, many therapists now include masturbation therapy as a first step in the treatment of inhibited female orgasm in order to make a woman more aware of her own body (LoPiccolo & Stock, 1986). The hope is that once a woman can reach orgasm during masturbation, she will be able to achieve it during sexual intercourse.

Performance anxiety can also contribute to orgasm problems. This can easily happen if a woman's partner expects or demands that she have an orgasm during sex. The subsequent spectatoring then makes the problem even worse. Just as with erectile disorders, it sometimes takes only a few instances of being unable to reach orgasm for a woman to develop performance anxiety.

> "My husband and I have a really good sex life, but I don't reach climax every time. This doesn't bother me, but it really bothers him. I've started worrying about it so much that I'm now having fewer orgasms and starting to fake more." (from the author's files)

Women (and their partners) should not expect to reach orgasm with every experience of sexual intercourse. This is an unrealistic expectation that can lead to unnecessary feelings of guilt (Davidson & Moore, 1994).

The behavioral and psychological factors that we have covered so far are really just generalities. In actuality, compared to men's responses very little research has been done regarding women's sexual responses (see

Leland, 2000b). Recently, however, there have been attempts to "medicalize" women's desire and orgasm problems, similar to what has happened with treatment of men's erectile disorders. For example, recall from Chapter 4 that the structure of the clitoris is very similar to the penis. Both consist of smooth muscle that becomes filled with blood during sexual arousal. Not surprisingly, then, there are currently attempts to increase women's sexual responsivity by treating them with the male impotence pill Viagra and other drugs, including testosterone (Bartlik et al., 1999; Leland, 2000b). In 2000, the government approved a hand-held device (called EROS-CTD) that uses a suction cup to draw blood into the clitoris, which supposedly would make a woman more responsive (see Leland, 2000b).

Figure 15–6 For any sexual problem, when the therapist allows the couple to resume sexual intercourse, it is almost always in the woman-on-top position. Women with orgasm problems are encouraged to touch their clitoris (or have their partners touch it) during intercourse.

To date, these medicalization approaches have not been very successful. Is that surprising? John Bancroft, head of the Kinsey Institute, stated, "We are still in a culture which has defined sexuality, sexual pleasure and [sexual goals] in male terms. Then we apply the same paradigm to women. That is a mistake" (quoted in Leland, 2000b, p. 50). All a man needs to have and enjoy intercourse is an erection, but women's sexual desire and pleasure is much more complex (see Basson, 2000) and depends to a large extent on the quality of the overall relationship. But before we consider that, let us first look at the behavior modification techniques used in traditional sex therapy.

What procedures are used in therapy to help a woman become more orgasmic? As explained earlier, if a woman has always had difficulty reaching orgasm (and particularly if she has never masturbated), the first thing that a therapist is likely to suggest is self-exploration. You don't necessarily need a therapist, but if you have never explored your body and responses before, some type of instruction will probably be necessary. A book by Heiman and LoPiccolo (1992), listed at the end of this chapter, is a good reference.

The next step is exploration with a partner—the widely used and popular sensate focus exercises. These nondemand exercises allow the woman and her partner to relax and learn what gives each maximum pleasure. The hand-riding technique is particularly useful here (Masters & Johnson, 1970). After several days of this, the therapist will probably instruct the partner to manually explore the woman's genitals, usually while both are sitting in the position shown in Figure 15–5.

When the couple is finally told that they may resume sexual intercourse, they will almost always be told to use a position that allows the woman a great deal of control, such as woman-on-top. She will decide when intromission begins and initiate pelvic movements once they start. By this point in therapy, both she and her partner will be comfortable with manual stimulation of the clitoris during intercourse. Remember, *manual stimulation of the clitoris during intercourse is not cheating.* Helen Kaplan (1974) has suggested that couples at first interrupt intercourse with periods of additional foreplay, but contrary to advice given in a popular book (Eichel & Nobile, 1992), no particular technique of intercourse can guarantee orgasms (Kaplan, 1992). The couple will have to try different techniques. With some practice, for example, the woman might be able to reach orgasm without manual stimulation by rubbing her clitoris against her partner's pubic bone, or vice versa (in a "high-ride" position). Recall from Chapter 2 that Kegel exercises may help some women with vaginal sensations and orgasmic responsiveness.

If at this point you are thinking that female orgasm problems have been treated rather mechanically, as if the solution is nothing more than finding the correct manner of physical stimulation, you are probably right. For many women, sexual satisfaction is closely related to how emotionally involved they are with their partners and how happy they are in their overall relationship

Box 15–A CROSS-CULTURAL PERSPECTIVES

Sex Therapy

The model of sex therapy presented in this chapter is based primarily on Western, middle-class values (Lavee, 1991). The two most important assumptions in the model are that people engage in sex primarily for (physical) pleasure, and that men and women can be viewed as equals. The model also assumes that men and women want to know about sex and that better communication makes for better sex.

Not all cultures share these attitudes. Recall from Box 4–A, for example, that in large parts of northern Africa and the Middle East (with primarily Islamic populations), sexual pleasure is reserved for the men, and women's pleasure is denied by clitoral circumcision and genital mutilation. Many Latin countries are also male-dominant to the point of denying women's sexual feelings (Guerrero Pavich, 1986). In these cultures, a woman's difficulty in reaching orgasm is not considered important, and certainly no grounds for therapy. Even painful intercourse (dyspareunia, vaginismus) is considered unimportant unless it interferes with a woman's ability to engage in sex. For women, the only purposes of sex are procreation and the pleasure of the husband. For men, premature ejaculation is not regarded as a problem. Men do regard difficulty in getting and maintaining an erection as a problem, and may seek therapy in order to engage in sexual intercourse (Osman & Al-Sawaf, 1995). However, both men and women reject the very idea of engaging in sensate focus exercises as a solution, for this is a mutual pleasuring technique (Lavee, 1991).

In sharp contrast to these attitudes (and our own) about sex are those held by many Hindu and Buddhist societies (Voigt, 1991). Tantric scriptures urge people to strive for the goal of transcendent unity and harmony, and thus sex is viewed as an opportunity for spiritual growth. While Western therapists emphasize the mutual physical pleasures of sex, these Asian societies emphasize the spiritual union. For example, in this chapter orgasm is presented as resulting from proper physical stimulation and effective technique. Those who follow Tantrism, on the other hand, "understand orgasm as a product of deep relaxation and a profound level of contact between partners" (Voigt, 1991). Western culture emphasizes doing, stimulation, activation, and outcome-focus, while Tantrism emphasizes being, stillness, meditation, and process-immersion. Good sex is not achieved by focusing on one or the other partner, but by focusing on the "between." Couples might be urged to follow five exercises (Voigt, 1991): (1) creation of a ceremonial sex ritual (a simple ceremony that sets the tone for shared sexual expression—for example, candles, flowers, a special room, massage, chanting together or joint meditation); (2) synchronized breathing while embracing or touching; (3) sustained, steady eye contact; (4) becoming motionless at the peak sensual experience during intercourse; and (5) refraining from orgasm at times in order to intensify the sexual-spiritual energy.

Sex therapy as we know it is geared, obviously, to our particular cultural beliefs, and perhaps to only part of our society. Nonwhite people, for example, are much less interested in going to sex therapy for an acknowledged sex problem than are white people (Perez et al., 1993). This may be due, in part, to a distrust of mental health professionals (Wilson, 1986), but it may also reflect different cultural attitudes about sex. Lavee (1991) has suggested that rather than trying to teach all people what healthy sex is (based on middle-class Western values), therapists would be wiser to fit the treatment to the individuals' cultural values.

(Hurlbert & Whittaker, 1991; Lawrance & Byers, 1995). These things are better predictors of a woman's sexual satisfaction than are frequency of sex and number of orgasms (Hurlbert et al., 1993). Conversely, the better a woman regards her emotional relationship with her partner, the more likely she is to judge her sex life satisfying (Jacoby, 1999; Kingsberg, 2000). In other words, for many women the therapy steps outlined in this section may do little good if the emotional aspects of their relationships are not satisfying.

SEXUAL PROBLEMS AMONG HOMOSEXUALS

Like some heterosexuals, homosexuals sometimes suffer from sexual problems, and they also seek sex therapy to deal with them. However, the types of problems and the focus of therapy is often different for homosexual men and women. Heterosexuals generally go to therapy for problems related to sexual intercourse, but homosexuals seeking sex therapy often have problems that arise from dealing with HIV and AIDS and/or sexual prejudice within society, which in some cases become internalized (Margolies et al., 1988; Nichols, 1988; Reece, 1988; Shannon & Woods, 1991). These problems can lead to depression (or, in the case of internalized homophobia, repression of sexuality) and consequent loss of sexual desire. Orgasm problems are not common among lesbians, but many lesbians who go to therapy have negative feelings about engaging in cunnilingus (Margolies et al., 1988). Similarly, many gay men in therapy have negative feelings about anal sex (Reece, 1988).

Masters and Johnson (1979) reported a 93 percent success rate for treating erectile disorders in male homosexuals as well as orgasm disorders in lesbians. Sensate focus exercises used with heterosexuals are similarly used with homosexuals. In fact, the success rate for homosexuals is generally higher than that for heterosexuals. This may be due to the fact that members of the same sex may be more understanding of the needs and pleasurable experiences of homosexual partners. In any case, an understanding partner who is sympathetic, willing to communicate, and not overly demanding is crucial to successful sex therapy for both heterosexual and homosexual individuals.

AVOIDING SEXUAL PROBLEMS

What have you learned in this and previous chapters that you could apply to your own life in order to minimize the chance that sexual problems will occur? First, establish an open, honest line of communication with your partner. Although you should learn to accentuate and reinforce the positive aspects of your relationship, this does not mean that you cannot say "no." A sexually healthy person, you remember, is free to make choices, but you must work any differences out with your partner.

In order to communicate, we must be properly educated. Sexual therapy, in fact, is really just sex education combined with a medical exam and counseling. Why did you have to wait until your age to receive sex education? When you have children, teach them the proper names for their body parts and instruct them about sexuality in such a way that they will grow up to think of the human body as something beautiful and good. A good sex life can contribute to a healthy and satisfying life. You can treat sexuality as something positive while at the same time teaching morals and sexual responsibility. Whatever you do, never equate sex with sin and guilt.

In the relationship with your partner, try to learn and grow together. Remember, a good relationship with your partner (i.e., sharing and caring) often carries over into sexual relations. Keep your sexual relations spontaneous and fun, and do not put pressure on yourself and set goals as if sex were an Olympic event. Remember, "Despite what the magazine covers at the supermarket checkout line may suggest, it is far from true that everyone is having more, better, hotter sex than you" (Howe, 1999).

Key Terms

benign coital cephalalgia 389
cognitive-behavioral therapy 377
dyspareunia 382
ejaculatory incompetence 389
erectile disorder 383
female orgasmic disorder 390
global sexual problem 383
hypersexuality 381
hypoactive sexual desire 379
male orgasmic disorder 389

medical history 377
medical model 377
performance anxiety 386
phimosis 382
PLISSIT model 377
premature ejaculation 388
priapism 389
primary sexual problem 383
psychosexual therapy 377
secondary sexual problem 383

self-awareness 378
sensate focus exercises 378
sexual addiction 381
sexual aversion 380
sexual history 377
sexual surrogate 378
situational sexual problem 383
spectatoring 386
systematic desensitization 377
vaginismus 390

Suggested Readings

Barbach, L. G. (1982). *For each other: Sharing sexual intimacy.* New York: Anchor/Doubleday.

Boston Women's Health Book Collective. (1998). *Our bodies, ourselves For the new century: A book by and for women.* New York: Simon & Schuster.

Heiman, J., & LoPiccolo, J. (1992). *Becoming orgasmic: A sexual and personal growth program for women.* New York: Simon & Schuster.

Kaplan, H. (1987). *The illustrated manual of sex therapy.* New York: Brunner/Mazel. Easy to read and tastefully written.

Kaplan, H. S. (1989). *PE: How to overcome premature ejaculation.* New York: Brunner/Mazel.

Kaplan, H. S. (1995). *Sexual desire disorders: Dysfunctional regulation of sexual motivation.* New York: Brunner/Mazel. Extensive coverage of hypoactive sexual desire and hypersexuality from the therapist who pioneered work in desire disorders.

Leland, J. (2000, May 29). The science of women & sex. *Newsweek.* A look at how science is attempting to "treat" orgasmic problems and low sexual desire in women.

Leland, J., et al. (1997, November 17). A pill for impotence? *Newsweek.* A good article on Viagra.

Schnarch, D. M. (1998). *Passionate marriage: Love, sex, and intimacy in emotionally committed relationships.* New York: Holt, Schnarch's earlier work written for the public.

Thayer, S. (1988, March). Close encounters. *Psychology Today.* Explores the role of touching in intimate relationships and examines gender and cultural differences.

Zilbergeld, B. (1999). *The new male sexuality.* New York: Bantam Books. A readable book about male sexuality and overcoming problems.

Study Guide

INTERACTIVE REVIEW

Studies have found that (1) _____ of all couples in the United States will eventually experience sexual problems. While some couples may grow apart and experience a variety of relationship problems (sex being just one indicator that there are other problems), even couples with a good relationship can experience sexual problems. It is common for two people in a relationship to differ in their preferences for frequency and type of sex. This often results from different expectations and assumptions about sex. When this happens, it is best to consider the problem as the (2) _____ problem. If the problem persists and is causing stress and anxiety, it is advisable to seek professional help.

Sex therapists are trained to (3) _____. They consider it unethical to (4) _____. Most sexual problems are treated with (5) _____, developed by Masters and Johnson; psychosexual therapy; or a combination of both. Sexual therapy programs generally have many things in common and follow the (6) _____ model, an acronym for permission, limited information, specific suggestions, and intensive therapy. Each represents a progressively deeper level of therapy. Most therapists will probably take a (7) _____ and (8) _____ history first. Some clients will need self-awareness exercises, but for most couples the first set of general exercises will be nondemand mutual pleasuring techniques called (9) _____. After completing these, the couple will then be assigned specific exercises.

Many therapists believe that the most common problem of couples seeking therapy is (10) _____. This refers to a persistent and pervasive inhibition of sexual desire. In its most extreme form, the avoidance of sex becomes phobic in nature and is called (11) _____. This generally requires psychosexual therapy. At the other extreme, hypersexual individuals are distinguished by the (12) _____ with which they engage in sex. A controversial term for these persons is (13) _____. Painful intercourse, or (14) _____, can occur in either men or women and can have a variety of causes, both organic and psychological.

The most common sexual problem specific to men is probably (15) _____, which is usually defined as a recurrent and persistent absence of (16) _____. Probably the most psychologically devastating male problem is (17) _____, which can have organic and/or psychological causes. The most common psychological cause is (18) _____. Difficulty reaching orgasm and ejaculating in a woman's vagina is called (19) _____ and usually has a psychological cause. Some men suffer from benign coital cephalalgia, or (20) _____, while others suffer from long-lasting (often painful) erections, a condition called (21) _____.

Some women experience involuntary contractions of the muscles surrounding the vaginal opening when they attempt intercourse, which results in pain. (22) _____, as it is called, usually has a psychological cause. The vast majority of women who go to sexual therapy do so because of problems (23) _____. This can be due to a variety of causes, including poor techniques by the partner, sexual repression during the woman's upbringing, and general relationship problems. When one member of a couple has a sexual problem, it is not unusual for the partner to develop a corresponding sexual difficulty.

Homosexuals can have many of the same sexual problems experienced by heterosexuals, but often experience additional problems that arise from dealing with (24) _____ and/or (25) _____.

SELF-TEST

A. TRUE OR FALSE

[T] [F] 26. Bob wants to have sex twice a week but is in a relationship with Sue, who wants to have sex every day. In this example, it is clear that Sue is hypersexual.

[T] [F] 27. The most frequent sexual problem for women seeking sex therapy is difficulty reaching orgasm.

[T] [F] 28. Stimulation of the clitoris during intercourse should not be necessary, and a woman should be able to be orgasmic through intercourse alone.

[T] [F] 29. Performance anxiety can cause sexual problems in men, but not women.

[T] [F] 30. The American Psychiatric Association defines a premature ejaculator as any man who usually reaches orgasm within 2 minutes of beginning sexual intercourse.

[T] [F] 31. Most women who have difficulty reaching orgasm do not enjoy sex.

[T] [F] 32. In order to help their clients, most sex therapists require them to stop masturbating.

[T] [F] 33. Dyspareunia is usually caused by a physical problem.

[T] [F] 34. Many men with psychologically caused erectile problems get full erections during sensate focus exercises.

[T] [F] 35. Sexual problems in one partner in a relationship often lead to sexual problems in the other partner.

[T] [F] 36. Female orgasm problems are always the result of insufficient stimulation.

[T] [F] 37. If it feels good to you, it must feel good to your partner.

[T] [F] 38. Most sex therapists today omit taking a medical history because most sex problems are psychologically caused.

[T] [F] 39. Therapists are in agreement that hypersexuality is a form of addiction similar to addiction to alcohol or drugs.

[T] [F] 40. Erectile problems are inevitable as men grow older.

[T] [F] 41. A majority of erectile problems have a physical basis.

[T] [F] 42. Headaches during orgasm occur mainly in men.

[T] [F] 43. The sex therapy model presented in this chapter is applicable to most peoples of the world.

B. MATCHING: FOR EACH OF THE SEXUAL PROBLEMS BELOW, MATCH WHICH TECHNIQUES THERAPISTS WOULD BE LIKELY TO USE (IN ORDER) ACCORDING TO THE TEXT. ANSWERS MAY BE USED MORE THAN ONCE.

_____ 44. hypoactive sexual desire

_____ 45. hypersexuality

_____ 46. dyspareunia

_____ 47. psychological erectile problem

_____ 48. premature ejaculation

_____ 49. male orgasmic disorder

a. sensate focus
b. psychosexual (or psycho-) therapy
c. Kegel exercises
d. bridge maneuver
e. use of dilators
f. resume woman-on-top position of intercourse
g. self-exploration and masturbation
h. tease technique

_____ 50. benign coital cephalalgia
_____ 51. vaginismus
_____ 52. female orgasmic disorder

i. treatment of the internal discomfort (antidepressants or stabilizing drugs)
j. treatment of specific organic cause (usually has organic cause)
k. squeeze technique or stop-start technique
l. relaxation techniques or medication for high blood pressure

C. FILL IN THE BLANKS

53. Most women need stimulation of the _____ in order to reach orgasm, even during intercourse.

54. Most therapists believe that the _____ position has the most erotic potential for both people during intercourse.

55. When a person begins to observe and evaluate his or her own sexual responses during sex, that is called _____, and it can be a cause of sexual problems.

56. PLISSIT is an acronym for _____, _____, _____ and _____.

57. The therapy technique used to reduce anxiety by slowly introducing elements of the anxiety-producing stimulus is called _____.

58. Sensate focus exercises are _____ techniques.

59. In men, painful intercourse can be caused by the foreskin of the penis being too tight, a condition called _____.

60. In men, a life stress such as unemployment could lead to _____.

61. If a man is totally unable to ejaculate in a woman's vagina, this is called _____.

62. Vaginismus is usually caused by _____.

63. Tantrism emphasizes _____ during sex.

64. Probably the most difficult sexual problem to treat successfully is _____.

Chapter 16

Paraphilias and Sexual Variants

*One fact about human behavior that is so obvious that it needs no research program to establish its truth
is that humans judge some sexual practices to be undesirable and changeworthy. . . . The particulars
surrounding these negative judgments made by mental health professionals about some sexual practices
are, unfortunately, not so clear. For example, it is not clear on what grounds humans in general,
or mental health professionals in particular, either do evaluate or should evaluate sexual practices.
That is, should sexual practices be evaluated on the grounds of whether they harm others (If so, what
kinds of harm, and how much harm, are necessary for the behavior to be regarded as a mental
disorder?), or whether the sexual practices are unhealthy (utilizing this criterion is clearly
problematic as it simply pushes the question to how properly healthy practices can be distinguished
from unhealthy ones), or whether the behaviors deviate from a statistical norm, or whether the
behaviors seem to be maladaptive in some evolutionary sense?*

(D. Richard Laws & William O' Donohue, 1997)

There are enormous individual differences among people in every aspect of human behavior. It should be obvious from the many references to other cultures throughout this book that this includes sexual behavior as well. Variety in behavior is usually considered to be good. We enjoy wearing different clothing, eating different foods, listening to different kinds of music—and, as you learned in Chapter 13, most of us enjoy practicing a variety of sexual behaviors.

What determines whether a behavior is designated "normal" or "conventional" as opposed to "abnormal" or "unconventional"? You may be surprised that what is considered to be normal or conventional is not always easy to define. Most of us would probably agree that someone who ate beetles was abnormal, but this is common in some African cultures. Obviously, cultural factors must be considered. Even within the same culture,

When you have finished studying this chapter, you should be able to:

1. Describe the various ways (i.e., statistical, sociological, and psychological approaches) one can define a behavior as being unconventional;

2. Explain the difference between a sexual variant and a paraphilia;

3. Define and discuss the following paraphilias: fetishism, transvestism, exhibitionism, obscene phone calls, voyeurism,

zoophilia, pedophilia, sadism, masochism, urophilia, coprophilia, mysophilia, frotteurism, klismaphilia, and necrophilia;

4. Discuss the various theories of how paraphilias develop and why nearly all paraphiliacs are men; and

5. Discuss the treatment (therapy) for individuals with a paraphilia.

what is believed to be normal today may not have been viewed as normal in the past, and may not be viewed as normal in the future. Here's an example. If a woman wears a string bikini on the beach today, she is considered normal. But if a woman living in 1900 (or maybe even 1950) had worn that outfit to a beach, she would have been arrested. On the other hand, if a woman wore a full-length swimsuit with bloomers to the beach today (the typical swimwear for American women in 1900), she might be considered sexually inhibited. Similarly, a man or woman can walk half-naked in New Orleans' French Quarter on Mardi Gras day and not get arrested. However, if he or she walked half-naked down the same streets the day before or the day after Mardi Gras, the person would be arrested.

Even at the same point in time in the same culture, normal behavior might be a matter of where it is observed. If someone tried to sunbathe in the nude at the local public swimming pool, he or she would probably be arrested. If this same person were sunning himself or herself on certain beaches on the West or East Coast, on the other hand, he or she could walk in naked splendor along with a whole beach full of other naked people. When does such behavior start being normal—before getting to the beach, after getting to the beach, never, or always? Again, the point is that "normal" is not an absolute thing. It can be determined by many factors, including where you are and when you are there.

Researchers have generally attempted to define "normal" or "abnormal" in one of three ways. One way is called the *statistical approach,* in which a behavior is considered normal or conventional if a large number of people engage in it, and abnormal or unconventional if only a few people do it (Pomeroy, 1966). Some professionals who use the statistical approach do not use "abnormal" or "unconventional" to describe behaviors, and instead use the label "sexual minorities" (Gagnon, 1977). There are, of course, some rather large minorities, and there are some behaviors that are so different that they represent a minority of one. However, the fact that only a minority of people have engaged in a behavior does not necessarily make that behavior bad or wrong, or the individuals disturbed or sick. Probably only a small minority of people in our culture, for example, have ever had sex outdoors (in private) at night under the stars, but most would agree that doing so would certainly not be a sign of mental illness. Because of the limitations of the statistical approach—defining normal and abnormal purely in terms of numbers—others have preferred a sociological or psychological approach.

The *sociological approach* calls a behavior unconventional if it is not customary within a society. Customs vary, not only from culture to culture but also within subcultures. Followers of the sociological approach are concerned with the social conditions that give rise to ab-

Figure 16–1 Walking on the beach naked might seem unusual and unacceptable to you, but if it is not done in front of unwilling observers, it is a sexual variant, not a paraphilia.

normal behavior as well as the interactions between people labeled abnormal and the rest of society.

The *psychological approach* focuses on the psychological health of the individual and the impact that behaviors have on this health (Buss, 1966). A sexual activity is considered to be a problem behavior if it makes an individual feel distressed or guilty or causes him or her problems in functioning efficiently in ordinary social and occupational roles.

This chapter will focus primarily on the psychological approach. Let us now take a look at how the psychiatric/psychological profession has dealt with the subject of sexual abnormalities.

HISTORICAL PERSPECTIVE

By the middle of the 11th century, Christian Church leaders had begun to regard sexual intercourse in any other position except the missionary position as an unnatural act, a sin against nature (Brundage, 1984). Shortly afterwards, Thomas Aquinas declared in his

Summa theologiae that there were four categories of un-natural acts: masturbation, bestiality, sodomy (which included homosexuality), and unnatural positions of intercourse (Murray, 1998).

In the Victorian era, sexual behaviors that were considered abnormal were referred to as "perversions" and later as "deviations." The first modern classification of sexual deviations was made by Richard von Krafft-Ebing in 1886 (*Psychopathia Sexualis*). His work was based on the premise that people are genetically predisposed toward sexual deviation; and although this theory has been discredited, Krafft-Ebing's case histories are still widely cited.

The Victorians were influenced by the "seminal theory," which can be traced back to Hippocrates in ancient Greece (Haller & Haller, 1977). According to this theory, the seed (the essence of life) was contained in semen. (The role of the ovum in reproduction was not understood until the 20th century.) As part of this theory, it was believed that semen contained cells that caused male maturation (Fitz-Gerald & Fitz-Gerald, 1998). Frequent sex (e.g., masturbation) could deplete a man of these critical cells and result in a stunting of both thought and secondary sex characteristics. Thus, masturbation was not only a perversion, but "self-abuse."

Sigmund Freud believed that any type of sexual behavior that took precedence over heterosexual vaginal intercourse was an indication of impaired psychosexual development (see Parsons, 2000). A person's sexual behavior was considered deviant if it was not directed toward an appropriate object (a heterosexual partner) and/or the aim was not sexual intercourse. According to this view, masturbation and oral-genital sex were considered very disturbed. (This is another excellent example of how what is considered abnormal depends on the time and culture.)

Simon (1994) has made an interesting distinction between the terms *deviance* and *perversion*. According to him, *sexual deviance* is "the inappropriate or flawed performance of a conventionally understood sexual practice." He uses rape as an example; we rarely refer to it as a perversion. Rape would be considered a perversion only if committed on someone whose inclusion in the act went beyond what we consider to be normal. Simon emphasizes that as sexual practices change, so do our definitions of deviance (oral sex being a good example). *Perversion,* on the other hand, "can be thought of as a disease of sexual desire not only in the sense that it appears to violate the sexual practices of a time and place, but also because it constitutes a violation of common understandings that render current sexual practice plausible. The 'pervert' is disturbing because, at the level of folk psychology, we have difficulty understanding why someone 'might want to do something like that.'" Thus, according to Simon, deviance is a problem of control, while perversion is a problem

of desire. Here, too, Simon emphasizes that our concept of perversion can change with time. Masturbation is a good example (see Chapter 13 for a history of attitudes). So, too, is homosexuality. Until the mid-1970s, the American Psychiatric Association regarded homosexuality as an official mental illness, a perversion (see Chapter 11).

Today, the American Psychiatric Association's handbook *Diagnostic and Statistical Manual of Mental Disorders* (DSM-IV, 1994) refers to psychosexual disorders of the type considered in this chapter as **paraphilias,** derived from the Greek *para* (meaning "besides," "beyond," or "amiss") and philia ("love"). Not all statistically or sociologically unusual behaviors are paraphilias. For a person's behavior to be called a paraphilia, the distinguishing feature must be that the person's sexual arousal and gratification *depend almost exclusively* on engaging in or thinking (fantasizing) about the behavior. The essential features of a paraphilia are that the fantasies and behaviors are recurrent (American Psychiatric Association DSM-IV, 1994).

As you read through the chapter, there will probably be one or more behaviors covered that you have either fantasized about or engaged in yourself on occasion (e.g., voyeurism, exhibitionism, bondage). This does not mean you have a paraphilia. It would be a paraphilia only if that was the preferred way in which you become sexually aroused. Otherwise, behaviors and fantasies are generally referred to as **sexual variants** (Stoller, 1977).

Some of the paraphilias covered in this chapter can result in physical harm to oneself (e.g., masochism) or physical or psychological harm to others (e.g., sadism, exhibitionism, voyeurism, pedophilia). Some can lead to arrest and prosecution. However, others would appear to be harmless—transvestism (cross-dressing) in the privacy of one's own home, for example. Some clinicians argue that harmless behaviors (this assumes that the behavior is engaged in without feelings of guilt, shame, or remorse) should not have a negative label, but others say that no paraphilia is harmless because, as the only source of sexual gratification, it deprives the individual of physically affectionate relations with others.

The following sections describe many, but not all, paraphilias. The chapter concludes with a discussion of causes and treatments.

FETISHISM

In anthropology, a fetish is an object that is believed to have magical powers (usually by capturing or embodying a powerful spirit). The term

paraphilias General term for a group of sexual disorders in which a person's sexual arousal and gratification depend almost exclusively on unusual behaviors.

sexual variant Unusual behaviors that are engaged in for variety and not as one's preferred manner of becoming sexually aroused.

erotic fetishism was coined by Alfred Binet (inventor of the first standardized intelligence test) in 1888. It generally refers to achieving sexual arousal and gratification almost exclusively by handling or fantasizing about an inanimate object or a particular part of the body.

Some of the more common fetishes involve women's undergarments (panties, bras, or stockings), shoes (usually high-heeled) or boots, hair, objects made of leather or rubber, and feet (Junginger, 1997). Fetishes involving hard objects such as boots, leather, or rubber objects are often associated with sadomasochistic practices and fantasies. Heterosexual male fetishists are aroused by the theme of "femininity" in their preferred object, while homosexual male fetishists are aroused by the theme of "masculinity" in the preferred objects (Weinberg et al., 1994). It is not uncommon for fetishists to be attracted to two or more objects (Junginger, 1997).

The large majority of known fetishists are men, and when their fetish involves clothing or shoes, they greatly prefer articles that have been used and have an odor. A man with a panty fetish, for example, would become highly aroused by a used pair of panties that retained vaginal odor, but would probably not be very aroused by the same panties if they were clean.

> "I work at a department store. One night I was folding towels when a man came over and started asking silly questions like, 'How often do you put rugs on sale?' I noticed that while he was talking, he kept glancing at my feet. He asked me where I got my shoes and if the inside was soft. He also asked if they held an odor. Not thinking, I said 'no' and took off a shoe. By this time, he had knelt down, picked up the shoe, and smelled it several times. He then gave it back and immediately left the store. Since my experience, he has been back in the store twice and has done the same thing to two other girls."

> "I know a married man in his late 20s who has a fetish. He goes around asking women (the ones he has affairs with) for a pair of their dirty underwear." (All examples are from the author's files.)

I chose to cover fetishism first because it provides an excellent example of the difference between a paraphilia and a variant. Most heterosexual men are aroused by women's panties, and many men have purchased sheer, lacy lingerie items for their partners. Most men have preferences about a partner's anatomy (breasts, buttocks, legs, shoulders). Many have

Figure 16–2 Edward Hyde, Governor of New York (1702–1709), chose to have his portrait painted while dressed in female clothing.

sucked their partner's toes, and some of you may have even sniffed a pair of panties sometime in your lifetime. For the large majority of men, none of these are the end goal; they merely serve to enhance sexual activity with their partners, not to compete with them. Thus, activities like buying lingerie or sucking a partner's toes are considered normal variants—they fall within the normal range of behavior. The fetishist, on the other hand, is focused exclusively on the object (e.g., panties) or body part (e.g., toes). The partner's personality or body as a whole cannot sustain arousal; her only role is to serve as a vehicle by which to enact the fantasy. In its most extreme form, the fetishist doesn't need or desire the partner at all.

Sexual arousal to specific objects or body parts has been explained in terms of a two-step learning process involving both classical and operant conditioning (Junginger, 1997). Other explanations will be considered later. Consider, for example, heterosexual men's arousal by women's panties. Most men's first exposure to women's panties comes during early necking or petting experiences, at which time they are highly sexually aroused. A few associations of panties with this emotional state, and panties themselves elicit some degree of arousal. This is an example of classical conditioning. A demonstration of this process was provided several years ago (Rachman, 1966). Under laboratory conditions, men were shown pictures of women's boots paired with pictures of nude women. After many pairings, pictures of the boots alone elicited sexual arousal (measured by penile blood volume). Men's sexual arousal can be classically conditioned to other objects as well (Lalumière & Quinsey, 1998).

Some clinicians have suggested that sexual arousal to an object or body part could develop into a fetish by a person's repeatedly reinforcing the behavior by including the object in fantasies during masturbation. This is an example of operant conditioning. Many men with fetishes were first attracted to their desired objects at an early age, perhaps as a result of the object's being associated with some of their first experiences of sexual arousal. The average age at which men first displayed paraphiliac interests is 16 years old (Abel & Rouleau, 1990).

How common is fetishism? We don't really know; fetishists rarely are arrested or seek therapy on their own. However, in a survey by Janus and Janus (1993) of people's attitudes about fetishes, 22 percent of the men and 18 percent of the women said that they thought fetishes were either "very normal" or "all

fetishism A condition in which sexual arousal occurs primarily when using or fantasizing about an inanimate object or a particular part of the body.

right" (as opposed to "unusual," "kinky," or "never heard of it"). Fewer than 2 percent said that this was their preferred way to achieve orgasm.

TRANSVESTISM

"He was an officer in the army (respected by his fellow officers and men), a devoted husband, and a father. He also wore women's clothing at home, often passing as a female relative, and was known as 'aunt' to his child when he assumed his womanly role." (cited in Hirschfeld, 1948, pp. 174–78)

Transvestism (from the Latin *trans,* meaning "across," and *vestia,* meaning "dress") refers to dressing as a member of the opposite sex *in order to achieve sexual arousal and gratification.* In fact, many experience orgasm while cross-dressing (Docter & Prince, 1997). Most researchers regard transvestism as very similar to a clothing fetish (and thus it is often called transvestic fetishism), except that the clothing is worn rather than just held and looked at (Zucker & Blanchard, 1997).

Figure 6–3 Transvestite talk-show host RuPaul (right) with comedian Joan Rivers.

Cross-dressing is not considered an example of transvestism if it is done for fashion (as in the case of most women who dress in "men's" clothing), if the clothes are worn as a party costume or for an act (as with female impersonators, for example), or as part of transsexualism (in which case individuals cross-dress not for sexual arousal but because they believe themselves to be members of the opposite sex).

Three large surveys of transvestites found that the large majority were heterosexual men and most were married (Buhrich, 1976; Docter & Prince, 1997; Prince & Bentler, 1972). In fact, the definition of transvestism in the American Psychiatric Association's DSM-IV (1994) focuses exclusively on heterosexual men. However, a few identify themselves as homosexual or bisexual, and over half of them prefer the masculine and feminine roles equally (Bullough & Bullough, 1997a; Docter & Prince, 1997).

A few men completely cross-dress as women and walk about in public for short periods of time, but most transvestites cross-dress secretly in the privacy of their own homes. Many wear only female undergarments under their male clothing during their cross-dressing. The transvestite may masturbate during a cross-dressing episode or during fantasies of cross-dressing, or may use the experience to become aroused enough to have sex with a partner. About one-fourth of the wives of transvestites accept their husbands' behaviors, but most only tolerate it, and many are distressed and resent it, especially if they discovered it only after they were married (Brown, 1994; Docter & Prince, 1997).

How many transvestites are there in the United States? Enough so that there exists an entire transvestite subculture, with clubs, magazines, and newsletters (transvestites generally identify themselves in underground newspapers by the abbreviation TV). In one survey, 2 percent of the men felt that cross-dressing was "very normal" and 6 percent thought it was "all right" (Janus & Janus, 1993). Other researchers estimate the prevalence of transvestism to be about 1 percent of the adult male population (Bullough & Bullough, 1993).

Why do some men dress in women's clothing? Transvestites are a very diverse group. Bullough (1991) says transvestism can be looked at "as an attempt for males to escape the narrow confines of the masculine role." Others hold the view that what transvestites have in common is a "comforting fantasy of the self as a girl or woman" (Levine, 1993). Most transvestites started cross-dressing before puberty (Buhrich, 1976; Docter & Prince, 1997), but most children have had experiences of cross-dressing (remember, children do not acquire the concept of gender

transvestism A condition in which sexual arousal is achieved primarily by dressing as a member of the opposite sex.

constancy until about age 7 [see Chapter 10] so most young boys will dress up as both Mom and Dad). Most research has found that transvestite men were not effeminate during childhood and did not display cross-gender behaviors or a tendency to play with girls as children (Zucker & Blanchard, 1997).

Is there anything that distinguishes the early childhood cross-dressing experiences of transvestites from those of others? Some transvestites report that they were punished by being made to dress as girls (Stoller, 1977), while some were encouraged to dress as girls (Bullough et al., 1983). Some clinicians believe that transvestism arises at an early age through association of opposite-sex clothing with sexual arousal (in the same manner that fetishes are acquired). However, explanations for transvestism (or for why there are many more male transvestites than female ones) range from the psychoanalytic (an attempt to conquer castration fears) and the anthropological-economic (Munroe, 1980) to the neurological (right-brain/left-brain differences; Flor-Henry, 1987) and the sociobiological (Wilson, 1987).

> *PERSONAL REFLECTIONS*
> *Do you believe that it is okay for consenting adults to engage in any sexual behavior in private as long as it does not cause physical and/or emotional injury and does not interfere with normal social and occupational activities? Why or why not?*

EXHIBITIONISM

"One day at sunset, I was walking back to my car in the . . . parking lot. As I was opening my car door I glanced over at the car facing mine. . . . This man was almost in a backbend over his driver seat masturbating at full speed. For a moment I was stunned and shocked. I just got in my car and drove off." (from the author's files)

In today's society, exposure of the body is highly glamorized and commercialized—in movies and television, books and magazines, and advertisements. Many people, including many celebrities, have posed naked for magazines, and some even star in sexually explicit films or "topless-bottomless" stage shows. Some of you may have gone to a nudist colony at one time or another. However, none of these are examples of exhibitionism because they involve willing observers. **Exhibitionism** (or indecent exposure) is defined as exposing one's genitals to unsuspecting strangers in order to obtain sexual arousal and gratification. Some of you may have "mooned" someone on occasion or participated in "streak-

exhibitionism Exposing one's genitals compulsively in inappropriate settings in order to obtain sexual gratification.

ing" (at one time a popular college prank). In a survey of college men, 21 percent said that they had exposed themselves in public on at least one occasion (Person et al., 1989). Although these acts involve involuntary observers, they are also generally not considered exhibitionism, for another characteristic of exhibitionists is that they engage in the behavior *compulsively*.

Most victims of exhibitionists, or "flashers," are women or children (Murphy, 1997). Some studies have found that as many as 33 to 48 percent of women have been victims of exhibitionism on at least one occasion (Cox, 1988; Riordan, 1999). One-fifth of the victims found the experience very distressing and another one-fourth said that their attitude about men or sex had been affected. Most victims say that the experience resulted in their limiting the number of places or areas they would go to alone.

Although there have been a few reported cases of women exposing their genitals (e.g., Grob, 1985), almost all exhibitionists are men. Most started exposing themselves in their midteens or 20s, and half or more either are or have been married (Murphy, 1997). The large majority of these men are described as shy and/or personally immature, but otherwise without serious emotional or mental disorders. They typically feel inadequate and insecure, fear rejection, and have problems forming close, intimate (including sexual) relations (Blair & Lanyon, 1981; Marshall et al., 1991).

Lance Rentzel was a star wide receiver for the Dallas Cowboys professional football team and had recently married one of the top young actresses in Hollywood. The Cowboys were headed to the Superbowl in 1970, but on November 19, while in the middle of a slump, Lance exposed himself to a 10-year-old girl. The media soon discovered that he had been arrested for the same thing 4 years earlier while playing for the Minnesota Vikings—and in the midst of another personal slump. Lance Rentzel had always been a hero on the football field and felt that he had to be highly successful to please his family. In his autobiography and account of his exhibitionism, *When All the Laughter Died in Sorrow* (1972), he says that he felt pressure to prove his masculinity over and over again, and as part of this he avoided close, intimate relations with women and instead proved his masculinity to himself by sexual conquests. During times of stress, when he wasn't a "winner," Lance Rentzel resorted to exposing himself as a way to prove his masculinity.

Although most exhibitionists are of normal or above-normal intelligence, some cases of exhibitionism occur among people who are intellectually impaired, either since birth or as a result of a neurological disorder or age. In these cases, the cause is usually an inability to understand what society considers (or the

"NO THANKS, I'M TRYING TO QUIT."

Bob Dayton.

Many of you may have made an obscene telephone call as a prank during adolescence. Although inappropriate, this behavior is different from that of the paraphiliac phone caller who makes obscene calls as his primary source of sexual arousal and gratification. **Telephone scatologia** (or *scatophilia,* from the Greek *skopein,* meaning "to view"), as it is called, is often considered a kind of exhibitionism (unique to the 20th century, of course; Matek, 1988). As with exhibitionists, the scatologist's arousal is proportionate to the victim's reaction of disgust, shock, and fear and to the sense of control it gives him. The scatologist often masturbates while making his calls. One difference between telephone scatologia and exhibitionism is that many scatologists want complete anonymity (Milner & Dopke, 1997).

In April, 1990, the president of American University resigned after police traced obscene phone calls to his office phone. His victims were women who had advertised home day-care services in the local newspaper. He had degrees from Ivy League schools and was a well-known civic activist who had appeared on television hundreds of times as a spokesman for higher education. (Gelman, 1990)

What can explain behavior like this on the part of an intelligent (and in this case, prominent) individual? Telephone scatologists feel inadequate and insecure and have difficulty maintaining normal sexual relations, much like exhibitionists (Matek, 1988). Most have anger toward women. They compulsively use the telephone for sexual interactions—it is safe (until recently, anyway), distant, and avoids intimacy. Of those who have been caught, a rather high proportion were sexually abused as children, as was the case with the university president (Gelman, 1990).

Over 1 million obscene phone calls are reported to phone companies or the police each year in the United States. Some callers boast about themselves and others just breathe heavily, while still others express their sexual intentions, sometimes in the form of threats. Some use the guise of taking a survey to get the victim to talk about herself. Many obscene callers know the names of the people they call, which can make the experience particularly frightening to the victim. It is rare, however, for scatologists to molest (or even approach) their victims. They prefer to keep their distance and masturbate either during or after the call.

individual previously considered) to be right as opposed to wrong (Zeiss et al., 1996).

Only about half of all exhibitionists have erections while exposing themselves, and they may or may not masturbate during the act (Langevin et al., 1979). But they usually do masturbate shortly afterwards, while fantasizing about the experience, and their erotic turn-on is directly related to the victim's reaction of shock, disgust, and fear (Blair & Lanyon, 1981). Exhibitionists rarely attempt to molest their victims (American Psychiatric Association, DSM-IV, 1994); thus, the best response (if you are ever a victim) is to give no facial or verbal reaction, leave the scene, and report the incident immediately. Interestingly, many exhibitionists compulsively expose themselves in the same location; perhaps the danger of being caught increases the arousal (Stoller, 1977). As a result, they are the most frequently caught paraphiliac offenders, comprising about one-third of all arrests for sexual offense.

OBSCENE PHONE CALLS

"The calls came three to four times a night. The caller would make obscene suggestions about his penis, oral sex, and bondage, and say that he was 'masturbating to the sound of my voice and the thought of my pussy.' Then he would start moaning. I was very shocked and disgusted." (from the author's files)

telephone scatologia A condition in which sexual arousal is achieved primarily by making obscene telephone calls.

If you should ever be a victim, the best advice is to say nothing and hang up *immediately* (remember, the scatologist is aroused by your reactions; even slamming the phone down can give him reinforcement). If the calls persist, your telephone company will cooperate in helping the police trace calls. Ask your phone company about Call Trace, a technology that allows the phone company to instantly record the source of a call made to you. Today, telephone caller ID machines are making obscene phone calls an increasingly risky behavior. When the caller is identified, do not be surprised if he turns out to be someone you know or have met; that is often the case.

VOYEURISM

> "Last month, I was sitting on my bed and I saw a shadow move across my window. I reluctantly peeked through the blinds and there was this man stroking his penis. . . . Last night I got a phone call from a neighbor telling me someone was looking in my window. I reported it. Apparently, they've been trying to catch this guy for a while. I'm very frightened right now."   (from the author's files)

What is a voyeur (from the French *voir,* meaning "to see")? Are men who like to look at naked women in magazines or at topless shows voyeurs? What about people who go to nudist colonies, or men who enjoy looking at women in string bikinis at the beach? What if a man sneaks a peak up a woman's skirt as she is sitting down, or, if he is innocently walking down the street, notices a woman undressing in her room and stops to watch? In their national survey, Laumann et al. (1994) reported that one-third of the men and 16 percent of the women found "watching others do sexual things" to be appealing. Although the word *voyeurism* is often used to describe such behavior, these are really just more examples of normal variants.

To be a **voyeur** (a paraphiliac), one must *repeatedly* seek sexual arousal by observing people undressing or in the nude *without their consent or knowledge.* The voyeur is aroused by the risk of discovery, and thus is not interested in going to nudist colonies or other places where people know that they are being watched (Tollison & Adams, 1979). A variation of voyeurism is *scoptophilia,* defined as repeatedly seeking sexual arousal by secretly watching sexual acts. In either case, voyeurism is the preferred means of sexual arousal. For example, a man was arrested in Louisiana for 341 reported cases of peeping in women's windows.

The great majority of voyeurs are men (thus the term *Peeping Tom* applies). Most

voyeurism Repeatedly seeking sexual arousal by observing nude individuals without their knowledge or consent.

Figure 16–4   Voyeurs repeatedly seek sexual arousal by secretly watching people undress.

voyeurs begin their deviant behavior before age 15. They have characteristics that resemble those of exhibitionists: feelings of inadequacy and insecurity, shyness and poor social skills, and a history of great difficulty in heterosexual relations (Kaplan & Krueger, 1997; Tollison & Adams, 1979).

> "I often 'do it' (masturbate) in my car while parked in areas where I can watch women. My social skills are poor, and I do not get on well with people easily."   (from the author's files)

Voyeurs may masturbate while observing their victims, or they may masturbate later while fantasizing about the incident. The large majority of voyeurs are not dangerous, preferring to keep their distance, but there are exceptions (Kaplan & Krueger, 1997). If you are ever a victim, you should consider a voyeur to be potentially dangerous if either he tries to draw attention to the fact that he is watching or he attempts to approach you or enters your building.

> *PERSONAL REFLECTIONS*
> *If you are ever victimized by a person with a paraphilia, what do you think you would do? Would you talk about it? To whom? Would you report it? To whom?*

BESTIALITY AND ZOOPHILIA

> "In my early teens my cousins and I penetrated a horse. I did it because of a dare. I've grown up now and have three children and a wife. Every now and then I think about what I've done and it makes me want to throw up."

> "One night several years ago myself and a few acquaintances were sharing some college experiences. One of the group stated that to become a

member of _____ he had to have sexual intercourse with a goat." (All examples are from the author's files.)

Bestiality is the act of having sexual contact with an animal. Greek mythology provides many stories of gods disguising themselves as animals and having sex with goddesses or humans. But is this type of sexual contact common for humans? Kinsey and his colleagues (1948, 1953) reported that about 8 percent of the men in his sample and over 3 percent of the women had had sexual contact with an animal on at least one occasion. Seventeen percent of boys raised on a farm admitted to such experiences. A more recent study confirms that a fair number of people have experienced sex with an animal on at least one occasion (Alvarez & Freinhar, 1991). For men, bestiality usually involves a farm animal, while household pets are more common for women. Men are most likely to engage in sexual intercourse with the animal; women usually have the animal lick their genitals, or they masturbate a male animal.

The large majority of people who have engaged in bestiality did so only once or a few times, often during adolescence (Tollison & Adams, 1979). It might have happened as a dare, as an initiation stunt, or out of curiosity. Bestiality becomes a paraphilia, called **zoophilia** (from the Greek *zoon,* meaning "animal"), only when it is the preferred means of sexual arousal (Perretti & Rowan, 1983). Zoophilia, however, is very rare and is usually a sign of severe psychological problems. Zoophiliacs are often withdrawn, have poor interpersonal skills, and frequently have other paraphilias (Milner & Dopke, 1997).

PEDOPHILIA

He was a man loved by children. He played a clown at birthday parties, and little ones loved to see him coming into their homes. Then he was caught molesting a child at a party where he had been hired to entertain. Interviews were conducted with children at parties he had worked before. They revealed that he had used his job as a means to repeatedly engage in sexual behavior with children. He was a pedophiliac. (summarized from news articles)

Pedophilia (from the Greek, meaning "love of children") is a condition in which an adult's sexual arousal and gratification depend primarily or exclusively on having sex with children. Although the legal age of consent differs from state to state (ranging from 14 to 18), sex researchers generally define a child as someone who is younger than 13 years old (Gebhard et al., 1965). Thus, we are discussing *sexual relations by an adult with prepubertal children.* To be considered an example of pedophilia, the adult must be at least 16 years old and at least 5 years older than the child (American Psychiatric Association, DSM-IV, 1994).

An isolated act of child molestation, although reprehensible, does not necessarily qualify as pedophilia. Remember, to be designated a pedophile, the molester must *repeatedly* seek sexual relations with children.

This is the most serious of the paraphilias, each year resulting in many thousands of victims who suffer long-term emotional and psychological problems. This section is intended only as an introduction to the problem of pedophilia. To learn about pedophiles and the effects of their behavior on the victims, see Chapter 17.

SADOMASOCHISM

Sadism refers to the infliction of pain on another person for sexual arousal and gratification. The term is named after the Marquis de Sade (1740–1814), a French aristocrat and novelist who wrote stories, supposedly based on his own experiences, of beating and torturing women while being sexually stimulated himself (his works include the novels *Justine* and *120 Days of Sodom*). **Masochism** refers to achieving sexual arousal by experiencing pain. It is named after Leopold von Sacher-Masoch (1835–1895), a practicing masochist who wrote novels (e.g., *Venus in Furs*) about people getting sexual pleasure by having pain inflicted on them. If the partner of a sadist participates willingly, as is usually the case, then he or she is, of course, a masochist, and the linkage of the two behaviors is indicated in the term **sadomasochism** (**S&M**).

The terms *sadism* and *masochism* were coined by Krafft-Ebing, who also was one of the first to report clinical cases:

There was a man who habitually attacked young girls on the street with a knife, wounding them in the upper arm. When arrested, he said that he did it because he would have an ejaculation at the moment he cut them. (cited in Krafft-Ebing, 1951, p. 223)

A 28-year-old man would have a woman tie him up with straps he brought for that purpose. Then he would have the woman take whips (which he had also brought) and beat him on the soles of his feet, the calves, and backside until he ejaculated. (cited in Krafft-Ebing, 1951, p. 261)

bestiality The act of having sexual contact with an animal.

zoophilia Using sexual contact with animals as the primary means of achieving sexual gratification.

pedophilia A condition in which sexual arousal is achieved primarily and repeatedly through sexual activity with children who have not reached puberty.

sadism A condition in which individuals repeatedly and intentionally inflict pain on others in order to achieve sexual arousal.

masochism A condition in which individuals obtain sexual pleasure primarily from having pain and/or humiliation inflicted on them.

sadomasochism (S&M) A term used to indicate the linkage of sadism with masochism.

Figure 16–5 Participants in S&M and D&S often wear leather garments and boots and use whips, chains, leashes, and collars in highly structured scenarios.

How common are sadism and masochism? In their mildest forms, they are probably very common. Many people, for example, enjoy being bitten, slapped (e.g., on the buttocks), pinched, scratched, or pinned down during sex.

> "I consider myself to be a normal sexual person. . . . I love to be spanked." (woman)

> "I figured I could ask you if it's 'normal' if you like to be bitten during sex? My arousal does not depend exclusively on biting nor does my boyfriend have to bite me hard, I just love it." (All examples are from the author's files.)

Kinsey and his associates (1948, 1953) found that over one-fourth of the men and women in their survey had erotic responses to being bitten during sex. Some people are sexually aroused by inflicting or experiencing pain that goes beyond love bites or spanking:

> "My best friend always talked about how he wanted to have anal sex with his girlfriend. All he really talked about was how he wanted to hear her let out a cry when he finally got to." (from the author's files)

Janus and Janus (1993) reported that 16 percent of the men and 12 percent of the women they surveyed agreed or strongly agreed that "pain and pleasure really go together in sex." However, only half as many felt that S&M was very normal or all right, indicating

domination Ruling over and controlling another individual. In sexual relations, it generally involves humiliation of the partner as well.

submission Obeying and yielding to another individual. In sexual relations, it generally involves being humiliated by the partner as well.

that many people do not regard their own behaviors as S&M. Where, then, do we draw the line as to what characterizes S&M?

To qualify as a paraphilia, sadomasochism must be the *preferred* means of sexual arousal. Until the 1980s, most of what was known about sadists and masochists was obtained from clinical case studies (such as Krafft-Ebing's) of individuals who had inflicted or experienced tremendous physical pain and harm. In the case of sadists, this often involved unwilling partners, as in the case of sadistic murderers (e.g., Ted Bundy, Jeffrey Dahmer, and John Wayne Gacy) or sadistic rapists (Hucker, 1997). Sadomasochism was thus viewed as a psychological abnormality, practiced by people with severe personality disorders. In its extreme form, sadism is less common than masochism (Gebhard et al., 1965), and male sadists far outnumber female sadists (Fiester & Gay, 1991). Sadists who act out their aggressive impulses share many features with other sexual aggressors (Langevin et al., 1988). Some of these features include abuse of alcohol and drugs, poor socialization, frequent history of abuse as children, tendency toward committing nonsexual crimes as well as sexual crimes, and long histories of antisocial behavior. Most experts feel that sadomasochistic activities involving severe pain are relatively uncommon.

More recent studies by sociologists and psychologists in nonclinical settings reveal that the majority of people who participate in sadomasochism differ substantially from individuals who have come to the attention of clinicians. Weinberg (1987) found that the distinctive feature in most sadomasochistic relations is not pain, but **domination** (or discipline) and **submission** *(D&S)*. The main features are pain (within well-defined limits), loss of control (e.g., bondage), and humiliation and/or embarrassment (Baumeister & Butler, 1997). Dominators ("master," "mistress," "tops") and submissives ("slaves," "bottoms") act out roles in highly structured scenarios (often involving *bondage*). This is usually done with a trusted partner (thus allowing them to explore dominance and submission safely), with both agreeing beforehand on the activities that follow.

> "My most favorite sexual activity is bondage. This is usually done with a partner with whom I have had sex enough times to develop a feeling of trust. I explain that I will tie her spread-eagle to

the bed and do anything to her that I want. After doing so, communication is active and only things that bring pleasure are done. At no time is fear or physical abuse implied. There has never been a bad experience to me or my partner during these adventures."

"The dominatrix (female dominator) commands me to clean a toilet, then 'rewards' me by allowing me to chew on one of her dirty socks." (All examples are from the author's files.)

The scenarios often include special clothing (e.g., leather garments, high-heeled shoes or boots) and gadgets (e.g., leashes, collars, whips, chains; see Figure 16–5), but pain-inducing behaviors are more symbolic than real. Sadomasochists may go to S&M establishments and pay to experience dominance or submission in structured role playing.

Dominators and submissives generally are not interested in injury or extreme pain, and pain is erotically arousing only when it is part of the agreed-upon ritual. (Male homosexual S&M tends to be more violent than heterosexual S&M; Breslow et al., 1986.) Activities preferred by a majority of both men and women include (in order of preference) spanking, master-slave relationships, oral sex, masturbation, bondage, humiliation, erotic lingerie, restraint, and anal sex (Breslow et al., 1985; Moser & Levitt, 1987; Sandnabba et al., 1999). People who participate in dominance and submission have a strong desire to control their environment, and the acting out of the highly structured D&S scenarios can become the preferred means of sexual arousal:

"Growing up I had fantasies about having a partner that would enjoy being on the submissive end of S&M. Well I found one and . . . I never knew my tendencies for that could become so everyday. We both fed on that behavior." (from the author's files)

Most nonclinical D&S participants are men (2-to-1 ratio over women), heterosexual, well educated (often with prominent jobs), and generally engage in ordinary consensual sex (Breslow et al., 1985; Moser & Levitt, 1987; Sandnabba et al., 1999). In their D&S activities, most have a strong preference for dominant or submissive roles, but many are able to switch between the two, and some change their preference over time (Sandnabba et al., 1999). Many female participants do so to please their male partners (Breslow et al., 1985). They, too, tend to be well educated, and while most prefer the submissive role, a sizable minority prefer the dominant role or have no preference (Ernulf & Innala, 1995; Levitt et al., 1994). Although most people who engage in D&S are socially well adjusted, close to a third report extreme nervous anxiety (Breslow et al., 1985). Today, some therapists believe that masochism (submission)

in particular "does not appear to be itself pathological or a symptom of deeper problems, nor does it generally involve wish for injury, punishment for sexual guilt, or self-destructive impulses" (Baumeister & Butler, 1997, p. 237).

Psychoanalytic explanations of sadism often focus on unconscious anger directed at one's mother, while masochism is sometimes explained as sadism directed at oneself. Behavior therapists, on the other hand, contend that S&M results from early associations of pain or aggression with orgasm (e.g., Kernberg, 1991). One study found that 80 percent of male sadomasochists and 40 percent of women attributed their interest in S&M to childhood or adolescent experiences (Breslow et al., 1985). However, a recent study found that the average age of first awareness of interest in D&S was 18 to 20 years old (Sandnabba et al., 1999). Weinberg (1987) believes that sadomasochism (dominance-submission) can be understood as a social phenomenon. Many men involved in S&M are submissives, and many are not only well educated but successful and prominent as well. The highly structured scripts with a trusted partner allow them to safely play a role that contradicts what our society says is appropriate for men. The dominator role, on the other hand, may be preferred by those who normally have little or no influence or power.

OTHER PARAPHILIAS

The sexual behaviors presented so far represent only the most common paraphilias. There are less common, more bizarre paraphilias, and I introduce a few of them here. For a description of others, see Money (1984).

Some of these paraphilias might be considered specific types of fetishes (urophilia, coprophilia, mysophilia, klismaphilia), as they involve sexual arousal by specific body discharges (Money, 1986). Behaviors such as urophilia and coprophilia are sometimes included in sadomasochistic acts as well.

"I personally know someone that was a urophiliac. He used to talk to one of my friends. She told me that every time they were together, he used to ask if he could urinate on her belly."

"My boyfriend likes to watch as I urinate. I even let him taste it one time." (All examples are from the author's files.)

Urophiliacs (from the Greek *ouron*, meaning "urine") are sexually aroused by the act of urination. They enjoy watching others urinate, and many are sexually aroused by urinating on their partner or having their partner

urophilia Sexual arousal caused by urine or the act of urination.

urinate on them (often called "golden showers"). Some even drink urine. The noted sexologist Henry Havelock Ellis admitted that he developed a mild form of urophilia during adolescence after witnessing his mother suffer several bouts of urinary incontinence.

Coprophiliacs (from the Greek *kropos*, meaning "dung") are sexually aroused by excrement. They may play with, masturbate with, or even eat feces *(coprophagia)*. In some brothels around the world, coprophiliac patrons can pay to watch from under a glass as prostitutes defecate. Although you might think that urophilia and coprophilia are extremely rare, they are common enough that there is a market for videocassettes showing people engaged in these behaviors. Janus and Janus (1993) found that 6 percent of the men in their survey, and 3 percent of the women, believed that the practice of "golden showers" was very normal or all right. Three percent of the men and 1 percent of the women said that being defecated on was very normal or all right.

Closely related to urophilia and coprophilia is **mysophilia** (from the Greek *mysos,* meaning "uncleanliness"), sexual arousal caused by filth. For example, there are documented cases of people who are sexually aroused by sweaty clothing or used menstrual products.

> "I know a man who has a very high position within a large company. His favorite thing sexually is to be given an enema containing Tabasco sauce. He would hold the fluid in and masturbate." (from the author's files)

Another paraphilia is **klismaphilia** (from the Greek *klusma,* meaning "enema"), obtaining sexual arousal by receiving an enema (Agnew, 2000). Individuals who are aroused by this often have an interest in sadomasochistic activities as well. Many klismaphiliacs self-administer the enema, but many others give and/or receive enemas with a partner. Many use warm water, while others use alcoholic solutions or coffee. Unlike most other paraphiliac behaviors, many klismaphiliacs are women.

> "A year ago I went with a small group of friends from my high school to London. Well, we were on a very crowded tube [subway] and were packed in so tight that we could barely move. But the guy behind me was able to move. He kept rubbing up and down against me the whole ride. I just thought that someone kept pushing him against me. My friends told me that he looked like he was 'getting off' by doing that. I never wore those pants again because I felt used and dirty." (from the author's files)

Frotteurism (from the French, meaning "rubbing") involves rubbing one's genitals against other people in public while fully clothed. In a study of college men, one-third admitted to having rubbed up against a woman in a crowded place (Templeman & Stinnett, 1991). Of course, most of these men are not frotteurists because this is not their preferred means of arousal. One study of nonincarcerated paraphiliacs found that the average number of acts of frottage was over 800 (Abel et al., 1987). Frotteurists seek out crowded buses or other places where bumping into strangers is less likely to cause them to be arrested. Again, it isn't unusual to get aroused by close physical contact with someone (as when you are dancing and holding your partner close to you). However, most people hope that they will get together after the dance for more intimate forms of contact. A frotteurist would not be interested in this, and prefers to escape before he is confronted.

Autoerotic asphyxiation (*asphyxiophilia* or *hypoxyphilia*) was introduced in Chapter 13. In this type of paraphilia, which some regard as a type of masochism (DSM-IV, 1994), individuals deprive themselves of oxygen when highly sexually aroused with the hope of intensifying their orgasm. This is often done with a rope, belt, or plastic bag.

> "A friend of mine was a bodyguard to a call girl. He went on a call with her once where the customer liked having plastic (plastic wrap) around his head while she squatted over his face naked. He said the sounds the man was making while he was gasping for breath made him sick to his stomach." (from the author's files)

This behavior results in an estimated 500 to 1,000 deaths every year (Saunders, 1989). Fatal autoerotic asphyxiation almost always occurs with young men masturbating alone (Milner & Dopke, 1997).

Perhaps the most bizarre paraphilia is **necrophilia** (from the Greek *necros,* meaning "dead")—obtaining sexual arousal and gratification by having sex with dead bodies. Almost all known cases involve men, although a few cases of female necrophiliacs have been reported (Rosman & Resnick, 1989). Janus and Janus (1993) found that only 1 percent of men, and no women, thought that this behavior was all right. Most experts consider these people to be severely emotionally disturbed or psychotic. Necrophiliacs often seek employment in mortuaries or morgues in order to have

---

coprophilia Sexual arousal caused by feces or the act of defecation.

mysophilia A condition in which sexual arousal is caused primarily by filth or filthy surroundings.

klismaphilia A condition in which sexual arousal is achieved primarily by being given an enema.

frotteurism A condition in which sexual arousal is achieved primarily by rubbing one's genitals against others in public places.

autoerotic asphyxiation Depriving oneself of oxygen during masturbation-induced orgasm.

necrophilia Sexual arousal by a dead body.

access to their "partners." Some necrophiliacs murder in order to obtain corpses (and often mutilate the corpse, as in the case of Jeffrey Dahmer), and thus can be regarded to be both sadists and necrophiliacs (Milner & Dopke, 1997).

MULTIPLE PARAPHILIAS

Many sexual offenders do not wish to describe their "private" lives. However, a study was conducted with outpatient sexual offenders in which the participants were guaranteed immunity from prosecution for any crimes they described in the research interviews (Abel et al., 1987, 1988a). In this study, 62 percent admitted to having committed a previously concealed deviant sexual behavior. Over half reported that they had engaged in more than one type of the previously described behaviors, with the average being three to four types. Most had developed their sexual interests and fantasies by age 12 or 13, but were afraid to discuss their arousal patterns with their parents.

Other studies have also found that individuals in treatment for one type of paraphilia often engage in other paraphilias (Bradford et al., 1992; Flor-Henry, 1987). In fact, some types of paraphilias tend to cluster together more often than others. Very serious sadistic offenders, for example, tend to engage in transvestism and fetishism as well (Hucker, 1997). Another group of paraphilias often seen together are known as **courtship disorders**—voyeurism, exhibitionism, and frotteurism (Freund et al., 1997). These studies indicate that the incidence of multiple paraphilias in individuals may be greater than previously believed, and explanations of the paraphilias must take this into account.

WHAT CAUSES PARAPHILIAS?

What causes people to become paraphiliacs? *Freudian* (psychoanalytic) *theorists* believe that paraphilias are the result of arrested psychosexual development, often due to a failure to resolve emotional conflicts. In this theory, paraphilias serve as defense mechanisms to reduce anxiety. One explanation of transvestism, for example, is that the behavior "functions to comfort, soothe, and alleviate unpleasant emotions" (Levine, 1993). Although Freudian theory has the advantage of being very flexible, the effectiveness of psychoanalysis as a therapy for paraphiliacs is very debatable, and is seldom used.

Learning theorists (behaviorists) attribute paraphilias to (usually early) learned associations. Conditioning of men's sexual responses to a specific stimulus has been demonstrated in the laboratory (Lalumière & Quinsey, 1998). Recall, too, the study by Rachman

(1966) regarding acquisition of a "fetish" to boots, or the fact that some sadists (dominators) had early associations of aggression with orgasm (Kernberg, 1991). Some individual case studies also lend credence to learning theory explanations. A man's fetish for plaster casts, for example, was traced to an experience he had at age 11 after he broke his leg (Tollison & Adams, 1979). He got an erection as the nurse held his leg, and later masturbated while fantasizing about it. His repeated fantasy/masturbation episodes led to the fetish.

Although both of these approaches have their advocates, an interesting question still remains: Why are most paraphiliacs men? With the exception of masochism, and perhaps klismaphilia, female paraphiliacs are relatively rare (Hunter & Mathews, 1997). Part of the answer can be explained by the social constructionist perspective you read about at the beginning of the chapter. What is considered to be abnormal depends on the particular time and place. Look, for example, at transvestism and exhibitionism. If women dress in men's clothing, few people today think anything about it—the women are simply being stylish. Similarly, if a woman exposes herself, she is likely to be viewed as "sexy." Thus, in our culture, only men who engage in these behaviors are regarded as behaving inappropriately

Nevertheless, of the nearly 90,000 arrests for sexual offenses other than forcible rape and prostitution that occur each year, over 90 percent are men. Most paraphiliacs describe themselves as heterosexual, but they generally have poor social skills, low self-esteem, histories of childhood abuse or neglect (or were raised in families where sex was thought of as evil and normal erotic development was inhibited), and anger at women (see previous sections for specific references). As a result, paraphiliacs have difficulties with intimacy, especially when they attempt to have sexual relationships. These characteristics are very common in men with the courtship disorders (voyeurism, exhibitionism, and frotteurism) and in some types of rapists (Freund et al., 1997).

Conventional sexual relationships are too complex and threatening for most paraphiliacs, who need to have a great deal of control in order to become sexually aroused. Think for a minute. What do a pair of panties, a dead body, an animal, a person being secretly watched, and a young child—all of them objects of paraphiliacs' fantasies—have in common? These objects are quiet, passive, and nonrejecting. Consider, for example, the following case history of necrophilia:

"Two males worked with me at _____. There we worked in the morgue and they used to always want me to watch one

courtship disorder A group of paraphilias (voyeurism, exhibitionism, and frotteurism) often seen together.

morgue while they watched another. Well, one day I went to their morgue after hearing about a young Puerto Rican female body which had been delivered after she died of a drug overdose. There was one guy on top of her and the other was waiting his turn. After talking with them, I found out that they had done this many times before. They tried to get me to do it but I refused, saying they were crazy. They said, 'No, you're crazy because this is the best. We have them any way we want, how we want and do whatever we want to them without any back talk!'"   (from the author's files)

In a *social systems perspective*, the need for some men to dominate women might encourage or sustain attempts to utilize unusual means of becoming sexually aroused in order to ensure against failure. Our society's often subtle but powerful expectation that men should be masculine and dominant may make it difficult for some men to form caring, normal relationships.

Did you notice a common element in all three explanations? In all three, childhood or early adolescent experiences play an important role. The manner in which one is raised is very important for healthy sexual development. John Money (1986) explains the impact of childhood experiences in terms of what he calls "lovemaps." "Lovemaps," according to Money, depict an idealized lover, a love scene, and erotic activities, and develop and are rehearsed during adolescence. For children whose rehearsals have been severely punished or restricted, the "lovemaps" become distorted, with one outcome being the paraphilias.

Today, many researchers are recognizing the similarity between paraphilias and other obsessive-compulsive disorders (e.g., Bradford, 1999). Recall from Chapter 15 the cycle of events that drives the individual who is hypersexual (or the sex addict, as some prefer to call such people). The individual is first preoccupied with obsessive thoughts, which lead to ritualistic behaviors, causing further sexual excitement, which eventually leads to the sexual act. The act, however, produces despair; and in order to reduce the anxiety, the individual becomes preoccupied again (Carnes, 1983, 1991). Hypersexuality is not recognized as a paraphilia in the American Psychiatric Association's diagnostic manual (DSM-IV, 1994), but the fact that a great many paraphiliacs engage in their behaviors compulsively cannot be denied. Men with paraphilias engage in sexual activities much more often than most people (Kafka, 1997). This often includes compulsive masturbation, protracted promiscuity, and heavy use of pornography (Kafka & Hennen, 1999). As sexologist Eli Coleman explains it, the paraphiliac's behavior "may initially be driven by the sexual excitement. . . . But the primary motivation is the reduction of stress and anxiety. There is usually a short-lived feeling of relief, followed by the recurrence of the anxiety" (quoted by Thompson, 1991; see also Coleman, 1991).

Recently, some researchers (e.g., Kafka, 1997) have suggested that men with paraphilias have abnormal brain chemistry. They base this on the observation that antidepressants, psychostimulants, and neuroleptic drugs often have sexual side effects and that many drugs used for psychiatric disorders also alleviate paraphiliac behavior. As you will now see, pharmacological interventions are playing an increasingly greater role in the treatment of paraphilias.

THERAPY

No one type of therapy has proven successful in treating paraphiliacs. Therapy often takes a multifaceted approach. Traditional *psychotherapy* or *group therapy* may be tried to get the individual to become aware of his feelings, while confrontational approaches are sometimes used to force the individual to see the effects his behavior has on others. Behavioral approaches often include *aversion therapy,* in which unpleasant stimuli are presented or associated with the undesired behavior, and *orgasmic reconditioning,* where pleasant stimuli (fantasies) are associated with orgasm.

Therapy is not completed once the paraphiliac's inappropriate urges have been controlled. Remember, paraphiliacs usually have anxieties about intimate relations and poor social skills. Unless these problems can be resolved, the inappropriate behaviors will eventually return. For anxieties, the most successful approach is *desensitization.* Here, the anxiety-causing stimuli (relations with women, in this case) are slowly introduced to the subject. Fantasies of normal relations with women are attempted first. Once this can be done in a relaxed state, thoughts of normal relations are gradually replaced with actual behaviors (e.g., being alone in a room with a woman, sitting next to a woman, and talking to a woman may be introduced in succession). *Social skills training* teaches these men skills, such as how to carry on a conversation and how to cope with rejection, that most of us (but not the paraphiliac) learned during adolescence. Nowadays paraphiliacs are increasingly being treated for hypersexual (compulsive) disorder (see Chapter 15).

No type of therapy for *any* problem (not just paraphilias) has a high success rate unless the individual wants to change. This is one reason that therapy ordered by criminal courts is often unsuccessful; the individual does not come to therapy on his own. For many paraphiliacs, the urge to engage in the behavior is so strong that it never seriously occurs to them to give it up (Money, 1986). As a result, behavioral therapy and insight-oriented psychotherapy usually are not successful (Kilmann et al., 1982). The recidivism rate (the rate at which treated individuals return to their behaviors) is very high (Feierman & Feierman, 2000).

Today, for those paraphiliacs who are considered to be hypersexual (many) or those who engage in behaviors that cause harm to others (e.g., pedophilia, sadism), *medical approaches* to reduce the sex drive are commonly being used. Earlier studies found that surgical castration greatly reduced both the sex drive and the recidivism rate (see Bradford, 1999). In place of surgical castration, therapists now use antiandrogen drugs (e.g., cyproterone acetate or medroxyprogesterone acetate) to reduce testosterone levels (see Balon, 1998, for a review). However, these drugs are not cures; they are used to curb the urge to engage in the behaviors while other therapies can be tried. The most promising advance is in pharmacological treatment with drugs that regulate a brain chemical called serotonin (see Bradford, 1999; Balon, 1998). These serotonergic antidepressant drugs (e.g., fluoxetine, sertraline) are also often used to treat obsessive-compulsive disorders, which again suggests a relationship between these two types of disorders.

The *social systems perspective* advocates a different approach to dealing with paraphilias. Rather than trying to change individuals, those who believe in this perspective advocate changing society's stereotypes about men's dominance over women. A prediction of the social systems perspective is that an early socialization process that did not place heavy expectations on men to control or dominate sexual relationships would lead to a sharp decline in the amount of paraphilia in our society. What do you think?

PERSONAL REFLECTIONS

Do you engage in sexual practices that may be physically or psychologically harmful to yourself or others (e.g., exhibitionism, obscene telephone calls, voyeurism, sadomasochism, pedophilia)? If so, have you sought therapy to help with your behavior? If you have not sought therapy, why not?

Key Terms

autoerotic asphyxiation   330, 410
bestiality   407
coprophilia   410
courtship disorders   411
domination   408
exhibitionism   404
fetishism   402
frotteurism   410

klismaphilia   410
masochism   407
mysophilia   410
necrophilia   410
paraphilia   401
pedophilia   407
sadism   407
sadomasochism (S&M)   407

sexual variant   401
submission   408
telephone scatologia   405
transvestism   403
urophilia   409
voyeurism   406
zoophilia   407

Suggested Readings

Garber, M. (1992). *Vested interests: Cross-dressing and cultural anxiety.* New York: Routledge. Interesting and provocative.
Laws, D. R., & O'Donohue, W. (Eds.). (1997). *Sexual deviance: Theory, assessment, and treatement.* New York: Guilford Press. Several up-to-date articles on all the various paraphilias.
Money, J., & Lamacz, M. (1989). *Vandalized lovemaps.* New York: Prometheus. Excellent case histories.

Weinberg, T. S. (1995). *S&M: Studies in dominance and submission.* Amherst, NY: Prometheus.
Wilson, G. (Ed.). (1986). *Variant sexuality: Research and theory.* Baltimore: Johns Hopkins University Press. Over 10 years old, but an excellent first source of information.

Study Guide

INTERACTIVE REVIEW

This chapter considers three different ways to define a behavior as unconventional or abnormal. The (1) _____ approach defines a behavior as normal if most people do it. Therefore, unconventional behaviors are those that are engaged in by relatively few people. The (2) _____ approach looks at various behaviors to determine if they are customary within a given society. The (3) _____ approach evaluates the behaviors with respect to whether or not they cause an individual to feel distressed or guilty, and/or cause the person problems in functioning efficiently in ordinary social and occupational roles. What is considered unconventional depends on the time and (4) _____ in which the behavior is displayed.

Paraphiliacs are individuals whose sexual arousal and gratification (5) _____ on behaviors (or fantasizing about behaviors) that are outside the usual and accepted sexual patterns for adults. Unusual behaviors that are used to enhance sexual activity with a partner, not to compete with him or her, are called (6) _____. (7) _____ refers to achieving sexual arousal when using or fantasizing about an inanimate object or a particular part of the body. (8) _____ refers to achieving sexual arousal and gratification from dressing as a member of the opposite sex. (9) _____ expose their genitals compulsively in inappropriate settings, while (10) _____ repeatedly make obscene phone calls for sexual arousal. (11) _____ prefer to seek sexual gratification by watching people undress(ed) without their knowledge or consent. Zoophiliacs prefer (12) _____ as sexual partners; pedophiliacs prefer (13) _____. (14) _____ intentionally inflict pain and/or humiliation on others for sexual arousal and gratification, while (15) _____ obtain sexual pleasure from having pain and/or humiliation inflicted on them.

Other paraphilias include (16) _____ (sexual arousal by the act of urination), (17) _____ (arousal by feces), (18) _____ (arousal by filth), (19) _____ (arousal by being given an enema), (20) _____ (rubbing one's genitals against others in public places), and necrophilia (sex with (21) _____). Recent studies have found that people who practice paraphilias often engage in more than one type.

The large majority of paraphiliacs are (22) _____. Most describe themselves as heterosexual, but have difficulty maintaining intimate (particularly erotic) relations. The paraphiliacs' behavior(s) allows them to have control over the objects of their sexual arousal. Therapy is generally unsuccessful in eliminating the paraphilia, often because the individual does not want to give it up. However, management of paraphiliacs is often possible by administering drugs that alter a brain chemical called (23) _____.

SELF-TEST

A. TRUE OR FALSE

- [T] [F] 24. Freud considered oral-genital sex to be a sign of impaired psychosexual development.
- [T] [F] 25. All abnormal behaviors are called paraphilias.
- [T] [F] 26. Most men who buy scanty, frilly panties for their female partners have a panty fetish.
- [T] [F] 27. Young children who occasionally dress up in clothing of the opposite sex usually grow up to be transvestites.
- [T] [F] 28. Most transvestites are heterosexual men and married.
- [T] [F] 29. Exhibitionists often behave as if they wish to be caught.
- [T] [F] 30. Strippers and nudists are the most common examples of exhibitionists.
- [T] [F] 31. The best way to react to an exhibitionist is to show disgust.
- [T] [F] 32. Most exhibitionists and voyeurs are harmless.
- [T] [F] 33. Voyeurs often like to go to nudist colonies to observe naked bodies.
- [T] [F] 34. A person may commit bestiality and not have a paraphilia.
- [T] [F] 35. Sadomasochists act out highly structured scenarios in which pain-inducing behaviors are more symbolic than real.
- [T] [F] 36. Many men involved in S&M prefer the submissive role, and are well educated and successful.
- [T] [F] 37. Most paraphiliacs have difficulties with intimacy.
- [T] [F] 38. Most paraphiliacs wish to be cured.

B. MATCHING (MATCH THE BEHAVIOR WITH THE NAME OF THE PARAPHILIA THAT BEST FITS IT)

_____ 39. bestiality

_____ 40. coprophilia

_____ 41. exhibitionism

_____ 42. fetishism

_____ 43. frotteurism

_____ 44. klismaphilia

_____ 45. masochism

_____ 46. mysophilia

_____ 47. necrophilia

_____ 48. pedophilia

_____ 49. sadism

_____ 50. sexual variant

_____ 51. telephone scatologia

_____ 52. autoerotic asphyxiation

_____ 53. transvestism

_____ 54. urophilia

_____ 55. voyeurism

a. Billy must seek crowded places in order to get away with this paraphilia.

b. Henry is trying to find employment in a morgue in order to act out his paraphiliac fantasies.

c. Joe has volunteered to serve as counselor at the elementary school's summer camp to have access to the objects of his sexual arousal.

d. John is highly aroused by watching his partner have a bowel movement.

e. Jim has sneaked out to the barn to find a four-footed sexual partner.

f. Allen peeks in windows in order to become aroused.

g. Bert is hanging around the laundromat hoping to steal the object of his sexual desire from an unwashed basket of clothing.

h. Carl is crawling on his hands and knees and being pulled by a leash in order to get sexually aroused.

i. Stan asks his partner to urinate on him whenever they have sex.

j. Greg is wearing frilly panties and a bra underneath his suit and tie.

k. Walter is waiting in his car in the grocery parking lot to show his penis to the first woman who walks by.

l. Susan gets highly aroused whenever she ties her partner up and orders him to lick her feet.

m. Sam gets highly aroused when his wife wears a negligee or teddy.

n. David is describing his erect penis to a woman in his class he has called but does not know.

o. Lenny is becoming highly aroused by his partner's nasal mucus.

p. Paul has paid a prostitute to give him an enema.

q. Larry puts a plastic bag over his head when he is highly sexually aroused.

C. FILL IN THE BLANKS

56. Transvestism is most closely related to _____.

57. The most frequently caught paraphiliac offenders are _____.

58. Telephone scatologia is most closely related to _____.

59. For pedophilia, sex researchers generally define a child as someone who is younger than _____.

60. Weinberg and others have found that the distinctive features in nonclinical sadomasochism are _____ and _____.

61. Urophilia, coprophilia, mysophilia, and klismaphilia involve sexual arousal by _____ and thus might be considered specific types of _____.

62. The objects of paraphiliacs' sexual arousal (e.g., a pair of used panties, a dead body, an animal, a young child) have in common that they are _____.

63. According to Simon, deviance is a problem of _____, while perversion is a problem of _____.

Sexual Victimization: Rape, Coercion, Harassment, and Abuse of Children

*Not only does [rape] harm the subordinated victim, those who care about her, and those whose fear
of rape is increased by her rape, but it also injures society, which loses the full participation of those
women who alter their behavior as a function of fear. Rape contributes to a social, emotional, and
political environment in which women's bodies, lives, experiences, and realities are improperly
restrained. It has meanings at the deepest level of human symbolism, and serves as an
excruciating reminder of how a culture that disinhibits the aggressive exercise of power
fosters callous oppression at the cost of female autonomy.*

(Owen D. Jones, 1999)

In the United States, 16 rapes are attempted every hour; on average, a woman is raped every 6 minutes. The United States has a rape rate 3 times greater than that of Sweden or Denmark, 5 times greater than that of Canada, 7 times greater than that of France, 13 times higher than that of England, and 20 times higher than that of Japan or Israel (U.S. Senate Judiciary Committee, 1990; United Nations/Economic Commission, 1995; see Figure 17–1). About 20 percent of girls and 12 percent of boys have been the victims of sexual abuse before the age of 13 (Kinsey et al., 1948; Laumann et al., 1994).

When you have finished studying this chapter, you should be able to:

1. Discuss, from a historical perspective, attitudes about rape and victims of rape;

2. Understand the prevalence of rape and describe some characteristics of rapists and their victims;

3. Describe acquaintance rape, date rape, sexual coercion, marital rape, gang rape, statutory rape, and the frequency of each;

4. Discuss why rape is common in some cultures and rare in others;

5. Compare and understand the psychodynamic, cultural, social learning, and interpersonal factors that contribute to rape;

6. Identify several myths about rape and appreciate why they are not true;

7. Describe post-rape posttraumatic stress disorder and other reactions to rape;

8. Discuss and evaluate three approaches to rape prevention;

9. Describe sexual harassment in the workplace and the classroom and ways to deal with it;

10. Describe the different types of child molesters and the situations in which sexual abuse of children is most likely to occur;

11. Discuss various forms of incest and describe the family dynamics that are typically found in cases of father-child incest; and

12. Understand the devastating long-term effects that can result from sexual abuse of children.

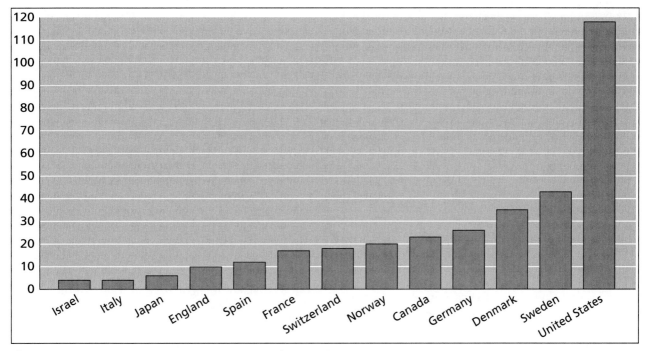

Figure 17–1 Rape rates per 100,000 women aged 15 to 59.

RAPE

HISTORICAL PERSPECTIVE

Compared to men in other cultures, men in the United States obviously have difficulty in their relations with women. Why?

> **"The difficult thing to explain is not why gender relations are so violent, but why violence is so gendered, so sexualized."** (Moore, 1994, p. 154)

We will examine rape in some detail and then return to this question.

Rape is "nonconsensual oral, anal, or vaginal penetration, obtained by force, by threat of bodily harm or when the victim is incapable of giving consent" (Koss, 1993b). The word *rape* comes from the Latin *rapere,* meaning "to steal" or "carry off." A story about the founding of Rome describes how the early Romans abducted women from a neighboring tribe in order to get wives (the "Rape of the Sabine Women"). Many cultures have ritualized the abduction of the bride-to-be by the groom as part of the marriage ceremony. In our own culture, for example, the practice of carrying a new bride across the threshold is a ceremonial re-creation of the Roman legend.

In biblical times, rape was viewed as a crime against a man's property rather than against a person (the woman), and fathers and husbands could do as they wished with their property. For example, the Old Testament (Genesis 19:1–8) tells of Lot, who lived in the town of Sodom. Two angels disguised as men came

to Sodom, and Lot invited them into his house. Later, the men of Sodom surrounded Lot's house and demanded that he send the angels outside. Lot instead offered to give the crowd his two virgin daughters to do with as they pleased if only the men would leave his guests alone.

The Old Testament (Deuteronomy 22:23–28) also describes different punishments for rape. If a married woman was raped, it was assumed that she had wanted it (and thus violated her husband), and both she and the rapist were put to death. If a betrothed virgin was raped inside the city walls, both the rapist and victim were then stoned to death, because it was assumed that the young woman could have cried out for help and been heard if she had wanted to resist. If a young woman was raped outside the city walls, the punishment was based on whether or not the woman was engaged. If she was, only the rapist was killed because it was assumed that the woman's cries for help could not have been heard. If she was not engaged, the rapist had to pay a fine to the young woman's father (it was his "property" that was damaged) and marry the woman (for who would want to marry "damaged goods"?).

It was not until the 13th century that English common law dropped its distinction between raping a married woman and raping a virgin, and also dropped the practice of forcing the rapist and victim to marry (Brownmiller, 1975). The idea that a

rape Nonconsensual oral, anal, or vaginal penetration, obtained by force, by threat of bodily harm, or when the victim is incapable of giving consent (Koss, 1993).

wife was property of her husband and that a husband could therefore do as he pleased with her continued for many centuries. You will learn of recent changes in the law regarding this in the section on marital rape.

Throughout history, men of victorious armies have raped the women of defeated nations. When the Japanese army invaded China in 1937, for example, the soldiers raped virtually every woman and girl in the wartime capital of Nanking. They later rounded up tens of thousands of Korean women to serve as sex slaves, with most of the women forced to have sex with dozens of soldiers everyday. In the 1990s in Bosnia, Serbian troops raped tens of thousands of Muslim women as part of their "ethnic cleansing" war. Wartime rapes generally are vicious gang rapes, and reports of American soldiers participating in such rapes appear in court-martial records during the Vietnam War.

Why do soldiers (men) engage in such atrocious behavior? It is done to demonstrate power—to destroy the national pride, the manhood, and the honor of the vanquished country. In the words of Susan Brownmiller (1993), the soldier rapes "to give vent to his submerged rage against all women *who belong to other men.* . . . In one act of aggression, the collective spirit of women and of the nation is broken, leaving a reminder long after the troops depart. And if she survives the assault [she becomes a] symbol of her nation's defeat. A pariah. Damaged property."

RAPE STATISTICS

FBI records show that there were over 300,000 rapes and sexual assaults in the United States in 2000. Although this is a large number, everyone agrees that the actual number of rapes committed each year is much higher than the number reported. The National Victims Center estimates there are as many as 683,000 rapes of adult women every year. In the national survey by Laumann et al. (1994), 22 percent of women said that they had been forced to have sex on at least one occasion. In 1998, the Justice Department estimated that 18 percent of American women had been the victim of rape or attempted rape. Koss (1993a,b) estimates that a woman living in the United States has a 1-in-5 chance of being raped in her lifetime.

Women between 16 and 24 years of age are the most frequently reported victims of rape (U.S. Department of Justice, 2000). However, the records show that anyone can be a victim of rape, including young children, elderly women, and men. For example, my grandmother was raped by a teenager when she was 85 years old.

> By the age of 80, Hazel's failing health no longer allowed her to make the trip next door to her daughter's house to prepare the family dinner. She was hunched over due to osteoporosis, and her hands were so arthritic that she had to give up playing the organ at church. Her face was heavily wrinkled, and her hair was gray and thin.
>
> When she was 85, a man in his late teens or early 20s broke into her room one night. He forced her to display herself, and he made her lean over his knees while he spanked her. This went on for 2 or 3 hours. He beat her up, permanently damaged one of her eyes, and raped her.

At least half of all rape victims are girls under the age of 19 (U.S. Department of Justice, 2000). However, these are reported rapes. A study by the National Victims Center, which included both reported and unreported rapes, found that nearly 62 percent of all victims were under the age of 18; 29.3 percent were under the age of 11. Karen Hanna of the National Victims Center says that young people are frequently the target of rape because "the youngest are the least likely to fight back and often don't realize they are victimized" (quoted in Sniffen, 1994).

Even infants can be the victims of rape:

> Eight-month-old "Susan" was placed in the care of her mother's boyfriend, "Joe," for a few hours. Upon returning home, her mother found Susan hemorrhaging badly. The baby was rushed to the emergency room of a local hospital, where evidence of vaginal penetration was found. Susan had to have an immediate operation, in which all of her reproductive organs except the vagina were removed in order to stop the bleeding. There were many vaginal lacerations, but the surgeons were able to stitch them up. This was an 8-month-old girl who would not be able to have children in the future and who would have to undergo repetitive reconstructive surgery. Anyone can be a victim of rape. (summarized from news releases)

The younger the rape victim, the more likely it is that the attacker is an acquaintance or relative (U.S. Department of Justice, 2000). Of rapes of girls under 12 years old, 96 percent were committed by a family member or acquaintance; the figure is 67 percent for women 18 or older. Women are much more likely to report a rape if they are raped by a stranger; thus, most men convicted of rape were strangers to their victims. If, prior to taking this course, you had been asked to describe a "typical" rape, chances are you, too, would have described a scenario in which a victim was raped by a stranger. However, *most rapes are committed by someone the victim knows* (U.S. Department of Justice, 2000; National Victims Center).

Some rapes are spontaneous, but rapists generally plan their assaults to some degree (see Ward et al., 1997). Even in rape cases committed by a stranger, the rapist often picks a particular place and/or time, with the victim simply being the first person to come along. Thus, being a victim of rape can simply be a matter of being in the wrong place at the wrong time. Rapists, however, often look for vulnerable women, such as those living alone or those who live in a place that can be easily entered (Selkin, 1975). Young women who have previously been raped (and suffer from long-term posttraumatic stress disorder) are especially vulnerable of being raped again (Acierno et al., 1999). One way that rapists may test for vulnerability is by asking a woman for help (e.g., asking the time, asking for directions). Selkin (1975) found that in 25 percent of the rape cases committed by a stranger, the woman had responded to a request for help.

SOME CHARACTERISTICS OF RAPISTS

Most rapists are young men who repeat the crime. About 23 percent are reconvicted, but the true repeat offense rate is much higher than this (Polaschek et al., 1997; Quinsey et al., 1995). The large majority of rapists have no more history of psychiatric illness than men convicted of other crimes, nor are their IQs any lower (see Polaschek et al., 1997).

There is no compelling evidence to show that rapists, in general, are either oversexed or deprived. Some studies have found higher than normal levels of testosterone in sex offenders, but this appears to be true only in the most aggressive of offenders (Rada et al., 1983). But, of course, not all men with high testosterone levels are rapists. Other studies have found that many rapists have sexual partners (wives or girlfriends) that they live with. One study, for example, found that one-third of their sample of rapists were married and having sexual intercourse regularly with their wives (Groth & Burgess, 1977). Convicted rapists who are extremely aggressive often have been found to have had earlier and more frequent childhood sexual experiences (Koss & Dinero, 1989) and to exhibit multiple paraphilias (Freund & Seto, 1998; Marshall, 1996). Sexually coercive (nonconvicted sexually aggressive) men also generally have had more extensive sexual histories than others (Lalumiere et al., 1996; Senn et al., 2000).

Are rapists highly aroused by rape-related stimuli? Early studies suggested this might be so, finding that rapists became sexually aroused while listening to audiotapes of rape, whereas nonrape sex offenders did not (Abel et al., 1977; Barbaree et al., 1979). They also found that rapists were less aroused by listening to tapes of consenting sex than were nonrapists (Quinsey et al., 1984). Later studies reported mixed results (see Polaschek et al., 1997). In two reviews, it was concluded that these findings held true mainly for the subgroup of rapists that use a great amount of violence in their attacks (Lalumiere & Quinsey, 1994; Marshall, 1992). However, a more recent study found that sexually coercive college men were more aroused than noncoercive men by scenes involving verbal pressure and threats (Lohr et al., 1997).

What about the developmental history of rapists? Studies show that two developmental factors differentiate rapists from other adult men: caregiver inconsistency (e.g., a distant or no relationship with parents) and sexual deviation and abuse in the family (Barbaree et al., 1998; Prentky et al., 1989). An unusually high number of sexual offenders were themselves physically and sexually abused as children (Dhawan & Marshall, 1996). Even if they were not abused themselves, the family environment in which they were raised often included a great deal of verbal or physical abuse by the father, directed at the mother. With this type of family history, a child may well come to view aggression toward women as normal. Psychologist Eugene Porter was quoted as saying, "I haven't seen a rapist who didn't have a childhood horror story" (quoted by Gelman et al., 1990b). As a result of this history, it is not surprising that rapists often have low self-esteem and difficulty forming intimate relationships, and even those with partners describe those relationships as lacking intimacy (Barbaree et al., 1998; Marshall et al., 1997).

Rapists may not have internal controls such as fear, guilt, or sympathy, or they may have learned to suppress them, in contrast to nonrapists. The majority of arrested rapists had been drinking prior to the assault (Seto & Barbaree, 1995), thus further releasing any inhibitions or internal controls. Men who force sex on women tend to have adversarial relationships with women in general. According to Neil Malamuth, "These men feel they have to be in control of their relationships with women, even in conversation" (quoted by Goleman, 1992).

Most rapists have distorted cognitive processes—distorted attitudes and beliefs about sex roles and female behavior, belief in rape myths (see later section), acceptance of violence toward women, and denial of responsibility (for reviews, see Polaschek et al., 1997; Ward et al., 1997). One thing that is clear is that most rapists lack empathy—the ability to see things from the victim's perspective (Barbaree et al., 1998; Marshall, 1996). Most are convinced that their victims wanted to have sex with them, or deserved to be raped (Blumenthal et al., 1999). As an example, psychiatrist Gene Abel, one of the foremost experts on rapists, related the story of a rapist (a patient) with a long arrest record for rape who said that he had never raped anyone. When asked how he knew when a woman wanted to have sex with him, Abel's patient responded that he knew a woman wanted sex if she spoke to him (cited in Gelman et al., 1990).

This section is intended only as a general introduction to the subject of rape. Keep in mind that much of what we know comes from studies of convicted rapists, most of whom were strangers to their victims. You will learn more about what makes some men rape in later sections. First let us look at some specific types of rape.

PERSONAL REFLECTIONS
Have you ever used sexual coercion to have sex with someone when she or he did not want to? This includes (but is not limited to) (a) purposely getting someone drunk to have sex; (b) physical coercion (e.g., persistent and relentless touching, holding, grabbing); and (c) verbal coercion (e.g., anger and/or threats to break up, other threats, put-downs). If so, why do you suppose you act like this? What effects might your behavior have on those you coerce?

DATE RAPE AND SEXUAL COERCION

One way to classify rapes is by the relationship that exists between the rapist and victim. I will use the term **stranger rape** to refer to a rape committed by someone the victim does not know. But remember that most rapes are committed by someone the victim knows, and thus are often called **acquaintance rape.** Acquaintance rape is called **date rape** if the rape occurs during a social encounter agreed to by the victim. The expression *date rape,* though purely descriptive in intent, has turned out to be unfortunate because many people believe that it is somehow different from rape by a stranger (see Krahé, 2000). Many people attribute more blame, and are less sympathetic, to victims of date rape than they are to victims of rape by a stranger (Barnett et al., 1992; Bridges & McGrail, 1989; Cowan, 2000). *Rape by a date or an acquaintance is no less real than rape by a stranger,* and we should simply refer to it as rape. Here are two examples:

"How many times have we heard our friends say, 'Go out with him, he is such a nice guy'? Well, I'm writing this letter to tell about a terrible occurrence that happened to me by a 'nice guy.'

"I met this guy in one of my college classes. We had four very fun dates. We would go to movies, dancing, parties, and he would always act like a perfect gentleman. He even told me that he did not date many girls at the university because they were only interested in sex. We had a great relationship, and I began to care for him. But my feelings soon changed.

"On our fifth date, he had a little too much to drink. Our friends dropped us at his apartment because he did not want to drive. I knew I was there for the night. I was not worried because he had always treated me with such respect. But that was soon to change. He became very aggressive with me. He told me he wanted to have sex with me because he cared for me so much. I begged him to leave me alone. I tried to fight him off, but I was not strong enough. That turned out to be the worst night of my life, because I was raped.

"I did not think I was leading him on by being in his apartment. I was in shock that such a 'nice guy' could do such a horrible thing to me."

"Robby (a grad student teacher at this university) lived around the corner while I was growing up. I thought of him like a brother, so when I was 17 and he asked me if I was still a virgin, I was not embarrassed to tell him that I was. About a month later a bunch of us went out and after too much to drink, I passed out. I thought I was safe since I was with friends, but he made them leave and I woke up with his fat 270 pound body on top of me. It was horrible and I passed out again. There went 5 1/2 years of friendship and trust. " (All examples are from the author's files.)

How commonly are women forced into unwanted sexual activity on a date (or during a mutually agreed upon social interaction)? Koss and Oros (1982) surveyed a group of university women and asked if they had ever been raped. Six percent answered "yes" to this question. They were then asked if any of them had had sex with men when they didn't want to, but were pressured into it. Twenty-one percent answered "yes" to this question. Again, one reason is that many women do not regard sexual assault as rape unless the assailant was a stranger (Krahé, 2000). In a later study, Koss et al. (1987) found that 25 percent of a national sample of college women had been pressured into sexual intercourse when they didn't want to have it. Others have reported similar results (e.g., Laumann et al., 1994).

Only about 5 percent of such rapes are ever reported to the police, and nearly half of the victims have never told anyone (Koss et al., 1988). Victims of rape often blame themselves (see later section), and this is particularly true when the rape was committed by a date or a close acquaintance.

"When I was 16 I was raped by four guys at a college frat party. In a way I still blame myself for being put in that position. . . . It was my fault for getting drunk. Especially at the age of 16. Guys take advantage of young 16-year-old girls."

"Exactly 6 months ago today, I was 'date raped.' Though before taking your course, I blamed myself, now I see it was him and not me who was in the wrong. I actually felt responsible and as if I had provoked it." (All examples are from the author's files.)

Laumann and colleagues (1994) found that only 3 percent of the men in their national survey felt that they had ever forced a woman into having sex. However, Koss et al. (1987) found that 4.4 percent of the men in their large survey admitted to acts that are legally defined as rape, and another 3.3 percent admitted having attempted rape. One-fourth admitted some form of sexual aggression. Another study found that 15 percent of a sample of college men admitted that they had forced intercourse on a date (Rapaport &

stranger rape Rape committed by someone who is not known by the victim.

acquaintance rape A rape committed by someone who is known by the victim.

date rape A type of acquaintance rape, committed during a social encounter agreed to by the victim.

Figure 17–2   Rubens's *The Rape of the Daughters of Leucippus* (1617), though a great work of art, has been criticized for glorifying rape.

Burkhart, 1984). Men often try to rationalize date rape and may claim, "She got me aroused and I couldn't stop," or say, "She came to my apartment, so she must have wanted it" (see Cowan & Campbell, 1995). Just because a woman goes out with a man, goes to his home or apartment, or engages in necking or petting does *not* mean that she wants to (or has to) engage in sexual intercourse.

Most people have no difficulty defining sex without consent of the partner as rape if the act involved physical force, violence, or the use of a weapon. But what about physical coercion? What about getting a partner heavily intoxicated (to the point of offering little or no resistance, as in the "Robby" case history) in order to have sex? In the mid-1990s, there was a big increase in the use of Rohypnol ("roofies") and other "date rape drugs" (odorless and tasteless but powerful tranquilizers) that were slipped into unknowing victims' drinks. Victims have no memory of any events that take place while under the drug's influence, including rape (Monroe, 1997). Federal law now allows up to 20 years to be added to the sentences of men who use these drugs in order to date-rape. What about verbal coercion (e.g., verbal pressure, anger, use of psychological power, or lying)?

"Many times my boyfriend forced me into having sex when I didn't want to. He thought that kissing always led to sex and when I said 'No,' he would become very angry." (from the author's files)

Koss and colleagues have been criticized for calling experiences like this rape (e.g., Gilbert, 1991) and fewer than half of the victims in Koss's studies viewed their own experiences as rape (Koss et al., 1988). A national survey taken for *Time*/CNN found that while over three-fourths of all women *and* men considered sex with an intoxicated partner rape, over half did not classify a man's use of verbal or emotional pressure to have sex as rape (Monroe et al., 1990). However, as women become more educated about date rape (and especially if they know someone who has been a victim), they are more likely to acknowledge such behavior as rape (Botta & Pingree, 1997). The question of what defines a rape has been addressed (Muehlenhard et al., 1992), but whether or not these behaviors are rape is not the real issue. The real issue is whether or not it is right to have sex with people against their will, and the answer to that is "No!"

I will refer to cases in which a person is forced into unwanted sexual activity through physical or verbal coercion as **sexual coercion.** If we define sexual coercion as nonconsensual sex, how do we determine whether a situation was consensual or not? The law uses the standard of how a *reasonable person* would have responded in the same situation (see Hubin & Haely, 1999). Others, such as Catherine Mackinnon (1989), have argued that a better standard would be the *reasonable woman.*

Some instances of coercive sex avoid the label "rape" only because the victims, fearing that they might be raped, "consent" to have sex. Studies have found that about two-thirds of all college men admit to having used sexual coercion of some type in order to have sex with a date (Rapaport & Burkhart, 1984).

However, studies have found that women, too, sometimes use sexual coercion with partners (see Anderson & Struckman-Johnson, 1998). At a West Coast university, 8.1 percent of the women surveyed admitted to such activity (Gwartney-Gibbs et al., 1987), while at Texas A&M University, 13.4 percent said that they had used verbal coercion and 6.5 percent said that they had used physical coercion to pressure a man into sex (Muehlenhard & Cook, 1988). Twelve percent of men sampled at the University of South Dakota said that they had been the victims of physical restraint or intimidation to have sex (Struckman-Johnson & Struckman-Johnson, 1994). In a more recent study, 21 percent of male college students interviewed at the University of Washington said that women had coerced them into unwanted sexual contact in the last year (Larimer et al., 1999).

In a series of studies, Muehlenhard (1998) found that nearly as many men as

sexual coercion The act of forcing another person into unwanted sexual activity by physical or verbal coercion (restraint or constraint).

women had been the victims of sexual coercion. However, there was an important difference: The coercion used by men was often physical, whereas the coercion used by women was generally verbal (see also Larimer et al., 1999). Verbal coercion often includes tactics such as persuasion, threats to withdraw love, and bribery, but a few women include physical restraint and intimidation as well. Anderson (1991) adds that there is also "the question of whether the male partners in the above studies can properly be viewed as 'victims' in the same manner as female victims of sexual abuse. Even if a woman is using verbal or physical force, it requires that he become aroused to engage in sexual intercourse."

Several of the previously cited researchers believe that *some* unwanted sexual experiences with social partners are due to poor communication skills. When it comes to conveying or interpreting sexual intentions, too many people rely on subtle cues (e.g., gestures or body language) that might be misunderstood. Without clear verbal communication in advance, some men misinterpret a woman's desire to engage in kissing and necking as meaning that she wants to "go all the way." Studies show that men who admit to engaging in sexually aggressive behavior are much more likely than others to misperceive women's sexual intent (Bondurant & Donat, 1999). When women openly communicate their sexual intentions early during a date, men are less likely to feel "led on" to attempt unwanted behaviors (Muehlenhard et al., 1996).

On the other hand, Muehlenhard and her colleagues found that over one-third of the college women surveyed admitted to having engaged in **token resistance**—saying "no" when they meant "yes"—during such encounters (Muehlenhard & Hollabaugh, 1989). In the survey for *Time*/CNN, 54 percent of the women indicated that they believed "some women like to be talked into having sex" (Monroe et al., 1990). Another form of ambiguous communication is **compliance**—agreeing to sexual intercourse when you don't really want to. About one-third to one-half of women report having engaged in compliance (Shotland & Hunter, 1995; Sprecher et al., 1994).

PERSONAL REFLECTIONS
Men: Have you ever ignored a date or acquaintance saying "no" to your sexual advances? Why? Women: Have you ever said "no" to a man's sexual advances when you did not mean it? Why? If you answered "yes," what are some possible repercussions of your behavior? Is there a better way to communicate with others about your sexual desires?

---

token resistance [to sex] Saying "no" to sex when one means "yes."

compliance Agreeing to sexual intercourse when you do not really want to engage in it.

Men who have had experiences with women who offer token resistance or who engage in compliance are likely to push ahead with another part-

ner when she says "no." Some men may even use a negative answer as a rationale to force sex on a partner. At the same time, women who engage in token resistance are more likely to be the victims of sexual aggression (Krahé, 2000).

Recent studies have found that just as many men as women have engaged in token resistance to sex (Muehlenhard & Rodgers, 1998; O'Sullivan & Allgeier, 1995). Most instances of token resistance occur in ongoing relationships, are done as expressive game-playing to increase sexual arousal (not for manipulative reasons), and are perceived as pleasant interactions by both partners. Nevertheless, there is still a danger that men who have had the experience of a partner engaging in token resistance may misinterpret sincere resistance by a future partner.

The use of alcohol further complicates interpersonal communication about sexual intentions (Abbey et al., 1998; Bernat et al., 1998). National surveys have found that about half of date rapists *and* their victims had been drinking before the attack (Ullman et al., 1999).

Unfortunately, many people, including many women, believe that it is okay for a man to force a woman into unwanted sexual intercourse in some circumstances (Goodchilds & Zellman, 1984; Monroe et al., 1990). These attitudes are learned early in life. For example, a survey was taken of 1,700 seventh- to ninth-graders who attended an assault awareness program presented by the Rhode Island Rape Crisis Center at schools throughout the state (Kikuchi, 1988). Opinions about male behavior toward a woman on a date included the following:

- Twenty-nine percent of the boys and 20 percent of the girls said that a man has a right to force his date to have sexual intercourse if she has had sexual intercourse with other men.
- Twenty-two percent of the boys and 10 percent of the girls said that a man has the right to have sexual intercourse without the woman's consent if he had spent a lot of money on her.
- Forty-eight percent of the boys believed that it was okay for a man to force a date to have sexual intercourse if she let him touch her above the waist.
- Fifty-seven percent of the boys and 38 percent of the girls believed it was okay for a man to force a date to have sexual intercourse if they had done it before.
- Sixty-seven percent of the boys and 59 percent of the girls said that a husband has the right to force his wife to have sexual intercourse against her will.

Is it any wonder that so many young woman have been forced into unwanted sexual activity (often forced intercourse) by a boyfriend or date?

PERSONAL REFLECTIONS

Is a man entitled to sexual intercourse when a woman agrees to go out with him, or because he spent money on her, or because she went to his house or apartment, or because she engaged in necking with him? Men: If you answered "yes," do you communicate these expectations to your dates before you go out?

It is best to make a firm decision about your sexual behavior for a social occasion *before* it begins (and before you start to drink alcohol), and then to communicate your sexual intentions clearly and verbally to your partner. This will prevent some unwanted sexual experiences. It will not, of course, stop someone who would use force to have sex, or who would take advantage of a defenseless (e.g., intoxicated) person. When this occurs, it is rape, and no less real than any other type of rape.

RAPE IN MARRIAGE

In the 17th century, a chief justice of England named Sir Matthew Hale wrote, "The husband cannot be guilty of rape committed by himself upon his lawful wife. For by their mutual consent and contract, the wife hath given herself up in this kind." There were two ideas in Hale's statement that found their way into the American system of justice (which is based on British common law). The first idea is that when two people marry, the marriage contract implies that the husband has a right to have sex with his wife even if she does not consent to it. The second idea is that this is justified because the wife is the property of the husband.

> "In the fifth year of my marriage I was raped by my husband after a violent physical attack. He blamed me for the attack and also said it was my obligation to provide sex whenever he desired it. . . . My marriage ended quite bitterly. For the last 3 1/2 years I was blaming myself for what happened."

> "My only form of sexual abuse was a one-time rape by my husband. I remember well; I thought that dying at the moment would be a blessing. After 10 years, the mental anguish and hurt still remain. To think that the man who promised to love, honor, and protect me was capable of such a violent act! How humiliating to have him stand there laughing at me while I lay crying. As far as I am concerned, the man belongs in jail." (All examples are from the author's files.)

Today, citizens and legislatures realize that laws based on such unfair and antiquated ideas must be changed. All 50 states now make **marital rape** a crime, but about half require that there be extraordinary violence before the rape is prosecuted. Only a third provide the same legal protection to wives as in other types of rape (Muehlenhard et al., 1992).

A 1992 report by the National Victims Center estimated that 9 percent of all women had been raped by their husbands or ex-husbands. Other studies have put the estimate even higher (Russell, 1990). Marital rape is often accompanied by severe beatings and other forms of physical abuse (Finkelhor & Yllo, 1985). Frieze (1983) reported that of 137 women beaten by their husbands, 34 percent were also raped as part of their "punishment." The male partners were often drinking heavily or taking drugs at the time of the abuse (Coker et al., 2000). Russell (1990) sees marital rape as being motivated by the same things as any other type of rape—power, anger, and sadism. There is no excuse for marital rape or abuse of a spouse; any rape is a real rape, regardless of who the rapist is.

GANG RAPE

In 1989, seven teenagers were arrested in Glen Ridge, New Jersey, for enticing a mentally impaired 17-year-old girl to perform sex acts while other teens watched. In 2000 in Georgia, at least 20 men and boys aged 12 to 27 raped a 13-year-old mentally disabled girl over a 12-hour period. In 1994, five men were charged with raping a woman in a bar after she had passed out from having too much to drink. In a highly publicized case, six teenagers in Manhattan attacked a lone 26-year-old jogger in Central Park. She was raped, beaten unconscious, and left for dead. This rape was not connected with drugs, robbery, or racial hatred. The only reason given was that it was "something to do" to escape boredom. The youths called their escapade "wilding."

Gang rape refers to cases in which a victim is assaulted by more than one attacker. There are several forms of gang rape. In prisons, weaker men are often gang-raped by other male inmates. On college campuses, many gang rapes are committed by fraternity members (with whom there is often an emphasis on heavy drinking and machismo; Sanday, 1990).

> "When I was 16, I was a very attractive and rebellious teenager. One Friday night my friends and I decided to go to a fraternity party. I did some drugs and I drank a lot of alcohol. I danced with a lot of guys and then a guy that I liked for some time asked me to dance. We danced for some time and he finally asked me to go to a little private party in the back room. When we went into the room, I saw four of his friends standing around a bed. The guy I was with started to kiss me while his friends began removing my clothes. I tried resisting, but with five pairs of hands holding me, it didn't do much good. After they each had a turn, they just left me there and told me if I told anyone, that they would kill me." (from the author's files)

marital rape Rape of a wife by her husband.

gang rape Rape in which a victim is assaulted by more than one attacker.

Box 17-A CROSS-CULTURAL PERSPECTIVES

Rape

At the beginning of this chapter, you learned that the rape rate in the United States is much higher than in other Western countries (see Figure 17–1). Rape of women is common in many other societies throughout the world as well. For example, there is a warlike tribe in Africa called the Gusii in which it is the custom for men to obtain brides by stealing young women from neighboring tribes. On the wedding night, the Gusii warrior rapes his new bride as many times as possible to prove his manhood to others (Levine, 1959). Some tribes use rape to punish women (Chappell, 1976). In the Mangaian culture in the South Pacific, for example, women who violate the sanctity of male-only gathering areas are taken into the forest and gang-raped (Marshall, 1971). Throughout history, mass rapes during wartime have routinely been committed by victorious soldiers to punish the defeated nation (see the "Historical Perspective" section).

As you can also see from Figure 17–1, rape is not common in all cultures. Rape is unheard of, for example, among the Arapesh, who raise boys to be caring, gentle, and nurturant (Mead, 1935). Anthropologist Peggy Sanday (1981) found over 40 societies that were free of rape. What do these societies have in common that results in this lack of violence by men toward women? Like the Arapesh, boys are raised to be nurturant, not aggressive, and to view women as equals who share power and responsibility within the society.

Rape of women is several hundred times more common in the United States than in societies like the Arapesh, but we are not alone; Sanday (1981) found over 50 "rape-prone" societies. Do these cultures have anything in common? The answer is yes. Sanday found that rape-prone societies like the United States promote and glorify male aggression, treat women as inferior and demean their nurturant roles (from which men remain aloof), view relationships between men and women as adversarial, and, to make matters worse, instill these attitudes in children early in their development.

A comparison of university students in the United States and Sweden found that U.S. women were three times as likely as Swedish women to be victims of physical sexual coercion (Lottes & Weinberg, 1996). Very few Swedish men had ever used physical force with a woman. The authors attributed the results to a difference in sex education in the two countries. In Sweden, boys and girls receive sex education in school beginning early in life, and this education emphasizes how to behave ethically. Few American children receive such guidance in school.

American culture is very heterogenous, and the prevalence of rape differs for different ethnic groups. Sexually aggressive behavior is lowest among Asian-Americans (Koss et al., 1987). Note also the low rape rate for Japan in Figure 17–1. Asian-American culture has a collectivist orientation (as compared to the American individualist orientation) that emphasizes group goals over individual goals and social support over individual competition. Hall and Barongan (1997) suggest that a collectivist orientation acts to protect against rape because interpersonal conflict is minimal and rape is viewed as a crime against the group, not just the individual.

The fact that rape is almost nonexistent in some societies proves that it can be eliminated, but for that to happen here we will have to raise boys to have different values than in the past. What type of values will you teach your sons?

In other instances, the victim may be chosen at random. A study by Amir (1971) found that 43 percent of the rape victims surveyed had been attacked by more than one assailant. Of the rapists studied, 71 percent had taken part in rapes with more than one assailant involved. Gang rapes were usually planned, although the specific victim was not always selected in advance. Victims usually lived in the same neighborhood as the rapists.

What motivates individuals to participate in gang rapes? Some of the reasons are the same reasons that single rapes are committed—to assert power and attempt to control others, to express anger, and to conform to the view—often reinforced by movies, television, and society in general—that men are the hunters or aggressors and that sexual relations involve conquering female victims. However, gang rapes often have a dynamic of their own. Individuals acting alone may not be capable of sexual assault, but being a member of a group creates special circumstances (O'Sullivan, 1991). For a group member, individuality is lost. This also means that individual responsibility for things a person does can be evaded or diffused while committing a rape as a member of a group. Furthermore, taking part in gang rape may be a way of demonstrating loyalty to the group in the eyes of group members, and hesitant individuals may decide to take part in order not to be seen as cowards (Sanday, 1990). Gang rapes are usually more violent than rapes committed by individuals because each member of the group is challenged to outdo the other (Gidycz & Koss, 1990). They may even bait one another into hideously shocking acts. In the Glen Ridge case, for example, the victim was sexually assaulted with a stick, a broom handle, and a miniature baseball bat.

Individuals who participate in gang rape tend to be younger than rapists who act alone (U.S. Bureau of Justice Statistics). Peer pressure is intense for teenagers. In a society where violence is a commonly portrayed means of interaction between men and women, it is not surprising that gang rapes occur. Only when society expects equality and nonviolence in relations between men and women will gang rape and other forms of rape begin to diminish in frequency.

STATUTORY RAPE

Most states have laws involving the crime **statutory rape,** sometimes referred to as *carnal knowledge of a juvenile.* These laws make it illegal for an adult to have sexual intercourse with anyone under a certain age, even if that person has consented to have sex. The legal "age of consent" varies from state to state, ranging from 14 to 18. The idea behind these laws is that underage individuals are not capable of giving informed consent (i.e., they are not capable of fully understanding the meaning and consequences of sexual relations).

The mentally handicapped are often protected by these laws as well. A landmark case was the Glen Ridge gang rape (see the section on gang rape). Although the 17-year-old victim allegedly agreed to have sex and had been sexually active since the age of 12, the defendants were convicted after the prosecution showed that she had an IQ of 64 and the social skills of an 8-year-old, and thus could not fully understand her actions. Thus, in some cases, a person can be found guilty of rape even if the victim was consenting.

Recall from Chapter 6 that half of the fathers of babies born to women aged 14 to 17 are at least 20 years old (Lindberg et al.,1997; Taylor et al., 1997). Today, some states are using statutory rape laws to prosecute these men with hopes that it will send a message to others and reduce the rate of teen pregnancies (Donovan, 1997).

SAME-SEX SEXUAL ASSAULT AND COERCION

The FBI's Uniform Crime Report doesn't even acknowledge that same-sex sexual assault exists—yet it does. The U.S. Department of Justice (2000) says that over 15,000 men a year report having been victims of rape or attempted rape. There are certainly many more unreported cases.

Many people assume that **male rape** occurs only in prison. Indeed, from 0.5 to 3 percent of all male inmates are sexually assaulted by other inmates (Moss et al., 1979). The victims are usually gang-raped by men who otherwise consider themselves heterosexual (Cotton & Groth, 1982). However, men are also raped by other men outside of prison. Laumann et al. (1994) reported that 1.9 percent of the men in their survey had had forced sex with a man. This includes college students (Scarce, 1997). About half of victims were raped when they were a child, and many were gang-raped, often by older boys they knew (King & Woollett, 1997).

> "I am a student in your class. I am a 24-year-old male. I am writing this because I feel it can help others in my situation. At 9 years of age, I was raped by three friends. They invited me in[to] their house to play 'strip poker.' I didn't know how to play, so I lost my shirt. Last, but not least, my underwear came off. At this point, the oldest, aged 16, told me to play with his penis. I refused and he punched me in the face. I started to cry and he hit me over and over. I still remember the look on his face. Well, anyway, they all took their penises and proceeded to rape me. They then took turns and at one point they made me perform oral sex on them. I still have nightmares about it. I still remember the blood, the pain, and the shame. What happened to them? Nothing. I never told anyone until this year." (from the author's files)

Grown men are also victims of rape by other men:

> On a stopover in St. Louis, he decided to stroll from the bus station to the Mississippi River. He was standing by the waves looking out at the water when a man approached and asked if he wanted to smoke some marijuana. Senter accepted the offer.
>
> He followed the man, then suddenly found himself being pushed into an empty tractor-trailer rig. . . . "He had his arm on my shoulder and his hand on my belt," Senter said. "I tried to get away once. He slammed me up on the side of the truck and told me not to do that again."
>
> At first, Senter tried to protest. His attacker told him that if he kept quiet, it would be over sooner. So Senter bit down on his thumb to keep from crying out. He bit so hard

statutory rape Sexual intercourse by an adult with a (consenting) partner who is not yet of the legal "age of consent." Sometimes called "carnal knowledge of a juvenile."

male rape Rape in which the victim is a man.

his thumb was left without feeling for days afterward.

Inwardly, though, his feelings exploded. (Read, 1993, p. E-3. Reprinted with permission.)

Several groups have published accounts of male rapes committed outside of prison (King & Woolett, 1997; Lipscomb et al., 1992; Mezey & King, 1989). Weapons were used in many of the assaults. Most of the rapists identified themselves as heterosexuals and so did the victims. One study found that there was nothing that distinguished the victims from other men and concluded that "all men are potential victims" (Lipscomb et al., 1992).

A substantial proportion of gay men also report being raped, by other gay men (Hickson et al., 1994). Similar to heterosexual sexual aggression, gay perpetrators use physical assault or threat of force, verbal coercion, or attempt to incapacitate their victims (e.g., alcohol) (Krahé et al., 2000). Within gay relationships, about one-fourth of men have experienced unwanted sex from a partner (Waldner-Haugrud, 1999).

What about lesbian relationships? Studies indicate that sexual coercion is at least as common, and perhaps more so, as in gay relationships (Waldner-Haugrud, 1999). This often involves forced sex, including penetration.

CAN A MAN BE RAPED BY A WOMAN?

Many people have difficulty believing that a man could get an erection while feeling great fear or terror, but it does happen. Sarrel and Masters (1982) reported 11 instances in which men had been kidnapped by a woman or a group of women who then forced them (often with use of a weapon) to engage in sexual intercourse. Anderson reported that some college women admitted to having used physical force or a weapon to have sex with a man (see Anderson & Struckman-Johnson, 1998). Others have also reported cases where men were victims of female sexual assault (King & Woollett, 1997; Smith et al., 1988). When victims were younger than 16, the perpetrator was often a family member, usually the mother (King & Woollett, 1997). These male victims of rape suffered long-term problems similar to those of female rape victims (see "Reactions to Rape") and generally felt guilt, or thought that something was wrong with them, because they were able to respond sexually under the circumstances (Masters, 1986; Sarrel & Masters, 1982).

EXPLANATIONS OF RAPE

power rapists Rapists who commit their attacks in order to overcome personal feelings of insecurity and inadequacy. Their rapes give them a sense of mastery and control.

Many years ago it was believed that men raped because of an overpowering sexual urge that women released by their looks, dress, or behavior. Then the pendulum swung so that rape

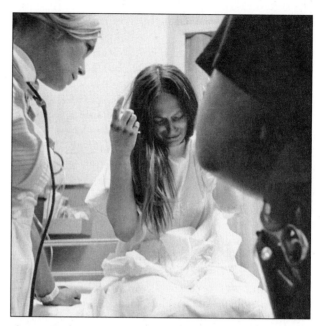

Figure 17–3 If you have ever been a victim of rape or child sexual molestation, just listening to a lecture about sexual abuse can bring back bad memories and upsetting emotions.

was considered as violence or anger at women expressed by a sexual act. Today, the prevailing view is that there are many types of rapists and that violence and sexual desires are present to differing degrees in different types of rape. Let us review some of the explanations of rape.

PSYCHODYNAMIC THEORIES. Psychodynamic theories view sexually deviant behavior as psychopathology—a character disorder that is very resistant to change. In the 1970s, two such theories about rapists were proposed that have had a substantial impact. Both attempted to classify offenders by their psychology or motivation. The first theory, by Cohen et al. (1971), classified rapists according to whether their aim was aggression, sexual, or sadism. I will focus on the second theory, by Groth, Burgess, and Holmstrom (1977). The two theories, however, have much in common.

Groth, Burgess, and Holmstrom describe three types of rapists. **Power rapists** commit premeditated attacks in order to overcome personal feelings of insecurity and inadequacy. The rape "is the means by which he [the rapist] reassures himself of his sexual adequacy and identity, of his strength and potency" (p. 1240). Rapes give power rapists a sense of mastery and control. These rapists seek to humiliate and degrade their victims through language and acts. Power rapists use whatever force is required to overcome the will of their victims, including threats and weapons. Although this sometimes can lead to injury, there is usually little physical harm to the victim beyond the act itself. The rape may last for an extended time.

Power rapists usually have great difficulty in relating to women and are often very awkward in their interpersonal relations. Groth (1979) estimated that 55 percent of all rapes are power rapes.

A second type commit what are called anger rapes. An **anger rapist** generally commits unplanned assaults in an attempt to express his hostility or anger about some wrong he feels has been done to him—by life or by his victim. His anger is often directed at women in general. Anger rapists often use more physical abuse than is necessary to commit the rape in an effort to punish their victims. The attack usually is of short duration. Groth estimated that 40 percent of all rapes are anger rapes, and more recent studies suggest that many rapists have problems controlling anger (see Ward et al., Hudson, & McCormack, 1997).

Finally, there is the sadistic rape. **Sadistic rapists** are erotically aroused by physical force and derive pleasure from inflicting physical pain on their victims. They may not be sexually satisfied if the victim does not resist, and may torture or even murder their victims to satisfy themselves. The attacks usually are of extended duration. Groth estimated that only 5 percent of all rapes are sadistic rapes.

Groth et al. (1977) concluded that although rape involves a sexual act, first and foremost it is an act of violence. Rape is motivated by the need to dominate, humiliate, and exert power over women. According to Groth, "We look at rape as the sexual expression of aggression, rather than as the aggressive expression of sexuality" (quoted by Gelman et al., 1990b).

There are many ways in which rape can be used to display dominance or power. In one case, a man known as the "ski mask rapist" committed several rapes in Texas and Louisiana. He always chose a female victim who lived with a man (husband or boyfriend). He would stake out her home, wait until the man left, and then break in when the woman was alone. He would then tie her up, wait until the man returned, and then tie up the man and force him to watch while the woman was raped. If sexual release had been the rapist's primary motivation, he would not have waited until the male partner returned home. In this case, the primary motive was clearly to dominate and humiliate both the woman and her male partner. Gang rapes, either of women or of men, provide another example of the use of rape to demonstrate power or domination.

There are many examples of anger rape as well. The following letter illustrates a clear case of rape used to act out the rapist's hostility toward women:

> Dear Ann Landers:
>
> You have printed letters from bartenders, secretaries, lawyers, musicians, housewives, lovesick teenagers . . . , but I have never seen a letter from a rapist. This may be your first, if you have the guts to publish it.
>
> I am 32 years old and started on this rotten road when I was 20. As of last week, I have raped 25 women, mostly in Oklahoma, Arizona, and California. I've never been caught. The system I use is virtually risk-free. I am highly intelligent—a college graduate from an Ivy League school.
>
> I am writing in the hope that you will print the letter and educate the public. They need to know why men rape. Perhaps if the reason were known, today's mothers of young children will do a better job and prevent another generation from growing up to be rapists who terrorize women of all ages. I hate what I am; but I know what caused me to be like this, and hope you will give my views as much coverage as possible.
>
> I have read repeatedly in your column, "Rape is not an act of lust. It is an act of violence." You are so right. Actually, rape has very little to do with sex. It has a lot to do with the way a male relates to females. Almost always, if you put it all together it spells M-O-T-H-E-R.
>
> I came from a well-to-do family and was raised by a domineering, overpowering mother (divorced). My miserable, cruel grandmother lived with us. Almost every day since I can remember, I was slapped, punched, kicked, beaten with a belt or a hairbrush. Once I suffered three broken ribs from being pushed down a flight of stairs. When I was taken to the doctor (Mom thought I might have a broken leg), I was instructed to say I fell off my bike.
>
> I have never had a girlfriend because I despise all women. I know I am sick in the head, but I have this uncontrollable urge to punish all females, and rape is the best way to get even. . . .
>
> No Name, No City, and No Fingerprints
> (Reprinted with permission of Ann Landers and Creators Syndicate.)

Groth et al.'s (1977) classification was based on in-depth research of convicted rapists. But recall that most convicted rapists are stranger rapists and that stranger rapists commit a minority of all rapes. On the basis of what we now know about acquaintance (including date) rapes, some researchers have proposed a fourth type of rapist—the **opportunistic rapist** (Prentky et al., 1988). Here, the primary motivation is sex, but these men have strongly distorted attitudes and beliefs about sex roles and female behavior that negate normal social inhibitions. These men rape impulsively when there is an opportunity, as on a date. They use only enough force to commit the act, and their only anger is at the victim's resistance. Opportunistic rapists probably account for the majority of date rapes.

Recent research has made it clear that rape cannot be

anger rapists Rapists who commit their attacks out of hostility or anger directed at their victims or at women in general.

sadistic rapists Rapists who are aroused by physical force and who derive pleasure by harming their victims.

opportunistic rapists Rapists motivated by a desire for sex who rape impulsively when there is an opportunity.

explained only by individual psychopathology, for rape is far more common in some cultures than others (see Box 17–A). Cultural, social learning, and interpersonal factors all play a role.

PERSONAL REFLECTIONS
Do you ever use sex to express power, dominance, control, or anger? If so, under what circumstances? Why do you use sex as an outlet for these desires and emotions?

FEMINIST (SEXUAL SCRIPT) THEORIES. Look again at the rape statistics at the very beginning of the chapter. Why is the incidence of rape so much higher in the United States than in many other countries? Studies have found that rape is most common in societies that glorify violence by men, particularly when the society is also sexually repressive (Baron et al., 1987; Sanday, 1981). These societies not only encourage boys to be aggressive (see Box 17–A) but have distinct gender roles for men and women, with men regarding women's roles as inferior. In our culture, the stereotypic gender role for male sexuality is "active, aggressive, thrusting and powerful," and for female sexuality it is "passive, powerless, submissive and receptive" (Moore, 1994). Feminist theory holds that the traditional sexual script "supports and condones male sexual coercion against women and that this sexual script remains the normative dating script in our society" (Byers, 1996). In this viewpoint, "rape is the logical and psychological extension of a dominant-submissive, competitive, sex-role stereotyped culture" (Burt, 1980, p. 229).

In fact, men who commit rape or engage in sexual coercion are likely to believe in stereotypic gender roles, to view men as dominant, to consider relations with women adversarial (very competitive), and to have male friends who believe that the use of physical force to have sex is okay in some situations (Harney & Muehlenhard, 1991; Malamuth, 1986; Rapaport & Burkhart, 1984). Men with callous attitudes about sex believe that women are here to serve their sexual interests. In short, these men believe that they are *entitled* to sex. As one researcher put it, "The ideological script of machismo is a hypermasculine variant of a traditional normative gender ideology that emphasizes destructive power rather than productive or integrative power" (Mosher, 1991, p. 201). Henrietta Moore (1994) argues that men's sexual violence toward women does not reflect a breakdown in the social order but is enacted in order to maintain the existing social order (as a "sign of a struggle for the maintenance of certain fantasies of identity and power").

You will learn about the effects of sexually violent pornography in the next chapter. One of the conclusions of research in this area is that men who look at scenes of aggression toward women—and the scenes do not need to be sexually explicit—become less sensitive to the victims of rape and more accepting of sexual violence (Donnerstein & Linz, 1984; Linz, 1989; Malamuth & Check, 1981). Nonsexually explicit rape scenes are exactly the type that are commonly shown on television.

One study found a strong positive correlation between men's attitudes about sexual relations (whether or not they held callous attitudes) and their use of sexual coercion with partners. The authors concluded by stating that "the socialization of the macho man, if it does not directly produce a rapist, appears to produce calloused sex attitudes toward women and rape and [the use of] forceful and exploitive tactics to gain sexual access to reluctant women" (Mosher & Anderson, 1986).

SOCIAL LEARNING THEORIES. These theories have much in common with cultural explanations. You have already read much about social learning research in previous sections, so this will serve mainly as a review. Recall that many rapists were either themselves abused as children or witnessed abuse within the family (Groth, 1979; Seghorn et al., 1987). Whatever type of family life a child experiences while growing up and accepts as "normal," it is likely that he or she will model the same behavior as an adult. Interestingly, women with a childhood experience of sexual abuse are more likely than others to be revictimized as adults, perhaps because the experience often lowers self-esteem and makes these women more vulnerable to being easily pressured into sex (Acierno et al., 1999). Thus, for both men and women, a past experience of sexual abuse (or, to a lesser extent, physical abuse) is predictive of the likelihood of inflicting or receiving such abuse when they are adults (Gwartney-Gibbs et al., 1987).

Learned gender roles are also important. Men who have learned extremely conservative stereotypes and who also believe that relationships between men and women are adversarial tend to believe the myths about rape that legitimize violence against women (see the next section) (Burt, 1980; Koss et al., 1985; Muehlenhard & Falcon, 1990).

INTERPERSONAL THEORIES. This section, too, will be review (see Spitzberg, 1998). Recall that a lack of shared meaning between men and women can lead to unwanted sexual aggression by men. Recall also that many men (and women) believe that rape is justified in some situations, including instances where a man has spent money on a date and feels that she has "led him on" (e.g., by engaging in necking or petting or going to his apartment) (Cook, 1995; Goodchilds & Zellman, 1984; Kikuchi, 1988). Men who accept extreme gender stereotypes of women are most likely to misinterpret behaviors like these as invitations for sex (Muehlenhard & Cook, 1988). The fact that some women engage in token resistance, initially saying "no" when they want the man to continue, compounds the misinterpretation of intentions (Muehlenhard &

Hollabaugh, 1989), not only on one date but on future dates with other women as well.

EVOLUTIONARY (SOCIOBIOLOGICAL) THEORIES.
Evolutionary theories of rape assume that the inclination of men to rape has a genetic basis (Ellis, 1993; Shields & Shields, 1983; Thornhill & Thornhill, 1992). Basically, these theories state that by having sex with many partners, men maximize their reproductive potential, and that evolution has favored sexually aggressive men by their producing more offspring. This view has received considerable attention with the publication of a book by Thornhill and Palmer (2000) in which they claim that rape is about sex and propagation (not violence) and that women can provoke rape. Others have pointed out that the book (and evolutionary theory) does not explain why men rape children, old women, and other men. Critics have also emphasized the dangers of generalizing from studies of animals and insects to humans and contend that other theories do a better job of explaining the specifics of rape behavior (see Polaschek et al., 1997).

In a thoughtful review, Jones (1999) has attempted to integrate biological and cultural feminist explanations of rape. He points out that evolutionary theory does *not* say that there is a gene responsible for directly heritable features specific to rape, but that rape is very possibly a by-product of other behaviors that are adaptive for organisms. For example, "If eager pursuit of possible sex partners on average increases reproductive success, and if such pursuit occasionally results in nonconsensual sex . . . then rape behavior could be a byproduct of a psychology evolved by direct selection to pursue eagerly, and persist in obtaining, possible sex partners." Jones points out that we must not confuse causation with motivation, and that is where cultural/feminist explanations come into play. The rapist does not have to consciously be aware of a desire to father children, but may be more immediately motivated by a desire to violate, humiliate, degrade, and dominate women.

COMPREHENSIVE THEORIES.
As you have seen, at various times the motivation for rape has been attributed to sex or to power. It is an ongoing debate fueled by politics as well as science. Today, more and more people are recognizing that there are probably multiple paths to sexual aggression, motivated by both sex and power to different degrees. Date rape, for example, is now often viewed as "the use of power to get sex" (Spitzberg, 1998).

For students, one of the most confusing aspects about research on rape is the lack of agreement on terminology. In addition to the types of rapists already presented in this chapter, you may also see references to *preferential rapists* (defined as a paraphiliac preference for rape/coercive sex), the *ritualistic sex offender* (also characterized by many paraphilias), and the *impulsive*

sex offender (not sophisticated criminally, but reactive to situations) (e.g., Freund and Seto, 1998; Hazelwood & Warren, 2000). Until researchers agree on a uniform terminology, I will avoid further use of new "types."

Malamuth and colleagues were among the first to offer a comprehensive theory (Malamuth, 1986; Malamuth et al., 1993). They say that sexual aggression results from several converging factors: motivation, elimination of the inhibitors (both internal and external) that normally prevent aggression, and opportunity. The social environment (including experiences during development such as parental violence and sexual abuse) then increases or decreases the chances that sexual aggression will proceed. Malamuth and colleagues provide six predictors for whether or not sexual aggression will proceed: sexual arousal, dominance as a motivation, hostile attitutudes toward women, aggressive attitudes toward women, antisocial personality, and promiscuous experience. The more of these features that a man possesses, the more likely that he will use aggression to obtain sex. In the end, two interacting pathways result in rape/sexual coercion: hypermasculinity with hostile attitudes and sexual promiscuity.

Marshall and Barbaree (1990) offer another integrated model that is very similar except that it gives greater importance to early developmental factors (e.g., abuse, family violence). Both theories acknowledge the importance of situational cues and socially created inhibitors. How important are these factors? Recall the research that found that convicted rapists, but not nonrapists, were sexually aroused by listening to tapes of or viewing rape scenes (see the section on characteristics of rapists). Are there any situations in which normal men might also respond to rape scenes, becoming aroused as rapists do? Barbaree and Marshall (1991) found that many men could become aroused by rape scenes when they had been drinking—remember, most date rapes occur when the man or both people have been drinking (Ullman et al., 1999). Barbaree's team also found that normal men's reactions to rape scenes became more like those of rapists if a woman had made them angry just before testing (this was done purposely as part of the research). How might these men behave if they incorrectly believed that a woman had "led them on"? As Barbaree concluded, "With the right combination of factors, most men can be aroused by violent sex" (cited in Goleman, 1992).

MISCONCEPTIONS ABOUT RAPE

By this point in the chapter, you have probably learned some facts about rapes and rapists that have challenged the beliefs you held before enrolling in the course. Mistaken beliefs about rape are widespread, so widespread that they are often referred to as **rape myths** (Burt, 1980). These myths serve the

rape myths Widespread mistaken beliefs about rape.

function of placing the blame on the victims. In general, men, especially young men, are more accepting of these myths than women (Johnson et al., 1997; Jones et al., 1998). This is particularly true of men who accept conservative gender-role stereotypes; and the combination of belief in stereotypes and belief in rape myths, you recall, is commonly found in men who engage in sexually coercive behavior. It is important, therefore, that we dispel these myths. Let us examine some of them.

MYTH #1: WOMEN WHO ARE RAPED USUALLY PROVOKED IT BY THEIR DRESS AND BEHAVIOR.

Read again the results of the study by Kikuchi (1988) at the end of the section on date rape. Many junior high school boys and girls believed that date rape was okay if the woman had engaged in certain behaviors. Many adults, especially men, continue to hold these beliefs. One-third to one-half of all people believe that a woman was at least partially to blame for rape if she wore a short skirt or went braless, went to the man's home or room, or was drinking alcohol (Burt, 1980; Goodchilds & Zellman, 1984; Monroe et al., 1990). As a result, many rape victims blame themselves. Here is the response of a young woman who was gang-raped at a party:

> " I still don't know exactly who to blame. I know that some of the blame goes to the guys who did it, but I do still feel that some of the blame should be placed on me because I was drinking." (from the author's files)

When rape cases go to trial, men are less likely than women to vote for conviction (Schutte & Hosch, 1997). A jury in Ft. Lauderdale, Florida, acquitted a drifter on trial for rape because his victim was wearing a lace miniskirt at the time (the jury foreman was quoted as saying, "She asked for it"). The man was a serial rapist who was later convicted of another rape. As a result of this case, the Florida legislature enacted a law that prevents discussion of a rape victim's clothing during court trials. Other states are now passing similar laws. Many women also blame female victims of rape, mistakenly believing that women can prevent themselves from being raped by behaving differently (e.g., by dressing conservatively).

When others put the blame for rape on the victim, it makes the emotional trauma all the worse:

> "I lost my virginity through rape at age 15. Even my parents thought it must have been my fault because I was at a party. Needless to say, this made matters worse. I had difficulty having a productive relationship until recently." (from the author's files)

Why is rape the only crime for which we have a tendency to blame the victims? Consider the following hypothetical scenario:

Steve wore his finest Italian suit and shoes to the company's reception. He was particularly proud of his new Rolex watch and felt sure it would make an impression on the brunette in Accounting. At the party he had two or three drinks. Steve enjoyed a drink on these occasions because it made him feel more sociable, but he often found that he had had one more than he wanted because of peer pressure—others made him feel like an outcast if he didn't have a drink in his hand. He intermingled freely, and toward the end of the evening finally struck up a conversation with the woman in Accounting. They made plans to get together for lunch the next day, so by the time Steve left, around midnight, he was feeling really good.

On the way home, Steve remembered he was out of bread and eggs, so he stopped at a convenience store, parking his BMW slightly off to the side. When he went to get back in his car, he was stopped by a man who said that he had a gun under his coat and that Steve had better give him his Rolex, wallet, and ring. Steve wanted to avoid injury and quickly handed over his valuables while pleading with the man not to hurt him. The man took the valuables and ran.

Steve called the police immediately, hoping to catch the robber. But when the police arrived, rather than asking for a description of the robber, they started to act suspicious about him. One asked why he was out so late. Didn't he know this was when most muggings take place? The other wanted to know how much he'd had to drink and made him take a breathalyzer test. When Steve finally got to tell them what the robber took, they were not sympathetic, but instead made comments that insinuated that he had invited the robbery by dressing so well and wearing a Rolex in public.

When Steve got home, his two male roommates couldn't believe that he hadn't resisted. They would have put up a fight, they said; it would never have happened to them. Steve went to bed feeling ashamed and guilty. The next day he didn't mention it at the office.

You probably found this scenario ridiculous, and well you should. So, if you have ever thought that it is women's behavior that leads to their being raped, stop for a moment and reexamine your attitude.

MYTHS #2 AND 3: WOMEN SUBCONSCIOUSLY WANT TO BE RAPED; NO WOMAN CAN BE RAPED IF SHE TRULY DOES NOT WANT IT.

These two closely related ideas are also widely believed (Burt, 1980; Holcomb et al., 1991). Although many women have had submission fantasies (Leitenberg & Henning, 1995; Meuwissen & Over, 1991), this does not mean that they actually wish to be raped. Most of us have fantasized about things we would never do in real life; the difference between fantasy and reality is that we are

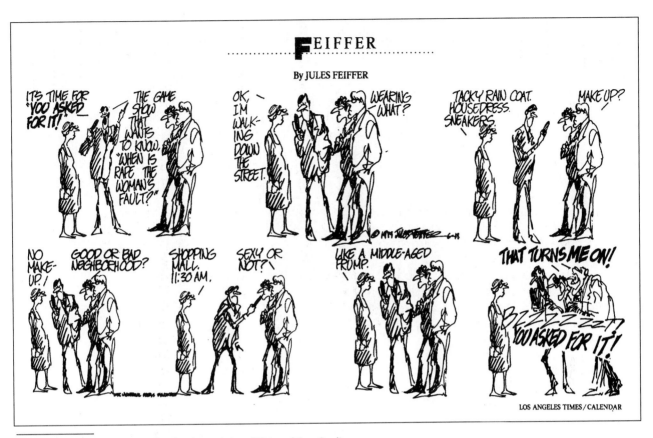

Feiffer © 1989 Jules Feiffer. Reproduced with permission of Universal Press Syndicate.

in control of our fantasies. Real rape involves someone else taking away all of your control. Women, unlike many men, are not sexually aroused by watching realistic rape scenes.

A common male phrase is "You can't thread a moving needle." However, most rapists are bigger and stronger than their victims, and many assaults involve more than one man. In our culture, most men are reinforced for their physical aggressiveness while growing up, while many women are reinforced for being passive. The end result is that most women wouldn't even know how to fight back if they were attacked. Nearly a third of all rapists use some kind of weapon (Bureau of Justice Statistics). The use of force and threats can result in anyone's being raped. If the myth were true, then we would certainly never expect men to be raped, but it happens every day, out of prison as well as in.

MYTH #4: WOMEN FREQUENTLY MAKE FALSE AC-CUSATIONS OF RAPE. This myth is based on the idea that a woman uses the accusation of rape to get even with a man—for revenge. Many men believe this (Holcomb et al., 1991). However, FBI statistics show that the percentage of reported rapes that are false is actually lower (2 percent) than for most other crimes. (When false accusations do occur, it is usually to pro-

vide an alibi, seek revenge, or obtain sympathy; Kanin, 1994.) We do not automatically doubt people when they claim that they were the victim of some other type of crime. So why do you suppose some people are so quick to doubt a woman's accusation of rape?

REACTIONS TO RAPE

In their initial reactions and long-term coping strategies, female victims of rape go through what has been called *rape trauma syndrome* (Burgess & Holmstrom, 1974). For most victims, it is probably better from a clinical and a legal aspect to consider it as a form of *posttraumatic stress disorder* (Boeschen et al., 1998; Foa & Riggs, 1995), now called **post-rape posttraumatic stress disorder.** First, there is an *acute phase,* which begins right after the rape and continues for several weeks. During this phase, the victim's body has to recover from the physical damage that may have been caused by the rape. About one-fourth of all rape victims suffer minor injuries, and about 4 percent are seriously injured (National Victims Center). In addition, the victim must begin to recover from the psychological damage that was done (Arata & Burkhart, 1996; Rynd, 1987). Some victims become very expressive about

post-rape posttraumatic stress disorder A group of clinical symptoms displayed by many victims of rape; previously called *rape trauma syndrome.*

their feelings and may cry and experience severe depression, become angry or fearful, and/or experience great anxiety. Others may have what is called a controlled reaction, as if they were trying to deny that the rapist had affected them in any way. However, these victims must also work through a great deal of anguish and may become expressive later. Many rape victims experience dissociative symptoms (restricted affect, detachment from other people, concentration problems) (Foa & Riggs, 1995). Many victims believed rape myths prior to the rape, and as a result experience guilt and self-blame, which makes the depression even worse (Frazier, 1991). Because the trauma for many victims is long term, rape victims may well be referred to as rape *survivors*.

Figure 17–4   Most communities now offer rape crisis counseling.

> "The lectures on rape were traumatic for me because I could remember everything so vividly. But I stuck with the lecture so I could find out if it was my fault. Now I don't feel as dirty." (from the author's files)

Next, the victim enters a *period of long-term reorganization*. In this stage, the rape victim attempts to regain control of her or his life (including taking steps to prevent rape from occurring again) and may move or change jobs. Each of us wants to believe that our world is a relatively safe, secure, and predictable place to live in and to feel that we have control over our lives and what happens to us. This belief allows us to reduce our fears and anxieties about the world we live in so that we can function efficiently and effectively in it. However, when a violent crime such as rape is committed, our belief system is shaken and our security is threatened. Rape victims often feel as if they no longer have any control over what is going to happen to them. Many of the reactions to rape are attempts by victims to reassert control over their lives.

Many victims lose their desire for sex and have trouble becoming sexually aroused (Burgess & Holmstrom, 1979; Gilbert & Cunningham, 1987). Reread the story of the teenage girl who was gang-raped. Here is part of her long-term reaction:

> "I talked to other rape victims and I worked through my guilt and blame. I still have a lot of fears about sexual relationships and have not had a sexual relationship since I was raped." (from the author's files)

Studies have found that many victims of sexual assault also suffer from long-term physical health problems (Golding, 1999). This may include poor general health, chronic pelvic pain and other gynecologic problems, headache, and gastrointestinal disorders.

The reactions of the victim's family are very important in this respect. Victims who experience negative social reactions have increased psychological problems (Ullman, 1996). For example, women whose partners respond warmly and sympathetically and do not pressure them to reestablish sexual relations have fewer long-term sexual problems. With rape victims who initially suppress their feelings, it is not unusual for symptoms to emerge months or even years after the incident.

> "The first thing I went and did after your class today was run to my car and cry for a half hour. Fourteen years ago I was raped." (from the author's files)

Just like female victims, men who are the victims of rape suffer long-term problems (Mezey & King, 1989). They frequently have sexual problems, difficulties in forming close relationships, and a damaged self-image. Unlike women who are victims, they are also likely to have doubts about their sexual self-identity and ask themselves whether the experience means that they are homosexual. Recovery is made more difficult because male victims are even less likely than female victims to tell anyone else, and thus are less likely to seek counseling.

The rates for child molestation, incest, and rape are high in our society, and thus, unfortunately, some victims of sexual abuse are later revictimized.

"When growing up, I was raped by five males in my neighborhood. . . . The speaker and your lectures helped me to realize that it wasn't my fault. . . . Recently, I was raped again . . . and it was very traumatic to me. When I told a close friend of mine, she reacted as if I had done it. She just couldn't understand how it could happen to me twice, and to be honest, neither can I."   (from the author's files)

Perhaps as many as 21 to 35 percent of rape victims have been sexually assaulted before (Acierno et al., 1999; Cohen & Roth, 1987; Ellis et al., 1982). Studies have found that some (but not all) people attribute greater blame to a repeat victim than to a first-time victim, regarding her as the type of person to get herself into rape situations (Schult & Schneider, 1991). Counseling to eliminate self-blame is very important for repeat victims.

PERSONAL REFLECTIONS
Have you ever been the victim of rape or sexual coercion? If so, has it affected how you feel about yourself and your relationships with others? If it has affected you in any way (including leaving you with any sense of self-blame), have you ever sought counseling? If you have not sought counseling, why not?

Box 17-B SEXUALITY AND HEALTH

Sexual Victimization, Pregnancy, and Sexually Transmitted Diseases

In addition to the immediate physical trauma that may occur during rape, the victim of sexual abuse is also burdened with the fear of possible pregnancy and/or sexually transmitted disease. A national survey found that about 32,000 pregnancies a year result from the rape of women aged 18 and older (Holmes et al., 1996). Many more pregnancies occur from the rape of younger girls. Half of these pregnancies are terminated by abortion.

Other studies have found that many rape victims have sexually transmitted infections as well. Between 2 and 13 percent of female rape victims have gonorrhea, while 2–17 percent have chlamydia and 6–20 percent have trichomoniasis (Beck-Sagué & Solomon, 1999; Glaser et al., 1991; Jenny et al., 1990). Fewer than 2 percent have syphilis.

STDs are very common, so not all of the infected victims in these studies had contracted the diseases during rape. In some, the infections had existed before the assault, while others had been acquired from new partners in the interval between the assault and the medical examination (see Beck-Sagué & Solomon, 1999). STDs that are found in the first 24 hours after the assault may represent preexisting conditions. Nevertheless, studies have verified that many rape victims do, in fact, acquire STDs at the time of the rape (Glaser et al., 1991; Jenny et al., 1990). In a recent review of child sexual abuse cases, 1–4.6 percent had gonorrhea, 0.4–11.1 percent had chlamydia, 2–33 percent had HPV, and many others had bacter-

ial vaginosis (Beck-Sagué & Solomon, 1999). As a result, authorities are saying that all rape victims should be treated with a variety of medications shortly after the rape (e.g., Glaser et al., 1991).

What about the possibility of becoming infected with HIV, the virus that causes AIDS, during a rape? Case reports indicate that HIV has been transmitted during sexual assault (Beck-Sagué & Solomon, 1999). Recall from Chapter 5 that the test for HIV (actually, for antibodies to HIV) cannot confirm the presence of the virus until many weeks after initial infection. So why not test the rapist if he's caught? In most states, victims and prosecutors are not allowed to see the results of rapists' HIV tests because of a defendant's right to privacy. This seems very unfair to victims (and most others), for worry about the possibility of HIV/AIDS adds to the trauma of many rape victims. At least one victim has allowed her attacker to have a reduced sentence in exchange for his HIV test results (see Salholz et al., 1990). However, remember that it is difficult to spread HIV from person to person—the odds of becoming infected during one act of unprotected vaginal intercourse with an infected partner is only about 1 in 500 (Hearst & Hulley, 1988). On the other hand, repeated abuse over an extended period or rape by multiple assailants (especially if there is genital trauma) greatly increases the risk (Murphy et al., 1989). Still, most AIDS experts believe that the chance of getting HIV during a rape is extremely low.

REACTIONS OF THE PARTNER

A rape victim's partner and family must also deal with their reactions and emotions. When a woman is raped, some male partners blame themselves for not being there to protect her. However, it is important that the man put this feeling aside and direct his attention and emotions to the real victim. He should let her recover from the assault at her own pace and allow her to make her own decisions. After all, one of the biggest steps on the road to recovery is regaining control of one's own life.

Perhaps the most devastating thing that can happen to a rape victim *after* the attack is if her partner and/or family blames her because they believe in rape myths. This will make recovery all the more difficult (Davis et al., 1991).

> "My girlfriend . . . about 1 year ago (3 years into the relationship) was walking alone on her college campus and was violently raped. I somehow held her responsible for 'letting' this happen to her. Both her parents also blamed her. I know I treated her with a little less respect after this happened. Now I feel like a complete schmuck. I realize that she had no control over what happened. Fortunately, her therapist convinced her that it was not her fault." (from the author's files)

If your partner is ever the victim of rape, do not ask questions such as "Why did you have to go there?" or "Why were you out so late?" or "What were you wearing?" Questions like these imply that the rape must have somehow been the victim's fault. Both the victim and the partner often find counseling very useful in learning how to cope with rape.

WHAT HAPPENS WHEN A RAPE IS REPORTED?

In most metropolitan areas, the police department has special units for dealing with the sexual abuse of children and rape victims. If a rape is reported, uniformed officers will arrive on the scene and determine whether a case of sexual abuse has occurred. They will search for the attacker, but the investigation of the case will be carried out by a detective from a special rape investigation unit, who will be next on the scene. These detectives are specially trained to deal with victims of rape. Most large cities now have *rape victim advocate programs* as well. These programs provide a specially trained counselor to be with the woman from the initial investigation through the prosecution. After the initial investigation, the victim is referred to a hospital for a medical exam.

To maximize the chance of a successful prosecution, it is very important to get a medical exam as soon as possible after a rape. It is crucial not to wash, douche, or change clothing after being raped, as doing so may destroy vital evidence (such as semen in the vagina) needed by the police to catch the rapist and prove that the crime was committed. Some victims are initially reluctant to prosecute, but later change their minds. If a medical exam has taken place, this option is still available. Without such medical attention, a successful prosecution (or even an attempted prosecution) is less likely.

Most hospitals today are much more sensitive to the trauma experienced by rape victims than they were in the past. Their emergency units are educated and trained to deal with rape victims, who are given the second highest priority for treatment (only life-and-death situations are given higher priority).

PREVENTING RAPE

In general, there are three basic perspectives or approaches regarding the prevention of rape. *The first approach focuses on the rapist.* Malamuth (1981) found that many men indicated that they would commit rape if they were certain they would not get caught. It was noted that watching films that showed violence toward women intensified this attitude (see Chapter 18). An approach focusing on the rapist would call for more policemen on patrol, more lights in dark parking lots, tougher laws that are more rigorously enforced, more arrests, and longer prison sentences for rapists. During its 1994 session, Congress passed the Violence against Women Act, which, among other things, increased penalties for sex offenses. About half of the 50 states have passed laws requiring that sex criminals released from prison register their addresses with police.

This first approach attempts to use legal deterrents to prevent rape. Almost everyone is in favor of strict law enforcement and a speedy and just court system. However, this approach deals with the symptom only (rape behavior), and not the cause (why does a man want to commit rape?). A law-and-order approach, by itself, may only make rapists more cautious in choosing the time, place, and victim.

The second approach focuses on the potential victim. Part of this approach involves decreasing the chances that a woman will be the target of a rape. Women are often urged to avoid settings or people that might increase the likelihood of rape (e.g., avoiding dark alleys and not picking up hitchhikers). They are also taught to keep dead bolts on doors, to avoid advertising the fact that they might live alone, not to trust door chains as a means of identifying strangers, and so on. When going to their cars, women are encouraged to look under and around the vicinity of the car from a distance and to check the back seat before getting in.

This approach also involves reacting to an attempted rape. Women are urged to learn at least a little bit about self-defense. Women who resist decrease the chance of the rape being completed by about 80 percent (Marchbanks et al., 1990). Surveys of victims of attempted rape have found that resistance is related to an increased chance of escape without serious harm (Bart, 1980; Ullman & Knight, 1991). Studies have also found that resistance does not increase the rapists' level of violence (Ullman, 1998).

Verbal assertiveness and aggression can also help prevent an attack, especially if a woman exhibits them when she is first approached. Brodsky (1976) reported that being assertive and fighting back are most likely to be successful when the rapist initially is polite, hesitant, or precedes the attack with conversation. Some women even get themselves to urinate, vomit, defecate, or tell their attacker that they have a sexually transmitted disease in order to make themselves repulsive. Other forms of trickery include trying to talk the rapist into going to a place where someone can recognize what's going on and help.

> "I was once approached by a rapist, who dragged me off into an alley. A part of me somehow remained calm. I simply told him that I would rather go to a motel, and that I would pay for it. And if we went to the phone company where I worked at the time, I would get my check and take the day off. He fell for it.
>
> "I kept calmly talking to him and assuring him how nice it was going to be and how lucky I was to be getting away from my husband. (Any and every lie I could conceive of, I verbalized casually.) At the phone company there was a guard with a gun. When I saw the guard, I began running in circles and screaming for help. The guard quickly pulled out his gun. What amazed me was that the rapist made no attempt to run, but instead told the guard we were going to a motel. His voice had degenerated into blubbering in anticipation. When the police came, he told them he was going to give me a baby in the alley, and I suggested a motel.
>
> "He was a notorious child molester, who had put eight little girls (aged 8 to 11 years old) in the hospital. I was the only one old enough to go to court against him—the kids were too young."
> (from the author's files)

There are some problems with this approach to rape prevention as well. The first problem is that by placing the responsibility for preventing rape in the hands of the victim, women who are raped may feel that they have somehow failed and that the rape was their fault. As noted earlier, a woman should never feel guilty for being raped, as she did not instigate or cause the action. Screaming, blowing a whistle, using Mace, or talking sometimes works very well, but may not work in every case. Techniques that drive away one rapist may do the reverse and anger another. There is no perfect defense against rape. Finally, these attempts to prevent rape do not deal with the underlying causes of rape.

A final approach is based on a *social systems perspective*. From this point of view, rape is caused by our society's belief that men should be sexually aggressive and dominant. The explanation of rape as resulting from sexual scripts fits this point of view (look again at the feminist theories of rape). In a society where violence has become both commonplace and acceptable (look at our TV and movie heroes), it should come as no surprise that men use violence as a means of subjugating women. From this perspective, rape can best be prevented by changing social attitudes about the way that men and women relate to each other. Sexual assault prevention programs on college campuses do, in fact, result in less belief in rape myths and rape-supportive attitudes (Breitenbecher, 2000). Even though this approach attempts to deal directly with the cause of rape, it may be the most difficult to implement. Nonetheless, although changing the values and attitudes of a society is hard, it is certainly not impossible. Recall that rape is much less common in many other civilized countries.

What do you think? Is a tougher law-and-order approach to rape needed? Should more women become prepared to deal with attempted rape? Is this enough? Will rape ever stop being a serious problem in our society? Why or why not?

SEXUAL HARASSMENT

Anita Hill's accusation of sexual harassment by U.S. Supreme Court nominee Clarence Thomas, similar charges against U.S. Senator Bob Packwood by several of his female staff and interns, and Paula Jones's charges against then-Governor Bill Clinton—all brought attention to an issue in the 1990s that many people (particularly men) had not taken seriously. Was sexual harassment something new? Of course not. Many surveys taken during the 1980s found that a large proportion of women (generally 40 to 60 percent) in all sorts of occupations felt that they had been the victims of sexual harassment at work (e.g., Gruber, 1990; see Gutek & Done, 2000, and O'Donohue et al., 1998, for reviews). Although it is not as common, men too can be the victims of sexual harassment at work (Stockdale et al., 1999; Waldo et al., 1998).

What is sexual harassment? In 1980, the Equal Employment Opportunity Commission (EEOC) established a legal definition of **sexual harassment** in the workplace:

> Unwelcome sexual advances, requests for sexual favors, and other verbal or physical conduct of a sexual nature

sexual harassment
Unwelcome sexual advances that persist after the recipient has indicated that they are unwanted. See text for an expanded definition.

Figure 17–5 Many women regard this type of behavior by a male supervisor to be inappropriate and a form of sexual harassment. Do you suppose that this man would behave the same way with a male employee?

constitute unlawful sexual harassment when (a) submission to such conduct is made either explicitly or implicitly a term or condition of an individual's employment, (b) submission to or rejection of such conduct by an individual is used as the basis for employment decisions affecting such individual, or (c) such conduct has the purpose or effect of unreasonably interfering with an individual's work performance or creating an intimidating, hostile, or offensive working environment.

Behavior is considered harassment when it *persists* after the recipient has indicated that it is unwanted. In 1986, the U.S. Supreme Court expanded the definition by ruling that harassment based on sex, which creates a hostile or offensive work environment, is also illegal (*Meritor Savings Bank v. Vinson,* 1986). In other words, *a victim does not have to prove that sexual favors were demanded in exchange for job benefits.* A hostile or offensive work environment can include such things as nude calendars, lewd jokes, touching, and obsessive staring. In 1993, the Court ruled that employees did not have to show that they were psychologically harmed to prove a claim of hostile work environment (*Harris v. Forklift,* 1993). How do the courts decide whether or not there is a hostile work environment? In a 1991 decision (*Ellison v. Brady*), the Court established the *"reasonable woman" standard:* When examining the particular workplace, would a reasonable woman conclude that there was sexual harassment that resulted in a hostile work environment (see Gutek et al., 1999). In 1998, the Court ruled that sexual harassment included same-sex harassment (e.g., a male employer and male employee) (*Oncale v. Sundowner Offshore Services, Inc.*). Men who are victims of same-sex sexual harassment are often targeted because they do not fit the harassers' gender-role masculine stereotype (Stockdale et al., 1999; Waldo et al., 1998).

These are legal definitions. Fitzgerald, Swan, and Magley (1997) have persuaded many that we should distinguish between legal definitions and psychological definitions. They provide the following psychological definition:

Unwanted sex-related behavior at work that is appraised by the recipient as offensive, exceeding her resources, or threatening her well-being.

The main difference from the legal definition is that it places the emphasis on the viewpoint of the victim.

The EEOC and the courts have also ruled that a company can be held liable for sexual harassment by its employees if it doesn't take "immediate and appropriate corrective action." Today, many large businesses have explicit policies against sexual harassment, as well as educational programs for their employees. Charges of sexual harassment are usually prosecuted as civil suits (rather than criminal cases) under Title VII of the Civil Rights Act of 1964, which bans discrimination in employment based on sex. The Civil Rights Act of 1991 expanded the limit of punitive and compensatory damages.

The legal definition of sexual harassment is still evolving. Many people think that the 40 to 60 percent prevalence rates reported in many studies seem high. Obviously, harassment can take many forms, some more serious than others. Gruber (1990) subdivided harassment of women into five types: pressure for dates/relationships (experienced by about 13 percent of women), sexual comments (28 percent), sexual posturing (24 percent), sexual touching (17 percent), and sexual assault (1 percent). O'Hare and O'Donohue (1999) found that 12 percent of women in the work force had been pressured to cooperate sexually in order to be treated well. One of the problems is that some behaviors are so common (e.g., sexual comments) that targeted individuals often do not label the behaviors as sexual harassment (see Gutek & Done, 2000).

Here are two examples of sexual harassment in the workplace provided to me by students:

"My boss started off saying nasty jokes. Then he began to relate the jokes to his own personal experiences. Next he started making comments about how big my breasts were or how my butt looked in jeans. At this time I got real scared."

"I started working as a legal assistant at the second largest law firm in New Orleans. I was assigned to two young associates. One of the associates was 28, engaged to be married, and took interest in helping me learn how the trial process is handled. I began to notice little things that 'Rich' did that were making me feel uncomfortable. First, compliments or personal remarks about my looks. Then he would make insinuations in front of others about how late we worked the night before, and how well we worked together. All of these were said in a manner that made me extremely uncomfortable.

"The last straw was the touching, at first on the back as I was typing or reading, but later on the thighs and calves. I went to my superior and we met with the head of personnel and the director of our law department. I quit that day without pressing charges or causing a big fuss. Why? Because the department I worked in was the Labor Department. 'Rich' defended sexual harassment cases and won. He actually defended employees against sexual harassment—he knew better."

It is obvious from this last case history that "some men just don't get it." Many more men than women feel that the problem of sexual harassment has been greatly exaggerated, and many men believe that women should not be so quickly offended when men show sexual interest in them (Dietz-Uhler & Murrell, 1992). Although men recognize certain overt behaviors as harassment (e.g., offering favors in return for sex), many men don't view less overt behaviors (e.g., sexual jokes and remarks) as harassment. Why? While women focus on the power relationship between them and the harasser, men attend to the sexual aspects of the situation, which they tend to define very broadly (Perry et al., 1998). Many men even blame the women for being sexually harassed (Jensen & Gutek, 1982). Thus, men generally take the issue of sexual harassment less seriously than women. The U.S. Supreme Court's application of the "reasonable woman" standard in hostile environment cases is a clear indication that the courts realize that many men and women see the same behaviors differently.

Why is this a serious issue to women? Sexual harassment usually *occurs in a relationship where there is unequal power,* such as employer-employee or teacher-student relationships (MacKinnon, 1979). This makes the victims of harassment very vulnerable, especially if they are economically dependent on their jobs. Not surprisingly, victims of harassment display a wide variety of responses, from passivity or leaving the field, to confrontation and reporting the behavior (O'Donohue et al., 1998). Victims may feel that there is no recourse. Who do you complain to if it is the boss who is doing the harassing? If a woman refuses sexual advances or objects to an offensive work environment, she might be the target of retaliation (e.g., she may be passed over for raises and promotions, given poor ratings, or even fired). If she quits, she may be ineligible for unemployment compensation. Whether she is fired or she quits, she will be unable to ask for references from this employer because he will no doubt invent reasons for her termination having to do with poor performance. The end result is that victims of sexual harassment often are left with feelings similar to those of other victims of sexual abuse—

feelings of helplessness, humiliation, shame, anger, and lower self-esteem (Gutek & Done, 2000; O'Donohue et al., 1998).

How do others view victims of sexual harassment? Gender-role stereotypes affect attitudes. Women who label behaviors of men as sexual harassment are often viewed more negatively by others (greater blame, less trustworthy), women as well as men (Marin & Guadagno, 1999). When the EEOC filed a sexual harassment suit against Mitsubishi Motor Manufacturer of America in Normal, Illinois, in 1996, almost all people living in the local area said that they were aware of the charges (e.g., male employees grabbing breasts and genitals, drawings of genitals, explicit photographs, managers calling women "sluts" and "bitches"). However, only one-third said that they would find the company guilty if they were a member of the jury (Simon et al., 1999). A recent study found that people have greater empathy for female victims if they are asked to look at the situation from the woman's point of view (Wiener & Hurt, 2000). Thus, again, the "reasonable woman" standard appears to have great merit.

SOME CAUSES OF SEXUAL HARASSMENT

Carlota Bustelo, of the United Nations Committee on the Elimination of Discrimination Against Women, said that sexual harassment "defines an ancient phenomenon that is frequent in the workplace but that remained undiscussed until the 1970s. Its disclosure, which began in the U.S., was due to changes taking place in the power relationships between men and women in society at large and, more particularly, on the job" (in *World Press Review,* February 1992). Research has shown that the more a man believes in traditional stereotypical roles for men and women, the more accepting he is of sexual harassment (Dietz-Uhler & Murrell, 1992). Sexual harassment is most common and most severe, for example, in blue-collar occupations in which women are underrepresented (Fitzgerald, 1993). Unlike women, most men cannot distinguish sexual attraction from power as motives for harassment (Popovich et al., 1996).

Academic studies of sexual harassment have considered several possible causes, including biological (e.g., men's high sex drive), organizational climate and authority relations, sociocultural factors, and situational and individual factors (see O'Donohue et al., 1998, for a review). One study of men's behaviors and attitudes concluded that sexual harassment and rape were both forms of sexual coercion (Pryor, 1987). Men who had a tendency to harass believed in rape myths and adversarial relations between the sexes.

Gender roles have changed considerably as more and more women have entered the work force over the last few decades; and in Chapter 10 you learned that our society has slowly evolved from stereotypical roles to a more androgynous state. Lately, however, there has been a disturbing increase in sexual harassment by teenaged boys. For example, many teenage boys try to "demonstrate their manhood" and gain popularity by yelling explicit propositions to girls or fondling girls as they walk by (Henneberger & Marriott, 1993). A survey of teenagers commissioned by the American Association of University Women and conducted by Louis Harris & Associates found that more than two-thirds of the girls (and a fair proportion of the boys) had been fondled, grabbed, or pinched in an explicitly sexual manner (AAUW, 1993). A more recent study of high school students found similar results (Fineran & Bennett, 1999). Girls are often the target of harassment by boys as early as elementary school (Murnen & Smolak, 2000). Although nearly as many teenaged boys as girls reported having experienced peer sexual harassment, girls were much more likely to have been the targets of overtly sexual forms of harassment. This behavior among young men portends a dim outlook for eliminating sexual harassment in the workplace in the future. "Raising awareness among men," according to one expert, "may be more important than getting women to complain" (Michelle Paludi, quoted in *New York Times,* October 22, 1991, p. C1).

Even in social situations, the signals between men and women are often ambiguous and the possibility of misunderstanding is great. A man may misinterpret how a woman is dressed or behaving as interest in him. Some men, however, construe every smile, gesture, or pleasantry as sexual interest. In our culture, men are also expected to be sexually aggressive, so if a man interprets a behavior as interest (correctly or incorrectly) he is likely to pursue it. Many men interpret initial resistance on the part of a woman as part of the "game," influenced perhaps by the fact that some women first say "no" even when they want to be pursued (Muehlenhard & Hollabaugh, 1988). When, then, does sexual interest become sexual harassment? When a woman has made it clear that sexual advances or comments are unwanted, then any persistence on the part of the man is clearly harassment. This should be true anywhere, but it is particularly true in the workplace.

SEXUAL HARASSMENT OF COLLEGE STUDENTS

Sexual harassment can occur in any setting in which there are power differences between people. College campuses are certainly an example of this. Several studies have found that many college women (17 to 33 percent, depending on the study) have been sexually harassed by an instructor (e.g., Fitzgerald et al., 1988; Popovich & Licata, 1986; Reilly et al., 1986). Female graduate students may be the most vulnerable to ha-

rassment by male faculty (Kelley & Parsons, 2000). On college campuses, men also are often the target of sexual harassment (e.g., Roscoe et al., 1987; Shepela & Levesque, 1998).

Harassment can be direct (offering "an A for a lay" or threatening to lower a grade unless the student agrees to sex) or less obvious (e.g., crude comments, hugs, insistence on seeing the student alone). As can happen in the workplace, an instructor can create an offensive environment for a student even if there are no direct propositions or threats:

"It was during my second semester in college when I became the target of sexual harassment from my instructor. The ordeal started when he began to stare at me in class for long periods of time. I grew uncomfortable and more importantly, self-conscious. I couldn't figure out why he was staring at me. He then began to approach me and make small talk. In between 'Hello' and 'How are you?' he would squeeze in a compliment. Eventually his compliments became suggestive, and before long, he was making blatant sexual innuendoes to me in front of the class. He would say 'I can't concentrate on my lectures with you sitting in the front row looking like that,' or, 'You sure do make it hard (emphasis on hard) on a guy.'

"Once, when I wore a skirt to class, he asked, 'Did you wear this for me?' as he fixed his eyes on my legs. On another occasion as I was picking up my school bag he tapped me on the shoulder and said, 'Don't bend over in those jeans like that.' Once he said he'd like to take me to lunch and have me for dessert.

"I finally had enough and I began to sit in the back of the lecture hall. He would come to me after class and tell me he 'missed me in the front row.' That was when I quit going altogether. I had four friends in class who knew what was going on and they insisted after about two weeks of absences that I come back to class. They begged me to press charges against him.

"The day I returned, my professor asked me where I'd been and told me that 'if I knew what he was thinking I could charge him with sexual harassment.' The next week I wore a tie to class and he touched my tie and commented, 'I'd like to tie you up.' A girl I didn't know approached me after class and offered herself as a witness if I wanted to file a formal complaint. I wanted to do just that. However, I was and still am very concerned about my grades; I was sure that if I charged him with this behavior he would have penalized me through my grade.

"This happened 2 years ago, and I saw this man again last week. (We haven't seen each other since I had his class.) The first thing he said to me—in front of my other professor and many students—was 'Hi honey, my place or yours?' This was the first impression my new professor had of me. This time I'm angry. I don't deserve to be talked to this way, nor does anyone else. My friends were right—he should be stopped!!"   (from the author's files)

It is *never* appropriate for an instructor to make sexual, or even romantic, overtures to a student presently enrolled in his class or under his supervision. As in the workplace, students who are the victims of sexual harassment may feel that there is no recourse, and the experience often results in negative emotional effects. Some victims feel so compromised that they change majors or drop out of school (Dziech & Weiner, 1984). Today, most colleges and universities have firm guidelines about harassment and grievance procedures that can be consulted by victims, and the U.S. Supreme Court ruled that under Title IX of the Education Amendment of 1972, schools can be held liable for not taking action (*Franklin v. Gwinnett County Public Schools*, 1992). The Court has also ruled that schools can be held liable if they ignore student-on-student sexual harassment (*Davis v. Monroe County Board of Education*, 1999). Do you know if your campus has established a policy about sexual harassment?

HOW TO DEAL WITH SEXUAL HARASSMENT

The number of sexual harassment cases reported to the EEOC doubled during the 1980s and more than doubled again in the 1990s. Currently about 15,000 to 16,000 cases are reported to the EEOC every year (Gutek & Done, 2000). Still, only 5 percent of victims ever decide to take formal action.

Sexual harassment can often be prevented if the recipient is assertive at the first sign of inappropriate behavior. Unfortunately, some women are uneasy about being assertive for fear that they will appear "unfriendly" or "impolite." Keep in mind that you are not the one who has behaved improperly. Giving the harasser a firm "no" (or saying that you will not tolerate being talked to like that) is expressing your right to personal dignity. If you are not assertive, some men may misinterpret that as a sign of interest.

If the harasser continues his behavior after you have delivered a clear message that it is not appreciated, then you will have to take other steps to deal with it. Most women choose to avoid it passively (e.g., by ignoring it, dropping the class, or quitting the job) or to defuse it by stalling tactics or making a joke out of it (Cochran et al., 1997).

When the harassment is blatant, persistent, and highly offensive, as in the example of the university professor in the case history, stronger measures are necessary. Talk to the harasser, or write a letter to him, relaying the facts and again expressing clearly and firmly that the behavior must stop. Document all the episodes of harassment (dates, places) and list all witnesses. The very next time the behavior occurs, follow the grievance procedure of your company or school and report it. Those companies and schools that have implemented grievance procedures will protect you against retaliation. If you should be treated unjustly, report the problem to the EEOC or file a civil suit (remember, companies and schools can now be held liable for not taking action).

For more information on how to deal with sexual harassment, contact one of the organizations listed in the "Resources" section following the text.

PERSONAL REFLECTIONS
Have you ever been the victim of sexual harassment by a supervisor, employer, or instructor? Did you report it? If not, why not? Are you familiar with your campus's procedures for dealing with sexual harassment? If you are not familiar with the procedures, where can you go to find out?

SEXUAL ABUSE OF CHILDREN

In 1992, a former priest was convicted of sexually molesting 32 children aged 10 to 14, some allegedly in church. In the same year, a former national "teacher of the year" was sentenced to a year in jail for molesting young boys at his cabin home. In 1997, a Nobel Prize–winning scientist was sentenced to jail for sexually molesting boys. In separate cases in the state of Washington, two men with long histories of sexual abuse were convicted of raping many young children and killing several of them, leading that state to pass a "sexual predator" law requiring that career molesters be confined for life.

Our culture has a long history of denial about sexual abuse of children (Olafson et al., 1993), but an abundance of research in the past few decades has made it clear that this is a serious, widespread problem. How common is sexual abuse of children? In a comprehensive review of many studies, Peters, Wyatt, and Finkelhor (1986) found that estimates of how many children had been sexually abused ranged from 6 to 62 percent for girls and from 3 to 31 percent for boys. Kinsey et al. (1953) found that 24 percent of the women in their survey were victims of sexual abuse. In the recent survey by Laumann and colleagues (1994), 17 percent of the women and 12 percent of the men reported having been victims of sexual touching (or worse) by an older person when they were younger than 13. For one-third of the female victims, the abuse occurred (or began) when they were less than 7 years old.

As these data show, nearly twice as many girls as boys are targeted as victims. Kinsey's group found that in 80 percent of the cases they studied, only one incident of molestation had occurred, but a 1985 *Los Angeles Times* poll found that for about 15 percent of all victims, the abuse continues for more than a year. Other studies have found that at least 10 to 15 percent of victims are abused by more than one adult (Conte et al., 1986; Tufts New England Medical Center, 1984).

Laumann et al. (1994) found that sexual contact with children usually involved fondling the genitals but that 10 percent of the girls and 30 percent of the boys who had been molested had been forced to perform oral sex. Fourteen percent of the girls had been forced into vaginal intercourse and 18 percent of the cases involving boys included anal intercourse.

WHAT IS CHILD SEXUAL ABUSE?

A recent review of many studies concluded that victims of child sexual abuse were, on average, only "slightly less well adjusted" than individuals who had not been abused, and even this was attributed to factors (e.g., family dysfunction) other than abuse (Rind et al., 1998). The authors found such little effect that they suggested that we quit calling the behavior child sexual abuse, and instead simply refer to it as "child-adult sex." Not surprisingly, the article was met with a storm of protest (see *Society,* May/June, 2000, for several responses). Columnists and others worried that it was an attempt to "normalize" pedophilia. Even some state legislatures voted to condemn the article (*New Orleans Times-Picayune,* 1999). To fuel the fire further, a few previous studies had even reported that some victims recall their experiences as having been positive or pleasurable (e.g., Bauserman & Rind, 1997; Haugaard & Emery, 1989; Okami, 1991).

One outcome of this controversy has been a reexamination of the term *child sexual abuse.* Haugaard (2000) points out that each word in this term has been defined and used differently by different groups. For example, what is a child? In some states the age of consent is 14, whereas in others it is 18. Similarly, some researchers define children as those younger than 18; others say 17, or 16. Within psychology and psychiatry, the term *children* refers to prepubescent children (before age 13), and most professionals also stipulate that the abuse must be by someone at least 5 years older (DSM-IV, 1994). The Kinsey (1953) and Laumann et al. (1994) surveys used this definition.

What is sexual (behavior)? This can include everything from an unwanted sexual advance, to inappropriate touching, to an incident of indecent exposure, to forced oral, vaginal, and anal intercourse. And abuse? There is no accepted definition here. Must there be physical or emotional harm, or merely violation of social norms?

Keep in mind that when we discuss adult-child sexual behavior, we must also consider the culture. As such, child sexual abuse can be considered a social concept. You have read in Chapter 11 (see Box 11-A) that sexual relations between adults and children (generally pederasty) is the norm in some cultures and has been so at times in Western culture as well. There is no question, however, that it is not normal or acceptable in Western culture today where children are dependent

on adults until late adolescence. The prevailing view was expressed well by sociology professor Julia Ericksen (2000):

> **We learn to be sexual in culture, and our sexuality is not unrelated to other aspects of our culture. In the West, children remain dependent on their parents and on adult society in general for a very long time. In such a society, children need protection from adult abuse. Child-adult sex cannot therefore be an activity to which both parties equally and freely consent. The most fruitful lines of inquiry about child-adult sexual activity in this culture must start with a discussion of the differences in power between adults and children.**

The end result is that the term *child sexual abuse* has gradually widened to become so broad that as a concept it presently has little discriminative power. Depending on how abusive behavior is defined, prevalence rates will be high or low. The effect of abuse will also depend on the type, or severity, of the abuse. In the Rind et al. (1998) article, many of the studies they reviewed were of inappropriate touching of adolescents or unwanted sexual advances. One would expect that the effects would be less negative than for forced intercourse. To deal with these problems, the National Institute for Child Health and Human Development is currently establishing a classification system for different types of child abuse. In this chapter, I have attempted to indicate when studies are referring to "severe" forms of abuse.

WHO MOLESTS CHILDREN?

The stereotype of a child molester is often that of a dirty old man who hangs around playgrounds offering candy to young boys and girls and who snatches the children away when their parents are not present. However, this is usually not the case. Studies have found that in the majority of molestation cases, the molester is an adult known to the victim, and often a relative (Laumann et al., 1994; see Table 17–1). In fact, the YWCA Rape Crisis Program estimates that about 80 percent of all molesters are known by their victims (Kikuchi, 1988).

"When I was 12 years old I was sexually molested by my sister's boyfriend. My mother and sister earlier that day had a doctor's appointment and he had offered to keep an eye on me while they were gone. . . . He dared me to do sexual things. If I refused he would then get forceful toward me and out of being scared I went along with it. He forced me to have oral sex on him. Finally, someone knocked at the door and they saved me from having to go through any more."

"When I was little (ages 5–7), I was molested. My parents worked but let me stay with our elderly neighbors. The old man did this to me. He taught me how to kiss and touch his penis. He did this when his

TABLE 17–1

RELATIONSHIP OF CHILD MOLESTERS TO THEIR VICTIMS, AS RECALLED BY ADULTS WHO HAD BEEN SEXUALLY ABUSED AS CHILDREN (AGED 12 OR YOUNGER)

Abuser	Abused[a]	
	Women (17%)	Men (12%)
Stranger	7%	4%
Acquaintance		
Family friend	29%	40%
Older brother	9	4
Stepfather or mother's boyfriend	9	2
Father	7	1
Other relative	29	13
Teacher	3	4
Other	20	21

[a]Total percentages exceed 100% because some victims were abused by more than one person.
Source: Laumann et al. (1994). Reprinted with the permission of The University of Chicago Press; adapted from Table 9.14, p. 343 from *The Social Organization of Sexuality.*

wife would either go to the store or leave out of the room. I hated it. He didn't like it when I'd fight him away from me. What I can't understand is why: why me. . . . " (All examples are from the author's files.)

Researchers have attempted to classify molesters in many different ways. For example, Groth, Hobson, and Gary (1982) proposed that molesters could be distinguished as *fixated* (having arrested psychosexual development) or *regressed* (under stress, after normal development). Howells (1981), Lanyon (1986), and others prefer a distinction between **preference molesters** (who have a primary sexual orientation toward children and are relatively uninterested in adult partners) and **situational molesters** (whose primary interest is toward adults and who consider their urges toward children, often done impulsively during stress, as abnormal). This last classification has much in common with the one in the American Psychiatric Association's DSM-IV (1994), which classifies molesters as pedophiles or nonpedophiles. You were introduced to the topic of pedophilia (from the Greek, meaning "love of children") in Chapter 16. A **pedophile** is a man for whom children provide the "repeatedly preferred or exclusive method of achieving sexual excitement." Thus, if a man were to commit an act of child molestation but was not repeatedly attracted to children, he would not be considered a pedophile (here the term *situational molester* is appropriate).

An older classification of incestuous molesters versus nonincestuous molesters, which assumed that the former limited their offenses to family members and were not a threat to the general community, is no longer regarded as a useful distinction. Both groups

have similar sexual preference patterns (Abel et al., 1981; Barsetti et al., 1998), and nearly half of all incestuous fathers and stepfathers have sexually abused other children during the same period when they were abusing their own children (Abel et al., 1988b).

"I am a victim of child sexual abuse. I was 6 years old and my godmother's fiance was the predator. . . . He made me do everything from vaginal penetration to oral-genital sex. . . . Later it was found that he did this to four of his six children, myself, two of my cousins and six other children." (from the author's files)

Pedophiles have been further classified according to their psychological characteristics (Cohen et al., 1969). The *personally immature pedophile* is the most common. He is attracted to children because he has never developed the social skills necessary to initiate and maintain a sexual relationship with an adult. A relationship with a child allows this individual to be in control, which he cannot achieve with an adult. Notice that the primary motivation here, control, is similar to the motivation in many rape cases. The *regressive pedophile,* on the other hand, is likely to engage in sexual relations in an impulsive manner, often with a child who is a stranger. These people describe their acts as the result of an uncontrollable urge. Unlike the personally immature pedophile, the regressive pedophile has a history of normal adult sexual relations. Regressive pedophiles begin turning to children as a result of developing feelings of sexual inadequacy, often due to stress. The problem is often complicated by alcohol abuse (Gebhard et al., 1965), which they often use as an excuse for their behavior. A third type, and fortunately the least common, is the *aggressive pedophile.* These people are not satisfied with just having sex with their young victims but are aroused by inflicting physical injury. Here, too, notice that the primary motivation, sadistic acts, is similar to the motivation in one of the classifications of rape discussed earlier. In fact, these men can be called child rapists (Groth et al., 1982), and they often show a variety of other antisocial behaviors. Seven to 15 percent of all child molestation cases include physical harm to the victims (Conte, 1991).

preference molesters (pedophiles) Child molesters who have a primary sexual orientation to children and who are relatively uninterested in adult partners.

situational molesters Child molesters who have a primary sexual orientation to adults. They have sex with children impulsively and regard their behavior as abnormal.

Pedophiles typically have molested many children before they are caught, if they are caught at all. For example, in one study of male pedophiles who were undergoing treatment, nonincestuous offenders who targeted girls had averaged 20 victims each, and those targeting boys had averaged nearly 200 victims each (Abel et al., 1987). Child molestation committed by men who are not pedophiles is usually within a father-daughter (or stepfather-stepdaughter) relationship and generally involves only one child (Freund et al., 1991).

Only a small minority of male sex offenders target both boys and girls (Groth & Birnbaum, 1978). Heterosexual men account for 95 percent of the cases of sexual abuse of girls, and "homosexual" men account for most cases involving boys (Finkelhor & Russell, 1984). (The word *homosexual* was placed in quotes because most molesters of boys do not have homosexual attractions to adults; see Freund & Langevin, 1976.) The ratio of female to male victims is 2 to 1, but because male offenders who target boys generally have many more victims, the ratio of heterosexual pedophiles to homosexual pedophiles has been estimated to be approximately 11 to 1 (Freund & Watson, 1992).

What is the child molester like personally? Most are respectable and otherwise law-abiding citizens (Lanyon, 1986). Many are shy, passive, and unassertive (Langevin, 1983), although incestuous fathers are generally very domineering and controlling within their own families (Meiselman, 1978). However, for the most part there are no reliable personality characteristics correlated with pedophilia (Lanyon, 1986; Okami & Goldberg, 1992). In short, there is no single personality profile; child molesters are a very heterogeneous group.

We do know that, unlike normal people, child molesters have the capacity to be sexually aroused by young children (Finkelhor & Araji, 1986; Marshall et al., 1986). This is generally acquired when molesters rehearse and fantasize what they will do to children while they masturbate, and this type of rehearsal often goes on for years. A majority of pedophiles were themselves the victims of sexual abuse as children (Freund & Kuban, 1994; Groth, 1979), and thus may never have learned that it is wrong to have sex with children. Recent work has found that child molesters have distorted cognitions (i.e., they truly believe that the act has positive effects on

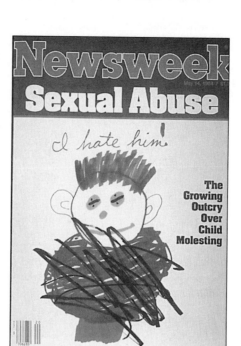

Figure 17–6

the children) (Blumenthal et al., 1999; Bumby, 1996). A study of online (Internet) pedophiles found that all of them justified their behavior, denying that it caused their child victims any harm (Durkin & Bryant, 1999). However, some experts believe that the molesters' sexual behaviors are primarily motivated by nonsexual needs, such as for affection or control (Groth et al., 1982; Lanyon, 1986). The pedophile, unlike most other paraphiliacs, usually does not display other paraphilias (Fedora et al., 1992).

One thing that is well established is that the deviant behavior often begins early in life. One study found that the median age for the first offense was 16 (Groth et al., 1982). Adolescents may be responsible for as many as 30 to 50 percent of child sexual abuse cases (Davis & Leitenberg, 1987; see Murphy et al., 1992). One study found that during childhood pedophiles had a much greater than normal curiosity in seeing naked children. They did not have a similar curiosity about adults (Freund & Kuban, 1993). Very young children (6 to 12 years old) who sexually abuse other children have generally been sexually abused themselves and/or have come from highly chaotic families (De Angelis, 1996).

Tragically, the true pedophile, in order to satisfy his sexual urges, often finds positions where he has access to children (teacher and "other" category in Table 17–1). Pedophiles have been found in positions as teachers, scout leaders, camp counselors, and even ministers or priests.

"I attended a very respectable summer camp during my junior high summers. Every session, about midway through the camp, the camp director took us to _____ Creek to go on the sliding rock. He would tell the kids if they slid down the rock 'skinny sliding' (nude) they would get to be in line first for the dinner buffet. The counselors were sharply divided on this. Some thought it was just funny and others thought it was odd. Two years ago, the director was caught for child molestation. He was convicted and served time in jail."

"I entered a monastery for boys. . . . As a novice, I was told to go to confession daily and the Father Superior would counsel me in both Christian education and my personal life. Confessions were very informal. The Father Superior heard them from 7:30 p.m. until midnight in his room. . . . One night he said, 'And do you know how they took oaths in the Old Testament? One would put his hand on the other man's genitals. But there was no sexual connotation intended. The Jews viewed sex differently than we do.' I was a little puzzled and didn't ask any questions.

"About a week later I went to see one of the brothers for confession, but he told me that the Father Superior wanted to see me. . . . He said, 'Do you want to take an oath like in the Old Testament?' I was stunned and didn't really know what he meant. Finally he took my hand and placed it under his robe on his penis. I was shocked and pulled my hand away immediately, but he said, 'Don't be afraid, there is no sexual intent here. You are keeping a very ancient form of taking an oath.' As he was saying this he took my hand again and placed it on his penis. I wanted to pull back, but I was afraid he would go into another temper tantrum. . . . He didn't do anything else that night, but he talked to me about how much we had to be obedient children. He often stressed obedience—total obedience. (This was how he set us up. We must be totally obedient.)

"Then it happened. One night we were talking and he said, 'Do you want to kiss my penis?'—I was so naive. I didn't know what he was talking about. He said, 'Do you want me to kiss your penis? That's how much I love you.' I said no, but then he said, 'Don't you think I love you? There is no sexual intent. It is a pure act of platonic love.' (He defined platonic love as love without passion—including sexual contact. He emphasized this: without passion. Passion is wrong. All passions. This passionless sex, he explained, could only be between him and his children.) Then he drew me closer to him, he opened my robe, unzipped my pants, put his hands into my underwear, brought my penis into the open and kissed it.

"It later turned into fellatio. . . . He taught me what he wanted done to him. He had orgasms every time that 'I went for confession.' I was instructed never to have orgasm. Never! 'That would not be good for me spiritually.'

"I have some very deep scars and am now receiving therapy."* (All examples are from the author's files.)

*Author's note: This young man later found out that many other boys had been victimized by the same man.

In today's technological world, pedophiles often use online chat rooms to find and seduce victims (Durkin, 1997; Thomas, 2000). The FBI has begun an Internet sting operation to trap these individuals and as of 2000 had initiated 1,500 investigations and made 532 arrests.

PERSONAL REFLECTIONS
Are you ever sexually aroused by children? If so, have you ever sought counseling? If you have not sought counseling, why not? Would it be better to seek counseling before you acted on an urge, or afterwards?

FEMALE PERPETRATORS OF CHILD SEXUAL ABUSE

Little is known about women who sexually abuse children. Most of what we know comes from clinical reports. However, two recent reviews have shed some light on this once unmentionable topic (Grayston & DeLuca, 1999; Lewis & Stanley, 2000).

Women commit less than 5 percent of sex crimes against children. Who are these women? There is considerable heterogeneity, but the "typical" female offender is young (20s and 30s), been a victim of prolonged sexual and/or physical abuse in her own childhood, has many problems in her present life, and has average to low intellectual ability. Unlike male molesters, who usually act alone, most female molesters have a male accomplice. Many are "passive" (supporting their male partner), but some are "active."

Who are the victims? They are almost always known to their female molesters, often their own children. Interestingly, in a majority of cases the victim is also female. This is consistent with feminist explanations of sexual abuse, which say that individuals in our culture with the least amount of power (women, and girls even more so) are the most likely to be abused, regardless of who the perpetrator may be.

To this point, the victims discussed were young children. Recently, much attention has been given to adult women who have sexual relations with adolescent boys. This was brought to the nation's attention with the case of Mary Kay LeTourneau, a married (with children) Seattle teacher who gave birth to two children by one of her teenaged students. California has seen dozens of cases like this in recent years (Masciola & Rams, 1999). Therapists say that the women are emotionally very needy, manipulative individuals who seek power and thrills. In this respect, they are much like male perpetrators. The boy victims often suffer long-term emotional devastation, just like girls who are molested by men.

EFFECTS OF ABUSE ON THE CHILDREN

Because of the strong social stigma against sexual relations between adults and children in our culture, it has traditionally been assumed that the effects on the child were always very negative and long-lasting. However, recall the review which concluded that child sexual abuse generally was not associated with long-term psychological harm (Rind et al., 1998). The children in those studies must have had a different experience than the many others who report anxiety, fear, depression, panic disorder, high prevalence of suicidal behavior, sexual dysfunctions, and other (often long-term) negative reactions (Beitchman et al., 1991, 1992; McCauley et al., 1997; Mina & Gallop, 1998).

What are we to conclude? Considerable research has now shown that, in fact, there is no single "post-sexual abuse syndrome" with a specific course or outcome (e.g., Beitchman et al., 1991, 1992). Instead, the effects of adult-child sexual relations represent a continuum of experiences. The results of many studies combined indicate that sexually abused children can be described as falling into one of four groups (Saywitz et al., 2000):

1. Children with no detectable problems (as many as one-third may be included in this group)
2. Children with a few symptoms (e.g., anxiety, low self-esteem) but not of a clinical nature
3. Children with major psychiatric symptoms (e.g., depression)
4. Children with posttraumatic stress disorder and other major psychiatric disorders (at least half of abused children are included in these last two groups)

Among children with no initial symptoms, about 30 percent develop problems later (Kendall-Tackett et al., 1993).

For many victims, not all of their problems can be attributed to the sexual abuse (Friedrich, 1998; Kendall-Tackett et al., 1993; Saywitz et al., 2000). Many experience other severely stressful life events that existed even before the sexual abuse began (e.g., dysfunctional family, generally maltreated in all other ways).

Several factors contribute to the particular response of a child. Some children are more resilient than others, and in some cases the abuse was minor. The greatest harm in terms of long-lasting negative effects is seen in cases where the abuse is frequent or long-lasting; where the abuse involves penetration, force, threats, or violence; where the abuser is the father or stepfather; and where there is little support from the mother (Bauserman & Rind, 1997; Beitchman et al., 1992; Kendall-Tackett et al., 1993; Rind & Tromovitch, 1997). Revictimization by others is not uncommon and substantially adds to psychological and emotional distress (Kellogg & Hoffman, 1997). The most frequent symptoms include fears, poor self-esteem, inappropriate sexual behavior, and depression. Some victims of severe sexual abuse later show promiscuity and increased sexual risk taking (Friedrich, 1993; Meston et al., 1999; Stock et al., 1997); they confuse sex with love or become sexually preoccupied or aggressive.

Figure 17–7 This self-portrait by a victim of sexual abuse shows the emotional suffering that is often experienced long after the crime.

Only about a third of all child victims inform their parents or another adult of the abuse (Finkelhor, 1979), and reactions that are perceived by the child as less than supportive can greatly add to the negativity of the experience. Consider, for example, the following three cases:

"When I was younger, I was sexually abused by one of my father's good friends. I told my mother . . . but they acted like they did not believe me. I felt very embarrassed." (woman)

"At the age of 9, I was molested by a man right outside of my neighborhood. I told my mother what had happened. I was very hurt and scared, but instead of talking to me, my mother refused to talk about it and acted as if it was my fault. Years later I discovered the man had done the same thing to other children. By then it was too late, I was already emotionally scarred." (woman)

"I was about 8 years old when I was sexually abused by a friend of my father. I refused, but he beat me up and made me have sexual intercourse with him. Later the same night I told my father, but my father, instead of going to the police as I thought, beat me very harshly with a wood stick." (man) (All examples are from the author's files.)

Like victims of rape, victims of child molestation have a tendency to blame themselves, which can greatly affect self-esteem (Hazzard et al., 1995).

"I was sexually abused for 9 years as a child by my older sister's husband. For years I believed it had happened because there was something wrong with me." (from the author's files)

A review of many studies concluded that about two-thirds of all victims of child sexual abuse show substantial recovery during the first 12 to 18 months (Kendall-Tackett et al., 1993). Even for these individuals, however, some symptoms, such as sexual preoccupation and aggressiveness, may worsen (Friedrich & Reams, 1987). From 10 to 24 percent of all abused female children not only fail to improve over time but actually get worse (see Kendall-Tackett et al., 1993). As adults, these women display problems (e.g., emotional distress, drug and alcohol abuse, suicide attempts) that are just as great as in women presently being abused (McCauley et al., 1997). Sexual dysfunctions are common among women who experienced childhood abuse involving penetration (Sarwer & Durlak, 1996).

Many adults who were sexually abused as children also have serious eating disorders (anorexia nervosa, bulimia) (Laws & Golding, 1996; Wonderlich et al., 1996).

RECOVERED (FALSE?) MEMORY SYNDROME

"For the first time, when I was 17 a boyfriend reached out to touch me in a sexual manner. In that split second, I flashed back to when I was 9 and my uncle (by marriage) was molesting me. Until that moment I had no conscious memory of that event. I began to scream and cry and the poor guy didn't know what to do other than bring me home.

"After 28 years, I still do not remember everything that happened that day. I am convinced that this was not the only occasion that he molested me. For many years I had a deep fear of the Christmas holidays, in particular the family Christmas Eve party.

"I recently found out that this man repeatedly molested all seven of my female cousins. When I finally asked my mother how this could have been going on . . . supposedly she and her three sisters did try to protect us by watching us and trying to keep him from being alone with us. She told me that they didn't tell because they didn't want to hurt their sister (his wife)."   (from the author's files)

One of the most bitter debates in the field of sexual abuse today is whether or not people can forget sexually traumatic past experiences and later remember them. On the one hand, there are therapists who believe that sexual abuse can be so traumatic that individuals, in order to cope, forget or suppress memories of the event, often for many years. Later, either spontaneously or while undergoing therapy, the individual remembers the past events. Many studies have documented that people can experience amnesia for nonsexual traumatic events (e.g., disasters, combat) (Arrigo & Pezdek, 1997). Many others have reported cases of sexual abuse victims who said that they also had experienced some degree of amnesia of the events for a period of time (e.g., Feldman-Summers & Pope, 1994; Gold et al., 1994; Herman, 1992). These studies find that, on average, about 50 percent of all victims report some amnesia (see Kristiansen et al., 1996).

On the other hand, others claim that most "recovered" memories are, in fact, false memories created by therapists working with vulnerable people (e.g., Loftus, 1997a, 1997b; Ofshe & Watters, 1994). These claims are bolstered by lab studies demonstrating that people can "remember" events which never occurred (Brainerd & Reyna, 1998). For example, many children can be led to falsely remember a serious animal attack (Porter et al., 1999). Sexually abused women with posttraumatic stress disorder are especially likely to show this in the lab (Bremner et al., 2000). Many of the disbelievers have even formed an organization, the False Memory Syndrome Foundation. According to Harvard psychiatrist Harrison Pope, "There are a certain number of therapists who see sexual abuse in every patient they see. And they can lead a patient by a thousand suggestions and implications, and by reinforcing what they do and don't listen to" (quoted by Cole, 1994). Accounts of abuse victims who have retracted their "memories" have been published (e.g., de Rivera, 1997), and some believe that the implanting of false memories has become epidemic.

Proponents of the theory of repressed memories cite evidence that few claims of amnesia are false (Hovdestad & Kristiansen, 1996) and that, in fact, claims of false memories are largely unsubstantiated (Pope, 1996). Some studies have verified that abuse actually occurred (Williams, 1994). The American Psychiatric Association's DSM-IV now includes repressed memory (under Dissociative Amnesia). It has even been claimed that those who believe that repressed memories are false memories do so because of their own personal needs and sociopolitical interests (Kristiansen et al., 1996).

Today, most people take a balanced view, accepting that in some cases memories of abuse are false, but that in other cases repressed memories are true. The role of the therapist is critical. To read more on both sides of this debate, see Pope (1996) and the replies in the September 1997 issue of *American Psychologist,* or Volume 5, number 2, of *Health Care Analysis* (1997).

INCEST

The term *incest* comes from a Latin word *(incestus)* meaning "impure." **Incest** refers to sexual activity between relatives who are too closely related to marry. It is illegal in all 50 states. One reason incest is illegal is that this type of mating has the highest probability of producing defective offspring (Thornhill, 1992). Until recently, many people thought that incest was rare, but it happens much more often than people might (or might not want to) believe. Look again at Table 17–1. About 8.5 percent of women and 2.4 percent of men in Laumann et al.'s (1994) national survey said that they had been sexually abused by a family member before the age of 13. Another study found that 3.3 percent of the men and 4.5 percent of the women surveyed reported having been molested by a relative as children, and in about 60 percent of these cases the molestation was "often" or "ongoing" (Janus & Janus, 1993). Only about 2 percent of adult-child incestuous relations ever get reported to authorities (Russell, 1984), and some victims do not understand that what happened to them was abuse (Kikuchi, 1988).

incest Sexual contact between two closely related persons.

Although they have received little attention by researchers, **polyincestuous families** are not uncommon (Faller, 1991). In these families, there are both multiple abusers and multiple victims, both across generations and within the same generation. Victims often become abusers, and in many cases view the activity as acceptable, or even expected. Unlike other cases of child molestation, much of the abuse in polyincestuous families is done by females (Faller, 1987; McCarty, 1986). In over half such families, there are also abusers and victims from outside the family (Faller, 1991).

Much more is known about specific types of incest. After you have read about these, we will return to a discussion of family dynamics in incest.

INCEST BETWEEN SIBLINGS

Brother-sister incest, or in some cases *brother-brother incest*, is believed to be five times more common than parent-child incest (Cole, 1982; Gebhard et al., 1965). Finkelhor (1980) surveyed college undergraduates and found that 15 percent of the women and 10 percent of the men in his sample had had some type of sexual experience with a sibling. This usually involves fondling, but sometimes includes sexual intercourse as well. In families in which sibling sexual activity occurs, the parents are often distant or inaccessible and/or create a sexual climate in the home.

> "I was a victim from age 4 until 13. My two brothers continually cornered me and forced me. My mother worked and was much too busy or tired to observe. She did not believe me when I tried to tell her. To this day, I still have problems sexually, emotionally, and mentally. My way of solving it was to move away (1200 miles away)."

> "When I was around 6, my oldest adoptive brother decided that he needed 'more fun.' Every week, about two or three times a week, he would pin me down, place a gag in my mouth, and rape me until he would say 'go shower, I'm done for now.' . . . One day Jimmy was careless and my parents came home early from work. My father banged my door down, threw him off me." (All examples are from the author's files.)

There is considerable debate among professionals about the long-term effects of sibling incest. Some believe that if the experience occurs between siblings of nearly the same age (less than a 4- to 5-year age difference), if there is no betrayal of trust, and if the children are not traumatized by adults in cases where their activity is discovered, then it is just "sex play" and "part of growing up" (Finkelhor, 1980; Steele & Alexander, 1981). However, as you can see from the previous case history, the

polyincestuous family
Families in which there are both multiple incestuous abusers and multiple victims, across generations and within the same generation.

effects can sometimes be quite negative. This is particularly so when the incest involves coercion, threats, force, or betrayal of trust (Canavan et al., 1992). Only about 12 percent of all people with childhood sibling incest experiences have ever told anyone, and "the pain of secrecy" adds to the negative experience (Finkelhor, 1980). In cases where physical pleasure is experienced in exploitative or abusive incest, the result can be confusion and guilt regarding sexuality (Canavan et al., 1992). Other long-term effects can include distrust of men in general, poor self-concept, depression, and confusing intimacy and sex (resulting in thinking that sex is the only way to relate to men; Canavan et al., 1992; Cole, 1982; Russell, 1986).

PARENT-CHILD INCEST

> "At the age of 5, I was the oldest of two children (my little sister was one year old). My mom would go to church and leave me in the care of my father. He would take out his penis and have me look at it and touch it, but I didn't know what was happening. It stopped for a while, but then he would try to put his tongue into my mouth. At the age of 8, after my mom had another baby, he would touch my vagina and lay on top of me (all 195 lbs.). At the age of 11, he got into my bed trying to take off my panties. I put up a fight but they were removed. He then took out his penis . . . I am a sophomore here at UNO, and it still hurts. I try to get over the hating of my father, but I don't really care what he thinks about me." (woman)

> "My father began to molest me when I was 12—on the night after my mother's funeral. I am an only child and he explained that since my mother was gone I was going to have to function as the 'woman' of the house. At first I was only required to function as a woman in the evenings (and most mornings too), sharing his bed as my mother had. As I grew older additional chores were added such as cooking and cleaning. It was always explained that if I truly loved him I would never hesitate to do his bidding—oral and anal sex, giving him showers, dressing him, etc. Finally I managed to get the courage to leave my father. . . . Throughout my entire adult life I have never had a successful relationship. I'm not gay, but I don't know how a man should act. I only know how to function as the 'lady of the house.'" (man) (All examples are from the author's files.)

Of all the types of incest, parent-child incest probably evokes the greatest emotional response in people. After all, most people believe that it is the role of parents to nurture, provide for, and protect their children, not turn them into sexual objects for their own selfish needs.

> " I realize that it wasn't just what he did to me physically. At that moment I lost my father. He was no longer a person to love and protect me. I was there to satisfy him." (from Spiegel, 2000)

Adults who commit incest with their children come from all walks of life. Former Miss America Marilyn Van Derbur focused much attention on this issue when she revealed that she had been repeatedly assaulted sexually beginning at age 5 by her father, a millionaire businessman, socialite, and philanthropist—a pillar of the community (Figure 17–8).

Although parent-child incest accounts for only 10 percent of all incest cases (Finkelhor, 1979), nearly 80 percent of arrests involve *father(stepfather)–daughter incest.* Stepfathers are more likely to victimize their children than are biological fathers (Finkelhor, 1979), but both types of cases are common. Fathers who commit incest are generally shy and publicly devoted family men who appear to be quite average, but in their own homes they are very domineering and authoritarian—"king of their castle" (Meiselman, 1978). They tend to be impulsive but generally are not psychotic. In relations with their children, they are often overprotective, selfish, and jealous.

Incestuous fathers, obviously, have the capacity to become sexually aroused by children (remember, nearly half of all incestuous fathers also molest other children; Abel et al., 1988b). Some incestuous fathers try to rationalize their behavior, saying that they are teaching their children in a loving way about life. Incestuous fathers who are caught often claim that the influence of alcohol or drugs caused them to commit incest, or that *they* were the ones who were seduced. Many of us have had too much to drink at times, but we didn't molest children while under the influence of alcohol. An incestuous father may have a drinking problem, but first and foremost he has a sexual problem.

The role of the mother in father-child incest is critical, and her response, or lack of any, is often as traumatizing to the child as the molestation. Consider, for example, the responses of the following four victims:

> "My mother didn't believe me. Even at age 19, I still feel resentment for her for not protecting me and for not believing me. At the time she was totally dependent on him (stepfather) and the thought of losing him was unthinkable."

> "I thought every father did that to their daughter. I thought it was a part of growing up, especially because my mom knew about it."

> "I eventually told my mother and she told me that it was nothing, that he probably thought it was her and she didn't mention it again."

> "I grabbed onto her leg saying—screaming, crying—'Don't leave me please. I don't want to be here with him!' She said I had to behave and then left without even looking at me. From this moment on I knew she was not going to listen to me, let alone protect me. This is why I am angry today."
> (All examples are from the author's files.)

Some mothers do call authorities when they become aware of the incest, but more than two-thirds do not try to protect their daughters (Herman & Hirschman, 1977). Although some mothers of incest victims have normal personalities (Groff, 1987), many are emotionally distant from their children and dependent on their husbands. They fear abandonment more than living with the fact that their children are victims of incest (Finkelhor, 1984). Many were victims of child abuse themselves (Summit & Kryso, 1978), and continue to suffer physical abuse within the marriage (Truesdell et al., 1986).

In some cases, the mother is the abuser. *Mother-child incest* has generally been regarded as rare. However, some believe that it may be underreported because surveys rarely ask specific questions about this type of incest (Lawson, 1993). Mother-son incest typically occurs in disrupted families where the mother seeks emotional support and physical closeness from her son rather than from other adults (Krug, 1989). However, recall from the previous section that daughters are as likely (or more likely) to be the victims as sons (Grayston & DeLuca, 1999). The mothers were generally the victims of sexual and/or physical abuse as children themselves.

Grandparents as incest perpetrators have also been found to be uncommon (e.g., Cupoli & Sewell, 1988;

Figure 17–8 Former Miss America Marilyn Van Derbur later announced that her father (seen here congratulating her) had sexually abused her when she was a child.

Kendall-Tackett & Simon, 1987), but may be on the increase because of the increased number of working parents leaving their children with the grandparents.

> "I only had to see him when we visited in the summer. He would get me downstairs in the cellar alone. . . . He would touch my vagina and I remember it hurting all of the time. He would sometimes take his penis out of his pants. . . . I never talked to anyone about it. One time I briefly talked to my sister about it at his funeral. She asked me why I did not seem sad. . . . She said it happened to her also. If it happened to me and my sister, it must have happened to all of the other grandchildren. I wonder if my mother was sexually abused as a child. I wonder if she knew or my grandmother knew." (from the author's files)

A large study of incestuous grandparents found that nearly all cases were *grandfather-granddaughter incest* (Margolin, 1992). Stepgranddaughters were at a higher risk than biological granddaughters. *Most of the abusive grandfathers had also been sexually abusive fathers.* One has to wonder what kind of mother would leave her children with an adult who had sexually abused her when she was a child.

EFFECTS OF INCEST ON CHILDREN

In this section, I will focus on the effects of father-child incest, although much of what you learn will be true of victims of other types of incest as well. Father-child incest generally involves frequent, long-term abuse, and in many cases there is vaginal and/or anal penetration. Recall that these are precisely the factors that often cause the greatest long-term harm in child molestation cases (Beitchman et al., 1992; Kendall-Tackett et al., 1993). A lack of support from the mother also substantially affects the victim's outcome.

Another important factor that leads to long-term problems in victims of father-child incest is that many victims blame themselves (often with encouragement from the father; Morrow, 1991). Thus, victims of incest are similar to rape victims in this respect. Consider, for example, the feelings of the following two victims:

> "I am 18 now and I believe that it was my fault. No matter how I look at it, I feel as though I could have prevented it."

> "[I] still question myself about if there was something I could have done to prevent it, or worse yet, if there was, somehow, something I did to cause it." (All examples are from the author's files.)

Victims can be very confused if they experienced any degree of physical pleasure during the abuse:

> "In my mind, I blamed me, not him. To make matters worse, somewhere along the way my 12-year-old adolescent body had my first orgasm. I hated it, hated myself, hated him. . . . I couldn't understand something I hated feeling good. Heavy, heavy guilt trip." (from the author's files)

Sadly, studies have found that many people, particularly men, also *incorrectly* blame the victims, especially if the victims were adolescents at the time of the abuse (Collings & Payne, 1991; Waterman & Foss-Goodman, 1984). If a victim tells someone of his or her experience and is met with this kind of response, this too contributes to a lasting negative outcome.

Children who are victims of incest often suffer from posttraumatic stress disorder (Lindberg & Distad, 1985). However, as with other types of child molestation, there is no definite or typical "incest syndrome" (Haesevoets, 1997). As adults, victims may have feelings of anxiety, helplessness, and powerlessness. Many victims suffer from low self-esteem and poor self-image (including a sense of separate selves or a loss of memory about the self; Cole & Putnam, 1992).

> "I've always felt alone, disassociated. Even when I'm with friends I don't feel like a part of the group. In class, I've never felt like I belonged."

> ". . . But deep down I feel really disgusted about my body." (All examples are from the author's files.)

Some victims later develop eating disorders (Hall et al., 1989), while others suffer from major depressive episodes and alcohol or drug abuse.

> "By the time I was 13, I had found alcohol and drugs as a safe haven from the immense pain inside me. By the age of 17, I was a full-blown alcoholic experiencing blackouts." (from the author's files)

Victims of child incest may also suffer from a variety of sexual problems. Some abused children may even victimize other children in an attempt to work out the distressing events (Johnson, 1989). As adults, they may be unable to form close, trusting relationships because they expect to be betrayed, rejected, and further abused (Cole & Putnam, 1992). This can lead to avoidance of relationships, or, at the other extreme, promiscuity. Victims are also a likely target for revictimization.

> "I find I cannot have open relationships with guys. It is hard for me to trust anyone. For the one time I tried to open up to a guy, I ended up even more hurt. I am 20 years old and I cannot even kiss a guy, much less give a simple hug to someone."

> "My relationships with men have all been abusive, even to the point that I have been battered and raped on several occasions. . . . I choose men that are very similar to my Dad . . . mainly because that's all I know." (All examples are from the author's files.)

Box 17-C CROSS-CULTURAL PERSPECTIVES

Incestuous Inbreeding—A Universal Taboo?

Incest has often been called the universal taboo, and there are many theories as to why it is supposedly banned throughout the world. One of the major theories comes from Freud (1913), who believed that most people prefer close kin as mating partners:

> [It is] beyond the possibility of doubt that an incestuous love choice is in fact the first and regular one. . . . (Freud, 1933/1953, pp. 220–221)

But inbreeding can lead to serious genetic defects in offspring (Thornhill, 1992) and would eventually ruin a society if it were practiced widely. Freud believed it was for this reason that societies make rules against incest.

A second, much different theory was proposed by Edward Westermarck in 1891. He believed that close physical contact between two people during childhood naturally results in loss of sexual attraction. Findings of several anthropological studies have been used as support for this theory (e.g., McCabe, 1983; Pastner, 1986; Shepher, 1971; Wolf, 1970). However, Nancy Thornhill (1991) has proposed that incest rules are not aimed at close family members (because of the Westermarck effect), but instead are directed at more distant kin (cousins) and special kinds of adultery (e.g., a man and his father's wife). Inbreeding between cousins, she says, "can concentrate wealth and power within families to the detriment of the powerful positions of (male) rulers in stratified societies."

Claude Lévi-Strauss (1969) offered yet a fourth explanation. His "alliance theory" says that the incest taboo exists not to prohibit marriage within the family, but is "a rule obliging the mother, sister, or daughter to be given to others." It ensures that women are exchanged between groups. According to Lévi-Strauss, "The incest taboo is where nature transcends itself. It brings about and is the advent of a new order."

There is no question that incestuous inbreeding is viewed very negatively in Western cultures (Ford & Beach, 1951). In the United States, marriage between first cousins is illegal in most states. Fewer than 0.5 percent of all marriages in North America and Western Europe are between first cousins. But what about elsewhere: Is inbreeding viewed with equal negativity in non-Western societies?

In times past in some cultures (e.g., Egyptian, Inca, Hawaiian), brothers and sisters married within royal families (Gregersen, 1982). For example, the Egyptian pharaoh Rameses II's wives included his younger sister and three of his daughters. Today, in areas that are primarily Muslim (northern Africa; western and southern Asia; Central Asian republics of the former Soviet Union; and northern, eastern, and central India), one-fourth to one-half of all marriages are between persons who are second cousins or closer (see Bittles et al., 1991, for a review). Marriages between parallel first cousins (a man and his father's brother's daughter) are particularly preferred. Among the Hindus of southern India, between 20 and 45 percent of marriages are between close relatives, with the preferred unions being uncle-niece or cross-first cousins (a man and his mother's brother's daughter). One-third to one-half of all marriages in sub-Saharan Africa are believed to be between relatives, and the practice is also thought to be very common in China.

Are there sociological or economic factors that might predict the acceptance of incestuous inbreeding? Yes: In those areas of the world where it is practiced, it is most common among either poor, uneducated rural people, or very rich land-owning families (see Bittles et al., 1991).

In conclusion, mother-son incestuous inbreeding is unheard of in any culture, and with rare exceptions, all cultures similarly frown upon father-daughter and brother-sister relations. However, outside Western culture, marriage between first cousins or between uncles and nieces is widely practiced.

Boys who are victims of incestuous mothers often experience such anxiety and disgust that as adults they emotionally reject all women (Krug, 1989).

In one study of the backgrounds of women in prison, it was found that over half of the prostitutes, over a third of the felons, and one-quarter of the child molesters had been incest victims (Hinds, 1981). In a more recent study of imprisoned male serial rapists, nearly half had been victims of father-son or stepfather-stepson incest (McCormack et al., 1992).

PERSONAL REFLECTIONS
Have you ever been the victim of child sexual abuse? If so, has it affected how you feel about yourself or your relationships with others? If it has affected you in any way (including leaving you with any sense of self-blame), have you ever sought counseling? If you have not sought counseling, why not?

FAMILY DYNAMICS

Father-child or stepfather-stepchild incest (and in many cases, sibling incest) typically occurs in certain family contexts (Canavan et al., 1992; Finkelhor, 1978). We have considered some of their characteristics, but let us review them here.

Within the home there is an all-powerful, authoritarian man (who may appear shy but otherwise normal to others) who sets hard, fixed gender roles for everyone and establishes an isolated, rigid system with strong external boundaries that separates the family from the outside world. However, boundaries within the family become blurred, and all emotional needs are met within the family. Independent thoughts and feelings are considered destructive as the family becomes isolated and family members become overdependent on one another. Although marital problems are common, the mother fails to protect her children, adding to their sense of abandonment and fear. Children who grow up in an environment like this may view it as normal and repeat the pattern when they become parents.

PREVENTING AND DEALING WITH CHILD SEXUAL ABUSE

The first thing to do to minimize the chance of your child's becoming a victim of sexual abuse is to *educate yourself*. You should be able to talk openly and candidly about sexual matters, including sexual abuse, with your child. You should be aware of the fact that young children who tell people about being molested are almost never making the stories up. Remember that most molesters are known to their victims, so do not doubt your child if he or she tells you that the molester is someone you know.

The next thing to do is to *educate your child*. As I have indicated in previous chapters, it is important that children know the correct names for the parts of their anatomy.

Dear Ann Landers:
    I have just spent a week on jury duty, hearing evidence in a sexual battery case. One victim was an 11-year-old girl in the sixth grade. She had difficulty describing what had happened because the poor child did not know the names of the parts of the human body. . . . When asked if she had ever seen a diagram of the human body, she replied, "No, we don't even get that till next year." (Reprinted with permission of Ann Landers and Creators Syndicate.)

Children should not be ashamed of their bodies, but they should also know which parts of their bodies are personal or private and should not be touched by other people. You must teach your children to be assertive and to know that it is all right to say "No!" to an adult who attempts to touch them in the genital area or on their breasts or buttocks. Discuss this with all family members present—incest is difficult in families in which there are no secrets. Your child must also know that he or she won't be punished for talking about being molested, no matter what the molester might say. Finally, it is crucial that your child know that he or she can communicate with you about sexual matters in general. If you are always open to discussion about sex, your child will be more likely to confide in you.

Know what to do if your child is molested or approached by a molester. Reassure him or her that talking to you about it was the right thing to do. Let your child know that being molested was not his or her fault and stress that it is the adult who was wrong. Don't confront the molester in front of your child, and if the molester is a family member or friend, let your child know that you want to help the molester get well. Let your child know that he or she will not be harmed by the molester. Finally, contact the police, even if you don't intend to press charges. By doing so, may help them prevent further child abuse.

There are certain signs to look for that may indicate that a child has been a victim of sexual abuse. A victim may suddenly begin to have episodes of depression, crying, or other out-of-character changes in mood or personality. He or she may begin to want to be alone or become afraid to go to a certain place or see a certain person. A victim may suddenly start to have problems at school or with discipline. Remember, if abuse is occurring, a victim may be unwilling or fearful to ask for help (abusers often threaten their victims). If you are a parent, do not write off these types of behaviors as a phase. Something serious might be hurting your child.

Even if you are not the parent, you can still help. Most states have a special office that people can contact if there is a suspected case of sexual abuse of a child. Staff answering the phone will ask for information, determine if an emergency exists, and have a social worker sent to investigate if action seems necessary. There are often several areas of specialization within these offices—for example, abuse and neglect, sexual abuse, and abuse within institutions (e.g., suspected abuse within a child day-care center). Investigators from this special office generally provide services for the families and children involved, and in extreme cases can have a child removed from home and put in foster care.

PROSECUTION OF SEXUAL OFFENDERS

RAPE

Almost half of all reported rapes are dismissed before trial (U.S. Senate Judiciary Committee report, May 1993). Most of the dismissed cases are acquaintance rapes, for which prosecutors traditionally have been hesitant to bring cases to trial. However, with increased education (of the public, police, and courts) there have been dramatic changes in the manner in which rape victims are treated by the courts. For example, the U.S. Supreme Court has upheld broad **rape-shield laws** that make prosecution easier and prevent the victim from feeling as if she (or he) is on trial. In 1991, the Court ruled that states can enact laws that bar an accused acquaintance rapist from introducing evidence that he and his victim had previously had consensual sex. In addition, a victim's past sexual history is no longer allowed to be introduced during trial. On the other hand, Congress passed the Federal Rules of Evidence (numbers 413–415) which allows rapists' and child molesters' past sexual offenses to be introduced in court (Eads et al., 2000).

Because many women delay reporting their rapes and many others appear calm and relaxed afterward—two common behaviors associated with post-rape post-traumatic stress disorders—many juries in the past have refused to believe victims' stories. Many states now allow expert testimony about post-rape posttraumatic stress syndrome to educate jurors about these behaviors (see Boeschen et. al., 1998). Previously, evidence of emission of semen had to be found before an assault could be called a rape. Today, many states no longer require evidence of ejaculation for rape to be charged. However, prosecution of rape is made easier when semen (in the vagina or on pubic hair or clothing) is found during the medical examination, especially now that there is genetic fingerprinting. In the past, semen could only reveal an attacker's blood type, but new technology now makes it possible to identify a person from fragments of DNA in their body cells, including semen and blood—much like a fingerprint.

CHILD SEXUAL ABUSE

In a case that went before the U.S. Supreme Court, the Court stated, "Child abuse is one of the most difficult crimes to detect and prosecute, in large part because there often are no witnesses except the victim" (*Pennsylvania v. Ritchie*, 1987). One of the greatest difficulties was that the Sixth Amendment of the U.S. Constitution guarantees that in all criminal cases, the accused has the right to confront all witnesses against him. Face-to-face confrontations were often very traumatic for children, who, in addition, were no match for shrewd and manipulative defense lawyers. However, in 1990 the Supreme Court ruled that individuals being prosecuted for child abuse had no guaranteed right to face-to-face confrontations with their young accusers if the children would suffer emotional trauma as a result. The Court upheld state laws that allowed use of video-taped testimony and testimony by one-way closed-circuit television. Most states have eliminated the corroboration rule as well (see Whitcomb, 1992, for a review of these legal changes). Courts are also allowing minors to testify with the aid of anatomically correct dolls so that they can show what happened to them, although there are still some unanswered questions as to the effectiveness of this method of assessment (Lamb et al., 1996). In 2000, the federal Child Abuse Prevention and Enforcement Act became law, which, among other things, provided court-appointed special advocates to help victims in court.

CONVICTION OF SEX OFFENDERS

Every state has laws that make it illegal to involve children in sexual activity or to fail to protect a child from sexual abuse. The goal of these laws is to protect the child and to see to it that the adult does not repeat the offense (see Conte, 1991). This goal would be best served by a coordinated effort among the police, the courts, and child welfare and community mental health programs, but attitudes in these four institutions often differ with regard to what to do about victims and offenders (Trute et al., 1992). Without a coordinated effort, many accused adults "fell out of the system" and received little therapy or confinement.

As the extent of sexual abuse of children has become better known, the states and federal government have taken a tougher stand. Washington was the first state to pass a *"sexual predator law"* that allows the state to confine pedophiles and rapists in mental institutions beyond their prison terms if it can be shown that it is likely that they will commit similar crimes again. The U.S. Supreme Court upheld this law in a 1997 decision (*Kansas v. Hendricks*) involving a Kansas man who had sexually abused children his entire adult life. The court upheld the law again in a 2000 case. As of 2000, 15 states had enacted similar laws. At least four states have passed laws that allow judges to order chemical castration (medroxyprogesterone acetate, or MPA) for repeat sex offenders but this is very controversial

rape-shield laws Laws that make the prosecution of rapists easier and that also prevent the victims from feeling as if they are on trial.

(see Miller, 1998). What about juvenile sex offenders, whose numbers are increasing every year? If they are not stopped early in their abusive careers, their behavior will only escalate. However, because of their age, should society focus on incarceration or therapy (see Martin & Pruett, 1998, for a thoughtful review)?

A U.S. Department of Justice study released in 1997 found that there were nearly a quarter of a million convicted sex offenders on probation nationwide. A federal law passed in 1996 established a nationwide registry to keep track of sex offenders, and the 2000 Federal Child Abuse Prevention and Enforcement Act increased the monitoring. Part of the law requires states to inform local communities whenever a sex offender moves into the neighborhood. "Megan's law," as it is called, resulted from the publicity that followed the rape and murder of 7-year-old Megan Kanka in 1994 by a convicted pedophile who was living across the street from the Kanka family. In 1998 the U.S. Supreme Court rejected a challenge to Megan's law that had been made by a group of sex offenders who claimed that the law amounted to a second punishment. Although well intentioned, the law has resulted in stigmatizing some people who were convicted of isolated nonviolent sex offenses, often decades ago.

As you will learn in the next chapter, hundreds of thousands of children in poor nations are pushed (and often sold) into prostitution every year and are exploited by pedophile tourists from rich nations. England and other European countries have passed laws that allow the prosecution of their citizens if they are involved in child sex tourism in other countries. Many people have already been convicted under these laws (Alldridge, 1997).

THERAPY

THERAPY FOR RAPISTS

One of the biggest problems in treating men arrested for rape is their tendency to deny or minimize their offenses. Recall that most rapists have distorted cognitive beliefs and attitudes and that it is not uncommon for rapists to believe that their victims wanted to have sex (see the section on rape). Early programs focused on deviant sexual arousal, but programs today take a multifaceted approach. Successful outcome depends on tailoring the type of therapy to the particular deficits and needs of the individual rapist. It is important, therefore, that there first be a comprehensive assessment of a rapist's developmental history, attitudes and beliefs about women and sex crimes, social competency, empathy, sexual knowledge and preferences, psychiatric history, substance abuse history, and offense variables (Ward et al., 1997).

Programs generally combine cognitive techniques with the traditional behavioral techniques, and many employ antiandrogen hormone treatment to reduce sex drive (Grossman et al., 1999; Marshall et al., 1993; Polaschek et al., 1997). Again, however, a big problem is that rapists are reluctant to engage in therapy, and even with those who do, the dropout rate is high (see Polaschek et al., 1997). There is also concern that the recidivisim rate (the percentage of offenders completing therapy who rape again), though improving, is still about 20 percent in the first 5 years (Greenberg, 1998; Hanson, 2000; Prentky et al., 1997). This is an underestimate because it is based on rapists who were caught again; many subsequent offenses are never detected. Some have suggested that better success can be achieved by adding empathy training (emotional recognition skills for the self and others) and by treating specific cognitive distortions related to issues of power and the desire to humiliate victims (Marshall, 1993; Polaschek et al., 1997).

THERAPY FOR CHILD MOLESTERS

For the incestuous molester, a family systems approach is often chosen as therapy. Here, therapy for each family member is combined with therapy for each pair of family members and is followed by therapy for all the family members together (Lanyon, 1986). Group therapy with other families is also often included. For positive change to occur, the father must accept responsibility for what he has done and the mother must also accept responsibility often for what she has not done. The child, on the other hand, must learn to believe that he or she is not responsible. The father must also give up his complete authoritarian rule, and each family member must learn to become more independent. Among rapists and child molesters, the recidivism rate is lowest for incestual child molesters (Greenberg et. al., 1998).

As for the nonpedophile (situational) molester, whose sexual attraction is primarily to adults, many experts believe that society is best served by seeing to it that he receives therapy. Most therapists use cognitive-behavioral approaches.

The outcome of therapy for pedophiles is less certain. For these men, sexual orientation is primarily and repeatedly directed toward children, and they have little or no sexual interest in adults. As you have already learned, many of these men have victimized dozens, and in some cases hundreds, of children (Abel et al., 1987), yet they typically display considerable denial and defensiveness (Grossman et al., 1992). The antiandrogen drugs cyproterone acetate and medroxyprogesterone acetate have proved effective in lowering sex drive, thus allowing clinicians to attempt therapy while the subject is not driven to commit his crimes (Bradford & Greenberg, 1997). As with rapists, a comprehensive cognitive/behavioral/social therapy approach is generally used today (Barbaree & Seto, 1997; Polaschek et al., 1997). However, the judicial system is full of examples of pedophiles who have been caught, confined, and undergone therapy time and time again. A recent study found that 14 percent of child molesters had been rearrested 3 years after release from prison, 30 percent after 10 years, and nearly half after 20 years (Prentky et al., 1997; see also Hanson, 2000). These types are often referred to as career pedophiles or, more recently, as career sexual predators. Prentky argues that simply allowing offenders to complete their prison terms and return to the community is dangerous and that community notification laws such as Megan's law are shortsighted. Instead, he believes that intensive long-term supervision and treatment are best.

PERSONAL REFLECTIONS

As you have learned, several states have passed sexual predator laws which require that molesters identified as career predators be confined for life. Our society will no doubt continue to debate this sensitive issue, weighing the rights of offenders against the rights of victims and future victims, for many years to come. What do you think is best?

THERAPY FOR VICTIMS

You have already learned that victims of rape or child abuse often suffer from a variety of symptoms indicating emotional distress (e.g., depression, anxieties, fears) and that they may exhibit substance abuse, sexual disorders, eating disorders, and relationship problems. Because of our society's attitudes, there is a tendency in part or in full to blame the victim, a feeling that even the victim may share. Additionally, male victims may have questions about their sexual orientation (Gartner, 1997).

For many victims, initial therapy may have to be geared to their posttraumatic stress (Mueser & Taylor, 1997). Cognitive-behavioral approaches have proven particularly effective in reducing the fear and distress experienced when recalling traumatic events (Saywitz et al., 2000). Eventually, however, the victim must overcome any self-blame, and the involvement of the victim's partner and family can be very beneficial here (Cohen & Mannarino, 2000; Grosz et al., 2000). In addition to individual therapy, programs such as those offered by the YWCA emphasize group sessions so that victims have an opportunity to share their experiences with others without fear of being judged negatively.

Sex is the closest form of communication between two people and can be one of life's most beautiful experiences. It is extremely important, therefore, for a person to get counseling and support from professionals and organizations if he or she is still feeling the effects of incest or child abuse as an adult or is suffering from the effects of being raped. Everyone should have the ability to enjoy sex in ways that are open and honest and that allow them to form healthy, intimate relationships.

RESOURCES FOR THOSE SEEKING HELP

For counseling, contact the *YWCA Rape Crisis Centers* nearest you. Services include a 24-hour rape crisis line; programs for victims of adult and child sexual assault and incest and for families and friends of victims; crisis and long-term counseling; weekly support groups; victim advocacy; information and referral services; training for medical personnel and police; agency consultation; community education, including assault prevention programs for people of all ages, from toddlers to senior citizens; and court monitoring.

For an extensive list of resources, see the "Resources" section following the text.

Key Terms

Suggested Readings

Parents: For an updated list of books and materials that are appropriate for children and adolescents, contact SIECUS, 130 West 42 Street, Suite 350, New York, NY 10036 (phone: 212-819-9770).

Anderson, P. B., & Struckman-Johnson, C. (Eds.). (1998). *Sexually aggressive women.* New York: Guilford Press.

Bass, E., & Davis, L. (1988). *The courage to heal: A guide for women survivors of child sexual abuse.* New York: Harper & Row.

Brownmiller, S. (1975). *Against our will: Men, women, and rape.* New York: Simon & Schuster. A key book in changing our society's attitudes about rape.

Crewdson, J. (1988). *By silence betrayed: Sexual abuse of children in America.* Boston: Little, Brown.

Gelman, D., et al. (1990, July 23). The mind of the rapist. *Newsweek.* Examines the motivations for rape.

Gilbert, B., and Cunningham, J. (1987, October). Women's post-rape sexual functioning: Review and implications for counseling. *Journal of Counseling and Development.* Discusses the effects of having been raped on long-term sexual functioning.

Grayston, A. D, & DeLuca, R. V. (1999). Female perpetrators of child sexual abuse: A review of the clinical and empirical literature. *Aggression and Violent Behavior, 4,* 93–106.

Groth, A. N. (1979). *Men who rape.* New York: Plenum Press. An excellent psychological and motivational profile of rapists.

Koss, M. B., et al. (Eds.). (1994). *No safe haven: Male violence against women at home, at work, and in the community.* Washington, DC: American Psychological Association.

Lew, M. (1990). *Victims no longer: Men recovering from incest and other sexual child abuse.* New York: Harper & Row.

Newsweek. (1993, October 25). Several articles and essays on date rape and sexual harassment.

Paludi, M. A. (Ed.). (1996). *Sexual harassment on college campuses., abusing the ivory power.* Albany: State University of New York Press. Updated chapters by many leading scholars.

Parrot, A., and Bechofer, L. (Eds.). (1991). *Acquaintance rape: The hidden crime.* New York: John Wiley. Many scholarly articles.

Sanday, P. R. (1990). *Fraternity gang rape.* New York: New York University Press. Analysis of a seldom-discussed type of sexual violence.

Scarce, M. (1997). *Male on male rape: The hidden toll of stigma and shame.* Insight Books (Plenum).

Volkman, E., and Rosenberg, H. L. (1985, June). The shame of the nation. *Family Weekly.* Discusses child pornography and its link to child abuse.

Study Guide

INTERACTIVE REVIEW

Historically, rape has been viewed as a violation of (1) _____ and victims were treated like "damaged goods." Even today, in the United States, many states will not prosecute a husband for raping his wife unless there is extreme physical harm to the victim.

There are about 100,000 reported cases of rape in the United States every year, but the actual number of rapes committed is many times greater. Most rapes are committed by (2) _____. Most victims are women between (3) _____ years of age, but anyone can be a victim of rape, including men. Rapists generally plan their crimes and seek victims who appear to be (4) _____.

Studies of convicted rapists reveal that most have (5) _____ IQs, have no more history of psychiatric illness than other criminals, are not oversexed, and have normal social skills. However, many were physically or sexually abused as children, or come from families in which they witnessed abuse of the mother by the father. Most rapists are (6) _____ men who repeat the crime and who lack internal controls and (7) _____.

Rape by a date or an acquaintance is no less real than rape by a stranger. Rape is rape. About 25 percent of all college women have been pressured into sex when they did not want to have it. About 7 to 15 percent of all men admit to using physical force in order to have sex on a date, while two-thirds admit to using (8) _____ to have sex. Women, too, often use coercion to have sex, but the coercion used by women is generally (9) _____, while that used by men is generally (10) _____. Many adolescents and young adults believe that a man has the right to force a date to have sexual intercourse under some circumstances. Poor communication skills regarding sexual intentions also contribute to unwanted sexual activities.

Many rapes involve more than one assailant, and these (11) _____ rapes are usually more violent than rapes committed by individuals. Marital rape, too, is often accompanied by severe beatings and physical abuse.

Most states have laws that make it illegal for an adult to have sex with anyone under the age of consent; this crime is generally called (12) _____. The mentally handicapped are often protected by these laws as well.

There are several explanations for rape. Psychodynamic theories explain rape as resulting from psychopathology. Studies of convicted rapists have found that rapists can be divided into three types, according to their motivation: (13) _____, (14) _____, and (15) _____. For these men, rape is not a crime of passion; it is a crime of violence and aggression. On the basis of what we now know of date rapists, some researchers have proposed a fourth type of rapist, the (16) _____ rapist, who has distorted cognitive processes and for whom the primary motivation is sex. Recent studies have shown that cultural factors, social learning, and interpersonal factors (a lack of shared meaning between men and women) also help explain why rape occurs. Rape is almost nonexistent in some societies, but is common in countries like the United States that promote and glorify (17) _____, and where large numbers of people conform to conservative stereotypic gender roles and men view relationships between the two sexes as (18) _____.

Many mistaken beliefs about rape are so widespread that they are called myths. This chapter considered four rape myths: (19) _____, (20) _____, (21) _____, and women frequently make false accusations of rape. None of these myths are true, but people who believe them tend to blame the victim for being raped.

Rape victims experience short- and long-term reactions in what is called (22) _____. In the acute phase, a victim's reactions may be either expressive or (23) _____. In the period of (24) _____, the victim attempts to regain control of her or his life. Long-term sexual problems are not uncommon. The reactions of a victim's partner and family are important to the recovery process, and it is crucial that they do not attribute blame to the victim.

If you are ever raped, it is important to report the crime immediately and get a medical exam as soon as possible. Do not wash, douche, or change clothes until the exam is completed. Today, most police forces have specially trained units, including counselors, to work with rape victims, and the U.S. Supreme Court has approved broad (25) _____ laws to protect victims from feeling as if they are on trial during court proceedings.

There are three basic approaches to rape prevention. One focuses on the rapists and advocates the creation of safer physical environments and tougher laws and punishments. Another focuses on potential victims and suggests educating women to be less vulnerable to assault. The third, a (26) _____ perspective, advocates changing society's values and its attitudes toward how men and women interact with one another.

Unwelcome sexual advances, requests for sexual favors, and other unwanted verbal or physical conduct of a sexual nature in the workplace or classroom is called (27) _____. The Supreme Court has ruled that this also includes the creation of a hostile or offensive work environment, and that a victim does not have to prove that sexual favors were demanded in exchange for job benefits. Companies and schools can be held liable for not taking immediate and appropriate corrective action.

We now know that sexual abuse of children is more widespread than previously believed. Most victims are molested by (28) _____. We can divide child molesters into two classifications: the (29) _____ molester, or pedophile, whose primary sexual orientation is to children, and the (30) _____ molester, whose primary sexual orientation is to adults. Pedophiles have been further classified according to their psychological characteristics as either (31) _____, (32) _____, or aggressive. Of pedophiles who have been caught, those who target girls average about 20 victims each, while those who target boys average nearly (33) _____ victims each. Heterosexual pedophiles outnumber homosexual pedophiles by 11 to 1. The effects of sexual abuse on children are often long-lasting, but there is no single "post-sexual-abuse-syndrome."

Sexual relations between relatives who are too closely related to marry is called incest. (34) _____ incest is five times more common than parent-child incest, although father-daughter and stepfather-stepdaughter incest account for 80 percent of all arrests. Incestuous fathers often appear to be shy and family-oriented publicly, but are dominating and authoritarian in their own homes. In these cases, the mothers are usually aware that the incest is going on. Because the abuse in father-child incest is usually frequent and long term, the victims generally have a variety of long-lasting problems. It is important for children who have been sexually abused to receive counseling and support from professionals and organizations familiar with sexual abuse.

SELF-TEST

A. TRUE OR FALSE

☐ T ☐ F   35. An adult woman cannot be raped if she truly does not want to be raped.

☐ T ☐ F   36. Rape was originally considered to be a crime against a man's property.

☐ T ☐ F   37. The percentage of reported rapes that are false is lower than for most other crimes.

☐ T ☐ F   38. Anyone can be a victim of rape, including any man.

☐ T ☐ F   39. If a woman willingly engages in necking or petting with a man, she cannot charge him with rape if he then forces her to have sexual intercourse.

☐ T ☐ F   40. Most rapists prefer victims who are feisty and who will try to physically resist.

☐ T ☐ F   41. Most rapists believe that their victims want to have sex with them, or deserve to be raped.

☐ T ☐ F   42. About 55 percent of all rapists are found to be psychotic.

☐ T ☐ F   43. Date rape is not as real as rape by a stranger.

☐ T ☐ F   44. Muehlenhard and colleagues found that over one-third of all college women had said "no" to a date when they really meant "yes" (to having sex).

☐ T ☐ F   45. Well over half of young adolescent boys and girls believe that a husband has the right to force his wife to have sexual intercourse against her will.

☐ T ☐ F   46. A man cannot be convicted of rape if the woman agreed to have sexual intercourse.

☐ T ☐ F   47. A man cannot be raped by a woman.

☐ T ☐ F   48. Women who are raped usually have done something to provoke it.

☐ T ☐ F   49. Many victims of rape do not show any emotional reactions afterwards.

☐ T ☐ F   50. A man who tells sexual jokes, makes sexual references, and/or stares obsessively at a female co-worker cannot be prosecuted for sexual harassment unless he demands sexual favors.

☐ T ☐ F   51. About 80 percent of all child molesters are known by their victims.

☐ T ☐ F   52. Most pedophiles were themselves sexually abused as children.

☐ T ☐ F   53. Pedophile is the term used by the American Psychiatric Association for all child molesters.

☐ T ☐ F   54. In families with father-child incest, the large majority of mothers do not try to protect their children.

☐ T ☐ F   55. Incestuous inbreeding (first cousins or closer in relation) is a universal taboo.

☐ T ☐ F   56. Victims of sexual abuse tend to blame themselves.

B. MATCHING

_____ 57. aggressive pedophile
_____ 58. anger rapist
_____ 59. opportunistic rapist
_____ 60. personally immature pedophile
_____ 61. power rapist
_____ 62. preference molester
_____ 63. regressive pedophile
_____ 64. sadistic rapist
_____ 65. sexual harasser
_____ 66. situational molester

a. Herbert feels insecure and inadequate. He commits rape to reassure himself of his sexual adequacy, strength, and potency.
b. Frank's sexual urges are primarily toward adults, but he has fondled a child and had the child touch his penis. He considers his behavior abnormal.
c. Jim tells crude sexual jokes and makes sexual references to his female employees.
d. Steve has sex with prepubescent boys and beats them before and afterwards.
e. Joe is sexually aroused and impulsively forces his date to have sex with him when they are alone.
f. Albert loves it when his rape victims try to resist and enjoys hurting them for a prolonged time.

g. David has never had a successful relationship with a woman and seeks out children, whom he can control, for sexual gratification.

h. Mike has no interest in adults as sexual partners. His sexual orientation is to children only.

i. Robert rapes because he despises all women, whom he blames for his lack of success.

j. Tom has always had sexual relations with adults, but work and marital problems have led him to drink, and when he feels sexually inadequate, he molests a child.

C. FILL IN THE BLANKS

67. People with mental disabilities are often protected against sexual abuse by the same laws that protect _____.

68. Koss (1993) estimated that a woman living in the United States had a 1-in-_____ chance of being raped in her lifetime.

69. Give four examples of sexually coercive behavior: _____, _____, _____, and _____.

70. Give two characteristics of cultures that are "rape-free": _____ and _____.

71. In _____ rape, the individual responsibility for things a person does can be diffused or forgotten.

72. Psychodynamic theories of rape explain it as resulting from _____.

73. The majority of date rapes are probably committed by _____ rapists.

74. Men who look at scenes of aggression toward women become _____.

75. Men who normally are not aroused by rape scenes are likely to become aroused by such scenes if _____ or _____.

76. In the _____ of post-rape posttraumatic stress disorder, victims attempt to regain control of their lives.

77. Charges of sexual harassment are usually prosecuted as civil suits under Title VII of the _____ of 1964.

78. Sexual harassment usually occurs in a relationship where there is _____.

79. Research has shown that the more a man believes in _____, the more accepting he is of sexual harassment.

80. A man who repeatedly prefers children for achieving sexual excitement is called a _____.

81. In the previous question, "children" refers to persons under the age of _____.

82. In _____ families there are both multiple abusers and multiple victims, both across generations and within the same generation.

Chapter 18

Sex and the Law

Morality is about right and wrong, and that's what laws attempt to put into legal form. Can you think of one law which doesn't declare one behavior right and its opposite wrong? The truth is, all laws legislate morality (even speed limits imply a moral right to safety on the roads). And everyone in politics—conservatives, libertarians and liberals—is trying to legislate morality. The only question is whose morality should be legislated?

(Frank Turek. From New Man Magazine, July/August 1999. Copyright 1999. Reprinted with permission of Strong Communications Company.)

Sex is an important part of most people's lives. Sex provides physical pleasure; it can be given and received as an expression of love and affection; and it can make us feel more masculine or feminine. People engage in a wide variety of sexual behaviors. In Chapter 13 you learned that most therapists take the view that any behavior between consenting adults that is done in private and does not cause physical, emotional, or psychological harm is okay. This text has treated sexual relations between consenting adults as something healthy, good, and positive, but there can be serious consequences (e.g., unwanted pregnancies or sexually transmitted diseases) if people do not act in a mature, responsible manner.

There are laws to prevent the sexual abuse of children and nonconsenting adults, as there should be (you learned about these in Chapter 17), but there are also laws that are designed to prevent or regulate sexual activity between consenting adults. As you might suspect, these laws are controversial, with many people objecting to attempts by others to regulate their

When you have finished studying this chapter, you should be able to:

1. Define and explain the different types of prostitution;

2. Describe the characteristics of prostitutes and their customers;

3. Evaluate the pros and cons of prostitution from a legal as well as a moral point of view;

4. Trace the history of sexually explicit material in the United States and the legal actions taken to control it;

5. Discuss the uses of sexually explicit material;

6. Compare and evaluate the effects of nonviolent and violent sexually explicit material; and

7. Explain sodomy laws and their implications for heterosexual and homosexual individuals.

private lives. Some of these laws were proposed and passed by politicians who were concerned about health-related issues (e.g., the spread of STDs), but some appear to be attempts by individuals to force the public to conform to their own moral standards. Many states, for example, once had laws that forbade the sale or distribution of contraceptive devices (these laws were finally ruled unconstitutional by the U.S. Supreme Court in *Griswold v. Connecticut* in 1965).

In this chapter, you will read about several topics for which there has been a long history of individuals attempting to regulate the sexual activity of others. I have purposely attempted not to show my own bias regarding these issues and have tried to take a neutral stand. My intent is to stimulate your own thinking by presenting both sides of an issue. You be the judge as to whether or not there should be laws regulating these activities.

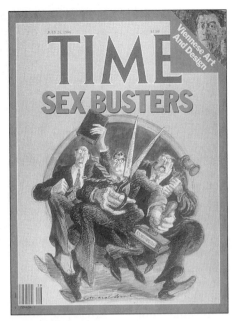

Figure 18–1

PROSTITUTION

Prostitution is often referred to as "the world's oldest profession." While this may or may not be true, the trade of sex for money or other favors has been around for as long as the recorded history of human beings. In the ancient Hebrew culture, it was not a crime for a father to prostitute his daughter, but if a daughter freely chose to have sex with a man (thus depriving her father of income), she could be put to death. Prostitution was very common in Roman society. In fact, the word **fornication** (sexual intercourse between a man and a woman who are not married to one another) is derived from *cellae fornicae,* the Latin term for the vaulted underground dwellings where prostitutes took their partners after the theater, circus, or gladiator contests.

In the Bible, Jesus told Mary Magdalene to "go, and sin no more," but prostitution flourished in Europe during the Middle Ages, and the Church had a somewhat tolerant attitude about it. St. Augustine believed that prostitution was necessary, as did St. Thomas Aquinas, who, though considered prostitution a sordid evil, reasoned that just as a palace would become polluted without sewers, the world would become immersed in lust without prostitution (see Bullough & Bullough, 1997b). Parisian prostitutes even adopted Mary Magdalene as their patron saint.

In Victorian times (mid-19th century to early 20th century), the upper class maintained a public attitude of purity and prudery, but prostitution was a common sexual outlet for husbands. The poverty and squalor of life in the lower class pushed many young women into prostitution, and it has been estimated that there were as many as 80,000 prostitutes in London at any one time. Prostitution was legalized and regulated by an act of the British Parliament in 1860.

In colonial America and the early years of the United States, Puritanism in the North and the availability of slaves in the South kept prostitution to a minimum. Immigration and industrialization, however, resulted in larger urban areas, and prostitution flourished in the latter half of the 19th century. Houses of prostitution (brothels) were commonplace, especially in the West, where men greatly outnumbered women. Ship captains imported thousands of women from the Orient and Central and South America to be forced into prostitution. San Francisco's population reached 25,000 in the early 1850s, and this included 3,000 prostitutes (Tannahill, 1980). Storyville, a 16-block district of legalized prostitution in New Orleans from 1897 to 1907, employed as many as 2,000 prostitutes at any one time (Warner, 1997).

Opposition to prostitution in the United States began to grow during the first part of the 20th century. Illinois became the first state to pass laws against prostitution in 1908. Federal laws passed at the start of World War I shut down many of the houses of prostitution that had existed near service bases (there were no cures for gonorrhea or syphilis at that time, and many men were being rejected for service because of infections).

These laws did not put a stop to prostitution. Kinsey and his colleagues (1948) found that 69 percent of the white men they surveyed had had at least one experience with a prostitute. Twenty-five percent of college-educated men and 54 percent of high school–educated men had had intercourse with a prostitute before marriage. Fewer men have their first sexual experience with prostitutes today than in the past. In a more recent survey, 20 percent of the male respondents indicated that they had paid for sex on at least one occasion (Janus & Janus, 1993). The percentage was the same for all income groups, and most of

fornication Sexual intercourse between a man and a woman who are not married to one another.

the men said that they did this occasionally. In the national survey by Laumann et al. (1994), 17 percent of the men and 2 percent of the women over the age of 18 said that they had paid someone for sex.

DEFINITION AND TYPES OF PROSTITUTION

We generally think of a prostitute as someone who exchanges sex for money. However, by this definition we would have to include people who allow someone to have sex with them for a job or career promotion, to gain a favor, or in return for a trip to Cancun or some other vacation spot. Some prostitutes bitterly complain that what they do is no different from what is done by a woman who remains married to and has sex with a man she does not care for just for the security. To get around these problems, legal definitions generally distinguish **prostitution** from other activities on the basis of the indiscriminate manner in which it occurs. The Oregon Supreme Court, for example, ruled that "the feature which distinguishes a prostitute from other women who engage in illicit intercourse is the indiscrimination with which she offers herself to men for hire."

How common is prostitution in the United States today? There are generally about 84,000 women working each year as full-time prostitutes (Potterat et al., 1990), not counting the women who have sex in exchange for drugs at crack houses and other such places. However, in a cross-sectional national survey, Janus and Janus (1993) found that over 4 percent of the women answered "yes" to the question "Have you ever had sex for money?" In other words, there are many women who have engaged in prostitution part time or for a short time. Estimates of the number of young teenage prostitutes, for example, range as high as 2.4 million (Joseph, 1995).

Prostitution in the United States was transacted primarily in brothels until the turn of the 20th century, but today it occurs in a variety of settings. Prostitutes can be divided roughly into three types according to status. On the lowest tier are **streetwalkers,** who solicit in public. Almost all of these women become prostitutes for financial reasons (e.g., to escape poverty or to support a drug habit) and not because of pathological sexual needs. Very few are forced into prostitution as in past centuries, but some are recruited. Most streetwalkers are protected by a pimp, who often takes a large share of the earnings. The sexual activity generally takes place in a room in a cheap hotel or apartment where the manager is aware of

Figure 18–2 Streetwalkers solicit in public and are the lowest paid type of prostitute. They typically have sex with four to five men a day.

what is occurring. The typical streetwalker has sex with four to five men a day, and the sexual activity usually involves giving oral-genital sex (Freund et al., 1989).

The once common house of prostitution is now legal only in some counties in Nevada. However, business at these legalized houses declined substantially during the 1980s, perhaps because of the fear of AIDS, but probably also owing to the increase in popularity of escort services.

Elsewhere, the **brothel prostitute** has been replaced by **B-girls,** who work in bars and hotels, generally with the approval of the ownership (which may take a cut of the profits or else benefit by the customers the prostitutes attract). Open solicitation, however, is generally frowned upon, so nonverbal messages are often used. The price is usually higher than for a streetwalker's services, and the sexual activity generally takes place in the customer's room.

"Candy" (her own fictitious name) is an attractive 33-year-old African-American B-girl. She solicits customers in New Orleans' French Quarter, in bars along Bourbon, Chartres, and Decatur Streets. Her minimum charge for sex is $50 for 15 minutes or $200 for a night. The vast majority of her customers are white men in town for conventions. She says that 75 percent of them are married. The sexual activity takes place either in the man's hotel room or in a neutral hotel. Whenever possible, however, she robs her customers rather than having sex with them. Candy says this is usually easy to do before they even get out of the

prostitution The exchange of sex for money. The feature that distinguishes a prostitute from other people who engage in illicit sexual intercourse is the indiscrimination with which she (or he) offers herself to others for hire.

streetwalker A prostitute who solicits in public.

brothel prostitutes Prostitutes who work in houses of prostitution.

B-girls Prostitutes who work in bars and hotels, generally with approval of the ownership.

bar. She rubs their genitals, and in their state of excitement they rarely notice that she is pick-pocketing them with the other hand. She doesn't worry about returning to the bar in a few days, because by then the "score" has left New Orleans. If she does have sex with a customer, afterwards she tries to relax them so that they fall asleep, and then she robs them of all their money and valuables.

Candy has four children and is on welfare. After high school she worked as a housekeeper and at other minimum-wage jobs. When she was 27, a pimp showed her the expensive nightclubs around town and said that she, too, could enjoy this life-style. After some deliberation, she paid him $300 to be "his lady" and now lives with him (her children live with her mother). She turns all the money that she makes as a prostitute and thief over to him. In return, he gives her protection, buys her nice clothing and jewelry, and lets her drive a Cadillac Seville.

Candy doesn't think about the future. She has been arrested 22 times on various charges in the past 7 years, and if convicted of prostitution again, she could be sentenced to 2 years in prison. She doesn't worry very much about AIDS or other sexually transmitted diseases either. Although she sometimes makes $3,000 to $4,000 in one month, none of it has been saved for when the time comes that she cannot prostitute anymore. She just enjoys the life-style that the money will buy now. (from the author's files)

More recently, sexual services have increasingly been offered through thinly disguised storefronts such as *massage parlors* (it should be noted, however, that some of these parlors are legitimate). Women who work in massage parlors are often called "hand whores" because toward the end of the massage (often given in the nude) they generally rub the thighs and groin area and let it be known that for a "tip" they will massage the genitals.

The highest-status prostitutes are the **call girls.** New customers are screened (recommendations from trusted sources are often required), and appointments are generally made by telephone. The call girl generally works out of her own apartment, but often offers her company for dinner and social occasions in addition to providing sexual services. The services do not come cheaply, however, with some of the most attractive call girls charging $1,500 per night or more. A more commercialized, and somewhat less expensive, variety of call girl prostitution today is offered through *escort services,* which advertise in newspapers. Judging by the increase in these advertisements, escort service prostitution increased by over 400 percent in the 1980s (Janus & Janus, 1993, p. 132).

Prostitution is not limited to women who cater to heterosexual men. Although not nearly as common as female prostitutes, men sometimes sell their bodies to

women as well. These men, called **gigolos,** are the male counterparts of call girls and often work as part of an escort service (generally used by wealthy, older, single women). For example, the following account is from a 22-year-old student working as a male escort. He said that most of his female clients are 30 to 45 years old and 80 percent are single.

"Being a male escort is not all that people perceive it to be. In this day and age you have women that are successful, and in order for them to stay that way they must constantly work harder than any man they're in competition with. This causes women to be subjected to long hours of work and devotion to their jobs, leaving them with no time at all for a personal life. Every time they attempt to have a relationship, they end up neglecting either work or their partner. That is the point where I come in. I am the individual that can be there for them when they need someone either as a friend or a lover. One of the misconceptions of being a male escort is that they only have sex with their clients. That may be true for females, but in the male's case, out of ten women, only five of them only want sex. Three of them want to be held while watching a movie or listening to music. And as for the other two, they want someone who they can go to events with, someone who can carry on intellectual conversation and stand by their side as their showpiece."

Homosexual prostitution is nearly as common as heterosexual prostitution in some large urban areas. Male prostitutes, called **hustlers,** are similar to female streetwalkers in that they generally solicit their customers on the street. Many hustlers do not regard themselves as homosexual (Earls & David, 1989), because in America the male prostitute generally plays a passive role (i.e., the customers pay to give oral sex to the prostitute, and not vice versa). Some studies estimate that there may be as many as 300,000 male child prostitutes in the United States (see Joseph, 1995). As many as 70 percent of hustlers do this only part time, with the primary motivation being financial and not sexual (Earls & David, 1989).

CHARACTERISTICS OF PROSTITUTES

In many parts of the world, women and girls have no choice; their families sell them into prostitution (Barry, 1995; Joseph, 1995). Even here, the primary reason given by persons engaging in prostitution is economics (Earls & David, 1989; Rio, 1991). Most prostitutes come from poor families and have little education, or they are young runaways with few or no skills (Bagley & Young, 1987). However, even for call girls or prostitutes who are

call girls The highest-status prostitutes, who generally work out of their own apartments by appointment only.

gigolos Male prostitutes who cater to women.

hustler A male prostitute who caters to men.

middle-class housewifes working part time, the main attraction is still money—their income is higher than that of other women matched for age and education (Exner et al., 1977).

Prostitution and the need for money are often fueled by drug use. The large majority of prostitutes are habitual users of addictive drugs such as heroin and crack cocaine (Potterat et al., 1998; Simon et al., 1992). Pimps often see to it that their prostitutes become addicted just so they will remain economically dependent. For the typical streetwalker or B-girl, prostitution does not turn out to be the gold mine it may have seemed at first, for most end up turning over most of their earnings to the pimp.

Economics may be their main motivation, but many prostitutes are attracted to the thrill and danger of "the life" (Potterat et al., 1985). In fact, Janus and Bess (see Janus & Janus, 1993) found that for some prostitutes, the life-style itself was addictive. Most people believe that prostitutes do not really enjoy sex with their customers and perform sex acts mechanically, but one study found that many prostitutes do, in fact, enjoy sex with their customers (including giving fellatio) at least sometimes (Savitz & Rosen, 1988).

Beyond the economic motives and aside from the frequent drug dependency is the fact that most prostitutes have very sad backgrounds. Many prostitutes—including the large majority of teenage prostitutes—were sexually abused as children (Bagley & Young, 1987; Potterat et al., 1998; Rio, 1991). Physical abuse by parents is also common, as are parents with alcohol or drug problems. Many prostitutes had trouble in school, had few friends, and generally felt rejected (Price et al., 1984). As a result, many grew up with severe self-esteem and self-identity problems, and generally are just less psychologically healthy than other people (Gibson-Ainyette et al., 1988). With this kind of background, it is not surprising that most teenage prostitutes are runaway or throwaway (not wanted even if they return) children who, with no other job options, have turned their first trick by the time they are 14 (Joseph, 1995).

"Jean" looks like most other 15-year-old girls. In fact, when her hair is in a ponytail she is often mistaken for 13 or 14 years old. The men, most of whom are married with daughters as old or older than she is, like her very young looks. They want to have sex with a "schoolgirl." Jean fulfills their fantasy by telling them that she is a sophomore at one of the local high schools. She charges them $30 to $50, depending on what they want (oral sex in their car is least expensive). Jean doesn't really go to school at all. She is a runaway. She ran away the last time at age 14 and found herself in New Orleans alone and hungry. That's when she met "Frank." He bought her a hamburger and offered her a place to stay. There were two other girls about her same age staying with Frank. He was particularly nice to Jean and bought her nice dresses. She felt wanted and cared for, and after a few days she and Frank had sex (her first time). He also introduced her to drugs. He told her that she was his special girl. Two weeks later he told her he needed money and asked her to go to bed with another man. The other girls told her it was easy. Jean was surprised to find out how easy it was, and within a short time she was having sex with up to six men a day. All she had to do was stand on a corner and within a short while older men would stop and talk to her. (from the author's files)

Unfortunately, there are some people who prefer to have sex with young teens, and thus the sexual exploitation of children will continue as long as there is a demand for and supply of destitute young runaway and throwaway children. The 1996 World Congress Against Commercial Sexual Exploitation of Children (Stockholm) estimated that 1 million children a year worldwide are drawn into prostitution. The total number of child prostitutes worldwide may be in the tens of millions, and sex tourism (going to foreign countries to have sex with young child prostitutes) is a big business (Joseph, 1995). In a world dominated by men—and especially in cultures where there are few opportunities for women to be employed—if a young woman does not have a father or husband to support her, prostitution may be the only way in which to survive (Bullough & Bullough, 1997b). The following organizations are devoted to helping these children get off the street:

Covenant House
1-800-999-9999
Provides counseling, shelter, and other referral services.
National Youth Crisis Hotline
1-800-448-4663
They will put you in touch with the nearest shelter program.
National Runaway Switchboard
1-800-621-4000
They encourage runaway children to reestablish contact with their families.

A study of adult male street prostitutes found that nearly all had serious problems with feelings of personal inadequacy, loneliness and social alienation (most said they had no friends), mistrust of others, and depression (Simon et al., 1992). All were drug users and felt that they were locked into their deviate careers. While the authors of the study acknowledge that the psychological problems may reflect the prostitutes' dangerous and chaotic environment, and probably their past, they also suggest that these psychological problems have led them to this particular life-style.

As bad as the developmental history of most prostitutes is, "on-the-job" conditions are often no better. A majority of prostitutes have been the victims of rape and assault. One study concluded, "Working as a streetwalker can be as traumatic as going to war. Two-thirds of the prostitutes surveyed suffered from post-traumatic stress disorders" (Farley et al., 1998).

THE CUSTOMER

Prostitution has continued to flourish for centuries despite laws, penalties, and the protests of outraged citizens. Part of the reason it has continued with unabated frequency is the fact that it is perceived as easy income by unskilled, financially destitute women; but without the demand for their services, of course, prostitution could not exist. In order for it to flourish as it has, the demand for sexual services must be great.

Customers are called *johns, tricks,* or *scores* by prostitutes. Most customers are white, middle-class, middle-aged, and married (Janus & Janus, 1993).

There are many reasons why men pay for sex. A few are able to function sexually only with prostitutes (Bess & Janus, 1976), but the reasons for many include lack of a partner (e.g., due to military service, traveling, or being unable to find a partner because of physical or social handicaps) and the desire for a new partner or a novel sexual act. Perhaps the major reason that many men pay for a prostitute's services is to enjoy sex without the time or effort required of an emotional involvement (Stein, 1977). Some men feel that they have to perform (i.e., please their partner) in their usual relationship, but sex with a prostitute allows them to receive pleasure without having to reciprocate. The majority of men who go to streetwalker prostitutes pay to have oral-genital sex performed on them (Leonard et al., 1989).

Men who pay to have sex with male prostitutes come from all walks of life (Morse et al., 1992). Most describe themselves as heterosexual or bisexual and are married. They are not part of the open gay community

Box 18–A SEXUALITY AND HEALTH

Prostitution and the AIDS Virus

You learned about the human immunodeficiency virus (HIV) and AIDS in Chapter 5. HIV infection, you recall, is the leading cause of death of Americans aged 25 to 44. Although once uncommon, heterosexual transmission is now the major cause of most new AIDS cases in women (Centers For Disease Control and Prevention, 2000).

Because of their sexual relations with multiple partners, as well as the high percentage who use drugs intravenously, prostitutes are at high risk for contracting HIV and are high-risk sexual partners for those who use them. Fewer than 1 percent of all U.S. citizens are infected with HIV, but what about prostitutes? The risk of HIV infection is greatest for prostitutes working on the street (Pyett & Warr, 1997). Studies have found that 25 to 50 percent of female prostitutes in many large U.S. cities may be infected with HIV (McKeganey, 1994; Turner et al., 1989, Weiner, 1996). The same percentage is found among male prostitutes (Boles & Elifson, 1994; Elifson et al., 1989). Several of these studies found high rates of infection with hepatitis B and syphilis as well.

You might think that men engaging in high-risk sexual behavior, such as sex with a prostitute, would use condoms. Regular use of condoms does substantially reduce the risk of getting HIV. For example, in legalized brothels in Nevada, where condom use is required (and almost all clients do, in fact, use them), no prostitute has tested positive for HIV (Albert et al., 1998). Condom use by men in the general population is quite low (Catania et al., 1995), but European studies have found that use of condoms is much higher among men who have sex with prostitutes (Barnard et al., 1993). However, this may not be true in the United States (Leonard et al., 1989; Weiner, 1996), and even in the European studies there were many clients of prostitutes who did not use condoms.

What can we conclude? By their use of prostitutes, especially when condoms are not used, many men are putting themselves *and their noncommercial partners* at high risk for infection with HIV.

and they use prostitutes in order to conceal their homosexual activities. Despite their married status, very few use condoms, although the behaviors they engage in put them at risk for sexually transmitted diseases.

PROSTITUTION AND THE LAW

Opponents of prostitution argue that it is often accompanied by drug addiction, a high risk of contracting sexually transmitted diseases (which the john can then spread to his wife or girlfriend[s]), and the possibility of assault and battery by the prostitute and her pimp (what do you suppose the chances are of a victimized john filing charges?). Studies in some cities, for example, found that many prostitutes are infected with the virus (HIV) that causes AIDS (see Box 18–A). The primary concern of many people, however, is the moral issue. They believe that prostitution is a sinful and degrading sexual activity, both for the individuals involved and for society as a whole. In some countries, such as China, the government uses aggressive, and often violent, punitive measures to fight prostitution (Gil & Anderson, 1998).

Many people, on the other hand, argue that prostitution is a victimless crime (see Rio, 1991). It is certainly true that very few prostitutes are reported by complainants. Instead, most are caught by undercover vice squad policemen posing as johns. Today, many researchers, feminists, and organized groups of prostitutes (e.g., COYOTE) have called for decriminalization or legalization of prostitution (Barry, 1995; Bullough & Bullough, 1997b). Prostitution is legal in some European countries (e.g., the Netherlands). It is certainly the case that local governments spend a great deal of money on a continually losing battle against prostitution. Proponents advocate the licensing and regulation of prostitutes, including regular required health checks for sexually transmitted diseases. This is already done in Nevada's legalized houses of prostitution, where customers are required to use condoms (see Albert et al., 1998). Proponents say that if prostitution were legalized everywhere, pimps and organized crime would become less influential, and the taxes collected on prostitutes' fees could be used to fight more serious crimes. In addition, some feminists argue that decriminalizing prostitution would give women more choice and allow many to leave the profession without social stigma.

The United States seems to have very ambivalent attitudes about prostitution. It is illegal in some places and legal in others. Although illegal in most places, many only halfheartedly prosecute it. While all states prosecute the sellers (prostitutes), very few seriously go after the buyers (johns who patronize them). Prostitution is the only sexual offense for which more women than men are prosecuted. If society does not curb the demand, the supply of prostitution will always be there, and thus our society's present treatment of prostitution probably assures that it will continue unabated.

> *PERSONAL REFLECTIONS*
> *How do you feel about prostitution: Should it remain illegal, or should we attempt to legalize and regulate it? Why? If you feel it should be illegal, should the "clients" be prosecuted?*

PORNOGRAPHY

Sexually explicit material is not new. It can be found in works of art in ancient cultures throughout the world. What is new is how readily available it is. Sexually explicit material seems to be everywhere today: on TV, in the movies, in books and magazines, over the telephone, and more and more so on the Internet. Only in the last few decades has there been such an eruption in the quantity of this material that even those who don't seek it out have difficulty avoiding it.

How did all this happen? The United States for a long time was a very puritanical country (and believe it or not, still is, compared to some other countries). The first real erotic literature by an American was Walt Whitman's *Leaves of Grass,* written in 1855. However, the **Comstock law,** passed in 1873, made the mailing of this or any other material considered obscene or lewd a felony. Moral crusader Anthony Comstock became a special agent of the U.S. Post Office and personally saw to it that the law named after him was enforced. Even information about birth control was not allowed to be mailed. Importation of James Joyce's novel *Ulysses* was banned when it was first published in 1922. The ban was lifted in 1933, but other novels, such as D. H. Lawrence's *Lady Chatterley's Lover* and Henry Miller's *Tropic of Cancer,* were banned in the United States and most other English-speaking countries until the late 1950s.

Censorship in movies was also very strict during this era. The movie industry was banned from filming erotica in 1935. Clark Gable's final words to Vivien Leigh (who played Scarlet O'Hara) in the movie *Gone with the Wind*—"Quite frankly, my dear, I don't give a damn!"—were shocking to many people. The brief love scene on the beach (with bathing suits on) in the 1953 movie *From Here to Eternity* was considered scandalous. Because it came into people's living rooms, TV was censored even more heavily than movies during the 1950s and 1960s. Many people were outraged when Lucy first used the word "pregnant" on the *I Love Lucy* show. Rock and roll was opposed by many parents in the 1950s, not only for its "suggestive" words (e.g., "Whole Lot of Shakin' Going On," "Let Me Be Your Teddy

Comstock law A law passed in 1873 that made it a felony to mail any material regarded as obscene or lewd.

Bear"), but also because of the performers' gyrations. Elvis Presley was shown only from the waist up when he appeared on the *Ed Sullivan Show* in 1956.

What about sexually explicit magazines? In the 1950s and 1960s there was really only *Playboy* (on a large scale, anyway). Hugh Hefner spent $600 in 1953 to publish the first issue, which featured nude photos of Marilyn Monroe, and sold it on the street himself. He turned *Playboy* into a multimillion-dollar publishing empire. Hefner really didn't have any competitors until the late 1960s and early 1970s, about the same time that movies and TV became more explicit.

Why the move toward more permissiveness in the middle and late 1960s? The story of Hugh Hefner's success pretty much tells the answer. It became obvious that despite efforts at censorship, there was a large demand for sexually oriented material. As a result, other magazines (e.g., *Penthouse, Hustler, Playgirl*) started to compete for a share of the market, and in an effort to outdo one another, these magazines continually expanded the borders of sexual license. At the same time, Americans flocked to see erotic European movies starring actresses like Brigitte Bardot, and their box office success led Hollywood to explore sexual boundaries as well.

So where are we in the 2000s? We can easily buy magazines that show hetero- or homosexual couples (or groups of people) having every imaginable kind of sex, using every position, having oral and anal sex, sex with violent themes, or sex with animals, and much more that is probably beyond your imagination. There is a booming $8 billion-a-year market in XXX-rated movies and video rentals (Schlosser, 1997). The XXX-rated movie *Deep Throat* cost only $24,000 to make in the early 1970s, but it earned over $25 million in profits within 10 years. You no longer have to turn to X-rated material for full frontal nudity and torrid sex scenes. R-rated movies such as 1992's *Body of Evidence* with Madonna and William Dafoe or *Basic Instinct* with Sharon Stone were clearly designed to shock us. But with all the sexually explicit material available, it takes a lot to shock us today. For hard-core fans, there's also dial-a-porn (telephone sex).

Today, sexually explicit material is readily available in the privacy of your own home at the touch of a mouse. The Internet has allowed greater accessibility to sexually explicit material for those embarrassed about going to stores to rent videos or buy magazines. Not only do companies like *Playboy* have a Web site (which averages 5 million hits a day; Schlosser, 1997), but anyone can start his or her own porn Web site, and for

Figure 18–3 Explicit sexual material was once available only in XXX movie theaters or video stores, but today it is readily available on the Internet.

a fee subscribers can watch live masturbation, oral sex, and anything else (Leland, 1999b). One-third of all use of the Internet is to porn sites, which together earn about $1 billion a year (*Newsweek*, 2000). Bulletin boards and chat rooms that cater to specific interests allow individuals to "talk" to each other and exchange sexual fantasies. Have a fetish? With the push of a few keys you can find many others with your same interest. Software (CD-ROMs) offers explicit material and even allows for some interaction. One group of researchers concluded, "The influence of the Internet on sexuality is likely to be so significant that it will ultimately be recognized as the next 'sexual revolution'" (Cooper et al., 2000). Experts predict that within 30 years people will be able to wear a special body suit, walk into a booth, and have virtual reality sex of any kind with anyone of their choice (Chang, 2000). Yes, explicit sex is everywhere today, and you would have to be a hermit living without computers, radio, TV, and magazines to avoid it.

Do we want it? Well, apparently many Americans do. In fact, when asked if they had seen an X-rated movie in the last year, about a third of all Americans said yes (Laumann et al., 1994). Nearly all college men and women have looked at an explicit magazine such as *Playboy* or *Playgirl* by the time they leave high school, and 85 to 90 percent have done so in junior high school (Bryant & Brown, 1989). The average college man spends about 6 hours a month looking at sexually explicit material, and the average college woman about 2 hours (Padgett et al., 1989). In short, a majority of

Americans now accept sexually explicit content in the mass media and believe that adults should have the right to obtain it (Winick & Evans, 1994). In fact, some universities now offer courses on hard-core pornography (Atlas, 1999).

Here are some representative views of students enrolled in my own course. Men were generally positive about sexually explicit material, with some qualifications about the availability to children.

"I do feel as though *Spice, Playboy,* and porn videos should be available. Reason being my parents didn't have that talk to me about the birds and bees. I learned from the streets, friends, and porn videos. I think that it should not be as easily available as it is, but if kids are curious they will find it or get it somewhere."

"I feel that porno is both a good and a bad product to sell. I think that some people need to see such things in order to place themselves on the creative side of the body. But I also think that it should be regulated very carefully because if it gets in the hands of children it could cause harmful ideas."

"I really don't have a problem with porn. There is a huge market for it and a ton of people enjoy it. The only problem is that the Internet has made it easy for kids to access it."

"I think that there is nothing at all wrong with sexually explicit material. It serves a need in our society, as evidenced by its success. If people didn't want it, they wouldn't buy it, and the companies providing it would collapse and become bankrupt. I don't think that these things should be censored or banned. If people don't like these items, it is easy enough to simply avoid purchasing them, rather than to engage in the ever-popular American pastime of attempting to shove their personal beliefs and biases down everybody else's throats."

Women were more variable in their views, though they too had concerns about access to children.

"I for one am bothered by sexually explicit material. Women are exploited while men are hardly shown. It bothers me to flip through the channels of the TV and see a naked woman bouncing across the screen."

"Pornography? If it's not violent, I don't have a problem with it. I used to think it was gross, but I've viewed it with my fiancé and we were actually educated. We were both pretty inexperienced and we learned many positions that we would like to try out and never thought of before. I don't think it should be banned. Just make it inaccessible to younger viewers."

"I personally think that sexually explicit magazines are degrading to women in that they reinforce feelings men have about women as mere sex objects, put on earth to please them."

"I don't particularly care for pornography. I've never looked at anything in great detail because it embarrasses me. . . I may be a prude, but I choose to be that way. Someone who wants to see pornography should have that right."

"I personally think that people should choose whether or not they view sexually explicit material. I think that if people would stop treating sex like a taboo, then it wouldn't be such a big business. . . the funny thing is that sex is something that we know we all do, but we like to pretend we don't or like to keep it secret from others."

PERSONAL REFLECTIONS
How would you respond if someone told you that this textbook was obscene and pornographic?

USES OF SEXUALLY EXPLICIT MATERIAL

Why do people look at, read, or listen to sexually explicit material? Bryant and Brown (1989) have identified four major reasons. Some people, they say, turn to sexually explicit material to learn about sex. In fact, many college students use sexually explicit material as a source of sexual information (Duncan & Nicholson, 1991):

"My boyfriend was very misinformed about females when I first started dating him. He didn't know what they like/dislike or what a woman's anatomy should look like. He now has a more accurate view of things. He got his info from porno movies." (from the author's files)

A second reason is that it allows people to rehearse sexual behaviors, much as fantasy does. A third, related reason is that today many people consider fantasy and masturbation while looking at sexually explicit material to be a form of safe sex (e.g., safe from sexually transmitted diseases).

Probably the foremost reason many people use sexually explicit material, however, is that they enjoy the sexual arousal it produces. Many people masturbate while using sexually explicit material. Many couples watch sexually explicit videos together to heighten their arousal, although in a few cases this results in dissatisfaction with a partner's sexual attraction and performance (Zillmann & Bryant, 1988). In short, most people regard sexually explicit material as a form of fantasy and use it to escape from the monotony of their daily routines.

EFFECTS OF NONVIOLENT SEXUALLY EXPLICIT MATERIAL

There have been many attempts to ban or censor sexually explicit material. People would not be concerned, of course, if they didn't believe that exposure to sexually explicit material has a negative effect on behavior.

In order to determine if this is true, President Lyndon Johnson in 1968 appointed an 18-member commission that spent 2 years collecting and studying evidence. The findings of the President's Commission on Obscenity and Pornography were released in 1970 and stimulated a decade of research (much of it originally funded by the commission). Here are some of the major conclusions from that era:

1. Looking at, reading, or listening to sexually explicit material (movies, pictures, books, tapes) produces physiological arousal in a majority of both men and women (e.g., Report of the Commission, 1970; Heiman, 1977; Henson et al., 1979; McConaghy, 1974). It was once believed that only men were aroused by sexually explicit material, but similar physiological responses were observed in both sexes. Many women may actively avoid sexually explicit material but still respond to it when they see or hear it.
2. People are more aroused by looking at sexual behaviors they consider to be normal than they are by unconventional behaviors. Sexually explicit material does not seem to create desires that were not already there (Report of the Commission, 1970).
3. When exposed to sexually explicit material, some people show an increase in sexual behavior, a smaller proportion show a decrease, but the majority of people report no change in their behaviors. Increases (almost always expressed as masturbation or sexual intercourse with the usual partner) are short-lived and disappear within 48 hours (Report of the Commission, 1970).
4. Continued exposure to sexually explicit material leads to a marked decrease in interest (indifference, boredom) in these materials (Report of the Commission, 1970; Lipton, 1983).
5. Contrary to many people's belief that sex offenders are generally obsessed with pornography, convicted sex offenders in prisons (e.g., rapists or child molesters) were often found to have had less exposure to sexually explicit materials (sex education as well as pornography) during adolescence than nonoffenders (Report of the Commission, 1970).
6. Consistent with the previous findings, it was found that when Denmark legalized the sale of hard-core pornographic material to adults in the mid-1960s, there was a lot sold at first as people satisfied their curiosity, but then sales dropped off considerably. There was over a 30 percent drop in sex crimes in the first few years after legalization, suggesting that pornography served as an outlet for some people who might otherwise have committed sex crimes (Report of the Commission, 1970; Kutchinsky, 1973).

The commission concluded that there was no significant link between exposure of adults to sexually explicit materials and sex crimes or other deviant or harmful behavior. They recommended the repeal of obscenity and pornography laws and the teaching of sex education in public schools:

> **Failure to talk openly and directly about sex has several consequences. It overemphasizes sex, gives it a magical, non-natural quality, making it more attractive and fascinating. It diverts the expression of sexual interest out of more legitimate channels, into less legitimate channels. . . . The Commission believes that interest in sex is normal, healthy, good.**

Richard Nixon was president when the commission's report was released in 1970. He dismissed it as "morally bankrupt" and rejected its findings.

Studies conducted since release of the report have generally supported the commission's conclusions. For example, studies that looked at the rate of sex crimes in states that had suspended prosecution of antipornography statutes have also concluded there is no link between exposure to sexually explicit material and sex offenses (Winick & Evans, 1996). However, the conclusion that sex offenders have had less exposure to sexually explicit material has proved to be somewhat controversial. Although most of the studies from that era found that there was no reliable difference between imprisoned sex offenders and nonoffenders in their rate of exposure to pornography (e.g., Cook & Fosen, 1970; Goldstein, 1973; Walker, 1970), others disagreed (Davis & Braught, 1970; Marshall, 1988). A later study found that child molesters had been exposed to sexually explicit material at a later age than were nonoffenders, and that adult sex offenders and nonoffenders did not differ in how often they looked at such material (Nutter & Kearns, 1993). The large majority of sex offenders in these studies did not believe that sexually explicit material caused them to commit their crimes.

The conclusion that women are aroused by sexually explicit material has also been found to be in need of some qualification. Early studies focused on physiological arousal (e.g., vasocongestion of genitals), but subsequent studies have shown that physiological arousal is not necessarily accompanied by subjective feelings of arousal (Laan & Everaerd, 1996). A review of many studies found that men report moderately greater arousal to sexual stimuli than do women and that the difference was greatest with very explicit material (Murnen & Stockton, 1997). Other studies have confirmed that most women's arousal to sexually explicit material is greater when the material is female-initiated/female-centered and romantic, as compared to male-initiated/male-centered and not romantic (Laan et al., 1994; Quackenbush et al., 1995).

EFFECTS OF VIOLENT AND DEGRADING SEXUALLY EXPLICIT MATERIAL

In the years after the President's Commission of 1970, there were concerns that the amount of sexually explicit material showing women being bound, chained, raped, and tortured had increased (e.g., Donnerstein & Linz, 1984). Sexual themes that include high-level types of violence (e.g., choking, punching, kicking, bondage, torture, weapons) have never accounted for more than a very small proportion (generally less than 10 percent) of sexually explicit videotapes and magazines (Barron & Kimmel, 2000; Scott & Cuvelier, 1993). In fact, by the 1990s explicit videos and magazines often showed women and men in egalitarian sexual roles, with any aggression being consensual (Barron & Kimmel, 2000; Davis & Bauserman, 1993; Schlosser, 1997). Most people today have a negative response to sexually explicit films that are violent or are degrading to women (Bauserman, 1998). Nevertheless there is still a small percentage of explicit magazines and videos that show sexually violent material. The percentage is much higher on the Internet newsgroup (Usenet), where close to half of the sexual scenes display high or extreme sexual violence, almost always with women as the victims (Barron & Kimmel, 2000). Thus, whether *violent sexually explicit material* is related to sex offenses is an important question. The President's Commission did not specifically examine this issue. Can looking at violent pornography cause some men to rape women?

In numerous studies designed to answer this question, volunteer subjects were shown films or heard tapes of (a) mutually consenting erotic behavior, (b) scenes of aggression toward women, or (c) scenes with both sexual explicitness and aggression. In many of the studies, violent sexually explicit material was found to cause arousal in male subjects (Malamuth & Donnerstein, 1984). In fact, they were often more aroused by violent sexually explicit scenes (e.g., of naked women bound and appearing distressed) than they were by scenes of women enjoying sex (Heilbrun & Seif, 1988; Malamuth, 1981). Men with lower IQs and those with rape-prone attitudes or high levels of aggressiveness are especially likely to be aroused by violent sexually explicit scenes (Bogaert et al., 1999; Davis & Bauserman, 1993; Linz, 1989).

Figure 18–4 With the bare-breasted *Spirit of Justice* in back of him, former U.S. Attorney General Edwin Meese accepts the Report of the 1986 Commission on Pornography. What is erotica to some people is pornography to others.

After watching violent sexually explicit films, many of the male subjects became less sympathetic toward female rape victims, showed greater belief in rape myths (viewing rape victims as more responsible for their assaults), displayed increased hostility to women in the lab, and were more likely to indicate that they would commit rape themselves if they were certain that they would not get caught (see Linz, 1989, or Malamuth & Donnerstein, 1984, or Donnerstein et al., 1987, for reviews). Donnerstein (1982) was startled to find that by the last day of looking at sexually explicit films showing violence toward women, many men found the material "less debasing and degrading of women, more humorous, more enjoyable, and claimed a greater willingness to see this type of film again." Similar results were found when men looked at *degrading sexually explicit material,* (i.e., nonviolent material showing women as sex objects where there is a clearly unequal balance of power) (Zillmann & Bryant, 1982). However, not all studies have found that violent pornography causes men to have antifemale thoughts or attitudes. While individual differences are important (e.g., IQ, attitudes about aggression), we are still not certain about the precise conditions that cause some men to react in such a manner (see Bogaert et al, 1999; Davies, 1997; Davis & Bauserman, 1993; Fisher & Grenier, 1994).

Unlike many men, women are not aroused by watching realistic rape scenes. However, childhood exposure to sexually explicit material can result in some women having attitudes more supportive of sexual violence against women (Corne et al., 1992).

Being aroused by fantasies of rape is not the same as actually committing a rape. None of the previous studies proved that looking at violent pornography really causes sex crimes to be committed (as far as we know, none of the volunteer subjects committed a rape after leaving the lab). To explore whether there really is a causal relationship between violent pornography and sex crimes, Edwin Meese, then attorney general of the United States, appointed an 11-member commission on pornography in 1985. They released their conclusions in the spring of 1986, less than a year after they were formed (see Figure 18–4). Their conclusion: A "causal relationship" exists between sexually violent pornography and violence toward women. They stated that these materials help foster the myth that women enjoy being raped and that "sexually explicit materials featuring violence [are] on the whole harmful to society." In contrast to the recommendations of the 1970 commission, they advocated stronger government enforcement of present obscenity laws and additional laws that would result in greater restrictions of sexually explicit material.

The 1986 commission funded no original research, but instead relied heavily on the findings of previously conducted laboratory experiments. However, the scientists who conducted that research accused the commission of drawing conclusions and making legal recommendations that did not follow from their data (see Linz et al., 1987). Even some of the commission members were critical of the report. Ellen Levine, editor of *Woman's Day* magazine, and Judith Becker, a clinical psychologist from New York State Psychiatric Institute, issued a formal statement of dissent. They both said that while they found pornography objectionable and offensive to women, the panel's report was flawed and rushed. Others questioned the objectivity of some of the commission's members, six of whom had previously called for greater government enforcement against pornographic materials. The commission's chairman, for example, was a U.S. attorney from Virginia who had made his reputation by prosecuting owners of adult bookstores. In summary, it would appear that some of the panelists were unable to distinguish between their own personal views and objective research.

Behavioral scientists conducting work in this area were brought together in their own conference in 1986. They agreed with the 1970 commission's conclusion that exposure to nudity alone has no detrimental effects on adult behavior (see Linz et al., 1987). They suggested that the real focus of concern should be depictions of violence toward women, regardless of whether or not it was in a sexually explicit context. Donnerstein, for example, was quoted as saying, "These conclusions [by the 1986 commission] seem bizarre to me. It is the violence more than the sex—and negative messages about human relationships—that are the problem. And these messages are everywhere" (*New York Times,* May 17, 1986, p. A6). Subsequent studies showed that it is violence-toward-women themes, more than sexual explicitness, that result in potentially harmful attitude and behavioral changes (Linz et al., 1987).

This type of potentially harmful material (violence toward women without sexual explicitness) is precisely the type of material that is common in R-rated movies and on TV today. Overall, 1 out of 8 Hollywood films shows a rape scene (National Coalition on Television Violence, 1990). In fact, rape is much more common in R-rated movies and TV shows than in X-rated movies or magazines like *Playboy* (Palys, 1986; Scott, 1986). Studies have consistently found, for example, that viewing nonexplicit movies showing violence toward women results in many men becoming less sensitive toward rape victims (Linz, 1989). So what is the conclusion of the leading behavioral scientists in the field?

> **The most clear and present danger . . . is all violent material in our society, whether sexually explicit or not, that promotes violence against women"** (Donnerstein & Linz, 1986)

In order to eliminate possible detrimental effects to society, we would have to suppress all materials showing violence toward women, not just sexually explicit material with violent themes. Scientists suggest that rather than imposing stricter laws, it might be easier to educate the public about the effects of viewing violence so that they can make better choices about which programs, movies, and books they choose to expose themselves and their children to.

SEXUALLY EXPLICIT MATERIAL INVOLVING CHILDREN

"Directly after high school I worked at a photo developing store. One day while sorting some pictures I noticed that the first six shots were of boys that looked to be no older than 10 having fellatio and sodomy with each other. The last eight pictures introduced an older man of about 40 years old. I, of course, showed my manager and he called the police. When the man's wife came to pick up the pictures she was arrested. She was charged with passing pornographic material through our store. Her husband was given a heavier sentence—20 years. He was a prestigious teacher at an uptown school and a career pedophile. In that year alone he had molested 12 boys." (from the author's files)

"I can watch as much crime and violence as I like as long as they keep their clothes on."

Herman® is reprinted with permission of LaughingStock Licensing Inc., Ottawa, Canada. All rights reserved.

The President's Commission of 1970 found no evidence that pornography was harmful to adults and suggested the repeal of laws prohibiting the sale and distribution of sexually explicit material. But what about photographs or films that show children nude or having sex with an adult or another child? Could looking at child pornography cause someone to molest children, or does this type of pornography provide an outlet for those who might otherwise abuse children? We cannot answer this, because for obvious ethical reasons there has been very little research in this area (Jarvie, 1992). Nevertheless, this is one type of pornography that nearly everyone feels should be banned. How can we do this and still protect First Amendment rights?

One way is to ask whether the "stars" of kiddie porn are capable of giving informed consent. Many are runaways who are coerced into participating by financial or other reasons. Some participants are so young that they could not possibly have any idea of what they are doing. They are obviously being exploited by adults (sometimes by their own parents or guardians). Children who are used in this manner generally grow up to feel like objects rather than people and often suffer a variety of emotional and sexual problems (Burgess et al., 1984). The U.S. Supreme Court ruled unanimously in 1982 (*New York v. Ferber*) that publishers and distributors of child pornography could be prosecuted for child abuse without requiring the prosecuters to prove that the material was obscene, thus avoiding arguments about First Amendment rights. The passage of the Protection of Children Against Sexual Exploitation Act in 1977, the Child Protection Act in 1984, and the Child Protection and Obscenity Enforcement Act in 1988 made it a federal crime to ship or receive, in interstate or foreign commerce or by mail, pictures of nude children or children (defined as any person under the age of 18) engaged in sexual acts. The maximum punishment for the first offense is 10 years in jail and a fine of $100,000 (except for participating parents and guardians, who can be sentenced to 20 years to life in prison). As a result of the legislation, prosecutions of child pornography increased more than 250 percent in the first few years after the Child Protection Act was passed. Adults who participate in child pornography in any capacity can be prosecuted. In 1990, the Supreme Court upheld an Ohio law that made it a crime even to possess pornography showing children under the age of 18. By the mid-1990s, over 15 percent of material downloaded from commercial bulletin boards was pedophilic material (Rimm, 1995). To counter this, the FBI has begun sting operations to trap on-line pedophiles.

This is presently the only type of sexually explicit material that is legally banned. The U.S. Customs Service has established a hotline for the National Center for Missing and Exploited Children to receive tips about pornography: 1-800-843-5678.

Even with this material, however, there is a question of where we should draw the line. Today, some bookstores and photography/art galleries sell photographs of nude children, resulting in considerable controversy as to whether this is art or pornography (Jones, 1998). What is child pornography? Authorities in programs for sex offenders have noted that there are men who become sexually aroused by watching diaper advertisements on TV. Should we ban all pictures of naked or partially clothed babies and children?

PERSONAL REFLECTIONS

Are you ever physically aroused by looking at sexually explicit photos or movies? What is your emotional reaction to this material and any arousal it causes? Why? Have you ever learned anything from photos of naked persons or by watching R-rated or X-rated sex scenes? If you had the power to do it, would you ban this material or allow unrestricted distribution to adults? Why?

COMPLETE LEGALIZATION OR CENSORSHIP?

What should we do about sexually explicit material? Should we remove all restrictions to the sale and distribution of hard-core material to adults (i.e., make it completely legal), or should we attempt to ban all such material? There are good arguments for both cases.

The President's Commission of 1970, you recall, found evidence that sexually explicit material served as an outlet to people with sexually criminal tendencies and might actually reduce sex crimes. It is probably difficult for you to believe that material you find offensive and repugnant may actually do some good, but that is because you are normal and have no deviant tendencies. Therapist John Money of Johns Hopkins University has noted that patients in clinics for sex offenders often say that they use pornography to fantasize about abnormal sexual activity so that they will not have to act out their desires in real life. In fact, most sex therapists still believe that socially unacceptable sexual behaviors often result from attempts to severely repress sexuality. Father Bruce Ritter, founder of Covenant House, is a possible example of this. A member of Meese's commission and an outspoken opponent of both pornography and sex for the purpose of pleasure, even within a marriage ("It wastes the seed," he said), Father Ritter resigned from Covenant House after being accused of sexual molestation by several male residents of the shelter for runaway children.

A national survey found that over half of all Americans feel that there is too much sexually explicit material in their neighborhood stores (Janus & Janus, 1993), and there have been numerous attempts by citizens, school boards, and local governments to ban

WHOAA... HOLD ON A SECOND!...

WHAT IF SOMEDAY SOMEBODY WANTS TO BURN A FLAG...OR..OR TAKE HOMO-EROTIC PICTURES OR SING EXPLICIT RAP LYRICS OR...

Jim Meddick; reprinted by permission of Newspaper Enterprise Association, Inc.

sexually oriented materials that they consider offensive. The producers or distributors of the materials, along with others, invariably protest on the grounds of First Amendment rights, and many cases have reached the U.S. Supreme Court. The First Amendment of our Constitution guarantees, among other things, that Congress "shall make no law . . . abridging the freedom of speech, or of the press." I suspect that the Founding Fathers never intended this to apply to explicit pictures of couples having anal sex, but the problem is deciding where to draw the line. Guess which of the following magazines and books have been targets of censorship by some communities in recent years:

The American Heritage Dictionary
The Bible
Brave New World
The Catcher in the Rye
Cinderella
Club magazine
The Diary of Anne Frank
Gorillas in the Mist
The Grapes of Wrath
Huckleberry Finn
Hustler magazine
Macbeth
Penthouse magazine
Playboy magazine
Romeo and Juliet
Sports Illustrated (swimsuit issues)
Stories about dinosaurs
The Wizard of Oz

If you guessed all of them, you were correct. Yes, there are some people who believe that parts of the Bible are too explicit for others to read. *The American Heritage Dictionary* was banned in some places because it included "bad words." High school teachers in Erie, Pennsylvania, blacked out passages in *Gorillas in the Mist* (by naturalist Dian Fossey) describing the mating habits of apes. Not all of these materials were banned because they were sexually explicit, however. *Cinderella,* for example, was banned from public schools in a Tennessee community in 1986 because it mentioned witchcraft, and *Macbeth* was banned by the same community because it mentioned magic (this ban was overturned by a decision of the U.S. Supreme Court). Attempts to censor or ban sexually explicit material continue today. The record album *As Nasty as They Wanna B* by the rap group 2 Live Crew became the first (in 1990) to be ruled obscene in federal court. In July 1990, the curator of Cincinnati's Contemporary Art Center was ordered to go to trial on obscenity charges for putting on an exhibit of homoerotic photos by photographer Robert Mapplethorpe.

With regard to sexually explicit material, the problem the Supreme Court has had to deal with (in cases appealed on First Amendment rights) is trying to distinguish between erotica and pornography. **Erotica** (from the Greek word *erotikos,* meaning "love poem") is any literature or art with a sexual theme, while **pornography** (from the Greek words *porne,* which means "prostitute," and graphos, meaning "depicting or writing about") is literature or art with a sexual theme that is designed to cause arousal. Many people use the terms *pornography* and *obscenity* interchangeably, while others feel that obscenity is a more limited term (see Penrod & Linz, 1984, for a history of this subject). The key, therefore, is how we define *obscene.* What is erotica to one person is pornography to another. The Venus de Milo may be regarded as a great work of art by most people (erotica), but to some it is just a statue of a nude woman (obscene and pornographic). Why are old paintings of nude persons or nude couples making love generally considered art, but modern photos of the same thing often considered pornographic? (See

erotica Any literature or art that has a sexual theme. This is a morally neutral term.

pornography Literature or art with a sexual theme that is designed to cause arousal and excitement and is considered to be obscene.

Figure 18–5 Why are many paintings with sexually explicit themes considered great art when modern photos with the same theme are often regarded to be pornographic? (Boucher's *Hercules and Omphale*, 1730s)

Figure 18–5.) Why are drawings of couples having sex considered educational if they appear in sexuality textbooks (such as those in Chapter 13 in this book), but pornographic if the same thing is found in magazines (see King & Lococo, 1990)?

After grappling with this issue for many years, the Supreme Court finally came up with a three-part definition of **obscenity** in 1973 (*Miller v. California*). Material was considered obscene if (1) by contemporary community standards it depicts patently offensive sexual conduct; (2) it lacks "serious literary, artistic, political, or scientific value"; and (3) it appeals to prurient interest (lustful craving) in sex.

Even the Supreme Court justices recognized problems with this definition, however. For example, in the following year (*Jenkins v. Georgia*, 1974) the Court ruled that local communities do not have "unbridled discretion" to decide what is obscene (a Georgia community had decided that the Hollywood movie *Carnal Knowledge* was obscene). On the other hand, the Court

obscenity In legal terminology, the classification of material that by contemporary community standards depicts patently offensive sexual conduct, lacks serious value, and appeals to prurient interests.

ruled in 2000 that cities and states could ban nude dancing (strip clubs) if they felt the clubs violated community standards.

Who determines what is patently offensive or which art or literature lacks serious value? Former Supreme Court Justice Potter Stewart admitted that he could not come up with a good definition of hard-core pornography, but said, "I know it when I see it" (*Jacobelis v. Ohio,* 1965). We all see things differently, however. You know what you find to be obscene, but do you want someone else to make that decision for you?

The Internet, with its easy accessibility to porn sites, bulletin boards, and chat rooms, has posed new problems for parents and others attempting to regulate sexually explicit material. One-fourth of teens have visited Internet porn sites, usually on their home computer (Leland, 1999b). In 1996, Congress passed the Communications Decency Act, which made it a crime to transmit sexually explicit images through the Internet. In a unanimous decision, the U.S. Supreme Court struck this down in 1997 *(Reno v. ACLU),* giving the Internet full protection under the First Amendment. So what are parents to do? A variety of Internet-blocking software (e.g., Cyber Patrol, Cyber sitter, Net Nanny, Net Shepherd, SurfWatch) are available that parents can use to block Web sites (Portelli & Meade, 1998). The Court concluded that this software is a "reasonably effective method by which parents can prevent their children from accessing material which the parents believe is inappropriate."

Even if it should eventually be proven that explicit hard-core material reduces sex crimes, it nevertheless is true that many people find it highly offensive and degrading. Some feminists oppose it on the grounds that it causes men to view women as sex objects and leads to sex discrimination (e.g., Dworkin, 1989). Although there are more sexually explicit videos today than in the past that show men and women in egalitarian sex roles (Davis & Bauserman, 1993; Schlosser, 1997), there are still many that do, in fact, emphasize the sexual desires and prowess of men while portraying women as sexually willing and available. Catherine MacKinnon (1993) argues that pornography perpetuates sexual inequality and that the antidiscrimination provisions of the Fourteenth Amendment of the Constitution should take precedence over the First Amendment. However, other feminists worry that attempts to ban sexually explicit material on grounds of discrimination reinforce a double standard. "It reasserts that women are sexually different from men and in need of special protection. Yet special protection inadvertently reinforces the ways in which women are legally and socially said to be different from men" (Vance, 1988; see also A. M. Smith, 1993).

We are one of the few countries in the world whose people have freedom of expression. Most people are offended by at least some of the sexually explicit material that is published or filmed today, but many worry that allowing others to have the power to ban certain materials might eventually infringe on their own presently enjoyed freedom of expression (after all, there are those who would ban passages in the Bible). What do you think should be done?

LAWS AGAINST FORNICATION, ADULTERY, AND SODOMY

What do you do behind closed and locked doors in your own home or apartment? You're right, it is none of my business. Is it anyone else's business? Well, you might be surprised to find out that many states have laws prohibiting certain sexual acts, even if done by consenting adults (including married couples) in private.

Seventeen states and the District of Columbia have laws that make *fornication* and/or *cohabitation* a crime. The maximum penalty is generally 3 to 6 months in jail and/or a fine. *Adultery,* which is a crime in 26 states, has historically been considered a more serious offense because it violates the sanctity of the family. Also, past attitudes held that women were property belonging to their husbands (and thus adultery was a violation of property rights). In *Griswold v. Connecticut* (the 1965 Supreme Court decision overruling Connecticut's ban on the sale of contraceptives to married persons), the justices held that the decision "in no way interferes with a State's proper regulation of sexual promiscuity or misconduct." Adultery is considered to be a very serious crime in many other countries (see Box 18–B). In Islamic countries, for example, women who commit adultery are often killed by their husbands or relatives for bringing shame to the family ("honor killings"), usually with little or no legal punishment (Jehl, 1999).

Are people in the United States ever prosecuted under these laws? Yes; in states that have laws forbidding adultery, for example, it is not uncommon for one member of a quarreling married couple to press charges against the other to gain an advantage during the settlement, or perhaps just for revenge (Sachs, 1990). In 1997, a North Carolina woman successfully sued her husband's lover for $1 million for breaking up their marriage. You may recall that in the same year the military charged Lt. Kelly Flinn, the first female B-52 pilot, with adultery (Vistica & Thomas, 1997). She subsequently resigned. Some states have begun prosecuting teenagers for fornication in order to prevent teen pregnancy. In Idaho, for example, several teens

WAIT... I THINK WE'D BETTER HAVE OUR LAWYER PRESENT.

© Tribune Media Services, Inc. All rights reserved. Reprinted with permission.

have been given 3 years' probation and community service for getting pregnant or getting someone pregnant. In 1998, a Louisiana woman was sentenced to 5 years' probation and fined $1,500 for selling adult sexual aids in her novelty shop, a violation of the state's Promotion of Obscene Devices Law.

More recently, there has been much attention devoted to **sodomy laws,** which ban specific behaviors between consenting adults. At one time, nearly all the states had laws that forbid oral or anal sex, which are often referred to as "crimes against nature" (see Eskridge, 1999). Today, 18 states (almost all of them in the South) still have sodomy laws. In Louisiana, for example, women are booked with prostitution, a misdemeanor, if they offered sexual intercourse for cash, but are booked with "unnatural carnal copulation" (sodomy), a felony that can result in 5 years in jail, if they offered oral sex for money. These laws reflect the early Judeo-Christian attitude that the only natural sexual act is heterosexual intercourse because it is the only sexual behavior that can result in reproduction (see Eskridge, 1999, for a history of these laws).

In five states (Arkansas, Kansas, Missouri, Oklahoma, and Texas), the sodomy laws are aimed specifically at homosexuals, but in 13 others the laws do not distinguish between heterosexual and homosexual couples. The existence of sodomy laws means, of course, that millions of married American couples are committing crimes for which they could potentially be put in jail (up to 5 years or more in 11 states). In the words of New Orleans lawyer John Rawls, who filed a lawsuit against Louisiana's law, "If oral sex were enforced as a 5-year felony, everyone from the president to the speaker of the house to your next-door neighbor would have to go to prison" (Bell, 1998). However, when the laws are enforced, which isn't too often, they are generally enforced only

sodomy laws Laws that prohibit oral and/or anal sex.

TABLE 18–1

LAWS REGULATING ORAL OR ANAL SEX BETWEEN CONSENTING ADULTS

State	Punishable Offense	Maximum Penalty
Alabama	Oral or anal sex with someone other than your spouse	1 year
Arizona	"Infamous crime against nature"	30 days and/or $500
Arkansas	Oral or anal sex with anyone of the same sex	1 year and/or $1000
Florida	"Unnatural and lascivious act"	60 days and/or $500
Idaho	"Infamous crime against nature"	Life (5 years minimum)
Kansas	Oral or anal sex with anyone of the same sex	6 months and/or $1000
Louisiana	"Unnatural carnal copulation"	5 years and/or $2000
Massachusetts	Sodomy and buggery	—
Michigan	Abominable and detestable crime against nature	15 years or $2500
Minnesota	Oral or anal sex	1 year and/or $3000
Mississippi	Detestable and abominable crime against nature	10 years
Missouri	Oral or anal sex with anyone of the same sex	1 year and $1000
North Carolina	Crime against nature	10 years
Oklahoma	Detestable and abominable crime against nature with anyone of the same sex	10 years
South Carolina	Abominable crime of buggery	5 years and/or $500
Texas	Oral or anal sex with anyone of the same sex	$200
Utah	Oral or anal sex with anyone other than your spouse	6 months or $299
Virginia	Oral or anal sex	20 years

Source: National Gay and Lesbian Task Force (2000).

against homosexuals. Homosexuals regard these laws as "legalized fag bashing" and have legally challenged a number of them.

Does the U.S. Constitution guarantee us the right to privacy? Apparently not. A Virginia law that forbids oral and anal sex between either hetero- or homosexual individuals was upheld by both a state and federal court in 1975. The U.S. Supreme Court refused to grant a hearing on the case (*Doe v. Commonwealth's Attorney*) in 1976 and thus upheld the right of states to regulate the private activity of its citizens. Basically, the ruling was that states have the right to regulate sexual behaviors just as they have the right to require you to use seat belts or anything else if it is "for your own good."

The case of a Georgia man focused national attention on the legality of sodomy laws. Michael Hardwick was arrested for having oral sex with another man in the privacy of his own bedroom (the arresting officer had come to the house about a traffic violation and was let in by another person). Hardwick, who could have served up to 20 years for this crime, sued the state of Georgia. The Supreme Court upheld the Georgia law by a 5–4 vote in June 1986 (*Bowers v. Hardwick*). Writing for the majority, Justice Byron White stated: "The proposition that any kind of private sexual conduct between consenting adults is constitutionally insulated from state proscription is unsupportable." In a dissenting opinion, Justice Harry Blackmun said: "What the court really has refused to recognize is the fundamental interest all individuals have in controlling the nature of their intimate associations." Justice Lewis Powell, Jr., later said that he regarded his vote with the majority position to have been a mistake (see Swisher & Cook, 1996). In 1997, the Georgia attorney general who prosecuted Hardwick admitted in court that he had had an adulterous affair (also a crime in Georgia). In 1998, the Georgia supreme court finally overturned the state's sodomy law after reviewing a case in which a man was serving a 5-year term for having consensual oral sex with a woman.

In the ruling, the Court avoided the larger issue of whether sodomy laws could be used to prosecute heterosexuals; the ruling was limited to "consensual homosexual sodomy." However, there was nothing in the language to cast doubt on the constitutionality of laws that forbid oral or anal sex between married heterosexual individuals. In 1992, Kentucky's supreme court struck down that state's sodomy law, which was aimed specifically at homosexuals, stating, "We need not sympathize, agree with, or even understand the sexual preference of homosexuals in order to recognize their right to equal treatment before the bar of criminal justice." Courts in Tennessee and Montana struck down those states' same-sex sodomy laws in 1996, and Maryland followed in 1998.

Box 18–B CROSS-CULTURAL PERSPECTIVES

Illegal Sex around the World

In the last part of this chapter you learned that many states prohibit and punish sexual behaviors such as fornication, cohabitation, adultery, and oral or anal sex. However, we are not the only country in which this is true. In fact, most countries make it illegal for consenting adults to engage in some forms of sex. The United States is more restrictive than some countries and more permissive than others. Here is a list of some of the countries around the world and the sexual activities that they consider illegal.

	Fornication	Cohabitation	Adultery	All Anal Sex	All Oral Sex	Homosexual Oral or Anal Sex
Mexico	—	—	√	—	—	√
Brazil	—	—	√	—	—	—
Argentina	—	—	√	—	—	—
Chile	—	—	√	—	—	√
England	—	—	—	—	—	—
France	—	—	—	—	—	—
Germany	—	—	—	—	—	—
Sweden	—	—	—	—	—	—
Italy	—	—	—	—	—	—
Russia	—	—	√	—	—	—
China	√	√	√	√	√	—
Japan	—	—	—	—	—	—
India	—	—	√	√	—	√
Australia	—	—	√	—	√	√
Saudi Arabia	√	√	√	√	√	
Iran	√	√	√	√	√	
Egypt	√	√	√	√	√	
Zaire	—	—	—	√	√	
Kenya	—	—	√	√	√	
South Africa	—	—	√	√	√	

Interestingly, the American Law Institute's Model Penal Code recommended as far back as 1962 that sexual behaviors between consenting adults (excluding prostitution) be decriminalized. Legislators tend to view *decriminalization* as a safer political route to take than legalization. They worry that any attempt to legalize sexual behaviors will be interpreted by voters as condoning them. Decriminalization simply means either that the acts will no longer be defined as criminal or that they will no longer be subject to penalties, and thus it is morally neutral.

Several states have followed the American Law Institute's recommendations and have decriminalized sexual acts between consenting adults. However, legislators in some states are still proposing restrictive laws. A bill proposed in the state of Washington in 1990, for example, would have made it a prosecutable offense (90 days in jail and a $5,000 fine) for anyone under the age of 18 to engage in necking or petting. Which approach do you believe is more correct?

PERSONAL REFLECTIONS

Do you believe that a couple should have the right to decide for themselves which sexual behaviors they engage in (assuming, of course, that it is done with mutual consent and does not cause physical or emotional harm to either person)? Or should a state serve as a higher moral authority and regulate the private consensual sexual activities of its citizens?

If you answered "no" to the second question, do you think that you or any other individual should pass judgment on others for their private consensual sexual behaviors?

Key Terms

adultery   473
B-girls   460
brothel prostitute   460
call girls   461
Comstock law   464
degrading sexually explicit
      material   468

erotica   471
fornication   459
gigolos   461
hustlers   461
johns   463
nonviolent sexually explicit
      material   466

obscenity   472
pornography   471
prostitution   460
sodomy laws   473
streetwalkers   460
violent sexually explicit
      material   468

Suggested Readings

Baxter, M. (1990, May 5). Flesh and blood. *New Scientist.* A short
      article about studies of the effects of violent pornography.
Bullough, V., and Bullough, B. (1988). *Women and prostitution: A
      social history.* Buffalo, NY: Prometheus Books. A sociological,
      historical, and cross-cultural examination. Very comprehensive.
Cooper, A., Boies, S., Maheu., M., and Greenfield, D. (2000).
      Sexuality and the Internet: The next sexual revolution. In L. T.
      Szuchman and F. Muscarella (Eds.), *Psychological perspectives on
      human sexuality* (pp. 519–545). New York: John Wiley.
      Addresses the question of whether the Internet will be the start
      of the new sexual revolution.
Donnerstein, E. J., and Linz, D. G. (1986, December). The ques-
      tion of pornography. *Psychology Today.* Authors of pornography
      research challenge the conclusions of the attorney general's
      commission and say that we should be more concerned with vi-
      olence in the media.
Heins, M. (1993). *Sex, sin, and blasphemy : A guide to America's cen-
      sorship wars.* New York: New Press. Takes the view that sexually

explicit material should be protected as a First Amendment
      right (see MacKinnon for an alternative viewpoint).
Joseph, C. (1995). Scarlet wounding: Issues of child prostitution.
      Journal of Psychohistory, 23, 2–17. Outstanding article on the
      history and prevalence of child prostitution.
MacKinnon, C. (1993). *Only words.* Cambridge, MA: Harvard
      University Press. Takes the view that pornography should be
      banned as discriminatory against women under the Fourteenth
      Amendment (see Heins for an alternative viewpoint).
Report of the Commission on Obscenity and Pornography. (1970).
      New York: Bantam Books. A paperback edition including the
      results and conclusions of the 1970 commission.
Tartaglione, R. (1996). Kids online: What parents can do to pro-
      tect their children from cyberspace. *SIECUS Report,* October/
      November.

Study Guide

INTERACTIVE REVIEW

In addition to laws that protect children and nonconsenting adults from sexual abuse, many states also have laws that attempt to regulate the sexual behaviors of consenting adults. Prostitution is illegal in all parts of the United States except for a few counties in (1) _____. In a recent survey, (2) _____ percent of the male re-spondents indicated that they had paid for sex on at least one occasion. Female prostitutes can be divided into three types according to status: (3) _____, who solicit in public; brothel prostitutes and (4) _____; and (5) _____, who generally work out of their own apartments. Male prostitutes who cater to homosexuals are called (6) _____. The primary reason most individuals engage in prostitution is (7) _____. Most prostitutes were sexually or physically abused as children and were loners. Most customers are white, (8) _____, and (9) _____. Opponents of prostitution argue that it spreads sexually transmitted diseases and is often as-sociated with other crimes. Proponents of legalization argue that licensing and required health checks would reduce both STDs (including HIV infection) and the influence of organized crime.

The sale of sexually explicit material is a multi-billion-dollar-a-year business. This could not have happened, of course, if there were not a large demand for such material. According to surveys, about (10) _____ of all Americans have seen an X-rated movie or video in the past year. One-third of all use of the Internet is to porn sites.

The President's Commission of 1970 and subsequent researchers have generally concluded that exposure to nonviolent sexually explicit material has (11) _____ effect on individuals. Subsequent research has shown that many men are aroused by sexually explicit material depicting violence toward women. Exposure to sexually explicit material with violent themes often results in men becoming (12) _____ toward rape victims, having greater belief in (13) _____, displaying (14) _____ to women, and being more likely to say that they would (15) _____. However, behavioral scientists have concluded that it is the (16) _____ in this material, not the (17) _____, that is potentially harmful.

Most people find some types of sexually explicit material offensive, but attempts to censor or ban this material raise questions about First Amendment rights. What is (18) _____ to one person is pornography to another, and who is to decide where to draw the line? The one exception is sexually explicit material involving (19) _____, for which persons can be prosecuted on the basis of abuse.

Several states have sodomy laws that prohibit (20) _____ and/or (21) _____ sex between consenting adults. Many people believe that they should have the right to decide for themselves what to do in privacy, but the Supreme Court has upheld the constitutionality of these laws.

Additional topics on the legality of sexual behavior are included in Chapters 7 (see the section on surrogate mothers), 11, and 17.

SELF-TEST

A. TRUE OR FALSE

T ☐ F ☐ 22. Most people who become prostitutes do so because of abnormal sexual needs.

T ☐ F ☐ 23. In the 1940s, Kinsey found that a majority of white males had had sex with a prostitute.

T ☐ F ☐ 24. When exposed to sexually explicit material, most people show an increase in sexual behavior.

T ☐ F ☐ 25. The 1970 President's Commission concluded that there was no significant link between exposure of adults to sexually explicit materials and sex crimes.

T ☐ F ☐ 26. In many states, a married couple caught having oral sex in the privacy of their own home can be sent to prison.

T ☐ F ☐ 27. Prostitution is the only sexual offense for which more women than men are prosecuted.

T ☐ F ☐ 28. Erotica and pornography are synonyms, and are really the same thing.

T ☐ F ☐ 29. When Denmark legalized the sale of hard-core pornographic material to adults, there was a marked decrease in sex crimes afterward.

T ☐ F ☐ 30. People are most aroused by looking at sexually explicit material showing behaviors they regard as normal.

T ☐ F ☐ 31. Adultery is a crime in nearly half of the 50 states.

T ☐ F ☐ 32. HIV infection is uncommon among prostitutes, probably because most have their customers use condoms.

T ☐ F ☐ 33. Nearly all junior high school boys and girls have looked at a sexually explicit magazine.

T ☐ F ☐ 34. A majority of both men and women are aroused by sexually explicit material.

T ☐ F ☐ 35. There is substantial evidence that sex offenders have had more exposure to sexually explicit material than have nonoffenders.

T ☐ F ☐ 36. Exposure to violent sexually explicit material often results in men adopting attitudes that are more supportive of sexual violence against women.

T ☐ F ☐ 37. There is more violence against women shown in X-rated movies than in R-rated movies.

T ☐ F ☐ 38. It is a crime to possess sexually explicit material (e.g., magazines, videos, photos) showing children.

T ☐ F ☐ 39. St. Augustine and St. Thomas Aquinas believed prostitution was necessary.

B. MATCHING

_____ 40. B-girl

_____ 41. brothel prostitute

_____ 42. call girl

_____ 43. gigolo

_____ 44. hustler

_____ 45. john

_____ 46. not a prostitute

_____ 47. pimp

_____ 48. streetwalker

a. Susan has sex for money at a legalized house in Nevada.

b. Joan has sex with her boss in the hope that it will get her a promotion.

c. Hank works out of an escort service and is paid by older women to have sex.

d. Stephanie works out of her own apartment, and her clients must make an appointment to have sex with her.

e. David takes 75 percent of the money earned by six women who do tricks on the west side of town.

f. Joe pays women to give him oral-genital sex.

g. Sam accepts money from men on the street who want to have sex with him.

h. Sally solicits for sex in a downtown bar.

i. Bonnie solicits men in public.

C. FILL IN THE BLANKS

49. The feature that distinguishes a prostitute from other women who engage in illicit sexual intercourse is the _____ with which she offers herself to men for hire.

50. Sexual intercourse between a man and a woman who are not married is called _____.

51. A hustler is on the same status level as a female _____.

52. Pornography is distinguished from erotica in that it is literature or art with a sexual theme that is considered to be _____.

53. Recent evidence suggests that it is exposure to _____, more than just sexual explicitness, that results in potentially harmful attitude and behavioral changes.

54. In *Miller v. California,* 1973, the Supreme Court ruled that material was obscene if (a) _____, (b) _____, and (c) _____.

55. The _____, passed in 1873, made the mailing of material considered to be obscene a felony.

56. Probably the foremost reason many people use sexually explicit material is that _____.

57. With regard to pornography, men and women rate themes in which there is _____ as the most degrading.

Glossary

abortion   Termination of pregnancy. Depending on how far the pregnancy has advanced, this can be done by taking a pill (RU 486); scraping the uterine lining (dilation and curettage); removing the uterine lining by suction (dilation and evacuation); or inducing labor (by injecting hypertonic saline or prostaglandins). (Ch. 6)

acquaintance rape   A rape committed by someone who is known by the victim. (Ch. 17)

adolescence (ad″ ′l es′ ′ns)   The time of life between puberty and adulthood. (Ch. 12)

adoption   Taking a child into one's family by legal process and raising the child as one's own. (Ch. 6, 7)

adrenal (ad- re′ nal) **glands**   Endocrine glands located near the kidneys that secrete steroid hormones and small amounts of gonadal hormones. (Ch. 3)

adrenarche (ad″ ren-ar′ke)   The maturation of the adrenal glands, usually between the ages of 6 and 8. (Ch. 12)

adrenogenital (ah-dre″ no-jen′ y-tal) **syndrome**   A condition in girls in which the adrenal glands excrete too much testosterone during fetal development, causing masculinization. This includes enlargement of the clitoris and labia, so that at birth the genitals are sometimes mistaken for those of a boy. Also called *congenital adrenal hyperplasia*. (Ch. 10)

adultery   Sexual intercourse with someone other than one's husband or wife. (Ch. 12, 18)

afterbirth   The expulsion of the placenta from the uterus after a baby is born. (Ch. 7)

agape (ah′ gah pā″)   A type of romantic love that puts the interest of the loved person ahead of one's own, even if it means great sacrifice. (Ch. 14)

aggressive pedophile   A pedophile who is sexually aroused by inflicting physical injury on victims. (Ch. 17)

AIDS (acquired immunodeficiency syndrome)   An often fatal disease caused by a virus (HIV) that destroys the immune system. It is spread by intimate sexual activity (the exchange of bodily fluids) or contaminated blood. (Ch. 5)

AIDS-related complex (ARC)   See **symptomatic HIV infection.**

amebiasis (am″ e-bi′ ah-sis)   Dysentery caused by infestation of amoebae, one-celled organisms. (Ch. 5)

amenorrhea (ah-men″ o-re′ ah)   The absence of menstruation. (Ch. 3)

amniocentesis (am″ ne-o-sen-te′ sis)   A technique for detecting fetal problems, involving collection of amniotic fluid after the 14th week of pregnancy. (Ch. 7)

amnion (am′ ne-on)   A thick-skinned sac filled with water that surrounds the fetus. (Ch. 7)

ampulla (am-pul′ lah)   The expanded end of the vas deferens where sperm are stored prior to ejaculation. (Ch. 2)

anabolic (an″ ah-bol′ ik) **steroids**   Synthetic steroid hormones that combine the growth (anabolic) effects of adrenal steroids with the masculinizing effects of androgenic steroids. (Ch. 3)

anal intercourse   Insertion of the penis into the anus and rectum of a sexual partner. (Ch. 13)

anaphrodisiacs (an″ af-ro-dĭz′ e-ak)   Substances that suppress sexual functioning. (Ch. 4)

androgen insensitivity syndrome   A condition in which the testicles secrete normal amounts of testosterone during male embryonic development, but the tissues do not respond to it. As a result, a clitoris, labia, and a short vagina develop, but the internal female structures do not develop because the testicles still secrete Mullerian duct–inhibitory substances. (Ch. 10)

androgens (an′ dro-jens)   Hormones that possess masculinizing properties. (Ch. 2)

androgyny (an-droj′ ĭ-ne)   The ability of an individual to display a variety of personality characteristics, both masculine and feminine, depending on whether a trait or behavior is appropriate in a given situation. It is often viewed as a positive characteristic that gives an individual greater adaptability. (Ch. 10)

anger rapists   Rapists who commit their attacks out of hostility or anger directed at their victims or at women in general. (Ch. 17)

anoxia (ah-nok′ se-ah)   An inability to get enough oxygen to the brain. (Ch. 7)

anxious-ambivalent   A style of attachment in which individuals have negative attitudes about themselves and are therefore insecure in their relationships. (Ch. 14)

aphrodisiacs (af″ ro-dĭz′ e-ak)   Substances that enhance sexual desire or performance. (Ch. 4)

areola (ah-re′ o-lah)   The darkened ring surrounding the nipple of a breast. (Ch. 2)

artificial insemination   A method of treating infertility caused by a low sperm count in men. Sperm are collected during several ejaculations and then inserted into the partner's vagina at the time of ovulation. (Ch. 7)

ascetic (ah set′ ik) **philosophy**   A philosophy that originated among the ancient Greeks. It emphasizes that virtue comes from wisdom and that these qualities can be achieved only by avoiding strong passions. (Ch. 1)

asymptomatic   Showing no symptoms. (Ch. 5)

attachment   Two meanings: (a) a drab, mundane form of companionship where one's partner gives few positive rewards, other than predictability, for remaining in the relationship; (b) the emotional tie between a parent and child, or between two adults. (Ch. 14)

attachment theory of love   The theory that the quality of the attachment between parents and child greatly affects the child's ability to form romantic relations as an adult. (Ch. 14)

autoerotic asphyxiation   Depriving oneself of oxygen during masturbation-induced orgasm. (Ch. 13, 16)

autoinoculation   The act of infecting oneself. (Ch. 5)

avoidant   A style of attachment in which individuals have negative attitudes about others and have difficulty with feelings of intimacy and letting another person get close to them. (Ch. 14)

B

bacteria   Small, single-celled organisms that lack a nuclear membrane, but have all the genetic material (RNA and DNA) to reproduce themselves. (Ch. 5)

bacterial vaginosis (vaj″ ĭ-no′ sis)   A type of vaginitis caused by the interaction of several vaginal bacteria (particularly *Gardnerella vaginalis*). (Ch. 5)

barrier (blockade) method   General term for contraceptive methods that block the passage of sperm. (Ch. 6)

Bartholin's (bar′ to-linz) **glands**   Glands located at the base of the labia minora in women that contribute a small amount of an alkaline fluid to their inner surfaces during sexual arousal. (Ch. 2)

basal body temperature   The temperature of the body while resting. It rises slightly after ovulation. (Ch. 6)

benign coital cephalalgia (sef ′ ah-lal′ je-ah)   Severe headaches that start during or slightly after orgasm, usually in men. (Ch. 15)

berdache (bar dash′)   See **two-spirit.**

bestiality (bes-te-al′ ĭ -te)   The act of having sexual contact with an animal. (Ch. 16)

beta-endorphins   Natural painkillers produced by the body. (Ch. 7)

B-girls   Prostitutes who work in bars and hotels, generally with the approval of the ownership. (Ch. 18)

Billings method   A fertility awareness method of birth control in which changes in the consistency and quantity of cervical mucus are used to tell when ovulation has occurred. (Ch. 6)

biological determinism   The belief that biological influences establish predetermined limits to the effects of cultural influences. (Ch. 10)

bisexual   An individual with a sexual orientation toward both men and women (Ch. 11)

blastocyst (blas′ to-sist)   The fluid-filled sphere that reaches the uterus after fertilization and which was created by the transformation of the morula through continued, rapid cell division. (Ch. 7)

blockade method   See **barrier (blockade) method.**

Bradley method   A method of prepared childbirth that emphasizes childbirth without medication; named after its founder, Robert Bradley. (Ch. 7)

Braxton-Hicks contractions   Uterine contractions experienced during the last trimester of pregnancy that are often incorrectly interpreted as the beginning of labor; also called *false labor.* (Ch. 7)

breast-feeding   In reference to contraception, the sucking response by a baby on the mother's nipple that inhibits release of follicle-stimulating hormone, thus preventing ovulation. (Ch. 6)

breasts   In women, glands that provide milk for infants; located at the front of the chest. (Ch. 2)

breech birth   A birth in which the baby is born feet or buttocks first. (Ch. 7)

brothel prostitutes   Prostitutes who work in houses of prostitution. (Ch. 18)

bulb (of penis)   The expanded inner end of the spongy body of the penis. (Ch. 2)

bulbocavernosus (bul″ bo-kav′ er-no′sus) **muscle**   A ring of sphincter muscles that surrounds the vaginal opening in women or the root of the penis in men. (Ch. 2)

bulbourethral (bul″ bo-u-re′ thral) **glands**   See **Cowper's glands.**

C

calendar method   A fertility awareness method of birth control that attempts to determine a woman's fertile period by use of a mathematical formula. (Ch. 6)

call girls   The highest-status prostitutes, who generally work out of their own apartments by appointment only. (Ch. 18)

candidiasis (kan″ dĭ-di′ ah-sis)   See **moniliasis.**

capacitation   A process that sperm undergo while traveling through the woman's reproductive tract in which their membranes become thin enough so that an enzyme necessary for softening the ovum's membrane can be released. (Ch. 7)

carnal knowledge of a juvenile   See **statutory rape.**

case study   An in-depth study of an individual. (Ch.1)

celocentesis (se″ lo-sen-te′ sis)   A technique used for detecting fetal abnormalities in which a needle is inserted between the placenta and the amniotic sac to retrieve cells. (Ch. 7)

cephalalgia   See **benign sexual cephalalgia.**

cervical cap   A contraceptive device that fits over the cervix by suction, thus blocking the passage of sperm into the uterus. (Ch. 6)

cervical mucus   The slimy secretion of mucous membranes located inside the cervix. (Ch. 6)

cervicitis (ser″ vĭ-si′ tis)   Inflammation of the cervix. (Ch. 5)

cervix (ser′ viks)   The narrow lower end of the uterus that projects into the vagina. (Ch. 2)

cesarean (se-sa′ re-an) **section** (C-section)   The surgical removal of a fetus through the mother's abdomen. (Ch. 7)

chancre (shang′ ker)   The painless sore that is the main symptom of the primary stage of syphilis. (Ch. 5)

chancroid (shang′ kroid)   A sexually transmitted disease, caused by the *Haemophilus ducreyi* bacterium, which is characterized by small, painful bumps. (Ch. 5)

child molestation   Sexual contact between an adult and a child. (Ch. 17)

chlamydia (klah-mid′ e-ah)   A sexually transmitted disease caused by the *Chlamydia trachomatis* bacterium, which lives on mucous membranes. (Ch. 5)

chorion (ko′ re-on)   The fourth membrane of the trophoblast; it develops into the lining of the placenta. (Ch. 7)

chorionic sampling   A technique used for detecting problems in a fetus during the 8th to 10th weeks of pregnancy. Hairlike projections (villi) of the chorion are collected and examined. (Ch. 7)

chromosomes (kro′mo-somz)   Rod-shaped structures containing the genetic material that determines a person's inherited characteristics. (Ch. 10)

circumcision (ser″ kum-sizh′ un)   In men, the removal of all or part of the foreskin of the penis. In women, the removal of the clitoral hood. (Ch. 2)

climacteric (kli-măk′ ter-ik)   The changes that occur in women in the few years that precede and the first year that follows menopause. (Ch. 12)

clitoral hood   The part of the labia minora that covers the clitoris in women. (Ch. 2)

clitoridectomy (klĭ″ to-rĭ-dek′ to-me)   Removal of the clitoris, often accompanied by removal of the labia minora. In an extreme form, called *infibulation,* the labia majora are also removed, and the sides of the vulva are then sewn together. (Ch. 4)

clitoris (klĭ′ to-ris)   A small, elongated erectile structure in women that develops from the same embryonic tissue as the penis. It has no known reproductive function other than to focus sexual sensations. (Ch. 2)

coach   In the Lamaze birthing technique, an individual (usually the woman's partner) who works with the expectant mother during labor to help her use her training and provide support and encouragement. (Ch. 7)

cognitive-behavioral therapy   Therapy that views problems as resulting from faulty learning and that focuses on specific behavioral problems. (Ch. 15)

cohabitation   Living together in an unmarried relationship. (Ch. 12, 18)

coitus (ko′ ĭ-tus)   Sexual intercourse. (Ch. 13)

coitus interruptus   See **withdrawal.**

colostrum (ko-los′ trum)   A thick, sticky liquid produced by a mother's breasts before milk starts to flow. (Ch. 7)

combination pill   An oral contraceptive that contains both synthetic estrogen and synthetic progesterone. (Ch. 6)

coming out   Disclosing to others one's homosexual orientation, from the expression "coming out of the closet." (Ch. 11)

communication   The exchange of information, thoughts, ideas, or feelings. (Ch. 8)

companionate love   Love based on togetherness, trust, sharing, and affection rather than passion. (Ch. 14)

compliance   Agreeing to sexual intercourse when you do not really want to engage in it. (Ch. 17)

Comstock law   A law passed in 1873 that made it a felony to mail any material regarded as obscene or lewd. (Ch. 18)

conception   The union of an egg and a sperm. (Ch. 7)

conditional love   Feelings of love that depend on the loved one satisfying needs and fulfilling desires. (Ch. 14)

condom   *For men,* a thin sheath made of latex rubber, lamb intestine, or polyurethane that fits over the penis. *For women,* a polyurethane intravaginal pouch held in place by two flexible rings. Condoms are effective as contraception and for prevention of sexually transmitted diseases. (Ch. 6)

congenital adrenal hyperplasia   See **adrenogenital syndrome.**

consummate love   According to Sternberg, the complete love found in relationships that include passion, intimacy, and commitment. (Ch. 14)

contraception   The prevention of conception. (Ch. 6)

contraceptive sponge   A contraceptive device made of polyurethane sponge that contains enough spermicide to be effective for 24 hours after being inserted into the vagina. (Ch. 6)

coprophilia (kop″ ro-fĭl′ e-ah)   Sexual arousal caused by feces or the act of defecation. (Ch. 16)

copulation (kop″ u-la′ shun)   Sexual intercourse. (Ch. 13)

corona (ko-ro′ nah)   The rounded border of the glans of the penis. (Ch. 2)

corpora cavernosa (kor′ po-rah kav″ er-no′ sah)   The two cavernous bodies of the penis or clitoris that fill with blood during sexual arousal. (Ch. 2)

corpus luteum (kor′ pus lew′ te-um)   The follicular cells that remain in the ovary after the follicle expels the ovum during ovulation. They begin to secrete progesterone in large quantities in the postovulatory stage. (Ch. 3)

corpus spongiosum (kor′ pus spun″ je-o′ sum)   The spongy body of the penis that fills with blood during sexual arousal; the urethra passes through it. (Ch. 2)

correlation   A mathematical measure of the degree of relationship between two variables. (Ch.1)

courtly love   In medieval times, when courtiers expressed their undying love for a woman who they worshipped from afar as the epitome of virtue. (Ch. 14)

courtship disorder   A group of paraphilias (voyeurism, exhibitionism, and frotteurism) often seen together. (Ch. 16)

couvade (koo-vahd′) **syndrome**   The experiencing of pregnancy symptoms by male partners; sometimes called "sympathy pains." (Ch. 7)

Cowper's (kow′ perz) **glands**   Two pea-shaped structures located beneath the prostate gland in men that secrete a few drops of an alkaline fluid prior to orgasm. (Ch. 2)

critical period   In relation to teratogens, the time during embryonic or fetal development during which a particular part of the body is most susceptible to damage. (Ch. 7)

crowning   The appearance of the fetus's head at the vaginal opening during childbirth. (Ch. 7)

crura (kroo′ rah)   The leglike ends of the cavernous bodies of the clitoris or penis that attach to the pubic bone. (Ch. 2)

cryptorchidism (krip-tor′ kĭ-dizm)   A defect in which the testes fail to descend into the scrotum. (Ch. 2)

culpotomy (kul-pot′ o-me)   A female sterilization technique in which the Fallopian tubes are approached through a small incision in the back of the vagina and then are cut or cauterized. (Ch. 6)

cunnilingus (kun″ ĭ-ling′ gus)   Oral stimulation of a woman's genitals. (Ch. 13)

cystitis (sis-ti′ tis)   A bacterial infection of the bladder (often caused by the bacterium *Escherichia coli*). (Ch. 2, 5)

D

date rape   A type of acquaintance rape, committed during a social encounter agreed to by the victim. (Ch. 17)

decision/commitment   One of the three basic components in Sternberg's theory of love; the decision that one loves another person and the commitment to maintain the relationship. (Ch. 14)

degrading sexually explicit material   Nonviolent sexually explicit material that shows women as sex objects and where there is a clear unequal balance of power. (Ch. 18)

delayed puberty   A condition in which the appearance of secondary sex characteristics and physical growth do not begin until well after they have begun in most children. (Ch. 12)

demand/withdraw A communication pattern often displayed during conflict, where one partner makes demands and the other withdraws. (Ch. 8)

Depo-Provera Market name for medroxyprogesterone acetate, a chemical that when injected suppresses ovulation for 3 months. (Ch. 6)

desensitization See **systematic desensitization.**

desire A state that "is experienced as specific sensations which move the individual to seek out, or become receptive to, sexual experiences" (Kaplan, 1979). (Ch. 4)

detumescence (de″ tu-mes′ ens) Loss of erection. (Ch. 4)

DHT deficiency syndrome A type of androgen insensitivity syndrome in which, because testosterone is not converted into dihydrotestosterone, boys' external genitals do not develop properly. Development occurs at puberty with the rise in testosterone. (Ch. 10)

diaphragm A dome-shaped rubber cup with a flexible rim that fits over the cervix and thus acts as a contraceptive device by serving as a barrier to the passage of sperm into the uterus. (Ch. 6)

dilation Becoming wider or larger. (Ch. 7)

dilation and curettage (D&C) An abortion technique in which the cervix is dilated and the endometrium is removed by scraping it with an instrument called a curette. (Ch. 6)

dilation and evacuation (D&E) An abortion technique in which the cervix is dilated and the endometrium is removed by suction. (Ch. 6)

dilation and extraction (D&X) See **intact dilation and evacuation.**

direct observation Observing and recording the activity of subjects as they conduct their activities. (Ch. 1)

domination Ruling over and controlling another individual. In sexual relations, it generally involves humiliation of the partner as well. (Ch. 16)

douching (doosh-ing) A feminine hygiene practice of rinsing out the vagina, usually with specifically prepared solutions. (Ch. 6)

dualism The belief that body and soul are separate and antagonistic. (Ch. 1)

dyke A slang term for a masculine lesbian. This is a stereotype that generally does not reflect how most lesbians look or behave. (Ch. 11)

dysmenorrhea (dĭs″ men-o-re′ ah) Painful menstruation. (Ch. 3)

dyspareunia (dĭs″ pah-roo′ ne-ah) Painful intercourse, usually resulting from organic factors (e.g., vaginal, prostate, or bladder infections). (Ch. 15)

E

eclampsia (e-klamp′ se-ah) An advanced case of toxemia of pregnancy, characterized by convulsions and coma. (Ch. 7)

ectoderm The layer of the embryo that forms the nervous system, skin, and teeth. (Ch. 7)

ectopic (ek-top′ ik) **pregnancy** The implantation of a fertilized egg outside of the endometrium of the uterus. (Ch. 7)

effacement The thinning of the cervix during labor. (Ch. 7)

effleurage (ef-loo-rahzh′) In the Lamaze birthing technique, a light self-massage of the abdomen that is used to counter the discomfort of labor contractions. (Ch. 7)

egocentric A term used by Jean Piaget in his theory of cognitive development referring to the inability of young children to consider another person's point of view. (Ch. 12)

ejaculation The expulsion of semen from the body. (Ch. 4)

ejaculatory ducts One-inch-long paired tubes that pass through the prostate gland. The third part of the duct system that transports sperm out of a man's body. (Ch. 2)

ejaculatory incompetence A condition in which a man is totally unable to ejaculate in a woman's vagina during sexual intercourse. (Ch. 15)

embryo (em′ bre-o) The term given to the blastocyst after it has implanted. (Ch. 7)

emergency contraception Methods that prevent contraception when used in the first few days *after* sexual intercourse. (Ch. 6)

emerging adulthood A developmental stage of life; an extended period of being a single adult that occurs between adolescence and young adulthood. (Ch. 12)

emission The first stage of an orgasm in men. Rhythmic muscular contractions in the vas deferens, prostate gland, and seminal vesicles force the sperm and prostate and seminal fluids into the ejaculatory ducts, thus forming semen. (Ch. 4)

empty love According to Sternberg, the emotion felt when there is decision and commitment to love another person, but no intimacy or passion. (Ch. 14)

endocrine system A network of ductless glands that secrete their chemical substances, called *hormones,* directly into the bloodstream, where they are carried to other parts of the body to exert their effects. (Ch. 3)

endoderm The layer of the embryo that forms the internal organs of the fetus. (Ch. 7)

endometriosis (en″ do-me′ tre-o′ sis) The growth of endometrial tissue outside of the uterus. (Ch. 3)

endometrium (en″-do-me′ tre-um) The inner mucous membrane of the uterus where a fertilized egg implants. Its thickness varies with the phase of the menstrual cycle. (Ch. 2, 3)

epididymis (ep″ ĭ-did′ ĭ-mis) The elongated cordlike structure on the back of a testicle. It is the first part of the duct system that transports sperm out of a man's body. (Ch. 2)

episiotomy (e-piz″ e-ot′ o-me) A surgical procedure performed on women just before giving birth to reduce the risk of tearing the perineum. (Ch. 2, 7)

erectile disorder A sexual problem in which a man has difficulty getting and maintaining an erection. (Ch. 15)

erection (of penis) The state of the penis during sexual arousal (i.e., hard and elongated) due to vasocongestion of tissues. (Ch. 4)

erogenous zone According to psychoanalytic theory, the part of the body where sexual energy is focused. (Ch. 10)

eros A highly idealized type of romantic love that is based mainly on physical beauty. Erotic lovers look for physical perfection. (Ch. 14)

erotica Any literature or art that has a sexual theme. This is a morally neutral term. (Ch. 18)

erotophilia (e-rah″ to fĭl″ e-ah) Having positive emotions about one's own sexuality. (Ch. 12)

erotophobia (e-rah′ to fo″ be-ah) Having negative emotions about one's own sexuality. (Ch. 12)

estrogen (es′ tro-jen) A hormone that is produced by the ovaries (and in very small amounts by the testes and adrenal glands). (Ch. 3)

estrous cycle The cycle of hormonal events that occurs in most nonhuman mammals. The females are sexually receptive ("in heat," or in estrus) to males only during ovulation. (Ch. 3)

ethnocentric The attitude that the behaviors and customs of one's own ethnic group or culture are superior to others. (Ch. 1)

excitement phase The first phase of the sexual response cycle as proposed by Masters and Johnson. The first signs are erection in men and vaginal lubrication in women. (Ch. 4)

exhibitionism Exposing one's genitals compulsively in inappropriate settings in order to obtain sexual gratification. (Ch. 16)

experiment A study in which an investigator attempts to establish a cause-and-effect relationship by manipulating a variable of interest (the independent variable) while keeping all other factors the same. (Ch. 1)

expressive A personality characteristic; a cognitive focus on "an affective concern for the welfare of others." (Ch. 10)

expulsion The second stage of an orgasm in men. Contractions in the urethra and muscles at the base of the penis force the semen from the penis (*ejaculation*). (Ch. 4)

F

Fallopian (fal-lo′ pe-an) **tubes** The passageways that eggs follow on their way to the uterus. (Ch. 2)

false labor A set of temporary contractions of the uterus that resemble the start of labor. (Ch. 7)

false memory syndrome False memories of childhood sexual abuse, often "inadvertently planted by therapists . . ." (Ch. 17)

fatuous love According to Sternberg, the emotion felt when a commitment is made on the basis of passion without the experience of intimacy. (Ch. 14)

fear-tension-pain cycle According to prepared childbirth advocates, the cycle of events that women experience during labor when they are not properly educated about labor and childbirth. (Ch. 7)

fecundity (fe kun′ deh te) The ability of a couple to conceive within a certain period of time. (Ch. 7)

fellatio (fe-la′ she-o) Oral stimulation of a man's genitals. (Ch. 13)

female orgasmic disorder A persistent or recurrent delay in, or absence of, orgasm following a normal sexual excitement phase. (Ch. 15)

fertility awareness methods Methods of birth control that attempt to prevent conception by having a couple abstain from sexual intercourse during the woman's ovulation. (Ch. 6)

fertility drugs Drugs that improve the chance of conception in women who are infertile owing to hormone deficiencies. The drugs either stimulate the pituitary gland to secrete FSH and LH or stimulate the ovaries directly. (Ch. 7)

fertilization Impregnation; the fusion of a sperm with an ovum. (Ch. 7)

fetal alcohol syndrome (FAS) A condition common to infants born to alcoholic mothers, involving physical and nervous system abnormalities. (Ch. 7)

fetal monitor A device attached to the expectant mother's abdomen during labor to monitor the heart rate of the fetus and the contractions of the uterus. (Ch. 7)

fetal surgery A surgical operation on the fetus while it is still in the uterus. (Ch. 7)

fetishism (fet′ ish-ĭ-zum) A condition in which sexual arousal occurs primarily when using or fantasizing about an inanimate object or a particular part of the body (such as the feet). (Ch. 16)

fetoscopy A procedure in which a tube containing fiberoptic strands is inserted into the amniotic sac to allow inspection of the fetus. (Ch. 7)

fetus The term given to the embryo after the 8th week of pregnancy. (Ch. 7)

fibrocystic (fi″ bro-sis′ tik) **disease** A benign overgrowth of fibrous tissue in the breast. (Ch. 2)

fimbria (fim′ bre-ah) The fingerlike processes at the ovarian end of the Fallopian tubes. (Ch. 2)

focal point In the Lamaze birthing technique, a point outside of the woman's body on which she focuses her concentration during labor contractions. (Ch. 7)

follicle (fol′ lĭ-k'l) A sac in the ovary containing an ovum and surrounding follicular cells. (Ch. 2, 3)

follicle-stimulating hormone (FSH) A gonadotropin hormone released by the pituitary gland that stimulates the development of a follicle in a woman's ovary and the production of sperm in a man's testicles. (Ch. 3)

follicular (proliferative) phase The preovulatory phase of the menstrual cycle, lasting from about day 5 to day 13 in a 28-day cycle. (Ch. 3)

foreskin The loose skin of the penis that folds over the glans and that is sometimes cut away in a procedure known as circumcision. (Ch. 2)

fornication (for′ nĭ ka′ shun) Sexual intercourse between a man and a woman who are not married to one another. (Ch. 18)

friendship A relationship that includes (a) enjoyment of each other's company, (b) acceptance of one another, (c) mutual trust, (d) respect for one another, (e) mutual assistance when needed, (f) confiding in one another, (g) understanding, and (h) spontaneity. (Ch. 14)

frigidity The common term used by men for women who have orgasm problems, but which is generally not used by therapists because it has negative connotations about emotional responsivity. (Ch. 15)

frotteurism (fro-tur′ izm) A condition in which sexual arousal is achieved primarily by rubbing one's genitals against others in public places. (Ch. 16)

fundus (fun′ dus) The broad end of the uterus. (Ch. 2)

G

galactorrhea (gah-lak″ to-re′ ah) The spontaneous flow of milk. (Ch. 2)

gamete intrafallopian transfer (GIFT) A procedure for treating female infertility in which sperm and eggs are gathered and placed directly into a Fallopian tube. (Ch. 7)

gang rape Rape in which a victim is assaulted by more than one attacker. (Ch. 17)

gay A term generally used to refer to male homosexuals, although in some places it is used to refer to homosexuals of either sex. (Ch. 11)

gender The social construction of femininity and masculinity. (Ch. 10)

gender constancy The knowledge that one's sex is constant and will not change. This knowledge is usually acquired by age 6 or 7. (Ch. 10)

gender dysphoria (dis-fo′ re-ah) The feeling of being trapped in a body of the opposite sex. (Ch. 10)

gender identity One's subjective sense of being a man (or boy) or a woman (or girl). This sense is usually acquired by the age of 3. (Ch. 10)

gender identity disorder A disorder whose criteria are (a) behaviors that indicate identification with the opposite gender, and (b) behaviors that indicate discomfort with one's own anatomy and gender roles. (Ch. 10)

gender role A set of culturally specific norms concerning the expected behaviors and attitudes of men and women. (Ch. 10)

gender-role identity The extent to which a person approves of and participates in feelings and behaviors deemed to be appropriate to his or her culturally constituted gender. (Ch. 10)

gender-role stereotypes Oversimplified, preconceived beliefs about the gender roles of men and women. (Ch. 10)

gender schemas (ske′ mahs) Ideas about gender roles that children create from their interactions with their environment. (Ch. 10)

genital herpes Herpes infection in the genital region. It can be caused by herpes simplex virus types 1 or 2. (Ch. 5)

genital warts Warts in the genital and anal regions caused by human papillomaviruses (mainly types 6 and 11). The warts are cauliflowerlike growths. (Ch. 5)

genitalia (jen″ ĭ-ta′ leah) The reproductive organs of the man or woman. (Ch. 2)

gigolos (jig′ ah-los) Male prostitutes who cater to women. (Ch. 18)

gland An organ or specialized group of cells that separates substances from the blood and secretes them for use by, or elimination from, the body. (Ch. 3)

glans (glanz) The rounded end of the penis or clitoris. (Ch. 2)

global moralities Values that are supposed to apply to all people under all circumstances. (Ch. 8)

global sexual problem A sexual problem that occurs in all sexual situations. (Ch. 8)

gonadarche (go″ nad-ar′ke) The maturation of the ovaries and testicles. (Ch. 12)

gonadotropin (gon″ ah-do-tro′ pin) A hormone that has a stimulating effect on the ovaries or testicles. (Ch. 3)

gonadotropin-releasing hormone (GnRH) A hormone released by the hypothalamus in the brain that causes the pituitary gland to release the hormones FSH and LH. (Ch. 3)

gonococcus (gon″ o-kok′ us) Common name for the bacterium that causes gonorrhea. (Ch. 5)

gonorrhea (gon″ o-re′ ah) A sexually transmitted disease caused by the *Neisseria gonorrhoeae* bacterium (often referred to as "the gonococcus"), which lives on mucous membranes. (Ch. 5)

Graafian (graf′ e-an) **follicle** A mature follicle. (Ch. 7)

Grafenberg (graf′ en-burg) **(G) spot** A small, sensitive area on the front wall of the vagina found in about 10 percent of all women. (Ch. 2, 4)

granuloma inguinale (gran″ u-lo′ mah ing′ gwĭ-nah le) A rare (in the United States) sexually transmitted disease that is characterized by ulceration of tissue. (Ch. 5)

growing apart Having fewer common interests over time. (Ch. 14)

growing together Maintaining common interests over time. (Ch. 14)

G-spot See **Grafenberg (G) spot.**

gumma (gum′ ah) A soft, gummy tumor that appears in late (tertiary) syphilis. (Ch. 5)

gynecomastia (jin″ ĕ-ko-mas′ te-ah) Excessive development of the male breasts. (Ch. 2, 12)

H

habituation Responding less positively to a stimulus with repeated exposure to it. (Ch. 14)

hand-riding A technique used to teach people how to touch in which the receiver places his or her hand over the giver's hand and guides it over the receiver's body. This is often included as part of sensate focus exercises. (Ch. 15)

HCG See **human chorionic gonadotropin (HCG).**

hepatitis (hep″ ah-ti′ tis) **A, B, and C** Liver infections caused by viruses. Type A is spread by direct or indirect contact with contaminated feces. Type B is transmitted by infected blood or body fluids, with 25 to 50 percent of the cases contracted during sex. Type C is spread mainly by contaminated blood, but may possibly be spread during sexual intercourse in some cases. (Ch. 5)

hermaphrodite (her-maf′ ro-dīt″) A person with both male and female reproductive systems as a result of failure of the primitive gonads to differentiate properly during embryonic development. (Ch. 10)

herpes (her′ pez) Painful blisters usually found on the mouth (fever blisters; cold sores) or genitals that are caused by a virus (herpes simplex virus type 1 or 2). Genital herpes is almost always contracted by intimate sexual activity, but oral herpes may be spread by casual kissing. (Ch. 5)

heterosexual An individual with a sexual orientation primarily to members of the opposite sex. (Ch. 11)

hierarchical model of love A theory that proposes that the structure of love consists of several levels (clusters) of features, with lower levels consisting of a larger number of smaller features. (Ch. 14)

HIV See **human immunodeficiency virus (HIV).**

homophobia An irrational fear of homosexual individuals and homosexuality. (Ch. 11)

homosexual An individual with a sexual orientation primarily to members of the same sex. (Ch. 11)

hormones Chemical substances that are secreted by ductless glands into the bloodstream. They are carried in the blood to other parts of the body, where they exert their effects on other glands or target organs. (Ch. 3)

hot flashes A warm feeling over the upper body experienced by menopausal women as a result of increased levels of FSH and LH. (Ch. 12)

HPV See **human papillomaviruses (HPV).**

human chorionic (ko" re-on' ik) **gonadotropin (HCG)** A hormone secreted by the chorion that stimulates the ovaries during pregnancy. (Ch. 3, 7)

human immunodeficiency virus (HIV) A virus that kills CD4+ cells, eventually resulting in AIDS. (Ch. 5)

human papillomaviruses (pap" ĭ-lo' mah) **(HPV)** Viruses that cause abnormal growths in epithelial cells. There are over 70 types. A few (types 6 and 11) cause genital warts, while others (types 16, 18, 31, 33, and 45) can lead to cancer of the cervix. (Ch. 5)

hustler A male prostitute who caters to men. (Ch. 18)

hyaluronidase (hi" ah-lu-ron'ĭ-das) An enzyme secreted by a sperm that allows the sperm to penetrate the surface of an ovum. (Ch. 7)

hymen (hi' men) The thin membrane that partially covers the vaginal opening in many sexually inexperienced women. Its presence or absence, however, is really a very poor indicator of prior sexual experience. (Ch. 2)

hypersexuality A term reserved for people who engage in sex compulsively, with little or no emotional satisfaction. Sometimes called *sexual addiction*. (Ch. 15)

hypoactive sexual desire A sexual problem characterized by a persisting and pervasive inhibition of sexual desire. (Ch. 15)

hypothalamus (hi" po-thal'ah-mus) A part of the brain that regulates the release of hormones from the pituitary gland. (Ch. 2, 3)

hysterectomy (his" tĕ-rek' to-me) Surgical removal of the uterus. (Ch. 2)

I

identification The adoption of the sex roles of the same-sex parent by a child. In Freudian theory, identification resolves the Oedipus complex. (Ch. 10)

ideology The mental frameworks that different classes and social groups use to make sense of the way society works. (Ch. 9)

"I" language Communicating your desires to another person by beginning sentences with "I," followed by your feelings, desires, or thoughts. (Ch. 8)

imitation Following the behaviors of someone taken as one's model. (Ch. 10)

immune system The bodily mechanisms involved in the production of antibodies in response to bacteria, viruses, and cancerous cells. (Ch. 5)

implantation The process by which the blastocyst attaches itself to the wall of the uterus. (Ch. 7)

impotence A common term for erectile disorders in men, but generally not used by therapists because it has negative connotations about a man's masculinity. (Ch. 15)

incest Sexual contact between two closely related persons. (Ch. 17)

incontinence The inability to control one's bladder. (Ch. 4)

individualist theory The theory that personality traits develop early in life and do not change much over the life cycle; these traits then determine an individual's expression of masculine or feminine behavior. (Ch. 10)

infatuated love According to Sternberg, the emotion felt when there is passion in the absence of intimacy and commitment. (Ch. 14)

infertility The inability of a couple to conceive. (Ch. 7)

infibulation See **clitoridectomy.**

inhibin (in-hib'in) A hormone produced by the testicles and ovaries that inhibits release of follicle-stimulating hormone from the pituitary gland. (Ch. 2, 3)

inhibited ejaculation See **male orgasmic disorder.**

inhibited female orgasm See **female orgasmic disorder.**

instrumental A personality characteristic; a cognitive focus on "getting the job done." (Ch. 10)

intact dilation and evacuation (intact D&E) An abortion procedure performed in very-late-term pregnancies in which the fetus's head is partially delivered and its brain is then removed by suction. Also called *dilation and extraction (D&X)*. (Ch. 6)

intersexual Individuals with a combination of male and female anatomical features. (Ch. 10)

intimacy Those feelings in a relationship that promote closeness or bondedness and the experience of warmth. (Ch. 14)

intracytoplasmic sperm injection A procedure used to treat men who have a low sperm count; injection of a single sperm directly into an egg. (Ch. 7)

intrauterine device (IUD) A birth control device, usually made of plastic with either a copper or progesterone coating, that is placed in the uterus to prevent conception and implantation. (Ch. 6)

introitus (in-tro'ĭ-tus) The entrance to the vagina. (Ch. 2)

in vitro fertilization A process in which a mature ovum is surgically removed from a woman's ovary, placed in a medium with sperm until fertilization occurs, and then placed in the woman's uterus. This is usually done in women who cannot conceive because of blocked Fallopian tubes. (Ch. 7)

IUD See **intrauterine device (IUD).**

J

jealousy An emotional state that is aroused by a perceived threat to a valued relationship or position. (Ch. 14)

john A street term for a man who pays for sex with a prostitute; johns are also called *tricks* or *scores*. (Ch. 18)

K

Kaposi's sarcoma (kap'-o-sez sar-ko'mah) A cancer of the capillary system that often occurs in people with AIDS. (Ch. 5)

Kegel exercises Exercises that are designed to strengthen the pubococcygeus muscle that surrounds the bladder and vagina. (Ch. 2)

Klinefelter's syndrome A condition in men in which there is one or more extra X chromosomes. (Ch. 10)

klismaphilia (kliz" mah-fil' e-ah) A condition in which sexual arousal is achieved primarily by being given an enema. (Ch. 16)

L

labia majora (la′ be-ah majo′ rah) Two elongated folds of skin extending from the mons to the perineum in women. Its outer surfaces become covered with pubic hair during puberty. (Ch. 2)

labia minora (la′be-ah mino′rah) Two hairless elongated folds of skin located between the labia majora in women. They meet above the clitoris to form the clitoral hood. (Ch. 2)

Lamaze A method of prepared childbirth; named after its founder, Fernand Lamaze. (Ch. 7)

lanugo (lah-nu′ go) Light hair that covers a newborn baby. (Ch. 7)

laparoscopy (lap″ ah-ros′ko-pe) A technique that involves inserting a slender, tubelike instrument (laparoscope) into a woman's abdomen to examine (via fiberoptics) her reproductive organs or a fetus. The procedure is often used to perform female sterilizations. (Ch. 6 and 7)

Leboyer method A method of prepared childbirth that advocates gentle birth; named after its founder, Frederick Leboyer, (Ch. 7)

lesbian (lez′ be-an) A female homosexual. (Ch. 11)

Leydig (li′ dig), **interstitial cells of** The cells in the testes that produce male hormones. (Ch. 2)

libido (lĭ-be′ do) In psychoanalytic theory, the sexual energy of an individual. (Ch. 10)

lightening Rotation of the fetus prior to childbirth so that its head is downward, resulting in decreased pressure on the mother's abdomen. (Ch. 7)

liking According to Sternberg, the emotion felt when there is intimacy without passion or commitment. (Ch. 14)

limerence "Head over heels" love in which one is obsessed with the loved one. (Ch. 14)

love Many possible definitions, and, according to researchers, many different types. For example, see **agape, companionate love, eros, ludus, mania, pragma, and storge.** (Ch. 14)

ludus A self-centered type of love. Ludic lovers avoid commitment and treat love as a game, often viewing the chase as more pleasurable than the prize. (Ch. 14)

lumpectomy A surgical procedure in which only a breast tumor and a small bit of surrounding tissue are removed. (Ch. 2)

luteal (lu′ te-al) **(secretory) phase** The postovulatory phase of the menstrual cycle, lasting from about day 15 to day 28 in a 28-day cycle. (Ch. 3)

luteinizing (lu′ te-in″ i-zing) **hormone (LH)** A gonadotropin hormone released by the pituitary gland that triggers ovulation in women and stimulates the production of male hormones in men. (Ch. 3)

lymphogranuloma venereum (lim″ fo-gran″ u-lo′ mah vene′ reum) (LGV) A sexually transmitted disease common in tropical countries that is caused by chlamydia. If left untreated, it causes swelling of the inguinal lymph nodes, penis, labia, or clitoris. (Ch. 5)

M

male orgasmic disorder A condition in which a man has difficulty reaching orgasm and ejaculating in a woman's vagina. (Ch. 15)

male rape Rape in which the victim is a man. (Ch. 17)

mammary glands Milk-producing glands of the breast. (Ch. 2)

mammogram Low-radiation X-rays used to detect breast tumors. (Ch. 2)

mania A type of love characterized by an intense emotional dependency on the attention and affection of one's lover. (Ch. 14)

marital rape Rape of a wife by her husband. (Ch. 17)

masochism (mas′ o-kizm) A condition in which individuals obtain sexual pleasure primarily from having pain and/or humiliation inflicted on them. (Ch. 16)

mastectomy (mas-tek′ to-me) Surgical removal of a breast. (Ch. 2)

masturbation Self-stimulation of one's genitals. (Ch. 12 and 13)

meatus (me-a′ tus) General term for an opening or passageway, as in *urinary meatus.* (Ch. 2)

medical abortion Abortion induced by taking a pill (see **RU 486**). (Ch. 6)

medical history One of the first steps used by most sex therapists. A complete medical history or exam is important because many sexual problems have an organic basis. (Ch. 15)

medical model Attributing sexual problems to organic causes and treating them with medical techniques. (Ch. 15)

menarche (mĕ-nar′ ke) The term for a girl's first menstrual period. (Ch. 3, 12)

menopause (men′ o-pawz) The term for a woman's last menstrual period. (Ch. 3, 12)

menstrual cycle The monthly cycle of hormonal events in a woman that leads to ovulation and menstruation. (Ch. 3)

menstrual taboos Incorrect negative attitudes about menstruating women. (Ch. 3)

menstruation (men″ stroo-a′ shun) The monthly discharge of endometrial tissue, blood, and other secretions from the uterus that occurs when an egg is not fertilized. (Ch. 3)

mesoderm The layer of the embryo that forms the muscles, skeleton, and blood vessels. (Ch. 7)

microstructural theory A theory that stresses the role of the external environment in shaping gender roles. (Ch. 10)

midwife See **nurse-midwife.**

minilaparotomy A female sterilization technique in which small incisions are made in the abdomen and the Fallopian tubes are then pulled to the opening and cut, tied, or blocked with clips. (Ch. 6)

minipill An oral contraceptive that contains only progestins. (Ch. 6)

miscarriage A spontaneous abortion. (Ch. 7)

missionary position A face-to-face position of sexual intercourse in which the woman lies on her back and the man lies on top with his legs between hers. It was called this because Christian missionaries instructed people that other positions were unnatural. (Ch. 1, 13)

Mittelschmerz (mit′ el-shmārts) Abdominal pain at the time of ovulation. (Ch. 3)

molluscum contagiosum (mo-lus′ kum contagio′ sum) A sexually transmitted virus whose symptom look like small pimples filled with kernels of corn. (Ch. 5)

moniliasis (mon-ĭ-lī′ ah-sis)   Sometimes called candidiasis. A type of vaginitis caused by the overgrowth of a microorganism (*Candida albicans*) that is normally found in the vagina. Moniliasis is a fungus or yeast infection and usually is a sexually related, rather than a sexually transmitted, disease. (Ch. 5)

mons veneris (monz ven′ eris)   The soft layer of fatty tissue that overlays the pubic bone in women. It becomes covered with pubic hair during puberty. (Ch. 2)

morning sickness   A symptom of early pregnancy involving nausea. (Ch. 7)

morula (mor′ u-lah)   The collection of cells formed when the zygote begins rapid cell division. (Ch. 7)

Mullerian-duct–inhibiting substance   A chemical secreted by the testes during embryonic development that causes the Mullerian ducts to shrink and disappear. (Ch. 10)

Mullerian (mil-e′ re-an) **duct system**   A primitive duct system formed in embryos, which, if allowed to develop, becomes the female reproductive system. (Ch. 10)

multiple orgasms   Having two or more successive orgasms without falling below the plateau level of physiological arousal. (Ch. 4)

myotonia (mi″ o-to′ ne-ah)   A buildup of energy in nerves and muscles resulting in involuntary contractions. (Ch. 4)

mysophilia (mi″ so-fil′ e-ah)   A condition in which sexual arousal is caused primarily by filth or filthy surroundings. (Ch. 16)

N

necking   Noncoital sexual contact above the waist. (Ch. 12)

necrophilia (nek″ ro-fil′ e-ah)   Sexual arousal by a dead body. (Ch. 16)

nipple   The protuberance on the breast that in women contains the outlets for the milk ducts. It consists of smooth muscle fibers. (Ch. 2)

nocturnal emission   An ejaculation that occurs during sleep in teenaged boys and men; a "wet dream." (Ch. 12)

nocturnal orgasm   An orgasm that occurs during sleep (sometimes called "wet dreams" in men). (Ch. 13)

nongonococcal (nonspecific) urethritis (NGU)   Any inflammation of the urethra that is not caused by the *Neisseria gonorrhoeae* (gonococcus) bacterium. (Ch. 5)

nonlove   According to Sternberg, the absence of all three components of love: intimacy, passion, and commitment. (Ch. 14)

nonoxynol-9   The active chemical in most spermicides. (Ch. 6)

nonverbal communication   Communicating with another person without using words. (Ch. 8)

nonviolent sexually explicit material   Sexually explicit material that does not show violent interactions between individuals. (Ch. 18)

Norplant   Six flexible silicone tubes containing a progestin that are implanted under the skin to prevent conception; they remain effective for 5 years. (Ch. 6)

nurse-midwife   A registered nurse, trained in obstetrical techniques, who delivers babies, often at the expectant mother's home. (Ch. 7)

O

obscenity   In legal terminology, the classification of material that by contemporary community standards depicts patently offensive sexual conduct, lacks serious value, and appeals to prurient interests. (Ch. 18)

observer bias   The prejudicing of observations and conclusions by the observer's own belief system. (Ch. 1)

Oedipus (ed′ ĭ-pus) **complex**   According to psychoanalytic theory, the sexual desire that a boy feels toward his mother (male Oedipus complex) or the sexual attraction that a girl feels toward her father (female Oedipus complex) during the phallic stage of psychosexual development. (Ch. 10, 11)

open marriage   A marital relationship in which the couple agrees that it is permissible to have sexual relations outside of the marriage. (Ch. 12)

operant conditioning   A type of learning in which an individual's behavior is modified by the consequences of the behavior. (Ch. 10)

opportunistic diseases   A variety of diseases that occur in individuals with a very weakened immune system, as in AIDS. (Ch. 5)

opportunistic rapists   Rapists motivated by a desire for sex who rape impulsively when there is an opportunity. (Ch. 17)

oral contraceptive   The birth control pill. (Ch. 6)

oral herpes   A herpes infection in or around the mouth. It can be caused by herpes simplex virus types 1 or 2. (Ch. 5)

orchiectomy (or″ ke-ek′ to-me)   Removal of one or both testicles. (Ch. 3)

orgasm   The brief but intense sensations (focused largely in the genitals but really a whole body response) experienced during sexual arousal. During orgasm, rhythmic muscular contractions occur in certain tissues in both the man and woman. The third phase of the sexual response cycle proposed by Masters and Johnson. (Ch. 4)

orgasmic disorder   See **male orgasmic disorder, female orgasmic disorder.**

orgasmic platform   The engorgement and consequent swelling of the outer third of the vagina during the plateau stage, causing the vaginal opening to narrow by 30 to 50 percent. (Ch. 4)

os   The opening of the cervix. (Ch. 2)

ovary (o′ vah-re)   The female gonad in which ova are produced. (Ch. 2)

ovulation (o″ vu-la′ shun)   The expulsion of an egg from one of the ovaries. (Ch. 3)

ovum   An egg; the female reproductive cell. (Ch. 2, 7)

oxytocin (ok″ se-to′sin)   A hormone released from the pituitary gland that causes the breasts to eject milk. (Ch. 2, 7)

P

Pap smear   A test for cancer of the cervix in women; named for Dr. Papanicolaou, who developed it. (Ch. 2)

paraphilias (par″ ah-fil′ e-ahs)   General term for a group of sexual disorders in which a person's sexual arousal and gratification depend almost exclusively on unusual behaviors. (Ch. 16)

passion   The drive leading to physical attraction, sexual relations, and romance. (Ch. 14)

passionate love "A state of intense longing for union with another. . . . A state of profound physiological arousal" (Hatfield, 1988). (Ch. 14)

pederasty (pehd′ ah ras″ te) A same-sex sexual behavior between adult men and boys. (Ch. 11)

pedophilia (pe″ do-fil′ e-ah) A condition in which sexual arousal is achieved primarily and repeatedly through sexual activity with children who have not reached puberty. (Ch. 16, 17)

peer pressure Expectations by one's peer group about how one is supposed to behave. (Ch. 12)

pelvic exam A necessary part of women's health care to check for cervical and vaginal infections; it includes a Pap smear. (Ch. 2)

pelvic inflammatory disease (PID) A bacterially caused inflammation of a woman's reproductive tract, particularly the Fallopian tubes, that can result in sterility. The most common (though not the only) cause is untreated gonorrhea and/or chlamydia. (Ch. 5)

penis (pe′ nis) The male organ for sexual intercourse and the passageway for sperm and urine. (Ch. 2)

penis envy According to psychoanalytic theory, the envy that a girl feels during the phallic stage of psychosexual development, when she realizes that she has no penis (and will never have one). (Ch. 10)

perfect-use pregnancy rate For a particular birth control technique, the percentage of pregnancies during the first year of use by couples who use the technique properly and consistently. See also **typical-use pregnancy rate.** (Ch. 6)

performance anxiety A fear of failure during sexual relations that can lead to erectile disorder in men and inhibited orgasm in women. (Ch. 15)

perineum (per″ ĭ-ne′ um) Technically, the entire pelvic floor, but more commonly used to refer to the hairless bit of skin between the anus and either the vaginal opening (in women) or the scrotum (in men). (Ch. 2)

personally immature pedophile A pedophile who is attracted to children because he never developed the social skills necessary to initiate and maintain a sexual relationship with an adult. (Ch. 17)

petting Noncoital sexual contact below the waist. (Ch. 12)

phallic (fal′ ik) **stage** According to psychoanalytic theory, the third stage of psychosexual development, in which a child's sexual desire for the parent of the opposite sex emerges and is resolved through the process of identification. (Ch. 10, 12)

pheromones (fer′ah monz) Chemical substances secreted externally by animals that convey information to, and produce specific responses in, members of the same species. (Ch. 3)

phimosis (fi-mo′ sis) A condition in uncircumcised men in which the foreskin of the penis is too tight, causing pain during erection. (Ch. 2 and 15)

PID See **pelvic inflammatory disease (PID).**

pill See **oral contraceptive.** (Ch. 6)

pinworms Small worms (*Enterobius vermicularis*) that live in the large intestine and are generally transmitted through nonsexual contact with the worms' eggs, but which can be transmitted sexually by manual or oral contact with the anus of an infected person. (Ch. 5)

pituitary (pĭ-tu′ ĭ-tar″ e) **gland** A gland located at the base of the brain that secretes eight hormones, including follicle-stimulating hormone and luteinizing hormone. (Ch. 3)

placenta (plah-sen′tah) An organ that serves as a connection or interface between the fetus's systems and those of the mother. (Ch. 7)

placenta previa A condition in which the placenta blocks the cervical opening. (Ch. 7)

plateau The second phase of the sexual response cycle proposed by Masters and Johnson. Physiologically, it represents a high state of arousal. (Ch. 4)

PLISSIT model An acronym for the four levels of treatment in sexual therapy: permission, limited information, specific suggestions, and intensive therapy. (Ch. 15)

PMS See **premenstrual syndrome (PMS).**

pneumocystis carinii (nu″ mo-sis′ tis cari′ nii) **pneumonia** A rare respiratory infection that often occurs in people with AIDS. (Ch. 5)

polyandry (pahl′ e an″ dre) The practice of allowing women to have more than one husband at the same time. (Ch. 12, 14)

polygamy (puh lig′ uh me) The practice of allowing men or women to have more than one mate at the same time. (Ch. 12)

polygyny (puh lij′ uh ne) The practice of allowing men to have two or more wives at the same time. (Ch. 12, 14)

polyincestuous family Families in which there are both multiple incestuous abusers and multiple victims, across generations and within the same generation. (Ch. 17)

population The complete set of observations about which a researcher wishes to draw conclusions. (Ch. 1)

pornography Literature or art with a sexual theme that is designed to cause arousal and excitement and is considered to be obscene. (Ch. 18)

postpartum blues A mild, transient emotional letdown experienced by a majority of women after giving birth. (Ch. 7)

postpartum depression A deep depression experienced by about 10 percent of women in the first few months after giving birth. (Ch. 7)

postpartum psychosis A psychotic state experienced by about 1 in 1,000 women after giving birth. (Ch. 7)

post-rape posttraumatic stress disorder A group of clinical symptoms displayed by many victims of rape; previously called *rape trauma syndrome.* (Ch. 17)

power rapists Rapists who commit their attacks in order to overcome personal feelings of insecurity and inadequacy. Their rapes give them a sense of mastery and control. (Ch. 17)

pragma A rational or practical type of love. Pragmatic lovers actively look for a "good match." (Ch. 14)

precocious puberty A condition in which puberty begins before the age of 9. (Ch. 12)

preeclampsia (pre″ e-klamp′se-ah) The early stage of toxemia of pregnancy, characterized by high blood pressure, weight gain, and swollen joints. (Ch. 7)

preference molesters (pedophiles) Child molesters who have a primary sexual orientation to children and who are relatively uninterested in adult partners. (Ch. 17)

premature ejaculation   A recurrent and persistent absence of reasonable voluntary control of ejaculation. (Ch. 15)

premenstrual dysphoric disorder (PMDD)   A severe form of PMS that markedly interferes with social relations, work, or education. (Ch. 3)

premenstrual syndrome (PMS)   A group of physical and/or emotional changes that many women experience in the last 3 to 14 days before the start of a menstrual period. (Ch. 3)

prenatal examination   A health checkup by a physician during pregnancy. (Ch. 7)

prepared childbirth   Courses or techniques that prepare women for labor and childbirth, with the goal of making it a positive experience. (Ch. 7)

prepping   The shaving of a woman's pubic hair prior to delivery of a baby. (Ch. 7)

preterm infant   An infant born weighing less than 5½ pounds and before week 37 of pregnancy. (Ch. 7)

priapism (pri′ ah-pizm)   A condition in which the penis remains erect for a prolonged period of time, sometimes days. (Ch. 15)

primary follicle   An immature ovum enclosed by a single layer of cells. (Ch. 2, 7)

primary HIV infection   The first few weeks of HIV infection, during which HIV reaches enormous levels in the blood and 50 to 75 percent of infected individuals experience flulike symptoms. (Ch. 5)

primary sexual problem   A sexual problem that has existed throughout an individual's life. (Ch. 15)

procreation   The act of producing offspring. (Ch. 1)

progesterone (pro-jes′ tĕ-ron)   A hormone that is produced in large amounts by the ovaries after ovulation. It prepares the endometrium of the uterus to nourish a fertilized egg. (Ch. 3)

progestin (proj-jes′ tin)   A synthetic form of progesterone. (Ch. 6)

prolactin (pro-lak′ tin)   A hormone released from the pituitary gland that stimulates milk production in the breasts. (Ch. 2 and 7)

proliferative phase   See **follicular (proliferative) phase.**

prophylactic   See **condom.**

prostaglandins (pros″ tah-glan′ dinz)   Chemical substances in the body that cause uterine contractions. (Ch. 3, 6)

prostate (pros′ tāt) **gland**   A gland in men that surrounds the origins of the urethra and neck of the bladder and contributes many substances to the seminal fluid. (Ch. 2, 5)

prostatitis (pros″ tah-ti′ tis)   Inflammation of the prostate gland. (Ch. 5)

prostitution   The exchange of sex for money. The feature that distinguishes a prostitute from other people who engage in illicit sexual intercourse is the indiscrimination with which she (or he) offers herself or himself to others for hire. (Ch. 18)

pseudohermaphroditism (su″ do-her-maf′ ro-di-tizm′)   A condition in which a person is born with ambiguous genitalia as a result of a hormonal abnormality. See also **adrenogenital syndrome** and **androgen insensitivity syndrome.** (Ch. 10)

psychosexual therapy   Therapy that attempts to provide insight into the historical cause of a client's problem. (Ch. 15)

puberty (pu′ ber-te)   The time in life when an individual first shows sexual attraction and becomes capable of reproduction. (Ch. 12)

pubic (pu′ bik) **hair**   Hair that grows in the genital region starting at puberty; a secondary sex characteristic. (Ch. 2)

pubic (pu′ bik) **lice**   An infestation of the parasite *Phthirus pubis,* which attach themselves to pubic hair and feed on blood. Also known as "crabs." (Ch. 5)

pubococcygeus (pu″ bo-kok-sij′ e-us) **muscle**   The major muscle in the pelvic region. In women, voluntary control over this muscle (to help prevent urinary incontinence or to enhance physical sensations during intercourse) is gained through Kegel exercises. (Ch. 2)

Q

quickening   The first time a pregnant woman experiences movement of the fetus, usually in the 5th month. (Ch. 7)

R

random sample   A sample in which observations are drawn so that all other possible samples of the same size have an equal chance of being selected. (Ch. 1)

rape   Nonconsensual oral, anal, or vaginal penetration, obtained by force, by threat of bodily harm, or when the victim is incapable of giving consent (Koss, 1993). (Ch. 17)

rape myths   Widespread mistaken beliefs about rape. (Ch. 17)

rape-shield laws   Laws that make the prosecution of rapists easier and that also prevent the victims from feeling as if they are on trial. (Ch. 17)

rape trauma syndrome   Older term for reactions of a rape victim, including an acute phase (involving initial physical and psychological recovery from the attack) and long-term psychological reorganization (involving attempts to deal with the long-term effects of the attack and to prevent a future rape). See **post-rape posttraumatic stress disorder** (Ch. 17)

recovered memory syndrome   The recovery of memories of childhood sexual abuse that were repressed (forgotten) and then later remembered. (Ch. 17)

Reformation   Sixteenth-century religious movement that was directed at reforming the Roman Catholic Church. (Ch. 1)

refractory period   In men, the period of time after an orgasm in which their physiological responses fall below the plateau level, thus making it impossible for them to have another orgasm (until the responses build back up to plateau). (Ch. 4)

regressive pedophile   A pedophile with a past history of normal adult sexual relations. (Ch. 17)

resolution   The fourth and final phase of the sexual response cycle proposed by Masters and Johnson. It refers to a return to the unaroused state. (Ch. 4)

respiratory distress syndrome   An illness common in premature infants; caused by insufficient levels of surfactin. (Ch. 7)

retarded ejaculation   See **male ogasmic disorder.**

retrograde ejaculation   An abnormal condition experienced by some men during orgasm in which the semen is forced into the bladder instead of out of the body. (Ch. 4)

Rh factor   A protein in the blood of most individuals. If a mother does not have it and the fetus she carries does, she can develop antibodies against the Rh factor. This is called an *Rh incompatibility problem*. (Ch. 7)

Rhogam   A drug used to treat *Rh incompatibility problems*, consisting of Rh-negative blood that already has Rh antibodies. (Ch. 7)

rhythm method   See **fertility awareness methods.**

romantic love   The idealization of another; the combination of passion and liking (intimacy). (Ch. 14)

root (of penis)   The part of the penis consisting of the crura and the bulb. (Ch. 2)

RU 486   A pill that chemically induces an abortion by blocking progesterone. (Ch. 6)

rubella (roo-bel′ ah)   A disease, also known as German measles, caused by a virus. If contracted during pregnancy, it can cause fetal abnormalities. (Ch. 7)

S

sadism (sad′ izm)   A condition in which individuals repeatedly and intentionally inflict pain on others in order to achieve sexual arousal. (Ch. 16)

sadistic rapists   Rapists who are aroused by physical force and who derive pleasure by harming their victims. (Ch. 17)

sadomasochism (S&M)   A term used to indicate the linkage of sadism with masochism. (Ch. 16)

safer sex   Sexual behaviors involving a low risk of contracting a sexually transmitted disease. These include consistent use of condoms and/or abstaining from sex until one enters a long-term monogamous relationship. (Ch. 5)

sample   A subset of a population of subjects. (Ch. 1)

scabies (ska′ bez)   A contagious infestation of parasitic mites (*Sarcoptes scabiei*) that burrow under the skin to lay their eggs. (Ch. 5)

schemas   See **gender schemas.**

scoptophilia (skop″ to-fil′ e-ah)   The practice of repeatedly seeking sexual arousal by secretly observing genitals and sexual intercourse. (Ch. 16)

scrotum (skro′ tum)   The pouch beneath the penis that contains the testicles. (Ch. 2)

secondary sex characteristics   Bodily changes that occur during puberty and differentiate men and women. (Ch. 12)

secondary sexual problem   A sexual problem occurring in an individual who has not had the problem in past sexual relations. (Ch. 15)

second stage of labor   The stage of labor that begins when the cervix is fully dilated and the fetus begins moving through the birth canal. It ends with birth. (Ch. 7)

secretory phase   See **luteal (secretory) phase.**

secure   A style of attachment in which individuals do not fear abandonment and find it easy to get close to others. (Ch. 14)

self-awareness   In sexual therapy, getting in touch with one's own physical responses. (Ch. 15)

self-disclosure   Revealing one's thoughts, feelings, and emotions to another. (Ch. 14)

self-esteem   The feeling one has about oneself. (Ch. 14)

semen (se′ men)   The fluid expelled from a man's penis during orgasm, consisting of sperm and fluids from the prostate gland and seminal vesicles. (Ch. 4)

seminal vesicles (sem″ ĭ-nal ves′ĭ-k'lz)   Two structures in a man that contribute many substances to the seminal fluid. (Ch. 2)

seminiferous (se″ mĭ-nif′ er-us) **tubules**   The tubules in the testicles that produce sperm. (Ch. 2)

sensate focus exercises   Exercises designed to reduce anxiety and teach mutual pleasuring through nongenital touching in nondemanding situations. (Ch. 15)

sensuality   The state of being sensual. It encompasses all of our senses and who we are as a total person. (Ch. 2)

serial monogamy   The practice of having a series of monogamous sexual relationships. (Ch. 5, 12)

Sertoli (ser-to′lēz) **cells**   Cells in the testicles that produce the hormone inhibin. (Ch. 2, 3)

sex ("had sex")   Many people limit this term to vaginal intercourse. In this text, unless otherwise specified, it refers to "any mutually voluntary activity with another person that involves genital contact and sexual excitement... even if intercourse or orgasm did not occur" (Laumann et al., 1994). (Ch. 1)

sex roles   Behaviors that are associated with being stereotypically masculine or feminine. (Ch. 10)

sex-tension flush   The rash that appears on the skin (due to vasocongestion) in 50–75 percent of all women and 25 percent of all men during the plateau phase of the sexual response cycle. (Ch. 4)

sexual addiction   See **hypersexuality.**

sexual aversion   An extreme form of hypoactive sexual desire in which an individual's avoidance of sex becomes phobic. (Ch. 15)

sexual coercion   The act of forcing another person into unwanted sexual activity by physical or verbal coercion (restraint or constraint). (Ch. 17)

sexual deviance   "The inappropriate or flawed performance of a conventionally understood sexual practice" (Simon, 1994). (Ch. 16)

sexual harassment   Unwelcome sexual advances that persist after the recipient has indicated that they are unwanted. See text for an expanded definition. (Ch. 17)

sexual history   One of the first steps in most sexual therapy programs. (Ch. 15)

sexuality   All of the sexual attitudes, feelings, and behaviors associated with being human. The term does not refer specifically to a person's capacity for erotic response or to sexual acts, but rather to a dimension of one's personality. (Ch. 1, 9)

sexual learning   Knowledge about sex that is received (usually informally) from family, friends, the media, and society in general. (Ch. 8)

sexually healthy person   Someone who feels comfortable with his or her sexuality and who feels free to choose whether or not to try a variety of sexual behaviors. (Ch. 13)

sexually related diseases   Diseases of the reproductive system or genitals that are not contracted through sexual activity. Often involve overgrowths of bacteria, yeasts, viruses, or fungal organisms that are found naturally in sexual and reproductive organs. (Ch. 5)

sexually transmitted diseases   Diseases that can be, but are not necessarily always, transmitted by sexual contact.

This term is generally preferred to the term *venereal diseases*. (Ch. 5)

sexual orientation A distinct preference for sexual partners of a particular sex in the presence of clear alternatives. (Ch. 11)

sexual perversion A problem of sexual desire, "not only in the sense that it appears to violate the sexual practices of a time and place, but also because it constitutes a violation of common understandings that render current sexual practice plausible" (Simon, 1994). (Ch. 16)

sexual prejudice Socially reinforced negative attitudes toward homosexuals, homosexual communities, and homosexual behaviors. (Ch. 11)

sexual response cycle The physiological responses that occur during sexual arousal, which many therapists and researchers have arbitrarily divided into different phases. (Ch. 4)

sexual revolution A period in U.S. history, beginning about 1960, of increased sexual permissiveness. (Ch. 1)

sexual self-schemas Cognitive views by individuals about sexual aspects of themselves. (Ch. 12)

sexual surrogate See **surrogate**.

sexual variant Unusual behaviors that are engaged in for variety and not as one's preferred manner of becoming sexually aroused. (Ch. 16)

shaft The long body of the penis or clitoris. (Ch. 2)

shigellosis (she″ gel-lo′ sis) A disease that can be contracted during sexual activity by exposure to feces containing the *Shigella* bacterium. (Ch. 5)

situational ethics Values or ethics that emphasize the proper thing to do in particular situations. (Ch. 8)

situational molesters Child molesters who have a primary sexual orientation to adults. They have sex with children impulsively and regard their behavior as abnormal. (Ch. 17)

situational sexual problem A sexual problem that occurs only in specific situations. (Ch. 15)

Skene's (skenz) **glands** Glands located in the urethras of some women that are thought to develop from the same embryonic tissue as the man's prostate, and that may be the source of a fluid emitted by some women during orgasm. (Ch. 4)

smegma (smeg′mah) The cheesy secretion of sebaceous glands that can cause the clitoris to stick to the clitoral hood or the foreskin of the penis to stick to the glans. (Ch. 2)

socialization The process of internalizing society's beliefs; the manner in which a society shapes individual behaviors and expectations of behaviors. (Ch. 9, 10)

socializing agent The social influences (e.g., parents, peers, the media) that shape behaviors. (Ch. 9)

sodomy (sod′ o-me) **laws** Laws that prohibit oral and/or anal sex. (Ch. 18)

spectatoring Observing and evaluating one's own sexual responses. This generally causes distraction, with subsequent erectile and/or orgasm problems. (Ch. 15)

sperm The germ cell of a man. (Ch. 2, 7)

spermatic (sper-mat′ ik) **cord** The cord that suspends a testicle in the scrotum. (Ch. 2)

spermatorrhea (sper″ mah-to-re′ ah) The Victorian name for male nocturnal emissions (wet dreams), so named because Victorian physicians believed it was caused by the same thing that caused gonorrhea. (Ch. 1, 13)

spermicides Chemicals that kill sperm. In most products, the chemical is nonoxynol-9. (Ch. 6)

start-up stage of labor The stage of labor that begins with uterine contractions pushing the fetus downward toward the cervix and ends when the cervix is fully dilated. (Ch. 7)

statistically normal A range of behaviors or values that encompasses a large number of individuals. (Ch. 13)

statutory rape Sexual intercourse by an adult with a (consenting) partner who is not yet of the legal "age of consent." Sometimes called "carnal knowledge of a juvenile." (Ch. 17)

stereotypes Oversimplified, preconceived beliefs that supposedly apply to anyone in a given group. (Ch. 10)

sterilization A general term for surgical techniques that render an individual infertile. (Ch. 6)

storge (stor′ ga) An affectionate type of love that grows from friendship. (Ch. 14)

straight A term used by homosexuals for a heterosexual. (Ch. 11)

stranger rape Rape committed by someone who is not known by the victim. (Ch. 17)

stratified random sample A sample in which subgroups are randomly selected in the same proportion as they exist in the population. Thus the sample is representative of the target population. (Ch. 1)

streetwalker A prostitute who solicits in public. (Ch. 18)

submission Obeying and yielding to another individual. In sexual relations, it generally involves being humiliated by the partner as well. (Ch. 16)

surfactin A liquid that lets the lungs transmit oxygen from the atmosphere to the blood. (Ch. 7)

surrogate A person, usually a woman, trained and skilled in sensate focus techniques who works under the direction of a therapist with a single partnerless client undergoing sexual therapy. (Ch. 15)

surrogate mother A woman who carries a fetus to full term for another couple, agreeing to give the infant to the other couple after it is born. The infant generally represents a union of the sperm from the man and either his partner's ovum or the ovum of the surrogate mother. (Ch. 7)

survey A study of people's attitudes, opinions, or behaviors. Responses are usually obtained either in a face-to-face interview or on a paper-and-pencil questionnaire. (Ch. 1)

swinging A type of open marriage relationship in which a couple has extramarital relations together with other couples. (Ch. 12)

swish A slang term for an effeminate gay. This is a stereotype that generally does not reflect how most gays look or behave. (Ch. 11)

symptomatic HIV infection Formerly called AIDS-related complex (ARC); the early symptoms of HIV infection, which eventually lead to AIDS. (Ch. 5)

sympto-thermal method A combination of the basal body temperature and Billings fertility awareness methods. (Ch. 6)

syphilis (sif′ ĭ-lis) A sexually transmitted disease caused by the *Treponema pallidum* bacterium (spirochete), which can also pass directly through any cut or scrape into the bloodstream. (Ch. 5)

systematic desensitization A therapy technique used to reduce anxiety by slowly introducing elements of the anxiety-producing theme. (Ch. 15, 16)

T

telephone scatologia (skat″ o-lo′ge-ah) A condition in which sexual arousal is achieved primarily by making obscene telephone calls. (Ch. 16)

teratogens (teh rat′ ojinz) Substances that can harm an embryo or fetus. (Ch. 7)

testicles (tes′ ty-k'ls) The male gonads that produce sperm and male hormones. (Ch. 2)

testicular torsion An uncommon condition in which the spermatic cord twists and cuts off the blood supply to the testicles. (Ch. 2)

testosterone (tes-tos′ te-ron) A hormone that is produced by the testicles (and in very small amounts by the ovaries and adrenal glands). (Ch. 2, 3, 10)

third stage of labor Detachment and expulsion of the placenta from the uterus after childbirth. (Ch. 7)

thrush A yeast infection (candidiasis) of the mouth. (Ch. 5)

token resistance [to sex] Saying "no" to sex when one means "yes." (Ch. 17)

toxemia of pregnancy A disease of pregnancy characterized in its early stage (preeclampsia) by high blood pressure, weight gain, swollen joints, and protein in the urine. Unless it is corrected, it can lead to convulsions and coma. (Ch. 7)

toxic shock syndrome A syndrome with symptoms of high fever, vomiting, diarrhea, and dizziness; caused by toxins produced by the *Staphylococcus aureus* bacterium. (Ch. 3)

transgender An individual whose gender roles are opposite of those that society expects based on his or her anatomy. (Ch. 10)

transition phase The last part of the start-up stage of labor, during which the cervix dilates to 10 cm in order for the baby to be able to enter the birth canal. (Ch. 7)

transsexual An adult whose gender identity does not match his or her biological sex. (Ch. 10)

transvestism A condition in which sexual arousal is achieved primarily by dressing as a member of the opposite sex. (Ch. 16)

triangular theory of love Sternberg's theory of love, which says that all of our different positive emotions are the result of different combinations of intimacy, passion, and decision/commitment. (Ch. 14)

trichomoniasis (trik″ o-mo-ni′ ah-sis) A type of vaginitis caused by a one-celled protozoan that is usually transmitted during sexual intercourse. (Ch. 5)

trimesters Three-month periods of pregnancy (months 1–3, 4–6, and 7–9), so labeled for descriptive purposes. (Ch. 7)

trophoblast (trof′ o-blast) The outer four cell layers of the embryo. (Ch. 7)

tubal ligation A female sterilization technique that originally referred only to the tying of the Fallopian tubes, but which is now often used as a general term for a variety of female sterilization techniques. (Ch. 6)

tubal pregnancy Implantation of a blastocyst in a Fallopian tube. (Ch. 7)

Turner's syndrome A condition in which women have only one X chromosome; as a result, their ovaries never develop properly. (Ch. 10)

two-spirit In North American Indian tribes of past centuries, a person, usually a man, who assumed the dress, occupations, and behavior of the other sex in order to effect a change in gender status. The term now preferred by Native Americans and anthropologists over *berdache*. (Ch. 10)

typical-use pregnancy rate For a particular birth control technique, the percentage of pregnancies during the first year of use by all couples who use the technique, regardless of whether or not they use it properly or consistently. See also **perfect-use pregnancy rate.** (Ch. 6)

U

ultrasound A noninvasive technique for examining the internal organs of a fetus; it uses sound waves like a radar or sonar scan to create a picture. (Ch. 7)

umbilical (um-bil′ ĭ-kal) **cord** The cord that connects an embryo or fetus to the mother's placenta. (Ch. 7)

unconditional love Feelings of love that do not depend on the loved one meeting certain expectations or desires. (Ch. 14)

undifferentiated Individuals who are low on both masculine and feminine traits. (Ch. 10)

urethra (u-re′ thrah) The passageway from the bladder to the exterior of the body. In men, it also serves as a passageway for semen during ejaculation. (Ch. 2)

urophilia (u″ ro-fil′ e-ah) Sexual arousal caused by urine or the act of urination. (Ch. 16)

uterus (u′ ter-us) The womb. The hollow, muscular organ in women where the fertilized egg normally implants. (Ch. 2)

V

vagina (vah-ji′ nah) The sheathlike canal in a woman that extends from the vulva to the cervix and that receives the penis during intercourse. (Ch. 2)

vaginal lubrication The first sign of sexual arousal in women; the result of the vaginal walls becoming engorged with blood. (Ch. 4)

vaginismus (vaj″ ĭ-niz′ mus) A sexual problem in women in which pain is experienced during attempted intercourse because of involuntary spasms in the muscles surrounding the outer third of the vagina. (Ch. 15)

vaginitis (vaj″ ĭ-ni′ tis) A general term that refers to any inflammation of the vagina. There are three general types: trichomoniasis, moniliasis, and bacterial vaginosis. (Ch. 5)

vas deferens (vas def′ er-enz) The second part of the duct system that transports sperm out of a man's body. (Ch. 2)

vasectomy (vah-sek′ to-me) The male sterilization technique in which the vas deferens is tied off and cut, thus preventing passage of sperm through the reproductive tract. (Ch. 2, 6)

vasocongestion (vas′ o kunjes′chun) The engorgement (filling) of tissues with blood. (Ch. 4)

venereal diseases Term originally used to refer to gonorrhea, syphilis, and three other diseases that are spread almost exclusively by sexual contact. (Ch. 5)

venereal warts See **genital warts.**

vernix caseosa A waxy bluish substance that covers a new-born baby. (Ch. 7)

vestibular (ves-tĭb′ u-lar) **area** A term used to refer to the area between the two labia minora. (Ch. 2)

vestibular (ves-tĭb′ u-lar) **bulbs** Structures surrounding the vaginal opening that fill with blood during sexual arousal, resulting in swelling of the tissues and a narrowing of the vaginal opening. (Ch. 2)

Victorian era The period during the reign of Queen Victoria of England (1819–1901). With regard to sexuality, it was a time of great public prudery (the pleasurable aspects of sex were denied) and many incorrect medical beliefs. (Ch. 1)

violent sexually explicit material Sexually explicit material that depicts violence, almost always showing men treating women violently. (Ch. 18)

viral load The amount of virus in the blood of an individual. (Ch. 5)

virus A protein shell around a nucleic acid core. Viruses have either RNA or DNA, but not both, and thus cannot reproduce themselves. They invade host cells that provide the material to manufacture new virus particles. (Ch. 5)

volunteer bias A bias in research results that is caused by differences between people who agree to participate and others who refuse. (Ch. 1)

voyeurism (voi′ yer-izm) Repeatedly seeking sexual arousal by observing nude individuals without their knowledge or consent. (Ch. 16)

vulva (vul′ vah) A term for the external female genitalia, including the mons veneris, labia majora, labia minora, clitoris, vaginal opening, and urethral opening. (Ch. 2)

W

wet dream An involuntary nocturnal emission of semen. This type of ejaculation often is a boy's first experience with ejaculation, as wet dreams generally begin at the onset of puberty. (Ch. 12, 13)

withdrawal (coitus interruptus) Withdrawal of the man's penis from his partner's vagina before ejaculation in order to avoid conception. It is sometimes ineffective because fluids from the Cowper's glands may contain sperm. (Ch. 6)

Wolffian duct system A primitive duct system found in embryos that, if allowed to develop, becomes the male reproductive system. (Ch. 10)

Z

zona pellucida (zo′nah pellu′ cĭda) The surface of an ovum. (Ch. 7)

zoophilia (zo″ ofil′ e-ah) Using sexual contact with animals as the primary means of achieving sexual gratification. (Ch. 16)

zygote (zi′ got) The one-celled organism created from the fusion of a sperm and egg. (Ch. 7)

zygote intrafallopian transfer (ZIFT) A method of treating infertility caused by blocked Fallopian tubes. An ovum taken from the infertile woman is fertilized by sperm from her partner and then transferred to the unblocked portion of a Fallopian tube. (Ch. 7)

Resources

GENERAL

American College Health Association
P.O. Box 28937
Baltimore, MD 21240-8937
(410) 859-1500
www.acha.org

Kinsey Institute For Research in Sex,
Gender, and Reproduction
Indiana University
Morrison Hall
Bloomington, IN 47405
www.indiana.edu/~kinsey
Kinsey Library (E-mail):
libknsy@indiana.edu

SIECUS (Sex Information and Education
Council of the U.S.)
130 West 42nd Street, Suite 350
New York, NY 10036
(212) 819-9770
www.siecus.org

Society for the Scientific Study of Sex
1248 Warwick Place
Allentown, PA 18104
(610) 530-2483
www.ssc.wisc.edu/ssss

ABORTION

National Abortion and Reproductive
Rights Action League
1156 15th Street, N.W., Suite 700
Washington, DC 20005
(202) 973-3000
www.naral.org
   The leading pro-choice abortion group.

National Right to Life Committee
419 7th Street, N.W., Suite 500
Washington, DC 20004
(202) 626-8800
www.nrlc.org
   The leading anti-abortion group.

BIRTH CONTROL/WOMEN'S
REPRODUCTIVE HEALTH

Advocates For Youth
1025 Vermont Avenue, NW
Suite 200
Washington, DC 20005
(202) 347-5700
www.advocatesforyouth.org

Alan Guttmacher Institute
120 Wall Street, 21st Floor
New York, NY 10005
(212) 248-1111
www.agi-usa.org

Association for Voluntary Surgical
Contraception (AVSC)
440 9th Avenue, 3rd Floor
New York, NY 10001
(212) 561-8000
www.avsc.org

Planned Parenthood Federation of
America
810 Seventh Avenue
New York, NY 10019
(212) 541-7800
www.ppfa.org/ppfa
   You can contact the national
   headquarters to get the address and
   phone number of the clinic closest to
   you.

The Population Institute
107 2nd Street, NE
Washington, DC 20002
(202) 544-3300
www.populationinstitute.org

CANCER

American Cancer Society
19 West 56th Street
New York, NY 10019
Information Center:
1(800) ACS-2345
   Local units can be found in your
   telephone directory.
www.cancer.org

National Cancer Institute Cancer
Information Service
1(800) 4-CANCER
www.cancer.gov

CHILD SEXUAL ABUSE/INCEST

CHILDHELP National Child Abuse
Hotline
1(800) 422-4453
www.childhelpusa.org
   Provides information, crisis intervention,
   and referrals to local services if you wish
   to report abuse.

Children's Defense Fund
25 E Street, N.W.
Washington, DC 20001
(202) 628-8787
www.childrensdefense.org
   Provides information about child abuse
   prevention.

Incest Survivors Anonymous
P.O. Box 17245
Long Beach, CA 90807-7245
(562) 428-5599
   For incest victims.

Incest Recovery Services of the Family
Place
P. O. Box 7999
Dallas, TX 75209
(214) 559-2170
www.familyplace.org
   For incest victims.

National Center for Missing and
Exploited Children
699 Prince Street
Alexandria, VA 22314
1(800) 843-5678
(703) 274-3900 (office)
www.missingkids.com
   For parents who wish to report missing
   children, and others who may have
   information about missing children,
   child pornography, or child prostitution.

RAINN (Rape, Abuse, and Incest
National Network)
1(800) 656-HOPE
   Contact them for the number and
   address of the rape crisis program nearest
   to you.

YWCA Rape Crisis Program
   Check your telephone directory for a
   program nearest to you, or call RAINN
   (see above).

GENDER AND WOMEN

Boston Women's Health Collective
240A Elm Street
Somerville, MA 02144
(617) 625-0271
www.ourbodiesourselves.org

Intersex Society of North America
P.O. Box 31791
San Francisco, CA 94131
E-mail: info@isna.org

Kinsey Institute For Research in Sex,
Gender, and Reproduction
Indiana University
Morrison Hall
Bloomington, IN 47405
www.indiana.edu/~kinsey
Kinsey library (E-mail):
libknsy@indiana.edu

National Organization for Women
1000 16th Street, NW, Suite 700
Washington, DC 20036
(202) 331-0066

HIV/AIDS

AIDS Information Exchange
U.S. Conference of Mayors
1620 I Street, N.W.
Washington, DC 20006
(202) 293-7330

American Red Cross AIDS Public
  Education Program
2131 K Street, NW
Washington, DC 20037
(202) 728-6400

ACLU Lesbian and Gay Rights/AIDS
  Project
American Civil Liberties Union
125 Broad Street, 18th Floor
New York, NY 10004 .
(212) 549-2500
www.aclu.org

National HIV/AIDS Hotline (Centers for
  Disease Control and Prevention)
1(800) 342-AIDS

National AIDS Information
  Clearinghouse
1(800) 458-5231
  Service provided by the Centers for
  Disease Control and Prevention.

National Association of People with AIDS
1413 K Street, N.W.
Seventh Floor
Washington, DC 20005
(202) 898-0414
www.napwa.org

See also listings under "homosexuality."

HOMOSEXUALITY

ACLU Lesbian and Gay Rights/AIDS
  Project
American Civil Liberties Union
125 Broad Street, 18th Floor
New York, NY 10004
(212) 549-2500
www.aclu.org

Federation of Parents and Friends of
  Lesbians and Gays (PFLAG)
1726 M Street, Suite 400
Washington, DC 20036
(202) 638-4200
www.pflag.org

Gay Men's Health Crisis
119 W. 24th Street, 6th Floor
New York, NY 10011
AIDS Hotline: (212) 807-6655
www.gmhc.org

Hetrick-Martin Institute
2 Astor Place
New York, NY 10003
(212) 674-2400
  Gay, lesbian, bisexual, and transgendered
  youth service agency.

Lambda Legal Defense and Education
  Fund, Inc.
6030 Wilshire Blvd., Suite 200
Los Angeles, CA 90036-3617
(213) 937-2728

National Gay and Lesbian Task
  Force
1700 Kalorama Road, NW
Washington, DC 20009
(202) 332-6483
www.ngltf.org

INFERTILITY/ADOPTION

American Society for Reproductive
  Medicine
1209 Montgomery Highway
Birmingham, AL 35216
(205) 978-5000
www.asrm.org
  Formerly called the American Fertility
  Society

National Council for Adoption
1930 17th Street, N.W.
Washington, DC 20009
(202) 328-1200
www.ncfa-usa.org
  Contact them for information about
  adoption services in your area.

Resolve, Inc.
1310 Broadway
Somerville, MA 02144-1779
(617) 623-0744
www.resolve.org
  Provides advice and help about
  infertility.

PREGNANCY/CHILDBIRTH

American College of Nurse-
  Midwives
818 Connecticut Avenue, N.W., Suite 900
Washington, DC 20006
(202) 728-9860
www.midwife.org

American College of Obstetricians and
  Gynecologists
409 12th Street, S.W.
Washington, DC 20024
(202) 638-5577
www.acog.org

Lamaze International
2025 M Street, NW
Washington, DC 20036
1(800) 368-4404
www.lamaze.org
  Contact them for the name and address
  of a certified Lamaze instructor in your
  area.

La Leche League International
1400 North Meacham Road
Schaumburg, IL 60173-4840
(800) LA-LECHE
  Advice about breast-feeding.

March of Dimes Birth Defects
  Foundation
1275 Mamaroneck Avenue
White Plains, NY 10605
(914) 428-7100
www.modimes.org
  Provides information on birth defects
  and gives referrals to genetic counseling
  and services in your area.

RAPE

Center for the Prevention of Sexual and
  Domestic Violence
936 North 34th Street, Suite 200
Seattle, Washington 98103
(206) 634-1903
www.cpsdv.org

National Clearinghouse on Marital and
  Date Rape
(510) 524-1582

National Resource Center on Domestic
  Violence
1(800) 537-2238

National Center For Victims of Crime
2111 Wilson Blvd., Suite 300
Arlington, VA 22201
(703) 276-2880
www.ncvc.org

RAINN (Rape, Abuse, and Incest
  National Network)
1(800) 656-HOPE
  Contact them for the number and
  address of the rape crisis program nearest
  to you.

U.S. Department of Justice
Office of Violence Against Women
810 7th Street, NW
Washington, DC 20531
(202) 307-6026
www.ojp.usdoj.gov.vawo

YWCA Rape Crisis Program
  Check your telephone directory for a
  program nearest to you, or call RAINN
  (see above).

RUNAWAY CHILDREN

Covenant House (Crisis Intervention
  Hotline)
1(800) 999-9999
  Provides counseling, shelter, and other
  referral services.

National Youth Crisis Hotline
1(800) 448-4663
  They will put you in touch with the
  nearest shelter program.

National Runaway Switchboard
1(800) 621-4000
  They encourage runaway children to
  reestablish contact with their families.

SEX/MARITAL THERAPY

AAMFT (American Association for
    Marriage and Family Therapy)
1133 15th Street, N.W., Suite 300
Washington, DC 20005
(202) 452-0109
www.aamft.org
    They will provide names and addresses
    of certified marriage and family
    therapists in your area.

AASECT (American Association of Sex
    Educators, Counselors and Therapists)
106 East Cary Street
Richmond, VA 23219
(804) 644-3288
www.aasect.org
    They will provide names and addresses
    of certified sex counselors and therapists
    in your area.

American Board of Sexology, and
    The American Academy of Clinical
    Sexologists
1929 18th Street, N.W., Suite 1166
Washington, DC 20009
(202) 462-2122
www.esextherapy.com
    They will provide names and addresses
    of certified sex therapists and sex
    educators in your area.

SEXUAL HARASSMENT

Center for Women in Government
State University of New York at Albany
Draper Hall, Room 302
135 Western Avenue
Albany, NY 12222
(518) 442-3900
www.cwig.albany.edu

National Organization for Women
733 15th Street, NW
2nd Floor
Washington, D.C. 20005
(202) 331-0066
www.now.org

SEXUALLY TRANSMITTED DISEASES
(OTHER THAN HIV/AIDS)

American Social Health Association
P.O. Box 13827
Research Triangle Park, NC 27709
www.ashastd.org

Herpes Resource Center (hotline)
(919) 361-8488
    Service provided by the American Social
    Health Association.

CDC National STD and AIDS Hotline
1 (800) 227-8922
    Service provided by the American Social
    Health Association, and funded by the
    Centers for Disease Control and
    Prevention.

Credits

Answers to Questions

CHAPTER 1

1. their friends
2. the media (e.g., TV)
3. 85
4. sexuality
5. the biblical Hebrews
6. Christians
7. St. Augustine
8. Queen Victoria
9. penicillin
10. the birth control pill and IUD
11. Sigmund Freud
12. Henry Havelock Ellis
13. Alfred Kinsey
14. Masters and Johnson
15. true
16. false
17. false
18. false
19. false
20. false
21. false
22. false
23. true
24. true
25. true
26. false
27. true
28. false
29. false
30. true
31. true
32. f
33. p
34. g
35. n
36. h
37. m
38. i
39. d
40. o
41. c
42. a
43. j
44. q
45. g
46. i
47. l
48. m
49. b
50. c
51. o
52. f
53. n
54. a
55. j
56. g
57. k
58. h
59. e
60. d
61. Inis Baeg
62. leisure time, mobility, birth control, antibiotics
63. each possible sample of that size
64. Plato
65. Puritans
66. freedom of belief
67. body, soul
68. spermatorrhea
69. St. Augustine
70. "Any mutually voluntary activity with another person that involves genital contact. . ."

CHAPTER 2

1. vulva
2. mons veneris
3. labia majora
4. labia minora
5. clitoris
6. vaginal opening
7. urethral opening
8. mons veneris
9. outer surfaces of the labia majora
10. clitoris
11. penis
12. labia minora
13. vestibular area
14. hymen
15. eight
16. vagina
17. uterus
18. Fallopian tubes
19. ovaries
20. vagina
21. vagina
22. Grafenberg (G) spot
23. ovary
24. Fallopian tube
25. uterus
26. endometrium
27. cancer of the cervix
28. scrotum
29. testicles
30. corpora cavernosa
31. corpus spongiosum
32. glans
33. foreskin
34. circumcision
35. testicles
36. testosterone
37. epididymis
38. vas deferens
39. ejaculatory ducts
40. urethra
41. prostate gland
42. seminal vesicles
43. semen
44. Cowper's glands
45. testicles
46. prostate gland
47. true
48. true
49. true
50. false
51. false
52. true
53. false
54. false
55. false
56. true
57. true
58. false
59. false
60. false
61. false
62. false
63. s
64. c
65. d
66. e
67. h
68. a
69. f
70. b
71. i
72. p
73. k
74. l
75. m
76. n
77. g
78. j
79. o
80. q
81. r
82. t
83. Pap smear; cervical
84. prostate gland
85. labia majora
86. endometrium
87. blood
88. Cowper's glands
89. amount of fatty tissue
90. just after menstruation
91. ejaculatory ducts
92. seminal vesicles
93. after a warm bath or shower
94. Bartholin's glands
95. seminiferous tubules
96. clitoris
97. pubococcygeus (PC)
98. front
99. prolactin
100. pituitary

CHAPTER 3

1. endocrine
2. testosterone
3. estrogen
4. progesterone
5. pituitary gland
6. 28
7. follicle-stimulating hormone (FSH)
8. follicle
9. follicular (or proliferative)
10. endometrium
11. FSH
12. luteinizing hormone (LH)
13. LH
14. ovulation
15. abdominal cavity
16. Fallopian tube
17. luteal (or secretory)
18. corpus luteum
19. endometrium
20. endometrium
21. menstruation
22. at least 8 days
23. estrous
24. estrus (ovulation)
25. taboos
26. sloughed off endometrial tissue
27. cervical mucus
28. blood

29. sperm production
30. luteinizing hormone
31. male hormones (e.g., testosterone)
32. high blood pressure; liver, prostate, and breast tumors; impaired reproductive function; masculinization in women; emotional or psychological problems
33. amenorrhea
34. 3 to 14
35. premenstrual syndrome (PMS)
36. with the start of menstruation
37. dysmenorrhea

38. prostaglandins
39. endometrial tissue grows outside the uterus
40. toxic shock syndrome
41. testosterone
42. estrogen
43. progesterone
44. testosterone
45. false
46. false
47. false
48. false (28 days is an average)
49. true
50. true
51. false
52. false (there is no strong evidence for this)

53. false
54. false
55. true
56. true
57. false
58. false
59. h
60. d
61. n
62. j
63. l
64. k
65. b
66. m
67. f
68. o
69. e
70. p
71. i

72. a
73. c
74. g
75. pituitary
76. pheromones
77. follicle
78. corpus luteum
79. progesterone
80. testosterone
81. human chorionic gonadotropin (HCG)
82. gonadotropin-releasing hormone (GnRH)
83. progesterone
84. testosterone
85. inhibin

CHAPTER 4

1. Masters and Johnson
2. more similar
3. excitement
4. plateau
5. orgasm
6. resolution
7. sexual response cycle
8. Helen Kaplan
9. desire
10. vasocongestive
11. penile erection
12. vaginal lubrication
13. plateau
14. orgasmic platform
15. pulls back against the pubic bone and disappears beneath the clitoral hood
16. 50 to 75
17. sex-tension flush

18. rhythmic muscular contractions
19. the brain
20. similar
21. emission
22. expulsion
23. ejaculation
24. refractory period
25. multiple orgasms
26. resolution
27. 30 to 50
28. clitoral
29. clitoral
30. vaginal
31. clitoris
32. front
33. Grafenberg (G) spot
34. emission of fluid
35. prostate gland
36. not important

37. aphrodisiacs
38. clitoridectomy
39. infibulation
40. false
41. true
42. false (not necessarily)
43. true
44. false
45. true
46. true
47. false
48. false
49. true
50. true
51. true
52. false
53. true
54. false
55. true
56. false

57. true
58. false
59. d
60. b, g, j, k, l, n, s
61. a, c, f, i, q, r, t
62. e, p, u
63. h, m, o
64. b, c, g, i, k, q, t
65. vasocongestion, myotonia
66. urethra
67. sex-tension flush
68. myotonia
69. emission
70. orgasmic platform
71. Grafenberg (G) spot
72. refractory period
73. labia minora

CHAPTER 5

1. 4
2. bacteria
3. viruses
4. parasites
5. gonorrhea
6. chlamydia
7. syphilis
8. gonorrhea
9. chlamydia
10. pelvic inflammatory disease (PID)
11. syphilis
12. antibiotics
13. skin, skin
14. recurrent
15. liver
16. feces
17. blood and other body fluids
18. human papilloma
19. human immunodeficiency virus (HIV)

20. CD4+
21. immune
22. opportunistic
23. 10
24. intimate sexual activity
25. blood
26. casual contact
27. men and women
28. infestations of parasites
29. trichomoniasis
30. monilial
31. bacterial vaginosis
32. false
33 true
34. false
35. false
36. false
37. true
38. false
39. true
40. false

41. true
42. false
43. false
44. false
45. true
46. false
47. true
48. false
49. false
50. false
51. false
52. false
53. false
54. true
55. true
56. true
57. true
58. false
59. true
60. true
61. false
62. a

63. l
64. c
65. q
66. h
67. f
68. o
69. i
70. m
71. j
72. e
73. n
74. g
75. b
76. d
77. p
78. k
79. parasites
80. vaginitis
81. pelvic inflammatory disease
82. human papillomavirus infection

83. human immunodeficiency virus (HIV) infection
84. types of vaginitis
85. hepatitis
86. acyclovir and 3 newer drugs
87. ectopic pregnancy, infertility
88. syphilis, human immunodeficiency virus, hepatitis
89. stress
90. mucous membranes
91. nongonoccoccal (or nonspecific) urethritis
92. yeast (moniliasis)
93. pinworms
94. chlamydia
95. CD4+ cells
96. during the first 60 days and late in the infection (AIDS)
97. HIV antibodies
98. gonorrhea, chlamydia, syphilis (the chancre is often internal), HPV infection, HIV infection
99. HPV infection, HIV infection, trichomoniasis
100. always use condoms, abstain from sex until you are in a long-term monogamous relationship

CHAPTER 6

1. over twice
2. half
3. calendar
4. basal body temperature
5. Billings
6. ovulation
7. spermicides
8. the diaphragm
9. the cervical cap
10. condoms
11. contraceptive sponge
12. uterus or vagina
13. offer some protection against sexually transmitted diseases
14. estrogen
15. progesterone
16. Depo-Provera
17. Norplant
18. 72
19. vas deferens
20. tubal ligation
21. laparoscopy
22. true
23. false
24. false
25. true
26. false
27. false
28. true
29. true
30. false
31. false
32. false
33. false
34. false
35. false
36. true
37. true
38. false
39. false
40. false
41. true
42. false
43. true
44. true
45. true
46. true
47. true
48. true
49. true
50. false
51. true
52. c
53. i
54. k
55. d
56. b, e
57. h
58. h
59. e
60. e
61. b, e, g
62. n
63. a, n
64. c, j, m
65. j
66. j
67. l
68. f
69. f
70. the Cowper's glands
71. he has had 12 to 16 ejaculations
72. 7, 20
73. rises slightly
74. clear and slippery
75. oil-based
76. in a stable monogamous relationship who have completed their families
77. male condom, female condom, contraceptive sponge
78. menstrual irregularities
79. male condom, female condom, diaphragm with spermicide, spermicides
80. The Yuzpe Method or implantation of a copper IUD
81. male condom with spermicide
82. 5 days
83. to abstain from sex

CHAPTER 7

1. 5
2. ovulation
3. 1
4. Fallopian tube
5. endometrium
6. ectopic
7. chlamydia and/or gonorrhea
8. human chorionic gonadotropin (HCG)
9. trimesters
10. embryo
11. 2
12. fetus
13. 7
14. quickening
15. 4th or 5th
16. teratogens
17. amniocentesis
18. fear-tension-pain
19. midwife
20. contractions
21. dilation
22. start-up
23. amniotic sac
24. transition phase
25. fully dilated
26. head
27. umbilical cord
28. placenta
29. cesarean (C-section)
30. proteins
31. postpartum blues or depression
32. 4 to 6
33. the sharing of childcare and housekeeping responsibilities
34. 10
35. 40
36. 40
37. 20
38. a low sperm count
39. artificial insemination
40. Fallopian tubes
41. ovulate
42. in vitro fertilization
43. zygote intrafallopian transfer
44. gamete intrafallopian transfer
45. false
46. false
47. true
48. false
49. true
50. false
51. false
52. false
53. false
54. true
55. false
56. false
57. true
58. true
59. false
60. false
61. false
62. true
63. false
64. false
65. d
66. j
67. f
68. l
69. c
70. b
71. h
72. k
73. m
74. i
75. a
76. g
77. e
78. d
79. morula, blastocyst
80. umbilical cord
81. preeclampsia
82. lightening
83. contractions are coming 10 minutes apart (or sooner) on a regular basis; contractions are at least 30 seconds long on a regular basis; cervix is dilated to at least two to three centimeters; cervix is at least 70 percent effaced
84. first
85. tubal
86. 25 to 35
87. blastocyst

88. the head
89. end of the first (beginning of the second)
90. 24 hours
91. amnion
92. episiotomies,
prepping, cesarean sections
93. 23 to 24 weeks
94. 2
95. 18 to 23 months
96. a failure to ovulate

CHAPTER 8

1. stereotypic gender roles
2. vocabulary
3. positive
4. negative
5. "you"
6. "why"
7. "we"
8. self-disclose
9. listener
10. eye contact
11. facial expressions
12. interpersonal distance
13. touch
14. sexual learning
15. no more
16. in early childhood
(preschool years)
17. how you say it
18. scare tactics
19. willingness to come to you when they have questions and problems
20. true
21. false
22. true
23. true
24. false
25. false
26. false
27. true
28. false
29. true
30. false (not true for all couples in all instances)
31. false
32. false
33. false
34. false
35. true
36. false
37. c
38. a
39. c
40. d
41. c or d
42. b
43. b
44. e
45. d
46. e
47. b
48. "I"
49. "communication"
50. verbal, nonverbal
51. age
52. behavior, character
53. your own pleasure
54. collaborative
55. mutual constructive, avoidance, demand/withdraw
56. their disagreements
57. open and comfortable
58. demand, withdraw

CHAPTER 9

1. sexuality
2. society
3. temptresses
4. virgin/whore
5. asexual
6. Freud
7. sex education courses
8. socialization
9. socializing agents
10. peers
11. school
12. religion
13. religion
14. the media
15. movies
16. radio
17. music
18. magazines
19. three-fourths
20. identification
21. Europe
22. false
23. true
24. true
25. false
26. true
27. true
28. true
29. true
30. true
31. false
32. true
33. true
34. false
35. false
36. true
37. false
38. ideology
39. sexuality
40. virgin/nymphomaniac
41. Islamic
42. television
43. 6.6

CHAPTER 10

1. gender identity
2. XX
3. XY
4. Klinefelter's
5. Turner's
6. testosterone
7. girl
8. intersexuals
9. gender dysphoria
10. gender identity disorder (transsexuals)
11. Freudian
12. social learning
13. gender constancy
14. 6 or 7
15. gender roles
16. individualist
17. microstructural
18. independent
19. androgyny
20. schemas
21. androgynous
22. false
23. true
24. true
25. true
26. true
27. true
28. false
29. true
30. true
31. true
32. true
33. true
34. true
35. true
36. false
37. false
38. true
39. true
40. true
41. false
42. f, g, n
43. e
44. i
45. p
46. q
47. b, j, l
48. b, d, j, l
49. c
50. f, g, o
51. a, l
52. m
53. k
54. h, j
55. gender constancy
56. 1800s (when the United States and other countries became industrialized)
57. microstructural
58. identification
59. socialization
60. stereotypes
61. undifferentiated
62. phallic
63. androgynous
64. testosterone
65. Oedipus
66. transvestites; transsexuals
67. imitation
68. biological determinism
69. expressive
70. 2
71. gender schema
72. testosterone
73. casual sex
74. two-spirit

CHAPTER 11

1. distinct preferences
2. 3 to 5
3. 1
4. 2, 3, or 4
5. gender identities
6. roles
7. Oedipus
8. domineering, overprotective
9. weak, detached
10. absent
11. cold, rejecting
12. social learning theory
13. Sambian
14. genetic
15. brains
16. hormones
17. interact
18. more
19. ancient Greeks

20. Romans
21. Thomas Aquinas
22. coming out
23. admitting to oneself that one has a homosexual orientation
24. sexual prejudice
25. commitment and romantic love
26. true
27. false
28. false
29. false
30. false
31. false
32. false
33. true

34. true
35. true
36. false
37. false
38. false
39. false
40. false
41. false
42. true
43. false
44. false
45. true
46. false
47. false
48. true
49. false
50. a

51. a
52. b
53. e
54. d
55. b
56. e
57. c
58. a
59. e
60. d
61. b
62. adolescence
63. Freud, Henry Havelock Ellis
64. latent homosexuals
65. hypothalamus
66. before or shortly after

birth
67. predispose
68. admitting a homosexual orientation to oneself; getting to know other homosexuals; telling family and friends of one's sexual orientation; complete openness about one's homosexuality
69. close-coupled
70. Socrates, Leonardo da Vinci, Michaelangelo, Gertrude Stein, Walt Whitman

CHAPTER 12

1. 3 through 5
2. modesty (and inhibitions about exposing their bodies in public)
3. puberty
4. reproduction
5. hormone
6. self-identity
7. half
8. peer pressure
9. serial monogamy
10. monogamy
11. lasting relationship
12. chastity
13. economic and physical protection
14. mid-20s to mid-30s
15. menopause
16. vaginal lubrication
17. estrogen
18. testosterone

19. refractory
20. their sexual activity when they were younger
21. true
22. false
23. true
24. false
25. true
26. false
27. true
28. false
29. true
30. false
31. true
32. true
33. false
34. false
35. true
36. false
37. true

38. false
39. false
40. false
41. false
42. true
43. true
44. false
45. true
46. false
47. true
48. false (true for men only)
49. false
50. false
51. true
52. a
53. b
54. e (caused by b)
55. c
56. a
57. c

58. e
59. d
60. a
61. d
62. d
63. f, c (from DHEA)
64. lack of a partner
65. the climacteric
66. self-exploration
67. phallic
68. secondary sex characteristics
69. emotional intimacy
70. test their virility
71. have multiple wives
72. emotional
73. opportunity, alienation
74. declines only slightly
75. adrenarche, gonadarche

CHAPTER 13

1. range
2. Kinsey
3. 92
4. 62
5. nocturnal orgasms
6. REM
7. have erections
8. vaginal lubrication
9. romantic and emotional
10. man
11. missionary
12. fellatio
13. cunnilingus
14. White

15. Latinos
16. African Americans
17. sexually healthy
18. false
19. false
20. true
21. false
22. false
23. false
24. true
25. false
26. true
27. false (not necessarily)
28. false
29. true

30. true
31. false
32. true
33. true
34. true
35. c, k, n
36. f, h, i, j, m
37. a, b, d, e, g, l
38. vaginal lubrication, penile erection
39. rectal bacteria
40. the replacement fantasy
41. variety
42. ritualized

43. vaginal intercourse, watching one's partner undress
44. a sexually active lifestyle
45. face-to-face
46. woman-on-top
47. feels comfortable with his or her sexuality; feels free to choose whether or not he or she wishes to try a variety of sexual behaviors
48. white; higher

CHAPTER 14

1. idealization
2. marriage
3. sexual desire
4. fascination (preoccupation with the other

person)
5. exclusiveness
6. sexual desire
7. cognitive component
8. companionate

9. a positive self-concept
10. self-disclosure
11. conditional
12. unconditional
13. jealousy

14. self-esteem
15. popularity, wealth, fame, and physical attractiveness
16. attachment

17. secure
18. avoidant
19. liking
20. romantic love
21. companionate love
22. consummate love
23. eros
24. storge
25. pragma
26. mania
27. ludus
28. agape
29. matches
30. intimacy
31. false
32. false
33. true
34. false
35. true
36. false
37. false

38. true
39. true
40. true
41. false
42. true
43. true
44. true
45. false
46. false (true for men only)
47. false
48. false
49. false
50. true
51. f
52. o
53. i
54. k
55. q
56. b
57. p

58. h
59. a
60. d
61. m
62. j
63. n
64. r
65. l
66. e
67. c
68. g
69. ludus
70. storge
71. mania
72. agape
73. realistic
74. emotional
75. (a) both individuals accepting themselves as they are, (b) each individual recogniz-

ing his or her partner for what they are, (c) each individual feeling comfortable to express himself or herself, (d) learning to deal with the partner's reactions.
76. habituation
77. sexual attraction/desire
78. idealization of another
79. passionate love
80. passionate love; companionate love
81. a deep friendship
82. obsessive review, emotional and social loneliness

CHAPTER 15

1. at least half
2. couple's
3. help people with sexual problems
4. have sex with a client
5. cognitive-behavioral therapy
6. PLISSIT
7. medical
8. sexual
9. sensate focus exercises
10. hypoactive sexual desire
11. sexual aversion
12. compulsiveness
13. sexual addicts
14. dyspareunia
15. premature ejaculation
16. reasonable voluntary control

17. erectile disorder
18. performance anxiety
19. orgasmic disorder
20. headaches after orgasm
21. priapism
22. vaginismus
23. reaching orgasm
24. HIV/AIDS
25. sexual prejudice attitudes within society
26. false
27. true
28. false (not necessarily)
29. false
30. false
31. false
32. false
33. true
34. true
35. true

36. false
37. false
38. false
39. false
40. false
41. true
42. true
43. false
44. a, b
45. i, b
46. j
47. a, h, f
48. a, k, f
49. g, d
50. l
51. a, e
52. g, a, f (possibly c as well)
53. clitoris
54. woman-on-top

55. spectatoring
56. permission, limited information, specific suggestions, intensive therapy
57. systematic desensitization
58. nondemand mutual pleasuring
59. phimosis
60. erectile disorder
61. ejaculatory incompetence
62. psychological problems
63. spiritual union
64. hypoactive sexual desire

CHAPTER 16

1. statistical
2. sociological
3. psychological
4. place
5. depend almost exclusively
6. sexual variants
7. fetishism
8. transvestism
9. exhibitionists
10. telephone scatologists
11. voyeurs
12. animals
13. prepubertal children
14. sadists
15. masochists
16. urophilia

17. coprophilia
18. mysophilia
19. klismaphilia
20. frotteurism
21. dead bodies
22. men
23. serotonin
24. true
25. false
26. false
27. false
28. true
29. true
30. false
31. false
32. true
33. false

34. true
35. true
36. true
37. true
38. false
39. e
40. d
41. k
42. g
43. a
44. p
45. h
46. o
47. b
48. c
49. l
50. m

51. n
52. q
53. j
54. i
55. f
56. fetishism
57. exhibitionists
58. exhibitionism
59. 13 years old
60. domination, submission
61. bodily discharges, fetishes
62. quiet, passive, and nonrejecting
63. control, desire

CHAPTER 17

1. property
2. someone the victim knows
3. 16 and 24
4. vulnerable
5. average
6. young
7. empathy
8. coercion
9. verbal
10. physical
11. gang
12. statutory rape
13. power
14. anger
15. sadism
16. opportunistic
17. violence by men
18. adversarial
19. women who are raped usually provoke it by their dress and behavior
20. women subconsciously want to be raped
21. no woman can be raped if she truly does not want it
22. post-rape posttrau-

matic stress disorder
23. controlled
24. long-term reorganization
25. rape shield
26. social systems
27. sexual harassment
28. someone they know
29. preference
30. situational
31. personally immature
32. regressive
33. 200
34. brother-sister
35. false
36. true
37. true
38. true
39. false
40. false
41. true
42. false
43. false
44. true
45. true
46. false
47. false
48. false
49. true
50. false

51. true
52. true
53. false
54. true
55. false
56. true
57. d
58. i
59. e
60. g
61. a
62. h
63. j
64. f
65. c
66. b
67. juveniles (persons under the legal "age of consent")
68. 5
69. getting a partner intoxicated in order to have sex, physical (relentless) pressure, verbal pressure (e.g., anger), emotional/psychological pressure (e.g., threatening to end the relationship)

70. boys are raised to be nurturant, not aggressive; boys are raised to view women as equals who share power and responsibility
71. gang
72. psychopathology (a character disorder)
73. opportunistic
74. less sensitive to the victims and more accepting of sexual violence
75. they had been drinking, if a woman had made them angry
76. period of long-term reorganization
77. Civil Rights Act
78. unequal power
79. traditional stereotypical gender roles
80. pedophile (preference molester)
81. 13
82. polyincestuous

CHAPTER 18

1. Nevada
2. 17 to 20
3. streetwalkers
4. B-girls
5. call girls
6. hustlers
7. economics (the need for money)
8. middle-class
9. married
10. one-third
11. no harmful
12. less sympathetic
13. rape myths
14. increased hostility
15. commit rape themselves if they were certain they would not get caught

16. depictions of violence toward women
17. sexual explicitness
18. erotica
19. children
20. oral
21. anal
22. false
23. true
24. false (not in the long-term)
25. true
26. true
27. true
28. false
29. true
30. true
31. true
32. false

33. true
34. true
35. false
36. true
37. false
38. true
39. true
40. h
41. a
42. d
43. c
44. g
45. f
46. b
47. e
48. i
49. lack of discrimination
50. fornication
51. streetwalker

52. obscene
53. material portraying violence toward women
54. (a) by contemporary community standards it depicts patently offensive sexual conduct; (b) it lacks serious literary, artistic, political, or scientific value; and (c) it appeals to prurient interests
55. Comstock law
56. they enjoy the sexual arousal it produces
57. active subordination of women

References

AARONSON, I. A. (1994). Micropenis: Medical and surgical implications. *Journal of Urology, 152,* 4–14.

AAUW. (1993). *Hostile hallways.* Washington, DC: American Association of University Women.

ABBEY, A., MCAUSLAN, P., & ROSS, L. T. (1998). Sexual assault perpetration by college men: The role of alcohol, misperception of sexual intent, and sexual beliefs and experiences. *Journal of Social and Clinical Psychology, 17,* 167–195.

ABDALLA, R. H. D. (1982). *Sisters in affliction: Circumcision and infibulation of women in Africa.* London: Zed Press (Westport, CT: L. Hill).

ABEL, E. L., & SOKOL, R. J. (1987). Incidence of fetal alcohol syndrome and economic impact of FAS-related anomalies. *Drug and Alcohol Dependency, 19,* 51–70.

ABEL, G. G., BARLOW, D. H., BLANCHARD, E. B., & GUILD, D. (1977). The components of rapists' sexual arousal. *Archives of General Psychiatry, 34,* 895–903.

ABEL, G. G., BECKER, J. V., MURPHY, W. D., & FLANAGAN, B. (1981). Identifying dangerous child molesters. In R. B. Stuard (Ed.), *Violent behavior: Social learning approaches to prediction, management, and treatment* (pp. 116–137). New York: Brunner/Mazel.

ABEL, G. G., & ROULEAU, J. L. (1990). The nature and extent of sexual assault. In W. L. Marshall, D. R. Laws, & H. E. Barbaree (Eds.), *Handbook of sexual assault* (pp. 9–20). New York: Plenum Press.

ABEL, G. G., et al. (1987). Self-reported sex crimes of non-incarcerated paraphiliacs. *Journal of Interpersonal Violence, 1,* 3–25.

ABEL, G. G., et al. (1988a). Multiple paraphiliac diagnoses among sex offenders. *Bulletin of the American Academy of Psychiatry and the Law, 16,* 153–168.

ABEL, G. G., et al. (1988b). Predicting child molesters' response to treatment. *Annals of the New York Academy of Sciences, 528,* 223–234.

ABMA, J., DRISCOLL, A., & MOORE, K. (1998). Young women's degree of control over first intercourse: An exploratory analysis. *Family Planning Perspectives, 30,* 12–18.

ABMA, J., et al. (1997). Fertility, family planning, and women's health: New data from the 1995 National Survey of Family Growth. *Vital Health Statistics, 23*(19). Hyattsville, MD: National Center for Health Statistics.

ACIERNO, R., et al. (1999). Risk factors for rape, physical assault, and post traumatic stress disorder in women: Examination of differential multivariate relationships. *Journal of Anxiety Disorders, 13,* 541–563.

ACKERMAN, M. D., & CAREY, M. P. (1995). Psychology's role in the assessment of erectile dysfunction: Historical precedents, current knowledge, and methods. *Journal of Consulting and Clinical Psychology, 63,* 862–876.

ADAMS, H. E., WRIGHT, L. W., & LOHR, B. A. (1996). Is homophobia associated with homosexual arousal? *Journal of Abnormal Psychology, 105,* 440–445.

ADDIEGO, F., et al. (1981). Female ejaculation: A case study. *Journal of Sex Research, 17,* 13–21.

ADDUCCI, C., & ROSS, L. (1991). Common urethral injuries in men. *Medical Aspects of Human Sexuality,* October, 32–44.

ADLER, J., et al. (1996). Adultery: A new furor over an old sin. *Newsweek,* September 30, 54–60.

ADLER, N. E., et al. (1990). Psychological responses after abortion. *Science, 248,* 41–44.

ADLERCREUTZ, H., et al. (1992). Dietary phyto-oestrogens and the menopause in Japan. *Lancet, 339,* 1233.

ADZICK, N. S., SUTTON, L. N., CROMBLEHOLME, T. M., & FLAKE, A. W. (1998). Successful fetal surgery for spina bifida. *Lancet, 352,* 1675–1676.

AFIFI, W. A. (1999). Harming the ones we love: Relational attachment and perceived consequences as predictors of safe-sex behavior. *Journal of Sex Research, 36,* 198–206.

AGNEW, J. (1986). Hazards associated with anal erotic activity. *Archives of Sexual Behavior, 15,* 307–314.

AGNEW, J. (2000). Klismaphilia. *Venereology, 13,* 75–79.

AHIA, R. N. (1991). Compliance with safer-sex guidelines among adolescent males: Application of the health belief model and protection motivation theory. *Journal of Health Education, 22,* 49–52.

AINSWORTH, M. D. S., BLEHAR, M. C., WATERS, E., & WALL, S. (1978). *Patterns of attachment: A psychological study of the strange situation.* Hillsdale, NJ: Erlbaum.

ALAN GUTTMACHER INSTITUTE (1999). Survey on teen peer pressure. www.teen pregnancy.org.

ALAN GUTTMACHER INSTITUTE (2001). *Sexually transmitted diseases latest statistics. Facts in brief.* New York: Author.

ALBERMAN, E. (1988). The epidemiology of repeated abortion. In R. W. Beard & F. Sharp (Eds.), *Early pregnancy loss: Mechanisms and treatment* (pp. 9–17). London: Royal College of Obstetricians and Gynaecologists.

ALBERT, A. E., WARNER, D. L., & HATCHER, R. A. (1998). Facilitating condom use with clients during commercial sex in Nevada's legal brothels. *American Journal of Public Health, 88,* 643–646.

ALEXANDER, C. J., SIPSKI, M. L., & FINDLEY, T. W. (1993). Sexual activities, desire, and satisfaction in males pre-and post-spinal cord injury. *Archives of Sexual Behavior, 22,* 217–228.

ALEXANDER, G. M., & HINES, M. (1994). Gender labels and play styles: Their relative contribution to children's selection of playmates. *Child Development, 65,* 869–879.

ALEXANDER, G. M., & SHERWIN, B. B. (1993). Sex steroids, sexual behavior, and selection attention for erotic stimuli in women using oral contraceptives. *Psychoneuroendocrinology, 18,* 91–102.

ALEXANDER, G. M., SHERWIN, B. B., BANCROFT, J., & DAVIDSON, D.W. (1990). Testosterone and sexual behavior in oral-contraceptive users and nonusers: A prospective study. *Hormones and Behavior, 24,* 388–402.

ALEXANDER, G. M., et al. (1997). Androgen-behavior correlations in hypogonadal men and eugonadal men. *Hormones and Behavior, 31,* 110–119.

ALEXANDER, N. J. (1994). Vaccines for contraception: A summary. *Reproduction Fertility Development, 6,* 417–419.

ALLDRIDGE, P. (1997). The Sexual Offenses (Conspiracy and Incitement) Act 1996. *Criminal Law Review,* January, 30–40.

ALLEN, D. J., & OLESON, T. (1999). Shame and internalized homophobia in gay men. *Journal of Homosexuality, 37,* 33–43.

ALLEN, L. S., & GORSKI, R. A. (1992). Sexual orientation and the size of the anterior commissure in the human brain. *Proceedings of the National Academy of Sciences of the U.S.A., 89,* 7199–7202.

ALLEN, M. C., DONAHUE, P. K., & DUSMAN, A. E. (1993). The limit of viability—Neonatal outcome of infants born at 22 to 25 weeks gestation. *New England Journal of Medicine, 329,* 1597–1601.

ALLGEIER, E. R. (1985). Are you ready for sex? Informed consent for sexual intimacy. *SIECUS Report, 13,* 8–9.

ALLGEIER, E. R., & MURNEN, S. K. (1985, March). Perception of parents as sexual beings: Pocs and Godow revisited. *SIECUS Report, 4,* 11–12.

ALTER, M. J., et al. (1999). The prevalence of hepatitis C virus infection in the United States, 1988 through 1994. *New England Journal of Medicine, 341,* 556–562.

ALVAREZ, W. A., & FREINHAR, J. P. (1991). A prevalence study of bestiality zoophilia in psychiatric in-patients, medical in-patients, and psychiatric staff. *International Journal of Psychosomatics, 38,* 45–47.

ALZATE, H., & LONDONO, M. L. (1984). Vaginal erotic sensitivity. *Journal of Sex & Marital Therapy, 10,* 49–56.

AMERICAN ACADEMY OF ALLERGY AND IMMUNOLOGY. (1986). Candidiasis hypersensitivity syndrome. *Journal of Allergy and Clinical Immunology, 78,* 271–273.

AMERICAN ACADEMY OF PEDIATRICS TASK FORCE ON CIRCUMCISION. (1999). Circumcision policy statement. *Pediatrics, 103,* 686–693.

AMERICAN CANCER SOCIETY. (2000). *Cancer facts and figures 2000.* Atlanta: Author.

AMERICAN COLLEGE OF PHYSICIANS AND INFECTIOUS DISEASES SOCIETY OF AMERICA. (1994). Human immunodeficiency virus (HIV) infection. *Annals of Internal Medicine, 120,* 310–319.

AMERICAN MEDICAL ASSOCIATION (AMA). (1994). Health care needs of gay men and lesbians in the U.S. Policy paper adopted December 6. Chicago: Author.

AMERICAN PSYCHIATRIC ASSOCIATION. (1994). *Diagnostic and statistical manual of mental disorder (DSM-IV)* (4th ed.). Washington, DC: Author.

AMES, T. R. H. (1991). Guidelines for providing sexuality-related services to severely and profoundly retarded individuals: The challenge for the nineteen-nineties. *Sexuality and Disability, 9,* 113–122.

AMIR, M. (1971). *Patterns in forcible rape.* Chicago: University of Chicago Press.

ANDERSEN, B. L., CYRANOWSKI, J. M., & ESPINDLE, D. (1999). Men's sexual self-scheme. *Journal of Personality and Social Psychology, 76,* 645–661.

505

ANDERSON, J. E., CAREY, J. W., & TAVERAS, S. (2000). HIV testing among the general US population and persons at increased risk: Information from national surveys, 1987–1996. *American Journal of Public Health, 90,* 1089–1095.

ANDERSON, J. E., & DAHLBERG, L. L. (1992). High-risk sexual behavior in the general population. *Sexually Transmitted Diseases, 19,* 320–325.

ANDERSON, P. A., ELOY, S. V., GUERRERO, L. K., & SPITZBERG, B. H. (1995). Romantic jealousy and relational satisfaction: A look at the impact of jealousy experience and expression. *Communication Reports, 8,* 77–85.

ANDERSON, P. B. (1991). Can men be the victim of unwanted sexual intercourse? In B. M. King, C. J. Camp, & A. Downey (Eds.), *Human sexuality today* (p. 370). Englewood Cliffs, NJ: Prentice Hall.

ANDERSON, P. B., & MATHIEU, D. A. (1996). College students' high-risk sexual behavior following alcohol consumption. *Journal of Sex & Marital Therapy, 22,* 259–264.

ANDERSON, P. B., & STRUCKMAN-JOHNSON, C. (1998). Sexually aggressive women—Current perspectives and controversies—Introduction. In P. B. Anderson & C. Struckman-Johnson (Eds.), *Sexually aggressive women* (pp. 1–8). New York: Guilford Press.

ANDERSON, P. B., et al. (1995). Changes in the telephone calling patterns of adolescent girls. *Adolescence, 30,* 779–784.

ANDERSON, R. A., BANCROFT, J., & WU, F. C. (1992). The effects of exogenous testosterone on sexuality and mood of normal men. *Journal of Clinical and Endocrinological Metabolism, 75,* 1503–1507.

ANGELL, M. (1991). A dual approach to the AIDS epidemic. *New England Journal of Medicine, 324,* 1498–1500.

ANGIER, N. (1991). The biology of what it means to be gay. *New York Times,* September 1, sec. 4, p. 1.

ANGIER, N. (1992). A male menopause? Jury is still out. *New York Times.*

ANLLO, L. M. (2000). Sexual life after breast cancer. *Journal of Sex & Marital Therapy, 26,* 241–248.

ANNAS, G. J., & GRODIN, M. A. (1998). Human rights and maternal-fetal HIV transmission prevention trials in Africa. *American Journal of Public Health, 88,* 560–563.

ANNON, J. (1974). *The behavioral treatment of sexual problems.* Honolulu: Enabling Systems.

APFELBAUM, B. (1989). Retarded ejaculation: A much misunderstood syndrome. In S. R. Leiblum & R. C. Rosen (Eds.), *Principles and practice of sex therapy: Update for the 1990s* (pp. 168–206). New York: Guilford Press.

APT, C., HURLBERT, D. F., & POWELL, D. (1993). Men with hypoactive sexual desire disorder: The role of interpersonal dependency and assertiveness. *Journal of Sex Education and Therapy, 19,* 108–116.

AQUINAS, T. (1968). Temperance. In T. Gilby (Ed. and Trans.), *Summa Theologiae* (Vol. 43). New York: McGraw-Hill.

ARAL, S. O., MOSHER, W. D., & CATES, W. (1991). Self-reported pelvic inflammatory disease in the United States, 1988. *Journal of the American Medical Association, 266,* 2570–2573.

ARATA, C. M., & BURKHART, B. R. (1996). Post-traumatic stress disorder among college student victims of acquaintance assault. *Journal of Psychology & Human Sexuality, 8,* 79–92.

ARIES, E. (1998). Gender differences in interaction: A re-examination. In D. J. Canary & K. Dindia (Eds.), *Sex differences and similarities in communication: Critical essays and empirical investigations of sex and gender in interaction* (pp. 65–81). Mahwah, NJ: Erlbaum.

ARIÈS, P. (1962). *Centuries of childhood.* London: Cape.

ARMSTRONG, K., EISEN, A., & WEBER, B. (2000). Assessing the risk of breast cancer. *New England Journal of Medicine, 342,* 564–571.

ARMSTRONG, P., & FELDMAN, S. (1990). *A wise birth.* New York: William Morrow.

ARNETT, J. J. (2000). Emerging adulthood: A theory of development from the late teens through the twenties. *American Psychologist, 55,* 469–480.

ARON, A., ARON, E. N., & ALLEN, J. (1998). Motivation for unreciprocated love. *Personality and Social Psychology Bulletin, 24,* 787–796.

ARON, A., & WESTBAY, L. (1996). Dimensions of the prototype of love. *Journal of Personality and Social Psychology, 70,* 535–551.

ARRIGO, J. M., & PEZDEK, K. (1997). Lessons from the study of psychogenic amnesia. *Current Directions in Psychological Science, 6,* 148–152.

ARRINDELL, W. A., & LUTEIJN, F. (2000). Similarity between intimate partners for personality traits as related to individual levels of satisfaction with life. *Personality and Individual Differences, 28,* 629–637.

ASCH, R. H., ELLSWORTH, L. R., BALMACEDA, J. P., & WONG, P. C. (1984). Pregnancy after translaparoscopic gamete intra-fallopian transfer [Letter]. *Lancet, 2,* 1034–1035.

ASKEW, M. W. (1965). Courtly love: Neurosis as institution. *Psychoanalytic Review, 52,* 19–29.

ATLAS, J. (1999). The loose canon: Why higher education has embraced pornography. *The New Yorker,* March 29, 60–65.

ATTANÉ, I. (2000). La Fécondité chinoise à l'aube du XXI Siècle: Constats et incertitudes. *Population, 55,* 233–264.

AUGENBRAUN, M. H., & ROLFS, R. (1999). Treatment of syphilis, 1998: Nonpregnant adults. *Clinical Infectious Diseases, 28* (Suppl. 1), S21–S28.

AUGER, J., KUNSTMANN, J. M., CZYGLIK, F., & JOUANNET, P. (1995). Decline in semen quality among fertile men in Paris during the past 20 years. *New England Journal of Medicine, 332,* 281–285.

AXINN, W. G., & BARBER, J. S. (1997). Living arrangements and family formation attitudes in early adulthood. *Journal of Marriage and the Family, 59,* 595–611.

AXINN, W. G., & THORNTON, A. (1992). The relationship between cohabitation and divorce: Selectivity or causal influence? *Demography, 29,* 357–374.

BACHMAN, G. A. (1989). Brief sexual inquiry in gynecologic practice. Pt. 1. *Obstetrics and Gynecology, 73,* 425–427.

BAGATELL, C. J., et al. (1994). Metabolic and behavioral effects of high-dose exogenous testosterone in healthy men. *Journal of Clinical and Endocrinological Metabolism, 79,* 561–567.

BAGLEY, C., & YOUNG, L. (1987). Juvenile prostitution and child sexual abuse: A controlled study. *Journal of Community Mental Health, 6,* 5–26.

BAILEY, J. M., DUNNE, M. P., & MARTIN, N. G. (2000). Genetic and environmental influences on sexual orientation and its correlates in an Australian twin sample. *Journal of Personality and Social Psychology, 78,* 524–536.

BAILEY, J. M., & PILLARD, R. C. (1991). A genetic study of male sexual orientation. *Archives of General Psychiatry, 48,* 1089–1096.

BAILEY, J. M., PILLARD, R. C., NEALE, M. C., & AGYEI, Y. (1993). Heritable factors influence sexual orientation in women. *Archives of General Psychiatry, 50,* 217–223.

BAILEY, J. M., & ZUCKER, K. J. (1995). Childhood sex-typed behavior and sexual orientation: A conceptual analysis and quantitative review. *Developmental Psychology, 31,* 43–55.

BAIRD, D. D., WEINBERG, C. R., VOIGHT, L. F., & DALING, J. R. (1996). Vaginal douching and reduced fertility. *American Journal of Public Health, 86,* 844–850.

BAKER, B. (1990). Birth control. *Common Cause Magazine, 16*(3), 11–14.

BAKER, R. R., & BELLIS, M. A. (1995). *Human sperm, competition, copulation, masturbation, and infidelity.* London: Chapman & Hall.

BALDWIN, J. D., & BALDWIN, J. I. (1988). Factors affecting AIDS-related sexual risk-taking behavior among college students. *Journal of Sex Research, 25,* 181–196.

BALDWIN, J. D., & BALDWIN, J. I. (1997). Gender differences in sexual interest. *Archives of Sexual Behavior, 26,* 181–210.

BALDWIN, J. I., & BALDWIN, J. D. (2000). Heterosexual anal intercourse: An understudied, high-risk sexual behavior. *Archives of Sexual Behavior, 29,* 357–373.

BALLARD-REISCH, D., & ELTON, M. (1992). Gender orientation and the Bem Sex Role Inventory: A psychological construct revisited. *Sex Roles, 27,* 291–306.

BALON, R. (1998). Pharmacological treatment of paraphilias with a focus on antidepressants. *Journal of Sex & Marital Therapy, 24,* 241–254.

BANCROFT, J. (1984). Hormones and human sexual behavior. *Journal of Sex & Marital Therapy, 10,* 3–21.

BANDURA, A., & WALTERS, R. H. (1963). *Social learning and personality development.* New York: Holt, Rinehart & Winston.

BARBACH, L. G. (1976). *For yourself: The fulfillment of female sexuality.* New York: Anchor/Doubleday.

BARBACH, L. G., (1980). *Women discover orgasm.* New York: Free Press.

BARBAREE, H. E., & MARSHALL, W. L. (1991). The role of male sexual arousal in rape: 6 models. *Journal of Consulting and Clinical Psychology, 59,* 621–630.

BARBAREE, H. E., MARSHALL, W. L., & LANTHEIR, R. (1979). Deviant sexual arousal in rapists. *Behavior Research and Therapy, 17,* 215–222.

BARBAREE, H. E., MARSHALL, W. L., & McCORMICK, J. (1998). The development of deviant sexual behavior among adolescents and its implications for prevention and treatment. *Irish Journal of Psychology, 19,* 1–31.

BARBAREE, H. E., & SETO, M. C. (1997). Pedophilia: Assessment and treatment. In D. R. Laws & W. O'Donohue (Eds.), *Sexual deviance: Theory, assessment, and treatment* (pp. 175–193). New York: Guilford Press.

BARBER, N. (1998). Ecological and psychosocial correlates of male homosexuality: A cross-cultural investigation. *Journal of Cross-Cultural Psychology, 29,* 387–401.

BARCUS, F. E. (1983). *Images of life on children's television: Sex roles, minorities, and families.* New York: Praeger.

BARDONI, B., et al. (1994). A dosage sensitive locus at chromosome XP21 is involved in male to female sex reversal. *Nature Genetics, 7,* 497–501.

BARNARD, M. A., MCKEGANEY, N. P., & LEYLAND, A. H. (1993). Risk behaviors among male clients of female prostitutes. *British Medical Journal, 307,* 361–362.

BARNER, M. R. (1999). Sex-role stereotyping in FCC-mandated children's educational television. *Journal of Broadcasting and Electronic Media, 43,* 551–564.

BARNES, M. L., & STERNBERG, R. J. (1997). A hierarchical model of love and its prediction of satisfaction in close relationships. In R. J. Sternberg & M. Hojjat (Eds.), *Satisfaction in close relationships* (pp. 79–101). New York: Guilford Press.

BARNES, R. H. (1999). Marriage by capture. *Journal of the Royal Anthropology Institute, 5,* 57–73.

BARNETT, M. A., et al. (1992). Factors affecting reactions to a rape victim. *Journal of Psychology, 126,* 609–620.

BARNHART, K., FURMAN, I., & DEVOTO, L. (1995). Attitudes and practice of couples regarding sexual relations during the menses and spotting. *Contraception, 51,* 93–98.

BARON, L., STRAUS, M., & JAFFEE, D. (1987). Legitimate violence, violent attitudes, and rape: A test of the cultural spillover theory. *Annals of the New York Academy of Sciences, SR121,* 1–23.

BARRATT, C. L. R., CHAUHAN, M., & COOKE, J. D. (1990). Donor insemination—A look to the future. *Fertility and Sterility, 54,* 375–387.

BARRON, N., & KIMMEL, M. (2000). Sexual violence in three pornographic media: Towards a sociological explanation. *Journal of Sex Research, 37,* 1–8.

BARROW, G., & SMITH, T. (1992). *Aging, ageism, and society.* St. Paul, MI: West.

BARRY, H., III, & SCHLEGEL, A. (1984). Measurements of adolescent sexual behavior in the standard sample of societies. *Ethnology, 23,* 315–329.

BARRY, K. (1995). *The prostitution of sexuality: The global exploitation of women.* New York: New York University Press.

BARSETTI, I., EARLS, C. M., LALUMIÈRE, M. L., & BÉLANGER, N. (1998). The differentiation of intrafamilial and extrafamilial heterosexual child molester. *Journal of Interpersonal Violence, 13,* 275–286.

BARSON, M. (1984). Penis size: A sexual or political issue? *Cosmopolitan,* March, 224–226.

BARSTOW, D. G. (1999). Female genital mutilation: The penultimate gender abuse. *Child Abuse & Neglect, 23,* 501–510.

BART, P. (1980). *Avoiding rape: A study of victims and avoiders. Final Report* (MH29311). Rockville, MD: National Institute of Mental Health.

BART, P. B. (1971). Depression in middle-aged women. In V. G. Gornick & B. K. Moran (Eds.), *Women in sexist society.* New York: Basic Books.

BARTELL, G. D. (1970). Group sex among the mid-Americans. *Journal of Sex Research, 6,* 113–130.

BARTHOLET, J., et al. (2000). The plague years. *Newsweek,* January 17, 32–37.

BARTHOLOMEW, K., & HOROWITZ, L. M. (1991). Attachment styles among young adults: A test of a four-category model. *Journal of Personality and Social Psychology, 61,* 226–244.

BARTLIK, B., LEGREE, R., & ANDERSSON, L. (1999). The combined use of sex therapy and testosterone replacement therapy for women. *Psychiatric Annals, 29,* 27–33.

BARTLIK, B., et al. (1999). Medications with the potential to enhance sexual responsivity in women. *Psychiatric Annals, 29,* 46–52.

BARTON, M. B., HARRIS, R., & FLETCHER, S. W. (1999). Does this patient have breast cancer? The screening clinical breast examination: Should it be done? How? *Journal of the American Medical Association, 282,* 1270–1280.

BARUCH, G. K., & BARNETT, R. (1986). Role quality, multiple role involvement, and psychological well-being in midlife women. *Journal of Personality and Social Psychology, 51,* 578–585.

BASOW, S. A., & JOHNSON, K. (2000). Predictors of homophobia in female college students. *Sex Roles, 42,* 391–404.

BASSON, R. (2000). The female sexual response: A different model. *Journal of Sex & Marital Therapy, 26,* 51–65.

BAUMEISTER, R. F. (2000). Gender differences in erotic plasticity: The female sex drive as socially flexible and responsive. *Psychological Bulletin, 126,* 347–374.

BAUMEISTER, R. F., & BUTLER, J. L. (1997). Sexual masochism: Deviance without pathology. In D. R. Laws & W. O. O'Donohue (Eds.), *Sexual deviance: Theory, assessment, and treatment* (pp. 225–239). New York: Guilford Press.

BAUSERMAN, R. (1998). Egalitarian, sexist, and aggressive sexual materials: Attitude effects and viewer responses. *Journal of Sex Research, 35,* 244–253.

BAUSERMAN, R., & DAVIS, C. (1996). Perceptions of early sexual experiences and adult sexual adjustment. *Journal of Psychology & Human Sexuality, 8*(3), 37–59.

BAUSERMAN, R., & RIND, B. (1997). Psychological correlates of male child and adolescent sexual experiences with adults: A review of the nonclinical literature. *Archives of Sexual Behavior, 26,* 105–141.

BAXTER, J., & WESTERN, M. (1998). Satisfaction with housework: Examining the paradox. *Sociology, 32,* 101–120.

BECK, U. (1995). *Ecological enlightenment: Essays on the politics of the risk society.* Atlantic Highlands, NJ: Humanities Press.

BECKMAN, L. J., HARVEY, S. M., & MURRAY, J. (1992). Perceived contraceptive attributes of current and former users of the vaginal sponge. *Journal of Sex Research, 29,* 31–42.

BECK-SAGUÉ, C. M., & SOLOMON, F. (1999). Sexually transmitted diseases in abused children and adolescent and adult victims of rape: Review of selected literature. *Clinical Infectious Diseases, 28,* S74–S83.

BEDEIAN, A. G., & PHILLIPS, A. S. (1998). PMS in the workplace: Myth or method? *Social Behavior and Personality, 26,* 357–362.

BEER, J., & HORN, J. M. (1999). The influence of rearing order on personality development within two adoption cohorts. *Journal of Personality, 68,* 789–819.

BEERNINK, F. J., DMOWSKI, W. P., & ERICSSON, R. J. (1993). Sex preselection through albumin separation of sperm. *Fertility and Sterility, 59,* 382–386.

BEGLEY, S. (2000). Sexuality among older women. *Journal of Women's Health & Gender-Based Medicine, 9,* 515–520.

BEGLEY, S. (2000). The risks of estrogen. *Newsweek,* May 29, 51.

BEGLEY, S., & GLICK, D. (1994). The estrogen complex. *Newsweek,* March 21, 76–77.

BEHNKE, M., et al. (1997). How fetal cocaine exposure increases neonatal hospital costs. *Pediatrics, 99,* 204–208.

BEITCHMAN, J. H., et al. (1991). A review of the short-term effects of child sexual abuse. *Child Abuse & Neglect, 15,* 537–556.

BEITCHMAN, J. H., et al. (1992). A review of the long-term effects of child sexual abuse. *Child Abuse & Neglect, 16,* 101–118.

BELCASTRO, P. (1985). Sexual behavior differences between African American and white students. *Journal of Sex Research, 21,* 55–67.

BELL, A. P., & WEINBERG, M. S. (1978). *Homosexualities.* New York: Simon & Schuster.

BELL, A. P., WEINBERG, M. S., & HAMMERSMITH, S. K. (1981). *Sexual preference: Its development in men and women.* Bloomington: Indiana University Press.

BELL, B. P., WASLEY, A., SHAPIRO, C. N., & MARGOLIS, H. S. (1999). Prevention of hepatitis A through active or passive immunization: Recommendations of the Advisory Committee on Immunization Practices (ACCP). *Morbidity and Mortality Weekly Reports, 48,* 1–37.

BELL, R. (1998). Felony status of sex offense fought. *Times-Picayune* (New Orleans), April 12, A1, A12.

BELZER, G. (1981). Orgasmic expulsions of women: A review and heuristic inquiry. *Journal of Sex Research, 17,* 1–12.

BEM, D. J. (1996). Exotic becomes erotic: A developmental theory of sexual orientation. *Psychological Review, 103,* 320–335.

BEM, S. L. (1974). The measurement of psychological androgyny. *Journal of Consulting and Clinical Psychology, 42,* 155–162.

BEM, S. L. (1979). Theory and measurement of androgyny: A reply to Pedhazur-Tetenbaum and Locksley-Colten critiques. *Journal of Personality and Social Psychology, 37,* 1047–1054.

BEM, S. L. (1981). Gender schema theory: A cognitive account of sex typing. *Psychological Review, 88,* 354–364.

BEM, S. L. (1983). Gender schema theory and its implications for child development: Raising gender-aschematic children in a gender-schematic society. *Signs, 8,* 598–616.

BENNINK, H. J. T. (1998). Presentation of clinical data on Implanon. *Contraception, 58* (Suppl. 6), 75S–76S.

BENTLER, P. M., & PEELER, W. H. (1979). Models of female orgasm. *Archives of Sexual Behavior, 8,* 405–424.

BERENBAUM, S. A., & SNYDER, E. (1995). Early hormonal influences on childhood sex-typed activity and playmate preferences: Implications for the development of sexual orientation. *Developmental Psychology, 31,* 31–42.

BERENSON, A. B. (1993). Appearance of the hymen at birth and one year of age: A longitudinal study. *Pediatrics, 91,* 820–825.

BERER, M. (2000). Making abortions safe: A matter of good public health policy and practice. *Bulletin of the World Health Organization, 78,* 580–592.

BERGER, G. S., WESTROM, L. V., & WOLNER-HANSSEN, P. (1992). Definition of pelvic inflammatory disease. In G. S. Berger & L. V. Weström (Eds.), *Pelvic inflammatory disease.* New York: Raven Press.

BERGER, R. M. (1982). The unseen minority: Older gays and lesbians. *Social Work, 27,* 236–242.

BERGERON, S., et al. (1997). The surgical treatment of vulvar vestibulitis syndrome: A follow-up study. *Journal of Sex & Marital Therapy, 23*, 317–325.

BERGLER, G., & KROGER, W. S. (1954). *Kinsey's myth of female sexuality.* New York: Grune & Stratton.

BERGMARK, K., et al. (1999). Vaginal changes and sexuality in women with a history of cervical cancer. *New England Journal of Medicine, 340*, 1383–1389.

BERGSTROM, R., et al. (1993). Detection of preinvasive cancer of the cervix and the subsequent reduction in invasive cancer. *Journal of the National Cancer Institute, 85*, 1050–1057.

BERLINER, D., MONTI-BLOCH, L., JENNINGS-WHITE, C., & DIAZ-SANCHEZ, V. (1996). The functionality of the human vomeronasal organ (VNO): Evidence for steroid receptors. *Steroid Biochemistry & Molecular Biology, 58*, 259–265.

BERMANT, G., & DAVIDSON, J. M. (1974). *Biological bases of sexual behavior.* New York: Harper & Row.

BERNAT, J. A., CALHOUN, K. S., & STOLP, S. (1998). Sexually aggressive men's responses to a date rape analogue: Alcohol as a disinhibiting cue. *Journal of Sex Research, 35*, 341–348.

BERSCHEID, E. (1982). Interpersonal attraction. In E. Aronson & G. Lindzey (Eds.), *Handbook of social psychology* (3rd ed.). Reading, MA: Addison-Wesley.

BERSCHEID, E., & WALSTER, E. (1974). A little bit about love. In T. L. Huston (Ed.), *Foundations of interpersonal attraction* (pp. 355–381). New York: Academic Press.

BERSCHEID, E., & WALSTER, E. (1978). *Interpersonal attraction* (2nd ed.). Reading, MA: Addison-Wesley.

BEYNE, Y. (1989). *Menarche to menopause: Reproductive lives of peasant women in two cultures.* Albany: State University of New York Press.

BIANCHI, S. M., & SPAIN, D. (1996). Women, work, and family in America. *Population Bulletin, 51*(3), 1–48.

BIEBER, I., et al. (1962). *Homosexuality: A psychoanalytic study.* New York: Basic Books.

BIERNAT, M. (1991). Gender stereotypes and the relationship between masculinity and femininity: A developmental analysis. *Journal of Personality and Social Psychology, 61*, 351–365.

BIGRIGG, A., et al. (1999). Depo Provera. Position paper on clinical use, effectiveness and side effects. *British Journal of Family Planning, 25*, 69–76.

BILLER, H., & BAHM, R. (1971). Father absence, perceived maternal behavior, and masculinity of self-concept among junior high school boys. *Developmental Psychology, 4*, 178–181.

BILLINGS, E. L., BILLINGS, J. J., & CATARINCH, M. (1974). *Atlas of the ovulation method.* Collegeville, MN: Liturgical Press.

BINDER, R. L. (1998). American Psychiatric Association resource document on controversies in child custody: Gay and lesbian parenting, transracial adoptions, joint versus sole custody, and custody gender issues. *Journal of the American Academy of Psychiatry and the Law, 26*, 267–276.

BING, E. (1990). Lamaze childbirth: Then and now. In S. J. Alt (Ed.), *Lamaze parents* (pp. 14–16). VA: ASPO/Lamaze.

BIRD, C. E. (1999). Gender, household labor, and psychological distress: The impact of the amount and division of housework. *Journal of Health and Social Behavior, 40*, 32–45.

BIRKHEAD, T. R. (2000). *Promiscuity: An evolutionary history of sperm competition.* Cambridge, MA: Harvard University Press.

BIRNS, B., & STERNGLANZ, S. H. (1983). Sex-role socialization: Looking back and looking ahead. In M. B. Liss (Ed.), *Social and cognitive skills: Sex roles and children's play.* New York: Academic Press.

BITTLES, A. H., MASON, W. M., GREENE, J., & RAO, N. A. (1991). Reproductive behavior and health in consanguineous marriages. *Science, 252*, 789–794.

BLACK, D., GATES, G., SANDERS, S., & TAYLOR, L. (2000). Demographics of the gay and lesbian population in the United States: Evidence from available systematic data sources. *Demography, 37*, 139–154.

BLACKBURN, M. (1995). Sexuality, disability and abuse: Advice for life . . . not just for kids: Annotation. *Childcare, Health and Development, 21*, 351–361.

BLACKMAN, D. K., BENNETT, E. M., & MILLER, D. S. (1999). Trends in self-reported use of mammograms (1989–1997) and Papanicolaou tests (1991–1997)—Behavioral risk factor surveillance system. *Morbidity and Mortality Weekly Report, 48*, 1–22.

BLACKWOOD, E. (2000). Culture and women's sexualities. *Journal of Social Issues, 56*, 223–238.

BLAIR, C. D., & LANYON, R. I. (1981). Exhibitionism: Etiology and treatment. *Psychological Bulletin, 89*, 439–463.

BLANCHARD, R. (1993). The she-male phenomenon and the concept of partial autogynephilia. *Journal of Sex & Marital Therapy, 19*, 69–76.

BLANCHARD, R., & BOGAERT, A. F. (1996a). Biodemographic comparisons of homosexual and heterosexual men in the Kinsey interview data. *Archives of Sexual Behavior, 25*, 551–579.

BLANCHARD, R., & BOGAERT, A. F. (1996b). Homosexuality in men and number of older brothers. *American Journal of Psychiatry, 153*, 27–31.

BLANCHARD-FIELDS, F., & SUHRER-ROUSSEL, L. (1992). Adaptive coping and social cognitive development of women. In E. E. Guice (Ed.), *Women and aging: Now and the future?* Westport, CT: Greenwood Press.

BLESKE, A. L., & BUSS, D. M. (2000). Can men and women be just friends? *Personal Relationships, 7*, 131–151.

BLOOD, R. O., JR. (1967). *Love match and arranged marriage.* New York: Free Press.

BLOOMFIELD, H., & VETTESE, S. (1989). *Lifemates: The love fitness program for a lasting relationship.* New York: New American Library.

BLUME, J. (1970). *Are you there God? It's me, Margaret.* Englewood Cliffs, NJ: Bradbury Press.

BLUMENTHAL, S., GUDJONSSON, G., & BURNS, J. (1999). Cognitive distortions and blame attribution in sex offenders against adults and children. *Child Abuse & Neglect, 23*, 129–143.

BLUMSTEIN, P. W., & SCHWARTZ, P. (1983). *American couples.* New York: William Morrow.

BLYTH, B., & DUCKETT, J. W. (1991). Gonadal differentiation: A review of physiological process and influencing factors based on recent experimental evidence. *Journal of Urology, 145*, 689–694.

BOESCHEN, L. E., SALES, B. D., & KOSS, M. P. (1998). Rape trauma experts in the courtroom. *Psychology, Public Policy, and Law, 4*, 414–432.

BOGAERT, A. F. (1996). Volunteer bias in human sexuality research: Evidence for both sexuality and personality differences in males. *Archives of Sexual Behavior, 25*, 125–140.

BOGAERT, A. F. (1997). Birth order and sexual orientation in women. *Behavioral Neuroscience, 111*, 1395–1397.

BOGAERT, A. F., & HERSHBERGER, S. (1999). The relation between sexual orientation and penile size. *Archives of Sexual Behavior, 28*, 213–221.

BOGAERT, A. F., WOODARD, V., & HAFER, C. L. (1999). Intellectual ability and reactions to pornography. *Journal of Sex Research, 36*, 283–291.

BOGART, L. M., et al. (2000). Is it "sex"? College students' interpretations of sexual behavior terminology. *Journal of Sex Research, 37*, 108–116.

BOHAN, J. S. (1993). Regarding gender: Essentialism, constructionism, and feminist psychology. *Psychology of Women Quarterly, 17*, 5–21.

BOHLEN, J. G., HELD, J. P., & SANDERSON, M. (1980). The male orgasm: Pelvic contractions measured by anal probe. *Archives of Sexual Behavior, 9*, 503–521.

BOHLEN, J. G., HELD, J. P., SANDERSON, M., & AHLGREN, A. (1982). The female orgasm: Pelvic contractions. *Archives of Sexual Behavior, 11*, 367–386.

BOLES, J., & ELIFSON, K. W. (1994). Sexual identity and HIV: The male prostitute. *Journal of Sex Research, 31*, 39–46.

BOLLING, D. R. (1988, November). *Survey of women and heterosexual anal intercourse.* Paper presented at the annual meeting of the Scientific Study of Sex, San Francisco.

BONDURANT, B., & DONAT, P. L. N. (1999). Perceptions of women's sexual interest and acquaintance rape. *Psychology of Women Quarterly, 23*, 691–705.

BONNET, M., et al. (1999). Detection of Epstein-Barr virus in invasive breast cancers. *Journal of the National Cancer Institute, 91*, 1376–1381.

BOSTON WOMEN'S HEALTH BOOK COLLECTIVE. (1984). *The new Our bodies, ourselves.* New York: Simon & Schuster.

BOSWELL, J. (1980). *Christianity, social tolerance, and homosexuality.* Chicago: University of Chicago Press.

BOTTA, R. A., & PINGREE, S. (1997). Interpersonal communication and rape: Women acknowledge their assaults. *Journal of Health Communication, 2*, 197–212.

BOUMAN, F. G. (1988). Sex reassignment surgery in male to female transsexuals. *Annals of Plastic Surgery, 21*, 526–531.

BOWDEN, F. J., & GARNETT, G. P. (2000). *Trichomonas vaginalis* epidemiology: Parameterising and analysing a model of treatment interventions. *Sexually Transmitted Infections, 76*, 248–256.

BOWLBY, J. (1969). *Attachment and loss: Vol. 1. Attachment.* New York: Basic Books.

BOZETT, F. W. (Ed.). (1987). *Gay and lesbian parents.* New York: Praeger.

BOZZETTE, S. A., et al. (1998). The care of HIV-infected adults in the United States. *New England Journal of Medicine, 339*, 1897–1904.

BRADFORD, J., RYAN, C., & ROTHBLUM, E. D. (1994). National lesbian health care survey: Implications for mental healthcare. *Journal of Consulting and Clinical Psychology, 62*, 228–242.

BRADFORD, J. M. W. (1999). The paraphilias, obsessive compulsive spectrum disorder, and the treatment of sexually deviant behavior. *Psychiatric Quarterly, 70,* 209–219.

BRADFORD, J. M. W., BOULET, J., & PAWLAK, A. (1992). The paraphilias: A multiplicity of deviant behaviors. *Canadian Journal of Psychiatry, 37,* 104–107.

BRADFORD, J. M. W., & GREENBERG, D. M. (1997). Pharmacological treatment of deviant sexual behavior. *Annual Review of Sex Research, 7,* 283–306.

BRADLEY, R. A. (1981). *Husband coached childbirth.* New York: Harper & Row.

BRADLEY, S. J., & ZUCKER, K. J. (1997). Gender identity disorder: A review of the past 10 years. *Journal of the American Academy of Child and Adolescent Psychology, 36,* 872–880.

BRADSHAW, C. (1994). Asia and Asian American women: Historical and political considerations in psychotherapy. In L. Comas-Diaz & B. Greene (Eds.), *Women of color.* New York: Guilford Press.

BRAINERD, C. J., & REYNA, V. F. (1998). When things that were never experienced are easier to "remember" than things that were. *Psychological Science, 9,* 484–489.

BRAZELTON, T. B. (1970). Effect of prenatal drugs on the behavior of the neonate. *American Journal of Psychiatry, 126,* 1261–1266.

BREEDLOVE, S. M. (1994). Sexual differentiation of the human nervous system. *Annual Review of Psychology, 45,* 389–418.

BREEDLOVE, S. M. (1997). Sex on the brain. *Nature, 389,* 801.

BREEDLOVE, S. M. (2000). Finger-length ratios and sexual orientation. *Nature, 404,* 455–456.

BREITENBECHER, K. H. (2000). Sexual assault on college campuses: Is an ounce of prevention enough? *Applied & Preventive Psychology, 9,* 23–52.

BREMNER, J. D., SHOBE, K. K., & KIHLSTROM, J. F. (2000). False memories in women with self-reported childhood sexual abuse: An empirical study. *Psychological Science, 11,* 333–337.

BRESLOW, N., EVANS, L., & LANGLEY, J. (1985). On the prevalence and roles of females in the sadomasochistic subculture. *Archives of Sexual Behavior, 14,* 303–317.

BRESLOW, N., EVANS, L., & LANGLEY, J. (1986). Comparisons among heterosexual, bisexual, and homosexual sadomasochists. *Journal of Homosexuality, 13,* 83–107.

BRETSCHNEIDER, J. G., & McCOY, N. L. (1988). Sexual interest and behavior in healthy 80- to 102-year-olds. *Archives of Sexual Behavior, 17,* 109–129.

BREWAEYS, A., & VAN HALL, E. V. (1997). Lesbian motherhood: The impact on child development and family functioning. *Journal of Psychosomatic Obstetrics and Gynecology, 18,* 1–16.

BREWER, S. S., & BREWER, T. (1985). *What every pregnant woman should know: The truth about diet and drugs in pregnancy.* New York: Penguin.

BREWSTER, K. L., & PADAVIC, I. (2000). Change in gender-ideology, 1977–1996: The contributions of intracohort change and population turnover. *Journal of Marriage and the Family, 62,* 477–487.

BREWSTER, K. L., et al. (1998). The changing impact of religion on the sexual and contraceptive behavior of adolescent women in the United States. *Journal of Marriage and the Family, 60,* 493–504.

BRIDGES, J. S., & McGRAIL, C. A. (1989). Attributions of responsibility for date and stranger rape. *Sex Roles, 21,* 273–286.

BRIGMAN, B., & KNOX, D. (1992). University students' motivation to have intercourse. *College Student Journal, 26,* 406–408.

BRINCAT, M. P. (2000). Hormone replacement therapy and the skin. *Maturitas, 35,* 107–117.

BRINGLE, R. G., & BUUNK, B. P. (1985). Jealousy and social behavior: A review of personal, relationship and situational determinants. In P. Shaver (Ed.), *Review of personality and social psychology* (Vol. 2, pp. 241–264). Beverly Hills, CA: Sage.

BRINTON, L. A., & BROWN, S. L. (1997). Breast implants and cancer. *Journal of the National Cancer Institute, 89,* 1341–1349.

BRISTOW, R. E., & KARLAN, B. Y. (1996). Ovulation induction, infertility, and ovarian cancer risk. *Fertility and Sterility, 66,* 499–507.

BRODSKY, S. L. (1976). Prevention of rape: Deterrence by the potential victim. In M. J. Walker & S. L. Brodsky (Eds.), *Sexual assault.* Lexington, MA: D. C. Heath.

BRODY, S. (1995). Lack of evidence for transmission of human immunodeficiency virus through vaginal intercourse. *Archives of Sexual Behavior, 24,* 383–393.

BROMBERGER, J. T., et al. (1997). Prospective study of the determinants of age at menopause. *American Journal of Epidemiology, 145,* 124–133.

BROMHAM, D. R. (1993). Intrauterine contraceptive devices—A reappraisal. *British Medical Bulletin, 49,* 100–123.

BROMWICH, P., COHEN, J., STEWART, I., & WALKER, A. (1994). Decline in sperm counts: An artifact of changed reference range of "normal"? *British Medical Journal, 309,* 19–22.

BROOKS-GUNN, J., & PAIKOFF, R. (1997). Sexuality and developmental transitions during adolescence. In J. Schulenberg, J. L. Maggs, & K. Hurrelmann (Eds.), *Health risks and developmental transitions during adolescence* (pp. 190–219). New York: Cambridge University Press.

BROUDE, G. J., & GREENE, S. J. (1976). Cross-cultural codes on twenty sexual attitudes and practices. *Ethnology, 15,* 409–429.

BROWN, D. (1990). The penis pin. In V. Sutlive (Ed.), *Female and male in Borneo: Contributions and challenges to gender studies* (pp. 435–454). Borneo: Borneo Research Council.

BROWN, G. R. (1994). Women in relationships with cross-dressing men: A descriptive study from a nonclincial setting. *Archives of Sexual Behavior, 23,* 515–530.

BROWN, J. D., CHILDERS, K. W., & WASZAK, C. S. (1990). Television and adolescent sexuality. *Journal of Adolescent Health Care, 11,* 62–70.

BROWN, J. D., & NEWCOMER, S. F. (1991). Televison viewing and adolescents' sexual behavior. *Journal of Homosexuality, 21,* 77–91.

BROWN, J. D., & STEELE, J. R. (1996). Sexuality and the mass media: An overview. *SIECUS Report, 24*(4), 3–9.

BROWN, T. J., YEN-MOORE, A., & TYRING, S. K. (1999). An overview of sexually transmitted diseases. Pt. II. *Journal of the American Academy of Dermatology, 41,* 661–677.

BROWN, Z. A., et al. (1997). The acquisition of herpes simplex virus during pregnancy. *New England Journal of Medicine, 337,* 509–515.

BROWNE, J., & MINICHIELLO, V. (1996). Condoms: Dilemmas of caring and autonomy in heterosexual safe sex practices. *Venereology, 9,* 24–33.

BROWNMILLER, S. (1975). *Against our will: Men, women, and rape.* New York: Simon & Schuster.

BROWNMILLER, S. (1993). Making female bodies the battlefield. *Newsweek,* January 4, 37.

BRUMBERG, J. J. (1997). *The body project.* New York: Random House.

BRUNDAGE, J. A. (1984). Let me count the ways: Canonists and theologians contemplate coital positions. *Journal of Medieval History, 10,* 81–93.

BRUNHAM, R. C., et al. (1988). Etiology and outcome of acute pelvic inflammatory disease. *Journal of Infectious Diseases, 158,* 510–517.

BRYANT, J., & BROWN, D. (1989). Uses of pornography. In Z. Dolf & B. Jennings (Eds.), *Pornography: Research advances and policy considerations.* Hillsdale, NJ: Erlbaum.

BRYANT, J., & ROCKWELL, S. C. (1994). Effects of massive exposure to sexually oriented prime-time television programming on adolescents' moral judgment. In D. Zillman, J. Bryant, & A. C. Huston (Eds.), *Media, children, and the family: Social scientific, psychodynamic, and clinical perspectives* (pp. 183–195). Hillsdale, NJ: Erlbaum.

BRYNER, C. (1989). Recurrent toxic shock syndrome. *American Family Physician, 39,* 157–164.

BUCHBINDER, S. P., et al. (1994). Long-term HIV-1 infection without immunologic progression. *AIDS, 8,* 1123–1128.

BUCK, G. M., SEVER, L. E., BATT, R. E., & MENDOLA, P. (1997). Life-style factors and female infertility. *Epidemiology, 8,* 435–441.

BUFFUM, J., et al. (1981). Drugs and sexual function. In H. Lief (Ed.), *Sexual problems in medical practice.* Monroe, WI: American Medical Association.

BUHRICH, N. (1976). A heterosexual transvestite club: Psychiatric aspects. *Australian and New Zealand Journal of Psychiatry, 10,* 331–335.

BULLOUGH, B., & BULLOUGH, V. L. (1997a). Are transvestites necessarily heterosexual? *Archives of Sexual Behavior, 26,* 1–12.

BULLOUGH, B., & BULLOUGH, V. L. (1997b). Female prostitution: Current research and changing interpretations. *Annual Review of Sex Research, 7,* 158–180.

BULLOUGH, V. L. (1981). Age at menarche: A misunderstanding. *Science, 213,* 365–366.

BULLOUGH, V. L. (1991). Transvestism: A reexamination. *Journal of Psychology & Human Sexuality, 4,* 53–67.

BULLOUGH, V. L. (1998). Alfred Kinsey and the Kinsey Report: Historical overview and lasting contributions. *Journal of Sex Research, 35,* 127–131.

BULLOUGH, V. L., & BULLOUGH, B. (1993). *Cross dressing, sex, and gender.* Philadelphia: University of Pennsylvania Press.

BULLOUGH, V., BULLOUGH, B., & SMITH, R. (1983). Comparative study of male transvestites, male to female transsexuals, and male homosexuals. *Journal of Sex Research, 19,* 238–257.

BUMBY, K. M. (1996). Assessing the cognitive distortions of child molesters and rapists: Development and validation of the MOLEST and RAPE scales. *Sexual Abuse, 8,* 37–54.

BUMPASS, L., & LU, H.–H. (2000). Trends in cohabitation and implications for children's family contexts in the United States. *Population Studies, 54,* 29–41.

BUMPASS, L. L., & SWEET, J. A. (1989). Children's experience in single-parent families: Implications of cohabitation and marital transitions. *Family Planning Perspectives, 21,* 256–260.

BUMPASS, L. L., SWEET, J. A., & CHERLIN, A. (1991). The role of cohabitation in declining rates of marriage. *Journal of Marriage and the Family, 53,* 913–927.

BUMPASS, L. L., THOMSON, E., & GODECKER, A. L. (2000). Women, men, and contraceptive sterilization. *Fertility and Sterility, 73,* 937–946.

BURGESS, A. W., HARMAN, C., McCAUSLAND, M., & POWERS, P. (1984). Response patterns in children and adolescents exploited through sex rings and pornography. *American Journal of Psychiatry, 141,* 656–662.

BURGESS, A. W., & HOLMSTROM, L. L. (1974). Rape trauma syndrome. *American Journal of Psychiatry, 131,* 981–986.

BURGESS, A. W., & HOLMSTROM, L. L. (1979). Rape: Sexual disruption and recovery. *American Journal of Orthopsychiatry, 49,* 648–657.

BURK, R. D., et al. (1996). Sexual behavior and partner characteristics are the prominent risk factors for genital human papillomavirus infection in young women. *Journal of Infectious Diseases, 174,* 679–689.

BURLING, K., TARVYDAS, V. M., & MAKI, D. R. (1994). Human sexuality and disability: A holistic interpretation of rehabilitation counseling. *Journal of Applied Rehabilitation Counseling, 25,* 10–16.

BURT, M. R. (1980). Cultural myths and supports for rape. *Journal of Personality and Social Psychology, 38,* 217–230.

BURTON, R. (1963). The anatomy of melancholy. In A. M. Witherspoon & F. Warnke (Eds.), *Seventeenth-century prose and poetry* (pp. 132–133). New York: Harcourt Brace Jovanovich. (Original work published 1651.)

BUSCAGLIA, L. F. (1972). *Love.* New York: Fawcett Crest.

BUSS, A. (1966). *Psychopathology.* New York: Wiley.

BUSS, D. M. (1985). Human mate selection. *American Scientist, 73,* 47–51.

BUSS, D. M. (1989). Sex differences in human mate selection: Evolutionary hypotheses tested in 37 cultures. *Behavioral and Brain Sciences, 12,* 1–49.

BUSS, D. M. (1999). *Evolutionary psychology: The new science of the mind.* Boston: Allyn & Bacon.

BUSS, D. M., & BARNES, M. F. (1987). Preferences in human mate selection. *Journal of Personality and Social Psychology, 50,* 559–570.

BUSS, D. M., LARSEN, R. J., WESTEN, D., & SEMMELROTH, J. (1992). Sex differences in jealousy: Evolution, physiology, and psychology. *Psychological Science, 3,* 251–255.

BUSS, D. M., & SCHMITT, D. P. (1993). Sexual strategies theory: An evolutionary perspective on human mating. *Psychological Review, 100,* 204–232.

BUSS, D. M., & SHACKELFORD, T. K. (1997). From vigilance to violence: Mate retention tactics in married couples. *Journal of Personality and Social Psychology, 72,* 346–361.

BUTLER, C. A. (1976). New data about female sexual response. *Journal of Sex & Marital Therapy, 2,* 40–46.

BUTLER, J. (1990). *Gender trouble: Feminism and the subversion of identity.* New York: Routledge.

BUTLER, J., et al. (1993). Supportive nurse-midwife care associated with a reduced incidence of cesarean section. *American Journal of Obstetrics & Gynecology, 168,* 1407–1413.

BYERS, E. S. (1996). How well does the traditional sexual script explain sexual coercion? Review of a program of research. *Journal of Psychology & Human Sexuality, 8,* 7–25.

BYERS, E. S., & DEMMONS, S. (1999). Sexual satisfaction and sexual self-disclosure within dating relationships. *Journal of Sex Research, 36,* 180–189.

BYNE, W., & PARSONS, B. (1993). Human sexual orientation: The biologic theories reappraised. *Archives of General Psychiatry, 50,* 228–239.

BYNE, W., & STEIN, E. (1997). Ethical implications of scientific research on the causes of sexual orientation. *Health Care Analysis, 5,* 136–148.

BYRNE, D., CLORE, G., & SMEATON, G. (1986). The attraction hypothesis: Do similar attitudes affect anything? *Journal of Personality and Social Psychology, 51,* 1167–1170.

BYRNE, D., & MURNEN, S. K. (1988). Maintaining loving relationships. In R. J. Sternberg & M. L. Barnes (Eds.), *The psychology of love.* New Haven, CT: Yale University Press.

CADO, S., & LEITENBERG, H. (1990). Guilt reactions to sexual fantasies during intercourse. *Archives of Sexual Behavior, 19,* 49–64.

CALDERONE, M. S. (1983a). Childhood sexuality: Approaching the prevention of sexual disease. In G. Albee et al. (Eds.), *Promoting sexual responsibility and preventing sexual problems.* Hanover, NH: University Press of New England.

CALDERONE, M. S. (1983b). Fetal erection and its message to us. *SIECUS Report, 11*(5/6), 9–10.

CALL, V., SPRECHER, S., & SCHWARTZ, P. (1995). The incidence and frequency of marital sex in a national sample. *Journal of Marriage and the Family, 57,* 639–652.

CALLE, E., MIRACLE-McMAHILL, H. L., THUN, M. J., & HEATH, C. W. (1994). Cigarette smoking and risk of fatal breast cancer. *American Journal of Epidemiology, 139,* 1001–1007.

CALLENDER, C., & KOCHEMS, L. (1987). The North American Berdache. *Current Anthropology, 24,* 443–456.

CAMERON, P. (1999). Homosexual parents: Testing "common sense"—A literature review emphasizing the Golombok and Tasker longitudinal study of lesbians' children. *Psychological Reports, 85,* 282–322.

CANAVAN, M. M., MEYER, W. J., III, & HIGGS, D. C. (1992). The female experience of sibling incest. *Journal of Marital and Family Therapy, 18,* 129–142.

CANAVAN, P., & HASKELL, J. (1977). The great American male stereotype. In C. Garney & S. McMahon (Eds.), *Exploring contemporary male/female roles: A facilitator's guide.* La Jolla, CA: University Associates.

CANCIAN, F. M. (1989). Love and the rise of capitalism. In B. J. Risman & P. Schwartz (Eds.), *Gender in intimate relationships: A microstructural approach.* Belmont, CA: Wadsworth.

CANO, A., & O'LEARY, K. D. (1997). Romantic jealousy and affairs: Research and implications for couple therapy. *Journal of Sex & Marital Therapy, 23,* 249–275.

CANTARELLA, E. (1992). *Bisexuality in the ancient world.* New Haven, CT: Yale University Press.

CAREY, M. P. (1999). Prevention of HIV infection through changes in sexual behavior. *American Journal of Health Promotion, 14,* 104–111.

CAREY, R. F., et al. (1992). Effectiveness of latex condoms as a barrier to human immunodeficiency-sized particles under conditions of simulated use. *Sexually Transmitted Diseases, 19,* 230–234.

CARLSEN, E., GIWERCMAN, A., KEIDING, N., & SKAKKEBACK, N. E. (1992). Evidence for decreasing quality of semen during past 50 years. *British Medical Journal, 305,* 609–613.

CARNES, P. J. (1983). *Out of the shadows: Understanding sexual addiction.* Minneapolis, MN: Compeare Publishers.

CARNES, P. J. (1991). *Don't call it love.* New York: Bantam Books.

CARPENTER, C. C. J., et al. (1997). Antiretroviral therapy for HIV infection in 1997. *Journal of the American Medical Association, 277,* 1962–1969.

CARRIER, J. M. (1980). Homosexual behavior in cross-cultural perspective. In J. Marmor (Ed.), *Homosexual behavior* (pp. 100–122). New York: Basic Books.

CARTER, J. A., McNAIR, L. D., CORBIN, W. R., & WILLIAMS, M. (1999). Gender differences related to heterosexual condom use: The influence of negotiation styles. *Journal of Sex & Marital Therapy, 25,* 217–225.

CARTER, J. J., et al. (1996). The natural history of human papillomavirus type 16 capsid antibodies among a cohort of university women. *Journal of Infectious Diseases, 174,* 927–936.

CARTER, S., & SOKOL, J. (1989). *What really happens in bed: A demystification of sex.* New York: M. Evans.

CASTLEMAN, M. (1997). Recipes for lust. *Psychology Today,* July/August, 50–56.

CASTRO, K. G., et al. (1988). Transmission of HIV in Belle Glade, Florida: Lessons for other communities in the United States. *Science, 239,* 193–197.

CATANIA, J. A., et al. (1993). Changes in condom use among black, Hispanic, and white heterosexuals in San Francisco: The AMEN cohort study. *Journal of Sex Research, 30,* 121–128.

CATANIA, J. A., et al. (1995). Risk factors for HIV and other sexually transmitted diseases and prevention practices among US heterosexual adults: Changes from 1990 to 1992. *American Journal of Public Health, 85,* 1492–1499.

CATES, JR., W. C., CHESNEY, M. A., & COHEN, M. S. (1997). Primary HIV infection—A public health opportunity. *American Journal of Public Health, 87,* 1928–1930.

CATES, JR., W., STEWART, F. H., & TRUSSELL, J. (1992). Commentary: The quest for women's prophylactic methods—Hopes vs. science. *American Journal of Public Health, 82,* 1479–1482.

CATES, JR., W., & STONE, K. M. (1992a). Family planning, sexually transmitted diseases and contraceptive choice: A literature update. Pt. I. *Family Planning Perspectives, 24*(2), 75–84.

CATES, JR., W., & STONE, K. M. (1992b). Family planning, sexually transmitted diseases and contraceptive choice: A literature update. Pt. II. *Family Planning Perspectives, 24*(3), 122–128.

CATOTTI, D. N., CLARKE, P., & CATOE, K. E. (1993). Herpes revisited: Still a cause of concern. *Sexually Transmitted Diseases, 20,* 77–80.

CATTERALL, R. D. (1974). *A short textbook of venereology.* Philadelphia: Lippincott.

CENTER FOR POPULATION OPTIONS. (1992). *Teenage pregnancy and too-early childbearing: Public costs, personal consequences.*

CENTERS FOR DISEASE CONTROL AND PREVENTION. (1992). Revised classification system for HIV infection and expanded surveillance case definitions for AIDS among adolescents and adults. *Morbidity and Mortality Weekly Report, 41,* 1–19.

CENTERS FOR DISEASE CONTROL AND PREVENTION. (1996). *Hepatitis surveillance report.* Atlanta: Author.

CENTERS FOR DISEASE CONTROL AND PREVENTION. (1996). Mortality attributable to HIV infection among persons aged 25–44 years—United States, 1994. *Morbidity and Mortality Weekly Report, 45,* 121–125.

CENTERS FOR DISEASE CONTROL AND PREVENTION. (1997a). Alcohol consumption among pregnant and childbearing-aged women—United States, 1991 and 1995. *Morbidity and Mortality Weekly Report, 46*(16), 346–350.

CENTERS FOR DISEASE CONTROL AND PREVENTION. (1997b). Rubella and congenital rubella syndrome—United States, 1994–1997. *Morbidity and Mortality Weekly Report, 46*(16), 350–354.

CENTERS FOR DISEASE CONTROL AND PREVENTION. (1999a). Update: Recommendations to prevent hepatitis B virus transmission—United States. *Morbidity and Mortality Weekly Report, 44,* 574–575.

CENTERS FOR DISEASE CONTROL AND PREVENTION. (1999b). Congenital syphilis—United States, 1998. *Morbidity and Mortality Weekly Report, 48,* 757–761.

CENTERS FOR DISEASE CONTROL AND PREVENTION. (1999c). Primary and secondary syphilis—United States, 1998. *Morbidity and Mortality Weekly Report, 48,* 875–878.

CENTERS FOR DISEASE CONTROL AND PREVENTION. (2000A). Abortion surveillance: Preliminary analysis—United States, 1997. *Morbidity and Mortality Weekly Report, 48,* 1171–1174.

CENTERS FOR DISEASE CONTROL AND PREVENTION. (2000b). Youth risk behavior surveillance—United States, 1999. *Morbidity and Mortality Weekly Report, 49,* SS-5.

CENTERS FOR DISEASE CONTROL AND PREVENTION. (2000c). *HIV/AIDS surveillance report, 11 (No. 2).*

CHANDRA, A., & STEPHEN, E. H. (1998). Impaired fecundity in the United States: 1982–1995. *Family Planning Perspectives, 30,* 34–42.

CHANG, H., & HOLT, G. (1991). The concept of yuan and Chinese interpersonal relationships. In S. Ting-Toomey & F. Korzenny (Eds.), *Cross-cultural interpersonal communication.* Newbury Park, CA: Sage.

CHANG, Y. (2000). Was it virtually good for you? *Newsweek,* January 1, 71.

CHAPPELL, D. (1976). Cross-cultural research on forcible rape. *International Journal of Criminology and Penology, 4,* 295–304.

CHAPPELL, K. D., & DAVIS, K. E. (1998). Attachment, partner choice, and perception of romantic partners: An experimental test of the attachment-security hypothesis. *Personal Relationships, 5,* 327–342.

CHASEN-TABER, L., et al. (1997). Oral contraceptives and ovulatory causes of delayed fertility. *American Journal of Epidemiology, 146,* 258–265.

CHEN, Z., et al. (1997). Human immunodeficiency virus type 2 (HIV-2) seroprevalence and characterization of a distinct HIV-2 genetic subtype 1133 from the natural range of simian immunodeficiency virus-infected sooty mangabeys. *Journal of Virology, 71,* 3953–3960.

CHI, I.-C. (1993a). Safety and efficacy issues of progestin-only oral contraceptives—An epidemiologic approach. *Contraception, 47,* 1–21.

CHI, I.-C. (1993b). What we have learned from recent IUD studies: A researcher's perspective. *Contraception, 48,* 81–108.

CHIANG, H.-S., WU, C.-C., & WEN, T.-C. (2000). 10 years of experience with penile prosthesis implantation in Taiwanese patients. *Journal of Urology, 163,* 476–480.

CHIAPPA, J. A., & FORISH, J. J. (1976). *The VD book.* New York: Holt, Rinehart & Winston.

CHIPOURAS, S., et al. (1979). *Who cares? A handbook on sex education and counseling services for disabled people.* Washington, DC: George Washington University.

CHIRAWATKUL, S., & MANDERSON, L. (1994). Perceptions of menopause in northeast Thailand: Contested meaning and practice. *Social Science Medicine, 39,* 1545–1554.

CHOI, K.-H., CATANIA, J. A., & DOLCINI, M. M. (1994). Extramarital sex and HIV risk behavior among US adults: Results from the National AIDS Behavioral Survey. *American Journal of Public Health, 84,* 2003–2007.

CHOI, K.-H., RICKMAN, R., & CATANIA, J. A. (1994). What heterosexual adults believe about condoms. *New England Journal of Medicine, 331,* 406–407.

CHRISTENSEN, A. (1988). Dysfunctional interaction patterns in couples. In P. Noller & M. A. Fitzpatrick (Eds.), *Perspectives on marital interaction* (pp. 31–52). Philadelphia: Multilingual Matters.

CHU, S. Y., et al. (1992). AIDS in bisexual men in the United States: Epidemiology and transmission to women. *American Journal of Public Health, 82,* 220–224.

CHUN, T. W., et al. (1999). Re-emergence of HIV after stopping therapy. *Nature, 401,* 874–875.

CLARK, D. (1987). *The new loving someone gay.* Berkeley, CA: Celestial Arts.

CLARK, J. T., SMITH, E. R., & DAVIDSON, J. M. (1984). Enhancement of sexual motivation in male rats. *Science, 224,* 847–849.

CLARK, R. D., & HATFIELD, E. (1989). Gender differences in receptivity to sexual offers. *Journal of Psychology & Human Sexuality, 2,* 39–55.

CLARKE, J. (1994). The meaning of menstruation in the elimination of abnormal embryos. *Human Reproduction, 9,* 1204–1207.

CLARKE, L. L., et al. (1998). Norplant selection and satisfaction among low-income women. *American Journal of Public Health, 88,* 1175–1181.

CLARKE, P. (1996/1997). Why do Americans find it easier to have sex than to talk about it? *STD News, 4*(2–3).

CLARKE, V. (2000). "Stereotype, attack, and stigmatize those who disagree": Employing scientific rhetoric in debates about lesbian and gay parenting. *Feminism & Psychology, 10,* 152–159.

CLARNETTE, T., SUGITA, Y., & HUTSON, J. (1997). Genital anomalies in human and animal models reveal the mechanisms and hormones governing testicular descent. *British Journal of Urology, 79,* 99–112.

CLEAVER, E. (1968). *Soul on ice.* New York: Dell.

CLEMENTS, M. (1994). Sex in America today. *Parade Magazine,* August 7, 4–6.

CLEMENTS, M. (1996). Sex after 65. *Parade Magazine,* March 17, 4–6.

CLIFFORD, D. B. (2000). Human immunodeficiency virus-associated dementia. *Archives of Neurology, 57,* 321–324.

COCHRAN, C. C., FRAZIER, P. A., & OLSON, A. M. (1997). Predictors of response to unwanted sexual attention. *Psychology of Women Quarterly, 21,* 207–226.

COCHRAN, S. D., & MAYS, V. M. (1990). Sex, lies, and HIV. *New England Journal of Medicine, 322,* 774–775.

COCHRAN, S. D., & MAYS, V. M. (2000). Lifetime prevalence of suicide symptoms and affective disorders among men reporting same-sex sexual partners: Results from NHANES III. *American Journal of Public Health, 90,* 573–578.

COCHRAN, S. D., & MAYS, V. M. (2000). Relation between psychiatric syndromes and behaviorally defined sexual orientation in a sample of the US population. *American Journal of Epidemiology, 151,* 516–523.

COCHRANE, J. (2000). Narrowing the gap: Access to HIV treatments in developing countries. A pharmaceutical company's perspective. *Journal of Medical Ethics, 26,* 47–50.

COCORES, J., DACKIS, C., & GOLD, M. (1986). Sexual dysfunction secondary to cocaine abuse. *Journal of Clinical Psychiatry, 47,* 384–385.

COENEN, M. E. (1998). Helping families with homosexual children: A model for counseling. *Journal of Homosexuality, 36,* 73–85.

COHEN, A. (2000). Excess female mortality in India: The case of Himachal Pradesh. *American Journal of Public Health, 90,* 1369–1371.

COHEN, J. A., & MANNARINO, A. P. (2000). Predictors of treatment outcome in sexually abused children. *Child Abuse & Neglect, 24,* 983–994.

COHEN, L. J., & ROTH, S. (1987). The psychological aftermath of rape: Long-term effects and individual differences in recovery. *Journal of Social and Clinical Psychology, 5,* 525–534.

COHEN, L. L., & SHOTLAND, R. L. (1996). Timing of first sexual intercourse in a relationship: Expectations, experiences, and perceptions of others. *Journal of Sex Research, 33,* 291–299.

COHEN, M. L., GAROFALO, R., BOUCHER, R., & SEGHORN, T. (1971). The psychology of rapists. *Seminars in Psychiatry, 3,* 307–327.

COHEN, M. L., SEGHORN, T., & CALMAS, W. (1969). Sociometric study of the sex offender. *Journal of Abnormal Psychology, 74,* 249–255.

COHEN, S. (1979). The volatile nitrates. *Journal of the American Medical Association, 241,* 2077–2078.

COHEN-KETTENIS, P. T., & GOOREN, L. J. G. (1999). Transsexualism: A review of etiology, diagnosis and treatment. *Journal of Psychosomatic Research, 46,* 315–333.

COHN, J. A. (1997). HIV infections—1. *British Medical Journal, 314,* 487–491.

COKER, A. L., SMITH, P. H., MCKEOWN, R. E., & KING, M. J. (2000). Frequency and correlates of intimate partner violence by type: Physical, sexual, and psychological battering. *American Journal of Public Health, 90,* 553–559.

COLAPINTO, J. (1997). The true story of John/Joan. *Rolling Stone,* December 11, 54–73, 92–96.

COLDITZ, G. A., et al. (1995). The use of estrogens and progestins and the risk of breast cancer in postmenopausal women. *New England Journal of Medicine, 332,* 1589–1593.

COLE, D. (1987). It might have been: Mourning the unborn. *Psychology Today,* July, 64–65.

COLE, E. (1982). Sibling incest: The myth of benign sibling incest. *Women and Therapy, 5,* 79–89.

COLE, P. M., & PUTNAM, F. W. (1992). Effect of incest on self and social functioning: A developmental psychopathology perspective. *Journal of Consulting and Clinical Psychology, 60,* 174–184.

COLE, R. (1994). Lawsuit challenges daughter's memory of sexual abuse. *Times-Picayune* (New Orleans), March 26, A-2.

COLEMAN, E. (1991). Compulsive sexual behavior: New concepts and treatment. *Journal of Psychology & Human Sexuality, 4*(2), 37–52.

COLEMAN, E., & EDWARDS, B. (1986, July). Sexual compulsion vs. sexual addiction: The debate continues. *SIECUS Report,* pp. 7–10.

COLEMAN, M., & GANONG, L. (1991). Remarriage and stepfamily research in the 1980s: Increased interest in an old form. In A. Booth (Ed.), *Contemporary families: Looking forward, looking back.* Minneapolis, MN: National Council on Family Relations.

COLEY, R. L., & CHASE-LANSDALE, P. L. (1998). Adolescent pregnancy and childhood: Recent evidence and future directions. *American Psychologist, 53,* 152–166.

COLLABORATIVE GROUP ON HORMONAL FACTORS IN BREAST CANCER. (1996). Breast cancer and hormonal contraceptives: Collaborative reanalysis of individual data on 53,297 women with and 100,239 women without breast cancer from 54 epidemiological studies. *Lancet, 347,* 1713–1727.

COLLABORATIVE GROUP ON HORMONAL FACTORS IN BREAST CANCER. (1997). Breast cancer and hormone replacement therapy: Collaborative reanalysis of data from 51 epidemiological studies of 52,705 women with breast cancer and 108,411 women without breast cancer. *Lancet, 350,* 1047–1059.

COLLAER, M. L., & HINES, M. (1995). Human behavioral sex differences: A role for gonadal hormones during early development? *Psychological Bulletin, 118,* 55–107.

COLLINGS, S. J., & PAYNE, M. F. (1991). Attribution of causal and moral responsibility to victims of father-daughter incest: An exploratory examination of five factors. *Child Abuse & Neglect, 15,* 513–521.

COLLINS, N. L., & MILLER, L. C. (1994). Self-disclosure and liking: A meta-analytic review. *Psychological Bulletin, 116,* 457–475.

COMFORT, A. (1995). *The new joy of sex.* New York: Random House.

COMHAIRE, F. H. (1994). Male contraception: Hormonal, mechanical and other. *Human Reproduction, 9,* 586–590.

COMISKEY, K. M. (1989). Relationship workshops: How "good marriages" can be strengthened. *Contemporary Sexuality, 1,* 10.

COMMISSION ON OBSCENITY AND PORNOGRAPHY. (1970). *The report of the Commission on Obscenity and Pornography.* Washington, DC: U.S. Government Printing Office.

CONDRY, J., & CONDRY, S. (1977). Sex differences: A study of the eye of the beholder. *Child Development, 47,* 812–819.

CONNERY, J. (1977). *Abortion: The development of the Roman Catholic perspective.* Chicago: Loyola University Press.

CONSTANTINOPLE, A. (1973). Masculinity-femininity: An exception to a famous dictum. *Psychological Bulletin, 80,* 389–407.

CONSUMER REPORTS. (1989). Can you rely on condoms? *Consumer Reports,* March, 135–141.

CONSUMER REPORTS. (1995). How reliable are condoms? *Consumer Reports,* May, 320–325.

CONTE, J. R. (1991). The nature of sexual offenses against children. In C. R. Hollin & K. Howells (Eds.), *Clinical approaches to sex offenders and their victims* (pp. 11–34). New York: Wiley.

CONTE, J. R., et al. (1986). Child sexual abuse and the family: A critical analysis. *Journal of Psychotherapy and the Family, 2,* 113–126.

COOK, R., & FOSEN, R. (1970). Pornography and the sex offender: Patterns of exposure and immediate arousal effects of pornographic stimuli. In *Technical report of the Commission on Obscenity and Pornography* (Vol. 7). Washington, DC: U.S. Government Printing Office.

COOK, S. L. (1995). Acceptance and expectation of sexual aggression in college students. *Psychology of Women Quarterly, 19,* 181–194.

COOPER, A., BOIES, S., MAHEU, M., & GREENFIELD, D. (2000). Sexuality and the Internet: The next sexual revolution. In L. T. Szuchman & F. Muscarella (Eds.), *Psychological perspectives on human sexuality* (pp. 519–545). New York: Wiley.

CORNE, S., BRIERE, J., & ESSES, L. M. (1992). Women's attitudes and fantasies about rape as a function of early exposure to pornography. *Journal of Interpersonal Violence, 7,* 454–461.

COSTE, J., et al. (1994). Sexually transmitted diseases as major causes of ectopic pregnancy: Results from a large case-control study in France. *Fertility and Sterility, 62,* 289–295.

COTTON, D., & GROTH, A. (1982). Innate rape: Prevention and intervention. *Journal of Prison and Jail Health, 2,* 45–57.

COUTINHO, E. M., et al. (2000). Gossypol blood levels and inhibition of spermatogenesis in men taking gossypol as a contraceptive. *Contraception, 61,* 61–67.

COUTTS, R. L. (1973). Love and intimacy: A psychological approach. San Ramon, CA: Consensus.

COWAN, G. (2000). Beliefs about the causes of four types of rape. *Sex Roles, 42,* 807–823.

COWAN, G., & CAMPBELL, R. R. (1995). Rape casual attitudes among adolescents. *Journal of Sex Research, 32,* 145–153.

COWAN. J. (1869). *The science of a new life.* New York: Cowan and Co.

COWLEY, G. (2000a). Fighting the disease: What can be done. *Newsweek,* January 17, 38.

COWLEY, G. (2000b). Looking beyond Viagra. *Newsweek,* April 24, 77–78.

COWLEY, G., GIDEONSE, T., & UNDERWOOD, A. (1997). Gender limbo. *Newsweek,* May 19, 64–66.

COWLEY, G., et al. (1996). Attention: Aging men. *Newsweek,* September 16, 68–75.

COX, A. D., HOLDEN, J. M., & SAGOVSKY, R. (1987). Detection of postnatal depression: Development of the 10 item Edinburgh postnatal depression scale. *Journal of Personality and Social Psychology, 150,* 782–786.

COX, D. J. (1988). Incidence and nature of male genital exposure behavior as reported by college women. *Journal of Sex Research, 24,* 227–234.

COXON, A. P. M., & McMANUS, T. J. (2000). How many account for how much? Concentration of high-risk sexual behavior among gay men. *Journal of Sex Research, 37,* 1–7.

CRANDALL, C. J. (1999). Estrogen replacement therapy and colon cancer: A clinical review. *Journal of Women's Health & Gender-Based Medicine, 8,* 1155–1166.

CROOK, W. G. (1983). *The yeast connection: A medical breakthrough.* Jackson, TN: Professional Books.

CROSBY, R. A., et al. (2000). Correlates of unprotected vaginal sex among African American female adolescents. *Archives Pediatric and Adolescent Medicines, 154,* 893–899.

CROSIGNANI, P. G., BIANCHEDI, D., RICCABONI, A., & VEGETTI, W. (1999). Management of anovulatory infertility. *Human Reproduction, 14,* (Suppl. 1), 108–119.

CROSS, S. E., & MADSON, L. (1997). Models of the self: Self-construals and gender. *Psychological Bulletin, 122,* 5–37.

CROWE, L. C., & GEORGE, W. H. (1989). Alcohol and human sexuality: Review and integration. *Psychological Bulletin, 105,* 374–386.

CROXATTO, H. B., & MAKARAINEN, L. (1998). The pharmacodynamics and efficacy of Implanon: An overview of the data. *Contraception, 58* (Suppl. 6), 91S–97S.

CUMMING, D. C., CUMMING, C. E., & KIEREN, D. K. (1991). Menstrual mythology and sources of information about menstruation. *American Journal of Obstetrics and Gynecology, 164,* 472–476.

CUNNINGHAM, F. G., et al. (1997). *Williams obstetrics* (20th ed.). Norwalk, CT: Appleton & Lange.

CUPACH, W. R., & METTS, S. (1991). Sexuality and communication in close relationships. In K. McKinney & S. Sprecher (Eds.), *Sexuality in close relationships.* Hillsdale, NJ: Erlbaum.

CUPACH, W. R., & SPITZBERG, B. H. (1998). Obsessive relational intrusion and stalking. In B. H. Spitzberg & W. R. Cupach (Eds.), *The dark side of close relationships* (pp. 233–263). Mahwah, NJ: Erlbaum.

CUPOLI, J. M., & SEWELL, P. M. (1988). One thousand fifty-nine children with a chief complaint of sexual abuse. *Child Abuse & Neglect, 12,* 151–162.

CURTIN, S. C. (1999). Recent changes in birth attendant, place of birth, and the use of obstetric interventions, United States, 1989–1997. *Journal of Nurse-Midwifery, 44,* 349–354.

CURTIS, R., & MILLER, K. (1988). Believing another likes or dislikes you: Behavior making the beliefs come true. *Journal of Personality and Social Psychology, 51,* 284–290.

CUTLER, W. B. (1999). Human sex-attractant pheromones: Discovery, research, development, and application in sex therapy. *Psychiatric Annals, 29,* 54–59.

CUTLER, W. B., FRIEDMAN, E., & McCOY, N. L. (1998). Pheromonal influences on sociosexual behavior in men. *Archives of Sexual Behavior, 27,* 1–13.

CUTLER, W. B., et al. (1985). Sexual behavior frequency and biphasic ovulatory-type menstrual cycles. *Physiology & Behavior, 34,* 805–810.

CUTLER, W. B., et al. (1986). Human axillary secretions influence women's menstrual cycles: The role of donor extract from men. *Hormones and Behavior, 20,* 463.

CYRANOWSKI, J. M., AARESTAD, S. L., & ANDERSEN, B. L. (1999). The role of sexual self-schema in a diathesis-stress model of sexual dysfunction. *Applied & Preventive Psychology: Current Scientific Perspectives, 8,* 217–228.

CYRANOWSKI, J. M., & ANDERSEN, B. L. (1998). Schemas, sexuality, and romantic attachment. *Journal of Personality and Social Psychology, 74,* 1364–1379.

DALTON, C., & BENNETT, N. G. (2000). Is biology destiny? Birth weight and life chances. *American Sociological Review, 65,* 458–467.

DALTON, K. (1964). *The premenstrual syndrome.* Springfield, IL: Charles C Thomas.

DALTON, K. (1980). Cyclical criminal acts in premenstrual syndrome. *Lancet, 2,* 1070–1071.

DALY, M., WILSON, M., & WEGHORST, S. J. (1982). Male sexual jealousy. *Ethology and Sociobiology, 3,* 11–27.

DARLING, C. A., DAVIDSON, J. K., & CONWAY-WELCH, C. (1990). Female ejaculation: Perceived origins, the Grafenberg spot/area, and sexual responsiveness. *Archives of Sexual Behavior, 19,* 29–47.

DARLING, C. A., DAVIDSON, J. K., & COX, R. P. (1991). Female sexual response and the timing of partner orgasm. *Journal of Sex & Marital Therapy, 17,* 3–21.

DARLING, C. A., DAVIDSON, J. K., & JENNINGS, D. A. (1991). The female sexual response revisited: Understanding the multi-orgasmic experience in women. *Archives of Sexual Behavior, 20,* 527–540.

DARROCH, J. E., LANDRY, D. J., & OSLAK, S. (1999). Age differences between sexual partners in the United States. *Family Planning Perspectives, 31,* 160–167.

DARROCH, J. E., LANDRY, D. J., & SINGH, S. (2000) Changing emphasis in sexuality education in U.S. public secondary schools, 1988–1999. *Family Planning Perspectives, 32,* 204–211 & 265.

D'AUGELLI, A. R., HERSHBERGER, S. L., & PILKINGTON, N. W. (1998). Lesbian, gay, and bisexual youth and their families: Disclosure of sexual orientation and its consequences. *American Journal of Orthopsychiatry, 68,* 361–371.

DAVEY, R. T., et al. (1999). HIV-1 and T cell dynamics after interruption of highly active antiretroviral therapy (HAART) in patients with a history of sustained viral suppression. *Proceedings of the National Academy of Sciences USA, 96,* 15109–15114.

DAVIDSON, J. K., & MOORE, N. B. (1994). Guilt and lack of orgasm during sexual intercourse: Myth versus reality among college women. *Journal of Sex Education and Therapy, 20,* 153–174.

DAVIES, K. A. (1997). Voluntary exposure to pornography and men's attitudes toward feminism and rape. *Journal of Sex Research, 24,* 131–137.

DAVIES, S., KATZ, J., & JACKSON, J. L. (1999). Sexual desire discrepancies: Effects on sexual and relationship satisfaction in heterosexual dating couples. *Archives of Sexual Behavior, 28,* 553–567.

DAVIS, C., & BAUSERMAN, R. (1993). Exposure to sexually explicit materials: An attitude change perspective. *Annual Review of Sex Research, 4,* 121–209.

DAVIS, G. E., & LEITENBERG, H. (1987). Adolescent sex offenders. *Psychological Bulletin, 101,* 417–427.

DAVIS, K. E. (1985). Near and dear: Friendship and love compared. *Psychology Today,* February, 22–28.

DAVIS, K. E., & BRAUGHT, G. N. (1970). Exposure to pornography, character, and sexual deviance: A retrospective study. In *Technical Report of the Commission on Obscenity and Pornography* (Vol. 7). Washington, DC: U.S. Government Printing Office.

DAVIS, K. E., & LATTY-MANN, H. (1987). Love styles and relationship quality: A contribution to validation. *Journal of Social and Personal Relationships, 4,* 409–428.

DAVIS, R. C., BRICKMAN, E., & BAKER, T. (1991). Supportive and unsupportive responses of others to rape victims: Effects on concurrent victim adjustment. *American Journal of Community Psychology, 19,* 443–451.

DAWOOD, K., et al. (2000). Familial aspects of male homosexuality. *Archives of Sexual Behavior, 29,* 155–163.

DE ANGELIS, T. (1996). Project explores sexual misconduct among children. *APA Monitor,* October, 43.

DE ANGELIS, T. (1997). Menopause symptoms may vary among ethnic groups. *APA Monitor,* November, 16–17.

DEAUX, K., & LEWIS, L. L. (1983). Components of gender role stereotypes. *Psychological Documents, 13,* 25.

DEEKS, S. G., SMITH, M., HOLODNIY, M., & KAHN, J. O. (1997). HIV-1 protease inhibitors: A review for clinicians. *Journal of the American Medical Association, 277,* 145–153.

DEJIN-KARLSSON, E., et al. (1998). Does passive smoking in early pregnancy increase the risk of small-for-gestational-age infants. *American Journal of Public Health, 88,* 1523–1527.

DE KRUIFF, M. E., et al. (2000). Vaginismus and dyspareunia: Is there a difference in clinical presentation? *Journal of Psychosomatic Obstetrics & Gynecology, 21,* 149–155.

DE KUYPER, E. (1993). The Freudian construction of sexuality: The gay foundation of heterosexuality and straight homophobia. In *If you seduce a straight person can you make them gay?* (pp. 137–144). New York: Haworth Press.

DELANEY, J., LUPTON, M. J., & TOTH, E. (1988). *The curse: A cultural history of menstruation.* Urbana: University of Illinois Press.

DeMARIS, A., & RAO, K. V. (1992). Premarital cohabitation and subsequent marital stability in the United States: A reassessment. *Journal of Marriage and the Family, 54,* 178–190.

DEMING, W. (1995). *Paul on marriage and celibacy: The Hellenistic background of 1 Corinthians 7.* Cambridge: Cambridge University Press.

DE MUNCK, V. C., & KOROTAYEV, A. (1999). Sexual equality and romantic love: A reanalysis of Rosenblatt's study on the function of romantic love. *Cross-Cultural Research, 33,* 265–277.

DENNERSTEIN, L., DUDLEY, E., & BURGER, H. (1997). Well-being and the menopausal transition. *Journal of Psychosomatic Obstetrics and Gynecology, 18,* 95–101.

DENNISTON, R. H. (1980). Ambisexuality in animals. In J. Marmor (Ed.), *Homosexual behavior* (pp. 25–40). New York: Basic Books.

DENNY, D. (1997). Transgender: Some historical, cross-cultural, and contemporary models and methods of coping and treatment. In B. Bullough, V. L. Bullough, & J. Elias (Eds.), *Gender blending.* New York: Prometheus Books.

DENNY, D. (1998). Rachel and me: A commentary on gender: An ethnomethodological approach. *Feminism & Psychology, 10,* 62–65.

DE RIVERA, J. (1997). The construction of false memory syndrome: The experience of retractors. *Psychological Inquiry, 8,* 271–292.

DERLEGA, V. J., & BARBEE, A. P. (1998). What is the impact of the HIV infection on individuals' social interactions and relationships? In V. J. Derlega and A. P. Barbee (Eds.), *HIV & social interaction* (pp. 1–11). Thousand Oaks, CA: Sage.

DERLEGA, V. J., METTS, S., PETRONIO, S., & MARGULIS, S. T. (1993). *Self-disclosure.* Newbury Park, CA: Sage.

DE ROUGEMENT, D. (1969). *Love in the Western world.* New York: Fawcett.

DE SADE, D., MARQUIS. (1965). *Justine* (R. Seaver & A. Wainhouse, Trans.). New York: Grove Press. (Original work published 1791.)

DESIGNER BABIES. (1998). *Newsweek,* November 9, 61–62.

DES JARLAIS, D. C., et al. (1996). HIV incidence among injecting drug users in New York City syringe-exchange programmes, *Lancet, 348,* 987–991.

DeSTENO, D. A., & SALOVEY, P. (1996). Evolutionary origins of sex differences in jealousy? Questioning the "fitness" of the model. *Psychological Science, 7,* 367–372.

DEUCHAR, N. (1995). Nausea and vomiting in pregnancy: A review of the problem with particular regard to psychological and social aspects. *British Journal of Obstetrics and Gynaecology, 102,* 6–8.

DE VILLIERS, E.-M. (1989). Heterogeneity of the human papillomavirus group. *Journal of Virology, 63,* 4898–4903.

DE VINCENZI, I., & EUROPEAN STUDY GROUP. (1994). A longitudinal study of human immunodeficiency virus transmission by heterosexual partners. *New England Journal of Medicine, 331,* 341–346.

DHAWAN, S., & MARSHALL, W. L. (1996). Sexual abuse histories of sexual offenders. *Sexual Abuse: A Journal of Research and Treatment, 8,* 7–15.

DIAMANT, A. L., SCHUSTER, M. A., McGUIGAN, K., & LEVER, J. (1999). Lesbians' sexual history with men: Implications for taking a sexual history. *Archives of Internal Medicine, 159,* 2730–2736.

DIAMOND, C., & BUSKIN, S. (1999). Continued risky behavior in HIV-infected youth. *American Journal of Public Health, 90,* 115–118.

DIAMOND, L. M. (2000). Sexual identity, attractions, and behavior among young sexual-minority women over a 2-year period. *Developmental Psychology, 36,* 241–250.

DIAMOND, M. (1993). Homosexuality and bisexuality in different populations. *Archives of Sexual Behavior, 22,* 291–310.

DIAMOND, M. (1997). Sexual identity and sexual orientation in children with traumatized or ambiguous genitalia. *Journal of Sex Research, 34,* 199–211.

DIAMOND, M. (1998). Sex and gender: Same or different? *Feminism & Psychology, 10,* 46–54.

DIAMOND, M., & KARLEN, A. (1980). *Sexual decisions.* Boston: Little, Brown.

DIAMOND, S., & MALISZEWSKI, M. (Eds.). (1992). *Sexual aspects of headaches.* Madison, CT: International University Press.

DICKEY, R., & STEPHENS, J. (1995). Female-to-male transsexualism, heterosexual type: Two cases. *Archives of Sexual Behavior, 24,* 439–445.

DICKINSON, G. M., et al. (1993). Absence of HIV transmission from an infected dentist to his patients. *Journal of the American Medical Association, 269,* 1802–1806.

DICK-READ, G. (1972). *Childbirth without fear* (4th ed.). New York: Harper & Row. (First published 1932)

DiCLEMENTE, R. J., et al. (1990). College students' knowledge and attitudes about AIDS and changes in HIV-preventive behaviors. *AIDS Education and Prevention, 2,* 201–212.

DIETZ-UHLER, B., & MURRELL, A. (1992). College students perceptions of sexual harassment: Are gender differences decreasing? *Journal of College Student Development, 33,* 540–546.

DiFRANZA, J. R., & LEW, R. A. (1995). Effect of maternal cigarette smoking on pregnancy complications and sudden infant death syndrome. *Journal of Family Practice, 40,* 385–394.

DIMMOCK, P. W., WYATT, K. M., JONES, P. W., & O'BRIEN, P. M. S. (2000). Efficacy of selective serotonin-reuptake inhibitors in premenstrual syndrome: A systematic review. *Lancet, 356,* 1131–1136.

DINDIA, K., & ALLEN, M. (1992). Sex differences in self-disclosure: A meta-analysis. *Psychological Bulletin, 112,* 106–124.

DITTMAN, R. W. (1998). Ambiguous genitalia, gender-identity problems, and sex reassignment. *Journal of Sex & Marital Therapy, 24,* 255–271.

DOCTER, R. F. (1985). Transsexual surgery at 74: A case report. *Archives of Sexual Behavior, 14,* 271–277.

DOCTER, R. F., & PRINCE, V. (1997). Transvestism: A survey of 1032 cross-dressers. *Archives of Sexual Behavior, 26,* 589–605.

DOMINIK, R., TRUSSELL, J., & WALSH, T. (2000). Failure rates among perfect users and during perfect use: A distinction that matters. *Contraception, 60,* 315–320.

DONAHEY, K. M., & CARROLL, R. A. (1993). Gender differences in factors associated with hypoactive sexual desire. *Journal of Sex & Marital Therapy, 19,* 25–40.

DONNERSTEIN, E. (1982). Pornography: Its effect on violence against women. In N. M. Malamuth & E. Donnerstein (Eds.), *Pornography and sexual aggression* (pp. 53–81). Orlando, FL: Academic Press.

DONNERSTEIN, E., & LINZ, D. (1984). Sexual violence in the media: A warning. *Psychology Today, 18,* 14–15.

DONNERSTEIN, E., & LINZ, D. (1986). The question of pornography. *Psychology Today,* December, 56–59.

DONNERSTEIN, E., LINZ, D., & PENROD, S. (1987). *The question of pornography: Research findings and policy implications.* New York: Free Press.

DONOVAN, P. (1997). Can statutory rape laws be effective in preventing adolescent pregnancy? *Family Planning Perspectives, 29,* 30–34.

DORNADULA, G., et al. (1999). Residual HIV-1 RNA in blood plasma of patients taking suppressive highly active antiretroviral therapy. *Journal of the American Medical Association, 282,* 1627–1632.

DORNER, G., et al. (1975). A neuroendocrine predisposition for homosexuality in men. *Archives of Sexual Behavior, 4,* 1–8.

DOUGLAS, M. (1966). *Purity and danger: An analysis of concepts of pollution and taboo.* New York: Praeger.

DOUGLASS, W. C. (1988). *WHO murdered Africa?* [Circulated booklet.]

DOWNEY, J. I., & FRIEDMAN, R. C. (1998). Female homosexuality: Classical psychoanalytic theory reconsidered. *Journal of the American Psychoanalytic Association, 46,* 471–506.

DOYLE, J. (1985). *Sex and gender: The human experiment.* Dubuque, IA: W. C. Brown.

DOYLE, J., & PALUDI, M. (1991). *Sex and gender* (2nd ed.). Dubuque, IA: Brown and Benchmark.

DOZORTSEV, D., DE SUTTER, P., RYBOUCH-KIN, A., & KHONT, M. (1995). Oocyte activation and intracytoplasmic sperm injection (ICSI). *Assisted Reproduction Review, 5,* 32–39.

DRAPER, E. S., MANKLELOW, B., FIELD, D. J., & JAMES, D. (1999). Prediction of survival for preterm births by weight and gestational age: Retrospective population based study. *British Medical Journal, 319,* 1093–1097.

DUBOIS-ARBER, F., JEANNIN, A., KONINGS, E., & PACCAUD, F. (1997). Increased condom use without other major changes in sexual behavior among the general population in Switzerland. *American Journal of Public Health, 87,* 558–566.

DUESBERG, P. H., & ELLISON, B. (1996). *Inventing the AIDS virus.* Lanhem, MD: Regnery.

DUMEZIL, G. (1979). *Mariages indo-européens.* Paris: Payot.

DUNCAN, D. F., & NICHOLSON, T. (1991). Pornography as a source of sex information for students at a southeastern state university. *Psychological Reports, 68,* 802.

DUNKLE, J. H., & FRANCIS, P. L. (1990). The role of facial masculinity/femininity in the attribution of homosexuality. *Sex Roles, 23,* 157–167.

DUNN, M. E., & CUTLER, N. (2000). Sexual issues in older adults. *AIDS Patient Care and STDs, 14,* 67–69.

DUNN, M. E., & TROST, J. E. (1989). Male multiple orgasms: A descriptive study. *Archives of Sexual Behavior, 18,* 377–387.

DURANT, L. E., & CAREY, M. P. (2000). Self-administered questionnaires versus face-to-face interviews in assessing sexual behavior in young women. *Archives of Sexual Behavior, 29,* 309–322.

DURKIN, K. F. (1997). Misuse of the Internet by pedophiles: Implications for law enforcement and probation practice. *Federal Probation, 61*(3), 14–18.

DURKIN, K. F., & BRYANT, C. D. (1999). Propagandizing pederasty: A thematic analysis of the on-line exculpatory accounts of unrepentant pedophiles. *Deviant Behavior: An Interdisciplinary Journal, 20,* 103–127.

DWORKIN, A. (1989). *Pornography: Men possessing women.* New York: Dutton.

DYKES, B. (2000). Problems in defining cross-cultural "kinds of homosexuality"—and a solution. *Journal of Homosexuality, 38,* 1–18.

DZIECH, B. W., & WEINER, L. (1984). *The lecherous professor: Sexual harassment on campus.* Boston: Beacon Press.

EADS, L. S., SHUMAN, D. W., DeLIPSEY, J. M. (2000). Getting it right: The trial of sexual assault and child molestation cases under Federal Rules of Evidence 413–415. *Behavioral Sciences and the Law, 18,* 169–216.

EAGLY, H. H., & WOOD, W. (1999). The origins of sex differences in human behavior: Evolved dispositions versus social roles. *American Psychologist, 54,* 408–423.

EARLS, C. M., & DAVID, H. (1989). A psychosocial study of male prostitution. *Archives of Sexual Behavior, 18,* 401–419.

EBI, K. L., PIZIALI, R. L., ROSENBERG, M., & WACHOB, H. F. (1996). Evidence against tail-strings increasing the rate of pelvic inflammatory disease among IUD users. *Contraception, 53,* 25–32.

EBRAHIM, S., et al. (2000). Trends in pregnancy-related smoking rates in the United States, 1987–1996. *Journal of the American Medical Association, 283,* 361–366.

ECKER, N. (1994). Culture and sexual scripts out of Africa: A North American trainer's view of taboos, tradition, trouble and truth. *SIECUS Report, 22*(2), 16–21.

ECKES, T., & TRAUTNER, H. M. (Eds.). (2000). *The developmental social psychology of gender.* Mahwah, NJ: Erlbaum.

EDWARDS, M. (1996). We have a responsibility to dialogue with the media. *SIECUS Report, 24*(5), 5–9.

EDWARDS, R. (1996). Can sexual orientation change with therapy? *APA Monitor,* September.

EFFAH, K. B. (1999). A reformation of the polygyny-fertility hypothesis. *Journal of Comparative Family Studies, 30,* 381–408.

EHRHARDT, A. A. (1992). Trends in sexual behavior and the HIV pandemic. *American Journal of Public Health, 82,* 1459–1461.

EHRLICH, P. R., & EHRLICH, A. H. (1990). *The population explosion.* New York: Simon & Schuster.

EHRLICHMAN, H., & EICHENSTEIN, R. (1992). Private wishes: Gender similarities and differences. *Sex Roles, 26,* 399–422.

EICHEL, E. W., & NOBILE, P. (1992). *The perfect fit: How to achieve mutual fulfillment and monogamous passion through the new intercourse.* New York: Donald Fine.

EINARSON, T. P., et al. (1990). Maternal spermicide use and adverse reproductive outcome: A meta-analysis. *American Journal of Obstetrics and Gynecology, 162,* 655–660.

EITZEN, D. S., & ZINN, M. B. (2000). *Social problems* (8th ed.). Boston: Allyn & Bacon.

EL HADI, A. (1997). A step forward for opponents of female genital mutilation in Egypt. *Lancet, 349,* 129–130.

ELIFSON, K. W., et al. (1989). Seroprevalence of human immunodeficiency virus among male prostitutes. *New England Journal of Medicine, 321,* 822–833.

ELLEN, J. M., et al. (1998). Individuals' perceptions about their sex partners' risk behaviors. *Journal of Sex Research, 35,* 328–332.

ELLIOTT, L., & BRANTLEY, C. (1997). *Sex on campus.* New York: Random House.

ELLIS, E. M., ATKESON, B. M., & CALHOUN, K. S. (1982). An examination of differences between multiple and single incident victims of sexual assault. *Journal of Abnormal Psychology, 91,* 221–224.

ELLIS, H. (1918). *Studies in the psychology of sex, Vol. II. Sexual inversion.* Philadelphia: Davis.

ELLIS, L. (1993). Rape as a biosocial phenomenon. In G. C. N. Hall et al. (Eds.), *Sexual aggression: Issues in etiology, assessment, and treatment* (pp. 17–41). Washington, DC: Taylor & Francis.

ELLIS, L., & AMES, M. A. (1987). Neurohormonal functioning and sexual orientation: A theory of homosexuality-heterosexuality. *Psychological Bulletin, 101,* 223–258.

ELSTER, N., et al. (2000). Less is more: The risks of multiple births. *Fertility and Sterility, 74,* 617–623.

ELWIN, U. (1968). *The kingdom of the young.* Oxford: Oxford University Press.

ENDELMAN, R. (1989). *Love and sex in twelve cultures.* New York: Psyche Press.

ENDICOTT, J. (2000). History, evolution, and diagnosis of premenstrual dysphoric disorder. *Journal of Clinical Psychiatry, 61,* (Suppl. 12), 5–8.

ENGLUND, J. A., et al. (1997). Zidovudine, didanosine, or both as the initial treatment for symptomatic HIV-infected children. *New England Journal of Medicine, 336,* 1704–1712.

EPSTEIN, E., & GUTTMAN, R. (1984). Mate selection in man: Evidence, theory, and outcome. *Social Biology, 31,* 243–278.

ERARD, J. R. (1988). Vaginal discharges: Diagnosis and therapy. *Diagnosis, 10*(6), 47.

ERICKSEN, J. A. (2000). Sexual liberation's last frontier. *Society,* May/June, 21–25.

ERIKSON, E. (1968). *Identity: Youth and crisis.* New York: Norton.

ERNST, E., & PITTLER, M. (1998). Yohimbine for erectile dysfunction: A systematic review and meta-analysis of randomized clinical trials. *Journal of Urology, 159,* 433–436.

ERNULF, K. E., & INNALA, S. M. (1995). Sexual bondage: A review and unobtrusive investigation. *Archives of Sexual Behavior, 24,* 631–654.

ERON JR., J. J. (2000) HIV-1 protease inhibitors. *Clinical Infectious Diseases, 30,* S160–S170.

ESCHENBACH, D. A. (1993). History and review of bacterial vaginosis. *American Journal of Obstetrics and Gynecology, 169,* 441–445.

ESKELAND, B., THOM, E., & SVENDSEN, K. (1997). Sexual desires in men: Effects of oral ingestion of a product derived from fertilized eggs. *Journal of International Medical Research, 25,* 62–70.

ESKRIDGE JR., W. N. (1999). *Hardwick* and historiography. *University of Illinois Law Review,* No. 2, 631–702.

ESPARZA, J., & BHAMARAPRAVATI, N. (2000). Accelerating the development and future availability of HIV-1 vaccines: Why, when, where, and how? *Lancet, 355,* 2061–2066.

ESPÍN, O. M. (1984). Cultural and historical influences on sexuality in Hispanic/Latin women: Implications for psychotherapy. In C. Vance (Ed.), *Pleasure and danger: Exploring female sexuality.* New York: Routledge & Kegan Paul.

ETHICS COMMITTEE OF THE AMERICAN SOCIETY OF REPRODUCTIVE MEDICINE. (1999). Sex selection and preimplantation genetic diagnosis. *Fertility and Sterility, 72,* 595–598.

EUROPEAN COLLABORATIVE STUDY. (1991). Children born to women with HIV-1 infection: Natural history and risk of transmission. *Lancet, 337,* 253–260.

EUROPEAN COLLABORATIVE STUDY. (1992). Risk factors for mother-to-child transmission of HIV-1. *Lancet, 339,* 1007–1012.

EUROPEAN COLLABORATIVE STUDY. (1994). Perinatal findings in children born to HIV-infected mothers. *British Journal of Obstetrics and Gynaecology, 101,* 136–141.

EVANS, M. (1998). "Falling in love with love is falling for make believe": Ideologies of romance in post-enlightenment culture. *Theory, Culture & Society, 15,* 265–275.

EVANS, R. B. (1969). Childhood parental relationships of homosexual men. *Journal of Counseling and Clinical Psychology, 33,* 129–135.

EVERETT. S. A., et al. (2000). Use of birth control pills, condoms, and withdrawal among U.S. high school students. *Journal of Adolescent Health, 27,* 112–118.

EWIGMAN, B. G., et al. (1993). Effect of prenatal ultrasound screening on perinatal outcome. *New England Journal of Medicine, 329,* 821–827.

EX, C. T. G. M., & JANSSENS, J. M. A. M. (1998). Maternal influences on daughters' gender role attitudes. *Sex Roles, 38,* 171–186.

EXNER, J. F., WYLIE, J., LEURA, A., & PARRILL, T. (1977). Some psychological characteristics of prostitutes. *Journal of Personality Assessment, 41,* 474–485.

EYLER, F., et al. (1998). Birth outcome from a prospective, matched study of prenatal crack cocaine use: I. Interactive and dose effects on health and growth. *Pediatrics, 101,* 229–237.

FAGOT, B. I. (1995). Psychosocial and cognitive determinants of early gender-role development. *Annual Review of Sex Research, 6,* 1–31.

FALLER, K. C. (1987). Women who sexually abuse children. *Victims and Violence, 2*(4), 23–27.

FALLER, K. C. (1991). Polyincestuous families: An exploratory study. *Journal of Interpersonal Violence, 6,* 310–321.

FARLEY, M., BARAL, I., KIREMIRE, M., SEZGIN, V. (1998). Prostitution in 5 countries: Violence and posttraumatic stress disorder. *Feminism & Psychology, 8,* 405–426.

FARQUHAR, C. M. (2000). Endometriosis. *British Medical Journal, 320,* 1449–1451.

FARR, G., GABELNICK, H., STURGEN, K., & DORFLINJER, L. (1994). Contraceptive efficacy and acceptability of the female condom. *American Journal of Public Health, 84,* 1960–1964.

FARROW, S. (1994). Falling sperm quality: Fact or fiction? *British Medical Journal, 309,* 1–2.

FAUCI, A. S. (1999). The AIDS epidemic: Considerations for the 21st century. *New England Journal of Medicine, 341,* 1046–1050.

FAUSTO-STERLING, A. (1993). The five sexes: Why male and female are not enough. *The Sciences, 33*(3), 20–24.

FAY, R. E., et al. (1989). Prevalence and patterns of same-gender sexual contact among men. *Science, 243,* 338–348.

FEDORA, O., et al. (1992). Sadism and other paraphelias in normal controls and aggressive and nonaggressive sex offenders. *Archives of Sexual Behavior, 21,* 1–15.

FEIERMAN, J. R., & FEIERMAN, L. A. (2000). Paraphilias. In L. T. Szuchman & F. Muscarella (Eds.), *Psychological perspectives on human sexuality* (pp. 480–518). New York: Wiley.

FEINGOLD, A. (1992). Gender differences in mate selection preferences: A test of the parental investment model. *Psychological Bulletin, 112,* 125–139.

FELDMAN-SUMMERS, S., & POPE, K. S. (1994). The experience of "forgetting" childhood abuse: A national survey of psychologists. *Journal of Consulting and Clinical Psychology, 62,* 636–639.

FERNSLER, K. (2000). Why I want a husband. In J. Selzer (Ed.), *Conversations: Readings for writing* (4th ed.). Boston: Allyn & Bacon.

FEUER, E. J., et al. (1993). The lifetime risk of developing breast cancer. *Journal of the National Cancer Institute, 85,* 892–897.

FIESTER, S. J., & GAY, M. (1991). Sadistic personality disorder: A review of data and recommendations for DSM-IV. *Journal of Personality Disorders, 5,* 376–385.

FINE, M. (1988). Sexuality, schooling, and adolescent females: The missing discourse of desire. *Harvard Educational Review, 58,* 29–53.

FINERAN, S., & BENNETT, L. (1999). Gender and power issues of peer sexual harassment among teenagers. *Journal of Interpersonal Violence, 14,* 626–641.

FINGER, W. R. (2000). Sex education helps prepare young adults. *Network, 20*(3), 10–15.

FINKELHOR, D. (1978). Psychological, cultural and family factors in incest and family sexual abuse. *Journal of Marriage and Family Counseling, 4,* 41–49.

FINKELHOR, D. (1979). *Sexually victimized children.* New York: Free Press.

FINKELHOR, D. (1980). Sex among siblings: A survey on prevalence, variety, and effects. *Archives of Sexual Behavior, 9,* 171–194.

FINKELHOR, D. (1984). *Child sexual abuse: New theory and research.* New York: Free Press.

FINKELHOR, D., & ARAJI, A. (1986). Explanations of pedophilia: A four-factor model. *Journal of Sex Research, 22,* 145–161.

FINKELHOR, D., & RUSSELL, D. (1984). The gender gap among perpetrators of child sexual abuse. In D. Russell (Ed.), *Sexual exploitation: Rape, child sexual abuse, and workplace harassment* (pp. 215–231). Beverly Hills, CA: Sage.

FINKELHOR, D., & YLLO, K. (1985). *License to rape: Sexual abuse of wives.* New York: Holt, Rinehart & Winston.

FINZI, D., et al. (1997). Identification of a reservoir for HIV-1 in patients on highly active antiretroviral therapy. *Science, 278,* 1295–1300.

FISCH, H., et al. (1995). Semen analyses in 1,283 men from the United States over a 25-year period: No decline in quality. *Fertility and Sterility, 65,* 1009–1014.

FISCHER, G. J. (1989). Sex words used by partners in a relationship. *Journal of Sex Education and Therapy, 15*(1), 50.

FISCHL, M. A., et al. (1989). Prolonged zidovudine therapy in patients with AIDS and advanced AIDS-related complex. *Journal of the American Medical Association, 262,* 2405–2410.

FISHER, B., et al. (1995). Reanalysis and results after 12 years of follow-up in a randomized clinical trial comparing total mastectomy and lumpectomy with or without irradiation in the treatment of breast cancer. *New England Journal of Medicine, 333,* 1456–1461.

FISHER, H. E. (1987). The four year itch. *Natural History, 10,* 22–29.

FISHER, H. E. (1989). Evolution of human sexual pairbonding. *American Journal of Physical Anthropology, 78,* 331–354.

FISHER, H. E. (1992). *Anatomy of love: The natural history of monogamy, adultery and divorce.* New York: Norton.

FISHER, H. E. (1997). Paper presented at the meeting of the American Association for the Advancement of Science.

FISHER, J. D., & FISHER, W. A. (1992). Changing AIDS-risk behavior. *Psychological Bulletin, 11,* 455–474.

FISHER, W. (1986). A psychological approach to human sexuality. In D. Byrne & K. K. Kelley (Eds.), *Alternative approaches to human sexuality.* Hillsdale, NJ: Erlbaum.

FISHER, W., & GRAY, J. (1988). Erotophobia-erotophilia and sexual behavior during pregnancy and postpartum. *Journal of Sex Research, 25,* 379–396.

FISHER, W. A., BRANSCOMBE, N. R., & LEMERY, C. R. (1983). The bigger the better?

Arousal and attributional responses to erotic stimuli that depict different size penises. *Journal of Sex Research, 19*, 337–396.

FISHER, W. A., & GRENIER, G. (1994). Violent pornography, antiwoman thoughts, and antiwoman acts: In search of reliable effects. *Journal of Sex Research, 31*, 23–38.

FITZGERALD, B. (1999). Children of lesbian and gay parents: A review of the literature. *Marriage & Family Review, 29*, 57–75.

FITZ-GERALD, D. R., & FITZ-GERALD, M. (1998). A historical review of sexuality education and deafness: Where have we been this century? *Sexuality and Disability, 16*, 249–268.

FITZGERALD, L. F. (1993). Sexual harassment: Violence against women in the workplace. *American Psychologist, 48*, 1070–1076.

FITZGERALD, L. F., SHULLMAN, S. L., BAILEY, N., & RICHARDS, M. (1988). The incidence and dimensions of sexual harassment in academia and the workplace. *Journal of Vocational Behavior, 32*, 152–175.

FITZGERALD, L. F., SWAN, S., & MAGLEY, V. J. (1997). But was it really sexual harassment? Legal, behavioral, and psychological definitions of the workplace victimization of women. In W. O'Donohue (Ed.), *Sexual harassment: Theory, research and therapy* (pp. 5–28). Boston: Allyn & Bacon.

FLAKE, A. W., et al. (1996). Treatment of X-linked severe combined immunodeficiency by in vitro transplantation of paternal bone marrow. *New England Journal of Medicine, 335*, 1806–1810.

FLAMM, B. L. (2000). Cesarean section: A worldwide epidemic? *Birth, 27*, 136–137.

FLAMM, B. L., BERWICK, D. M., & KABCENELL, A. (1998). Reducing cesarean section rates safely: Lessons from a "breakthrough" collaborative. *Birth, 25*, 117–124.

FLEMING, D. T., et al. (1997). Herpes simplex virus type 2 in the United States, 1976 to 1994. *New England Journal of Medicine, 337*, 1105–1111.

FLINT, M. P. (1997). Secular trends in menopause age. *Journal of Psychosomatic Obstetrics and Gynecology, 18*, 65–72.

FLOR-HENRY, P. (1987). Cerebral aspects of sexual deviation. In G. D. Wilson (Ed.), *Variant sexuality: Research and theory*. Baltimore: Johns Hopkins University Press.

FOA, E. B., & RIGGS, D. S. (1995). Posttraumatic stress disorder following assault: Theoretical considerations and empirical findings. *Current Directions in Psychological Science, 4*, 61–65.

FOLDSPANG, A., MOMMSEN, S., & DJURHUUS, J. C. (1999). Prevalent urinary incontinence as a correlate of pregnancy, vaginal childbirth, and obstetric techniques. *American Journal of Public Health, 89*, 209–212.

FONDA, G. (1994). Local estrogen replacement for local symptoms in older community dwelling women. *Gerontology, 40*(Suppl.), 9–13.

FOOTE, D. (1998). And baby makes one. *Newsweek,* February 2, 68, 70.

FORD, C. S., & BEACH, F. A. (1951). *Patterns of sexual behavior*. New York: Harper & Brothers.

FORD, W. C. L., et al. (2000). Increasing paternal age is associated with delayed conception in a large population of fertile couples: Evidence for declining fecundity in older men. *Human Reproduction, 15*, 1703–1708.

FOREHAND, R., & KOTCHICK, B. A. (1996). Cultural diversity: A wake-up call for parent training. *Behavior Therapy, 27*, 187–206.

FORMAN, D., & MOLLER, H. (1994). Testicular cancer. *Cancer Surveillance, 19–20*, 323–341.

FOSTER, C. (2000). The limits to low fertility: A biosocial approach. *Population and Development Review, 26*, 209–234.

FOXMAN, B., et al. (1997). Condom use and first-time urinary tract infection. *Epidemiology, 8*, 637–641.

FRANCE, D. (2000). The HIV disbeliever. *Newsweek,* August 28, 46–48.

FRANCE, D., & ROSENBERG, D. (2000). The abortion pill. *Newsweek,* October 9, 26–30.

FRANK, E., ANDERSON, C., & RUBENSTEIN, D. (1978). Frequency of sexual dysfunction in "normal" couples. *New England Journal of Medicine, 299*, 111–115.

FRANK, P., et al. (1993). The effect of induced abortion on subsequent fertility. *British Journal of Obstetrics and Gynaecology, 100*, 575–580.

FRANKLIN, D. (1984). Rubella threatens unborn in vaccine gap. *Science News, 125*, 186.

FRANKLIN, K. (2000). Antigay behaviors among young adults: Prevalence, patterns, and motivators in a noncriminal population. *Journal of Interpersonal Violence, 15*, 339–362.

FRASER, C. M., et al. (1998). Complete genome sequence of *Treponema pallidum*, the syphilis spirochete. *Science, 281*, 375–388.

FRAYSER, S. (1985). *Varieties of sexual experience: An anthropological perspective on human sexuality*. New Haven, CT: Human Relations Area Files Press.

FRAYSER, S. (1994). Defining normal childhood sexuality: An anthropological approach. *Annual Review of Sex Research, 5*, 173–217.

FRAZER, I. H. (1996). The role of vaccines in the control of STDs: HPV vaccines. *Genitourinary Medicine, 72*, 398–403.

FRAZIER, P. A. (1991). Self-blame as a mediator of postrape depressive symptoms. *Journal of Social and Clinical Psychology, 10*, 47–57.

FREUD, S. (1905). *Three essays on the theory of sexuality*. In Standard edition, Vol. VII, pp. 125–245. London: Hogarth Press, 1953.

FREUD, S. (1913). *Totem and taboo*. New York: Vintage Books.

FREUD, S. (1924). *The sexual life of man*. *In E. Jones (Trans.), A general introduction to psychoanalysis,* (pp. 312–328). New York: Washington Square Press.

FREUD, S. (1953). Contributions to the psychology of love: A special type of choice of objects made by men. In E. Jones (Ed.), *Collected papers* (Vol. 4, pp. 192–202). London: Hogarth Press. (Originally published 1933.)

FREUD, S. (1965). *New introductory lectures on psychoanalysis*. New York: Norton.

FREUND, K., & KUBAN, M. (1993). Toward a testable developmental model of pedophilia: The development of erotic age preference. *Child Abuse & Neglect, 17*, 315–324.

FREUND, K., & KUBAN, M. (1994). The basis of the abused abuser theory of pedophilia: A further elaboration on an earlier study. *Archives of Sexual Behavior, 23*, 553–563.

FREUND, K., & LANGEVIN, R. (1976). Bisexuality in homosexual pedophilia. *Archives of Sexual Behavior, 5*, 415–423.

FREUND, K., & SETO, M. C. (1998). Preferential rape in the theory of courtship disorder. *Archives of Sexual Behavior, 27*, 433–443.

FREUND, K., SETO, M.C., & KUBAN, M. (1997). Frotteurism and the theory of courtship disorder. In D. R. Laws & W. O'Donohue (Eds.), *Sexual deviance: Theory, assessment, and treatment* (pp. 111–130). New York: Guilford Press.

FREUND, K., & WATSON, R. J. (1992). The proportions of heterosexual and homosexual pedophiles among sex offenders against children: An exploratory study. *Journal of Sex & Marital Therapy, 18*, 34–43.

FREUND, K., WATSON, R., & DICKEY, R. (1991). Sex offenses against female children perpetrated by men who are not pedophiles. *Journal of Sex Research, 28*, 409–423.

FREUND, M., LEONARD, T. L., & LEE, N. (1989). Sexual behavior of resident street prostitutes with their clients in Camden, New Jersey. *Journal of Sex Research, 26*, 460–478.

FRIEDMAN, C. I., & KIM, M. H. (1985). Obesity and its effect on reproductive function. *Clinical Obstetrics and Gynecology, 28*, 645–663.

FRIEDMAN, R. (1947). *The story of scabies* (Vol. I). New York: Froben Press.

FRIEDMAN, R. C., & DOWNEY, J. (1995). Biology and the Oedipus complex. *Psychoanalytic Quarterly, 64*, 234–264.

FRIEDRICH, W. N. (1993). Sexual victimization and sexual behavior in children: A review of recent literature. *Child Abuse & Neglect, 17*, 59–66.

FRIEDRICH, W. N. (1998). Behavioral manifestations of child sexual abuse. *Child Abuse & Neglect, 22*, 523–531.

FRIEDRICH, W. N., & REAMS, R. A. (1987). Course of psychological symptoms in sexually abused young children. *Psychotherapy, 24*, 160–170.

FRIEDRICH, W. N., et al. (1991). Normative sexual behavior in children. *Pediatrics, 88*, 456–464.

FRIEZE, I. H. (1983). Investigating the causes and consequences of marital rape. *Signs, 8*, 532–553.

FROMM, E. (1956). *The art of loving*. New York: Harper & Row.

FURNHAM, A., & MAK, T. (1999). Sex-role stereotyping in television commercials: A review and comparison of fourteen studies done on five continents over 25 years. *Sex Roles, 41*, 413–437.

FURSTENBERG, JR., F. F., et al. (1984). Family communication and teenagers' contraceptive use. *Family Planning Perspectives, 16*, 163–170.

FURTADO, M. R., et al. (1999). Persistance of HIV-1 transcription in peripheral-blood mononuclear cells in patients receiving potent antiretroviral therapy. *New England Journal of Medicine, 340*, 1614–1622.

GABRIEL, S. E., et al. (1997). Complications leading to surgery after breast implantation. *New England Journal of Medicine, 336*, 677–682.

GAGNON, J. H. (1977). *Human sexualities*. Glenview, IL: Scott, Foresman.

GAGNON, J. H. (1985). Attitudes and responses of parents to preadolescent masturbation. *Archives of Sexual Behavior, 14*, 451–466.

GAGNON, J. H., & SIMON, W. (1973). *Sexual conduct: The social origins of human sexuality*. Chicago: Aldine.

GALLAGHER, W. (1986). The etiology of orgasm. *Discover,* February, 51–59.

GANNON, C. L. (1998). The deaf community and sexuality education. *Sexuality and Disability, 16*, 283–293.

GANONG, L., & COLEMAN, M. (1989). Preparing for remarriage: Anticipating the issues, seeking solutions. *Family Relations, 38,* 28–33.

GAO, F., et al. (1992). Human infection by genetically diverse SIVSM-related HIV-2 in West Africa. *Nature, 358,* 495–499.

GAO, F., et al. (1999). Origin of HIV-1 in the chimpanzee *Pan troglodytes troglodytes. Nature, 397,* 436–441.

GARBER, L. (1991). *Vested interests.* Boston: Little, Brown.

GARNER, D. M. (1997). The 1997 body image survey results. *Psychology Today,* January/February, 30–36, 38–40, 42–44, 75, 76, 78, 84.

GARTNER, R. B. (1997). Considerations in the psychoanalytic treatment of men who were sexually abused as children. *Psychoanalytic Psychology, 14,* 13–41.

GATES, D., & MILLER, M. (2000). Dr. Laura, talk radio celebrity. *Newsweek,* March 20, 52.

GATES, G. J., & SONENSTEIN, F. L. (2000). Heterosexual genital sexual activity among adolescent males: 1988 and 1995. *Family Planning Perspectives, 32,* 295–297 & 304.

GAYLE, H. (2000). Paper presented at a briefing hosted by the American Medical Association before the start of the 13th International Conference on AIDS, Durban, South Africa.

GEARY, D. C. (1999). Evolution and developmental sex differences. *Current Directions in Psychological Science, 8,* 115–120.

GEBHARD, P. H. (1985). Sexuality in cross-cultural perspective. In W. Masters, V. Johnson, & R. Kolodny (Eds.), *Human Sexuality* (2nd ed., pp. 620–637). Boston: Little, Brown.

GEBHARD, P. H., GAGNON, J. H., POMEROY, W. B., & CHRISTENSON, C. V. (1965). *Sex offenders: An analysis of types.* New York: Harper & Row.

GEER, J. H., & BELLARD, H. S. (1996). Sexual content induced delays in unprimed lexical decisions: Gender and content effects. *Archives of Sexual Behavior, 25,* 379–395.

GEGAX, T. T. (1997) The AIDS predator. *Newsweek,* November 10, 52–59.

GELFAND, M. M. (2000). Sexuality among older women. *Journal of Women's Health & Gender-Based Medicine, 9,* 515–520.

GELMAN, D. (1990). Was it illness or immorality? *Newsweek,* June 11, 55.

GELMAN, D., FOOTE, D., BARRETT, T., & TALBOT, M. (1992). Born or bred? *Newsweek,* February 24, 46–53.

GELMAN, D., & ROGERS, P. (1993). Mixed messages. *Newsweek,* April 12, 28–29.

GELMAN, D., et al. (1990). The mind of a rapist. *Newsweek,* July 23, 46–52.

GENEVIE, L., & MARGOLIES, E. (1987). *The motherhood report: How women feel about being mothers.* New York: Macmillan.

GIAMPAOLI, S. (2000). Epidemiology of major age-related diseases in women compared to men. *Aging Clinical and Experimental Research, 12,* 93–105.

GIBBONS, J. L. (2000). Gender development in cross-cultural perspective. In T. Eckes & H. M. Trautner (Eds.), *The developmental social psychology of gender* (pp. 389–415). Mahwah, NJ: Erlbaum.

GIBBS, N., et al. (1990). The dreams of youth. *Time,* Special Issue (Fall), 10–14.

GIBSON-AINYETTE, I., TEMPLER, D. I., BROWN, R., & VEACO, L. (1988). Adolescent female prostitutes. *Archives of Sexual Behavior, 17,* 431–438.

GIDYCZ, C. A., & KOSS, M. P. (1990). A comparison of group and individual sexual assault

victims. *Psychology of Women Quarterly, 14,* 325–342.

GIFFORD, S. M. (1994). The change of life, the sorrow of life: Menopause, bad blood and cancer among Italian-Australian working class women. *Culture, Medicine, Psychiatry, 18,* 299–321.

GIL, V. E., & ANDERSON, A. F. (1998). State-sanctioned aggression and the control of prostitution in the people's republic of China: A review. *Aggression and Violent Behavior, 3,* 129–142.

GILBERT, B., & CUNNINGHAM, J. (1987). Women's post rape sexual functioning: Review and implications for counseling. *Journal of Counseling and Development, 65,* 71–73.

GILBERT, N. (1991). The phantom epidemic of sexual assault. *The Public Interest, 103,* 54–65.

GILBERT, W. M., NESBITT, T. S., & DANIEL-SEN, B. (1999). Childbearing beyond age 40: Pregnancy outcome in 24,032 cases. *Obstetrics & Gynecology, 93,* 9–14.

GILLMORE, M. R., et al. (1997). Repeat pregnancies among adolescent mothers. *Journal of Marriage and the Family, 59,* 536–550.

GIOVANNUCCI, E., et al. (1993). A prospective cohort study of vasectomy and prostate cancer in United States men. *Journal of the American Medical Association, 269,* 873–877.

GLADUE, B. A. (1988). Hormones in relationship to homosexual/bisexual/heterosexual gender orientation. In J. M. A. Sitesen (Ed.), *Handbook of sexology: Vol. 6. The pharmacology and endocrinology of sexual function.* Amsterdam: Elsevier.

GLADUE, B. A. (1994). The biopsychology of sexual orientation. *Current Directions in Psychological Science, 3,* 150–154.

GLADUE, B. A., GREEN, R., & HELLMAN, R. E. (1984). Neuroendocrine response to estrogen and sexual orientation. *Science, 225,* 1496–1498.

GLASER, J. B., et al. (1991). Sexually transmitted diseases in postpubertal female rape victims. *Journal of Infectious Diseases, 164,* 726–730.

GLASIER, A. (1997). Emergency postcoital contraception. *New England Journal of Medicine, 337,* 1058–1064.

GLYNN, S. A. (2000). Trends in incidence and prevalence of major transfusion-transmissible viral infections in US blood donors, 1991 to 1996. *Journal of the American Medical Association, 284,* 229–235.

GOCHROS, H., GOCHROS, J. S., & FISHER, J. (Eds.). (1986). *Helping the sexually oppressed.* Englewood Cliffs, NJ: Prentice Hall.

GOERGE, R. M., & LEE, B. J. (1997). Abuse and neglect of the children. In R. A. Maynard (Ed.), *Kids having kids: Economic costs and social consequences of teen pregnancy* (pp. 205–230). Washington, DC: Urban Institute Press.

GOERGEN, D. (1975). *The sexual celibate.* New York: Seabury.

GOLD, S. N., HUGHES, D., & HOHNECKER, L. (1994). Degrees of repression of sexual abuse memories. *American Psychologist, 49,* 441–442.

GOLDBERG, C., & ELDER, J. (1998). Public still backs abortion, but wants limits, poll says. A notable shift from general acceptance. *New York Times,* January 16, A1, A16.

GOLDBERG, H. (1979). *The new male.* New York: William Morrow.

GOLDBERG, H., et al. (1998). *1996 Russian women's reproductive health survey: A study of*

three sites—Final report. Atlanta: Centers for Disease Control and Prevention.

GOLDEN, C. R. (2000). Still seeing differently, after all these years. *Feminism & Psychology, 10,* 30–35.

GOLDENBERG, R. L., et al. (1998). The preterm prediction study: The value of new vs standard risk factors in predicting early and all spontaneous preterm births. *American Journal of Public Health, 88,* 233–238.

GOLDHABER, M. K., et al. (1993). Long-term risk of hysterectomy among 80,007 sterilized and comparison women at Kaiser Permanente, 1971–1987. *American Journal of Epidemiology, 138,* 508–521.

GOLDING, J. M. (1999). Sexual-assault history and long-term physical health problems: Evidence from clinical and population epidemiology. *Current Directions in Psychological Science, 8,* 191–194.

GOLDMAN, B., BUSH, P., & KLATZ, R. (1987). *Death in the locker room: Steroids, cocaine, and sports.* Tucson, AZ: Body Press.

GOLDSTEIN, B. (1976). *Human sexuality.* New York: McGraw-Hill.

GOLDSTEIN, D. (1994). AIDS and women in Brazil: The emerging problem. *Social Science and Medicine, 39,* 919–929.

GOLDSTEIN, I., et al. (1998). Oral sildenafil in the treatment of erectile dysfunction. *New England Journal of Medicine, 338,* 1397–1404.

GOLDSTEIN, M. J. (1973). Exposure to erotic stimuli and sexual deviance. *Journal of Social Issues, 29,* 197–220.

GOLEMAN, D. (1990). Homophobia: Scientists find clues to its roots. *New York Times,* July 10, C1, C11.

GOLEMAN, D. (1992). New studies map the mind of the rapist. *New York Times.*

GOLLUB, E. L. (2000). The female condom: Tool for women's empowerment. *American Journal of Public Health, 90,* 1377–1381.

GOODCHILDS, J., & ZELLMAN, G. (1984). Sexual signaling and sexual aggression in adolescent relationships. In N. Malamuth & E. Donnerstein (Eds.), *Pornography and sexual aggression.* Orlando, FL: Academic Press.

GOODMAN, A. (1992). Sexual addiction: Designation and treatment. *Journal of Sex & Marital Therapy, 18,* 304–314.

GOODMAN, A. (1998). *Sexual addiction: An integrated approach.* Madison, CT: International Universities Press.

GOODSON, P., EVANS, A., & EDMUNDSON, E. (1997). Female adolescents and onset of sexual intercourse: A therapy-based review of research from 1984 to 1994. *Journal of Adolescent Health, 21,* 147–155.

GORDON, C. M., CAREY, M. P., & CAREY, K. B. (1997). Effects of a drinking event on behavioral skills and condom attitudes in men: Implications for HIV risk from a controlled experiment. *Health Psychology, 16,* 490–495.

GORDON, S. (1989). *Raising your child conservatively in a sexually permissive world.* New York: Fireside.

GORDON, S., & SNYDER, C. W. (1989). *Personal issues in human sexuality: A guidebook for better sexual health* (2nd ed.). Boston: Allyn & Bacon.

GORSKI, R., GORDON, J., SHRYNE, J., & SOUTHAM, A. (1978). Evidence for a morphological sex difference within the medial preoptic area of the rat brain. *Brain Research, 148,* 333–346.

GOTTLIEB, J. (2000). Gun control, gay issues: O.C. surprisingly liberal. *Los Angeles Times,* June 27, B4.

GOTTMAN, J. M., & KROKOFF, L. J. (1989). Marital interaction and satisfaction: A longitudinal view. *Journal of Consulting and Clinical Psychology, 57,* 47–52.

GOULD, L. (1989). Impact of cardiovascular disease on male sexual function. *Medical Aspects of Human Sexuality,* April, 24–27.

GRABER, B. (Ed.). (1982). *Circumvaginal musculature and sexual function.* New York: Karger.

GRADY, W. R., HAYWARD, M. D., & FLOREY, F. A. (1988). Contraceptive discontinuation among married women in the United States. *Studies in Family Planning, 19,* 227–235.

GRAFENBERG, E. (1950). The role of the urethra in female orgasm. *International Journal of Sexology, 3,* 145–148.

GRAHAM, S.(1834). *A lecture to young men.* Providence, Rhode Island: Weeden and Corey.

GRAM, I., AUSTIN, H., & STALSBERG, H. (1992). Cigarette smoking and the incidence of cervical intraepithelial neoplasia, grade III, and the cancer of the cervix uteri. *American Journal of Epidemiology, 135,* 341–346.

GRAVHOLT, C. H., JUUL, S., NAERAA, R. W., & HANSEN, J. (1996). Prenatal and postnatal prevalence of Turner's syndrome: A registry study. *British Medical Journal, 312,* 16–21.

GRAY, J. (1992). *Men are from Mars, women are from Venus: A practical guide to improving communication and getting what you want in your relationships.* New York: HarperCollins.

GRAY, P. (1993a). What is love? *Time,* February 15, 46–49.

GRAY, P. (1993b). The assault on Freud. *Time,* November 29, 46–51.

GRAYSTON, A. D., & DELUCA, R. V. (1999). Female perpetrators of child sexual abuse: A review of the clinical and empirical literature. *Aggression and Violent Behavior, 4,* 93–106.

GREEN, R. (1987). *The "sissy boy syndrome" and the development of homosexuality.* New Haven, CT: Yale University Press.

GREEN, R., & FLEMING, D. T. (1990). Transsexual surgery follow-up: Status in the 1990s. *Annual Review of Sex Research, 1,* 163–174.

GREENBERG, B. S., & BUSELLE, R. (1996). Soap operas and sexual activity: A decade later. *Journal of Communication, 46,* 153–160.

GREENBERG, B. S., & HOFSCHIRE, L. (2000). Sex on entertainment television. In D. Zillman & P. Vorderer (Eds.), *Media entertainment: The psychology of its appeal* (pp. 93–111). Mahwah, NJ: Erlbaum.

GREENBERG, B. S., & WOODS, M. G. (1999). The soaps: Their sex, gratifications, and outcomes. *Journal of Sex Research, 36,* 250–257.

GREENBERG, D., BRADFORD, J., FIRESTONE, P., & CURRY, S. (2000). Recidivism of child molesters: A study of victim relationship with the perpetrator. *Child Abuse & Neglect, 24,* 1485–1494.

GREENBLATT, C. S. (1983). The salience of sexuality in the early years of marriage. *Journal of Marriage and the Family, 45,* 289–299.

GREENDALE, G. A., et al. (1993). The relationship of *Chlamydia trachomatis* infection and male infertility. *American Journal of Public Health, 83,* 996–1001.

GREGERSEN, E. (1982). *Sexual practices.* New York: Franklin Watts.

GREGOR, T. (1985). *Anxious pleasures: The sexual lives of an Amazonian people.* Chicago: University of Chicago Press.

GREGORY, J. G., & PURCELL, M. M. (1989). Penile curvature: Assessment and treatment. *Medical Aspects of Human Sexuality, 23,* 64.

GREILING, H., & BUSS, D. M. (2000). Women's sexual strategies: The hidden dimension of extra-pair mating. *Personality and Individual Differences, 28,* 929–963.

GRIMAL, P. (1986). *Love in ancient Rome.* Norman: University of Oklahoma Press.

GRIMES, D. A. (1992). The intrauterine device, pelvic inflammatory disease, and infertility: The confusion between hypothesis and knowledge. *Fertility & Sterility, 58,* 670–673.

GRIMES, D. A. (1997). Medical abortion in early pregnancy: A review of the evidence. *Obstetrics and Gynecology, 89,* 790–796.

GRISEZ, G. G. (1970). *Abortion: The myths, the realities, and the arguments.* New York: Corpus Books.

GROB, C. S. (1985). Female exhibitionism. *Journal of Nervous and Mental Disease, 173,* 253.

GRODSTEIN, F., et al. (1996). Postmenopausal estrogen and progestin use and the risk of cardiovascular disease. *New England Journal of Medicine, 335,* 453–461.

GRODSTEIN, F., et al. (1997). Postmenopausal hormone therapy and mortality. *New England Journal of Medicine, 336,* 1769–1775.

GROENENDIJK, L. F. (1997). Masturbation and neurasthenia: Freud and Stekel in debate on the harmful effects of autoerotism. *Journal of Psychology and Human Sexuality, 91,* 71–94.

GROFF, M. G. (1987). Characteristics of incest offenders' wives. *Journal of Sex Research, 23,* 91–96.

GROSS, L. (1996). Lesbians and gays in the broadcast media. *SIECUS Report, 24*(4), 10–14.

GROSSMAN, L. S., HAYWOOD, T. W., & WASYLIW, O. E. (1992). The evaluation of truthfulness in alleged sex offenders' self-reports: 16 PF and MMPI validity scales. *Journal of Personality Assessment, 59,* 264–275.

GROSSMAN, L. S., MARTIS, B., & FICHTNER, C. G. (1999). Are sex offenders treatable? A research overview. *Psychiatric Services, 50,* 349–361.

GROSZ, C. A., KEMPE, R. S., & KELLY, M. (2000). Extrafamilial sexual abuse: Treatment for child victims and their families. *Child Abuse & Neglect, 24,* 9–23.

GROTH, A. N. (1979). *Men who rape.* New York: Plenum Press.

GROTH, A. N., & BIRNBAUM, H. J. (1978). Adult sexual orientation and attraction to underage persons. *Archives of Sexual Behavior, 7,* 175–181.

GROTH, A. N., & BURGESS, A. W. (1977). Sexual dysfunction during rape. *New England Journal of Medicine, 297,* 764–766.

GROTH, A. N., BURGESS, A. W., & HOLMSTROM, L. (1977). Rape: Power, anger, and sexuality. *American Journal of Psychiatry, 134,* 1239–1243.

GROTH, A. N., HOBSON, W. F., & GARY, T. S. (1982). The child molester: Clinical observations. In J. Conte & D. A. Shore (Eds.), *Social work and child sexual abuse* (pp. 129–144). New York: Haworth Press.

GRUBER, J. E. (1990). Methodological problems and policy implications in sexual harassment research. *Population Research and Policy Review, 9,* 235–254.

GRUENBAUM, E. (1996). The cultural debate over female circumcision: The Sudanese are arguing this one out for themselves. *Medical Anthropology Quarterly, 10,* 455–475.

GRUNDLACH, R. (1977). Sexual molestation and rape reported by homosexual and heterosexual women. *Journal of Homosexuality, 2,* 367–384.

GRUNSEIT, A., et al. (1997). Sexuality education and young people's sexual behavior: A review of studies. *Journal of Adolescent Research, 12,* 421–453.

GUAY, L. A., et al. (1999). Intrapartum and neonatal single-dose nevirapine compared with zidovudine for prevention of mother-to-child transmission of HIV-1 in Kampala, Uganda: HIVNET 012 randomised trial. *Lancet, 354,* 795–802.

GUDYKUNST, W., et al. (1996). The influence of cultural individualism-collectivism, self construals, and individual values on communication styles across cultures. *Human Communication Research, 22,* 510–543.

GUERRERO, L. K. (1996). Attachment-style differences in intimacy and involvement: A test of the four-category model. *Communication Monographs, 63,* 269–292.

GUERRERO, L. K. (1998). Attachment-style differences in the experience and expression of romantic jealousy. *Personal Relationships, 5,* 273–291.

GUERRERO, L. K., & ANDERSON, P. A. (1998). The dark side of jealousy and envy: Desire, delusion, desperation, and destructive communication. In B. H. Spitzberg & W. R. Cupach (Eds.), *The dark side of close relationships* (pp. 33–70). Mahwah, NJ: Erlbaum.

GUERRERO PAVICH, E. (1986). A Chicano perspective on Mexican culture and sexuality. In L. Lister (Ed.), *Human sexuality, ethnoculture, and social work.* New York: Haworth Press.

GUITERMAN, A. (1992). Poem. In *Bartlett's familiar quotations* (15th ed.).

GURA, T. (1994). Mating study: Men seek variety, women security. *Times-Picayune* (New Orleans), July 31, A-7.

GURALNIK, J. M., BALFOUR, J. L., & VOLPATO, S. (2000). The ratio of older women to men: Historical perspectives and cross-national comparisons. *Aging Clinical and Experimental Research, 12,* 65–76.

GUTEK, B. A., & DONE, R. S. (2000). Sexual harassment. In R. K. Unger (Ed.), *Handbook of the psychology of women and gender.* New York: Wiley.

GUTEK, B. A., et al. (1999). The utility of the reasonable woman legal standard in hostile environment sexual harassment cases. *Psychology, Public Policy, and Law, 5,* 596–629.

GUZICK, D. S., et al. (1999). Efficacy of superovulation and intrauterine insemination in the treatment of infertility. *New England Journal of Medicine, 340,* 177–183.

GWARTNEY-GIBBS, P., STOCKARD, J., & BOHMER, S. (1987). Learning courtship aggression: The influence of parents, peers, and personal experience. *Family Relations, 36,* 276–282.

HAAVIO-MANNILA, E., & KONTULA, O. (1997). Correlates of increased sexual satisfaction. *Archives of Sexual Behavior, 26,* 399–419.

HACK, M., et al. (1994). School-age outcomes in children with birth weights under 750g. *New England Journal of Medicine, 331,* 753–759.

HACKEL, L. S., & RUBLE, D. N. (1992). Changes in marital relationship after the first baby is born: Predicting the impact of expectancy disconfirmation. *Journal of Personality and Social Psychology, 62,* 944–957.

HAESEVOETS, Y.-H. (1997). L'enfant victime d'inceste: Symptomatologie spécifique ou aspécifique? (Essai de conceptualisation clinique). *Psychiatrie de l'enfant, XL*(1), 87–119.

HAFFNER, D. W., & CASSELMAN, M. (1996). Toy story: A look into the gender-stereotyped world of children's catalogs. *SIECUS Report, 24*(4), 20–21.

HAGAN, E. H. (1999). The functions of postpartum depression. *Evolution and Human Behavior, 20,* 325–359.

HAGE, J. J., BLOEM, J. J. A. M., & SULIMAN, H. M. (1993). Review of the literature on techniques for phalloplasty with emphasis on the applicability in female-to-male transsexuals. *Journal of Urology, 150,* 1093–1098.

HAGLUND, B., et al. (1990). Cigarette smoking as a risk factor for sudden infant death syndrome: A population-based study. *American Journal of Public Health, 80,* 29–32.

HAHN, B. H., SHAW, G. M., DE COCK, K. M., & SHARP, P. M. (2000). AIDS as a zoonosis: Scientific and public health implications. *Science, 287,* 607–614.

HAHN, J., & BLASS, T. (1997). Dating partner preferences: A function of similarity of love styles. *Journal of Social Behavior and Personality, 12,* 595–610.

HAIGNERE, C. S., et al. (2000). High-risk adolescents and female condoms: Knowledge, attitudes, and use patterns. *Journal of Adolescent Health, 26,* 392–398.

HAJCAK, F., & GARWOOD, P. (1988). Quick-fix sex: Pseudosexuality in adolescents. *Adolescence, 23,* 755–760.

HALDEMAN, D. (1994). The practice and ethics of sexual orientation conversion therapy. *Journal of Consulting and Clinical Psychology, 62,* 221–227.

HALL, G. C. N., & BARONGAN, C. (1997). Prevention of sexual aggression: Socioculture risk and protective factors. *American Psychologist, 52,* 5–14.

HALL, G. S. (1904). *Adolescence: Its psychology and the relation to physiology, anthropology, sociology, sex, crime, religion and education* (Vols. 1–2). New York: Appleton.

HALL, L. A. (1992). Forbidden by God, despised by men: Masturbation, medical warnings, moral panic, and manhood in Great Britain, 1850–1950. *Journal of the History of Sexuality, 2,* 365–387.

HALL, R. C., et al. (1989). Sexual abuse in patients with anorexia nervosa and bulimia. *Psychosomatics, 30,* 73–79.

HALL, S. (1986). The problem of ideology: Marxism without guarantees. *Journal of Communication Inquiry, 10,* 28–44.

HALLER, J. S., & HALLER, R. M. (1977). *The physician and sexuality in Victorian America.* New York: Norton.

HALLSTROM, T., & SAMUELSSON, S. (1990). Changes in women's sexual desire in middle life: The longitudinal study of women in Gothenburg (Sweden). *Archives of Sexual Behavior, 19,* 259–267.

HALMAN, L. J., ABBEY, A., & ANDREWS, F. M. (1992). Attitudes about infertility interventions among fertile and infertile couples. *American Journal of Public Health, 82,* 191–194.

HALPERIN, D. (1998). HIV, STDs, anal sex and HIV prevention policy in a northeastern Brazilian city. *International Journal of STD and AIDS, 9,* 294–298.

HALPERIN, D. T. (1999). Heterosexual anal intercourse: Prevalence, cultural factors, and HIV infection and other health risks. Pt. I. *AIDS Patient Care and STDs, 13,* 717–730.

HALPERN, C. T., UDRY, J. R., & SUCHINDRAN, C. (1998). Monthly measures of salivary testosterone predict sexual activity in adolescent males. *Archives of Sexual Behavior, 27,* 445–465.

HALPERN, C. T., et al. (1994). Testosterone and religiosity as predictors of sexual attitudes and activity among adolescent males: A biosocial model. *Journal of Biosocial Science, 26,* 217–234.

HALPERN, S. H., et al. (1998). Effect of epidural vs. parenteral opioid analgesia on the progress of labor. A meta-analysis. *Journal of the American Medical Association, 280,* 2105–2110.

HALSTEAD, J. M. (1997). Muslims and sex education. *Journal of Sex Education, 26,* 317–330.

HAMER, D. H., et al. (1993). A linkage between DNA markers on the X chromosome and male sexual orientation. *Science, 261,* 321–327.

HAMILTON, J. D., et al. (1992). A controlled trial of early versus late treatment with zidovudine in symptomatic human immunodeficiency virus infection. *New England Journal of Medicine, 326,* 437–443.

HAN, J. H., PARK, S. H., LEE, B. S., & CHOI, S. V. (1999). Erect penile size of Korean men. *Venereology, 12,* 135–139.

HANRAHAN, S. N. (1994). Historical review of menstrual toxic shock syndrome. *Women & Health, 21,* 141–165.

HANSON, R. K. (2000). Will they do it again? Predicting sex-offense recidivism. *Current Directions in Psychological Science, 9,* 106–109.

HARDIE, E. A. (1997). PMS in the workplace: Dispelling the myth of cyclic dysfunction. *Journal of Occupational and Organizational Psychology, 70,* 97–102.

HARDING, S. (1986). *The science question in feminism.* Ithaca, NY: Cornell University Press.

HARLOW, B. L., & SIGNORELLO, L. B. (2000). Factors associated with early menopause. *Maturitas, 35,* 3–9.

HARLOW, S. D., & EPHROSS, S. A. (1995). Epidemiology of menstruation and its relevance to women's health. *Epidemiologic Reviews, 17,* 265–286.

HARNEY, P., & MUEHLENHARD, C. (1991). Rape. In E. Graverholz & M. Korlewski (Eds.), *Sexual coercion: A sourcebook on its nature, causes, and prevention.* Lexington, MA: Lexington Books.

HARNISH, S. (1988). Congenital absence of the vagina: Clinical issues. *Medical Aspects of Human Sexuality,* July, 54–60.

HARRIS, C. R., & CHRISTENFELD, N. (1996). Gender, jealousy, and reason. *Psychological Science, 7,* 364–366.

HARRISON, M. R., et al. (1990). Successful repair in utero of a fetal diaphragmatic hernia after removal of herniated viscera from the left thorax. *New England Journal of Medicine, 322,* 1582–1584.

HARRISON, P. F. (2000). Microbicides: Forging scientific and political alliances. *AIDS Patient Care and STDs, 14,* 199–205.

HARRISON, P. F., & ROSENFIELD, A. (Eds.). (1996). *Contraceptive research and development: Looking to the future.* Washington, DC: National Academy Press.

HASSETT, J. (1978). Sex and smell. *Psychology Today, 11,* 40–42, 45.

HATCH, M., LEVIN, B., SHU, X-O., & SUSSER, M. (1998). Maternal leisure-time exercise and timely delivery. *American Journal of Public Health, 88,* 1528–1533.

HATCHER, R. A., et al. (1998). *Contraceptive technology* (17th ed.). New York: Ardent Media.

HATFIELD, E. (1984). The dangers of intimacy. In V. Derlaga (Ed.), *Communication, intimacy, and close relationships* (pp. 207–220). New York: Academic Press.

HATFIELD, E. (1988). Passionate and companionate love. In R. J. Sternberg & M. L. Barnes (Eds.), *The psychology of love* (pp. 191–217). New Haven, CT: Yale University Press.

HATFIELD, E., & RAPSON, R. L. (1993). *Love, sex, and intimacy: Their psychology, biology, and history.* New York: HarperCollins.

HATHAWAY, S. R., & McKINLEY, J. C. (1943). *The Minnesota Multiphasic Personality Inventory.* New York: Psychological Corporation.

HAUGAARD, J. J. (2000). The challenge of defining child sexual abuse. *American Psychologist, 55,* 1036–1039.

HAUGAARD, J. J., & EMERY, R. E. (1989). Methodological issues in child sexual abuse research. *Child Abuse & Neglect, 13,* 89–100.

HAWKESWORTH, M. (1997). Confounding gender. *Signs: Journal of Women in Culture and Society, 22,* 649–684.

HAWKINS, J. L., et al. (1997). Obstetric anesthesia work force survey, 1981 versus 1992. *Anesthesiology, 87,* 135–143.

HAWTON, K., CATALAN, J., & FAGG, J. (1991). Low sexual desire: Sex therapy results and prognostic factors. *Behavior Research and Therapy, 29,* 217–224.

HAYS, D., & SAMUELS, A. (1989). Heterosexual women's perceptions of their marriages to bisexual or homosexual men. *Journal of Homosexuality, 18,* 81–100.

HAZAN, C., & SHAVER, P. (1987). Love conceptualized as an attachment process. *Journal of Personality and Social Psychology, 52,* 511–524.

HAZELWOOD, R .R., & WARREN, J. J. (2000). The sexually violent offender: Impulsive or ritualistic? *Aggression and Violent Behavior, 5,* 267–279.

HAZZARD, A., et al. (1995). Predicting symptomatology and self-blame among child sex abuse victims. *Child Abuse & Neglect, 19,* 707–714.

HEARST, N., & HULLEY, S. B. (1988). Preventing the heterosexual spread of AIDS: Are we giving our patients the best advice? *Journal of the American Medical Association, 259,* 2428–2432.

HEATH, D. (1984). An investigation into the origins of a copious vaginal discharge during intercourse—"enough to wet the bed"—that "is not urine." *Journal of Sex Research, 20,* 194–215.

HEAVEY, C. L., CHRISTENSEN, A., & MALAMUTH, N. M. (1995). The longitudinal impact of demand and withdrawal during marital conflict. *Journal of Consulting and Clinical Psychology, 63,* 797–801.

HECHT, M. RIBEAU, S., & SEDANO, M. (1990). A Mexican American perspective on interethnic communication. *International Journal of Intercultural Relations, 14,* 31–55.

HEDRICKS, C. A. (1995). Female sexual activity across the human menstrual cycle. *Annual Review of Sex Research, 5,* 122–172.

HEIDER, K. G. (1979). *Grand Valley Dani: Peaceful warriors.* New York: Holt, Rinehart & Winston.

HEILBRUN, A., & SEIF, D. (1988). Erotic value of female distress in sexually explicit photographs. *Journal of Sex Research, 24,* 47–57.

HEIMAN, J. (1977). A psychophysiological exploration of sexual arousal patterns in females and males. *Psychophysiology, 14,* 266–274.

HEIMAN, J., & LOPICCOLO, J. (1992). *Becoming orgasmic: A sexual growth program for women.* Englewood Cliffs, N.J.: Prentice Hall

HEIMAN, M. L., LEIBLUM, S., ESQUILIN, S. C., & PALLITTO, L. M. (1998). A comparative survey of beliefs about "normal" childhood sexual behaviors. *Child Abuse & Neglect, 22,* 289–304.

HEIN, H. A., BURMEISTER, L. F., & PAPKE, K. R. (1990). The relationship of unwed status to infant mortality. *Obstetrics and Gynecology, 76,* 763–768.

HELMREICH, R., SPENCE, J., & HOLAHAN, C. (1979). Psychological androgyny and sex role flexibility: A test of two hypotheses. *Journal of Personality and Social Psychology, 37,* 1631–1644.

HELWIG-LARSEN, M., & COLLINS, B. E. (1997). A social psychological perspective on the role of knowledge about AIDS in AIDS prevention. *Current Directions in Psychological Science, 6,* 23–26.

HENDERSON, D. J., BOYD, C. J., & WHITMARSH, J. (1995). Women and illicit drugs: Sexuality and crack cocaine. *Health Care for Women International, 16,* 113–124.

HENDERSON, M. G. (1998). Disclosure of sexual orientation: Comments from a parental perspective. *American Journal of Orthopsychiatry, 68,* 372–375.

HENDERSON, R. (1990). Parents need right words, right time to talk kids about sex. *Los Angeles Times,* November 22, X1.

HENDRICK, C., & HENDRICK, S. (1983). *Liking, loving and relating.* Monterey, CA: Brooks/Cole.

HENDRICK, C., & HENDRICK, S. (1986). A theory and method of love. *Journal of Personality and Social Psychology, 50,* 392–402.

HENDRICK, C., & HENDRICK, S. S. (1989). Research or love: Does it measure up? *Journal of Personality and Social Psychology, 56,* 784–794.

HENDRICK, C., HENDRICK, S., & ADLER, N. (1988). Romantic relationships: Love, satisfaction, and staying together. *Journal of Personality and Social Psychology, 54,* 980–988.

HENDRICK, S. S., & HENDRICK, C. (1993). Lovers as friends. *Journal of Social and Personal Relationships, 10,* 459–466.

HENNEBERGER, M., & MARRIOTT, M. (1993). What teens call flirting, adults call sex harassment. *New York Times.*

HENNESSEY, K. A., et al. (2000). AIDS onset at high CD4+ cell levels is associated with high HIV load. *AIDS Research and Human Retroviruses, 16,* 103–107.

HENRIKSEN, T. B., BEK, K. M., HEDEGAARD, M., & SECHER, N. J. (1994). Methods and consequences of changes in use of episiotomy. *British Medical Journal, 309,* 1255–1258.

HENSHAW, S. K. (1998a). Unintended pregnancy in the United States. *Family Planning Perspectives, 30,* 24–29, 46.

HENSHAW, S. K. (1998b). Abortion incidence and services in the United States, 1995–1996. *Family Planning Perspectives, 30,* 263–270, 287.

HENSHAW, S. K., & KOST, K. (1996). Abortion patients in 1994–1995: Characteristics and contraceptive use. *Family Planning Perspectives, 28,* 140.

HENSON, C., RUBIN, H. B., & HENSON, D. E. (1979). Women's sexual arousal concurrently assessed by three genital measures. *Archives of Sexual Behavior, 8,* 459–479.

HERDT, G. (1990). Mistaken gender: 5-Alpha reductase hermaphroditism and biological reductionism in sexual identity reconsidered. *American Anthropologist, 92,* 433–446.

HERDT, G., & McCLINTOCK, M. (2000). The magical age of 10. *Archives of Sexual Behavior, 29,* 587–606.

HERDT, G. H. (1993). Semen transactions in Sambia culture. In D. N. Suggs & A. W. Miracle (Eds.), *Culture and human sexuality* (pp. 298–327). Pacific Grove, CA: Brooks/Cole.

HEREK, G. M. (1988). Heterosexuals' attitudes toward lesbian and gay men: Correlates and gender differences. *Journal of Sex Research, 25,* 451–477.

HEREK, G. M. (1989). Hate crimes against lesbian and gay men: Issues for research and policy. *American Psychologist, 44,* 948–955.

HEREK, G. M. (1998). Bad science in the service of stigma: A critique of the Cameron Group's survey studies. In G. M. Herek (Ed.), *Stigma and sexual orientation: Understanding prejudice against lesbians, gay men, and bisexuals* (pp. 223–255). Thousand Oaks, CA: Sage.

HEREK, G. M. (2000). The psychology of sexual prejudice. *Current Directions in Psychological Science, 9,* 19–22.

HEREK, G. M. (2000). Sexual prejudice and gender: Do heterosexuals' attitudes toward lesbians and gay men differ? *Journal of Social Issues, 56,* 251–266.

HERMAN, J., & HIRSCHMAN, L. (1977). Father-daughter incest. *Journal of Women in Culture and Society, 2,* 735–756.

HERMAN, J. L. (1992). *Trauma and recovery.* New York: Basic Books.

HERMAN-GIDDENS, M. E., et al. (1997). Secondary sexual characteristics and menses in young girls seen in office practice: A study from the pediatric research in office settings network. *Pediatrics, 99,* 505–512.

HERRINGTON, D. M., et al. (2000). Effects of estrogen replacement on the progression of coronary-artery atherosclerosis. *New England Journal of Medicine, 343,* 522–529.

HERSHBERGER, S. L. (1997). A twin registry study of male and female sexual orientation. *Journal of Sex Research, 34,* 212–222.

HETEROSEXUAL AIDS: Setting the odds. (1988). *Science, 240,* 597.

HEWITT, C. (1998). Homosexual demography: Implications for the spread of AIDS. *Journal of Sex Research, 35,* 390–396.

HICKMAN, S. E., & MUEHLENHARD, C. L. (1999). "By the semi-mystical appearance of a condom": How young women and men communicate sexual consent in heterosexual situations. *Journal of Sex Research, 36,* 258–272.

HICKSON, F. C. I., et al. (1994). Gay men as victims of nonconsensual sex. *Archives of Sexual Behavior, 23,* 281–294.

HILL, C. A. (1997). The distinctiveness of sexual motives in relation to sexual desire and desirable partner attributes. *Journal of Sex Research, 34,* 139–153.

HILL, C. A., & PRESTON, L. K. (1996). Individual differences in the experience of sexual motivation: Theory and measurement of dispositional sexual motives. *Journal of Sex Research, 33,* 27–45.

HILL, C. T., & PEPLAU, L. A. (1998). Premarital predictors of relationship outcomes: A 15-year follow-up of the Boston Couples Study. In T. N. Bradbury (Ed.), *The developmental course of marital dysfunction* (pp. 237–278). New York: Cambridge University Press.

HILLIER, L., HARRISON, L., & WARR, D. (1998). "When you carry condoms all the boys think you want it": Negotiating competing discourses about safe sex. *Journal of Adolescence, 21,* 15–29.

HILLIS, S. D., et al. (1998). Higher hysterectomy risk for sterilized than nonsterilized women: Findings from the U.S. collaborative review of sterilization. *Obstetrics & Gynecology, 91,* 241–246.

HINDS, M. C. (1981). The child victim of incest. *New York Times,* June 15.

HINES, M., & COLLAER, M. L. (1993). Gonadal hormones and sexual differentiation of human behavior: Developments from research on endocrine syndromes and studies of brain structure. *Annual Review of Sex Research, 4,* 1–48.

HINES, M., & GREEN, R. (1991). Human hormonal and neural correlates of sex-typed behaviors. *Review of Psychiatry, 10,* 536–555.

HINGSON, R., et al. (1982). Effects of maternal drinking and marijuana use on fetal growth and development. *Pediatrics, 70,* 539–546.

HIORT, O., & HOLTERHUS, P.-M. (2000). The molecular basis of male sexual differentiation. *European Journal of Endocrinology, 142,* 101–110.

HIRSCHEL, B., & OPRAVIL, M. (1999). The year in review: Antiretroviral treatment. *AIDS, 13* (Suppl. A), S177–S187.

HIRSCHFELD, M. (1948). *Sexual anomalies.* New York: Emerson.

HITE, S. (1976). *The Hite report.* New York: Macmillan.

HITE, S. (1981). *The Hite report on male sexuality.* New York: Knopf.

HITE, S. (1987). *Women and love: A cultural revolution in progress.* New York: Knopf.

HOCKENBERRY, S. L., & BILLINGHAM, R. (1987). Sexual orientation and boyhood gender conformity. *Archives of Sexual Behavior, 16,* 475–493.

HOCKEY, J., & JAMES, A. (1993). *Growing up and growing old.* London: Sage.

HOCKING, J. E., TURK, D., & ELLINGER, A. (1999). The effects of partner insistence of condom usage on perceptions of the partner, the relationship, and the experience. *Journal of Adolescence, 22,* 355–367.

HODES, M. (Ed.). (1999). *Sex, love, race: Crossing boundaries in North American history.* New York: New York University Press.

HOLCOMB, D. R., et al. (1991). Gender differences among college students. *College Student Journal, 25,* 434–439.

HOLMES, M. M., et al. (1996). Rape-related pregnancy: Estimates and descriptive characteristics from a national sample of women. *American Journal of Obstetrics and Gynecology, 175,* 320–325.

HOLT, C. L., & ELLIS, J. B. (1998). Assessing the current validity of the Bem Sex-Role Inventory. *Sex Roles, 39,* 929–941.

HOLT, V. L., et al. (1989). Induced abortion and the risk of subsequent ectopic pregnancy. *American Journal of Public Health, 79,* 1234–1238.

HONORÉ, G. M., HOLDEN, A. E. C., & SCHENKEN, R. S. (1999). Pathophysiology and management of proximal tubal blockage. *Fertility and Sterility, 71,* 785–795.

HOOKER, E. (1957). The adjustment of the male overt homosexual. *Journal of Projective Techniques, 21,* 18–31.

HOOKER, E. (1965). An empirical study of some relations between sexual patterns and gender identity in male homosexuals. In J. Money (Ed.), *Sex research: New developments.* New York: Henry Holt.

HOOKER, E. (1993). Reflections of a 40-year exploration: A scientific view on homosexuality. *American Psychologist, 48,* 1–4.

HOOTON, T. M., et al. (1996). A prospective study of risk factors for symptomatic urinary tract infection in young women. *New England Journal of Medicine, 335,* 468–474.

HOOVER, D. R., et al. (1995). Long-term survival without clinical AIDS after CD41 cell counts fall below 200 × 106/l. *AIDS, 9,* 145–152.

HORT, B. E., LEINBACH, M. D., & FAGOT, B. I. (1991). Is there coherence among the cognitive components of gender acquisition? *Sex Roles, 24,* 195–207.

HORWITZ, A. V., WHITE, H. R., & HOWELL-WHITE, S. (1996). Becoming married and mental health: A longitudinal study of a cohort of young adults. *Journal of Marriage and the Family, 58,* 895–907.

HORWITZ, S. M., KLERMAN, L. V., KUO, H. S., & JEKEL, J. F. (1991). Intergenerational transmission of school-age parenthood. *Family Planning Perspectives, 23,* 168–177.

HOVDESTAD, W. E., & KRISTIANSEN, C. M. (1996, Summer). A field study of "false memory syndrome": Construct validity and incidence. *Journal of Psychiatry & Law,* 299–338.

HOWARD, C. R., HOWARD, F. M., & WEITZMAN, M. L. (1994). Acetaminophen analgesia in neonatal circumcision: The effect on pain. *Pediatrics, 93,* 641–646.

HOWARDS, S. S. (1995). Treatment of male infertility. *New England Journal of Medicine, 332,* 312–317.

HOWE, J. E., MINKOFF, H. L., & DUERR, A. C. (1994). Contraceptives and HIV. *AIDS, 8,* 861–871.

HOWE, P. J. (1999). Sexual problems plague many. *Times-Picayune* (New Orleans), February 10, A-10.

HOWELLS, K. (1981). Adult sexual interest in children: Considerations relevant to theories of etiology. In M. Cook & K. Howells (Eds.), *Adult sexual interest in children* (pp. 55–94). New York: Academic Press.

HOYERT, D. L, DANEL, I., & TULLY, P. (2000). Maternal mortality, United States and Canada, 1982–1987. *Birth, 27,* 4–11.

HSU, F. (1983). Eros, affect and pao. In F. Hsu (Ed.), *Rugged individualism reconsidered.* Knoxville: University of Tennessee Press.

HSU, F. L. K. (1981). *Americans and Chinese: Passage to difference* (3rd ed.). Honolulu: University Press of Hawaii.

HU, S., et al. (1995). Linkage between sexual orientation and chromosome Xq 28 in males but not in females. *Nature Genetics, 11,* 248–256.

HUANG, Z., et al. (1997). Dual effects of weight and weight gain on breast cancer risk. *Journal of the American Medical Association, 278,* 1407–1411.

HUBIN, D. C, & HAELY, K. (1999). Rape and the reasonable man. *Law and Philosophy, 18,* 113–139.

HUCKER, S. J. (1997). Sexual sadism: Psychopathology and theory, In D. R. Laws & W. O'Donohue (Eds.), *Sexual deviance: Theory, assessment, and treatment* (pp. 194–209). New York: Guilford Press.

HUDSON, B., PEPPERELL, R., & WOOD, C. (1987). The problem of infertility. In R. Pepperell, B. Hudson, & C. Wood (Eds.), *The infertile couple.* Edinburgh: Churchill-Livingstone.

HUHNER, M. (1916). *Disorders of the sexual function.* Philadelphia: Davis.

HULKA, B., et al. (1982). Protection against endometrial carcinoma by combination-product oral contraceptives. *Journal of the American Medical Association, 247,* 475–477.

HUMPHREYS, L. (1970). *Tearoom trade: Impersonal sex in public places.* Chicago: Aldine.

HUNT, M. (1959). *The natural history of love.* New York: Knopf.

HUNT, M. (1974). *Sexual behavior in the 1970s.* Chicago: Playboy Press.

HUNTER, J. A., & MATHEWS, R. (1997). Sexual deviance in females. In D. R. Laws & W. O'Donohue (Eds.), *Sexual deviance: Theory, assessment, and treatment* (pp. 465–480). New York: Guilford Press.

HUPKA, R. B. (1981, August). Cultural determinants of jealousy. *Alternative Life Styles,* p. 4.

HURLBERT, D. F. (1991). The role of assertiveness in female sexuality: A comparative study between sexually assertive and sexually non-assertive women. *Journal of Sex & Marital Therapy, 17,* 183–190.

HURLBERT, D. F., APT, C., & RABEHL, S. M. (1993). Key variables to understanding female sexual satisfaction: An examination of women in nondistressed marriages. *Journal of Sex & Marital Therapy , 19,* 154–165.

HURLBERT, D. F., & WHITTAKER, K. E. (1991). The role of masturbation in marital and sexual satisfaction: A comparative study of female masturbators and nonmasturbators. *Journal of Sex Education and Therapy, 17,* 272–282.

HUSTON, A. C. (1983). Sex-typing. In E. M. Hetherington (Ed.), *Handbook of child psychology: Vol. 4. Socialization, personality, and social development* (pp. 387–468). New York: Wiley.

HUSTON, A. C., WARTELLA, E., & DONNERSTEIN, E. (1998). *Measuring the effects of sexual content in the media: A report to the Kaiser Family Foundation.* Menlo Park, CA: Kaiser Family Foundation.

HYDE, J. S., DELAMATER, J. D., PLANT, E. A., & BYRD, J. M. (1996). Sexuality during pregnancy and the year postpartum. *Journal of Sex Research, 33,* 143–151.

HYLAN, T. R., SUNDELL, K., & JUDGE, R. (1999). The impact of premenstrual symptomatology on functioning and treatment-seeking behavior: Experience from the United States, United Kingdom, and France. *Journal of Women's Health & Gender-Based Medicine, 8,* 1043–1052.

HYNIE, M., LYDON, J. E., CÔTÉ, S., & WIENER, S. (1998). Relational sexual scripts and women's condom use: The importance of internalized norms. *Journal of Sex Research, 35,* 370–380.

IMBER, M. (1994). Toward a theory of educational origins: The genesis of sex education. *Educational Theory, 34,* 275–286.

IMPERATO-MCGINLEY, J., PETERSON, R. E., GAUTIER, T., & STURLA, E. (1979). Androgens and the evolution of male-gender identity among male pseudohermaphrodites with 5-reductase deficiency. *New England Journal of Medicine, 300,* 1233–1237.

INAZU, J. K., & FOX, G. L. (1980). Maternal influence on the sexual behaviors of teenage daughters. *Journal of Family Issues, 1,* 81–99.

INSTITUTE OF MEDICINE. (1990). *Nutrition during pregnancy.* Washington, DC: National Academy of Sciences, Subcommittee on Nutritional Status and Weight Gain during Pregnancy.

INSTITUTE OF MEDICINE. (1991). *Nutrition during lactation.* Washington, DC: National Academy Press.

INSTITUTE OF MEDICINE. (1997). Committee on Prevention and Control of Sexually Transmitted Diseases. *The hidden epidemic: Confronting sexually transmitted diseases.* Washington, DC: National Academy Press.

INTERNATIONAL PERINATAL HIV GROUP. (1999). The mode of delivery and the risk of vertical transmission of human immunodeficiency virus, type 1. *New England Journal of Medicine, 340,* 977–987.

IPPOLITO, G., et al. (1999). Occupational human immunodeficiency virus infection in health care workers: Worldwide cases through September 1997. *Clinical Infectious Diseases, 28,* 365–383.

IRVINE, S., et al. (1996). Evidence of deteriorating semen quality in the United Kingdom: Birth cohort study in 577 men in Scotland over 11 years. *British Medical Journal, 312,* 467–471.

ISAY, R. A. (1998). Heterosexually married homosexual men: Clinical and developmental issues. *American Journal of Orthopsychiatry, 68,* 424–432.

IYASU, S., et al. (1993). The epidemiology of placenta previa in the United States, 1979 through 1987. *American Journal of Obstetrics and Gynecology, 168,* 1424–1429.

JACKLIN, C. N., & MACCOBY, E. E. (1983). Issues of gender differentiation in normal development. In M. D. Levine, W. B. Carey, A. C. Crocker, & R. T. Gross (Eds.), *Developmental-behavioral pediatrics.* Philadelphia: Saunders.

JACOB, K. A. (1981). The Mosher report. *American Heritage, 32*(4), 56–64.

JACOBS, S.-H., & THOMAS, W. (1994). Native American two-spirits. *Anthropology Newsletter, 35*(8), 7.

JACOBY, S. (1999). Great sex: What's age got to do with it? *Modern Maturity,* September–October, 40–45, 91.

JAIN, A. K. (1969). Pregnancy outcome and the time required for next conception. *Population Studies, 23,* 421–433.

JAMES, A., et al. (1998). *Theorizing childhood.* Cambridge: Potity.

JAMISON, P. L., & GEBHARD, P. H. (1988). Penis size increase between flaccid and erect states: An analysis of the Kinsey data. *Journal of Sex Research, 24,* 177–183.

JANKOWIAK, W. R., & FISCHER, E. F. (1992). A cross-cultural perspective on romantic love. *Ethnology, 31,* 149–155.

JANOWSKY, E. C., KUPPER, L. L., & HULKA, B. S. (2000). Meta-analyses of the relation between silicone breast implants and the risk of connective-tissue diseases. *New England Journal of Medicine, 342,* 781–790.

JANUS, S. S., & JANUS, C. L. (1993). *The Janus report on sexual behavior.* New York: Wiley.

JARVIE, I. C. (1992). Child pornography and prostitution. In W. O'Donohue & J. H. Geer (Eds.), *The sexual abuse of children: Theory and research* (Vol. 1, pp. 307–328). Hillsdale, NJ: Erlbaum.

JEHL, D. (1999). The price of Arab honor is the blood of women. *Times-Picayune* (New Orleans), June 20, A24–A25. Syndicated from the *New York Times.*

JENKS, R. J. (1998). Swinging: A review of the literature. *Archives of Sexual Behavior, 27,* 507–521.

JENNY, C., et al. (1990). Sexually transmitted diseases in victims of rape. *New England Journal of Medicine, 322,* 713–716.

JENSEN, J. T., ASTLEY, S. J., MORGAN, E., & NICHOLS, M. D. (1999). Outcomes of suction curettage and mifepristone abortion in the United States: A prospective comparison study. *Contraception, 59,* 153–159.

JENSEN, J. W., & GUTEK, B. A. (1982). Attributions and assignment of responsibility in sexual harassment. *Journal of Social Issues, 38,* 121–136.

JOESOEF, M. R., SCHMID, G. P., & HILLIER, S. L. (1999). Bacterial vaginosis: Review of treatment options and potential clinical indications for therapy. *Clinical Infectious Diseases, 28* (Suppl. 1), S57–S65.

JOFFE, G. P., et al. (1992). Multiple partners and partner choice as risk factors for sexually transmitted disease among female college students. *Sexually Transmitted Diseases, 19,* 272–278.

JOHANSSON, J. E., et al. (1997). Fifteen-year survival in prostate cancer: A prospective, population-based study in Sweden. *Journal of the American Medical Association, 277,* 467–471.

JOHN, D., & SHELTON, B. A. (1997). The production of gender among black and white women and men: The case of household labor. *Sex Roles, 36,* 171–193.

JOHN, G. C., & KREISS, J. (1996). Mother-to-child transmission of human immunodeficiency virus type 1. *Epidemiologic Reviews, 18,* 149–157.

JOHNSON, B. E., KUCK, D. L., & SCHANDER, P. R. (1997). Rape myth acceptance and sociodemographic characteristics: A multidimensional analysis. *Sex Roles, 36,* 693–707.

JOHNSON, J. W. C., LONGMATE, J. A., & FRENTZEN, B. (1992). Excessive maternal weight and pregnancy outcome. *American Journal of Obstetrics and Gynecology, 167,* 353–372.

JOHNSON, T. C. (1989). Female child perpetrators: Children who molest other children. *Child Abuse & Neglect, 13,* 571–585.

JONES, C. A., KNAUP, R. C., HAYES, M., & STONER, B. P. (2000). Urine screening for gonococcal and chlamydial infections at community-based organizations in a high-morbidity area. *Sexually Transmitted Diseases, 27,* 146–151.

JONES, JR., M. (1998). Can art photography be kiddie porn? *Newsweek,* March 9, 58.

JONES, M. E., RUSSELL, R. L., & BRYANT, F. B. (1998). The structure of rape attitudes for men and women: A three-factor model. *Journal of Research in Personality, 32,* 331–350.

JONES, O. D. (1999). Sex, culture, and the biology of rape: Toward explanation and prevention. *California Law Review, 87,* 827–941.

JONES, W. K., SMITH, J., & KIEKE, JR., B., & WILCOX, L. (1997). Female genital mutilation/female circumcision: Who is at risk in the United States? *Public Health Reports, 112,* 368–377.

JOSEPH, C. (1995). Scarlet wounding: Issues of child prostitution. *Journal of Psychohistory, 23,* 2–17.

JOSEPH, C. (1996). Compassionate accountability: An embodied consideration of female genital mutilation. *Journal of Psychohistory, 24,* 2–17.

JOURARD, S. M., & LASAKOW, P. (1958). Some factors in self-disclosure. *Journal of Abnormal and Social Psychology, 56,* 91–98.

JOW, W., & GOLDSTEIN, M. (1994, May). No-scalpel vasectomy offers minimal invasiveness. *Contemporary Ob/Gyn,* 83–96.

JUNGINGER, J. (1997). Fetishism: Assessment and treatment. In D. R. Laws & W. O'Donohue (Eds.), *Sexual deviance: Theory, assessment, and treatment* (pp. 92–110). New York: Guilford Press.

JURKOVIC, D., et al. (1993). Coelocentesis: A new technique for early prenatal diagnosis. *Lancet, 341,* 1623–1624.

KAESER, L. (1989). Reconsidering the age limits on pill use. *Family Planning Perspectives, 21,* 273–274.

KAFKA, M. P. (1997). A monoamine hypothesis for the pathophysiology of paraphilic disorders. *Archives of Sexual Behavior, 26,* 343–358.

KAFKA, M. P., & HENNEN, J. (1999). The paraphilia-related disorders: An empirical investigation of nonparaphilic hypersexuality disorders in outpatient males. *Journal of Sex & Marital Therapy, 25,* 305–319.

KAGAN-KRIEGER, S. (1998). Women with Turner syndrome: A maturational and developmental perspective. *Journal of Adult Development, 5,* 125–135.

KAHN, J. G., et al. (2000). The efficacy of medical abortion: A meta-analysis. *Contraception, 61,* 29–40.

KAISER FAMILY FOUNDATION. (1996, June 24). Survey on teens and sex: What they say teens today need to know, and who they listen to. [News release].

KAISER FAMILY FOUNDATION. (1998). *Kaiser Family Foundation and YM Magazine national survey of teens: Teens talk about dating, intimacy, and their sexual experiences.* Menlo Park, CA: Author.

KAISER FAMILY FOUNDATION. (2000). *Sex education in America: A view from inside the nation's classrooms.* Menlo Park, CA: Author.

KAISER FAMILY FOUNDATION. (2001). *Sex on TV: Content and context.* Menlo Park, CA: Author.

KALB, C. (1997). How old is too old? *Newsweek,* May 5, 64.

KALICHMAN, S. C. (1995). Magic Johnson and public attitudes toward AIDS: A review of empirical studies. *AIDS Education and Prevention, 6,* 542–557.

KALICHMAN, S. C., CAREY, M. P., & JOHNSON, B. T. (1996). Prevention of sexually transmitted HIV infection: A meta-analytic review of the behavioral outcome literature. *Annals of Behavioral Medicine, 18,* 6–15.

KALICHMAN, S. C., & SIKKEMA, K. J. (1994). Psychological sequelae of HIV infection and AIDS: Review of empirical findings. *Clinical Psychology Reviews, 7,* 611–632.

KALLMAN, F. J. (1952). Comparative twin study on the genetic aspects of male homosexuality. *Journal of Nervous and Mental Disease, 115,* 283–298.

KAMISCHKE, A., & NIESCHLAG, E. (1999). Analysis of medical treatment of male infertility. *Human Reproduction, 14,* 1–23.

KAMWENDO, F., FORSLIN, L., BODIN, L., & DANIELSSON, D. (2000). Epidemiology of ectopic pregnancy during a 28 year period and the role of pelvic inflammatory disease. *Sexually Transmitted Infections, 76,* 28–32.

KANDEL, D. B. (1990). Early onset of adolescent sexual behavior and drug involvement. *Journal of Marriage and the Family, 52,* 783–798.

KANE, M. A. (1995). Global programme for control of hepatitis B infection. *Vaccine, 13* (Suppl. 1), S47–S49.

KANIN, E. J. (1994). False rape allegations. *Archives of Sexual Behavior, 23,* 81–92.

KAPLAN, H. S. (1974). *The new sex therapy.* New York: Brunner/Mazel.

KAPLAN, H. S. (1977). Hypoactive sexual desire. *Journal of Sex & Marital Therapy, 3,* 3–9.

KAPLAN, H. S. (1979). *Disorders of desire.* New York: Brunner/Mazel.

KAPLAN, H. S. (1983). *The evaluation of sexual disorders: Psychological and medical aspects.* New York: Brunner/Mazel.

KAPLAN, H. S. (1987). *Sexual aversion, sexual phobias, and panic disorders.* New York: Brunner/Mazel.

KAPLAN, H. S. (1989). *How to overcome premature ejaculation.* New York: Brunner/Mazel.

KAPLAN, H. S. (1992). Does the CAT technique enhance female orgasm? *Journal of Sex & Marital Therapy, 18,* 285–291.

KAPLAN, H. S. (1993). Post-ejaculatory pain syndrome. *Journal of Sex & Marital Therapy, 19,* 91–103.

KAPLAN, H. S., & OWETT, T. (1993). The female androgen deficiency syndrome. *Journal of Sex & Marital Therapy, 19,* 3–24.

KAPLAN, L. (1996). Sexual and institutional issues when one spouse resides in the community and the other lives in a nursing home. *Sexuality and Disability, 14,* 281–293.

KAPLAN, M. S., & KRUEGER, R. B. (1997). Voyeurism: Psychopathology and theory. In D. R. Laws & W. O'Donohue (Eds.), *Sexual deviance: Theory, assessment, and treatment* (pp. 297–310). New York: Guilford Press.

KARLSON, P., & LUSCHER, M. (1959). Pheromones: A new term for a class of biologically active substances. *Nature, 183,* 55–56.

KARMEL, M. (1959). *Thank you Dr. Lamaze.* Philadelphia: Lippincott.

KATLAMA, C., & DICKINSON, G. M. (1993). Update on opportunistic infections. *AIDS, 7,* S185–S194.

KATZ, J. (1976). *Gay American history: Lesbian and gay men in the U.S.A.* New York: Crowell.

KATZ, M. G., & VOLLENHOVEN, B. (2000). The reproductive endocrine consequences of anorexia nervosa. *British Journal of Obstetrics and Gynaecology, 107,* 707–713.

KATZ, S., SHEMESH, T., & BIZMAN, A. (2000). Attitudes of university students towards the sexuality of persons with mental retardation and persons with paraplegia. *British Journal of Developmental Disabilities, 46,* 109–117.

KAUFERT, P. A., & LOCK, M. (1997). Medicalization of women's third age. *Journal of Psychosomatic Obstetrics and Gynecology, 18,* 81–86.

KAWACHI, I., COLDITZ, G. A., & HANKINSON, S. (1994). Long-term benefits and risks of alternative methods of fertility control in the United States. *Contraception, 50,* 1–16.

KAWAS, C., et al. (1997). A prospective study of estrogen replacement therapy and the risk of developing Alzheimer's disease: The Baltimore Longitudinal Study of Aging. *Neurology, 48,* 1517–1521.

KEGEL, A. (1952). Sexual functions of the pubococcygeus muscle. *Western Journal of Surgery, Obstetrics, and Gynecology, 60,* 521–524.

KELLETT, J. M. (1991). Sexuality and the elderly. *Sexual and Marital Therapy, 6,* 147–155.

KELLETT, J. M. (2000). Older adult sexuality. In L. T. Szuchman and F. Muscarella (Eds.), *Psychological perspectives on human sexuality* (pp. 355–379). New York: Wiley.

KELLEY, M. L., & PARSONS, B. (2000). Sexual harassment in the 1990s. *Journal of Higher Education, 71,* 548–568.

KELLOGG, J. H. (1887). *Plain facts for old and young: Embracing the natural history and hygiene of organic life.* Burlington, IA: I. F. Segner.

KELLOGG, N. D., & HOFFMAN, T. J. (1997). Child sexual revictimization by multiple perpetrators. *Child Abuse & Neglect, 21,* 953–964.

KELLY, J. A., & WORELL, J. (1977). New formulations of sex roles and androgyny: A critical review. *Journal of Consulting and Clinical Psychology, 45,* 1101–1115.

KELLY, M. A., & McGEE, M. (1999). Report from a study tour: Teen sexuality education in the Netherlands, France, and Germany. *SIECUS Report, 27*(2), 11–14.

KELLY, M. P., STRASSBERG, D. S., & KIRCHER, J. R. (1990). Attitudinal and experiential correlates of anorgasmia. *Archives of Sexual Behavior, 19,* 165–177.

KELLY, S. J., OSTROWSKI, N. L., & WILSON, M. A. (1999). Gender differences in brain and behavior: Hormonal and neural bases. *Pharmacology Biochemistry & Behavior, 64,* 655–664.

KEMPNER, M. (1998). 1997–98 sexuality education controversies in the United States. *SIECUS Report, 26*(6), 16–26.

KENDALL-TACKETT, K. A., & SIMON, A. F. (1987). Perpetrators and their acts: Data from 365 adults molested as children. *Child Abuse & Neglect, 11,* 237–245.

KENDALL-TACKETT, K. A., WILLIAMS, L. M., & FINKELHOR, D. (1993). Impact of sexual abuse on children: A review and synthesis of recent empirical studies. *Psychological Bulletin, 113,* 164–180.

KENDLER, K. S., THORNTON, L. M., GILMAN, S. E., & KESSLER, R. C. (2000). Sexual orientation in a U.S. national sample of twin and nontwin sibling pairs. *American Journal of Psychiatry, 157,* 1843–1846.

KENDRICK, D. T., & KEEFE, R. C. (1992). Age preferences in mates reflect sex differences in reproductive strategies. *Behavioral and Brain Sciences, 15,* 75–133.

KENNEDY, G. J., HAQUE, M., & ZARANKOW, B. (1997). Human sexuality in late life. *International Journal of Mental Health, 26,* 35–46.

KEPHART, W. M. (1967). Some correlates of romantic love. *Journal of Marriage and the Family, 29,* 470–474.

KERNBERG, O. F. (1991). Sadomasochism, sexual excitement, and perversion. *Journal of the American Psychoanalytic Association, 39,* 333–362.

KERRIGAN, C. (1999). Paper presented at the annual meeting of the American Society of Plastic and Reconstructive Surgeons, New Orleans, October.

KESSLER, S. J., & McKENNA, W. (1978). *Gender: An ethnomethodological approach.* New York: Wiley.

KESTELMAN, P., & TRUSSELL, J. (1991). Efficacy of the simultaneous use of condoms and spermicides. *Family Planning Perspectives, 23,* 226–232.

KIKUCHI, J. J. (1988). Rhode Island develops successful intervention program for adolescents. *NCASA News,* Fall, 26.

KILMANN, P. R., et al. (1982). The treatment of sexual paraphilias: A review of the outcome research. *Journal of Sex Research, 18,* 193–252.

KILMARX, P. H., et al. (1997). Sociodemographic factors and the variation in syphilis rates among US counties, 1984 through 1993: An ecological analysis. *American Journal of Public Health, 87,* 1937–1943.

KIM, S. H., et al. (1997). Microsurgical reversal of tubal sterilization: A report on 1,118 cases. *Fertility and Sterility, 68,* 865–870.

KIMMEL, M. S. (1989). From separate spheres to sexual equality: Men's responses to feminism at the turn of the century. In B. J. Risman & P. Schwartz (Eds.), *Gender in intimate relationships: A microstructural approach.* Belmont, CA: Wadsworth.

KING, B. M., & ANDERSON, P. B. (1994). A failure of HIV education: Sex can be more important than a long life. *Journal of Health Education, 25,* 13–18.

KING, B. M., & LOCOCO, G. C. (1990). Effects of sexually explicit textbook drawings on enrollment and family communication. *Journal of Sex Education and Therapy, 16,* 38–53.

KING, B. M., & LoRUSSO, J. (1997). Discussions in the home about sex: Different recollections by parents and children. *Journal of Sex & Marital Therapy, 23,* 52–60.

KING, B. M., PARISI, L. S., & O'DWYER, K. R. (1993). College sexuality education promotes future discussions about sexuality between former students and their children. *Journal of Sex Education and Therapy, 19,* 285–293.

KING, M., & WOOLLETT, E. (1997). Sexually assaulted males: 115 men consulting a counseling service. *Archives of Sexual Behavior, 26,* 579–588.

KINGSBERG, S. A. (2000). The psychological impact of aging on sexuality and relationships. *Journal of Women's Health & Gender-Based Medicine, 9,* S33–S38.

KINSEY, A. C., POMEROY, W., & MARTIN, C. (1948). *Sexual behavior in the human male.* Philadelphia: Saunders.

KINSEY, A. C., POMEROY, W., MARTIN, C., & GEBHARD, P. (1953). *Sexual behavior in the human female.* Philadelphia: Saunders.

KIRBY, D., KORPI, M., BARTH, R. P., & CAGAMPANG, H. H. (1997). The impact of the Postponing Sexual Involvement curriculum among youths in California. *Family Planning Perspectives, 29,* 100–108.

KIRBY, D., et al. (1999). The impact of condom distribution in Seattle schools on sexual behavior and condom use. *American Journal of Public Health, 89,* 182–187.

KIRK, M., & MADSEN, H. (1989). *How America will conquer its fear and hatred of homosexuals in the '90s.* New York: Doubleday.

KIRKMAN, R. J. E., BROMHAM, D. R., O'CONNOR, T. P., & SAHOTA, J. E. (1999). Prospective multicentre study comparing levonorgestrel implants with a combined contraceptive pill: Final results. *British Journal of Family Planning, 25,* 36–40.

KIRKPATRICK, L. A., & DAVIS, K. E. (1994). Attachment style, gender, and relationship stability: A longitudinal analysis. *Journal of Personality and Social Psychology, 66,* 502–512.

KITAZAWA, K. (1994). Sexuality issues in Japan: A view from the front on HIV/AIDS and sexuality education. *SIECUS Report, 22*(2), 7–11.

KITE, M. E., & WHITLEY, JR., B. E. (1996). Sex differences in attitudes toward homosexual persons, behaviors and civil rights: A meta-analysis. *Personality and Social Psychology Bulletin, 22,* 336–352.

KJERSGAARD, A. G., et al. (1989). Male or female sterilization: A comparative study. *Fertility and Sterility, 51,* 439–443.

KLEIN, M. (1999). AIDS and HIV vaccines. *Vaccine, 17,* 565–570.

KLEINPLATZ, P. J. (1998). Sex therapy for vaginismus: A review, critique, and humanistic alternative. *Journal of Humanistic Psychology, 38,* 51–81.

KLEPINGER, D. H., BILLY, J. O. G., TANFER, K., & GRADY, W. R. (1993). Perception of AIDS risk and severity and their association with risk-related behavior among U.S. men. *Family Planning Perspectives, 25,* 74–82.

KLIEWER, E. U., & SMITH, K. R. (1995). Breast cancer mortality among immigrants in Australia and Canada. *Journal of the National Cancer Institute, 87,* 1154–1161.

KLIGMAN, E. W., & PEPIN, E. (1992). Prescribing physical activity for older patients. *Geriatrics, 47*(8), 33–47.

KLINETROB, N. A., & SMITH, D. A. (1996). Demand-withdraw communication in marital interaction: Tests of interspousal contingency and gender role hypotheses. *Journal of Marriage and the Family, 58,* 945–957.

KLITSCH, M. (1993). Vasectomy and prostate cancer: More questions than answers. *Family Planning Perspectives, 25,* 133–135.

KLONOFF-COHEN, H. S., SAVITZ, D. A., CEFALO, R. C., & McCANN, M. F. (1989). An epidemiologic study of contraception and preeclampsia. *Journal of the American Medical Association, 262,* 3143–3147.

KNOLL, J. (1997). Sexual performance and longevity. *Experimental Gerontology, 32,* 539–552.

KOBLIN, B. A., et al. (1999). Long-term survival after infection with human immunodeficiency virus type 1 (HIV-1) among homosexual men in hepatitis B vaccine trial cohorts in Amsterdam, New York City, and San Francisco, 1978–1995. *American Journal of Epidemiology, 150,* 1026–1030.

KOHLBERG, L. (1966). A cognitive-developmental analysis of children's sex-role concepts and attitudes. In E. E. Maccoby (Ed.), *The development of sex differences* (pp. 82–173). Stanford, CA: Stanford University Press.

KOHLBERG, L., & ULLIAN, D. Z. (1974). Stages in the development of psychosexual concepts and attitudes. In R. C. Friedman, R. M. Richart, & R. L. Van de Wiele (Eds.), *Sex differences in behavior* (pp. 209–222). New York: Wiley.

KOLODNY, R. C., MASTERS, W. H., & JOHNSON, V. E. (1979). *Textbook of sexual medicine.* Boston: Little, Brown.

KOLODNY, R. C., MASTERS, W. H., KOLODNY, W. H., & TORO, G. (1974). Depression of plasma testosterone levels after chronic intensive marijuana use. *New England Journal of Medicine, 290,* 872–874.

KOPLAN, J. (2000). National syphilis elimination launch: Nashville, Tennessee, October 7, 1999. Syphilis elimination: History in the making— Opening remarks. *Sexually Transmitted Diseases, 27,* 63–65.

KORBER, B., et al. (2000). Timing the ancestor of the HIV-1 pandemic strains. *Science, 288,* 1789–1796.

KOSS, M. P. (1993a). Detecting the scope of rape: A review of prevalence research methods. *Journal of Interpersonal Violence, 8,* 198–222.

Koss, M. P. (1993b). Rape: Scope, impact, interventions, and public policy responses. *American Psychologist, 48,* 1062–1069.

Koss, M. P., & Dinero, T. E. (1989). Predictors of sexual aggression among a national sample of male college students. In R. A. Prentky & V. L. Quinsley (Eds.), *Human sexual aggression: Current perspectives* (pp. 133–146). New York: New York Academy of Sciences.

Koss, M. P., Dinero, T. E., Seibel, C. A., & Cox, S. L. (1988). Stranger and acquaintance rape: Are there differences in the victim's experience? *Psychology of Women Quarterly, 12,* 1–23.

Koss, M. P., Gidycz, C. A., & Wisniewski, N. (1987). The scope of rape: Incidence and prevalence of sexual aggression and victimization in a national sample of higher education students. *Journal of Consulting and Clinical Psychology, 55,* 162–170.

Koss, M. P., Leonard, K., Beezley, D., & Oros, C. (1985). Nonstranger sexual aggression: A discriminant analysis of the psychological characteristics of undetected offenders. *Sex Roles, 12,* 981–982.

Koss, M. P., & Oros, C. J. (1982). Sexual experiences survey: A research instrument investigating sexual aggression and victimization. *Journal of Consulting and Clinical Psychology, 50,* 455–457.

Krafft-Ebing, R. von. (1927). *Psychopathia sexualis: A medico-forensic study.* London: Heinemann.

Krafft-Ebing, R. von. (1951). *Aberrations of sexual life.* New York: Staples Press.

Krafft-Ebing, R. von. (1978; originally 1886). *Psychopathia sexualis.* New York: Stein & Day.

Krahé, B. (2000). Sexual scripts and heterosexual aggression. In T. Eckes & H. M. Trautner (Eds.), *The developmental social psychology of gender* (pp. 273–292). Mahwah, NJ: Erlbaum.

Krahé, B., Schütze, S., Fritsche, I., & Waizenhöfer, E. (2000). The prevalence of sexual aggression and victimization among homosexual men. *Journal of Sex Research, 37,* 142–150.

Krieger, J. N. (2000). Consider diagnosis and treatment of trichomoniasis in men. *Sexually Transmitted Diseases, 27,* 241–242.

Krieger, W. G. (1976). Infant influences and the parent sex by child sex interaction in the socialization process. *JSAS Catalogue of Selected Documents in Psychology, 6,* 36.

Kristiansen, C. M., Felton, K. A., & Hovdestad, W. E. (1996). Recovered memories of child abuse: Fact, fantasy or fancy? *Women & Therapy, 19,* 47–59.

Kronenberg, F. (1994). Hot flashes. In R. A. Lobo (Ed.), *Treatment of the postmenopausal woman: Basic and clinical aspects* (pp. 97–117). New York: Raven Press.

Krug, R. S. (1989). Adult male report of childhood sexual abuse by mothers: Case descriptions and long-term consequences. *Child Abuse & Neglect, 13,* 111–119.

Ku, L., et al. (1998). Understanding changes in sexual activity among young metropolitan men: 1979–1995. *Family Planning Perspectives, 30,* 256–262.

Ku, L. C., Sonenstein, F. L., & Pleck, J. H. (1993). Young men's risk behaviors for HIV infection and sexually transmitted diseases, 1988 through 1991. *American Journal of Public Health, 83,* 1609–1615.

Kuhn, D., Nash, S., & Brucken, L. (1978). Sex role concepts of two- and three-year olds. *Child Development, 49,* 445–451.

Kulhanjian, J. A., et al. (1992). Identification of women at unsuspected risk of primary infection with herpes simplex virus type 2 during pregnancy. *New England Journal of Medicine, 326,* 16–20.

Kulin, H. E. (1996). Extensive personal experience: Delayed puberty. *Journal of Clinical Endocrinology and Metabolism, 81,* 3460–3464.

Kunce, L. J., & Shaver, P. R. (1994). An attachment-theoretical approach to caregiving in romantic relationships. In K. Bartholomew & D. Perlman (Eds.), *Advances in personal relationships: Vol. 5 Attachment process in adulthood* (pp. 205–237). Bristol, PA: Kingsley.

Kunkel, D., Cope, K. M., & Biely, E. (1999). Sexual messages on television: Comparing findings from three studies. *Journal of Sex Research, 36,* 230–236.

Kurdek, L. A. (1995). Assessing multiple determinants of relationship commitment in cohabiting gay, cohabiting lesbian, dating heterosexual and married heterosexual couples. *Family Relations, 44,* 261–266.

Kusseling, F. S., Shapiro, M. F., Greenberg, J. M., & Wenger, N. S. (1996). Understanding why heterosexual adults do not practice safer sex: A comparison of two samples. *AIDS Education and Prevention, 8,* 247–257.

Kutchinsky, B. (1973). The effect of easy availability of pornography on the incidence of sex crimes. *Journal of Social Issues, 29,* 163–182.

Kutchinsky, B. (1996). A case for testing: The roles of safer sex and HIV testing in AIDS prevention. In P. B. Anderson, D. de Mauro, & R. J. Noonan (Eds.), *Does anyone still remember when sex was fun?* (3rd ed., pp. 44–70). Dubuque, IA: Kendall/Hunt.

Kyman, W. (1998). Into the 21st century: Renewing the campaign for school-based sexuality education. *Journal of Sex & Marital Therapy, 24,* 131–137.

Laan, E., & Everaerd, W. (1996). Determinants of female sexual arousal: Psychophysiological theory and data. *Annual Review of Sex Research, 6,* 32–76.

Laan, E., Everaerd, W., Van Bellen, G., & Hanewald, G. (1994). Women's sexual and emotional responses to male- and female-produced erotica. *Archives of Sexual Behavior, 23,* 153–169.

Labbok, M. H., et al. (1997). Multicenter study of the lactational amenorrhea method (LAM): I. Efficacy, duration, and implications for clinical application. *Contraception, 55,* 327–336.

Labouvie-Vief, G. (1990). Modes of knowledge and the organization of development. In M. L. Commons et al. (Eds.), *Adult development models and methods in the study of adolescents and adult thought.* New York: Praeger.

Ladas, A. K., Whipple, B., & Perry, J. D. (1982). *The G spot and other recent discoveries about human sexuality.* New York: Holt, Rinehart & Winston.

Laga, M., Meheus, A., & Piot, P. (1989). Epidemiology and control of gonococcal ophthalmia neonatorum. *Bulletin of the World Health Organization, 67,* 471–478.

Lalumiere, M. L., Blanchard, R., & Zucker, K. J. (2000). Sexual orientation and handedness in men and women: A meta-analysis. *Psychological Bulletin, 126,* 575–592.

Lalumiere, M. L, Chalmers, L. J., Quinsey, V. L., & Seto, M. C. (1996). A test of the male deprivation hypothesis of sexual coercion. *Ethology and Sociobiology, 17,* 299–318.

Lalumiere, M. L., & Quinsey, V. L. (1994). The discriminability of rapists from non-sex offenders using phallometric measures: A meta-analysis. *Criminal Justice and Behavior, 21,* 150–175.

Lalumiere, M. L., & Quinsey, V. L. (1998). Pavlovian conditioning of sexual interests in human males. *Archives of Sexual Behavior, 27,* 241–252.

Lamaze, F. (1970). *Painless childbirth.* Chicago: Regnery. (Originally published 1956.)

Lamb, M. E., et al. (1996). Investigative interviews of alleged sexual abuse victims with and without anatomical dolls. *Child Abuse & Neglect, 20,* 1251–1259.

Lambert, J. D. (1995). A legacy of pleasure. In P. B. Anderson, D. de Mauro, & R. J. Noonan (Eds.), *Does anyone still remember when sex was fun?* (3rd ed., pp. 13–30). Dubuque, IA: Kendall/Hunt.

Landesman, S. H., et al. (1996). Obstetrical factors and the transmission of human immunodeficiency virus type 1 from mother to child. *New England Journal of Medicine, 334,* 1617–1623.

Laner, M. R. (2000). "Sex" versus "gender": A renewed plea. *Sociological Inquiry, 70,* 462–474.

Laner, M. R., & Russell, J. N. (1998). Desired characteristics of spouses and best friends: Do they differ by sex and/or gender? *Sociological Inquiry, 68,* 186–202.

Langenberg, A. G. M., et al. (1999). A prospective study of new infections with herpes simplex virus type 1 and type 2. *New England Journal of Medicine, 341,* 1432–1438.

Langevin, R. (1983). *Sexual strands.* Hillsdale, NJ: Erlbaum.

Langevin, R., et al. (1979). Experimental studies of the etiology of genital exhibitionism. *Archives of Sexual Behavior, 8,* 307–332.

Langevin, R., et al. (1988). Sexual sadism: Brain, blood, and behavior. *Annals of the New York Academy of Sciences, 528,* 163–171.

Langfeldt, T. (1981). Sexual development in children. In M. Cook & K. Howells (Eds.), *Adult sexual interest in children.* London: Academic Press.

Langlois, J. H., & Downs, A. C. (1980). Mothers, fathers, and peers as socialization agents of sex-typed play behaviors in young children. *Child Development, 51,* 1237–1247.

Langmyhr, G. J. (1976). Varieties of coital positions: Advantages and disadvantages. *Medical Aspects of Human Sexuality,* June, 128–139.

Lanyon, R. I. (1986). Theory and treatment in child molestation. *Journal of Consulting and Clinical Psychology, 54,* 176–182.

Larimer, M. E., Lydum, A. R., Anderson, B. K., & Turner, A. P. (1999). Male and female recipients of unwanted sexual contact in a college student sample: Prevalence rates, alcohol abuse, and depression symptoms. *Sex Roles, 40,* 295–308.

Larimore, W. (1995). Family-centered birthing: History, philosophy, and need. *Family Medicine, 27,* 132–137.

Laumann, E. O., Masi, C. M., & Zuckerman, E. W. (1997). Circumcision in the United States: Prevalence, prophylactic effects, and sexual practice. *Journal of the American Medical Association, 277,* 1052–1057.

LAUMANN, E. O., MICHAEL, R., GAGNON, J., & MICHAELS, S. (1994). *The social organization of sexuality: Sexual practices in the United States.* Chicago: University of Chicago Press.

LAUMANN, E. O., PAIK, A., & ROSEN, R. C. (1999). Sexual dysfunction in the United States: Prevalence and predictors. *Journal of the American Medical Association, 281,* 537–544.

LAUPER, U. (1996). Genital candidosis. In P. Elsner & A. Eichmann (Eds.), *Sexually transmitted diseases. Advances in diagnosis and treatment* (pp. 123–131). Basel: Karger.

LAVEE, Y. (1991). Western and non-Western human sexuality: Implications for clinical practice. *Journal of Sex & Marital Therapy, 17,* 203–213.

LAWRANCE, K., & BYERS, E. S. (1995). Sexual satisfaction in long-term heterosexual relationships: The interpersonal exchange model of sexual satisfaction. *Personal Relationships, 2,* 267–285.

LAWRENCE, D. H. (1930). *Lady Chatterley's lover.* New York: Faro.

LAWS, A., & GOLDING, J. M. (1996). Sexual assault history and eating disorder symptoms among white, Hispanic and African-American women and men. *American Journal of Public Health, 86,* 579–582.

LAWS, D. R., & O'DONOHUE, W. (1997). Fundamental issues in sexual deviance. In D. R. Laws & W. O'Donohue (Eds.), *Sexual deviance: Theory, assessment, and treatment* (pp. 1–21). New York: Guilford Press.

LAWSON, C. (1993). Mother-son sexual abuse: Rare or underreported? A critique of the research. *Child Abuse & Neglect, 17,* 261–269.

LAZAR, P. (1996). Maturation folliculaire, conceptions gémellaires dizygotes et âge maternal. *Comptes Rendus Académie des Sciences, Paris, 319,* 1139–1144.

LAZARUS, J. A. (1992). Sex with former patients almost always unethical. *American Journal of Psychiatry, 149,* 855–857.

LEBOYER, F. (1975). *Birth without violence.* New York: Knopf.

LEDE, R. L., BELIZAN, J. M., & CARROLI, G. (1996). Is routine use of episiotomy justified? *American Journal of Obstetrics and Gynecology, 174,* 1399–1402.

LEDERMAN, M. M., & VALDEZ, H. (2000). Immune restoration with antiretroviral therapies: Implications for clinical management. *Journal of the American Medical Association, 284,* 223–228.

LEE, J. A. (1974). The styles of loving. *Psychology Today,* October, 8, 43–50.

LEE, J. A. (1976). *The colors of love.* Englewood Cliffs, NJ: Prentice Hall.

LEE, J. A. (1988). Love-styles. In R. J. Sternberg & M. L. Barnes (Eds.), *The psychology of love* (pp. 38–67). New Haven, CT: Yale University Press.

LEFKOWITZ, E. S., et al. (2000). How Latino American and European American adolescents discuss conflicts, sexuality, and AIDS with their mothers. *Developmental Psychology, 36,* 315–325.

LEIBLUM, S. R., PERVIN, L., & CAMPBELL, E. H. (1989). The treatment of vaginismus: Success and failure. In S. R. Leiblum & R. C. Rosen (Eds.), *Principles and practice of sex therapy: Update for the 1990s* (pp. 113–138). New York: Guilford Press.

LEIBLUM, S. R., & ROSEN, R. C. (Eds.). (1988). *Sexual desire disorders.* New York: Guilford Press.

LEIBLUM, S. R., & ROSEN, R. C. (1989). *Principles and practice of sex therapy: An update for the 1990s.* New York: Guilford Press.

LEIBLUM, S. R., & ROSEN, R. C. (1991). Couples therapy for erectile disorders: Conceptual and clinical considerations. *Journal of Sex and Marital Therapy, 17,* 147–159.

LEIBLUM, S. R., et al. (1983). Vaginal atrophy in the post menopausal woman: The importance of sexual activity and hormones. *Journal of the American Medical Association, 249,* 2195–2198.

LEIGH, B. (1989). Reasons for having and avoiding sex: Gender, sexual orientation, and relationship to sexual behavior. *Journal of Sex Research, 26,* 199–208.

LEINWAND, D., & FIELDS, G. (2000). Feds crack down on Ecstasy. *USA Today,* April 19, 1A-2A.

LEITENBERG, H., DETZER, M. J., & SREBNIK, D. (1993). Gender differences in masturbation and the relation of masturbation experience in preadolescence and/or early adolescence to sexual behavior and sexual adjustment in young adulthood. *Archives of Sexual Behavior, 22,* 87–98.

LEITENBERG, H., & HENNING, K. (1995). Sexual fantasy. *Psychological Bulletin, 117,* 469–496.

LEITENBERG, H., & SALTZMAN, H. (2000). A statewide survey of age at first intercourse for adolescent females and age of their male partners: Relation to other risk behaviors and statutory rape implications. *Archives of Sexual Behavior, 29,* 203–215.

LELAND, J. (1995). Bisexuality. *Newsweek,* July 17, 44–50.

LELAND, J. (1999a). Bad news in the bedroom. *Newsweek,* February, 22, 47.

LELAND, J. (1999b). More buck for the bang. *Newsweek,* September 20, 1999.

LELAND, J. (2000b). The science of women & sex. *Newsweek,* May 29, 48–54.

LELAND, J., & MILLER, M. (1998). Can gays "convert"? Newsweek, August 17, 46–50.

LELAND, J., et al. (1997). A pill for impotence? *Newsweek,* November 17, 62–68.

LELAND, J., et al. (2000a). Shades of gay. *Newsweek,* March 20, 46–49.

LELAND, N. L., & BARTH, R. P. (1993). Characteristics of adolescents who have attempted to avoid HIV and who have communicated with parents about sex. *Journal of Adolescent Research, 8,* 58–76.

LEMONICK, M. D. (2000). Teens before their time. *Time,* October 30, 66–74.

LEONARD, T. L., FREUND, M., & PLATT, J. J. (1989). Behavior of clients of prostitutes. *American Journal of Public Health, 79,* 903.

LERMAN, H. (1986). *A mote in Freud's eye: From psychoanalysis to the psychology of women.* New York: Springer.

LESERMAN, J., et al. (2000). Impact of stressful life events, depression, social support, coping, and cortisol on progression to AIDS. *American Journal of Psychiatry, 157,* 1221–1228.

LESSEY, B. A. (2000). Medical management of endometriosis and infertility. *Fertility and Sterility, 73,* 1089–1096.

LEVAY, S. (1991). A difference in hypothalamic structure between heterosexual and homosexual men. *Science, 253,* 1034–1037.

LEVE, L. D., & FAGOT, B. I. (1997). Gender-role socialization and discipline processes in one- and two-parent families. *Sex Roles, 36,* 1–21.

LEVER J. (1994). Sexual revelations: The 1994 Advocate survey of sexuality and relationships: The men. *The Advocate,* August 23, 16–24.

LEVER, J., et al. (1992). Behavior patterns and sexual identity of bisexual males. *Journal of Sex Research, 29,* 141–167.

LEVIN, R. J., & LEVIN, A. (1975). Sexual pleasure: The surprising performances of 100,000 women. *Redbook,* September, 51.

LEVIN, R. J., & WAGNER, G. (1985). Orgasm in women in the laboratory—Quantitative studies on duration, intensity, latency, and vaginal blood flow. *Archives of Sexual Behavior, 11,* 367–386.

LEVINE, M. P., & TROIDEN, R. R. (1988). The myth of sexual compulsivity. *Journal of Sex Research, 25,* 347–363.

LEVINE, P. B., STAIGER, D., KANE, T. J., & ZIMMERMAN, D. J. (1999). *Roe v. Wade* and American fertility. *American Journal of Public Health, 89,* 199–203.

LEVINE, R., SATO, S., HASHIMOTO, T., & VERMA, J. (1995). Love and marriage in eleven cultures. *Journal of Cross-Cultural Psychology, 26,* 554–571.

LEVINE, R. A. (1959). Gussi sex offenses: A study in social control. *American Anthropologist, 61,* 965–990.

LEVINE, R. A. (1974). Gussi sex offenses: A study in social control. In N. N. Wagner (Ed.), *Perspectives on human sexuality* (pp. 308–352). New York: Behavioral Publishers.

LEVINE, S. B. (1993). Gender-disturbed males. *Journal of Sex & Marital Therapy, 19,* 131–141.

LEVINE, S. B. (1995). The vagaries of sexual desire. In R. C. Rosen & S. R. Leiblum (Eds.), *Case studies in sex therapy* (pp. 96–109). New York: Guilford Press.

LEVINE, S. B., & ALTHOF, S. E. (1991). The pathogenesis of psychogenic erectile dysfunction. *Journal of Sex Education and Therapy, 17,* 251–266.

LEVINGER, G. (1988). Can we picture "love"? In R. J. Sternberg & M. L. Barnes (Eds.), *The psychology of love* (pp. 139–158). New Haven, CT: Yale University Press.

LÉVI-STRAUSS, C. (1969). *The elementary structures of kinship.* Boston: Beacon Press.

LEVITT, E. E., MOSER, C., & JAMISON, K. V. (1994). The prevalence and some attributes of females in the sadomasochistic subculture: A second report. *Archives of Sexual Behavior, 23,* 465–473.

LEVRAN, D., et al. (1990). Pregnancy potential of human oocytes—The effect of cryopreservation. *New England Journal of Medicine, 323,* 1153–1156.

LEWIS, C. F., & STANLEY, L. C. S. W. (2000). Women accused of sexual offenses. *Behavioral Sciences and the Law, 18,* 73–81.

LEWIS, D. K., WATTERS, J. K., & CASE, P. (1990). The prevalence of high-risk sexual behavior in male intravenous drug users with steady female partners. *American Journal of Public Health, 80,* 465–466.

LEWIS, M., & BUTLER, R. (1994). *Love and sex after 60.* New York: Ballantine.

LEWIS, W. J. (1997). Factors associated with post-abortion adjustment problems: Implications for triage. *Canadian Journal of Human Sexuality, 6,* 9–16.

LI, D.-K., & WI, S. (2000). Changing paternity and the risk of preeclampsia/eclampsia in the subsequent pregnancy. *American Journal of Epidemiology, 151,* 57–62.

LICHTENSTEIN, P., et al. (2000). Environmental and heritable factors in the causation of cancer: Analyses of cohorts of twins from Sweden, Denmark, and Finland. *New England Journal of Medicine, 343,* 78–85.

LIDSTER, C., & HORSBURGH, M. (1994). Masturbation—Beyond myth and taboo. *Nursing Forum, 29*(3), 18–26.

LIEBOWITZ, M. (1983). *The chemistry of love.* Boston: Little, Brown.

LIEF, H. J. (1977). Inhibited sexual desire. *Medical Aspects of Human Sexuality, 7,* 94–95.

LINDBERG, F. H., & DISTAD, L. J. (1985). Post-traumatic stress disorders in women who experienced childhood incest. *Child Abuse & Neglect, 9,* 329–334.

LINDBERG, L. D., SONENSTEIN, F. L., KU, L., & MARTINEZ, G. (1997). Age differences between minors who give birth and their adult partners. *Family Planning Perspectives, 29,* 61–66.

LINDEGREN, M. L., et al. (1999). Trends in perinatal transmission of HIV/AIDS in the United States. *Journal of the American Medical Association, 282,* 531–538.

LINDHOLM, C. (1998). Love and structure. *Theory, Culture & Society, 15,* 243–263.

LINDHOLM, C., & LINDHOLM, C. (1980). Life behind the veil. *Science Digest Special,* Summer.

LINTON, R. (1936). *The study of man.* New York: Appleton-Century.

LINZ, D. (1989). Exposure to sexually explicit materials and attitudes toward rape: A comparison of study results. *Journal of Sex Research, 26,* 50–84.

LINZ, D., DONNERSTEIN, E., & PENROD, S. (1987). The findings and recommendations of the Attorney General's Commission on Pornography: Do the psychological "facts" fit the political fury? *American Psychologist, 42,* 946–953.

LIPS, H. (1992). *Sex and gender.* Mountain View, CA: Mayfield.

LIPSCOMB, G. H., MURAM, D., SPECK, P. M., & MERCER, B. M. (1992). Male victims of sexual assault. *Journal of the American Medical Association, 267,* 3064–3066.

LIPTON, M. A. (1983). The problem of pornography. In W. E. Fann et al. (Eds.), Phenomenology and treatment of psychosexual disorders (pp. 113–134). New York: Spectrum.

LIPWORTH, L., BAILEY, L. R., & TRICHOPOULAS, D. (2000). History of breast-feeding in relation to breast cancer risk: A review of the epidemiologic literature. *Journal of the National Cancer Institute, 92,* 302–312.

LITTLE, R. E., et al. (1989). Maternal alcohol use during breastfeeding and infant mental and motor development at one year. *New England Journal of Medicine, 321,* 425–430.

LOCK, M. (1994). Menopause in cultural context. *Experimental Gerontology, 29,* 307–317.

LOFTUS, E. F. (1997a). Creating false memories. *Scientific American, 277,* 70–75.

LOFTUS, E. F. (1997b). Memory for a past that never was. *Current Directions in Psychological Science, 6,* 60–65.

LOHR, B. A., ADAMS, H. E., & DAVIS, J. M. (1997). Sexual arousal to erotic and aggressive stimuli in sexually coercive and noncoercive men. *Journal of Abnormal Psychology, 106,* 230–242.

LONGNECKER, M. P., et al. (1992). Risk of breast cancer in relation to past and recent alcohol consumption. *American Journal of Epidemiology, 136,* 1001.

LOPICCOLO, J., & FRIEDMAN, J. (1988). Broad-spectrum treatment of low sexual desire: Integration of cognitive, behavioral, and systemic therapy. In S. R. Leiblum & R. C. Rosen (Eds.), *Sexual desire disorders.* New York: Guilford Press.

LOPICCOLO, J., & STOCK, W. (1986). Treatment of sexual dysfunction. *Journal of Consulting and Clinical Psychology, 54,* 158–167.

LOPICCOLO, L. (1980). Low sexual desire. In S. R. Leiblum & L. A. Pervin (Eds.), *Principles and practice of sex therapy* (pp. 29–64). New York: Guilford Press.

LOTTES, I. L., & WEINBERG, M. S. (1996). Sexual coercion among university students: A comparison of the United States and Sweden. *Journal of Sex Research, 34,* 67–76.

LOUDERBACK, L. A., & WHITLEY, JR., B. E. (1997). Perceived erotic value of homosexuality and sex-role attitudes as mediators of sex differences in heterosexual college students' attitudes toward lesbians and gay men. *Journal of Sex Research, 34, 175–182.*

LOW, L. K., SENG, J. S., MURTLAND, T. L., & OAKLEY, D. (2000). Clinician-specific episiotomy rates: Impact on perineal outcomes. *Journal of Midwifery & Women's Health, 45,* 87–93.

LOWIE, R. H. (1931). Sex and marriage. In J. F. McDermott (Ed.), *The sex problem in modern society* (pp. 146–160). New York: Modern Library.

LOWN, J., & DOLAN, E. (1988). Financial challenges in remarriage. *Lifestyles: Family and Economic Issues, 9,* 73–88.

LUCKE, J. C. (1998). Gender roles and sexual behavior among young women. *Sex Roles, 39,* 273–297.

LUCKEY, E. B., & BAIN, J. K. (1970). Children: A factor in marital satisfaction. *Journal of Marriage and the Family, 32,* 43–44.

LUGER, A. (1993). The origin of syphilis. *Sexually Transmitted Diseases, 20,* 110–117.

LUKE, B., et al. (1994). The changing pattern of multiple births in the United States: Maternal and infant characteristics, 1973 and 1990. *Obstetrics and Gynecology, 84,* 101–106.

LURIE, N. O. (1953). Winnebago berdache. *American Anthropologist, 55,* 708–712.

LYNCH, H. T., & LYNCH, J. F. (1992). Hereditary ovarian carcinoma. *Hematology/Oncology Clinics of North America, 6,* 783–811.

MACALUSO, M., et al. (1999). Mechanical failure of the latex condom in a cohort of women at high STD risk. *Sexually Transmittted Diseases, 26,* 450–458.

MACALUSO, M., et al. (2000). Female condom use among women at high risk of sexually transmitted diseases. *Family Planning Perspectives, 32,* 138–144.

MACDONALD, A. P. (1981). Bisexuality: Some comments on research and theory. *Journal of Homosexuality, 6,* 21–35.

MACDONALD, A. P. (1982). Research on sexual orientation: A bridge which touches both shores but doesn't meet in the middle. *Journal of Sex Education and Therapy, 8,* 9–13.

MACKENZIE, W. R., et al. (1992). Multiple false-positive serologic tests for HIV, HTLV-1, and hepatitis C following influenza vaccination, 1991. *Journal of the American Medical Association, 268,* 1015–1017.

MACKINNON, C. A. (1979). *Sexual harassment of working women.* New Haven, CT: Yale University Press.

MACKINNON, C. (1989). *Toward a feminist theory of the state.* Cambridge, MA: Harvard University Press.

MACKINNON, C. (1993). *Only words.* Boston: Harvard University Press.

MADDOCK, J. W., et al. (1983). *Human sexuality and the family.* New York: Haworth Press.

MADON, S. (1997). What do people believe about gay males? A study of stereotype content and strength. *Sex Roles, 37,* 663–685.

MAGNANI, R. J., et al. (1999). Vasectomy in the United States, 1991 and 1995. *Amerian Journal of Public Health, 89,* 92–94.

MAJOR, B., et al. (2000). Psychological responses of women after first trimester abortion. *Archives of General Psychiatry, 57,* 777–784.

MALAMUTH, N. (1981). Rape proclivity among males. *Journal of Social Issues, 37,* 138–157.

MALAMUTH, N. (1986). Predictors of naturalistic sexual aggression. *Journal of Personality and Social Psychology, 50,* 953–962.

MALAMUTH, N., & CHECK, J. (1981). The effects of mass media exposure on acceptance of violence against women: A field experiment. *Journal of Research in Personality, 15,* 436–446.

MALAMUTH, N., & DONNERSTEIN, E. (Eds.). (1984). *Pornography and sexual aggression.* New York: Academic Press.

MALAMUTH, N. M., HEAVEY, C. L., & LINZ, D. (1993). Predicting men's antisocial behavior against women: The interaction model of sexual aggression. In G. C. N. Hall, R. Hirschman, J. R. Graham, & M. S. Zaragoza (Eds.), *Sexual aggression: Issues in etiology, assessment and treatment* (pp. 63–97). Washington, DC: Taylor & Francis.

MALATESTA, V. J. (1979). Alcohol effects on the orgasmic-ejaculatory response in human males. *Journal of Sex Research, 15,* 101–107.

MALATESTA, V. J., et al. (1982). Acute alcohol intoxication and female orgasmic response. *Journal of Sex Research, 18,* 1–17.

MANDOKI, M. W., SUMNER, G. S., HOFFMAN, R. P., & RICONDA, D. L. (1991). A review of Klinefelter's syndrome in children and adolescents. *Journal of the American Academy of Child and Adolescence Psychiatry, 30,* 167–172.

MANNICHE, L. (1987). *Sexual life in ancient Egypt.* London: KPI.

MANNINO, D. M., KLEVENS, R. M., & FLANDERS, W. D. (1994). Cigarette smoking: An independent risk factor for impotence? *American Journal of Epidemiology, 140,* 1003–1008.

MARCHANT, S., et al. (1999). A survey of women's experiences of vaginal loss from 24 hours to three months after childbirth (the BLIPP study). *Midwifery, 15,* 72–81.

MARCHBANKS, P. A., KUNG-JONG, L., & MERCY, J. A. (1990). Risk of injury from resisting rape. *American Journal of Epidemiology, 132,* 540–549.

MARGOLIES, L., BECHER, M., & JACKSON-BREWER, K. (1988). Internalized homophobia: Identifying and treating the oppressor within. In Boston Lesbian Psychologies Collective (Ed.), *Lesbian psychologies.* Urbana: University of Illinois Press.

MARGOLIN, L. (1992). Sexual abuse by grandparents. *Child Abuse & Neglect, 16,* 735–742.

MARIN, A. J., & GUADAGNO, R. E. (1999). Perceptions of sexual harassment victims as a function of labeling and reporting. *Sex Roles, 41,* 921–940.

MARIN, G., & VAN OSS MARIN, B. (1991). *Research with Hispanic populations, applied social research methods.* Newbury Park, CA: Sage.

MARKS, G., RICHARDSON, J. L., & MALDONADO, N. (1991). Self-disclosure of HIV infection to sexual partners. *American Journal of Public Health, 81,* 1321–1323.

MARMOR, J. (1980). Clinical aspects of male homosexuality. In J. Marmor (Ed.), *Homosexual behavior: A modern reappraisal* (pp. 267–279). New York: Basic Books.

MARSHALL, D. S. (1971). Sexual behavior on Mangaia. In D. S. Marshall & R. C. Suggs (Eds.), *Human sexual behavior* (pp. 103–162). New York: Basic Books.

MARSHALL, W. L. (1988). The use of sexually explicit stimuli by rapists, child molesters, and nonoffenders. *Journal of Sex Research, 25,* 267–268.

MARSHALL, W. L. (1992). Pornography and sex offenders. In D. Zillman & J. Bryant (Eds.), *Pornography: Recent research, interpretation, and policy considerations* (pp. 185–214). Hillsdale, NJ: Erlbaum.

MARSHALL, W. L. (1993). A revised approach to the treatment of men who sexually asault adult females. In G. C. N. Hall et al. (Eds.), *Sexual aggression: Issues in etiology, assessment, and treatment* (pp. 143–165). Washington, DC: Taylor & Francis.

MARSHALL, W. L. (1996). Assessment, treatment, and theorizing about sex offenders. *Criminal Justice and Behavior, 23,* 162–199.

MARSHALL, W. L., ANDERSON, D., & CHAMPAGNE, F. (1997). Self-esteem and its relationship to sexual offending. *Psychology, Crime and Law, 3,* 161–186.

MARSHALL, W. L., & BARBAREE, H. E. (1990). An integrated theory of the etiology of sexual offending. In W. L. Marshall, D. R. Laws, & H. E. Barbaree (Eds.), *Handbook of sexual assault: Issues, theories, and treatment of the offender* (pp. 257–275). New York: Plenum Press.

MARSHALL, W. L., BARBAREE, H. E., & CHRISTOPHE, D. (1986). Sexual offenders against female children: Sexual preferences for age of victims and type of behavior. *Canadian Journal of Behavioral Science, 18,* 424–439.

MARSHALL, W. L., ECCLES, A., & BARBAREE, H. (1991). The treatment of exhibitionists: A focus on sexual deviance versus cognitive and relationship features. *Behavior Research and Therapy, 29,* 129–135.

MARSHALL, W. L., ECCLES, A., & BARBAREE, H. E. (1993). A three-tiered approach to the rehabilitation of incarcerated sex offenders. *Behavioral Sciences and the Law, 11,* 441–455.

MARSIGLIO, W. (1993a). Adolescent males' orientation toward paternity and contraception. *Family Planning Perspectives, 25,* 22–31.

MARSIGLIO, W. (1993b). Attitudes toward homosexual activity and gays as friends: A national survey of heterosexual 15- to 19-year-old males. *Journal of Sex Research, 30,* 12–17.

MARSIGLIO, W., & DONNELLY, D. (1991). Sexual relations in later life: A national study of married persons. *Journal of Gerontology, 46,* S338–S344.

MARTIN, A.-M., & WEBER, B. L. (2000). Genetic and hormonal risk factors in breast cancer. *Journal of the National Cancer Institute, 92,* 1126–1135.

MARTIN, C. L., & RUBLE, D. N. (1997). A developmental perspective of self-construals and sex differences: Comment on Cross and Madson (1997). *Psychological Bulletin, 122,* 45–50.

MARTIN, E. F., & PRUETT, M. K. (1998). The juvenile sex offender and the juvenile justice system. *American Criminal Law Review, 35,* 279–332.

MARTIN, J. N., et al. (1998). Sexual transmission and the natural history of human herpes virus 8 and infection. *New England Journal of Medicine, 338,* 948–954.

MASCIOLA, C., & RAMS, B. (1999). Reasons women molest adolescent boys unclear. National article from the *Orange County Register,* August.

MASLAND, T., & KING, P. (2000). Flirting with strange ideas. *Newsweek,* April 17, 36.

MASLAND, T., & NORDLAND, R. (2000). 10 million orphans. *Newsweek,* January 17, 42–45.

MASLOW, A. H. (1968). *Toward a psychology of being* (2nd ed.). Princeton, NJ: Van Nostrand.

MASTERS, W. H. (1986). Sexual dysfunction as an aftermath of sexual assault of men by women. *Journal of Sex & Marital Therapy, 12,* 35–45.

MASTERS, W. H., & JOHNSON, V. E. (1966). *Human sexual response.* Boston: Little, Brown.

MASTERS, W. H., & JOHNSON, V. E. (1970). *Human sexual inadequacy.* Boston: Little, Brown.

MASTERS, W. H., & JOHNSON, V. E. (1979). *Homosexuality in perspective.* Boston: Little, Brown.

MASTROYANNIS, C. (1993). Gamete intrafallopian transfer: Ethical considerations, historical development of the procedure, and comparison with other advanced reproductive technologies. *Fertility and Sterility, 60,* 389–402.

MASUR, F. T. (1979). Resumption of sexual activity following myocardial infarction. *Sexuality and Disability, 2,* 98–114.

MATEK, O. (1988). Obscene phone callers. *Journal of Social Work and Human Sexuality, 7,* 113–130.

MATHIAS-RIEGEL, B. (1999). Intimacy 101: A refresher course in the language of love. *Modern Maturity,* September–October, 46–49, 84.

MATHUR, R., & BRAUNSTEIN, G. D. (1997). Gynecomastia: Pathomechanisms and treatment strategies. *Hormone Research, 48,* 95–102.

MATTHIAS, R. E., LUBBEN, J. E., ATCHISON, K. A., & SCHWEITZER, S. O. (1997). Sexual activity and satisfaction among very old adults: Results from a community-dwelling Medicare population survey. *The Gerontologist, 37,* 6–14.

MAUCK, C., et al. (1996). Lea's Shield: A study of the safety and efficacy of a new vaginal barrier contraceptive used with and without spermicide. *Contraception, 53,* 329–335.

MAULDON, J., & DELBANCO, S. (1997). Public perceptions about unplanned pregnancy. *Family Planning Perspective, 29,* 25–29, 40.

MAZUR, A., & BOOTH, A. (1998). Testosterone and dominance in men. *Behavioral and Brain Sciences, 21,* 353–397.

MCCABE, M. (1987). Desired and experienced levels of premarital affection and sexual intercourse during dating. *Journal of Sex Research, 23,* 23–33.

MCCABE, M. P., & CUMMINS, R. A. (1998). Sexuality and quality of life among young people. *Adolescence, 33,* 761–770.

MCCABE, S. (1983). FBD marriage: Further support for the Westermarck hypothesis of the incest taboo? *American Anthropologist, 85,* 50–69.

MCCARTHY, B. W. (1997). Strategies and techniques for revitalizing a nonsexual marriage. *Journal of Sex & Marital Therapy, 23,* 231–240.

MCCARTHY, B. W. (1999). The nonsexual marriage: Assessing viability and treatment options. *Journal of Sex & Marital Therapy, 25,* 227–236.

MCCARTON, C. M., et al. (1997). Results at age 8 years of early intervention for low-birth-weight premature infants. *Journal of the American Medical Association, 277,* 126–132.

MCCARTY, L. (1986). Mother-child incest: Characteristics of the offender. *Child Welfare, 6,* 447–458.

MCCAULEY, J., et al. (1997). Clinical characteristics of women with a history of childhood abuse: Unhealed wounds. *Journal of the American Medical Association, 277,* 1362–1368.

MCCLINTOCK, M. (1971). Menstrual synchrony and suppression. *Nature, 229,* 244–245.

MCCLINTOCK, M. K. (1999). Whither menstrual synchrony? *Annual Review of Sex Research, 9,* 77–95.

MCCLINTOCK, M. K., & HERDT, G. (1996). Rethinking puberty: The development of sexual attraction. *Current Directions in Psychological Science, 5,* 178–183.

MCCONAGHY, N. (1974). Penile volume responses to moving and still pictures of male and female nudes. *Archives of Sexual Behavior, 3,* 566–570.

MCCONAGHY, N., BUHRICH, N., & SILOVE, D. (1994). Opposite sex-linked behaviors and homosexual feelings in the predominantly heterosexual male majority. *Archives of Sexual Behavior, 23,* 565–577.

MCCORMACK, A., ROKDUS, F. E., HAZELWOOD, R. R., & BURGESS, A. W. (1992). An exploration of incest in the childhood development of serial rapists. *Journal of Family Violence, 7,* 219–228.

MCCOY, N. L., & MATYAS, J. R. (1996). Oral contraceptives and sexuality in university women. *Archives of Sexual Behavior, 25,* 73–90.

MCFADDEN, D., & PASANEN, E. G. (1998). Comparison of the auditory systems of heterosexuals and homosexuals: Click-evoked otoacoustic emissions. *Proceedings of the National Academy of Sciences, USA, 95,* 2709–2713.

MCGEE, E. A., & HSUEH, A. J. W. (2000). Initial and cyclic recruitment of ovarian follicles. *Endocrine Reviews, 21,* 200–214.

MCHALE, S. M., & CROUTER, A. C. (1992). You can't always get what you want: Incongruence between sex-role attitudes and family work roles and its implications for marriage. *Journal of Marriage and the Family, 54,* 537–547.

MCKAIN, T. L. (1996). Acknowledging mixed-sex people. *Journal of Sex & Marital Therapy, 22,* 265–274.

MCKAY, A. (1997). Accommodating ideological pluralism is sexuality education. *Journal of Moral Education, 26,* 285–300.

MCKEGANEY, N. P. (1994). Prostitution and HIV: What do we know and where might research be targeted in the future? *AIDS, 8,* 1215–1226.

MCKIRNAN, D. J., STOKES, J. P., DOLL, L., & BURZETTE, R. G. (1995). Bisexually active men: Social characteristics and sexual behavior. *Journal of Sex Research, 32,* 65–76.

MCMAHON, M. J., LUTHER, M. P. H., BOWES, W. A., & OLSHAN, A. F. (1996). Comparison of a trial of labor with an elective second cesarean section. *New England Journal of Medicine, 355,* 689–695.

MCQUILLAN, G. M., et al. (1999). Prevalence of hepatitis B virus infection in the United States: The National Health and Nutrition Examination Surveys, 1976 through 1994. *American Journal of Public Health, 89,* 14–18.

MEAD, M. (1935). *Sex and temperament in three primitive societies.* New York: William Morrow.

MEAD, M. (1975). *Male and female.* New York: William Morrow.

MEDIA REPORT TO WOMEN. (1993). Muppet gender gap. *Media Report to Women, 21,* 8.

MEDLAR, T. (1998). The sexuality education program of the Massachusetts statewide head injury program. *Sexuality and Disability, 16,* 11–19.

MEEKS, B. S., HENDRICK, S. S., & HENDRICK, C. (1998). Communication, love and relationship satisfaction. *Journal of Social and Personal Relationships, 15,* 755–773.

MEHREN, E. (1991). What we really think about adultery. *Los Angeles Times,* June 2, E1, E8.

MEINKING, T. L., & TAPLIN, D. (1996). Infestations: Pediculosis. In P. Elsner & A. Eichmann (Eds.), *Sexually transmitted diseases: Advances in diagnosis and treatment* (pp. 157–163). Basel: Karger.

MEINKING, T. L., et al. (1995). The treatment of scabies with ivermectin. *New England Journal of Medicine, 333,* 26–30.

MEISELMAN, K. (1978). *Incest: A psychological study of causes and effects with treatment recommendations.* San Francisco: Jossey-Bass.

MELBYE, M., et al. (1997). Induced abortion and the risk of breast cancer. *New England Journal of Medicine, 336,* 81–85.

MELENDY, M. R. (1903). *Perfect womanhood: For maidens-wives-mothers.* Philadelphia: K. T. Boland.

MELLORS, J. W., et al. (1996). Prognosis in HIV-1 infection predicted by the quantity of virus in plasma. *Science, 272,* 1167–1170.

MELLORS, J. W., et al. (1997). Plasma viral load and CD4+ lymphocytes as prognostic markers of HIV-1 infection. *Annals of Internal Medicine, 126,* 946–954.

MENDEZ, Z. M. (1996). Colombia's "National Project for Sex Education." *SIECUS Report, 24*(3), 13.

MENEZO, Y. J. R., & JANNY, L. (1996). Is there a rationale for tubal transfer in human ART? *Human Reproduction, 11,* 1818–1820.

MEREDITH, N. (1984). The gay dilemma. *Psychology Today, 18,* 56–62.

MERIGGIOLA, M. C., et al. (1997). An oral regimen of cyproterone acetate and testosterone undecanoate for spermatogenic suppression in men. *Fertility and Sterility, 68,* 844–850.

MERSKIN, D. (1999). Adolescence, advertising, and the ideology of menstruation. *Sex Roles, 40,* 941–957.

MESSENGER, J. (1971). Sex and repression in an Irish folk community. In D. Marshall & R. Suggs (Eds.), *Human sexual behavior* (pp. 3–37). New York: Basic Books..

MESSIAH, A., et al. (1995). Sociodemographic characteristics and sexual behavior of bisexual men in France: Implications for HIV prevention. *American Journal of Public Health, 85,* 1543–1546.

MESSIAH, A., et al. (1997). Condom breakage and slippage during heterosexual intercourse: A French national survey. *American Journal of Public Health, 87,* 421–424.

MESTON, C. M., HEIMAN, J. R., & TRAPNELL, P. D. (1999). The relation between early abuse and adult sexuality. *Journal of Sex Research, 36,* 385–395.

MESTON, C. M., HEIMAN, J. R., TRAPNELL, P. D., & PAULHUS, D. L. (1998). Socially desirable responding and sexuality self-reports. *Journal of Sex Research, 35,* 148–157.

METTLER, F. A. (1996). Benefits versus risks from mammography. *Cancer, 77,* 903–909.

METTS, S., & FITZPATRICK, M. A. (1992). Thinking about safer sex: The risky business of "Know your partner" advice. In T. Edgar, M. A. Fitzpatrick, & V. S. Freimuth (Eds.), *AIDS: A communication perspective.* Hillsdale, NJ: Erlbaum.

METZ, M. E., et al. (1997). Premature ejaculation: A psychophysiological review. *Journal of Sex & Marital Therapy, 23,* 3–23.

MEUWISSEN, I., & OVER, R. (1991). Multidimensionality of the content of female sexual fantasy. *Behavior Research and Therapy, 29,* 179–189.

MEYENBURG, B. (1999). Gender identity disorder in adolescence: Outcomes of psychotherapy. *Adolescence, 34,* 305–313.

MEYER-BAHLBURG, H. F. L., et al. (1995). Prenatal estrogens and the development of homosexual orientation. *Developmental Psychology, 31,* 12–21.

MEYEROKOWITZ, B. E., et al. (1999). Sexuality following breast cancer. *Journal of Sex & Marital Therapy, 25,* 237–250.

MEYERS, S. A., & BERSCHEID, E. (1997). The language of love: The difference a preposition makes. *Personality and Social Psychology Bulletin, 23,* 347–362.

MEZEY, G., & KING, M. (1989). The effects of sexual assault on men: A survey of 22 victims. *Psychological Medicine, 19,* 205–209.

MICHAEL, R., GAGNON, J., LAUMANN, E., & KOLATA, G. (1994). *Sex in America: A definitive survey.* Boston: Little, Brown.

MICHAELS, R. H., & MELLIN, G. W. (1960). Prospective experience with maternal rubella and the associated congenital malformations. *Pediatrics, 26,* 200–209.

MIKACH, S. M., & BAILEY, J. M. (1999). What distinguishes women with unusually high numbers of sex partners? *Evolution and Human Behavior, 20,* 141–150.

MIKULINCER, M., & NACHSHON, O. (1991). Attachment styles and patterns of self-disclosure. *Journal of Personality and Social Psychology, 61,* 321–331.

MILLER, B. C., NORTON, M. C., FAN, X., & CHRISTOPHERSON, C. R. (1998). Pubertal development, parental communication, and sexual values in relation to adolescent sexual behaviors. *Journal of Early Adolescence, 18,* 27–52.

MILLER, E. M. (2000). Homosexuality, birth order, and evolution: Toward an equilibrium reproductive economics of homosexuality. *Archives of Sexual Behavior, 29,* 1–34.

MILLER, K. S., et al. (1998a). Family communication about sex: What are parents saying and are their adolescents listening? *Family Planning Perspectives, 30,* 218–222, 235.

MILLER, K. S., LEVIN, M. L., WHITAKER, D. J., & XU, X. (1998b). Patterns of condom use among adolescents: The impact of mother-adolescent communication. *American Journal of Public Health, 88,* 1542–1544.

MILLER, M., et al. (2000). Sexual behavior changes and protease inhibitor therapy. *AIDS, 14,* F33–F39.

MILLER, R. D. (1998). Forced administration of sex-drive reducing medications to sex offenders: Treatment or punishment? *Psychology, Public Policy, and Law, 4,* 175–199.

MILNER, J. S., & DOPKE, C. A. (1997). Paraphilia not otherwise specified: Psychopathology and theory. In D. R. Laws & W. O'Donohue (Eds.), *Sexual deviance: Theory, assessment, and treatment* (pp. 394–423). New York: Guilford Press.

MILSOM, I., SUNDELL, G., & ANDERSCH, B. (1990). The influence of different combined oral contraceptives on the prevalence and severity of dysmenorrhea. *Contraception, 42,* 497–506.

MINA, E. E., & GALLOP, R. M. (1998). Childhood sexual and physical abuse and adult self-harm and suicidal behavior: A literature review. *Canadian Journal of Psychiatry, 43,* 793–800.

MINIUM, E. W., KING, B. M., & BEAR, G. (1993). *Statistical reasoning in psychology and education* (3rd ed.) New York: Wiley.

MIRACLE-MCMAHILL, H. L., et al. (1997). Tubal ligation and fatal ovarian cancer in a large prospective cohort study. *American Journal of Epidemiology, 145,* 349–357.

MIRKIN, G., & HOFFMAN, M. (1978). *The sportsmedicine book.* Boston: Little, Brown.

MISHELL, JR., D. R. (1989). Medical progress: Contraception. *New England Journal of Medicine, 320,* 777–787.

MISHELL, JR., D. R. (1999). Cardiovascular risks: Perception versus reality. *Contraception, 59,* 215–245.

MISHU, B., et al. (1990). A surgeon with AIDS: Lack of evidence of transmission to patients. *Journal of the American Medical Association, 264,* 467–470.

MOFENSON, L. M., et al. (1999). Risk factors for perinatal transmission of human immunodeficiency virus type 1 in women treated with zidovudine. *New England Journal of Medicine, 341,* 385–393.

MOL, B. W. J., et al. (2000). Cost-effectiveness of in vitro fertilization and embryo transfer. *Fertility and Sterility, 73,* 748–754.

MOLLER, L. C., HYMEL, S., & RUBIN, K. H. (1992). Sex typing in play and popularity in middle childhood. *Sex Roles, 26,* 331–335.

MONEY, J. (1970). Clitoral size and erotic sensation. *Medical Aspects of Human Sexuality, 4,* 95.

MONEY, J. (1975). Ablatio penis: Normal male infant sex-reassigned as a girl. *Archives of Sexual Behavior, 4,* 65–72.

MONEY, J. (1984). Paraphilias: Phenomenology and classification. *American Journal of Psychotherapy, 38,* 164–179.

MONEY, J. (1986). *Lovemaps: Clinical concepts of sexual/erotic health and pathology, paraphilia, and gender transposition in childhood, adolescence, and maturity.* New York: Irvington.

MONEY, J. (1994). *Sex errors of the body and related syndromes.* Baltimore: Paul H. Brookes.

MONEY, J., & EHRHARDT, A. E. (1972). *Man & woman, boy & girl.* Baltimore: Johns Hopkins University Press.

MONEY, J., & SCHWARTZ, M. (1977). Dating, romantic and nonromantic friendships, and sexuality in 17 early-treated adrenogenital females, aged 16–25. In P. A. Lee et al. (Eds.), *Congenital adrenal hyperplasia.* Baltimore: University Park Press.

MONROE, J. (1997). Roofies: Horror drug of the '90s. *Current Health, 2,* 24–27.

MONROE, S., PAINTON, P., & TOUFEXIS, A. (1990). When is it rape? *Time,* June 3, 48–54.

MONTO, M. A. (1996). Lamaze and Bradley childbirth classes: Contrasting perspectives toward the medical model of birth. *Birth, 23,* 193–201.

MOORE, H. (1994). In P. Harvey & P. Gow (Eds.), *Sex and violence: Issues in representation and experience.* New York: Routledge.

MOORE, K. (1993). *The developing human: Clinically oriented embryology* (5th ed.). Philadelphia: Saunders.

MOORE, N. B., & DAVIDSON, J. K. (1997). Guilt about first intercourse: An antecedent of sexual dissatisfaction among college women. *Journal of Sex & Marital Therapy, 23,* 29–46.

MORGAN, S. P., LYE, D. N., & CONDRAN, G. A. (1988). Sons, daughters, and the risk of marital disruption. *American Journal of Sociology, 94,* 110–129.

MOROKOFF, P. J., & GILLILLAND, R. (1993). Stress, sexual functioning, and marital satisfaction. *Journal of Sex Research, 30,* 43–53.

MORROW, K. B. (1991). Attributions of female adolescent incest victims regarding their molestation. *Child Abuse & Neglect, 15,* 477–483.

MORSE, E. V., SIMON, P. M., BALSON, P. M., & OSOFSKY, H. J. (1992). Sexual behavior patterns of customers of male street prostitutes. *Archives of Sexual Behavior, 21,* 347–357.

MOSER, C., & LEVITT, E. (1987). An exploratory-descriptive study of a sadomasochistically oriented sample. *Journal of Sex Research, 23,* 322–337.

MOSGAARD, B. J., et al. (1997). Infertility, fertility drugs, and invasive ovarian cancer: A case-control study. *Fertility and Sterility, 67,* 1005–1012.

MOSHER, D. L. (1991). Macho men, machismo, and sexuality. *Annual Review of Sex Research, 2,* 199–249.

MOSHER, D., & ANDERSON, R. (1986). Macho personality, sexual aggression, and reactions to guided imagery of realistic rape. *Journal of Research in Personality, 20,* 77–94.

MOSHER, W. D., & PRATT W. F. (1991). Fecundity and infertility in the United States: Incidence and trends. *Fertility and Sterility, 56,* 192–193.

MOSS, C., HOSFORD, R., & ANDERSON, W. (1979). Sexual assault in prison. *Psychological Reports, 44,* 823–828.

MOSTAD, S. B., & KREISS, J. K. (1996). Shedding of HIV-1 in the genital tract. *AIDS, 10,* 1305–1315.

MOSTAD, S. B., et al. (1997). Hormonal contraception, vitamin A deficiency, and other risk factors for shedding of HIV-1 infected cells from the cervix and vagina. *Lancet, 350,* 922–927.

MOSURE, D. J., et al. (1997). Genital chlamydia infections in sexually active female adolescents: Do we really need to screen everyone? *Journal of Adolescent Health, 20,* 6–13.

MOYER, A. (1997). Psychosocial outcomes of breast-conserving surgery versus mastectomy: A meta-analytic review. *Health Psychology, 16,* 284–298.

MUEHLENHARD, C. L. (1998). The importance and danger of studying sexually aggressive women. In P. B. Anderson & C. Struckman-Johnson (Eds.), *Sexually aggressive women* (pp. 19–48). New York: Guilford Press.

MUEHLENHARD, C. L., ANDREWS, S. L., & BEAL, G. K. (1996). Beyond "just saying no": Dealing with men's unwanted sexual advances in heterosexual dating contexts. *Journal of Psychology and Human Sexuality, 8,* 141–168.

MUEHLENHARD, C. L., & COOK, S. W. (1988). Men's self-reports of unwanted sexual activity. *Journal of Sex Research, 24,* 58–72.

MUEHLENHARD, C. L., & FALCON, P. (1990). Men's heterosexual skill and attitudes toward women as predictors of verbal and sexual coercion and forceful rape. *Sex Roles, 23,* 241–259.

MUEHLENHARD, C. L., & HOLLABAUGH, L. (1989). Do women sometimes say no when they mean yes? The prevalence and correlates of women's token resistance to sex. *Journal of Personality and Social Psychology, 54,* 872–879.

MUEHLENHARD, C. L., & MCCOY, M. L. (1991). Double standard/double blind: The sexual double standard and women's communication about sex. *Psychology of Women Quarterly, 15,* 447–461.

MUEHLENHARD, C. L., POWCH, I. G., PHELPS, J. L., & GIUSTI, L. M. (1992). Definitions of rape: Scientific and political implications. *Journal of Social Issues, 48,* 23–44.

MUEHLENHARD, C. L., & RODGERS, C. S. (1998). Token resistance to sex: New perspectives on old stereotypes. *Psychology of Women Quarterly, 22,* 443–463.

MUEHLENHARD, C. L., & SCHRAG, J. (1990). Nonviolent sexual coercion. In A. Parrot & L. Bechhofer (Eds.), *Hidden rape: Sexual assault among acquaintances, friends, and intimates.* New York: Wiley.

MUESER, K. T., & TAYLOR, K. L. (1997). A cognitive-behavioral approach. In M. Harris & C. L. Landis (Eds.), *Sexual abuse in the lives of women diagnosed with serious mental illness* (pp. 67–90). Amsterdam: Harwood Academic Publishers.

MUKHERJEE, A. B., & HODGEN, G. D. (1982). Maternal ethanol exposure induces transient impairment of umbilical circulation and fetal hypoxia in monkeys. *Science, 218,* 700–702.

MULLER, J. E., et al. (1996). Triggering myocardial infarction by sexual activity: Low absolute risk and prevention by regular physical exertion. *Journal of the American Medical Association, 275,* 1405–1409.

MULNARD, R. A., et al. (2000). Estrogen replacement therapy for treatment of mild to moderate Alzheimer disease: A randomized controlled trial. *Journal of the Amerian Medical Association, 283,* 1007–1015.

MUNJACK, D. J., & KANNO, P. H. (1979). Retarded ejaculation: A review. *Archives of Sexual Behavior, 8,* 139–150.

MUNOZ, A., & XU, J. (1996). Models for the incubation of AIDS and variations according to age and period. *Statistics in Medicine, 15,* 2459–2473.

MUNROE, R. L. (1980). Male transvestism and the couvade: A psychocultural analysis. *Ethos, 8,* 49–59.

MURDOCK, G. P. (1967). *Ethnographic atlas.* Pittsburgh: University of Pittsburgh Press.

MURNEN, S. K., & SMOLAK, L. (2000). The experience of sexual harassment among grade-school students: Early socialization of female subordination. *Sex Roles, 43,* 1–17.

MURNEN, S. K., & STOCKTON, M. (1997). Gender and self-reported sexual arousal in response to sexual stimuli: A meta-analytic review. *Sex Roles, 37,* 135–153.

MURPHY, J. J., & BOGGESS, S. (1998). Increased condom use among teenage males, 1988–1995: The role of attitudes. *Family Planning Perspectives, 30,* 276–280, 303.

MURPHY, S., KITCHEN, V., & HARRIS, J. R. W. (1989). Rape and subsequent seroconversion to HIV. *British Medical Journal, 299,* 718–722.

MURPHY, T. F. (1992). Redirecting sexual orientation: Techniques and justifications. *Journal of Sex Research, 29,* 501–523.

MURPHY, W. D. (1997). Exhibitionism: Psychopathology and theory. In D. R. Laws & W. O'Donohue (Eds.), *Sexual deviance: Theory, assessment, and treatment* (pp. 22–39). New York: Guilford Press.

MURPHY, W. D., HAYNES, M. R., & PAGE, I. J. (1992). Adolescent sex offenders. In W. O'Donohue & J. H. Geer (Eds.), *The sexual abuse of children: Clinical issues* (Vol. 2, pp. 394–429). Hillsdale, NJ: Erlbaum.

MURRAY, B. (1999). Boys to men: Emotional miseducation. *APA Monitor, 30*(7), 1, 38–39.

MURRAY, J. (1995). Thinking about gender. The diversity of medieval perspectives. In J. Carpenter & S.-B. MacLean (Eds.), *Power of the weak. Women in the Middle Ages* (pp. 1–26). Chicago: University of Illinois.

MURRAY, J. (1998). Men's bodies, men's minds: Seminal emissions and sexual anxiety in the Middle Ages. *Annual Review of Sex Research, 8,* 1–26.

MURRAY, L. (1992). The impact of postnatal depression on infant development. *Journal of Child Psychology and Psychiatry, 33,* 543–561.

MURRAY, L., & COOPER, P. J. (1997). Postpartum depression and child development. *Psychological Medicine, 27,* 253–260.

MURRAY, S. (1992). *Oceanic homosexualities.* New York: Garland.

MURRAY, S. L., HOLMES, J. G., & GRIFFIN, D. W. (1996). The self-fulfilling nature of positive illusions in romantic relationships: Love is not blind, but prescient. *Journal of Personality and Social Psychology, 71,* 1155–1180.

MURSTEIN, B. I. (1978). Swinging, or comarital sex. In B. I. Murstein (Ed.), *Exploring intimate life styles* (pp. 109–130). New York: Springer.

MURSTEIN, B. I. (1988). A taxonomy of love. In R. J. Sternberg & M. L. Barnes (Eds.), *The psychology of love* (pp. 13–37). New Haven, CT: Yale University Press.

MYERS, G., MACINNES, K., & KORBER, B. (1992). The emergence of simian/human immunodeficiency viruses. *AIDS Research and Human Retroviruses, 8,* 373–386.

MYERS, L., et al. (1990). Effects of estrogen, androgen, and progestin on sexual psychophysiology and behavior in postmenopausal women. *Journal of Clinical Endocrinology and Metabolism, 70,* 1124–1131.

NABRINK, M., BIRGERSSON, L., COLLING-SALTIN, A.-S., & SOLUM, T. (1990). Modern oral contraceptives and dysmenorrhea. *Contraception, 42,* 275–283.

NACHTIGALL, L. E. (1994). Sexual function in menopause and postmenopause. In B. A. Lobo (Ed.), *Treatment of the postmenopausal woman: Basic and clinical aspects* (pp. 301–306). New York: Raven Press.

NANNINI, D. K., & MEYERS, L. S. (2000). Jealousy in sexual and emotional infidelity: An alternative to the evolutionary explanation. *Journal of Sex Research, 37,* 117–122.

NANSON, J. (1997). Binge drinking during pregnancy: Who are the women at risk? *Canadian Medical Association Journal, 156,* 807–808.

NARAL. (1995). *Sexuality education in America: A state-by-state review.* National Abortion and Reproductive Rights Action League.

NATIONAL INSTITUTE ON DRUG ABUSE. (2000). *Community drug alert bulletin: Hepatitis C.* NIH Publication No. 00-4663. Bethesda, MD.

NATIONAL INSTITUTES OF HEALTH (NIH). (1992). Impotence. *NIH Consensus Statement, 10*(4), 1–33.

NATIONAL INSTITUTES OF HEALTH. (1997) Concensus Development Conference Statement, February, 11–13.

NATIONAL SPINAL CORD STATISTICAL CENTER. (1995). *Spinal cord injury: Facts and figures at a glance.* Birmingham: University of Alabama Press.

NAY, R., & GORMAN, D. (1999). Sexuality in aged care. In R. Nay & S. Garratt (Eds.), *Nursing older people: Issues and innovations* (pp. 193–211). Sydney, Australia: MacLennan & Petty.

NAYAK, J., & BOSE, R. (1997). Making sense, talking sexuality: India reaches out to its youth. *SIECUS Report, 25*(2), 19–21.

NAZ, R. K. (1999). Vaccine for contraception targeting sperm. *Immunological Reviews, 171,* 193–202.

NAZARIO, S. L. (1990). Midwifery is staging revival as demand for prenatal care, low-tech births rises. *Wall Street Journal,* September 9, B1, B4.

NDUATI, R., et al. (2000). Effect of breastfeeding and formula feeding on transmission of HIV-1: A randomized clinical trial. *Journal of the American Medical Association, 283,* 1167–1174.

NESS, R. B., et al. (1993). Number of pregnancies and the subsequent risk of cardiovascular disease. *New England Journal of Medicine, 328,* 1528–1533.

NESS, R. B., et al. (1999). Cocaine and tobacco use and the risk of spontaneous abortion. *New England Journal of Medicine, 340,* 333–339.

NESS, R. B., et al. (2000). Risk of ovarian cancer in relation to estrogen and progestin dose and use characteristics of oral contraceptives. *American Journal of Epidemiology, 152,* 233–241.

(NEW ORLEANS) *TIMES-PICAYUNE.* (1999). Against pedophilia. May 28, A-3.

NEWSWEEK. (1989). Pregnancy + alcohol = problems. July 31, 57–59.

NEWSWEEK. (2000a). Selling sex on the Web. June 12, 76J.

NEWSWEEK. (2000b). There's something about sex. *Newsweek,* May 8, 59.

NHU, T. T. (1997). Sex surrogate offers healing. *Times-Picayune* (New Orleans), October 5, A-20.

NICHOLS, M. (1988). Bisexuality in women: Myths, realities, and implications for therapy. *Women and Therapy, 7,* 235–252.

NIELSON, J., & WOHLERT, M. (1991). Chromosome abnormalities found among 34,910 newborn children: Results from a 13-year incidence study in Arhus, Denmark. *Human Genetics, 87,* 81–83.

NOCK, S. (1987). The symbolic meaning of childbearing. *Journal of Family Issues, 8,* 373–393.

NORDENTOFT, M., et al. (1996). Intrauterine growth retardation and premature delivery: The influence of maternal smoking and psychosocial factors. *American Journal of Public Health, 86,* 347–354.

NORWITZ, E. R., ROBINSON, J. N., & CHALLIS, J. R. G. (1999). The control of labor. *New England Journal of Medicine, 341,* 660–666.

NOTARIUS, C. I., LASHLEY, S. L., & SULLIVAN, D. J. (1997). Angry at your partner? Think again. In R. J. Sternberg & M. Hojjat (Eds.), *Satisfaction in close relationships* (pp. 219–248). New York: Guilford Press.

NOTARIUS, C. I., & MARKMAN, H. J. (1993). *Love can work it out: Making sense of marital conflict.* New York: Putnam's.

NUTTER, D. E., & KEARNS, M. E. (1993). Patterns of exposure to sexually explicit material among sex offenders, child molesters, and controls. *Journal of Sex & Marital Therapy, 19,* 77–85.

NYGREN, A. (1982). *Agape and eros.* Chicago: University of Chicago Press.

O'BRIEN, M., & HUSTON, A. C. (1985). Development of sex-typed play behavior in toddlers. *Developmental Psychology, 21,* 866–871.

O'BRIEN, W. A., et al. (1996). Changes in plasma HIV-1 RNA and CD4+ lymphocyte counts and the risk of progression to AIDS. *New England Journal of Medicine, 334,* 426–431.

O'CAMPO, P., et al. (1992). Prior episode of sexually transmitted disease and subsequent sexual risk-reduction practices: A need for improved risk-reduction interventions. *Sexually Transmitted Diseases, 19,* 326.

ODDEN, T., & FICK, D. (1998). Identifying and managing exercise-induced amenorrhea. *Journal of the American Academy of Physician Assistants, 11,* 59–80.

ODDENS, B. J. (1999). Women's satisfaction with birth control: A population survey of physical and psychological effects of oral contraceptives, intrauterine devices, condoms, natural family planning, and sterilization among 1466 women. *Contraception, 59,* 277–286.

O'DONOHUE, W., DOWNS, K., & YEATER, E. A. (1998). Sexual harassment: A review of the literature. *Aggression and Violent Behavior, 3,* 111–128.

O'DOWD, G. J., et al. (1997). Update on the appropriate staging evaluation for newly diagnosed prostate cancer. *Journal of Urology, 158,* 687–698.

OFSHE, R., & WATTERS, E. (1994). *Making monsters.* New York: Scribner's.

OGDEN, S. R., & BRADBURN, N. M. (1968). Dimensions of marriage happiness. *American Journal of Sociology, 73,* 715–731.

O'HARA, M. W. (1997). The nature of postpartum depression. In L. Murray & P. Cooper (Eds.), *Postpartum depression and child development* (pp. 3–31). New York: Guilford Press.

O'HARE, E. H., & O'DONOHUE, W. (1999). Sexual harassment: Identifying risk factors. *Archives of Sexual Behavior, 27,* 561–580.

OKAMI, P. (1991). Self-reports of "positive" childhood and adolescent sexual contacts with older persons: An exploratory study. *Archives of Sexual Behavior, 20,* 437–457.

OKAMI, P., & GOLDBERG, A. (1992). Personality correlates of pedophilia: Are they reliable indicators? *Journal of Sex Research, 29,* 297–328.

OLAFSON, E., CORWIN, D. L., & SUMMIT, R. C. (1993). Modern history of child sexual abuse awareness: Cycles of discovery and suppression. *Child Abuse & Neglect, 17,* 7–24.

OLDHAM, J. D., & KASSER, T. (1999). Attitude change in response to information that male homosexuality has a biological basis. *Journal of Sex & Marital Therapy, 25,* 121–124.

OLDS, J. (1958). Self-stimulation of the brain. *Science, 127,* 315–324.

OLIVER, M. B., & HYDE, J. S. (1993). Gender differences in sexuality: A meta-analysis. *Psychological Bulletin, 114,* 29–51.

OLSEN, O. (1997). Meta-analysis of the safety of home birth. *Birth, 24,* 4–13.

ONCALE, R. M., & KING, B. M. (2001). Comparison of men's and women's attempts to dissuade sexual partners from the couple using condoms. *Archives of Sexual Behavior,* in press.

O'NEILL, N., & O'NEILL, G. (1972). *Open marriage: A new life style for couples.* New York: M. Evans.

ORGEBIN-CRIST, M.-C. (1998). The epididymis across 24 centuries. *Journal of Reproduction and Fertility, 53* (Suppl.), 285–292.

ORY, H. W., ROSENFELD, A., & LANDMAN, L. C. (1980). The pill at 20: An assessment. *Family Planning Perspectives, 12,* 278–283.

OSMAN, A., & AL-SAWAF, M. (1995). Cross-cultural aspects of sexual anxieties and the associated dysfunction. *Journal of Sex Education and Therapy, 21,* 174–181.

OSTERGAARD, J., & KRAFT, M. (1992). Natural course of benign coital headache. *British Medical Journal, 305,* 1129.

O'SULLIVAN, C. S. (1991). Acquaintance gang rape on campus. In A. Parrot & L. Bechhofer (Eds.), *Acquaintance rape: The hidden crime.* New York: Wiley.

O'SULLIVAN, L. F., & ALLGEIER, E. R. (1994). Disassembling a stereotype: Gender differences in the use of token resistance. *Journal of Applied Social Psychology, 24,* 1035–1055.

O'SULLIVAN, L. F., & BYERS, E. S. (1992). College students' incorporation of imitation and restrictor roles in sexual dating interactions. *Journal of Sex Research, 29,* 435–446.

OUDSHOORN, N. E. J. (1997). Menopause, only for women? The social construction of menopause as an exclusively female condition. *Journal of Psychosomatic Obstetrics and Gynecology, 18,* 137–144.

OWEN, L. (1993). *Her blood is gold.* San Francisco: HarperCollins.

PADGETT, V. R., BRISLUTZ, J. A., & NEAL, J. A. (1989). Pornography, erotica, and attitudes toward women: The effects of repeated exposure. *Journal of Sex Research, 26,* 479–491.

PAGE, T. (1999). The graduate. *Washington Post Magazine, 152,* May 16, 18, 20.

PAIGE, K. E. (1978). The declining taboo against menstrual sex. *Psychology Today, 12*(7), 50–51.

PAIGE, K. E., & PAIGE, J. M. (1981). The politics of reproductive ritual. Berkeley: University of California Press.

PAINTER, K. (1999). Earlier, easier abortions. *USA Today,* August 4, D1–D2.

PALACE, E. M., & GORZALKA, B. B. (1992). Differential patterns of arousal in sexually functional and dysfunctional women: Physiological and subjective components of sexual response. *Archives of Sexual Behavior, 21,* 135–159.

PALMER, L. D. (1999). Hermaphrodite activists urge medical reforms. *Times-Picayune* (New Orleans), December 12, A28–A30. Newhouse News Service nationally released article.

PALMLUND, I. (1997). The social construction of menopause as risk. *Journal of Psychosomatic Obstetrics and Gynecology, 18,* 87–94.

PALYS, T. S. (1986). Testing the common wisdom: The social content of video pornography. *Canadian Psychology, 27,* 22–35.

PAN, E. (1999). Not Mother Nature's way. *Newsweek,* November 29, 106–108.

PANCHAUD, C., SINGH, S., FEIVELSON, D., & DARROCH, J. E. (2000). Sexually transmitted diseases among adolescents in developed countries. *Family Planning Perspectives, 32,* 24–32, 45.

PANSER, L. A., & PHIPPS, W. R. (1991). Type of oral contraceptive in relation to acute, initial episodes of pelvic inflammatory disease. *Contraception, 43,* 91–99.

PAPE, J. W., & WARREN, W. D., JR. (1993). AIDS in Haiti, 1982–1992. *Clinical Infectious Diseases, 17,* S341–S345.

PAPE, J. W., et al. (1990). Prevalence of HIV infection and high-risk activities in Haiti. *Journal of Acquired Immune Deficiency Syndromes, 3,* 995–1001.

PARDUN, C. J., & MCKEE, K. B. (1995). Strange bedfellows: Images of religion and sexuality on MTV. *Youth and Society, 26,* 438–449.

PARER, J. T., & KING, T. (2000). Fetal heart rate monitoring: Is it salvageable? *American Journal of Obstetrics and Gynecology, 182,* 982–987.

PARHAM, T., WHITE, J. L, & AJAMU, A. (1999). *The psychology of blacks: An African-centered perspective* (3rd ed.). Upper Saddle, NJ: Prentice Hall.

PARSONS, M. (2000). Sexuality and perversion a hundred years on: Discovering what Freud discovered. *International Journal of Psychoanalysis, 81,* 37–51.

PASTNER, C. M. (1986). The Westermarck hypothesis and first cousin marriage: The cultural modification of negative imprinting. *Journal of Anthropological Research, 24,* 573–586.

PATTATUCCI, A. M. L., & HAMER, D. H. (1995). Development and familiarity of sexual orientation in females. *Behavior Genetics, 25,* 407–420.

PATTERSON, C. J. (1992). Children of lesbian and gay parents. *Child Development, 63,* 1025–1042.

PATTERSON, C. (1997). Children of lesbian and gay parents. In T. Ollendick & R. Prinz (Eds.), *Advances in clinical child psychology,* Vol. 19. New York: Plenum Press.

PATTON, M. (1986). Twentieth-century attitudes toward masturbation. *Journal of Religion and Health, 25,* 291–302.

PAULOZZI, L. J., ERICKSON, J. D., & JACKSON, R. J. (1997). Hypospadias trends in two US surveillance systems. *Pediatrics, 100,* 831–834.

PAULSEN, C. A., BERMAN, N. G., & WANG, C. (1996). Data from men in greater Seattle area reveals no downward trend in semen quality: Further evidence that deterioration of semen quality is not geographically uniform. *Fertility and Sterility, 65,* 1015–1020.

PAULY, I. B. (1985). Gender identity disorder. In M. Farber (Ed.), *Human sexuality: Psychosexual effects of disease* (pp. 295–316). New York: Macmillan.

PECK, M. S. (1978). *The road less traveled: A new psychology of love, traditional values and spiritual growth.* New York: Touchstone.

PEELE, S. (1988). Fools for love: The romantic ideal, psychological theory, and addictive love. In R. J. Sternberg & M. L. Barnes (Eds.), *The psychology of love* (pp. 159–188). New Haven, CT: Yale University Press.

PEETERS, M., & SHARP, P. M. (2000). Genetic diversity of HIV-1: The moving target. *AIDS, 14,* S129–S140.

PELLETIER, L., & HAROLD, E. (1988). The relationship of age, sex guilt, and sexual experience with female sexual fantasies. *Journal of Sex Research, 24,* 250–256.

PENLAND, L. (1981). Sex education in 1900, 1940, and 1980: A historical sketch. *Journal of School Health, 51,* 305–309.

PENROD, S., & LINZ, D. (1984). Using psychological research on violent pornography to inform legal change. In N. M. Malamuth & E. Donnerstein (Eds.), *Pornography and sexual aggression* (pp. 247–275). Orlando, FL: Academic Press.

PENTON-VOAK, I. S., et al. (1999). Menstrual cycle alters face preference. *Nature, 399,* 741–742.

PEPLAU, L. A. (1988). Research on homosexual couples. In J. De Cecco (Ed.), *Gay relationships.* New York: Haworth Press.

PERELSON, A. S., et al. (1996). HIV-1 dynamics in vivo: Virion clearance rate, infected cell life-span, and viral generation time. *Science, 271,* 1582–1586.

PEREZ, E. D., MULLIGAN, T., & WAN, T. (1993). Why men are interested in an evaluation for a sexual problem. *Journal of the American Geriatric Society, 41,* 233–237.

PERRETTI, P. O., & ROWAN, M. (1983). Zoophilia: Factors related to its sustained practice. *Panminerva Medicine, 25,* 127.

PERRY, E. L., SCHMIDTKE, J. M., & KULIK, C. T. (1998). Propensity to sexually harass: An exploration of gender differences. *Sex Roles, 38,* 443–460.

PERRY, J. D., & WHIPPLE, B. (1981). Pelvic muscle strength of female ejaculators: Evidence in support of a new theory of orgasm. *Journal of Sex Research, 17,* 22–39.

PERSKY, H., et al. (1982). The relation of plasma androgen levels to sexual behavior and attitudes of women. *Psychosomatic Medicine, 44,* 305–319.

PERSON, E. S., et al. (1989). Gender differences in sexual behaviors and fantasies in a college population. *Journal of Sex & Marital Therapy, 15,* 187–198.

PETERS, S. D., WYATT, G. E., & FINKELHOR, D. (1986). Prevalence. In D. Finkelhor (Ed.), *A sourcebook on child sexual abuse* (pp. 15–59). Beverly Hills, CA: Sage.

PETERSON, H. B., et al. (2000). The risk of menstrual abnormalities after tubal sterilization. *New England Journal of Medicine, 343,* 1681–1687.

PETERSON, J. L., MOORE, K. A., & FURSTENBERG, F. F. (1991). Television viewing and early initiation of sexual intercourse: Is there a link? *Journal of Homosexuality, 21,* 93–119.

PETERSON, L. S., OAKLEY, D., POTTER, L. S., & DARROCH, J. E. (1998). Women's efforts to prevent pregnancy: Consistency of oral contraceptive use. *Family Planning Perspectives, 30,* 19–23.

PETITTI, D. B. (1992). Reconsidering the IUD. *Family Planning Perspectives, 24,* 33–35.

PETRI, JR., W. A., & SINGH, V. (1999). Diagnosis and management of amebiasis. *Clinical Infectious Diseases, 29,* 1117–1125.

PETROVIC, J. E. (1999). Moral democratic education and homosexuality: Censoring morality. *Journal of Moral Education, 28,* 201–209.

PETRUCCI, A., et al. (1997). How many HIV-infected individuals may be defined as long-term nonprogressors? A report from the Italian seroconversion study. *Journal of Acquired Immune Deficiency Syndromes and Human Retrovirology, 14,* 243–248.

PHELPS, D. L., et al. (1991). 28–day survival rates of 6676 neonates with birth weights of 1250 grams or less. *Pediatrics, 87,* 7–17.

PHI DELTA KAPPA/GALLUP POLL. (1998). The 30th annual Phi Delta Kappa/Gallup Poll of the public's attitudes toward the public schools. *Phi Delta Kappan,* September , 54.

PHILLIPS, G., & OVER, R. (1995). Differences between heterosexual, bisexual, and lesbian women in recalled childhood experiences. *Archives of Sexual Behavior, 24,* 1–10.

PIATUK, M. P., LUK, K.-C., WILLIAMS, B., & LIFSON, J. D. (1993). Quantitative competitive polymerase chain reaction of accurate quantitation of HIV DNA and RNA species. *BioTechniques, 14,* 70–77.

PICCININO, L. J., & MOSHER, W. D. (1998). Trends in contraceptive use in the United States. *Family Planning Perspectives, 30,* 4–10, 46.

PIMENTEL, D. (1998). Too many people for food resources and the environment. *Politics and the Life Sciences, 16,* 217–219.

PINES, A., & ARONSON, E. (1983). Antecedents, correlates, and consequences of sexual jealousy. *Journal of Personality, 51,* 108–136.

PLANNED PARENTHOOD. (1991). *Human sexuality: What children should know and when they should know it.* New York: Author.

PLANT, E. A., HYDE, J. S., KELTNER, D., & DEVINE, P. G. (2000). The gender stereotyping of emotions. *Psychology of Women Quarterly, 24,* 81–92.

PLANT, T. M., WINTERS, S. J., ATTARDI, B. J., & MAJUMDAR, S. S. (1993). The follicle stimulating hormone–inhibin feedback loop in male primates. *Human Reproduction, 8* (Suppl. 2), 41–44.

PLATT, R., RICE, P. A., & MCCORMICK, W. M. (1983). Risk of acquiring gonorrhea and prevalence of abnormal adnexal findings among women recently exposed to gonorrhea. *Journal of the American Medical Association, 250,* 3205–3209.

PLECK, J. H. (1976). The male sex role: Definitions, problems and sources of change. *Journal of Social Issues, 32*(3), 155–164.

POCS, O., & GODOW, A. G. (1977). Can students view parents as sexual beings? *Family Coordinator, 26,* 31–36.

POIRIER, J. C., & FRANKOVIC, J. (1996). Celibacy and charism in 1 Corinthians 7:5–7. *Harvard Theological Review, 89,* 1–19.

POLAND, R. L. (1990). The question of routine neonatal circumcision. *New England Journal of Medicine, 322,* 1312–1315.

POLASCHEK, D. L. L., WARD, T., & HUDSON, S. M. (1997). Rape and rapists: Theory and treatment. *Clinical Psychology Review, 17,* 117–144.

POMEROY, W. B. (1966). Normal vs. abnormal sex. *Sexology, 32,* 436–439.

POMEROY, W. B. (1972). *Dr. Kinsey and the Institute for Sex Research.* New York: Harper & Row.

POMEROY, W. B. (1975). The diagnosis and treatment of transvestites and transsexuals. *Journal of Sex & Marital Therapy, 1,* 215–224.

POPE, JR., H. G., & KATZ, D. L. (1988). Affective and psychotic symptoms associated with anabolic steroid use. *American Journal of Psychiatry, 145,* 487–490.

POPE, K. S. (1996). Memory, abuse, and science: Questioning claims about false memory syndrome epidemic. *American Psychologist, 51,* 957–974.

POPOVICH, P. M., & LICATA, B. J. (1986). Assessing the incidence and perceptions of sexual harassment behaviors among American undergraduates. *Journal of Psychology, 120,* 387–396.

POPOVICH, P. M., et al. (1996). Physical attractiveness and sexual harassment: Does every picture tell a story or every story draw a picture? *Journal of Applied Social Psychology, 26,* 520–542.

POPULATION COUNCIL. (1994, September 27). Copper T380A Intrauterine Device is effective for 10 years [News release].

PORTELLI, C. J., & MEADE, C. W. (1998). Censorship and the Internet: No easy answers. *SIECUS Report, 27,* 4–8.

PORTER, S., YUILLE, J. C., & LEHMAN, D. R. (1999). The nature of real, implanted, and fabricated childhood emotion events: Implications for the recovered memory debate. *Law and Human Behavior, 23,* 517–537.

POTTERAT, J. J., PHILLIPS, L., ROTHENBERG, R. B., & DARROW, W. V. (1985). On becoming a prostitute: An explanatory case-comparison study. *Journal of Sex Research, 21,* 329–335.

POTTERAT, J. J., WOODHOUSE, D. E., MUTH, J. B., & MUTH, S. Q. (1990). Estimating the prevalence and career longevity of prostitute women. *Journal of Sex Research, 27,* 233–243.

POTTERAT, J. J., et al. (1998). Pathways to prostitution: The chronology of sexual and drug abuse milestones. *Journal of Sex Research, 35,* 333–340.

POTTS, M. (2000). The unmet need for family planning. *Scientific American,* January, 88–93.

POWLISHTA, K., SERBIN, L., & MOLLER, L. (1993). The stability of individual differences in gender typing: Implication for understanding gender segregation. *Sex Roles, 29,* 723–737.

PRENTKY, R. A., KNIGHT, R. A., & ROSENBERG, R. (1988). Validation analysis on a taxonomic system for rapists: Disconfirmation and reconceptualization. *Annals of the New York Academy of Sciences, 528,* 21–40.

PRENTKY, R. A., LEE, A. F. S., KNIGHT, R. A., & CERCE, D. (1997). Recidivism rates among child molesters and rapists: A methodological analysis. *Law and Human Behavior, 21,* 635–659.

PRENTKY, R. A., et al. (1989). Developmental antecedents of sexual aggression. *Development and Psychopathology, 1,* 153–169.

PRETI, G., et al. (1986). Human axillary secretions influence women's menstrual cycles: The role of donor extract of females. *Hormones and Behavior, 20,* 474–482.

PRICE, V., SCANLON, B., & JANUS, M.-D. (1984). Social characteristics of adolescent male prostitution. *Victimology, 9,* 211–221.

PRINCE, V., & BENTLER, P. M. (1972). Survey of 504 cases of transvestism. *Psychological Reports, 31,* 903–917.

PROFET, M. (1993). Menstruation as a defense against pathogens transported by sperm. *Quarterly Review of Biology, 68,* 335–381.

PRYOR, J. B. (1987). Sexual harassment proclivities in men. *Sex Roles, 17,* 269–289.

PURCELL, D. W., BLANCHARD, R., & ZUCKER, K. J. (2000). Birth order in a contemporary sample of gay men. *Archives of Sexual Behavior, 29,* 349–356.

PURNINE, D. M., & CAREY, M. P. (1997). Interpersonal communication and sexual adjustment: The roles of understanding and agreement. *Journal of Consulting and Clinical Psychology, 65,* 1017–1025.

PYETT, P. M., & WARR, D. J. (1997). Vulnerability on the streets: Female sex workers and HIV risk. *AIDS Care, 9,* 539–547.

QUADAGNO, D., et al. (1998). Ethnic differences in sexual decisions and sexual behavior. *Archives of Sexual Behavior, 27,* 57–75.

QUAKENBUSH, D. M., STRASSBERG, D. S., & TURNER, C. W. (1995). Gender effects of romantic themes in erotica. *Archives of Sexual Behavior, 24,* 21–35.

QUEEN, S., HABENSTEIN, R., & QUADAGNO, J. (1985). *The family in various cultures* (5th ed.). New York: Harper & Row.

QUINN, T. C., et al. (2000). Viral load and heterosexual transmission of human immunodeficiency virus type 1. *New England Journal of Medicine, 342,* 921–929.

QUINSEY, V., CHAPLIN, T., & UPFOLD, D. (1984). Sexual arousal to nonsexual violence and sadomasochistic themes among rapists and non-sex-offenders. *Journal of Consulting and Clinical Psychology, 52,* 651–657.

QUINSEY, V. L., et al. (1995). Predicting sexual offenses. In J. C. Campbell (Ed.), *Assessing dangerousness: Violence by sexual offenders, batterers, and child abusers* (pp. 114–137). Thousand Oaks, CA: Sage.

RABKIN, J. G., & CHESNEY, M. (1999). Treatment adherence to HIV medications—The Achilles heel of the new therapeutics. In D. G. Ostrow & S. C. Kalichman (Eds.), *Psychosocial and public health impacts of new HIV therapies* (pp. 61–82). New York: Plenum Press.

RABOCH, J., & RABOCH, J. (1992). Infrequent orgasms in women. *Journal of Sex & Marital Therapy, 18,* 114–120.

RACHMAN, S. (1966). Sexual fetishism: An experimental analogue. *Psychological Record, 16,* 293–296.

RADA, R. T., et al. (1983). Plasma androgens in violent and nonviolent sex offenders. *Bulletin of the American Academy of Psychiatry and the Law, 11,* 149–158.

RAFFAELLI, M., BOGENSCHNEIDER, L., & FLOOD, M. F. (1998). Parent-teen communication about sexual topics. *Journal of Family Issues, 19,* 315–333.

RAISLER, J., ALEXANDER, C., & O'CAMPO, P. (1999). Breast-feeding and infant illness: A dose-response relationship? *American Journal of Public Health, 89,* 25–30.

RAKIC, Z., STARCEVIC, V., STARCEVIC, V. P., & MARINKOVIC, J. (1997). Testosterone treatment in men with erectile disorder and low levels of total testosterone in serum. *Archives of Sexual Behavior, 26,* 495–504.

RAKO, S. (1996). *The hormone of desire: The truth about sexuality, menopause, and testosterone.* New York: Harmony Books.

RANGARAJAN, A., & GLEASON, P. (1998). Young unwed fathers of AFDC children: Do they provide support? *Demography, 35,* 175–186.

RAPAPORT, K., & BURKHART, B. R. (1984). Personality and attitudinal characteristics of sexually coercive college males. *Journal of Abnormal Psychology, 93,* 216–221.

RAPHAEL, S., & ROBINSON, M. (1980). The older lesbian: Love relationships and friendship patterns. *Alternate Lifestyles, 3,* 207–229.

RAPOPORT, N. (1994). *A woman's book of grieving.* New York: William Morrow.

RAUBE, K., & MERRELL, K. (1999). Maternal minimum-stay legislation: Cost and policy implications. *American Journal of Public Health, 89,* 922–923.

READ, K. (1993). Male rape: One of the last taboo topics. *Times-Picayune* (New Orleans), April 27, E-1, E-3.

RECUR, P. (1993). Study: Male homosexual gene pattern is found. *Times-Picayune* (New Orleans), July 17, G-20.

REECE, R. (1988). Special issues in the etiologies and treatments of sexual problems among gay men. *Journal of Homosexuality, 15,* 43–57.

REGAN, P. C. (1998). Of lust and love: Beliefs about the role of sexual desire in romantic relationships. *Personal Relationships, 5,* 139–157.

REGAN, P. C., & BERSCHEID, E. (1997). Gender differences in characteristics desired in a potential sexual and marriage partner. *Journal of Psychology & Human Sexuality, 9,* 25–37.

REICHERT, T., et al. (1999). Cheesecake and beefcake: No matter how you slice it, sexual explicitness in advertising continues to increase. *Journalism & Mass Communication Quarterly, 76,* 7–20.

REILLY, M. E., LOTT, B., & GALLOGLY, S. M. (1986). Sexual harassment of university students. *Sex Roles, 15,* 333–358.

REINEKE, M. J. (1995). Out of order: A critical perspective on women in religion. In J. Freeman (Ed.), *Women: A feminist perspective* (5th ed., pp. 395–414). Mountain View, CA: Mayfield.

REINHOLTZ, R. K., & MUEHLENHARD, C. L. (1995). Genital perceptions and sexual activity in a college population. *Journal of Sex Research, 32,* 155–165.

REINISCH, J. M. (1990). *The Kinsey Institute new report on sex.* New York: St. Martin's.

REISMAN, J. A., & EICHEL, E. W. (1990). *Kinsey, sex and fraud: The indoctrination of a people.* Lafayette, LA: Huntington House.

REISS, I. L. (1980). *Family systems in America.* New York: Holt, Rinehart & Winston.

REISS, I. L., & LEIK, R. K. (1989). Evaluating strategies to avoid AIDS: Number of partners versus use of condoms. *Journal of Sex Research, 4,* 411–433.

REISS, M. J. (1995). Conflicting philosophies of school sex education. *Journal of Moral Education, 24,* 371–382.

REISS, M. J. (1999). How should we teach in schools about sexual orientation? A rejoinder to Petrovic. *Journal of Moral Education, 28,* 211–214.

RENSHAW, D. (1990). Short-term therapy for sexual dysfunction: Brief counseling to manage vaginismus. *Clinical Practice in Sexuality, 6*(5), 23–29.

RENTZEL, L. (1972). *When all the laughter died in sorrow.* New York: Saturday Review Press.

REPORT OF THE COMMISSION ON OBSCENITY AND PORNOGRAPHY. (1970). New York: Bantam Books.

RESNICK, M., et al. (1997). Protecting adolescents from harm: Findings from the National Longitudinal Study on Adolescent Health. *Journal of the American Medical Association, 278,* 823–832.

REUTER, S. (1999). Barriers to the use of IUDs as emergency contraception. *British Journal of Family Planning, 25,* 63–68.

RHODES, J. C., KJERULFF, K. H., LANGENBERG, P. W., & GUZINKSI, G. M. (1999). Hysterectomy and sexual functioning. *Journal of the American Medical Association, 282,* 1934–1941.

RICE, G., ANDERSON, C., RISCH, N., & EBERS, G. (1999). Male homosexuality: Absence of linkage to microsatellite markers at Xq28. *Science, 284,* 665–667.

RICE, P. A., & SCHACHTER, J. (1991). Pathogenesis of pelvic inflammatory disease. *Journal of the American Medical Association, 266,* 2587–2593.

RICHARDS, E., TEPPER, M., WHIPPLE, B., & KOMISARUK, B. R. (1997). Women with complete spinal cord injury: A phenomenological study of sexuality and relationship experiences. *Sexuality and Disability, 15,* 271–283.

RICHARDS, R., & AMES, J. (1983). *Second serve.* New York: Stein & Day.

RICHMAN, K. M., & RICKMAN, L. S. (1993). The potential for transmission of human immunodeficiency virus through human bites. *Journal of Acquired Immune Deficiency Syndromes, 6,* 402–406.

RICHTERS, J., GEROFI, J., & DONOVAN, B. (1995). Are condoms the right size(s)? A method for self-measurement of the erect penis. *Venereology, 8,* 77–81.

RICHTERS, J. M. A. (1997). Menopause in different cultures. *Journal of Psychosomatic Obstetrics and Gynecology, 18,* 73–80.

RIGHETTI-VELTEMA, M., CONNE-PERRÉARD, E., BOUSQUET, A., & MANZANO, J. (1998). Risk factors and predictive signs of postpartum depression. *Journal of Affective Disorders, 49,* 167–180.

RIMM, M. (1995). Marketing pornography on the information superhighway: A survey of 917, 410 images. *Georgetown Law Review, 83,* 1849–1925.

RIND, B. (1998). Biased use of cross-cultural and historical perspectives on male homosexuality in human sexuality textbooks. *Journal of Sex Research, 35,* 397–407.

RIND, B., & TROMOVITCH, P. (1997). A meta-analytic review of findings from national samples on psychological correlates of child sexual abuse. *Journal of Sex Research, 34,* 237–255.

RIND, B., TROMOVITCH, P., & BAUSERMAN, R. (1998). A meta-analytic examination of assumed properties of child sexual abuse using college samples. *Psychological Bulletin, 124,* 22–53.

RINEHART, W., & PIOTROW, P. T. (1979). OCs: Update on usage, safety, and side effects. *Population Reports,* Series A, January.

RIO, L. (1991). Psychological and sociological research and the decriminalization or legalization of prostitution. *Archives of Sexual Behavior, 20,* 205–217.

RIORDAN, S. (1999). Indecent exposure: The impact upon the victim's fear of sexual crime. *Journal of Forensic Psychiatry, 10,* 309–316.

RISMAN, B. J., & SCHWARTZ, P. (1989). Being gendered: A microstructural view of intimate relationships. In B. J. Risman & P. Schwartz (Eds.), *Gender in intimate relationships: A microstructural approach.* Belmont, CA: Wadsworth.

RIVKIN-FISH, M. (1999). Sexuality education in Russia: Defining pleasure and danger for a fledgling democratic society. *Social Science & Medicine, 49,* 801–814.

ROAN, S. (1995). Are we teaching too little, too late? *Los Angeles Times,* July 12, E1, E4.

ROBBINS, M., & JENSEN, G. (1978). Multiple orgasm in males. *Journal of Sex Research, 14,* 21–26.

ROBERTS, C., GREEN, R., WILLIAMS, K., & GOODMAN, M. (1987). Boyhood gender identity development: A statistical contrast of two family groups. *Developmental Psychology, 23,* 544–557.

ROBERTS, T. W. (1992). Sexual attraction and romantic love: Forgotten variables in marital therapy. *Journal of Marital and Family Therapy, 18,* 357–364.

ROBINSON, A. J., & RIDGWAY, G. L. (1994). Sexually transmitted diseases in children: Non viral including bacterial vaginosis, *Gardnerella vaginalis,* mycoplasmas, *Trichomonas vaginalis, Candida albicans,* scabies and pubic lice. *Genitourinary Medicine, 70,* 208–214.

ROBINSON, H. (1992). Sex, marriage, and divorce. *Christianity Today, 36*(15), 29–33.

ROBINSON, O. G., BRADLEY, E. L., & WILSON, D. S. (1995). Analysis of explanted silicone implants: A report of 300 patients. *Annals of Plastic Surgery, 34,* 1–6.

RODRIGUEZ, M., et al., (1996). Teaching our teachers to teach: A SIECUS study on training and preparation for HIV/AIDS prevention and sexuality education. *SIECUS Report, 28*(2), 3–11.

ROEHRBORN, C. G., & McCONNELL, J. D. (1991). *Benign prostatic hyperplasia guideline panel, 1991.* Agency for Health Care Policy and Research.

ROGERS, A. S., et al. (1993). Investigation of potential HIV transmission to the patients of an HIV-infected surgeon. *Journal of the American Medical Association, 269,* 1795–1801.

ROGERS, D. E. (1992). Report card on our national response to the AIDS epidemic—some A's, too many D's. *American Journal of Public Health, 82,* 522–524.

ROGERS, S. M., & TURNER, C. F. (1991). Male-male sexual contact in the U.S.A.: Findings from five sample surveys, 1970–1990. *Journal of Sex Research, 28,* 491–519.

ROMIEU, I., BERLIN, J. A., & COLDITZ, G. (1990). Oral contraceptives and breast cancer: Review and meta-analysis. *Cancer, 66,* 2253–2263.

ROSARIO, M., et al. (1996). The psychosexual development of urban lesbian, gay, and bisexual youths. *Journal of Sex Research, 33,* 113–126.

ROSCOE, B., GOODWIN, M., REPP, S., & ROSE, M. (1987). Sexual harassment of university student and student-employees: Findings and implications. *College Student Journal, 12,* 254–273.

ROSE, M. K., & SOARES, H. H. (1993). Sexual adaptations of the frail elderly: A realistic approach. *Journal of Gerontological Social Work, 19,* 167–178.

ROSEN, M. G., DICKINSON, J. C., & WESTHOFF, C. L. (1991). Vaginal birth after cesarean: A meta-analysis of morbidity and mortality. *Obstetrics and Gynecology, 77,* 465–470.

ROSEN, R. C. (1991). Alcohol and drug effects on sexual response: Human experimental and clinical studies. *Annual Review of Sex Research, 2,* 119–179.

ROSEN, R. C., LANE, R. M., & MENZA, M. (1999). Effects of SSRIs on sexual function: A critical review. *Journal of Clinical Psychopharmacology, 19,* 67–85.

ROSENBERG, H. M., et al. (1996). Birth and deaths: United States, 1995. *Monthly Vital Statistics Report, 45*(3), Suppl. 2.

ROSENBERG, M. (1998). Weight change with oral contraceptive use during the menstrual cycle: Results of daily measurements. *Contraception, 58,* 345–349.

ROSENBERG, M. J., & GOLLUB, E. L. (1992). Methods women can use that may prevent sexually transmitted diseases, including HIV. *American Journal of Public Health, 82,* 1473–1478.

ROSENBERG, M. J., WAUGH, M. S., SOLOMON, H. M., & LYSZKOWSKI, A. D. L. (1996). The male polyurethane condom: A review of current knowledge. *Contraception, 53,* 141–146.

ROSENBERG, M. J., et al. (1992). Barrier contraceptives and sexually transmitted diseases in women: A comparison of female-dependent methods and condoms. *American Journal of Public Health, 82,* 669–674.

ROSENBLATT, K. A., et al. (1996). Intrauterine devices and endometrial cancer. *Contraception, 54,* 329–332.

ROSENFIELD, J. A., ZAHORIK, P. M., SAINT, W., & MURPHY, G. (1993). Women's satisfaction with birth control. *Journal of Family Practice, 36,* 169–173.

ROSENTHAL, D. A., & FELDMAN, S. S. (1999). The importance of importance: Adolescents' perceptions of parental communication about sexuality. *Journal of Adolescence, 22,* 835–851.

ROSMAN, J. P., & RESNICK, P. J. (1989). Sexual attraction to corpses: A psychiatric review of necrophilia. *Bulletin of the American Academy of Psychiatry and the Law, 17,* 153–163.

ROSS, J. A. (1989). Contraception: Short-term vs. long-term failure rates. *Family Planning Perspectives, 21,* 275–277.

ROTHERAM, M. J., & WEINER, N. (1983). Androgyny, stress, and satisfaction: Dual-career and traditional relationships. *Sex Roles, 9,* 151–158.

ROTHMAN, E. K. (1984). *Hands and hearts: A history of courtship in America.* New York: Basic Books.

ROTHMAN, K. J., et al. (1995). Teratogenicity of high vitamin A intake. *New England Journal of Medicine, 333,* 1369–1373.

ROTHSCHILD, B. S., FAGAN, P. J., WOODALL, C., & ANDERSON, A. E. (1991). Sexual functioning of female-disordered patients. *International Journal of Eating Disorders, 10,* 389–394.

ROWLAND, D. L. (1998). Penile sensitivity in men: A composite of recent findings. *Urology, 52,* 1101–1105.

ROWLAND, D. L., & BURNETT, A. L. (2000). Pharmacotherapy in the treatment of male sexual dysfunction. *Journal of Sex Research, 37,* 226–243.

ROWLAND, D. L., COOPER, S. E., & SCHNEIDER, M. (2000). Defining premature ejaculation for experimental and clinical investigations. *Archives of Sexual Behavior, 30,* 235–253.

ROWLAND, D. L., KALLAN, K., & SLOB, A. (1997). Yohimbine, erectile capacity, and sexual response in men. *Archives of Sexual Behavior, 26,* 49–62.

ROWLAND, D. L., et al. (1987). Endocrine, psychological and genital response to sexual arousal in men. *Psychoneuroendocrinology, 12,* 149–158.

ROZEMA, H. J. (1986). Defensive communication climate as a barrier to sex education in the home. *Family Relations, 35,* 531–537.

ROZENBERG, S., et al. (1994). Osteoporosis prevention with sex hormone replacement therapy. *International Journal of Fertility, 39,* 262–271.

RUBIN, A. M., & ADAMS, J. R. (1986). Outcomes of sexually open marriages. *Journal of Sex Research, 22,* 311–319.

RUBIN, R. T., REINISCH, J. M., & HASKETT, R. F. (1981). Postnatal gonadal steroid effects on human behavior. *Science, 211,* 1318–1324.

RUBIN, Z. (1988). Preface. In R. J. Sternberg & M. L. Barnes (Eds.), *The psychology of love* (pp. vii–xii). New Haven, CT: Yale University Press.

RUBIN, Z., et al. (1980). Self-disclosure in dating couples: Sex roles and the ethic of openness. *Journal of Marriage and the Family, 42,* 305.

RUDLINGER, R., & NORVAL, M. (1996). Human papillomavirus infections. In P. Elsner & A. Eichmann (Eds.), *Sexually transmitted diseases. Advances in diagnosis and treatment* (pp. 67–76) Basel: Karger.

RUGPAO, S., et al. (1997). Multiple condom use and decreased condom breakage and slippage in Thailand. *Journal of Acquired Immune Deficiency Syndromes and Human Retrovirology, 14,* 169–173.

RUSSELL, C. D., & ELLIS, J. B. (1991). Sex-role development in single parent households. *Social Behavior and Personality, 19,* 5–9.

RUSSELL, D. E. H. (Ed.). (1984). *Sexual exploitation: Rape, child sexual abuse and workplace harassment.* Beverly Hills, CA: Sage.

RUSSELL, D. E. H. (1986). *The secret trauma: Incest in the lives of girls and women.* New York: Basic Books.

RUSSELL, D. E. H. (1990). *Rape in marriage* (rev. ed.). Bloomington: Indiana University Press.

RUSSO, N. F., & DABUL, A. J. (1997). The relationship of abortion to well-being: Do race and religion make a difference. *Professional Psychology: Research and Practice, 28,* 23–31.

RUTHERFORD, G. W., et al. (1990). Course of HIV-1 infection in a cohort of homosexual and bisexual men: An 11 year follow up study. *British Medical Journal, 301,* 1183–1188.

RYAN, A. S. (1997). The resurgence of breast-feeding in the United States. *Pediatrics, 99,* E12.

RYAN, G. (2000). Childhood sexuality: A decade of study. Pt. I. Research and curriculum development. *Child Abuse & Neglect, 24,* 33–48.

RYND, N. (1987). Incidence of psychosomatic symptoms in rape victims. *Journal of Sex Research, 24,* 155–161.

SACHS, A. (1990). Handing out scarlet letters. *Time,* October 1, 98.

SADKER, M., & SADKER, D. (1994). *Failing at fairness: How America's schools cheat girls.* New York: Scribner's.

SALHOLZ, E., SPRINGEN, K., DE LA PEÑA, N., & WITHERSPOON, D. (1990). A frightening aftermath: Concern about AIDS adds to the trauma of rape. *Newsweek,* July 23, 53.

SALOVEY, P., & RODIN, J. (1985). The heart of jealousy. *Psychology Today,* September, 22–29.

SALT, R. E. (1991). Affectionate touch between fathers and preadolescent sons. *Journal of Marriage and the Family, 53,* 545–554.

SALUTER, A. F. (1996). Marital status and living arrangements: March 1994. *Current Population Reports.*

SANCHEZ, Y. M. (1997). Families of Mexican origin. In M. K. DeGenova (Ed.), *Families in cultural context: Strengths and challenges in diversity.* Mountain View, CA: Mayfield.

SANDAY, P. (1981). The socio-cultural context of rape: A cross-cultural study. *Journal of Social Issues, 37,* 5–27.

SANDAY, P. (1990). *Fraternity gang rape: Sex, brotherhood and privilege on campus.* New York: New York University Press.

SANDBERG, D. E., & MEYER-BAHLBURG, H. F. L. (1994). Variability in middle childhood play behavior: Effects of gender, age, and family background. *Archives of Sexual Behavior, 23,* 645–663.

SANDERS, G., & WRIGHT, M. (1997). Sexual orientation differences in cerebral asymmetry and in the performances of sexually dimorphic and motor tasks. *Archives of Sexual Behavior, 26,* 463–480.

SANDERS, S. A., & REINISCH, J. M. (1999). Would you say you "had sex" if . . . ? *Journal of the American Medical Association, 281,* 275–277.

SANDNABBA, N. K., SANTTILA, P., & NORDLING, N. (1999). Sexual behavior and social adaptation among sadomasochistically-oriented males. *Journal of Sex Research, 36,* 273–282.

SANGI-HAGHPEYKAR, H., et al. (1996). Experiences of injectable contraceptive users in urban setting. *Obstetrics and Gynecology, 88,* 227–233.

SANGRADOR, J. L., & YELA, C. (2000). "What is beautiful is loved": Physical attractiveness in love relationships in a representative sample. *Social Behavior and Personality, 28,* 207–218.

SANTELLI, J. S., et al. (1998). Multiple sexual partners among U.S. adolescents and young adults. *Family Planning Perspectives, 30,* 271–275.

SARREL, P., & MASTERS, W. (1982). Sexual molestation of men by women. *Archives of Sexual Behavior, 11*(2), 117–131.

SARREL, P. M. (2000). Effects of hormone replacement therapy on sexual psychophysiology and behavior in postmenopause. *Journal of Women's Health & Gender-Based Medicine, 9,* S25–S32.

SARVELA, P. D., et al. (1992). Connotative meanings assigned to contraceptive options. *Journal of American College Health, 41,* 91–97.

SARWER, D. B., et al. (1993). Sexual aggression and love styles: An exploratory study. *Archives of Sexual Behavior, 22,* 265–275.

SARWER, D. B., & DURLAK, J. A. (1996). Childhood sexual abuse as a predictor of adult female sexual dysfunction: A study of couples seeking sex therapy. *Child Abuse & Neglect, 20,* 963–972.

SATTIN, R. W., et al. (1986). Oral-contraceptive use and the risk of breast cancer: The Cancer and Steroid Hormone Study of the Centers for Disease Control and the National Institute of Child Health and Human Development. *New England Journal of Medicine, 315,* 405–411.

SAUER, M. V., PAULSON, R. J., & LOBO, R. A. (1992). Reversing the natural decline in human fertility. *Journal of the American Medical Association, 268,* 1275–1279.

SAUER, M. V., PAULSON, R. J., & LOBO, R. A. (1993). Pregnancy after age 50: Application of oocyte donation to women after natural menopause. *Lancet, 341,* 321–323.

SAUNDERS, E. J. (1989). Life-threatening autoerotic behavior: A challenge for sex educators and therapists. *Journal of Sex Education and Therapy, 15*(2), 77–81.

SAUNDERS, N. (1997). Pregnancy in the 21st century: Back to nature with a little assistance. *Lancet, 349,* 517–519.

SAVITZ, L., & ROSEN, L. (1988). The sexuality of prostitutes: Sexual enjoyment reported by streetwalkers. *Journal of Sex Research, 24,* 200–208.

SAYWITZ, K. J., MANNARINO, A. P., BERLINER, L., & COHEN, J. A. (2000). Treatment for sexually abused children and adolescents. *American Psychologist, 55,* 1040–1049.

SCARCE, M. (1997). Same-sex rape of male college students. *Journal of American College of Health, 45,* 171–173.

SCHACHTER, J., et al. (1986). Prospective study of perinatal transmission of *Chlamydia trachomatis. Journal of the American Medical Association, 255,* 3374–3377.

SCHACHTER, M., & SHOHAM, Z. (1994). Amenorrhea during the reproductive years—Is it safe? *Fertility and Sterility, 62,* 1–16.

SCHACTER, S., & SINGER, J. (1962). Cognitive, social and physiological determinants of emotional state. *Psychological Review, 69,* 379–399.

SCHAEFFER, K. W., et al. (1999). Religiously-motivated sexual orientation change: A follow-up study. *Journal of Psychology and Theology, 27,* 329–337.

SCHAFF, E. A., et al. (2000). Low-dose mifepristone followed by vaginal misoprostol at 48 hours for abortion up to 63 days. *Contraception, 61,* 41–46.

SCHAIRER, C., et al. (2000). Menopausal estrogen and estrogen-progestin replacement therapy and breast cancer risk. *Journal of the American Medical Association, 283,* 485–491.

SCHIAVI, R. C. (1990). Sexuality and aging in men. *Annual Review of Sex Research, 1,* 227–249.

SCHIEVE, L. A., et al. (1999). Live-birth rates and multiple-birth risk using in vitro fertilization. *Journal of the American Medical Association, 282,* 1832–1838.

SCHIFFMAN, M., et al. (2000). HPV DNA testing in cervical cancer screening: Results from women in a high-risk province of Costa Rica. *Journal of the American Medical Association, 283,* 87–93.

SCHIFFMAN, M. H., & BRINTON, L. A. (1995). The epidemiology of cervical carcinogenesis. *Cancer, 76,* 1888–1901.

SCHLEGEL, A., & BARRY III, H. (1980). The evolutionary significance of adolescent initiation ceremonies. *American Ethnologist, 7,* 696–715.

SCHLEGEL, W. S. (1962). Die konstitutionbiologischen grundlagen der homosexualitat. *Zeitschrift fuer Menschliche Vererbungs und Konstitutionslehre, 36,* 341–364.

SCHLOSSER, E. (1997). The business of pornography. *Newsweeek,* February 10, 42–52.

SCHNEIDER, D., BARRETT-CONNOR, E., & MORTON, D. (1997). Timing of postmenopausal estrogen for optimal bone mineral density. *Journal of the American Medical Association, 277,* 543–547.

SCHNYDER, V., SCHNYDER-LUTHI, C., BALLINARI, P., & BLASER, A. (1998). Therapy for vaginismus: In vivo versus in vitro desensitization. *Canadian Journal of Psychiatry, 43,* 941–944.

SCHOBEL, H. P., et al. (1996). Preeclampsia—a state of sympathetic overactivity. *New England Journal of Medicine, 335,* 1480–1485.

SCHOEN, E. J. (1990). The status of circumcision of newborns. *New England Journal of Medicine, 322,* 1308–1312.

SCHOLES, D., DALING, J. R., & STERGACHIS, A. S. (1992). Current cigarette smoking and risk of acute pelvic inflammatory disease. *American Journal of Public Health, 82,* 1352–1355.

SCHOPENHAVER, A. (1966). *The world as will and representation,* Vol. 2. New York: Dover.

SCHOVER, L. R., & JENSEN, S. B. (1988). *Sexuality and chronic illness: A comprehensive approach.* New York: Guilford Press.

SCHOVER, L. R., & LEIBLUM, S. R. (1994). Commentary: The stagnation of sex therapy. *Journal of Psychology & Human Sexuality, 6*(3), 5–30.

SCHOVER, L. R., et al. (1982). Multiaxial problem-oriented system for sexual dysfunctions. *Archives of General Psychiatry, 39,* 614–619.

SCHULT, D. G., & SCHNEIDER, L. J. (1991). The role of provocativeness, rape history, and observer sex in attributions of blame in sexual assault. *Journal of Interpersonal Violence, 6,* 94–101.

SCHULTZ, W. C. M., et al. (1989). Vaginal sensitivity to electric stimuli: Theoretical and practical implications. *Archives of Sexual Behavior, 18,* 87–95.

SCHUSTER, M. A., BELL, R. M., BERRY, S. H., & KANOUSE, D. E. (1998). Impact of a high school condom availability program on sexual attitudes and behaviors. *Family Planning Perspectives, 30,* 67–72, 88.

SCHUSTER, M. A., BELL, R. M., & KANOUSE, D. E. (1996). The sexual practices of adolescent virgins: Genital sexual activities of high school students who have never had vaginal intercourse. *American Journal of Public Health, 86,* 1570–1576.

SCHUSTER, M. A., BELL, R. M., PETERSEN, L. P., & KANOUSE, D. E. (1996). Communication between adolescents and physicians about sexual behavior and risk prevention. *Archives of Pediatrics and Adolescent Medicine, 150,* 906–913.

SCHUTTE, J. W., & HOSCH, H. M. (1997). Gender differences in sexual assault verdicts: A meta-analysis. *Journal of Social Behavior and Personality, 12,* 759–772.

SCHWARTZ, G. (1973). Devices to prevent masturbation. *Medical Aspects of Human Sexuality,* May, 141–153.

SCHWARTZ, P. (1994). *Peer marriage.* New York: Free Press.

SCHWINGL, P. J., & GUESS, H. A. (2000). Safety and effectiveness of vasectomy. *Fertility and Sterility, 73,* 923–936.

SCOTT, J. E. (1986). An updated longitudinal content analysis of sex references in mass circulation magazines. *Journal of Sex Research, 22,* 385–392.

SCOTT, J. E., & CUVELIER, S. J. (1993). Violence and sexual violence in pornography: Is it really increasing? *Archives of Sexual Behavior, 22,* 357–371.

SCOTTI, J. R., SLACK, B. S., BOWMAN, R. A., & MORRIS, T. L. (1996). College student attitudes concerning the sexuality of persons with mental retardation: Development of the perceptions of sexuality scale. *Sexuality and Disability, 14,* 249–263.

SEAL, A. (1996). Women, STDs and safe sex: A review of the evidence. *Venereology, 9,* 48–53.

SEAMAN, B. (1972). *Free and female.* New York: Coward, McGann & Geoghegan.

SEGHORN, T. K., PRENTKY, R. A., & BOUCHER, R. J. (1987). Childhood sexual abuse in the lives of sexually aggressive offenders. *Journal of the American Academy of Child and Adolescent Psychiatry, 26,* 262–267.

SEGRAVES, R. T., & SEGRAVES, K. B. (1995). Human sexuality and aging. *Journal of Sex Education and Therapy, 21,* 88–102.

SEIDMAN, S. N., & RIEDER, R. O. (1994). A review of sexual behavior in the United States. *American Journal of Psychiatry, 151,* 330–341.

SELKIN, J. (1975). Rape. *Psychology Today, 8,* 70–76.

SELL, R. L. (1997). Defining and measuring sexual orientation: A review. *Archives of Sexual Behavior, 26,* 643–658.

SELL, R. L., WELLS, J. A., & WYPIJ, D. (1995). The prevalence of homosexual behavior and attraction in the United States, the United Kingdom and France: Results of national population-based samples. *Archives of Sexual Behavior, 24,* 235–248.

SEMANS, J. H. (1956). Premature ejaculation: A new approach. *Journal of Southern Medicine, 79,* 353–361.

SENANAYAKE, P. (1990). IUDs: A global review. XVIIth Current Fertility Control Symposium. *British Journal of Family Planning, 15* (Suppl.), 8–12.

SENN, C. Y., DESMARAIS, S., VERBERG, N., & WOOD, E. (2000). Predicting coercive sexual behavior across the lifespan in a random sample of Canadian men. *Journal of Social and Personal Relationships, 17,* 95–113.

SETO, M. C., & BARBAREE, H. E. (1995). The role of alcohol in sexual aggression. *Clinical Psychology Review, 15,* 545–566.

SEVERY, L. J., & SPIELER, J. (2000). New methods of family planning: Implications for intimate behavior. *Journal of Sex Research, 37,* 258–265.

SHACKELFORD, T. K., & BUSS, D. M. (1997). Marital satifaction in evolutionary perspective. In R. J. Sternberg & M. Hojjat (Eds.), *Satisfaction in close relationships* (pp. 7–25). New York: Guilford Press.

SHANNON, J. W., & WOODS, W. J. (1991). Affirmative psychotherapy for gay men. *Counseling Psychologist, 19,* 197–215.

SHANTHA, T. R., SHANTHA, D. T., & BENNETT, J. K. (1990). Priapism. *Medical Aspects of Human Sexuality,* April, 63–67.

SHAPIRO, L. (1990). Guns and dolls. *Newsweek,* May 28, 54–65.

SHAPIRO, M. F., et al. (1999). Variations in the care of HIV-infected adults in the United States: Results from the HIV cost and utilization study. *Journal of the American Medical Association, 281,* 2305–2315.

SHARLAND, M., et al. (1997). Paediatric HIV infections. *Archives of Disease in Childhood, 76,* 293–297.

SHARPSTEEN, D. J. (1991). Organization of jealousy knowledge: Romantic jealousy as a blended emotion. In P. Salovey (Ed.), *The psychology of jealousy and envy* (pp. 31–51). New York: Guilford Press.

SHAUGHNESSY, M. F., & SHAKESBY, P. (1992). Adolescent sexual and emotional intimacy. *Adolescence, 27,* 475–480.

SHAVER, P., HAZAN, C., & BRADSHAW, D. (1988). Love as attachment. In R. J. Sternberg & M. L. Barnes (Eds.), *The psychology of love* (pp. 68–99). New Haven, CT: Yale University Press.

SHAW, J. (1994). Aging and sexual potential. *Journal of Sex Education and Therapy, 20,* 134–139.

SHAW, J. (1997). Treatment rationale for internet infidelity. *Journal of Sex Education and Therapy, 22,* 29–34.

SHEERAN, R., ABRAHAM, C., & ORBELL, S. (1999). Psychosocial correlates of heterosexual condom use: A meta-analysis. *Psychological Bulletin, 125* 90–132.

SHEPELA, S. T., & LEVESQUE, L. L. (1998). Poisoned waters: Sexual harassment and the college climate. *Sex Roles, 38,* 589–611.

SHEPHER, J. (1971). Mate selection among second generation kibbutz adolescents and adults: Incest avoidance and negative imprinting. *Archives of Sexual Behavior, 1,* 293–307.

SHERR, L. (1990). Fear arousal and AIDS: Do shock tactics work? *AIDS, 4,* 361–364.

SHERWIN, B. B. (1988). A comparative analysis of the role of androgens in human male and female sexual behavior: Behavior specificity, critical thresholds and sensitivity. *Psychobiology, 16,* 416–425.

SHIELDS, W. M., & SHIELDS, L. M. (1983). Forcible rape: An evolutionary perspective. *Ethology and Sociobiology, 4,* 115–136.

SHIPLEY, W. U., et al. (1999). Radiation therapy for clinically localized prostate cancer: A multi-institutional pooled analysis. *Journal of the American Medical Association, 281,* 1598–1604.

SHORTRIDGE, J. L. (1997). Nigerian guidelines for sexuality education introduced at ceremony in Lagos. *SIECUS Report, 25*(2), 4–7.

SHOSTAK, M. (1981). *Kalahari hunter-gatherers.* Cambridge, MA: Harvard University Press.

SHOTLAND, R. L., & HUNTER, B. A. (1995). Women's "token resistant" and compliant sexual behaviors are related to uncertain sexual intentions and rape. *Personality and Social Psychology Bulletin, 21,* 226–236.

SHUGARS, D. C., ALEXANDER, A. L., FU, K., & FREEL, S. A. (1999). Endogenous salivary inhibitors of human immunodeficiency virus. *Archives of Oral Biology, 44,* 445–453.

SHY, K., et al. (1989). Papanicolaou smear screening interval and risk of cervical cancer. *Obstetrics and Gynecology, 74,* 838–843.

SIECUS. (1992). Sexuality education and the schools: Issues and answers. *SIECUS Report* (Fact Sheet No. 3), August/September, 13–14.

SIECUS. (1998). The truth about latex condoms. *SIECUS Report, 27* (1), 21–22.

SIECUS. (2000). SIECUS position statement on sexuality of persons with disabilities. www.siecus.org.

SIECUS/ADVOCATES FOR YOUTH. (1999). *SIECUS/Advocates for youth survey of Americans' views on sexuality education.* Washington, DC: Sexuality Information and Education Council of the United States and Advocates for Youth.

SIECUS NATIONAL GUIDELINES TASK FORCE. (1996). *Guidelines for comprehensive sexuality education* (2nd ed.). New York: Author.

SIGELMAN, C.K., et al. (1995). Parents' contributions to children's knowledge and attitudes regarding AIDS: Another look. *Journal of Pediatric Psychology, 20,* 61–77.

SILVERMAN, B. G., & GROSS, T. P. (1997). Use and effectiveness of condoms during anal intercourse. *Sexually Transmitted Diseases, 24,* 11–17.

SIMON, P. M., et al. (1992). Psychological characteristics of a sample of male street prostitutes. *Archives of Sexual Behavior, 21,* 33–44.

SIMON, R. J., SCHERER, J., & RAU, W. (1999). Sexual harassment in the heartland? Community opinion on the EEOC suit against Mitsubishi Motor Manufacturing of America. *Social Science Journal, 36,* 487–495.

SIMON, W. (1994). Deviance as history: The future of perversion. *Archives of Sexual Behavior, 23,* 1–20.

SIMPSON, J. A., CAMPBELL, B., & BERSCHEID, E. (1986). The association between romantic love and marriage: Kephart (1967) twice revisited. *Personality and Social Psychology Bulletin, 12,* 363–372.

SINCLAIR, A. H., et al. (1990). A gene from the human sex-determining region encodes a protein with homology to a conserved DNA binding motif. *Nature, 346,* 240–244.

SINGER, A. G. (1991). A chemistry of mammalian pheromones. *Journal of Steroid Biochemistry, 39,* 627–632.

SINGER, I. (1984). *The nature of love, Vol. 1: Plato to Luther*. Chicago: University of Chicago Press.

SINGER, I. (1984–1987). *The nature of love* (Vols. 1–3). Chicago: University of Chicago Press.

SINGER, L., FARKAS, K., & KLIEGMAN, R. (1992). Childhood medical and behavioral consequences of maternal cocaine use. *Journal of Pediatric Psychology, 17,* 389–406.

SINGH, D., MEYER, W., ZAMBARANO, R. J., & HULBERT, D. F. (1998). Frequency and timing of coital orgasm in women desirous of becoming pregnant. *Archives of Sexual Behavior, 27,* 15–29.

SINGH, G. K., & YU, S. M. (1995). Infant mortality in the United States: Trends, differentials, and projections, 1950 through 2010. *American Journal of Public Health, 85,* 957–964.

SINGH, S., & DARROCH, J. E. (1999). Trends in sexual activity among adolescent American women: 1982–1995. *Family Planning Perspectives, 31,* 212–219.

SINGH, S., & DARROCH, J. E. (2000). Adolescent pregnancy and childbearing: Levels and trends in developed countries. *Family Planning Perspectives, 32,* 14–23.

SINGH, S., WULF, D., SAMARA, R., & CUCA, Y. P. (2000). Gender differences in the timing of first intercourse: Data from 14 countries. *International Family Planning Perspectives, 26,* 21–28, 43.

SINICCO, A., et al. (1993). Risk of developing AIDS after primary acute HIV-1 infection. *Journal of Acquired Immune Deficiency Syndromes, 6,* 575–581.

SIPSKI, M. L., ALEXANDER, C. J., & ROSEN, R. C. (1999). Sexual response in women with spinal cord injuries: Implications for our understanding of the able bodied. *Journal of Sex & Marital Therapy, 25,* 11–22.

SISKIND, V., GREEN, A., BAIN, C., & PURDIE, D. (1997). Breastfeeding, menopause, and epithelial ovarian cancer. *Epidemiology, 8,* 188–191.

SIVIN, I. (1989). IUDs are contraceptives, not abortifacients: A comment on research and belief. *Studies in Family Planning, 20,* 355–359.

SIVIN, I. (1993). Another look at the Dalkon Shield: Meta-analysis underscores its problems. *Contraception, 48,* 1–12.

SIVIN, I., et al. (2000). Prolonged effectiveness of Norplant capsule implants: A 7-year study. *Contraception, 61,* 187–194.

SLEEK, S. (1998). Chinese psychiatrists debate meaning of sex orientation. *APA Monitor,* September, 33.

SLIJPER, F. M. E., DROP, S. L. S., MOLENAAR, J. C., & KEIZER-SCHRAMA, S. M. P. F. (1998). Long-term psychological evaluation of intersex children. *Archives of Sexual Behavior, 27,* 125–143.

SMITH, A. M. (1993). "What is pornography?": An analysis of the policy statement of the campaign against pornography and censorship. *Feminist Review, 43,* 71–87.

SMITH, A. M. A., ROSENTHAL, D. A., & REICHLER, H. (1996). High schoolers' masturbatory practices: Their relationship to sexual intercourse and personal characteristics. *Psychological Reports, 76,* 499–509.

SMITH, G., KIPPAX, S., & CHAPPLE, M. (1998). Secrecy, disclosure, and closet dynamics. *Journal of Homosexuality, 35,* 53–73.

SMITH, G. D., FRANKEL, S., & YARNELL, J. (1997). Sex and death: Are they related?

Findings from the Caerphilly cohort study. *British Medical Journal, 315,* 1641–1645.

SMITH, J. I. (1987). Islam. In A. Sharma (Ed.), *Women in world religions*. Albany: State University of New York Press.

SMITH, J. I., & HADDAD, Y. (1975). Women in the afterlife: The Islamic view as seen from the Qur'an and tradition. *Journal of the American Academy of Religion, 43,* 39–50.

SMITH, L. (1993). Saying no to birth control. *Los Angeles Times*, January 6, A1, A12.

SMITH, R., PINE, C., & HAWLEY, M. (1988). Social cognitions about adult male victims of female sexual assault. *Journal of Sex Research, 24,* 101–112.

SMITH, T. W. (1999). The JAMA controversy and the meaning of sex. *Public Opinion Quarterly, 63,* 385–400.

SNIFFEN, M. J. (1994). Study: Most rape victims young. *Times-Picayune* (New Orleans), June 23, A-9.

SOCARIDES, C. W. (1996). *Homosexuality: A freedom too far*. Phoenix, AZ: Adam Margrave Books.

SOCIETY FOR ASSISTED REPRODUCTIVE TECHNOLOGY, AMERICAN FERTILITY SOCIETY. (1993). Assisted reproductive technology in the United States and Canada: 1991 results from the Society for Assisted Reproductive Technology generated from the American Fertility Society Registry. *Fertility and Sterility, 59,* 956–962.

SOCIETY FOR ASSISTED REPRODUCTIVE TECHNOLOGY, et al. (1997). *The 1995 assisted reproductive technology success rate: National survey and fertility clinics report*. Atlanta: U.S. Department of Health and Human Services.

SOLER, H., et al. (2000). Relationship dynamics, ethnicity and condom use among low-income women. *Family Planning Perspectives, 32,* 82–88, 101.

SONENSTEIN, F. L., et al. (1998). Changes in sexual behavior and condom use among teenaged males: 1988 to 1995. *American Journal of Public Health, 88,* 956–959.

SOWERS, M. F. R. (2000). The menopause transition and the aging process: A population perspective. *Aging Clinical and Experimental Research, 12,* 85–92.

SPARLING, J. (1997). Penile erections: Shape, angle, and length. *Journal of Sex & Marital Therapy, 23,* 195–207.

SPARLING, P. F., ELKINS, C., WYRICK, P. B., & COHEN, M. S. (1994). Vaccines for bacterial sexually transmitted infections: A realistic goal. *Proceedings of the National Academy of Sciences of the U.S.A., 91,* 2456–2463.

SPEAR, L. P. (2000). Neurobehavioral changes in adolescence. *Current Directions in Psychological Science, 9,* 111–114.

SPECTOR, I., & CAREY, M. (1990). Incidence and prevalence of the sexual dysfunctions: A critical review of the empirical literature. *Archives of Sexual Behavior, 19,* 389–408.

SPECTOR, I. P., & FREMETH, S. M. (1996). Sexual behaviors and attitudes of geriatric residents in long-term care facilities. *Journal of Sex & Marital Therapy, 22,* 235–246.

SPENCE, J. T., & HAHN, E. D. (1997). The Attitude Toward Women Scale and attitude change in college students. *Psychology of Women Quarterly, 21,* 17–34.

SPENCE, J. T., & HELMREICH, R. L. (1972). Who likes competent women? Competence, sex-role congruence of interests, and attitudes towards women as determinants of interper-

sonal attraction. *Journal of Applied and Social Psychology, 2,* 197–213.

SPENCE, J. T., & HELMREICH, R. L. (1978). *Masculinity & femininity: Their psychological dimensions, correlates, and antecedents*. Austin: University of Texas Press.

SPENCE, J. T., HELMREICH, R. L., & STAPP, J. (1974). The personal attributes questionnaire: A measure of sex role stereotypes and masculinity-femininity. *JSAS Catalog of Selected Documents in Psychology, 4,* 43.

SPENCE, J. T., HELMREICH, R. L., & STAPP, J. (1975). Ratings of self and peers on sex role attributes and their relation to self-esteem and conceptions of masculinity and femininity. *Journal of Personality and Social Psychology, 32,* 29–39.

SPIEGEL, D. (2000). Suffer the children: Long-term effects of sexual abuse. *Society,* May/June, 18–20.

SPINNATO II., J. A. (1997). Mechanism of action of intrauterine contraceptive devices and its relation to informed consent. *American Journal of Obstetrics and Gynecology, 176,* 503–506.

SPITZ, R. A. (1945). Hospitalism: An inquiry into the genesis of psychiatric conditioning in early childhood. In D. Fenschel & A. Freud (Eds.), *Psychoanalytic studies of the child* (Vol. 1). New York: International Universities Press.

SPITZ, R. A. (1946). Hospitalism: A follow-up report. In D. Fenschel, P. Greenacre, & A. Freud (Eds.), *Psychoanalytic studies of the child* (Vol. 2, pp. 113–117). New York: International Universities Press.

SPITZBERG, B. H. (1998). Sexual coercion in courtship relations. In B. H. Spitzberg & W. R. Cupach (Eds.), *The dark side of close relationships* (pp. 179–232). Mahwah, NJ: Erlbaum.

SPRAUVE, M., LINDSAY, M., HERBERT, S., & GRAVES, W. (1997). Adverse outcome in parturients who use crack cocaine. *Obstetrics & Gynecology, 89,* 674–678.

SPRECHER, S., BARBEE, A., & SCHWARTZ, P. (1995). "Was it good for you, too?": Gender differences in first sexual intercourse experiences. *Journal of Sex Research, 32,* 3–15.

SPRECHER, S., & REGAN, P. C. (1998). Passionate and companionate love in courting and young married couples. *Sociological Inquiry, 68,* 163–185.

SPRECHER, S., REGAN, P. C., & McKINNEY, K. (1998). Beliefs about the outcomes of extramarital sexual relationships as a function of the gender of the "cheating spouse." *Sex Roles, 38,* 301–311.

SPRECHER, S., et al. (1994). Token resistance to sexual intercourse and consent to unwanted sexual intercourse: College students' dating experiences in 3 countries. *Journal of Sex Research, 31,* 125–132.

SPRUANCE, S. L., et al. (1997). Penciclovir cream for the treatment of herpes simplex labialis. *Journal of the American Medical Association, 277,* 1374–1379.

SPRUYT, A., et al. (1998). Identifying condom users at risk for breakage and slippage: Findings from three international sites. *American Journal of Public Health, 88,* 239–244.

STACK, S., & GUNDLACH, J. H. (1992). Divorce and sex. *Archives of Sexual Behavior, 21,* 359–368.

STAGNOR, C., & RUBLE, D. N. (1987). Development of gender knowledge and gender constancy. In L. S. Lieben & M. L. Signorella (Eds.), *Children's gender schemata*. San Francisco: Jossey-Bass.

STALL, R. D., et al. (2000). The gay '90s: A review of research in the 1990s on sexual behavior and HIV risk among men who have sex with men. *AIDS, 14,* S101–S114.

STAMPFER, M. J., et al. (1991). Postmenopausal estrogen therapy and cardiovascular disease. *New England Journal of Medicine, 325,* 756–762.

STANBERRY, L. R. (1998). Control of STDs—The role of prophylactic vaccines against herpes simplex virus. *Sexually Transmitted Infections, 74,* 391–394.

STANFORD, J. L., et al. (1995). Combined estrogen and progestin hormone replacement therapy in relation to risk of breast cancer in middle-aged women. *Journal of the American Medical Association, 274,* 137–142.

STANFORD, J. L., et al. (2000). Urinary and sexual function after radical prostatectomy for clinically localized prostate cancer: The prostate cancer outcomes study. *Journal of the American Medical Association, 283,* 354–360.

STANTON, H. (1922). *Sex: Avoided subjects discussed in plain English*. New York: Social Mentor.

STAPLETON, A., LATHAM, R. H., JOHNSON, C., & STAMM, W. E. (1990). Postcoital antimicrobial prophylaxis for recurrent urinary tract infection. *Journal of the American Medical Association, 264,* 703–706.

STEELE, B. F., & ALEXANDER, H. (1981). Long-term effects of sexual abuse in childhood. In P. B. Mzazek & C. H. Kempe (Eds.), *Sexually abused children and their families* (pp. 223–233). New York: Pergamon.

STEELE, J. R. (1999). Teenage sexuality and media practice: Factoring in the influences of family, friends, and school. *Journal of Sex Research, 36,* 331–341.

STEIN, M. L. (1977). Prostitution. In J. Money & H. Musaph (Eds.), *Handbook of sexology*. Amsterdam: Elsevier/North-Holland.

STEINBERG, K. K., et al. (1991). A meta-analysis of the effect of estrogen replacement therapy on the risk of breast cancer. *Journal of the American Medical Association, 265,* 1985–1990.

STEINEM, G. (1983). *Outrageous acts and everyday rebellions*. New York: Holt, Rinehart & Winston.

STEINER, M. (2000). Premenstrual syndrome and premenstrual dysphoric disorder: Guidelines for management. *Journal of Psychiatry & Neuroscience, 25,* 459–468.

STEINER, M., DOMINIK, R., TRUSSELL, J., & HERTZ-PICCIOTTO, I. (1996). Measuring contraceptive effectiveness: A conceptual framework. *Obstetrics and Gynecology, 88* (3 Suppl.), 24S–30S.

STEINER, M. J., et al. (1998). Measuring true contraceptive efficacy: A randomized approach—Condom vs. spermicide vs. no method. *Contraception, 58,* 375–378.

STEPHEN, E. H., & CHANDRA, A. (2000). Use of fertility services in the United States: 1995. *Family Planning Perspectives, 32,* 132–137.

STEPHENSON, P., WAGNER, M., BADEA, M., & SERBANESCU, F. (1992). Commentary: The public health consequences of restricted induced abortion—Lessons from Romania. *American Journal of Public Health, 82,* 1328–1331.

STEPTOE, P. C., & EDWARDS, R. G. (1978). Birth after the implantation of a human embryo [letter]. *Lancet, 2,* 366.

STERN, K., & MCCLINTOCK, M. K. (1998). Regulation of ovulation by human pheromones. *Nature, 392,* 177–179.

STERNBACH, H. (1998). Age-associated testosterone decline in men: Clinical issues for psychology. *American Journal of Psychiatry, 155,* 1310–1318.

STERNBERG, R. J. (1986). A triangular theory of love. *Psychological Review, 93,* 119–135.

STERNBERG, R. J. (1987). Liking vs. loving: A comparative evaluation of theories. *Psychological Bulletin, 102,* 331–345.

STERNBERG, R. J. (1988). Triangulating love. In R. J. Sternberg & M. L. Barnes (Eds.), *The psychology of love* (pp. 119–138). New Haven, CT: Yale University Press.

STERNBERG, R. J., & GRAJEK, S. (1984). The nature of love. *Journal of Personality and Social Psychology, 47,* 312–329.

STICK, S. M., et al. (1996). Effects of maternal smoking during pregnancy and a family history of asthma on respiratory function in newborn-infants. *Lancet, 348,* 1060–1064.

STOCK, J. L., BELL, M. A., BOYER, D. K., & CONNELL, F. A. (1997). Adolescent pregnancy and sexual risk-taking among sexually abused girls. *Family Planning Perspectives, 29,* 200–203, 207.

STOCKARD, J., & JOHNSON, M. M. (1980). *Sex roles, sex inequality and sex role development*. Englewood Cliffs, NJ: Prentice Hall.

STOCKDALE, M. S., VISIO, M., & BATRA, L. (1999). The sexual harassment of men: Evidence for a broader theory of sexual harassment and sex discrimination. *Psychology, Public Policy, and Law, 5,* 630–664.

STODGHILL II, R. (1998). Where'd you learn that? *Time,* June 15, 52–59.

STOKES, J. P., DAMON, W., & MCKIRNAN, D. J. (1997). Predictors of movement toward homosexuality: A longitudinal study of bisexual men. *Journal of Sex Research, 34,* 304–312.

STOKES, J., MCKIRNAN, D., DOLL, L., & BURZETTE, R. (1996). Female partners of bisexual men: What they don't know might hurt them. *Psychology of Women Quarterly, 20,* 267–284.

STOLLER, R. J. (1977). Sexual deviations. In F. Beach (Ed.), *Human sexuality in four perspectives* (pp. 190–214). Baltimore: Johns Hopkins University Press.

STONE, K. M., et al. (1989). National surveillance for neonatal herpes simplex virus infections. *Sexually Transmitted Diseases, 16,* 152–160.

STONER, B. P., et al. (2000). Comparative epidemiology of heterosexual gonococcal and chlamydial networks. *Sexually Transmitted Diseases, 27,* 215–223.

STORMS, M. (1980). Theories of sexual orientation. *Journal of Personality and Social Psychology, 38,* 783–792.

STRASSBERG, D. S., & LOCKERD, L. K. (1998). Force in women's sexual fantasies. *Archives of Sexual Behavior, 27,* 403–414.

STRASSBERG, D. S., & LOWE, K. (1995). Volunteer bias in sexuality research. *Archives of Sexual Behavior, 24,* 369–382.

STRATHDEE, S. A., et al. (1997). Needle exchange is not enough: Lessons from the Vancouver injecting drug use study. *AIDS, 11,* F59–F65.

STREICHER, H. W. (1974). The girls in the cartoons. *Journal of Communication, 24,* 125–129.

STRIAR, S., & BARTLIK, B. (1999). Stimulation of the libido: The use of erotica in sex therapy. *Psychiatric Annals, 29,* 60–62.

STRONG, E. K. (1936). Interests of men and women. *Journal of Social Psychology, 7,* 49–67.

STROUSE, J., & FABES, R. A. (1985). Formal versus informal sources of sex education: Competing forces in the sexual socialization of adolescents. *Adolescence, 20,* 251–263.

STROUSE, J. S., BUERKEL-ROTHFUSS, N., & LONG, E. C. (1995). Gender and family as moderators of the relationship between music video exposure and adolescent sexual permissiveness. *Adolescence, 30,* 505–521.

STRUCKMAN-JOHNSON, C., & STRUCKMAN-JOHNSON, D. (1994). Men pressured and forced into sexual experience. *Archives of Sexual Behavior, 23,* 93–114.

SULIGOI, B. (1997). The natural history of human immunodeficiency virus infection among women as compared with men. *Sexually Transmitted Diseases, 24,* 77–83.

SULIK, K. K., JOHNSON, M. C., & WEBB, M. A. (1981). Fetal alcohol syndrome: Embryogenesis in a mouse model. *Science, 214,* 936–938.

SUMMIT, R., & KRYSO, J. (1978). Sexual abuse of children: A clinical spectrum. *American Journal of Orthopsychiatry, 48,* 237–251.

SUTTIE, I. D. (1952). *The origins of love and hate*. New York: Julian Press.

SWAAB, D. F., GOOREN, L. J. G., & HOFMAN, M. A. (1992). The human hypothalamus in relation to gender and sexual orientation. *Progress in Brain Research, 93,* 205–219.

SWAAB, D. F., & HOFMAN, M. A. (1990). An enlarged suprachiasmatic nucleus in homosexual men. *Brain Research, 537,* 141–148.

SWISHER, P. N., & COOK, N. D. (1996). Bottoms v. Bottoms: In whose best interest? Analysis of a lesbian mother child custody dispute. *University of Louisville Journal of Family Law, 34,* 843–895.

SYFERS, J. (1972). Why I want a wife. *Ms., 1,* July, 56.

SYMONS, D. (1979). *The evolution of human sexuality*. New York: Oxford University Press.

TANG, M.-X., et al. (1996). Effect of estrogen during menopause on risk and age at onset of Alzheimer's disease. *Lancet, 348,* 429–432.

TANNAHIL, R. (1980). *Sex in history*. New York: Stein & Day.

TANNEN, D. (1990). *You just don't understand: Women and men in conversation*. New York: William Morrow.

TARDIF, G. S. (1989). Sexual activity after a myocardial infarction. *Archives of Physical Medicine and Rehabilitation, 70,* 763–766.

TARIS, T. W., & SEMIN, G. R. (1997a). Gender as a narrative of the effects of the love motive and relational context on sexual experience. *Archives of Sexual Behavior, 26,* 159–180.

TARIS, T. W., & SEMIN, G. R. (1997b). Passing on the faith: How mother-child communication influences transmission of moral values. *Journal of Moral Education, 26,* 211–221.

TAY, J. I., MOORE, J., & WALKER, J. J. (2000). Ectopic pregnancy. *British Medical Journal, 320,* 916–919.

TAYLOR, D., et al. (1997). Risk factors for adult paternity in births to adolescents. *Obstetrics and Gynecology, 89,* 199–205.

TAYLOR, M. C., & HALL, J. A. (1982). Psychological androgyny: Theories, methods, and conclusions. *Psychological Bulletin, 92,* 347–366.

TEMPLEMAN, T. L., & STINNETT, R. D. (1991). Patterns of sexual arousal and history in a "normal" sample of young men. *Archives of Sexual Behavior, 20,* 137–150.

TENNOV, D. (1979). *Love and limerence.* New York: Stein and Day.

TEPPER, M. S., & LAWLESS, B. (1997). Relevant resources for sexuality and spinal cord injury. *Sexuality and Disability, 15,* 203.

TERMAN, L., & MILES, C. C. (1936). *Sex and personality.* New York: McGraw-Hill.

TERZIAN, H., & ORE, G. (1955). Syndrome of Kluver and Bucy reproduced in man by bilateral removal of the temporal lobes. *Neurology, 5,* 373–380.

THAYER, L. (1986). *On communication.* Norwood, NJ: Ablex.

THEIM, R. (1994). Gay parents' custody rights debated by lawyers. *Times-Picayune* (New Orleans), August 6, A-7.

THOMAS, K. (2000). Girlhood, interrupted. *USA Today,* April 19, D1–D2.

THOMPSON, A. (1984). Emotional and sexual components of extramarital relations. *Journal of Marriage and the Family, 46,* 35–42.

THOMPSON, H. B. (1903). *The mental traits of sex.* Chicago: University of Chicago Press.

THOMPSON, L. (1991). Paraphilia spans extremes of sexual disorders. *Washington Post.*

THOMPSON, S. (1990). Putting a big thing into a little hole: Teenage girls' accounts of sexual initiation. *Journal of Sex Research, 27,* 341–361.

THOMPSON, T. L., & ZERBINOS, E. (1997). Television cartoons: Do children notice it's a boy's world? *Sex Roles, 37,* 415–432.

THORNHILL, N. W. (1991). An evolutionary analysis of rules regulating human inbreeding and marriage. *Behavioral and Brain Sciences, 14,* 247–293.

THORNHILL, N. W. (1992). Human inbreeding. In N. W. Thornhill (Ed.), *The natural history of inbreeding and outbreeding: Theoretical and empirical perspectives.* Chicago: University of Chicago Press.

THORNHILL, R., & GRAMMER, K. (1999). The body and face of woman: One ornament that signals quality? *Evolution and Human Behavior, 20,* 105–120.

THORNHILL, R., & PALMER, C. T. (2000). *A natural history of rape: Biological bases of sexual coercion.* Cambridge, MA: MIT Press.

THORNHILL, R., & THORNHILL, N. W. (1992). The evolutionary psychology of men's coercive sexuality. *Behavioral and Brain Sciences, 15,* 363–421.

THUNE, I., et al. (1997). Physical activity and the risk of breast cancer. *New England Journal of Medicine, 336,* 1269–1275.

TIEFER, L. (1991). Historical, scientific, clinical and feminist criticisms of "The human sexual response" model. *Annual Review of Sex Research, 2,* 1–23.

TIEFER, L. (1994). Might premature ejaculation be organic? The perfect penis takes a giant step forward. *Journal of Sex Education and Therapy, 20,* 7–8.

TIEFER, L. (2000). Sexology and the pharmaceutical industry: The threat of co-optation. *Journal of Sex Research, 37,* 273–283.

TIEZZI, L., et al. (1997). Pregnancy prevention among urban adolescents younger than 15: Results of the 'In Your Face' program. *Family Planning Perspectives, 29,* 176–186, 197.

TIME ESSAY. (1966). The homosexual in America. *Time,* January 21, 40–41.

TOLLISON, C. D., & ADAMS, H. E. (1979). *Sexual disorders: Treatment, theory, and research.* New York: Gardner Press.

TOPPARI, J., & KALEVA, M. (1999). Maldescendus testis. *Hormone Research, 51,* 261–269.

TORASSA, U. (2000). "Maternal choice caesareans." *Times-Picayune* (New Orleans), May 27, E1, E4.

TOSTESON, A. N. A., et al. (2000). Has the impact of hormone replacement therapy on health-related quality of life been undervalued? *Journal of Women's Health & Gender-Based Medicine, 9,* 119–130.

TOUBIA, N. (1988). Women and health in Sudan. In N. Toubia (Ed.), *Women of the Arab world* (pp. 98–109). London: Zed Books.

TOUBIA, N. (1994). Female circumcision as a public health issue. *New England Journal of Medicine, 331,* 712–716.

TOUFEXIS, A. (1993). The right chemistry. *Time,* February 15, 49–51.

TOWNSEND, J. M. (1995). Sex without emotional involvement: An evolutionary interpretation of sex differences. *Archives of Sexual Behavior, 24,* 173–206.

TRELOAR, A. E., BOYNTON, R. E., BEHN, D. E., & BROWN, B. W. (1967). Variation of the human menstrual cycle through reproductive life. *International Journal of Fertility, 12,* 77–126.

TREVATHAN, W. R., BURLESON, M. H., & GREGORY, W. L. (1993). No evidence for menstrual synchrony in lesbian couples. *Psychoneuroendocrinology, 18,* 425–435.

TRUDGILL, E. (1976). *Madonnas and Magdalens: The origins and development of Victorian sexual attitudes.* New York: Holmes & Meier.

TRUESDELL, D., McNEIL, J., & DESCHNER, J. (1986). Incidence of wife abuse in incestuous families. *Social Work, 31,* 138–140.

TRUSSELL, J., DURAN, V., SHOCHET, T., & MOORE, K. (2000). Access to emergency contraception. *Obstetrics & Gynecology, 95,* 267–270.

TRUSSELL, J., & GRUMMER-STRAWN, L. (1990). Contraceptive failure of the ovulation method of periodic abstinence. *Family Planning Perspectives, 2*(2), 65–75.

TRUSSELL, J., KOENIG, J., ELLERTSON, C., & STEWART, F. (1997) Preventing unintended pregnancy: the cost-effectiveness of three methods of emergency contraception. *American Journal of Public Health, 87,* 932–937.

TRUSSELL, J., RODRIGUEZ, G., & ELLERTSON, C. (1999). Updated estimates of the effectiveness of Yuzpe regimen of emergency contraception. *Contraception, 59,* 147–151.

TRUSSELL, J., & STEWART, F. (1992). The effectiveness of postcoital contraception. *Family Planning Perspectives, 24,* 262–264.

TRUSSELL, J., STRICKLER, J., & VAUGHAN, B. (1993). Contraceptive efficacy of the diaphragm, the sponge and the cervical cap. *Family Planning Perspectives, 25,* 100–105, 135.

TRUSSELL, J., STURGEN, K., STRICKLER, J., & DOMINIK, R. (1994). Comparative contraceptive efficacy of the female condom and other barrier methods. *Family Planning Perspectives, 26,* 66–72.

TRUSSELL, J., WARNER, D. L., & HATCHER, R. A. (1992). Condom slippage and breakage rates. *Family Planning Perspectives, 24,* 20–23.

TRUSSELL, J., et al. (1990). Contraceptive failure in the U.S.: An update. *Studies in Family Planning, 21*(1), Table 1.

TRUTE, B., ADKINS, E., & MACDONALD, G. (1992). Professional attitudes regarding the sexual abuse of children: Comparing police, child welfare and community mental health. *Child Abuse & Neglect, 16,* 359–368.

TUCKER, M. B., TAYLOR, R. J., & MITCHELL-KERNAN, C. (1993). Marriage and romantic involvement among aged African Americans. *Journal of Gerontology, 48,* S123–S132.

TUFTS NEW ENGLAND MEDICAL CENTER. (1984). *Sexually exploited children: Services and research project.* Boston: Author.

TUITEN, A., et al. (2000). Time course of effects of testosterone administration on sexual arousal in women. *Archives of General Psychiatry, 57,* 149–153.

TUREK, F. (1999). Legislating morality. *New Man Magazine,* July/August, 50–55.

TURNBULL, D., et al. (1996). Randomized, controlled trial of efficacy of midwife-managed care. *Lancet, 348,* 213–218.

TURNER, C. F., MILLER, H. G., & MOSES, L. E. (Eds.). (1989). *AIDS: Sexual behavior and intravenous drug use.* Washington, DC: National Academy Press.

TURNER, W. J. (1995). Homosexuality, type 1: An Xq28 phenomenon. *Archives of Sexual Behavior, 24,* 109–134.

TWENGE, J. M. (1997). Changes in masculine and feminine traits over time: A meta-analysis. *Sex Roles, 36,* 305–325.

ULLMAN, S. E. (1996). Social reactions, coping strategies, and self-blame attributions in adjustment to sexual assault. *Psychology of Women Quarterly, 20,* 505–526.

ULLMAN, S. E.(1998). Does offender violence escalate when rape victims fight back? *Journal of Interpersonal Violence, 13,* 179–192.

ULLMAN, S. E., KARABATSOS, G., & KOSS, M. P. (1999). Alcohol and sexual aggression in a national sample of college men. *Psychology of Women Quarterly, 23,* 673–689.

ULLMAN, S. E., & KNIGHT, R. A. (1991). A multivariate model for predicting rape and physical injury outcomes during sexual assaults. *Journal of Consulting and Clinical Psychology, 59,* 724–731.

ULLRICH, H. E. (1992). Menstrual taboos among Havik Brahmin women: A study of ritual change. *Sex Roles, 26,* 19–40.

UNGER, R., & CRAWFORD, M. (1992). Images of women (Ch. 4). In *Women & gender: A feminist psychology.* New York: McGraw-Hill.

UNITED KINGDOM TESTICULAR CANCER SOCIETY STUDY GROUP. (1994). Aetiology of testicular cancer: Association with congenital abnormalities, age at puberty, infertility, and exercise. *British Medical Journal, 308,* 1393–1399.

UNITED NATIONS, DEPARTMENT OF ECONOMICS AND SOCIAL AFFAIRS. (1999). *The demographic impact of HIV/AIDS.* New York: Author.

UNITED NATIONS DEVELOPMENT PROGRAMME, et al. (2000). Efficacy and side effects of immediate postcoital levonorgestral used repeatedly for contraception. *Contraception, 61,* 303–308.

UNITED NATIONS/ECONOMIC COMMISSION FOR EUROPE. (1995). *Trends in Europe and North America: The statistical yearbook of the Economic Commission for Europe.* Author.

UNITED NATIONS PROGRAMME ON HIV/AIDS. (2000). Report on the global HIV/AIDS epidemic. December 2000. Geneva, Switzerland: United Nations.

UPCHURCH, D. M., LEVY-STORMS, L., SUCOFF, C. A., & ANESHENSEL, C. S. (1998). Gender and ethnic differences in the timing of first sexual intercourse. *Family Planning Perspectives, 30,* 121–127.

URSIN, G., et al. (1994). Oral contraceptive use and adenocarcinoma of cervix. *Lancet, 344,* 1390–1394.

U.S. ATTORNEY GENERAL'S COMMISSION ON PORNOGRAPHY. (1986). *Final Report of the Attorney General's Commission on Pornography.* Washington, DC: U.S. Justice Department.

U.S. DEPARTMENT OF HEALTH AND HUMAN SERVICES. (1997). Fertility, family planning, and women's health: New data from the 1995 National Survey of Family Growth. *Vital and Health Statistics,* Series 23, No. 19.

U.S. DEPARTMENT OF JUSTICE. (1996). *Hate crime statistics. Uniform Crime Reports.* Washington, DC: Federal Bureau of Investigation.

U.S. DEPARTMENT OF JUSTICE. (2000). *Bureau of Justice statistics sourcebook of criminal justice statistics—1999.* Washington, DC: U.S. Government Printing Office.

U.S. GENERAL ACCOUNTING OFFICE. (1990). *Drug exposed infants: A generation at risk.* Publication GAO/HRD-90-138. Washington, DC: Author.

UTIAN, W. (1997). Women's experience and attitudes toward menopause. Paper presented at the annual meeting of the North American Menopause Society, Boston.

VALENTICH, M., & GRIPTON, J. (1989). Teaching children about AIDS. *Journal of Sex Education and Therapy, 15*(2), 92.

VALLEROY, L. A., et al. (2000). The HIV prevalence and associated risks in young men who have sex with men. *Journal of the American Medical Association, 284,* 198–204.

VANCE, C. S. (1988). Ordinances restricting pornography could damage women. In R. T. Francoeur (Ed.), *Taking sides: Clashing views on controversial issues in human sexuality.* Guilford, CT: Dushkin.

VANCE, E. B., & WAGNER, N. N. (1976). Written descriptions of orgasm: A study of sex differences. *Archives of Sexual Behavior, 5,* 87–98.

VAN DAMME, L., & ROSENBERG, Z. F. (1999). Microbicides and barrier methods in HIV prevention. *AIDS, 13* (Suppl. A), S85–S92.

VAN DAMME, L., et al. (2000). Paper presented at the 13th International AIDS Conference, Durban, South Africa.

VAN DER LOEFF, M. F. S., & AABY, P. (1999). Towards a better understanding of the epidemiology of HIV-2. *AIDS, 13* (Suppl. A), S69–S84.

VAN DE VELDE, T. H. (1930). *Ideal marriage: Its physiology and technique.* New York: Couici-Friede.

VAN HALL, E. V. (1997). The menopausal misnomer. *Journal of Psychosomatic Obstetrics and Gynecology, 18,* 59–62.

VAN NOORD-ZAADSTRA, B., et al. (1991). Delaying childbearing: Effect of age on fecundity and outcome of pregnancy. *British Medical Journal, 302,* 1361–1365.

VANNOY, R. (1980). *Sex without love: A philosophical exploration.* Buffalo, NY: Prometheus Books.

VAN OSS MARIN, B., & GOMEZ, C. (1994). Latinos, HIV disease, and culture: Strategies for HIV prevention. In P. Cohen, M. Sande,

& P. Volberding (Eds.), *The AIDS knowledge base* (pp. 10.8-1–10.8-13). New York: Little, Brown.

VAN WYK, P. (1984). Psychosocial development of heterosexual, bisexual, and homosexual behavior. *Archives of Sexual Behavior, 13,* 505–544.

VENTURA, J. N. (1987). The stresses of parenthood reexamined. *Family Relations, 36,* 26–29.

VENTURA, S. J., CURTIN, S. C., & MATHEWS, T. J. (2000). Variations in teenage birth rates, 1991–1998: National and state trends. *National Vital Statistics Report, 48*(6), 1–16.

VENTURA, S. J., MATHEWS, T. J., & CURTIN, S. C. (1999). Declines in teenage birth rates, 1991–1998: Update of national and state trends. *National Vital Statistics Report, 47*(26), 1–12.

VENTURA, S. J., MOSHER, W. D., CURTIN, S. C., & AABMA, J. C. (1999). Highlights of trends in pregnancies and pregnancy rates by outcome: Estimates for the United States, 1976–1996. *National Vital Statistics Reports, 47*(29), 1–12.

VENTURA, S. J., et al. (1997). Report of final natality statistics, 1995. National Center for Health Statistics. *Monthly Vital Statistics Report, 45*(11).

VERNAZZA, P. L., ERON, J. J., FISCUS, S. A., & COHEN, M. S. (1999). Sexual transmission of HIV: Infectiousness and prevention. *AIDS, 13,* 155–166.

VESSEY, M. P., & PAINTER, R. (1994). Oral contraceptive use and benign gallbladder disease; revisited. *Contraception, 50,* 167–173.

VISNESS, C. M., & KENNEDY, K. I. (1997). The frequency of coitus during breastfeeding. *Birth, 24,* 253–257.

VISTICA, G. (2000). One, two, three, out. *Newsweek,* March 20, 57–58.

VISTICA G. L., & THOMAS, E. (1997). Sex and lies. *Newsweek,* June 2, 26–31.

VITTENGL, J. R., & HOLT, C. S. (2000). Getting acquainted: The relationship of self-disclosure and social attraction to positive affect. *Journal of Social and Personal Relationships, 17,* 53–66.

VLAJINAC, H. D., et al. (1997). Effect of caffeine intake during pregnancy on birth weight. *American Journal of Epidemiology, 145,* 335–338.

VOELLER, B. (1991). AIDS and heterosexual anal intercourse. *Archives of Sexual Behavior, 201,* 233–269.

VOGEL, D. L., WESTER, S. R., & HEESACKER, M. (1999). Dating relationships and the demand/withdraw pattern of communication. *Sex Roles, 41,* 297–306.

VOIGHT, D. Q. (1984). A tankard of sporting taboos. In R.B. Brown (Ed.), *Forbidden fruits: Taboos and tabooism in culture.* Bowling Green, OH: Bowling Green University Popular Press.

VOIGT, H. (1991). Enriching the sexual experience of couples: The Asian traditions and sexual counseling. *Journal of Sex & Marital Therapy, 17,* 214–219.

VOLPE, A., SILFERI, M., GENAZZANI, A. D., & GENAZZANI, A. R. (1993). Contraception in older women. *Contraception, 47,* 229–239.

VON KROGH, G., et al. (2000). European course on HPV associated pathology: Guidelines for primary care physicians for the diagnosis and management of anogenital warts. *Sexually Transmitted Infections, 76,* 162–168.

VON SYDOW, K. (1999). Sexuality during pregnancy and after childbirth: A metacontent analysis of 59 studies. *Journal of Psychosomatic Research, 47,* 27–49.

VROEGE, J. A., GIJS, L., & HENGEVELD, M. W. (1998). Classification of sexual dysfunction: Towards DSM-V and ICD-11. *Comprehensive Psychiatry, 39,* 333–337.

WALBOOMERS, J. M., et al. (1999). Human papillomavirus is a necessary cause of invasive cervical cancer worldwide. *Journal of Pathology, 189,* 12–19.

WALD, A. (1999). New therapies and prevention strategies for genital herpes. *Clinical Infectious Diseases, 28* (Suppl. 1), S4–S13.

WALD, A., et al. (2000). Reactivation of genital herpes simplex virus type 2 infection in asymptomatic seropositive persons. *New England Journal of Medicine, 342,* 844–850.

WALDENSTRÖM, U. (1996). Modern maternity care: Does safety have to take the meaning out of birth? *Midwifery, 12,* 165–173.

WALDENSTRÖM, U., & NILSSON, C.-A. (1997). A randomized controlled study of birth center care versus standard maternity care: Effects on women's health. *Birth, 24,* 17–26.

WALDMAN, T. N. (1998). Menopause: When hormone replacement therapy is not an option. *Journal of Women's Health, 7,* 673–683.

WALDNER-HAUGRUD, L. K. (1999). Sexual coercion in lesbian and gay relationships; A review and critique. *Aggression and Violent Behavior, 4,* 139–149.

WALDO, C. R., BERDAHL, J. L., & FITZGERALD, L. F. (1998). Are men sexually harassed? If so, by whom? *Law and Human Behavior, 22,* 59–79.

WALKER, B. D., & GOULDER, P. J. R. (2000). Escape from the immune system. *Nature, 407,* 313–314.

WALKER, C. E. (1970). Erotic stimuli and the aggressive sexual offender. In *Technical Report of the Commission on Obscenity and Pornography* (Vol. 7, pp. 91–147). Washington, DC: U.S. Government Printing Office.

WALSTER, E., ARONSON, V., ABRAHAMS, D., & ROTTMAN, L. (1966). Importance of physical attractiveness in dating behavior. *Journal of Personality and Social Psychology, 4,* 508–516.

WALSTER, E., & WALSTER, G. W. (1978). *A new look at love.* Reading: MA: Addison-Wesley.

WARD, L. M., & RIVADENEYRA, R. (1999). Contributions of entertainment television to adolescents' sexual attitudes and expectations: The role of viewing amount versus viewer involvement. *Journal of Sex Research, 36,* 237–249.

WARD, M. C. (1989). *Nest in the wind: Adventures in anthropology on a tropical island.* Prospect Heights, IL: Waveland Press.

WARD, T., HUDSON, S. M., & McCORMACK, J. (1997). The assessment of rapists. *Behaviour Change, 14,* 39–54.

WARDLE, L. D. (1997). The potential impact of homosexual parenting on children. *University of Illinois Law Review, 1997,* 832–920.

WARNER, C. (1997). Storied history. *Times-Picayune* (New Orleans), September 29, A1, A6–A7.

WASHINGTON, A. E., CATES, W., & WASSERHEIT, J. N. (1991). Preventing pelvic inflammatory disease. *Journal of the American Medical Association, 266,* 2574–2580.

WASHTON, A. M. (1989). Cocaine abuse and compulsive sexuality. *Medical Aspects of Human Sexuality,* December, *23,* 32–39.

WASOW, M., & LOEB, M. (1979). Sexuality in nursing homes. *Journal of the American Geriatrics Society, 27,* 73–79.

WASSON, J. H., et al. (1995). A comparison of transurethral with watchful waiting for moderate symptoms of benign prostatic hyperplasia. *New England Journal of Medicine, 332,* 1995.

WATERMAN, C. K., & FOSS-GOODMAN, D. (1984). Child molesting: Variables relating to attribution of fault to victims, offenders and nonparticipating parents. *Journal of Sex Research, 20,* 329–349.

WEBER, A. L. (1998). Losing, leaving, and letting go: Coping with nonmarital breakups. In B. H. Spitzberg & W. R. Cupach (Eds.), *The dark side of close relationships* (pp. 267–306). Mahwah, NJ: Erlbaum.

WEBER, M. (1993). Images in clinical medicine: Pinworms. *New England Journal of Medicine, 328,* 927.

WEED, S. S. (1999). Menopause and beyond: The wise woman way. *Journal of Nurse-Midwifery, 44,* 267–279.

WEG, R. B. (1996). Sexuality, sensuality, and intimacy. In G. L. Maddox (Ed.), *The encyclopedia of aging* (2nd ed., pp. 479–488). New York: Springer.

WEGESIN, D. J. (1998). A neuropsychologic profile of homosexual and heterosexual men and women. *Archives of Sexual Behavior, 27,* 91–108.

WEINBERG, M., & WILLIAMS, C. (1988). African American sexuality: A test of two theories. *Journal of Sex Research, 25,* 197–218.

WEINBERG, M. S., WILLIAMS, C. J., & CALHAN, C. (1994). Homosexual foot fetishism. *Archives of Sexual Behavior, 23,* 611–626.

WEINBERG, T. (1987). Sadomasochism in the United States: A review of recent sociological literature. *Journal of Sex Research, 23,* 50–69.

WEINER, A. (1996). Understanding the social needs of streetwalking prostitutes. *Journal of the National Association of Social Workers, 41,* 97–105.

WEINHARDT, L. S., CAREY, M. P., JOHNSON, B. T., & BICKHAM, N. L. (1999). Effects of HIV counseling and testing on sexual risk behavior: A meta-analytic review of published research, 1985–1997. *American Journal of Public Health, 89,* 1397–1405.

WEINSTOCK, H., et al. (1994). *Chlamydia trachomatis* infections. *Infectious Disease Clinics of North America, 8,* 797–819.

WEIS, D. L. (1983). Affective reactions of women to their initial experience of coitus. *Journal of Sex Research, 19,* 209–237.

WEIS, D. L. (1985). The experience of pain during women's first sexual intercourse: Cultural mythology about female sexual initiation. *Archives of Sexual Behavior, 14,* 421–428.

WEIS, H. A., QUIGLEY, M. A., & HAYES, R. J. (2000). Male circumcision and risk of HIV infection in sub-Saharan Africa: A systematic review and meta-analysis. *AIDS, 14,* 2361–2370.

WEISS, R. S. (1975). *Marital separation.* New York: Basic Books.

WELLER, A., & WELLER, L. (1993). Menstrual synchrony between mothers and daughters and between roommates. *Physiology & Behavior, 53,* 943–949.

WELLER, A., & WELLER, L. (1997). Menstrual synchrony under optimal conditions: Bedouin families. *Journal of Comparative Physiology, 111,* 143–151.

WELLS, B. L. (1986). Predictors of female nocturnal orgasms. *Journal of Sex Research, 22,* 421–437.

WESSELLS, H., LUE, T. F., & MCANINCH, J. W. (1996). Penile length in the flaccid and erect states: Guidelines for penile augmentation. *Journal of Urology, 156,* 995–997.

WEST, J. (1999). (Not) talking about sex: Youth, identity, and sexuality. *Sociological Review, 47,* 525–547.

WESTERMARCK, E. A. (1891). *The history of human marriage.* New York: Macmillan.

WESTFALL, J. M., MAIN, D. J., & BARNARD, L. (1996). Continuation rates among injectable contraceptive users. *Family Planning Perspectives, 28,* 275–277.

WESTROM, L. (1980). Incidence, prevalence, and trends of acute pelvic inflammatory disease and its consequences in industrialized countries. *American Journal of Obstetrics and Gynecology, 138,* 880.

WETZEL, C., & INSKO, C. (1982). The similarity-attraction relationship: Is there an ideal one? *Journal of Experimental Social Psychology, 18,* 253–276.

WHALEN, R. (1977). Brain mechanisms controlling sexual behavior. In F. A. Beach (Ed.), *Human sexuality in four perspectives.* Baltimore: Johns Hopkins University Press.

WHIPPLE, B., & KOMISARUK, B. R. (1999). Beyond the G spot: Recent research on female sexuality. *Psychiatric Annals, 29,* 34–37.

WHIPPLE, B., OGDEN, G., & KOMISARUK, B. R. (1992). Physiological correlates of imagery-induced orgasm in women. *Archives of Sexual Behavior, 21,* 121–133.

WHITAKER, D. J., MILLER, K. S., MAY, D. C., & LEVIN, M. L. (1999). Teenage partners' communication about sexual risk and condom use: The importance of parent-teenager discussions. *Family Planning Perspectives, 31,* 117–121.

WHITAM, F. L. (1983). Culturally invariable properties of male homosexuality: Tentative conclusions from cross-cultural research. *Archives of Sexual Behavior, 12,* 207–226.

WHITAM, F. L., DASKALOS, C. T., & MATHY, R. M. (1995). A cross-cultural assessment of familial factors in the development of female homosexuality. *Journal of Psychology and Human Sexuality, 7*(4), 59–76.

WHITAM, F. L., DIAMOND, M., & MARTIN, J. (1993). Homosexual orientation in twins: A report on 61 pairs and three triplet sets. *Archives of Sexual Behavior, 22,* 187–205.

WHITAM, F. L., & MATHY, R. M. (1986). *Male homosexuality in four societies: Brazil, Guatemala, the Philippines, and the United States.* New York: Praeger.

WHITBECK, L. B., CONGER, R. D., & SIMONS, R. L. (1993). Minor deviant behaviors and adolescent sexual activity. *Youth and Society, 25,* 24–37.

WHITCOMB, D. (1992). Legal reforms on behalf of child witnesses: Recent developments in the American courts. In H. Dent & R. Flin (Eds.), *Children as witnesses* (pp. 151–165). Chichester, England: Wiley.

WHITE, D. R., & BURTON, M. L. (1988). Causes of polygyny: Ecology, economy, kinship, and warfare. *American Anthropologist, 90,* 871–887.

WHITE, G. L. (1980). Inducing jealousy: A power perspective. *Personality and Sexual Psychology Bulletin, 6,* 222–227.

WHITE, G. L. (1981). Relative involvement, inadequacy, and jealousy: A test of a causal model. *Alternative Lifestyles, 4,* 291–309.

WHITEHEAD, B. D. (1994). The failure of sex education. *Atlantic Monthly, 274,* 55–80.

WHITEHURST, R. N. (1972). Extramarital sex: Alienation or extension of normal behavior. In J. N. Edwards (Ed.), *Sex and society.* Chicago: Rand McNally.

WHITING, B. (1979). Contributions of anthropology to the study of gender identity, gender role, and sexual behavior. In H. Katchadourian (Ed.), *Human sexuality: A comparative and developmental perspective.* Berkeley: University of California Press.

WHITLEY, JR., B. E. (1998). False consensus on sexual behavior among college women: Comparison of four theoretical explanations. *Journal of Sex Research, 35,* 206–214.

WHITTEMORE, A. S., HARRIS, R., ITNYRE, J., & COLLABORATIVE OVARIAN CANCER GROUP. (1992a). Characteristics relating to ovarian cancer risk: Collaborative analysis of 12 U.S. case-control studies. II: Invasive epithelial ovarian cancers in white women. *American Journal of Epidemiology, 136,* 1184–1203.

WHO COLLABORATIVE STUDY OF CARDIOVASCULAR DISEASE AND STEROID HORMONE CONTRACEPTION. (1996a). Haemorrhagic stroke, overall stroke risk, and combined oral contraceptives: Results of an international, multicentre, case-control study. *Lancet, 348,* 505–510.

WIDMER, E. D., TREAS, J., & NEWCOMB, R. (1998). Attitudes toward nonmarital sex in 24 countries. *Journal of Sex Research, 35,* 349–358.

WIEDERMAN, M. W. (1997a). Pretending orgasm during sexual intercourse: Correlates in a sample of young adult women. *Journal of Sex & Marital Therapy, 23,* 131–139.

WIEDERMAN, M. W. (1997b). Extramarital sex: Prevalence and correlates in a national survey. *Journal of Sex Research, 34,* 167–174.

WIEDERMAN, M. W. (1997c). The truth must be in here somewhere: Examining the gender discrepancy in self-reported lifetime number of sex partners. *Journal of Sex Research, 34,* 375–386.

WIEDERMAN, M. W., & HURST, S. R. (1998). Body size, physical attractivness and body image among young adult women: Relationships to sexual experience and sexual esteem. *Journal of Sex Research, 35,* 272–281.

WIEDERMAN, M. W., & KENDALL, E. (1999). Evolution, sex, and jealousy: Investigation with a sample from Sweden. *Evolution and Human Behavior, 20,* 121–128.

WIELANDT, H., & KNUDSEN, L. B. (1997). Birth control: Some experiences from Denmark. *Contraception, 55,* 301–306.

WIENER, R. L., & HURT, L. E. (2000). How do people evaluate social sexual conduct at work: A psychological model. *Journal of Applied Psychology, 85,* 75–85.

WIEST, W. (1977). Semantic differential profiles of orgasm and other experiences among men and women. *Sex Roles, 3,* 399–403.

WIGHT, D. (1992). Impediments to safer heterosexual sex: A review of research with young people. *AIDS Care, 4,* 11–23.

WILCOX, A. J., BAIRD, D. D., & WEINBERG, C. R. (1999). Time of implantation of the conceptus and loss of pregnancy. *New England Journal of Medicine, 340,* 1796–1799.

WILCOX, A. J., WEINBERG, C. R., & BAIRD, D. D. (1995). Timing of sexual intercourse in relation to ovulation: Effects on the probability of conception, survival of the pregnancy, and sex of the baby. *New England Journal of Medicine, 333,* 1517–1521.

WILCOX, A. J., et al. (1988). Incidence of early loss of pregnancy. *New England Journal of Medicine, 319,* 189–194.

WILLIAMS, J. E., & BEST, D. L. (1990). *Measuring sex stereotypes: A multinational study.* Newbury Park, CA: Sage.

WILLIAMS, L., & SOBIESZCZYK, T. (1997). Attitudes surrounding the continuation of female circumcision in the Sudan: Passing the tradition to the next generation. *Journal of Marriage and the Family, 59,* 966–981.

WILLIAMS, L. M. (1994). Recall of childhood trauma: A prospective study of women's memories of child sexual abuse. *Journal of Consulting and Clinical Psychology, 62,* 1167–1176.

WILLIAMS, N., CHELL, J., & KAPILA, L. (1993). Why are children referred for circumcision? *British Medical Journal, 306,* 28.

WILSON, G. D., (1987). An ethological approach to sexual deviation. In G. D. Wilson (Ed.), *Variant sexuality: Research and theory.* Baltimore: Johns Hopkins University Press.

WILSON, H. C., KIEFHABER, S. H., & GRAVEL, V. (1991). Two studies of menstrual synchrony: Negative results. *Psychoneuroendocrinology, 16,* 353–359.

WILSON, P. (1986). Black culture and sexuality. *Journal of Social Work and Human Sexuality, 4,* 29–46.

WILSON, R. (1998). Randomised trial to assess safety and fetal outcome of early and midtrimester amniocentesis. *Lancet, 351,* 242–247.

WINCZE, J., & CAREY, M. (1991). *Sexual dysfunction: A guide for assessment and treatment.* New York: Guilford Press.

WINGOOD, G. M., & DICLEMENTE, R. J. (1998). Gender-related correlates and predictors of consistent condom use among young adult African-American women: A prospective analysis. *International Journal of STD & AIDS, 9,* 139–145.

WINICK, C., & EVANS., J. T. (1994). Is there a national standard with respect to attitudes toward sexually explicit media material? *Archives of Sexual Behavior, 23,* 405–419.

WINICK, C., & EVANS, J. T. (1996). The relationship between nonenforcement of state pornography laws and rates of sex crimes arrests. *Archives of Sexual Behavior, 25,* 439–453.

WINN, R., & NEWTON, N. (1982). Sexuality in aging: A study of 106 cultures. *Archives of Sexual Behavior, 11,* 283–298.

WITHERINGTON, R. (1990). External penile appliances for management of impotence. *Seminars in Urology, 8,* 124–128.

WITLIN, A. G., & SIBAI, B. M. (1997). Hypertension in pregnancy: Current concepts of preeclampsia. *Annual Review of Medicine, 48,* 115–127.

WITT, S. D. (1996). Traditional or androgynous: An analysis to determine gender role orientation of basal readers. *Child Study Journal, 26,* 303–318.

WOLF, A. P. (1970). Childhood association and sexual attraction: A further test of the Westermarck hypothesis. *American Anthropologist, 72,* 503–515.

WOLFE, P. S. (1997). The influence of personal values on issues of sexuality and disability. *Sexuality and Disability, 15,* 69–90.

WOLFF, C. (1971). *Love between women.* New York: Harper & Row.

WOLNER-HANSSEN, P., KIVIAT, N. K., & HOLMES, K. K. (1990). Atypical pelvic inflammatory disease: Subacute, chronic, or subclinical upper genital tract infection in women. In K. K. Holmes et al. (Eds.), *Sexually transmitted diseases* (2nd ed.). New York: McGraw-Hill.

WONDERLICH, S. A., WILSNACK, R. W., WILSNACK, S. C., & HARRIS, T. R. (1996). Childhood sexual abuse and bulimia behavior in a nationally representative sample. *American Journal of Public Health, 86,* 1082–1086.

WONG, J. K., et al. (1997). Recovery of replication-competent HIV despite prolonged suppression of plasma viremia. *Science, 278,* 1291–1295.

WOOD, E., et al. (2000). Extent to which low-level of antiretroviral treatment could curb the AIDS epidemic in sub-Saharan Africa. *Lancet, 355,* 2095–2100.

WORLD HEALTH ORGANIZATION. (1978). *Special Programme of Research, Development and Research Training: Seventh annual report.* Geneva: Author.

WORLD HEALTH ORGANIZATION. (1981). A prospective multicentre trial of the ovulation method of natural family planning: II. The effectiveness phase. *Fertility and Sterility, 36,* 591–598.

WORLD HEALTH ORGANIZATION. (1984). Mental health and female sterilization: Report of a WHO collaborative prospective study. *Journal of Biosocial Sciences, 16,* 1–21.

WORLD HEALTH ORGANIZATION. (1985). Mental health and female sterilization: A follow-up. *Journal of Biosocial Sciences, 17,* 1–18.

WORLD HEALTH ORGANIZATION. (1992). *The ICD-10 classification of mental and behavioral disorders.* Geneva: Author.

WORLD HEALTH ORGANIZATION. (1995). The World Health Organization's infant-feeding recommendation. *Weekly Epidemiology Record, 70,* 119–120.

WORLD HEALTH ORGANIZATION. (1996). *Revised 1990 estimates of maternal mortality— A new approach by WHO and UNICEF.* WHO/FRH/MSM 96.11: UNICEF? PLN? 96.1. Geneva: Author.

WORLD HEALTH ORGANIZATION. (1999). Task Force on Methods for the Natural Regulation of Fertility. The World Health Organization multinational study of breastfeeding and lactational amenorrhea: III. Pregnancy during breast-feeding. *Fertility and Sterility, 72,* 431–440.

WRIGHT, A. L. (1983). A cross-cultural comparison of menopause symptoms. *Medical Anthropology, 7,* 20–36.

WRITING GROUP FOR THE PEPI TRIAL. (1996). Effects of hormone therapy on bone mineral density. *Journal of the American Medical Association, 276,* 1389–1396.

YANG, A. S. (1997). Attitudes toward homosexuality. *Public Opinion Quarterly, 6,* 477–507.

YESALIS, C. E., BARSUKIEWICZ, C. K., KOPSTEIN, A. N., & BAHRKE, M. S. (1997). Trends in anabolic-androgenic steroid use among adolescents. *Archives of Pediatric and Adolescent Medicine, 151,* 1197–1206.

ZANJANI, E. D., & ANDERSON, W. F. (1999). Prospects for in utero human gene therapy. *Science, 285,* 2084–2088.

ZAVIACIC, M., & WHIPPLE, B. (1993). Update on the female prostate and the phenomenon of female ejaculation. *Journal of Sex Research, 30,* 148–151.

ZAVIACIC, M., ZAVIACICOVA, A., HOLOMAN, I. K., & MOLCAN, J. (1988). Female urethral expulsions evoked by local digital stimulation of the G-spot: Differences in the response patterns. *Journal of Sex Research, 24,* 311–318.

ZAVIACIC, M., et al. (1988). Concentrations of fructose in female ejaculate and urine: A comparative biochemical study. *Journal of Sex Research, 24,* 319–325.

ZEISS, A. M., DAVIES, H. D., & TINKLENBERG, J. R. (1996). An observational study of sexual behavior in demented male patients. *Journal of Gerontology: Medical Sciences, 51A,* M325–M329.

ZEVIN, D. (1992). The pleasure people. *US,* August, 32–36.

ZHANG, J., THOMAS, A. G., & LEYBOVICH, E. (1997). Vaginal douching and adverse health effects: A meta-analysis. *American Journal of Public Health, 87,* 1207–1211.

ZHOU, J., HOFMAN, M. A., GOOREN, L. J. G., & SWAAB, D. F. (1995). A sex difference in the human brain and its relation to transsexuality. *Nature, 378,* 68–70.

ZHOU, Q., O'BRIEN, B., & RELYEA, J. (1999). Severity of nausea and vomiting during pregnancy: What does it predict? *Birth, 26,* 108–114.

ZHU, B.-P., ROLFS, R. T., NANGLE, B. E., & HORAN, J. M. (1999). Effect of the interval between pregnancies on perinatal outcomes. *New England Journal of Medicine, 340,* 589–594.

ZHU, T. F., et al. (1998). An African HIV-1 sequence from 1959 and implications for the origin of the epidemic. *Nature, 391,* 594–597.

ZILBERGELD, B. (1978). *Male sexuality: A guide to sexual fulfillment.* Boston: Little, Brown.

ZILBERGELD, B., & KILMANN, P. (1984). The scope and effectiveness of sex therapy. *Psychotherapy, 21,* 319–326.

ZILLMANN, D., & BRYANT, J. (1982). Pornography, sexual callousness, and the trivialization of rape. *Journal of Communication,* Autumn, 10–21.

ZILLMANN, D., & BRYANT, J. (1988). Pornography's impact on sexual satisfaction. *Journal of Applied Social Psychology, 18,* 438–453.

ZUCKER, K. J., & BLANCHARD, R. (1997). Transvestic fetishism: Psychopathology and theory. In D. R. Laws & W. O'Donohue (Eds.), *Sexual deviance: Theory, assessment, and treatment* (pp. 253–279). New York: Guilford Press.

ZUCKER, K. J., & Bradley, S. J. (1995). *Gender identity disorder and psychosexual problems in children and adolescents.* New York: Guilford Press.